Readings In Artificial Intelligence

Readings In Artificial Intelligence

a collection of articles by

Amarel • Barstow • Berliner • Bledsoe • Buchanan • Chang • Cohen • Davis • Doyle • Duda • Erman • Feigenbaum • Fikes • Gaschnig • Green • Hart • Hayes • Hayes-Roth • Lesser • Mackworth • Manna • McCarthy • Mitchell • Moore • Nilsson • Perrault • Reddy • Reiter • Shortliffe • Slagle • Stefik • Waldinger • Weyhrauch • Wilkins • Woods

edited by

Bonnie Lynn Webber
University of Pennsylvania

and

Nils J. Nilsson
SRI International

Library of Congress Cataloging in Publication Data
Readings in artificial intelligence
Includes index.
1. Artificial intelligence—articles, papers, lectures.
I. Webber, Bonnie Lynn, 1946- . II. Nilsson, Nils J., 1933-
Q335.5.R3 001.53'5 81-13630
ISBN 0-935382-03-8 AACR2

P.O. Box 98, Palo Alto, California 94302

ISBN 0-935382-03-8

BCDEFG-C-76543

TABLE OF CONTENTS

PREFACE

We regard artificial intelligence (AI) as a branch of computer science whose objective is to endow machines with reasoning and perceptual abilities. Artificial intelligence is a young discipline. Born in the 1950s, it gathered momentum and adolescent confidence in the 60s, and began to mature and show promise in the 70s. Like many other young subjects, AI is difficult to teach and learn because it has not yet accumulated a large body of established theory. Although several authors (including one of us—NJN) have written AI textbooks, these books give somewhat differing perspectives of AI. To avoid complete dependence on any one point of view, it is essential for students of AI to supplement textbook study by reading some original papers on AI theory and experiment. The purpose of this volume is to make a number of these important papers more accessible—not only to present and future specialists, but to all those for whom the problems of artificial intelligence hold particular fascination and interest.

Many of the papers included here are rather difficult to find. Some appeared originally in limited-edition conference proceedings that are now available in microfiche only. Some are published in collections or journals that college and university libraries might have in single copies only—or none whatsoever. To keep the price of the volume within the reach of students, we have arranged with the publisher to print it from photocopies of the original sources—thus saving the cost of retypesetting.

The papers assembled here cover a variety of topics and viewpoints. Some are theoretical, some experimental. Most of the papers are frequently cited by AI textbooks and current research articles. Although we might not be able to give compelling arguments for each of the papers included or against those not contained herein, we believe that, on the whole, this volume may be considered representative of some of the best thinking and research in AI.

We have organized the papers into five major chapters: Search and Search Representations, Deduction, Problem-Solving and Planning, Expert Systems and AI Applications, and Advanced Topics. Each section is preceded by a brief description of the papers it contains. A subject index is included at the end of the volume.

We thank all of the authors and publishers for giving us permission to reproduce their papers.

Bonnie Lynn Webber
Nils J. Nilsson

ACKNOWLEDGMENTS

The editors are pleased to thank the following authors and publishers for permission to include copyrighted material in the present volume:

Amarel, S., "On Representations of Problems of Reasoning About Actions," from MACHINE INTELLIGENCE 3, D. Michie (ed.), pages 131-171, Edinburgh University Press, 1968. Copyright 1968 by Edinburgh University Press.

Gaschnig, J., "A Problem Similarity Approach to Devising Heuristics: First Results," from PROC. 6TH INTL. JOINT CONF. ON ARTIFICIAL INTELLIGENCE, 301-307, 1979. Copyright 1979 by International Joint Conferences on Artificial Intelligence.

Woods, W. A., "Optimal Search Strategies for Speech Understanding Control," to appear in ARTIFICIAL INTELLIGENCE. Copyright 1981 by North-Holland Publishing Co.

Mackworth, A., "Consistency in Networks of Relations," from ARTIFICIAL INTELLIGENCE, 8(1):99-118, 1977. Copyright 1977 by North-Holland Publishing Co.

Berliner, H., "The B* Tree Search Algorithm: A Best-First Proof Procedure," from ARTIFICIAL INTELLIGENCE, 12(1):23-40, 1979. Copyright 1979 by North-Holland Publishing Co.

Bledsoe, W. W., "Non-Resolution Theorem Proving," from ARTIFICIAL INTELLIGENCE, 9(1):1-35, 1977. Copyright 1977 by North-Holland Publishing Co.

Chang, C. and J. Slagle, "Using Rewriting Rules for Connection Graphs to Prove Theorems," from ARTIFICIAL INTELLIGENCE, 12(2):159-178, 1979. Copyright 1979 by North-Holland Publishing Co.

Reiter, R., "On Closed World Data Bases," from LOGIC AND DATA BASES, 55-76, H. Gallaire and J. Minker (eds.), Plenum Press, 1978. Copyright 1978 by Plenum Press.

Manna, Z. and R. Waldinger, "A Deductive Approach to Program Synthesis," from ACM TRANSACTIONS ON PROGRAMMING LANGUAGES AND SYSTEMS, 2(1):120-121, ACM, 1980. Copyright 1980 by the Association for Computing Machinery, Inc.

Weyhrauch, R., "Prolegomena to a Theory of Mechanized Formal Reasoning," from ARTIFICIAL INTELLIGENCE, 13(1,2):133-170, 1980. Copyright 1980 by North-Holland Publishing Co.

Duda, R., Hart, P. and N. Nilsson, "Subjective Bayesian Methods for Rule-Based Inference Systems," in PROCEEDINGS 1976 NATIONAL COMPUTER CONFERENCE, 1075-1082, AFIPS, vol. 45, 1976. Copyright 1976 by AFIPS Press.

Green, C., "Application of Theorem Proving to Problem Solving," in PROC. 1ST INTL JOINT CONF. ON ARTIFICIAL INTELLIGENCE, 219-239, 1969. Copyright 1969 by International Joint Conferences on Artificial Intelligence.

Hayes, P., "The Frame Problem and Related Problems in Artificial Intelligence," from ARTIFICIAL AND HUMAN THINKING, 45-59, A. Elithorn and D. Jones (eds.), Jossey-Bass, 1973. Copyright 1973 by Jossey-Bass, Inc. and Elsevier Scientific Publishing Company.

Fikes, R., Hart, P. and N. Nilsson, "Learning and Executing Generalized Robot Plans," from ARTIFICIAL INTELLIGENCE, 3(4):251-288, 1972. Copyright 1972 by North-Holland Publishing Co.

Waldinger, R., "Achieving Several Goals Simultaneously," from MACHINE INTELLIGENCE 8, 94-136, E. Elcock and D. Michie (eds.), Ellis Horwood, 1977. Copyright 1977 by E. W. Elcock and D. Michie/Ellis Horwood, Limited.

Stefik, M., "Planning and Meta-Planning," from ARTIFICIAL INTELLIGENCE, 16(2):141-170, 1981. Copyright 1981 by North-Holland Publishing Co.

Barstow, D., "An Experiment in Knowledge-Based Automatic Programming," from ARTIFICIAL INTELLIGENCE, 12(2):73-119, 1979. Copyright 1979 by North-Holland Publishing Co.

Buchanan, B. and E. Feigenbaum, "Dendral and Meta-Dendral: Their Applications Dimension," from ARTIFICIAL INTELLIGENCE, 11(1,2):5-24, 1978. Copyright 1978 by North-Holland Publishing Co.

Shortliffe, E., "Consultation Systems for Physicians," from PROC. CANADIAN SOC. FOR COMPUTATIONAL STUDIES OF INTELLIGENCE (CSCSI), University of Victoria, Victoria B.C., 1980. Copyright 1980 by Canadian Society for Computational Studies of Intelligence.

Duda, R., Gaschnig, J. and P. Hart, "Model Design in the Prospector Consultant System for Mineral Exploration," from EXPERT SYSTEMS IN THE MICROELECTRONIC AGE, 153-167, D. Michie (ed.), Edinburgh University Press, 1979. Copyright 1979 by Edinburgh University Press.

Erman, L., Hayes-Roth, F., Lesser, V., and D. Reddy, "The Hearsay-II Speech Understanding System: Integrating Knowledge to Resolve Uncertainty," from COMPUTING SURVEYS 12(2)213-253, 1980. Copyright 1980 by the Association for Computing Machinery, Inc.

Wilkins, D., "Using Patterns and Plans in Chess," from ARTIFICIAL INTELLIGENCE, 14(2):165-203, 1980. Copyright 1980 by North-Holland Publishing Co.

Davis, R., "Interactive Transfer of Expertise: Acquisition of New Inference Rules," from ARTIFICIAL INTELLIGENCE, 12(2):121-157, 1979. Copyright 1979 by North-Holland Publishing Co.

McCarthy, J. and P. Hayes, "Some Philosophical Problems from the Standpoint of Artificial Intelligence," from MACHINE INTELLIGENCE 4, 463-502, B. Meltzer and D. Michie (eds.), Edinburgh University Press, 1969. Copyright 1969 by Edinburgh University Press.

Hayes, P., "The Logic of Frames," from FRAME CONCEPTIONS AND TEXT UNDERSTANDING, D. Metzing (ed.), de Gruyter, pages 46-61, 1979. Copyright 1979 by Walter de Gruyter & Co.

McCarthy, J., "Epistemological Problems of Artificial Intelligence," from PROC. 5TH INTL. JOINT CONF. ON ARTIFICIAL INTELLIGENCE, 1038-1044, 1977. Copyright 1977 by International Joint Conferences on Artificial 1ntelligence.

McCarthy, J., "Circumscription—A Form of Non-Monotonic Reasoning," from ARTIFICIAL INTELLIGENCE, 13(1,2):27-39, 1980. Copyright 1980 by North-Holland Publishing Co.

Moore, R. C., "Reasoning About Knowledge and Action," from PROC. 5TH INTL. JOINT CONF. ON ARTIFICIAL INTELLIGENCE, 223-227, 1977. Copyright 1977 by International Joint Conferences on Artificial Intelligence.

Cohen, P. and C. R. Perrault, "Elements of a Plan-Based Theory of Speech Acts," from COGNITIVE SCIENCE, 3(3):177-212, 1979. Copyright 1979 by Ablex Publishing Corporation.

Doyle, J., "A Truth Maintenance System," from ARTIFICIAL INTELLIGENCE, 12(3):231-272, 1979. Copyright 1979 by North-Holland Publishing Co.

Mitchell, T., "Generalization as Search," to appear in ARTIFICIAL INTELLIGENCE, Copyright 1981 by North-Holland Publishing Co.

1 / Search and Search Representations

Search processes play a fundamental role in artificial intelligence. In familiarizing oneself with a complex AI system, there are several things one would want to know that have to do with search. First, does the system use search at all? If so, does it do so by backtracking, or by scanning breadth-first or best-first? What is the search space? What heuristics are used in ordering the search? Does the system use constraint satisfaction techniques to help reduce the magnitude of the search? Much important information about search and search representations is contained in standard AI textbooks, and these topics continue to be subjects of active research in AI. The five papers included in this section will introduce the reader to some of the important research issues related to search.

Amarel's paper is a case study on how shifts in problem representation can drastically reduce the size of the search space. It is the classic paper on this topic and contains many intriguing ideas for continuing research.

The use of heuristic estimating functions for controlling search raises the question of how to obtain these functions. Gaschnig's paper addresses this problem in a clear and inviting manner, laying a nice foundation for future work in this area.

Woods's paper views recognition as a search problem. Rather than follow the usual approach of searching for a minimal-cost path to a goal state, Woods seeks the final state with the highest score (regardless of the cost of the path to that state). Applied to recognition problems, the highest-scoring state is the (consistent) interpretation of the perceptual input data that is most strongly supported by the input evidence.

Constraints on possible problem solutions can often be used to reduce the size of the search space before search begins. Sometimes these constraints are so confining that very little search effort is needed after the constraint computations are performed. In some cases, the complete set of constraints is assumed to be known at the outset, while, in other cases, constraints are acquired and integrated incrementally. Mackworth's paper, written several years ago, provides a clear introduction to constraint satisfaction and network consistency algorithms. It is fundamental to understanding more recent work in this area.

Much of the early work on developing search methods was done in the context of puzzle-solving and game-playing. Chess has posed particularly challenging problems. Berliner's paper describes an algorithm, called B*, for searching game and proof trees. In addition to the optimistic bound on the cost function used by the classical A* algorithm, B* uses a pessimistic bound as well. Search can be terminated below those nodes whose bounds conflict.

On Representations of Problems of Reasoning about Actions

Saul Amarel
RCA Laboratories
Princeton, N.J.

1. INTRODUCTION

The purpose of this paper is to clarify some basic issues of choice of representation for problems of reasoning about actions. The general problem of representation is concerned with the relationship between different ways of formulating a problem to a problem solving system and the efficiency with which the system can be expected to find a solution to the problem. An understanding of the relationship between problem formulation and problem solving efficiency is a prerequisite for the design of procedures that can automatically choose the most 'appropriate' representation of a problem (they can find a 'point of view' of the problem that maximally simplifies the process of finding a solution).

Many problems of practical importance are problems of reasoning about actions. In these problems, a course of action has to be found that satisfies a number of specified conditions. A formal definition of this class of problems is given in the next section, in the context of a general conceptual framework for formulating these problems for computers. Everyday examples of reasoning about actions include planning an airplane trip, organizing a dinner party, etc. There are many examples of industrial and military problems in this category, such as scheduling assembly and transportation processes, designing a program for a computer, planning a military operation, etc.

We shall analyze in detail a specific problem of transportation scheduling–the 'missionaries and cannibals' problem (which is stated in section 3)–in order to evaluate the effects of alternative formulations of this problem on the expected efficiency of mechanical procedures for solving it, and also in order to examine the processes that come into play when a transition takes place from a given problem formulation into a better one. After the initial verbal formulation of the missionaries and cannibals problem in section 3, the problem undergoes five changes in formulation, each of which increases the ease with which it can be solved. These reformulations are discussed in sections 4 to 11. A summary of the main ideas in the evolution of formulations, and comments on the possibility of mechanizing the transitions between formulations are given in section 12.

2. PROBLEMS OF REASONING ABOUT ACTIONS

A problem of reasoning about actions (Simon, 1966) is given in terms of an initial situation, a terminal situation, a set of feasible actions, and a set of constraints that restrict the applicability of actions; the task of the problem solver is to find the 'best' sequence of permissible actions that can transform the initial situation into the terminal situation. In this section, we shall specify a *system of productions*, P, where problems of reasoning about actions can be naturally formulated and solved.

In the system P, a basic description of a situation at one point in time is a listing of the basic features of the situation. The basic features are required for making decisions about actions that can be taken from the situation. We call a situation a *state of nature* (an N-state). The language in which N-states are described is called an *N-state language*. Such a language is defined by specifying the following:

(i) a non-empty set U_0 called the *basic universe*; this set contains the basic elements of interest in situations (the individuals, the objects, the places);

(ii) a set of basic predicates defined for elements of U_0 (properties of elements and relations between elements);

(iii) a set of rules of formation for expressions in the language.

The rules of formation determine whether an N-state language is a linear language, a two-dimensional (graphic) language, or it has some other form. Regardless of the form taken by an expression in an N-state language, such an expression is meant to assert that a given element in U_0 has a certain property or that a given subset of elements in U_0 are related in a specified manner. Thus, an expression in an N-state language has the logical interpretation of a true proposition about a basic feature of the situation. A finite set (possibly empty) of expressions in an N-state language is called a *configuration*. The empty configuration will be written Λ. In the logic interpretation, a (non-empty) configuration is a conjunction of the true assertions made by its component expressions. The set union of two configurations is itself a

The research presented in this paper was sponsored in part by the Air Force Office of Scientific Research, under Contract Number AF49(638)-1184. Part of this work was done while the author was on a visiting appointment at the Computer Science Department of the Carnegie Institute of Technology, Pittsburgh, Pa. At Carnegie Tech. this research was sponsored by the Advanced Research Projects Agency of the Office of the Secretary of Defense under Contract Number SD-146.

configuration. If α and β are configurations, then their union will be written α, β. A *basic description*, s, of an N-state is a configuration from which all true statements about the N-state (that can be expressed in the terms of the N-state language) can be directly obtained or derived. Thus a basic description completely characterizes an N-state. Henceforth we shall refer to an N-state by its basic description.

A derived description of an N-state at one point in time is a listing of compound features of the N-state. Compound features are defined in terms of the basic features, and they are intended to characterize situations in the light of the problem constraints, so that decisions about the legality of proposed actions can be made. We denote by $d(s)$ a derived description that is associated with an N-state s. The language in which derived descriptions are formulated is an extension of the N-state language, and it is called the *extended description language*. Such a language is defined by the following:

(i) a set U_1 called the *extended universe*, where $U_0 \subset U_1$ (this is not necessarily a proper inclusion); the extension of U_0 contains compound elements of interest (definable in terms of the basic elements in U_0), and possibly new elements (not obtainable from U_0) that are used for building high level descriptions;

(ii) a set of new predicates defined for elements of U_1 (properties and relations that are required for expressing the constraining conditions of the problem);

(iii) a set of rules of formation for expressions in the language.

The rules of formation in this language are identical with those of the N-state language. Each expression in the extended description language has the logical interpretation of a proposition about a compound feature in a situation. A derived description $d(s)$ is a set of expressions in the extended description language (it is a configuration in the language). In the logical interpretation, $d(s)$ is a conjunction of the propositions that are specified by its constituent expressions.

The *rules of action* in the system P specify a possible next situation (next in time with respect to a given time scale) as a function of certain features in previous situations. The complexity of a problem about actions is determined by the nature of this dependence. There is a sequential and a local component in such a dependence. The sequential part is concerned with dependencies of the next situation on features of sequences of past situations. We will not be concerned with such dependencies in this paper. The local part is concerned with the amount of local context that is needed to determine a change of a basic feature from one situation to the next.

In the specification of a rule of action, an N-state is given in terms of a *mixed description* s', which is written as follows:

$$s' = s;\ d(s), \qquad (2.1)$$

where s is the basic description of the N-state, and $d(s)$ is its associated derived description. Let A be a feasible action and let (A) denote the rule of action that refers to A. A rule of action is given as a transition schema between mixed descriptions of N-states, and it has the following form:

$$(A)\colon s_a;\ d(s_a) \rightarrow s_b;\ d(s_b) \qquad (2.2)$$

The feasible action A is defined as a transformation from the N-state s_a to the N-state s_b. If A is applied at s_a, then the next N-state will be s_b. The rule (A) specifies the condition under which the application of A at s_a is permissible. This is to be interpreted as follows: 'If $d(s_a)$ and $d(s_b)$ are both satisfied, then the application of A at s_a is permissible.' A derived description $d(s)$ is satisfied if it is true under the logical interpretation. The rule (A) imposes a restriction on the mapping $A\colon s_a \rightarrow s_b$, i.e. it restricts the domain of the feasible action. Thus, given an N-state s_a for which A is a feasible action, A can be applied at s_a only if the N-state s_b that results from the application of A has certain compound features that are specified in $d(s_b)$.

Let $\{(A)\}$ be the (finite) set of rules of action and let $\{s\}$ be the set of all possible N-states. The set $\{(A)\}$ specifies a relation of *direct attainability* between the elements of $\{s\}$. Given any two states s_x, s_y from $\{s\}$, the N-state s_y is directly attainable from s_x if and only if there exists a permissible action in $\{(A)\}$ that can take s_x to s_y. Let us denote by T the relation of direct attainability.[1] The expression $s_x T s_y$ asserts that the N-state s_x can occur *just earlier than* s_y in a possible evolution of the system. Thus, the relation T represents local time order for the system P.

A *trajectory* from an N-state s_a to an N-state s_b is a finite sequence $s_1, s_2, \ldots, s_m$ of N-states such that $s_1 = s_a$, $s_m = s_b$, and for each i, $1 < i \leqslant m$, s_i is directly attainable from s_{i-1}. For any pair of N-states s_a, s_b, we say that s_b *is attainable from* s_a if and only if $s_a = s_b$ or there exists a trajectory from s_a to s_b. We denote the relation of attainability from s_a to s_b by $s_a \Rightarrow s_b$. The notion of a schedule is close to the notion of a trajectory; it is the sequence of actions that are taken in moving over the trajectory.

Now a problem of reasoning about actions can be formulated in the system P as follows: Given

(i) an N-state language

(ii) an extended description language

(iii) a set of rules of action

(iv) an initial N-state and a terminal N-state,

find the shortest schedule (or the shortest trajectory) from the initial N-state to the terminal N-state (if a schedule exists at all).

The set of all N-states, partly ordered under the relation T, defines a space σ that we call the N-state space. The search for a solution trajectory takes place in this space.

[1] This relation is very close to the relation 'earlier' introduced by Carnap (1958), and denoted T, in his language for space-time topology. In Carnap's case, T represents time order between two world points that are on the same trajectory.

Commonly, the initial formulation of a problem of reasoning about actions is a *verbal formulation*. Given the initial verbal formulation, there are several possible N-state languages and extended description languages that can be used for formulating the problem in the system of productions P. The choice of the universe U_1 and of the features in terms of which situations are described can strongly influence the amount of effort that is needed in order to find a solution in the formulation P. Here is an important decision point where problem solving power is affected by the choice of a problem representation. In addition, strong improvements in problem solving power may result from the discovery and exploitation of regularities in N-state space. The discovery of such regularities is facilitated by appropriate representations of N-state space. We shall illustrate these points by discussing in detail in the following sections a sequence of formulations of an extended version of the Missionary and Cannibals problem.

3. TRANSPORTATION PROBLEMS: INITIAL FORMULATION, F_1, OF M&C PROBLEMS

Many transportation scheduling problems are problems of reasoning about actions. Such problems can be formulated as follows. Given a set of space points, an initial distribution of objects in these points, and transportation facilities with given capacities; find an optimal sequence of transportations between the space points such that a terminal distribution of objects in these points can be attained without violating a set of given constraints on possible intermediate distribution of objects.

An interesting subclass of these transportation scheduling problems is the class of 'difficult crossing' problems, typified by the 'Missionaries and Cannibals' problem. This problem appears frequently in books on mathematical recreations. It has also received attention in the dynamic programming literature (Bellman and Dreyfus, 1962) and in the literature on computer simulation of cognitive processes. (Simon and Newell, 1961). The following is a verbal formulation of the 'missionaries and cannibals' problem (we call it formulation F_1). Three missionaries and three cannibals seek to cross a river (say from the left bank to the right bank). A boat is available which will hold two people, and which can be navigated by any combination of missionaries and cannibals involving one or two people. If the missionaries on either bank of the river, or 'en route' in the river, are outnumbered at any time by cannibals, the cannibals will indulge in their anthropophagic tendencies and do away with the missionaries. Find the simplest schedule of crossings that will permit all the missionaries and cannibals to cross the river safely.

In a more generalized version of this problem, there are N missionaries and N cannibals (where $N \geqslant 3$) and the boat has a capacity k (where $k \geqslant 2$). We call this problem the M&C *problem*. We shall refer to the specific problem that we have formulated above (where $N=3, k=2$) as *the elementary* M&C *problem*.

4. FORMULATION F_2 OF THE M&C PROBLEM IN ELEMENTARY SYSTEMS OF PRODUCTIONS

We shall formulate now the M&C problem in a system of productions of the type described in section 2. We start by specifying a simple but straightforward N-state language.

The universe U_0 of the N-state language contains the following basic elements:

(i) N individuals $m_1, m_2, \ldots, m_N$ that are missionaries and N individuals $c_1, c_2, \ldots, c_N$ that are cannibals,

(ii) an object (a transportation facility)–the boat b_k with a carrying capacity k,

(iii) two space points p_L, p_R for the left bank and the right bank of the river respectively.

The basic relations between basic elements in U_0 are as follows:

(i) *at*; this associates an individual or the boat with a space point (example: *at* (m_1, p_L) asserts that the missionary m_1 is at the left bank),

(ii) *on*; this indicates that an individual is aboard the boat (example: *on* (c_1, b_k) asserts that the cannibal c_1 is on the boat).

A set of expressions, one for each individual and one for the boat (they specify the positions of all the individuals and of the boat) provides a basic description of a situation, i.e. it characterizes an N-state. Thus, the initial N-state for the M&C problem can be written as follows:

$$s_0 = at(b_k, p_L), at(m_1, p_L), at(m_2, p_L), \ldots, at(m_N, p_L), at(c_1, p_L), at(c_2, p_L), \ldots, at(c_N, p_L). \qquad (4.1)$$

The terminal N-state is attained from (4.1) by substituting p_R for p_L throughout.

The verbal statement of the M&C problem induces the formulation of an extended description language where a non-empty extension of U_0 is introduced together with certain properties and relations for the elements of this extension. The compound elements in the extension of U_0 are defined in terms of notions in the N-state language. These compound elements are the following six subsets of the total set $\{m\}$ of missionaries and the total set $\{c\}$ of cannibals:

$\{m\}_L = \{x \mid x \in \{m\}, at\ (x, p_L)\}$; the subset of missionaries at left,
$\{m\}_R = \{x \mid x \in \{m\}, at\ (x, p_R)\}$; the subset of missionaries at right,
$\{m\}_b = \{x \mid x \in \{m\}, on\ (x, b_k)\}$; the subset of missionaries aboard the boat.

The three remaining compound elements $\{c\}_L, \{c\}_R, \{c\}_b$ are subsets of the total set of cannibals that are defined in a similar manner.

In the M&C problem, the properties of interest for the specification of permissible actions are the sizes of the compound elements that we have just introduced, i.e. the number of elements in the subsets $\{m\}_L$, $\{m_R\}$, etc. Let $M_L, M_R, M_b, C_L, C_R, C_b$ denote the number of individuals in the sets $\{m\}_L$, $\{m\}_R, \ldots, \{c\}_b$ respectively. These are variables that take values from the finite set of nonnegative integers $J_0{}^N=\{0, 1, 2, \ldots, N\}$. These integers are also elements of the extension of U_0. They bring with them in the extended description language the arithmetic relations $=, >, <$, as well as compound relations that are obtainable from them via the logical connectives $\sim, \vee, \wedge$, and also the arithmetic functions $+, -$. A derived description $d(s)$ which is associated with an N-state s is a set of expressions that specify certain arithmetic relations between the variables M_L, M_R, etc. whose values are obtained from s.

The rules of formation that we shall use for description languages are of the type conventionally used in logic; they yield linear expressions. Expressions are concatenated (with separating commas) to form configurations. The basic description given in (4.1) is an example of a configuration in the linear language.

The verbal statement of the M & C problem does not induce a unique choice of a set of feasible actions. We shall consider first a 'reasonable' set of *elementary* actions that are assumed to be feasible and that satisfy the given constraints on boat capacity and on the possible mode of operating the boat. The set of permissible actions is a subset of this set that can be obtained by specifying the appropriate restrictions on the relative number of missionaries and cannibals in the two river banks as well as '*en route*'.

$\{(A)'\}_1$: *Elementary feasible actions in Formulation F_2 that are sensitive to boat constraints.* In the following transition schemata, α denotes an arbitrary configuration that completes a basic description of an N-state:

Load boat at left, one individual at a time $(LBL)'$

For any individual x,

$(LBL)'$: $\alpha, at(b_k, p_L), at(x, p_L); (M_b+C_b \leqslant k-1) \rightarrow \alpha, at(b_k, p_L), on(x, b_k); \Lambda$

Move boat across the river from left to right $(MBLR)'$

$(MBLR)'$: $\alpha, at(b_k, p_L); (M_b+C_b>0) \rightarrow \alpha, at(b_k, p_R); \Lambda$

Unload boat at right, one individual at a time $(UBR)'$.

For any individual x,

$(UBR)'$: $\alpha, at(b_k, p_R), on(x, b_k); \Lambda \rightarrow \alpha, at(b_k, p_R)\ at(x, p_R); \Lambda$

In addition, we have the three following elementary actions in $\{(A)'\}_1$ 'Load boat at right one individual at a time $(LBR)'$', 'Move boat across the river from right to left $(MBRL)'$', and 'Unload boat at left one individual at a time $(UBL)'$'. The definitions of these actions are obtained from the previous definitions by substituting p_L for p_R and p_R for p_L in the corresponding actions. For example, the definition of $(MBRL)'$, is as follows:

$(MBRL)'$: $\alpha, at(b_k, p_R); (M_b+C_b>0) \rightarrow \alpha, at(b_k, p_L); \Lambda$

The six elementary actions that we have just introduced can be used together in certain sequences to form macro-actions for transfering *sets* of individuals from one river bank to the other. A transfer of r individuals from left to right, where $1 \leqq r \leqq k$; can be effected by a sequence

$$\underbrace{(LBL)', (LBL)', \ldots, (LBL)'}_{r \text{ times}}, (MBLR)', \underbrace{(UBR)', (UBR)', \ldots, (UBR)'}_{r \text{ times}} \tag{4.2}$$

This sequence of actions starts with an empty boat at left and ends with an empty boat at right.

We can view the sequence of elementary actions in (4.2) as a transfer macroaction that is composed of two parts: the first part consists of the initial loading sequence for the boat, or equivalently the unloading sequence for the place that is the origin of the transfer. The second part starts with the river crossing and is followed by an unloading sequence for the boat, or equivalently by the loading sequence for the place that is the destination of the transfer. Since the constraints of the problem are given in terms of the relative sizes of various sets of individuals at points that can be considered as ends of loading (or unloading) sequences, then it is reasonable to attempt the formulation of actions as transitions between such points. We use these considerations in the formulation of a set of feasible compound actions that are only sensitive to boat constraints.

$\{(A)'\}_2$: *Compound feasible actions in formulation F_2 that are sensitive to boat constraints,*

Load empty boat at left with r individuals, $1 \leqslant r \leqslant k$, $^r(L^rBL)'$.

Here we have a class of transition schemas that can be specified as follows:

For a set of r individuals $x_1, \ldots, x_r$, where $1 \leqq r \leqq k$,

$(L^rBL)'$: $\alpha, at(b_k, p_L), at(x_1, p_L), \ldots, at(x_r, p_L); (M_b+C_b=0) \rightarrow \alpha, at(b_k, p_L), on(x_1, b_k), \ldots, on(x_r, b_k); \Lambda$

In these transitions, r is the number of individuals from the left bank that board the boat for a crossing.

Move boat (loaded with r individuals) across the river from left to right and unload all its passengers at right $(MBLR+U^rBR)'$.

Here also we have a class of transition schemas which is defined as follows:

For a set of r individuals $x_1, \ldots, x_r$, $1 \leqslant r \leqslant k$,

$(MBLR+U^rBR)'$: $\alpha[e], at(b_k, p_L), on(x_1\ b_k), \ldots, on(x_r, b_k); \Lambda \rightarrow \alpha\ [e], at(b_k, p_R), at(x_1, p_R), \ldots, at(x_r, p_R); \Lambda$,

where $\alpha\ [e]$ stands for a configuration that is constrained by the condition e, which is as follows: no expression in the form *on* (y, b_k), for any individual y is included in α. This is a way of saying that, after the crossing, all the r

passengers that have initially boarded the boat in the left bank, have to leave the boat and join the population of the right bank.

In addition to the two compound actions defined above, we have the two following compound actions in $\{(A)'\}_2$: 'Load empty boat at right with r individuals, $(L'BR)'$,' and 'Move boat (loaded with r individuals) across the river from right to left and unload all its passengers at left $(MBRL+U'BL)$''. The definitions of these compound actions are obtained from the definitions for $(L'BL)'$ and $(MBLR+U'BR)'$ by substituting p_L for p_R and p_R for p_L in the corresponding compound actions.

The compound actions that we have just introduced define the feasible transitions between N-states that are constrained only by the conditions on the transportation facility. Consider now a restriction on these compound actions that provides a set of rules of action where consideration is given to all the constraints of the M&C problem.

$\{(A)\}_2$: *First set of rules of action in formulation* F_2.

$(L'BL)$.

For a set of r individuals $x_1, \ldots, x_r$, where $1 \leqslant r \leqslant k$,

$$(L'BL): \alpha, at(b_k, p_L), at(x_1, p_L), \ldots, at(x_r, p_L); (M_b+C_b=0) \rightarrow \alpha, at(b_k, p_L), on(x_1, b_k), \ldots, on(x_r, b_k); ((M_L=0) \vee (M_L \geqslant C_L)), ((M_b=0) \vee (M_b \geqslant C_b)).$$

These compound actions are a subset of the compound actions $(L'BL)'$, where a valid next N-state is such that if any missionaries remain in the left bank then their number is no smaller than the number of cannibals remaining there, and also if any missionaries board the boat, then their number is no smaller than the number of cannibals that have also boarded the boat. Note that if an individual, say a missionary, is aboard the boat and the boat is at p_L, then the individual is not considered as a member of $\{m\}_L$, and therefore he is not counted in M_L.

$(MBLR+U'BR)$.

For any r, where $1 \leqslant r \leqslant k$,

$$(MBLR+U'BR): \alpha\,[e], at(b_k, p_L), on(x_1, b_k), \ldots, on(x_r, b_k); \Lambda \rightarrow \alpha\,[e], at(b_k, p_R), at(x_1, p_R), \ldots, at(x_r, p_R), ((M_R=0) \vee (M_R \geqslant C_R)).$$

Here the restricted configuration $\alpha[e]$ has the same meaning as in $(MBLR+U'BR)'$. The present compound actions are a subset of $(MBLR+U'BR)'$, where a valid next N-state is such that if any missionaries are present in the right bank then their number is no smaller than the number of cannibals there.

In addition to the transitions $(L'BL)$ and $(MBLR+U'BR)$, we also have the two transitions $(L'BR)$ and $(MBRL+U'BL)$, that are obtained from the previous ones by appropriately interchanging the places p_L and p_R throughout the definitions.

With the formulation of the permissible transitions between N-states, it is now possible to specify a procedure for finding a schedule of transfers that would solve the general M&C problem. Each transfer from left to right will be realized by a sequence $(L'BL)$, $(MBLR+U'BR)$, and each transfer from right to left will be realized by a sequence $(L'BR)$, $(MBRL+U'BL)$. Essentially, the selection of compound actions for each transfer amounts to finding r-tuples of individuals from a river bank that could be transferred to the opposite bank in such a way that cannibalism can be avoided in the source bank, in the destination bank and in the boat; i.e. the *non-cannibalism conditions*

$$((M_L=0) \vee (M_L \geqslant C_L)), ((M_b=0) \vee (M_b \geqslant C_b)), ((M_R=0) \vee (M_R \geqslant C_R)) \quad (4.3)$$

are all satisfied at the end of each of the two compound actions that make a transfer.

The formulation of compound actions and of problem solving procedures can be simplified *via* the utilization of the following property of our problem:

Theorem. If at both the beginning and the end of a transfer the non-cannibalism conditions $((M_L=0) \vee (M_L \geqslant C_L))$ and $((M_R=0) \vee (M_R \geqslant C_R))$ are satisfied for the two river banks, then the non-cannibalism condition for the boat, i.e. $((M_b=0) \vee (M_b \geqslant C_b))$, is also satisfied.

Proof. At the beginning and the end of each transfer we have $M_L+M_R=C_L+C_R=N$; also, by supposition, the following two conditions hold simultaneously both at the beginning and at the end of a transfer:

$$(1)\ ((M_L=0) \vee (M_L=C_L) \vee (M_L>C_L)),$$
$$(2)\ ((N-M_L=0) \vee (N-M_L=N-C_L) \vee (N-M_L>N-C_L)). \quad (4.4)$$

The conjunction of the above two conditions is equivalent to the following condition:

$$(M_L=0) \vee (M_L=N) \vee (M_L=C_L). \quad (4.5)$$

But now in order to maintain this condition over a transfer, the boat can either carry a pure load of cannibals (to conserve $(M_L=0)$ or $(M_L=N)$) or a load with an equal number of missionaries and cannibals (to conserve $(M_L=C_L)$) or a load with a number of missionaries that exceeds the number of cannibals (for a transition from $(M_L=N)$ to $(M_L=C_L)$ or $(M_L=0)$, or a transition from $(M_L=C_L)$ to $(M_L=0)$). This conclusion is equivalent to asserting the non-cannibalism condition for the boat, i.e. $((M_b=0) \vee (M_b \geqslant C_b))$.

The previous theorem enables us to eliminate the non-cannibalism condition for the boat when we formulate permissible actions for realizing a transfer from one side of the river to the other. This permits the introduction of a single compound action per transfer. We can write then a new set of rules of action as follows:

$\{(A)\}_3$: *Second set of rules of action in formulation* F_2

Transfer safely a set of r individuals from left to right ($T'LR$).

For a set of r individuals $x_1, \ldots, x_r$, where $1 \leqslant r \leqslant k$,

$(T'LR)$: α, $at(b_k, p_L)$, $at(x_1, p_L)$, $\ldots$, $at(x_r, p_L)$; $(M_b + C_b = 0) \rightarrow$
α, $at(b_k, p_R)$, $at(x_1, p_R)$, $\ldots$, $at(x_r, p_R)$; $(M_b + C_b = 0)$,
$((M_L = 0) \vee (M_L \geqslant C_L))$, $((M_R = 0) \vee (M_R \geqslant C_R))$

Transfer safely a set of r individuals from right to left ($T'RL$).

The definition of this transfer action is obtained from ($T'LR$) by interchanging the places p_L and p_R throughout the definition.

It is clear that the formulation of the second set of rules of action has the effect of appreciably reducing the size of the N-state space that has to be searched, relative to the search space for the first set of rules of action. The transfers act as macro-actions, on basis of which the solution can be constructed without having to consider the fine structure of their component actions (loading the boat, unloading, crossing the river), thus without having to construct and consider intermediate N-states that are not needed for the key decisions that lead to the desired schedule.

Note that the reduction of the search space becomes possible because of the use of a formal property of our problem that enables the elimination of a redundant condition. The examination of the set of conditions of a problem, with the objective of identifying eliminable conditions and of reformulating accordingly the N-state space over which search proceeds, is one of the important approaches towards an increase in problem solving power.

5. FORMULATION F_3 OF THE M&C PROBLEM IN AN IMPROVED SYSTEM OF PRODUCTIONS

The notions that we have initially introduced in the description languages of the production systems of the previous sections reflect a general *a priori* approach to problems of reasoning about actions (i.e. consider as basic elements the individuals, the objects and the places that are specified in the problem, and consider as basic relations the elementary associations of individuals to places, etc), and also a problem-specific process of formulating concepts and attributes that are suggested from the verbal statement of the problem and that appear necessary for the expression of permissible transitions in the N-state space (notions such as M_L, C_L, etc. and the associated integers and arithmetic relations).

After several formulations of the problem, it becomes apparent that the description languages can be *restricted* and the formulation of N-states and of transitions between N-states can be considerably simplified. First, it is obvious that there is no need to use distinct individuals in the formulations. It suffices to use the compound elements, i.e. the sets $\{m\}_L$, $\{m\}_R$, $\{m\}_b$, $\{c\}_L$, $\{c\}_R$, $\{c\}_b$. Furthermore, since the conditions of the problem are expressed as arithmetic properties of the sizes of the compound elements, it suffices to consider the entities M_L, M_R, M_b, C_L, C_R, C_b, the set of integers $J_0{}^n$ and the arithmetic relations and operations. The main idea in this language restriction is that only those elements are to remain that are necessary for expressing the rules of action–that define the permissible transitions between N-states.

Because of the conservation of the total number of missionaries and the total number of cannibals throughout the transportation process, we have for each N-state (i.e. for each beginning and end of a transfer action) the following relationships:

$$M_L + M_R = C_L + C_R = N. \tag{5.1}$$

Thus, it is sufficient to consider explicitly either the set M_L, M_b, C_L, C_b or the set M_R, M_b, C_R, C_b; we choose to consider the former. Finally, we introduce two variables B_L, B_R in the restricted language such that

$$\begin{aligned} &at(b_k, p_L) \equiv (B_L = 1) \equiv (B_R = 0) \\ &at\,(b_k, p_R) \equiv (B_L = 0) \equiv (B_R = 1). \end{aligned} \tag{5.2}$$

In the restricted N-state language the basic description of an N-state has the form

$$(M_L = i_1),\ (C_L = i_2),\ (B_L = i_3),$$

where i_1, i_2 are integers from J_0^N, and i_3 is 1 or 0. Such a description can be abbreviated to take the form of a vector (M_L, C_L, B_L), whose components are the numerical values of the key variables. The vector description shows explicitly the situation at the left river bank. Thus, the initial N-state of the M&C problem–expressed in the abbreviated vector notation–is $(N,N,1)$, and the terminal N-state is $(0,0,0)$.

We can now express the rules of action as follows:

$\{(A)\}_4$: *Set of rules of action in Formulation* F_3.

Transfer safely a mix (M_b, C_b) *from left to right* (TLR, M_b, C_b).

Any pair (M_b, C_b) such that $1 \leqslant M_b + C_b \leqslant k$, specifies a feasible action; for each such pair, we have a transition:

(TLR, M_b, C_b): $(M_L, C_L, 1)$; $\Lambda \rightarrow (M_L - M_b, C_L - C_b, 0)$;
$((M_L - M_b = 0) \vee (M_L - M_b \geqslant C_L - C_b))$,
$((N - (M_L - M_b) = 0) \vee (N - (M_L - M_b) \geqslant N - (C_L - C_b)))$.

Here M_b, C_b are the number of missionaries and the number of cannibals respectively that are involved in the transfer.

Transfer safely a mix (M_b, C_b) *from right to left* (TRL, M_b, C_b).

Again, any pair (M_b, C_b) such that $1 \leqslant M_b + C_b \leqslant k$,
specifies a feasible action; for each such pair, we have a transition:

(TRL, M_b, C_b): $(M_L, C_L, 0)$; $\Lambda \rightarrow (M_L + M_b, C_L + C_b, 1)$;
$((M_L + M_b = 0) \vee (M_L + M_b \geqslant C_L + C_b))$,
$((N - (M_L + M_b) = 0) \vee (N - (M_L + M_b) \geqslant N - (C_L + C_b)))$.

The restriction of the N-state language, and the introduction of new basic descriptions for N-states and of new rules of transitions between N-states has a significant effect on the relative ease with which a solution of the M&C problem can be found. The irrelevant variety of transitions that is possible when individuals are considered, is now reduced to a meaningful variety that depends on the relative sizes of appropriately defined groups of individuals. In reasoning about the M&C problem, a completely different viewpoint can now be used. We do not have to think of individuals that are being run through a sequence of processes of loading the boat, moving the boat, etc. but we can concentrate on a sequence of vector additions and subtractions that obey certain special conditions and that should transform a given initial vector to a given terminal vector. The construction of a solution amounts to finding such a sequence of vector operations. The transition to the present formulation of the M&C problem illustrates an important process of improving a problem solving system by choosing an 'appropriate' N-state language and by using this language in an 'appropriate' way to define N-states and transitions between them.

6. FORMULATION F_4 OF THE M&C PROBLEM IN A REDUCTION SYSTEM

The previous formulations F_2 and F_3 of the M&C problem were in systems of productions. A solution to our problem in these systems amounts to finding the shortest schedule (or the shortest trajectory) from the intial N-state to the terminal N-state, if there exists a trajectory between these states (i.e. if there exists a solution at all). Note that this is a typical problem of derivation.

Let us formulate now the problem in a form that will permit us to specify a reduction procedure[1] for its solution. To specify the search space for the reduction procedure we need the notions of problem states (P-states) and the set of relevant moves – terminal and nonterminal. These notions correspond respectively to formulas, axioms and rules of inference in some natural inference system (Amarel, 1967).

P-states are expressions of the form $S=(s_a \Rightarrow s_b)$. In its logic interpretation, such an expression is a proposition that means 's_b is attainable from s_a'. Thus, it is equivalent to the logical notion CAN (s_a, s_b) that has been used by McCarthy (1963) and Black (1964) (in their formalization of problems of 'ordinary reasoning'), and that has been recently discussed by Newell (1966) and Simon (1966).

In the following, we consider the formulation F_3 in the improved system of productions as the starting point for the present formulation F_4. Thus, the initial P-state for the general M&C problem is

$$S_0=((N,N,1)\Rightarrow(0,0,0)). \qquad (6.1)$$

A relevant *nonterminal move* corresponds to the application of a permissible action at the left N-state of a P-state. Thus, given a P-state $S_i=(s_a \Rightarrow s_b)$, and a permissible action A that takes s_a to s_c, then the application of the action at s_a corresponds to the application of a move (call it A also) that reduces S_i to the P-state $S_j=(s_c \Rightarrow s_b)$. We can represent such a move application as follows:

$$\begin{array}{l} S_i=(s_a \Rightarrow s_b) \\ \quad \updownarrow A \text{ (a permissible action that takes } s_a \text{ to } s_c) \\ S_j=(s_c \Rightarrow s_b) \end{array}$$

In the logic interpretation, such a move corresponds to the inference 'S_j implies S_i' (this is the reason for the direction of the arrows). In other words, 'if s_b is attainable from s_c, then s_b is also attainable from s_a (because s_c is known to be attainable from s_a)'.

A terminal move in the present formulation, is a move that recognizes that the left and right sides of a P-state are identical; we call it M_t. Logically, such a move corresponds to the application of an axiom scheme for validation in the natural inference system.

A solution is a sequence of P-states, attained by successive applications of nonterminal moves, starting from the initial state and ending in a state where the terminal move applies. In the logic interpretation, a solution is a proof that the initial P-state is valid, i.e. that the terminal N-state is attainable from the initial N-state. From a solution in the reduction system, it is straightforward to attain a trajectory in the system of productions or the schedule of actions that is associated with such a trajectory.

7. THE SEARCH FOR SOLUTION IN THE REDUCTION SYSTEM

A simple search process by successive reductions can be used to obtain the solution. All relevant nonterminal moves are taken from a P-state. If a new P-state is obtained which is identical to a parent P-state in the search tree, then the development below that P-state stops. This guarantees the attainment of a simplest schedule if one exists and it provides a basis for a decision procedure, i.e. if all possible lines of development from the initial P-state are stopped, then no solution exists.

The search graphs for the cases ($N=3$, $k=2$) and ($N=5$, $k=3$) are shown in figure 7.1. These are condensations of search trees that are obtained by retaining only one copy of a P-state and its continuations. For simplicity, except for the initial and terminal P-states, all the P-states are represented by their left N-states (they all share the same right side; i.e. the desired terminal

[1] We have studied previously reduction procedures in the context of theorem-proving problems (Amarel, 1967) and syntactic analysis problems (Amarel, 1965). In these cases, the initial formulation of the problem was assumed to be in a system of productions. However, in the M&C problem, a formulation in a system of productions is a derived formulation that results from the translation of an initial verbal formulation.

N-state). The branches of the graphs represent move applications. The arrows indicate the direction of transfer actions for move applications. A solution is indicated in figure 7.1 a path in heavy lines. The schedule associated with a solution path is shown at the left of each graph as a sequence of transfer actions. Thus one (of the four possible) optional schedules for the elementary M&C problem (N=3, $k=2$) reads as follows:

(1) Transfer two cannibals from left to right.
(2) Transfer back one cannibal to the left.
⋮
(6) Transfer one missionary and one cannibal from right to left.
⋮
(11) Transfer two cannibals from left to right.

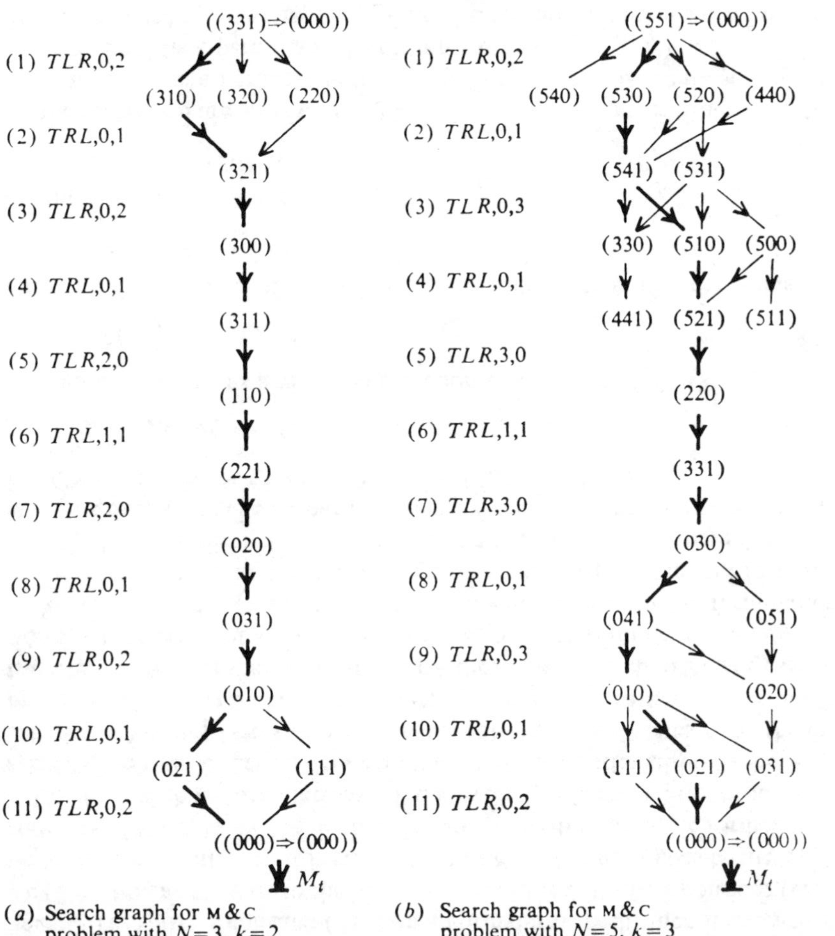

(*a*) Search graph for M&C problem with $N=3$, $k=2$

(*b*) Search graph for M&C problem with $N=5$, $k=3$

Figure 7.1. Search graphs for M & C problems in formulation F_4

In each case shown in figure 7.1 there is more than one solution. However, it is interesting to note that even if there is a certain amount of variety at the ends of the solution paths, the central part of the path has no variety (in the cases presented here, the center of the path is unique, in some other cases there may be two alternatives at the graph's neck, as we shall see in a subsequent example for $N=4$, $k=3$).

It should be evident from these search graphs that the M&C problem is a relatively simple problem that can be easily handled in an exhaustive search with a procedure of reduction type. There is no need for heuristics and complex rules for selecting moves and organizing the search. It is noteworthy that such a problem, while easily handled by computer procedures, is a relatively difficult problem for people. If one's approach is to try alternative sequences in some systematic manner (the computer approach that was just described) he becomes quickly memory limited. Also, people tend not to consider moves that, even though applicable to a situation, appear to be *a priori* bad moves on basis of some gross criterion of progress. In the elementary M&C problem, the sixth move in the schedule is such a stumbling block–yet it is the only move applicable.

Because of the one-sided development of the solution (from the initial N-state forward in time), and because of the exhaustiveness of the search, the process of searching for a solution would be the same if a reduction procedure (as described here) or a *generation procedure*, based directly on the formulation F_3, were used. In a generation procedure, all the sequences of N-states that are attainable from the initial N-state are constructed. The system is actually made to run over its permissible trajectories. The reduction approach was introduced at this stage, in order to show the equivalence between the generational approach (where the system is made to run between two given points) and the reductionist-logical approach (where essentially a proof is constructed that a trajectory exists between the two given points). While the reduction-logical approach has no advantage over the generational approach in the present formulation, there are cases where such an approach is especially useful. For example, in the next stage of formulation of the M&C problem it is convenient and quite natural to develop the approach to solution *via* a reduction procedure and its associated logical interpretation.

8. DISCOVERY AND UTILIZATION OF SYMMETRIES IN THE SEARCH SPACE. FORMULATION F_5 OF THE M&C PROBLEM

From an analysis of the search graphs for M&C problems (such as those in figure 7.1), it becomes apparent that the situation in search space is *symmetric with respect to time reversal.* Roughly, if we run a movie of a schedule of transportations forwards or backwards, we can't tell the difference. Consider two N-states (M_L,C_L,B_L) and $(N\text{-}M_L,N\text{-}C_L,1\text{-}B_L)$ in N-state space. When the space is viewed from the vantage point of each N-state in this pair, it appears identical, provided that the direction of transitions is 'perceived' by one N-

state as opposite to the direction 'perceived' by the other N-state. For example, consider the points (311) and (020) in the elementary M&C problem (see figure 7.1(a)). If we consider (311) on a normal time path, then it is reached *via* $(TRL,0,1)$ and it goes to the next state *via* $(TLR,2,0)$; if we consider (020) under time reversal, then it is reached *via* $(TRL,0,1)$ and it goes to the 'next' state *via* $(TLR,2,0)$. We shall consider now this situation more formally.

In our previous formulations of the M&C problem within production systems, the rules of action define a relation of direct attainability T between successive N-states (see section 2). Thus, for any two N-states s_a, s_b, the expression $s_a T s_b$ asserts that the N-state s_a occurs just earlier than s_b on a trajectory in N-state space. Consider now the converse relation $\check{T}$. The expression $s_a \check{T} s_b$ asserts that s_a occurs *just after* s_b on a trajectory.

We shall consider specifically in the following discussion the formulation of the M&C problem in the improved system of productions, i.e., the formulation F_3. Let σ be the space of N-states, partly ordered under the relation T, and $\check{\sigma}$ its dual space (i.e., $\check{\sigma}$ has the same elements of σ, partly ordered under $\check{T}$). Consider now the following mapping θ between N-states:

$$\theta\colon (M_L, C_L, B_L) \rightarrow (N\text{-}M_L, N\text{-}C_L, 1\text{-}B_L) \tag{8.1}$$

We can also write θ as a vector subtraction operation as follows:

$$\theta(s) = (N,N,1) - s. \tag{8.2}$$

Theorem. For any pair of N-states s_a, s_b the following equivalence holds:

$$s_a T s_b \equiv \theta(s_a)\, \check{T}\, \theta(s_b),$$

or equivalently

$$s_a T s_b \equiv \theta(s_b)\, T\, \theta(s_a);$$

i.e. the spaces σ, $\check{\sigma}$ are anti-isomorphic under the mapping θ. Furthermore, the move that effects a permissible transition from s_a to s_b is identical with the move that effects a permissible transition from $\theta(s_b)$ to $\theta(s_a)$.

Proof. Consider any permissible N-state (i.e. the non-cannibalism conditions are satisfied at this state) with the boat at left; suppose that this N-state is described by the vector $s_a = (M_L, C_L, 1)$. Corresponding to s_a we have an N-state described by $\theta(s_a) = (N\text{-}M_L, N\text{-}C_L, 0)$. Note that, in general, the non-cannibalism conditions (stated in (4.4)) are invariant under θ. Thus, the N-state described by $\theta(s_a)$ is also permissible. We can also write in vector notation,

$$\theta(s_a) = (N,N,1) - s_a. \tag{8.3}$$

Consider now a transition from left to right at s_a, defined by some pair (M_b, C_b) such that $1 \leqslant M_b + C_b \leqslant k$. A transition of ths type is always *a priori* possible if $M_L + C_L \neq 0$ in s_a (i.e. if there is *somebody* at left when the boat is there–a condition which we are obviously assuming); however the *a priori* possible transition is not necessarily permissible–in the sense of satisfying the non-cannibalism conditions at the resulting N-state. The transition defined by (M_b, C_b) yields a new vector s_b that is related to s_a by vector subtraction as follows:

$$s_b = s_a - (M_b, C_b, 1). \tag{8.4}$$

This can be verified by examining the rules of action. Corresponding to s_b we have via the mapping θ,

$$\begin{aligned}\theta(s_b) &= (N,N,1) - s_b = (N,N,1) - s_a + (M_b, C_b, 1)\\ &= \theta(s_a) + (M_b, C_b, 1).\end{aligned} \tag{8.5}$$

Suppose first that s_b is permissible (which means that the move defined by the pair (M_b, C_b) is permissible, and the relation $s_a\, T\, s_b$ holds); then $\theta(s_b)$ is also permissible because of the invariance of the non-cannibalism conditions under θ. Now in the N-state described by $\theta(s_b)$ the boat is at left and a left to right transition defined by (M_b, C_b) is possible (in view of (8.5) and noting that the components of $\theta(s_a)$ cannot be negative). This transition yields a vector $\theta(s_b) - (M_b, C_b, 1)$, which is identical with $\theta(s_a)$. Since $\theta(s_a)$ is permissible, then the transition defined by (M_b, C_b) (which takes $\theta(s_b)$ to $\theta(s_a)$) is permissible, and the relation $\theta(s_b)\, T\, \theta(s_a)$ holds. It is inherent in this argument that the same move that takes s_a to s_b, also takes $\theta(s_b)$ to $\theta(s_a)$.

Suppose now that s_b is not permissible (which means that the relation $s_a\, T\, s_b$ does not hold); then $\theta(s_b)$ is not permissible either, and the relation $\theta(s_b)\, T\, \theta(s_a)$ does not hold.

A similar argument can be developed for a right to left transition. This establishes the anti-isomorphism and the relationship between symmetric moves.

The situation can be represented diagramatically as follows:

$$\begin{array}{ccc} & \theta & \\ s_a & \longrightarrow\!\!\longrightarrow\!\!\longrightarrow & \theta(s_a) \\ T\downarrow & \theta & T\uparrow\,\downarrow\check{T} \\ s_b & \longrightarrow\!\!\longrightarrow\!\!\longrightarrow & \theta(s_b) \end{array} \tag{8.7}$$

Corollary. For any pair of N-states s_a, s_b, the following equivalence holds:

$$(s_a \Rightarrow s_b) \equiv (\theta(s_b) \Rightarrow \theta(s_a)).$$

The proof is an extension of the previous proof.

The recognition of the anti-isomorphism permits us to approach the problem simultaneously, and in a relatively simple manner, both in the space σ and in its dual space. The reasoning behind this dual approach relies on the logical properties of the attainability relation $\Rightarrow$, and on the properties of the anti-isomorphism.

Consider an attainability relation $(s_0 \Rightarrow s_b)$, where s_0 is the initial N-state and s_b is an arbitrary N-state such that $s_b \neq s_0$. Let us denote by $\{s_1\}$ the set of all N-states that are directly attainable from s_0; thus

$$\{s_1\} = \{s | s_0 T s \text{ holds}\}. \tag{8.8}$$

We have then

$$(s_0 \Rightarrow s_b) \equiv \bigvee_{s \in \{s_1\}} (s \Rightarrow s_b). \tag{8.9}$$

If $s_b = s_t$, where s_t is the desired terminal N-state, then we have as a special case of (8.9),

$$(s_0 \Rightarrow s_t) \equiv \bigvee_{s \in \{s_1\}} (s \Rightarrow s_t). \tag{8.10}$$

From the previous corollary, and since $\theta(s_t) = s_0$ in the M&C problem, we can write the equivalence (8.10) as follows:

$$(s_0 \Rightarrow s_t) \equiv \bigvee_{s \in \{s_1\}} (s_0 \Rightarrow \theta(s)). \tag{8.11}$$

By using (8.9) in (8.11) we obtain:

$$(s_0 \Rightarrow s_t) \equiv \bigvee_{s_i \in \{s_1\}} \Big(\bigvee_{s_j \in \{s_1\}} (s_j \Rightarrow \theta(s_i)) \Big). \tag{8.12}$$

The situation can be shown schematically as follows:

$$\begin{array}{ccc} s_0 & \Rightarrow & s_t \\ T \swarrow \swarrow \downarrow & & \nearrow \uparrow \nwarrow T \\ \{s_1\} = \{s_{1,1}\ s_{1,2}\ \ldots\ s_{1,n}\} & & \theta\{s_1\} = \{\theta(s_{1,1})\ \theta(s_{1,2})\ \ldots\ \theta(s_{1,n})\} \\ & \text{find link} & \end{array} \tag{8.13}$$

The terminal N-state s_t is attainable from s_0 if and only if any of the N-states from which s_t is directly attainable is itself attainable from any N-state that is directly attainable from s_0.

Now for each growth below $s_{1,i} \epsilon \{s_1\}$, there is a corresponding *image growth* below $\theta(s_{1,i})$. Let us denote the set of all N-states that are directly attainable from elements of $\{s_1\}$ by $\{s_2\}$; thus

$$\{s_2\} = \{s | s_a \in \{s_1\},\ s_a T s \text{ holds}\}. \tag{8.14}$$

Let us call the image of $\{s_2\}$ under θ, $\theta\{s_2\}$. Repeating the previous argument we obtain that s_t is attainable from s_0 if and only if any of the N-states in $\theta\{s_2\}$ is attainable from any of the N-states in $\{s_2\}$. This type of argument can be continued until either a set $\{s_n\}$ at some level n does not have any new progeny, or an N-state in $\theta\{s_n\}$ is directly attainable from an N-state in $\{s_n\}$.

From the preceding discussion, it is clear that we can develop the search for solution simultaneously, both forward from the initial N-state and backward from the terminal N-state, without having to spend search effort in both sides. Only the sets $\{s_1\}, \{s_2\}, \ldots \{s_n\}$, that represent the forward exploration of the search space from the initial N-state, have to be constructed. The exploration from the terminal N-state backwards is directly obtainable as the image of the forward exploration under time reversal (i.e. under the anti-isomorphism). This means that the knowledge of the symmetry property permits us to cut the depth of search by a factor of two – which is a substantial reduction in expected search effort. Note, however, that as is the case in any two-sided approach to search, new problems of coordination and recognition arise because of the need to find links between the forward moving search front and its backward moving image. In our present problem, because of the relative narrowness of the moving fronts, this problem of recognizing a linking possibility is not too difficult.

Let us formulate now a reduction procedure for carrying out the two-sided solution construction activity that we have just described. We introduce here a broader concept of a problem state, the *total P-state*, Σ:

$$\Sigma_i = (\{s_i\} \Rightarrow \theta\{s_i\}),\ i = 0,1,2, \ldots$$

where i indicates the number of transitions from one of the schedule terminals (initial or terminal N-state) and the current total P-state. In its logic interpretation, an expression Σ_i stands for the proposition 'there exists an N-state in $\{s_i\}$ from which some N-state in $\theta\{s_i\}$ is attainable'.

A *nonterminal move* in the present formulation is a broader notion than a nonterminal move in our previous reduction procedure. Here, a nonterminal move effects a transition between Σ_i and Σ_{i+1} in such a manner that $\Sigma_i \equiv \Sigma_{i+1}$. Such a move represents a combination of parallel transfers, half of which are source-based and they are found by direct search, and the other half are destination-based and they are computed on basis of the symmetry property.

A *terminal move* in the present formulation establishes links between N-states in $\{s_i\}$ and N-states in $\theta\{s_i\}$ that are directly attainable from them.

A *solution* (or correspondingly an attainability proof) has the form of a chain of total P-states that start with $\Sigma_0 = (s_0 \Rightarrow s_t)$ and that ends with a total P-state Σ_n where a terminal move applies. A trajectory (or a schedule) is obtained from this solution by tracing a sequence of N-states that starts with s_0; it is followed by a directly attainable N-state in $\{s_1\}$; it continues this way up to $\{s_n\}$, and then it goes to $\theta\{s_n\}, \theta\{s_{n-1}\}, \ldots$ up to $\theta(s_0) = s_t$.

The development of the solution for the elementary M&C problem in the present formulation is shown in figure 8.1.

The total P-state Σ_5 is valid because there is a link (*via TRL*, 1,1) between 110 and 221. The darkened path shows a solution trajectory. The schedule associated with the trajectory is given at left. The same transfer actions apply at points of the trajectory that are equidistant from the terminals. Thus, in the

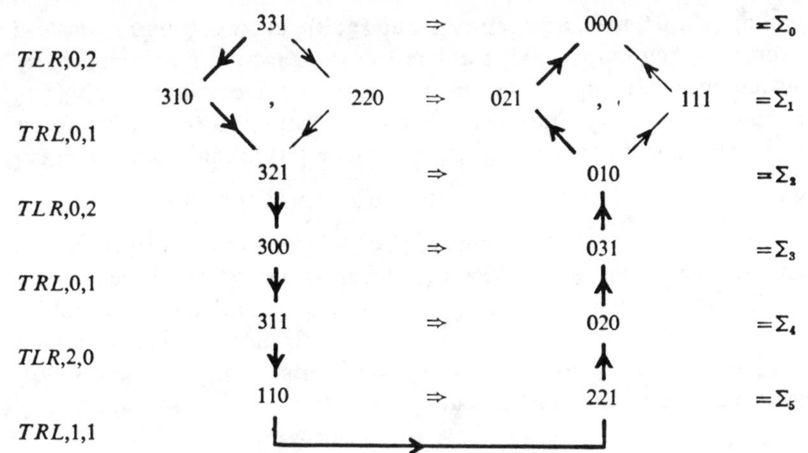

Figure 8.1. Search graph for the elementary M & C problem in the formulation F_5

present case, we have a schedule which is symmetrical with respect to its middle point. Note that the solution development given in figure 8.1 is a folded version of the solution development which is given in figure 7.1(a).

It is of interest to develop the solution for the case $N=4$, $k=3$ within the present formulation; this is given next in figure 8.2.

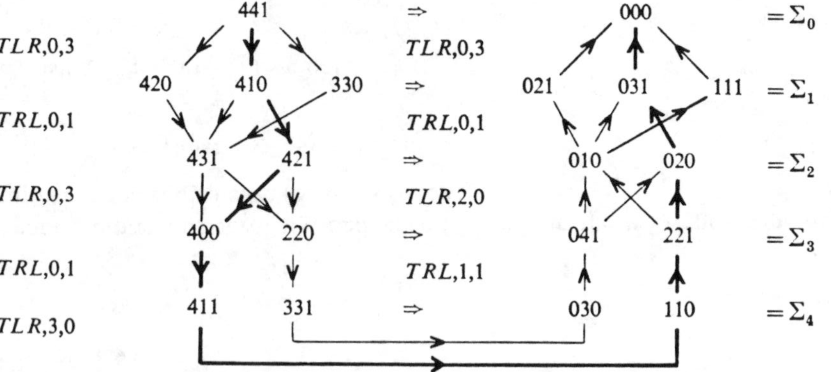

Figure 8.2. Search graph for the M & C problem ($N=4$, $k=3$) in the formulation F_5

The total P-state Σ_4 is valid, since a terminal move composed of two links applies at Σ_4. The darkened path in figure 8.2 shows one solution trajectory. The schedule associated with the trajectory is shown in the sides of the solution graph. Note that in the present case the trajectory is not symmetrical. While the two halves of the search graph are images of each other under θ, the two halves of a trajectory are not. Roughly the situation is as follows: Two main sequences of N-states grow from each of the two sides; these two sequences are images of each other under θ; a solution trajectory starts with one of these sequences from the one side, and then at its middle point, rather than continuing with the image of the initial sequence, it flips over to the image of the second sequence.

In the present formulation, it is possible again to develop a solution *via* a generation procedure that would operate in an equivalent manner to the reduction procedure that we have described here. However, the direct correspondence between the logic of the solution and the elements of the reduction procedure make the latter more convenient to use.

9. DISCOVERY OF SOLUTION PATTERNS IN AN APPROPRIATE REPRESENTATION OF N-STATE SPACE

One of the significant ways of increasing the power of a problem solving system for the M & C problem is to look for some characteristic patterns in its search space that go beyond the properties that we have discussed so far. To this end, it is extremely important to find a representation of the search space that enables a global view of the situation, so that reasoning about a solution can first proceed in broad terms and it can then be followed by the detailed scheduling of actions. We shall present next such a representation of the space of N-states. This representation utilizes the basic description of N-states that was introduced in the formulation F_3 of the M & C problem.

The number of possible N-states for an M & C problem equals the number of possible valuations of the vector (M_L, C_L, B_L); this number is $2(N+1)^2$. We represent the space of N-states by a limited fragment of three-dimensional space with coordinates M_L, C_L and B_L. This fragment consists of two parallel square arrays of points, that are disposed as follows: One array is on the plane $B_L=0$ and the other on the plane $B_L=1$; the points on each array have coordinates (M_L, C_L), where the values of M_L, C_L are 0, 1, 2, . . ., N. Thus, each point corresponds to a possible N-state. Such a representation for the N-state space of the elementary M & C problem is shown in figure 9.1. The blackened points stand for non-permissible N-states (i.e. the non-cannibalism conditions are violated in them). The feasible transitions from an N-state s in a given B_L plane to other N-states in the same plane are shown in figure 9.2. These feasible transitions reflect mainly boat capacity. A feasible transition is not permissible if it leads to a non-permissible N-state. Thus, starting from an N-state in the $B_L=1$ plane, a transition can be made to any permissible point within a 'distance' of 2 lattice steps in the plane, in a general southwestern direction; after the movement in the plane is carried out (it represents 'load-in the boat' at left) a left-to-right transfer action is completed by jumping from the $B_L=1$ array to the $B_L=0$ array in a direction parallel to the B_L axis. A right-to-left transfer starts from an N-state in the $B_L=0$ plane; a transition is first made to a permissible point within a 'distance' of 2 lattice steps in the plane, in a general northeastern direction; after this transition, the transfer is completed by jumping across to the $B_L=1$ array.

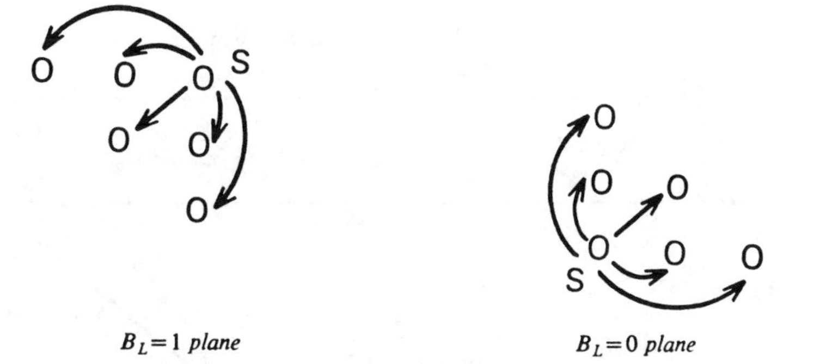

Figure 9.1 Feasible transitions in space of N-states

A solution for the elementary M & C problem is shown in figure 9.1 as a path in N-state space. It is suggestive to regard the solution path as a thread entering the initial N-state, leaving the terminal N-state, and woven in a specific pattern of loops that avoids going through the non-permissible points in N-space. Furthermore, the solution shown in figure 9.1 requires the 'least

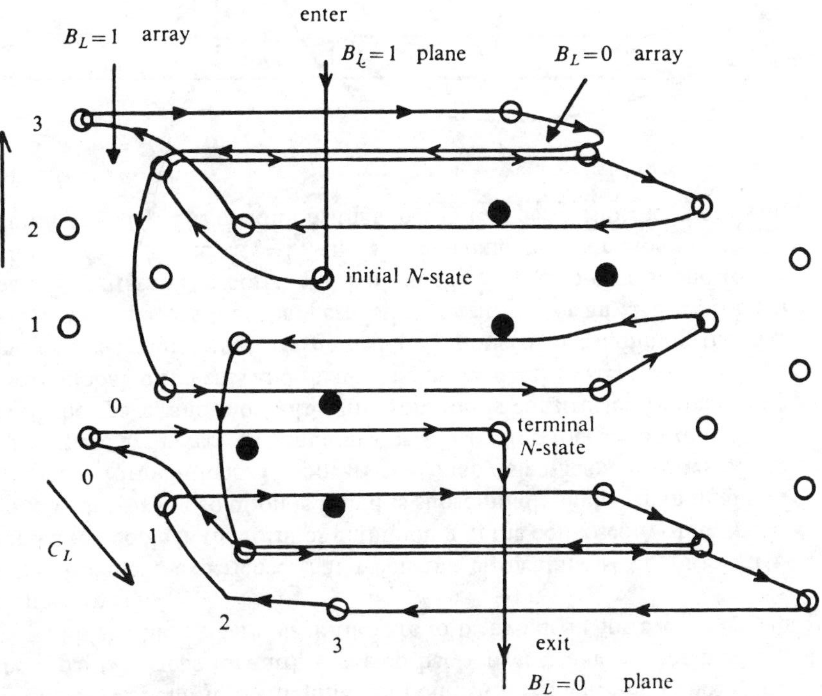

Figure 9.2. Space of N-states for elementary M & C problem

amount of thread' to go from the initial N-state to the terminal N-state within the imposed constraints in the weaving pattern. It is easy to see that the solution trajectory shown in figure 9.2 is the same as the solution shown in figure 7.1(a).

We can simplify the representation of N-state space by collapsing it into a single square array of $(N+1)^2$ points (figure 9.3). This requires a more complex specification of the possible transitions. We represent a left-to-right transfer by an arrow with a black arrowhead, and a right-to-left transfer by an arrow with a white arrowhead. In the previous two-array representation, a black arrow corresponds to a movement in the $B_L=1$ plane that is followed by a jump across planes, and a white arrow corresponds to a movement in the $B_L=0$ plane followed by a jump across planes. A point in the collapsed space is given by two coordinates (M_L,C_L), and it can represent either of the two N-states $(M_L, C_L, 1)$ or $(M_L, C_L, 0)$. The point (M_L, C_L) in association with an entering black arrowhead represents $(M_L,C_L,0)$; in association with an entering white arrowhead, it represents $(M_L,C_L,1)$. A sequence of two arrows →‒▷ represents a round trip left-right-left. A sequence of arrows, with alternating arrowhead types, that starts at the initial point (N,N) and ends at the terminal point (0,0) represents a solution to the M & C problem.

The collapsed N-state space for the elementary M & C problem is shown in figure 9.3. The solution path shown in this figure represents the same solution

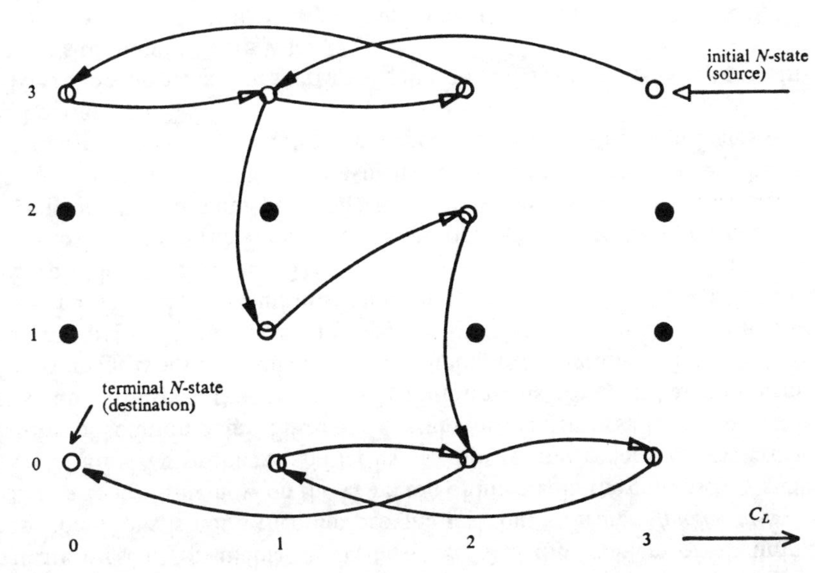

Figure 9.3. Collapsed N-space for elementary M & C problem

that is shown (in different forms) in the figures 7.1(*a*) and 9.2. The solution path in the collapsed *N*-state space suggests a general movement forward from the source point to the destination point by a sequence of 'dance steps' of the type 'two steps forward, one step back' over a dance floor made of white and black tiles, where black tiles are to be avoided (however, they can be skipped over).

It has been our experience that when the elementary M&C problem is presented to people in the form of pathfinding in the collapsed *N*-state space, the ease with which a solution is found is substantially higher than in any of the previous formulations. It appears that many significant features of the solution space are perceived simultaneously, attention focuses on the critical parts of the space, and most often the solution is constructed by reasoning first with global arguments and then filling in the detailed steps.

One of the features that are immediately noticed in examining the collapsed *N*-state space is that the 'permissible territory' for any M&C problem forms a **Z** pattern. The horizontal bars of the **Z** region correspond to the conditions $M_L=N$ and $M_L=0$, and the diagonal line corresponds to the condition $M_L=C_L$. The conditions that specify the 'permissible territory' can

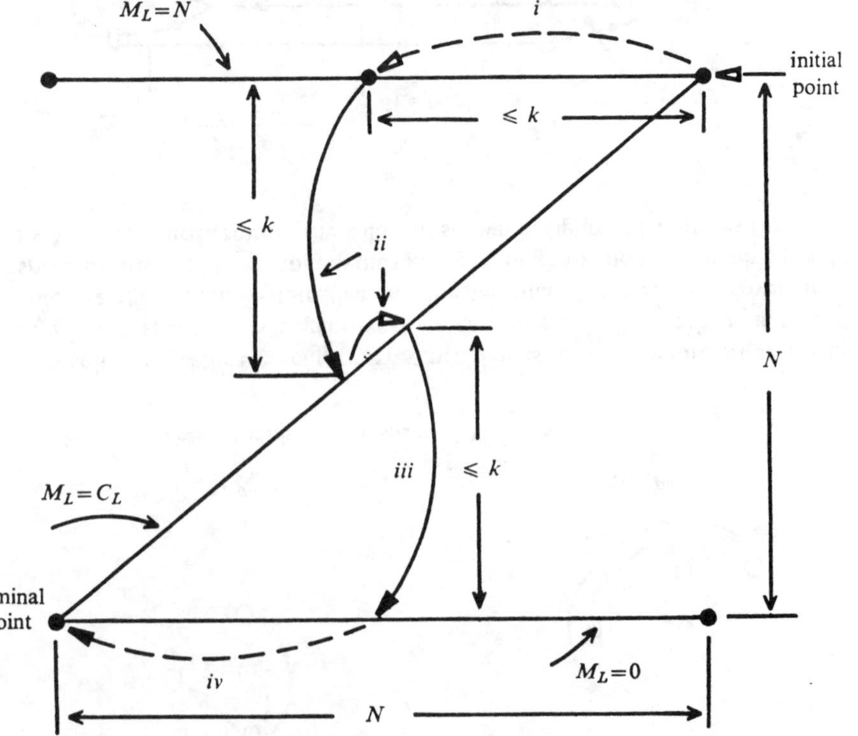

Figure 9.4. The 'permissible territory' in the M & C problem

be obtained directly as consequences of the problem constraints; we have used them in the proof of the eliminability of the 'boat condition' in section 4, and it is conceivable that they could be derived mechanically with techniques that are presently available. Note, however, that the problem of obtaining these conditions is not a theorem proving task but a *theorem finding task*.

Let us concentrate now on the **Z** region of interest in the collapsed *N*-state space of an M&C problem, and let us attempt to find general characteristic features of solution paths. Since the **Z** region is the permissible territory, it is reasonable to expect that features of solution paths are describable in terms of movement types over this **Z**. By examining the diagram in figure 9·4 we shall try first to identify certain properties of solution paths that will permit us to characterize the solution schema that we have used in the elementary M&C problem (see figure 9.3).

In the diagram of the **Z** region, this solution schema can be seen to consist in general of four main parts, (i) to (iv). An arrow ◁– – – denotes a sequence of transitions the last of which brings the boat to the left river bank, and an arrow ◀– – – denotes a sequence of transitions that terminates with the boat at right.

The following general properties of solution paths are suggested by examining the situation in figure 9.4:

(i) On the $M_L=N$ line, any of the points $(N, x, 1)$, where $1<x<N$, are attainable from the initial point $(N,N,1)$ by a 'horizontal' sequence of transitions of the following type:

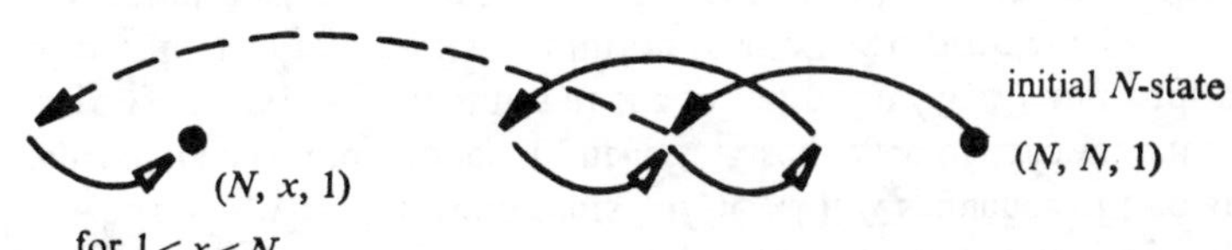

More generally, any point $(N, x, 1)$, where $1\leqslant x\leqslant N$, can be attained from any other point $(N, y, 1)$, where $1\leqslant y\leqslant N$, by some 'horizontal' sequence of transitions that is similar to the one just shown. Roughly, this indicates that 'horizontal' movements over the $M_L=N$ line are *easily achievable* by a known routine of steps.

(ii) If k is the boat capacity, and if $k\geqslant 2$, then any of the points $(N, N-x, 1)$, where $0<x\leqslant k$, can reach, *via* a single transition $(TLR, x, 0)$, a point $(N-x, N-x, 0)$ on the diagonal of the **Z** region. From this point, a $(TRL, 1, 1)$ transition can lead to a point $(N-x+1, N-x+1, 1)$ on the diagonal. While the first transition in this pair determines the size of the 'jump' from the $M_L=N$ line to the diagonal, the second transition is necessary for

'remaining' on the diagonal. Thus, we can regard this pair of transitions as a way of achieving a 'stable jump' from the line $M_L=N$ to the diagonal. It is clear from this discussion that a boat capacity of at least two is necessary for realizing a 'stable jump'. Note that the second transition in the pair corresponds to the critical move of returning one missionary and one cannibal–in general, an equal number of missionaries and cannibals–to the left, in mid schedule. As we have observed before, this is an unlikely move choice if the problem solver has a general notion of progress that guides his move preferences uniformly over all parts of the solution space. Only after knowing the local structure of this space, is it possible to see immediately the inevitability of this move. Now, the remotest point of the diagonal (from the initial point) that can be reached by this pair of transitions is $(N-k+1, N-k+1, 1)$.

(iii) A point on the diagonal can directly attain a point on the line $M_L=0$ if its distance from that line does not exceed k. Thus, to move from the $M_L=N$ line to the $M_L=0$ line in two 'jumps', by using the diagonal as an intermediate support, we need a boat capacity that satisfies the following condition:

$$k \geqslant \frac{N+1}{2}. \tag{9.1}$$

(Thus, for $N=5$ and $k=2$ there is no solution. This specific result could have been obtained in any of our previous formulations by recognizing that a definite dead end is attained in the course of searching for a solution. However, it is obtained much more directly from our present analysis; furthermore, we can easily assign the reason for the unsolvability to the low capacity of the boat.)

(iv) On the $M_L=0$ line, any of the points to the right of the terminal point, can reach the terminal point (0,0,0) by a 'horizontal' sequence of transitions of the type shown in (i). More generally, any point $(0,x,0)$, where $0 \leqslant x < N$, can be attained from any other point $(0,y,0)$, where $0 \leqslant y < N$, by some 'horizontal' sequence of transitions. Again, this indicates roughly that 'horizontal' movement over the $M_L=0$ line are easily achieved by a known routine of steps.

From the general properties just discussed we can characterize a general solution pattern, which we call the *zig-zag pattern*, by the following sequence of global actions: (i) starting from the initial point, slide on the $M_L=N$ line, over a 'horizontal' transition sequence, up to the point $(N, N-k, 1)$; (ii) jump on the diagonal, *via* two transitions, to the point $(N-k+1, N-k+1, 1)$; (iii) jump off the diagonal to the $M_L=0$ line; (iv) slide on the $M_L=0$ line, *via* a 'horizontal' transition sequence, to the terminal point.

It can be easily verified that the solutions to the three cases that we have presented previously, i.e. $(N=3, k=2)$, $(N=4, k=3)$ and $(N=5, k=3)$, follow precisely the zig-zag pattern that we have outlined. If $N=6$, then in order to use the present solution scheme, a boat of capacity 4 is needed (see the condition (9.1)). When a boat capacity of 4 (or more) is available, then *any* M & C problem is solvable. This property is due to the fact that the following pattern of transitions, that allows one 'to slide along the diagonal', is possible when $k \geqslant 4$:

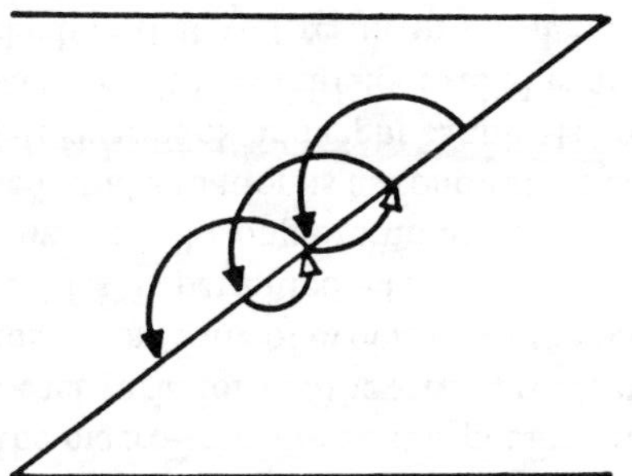

The 'sliding along the diagonal' for $k=4$ is realized by a 'diagonal' sequence of round trips of the type: $(TLR, 2, 2), (TRL, 1, 1), (TLR, 2, 2), (TRL, 1, 1)$, etc., where each round trip realizes a net transfer of two individuals from left to right.

For cases with $k \geqslant 4$ it is possible to use a simple and efficient solution pattern, the *diagonal pattern*, that has a single global action, as follows: starting from the initial point slide down the diagonal via a 'diagonal' transition sequence that takes in each round trip $\frac{k}{2}$ missionaries and $\frac{k}{2}$ cannibals to the right (when k is even–otherwise it takes $\frac{k-1}{2}$ of each) and it returns one missionary and one cannibal back, except in the last trip, until the terminal point is reached. It is also possible to construct solution patterns that combine parts of the zig-zag pattern with parts of the diagonal pattern. Such a combined solution scheme is shown in figure 9.5.

For the M & C problem (i.e. find a path from $(N,N,1)$ to $(0,0,0)$), it can be shown that if the boat capacity k is high, and if k is even, then the pure diagonal pattern of solution is always better than any combined pattern (in terms of number of trips required for a schedule); if k is odd, then there are cases where a small advantage is gained by starting the schedule with the first two round trips of the zig-zag pattern; if $k=4$, and $N \geqslant 6$, then the diagonal solution pattern, the zig-zag pattern or the combined pattern of figure 9.5, when it applies, are all of equivalent quality.

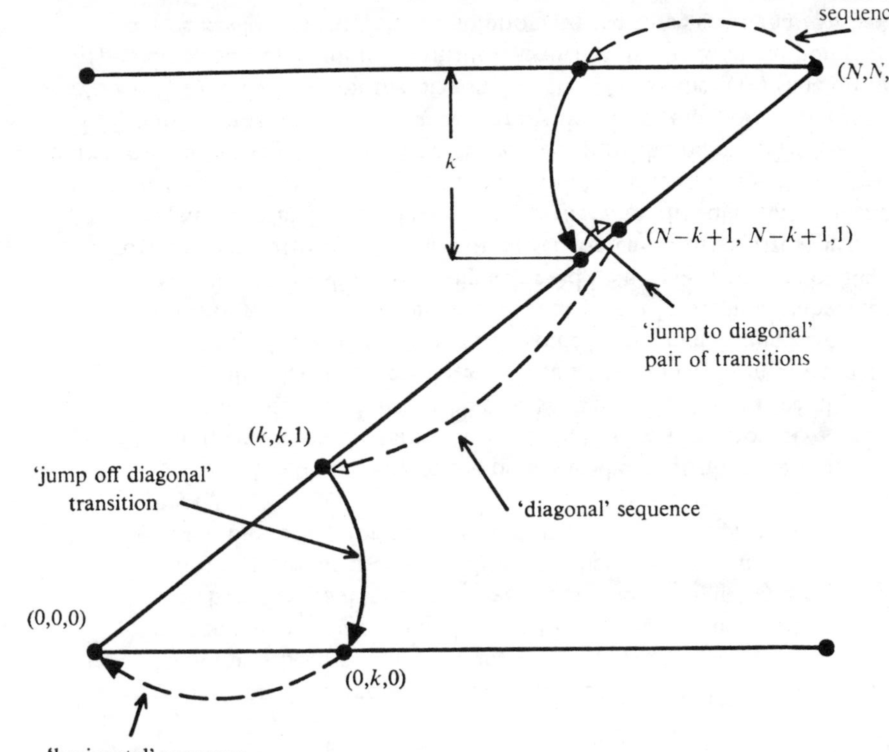

Figure 9.5. Combined scheme of solution shown on the Z region

10. FORMULATION F_6 OF EXTENDED M&C PROBLEM IN A MUCH IMPROVED PRODUCTION SYSTEM THAT CORRESPONDS TO A HIGHER LEVEL SEARCH SPACE

After the exploration of solution patterns in our array representation of N-state space, and after new global transition concepts are developed, it is possible to re-formulate the M&C problem (in fact, an extended version of this problem) in a new and much improved system of productions to which there corresponds an N-state space that has many fewer points than in any of the previous spaces.

From the analysis of possible global movements in the N-state space, we can now formulate the following set of *macro-transitions*:

$\{(A)\}_6$: *set of rules of (macro) action in formulation* F_6.

$$\begin{aligned}
&(H_1): (N,C_L,1);\ 0<C_L<N,\ k\geqslant 2\rightarrow(N,N,1)\\
&(H_1,J_1): (N,C_L,1);\ 0<C_L\leqslant N,\ k\geqslant 2\rightarrow(N-k+1,\ N-k+1,\ 1)\\
&(D): (M_L,C_L,1);\ 0<M_L=C_L\leqslant N,\ k\geqslant 4\rightarrow(0,0,0) \qquad (10.1)\\
&(J_2): (M_L,C_L,1): 0<M_L=C_L\leqslant k\rightarrow(0,C_L,0)\\
&(D,J_2): (M_L,C_L,1);\ M=C_L>k\geqslant 4\rightarrow(0,k,0)\\
&(H_2): (0,C_L,0);\ 0\leqslant C_L<N,\ k\geqslant 2\rightarrow(0,C'_L,0);\ 0\leqslant C'_L<N,\ C_L\neq C'_L
\end{aligned}$$

Each of these macro-transitions is realized by a routine of elementary transitions. Thus, (H_1) is realized by a 'horizontal' sequence of transitions that slides a point on the $M_L=N$ line to the corner point $(N,N,1)$, with the least number of steps; (H_1,J_1) is realized by a 'horizontal' sequence of transitions that takes a point on the $M_L=N$ line to the point $(N,N-k,\ 1)$ on that line, and then it is followed by a pair of transitions that effects a 'stable jump' to the point $(N-k+1,\ N-k+1,\ 1)$ on the diagonal, all this with the least number of steps; (D) is realized by a 'diagonal' sequence of transitions that takes a point on the diagonal to the bottom of that diagonal, in the least number of steps; (J_2) is realized by a single transition that effects a 'jump' from a point on the diagonal to the $M_L=0$ line; (D,J_2) is realized by a 'diagonal' sequence of transitions that takes a point along the diagonal to the point $(k,k,1)$, and then it is followed by a transition that effects a 'jump' to the point $(0,k,0)$ on the $M_L=0$ line, all this with the least number of steps; (H_2) is realized by a 'horizontal' sequence of transitions that takes a point on the $M_L=0$ line to another point on that line, in the smallest number of steps.

The formulation of the macro-transitions enables us to approach a problem of finding the best schedule for an M&C problem (or extensions of this problem) by first solving the problem in a higher order space, where we obtain a set of possible *macro-schedules*–that are defined in terms of macro-transitions–and then converting the macro-schedules to schedules by compiling in the appropriate way the macro-transition routines. Note that the present formulation is suitable for handling conveniently a class of problems which is larger than the strict class of M&C problems that we have defined in section 3; specifically, an arbitrary distribution of cannibals at left and right can be specified for the initial and terminal N-states. By certain changes in the specification of the macro-transitions, it is possible to consider within our present framework other variations of the M&C problem, e.g. cases where the boat capacity depends on the state of evolution of the schedule, cases where a certain level of 'casualties' is permitted, etc.

Let us consider now the following example:

Example 10.1. The initial situation is as follows: nine missionaries and one cannibal are at the left river bank and eight cannibals are at the right bank; a boat that has a capacity of four is initially available at left. We wish to find the simplest safe schedule that will result in an interchange of populations between the two river banks.

The search graph in the higher order space gives all the macro-schedules for the case of a constant boat capacity of four; this graph is shown in figure 10.1. The macro-transitions are applied on the left side of a P-state (i.e., the macro-schedule is developed forward in time) until a conclusive P-state is reached. The number within square brackets that is associated with a macro-transition indicates its 'weight', i.e., the number of trips in the routine that realizes the macro-transition. Thus, we have macro-schedules of weights 15, 21, and 27. The simplest macro-schedule is given by the sequence

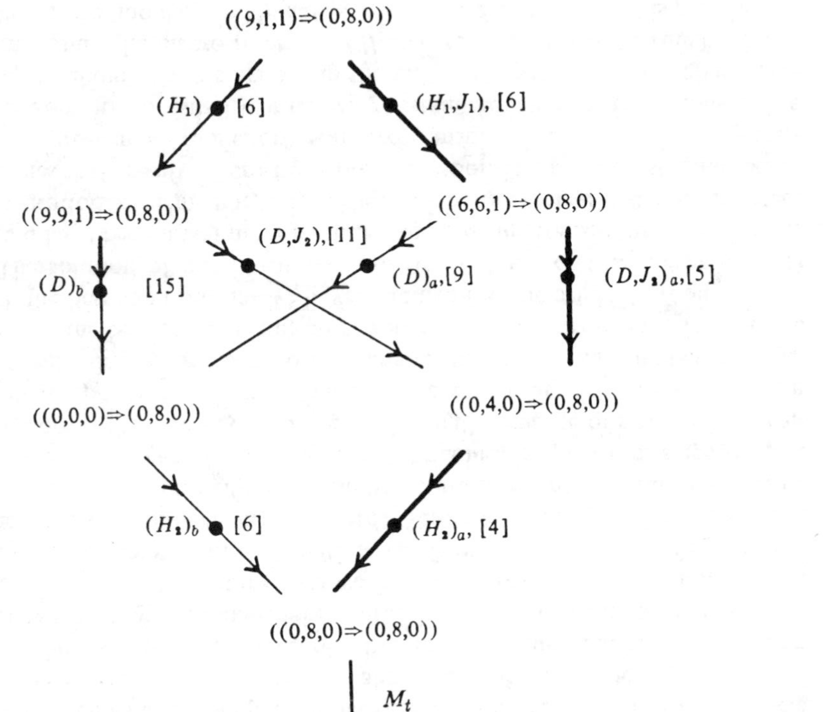

Figure 10.1 Search graph in higher order space for the example 10.1

(H_1,J_1), $(D,J_2)_a$, $(H_2)_a$ of macro-transitions, which corresponds to the darkened path in figure 10.1.

The situation in the collapsed N-state space is shown in figure 10.2. The patterns of the alternative macro-schedules are shown schematically in the lower part of the figure.

After a macro-transition is specified, its realization in terms of elementary transitions is easily carried out by a compiling routine. For example, the macro-transition (H_1,J_1) in our problem is realized as follows by a routine (H_1,J_1) with initial N-state (9,1,1) and a terminal N-state (6,6,1):

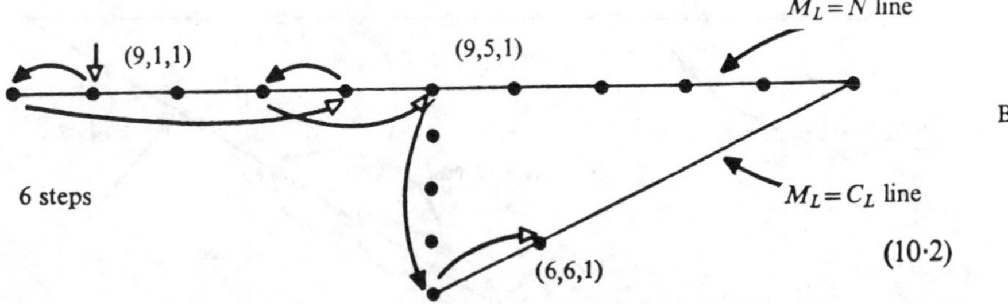

(10·2)

As a second example, consider next the realization of the macro-transition $(D,J_2)_a$, by a routine (D,J_2) from (6.6.1) to (0,4,0); *see* (10.3).

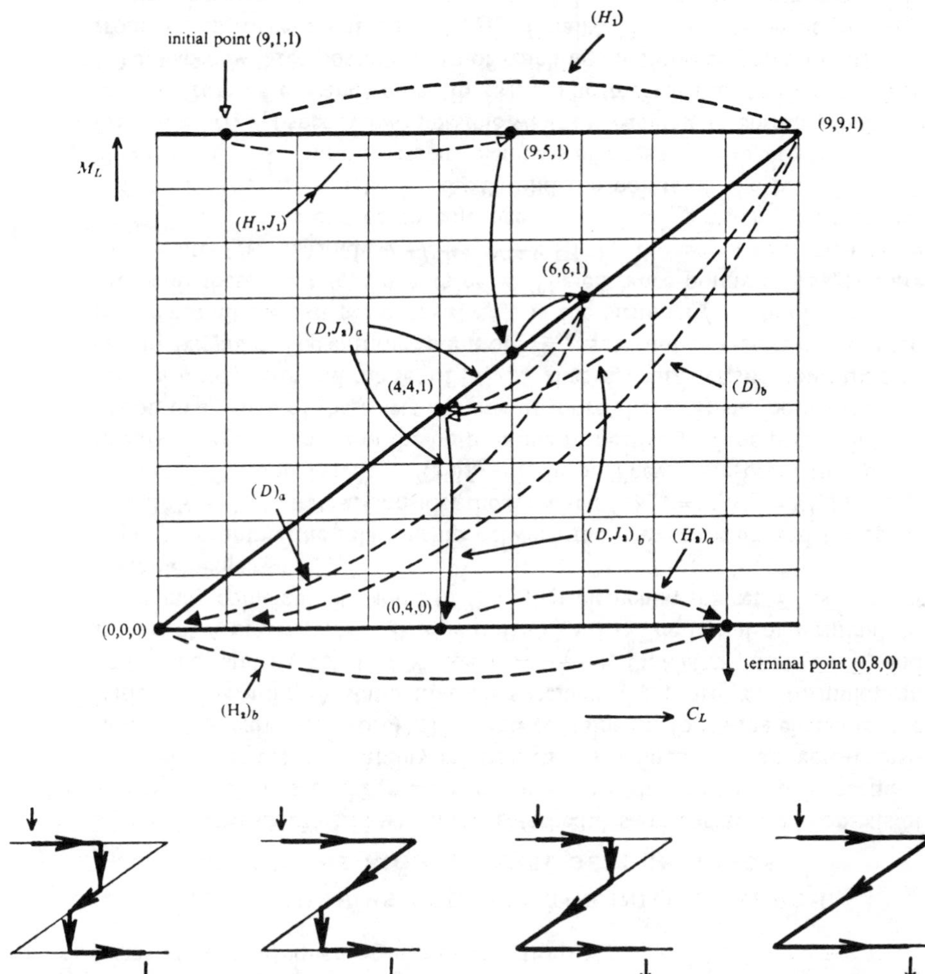

Figure 10.2. Collapsed N-state space for the example (10.1)

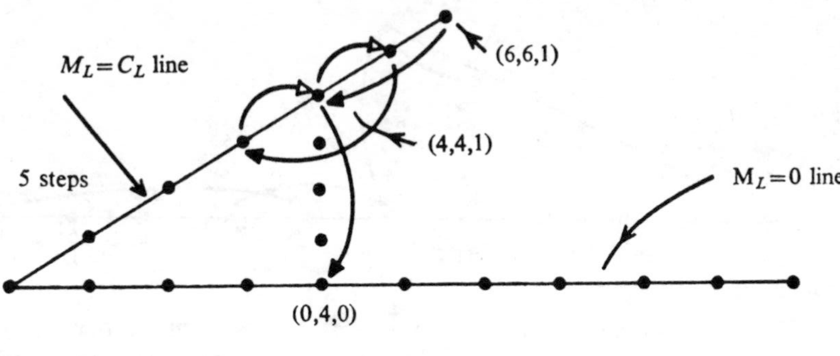

(10·3)

If we think of the problem in terms of path finding in the **Z** region of the collapsed N-state space, we can immediately see analogies with simple 'monkey problems'. These are problems suggested by McCarthy (1963), where a schedule of actions has to be found for a monkey that has to reach certain specified goals by moving in three-dimensional space, transferring objects from place to place, reaching objects, etc. It is clear that 'monkey problems' are simple prototypes of problems of reasoning about actions in the real world, such as assembling a physical object from parts, navigating a vehicle in a heavy traffic, etc. We can visualize our problem in the following way: a monkey is at the upper level of a two-level structure that has in its side an inclined stairway, and his goal is to reach a bunch of bananas that is at the lower level and at a certain distance from the stairway landing; suppose that the detailed geometry of the situation is as shown in the diagram of figure 10.2, where the scale of distances is in yards; suppose further that the monkey can always see the entire situation (the structure is essentially transparent): he can move over each level by using a 'horizontal' sequence of steps, he can move down the stairway by using a 'diagonal' sequence of steps, and he can safely jump vertical distances that do not exceed four yards; find a safe path that will bring the monkey to the bananas in the smallest number of steps. Clearly, the best solution trajectory for this monkey problem is isomorphic with the best solution that we have obtained for our original problem.

The solution of our illustrative problem (in any of the interpretations) would have been much more painful if the possible transitions were given as specifications of elementary steps. The availability of integrated, goal oriented, routines that specify macro-transitions is responsible for a substantial reduction in problem solving effort. A macro-transition is an expression of knowledge about the possibility of realizing certain sequences of transitions. It is a theorem about possible actions in the universe in which we are solving problems. Thus, the macro-transition (H_1,J_1) (see (10.1)) can be roughly interpreted in the 'monkey and bananas' context as asserting that it is possible for the monkey to go from *any* place on the upper level (except one corner point) to a place on the stairway which is four yards below the upper level. The proof of this assertion consists in exhibiting a sequence of realizable elementary steps that can be used by the monkey for going from any of the initial places at the upper level to the terminal place. Note that the elementary steps have themselves the status of macro-steps with respect to a lower level of possible actions. For example, in the M & C problem, we are using now a transfer across the river as an elementary step, and this transfer is realized by more elementary actions of loading the boat, moving it, and unloading it; in the 'monkey and bananas' interpretation, an elementary step may be realized in terms of certain sequences of muscle actions.

11. RELATIONSHIPS BETWEEN THE INITIAL SEARCH SPACE AND THE HIGHER LEVEL SEARCH SPACE

The high level space σ^* in which macro-schedules are constructed consists of a subset α of the set of $2(n+1)^2$ N-states, with the elements of α partially ordered under the attainability relation that is defined by the macro-transitions $\{(A)\}_5$ (given in (10.1)). The set α contains the following elements: the initial and terminal N-states that are specified in the problem formulation, and four N-states $(N,N,1)$, $(N-k+1, N-k+1, 1)$, $(0,0,0)$, and $(0,k,0)$ and the set of N-states $\{s|M_L=0,\ B_L=0,\ 0<C_L<k\}$. The initial or terminal N-states may coincide with some of the other elements; the set α has at most $5+k$ elements.

Let us examine the relationship between the new space σ^* and the space σ of $2(N+1)^2$ N-states. Consider the three sets $\{s\}_{top}=\{s|M_L=N\}$, $\{s\}_{diagonal}=\{s|M_L=C_L\}$ and $\{s\}_{bottom}=\{s|M_L=0\}$ in σ. They correspond to the top line, the diagonal line, and the bottom line respectively of the permissible **Z** region in σ. Each of these sets has one or more characteristic points that we call *entrance points* and the set of $\{s\}_{bottom}$ has a characteristic point that we call an *exit point*. The entrance point of $\{s\}_{top}$ is the initial N-state of the M & C problem, and the exit point of $\{s\}_{bottom}$ is the terminal N-state of the M & C problem; these are two elements of α. The entrance points of $\{s\}_{middle}$ are the N-states $(N,N,1)$ and $(N-k+1, N-k+1, 1)$; these are two elements of α (note that $(N,N,1)$ can be an entrance point of $\{s\}_{top}$ also). The entrance points of $\{s\}_{bottom}$ are $(0,0,0)$ $(0,k,0)$ and the points of the set $\{s|M_L=0,\ B_L=0,\ 0<C_L<k\}$; all of these are elements of α also. The macro-transitions (H_1) and (H_1,J_1) specify two possible ways of reaching an entrance point in $\{s\}_{middle}$ from an entrance point in $\{s\}_{top}$ The macro-transitions (D), (J_2), (D,J_2) specify three possible ways of reaching an entrance point in $\{s\}_{bottom}$ from an entrance point in $\{s\}_{middle}$. Finally, the macro-transition (H_2) specifies a way of reaching an exit point of $\{s\}_{bottom}$ from an entrance point in the same set.

We can think of the three sets $\{s\}$ as *easily traversable areas*, where a path for going from one point to another can be found with relative ease. However, the critical points of the problem occur at the points of transition, the '*narrows*', between easily traversable areas. These are represented by the intermediate entrance points. A substantial increase in problem solving power is obtained when such 'narrows' are identified, and when general ways of going from 'narrow' to 'narrow' are developed. Our macro-transitions provide precisely the capability of going from one 'narrow' into an easily traversable area, and then through that area to another 'narrow' that leads to the next easily traversable area or to the desired terminal exit.

The space σ^* is an *abstraction* of the space σ. Formally, a simplest solution to an M&C problem is attainable in σ^* if and only if it is attainable in σ. Furthermore, the minimal path linking two points in σ^* is identical with the minimal path between the same two points in σ. In σ^* attention is focused on a small number of well chosen critical points of σ. By looking for paths between points in σ^*, we solve the problem in at most three 'leaps', and then we can 'fill in' the details with the help of the definitions for the macro-transitions.

The main difficulty in finding an appropriate abstraction for the problem space lies in the discovery of the critical 'narrows' in that space, or more generally, of the topology of easily traversable areas and their connections in the problem space. After the 'narrows' are found, it is possible to build an abstract problem space that is based on them and that has ways of moving among them. It appears significant for the discovery of features in problem space–that lead to a formulation of an abstracted space–to have an appropriate representation of the space. Such is, we feel, the array representation that we have used for σ.

12. SUMMARY AND CONCLUDING COMMENTS

It is reasonable to expect that most 'real life' problems of reasoning about actions will not be formulated at the outset within a formal system. In many cases, the problem will have an initial verbal formulation. If such a problem is to be solved by a computer system, then the system must be able to accept a verbal formulation of the problem, and to convert this formulation into a form that is acceptable to a suitable problem solving subsystem. We have not considered in this paper the linguistic problem of *translating* from the natural language input into an 'internal' machine language that is acceptable to a problem solving program. This problem is receiving considerable attention at present (*see* Simmons, 1965). However, the question of choosing an 'appropriate' machine language, into which the verbal statement of the problem is to be translated, has received much less attention to date. In this paper, we are taking a first step towards understanding the nature of this question. Our notion of 'appropriateness' here is meant in the sense of suitability with respect to the *efficiency* of the problem solving process. In order to approach such a question of optimal choice of language, it is important to clarify the relationships between the language in which a problem is formulated for a problem solving system and the efficiency of the system. The systems of production P (introduced in section 2) provide a conceptual framework where such relationships can be studied. The 'internal' formulation of a problem amounts to specifying a system P, i.e. specifying the N-state language, the extended description language, the rules of action, and the two N-states that correspond to the initial and terminal situations between which the problem solving system is to find a solution trajectory. There exists considerable experience at present with computer realizations of problem solvers that work with formulations of problems in systems of production. GPS is an important prototype of such a problem solving system (see Newell, Shaw and Simon, 1960). To each system P there corresponds an N-state space over which the search for solution takes place. A good measure of the difficulty of the problem task is given by the size of the N-state space that must be searched to find a solution. Therefore, given a certain class of problems, we can evaluate the relative merits of languages for representing these problems in systems of productions by comparing the sizes of their associated N-state spaces that must be searched to obtain solutions.

In the specification of description languages for a system of productions where a given problem is to be formulated, the choice of basic elements (the universe U_0) and of basic predicates (properties and relations of the basic elements) is critical. This choice should provide enough expressive power for formulating the rules of action in a manner that reflects all the conditions of the problem. This is always possible if the elements and the predicates are chosen at a low enough, atomic, level; unfortunately, descriptions built of atomic elements have astronomical N-state spaces. Thus, we are confronted with the problem of finding the coarsest possible elements and predicates that can form descriptions that are fine enough for expressing the rules of action in the required detail. This is a difficult problem for people; at present, it is still more difficult for machines. In the M&C problem, we see that the initial formulation F_2 in a system of productions is much poorer than the formulation F_3 where instead of using individuals as elements, the sizes of certain sets of individuals (a much coarser notion) are considered to be the basic elements of the problem universe.

It appears desirable at present that an automatic translator whose task is to convert a verbal statement of a problem about actions to a machine formulation of the problem should have as its target language a language of descriptions that is atomic enough to accept quickly a great variety of problems about actions. The design of such a language seems possible and is now under study. The task of taking a possibly cumbersome system of productions P_1 from the output of such a translator and producing a better system P_2–in which the search for solution takes place–should then be delegated to the problem solving system. This is in accordance with our general thesis that it is an important function of the problem solver to find the most appropriate representation of his (its) problem. The separation of the initial translation process and the process of finding the most appropriate internal language for a problem appears to be methodologically desirable at present – given our state of knowledge about problem representations and conversions between them. It is conceivable, however, that the design of these two processes will be combined in the future. Undoubtedly, a unified approach to these two processes will strengthen both.

The rules of action of a system P play the role of the *laws of motion* that govern action sequences in the space of N-states. They are analogous to the differential equations that specify the possible time traces of a physical dynamic system. They are also analogous to the productions of combinatorial systems. Different types of problem conditions are reflected in different *forms* of rules of action. The non-cannibalism conditions of the M & C problem are easily expressible in the form of required derived descriptions for consequence of actions. As in the cases of differential equations and combinatorial systems, it is to be expected that there are classes of forms of rules of action to which there correspond problem spaces with certain special properties, characteristic patterns, etc. The identification and study of such classes would be an important contribution to the theory of problem solving processes. Even though such knowledge may not have direct implications for the design of problem solving systems that attempt to find a solution by intelligent search in a *given* problem space, it is most likely that it will be of great significance for the design of a system that would attempt to discover regularities in a problem space and that would subsequently use them for formulating new spaces where the process of searching for a solution becomes much easier.

An initial improvement in the formulation of the M & C problem came from the recognition that one of the conditions of the problem (non-cannibalism in the boat) is redundant. This permitted the formulation of new actions, as sequences of elementary actions, and it resulted in the effective elimination of many intermediate N-states. Hence, knowledge of the redundancy property permits a shrinkage of N-state space, i.e. an increase in problem solving efficiency. As shown in section 4, the redundancy of the boat condition can be established by deductive reasoning from the rules of action. Such reasoning can be carried out by machine theorem proving processes that are within the present state of the art. However, the process of *looking for* a redundant condition among the conditions of the problem is not a simple deductive process. It is a process of logical minimization. This also could be mechanized without much difficulty at present. The idea of eliminating redundant, irrelevant, conditions in a problem is an old and useful idea in the art of problem solving. It would pay then to have enough logical capabilities in a problem solving system in order to effectively attempt such eliminations.

In the M & C problem, an automatic conversion from the formulation F_2 to F_3 seems possible within the present state of the art. The conversion is based on the elimination of the redundant boat condition, the specification of compound transfer actions as sequences of the previous elementary actions (this is made possible by the previous elimination) and the formulation of new basic elements for the N-state language; this latter formulation can be guided by the form of the derived descriptions in the rules of action.

In section 6 we have shown that the formulation of the M & C problem in a production system is strongly equivalent to its formulation in a reduction system (which is a theorem proving system). A rule in the system of productions directly corresponds to a move (or a rule of inference) in the reduction system; the search trees are identical in the two systems. The reduction system has the advantage of showing clearly the logic of the attainability relations, as the search for solution evolves.

For each formulation of a problem in a system of productions it is always possible to specify an equivalent formulation in a reduction system. At worst, the search for solution in the reduction system will be identical with the search in the production system. In some cases, where the rules of action are *context free*, it is possible to specify stronger rules of inference in the reduction system, and to obtain as a consequence searches for solution that are faster than in a production system. A context free rule of action has the property that a given subconfiguration of an N-state can go to a specified subconfiguration of the next N-state regardless of the context of these subconfigurations in their respective N-states. In the M & C problem, the rules of action are strongly *context dependent*.

For example, no decision on the transfer of missionaries can be made independently of a decision on the transfer of cannibals or on the position of the boat. Thus, a reduction system cannot give an essential advantage in the M & C problem. An example where a reduction approach has considerable advantage for the solution of a problem that is formulated in a system of productions is the syntactic analysis of context free languages (*see* Amarel, 1965).

After the language of descriptions of a problem in a system of productions becomes reasonably efficient – as in the formulation F_3 in the M & C case – then the main improvements in problem solving power come from the discovery and exploitation of *useful properties* in the search space. An important property of this type is the *symmetry under time reversal* that we have found in the M & C problem. This property enables us to cut the depth of search for solution in N-state space by a factor of 2 – a significant reduction, hence a significant increase in problem solving efficiency. The symmetry property can be utilized by thinking in terms of a combined development of the search both from the initial N-state ahead in time, and from the terminal N-state back in time. However, only the development from one side is actually carried out. As soon as a search front reaches a point where there are linking possibilities between it and its image, then the search stops and a solution is found. In the present case, the formulation of the problem in a reduction system enables a clear development of the logic of search.

The symmetry property is strongly suggested by observing search graphs of the M & C problem (such as in figure 7.1) and also by examining the array representation of the N-state space. To establish the symmetry property (in section 8) we have used reasoning that is based on properties of the expressions for the rules of action. Again, such deductive reasoning is mechanizable at present. The mechanization of the more difficult task of *looking for* symmetries of certain type, given appropriate representations of solutions is also within sight. Given a newly discovered symmetry property, its utilization for problem solving requires reasoning *about* the problem solving process at a meta-level. This can be carried out with relative ease if the process is considered from the viewpoint of a reduction procedure and its logic interpretation.

In order to discover useful properties in the *N*-state space it is very important to have 'appropriate' representations of that space. In the M&C problem, the array representation (introduced in section 9) of *N*-state space has proved extremely fruitful. People have found the solution of M&C problems much easier when formulated as path finding in the array. Also, it is relatively easy for people to discover the properties that lead to the definition of macro-transitions. Is the 'appropriateness' of our array representation due solely to certain properties of the perceptual and reasoning processes of humans? Would this representation be as appropriate for (some) machine processes of pattern discovery? These remain open questions at present. In general, the problem of *choosing* a representation of *N*-state space, and of *discovering useful regularities* of solution trajectories in this representation, require much more study. Further exploration of these problems in the context of the 'dance floor' array representation of our M&C problem may provide interesting insights into them.

The definition of macro-transitions enables the formulation of the M&C problem in an extremely powerful system of productions (formulation F_6). The size of the *N*-state space is drastically reduced and a solution is obtained with practically no search, regardless of the size of the problem (sizes of populations to be transported and boat capacity). Macro-transitions act as well-chosen lemmas in a mathematical system; they summarize knowledge about the possibility of reaching certain critical intermediate points in the search space from some other points. The new *N*-state space that is based on macro-transitions is an *abstraction* of the previous *N*-state space. Only certain *critical points* of the lower level space appear in the abstracted space. We can reason in broad lines about the solution–and construct in the process a macro-schedule–by trying to establish a path, made of macro-transitions, that goes through some of these critical points. Once the macro-schedule is built, it is straightforward to obtain a detailed schedule by compiling the routines of action sequences that define the macro-transitions. The idea of finding a small set of points in the search space that are necessary and sufficient for the construction of the solution, is central in our last approach. In discussing the importance of such an approach, Simon (1966) brings the example of the simplex method in linear programming, where only the subspace made of the boundary points of the space of feasible points is searched for a solution.

The evolution of formulations of the M&C problem from its verbal statement to its last formulation in the abstracted subspace of the *N*-space is accompanied by a continuous and sizable increase in problem solving efficiency. This evolution demonstrates that the choice of appropriate representations is capable of having spectacular effects on problem solving efficiency. The realization of this evolution of formulations requires solutions to the following four types of problems:

(i) The choice of 'appropriate' basic elements and attributes for the *N*-state language.

(ii) The choice of 'appropriate' representations for rules of action and for the *N*-state space.

(iii) The discovery of useful properties of the problem that permit a reduction in size of the *N*-state space. Specifically, the discovery of a redundant condition in the problem, the discovery of symmetry in the problem space, and the discovery of critical points in the problem space that form a useful higher level subspace.

(iv) The utilization of new knowledge about problem properties in formulating better problem solving procedures.

Given solutions to (i) and (ii), it is conceivable that the approach to the solution of (iii) and (iv) is mechanizable–assuming good capabilities for deductive processing. There is very little knowledge at present about possible mechanizations of (i) and (ii). However, if experience in problems of type (iii) and (iv) is gained, then at least the notions of 'appropriateness' in (i) and (ii) will become clearer.

Acknowledgment

This work was greatly stimulated by discussions with A. Newell and H. A. Simon.

REFERENCES

Amarel, S. (1965), Problem solving procedures for efficient syntactic analysis, *ACM 20th National Conference.*

Amarel, S. (1967), An approach to heuristic problem solving and theorem proving in Propositional Calculus, *Computer Science and Systems.* Toronto: University of Toronto Press.

Bellman, R. & Dreyfus, S. (1962), *Applied Dynamic Programming.* Princeton: Princeton University Press.

Black, F. (1964), *A Deductive Question Answering System.* Unpublished Doctoral Dissertation, Harvard University.

Carnap, R. (1958), *Introduction to Symbolic Logic and its Application.* New York: Dover Publications.

McCarthy, J. (1963), Situations, actions, and causal laws. *Stanford Artificial Intelligent Project, Memo No.* 2.

Newell, A. (1966), Some examples of problems with several problem spaces, *Seminar Notes,* CIT, Feb. 22.

Newell, A., Shaw, T. & Simon, H.A. (1960), Report on a General Problem-Solving program for computer, *Proceedings of the International Conference on Information Processing*, pp. 256–64. Paris: UNESCO.

Simmons, R.F. (1965), Answering English questions by computer: a survey, *Communications of the ACM*, **8**.

Simon, H.A. (1966), On reasoning about actions, CIT # 87, Carnegie Institute of Technology.

Simon, H.A. & Newell, A. (1961), Computer simulation of human thinking and problem solving. *Datamation*, June–July. 1961.

A PROBLEM SIMILARITY APPROACH TO DEVISING HEURISTICS: FIRST RESULTS

John Gaschnig
Department of Computer Science
Carnegie-Mellon University
Pittsburgh, PA 15213

Abstract

Here we describe an approach, based upon a notion of problem similarity, that can be used when attempting to devise a heuristic for a given search problem (of a sort represented by graphs). The proposed approach relies on a change in perspective: instead of seeking a heuristic directly for a given problem P1, one seeks instead a problem P2 easier to solve than P1 and related to P1 in a certain way. The next step is to find an algorithm for finding paths in P2, then apply this algorithm in a certain way as a heuristic for P1. In general, the approach is to consider as candidates problems P2 that are "edge subgraphs" or "edge supergraphs" of the given problem P1. As a non-trivial application, we show that a certain restricted form of sorting problem (serving as P2) is an edge supergraph of the 8-puzzle graph (P1). A simple algorithm for solving this sorting problem is evident, and the number of swaps executed in solving an instance thereof is taken as a heuristic estimate of distance between corresponding points in the 8-puzzle graph. Using the A* algorithm, we experimentally compare the performance of this "maxsort" heuristic for the 8-puzzle with others in the literature. Hence we present evidence of a role for exploiting certain similarities among problems to transfer a heuristic from one problem to another, from an "easier" problem to a "harder" one.

1. Introduction *, **

Many combinatorially large problems cannot be solved feasibly by exhaustive case analysis or brute force search, but can be solved efficiently if a heuristic can be devised to guide the search. Finding such a heuristic for a given problem, however, usually requires an exercise of creativity on the part of the researcher.

Research to date on devising heuristics has spanned several problem-solving domains and several approaches. In some efforts, the objective has been to optimize, using some adaptation scheme over a number of trials, the values of coefficients determining the relative weighting of several preselected terms in an evaluation function, so as to maximize the overall performance (e.g., [Samuel 1959], [Samuel 1967], [Rendell 1977]). Other approaches to automatic generation of heuristics include [Ernst, et al., 1974] and [Rendell, 1976]. Related efforts have focused on what might be called "disciplined creativity", enunciating general principles or rules of thumb that a person may apply to the problem at hand (e.g., [Polya 1945], [Wickelgren 1974]).

The approach to devising heuristics proposed here differs in perspective from these previous efforts: instead of seeking a heuristic directly, one seeks instead a problem P2 that is easier to solve than the given problem P2 and is related to P2 in a certain way. * The next step is to find an algorithm for finding paths in P2, then apply this algorithm in a certain way as a heuristic for P1. As an elementary example, the rectilinear distance function is an efficient heuristic for finding paths in a "Manhattan street pattern" graph even when some (but not too many) of the streets have been blockaded (i.e., some edges are removed from the graph). Generalizing, the approach is to consider as candidates problems P2 that are "edge subgraphs" or "edge supergraphs" of the given problem P1. As a non-trivial application, we show that a certain restricted form of sorting problem (serving as P2) is an edge supergraph of the 8-puzzle graph (P1). A simple algorithm for solving this sorting problem is evident, and the number of swaps executed in solving an instance thereof is taken as a heuristic estimate of distance between corresponding points in the 8-puzzle graph. Using the A* algorithm, we experimentally compare the performance of this "maxsort" heuristic for the 8-puzzle with others in the literature.

The general class of problems to which the present approach can be applied are those state space problems that can be represented as graphs, in which the objective is to find a path from a given initial node in the graph to

---

* This research was sponsored by the Defense Advanced Research Projects Agency (DOD), ARPA Order No. 3597, monitored by the Air Force Avionics Laboratory Under Contract F33615-78-C-1551.

The views and conclusions contained in this document are those of the author and should not be interpreted as representing the official policies, either expressed or implied, of the Defense Advanced Research Projects Agency or the U.S. Government.

** Author's present address: Artificial Intelligence Center, SRI International, 333 Ravenswood Ave., Menlo Park, CA 94025

* This perspective is somewhat akin to that on which are based the results of backward error analysis (as defined in the numerical analysis literature), in which one asks of a matrix inversion algorithm, for example, not how accurate are the answers that it computes, but rather how different from the given problem is the problem for which the computed answers are the exact answers.

a given goal node.* Such problems can be solved using the A* best-first search algorithm, which iteratively grows a tree or graph of partial paths from the initial node, at each step expanding the node (along the edge of this tree or graph) that appears to be "best".** The definition of "best" is specified by assigning a number to each node generated, whose computation typically involves the value of a heuristic function K(s, t) used to estimate the distance in the graph from an arbitrary node s in the graph to another arbitrary node t (where t is taken to be the goal node in a particular instance of search). Devising heuristic functions that estimate distance between points in a given graph is the present practical objective.

Additional theoretical objectives motivated this work: to investigate how "similar" or "dissimilar" problems differ in structural properties, and how such structural differences relate to difference in difficulty to solve the problem. Investigations of relatively simple problems serve this purpose well. Note that we are not interested in the 8-puzzle (our principal example) per se, but as a concrete instance with which to investigate general principles.

Section 2 defines the notions of "edge subgraph" and "edge supergraph", and illustrates their relation to heuristic transfer using a simple example -- a "Manhattan street pattern" graph and variants thereof. Section 3 applies the basic approach to a larger problem -- the 8-puzzle. Section 4 discusses the generality of the results and poses future tasks.

2. Problem Similarity: Edge Subgraphs and Supergraphs

The basic idea considered in this paper can be illustrated using a simple example. Consider the graphs depicted in Figures 1a, 1b, and 1c, which we shall refer to as MSUB44, M44, MSUP44, respectively. We note that these three graphs have identical numbers of nodes, and that the edges of MSUB44 comprise a subset of those of M44; similarly the edges of M44 comprise a subset of those of MSUP44. We shall say therefore that MSUB44 is an <u>edge subgraph</u> of M44 and that similarly M44 is an edge subgraph of MSUP44. Likewise we also say that M44 is an <u>edge supergraph</u> of MSUB44 and that MSUP44 is an edge supergraph of M44. These relations of edge subgraph and edge supergraph generalize formally in the obvious way for the class of <u>problem graphs</u>, which we define to be any finite, strongly connected graph G = (V, E) having no self-loops and no multiple edges. This definition includes the familiar problems cited in the preceding section.*

To illustrate how edge subgraph or edge supergraph similarity between problem graphs is related to heuristic transfer, we now consider three cases in turn: (1) that M44 is the given problem to be solved; (2) that MSUB44 is the given problem; and (3) that MSUP44 is the given problem. In general we wish to solve an arbitrary instance of a given problem graph P, that is to find a path from an arbitrary initial node s_r in P to an arbitrary goal node s_g. (We denote such a <u>problem instance</u> I of a problem graph P thus: I = (s_r, s_g).) This trivial example serves as a vehicle for introducing several general concepts.

The task of finding a path between arbitrary initial and goal nodes in the M44 graph (or in some larger version of this "Manhattan street pattern" graph) is trivial. A simple algorithm for solving instances of this problem graph is readily evident: comparing the coordinates of the current node (starting with the initial node s_r), move iteratively up (or down as the case may be) until the vertical coordinate of the goal node is reached, then move right (or left) iteratively until the goal node is reached. Call this algorithm L (for "L-shaped solution path").

If MSUB44 is taken instead of M44 as the problem to be solved, the A* approach seems more attractive than attempting to devise an algorithm like algorithm L, because of the additional cases an algorithm of the latter sort must account for: besides comparing the coordinates of the current node with those of the goal node, it must also be prepared to make detours when necessary.

To use A* to solve MSUB44, one must supply a heuristic function K(s, t) that estimates distance from node s to node t. Let $h_P(s, t)$ denote the actual distance in P from s to t, assuming edges have unit weight. In the case K(s, t) = h(s, t) the distance estimate is exact; it is well known [Hart et al. 1968] that this case minimizes the number of nodes expanded -- the number is exactly $h(s_r, s_g)$, the distance from initial node to goal node.** For M44, it is evident that $h_{M44}(s, t) = |x_s - x_t| + |y_s - y_t|$, where x_s and y_s are the x and y coordinates, respectively, of node s. For MSUB44 a symbolic formula for h(s, t) is not so compact, since it must distinguish more cases. An alternative to enunciating h(s, t) for MSUB44 is to use $K(s, t) = h_{M44}(s, t)$, i.e., use the distance function of M44 to approximate the distance function of MSUB44.

It is easy to show, as follows, that solution paths found for an arbitrary problem instance of MSUB44 using

---

* Elementary examples of such problems include the 8-puzzle, The Tower of Hanoi, the water jug problem, missionaries and cannibals problem and other "toy" problems familiar in the literature [Nilsson 1971, pp. 39-41, 77-78], [Jackson 1974, pp. 81-84, 110-115], [Raphael 1976, pp. 79-86], [Wickelgren 1974, pp. 49-57, 78-80 cf.]. Somewhat less frivolous examples include certain algebraic manipulation problems [Doran & Michie 1966, pp. 254-255], [Doran 1967, pp. 114-115], and a version of the traveling salesperson problem [Doran 1968], [Harris 1974].

** The Graph Traverser algorithm [Doran & Michie 1966] and the HPA algorithm [Pohl 1970a] are essentially the same as A*.

* Note that the 8-puzzle graph consists of two disjoint components. For present purposes, we consider search within one such component. Also, we assume that a problem graph is specified in practice by a successors function: SUC(s) denotes, for any node s in the graph, the of nodes v_i for which there exists an edge from s to v_i. Typically SUC(s) is implemented by a set of operators, each of which transforms a given state s into another state v_i, provided the operator's precondition is satisfied. In the 8-puzzle context, one such operator might have the effect of moving the hole upward if it is not in the top row of the board.

** To achieve this bound, one must be careful in selecting a strategy for resolving ties among nodes for which equal values were assigned.

$K(s, t) = h_{M44}(s, t)$ will be of minimal length. If P1 and P2 are any problem graphs such that P1 is an edge subgraph of P2 (denoted $P1 \subseteq_e P2$), then the distance between arbitrary nodes s and t in P2 is never more than the distance between the corresponding points in P1, i.e., $h_{P2}(s, t) \leq h_{P1}(s, t)$. Hence using the heuristic function $K(s, t) = h_{P2}(s, t)$ for solving P1 it follows that $K(s, t) \leq h_{P1}(s, t)$. Hence by the A* admissibility theorem ([Hart, et al. 1968], [Gelperin 1977]) the solution path found is always of minimum length when using $K(s, t) = h_{P2}(s, t)$ in solving P1.*

As a third case, take MSUP44 as the problem to be solved. Now $h_{MSUP44}(s, t) \leq h_{M44}(s, t)$, hence taking $K(s, t) = h_{M44}(s, t)$ overestimates the distance from s to t in MSUP44. Instead of using A*, however, note that algorithm L can be used to find paths in MSUP44, although they will not necessarily be of minimum length. (Whether this is important depends on the application.) In general, if $P2 \subseteq_e P1$ then an algorithm that finds paths in P2 can also be used to find paths in P1 (assuming the same encoding scheme is used for identifying corresponding nodes in P1 and P2).

These simple examples illustrate a general approach: given a problem graph P1 to be solved, first identify a problem graph P2 that is an edge subgraph or edge supergraph of P1. We call P1 the <u>given problem</u> and P2 the <u>transfer problem</u>. Then find a way of computing $h_{P2}(s, t)$. (In the preceding examples a simple formula for h_{M44} was readily evident. When a formula for h_{P2} is not evident, we instead attempt to devise an algorithm for computing the values of $h_{P2}(s, t)$ by finding a path in P2 from s to t and counting the number of steps in the path. See section 3.) Then use $h_{P2}(s, t)$ as a heuristic function for solving instances of P1: given a goal node s_g, whenever A* calls for a value to be assigned to a node s in P1, compute $h_{P2}(s,s_g)$.

3. Example: A Sorting Algorithm Used as Heuristic for the 8-Puzzle

Section 3.1 defines the "9MAXSWAP" graph and shows it to be an edge supergraph of the 8-puzzle graph. Section 3.2 defines an algorithm, called MAXSORT, for finding paths in the 9MAXSWAP problem graph. Section 3.3 reports experimental results measuring the performance of MAXSORT when used as the basis of a heuristic distance-estimating function for the 8-puzzle, and compares this observed performance with those of other known heuristics for the 8-puzzle. This section also proposes and tests another related heuristic for the 8-puzzle. Section 3.4 reports experimental measurements of how closely the heuristic function based on MAXSORT approximates the distance function of the 8-puzzle. This larger example serves as a non-trivial application and as a vehicle for introducing additional concepts.

3.1. The MAXSWAP problem

The 8-puzzle is a one-person game the objective of which is to rearrange a given configuration of eight tiles on a 3x3 board into another given configuration by iteratively sliding a tile into the orthogonally adjacent empty location, like so:

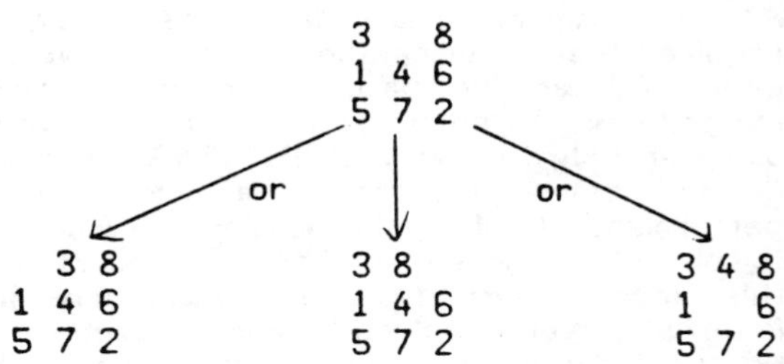

To apply the present approach (which might be called the "edge subgraph/supergraph transfer" approach) to the 8-puzzle, first we must identify a suitable edge subgraph or edge supergraph of the 8-puzzle. Toward this end we note that an 8-puzzle tile configuration can be considered a permutation of the sequence 1,2,...,9, letting 9 correspond to the hole in the 8-puzzle, and numbering the nine locations of the 8-puzzle board in left to right, top to bottom manner, say. Hence the topmost of the four configurations depicted above corresponds to the sequence 398146572.

Now we define the "N-swap" graph to have N! nodes, corresponding to the N! permutations of the sequence 1,2,...,N. An edge connects two vertices of this graph iff the corresponding permutations differ by a single swap. In an obvious way, the behavior of any sorting algorithm which operates by sequentially interchanging pairs of array elements can be mapped into sets of paths in this graph. Taking N = 9, there is evident a one-to-one correspondence between the nodes of 9-Swap (but not the edges) and those of the 8-puzzle graph.

By noting that the effect of moving a tile in the 8-puzzle graph is to exchange two elements of a 9 element vector, it is easy to see that the 8-puzzle graph is an edge subgraph of 9SWAP. Hence the 8-puzzle can be viewed as a restricted version of permutation sorting, such that every swap must include the largest element (i.e., 9), and that certain swaps are forbidden, depending on the location of the largest element.

If we impose the restriction on sorting N-element permutations that every swap must exchange the largest element, N, with some other element, we obtain what might be called the "N-MAXSWAP" graph. For illustrative purposes, Figure 2 depicts the 4MAXSWAP graph. Note that 8-puzzle $\subseteq_e$ 9MAXSWAP $\subseteq_e$ 9SWAP, hence for arbitrary nodes s and t, $h_{9SWAP}(s, t) \leq h_{9MAXSWAP}(s, t) \leq h_{8\text{-puzzle}}(s, t)$. Hence the distance functions of both 9SWAP and 9MAXSWAP underestimate the distance function of the 8-puzzle, but that of 9MAXSWAP is a closer approximation of the

* A* is analyzed mathematically in [Hart, et al. 1978], [Pohl 1970a], [Pohl 1970b], [Nilsson 1971], [Harris 1974], [Vanderbrug 1976], [Munyer 1976], [Munyer & Pohl 1976], [Ibaraki 1977], [Pohl 1977], [Gelperin 1977], [Martelli 1977], [Gaschnig 1979], and elsewhere. Attempting to apply such analytic results is not a major concern here; in Section 3.3 we measure heuristic performance experimentally.

8-puzzle's distance function than that of 9SWAP. * We will use 9MAXSWAP as the transfer problem for the 8-puzzle in this example; next, we must demonstrate the transfer.

3.2. The MAXSORT algorithm

We describe now what seems to be a most peculiar way of solving the 8-puzzle. Given a problem instance, A* iteratively expands nodes in the 8-puzzle graph and requires that a number be assigned to every new node generated, as the basis for deciding which node to expand next. To obtain each such number we propose to solve an entire instance of 9MAXSWAP using an algorithm defined below, and return a number measuring its performance (in fact, the number of swaps it executes). If solving instances of 9MAXSWAP itself required search, this approach might consume more time than if the 8-puzzle were solved using breadth-first search. However, the point of this example is that the 9-Maxswap problem is simpler than the 8-puzzle --- one can readily devise an efficient algorithm for it, as follows.

The basis for an algorithm which we call "MAXSORT" (defined by a SAIL procedure in the `test`) for finding paths in an N-MAXSWAP graph is the observation that the largest element, N, in the permutation can always be swapped with the element whose proper place in the permutation it occupies, except when N is in the N'th position of the permutation. We illustrate using N = 4. To sort the permutation P = 2341 (into 1234), the algorithm first swaps 3 and 4 producing 2431, in which the element 3 now occupies its proper place. Next swapping 2 and 4 puts 2 in its proper place and then swapping 4 and 1 puts both those elements in their proper places and the algorithm terminates. To implement this policy of simply swapping the largest element 4 with the element whose proper place 4 is occupying, MAXSORT uses an internal auxiliary array B, and begins by assigning to B[i] the location of element i in the input permutation, i.e., B[1:4] = 4123 for the above example. Then MAXSORT simply swaps iteratively P[B[4]] with P[B[B[4]]], updating both P and B at each iteration, until the sort is complete, with the followng exception to this rule.

Sorting 4321 using MAXSORT, the first swap produces 1324, but now 4 is in its proper place, and so we must do something other than swap 4 with itself indefinitely. Instead, the algorithm swaps 4 with the leftmost element of P that is not in its proper place, i.e., 3 in this case, and we proceed as before. (Determining this leftmost element is accomplished efficiently -- using the variable called avail for bookkeeping, the block named "available-spot-found" is executed at most N/3 times.) So each swap executed by MAXSORT moves zero or one new element, other than N, into its proper place and never moves an element, other than N, from its proper place. Table 1 shows the current permutation, the contents of the elements of B, and the value of the variable avail for each step in the above example.

(Trace this sequence as a path in the graph in Figure 2.) *

iteration	permutation	b array	avail
	4 3 2 1	4 3 2 1	1
1			
	1 3 2 4	1 3 2 4	2
2			
	1 4 2 3	1 3 4 2	2
3			
	1 2 4 3	1 2 4 3	3
4			
	1 2 3 4	1 2 3 4	4

Table 1. MAXSORT trace for permutation 4321

To apply MAXSORT as a heuristic for the 8-puzzle, we take N = 9. Let $K_{MAXSORT}(p)$ denote the number of swaps executed by MAXSORT given permutation p. Then given an 8-puzzle instance with arbitrary initial node p and goal node q = 123456789, the function $K_{MAXSORT}$ can serve as a heuristic for the 8-puzzle: we take $K(s) = K_{MAXSORT}(s)$, obtained for any state s by executing MAXSORT on s and counting the number of swaps it executes. For example if p = 296134758 and q = 123456789, then MAXSORT executes seven swaps when sorting p, hence K(p) = 7. (It happens that $h_{8\text{-puzzle}}(p,q) = 9$ in this case.) For other goal nodes q, we compute $K_{MAXSORT}(p, q)$ by simply using MAXSORT to sort p into q by first transforming the instance (p, q) into the canonical form (p', 123456789) and then sorting p' by MAXSORT. The permutation p' is the image of p under the transformation that maps q into 123456789, e.g., if p = 258491367 and q = 485297361, then 4 in p becomes 1 in p', 8 in p becomes 2 in p', and so on, so that p' = 4 32159786. Note that every swap must include as one of its elements not 9, but rather the image of 9 under this transformation, i.e., 5 in this example. (The trivial generalization of the MAXSORT code to accomplish this transformation is omitted here for brevity.)

Since 8-puzzle $\subseteq_e$ 9MAXSWAP it follows that $h_{9MAXSWAP}(s, t) \le h_{8puzzle}(s, t)$. Hence if $K_{MAXSORT}(s, t) = h_{9MAXSWAP}(s, t)$ it follows from the A* admissibility theorem that solution paths found using $K_{MAXSORT}(s)$ as heuristic function for the 8-puzzle are

---

* If the number of edges in 9MAXSWAP were close to the number in the 8-puzzle we could infer that the distance function of the former is a close approximation of that of the latter, but such is not the case: The 8-puzzle, 9MAXSWAP, and 9SWAP each has 9! = 362,880 nodes. The 9MAXSWAP graph has 4·9! = 1,451,520 edges. (The number of edges in the N-MAXSWAP graph is N! (N-1)/2.) Nodes in the 8-puzzle graph are incident to 2, 3, or 4 edges, in the proportion 4:4:1, respectively. Hence the number of edges is 9!(2·4/9 + 3·4/9 + 4·1/9) / 2 = 9!·4/3 = 483,840, a factor of 3 fewer than in 9MAXSWAP. By comparison, the 9SWAP graph has 18·9! = 6,531,840 edges, a factor of 3.375 more than in 9MAXSWAP. (The number of edges in N-SWAP is N! N(N-1)/4.)

* The general behavior of MAXSORT for 4MAXSWAP can be depicted graphically as follows. Since the execution of MAXSORT for an arbitrary 4 element permutation corresponds to a path in the 4MAXSWAP graph (see Figure 2), the union over all 4-element permutation of the execution paths of MAXSORT (i.e., to sort into ascending order) is a subgraph of 4MAXSWAP. In fact this subgraph is a spanning tree of 4MAXSWAP (see Figure 3.)

of minimal length. * In words, to prove the premise is to show that for any 9-element permutations p and q, the number of swaps executed by MAXSORT in sorting p into q is minimal, i.e., it equals the minimum distance from p to q in the 9-MAXSWAP graph. Instead of attempting to prove this (its relevance beyond the example at hand being minimal), we note that it has been observed that heuristic functions that overestimate distance in a graph often are more efficient than similar functions that always underestimate the true distance ([Doran & Michie 1966], [Nilsson 1971], [Gaschnig 1977], [Gaschnig 1979]). Hence it may advantageous for efficiency in solving the 8-puzzle if $K_{MAXSORT}$ does not find minimal length paths in 9MAXSWAP, provided that a guarantee of minimal length solution paths in the 8-puzzle is not mandatory.

3.3. Experimental Performance Measurement Results

How efficient is the function $K_{MAXSORT}$ as a heuristic function for the 8-puzzle? To find out, we selected randomly a set of over 800 problem instances of the 8-puzzle, and solved each of these with A* using $K_{MAXSORT}$ as the heuristic function. As a measure of search efficiency, for each such problem instance (s_r, s_g) we measured the value of $X(s_r, s_g)$, the number of nodes expanded before a solution path is found to problem instance (s_r, s_g) when using $K_{MAXSORT}$ as a heuristic function with A*. This sample of problem instances is identical to the one used in [Gaschnig 1977] and [Gaschnig 1979], as is the experimental procedure followed, hence those results and the present results are comparable. The problem instances (s_r, s_g) in this sample are grouped together according to the value of $h(s_r, s_g)$, the length of a minimum length path in the graph from s_r to s_g.

Figure 4 plots the observed values of XMEAN(N), the mean number of nodes expanded as a function of depth of the goal node (i.e., the mean over all instances (s_r, s_g) in the sample such that $h(s_r, s_g) = N$). Superimposed in Figure 4 for comparison purposes are the analogous experimental data reported in Figure 1 of [Gaschnig 1977] and [Gaschnig 1979] for three particular 8-puzzle heuristic functions there called K_1, K_2, and K_3. Figure 4 shows that $K_{MAXSORT}$ is slightly better than $K_1(s)$, which computes the number of tiles out of place in tile configuration s with respect to the goal node. Figure 4 shows also that $K_{MAXSORT}$ usually expands many more nodes than do K_2 or K_3.** So it turns out that $K_{MAXSORT}$ is a relatively inefficient heuristic for the 8-puzzle, compared with these other known heuristic functions, but inspection of Figure 4 reveals that it expands far fewer nodes in solving the 8-puzzle than does breadth-first search.

* As a matter of convenience, we sometimes write K(s) instead of K(s, t) when t is understood implicitly. For example, in any given A* search node t is understood to be the goal node.

** K_2 computes the number of tiles out of place, each weighted by the orthogonal distance the tile must move to its desired spot, assuming no other tiles block the path; K_3 equals K_2 plus another term measuring the degree to which the outer tiles in s agree in rotational order to those in the goal node. See [Doran & Michie 1966], [Nilsson 1971], [Gaschnig 1977], or [Gaschnig 1979] for additional details.

4. Analysis of Distance Function Approximation

The experimental results in Figure 4 pose a challenge: why is $K_{MAXSORT}$ a relatively inefficient heuristic for the 8-puzzle, and is it coincidental that its performance is comparable to that of K_1? One approach to answering such questions is to determine how closely $K_{MAXSORT}(s, t)$ approximates $h_{8\text{-puzzle}}(s, t)$. Figure 5 plots experimental measurements of the range of $K_{MAXSORT}$'s estimates of distance to the goal node in the 8-puzzle vs. the actual distance to the goal. KMIN(i) is defined with respect to $K_{MAXSORT}$ to be the minimum value of $K_{MAXSORT}(s, t)$ over all node pairs (s, t) such that h(s, t) = i, and similarly KMAX(i) is the maximum of these values. Hence KMIN(i) and KMAX(i) bound the values computed by $K_{MAXSORT}$ for nodes that happen to be distance i from the goal. The data plotted in Figure 5 were recorded during the same experiment represented in Figure 4, in the following way. The value of $K_{MAXSORT}(s_r, s_g)$ was recorded for each problem instance (s_r, s_g) in the sample set. The value of $h(s_r, s_g)$ equals the length of the solution path found, which is of minimum length since $K_{MAXSORT}$ underestimates distance in the 8-puzzle graph. In addition we measured the value of $K_{MAXSORT}(s,s_g)$ for each node s along the solution path found for each problem instance in the sample set. Since the solution path found is of minimum length, the value of $h(s,s_g)$ is known for each such node s. In all, Figure 5 represents over 10,000 distinct observations of $K_{MAXSORT}(s, t)$ vs. $h_{8\text{-puzzle}}(s, t)$. Superimposed for comparison in Figure 5 are analogous experimental measurements of KMIN(i) and KMAX(i) for K_1, taken from Figure 2 in [Gaschnig 1977] or [Gaschnig 1979].

Figure 5 shows both that $K_{MAXSORT}$ is a poor approximation of $h_{8\text{-puzzle}}$, and that the approximation is only slightly better than that of K_1.

5. Discussion

We have described a general principle of problem similarity for path-finding state-space problems -- the edge subgraph and edge supergraph relations. We have demonstrated, using the 8-puzzle as case study, how this principle of "edge subgraph/supergraph transfer" can be exploited to aid in devising a heuristic function for a given problem, by transferring a heuristic from an "easier" problem to a related "harder" one. We have measured experimentally the efficiency of the resulting heuristic function devised for the 8-puzzle, demonstrating at least a limited practical utility.

These first results leave many questions unanswered. Our intention here has been merely to introduce the idea for further consideration. Hence the remainder of this discussion focusses on extensions to the present efforts.

Additional insight might be obtained by applying the transfer approach to additional problem graphs, including some in which the transfer problem is an edge subgraph of the given problem instead of an edge supergraph, as in the 8-puzzle case study. In particular, we note of the 8-puzzle case study that a transfer problem (9MAXSWAP) was readily apparent, that an efficient algorithm for 9MAXSWAP was readily devised, and that this algorithm proved to be a relatively inefficient heuristic function for the 8-puzzle. How formidable these hurdles are for other problems remains to be determined.

Another objective is to attempt to devise for the 8-puzzle another transfer problem which is a closer approximation to it than is the 9MAXSWAP graph, that is to identify a problem graph that is an edge supergraph of the 8-puzzle and an edge subgraph of 9MAXSWAP.

It may be interesting to apply this transfer concept in reverse fashion: given a particular heuristic function for a given problem, identify the graph to which it is equivalent. For example, one might attempt to determine whether a graph corresponding to the K_1 function is an edge supergraph of the 9MAXSWAP graph, or to identify a graph corresponding to the function K_2.* A theory about the equivalence of problem graphs and heuristic functions along these lines is conceivable.

Acknowledgement. Richard Korf offered helpful comments on an earlier draft of this paper.

6. References

Doran, J., "An Approach to Automatic Problem Solving," in Machine Intelligence 1, N. Collins and D. Michie (eds.), American Elsevier Publ. Co., New York 1967.

Doran, J., "New Developments of the Graph Traverser," in Machine Intelligence 2, E. Dale and D. Michie (eds.), American Elsevier Publ. Co., New York 1968.

Doran, J., and D. Michie, "Experiments with the Graph Traverser Program," Proc. Royal Society of London, Series A, Vol. 294, 1966, pp. 235-259.

Ernst, G.W., Banerji, R.B., Hookway, R.J., Oyen, R.A., and Shaffer, D.E., "Mechanical Discovery of Certain Heuristics", Report 1136-A, Jennings Computing Center, Case Western Reserve Univ., Cleveland, Ohio, January 1974.

Gaschnig, J., "Exactly How Good are Heuristics?: Toward a Realistic Predictive Theory of Best First Search", Proc. Intl. Joint Conf. on Artificial Intelligence, Cambridge, Mass., August 1977, pp. 434-441.

Gaschnig, J., Performance Measurement and Analysis of Certain Search Algorithms, Ph.D. thesis, Dept. of Computer Science, Carnegie-Mellon University, Pittsburgh, Pa., May 1979.

Gelperin, D., "On the Optimality of A*," Artificial Intelligence, Vol. 8, 1977, pp. 69-76.

Harris, L., "Heuristic SEarch under Conditions of Error," Artificial Intelligence, Vol. 5, No. 3, North Holland Publ. Co., Amsterdam, 1974, pp. 217-234.

Hart, P., N. Nilsson and B. Raphael, "A Formal Basis for the Heuristic Determination of Minimum Cost Paths," IEEE Trans. Sys. Sci. Cybernetics, Vol. 4, No. 2, 1968.

Ibaraki, T., "Theoretical Comparisons of Search Strategies in Branch-and-Bound Algorithms," International Journal of Computer and Information Sciences, Vol. 5, No. 4, December 1976, pp. 315-344.

Jac' on, P. Introduction to Artificial Intelligence, Petrocelli Books, New York 1974.

Martelli, A., "On the Complexity of Admissible Search Algorithms," Artificial Intelligence, Vol. 8, 1977, pp. 1-13.

Munyer, J., "Some Results on the Complexity of Heuristic Search in Graphs," Technical report HP-76-2, Information Sciences Dept., U. Cal. Santa Cruz, September 1976.

Munyer, J., and I. Pohl, "Adversary Arguments for the Analysis of Heuristic Search in General Graphs," Technical report HP-76-1, Information Sciences Dept., U. Cal. Santa Cruz, July 1976.

Nilsson, N., Problem Solving Methods in Artificial Intelligence, 1971.

Pohl, I., "First Results on the Effect of Error in Heuristic Search," Machine Intelligence 5, B. Meltzer and D. Michie (eds.), Edinburgh University Press, Edinburgh 1970 (1970a).

Pohl, I., "Heuristic Search Viewed as Path-Finding in a Graph", Artificial Intelligence, Vol. 1, 1970 (1970b).

Pohl, I., "Practical and Theoretical Consideration in Heuristic Search Algorithms," in Machine Intelligence 8, E. Elcock and D. Michie (eds.), Ellis Howard Ltd., Chichester, England 1977.

Polya, G., How to Solve It, Princeton University Press, Princeton, N. J. 1945.

Raphael, B., The Thinking Computer: Mind Inside Matter, W. H. Freeman & Co., San Francisco 1976.

Rendell, L., "A Method for Automatic Generation of Heuristics for State-Space Problems", Report CS-76-10, Department of Computer Science, University of Waterloo, Waterloo, Ontario, Canada, February 1976.

Rendell, L., "A Locally Optimal Solution of the Fifteen Puzzle Produced by an Automatic Evaluation Function Generator," Report CS-77-36, Dept. of Computer Science, University of Waterloo, December 1977.

Samuel, A., "Some Studies in Machine Learning Using the Game of Checkers," in E. Feigenbaum and J. Feldman (eds.), Computers and Thought, McGraw-Hill 1963, pp. 71-105.

Samuel, A., "Some Studies in Machine Learning Using the Game of Checkers II. Recent Progress", IBM J. Research and Development, Vol. 11, No. 6, (1967), pp. 601-617.

Schofield, P. "Complete Solution of the Eight Puzzle," in Machine Intelligence 1, N. Collins and D. Michie (eds.), American Elsevier Publ. Co., New York 1967.

Slagle, J., and Farrell, C., "Experiments in Automatic Learning for a Multipurpose Heuristic Program," Communications A.C.M., Vol. 14, No. 2, pp. 91-99.

Swinehart, D., and B. Sproull, SAIL, Stanford Artificial Intelligence Laboratory Operating Note 57.2, January 1971.

Vanderbrug, G., "Problem Representations and Formal Properties of Heuristic Search," Information Science, Vol. 11, No. 4, 1976.

Wickelgren, W., How to Solve Problems, W. H. Freeman and Co., San Francisco 1974.

*Given a heuristic function K for a given problem graph P1, one can define another graph P2 thus: the nodes in P2 correspond to the nodes in P1; an edge connects two nodes s and t in P2 iff K(s, t) = 1. Whether or not P2 satisfies the conditions of problem graph depends on the value computed by K.

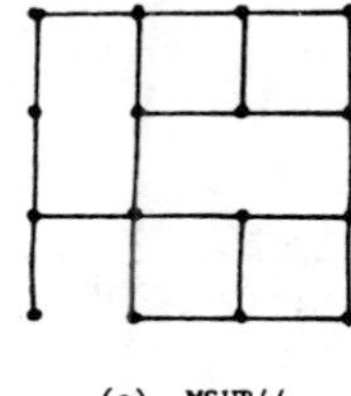

(a) MSUB44

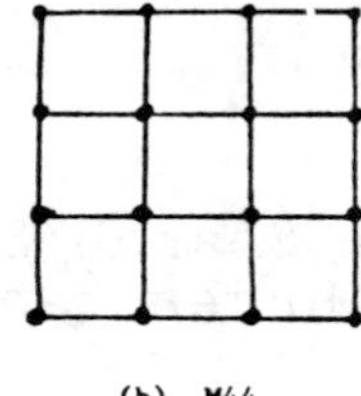

(b) M44

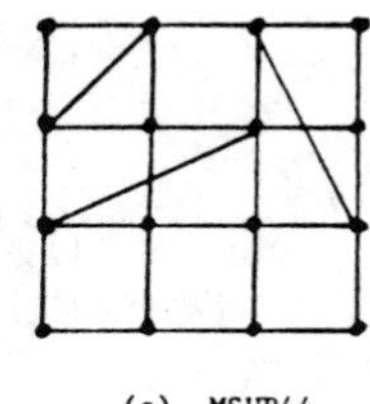

(c) MSUP44

Figure 1. A "Manhattan street pattern" graph and two variants thereof

Note that MSUB44 $\leq_e$ M44 $\leq_e$ MSUP44

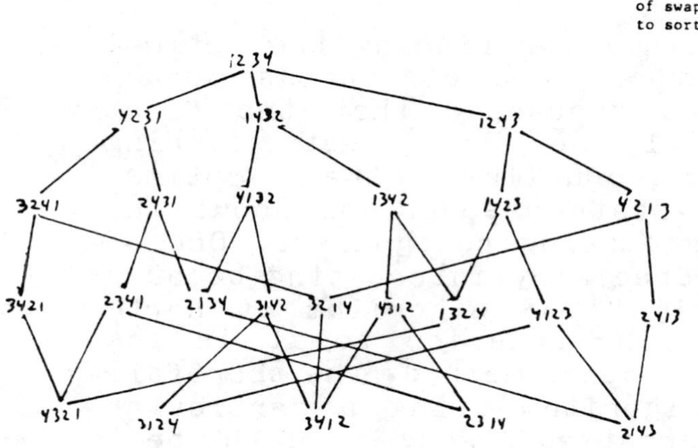

Figure 2 4MAXSWAP graph

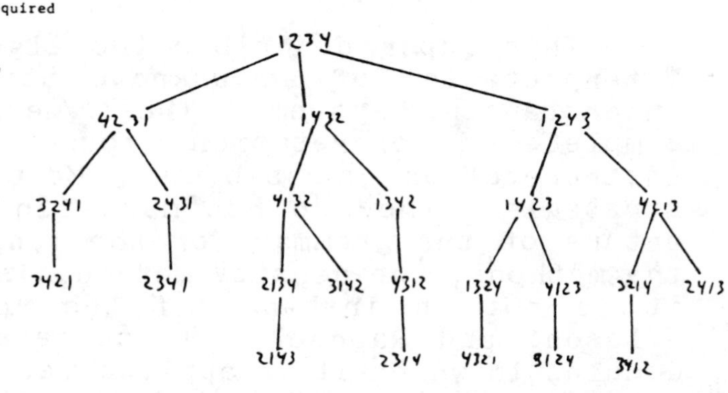

Figure 3. The union of the paths taken by MAXSORT in sorting any 4-element permutation is a spanning tree of 4MAXSWAP (and hence an edge subgraph of 4MAXSWAP; compare with Figure 2)

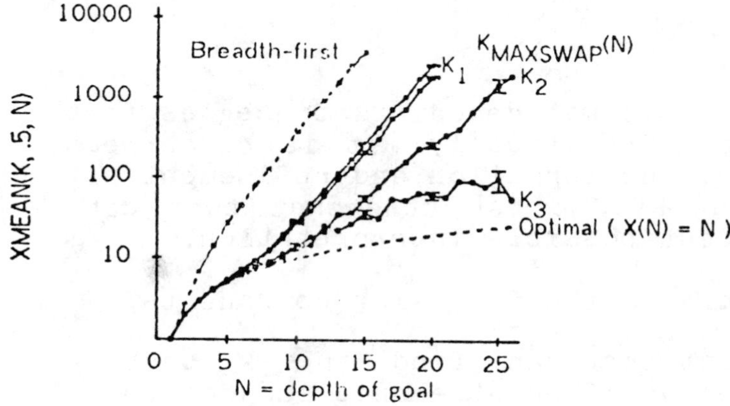

Figure 4 Mean number of nodes expanded vs. depth of goal
A* search of the 8-puzzle, comparing heuristic K_{MAXSAP} and $K_{WMAXSWAP}$ with heuristics K_1, K_2, and K_3
40 problem instances for most values of N
760 to 895 algorithm executions per heuristic function

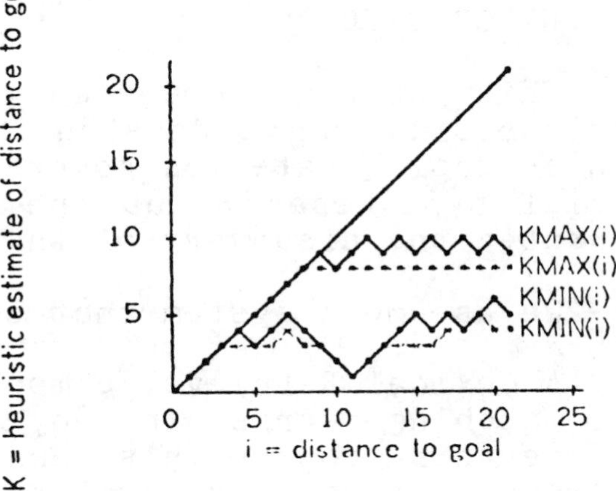

Figure 5
Heuristic estimate of distance to goal vs. actual distance
8-puzzle heuristic $K_{MAXSWAP}$ (solid) compared with heuristic K_1 (dash)

Optimal Search Strategies for Speech Understanding Control

W. A. Woods
Bolt Beranek and Newman Inc.
Cambridge, MA 02238

Abstract

This paper describes two algorithms for finding the optimal interpretation of an unknown utterance in a continuous speech understanding system. These methods guarantee that the first complete interpretation found will be the best scoring interpretation possible. Moreover, unlike other optimal strategies, they do not make finite-state assumptions about the nature of the grammar for the language being recognized. One of the methods, the density method, is especially interesting because it is not an instance of the "optimal" A* algorithm of Hart, Nilsson, and Raphael, and appears to be superior to it in the domains in which it is applicable. The other method, the shortfall method, is an instance of the A* algorithm using a particular heuristic function. Proofs of the guaranteed discovery of the best interpretation and some empirical comparisons of the methods are given. The relationship of these methods to strategies used in existing speech understanding systems is also discussed. Although presented in the speech context, the algorithms are applicable to a general class of optimization and heuristic search problems.

1. INTRODUCTION

This paper is concerned with optimal decoding strategies for continuous speech understanding. Specifically, it is concerned with control strategies governing the formation and refinement of partial hypotheses about the identity of an utterance that can guarantee the discovery of the best possible interpretation.

We assume a system that contains the following components:

a) A Lexical Retrieval component that can find the k best matching words in any region of an utterance subject to certain constraints and can be recalled to continue enumerating word matches in decreasing order of goodness (where possible constraints include anchoring the left or right end of the word to particular points in the utterance or to particular adjacent word matches). We assume that this component is interfaced to appropriate signal processing, acoustic-phonetic and phonological analysis components as in (Woods et al., 1976), and that it assigns a "quality" score to each word match reflecting the goodness of the match.

b) A Linguistic component that, given any sequence of words, can determine whether that sequence can be parsed as a possible initial, final, or internal subsequence of a syntactically correct and semantically and pragmatically appropriate utterance, and can propose compatible classes of words at each end of such a sequence.

The HWIM speech understanding system developed at BBN (Woods et al., 1976; Wolf and Woods, 1977) has such capabilities. A control strategy for such a system must answer questions such as:

a) At which points in the utterance to call the Lexical Retrieval component, and when,

b) What number of words to ask for,

c) When to give subsequences of the results to the Linguistic component, and

d) When to recall the Lexical Retrieval component to continue enumerating words at a given point.

The goal of the control strategy is to <u>discover the best scoring sequence of words that covers the entire utterance and is acceptable to the Linguistic component</u>. We will consider here a particular class of control strategies which we refer to as "island-driven".

2. ISLAND-DRIVEN STRATEGIES

In an island-driven control strategy, partial hypotheses about the possible identity of the utterance are formed around initial "seed" words somewhere in the utterance and are grown into larger and larger "island" hypotheses by the addition of words to one or the other end of the island. Occasionally, two islands may "collide" by proposing and discovering the same word in the gap between them and may then be combined into a single larger island.

Each island hypothesis is evaluated by the Lexical Retrieval component to determine its degree of match with the acoustic evidence and is checked for syntactic, semantic, and pragmatic consistency by the Linguistic component. We will refer to a partial hypothesis that has been so evaluated and checked for consistency as a "theory". The strategies that we will consider operate by successively processing "events" on an event queue, where events correspond to suspended or dormant processes that may result in the creation of theories.

The general algorithm operates as follows:

(1) An initial scan of the utterance is performed by the Lexical Retrieval component to discover the n best matching words anywhere in the utterance according to some criterion of "best" and for some value n.* An initial seed event is created for each such word and placed on the event queue. In addition, one or more continuation events, which can be processed to continue the enumeration of successively lower scoring words (regardless of position in the utterance), is created and placed on the queue. Each seed event is assigned a priority score (derived, in one of several ways to be described shortly, from the quality score that the Lexical Retrieval component gave it). Each continuation event is assigned a priority score that can be guaranteed to bound the priority score of any word that can be generated by that event (e.g., derived from the score of the last word enumerated prior to the continuation). The events are ordered on the event queue by their priority scores and are processed in order of priority.

(2) The highest priority event is selected for processing. This consists of (i) creating the corresponding theory (a one-word theory in the case of a seed event), (ii) calling the Linguistic component to check the consistency of the theory and to make predictions for words and/or word classes that can occur adjacent to it, at each end of the theory, (iii) calling the Lexical Retrieval component to enumerate the k best matching words satisfying these predictions at each end of the theory, and (iv) generating a "word" event for each such word found. A word event is an event that will add one word to a theory to create a larger theory. Continuation events are also created that will continue the enumeration of successively lower scoring words adjacent to the theory. If island-collision is permitted as an operation (island collision is a feature than can be enabled or disabled by a flag), then each word event generated is checked against an island table

---

* The HWIM system also has the ability to execute left-fo-right, right-to-left, and various hybrid strategies by appropriately constraining this initial search (e.g., confining it to the left end).

to see if the same word (at the same position in the input) has been proposed and found in the other direction by some theory. If so, an "island-collision" event is created that will combine the new word and the two theories on either side of it. Both word and island-collision events are assigned priority scores derived from the quality scores of the words that they contain and are inserted into the event queue according to their priorities.

(3) Continue selecting the top priority event from the event queue (step 2) until a theory is discovered that spans the entire utterance and is syntactically, semantically, and pragmatically acceptable as a complete sentence.

The main topic in this paper is the assignment of priority scores to the events in the above algorithm in order to guarantee that the first complete theory found will be the best scoring one that can be found. Using the quality scores assigned by the Lexical Retrieval component directly as priority scores does not ordinarily provide such a guarantee. That is, a straightforward "best-first" search strategy does not guarantee discovery of the best overall hypothesis.

Note: Although the basic island-driven strategies are presented here as involving an initial scan of the entire utterance before beginning the processing of events, there is nothing to prevent an implementation from dovetailing this initial scan with the event processing so that, for example, event processing on the early portions of an utterance could begin before the entire utterance had been heard.

3. THE SHORTFALL SCORING METHOD

3.a <u>Assumptions</u>

The shortfall method assumes that the quality scores assigned to word matches by the Lexical Retrieval component are additive, so that theories are appropriately assigned scores that are the sums of the scores of the word matches contained in them (scores that are basically multiplicative can be handled by using their logarithms). It also assumes that word matches have associated beginning and ending positions that correspond to boundary positions in the input utterance. In the HWIM system, the quality scores are logarithms of estimates of the relative probabilities of the correctness of theories given the acoustic evidence.

3.b The Basic Shortfall Scoring Procedure

Assume the utterance is divided by an acoustic-phonetic processor into phonetic or subphonetic segments separated by boundaries numbered logically from the beginning of the utterance. Let t(i) be the time in milliseconds of the i-th boundary in the utterance; nsegs, the number of segments in the utterance; and seg(i) be the region of the input utterance from t(i-1) to t(i), for i from 1 to nsegs.

For a word match from position i to j with score q, we will, in some systematic way, allocate the total word score q to the segments seg(i+1) ... seg(j) covered by the word match. For this discussion, let us allocate it proportional to the durations of the segments.

For a given utterance, we will determine for each segment seg(i) the maximum score maxseg(i) that can be allocated to that segment by any word match that covers the segment.* The score for any word match from i to j will hence be bounded by the sum maxseg(i+1)+ ... +maxseg(j), and the maximum score for any complete theory will be bounded by T = the sum from 1 to nsegs of maxseg(i).

Every partial theory will consist of a sequence of contiguous word matches spanning a region from some boundary i to some boundary j. Each such theory will carry with it two scores m and q, where m is the sum of the maxseg(i) for the segments covered by the sequence and q is the sum of the word scores of the theory. We will assign each theory a priority score p = T - m + q, which can be thought of as the maximum total score T for any theory minus the <u>shortfall</u> from this ideal to which one is committed by choosing this particular sequence of words (i.e., p = T-(m-q)). Alternatively, p can be thought of as the estimated best possible future score consisting of the score q which has already been achieved for the region covered plus the best potential score T-m for the region not yet covered (i.e., p = q+(T-m)). Because T-m is an upper bound on the possible score that can be achieved on the region not covered, the priority scores p have the characteristic that they are non-increasing as theories grow.

---

* There are several ways to actually compute such an upper bound. The simplest involves using the best possible phoneme scores assigned by the acoustic phonetic recognizer. The tightest bound comes from accumulating the maxsegs from allocated scores of actual word matches. See Section 3.j for further discussion.

3.c Strategy

In the shortfall scoring strategy, the priority scores of the individual seed events are simply the shortfall scores of the words. A priority score for a continuation event that will be an upper bound on the priority score of any words that might result from the continuation can be computed as follows: Since the Lexical Retrieval component enumerates words in decreasing order of score, the quality score of any word that results from the continuation will be no greater than that of the last word enumerated so far. Moreover, we can derive from the lexicon a lower bound on the length of a word and from this we can deduce the shortest region of the utterance that such a word could cover, and hence the smallest possible m score that such a word could have. From these two numbers, we can bound the priority score (T-m+q) of any future word and use that as the priority score of the continuation event. (This bound is excessively conservative, and in actual practice it should be possible to derive a much tighter bound. However, this argument is sufficient to guarantee that such a bound can be computed.) A preferred alternative in this case would be to have a lexical retrieval component that enumerated words directly in increasing order of shortfall. This could be done by another instantiation of the same shortfall method, recognizing words as sequences of phonemes. The lexical retrieval component in HWIM, however, did not do this.

As new theories arise from processing events linking an existing theory with a new word match, the m and q scores of an event and the new theory that it will create are simply the respective sums of the m and q scores of the old theory and the word being added to it. Thus, after assigning an m score to a word match by summing the max numbers for the segments that it covers, the m score of any new theory that includes it can be computed by a single addition.

3.d Admissibility of the Method

Claim:

The first complete spanning theory found by the shortfall scoring method will be one of the best scoring complete theories (there could be more than one) that can be found by any strategy (i.e., the algorithm is "admissible" in the conventional terminology of heuristic search).

Proof:

At the time the first complete spanning theory has been processed, every other event on the event queue (including continuation events for finding lower scoring seeds or lower scoring words to add to the ends of islands) will already have fallen low enough in its partial score (q score) that no possible match sequence in the remaining region of the utterance can bring its total score above that of the spanning theory. Also, the presence of the continuation events in the queue makes the search process complete in the sense that any word in the vocabulary would be enumerated if the process were continued long enough. Thus there is no possible word sequence across the utterance that would not be considered by this search algorithm if it were run sufficiently far. Hence, any complete theory of the utterance will have a shortfall (m-q) at least as great as that of the first complete theory discovered. Since all spanning theories have the same maxscore m = T, it follows that the first spanning theory also has the maximum possible quality score (q) of any spanning theory.

3.e Notes

Note that the process can be continued to obtain the second best complete theory, and so on. Note also that the admissibility holds for this method whether the process is left-to-right (i.e., seeds only at the left end of the utterance) or middle-out (seeds anywhere in the utterance), and that it does not require any island collision feature.

The shortfall method works with almost any type of grammar. It makes no assumptions that the grammar is finite-state, as do Markovian strategies. In the middle-out modes, it does require the linguistic consultant to have a parser (such as the bidirectional ATN parser in the HWIM system) that can take an arbitrary island fragment in the middle of an utterance and judge whether it is a possible subsequence of an acceptable sentence. In practice, it also helps if the parser can use the grammar to predict the acceptable words and classes adjacent to an island, and if the Lexical Retrieval component can use such predictions to constrain its search (as in HWIM), but this is not essential to the formal admissibility of the algorithm.

3.f Avoiding Duplicate Theories

Note that in the middle-out, island-driven strategies there are many different ways of eventually arriving at the same theory.

For example, if we have an island w with a possible word x on the left and a possible word y on the right, then we can first form the theory (xw) and then (xwy) or we can form the theory (wy) and then derive (xwy) from that. Which of these two routes is taken will depend on the scores of the words, but it is quite possible (in fact, likely) that in the course of working toward a complete theory a strategy will arrive at the same subtheory several different times by alternate routes.

If we do not include checks for the duplication of theories, then we would often get two copies of the same theory. These would forever duplicate the same predictions and theory formations, giving rise to an exponential explosion of the search process. If we include a test each time a theory is formed to determine whether that theory has been formed previously, then we can avoid this exponential process. In fact, if each time we are about to put a word event on the event queue we check the event to see if the set of word matches that it uses is the same as that of some other event, then we can terminate this duplication before making the entry on the queue and consuming the queue space (and certainly before calling the Linguistic component to check it out and make further predictions).

The check for duplication among all the events that have been created can constitute a considerable amount of testing if done in a brute force exhaustive test. However, it can be considerably reduced by indexing events by their beginning and end points or other tricks. Moreover, if one can rely on the events being generated in the order determined by the basic shortfall strategy, then the following simple check based only on the word matches at each end of an event can be used to determine whether an event is redundant (i.e., will produce the same theory as some event already generated):

> If the new word is at the left end and has the same or smaller shortfall as the rightmost word in the theory, then this event is redundant.
>
> If the new word is at the right end and has strictly smaller shortfall than the leftmost word in the theory, then this event is redundant.

The argument for the validity of this test is as follows:

In the search space we are considering, it is possible, without a check for duplication, to derive a given theory with words $w_1, w_2, \ldots, w_k$ in 2^{k-1} different ways - one corresponding to each of the possible binary derivation trees starting with some one of the w_i as a seed, and then successively adding words either to the right or the left end. (Proof - either w_1 or w_k was chosen last, hence there are two ways to derive a string of length k for every possible derivation of a string of length k-1. There is one possible way - i.e., as a seed - to derive a string of length 1.) Of all these derivation trees, the first one that will be found is the one that uses the w_i with the smallest shortfall as a seed, and at subsequent steps adds the better (in terms of shortfall) of the two words at either end (assume for the moment that no two of the words have exactly the same score). Hence, any derivation that attempts to add a word to one end of an island when that word has a smaller shortfall than the word at the other end of the island will be duplicating a theory that has already been derived (or at least already has an event for it on the event queue). In the case of two competing seeds with the same shortfall or words at each end of an island that have the same shortfall, we have arbitrarily picked the leftmost as the preferred one, which we will permit the algorithm to follow fully, and we block the derivation of duplicates from the other one. Thus, if we have a word being added to the left end of a theory that has the same shortfall as the word at the right end, then this event is redundant, since the preferred order will generate an equivalent event that adds the left end word first.

Thus, a very simple check between the score of the word being added to a theory and the score of the word at the other end of the theory will suffice to eliminate the formation of redundant events.

3.g Fuzzy Word Matches

The above discussion does not explicitly mention the problem of finding the same word in essentially the same place but with slightly different end points and different scores. We have observed this kind of output from the Lexical Retrieval component of HWIM and indeed find it desirable to know the degree of variation possible in the end points of a word match and the appropriate degradation in score for each. However, it is wasteful to give several different events to the Linguistic component, all of which are adding word matches to a given theory that differ only in their endpoints and scores. For this reason, we have introduced a structure that groups together multiple equivalent word matches into a single entity called a <u>fuzzy word match</u> (or "fuzzy" for short), which is given the score of its best member. A theory containing fuzzy word matches actually represents a class of grammatically equivalent theories and carries the score of the best one.

When an event is created to add a word match to a theory containing a fuzzy word match at that end, the score of the event must be computed using a "rectified" score that takes into account the best member of the fuzzy that is compatible with the new word (i.e., has boundaries that hook up to the new word and satisfies appropriate phonological word boundary constraints). In general, when several fuzzies are adjacent, the best compatible sequence of word matches must be chosen, and when the new word match is itself a fuzzy, the best combination of one of its members with a sequence of word matches from the theory must be taken. The event is thus given the score of the best of the grammatically equivalent, non-fuzzy events for which it stands. (Note that the score for an event is the same as the score for the theory which will result from it.)

If word matches returned by the Lexical Retrieval component are grouped into fuzzy matches whenever possible, and word events are given appropriately rectified scores, then the above admissibility result still holds (i.e., the first complete theory processed will be the best). The only difference (aside from the elimination of separate processing for grammatically equivalent theories) will be that certain word events (i.e., those whose new word(s) is (are) compatible only with a less-than-best path through the existing theory) will be formed earlier than they otherwise would have. However, these events will still be placed on the queue with the correct score (i.e., the score of the best path through the resulting theory) so that they will reach the top and be processed in exactly the same order as they would in the strategy without fuzzies.

3.h Comparison with Known Optimal Algorithms

The shortfall scoring method is similar in some respects to the well-known branch and bound technique, except for the fact that the space of possible solutions is determined by a grammar, and the characteristic in the middle-out version that the same partial interpretation may be reached by many different paths. It can also be modeled as an example of the A* algorithm of Hart, Nilsson, and Raphael (1968) for finding the shortest path through a graph, where, in this case, the nodes in the graph are partial interpretations of the utterance, and the connections in the graph correspond to the seed and word events. Consequently, it shares with that algorithm a certain kind of optimality that Hart, Nilsson, and Raphael prove - i.e., among other algorithms in its class, it explores the fewest hypotheses possible for a given bounding function while still assuring the discovery of the best hypothesis. It is simpler than the general A* algorithm, however, in that we are looking for the best scoring node, and we are not interested in scores of paths leading to that node (in fact all such paths have the same score in our case). The simple argument given previously suffices to show the admissibility of the shortfall method, whereas the general A* algorithm is more complicated.

3.i Computing the MAXSEG Profile

Measuring the shortfall from any maxseg profile that is a per word upper bound of quality score would be sufficient to assure the theoretical admissibility of the shortfall method. However, the tightness of the upper bound affects the number of events tried and partial theories created in the search for a successful interpretation (i.e., the "breadth" of the search). By assigning the upper bound as a segment-by-segment profile determined by allocated shares of actual word match scores, a fairly tight upper bound can be achieved, which tends to minimize the breadth of search. In HWIM, the maxseg profile was computed from the word matches found so far (the best of which are found first). When occasionally a word match is found that raises the maxseg for some segment, all events are appropriately rescored.

3.j Discussion

When using the shortfall method, the overwhelming tendency is that an event adding a new word to an island will pick up additional shortfall and fall some distance down in the queue. The result is that other events are processed before any additional work is done on that island. (Occasionally, the new word is the best word in its region and buys no additional shortfall, but this is a rarity.) The distance that this new event falls down the queue is determined by the amount of additional shortfall that it has just picked up and the shortfalls of the events that are competing with it on the queue. This distance directly affects the degree of "depth-first" vs. "breadth-first" processing done by the algorithm. If the new word scores well, the event falls only slightly, and few, if any, alternate events are processed before it. In this case the algorithm is relatively depth first. If the new word scores badly, the event falls further down the queue, many more alternative events have priority over it and the algorithm is more breadth first.

The above characterization is only an intuitive approximation, since the actual number of events processed before the new event is considered depends on the number of new events that will be generated by the intervening events that will also score higher than this one. In some cases, the number of such events can be extensive. The general effect, however, is that the shortfall scoring method provides a dynamically varying combination of depth-first and breadth-first search which is determined by the relative qualities of the events that are in competition.

Unfortunately, experience with the HWIM system has shown that the shortfall algorithm is excessively conservative. It amounts to assuming that any theory will obtain the maximum possible scores in the regions not yet covered. This is clearly overly optimistic in almost all cases, and it in fact leads to an excessively breadth first search. (For more details, see Section 7.)

4. DENSITY SCORING WITH ISLAND COLLISIONS

Density scoring is a fundamentally different priority scoring method. It uses a priority score which is the quality score of a theory divided by the duration of the region that it covers. One way to view this strategy is to consider again the task of estimating the expected score to be achieved in the region not covered by a theory and consider estimating this score as a direct extrapolation of the same score per millisecond that has already been achieved - i.e., add to the current score an estimated potential score consisting of the score density of the current theory times the duration of the region not covered by that theory. Since the resulting total estimated score is just the score density of the theory times the total duration of the utterance, and the total duration of the utterance is a constant, we can compare only the score densities of the theories themselves and achieve the same decisions.

When we think of the score density as an extrapolation of the score already achieved by a theory into the region not yet covered we are clearly no longer obtaining an upper bound on the possible future score an event might lead to. Hence, the previous proof of admissibility used for the shortfall method no longer applies. In particular, whereas T minus the shortfall is a monotonically decreasing function as an island grows, the score densities can get smaller when a bad word is picked up and then get larger again as the theory grows and picks up better words (thus averaging the score of the bad word over a larger duration). Hence, it is not true that the score density of descendants of an event must be no greater than that of the event itself.

However, when used with an island collision feature that allows one to combine together in one step the word lists of two different theories that are noticing the same word from opposite directions, the density method also guarantees that the first complete theory found is the best one. To prove this, we must use a different argument than for the basic shortfall strategy. The argument depends on the ability to derive subparts of a theory independently from different seeds - i.e., the middle-out control strategy is essential for the admissibility of the density scoring method.

<u>Lemma</u>:

Using the density scoring method in a middle-out strategy with island collision events, any theory covering any region of the utterance can be derived by a sequence of events all of which have a score density no less than that of the theory itself.

<u>Proof</u>:

By induction on the number of words in the theory:

(1) The hypothesis is trivially true for one-word theories by means of a seed event.

(2) Suppose that the hypothesis is true for theories of k or fewer words and that we have a theory of k+1 words with density d. Assume that the theory consists of the sequence of words $w_0 w_1 \ldots w_k$.

Case a. If the theory $w_1 \ldots w_k$ (i.e., all but w_0) has density not less than d, then by the inductive hypothesis it has a derivation whose events all have density not less than d, and this derivation plus the event to add w_0 will constitute the desired derivation of the complete theory.

Case b. Similarly if the theory $w_0 \ldots w_{k-1}$ has a density no less than d, there is a suitable derivation of that theory that can be extended to a derivation of the complete theory with density no less than d by adding w_k.

Case c. If neither a nor b is the case, then since $w_1 \ldots w_k$ has density less than d, therefore w_0 must have density greater than d. Let j be the smallest integer such that $w_0 \ldots w_j$ has density less than d. Such a j, smaller than k, must exist since the theory $w_0 \ldots w_{k-1}$ has density less than d. Also, j must be larger than 0 since w_0 has density greater than d. Now since the density of $w_0 \ldots w_j$ is less than d, the remaining theory $w_{j+1} \ldots w_k$ must have density greater than d. Also, since j is the smallest such, the theory $w_0 \ldots w_{j-1}$ has density greater than or equal to d.

Since these last two theories each have length smaller than k and density no less than d, by the inductive hypothesis they each have derivations using events of density no less than d. Therefore, before any events of density less than d can reach the top of the stack, both of these theories would have been processed, and both would have noticed the word w_j from opposite sides; hence an island collision event would have been constructed for the combined theory and would have the combined density d.

Corollary:

When a spanning theory of some density has been found by the middle-out density scoring method with island collisions, any spanning theory of higher density could have been completely derived using events of higher density, and thus would have been found before the theory in question. Hence, the first complete spanning theory found will be one of the best possible interpretations.

Corollary (dual algorithm):

A dual of the above lemma shows that a density algorithm that prefers the smallest rather than the largest density will guarantee the discovery of the lowest scoring theory.

5. SHORTFALL DENSITY

The above proof of the admissibility of density scoring makes no assumptions about the scoring metric whose density is being taken other than that it be additive. Hence, the density method can be applied to either the original quality score assigned by the Lexical Retrieval component, or to the local shortfall described previously, giving rise to strategies which we refer to as quality density and shortfall density, respectively. Initial experimental comparison of the algorithms (see Sec. 7) suggests that the shortfall density method is superior to quality density, which is in turn superior to the shortfall method alone. The superiority of the density methods over the shortfall method can be accounted for by the excessive conservatism (over optimistic scoring of alternative hypotheses) of the shortfall method. The superiority of the combined shortfall density method can be attributed to an improved "focus of attention" strategy as follows:

5.a Focus of Attention by a MAXSEG Profile

A major effect of scoring the shortfall from a maxseg profile is that the score differences in different parts of the utterance are effectively leveled out, so that events in a region of the utterance where there are not very good quality words can hold their own against alternative interpretations in regions where there are high quality words. This promotes the refocusing of attention from a region where there may happen to be high quality accidental word matches to events whose word match quality may not be as great, but are the best matches in their regions. If this were not done, then many second best, third best, etc. matches in the high scoring region could be considered before any theories worked their way across the low scoring regions. Thus, an apparently satisfactory and intuitively reasonable strategy for focusing attention emerges from the same strategy that guarantees to get the best scoring theory first.

Notice that in the shortfall density method, the maxseg profile is no longer serving the role of guaranteeing admissibility that it did in the shortfall method. In this case, the admissibility is guaranteed by the nature of densities and island collisions. Rather, in this method the maxseg profile is used only to provide this leveling of effort over portions of the utterance to promote the refocusing of attention from regions where there are many good quality matches to regions where the best matching possibility may not be as great. In fact, it is no longer necessary that the maxseg profile be an upper bound (although there are undesirable effects when the shortfall density goes negative).

As long as shortfall is positive, the addition of a word with no shortfall to a hypothesis will produce a longer duration hypothesis and consequently a smaller shortfall density (which counts as a better hypothesis). Consequently, such a hypothesis will be encouraged. However, when the shortfall is negative, the addition of a new word with no shortfall will similarly produce a hypothesis with longer duration and will spread the negative shortfall over a longer period producing a density score with smaller magnitude but (since it is negative) a larger value. Consequently, such a hypothesis will be discouraged and there will be a tendency to shift attention to other negative shortfall hypotheses that are shorter. Thus, when shortfall is positive, the ordering tends to prefer hypotheses that are longer (shortfall being equal), while when the shortfall is negative, the ordering prefers hypotheses that are shorter. Hence, in a collection of hypotheses whose shortfall is negative, the search strategy will strongly favor shifting attention back to shorter hypotheses rather than pursuing longer hypotheses. This will not affect the admissibility of the algorithm, but will exacerbate the breadth of the search in the region of negative shortfall.

6. EFFICIENCY TECHNIQUES

In addition to the basic choice of priority scoring metric used for ranking the event queue, there are several efficiency techniques that can be used to improve the performance of the island-driven strategy, frequently without loss of admissibility guarantees. Two of these are the use of "ghost" words, and the selection of a preferred direction for events from a given theory.

6.a Ghost Words

Every time a theory is given to the linguistic consultant for evaluation, proposals are made for new words on both sides of the resulting island (unless the island is already against one end of the utterance). Although events can add only one word at a time to the island, and this must be at one end or the other, eventually a word will have to be added to the other end, and that word cannot score better than the best word that was found at that end the first time. The ghost words feature consists of remembering with each event the list of words found by the Lexical Retrieval component at the other end and scoring the event using the best of the ghost words as well as the words in the event proper. The result is that bad partial interpretations tend to get bad twice as fast, since they have essentially a one-word look-ahead at the other end that comes free each time an event is processed. On the other hand, an event that has a good word match at the other end gets credit for it early, so that it gets processed sooner. The ghost words feature, thus, is an accelerator that causes extraneous events to fall faster down the event queue and allows the desired events to rise to the top faster. Experimental use of this feature has shown it to be very effective in reducing the number of events that must be processed to find the best spanning event. Its addition to the shortfall algorithm does not sacrifice admissibility. It is not theoretically admissible when added to the density methods, but it appears in practice not to sacrifice much.

6.b Choosing a Preferred Direction

Again, recall that when a theory is evaluated by the linguistic consultant, predictions are made at both ends of the island. When one of the events resulting from these predictions is later processed, adding a new word to one end of the island, the predictions at the other end of the new island will be a subset of the predictions previously made at that end of the old island. In general, words found by this new island at that end will also have been found by the old island, and if the score of the new island is slightly worse than that of the old island (the normal situation), then the strategy will tend to revert to the old island to try events picking up a word at the other end. This leads to a rather frustrating derivation of a given theory by first enumerating a large number of different subsequences of its final word sequence.

Since any eventual spanning theory must eventually pick some word at each end of the island, one could arbitrarily pick either direction and decide to work only in that direction until the end of the utterance is encountered, and only then begin to consider events in the other direction. This would essentially eliminate the duplication described above, but could cause the algorithm to work into a region of the utterance where the correct word did not score very well without the benefit of additional syntactic support that could have been obtained by extending the island further in the other direction for a while.

Without sufficient syntactic constraint at the chosen end, there may be too many acceptable words that score fairly well for the correct poorly scoring word to occur within a reasonable distance from the top of the queue. By working on the other end, one may tighten that constraint and enable the desired word to appear (although this can never cause a better scoring word to appear than those that appeared for the shorter island).

A flag in the HWIM system causes the algorithm to pick a preferred or "chosen" direction for a given theory as the direction of the best scoring event that extends that theory, and to mark the events going in the other direction from that theory so that they can be used only for making tighter predictions for words at the chosen end. This is accomplished by blocking any events noticing one of the ghost words at the inactive end of an event if that event is going counter to the chosen direction. This blocking, alone, eliminates a significant number of redundant generations of different ways to get to the same theory. An even greater improvement is obtained by rescoring the events that are going counter to the chosen direction by using the worst ghost at the other end rather than the best ghost. Since only word matches that score worse than any of the ghosts at that end are being sought by these events, this is a much better estimate of the potential score of any spanning theories that might result from these events.

The effect of rescoring the events in the non-chosen direction using the worst ghost is that, in most cases, these events fall so low in the event queue as to be totally out of consideration. Only in those cases where there was little syntactic constraint in the chosen direction and the worst matching word at that point was still quite good, do these events stay in contention, and in those cases, the use of the worst ghost score provides an appropriate ranking of these events in the event queue.

6.c Nearly Admissible Algorithms

The heuristics of ghosts and preferred direction when added to the basic shortfall algorithm improve efficiency without affecting the formal admissibility of the algorithm. Similarly the combination of the shortfall and density algorithms does not affect the formal admissibility of the density algorithm. When adding ghosts and direction preference to the density algorithms, however, this is not necessarily the case (at least the Lemma proving the admissibility of the density method no longer goes through). It is not obvious whether these variations of the density algorithm are admissible or not. However, the basic admissibility characteristics of the algorithm remain in effect in any case, with at worst a slight chance of a non-optimal interpretation being found in pathological circumstances. We can characterize such algorithms as "nearly" admissible -- i.e., adaptations of admissible algorithms that guarantee to get the best interpretation except possibly in very low probability exceptional circumstances. Empirically, as shown below, these nearly admissible algorithms appear to have all of the advantages of the provably admissible ones (i.e., not finding incorrect interpretations) while gaining the advantages of the efficiency heuristics.

7. EMPIRICAL COMPARISON OF THE DIFFERENT STRATEGIES

In the HWIM Speech understanding system, approximations to the shortfall and density algorithms have been implemented and tested. The major approximation is that continuation events are not implemented, but instead the initial values of n and k are chosen large enough that one believes that the correct interpretation of the utterance is found before any of the continuation events would have reached the top of the queue. If such is the case, then all of the decisions made by the approximation are the same as those of the admissible theoretical algorithm, and hence the first complete theory found will still be guaranteed to be the best. There are other approximations that are less justifiable, due to bugs and some rectifiable (but not rectified) discrepancies between the actual implementation and the theoretical algorithm. These differences are believed to be minor.

Details of the system's general performance are found in (Woods et al., 1976). Comparative performance results on a set of 10 utterances for the shortfall (S), shortfall density (SD), and quality density (QD) scoring strategies are shown in Table 1 below. The option of using the quality score (Q) alone as a priority score is given for comparison.

	Q	QD	S	SD
Correct first interpretation	4	3	0	5
Incorrect first interpretation	2	0	0	0
No response	4	7	10	5
Average number of theories processed *	49	82	100	73

Table 1. Comparison of different priority scoring functions.

These experiments were run using the ghosts, island-collision, and preferred direction heuristics with a resource limit of 100 theories to process before the system would give up with no response. The ten sentences used for the test were chosen at random from a test set of 124 recorded sentences.

Although a test set of only ten utterances is admittedly too small, I believe that the trends indicated in the figure are generally correct. Specifically, while using the quality score alone leads to a spanning interpretation in relatively few theories, it does so without much assurance of getting the best interpretation. In this case, only two-thirds of its answers are correct. All of the other methods consider more theories in an effort to make sure that the best interpretation is found. Consequently they found fewer spanning interpretations within the resource limitation but found no incorrect interpretations. We did not try running the quality scoring strategy beyond the first interpretation to see if a better interpretation could be found

* This average is computed over 9 sentences, omitting one for which the system broke due to a bug.

since, among other things, it is nontrivial to decide when to terminate such a process.* Running in this mode, one could easily enumerate more theories than the other methods and still not have any guarantee that the best interpretation had been discovered.

None of the versions of admissible algorithms found incorrect interpretations, so the reliability of their interpretations, when they get them, is 100% (providing the acoustic phonetic analysis of the input utterance does not cause some incorrect interpretation to score higher than the correct one, a situation that occurs sometimes in the HWIM system, but was not a factor in this experiment). Unfortunately, the shortfall strategy alone is so conservative in doing this that it failed to find any interpretations within the resource limit. Both of the density methods are clearly superior to the straight shortfall method. (Incidentally, the left-to-right shortfall strategy also failed to get any interpretations within the resource limit.)

The shortfall density strategy ranked superior to the quality density strategy in terms of the number of events that needed to be processed to find the first spanning interpretation and consequently found more correct interpretations within the resource limitations.

The effects of the island collision (C), ghosts (G), and preferred direction (D) heuristics are shown in Table 2 (where SD+0 means shortfall density without collisions, ghosts, or chosen direction, SD+C means shortfall density with island collisions, etc.). The inclusion of a heuristic does not always guarantee that the system will understand an utterance in fewer theories, but the pooled results shown (note especially the series SD+0, SD+G, SD+GD,

* Mostow (1977) gives a partial description of the criteria used in the Hearsay II system for making this decision, but the method is not algorithmic and is based on the assumption that any partial solution that is locally better than a found solution I (and that can be extended to a globally superior solution I") can be extended step by step into I" so that the partial solution I' at each step is locally superior to I. He makes no attempt to prove that such a sequence of partial solutions exists and appears only concerned with whether a search strategy can find one. In fact, there are situations in which no such sequence of stepwise extensions exists, as can be determined by reflecting on the proof of the admissibility of the density method and the necessity of the island collision feature for the admissibility result. One can then easily construct counterexamples to Mostow's assumption.

SD+GDC) suggest that the successively added heuristics produce improvements in both accuracy and number of theories required. (Note that our formal admissibility results have been shown only for the SD+C case. The SD+GDC case is at least nearly admissible.)

	SD+0	SD+C	SD+G	SD+GD	SD+GDC
Correct	3	3	3	4	5
Incorrect	0	0	0	0	0
No response	7	7	7	6	5
Average number of theories processed *	83	78	81	76	69

Table 2. The effects of island collisions, ghosts, and direction preference.

8. COMPARISON WITH EXISTING SPEECH UNDERSTANDING SYSTEMS

8.a BBN HWIM

The variations on admissible strategies discussed above are only some of the control strategy options implemented in the BBN HWIM speech understanding system. In addition there are a large number of strategy variations that result in deliberately inadmissible strategies, including strictly left-to-right density strategies and "hybrid" strategies that start near the left end of an utterance and work left to the end and then left-to-right across the rest of the utterance. For reasons of time and resource limitations, the final test run of the HWIM system was made using one of the inadmissible hybrid left-to-right strategies (Woods, et al., 1976). Subsequently, a much smaller experiment was run to compare various control strategies on a set of ten utterances chosen at random from the larger set. Although this sample is much too small to be relied on, the results are nevertheless suggestive. For two comparable experiments using our best left-to-right method (left-hybrid shortfall density) and our best nearly admissible method (shortfall density with ghosts, island collisions, and direction preference), both with a resource limitation of 100 theories and without using a facility for analysis-by-synthesis word verification, the results were as follows:

---

* This average is computed over 8 sentences, omitting two for which the system broke due to bugs.

	LHSDNV	SD+GCD
Correct interpretation	6	5
Incorrect interpretation	2	0
No interpretation	2	5
Average number of theories evaluated	51	76

That is, the inadmissible left-hybrid strategy found the best (and in these cases the correct) interpretation within the resource limitation in 6 of the 10 cases, while the nearly admissible shortfall density strategy found only 5 (not necessarily a significant difference for this size sample). On the other hand, the left-hybrid method misinterpreted two additional utterances with no indication to distinguish them from the other 6. If this strategy were used in an actual application with comparable degrees of acoustic degradation (e.g., due to a noisy environment), the system would claim to understand 80% of its utterances, but would actually misunderstand 25% of those. The shortfall density strategy, on the other hand, would only claim to understand 50% of the utterances, but would misunderstand a negligible fraction.

The middle-out shortfall density algorithm in the above experiments expanded only 50% more theories (and incidentally used only 30% more cpu time) than did the left-hybrid strategy. Although as we said before, this test set is much too small to draw firm conclusions, the success rate of the two methods are not much different, except that the middle-out method is clearly less likely to make an incorrect interpretation. Moreover, the numbers of theories considered and the computation times are not vastly different. If one considers proposals to improve the performance of inadmissible strategies by having them continue to search for additional interpretations after the first one is found (and thus take the best of several), then the time difference shown above could easily be reversed and there would still be no guarantee that the interpretation found would be the best one.

8.b DRAGON

The DRAGON system (Baker, 1975) is the only other speech understanding system in the ARPA project that provides a guaranteed best matching solution. It does this by using a dynamic programming algorithm that depends on the grammar being a Markov process (i.e., a finite-state grammar). It operates by incrementally constructing, for each position in the input and each state in the grammar, the best path from the beginning of the utterance ending in that state at that position. The computation of the best paths at position i+1 from those at position i is a relatively straightforward local computation, although for a grammar with n states, the number of operations for each such step is n times the branching ratio (i.e., the average number of transitions with non-zero probability leaving a state). DRAGON performs such a step for each 10 millisecond portion of the utterance using a state transition that "consumes" an individual allophonic segment of a phoneme.

The optimality of the solution found by this algorithm depends on the property of finite state grammars that one sequence of words (or phonemic segments) leading to a given state is equivalent to any other such sequence as far as compatibility with future predictions is concerned (regardless of the particular words used). * It is this property that permits the algorithm to ignore all but the best path leading to each state (even if competing paths score quite well!), and therefore permits it to find the best solution by progressively extending a bounded number of paths across the utterance from left to right. (This is a very attractive property, although in this case it requires one such path for each state in the grammar.) For more general grammars, where there may be context-sensitive checking between two different parts of the utterance (e.g., person and number agreement and semantic constraints between a subject and a verb), the best path leading to a given state at a given position may not be compatible with the best path following it. In this case, second best (and worse) paths leading to a given state may have to be considered in order to find any complete paths at all (much less an optimum).

Although only applicable to finite-state languages, DRAGON's dynamic programming method has the advantage of taking an amount of time proportional to the length of the utterance, being simple to compute, and guaranteeing to obtain the optimal solution. The only difficulty (aside from estimating the necessary transition probabilities) is that for a large number of states in the grammar (e.g., thousands for a reasonable size grammar) the amount of computation required is expensive. Except to the extent that the finite-state grammar permits one to eliminate from consideration

* I am using the term "state" a little casually here in roughly the sense that it is used in an ATN grammar (Woods, 1970). If one takes the condition of having equivalent future predictions as the definition of a "state" of a grammar, then what the finite-state grammar does is guarantee that there are only a finite number of such states, which can therefore be enumerated and named ahead of time. For a more general grammar, the number of such states is open-ended.

any path that is not the best one leading to its state, the algorithm exhaustively enumerates all other possibilities.

Although DRAGON's scores are estimates of probabilities of interpretations, its guarantee of optimality does not depend on that, but only on the fact that its grammar is finite-state and that therefore it suffices to carry a record of the best path leading to each state. The same dynamic programming algorithm can be applied at the level of phonemes or words, and can be generalized to apply to an input lattice such as the BBN segment lattice (Woods et al., 1976).

An unfortunate disadvantage of the dynamic programming algorithm is that it cannot be continued to obtain the second best interpretation. It loses this ability when it throws away all but the best path leading to each state. Hence a system like DRAGON can have no way of knowing if there are two competing interpretations with very similar scores.

8.c HARPY

The CMU HARPY system (Lowerre, 1976) is a development on the DRAGON theme which gives up the theoretical guarantee of optimality in exchange for computation speed. Like DRAGON, it takes advantage of the unique characteristic of finite-state grammars cited above, so that only the best path leading to a given state need be considered. However, it uses an adaptation of the dynamic programming algorithm in which not all of the paths ending at a given position are constructed. Specifically, at each step of the computation, those paths scoring less than a variable threshold are pruned from further consideration. This gives an algorithm that carries a number of paths in parallel (the number varying depending on the number of competitors above the threshold at any given point) but is not exhaustive. If the threshold is chosen appropriately, the performance can closely approximate that of the optimal algorithm, although there is a tradeoff between the speed efficiency gained and the chances of finding a less than optimal path. In practice, HARPY's threshold is set so that it introduces negligible likelihood of missing the best interpretation, thus achieving a nearly admissible algorithm in the terminology introduced above. Like the DRAGON algorithm, it cannot be continued to produce the second best interpretation.

The HARPY system has the best demonstrated performance statistics of any of the ARPA continuous speech understanding systems. However, it derives this performance in large part from the use of a highly constraining (and advantageously structured) finite-state grammar (see Wolf and Woods, 1980). This grammar has an average branching ratio of approximately 10, and characterizes a non-habitable, finite set of sentences, with virtually no "near miss" sentence pairs included.* For example, "What are their affiliations" is in the grammar, but no other sentences starting with "What are their" are possible. The only two sentences starting with "What are the" are "What are the titles of the recent ARPA surnotes," and "What are the key phrases." These three sentences will almost certainly find some robust difference beyond the initial three words that will reliably tell them apart. Similarly, the grammar permits sentences of the form "We wish to get the latest forty articles on <topic>," but one cannot say a similar sentence with "I" for "we", "want" for "wish", "see" for "get", "a" for "the", "thirty" for "forty", or any similar deviation from exactly the word sequence given above.) Most of HARPY's grammar patterns (such as the last one) consist of a particular sentence with one single open category for either an author's name or a topic. A large number of them are particular sentences with no open categories (like the first three above). Such grammar patterns significantly reduce the number of possible "distractor" hypotheses that can compete with the correct interpretation of a test sentence, even when they are not used as test sentences themselves.

The HARPY algorithm makes no guarantee that the correct path will not be pruned from consideration if it starts out poorly, but at least for the structure of HARPY's current grammar (most of whose sentences start with stressed imperative verbs or interrogative pronouns), the correct interpretation is usually found.

---

* Later references to this grammar refer to a "dynamic" branching ratio of 30. This ratio is computed by averaging the branching ratio along the paths of the correct interpretations of utterances, whereas the branching ratio of 10 results from averaging uniformly over the grammar as a whole. As a measure of the difficulty of a grammar for speech understanding, the average over the entire grammar is more appropriate, since it measures the potential for the grammar to permit viable "distractor" hypotheses that might be confused with a correct interpretation. In the actual searching of the hypothesis space for a correct interpretation, most of the hypotheses considered will in fact be such distractor hypotheses and not partial hypotheses along the correct path.

The HARPY technique appears to be the algorithm of preference at present for applications involving carefully structured artificial languages with finite-state grammars and small branching ratios (on the order of 10 possible word choices at each position in an utterance). However, it does not conveniently extend to larger and more habitable grammars. This is due to a number of factors, the most important of which is the combinatorics of expanding a large habitable grammar into a finite-state network. For example, the incorporation of a single context sensitive feature (such as number agreement between subjects and verbs) into a finite-state grammar requires the doubling of the number of states in a large sub net of the grammar, the incorporation of two such features requires a quadrupling of states, and so on. In the worst case, implementing the constraint of a context free grammar that the number of "pushes" for self-embedding constituents must match the number of "pops" cannot be represented with any finite number of states, necessitating finite-state approximations tat either accept sentences that the original grammar doesn't or fail to accept some that it does. Such finite-state grammars also have difficulty dealing with dynamically changing situations such as constraints on utterances that depend on previous utterances.

Neither the DRAGON nor the HARPY system use density normalization or any method to attempt to estimate the potential score that is achievable on the as yet unanalyzed portion of the utterance. Such normalization is not necessary, since they follow paths in parallel, all of which start and end at the same point in the utterance, and therefore never have to compare paths of different lengths or in different parts of the utterance. Again, it is worth emphasizing that the ability of these algorithms to keep the number of paths that need to be considered manageable depends on the unique characteristic of finite-state languages that requires only the best path to each state be considered.

8.d IBM

A group at IBM (Bahl et al., 1976) has a speech understanding system based on Markov models of language, which has implemented two control strategies: a Viterbi algorithm (essentially the same dynamic programming algorithm used by DRAGON) and a "stack decoder", a left-to-right algorithm with a priority scoring function that attempts to estimate the probability that a given partial hypothesis will lead to the correct overall hypothesis. The latter apparently does not guarantee the optimal interpretation, but somehow is reported as getting more sentences correct than the other (a circumstance that can happen if there are acoustic-phonetic scoring errors such that the best scoring interpretation is not correct or if the transition probabilities of the Markov model do not agree with the test set).

Recent experiments with an improved version of one of the IBM systems, incorporating the CMU technique of bypassing a phonetic segmentation to do recognition on fixed length acoustic segments (Bahl et al., 1978), reported performance on the same grammar used in the HARPY system (the "CMU-AIX05 Language") of 99% correct sentence understanding. (This performance is based on recordings in a noise-free environment, however, compared to a rather casual environment for the CMU results). They also report performance of 81% correct sentence understanding on a more difficult, but still small branching ratio, finite-state grammar (their "New Raleigh Language"). Both of these results were obtained in experiments with the system trained for a single speaker and tested on that same speaker. Performance of the system when tested with a different speaker is significantly less.

8.e Hearsay II

The Hearsay II system (Erman et al., 1980) permits the kind of generalized middle-out parsing described in this paper, and does so for context free grammars (although apparently not for context-sensitive or more powerful grammars). Moreover, it has a capability for the kind of island collisions described here. However, the control strategies with which it has been run are substantially different.

The major emphasis of the Hearsay-II work has been architectural rather than algorithmic, resulting in a general system of knowledge sources (KS's) which communicate with each other via a cross referenced structure called a "blackboard." Each KS is invoked by the satisfaction of a condition called a stimulus frame (SF) associated with the KS. When a KS is invoked, it performs actions specified in a response frame (RF) which make or change entries on the blackboard, thus triggering additional KS's until a stopping condition is realized. At that time, the best overall hypothesis yet found is taken as the interpretation of the utterance, or if not complete hypothesis has been found, a combination of partial hypotheses is chosen and the system attempts to construct a semantic interpretation from that. The blackboard of the system is divided into parametric, segment, syllable, word, word-sequence, phrase, and semantic interpretation levels.

Compared to HWIM, the Hearsay-II architecture appears to encourage a kind of "pandemonium" strategy versus HWIM's emphasis on specific components interacting in specific ways with specified orderings of queues of events. In fact the differences between HWIM and Hearsay-II in this respect are more apparent than real. The Hearsay-II system also maintains queues of things to do, and the HWIM system does in fact maintain pointers connecting data structures at different levels. A substantial architectural difference is that the structures in HWIM are tailored to the classes of algorithms being executed rather than using a very general common data structure throughout as in Hearsay.* The major difference comes down to the former's emphasis on an architecture to support a nonspecific control strategy versus HWIM's emphasis on the discovery of effective control algorithms.

The details of the algorithms used in Hearsay-II are largely relegated to the "contents of the KS's" and have been difficult to extract from available publications. As of 1976, when this paper was first written, the best available description of the Hearsay-II algorithm was extremely sketchy, reflecting the extreme of the architectural vs algorithmic emphasis. In Hayes-Roth and Lesser (1976), even the idea of formulating an explicit control strategy was rejected as "inappropriate" (because it "destroys the data-directed nature and modularity of knowledge source activity").

Hearsay-II's scoring function for hypotheses, which its authors refer to as the "desirability" of a KS, is an ad hoc combination of functions reflecting intuitive notions of "value", "reliability", "validity", "credibility", "significance", "utility", etc. Specifically, they state: "the desirability of a KS invocation is defined to be an increasing function of the following variables: the estimated value of its RF (an increasing function of the reliability of the KS and the estimated level, duration, and validity credibility of the hypothesis to be created or supported); the ratio of the estimated RF value to the minimum current state in the time region of the RF; and the probability that the KS invocation will directly satisfy or indirectly contribute to the satisfaction of a goal as well as the utility of the potentially satisfied goal." (Hayes-Roth & Lesser, 1976).

They go on to say that the above is not "complex enough" to "provide precise control in all of the situations that arise," and proceed to describe various further elaborations. Although it is

---

* The latter has aesthetic appeal, but the former is more efficient, as evidenced by the historical trend in Hearsay development toward moving information out of the blackboard and into specialized data structures within the different components (see Erman et al., 1980).

not possible to tell from this description exactly what Hearsay II does, we can infer some characteristics of its behavior. First of all, the fact that the desirability of a KS invocation is an increasing function of its duration definitely rules out any interpretation of it as implementing the shortfall or density methods.

The above allusion to the "current state in the time region of the RF" refers to a function S(t) that for each point t in the utterance specifies the maximum of the "values" of all hypotheses "which represent interpretations containing the point t." This "state" function at first glance seems similar to the maxseg profile used in the shortfall algorithm (and indeed was what caused me to start thinking along those lines), but in actuality it is quite different. Instead of being an estimate of the maximum possible portion of a score that can be attributed to a segment, Hearsay-II's state is the maximum total score of any hypothesis found so far that covers it (recall that such scores increase with length of the theory). Its contribution to the desirability of a hypothesis is described as the ratio of the "value" of that hypothesis to the smallest value of the state parameter in its region.

Since the smallest state value in the region of a hypothesis will always be at least as great as that of the hypothesis being valued (each state is the max value of all covering hypotheses), this ratio is always less than or equal to one, and is strictly less only when every portion of the region covered by the hypothesis has some better covering hypothesis (although not necessarily a single hypothesis that covers the whole region). Consequently, this "state" component of the score has the effect of inhibiting a hypothesis that at every point has a better competitor. Since the values of hypotheses grow with the length of the region covered, the effect will be that hypotheses that get big early will inhibit alternative hypotheses on the regions they cover. With shortfall scoring, on the other hand, the tendency is for big hypotheses to pick up additional shortfall and increase the likelihood of a shift to a competing hypothesis. Hearsay-II's use of the "state" parameter, is more reminiscent of SRI's "focus by inhibition" technique discussed below, which was found to have generally undesirable effects, although it did offset some of the costs of their island driving strategy (Paxton, 1976).

Since this paper was originally written, a newer paper (Hayes-Roth and Lesser, 1977) has presented additional details of the above strategy (which they call "phrase specific") and a newer control strategy called "word specific". Among the things made clearer in the later paper are that the duration bias discussed above is parameterized and that the current state function S(t) (and a related "implicit goal state" I(t)) participate in the overall desirability calculation as separate components of a weighted sum. By appropriate settings of parameters, one could eliminated the duration bias and any of three different terms that exploit the "state": one involving a ratio of the hypothesis's "RF validity" to the smallest state in its region (discussed above), one involving the difference between the RF validity and the state (not the same as my shortfall, however), and one proportional to the maximum I(t) in the region (I(t) is specified in the paper only to the extent that "it is only a slight oversimplification to think of I(t) as the arithmetic inverse of the current state S(t)").

The "word specific" strategy differs from the "phrase specific" strategy in several ways, one of which is that the current state function S(t) represents the highest value of any word hypothesis that is incorporated into any grammatical sequence. This makes the state function very similar to the maxseg profile at a slightly larger "grain size" (i.e., in word sized pieces rather than phoneme sized pieces). However, it is not used in the same way as the maxseg profile. Both terms that use the S(t) function in the desirability computation are measures of how much a hypothesis is better than the worst value of S(t) in its region. (The maxseg profile is used to measure how much a hypothesis is worse than an estimated best covering of its region.) The word specific strategy also drops the duration biasing from several components of the desirability computation, but still retains (and increases) the duration bias in the component which their tuning parameters give the most importance. The values of the tuning parameters are also changed in the word specific case, and the paper is somewhat ambiguous about what "value" is actually used to construct the current state function in this case.

There are sufficient omissions and ambiguities even in the later paper that it is still difficult to tell how the overall control strategy actually works. One can determine, however, that the word specific strategy is somewhat more similar to the density method than the phrase specific strategy is, although it is still substantially different. Given their description, it would be possible to set the parameters of the desirability calculation to be very similar to the quality density method (although not the shortfall density method). However, depending on details of the way the desirability of KS invocations is used in the overall system, the resulting control strategy might still not be comparable to the method presented here. At any rate, they do not appear to have tried this option. The paper reports one experiment that shows the word specific strategy to be superior to the phrase specific one, but does not discuss the effects of varying the tuning parameters to assess the relative utilities of the various components of the desirability computation. It would be nice to see a systematic study a la Paxton (see below) of the relative merits of the different options.

In summary, the emphasis of the Hearsay-II has been largely architectural and there has apparently been little success in determining the importance of the various components of their scoring functions or in uncovering the essential elements of an effective control strategy. They report that "A significant amount of tuning of the focusing parameters has been attempted. Nevertheless, the current parameter values are probably not optimal, and it seems clearly impossible to determine what the optimal values are." (Hayes-Roth and Lesser, 1977). One can speculate, given the optimality results of this paper, that the optimum parameter values may lie in a direction much closer to the density method. The relative performance of their word specific and phrase specific strategies is consistent with this conjecture. However, it is possible that some nonobvious characteristic of the Hearsay-II architecture might block their fully exploiting the density method.

8.f The SRI experiments

At SRI, Paxton (1977) performed a number of experiments on control strategy options, using a simulated word matching component based on performance statistics of the SDC word matching component to which a speech understanding system at SRI was originally intended to be coupled. Paxton's system is well-documented, and contains a number of interesting and well-done capabilities. He has worked out a very clean representation of the SRI grammar as a collection of small ATN networks (although he doesn't call them that) which do not have the directional left-to-right orientation that conventional ATN's do and in which the association of augments with transitions is more systematized and less procedural. The capabilities of this system for syntactic/semantic/pragmatic constraint are comparable in power to that of HWIM's general ATN grammar, and in several respects the notations used are cleaner and more perspicuous. Moreover, the implementation of these grammars contains some very elegant efficiency techniques. The system has a capability for middle-out parsing making use of the semantic/pragmatic augments in the grammar, although it doesn't seem to have a capability for island collisions and doesn't construct islands for arbitrary sentence fragments.

In terms of the control strategy framework set up in this paper (as opposed to the terms that he himself uses), Paxton's system makes a distinction between a quality score for a hypothesis and a priority score for an event, although the kinds of hypotheses and events that his system creates are somewhat different than those in HWIM. One way of viewing his system in the terms presented here is that his hypotheses are always partially completed constituents (what he calls "phrases"), which can make predictions for the kinds of words or constituent phrases that they can use. These phrases are incorporated into a structure called a "parse net" in which explicit "producer" and "consumer" links associate such hypotheses to each other, but partially completed phrases are not combined into larger sentence fragments corresponding to HWIM's notion of islands. His events are of two types: operations to look for a word or words at a point (which he calls a "word task", comparable to our proposals to the lexical retrieval component), and events to create such predictions from a phrase (which he calls a "predict task"). Every phrase is implicitly an event for a predict task, and he has a special data type called a "prediction" to represent events for word tasks.

Whereas HWIM, when it processes a hypothesis, will always make all predictions, then call the Lexical Retrieval component to find all matching words, and then create word events for each such found word, Paxton's system breaks this cycle up differently. His system schedules separate events for each of the individual word predictions generated by a hypothesis, and whenever a word or completed phrase is found he distributes it immediately to all its "consumers" without waiting. (This difference is perhaps motivated by his lack of a word matcher that could efficiently find the best matching words at a given position without exhaustively considering each word in the dictionary.) The success of such a method would appear to depend on the ability to judge a priori, without local acoustic evidence what words were likely to appear. That is, it demands exceptionally strong syntactic/semantic predictions.

Paxton's system makes no attempt to guarantee the best interpretation, nor does it stop with the first complete interpretation it finds. Rather it runs until one of several stopping conditions is satisfied (such as running out of storage), after which it takes the best interpretation that it has found so far.

Paxton performed a systematic set of experiments varying four control strategy choices, which he called "focus by inhibition," "map all at once," "context checking," and "island driving." The first was a strategy for focusing on a set of words that occur in high scoring hypotheses and decreasing the scores of all tasks for hypotheses incompatible with those words.

The "map all at once" strategy referred to a "bottom up" lexical retrieval strategy that found all possible words at a given point and ranked them taking their word mapper scores into account, rather than proposing such words one at a time in the order in which their proposing hypothesis ranked them (i.e., rather than ranking such words according to *a priori* preferences assigned by the grammar). This is more similar to the way the lexical retrieval component is used in HWIM and the algorithms presented in this paper.

"Context checking" referred to a technique of assigning a priority score to predictions of a partial phrase on the basis of a heuristic search for the best possible combinations of higher level constituents that can use it, rather than by basing such priority scores solely on the local quality of the partial phrase alone. (This mechanism gives part of the effect of our use of theories that include arbitrary fragments of a sentence that may cross several levels of phase boundary, but apparently does not permit a fragment that has incomplete phrases at both ends to be assigned a priority as a whole. It assigns the resulting priority score just to the phrase doing the prediction without apparently remembering the context that justified this score.)

"Island driving," in Paxton's system, referred to the use of a middle-out strategy that looked for a best word somewhere in the utterance to start a seed, and if all hypotheses from that seed scored badly enough would look for another such seed, and so on. However, his system contained none of the features such as island collisions, ghosts, preferred directions, shortfall, or density scoring techniques discussed in this paper (although it may have had something amounting to an absolute direction preference - the documentation is not totally clear on whether both ends of an island can be worked on independently). Hence its version of island driving seems to have all of the disadvantages of a middle-out strategy with almost none of the compensating advantages.

The experiments indicated that the "main effects" of focus by inhibition (i.e., the net effects averaged over all combinations of other strategy options) were negative both in accuracy of the recognition and in number of events processed, and that the main effects of mapping all at once and context checking were positive (the former was more expensive in run time in their system, but might not have been with a suitable lexical retrieval component such as that of HWIM). All three of these experiments showed a statistically significant effect. In addition, the main effect of Paxton's island driving feature was found to be negative in time and accuracy, although the result was not statistically significant "because of a large interaction with sentence length." Specifically, Paxton found that island driving improved performance for short utterances, but decreased performance for longer ones, largely due to exceeding the storage limitations before finding the best interpretation. Consequently, it is possible that the implementation of some of the features described in this paper might have improved the performance of the island driving strategy sufficiently to gain a net improvement.

Paxton's results with the focus by inhibition strategy reflect what seems to have been a common experience of the various speech understanding groups in the ARPA project. Although it seemed natural to expect that some word match scores should be good enough that they could be considered correct, thereby eliminating attempts to find alternatives to them, in fact all attempts to implement such an intuition seem to have led to at best indifferent results and usually to positive degradation. In retrospect, the fact that perfect matches of other words or short word sequences can occur by accident in completely accurate transcriptions of sentences (e.g., "four" within "California") should suggest that there is no magic threshold above which one can consider a given hypothesis correct without verifying its consistent extension to a complete spanning theory. It seems, therefore, that the absolute value of the local quality score is not what matters in deciding the most likely interpretation. The relative scores of competing hypotheses are more relevant, but what really counts is the eventual quality of the complete spanning theory.

9. COST/BENEFITS OF OPTIMALITY

There is a "folk theorem" in some AI circles that admissible strategies are more expensive than approximate ones and therefore to be avoided. Our experience with various control strategies in HWIM appears to indicate that at least in the case of speech and for the island-driven shortfall density method with island collisions, the admissible method is only 30-50% less "efficient" than a straightforward "best-first" strategy and has substantial performance advantages in minimizing false interpretations.* An

* Erman et al.'s statement (Erman et al., 1980) that BBN's experiments substantiated SRI's claim that island driving was inferior to some forms of left-to-right search is incorrect.

additional characteristic of the shortfall density method with respect to efficiency is that the combinatorics of the search depend on the amount of shortfall and not directly on the length of the input. Thus as the quality of the acoustic phonetic components improve, the combinatorics of the shortfall density algorithm improve dramatically.

One might be tempted to take the performance comparisons of the HWIM system versus the Hearsay-II system (Lea, 1980) as evidence of the superiority of approximate strategies over admissible ones. However, it is more likely that the difference in performance is due to the differences in difficulty of the two grammars or to differences in their acoustic "front end."* Hearsay-II can in principle explore all the alternative hypotheses that the quality density strategy would and should in fact explore at least these if functioning according to its design philosophy of finding a first interpretation and then exploring further any hypotheses that could produce something better.

When speaking of nonadmissible strategies, one should be careful to distinguish between arbitrary, ad hoc strategies and what I have called "nearly admissible strategies." The latter can often have all the advantages of both. In further support of the advantages of admissibility, or at least near admissibility, over

---

Their statement is apparently based on the fact that HWIM's final performance run was made using a left-to-right, nonadmissible strategy (which we believed at the time to be expedient). (See also the discussion of Paxton's result in 8.f above.) Incidentally, their statement that the HWIM system had an explicit control strategy is also incorrect. HWIM had an explicit interconnection of components, but many different control strategies were explored within this basic architecture.

* The best reported performance results of the Hearsay II system are based on the same highly constrained, branching ratio 10 grammar used by HARPY (see section 8.c above). HWIM, on the other hand, used a general ATN grammar with estimated average branching ratio of 196, permitting a relatively habitable subset of English which includes such minimal pairs as "What is the registration fee" and "What is their registration fee." Another factor affecting the relative performance of HWIM versus both HARPY and Hearsay-II is that the latter take their dictionary pronunciations from averaged actual speech of specific speakers. HWIM attempts the more difficult task of synthesizing them by rule from phonetic pronunciations from a pronouncing dictionary of American English. HWIM consequently neither requires nor uses any speaker training.

ad hoc search strategies, I should point out that the performance of the HARPY system was consistently superior both in speed and accuracy to that of Hearsay-II on the same grammar and vocabulary and with the same acoustic front end. (This is not entirely fair since Hearsay-II carried a lot of architectural baggage and was not as finely tuned as HARPY. However, it is clearly not a victory for the ad hoc approach.) Although the HARPY developers make much of the fact that their "beam search" technique gives up the guarantee of admissibility for efficiency, the HARPY algorithm in fact owes much of its success to being a nearly admissible algorithm, derived as discussed above from an admissible dynamic programming algorithm.

I would argue therefore that it is premature to rule out admissible algorithms as undesirable or inappropriate for speech understanding. In fact, preliminary evidence suggests that admissible algorithms or at least "nearly admissible" algorithms are to be preferred.

10. CONCLUSIONS

We have presented two basic priority scoring methods, <u>shortfall</u> and <u>density</u> scoring, that provide admissible search strategies for finding the best matching interpretation of a continuous speech utterance, with no limitations to finite-state grammars and without exhaustively enumerating all possible interpretations. Moreover, the two methods can be used in conjunction, and the combined method appears to be more efficient than either of the methods by themselves. We have also presented several heuristics that can be used with these basic strategies to produce admissible or nearly admissible algorithms that appear to have all of the advantages of the provably admissible ones while exploring fewer hypotheses. Although the methods are presented here in the context of speech understanding systems, analogous methods are applicable to other perceptual tasks such as vision, with appropriate generalizations of segment, word, and phrase.

The density scoring method is especially interesting, since it is not an instance of the "optimal" A* algorithm and (at least for the speech understanding problem) appears to be superior to the corresponding A* algorithm (the shortfall method) in the number of hypotheses that need to be explored to obtain the best matching solution. It apparently gains this superiority from its ability to work on different parts of the solution independently and combine them by the mechanism of island collision. This is similar in some respects to the use of lemmas in a theorem proving system. The density method is not applicable to as wide a class of problems as the general A* algorithm, but should be applicable to any "covering" problem where scores are accumulated from partial hypotheses that can be said to "cover" some analog of a region.

Acknowledgment

This research was supported in part by the Advanced Research Projects Agency of the Department of Defense and was monitored by ONR under Contract No. N00014-75-0533.

References

Bahl, L.R., Baker, J.K., Cohen, P.S., Cole, A.G., Jelinek, F., Lewis, B.L., and Mercer, R.L. (1978) "Automatic Recognition of Continuously Spoken Sentences from a Finite State Grammar." Conference Record, 1978 IEEE Int'l Conf. on Acoustics, Speech and Signal Processing, IEEE 78CH1285-6 ASSP, Tulsa, OK, April, 1978.

Bahl, L.R., Baker, J.K., Cohen, P.S., Dixon, N.R., Jelinek, F., Mercer, R.L., and Silverman, H.F. (1976) "Preliminary Results on the Performance of a System for the Automatic Recognition of Continuous Speech," Conference Record, IEEE Int'l Conf. on Acoustics, Speech and Signal Processing, ICASSP-76, Philadelphia, Pa., April, 1976.

Baker, J.K. (1975) "The DRAGON System -- An Overview," IEEE Trans. Acoustics, Speech and Signal Processing, Vol. ASSP-23, No. 1, February, 1975, pp. 24-29.

Erman, L.D., Hayes-Roth, F, Lesser, V.R., and Reddy, D.R. (1980) "The Hearsay-II Speech-Understanding System: Integrating Knowledge to Resolve Uncertainty," Computing Surveys 12 (2), June, 1980, pp. 213-253.

Hart, P., Nilsson, N., and Raphael, B. (1968) "A Formal Basis for the Heuristic Determination of Minimum Cost Paths," IEEE Trans. Sys. Sci. Cybernetics, July, Vol. SSC-4, No. 2, pp. 100-107.

Hayes-Roth, F, and Lesser, V.R. (1976) "Focus of Attention in a Distributed-Logic Speech Understanding System," Conference Record, IEEE Int'l Conf. on

Acoustics, Speech and Signal Processing, ICASSP-76, Philadelphia, Pa., April, 1976.

Hayes-Roth, F. and Lesser, V.R. (1977)
"Focus of Attention in the Hearsay-II Speech Understanding System," in Proc. 5th Int'l Joint Conf. on Artificial Intelligence, Cambridge, Mass., 1977, pp. 27-35.

Lea, Wayne (1980)
Trends in Speech Recognition, Prentice-Hall, Engelwood Cliffs, N.J.

Lowerre, Bruce T. (1976)
"The HARPY Speech Recognition System," Technical Report, Department of Computer Science, Carnegie-Mellon Univ., April, 1976.

Mostow, D.J. (1977)
"A Halting Condition and Related Pruning Heuristic for Combinatorial Search," in CMU Computer Science Speech Group, Summary of the CMU Five-year ARPA Effort in Speech Understanding Research, Carnegie-Mellon University, Computer Science Department, Technical Report, 1977.

Paxton, W.H. (1977)
"A Framework for Speech Understanding," Stanford Research Institute Artificial Intelligence Center, Technical Note 142, June, 1977.

Wolf, J.J. and Woods, W.A. (1977)
"The HWIM Speech Understanding System," Conference Record, IEEE Int'l Conf. on Acoustics, Speech and Signal Processing, Hartford, Conn., May, 1977.

Wolf, J.J. and Woods, W.A. (1980)
"The HWIM Speech Understanding System" in Wayne Lea (Ed.) Trends in Speech Recognition, Prentice-Hall, Engelwood Cliffs, N.J.

Woods, W.A. (1970)
"Transition Network Grammars for Natural Language Analysis," Communications of the ACM, Vol. 13, No. 10, October, 1970, pp. 591-606.

Woods, W.A. (1978)
"Theory Formation and Control in a Speech Understanding System with Extrapolations Toward Vision," in A.R. Hanson and

E.M. Riseman (Eds.) Computer Vision Systems, Academic Press, New York, pp. 379-390.

Woods, W., M. Bates, G. Brown, B. Bruce, C. Cook, J. Klovstad, J. Makhoul, B. Nash-Webber, R. Schwartz, J. Wolf, V. Zue (1976) "Speech Understanding Systems - Final Technical Progress Report," BBN Report No. 3438 Vols. I-V, Bolt Beranek and Newman Inc., Cambridge, Ma.

Consistency in Networks of Relations

Alan K. Mackworth

Department of Computer Science, University of British Columbia, Vancouver, B.C., Canada

ABSTRACT

Artificial intelligence tasks which can be formulated as constraint satisfaction problems, with which this paper is for the most part concerned, are usually solved by backtracking. By examining the thrashing behavior that nearly always accompanies backtracking, identifying three of its causes and proposing remedies for them we are led to a class of algorithms which can profitably be used to eliminate local (node, arc and path) inconsistencies before any attempt is made to construct a complete solution. A more general paradigm for attacking these tasks is the alternation of constraint manipulation and case analysis producing an OR problem graph which may be searched in any of the usual ways.

Many authors, particularly Montanari and Waltz, have contributed to the development of these ideas; a secondary aim of this paper is to trace that history. The primary aim is to provide an accessible, unified framework, within which to present the algorithms including a new path consistency algorithm, to discuss their relationships and the many applications, both realized and potential, of network consistency algorithms.

1. Introduction

A concern for the efficiency of our programs is not a major component of the current artificial intelligence zeitgeist, and yet, as the focus shifts from small, toy problems to large ones, that concern should become more central. Even if, as some claim by way of excuse, the technology is advanced at an exponential rate, if our programs consume a quantity of resources that is exponential in the size of the task, $O(k^n)$, then each doubling of available resources only means an additional $(\ln 2/\ln k)$ words, regions or clauses can be handled. This paper is concerned with the effectiveness of algorithms designed to solve a certain class of problems.

2. The Task

Many tasks can be seen as constraint satisfaction problems. In such a case the task specification can be formulated to consist of a set of variables, each of which must be instantiated in a particular domain and a set of predicates that the values of the variables must simultaneously satisfy. Restricting the discussion for the moment to unary and binary predicates the task consists, then, of providing a constructive proof for the wff:

$$(\exists x_1)(\exists x_2)\ldots(\exists x_n)P_1(x_1) \wedge P_2(x_2) \wedge \ldots \wedge P_n(x_n) \wedge P_{12}(x_1, x_2) \wedge P_{13}(x_1, x_3) \wedge \ldots \wedge P_{n-1,n}(x_{n-1}, x_n),$$

where P_{ij} is only included in the wff if $i < j$ for we require $P_{ji}(v_j, v_i) = P_{ij}(v_i, v_j)$. Imposing a further restriction that the variable domains each consist of a finite number of discrete values then there are several candidate solution schemes. Among these are generate-and-test, formal theorem-proving methods and backtracking.

3. Backtracking and Three of its Maladies

Backtracking consists, in general, of the sequential instantiation of the variables from ordered representations of their domains. As soon as all of the variables of any predicate are instantiated its truth value is tested. If it is true the process of instantiation and testing continues but if it is false the process fails back to the last variable instantiated that has untried values in its domain and reinstantiates it to its next value. The intrinsic merit of backtracking is that substantial subspaces of the generate-and-test search space, the Cartesian product of all the variable domains, are eliminated from further consideration by a single failure.

On the other hand, backtracking can still be grotesquely inefficient. See Sussman and McDermott [19] and Gaschnig [10] for particular samples of pathological behavior. Bobrow and Raphael [2] have labeled this class of behavior "thrashing". In particular, the time taken to find a solution tends to be exponential in the number of variables both in the worst-case and on the average. It is important to identify the causes of this poor behavior and to suggest remedies.

(A) The most obvious source of inefficiency and the easiest to prevent concerns the unary predicates. If the domain for variable v_i, D_i, includes a value that does not satisfy $P_i(x)$ then it will be the cause of repeated instantiation and failure which could be eliminated by simply discarding once and for all those domain elements that do not satisfy the corresponding unary predicate.

(B) A second source of inefficiency occurs in the following situation. Suppose the variables are instantiated in the order $v_1, v_2, \ldots, v_n$ and for $v_i = a$, $P_{ij}(a, v_j)$ (where $j > i$) does not hold for any value of v_j. Backtracking will try all values of v_j, fail and try all values of v_{j-1} (and for each of these try all values of v_j) and so on until it tries all combinations of values for $v_{i+1}, v_{i+2}, \ldots, v_j$ before finally discovering that a is not a possible value for v_i. What's worse this identical failure process may be repeated for all other sets of values for $v_1, v_2, \ldots v_{i-1}$ with $v_i = a$.

(C) A third phenomenon that causes gross inefficiency and replication of effort occurs when $v_i = a$, $v_j = b$, and $P_i(a)$, $P_j(b)$ and $P_{ij}(a, b)$ do hold but there is no value x for a third variable v_k such that $P_{ik}(a, x)$, $P_k(x)$ and $P_{kj}(x, b)$ are simultaneously satisfied as they must be in any solution. As in the previous case, this is not only expensive to discover but may also be rediscovered many times by a backtracking solution process.

It is the purpose of this paper to provide a unified treatment of these phenomena and algorithms designed to prevent their occurrence thereby leading to solution strategies that do not require exponential time for particular task domains.

It is convenient to view the task specification as a network which consists of a labeled, directed graph in which the variables are represented by the nodes each with an associated set representing the variable's domain, the unary predicates are represented by loops on the nodes, and the binary predicates by labeled, directed arcs. For each arc from node i to node j corresponding to $P_{ij}(i < j)$ there is an arc from node j to node i corresponding to $P_{ji}(v_j, v_i) = P_{ij}(v_i, v_j)$. Suitable terms to name each of the state of affairs that lead to the three phenomena described above are, respectively, node inconsistency, arc inconsistency, and path inconsistency.

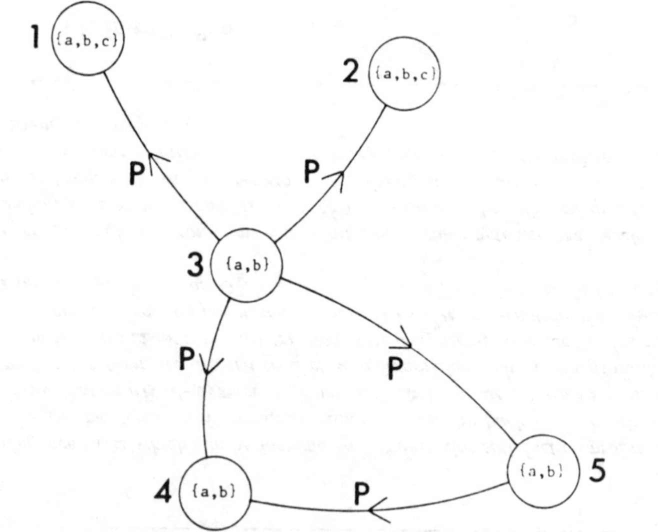

FIG. 1. A network exhibiting inconsistency.

As an example of arc and path inconsistencies consider the network of Fig. 1. The domains associated with the nodes are $D_1 = D_2 = \{a, b, c\}$ and $D_3 = D_4 = D_5 = \{a, b\}$. The binary predicate P denotes strict lexicographic ordering of its arguments so that $P(a, b) = P(a, c) = \ldots = T$ and $P(a, a) = P(b, a) = \ldots = F$. The arcs for $P^T(x, y) = P(y, x)$ are omitted. A backtrack search demonstrating that no solution exists is shown in Fig. 2. The network nodes are treated in the order 1, 2, 3, 4, 5. Each node in the search tree is labeled with the partial solution developed to that node. As usual, as soon as a partial solution fails to satisfy one of the network relations backtracking occurs.

Arc inconsistency appears at, for example, arc 2–3. The value $a \in D_2$ has no corresponding $x \in D_3$ such that $P(x, a)$. In the search tree this is reflected as one of the reasons for the failure of the subtree rooted at *aa*, (*aa*(*aaa*)(*aab*)), and rediscovered in the failure of the subtree (*ba*(*baa*)(*bab*)) and again in the subtree (*ca*(*caa*)(*cab*)).

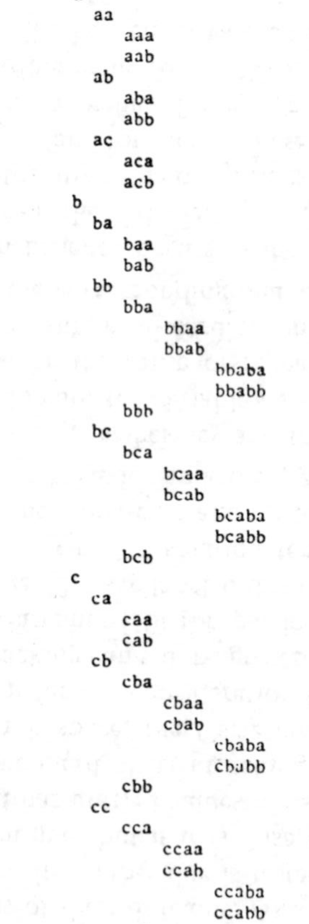

FIG. 2. A backtracking search of the solution space of the network in Fig. 1.

Path inconsistency appears on the path 3–5–4. The values $a \in D_3$ and $b \in D_4$ satisfy the vacuous unary predicates and the non-vacuous binary predicate $P(a, b)$; however, there is no value $x \in D_5$ such that $P(a, x) \wedge P(x, b)$. This is discovered in the search tree in the failure of the subtree (*bbab*(*bbaba*)(*bbabb*)) and rediscovered three more times in the failure of the subtrees rooted at nodes *bcab*, *cbab*, and *ccab*.

This example was chosen to be as small as possible and yet still demonstrate these effects. Clearly with larger domains and larger networks these problems multiply. In particular, in this example there are no nodes intervening between the nodes causing the failure. If there are such intervening nodes that are irrelevant to the failure then the failed subtrees can be very much larger besides reoccurring often. It should also be clear that although here the ordering of the nodes was somewhat malicious in intent (although it could have been worse: consider 1, 2, 4, 5, 3) these inefficiencies of backtracking cannot be removed by such minor palliatives as reordering the nodes.

4. Consistency: A State of Affairs that Forestalls Thrashing

The state of affairs that ensures that those phenomena do not occur can be defined as follows:

(A) *Node consistency*

Node i is node consistent iff for any value $x \in D_i$, $P_i(x)$ holds.

(B) *Arc consistency*

Arc (i, j) is arc consistent iff for any value $x \in D_i$ such that $P_i(x)$, there is a value $y \in D_j$ such that $P_j(y)$ and $P_{ij}(x, y)$.

(C) *Path consistency*

A path of length m through the nodes $(i_0, i_1, \ldots, i_m)$ is path consistent iff for any values $x \in D_{i_0}$ and $y \in D_{i_m}$ such that $P_{i_0}(x)$ and $P_{i_m}(y)$ and $P_{i_0 i_m}(x, y)$, there is a sequence of values $z_1 \in D_{i_1}, \ldots, z_{m-1} \in D_{i_{m-1}}$ such that

(i) $P_{i_1}(z_1)$ and . . . and $P_{i_{m-1}}(z_{m-1})$,

(ii) $P_{i_0 i_1}(x, z_1)$ and $P_{i_1 i_2}(z_1, z_2)$ and . . . and $P_{i_{m-1} i_m}(z_{m-1}, y)$.

The definition and example of path inconsistency given in Section 3 was only for path length $m = 2$. This definition of path consistency does not require that the nodes $(i_0, i_1, \ldots, i_m)$ all be distinct. That is, path consistency applies to both simple and non-simple paths. Moreover, a non-simple path may be consistent even though different occurrences of the same node on the path correspond to different occurrences of the associated variable.

A network is said to be node, arc or path consistent iff every node, arc or path of its graph is consistent.

5. How to Achieve Node Consistency

Since node consistency is concerned only with the unary predicates, in achieving it there is no interaction between the nodes; thus, it is achieved by a simple one-pass algorithm NC-1 that applies the node consistency procedure NC to each node i.

```
procedure NC(i):
D_i ← D_i ∩ {x | P_i(x)}
begin
  for i ← 1 until n do NC(i)
end
```

NC-1: the node consistency algorithm

6. How to Achieve Arc Consistency

The algorithms in this section are all based on the following observation (first made by Fikes [6]): given discrete domains, D_i and D_j, for two variables v_i and v_j which are node consistent, if $x \in D_i$ and there is no $y \in D_j$ such that $P_{ij}(x, y)$ then x can be deleted from D_i. When that has been done for each $x \in D_i$ then arc (i, j) (but not necessarily (j, i)) is consistent. As this is the basic action of the arc consistency algorithms we embody it in a Boolean procedure:

```
procedure REVISE((i, j)):
begin
  DELETE ← false
  for each x ∈ D_i do
    if there is no y ∈ D_j such that P_ij(x, y) then
      begin
        delete x from D_i;
        DELETE ← true
      end;
  return DELETE
end
```

Note that immediately after applying REVISE to arc (i, j) it must be consistent; however, it may not remain consistent because values in D_j may subsequently be removed by applications of REVISE to some arc (j, k). A single pass through all the arcs applying REVISE to each is not sufficient. The simplest algorithm to achieve arc consistency, AC-1, iterates such a pass until there is no change on an entire pass at which point the network must be arc consistent.

```
begin
  for i ← 1 until n do NC(i);
  Q ← {(i, j) | (i, j) ∈ arcs (G), i ≠ j}
  repeat
    begin
      CHANGE ← false
      for each (i, j) ∈ Q do CHANGE ← (REVISE ((i, j)) or CHANGE)
    end
  until ¬ CHANGE
end
```

AC-1: the first arc consistency algorithm

The obvious inefficiency in AC-1 is that a single, successful revision of an arc on a particular iteration causes all the arcs to be revised on the next iteration whereas in fact only a small fraction of them could possibly be affected.

In noting this fact Waltz [24] implemented an elegant algorithm that he described as follows: (to convert to our framework, for "junction" read "node", for "label" read "value" and for "branch" read "arc").

"[The result] is obtained by going through the junctions in numerical order and:

(1) Attaching to a junction all labels which do not conflict with junctions previously assigned, i.e., if it is known that a branch must be labeled from the set S, do not attach any junction labels which would require that the branch be labeled with an element not in S.

(2) Looking at the neighbors of this junction which have already been labeled; if any label does not have a corresponding assignment for the same branch, then eliminate it.

(3) Whenever any label is deleted from a junction, look at all its neighbors in turn, and see if any of their labels can be eliminated. If they can, continue this process iteratively until no more changes can be made. Then go on to the next junction (numerically)."

The idea behind this algorithm is that arc consistency can be achieved in one pass through the nodes by ensuring that following the introduction of node i all arcs (k, m) where $k, m \leqslant i$ and $k \neq m$ are made consistent. When node $i+1$ is introduced all arcs leading from it and all arcs leading to it (to and from nodes introduced earlier) may be inconsistent and so must be revised. If a REVISE((k, m)) is successful (i.e., modifies D_k) then the only additional arcs that need to be reconsidered are all those that lead to k, $\{(p, k)\}$, with the important exception of (m, k). (m, k) is excepted because it cannot have become inconsistent as a direct result of the deletions made in D_k by REVISE((k, m)): any deletions were made precisely because there was no corresponding value in D_m.

These notions are captured in AC-2 which follows that Waltz' filtering algorithm in spirit (see p. 106).

When node i is introduced on the ith iteration of lines 3–18, Q and Q' are initialized on lines 5 and 6 to contain all arcs directed away from and toward node i respectively. When Q is exhausted by the iteration of lines 10–14, Q is set to Q' and Q' emptied ready to hold all arcs directed at nodes one arc removed from node i that need to be revised. At the start of the sth ($s > 2$) iteration of lines 8–17, Q consists of all arcs directed at nodes $(s-2)$ arcs removed from i that are to be revised while Q' is ready to hold all the arcs directed at nodes $(s-1)$ arcs removed from i that need to be revised as a result of the revising of the arcs on Q. This process initially spreads out from node i but may return to it if there are any cycles in the graph of arc length greater than 2. The particular form of AC-2 derives, in part, from considering just such a situation in which the spreading wave of arc revision will cross itself.

Another approach to the arc consistency problem abandons the idea of making the network arc consistent on a single pass through the nodes. Instead simply make a queue of all the arcs in the network and apply REVISE to them sequentially. If

```
1  begin
2    for i ← 1 until n do
3      begin
4        NC(i);
5        Q ← {(i,j) | (i,j) ∈ arcs(G), j < i}
6        Q' ← {(j,i) | (j,i) ∈ arcs(G), j < i}
7        while Q not empty do
8          begin
9            while Q not empty do
10             begin
11               pop (k,m) from Q
12               if REVISE((k,m)) then
13                 Q' ← Q' ∪ {(p,k) | (p,k) ∈ arcs (G), p ≤ i, p ≠ m}
14             end
15           Q ← Q'
16           Q' ← empty
17         end
18     end
19 end
```

AC-2: the second arc consistency algorithm

REVISE is successful on any arc (reduces a node domain) then one need only (re)apply REVISE to those arcs that could possibly have the result of applying REVISE changed from *false* to *true*. (Contrast this with AC-1 which would subsequently reapply REVISE to all the arcs.) Some of these arcs may already be waiting on the queue. If so, they should not be reentered on it. AC-3 embodies this approach.

```
begin
  for i ← 1 until n do NC(i);
  Q ← {(i,j) | (i,j) ∈ arcs(G), i ≠ j}
  while Q not empty do
    begin
      select and delete any arc (k, m) from Q;
      if REVISE ((k, m)) then Q ← Q ∪ {(i, k) | (i, k) ∈ arcs(G), i ≠ k, i ≠ m}
    end
end
```

AC-3: the third arc consistency algorithm

Although AC-2 appears more complex than AC-3 it is just a special case of the latter algorithm corresponding to the choice of a particular ordering of AC-3's priority queue, with the exception of one minor discrepancy. The discrepancy is that in AC-2 it is possible if the graph has cycles of arc length greater than 2 for an arc to be waiting on both Q and Q' simultaneously.

7. How to Achieve Path Consistency

Montanari [14] has provided an elegant, formal treatment of the concept of path consistency. The purpose of this section is to introduce some of Montanari's notation and theorems and his algorithm for achieving path consistency and, furth.rmore, to show how the same result can be achieved by doing considerably less computation by refining the algorithm in a manner somewhat analogous to the progression from AC-1 to AC-3.

7.1. Representing relations

The arc consistency algorithms operate on an explicit data structure representation of the unary predicates, (i.e., the sets of all values that satisfy them, D_i) deleting values that cannot be part of a complete solution because of the restrictions imposed on adjacent nodes by the binary predicates. However, it is a matter of indifference to those algorithms whether the binary predicates are represented by a data structure or a procedure. The path consistency algorithms can be seen as generalizations in that although the predicate $P_{13}(x, y)$ may allow a pair of values, say, $P_{13}(a, b)$ that pair may actually be forbidden because there is an indirect constraint on v_1 and v_3 imposed by the fact that there must be a value, c, for v_2 that satisfies $P_{12}(a, c)$, $P_2(c)$ and $P_{23}(c, b)$. If there is no such value then that fact may be recorded by deleting the pair (a, b) from the set of value pairs allowed initially by P_{13}, in a fashion directly analogous to the deletion of individual values from the variable domains in the arc consistency algorithms. In order to perform that deletion it is necessary to have a data representation for the set of pairs allowed by a binary predicate. If the variable domains are finite and discrete then a relation matrix with binary entries is such a representation. Predicate P_{ij} is represented by a relation matrix R_{ij} whose m_i rows correspond to the m_i values of v_i and whose m_j columns correspond to the m_j values of v_j.

A useful example of the concepts involved is the set of n-queens problems. Used by Floyd [7], Fikes [6] and Djikstra [4] to illustrate backtrack programming, REF–ARF and structured programming respectively, this example is also of historical and comparative interest. The task is to place n queens on an $n \times n$ chessboard so that no queen is on the same row, column or diagonal as any other. Since each queen must be in a different column the task can be put in the constraint satisfaction paradigm by creating n variables $(v_1, v_2, \ldots, v_n)$, one for each column. The value of each variable is the row number of the queen in that column. Consider the 5-queens problem of Fig. 3(a). The queen shown in column 2, $(v_2 = 3)$, forbids the values $v_1 = 2$, $v_1 = 3$ and $v_1 = 4$ hence column 3 of the initial value of R_{12} is as shown in Fig. 3(b). For uniformity the currently permitted values for each variable are not given by a set D_i as for the arc consistency algorithms but by a matrix R_{ii} whose off-diagonal entries are required to be zero.

Columns

Rows	1	2	3	4	5
1				x	
2	x		x		
3	x	Q	x	x	x
4	x		x		
5				x	

(a)

$$R_{12} = \begin{pmatrix} 0 & 0 & 1 & 1 & 1 \\ 0 & 0 & 0 & 1 & 1 \\ 1 & 0 & 0 & 0 & 1 \\ 1 & 1 & 0 & 0 & 0 \\ 1 & 1 & 1 & 0 & 0 \end{pmatrix}$$

(b)

FIG. 3. Illustrating the 5-queens problem.

7.2. Operations on relations

Two operations on relations are needed: intersection and composition.

7.2.1. *Intersection of relations*

If two separate relations are both required to hold between v_i and v_j, R'_{ij} and R''_{ij}, then their intersection is written $R_{ij} = R'_{ij}$ & R''_{ij} where the entry in the rth row and sth column of R_{ij}: $R_{ij,rs} = R''_{ij,rs} \wedge R''_{ij,rs}$.

7.2.2. *Composition of relations*

Suppose relation R_{12} holds between v_1 and v_2 and R_{23} between v_2 and v_3 then the induced relation transmitted by v_2 is the composite relation $R_{13} = R_{12} \cdot R_{23}$. A pair (a, c) is allowed by R_{13} only if there is a pair (a, b) allowed by R_{12} and a pair (b, c) allowed by R_{23}. That is,

$$R_{13} = R_{12} \cdot R_{23}$$

iff

$$R_{13,rs} = \bigvee_{t-1}^{m_2} (R_{12,rt} \wedge R_{23,ts}).$$

In the matrix representation, composition is simply binary matrix multiplication. Composition of relation matrices takes precedence over intersection.

7.3. Direct and induced relations

If, in the example above, R^0_{13} was the original direct relation between v_1 and v_3 then it can be intersected with the induced relation $R_{12} \cdot R_{23}$ to give a new and possibly more restrictive constraint $R'_{13} = R^0_{13}$ and $R_{12} \cdot R_{23}$.

7.3.1. *Two examples of induced relations*

7.3.1.1. 5-*queens*. In Fig. 4, R^0_{25} permits the pair of queens shown but there is no value of v_1 that satisfies both R_{21} and R_{15} so $R'_{25} = R^0_{25}$ and $R_{21} \cdot R_{15}$ forbids the pair of queens shown. In the matrix notation $R^0_{25,31} = 1$ but $(R_{21} \cdot R_{15})_{31} = 0$ hence $R'_{25,31} = 0$.

Rows \ Columns	1	2	3	4	5
1	X	X	X	X	Q
2	X		X	X	
3	X	Q	X	X	X
4	X	X	X		
5	X			X	

FIG. 4. Induced relations in the 5-queens problem.

7.3.1.2. *Arc consistency*. The basic arc consistency procedure of Section 6, REVISE $((i,j))$, can be written in the current notation as:

$$R'_{ii} = R^0_{ii} \ \& \ R_{ij} \cdot R_{jj} \cdot R_{ji} \tag{7.1}$$

To see that this is so, note that $R_{ji} = R^T_{ij}$ and $R_{jj} = R_{jj} \cdot R_{jj}$ so (7.1) can be written as

$$R'_{ii} = R^0_{ii} \ \& \ R_{ij} \cdot R_{jj} \cdot R^T_{ij}$$

$$R'_{ii} = R^0_{ii} \ \& \ (R_{ij} \cdot R_{jj}) \cdot (R_{ij} \cdot R_{jj})^T$$

Each row of R_{ij}, corresponding to each value of v_i, has a 1 for each value of v_j allowed. $R_{ij} \cdot R_{jj}$ is the same except that all columns corresponding to non-permitted values of v_j will be zeroed. $(R_{ij} \cdot R_{jj}) \cdot (R_{ij} \cdot R_{jj})^T$ will have a 1 at position rr on the main diagonal iff $R_{ij} \cdot R_{jj}$ has at least one 1 in row r (that is, there is at least one value for v_j for the rth value of v_i). R^0_{ii} is zero off the diagonal and 1 at position rr if the rth value of v_i was previously allowed; this position is zero in R'_{ii} iff there is no corresponding value of v_j. Thus the effect of (7.1) parallels exactly the side effect of REVISE$((i,j))$.

7.4. The minimal network

Having introduced the notion of induced relations it is natural to enquire if there is an algorithm that makes explicit all the induced relations implicit in a network. To specify the task properly we need two definitions:

(a) Two networks N_1 and N_2 each with n nodes are *equivalent* iff the set of n-tuples satisfying N_1 is identical to the set of n-tuples satisfying N_2

(b) A network M is *minimal* iff

$$(R_{ij,x_ix_j} = 1) \rightarrow (\exists v_1)(\exists v_2) \ldots (\exists v_n)(v_i = x_i)(v_j = x_j)(\forall k)(\forall p)(R_{kp,v_kv_p} = 1).$$

In English, in a minimal network the remainder of the network does not add any further constraint to the direct constraint R_{ij} between v_i and v_j. If any pair of values is permitted by its direct constraint then it is part of at least one solution. The task that Montanari calls the central problem is to compute for a given network N, a network M that is minimal and equivalent to N. The central problem is clearly solvable: generate the set of all solutions by backtracking and then for all i and j set $R_{ij,ab} = 1$ iff there is a solution $(x_1, x_2, \ldots, x_n)$ where $x_i = a$ and $x_j = b$. However, that is expensive.

In fact, the central problem is NP-complete, that is, putatively exponential. (Montanari [15] credits this observation to a private communication from R. M. Burstall.) It is easy to see that this must be so. If it is solvable in polynomial time then so is the problem of deciding if a planar, undirected graph with at most four edges incident at a node has a chromatic number of at most 3 which in turn is known to imply that P = NP (which conjecture is thought unlikely to be true) [9, 1]. The chromatic number of a graph is the minimum number of different colours needed to paint the nodes so that each node is a different colour from every adjacent node. To put the chromatic number problem into our framework, the relations R can all be 3×3 Boolean matrices. R_{ii} is the 3×3 identity matrix while R_{ij} $(i \neq j)$ is 0 on the main diagonal and 1 off it if there is an arc (i,j) otherwise the entries of R_{ij} $(i \neq j)$ are all 1. If the central problem for this network can be solved in polynomial time then one can simply inspect any R_{ii}: if there is a non-zero entry then the 3-colorability decision problem is answered affirmatively otherwise negatively. This sharp result, due to Garey, Johnson and Stockmeyer in [9], shows that even quite restricted network consistency problems can be inherently exponential; here, for example, we have domains of size 3 and only four non-vacuous relations out of each node.

7.5. Path consistency

Given that the central problem is not likely to admit of an efficient (polynomial time) solution, it seems judicious to attack an easier problem: the task of computing a path consistent network equivalent to a given network. To recall, a network is path consistent iff any pair allowed by any direct relation R_{ij} is also allowed by all paths from v_i to v_j. A pair is allowed by a path from v_i to v_j if at every intermediate vertex values can be found that satisfy the unary and binary predicates along the path. The following theorem due to Montanari [14] can be used to justify the first path consistency algorithm.

THEOREM. *If every path of length 2 of a network with a complete graph is path consistent the network is path consistent.*

Proof. By straightforward induction on the length of the path.

Observe that in our notation a path of length 2 from node i through node k to node j is consistent iff $R_{ij} = R_{ij} \,\&\, R_{ik} \cdot R_{kk} \cdot R_{kj}$. The algorithm given by Montanari to compute a path consistent network equivalent to R is then as follows:

```
1  begin
2    Y^n ← R
3    repeat
4      begin
5        Y^0 ← Y^n
6          for k ← 1 until n do
7            for i ← 1 until n do
8              for j ← 1 until n do
9                Y^k_ij ← Y^(k-1)_ij & Y^(k-1)_ik · Y^(k-1)_kk · Y^(k-1)_kj
10     end
11   until Y^n = Y^0;
12   Y ← Y^n
13 end
```

PC-1: the first path consistency algorithm

Montanari [14] gives an inductive proof for the correctness of PC-1. Another justification derives directly from the theorem above. To see that the algorithm halts observe that the & operation of line 9 has a monotonic effect on Y_{ij}. On the iteration of lines 4–10 that the algorithm halts on, $Y = Y^n = Y^0 = Y^k\,(1 \leqslant k \leqslant n)$ and so line 9 has had no effect at all: for all i, j, k, $Y_{ij} = Y_{ij} \,\&\, Y_{ik} \cdot Y_{kk} \cdot Y_{kj}$. All paths of length 2 (v_i, v_j, v_k) are consistent so Y is path consistent.

Parenthetically, Algorithm PC-1 should be compared to Algorithm 5.5 of Aho, Hopcroft and Ullman [1] which is a generalization of Warshall's [25] transitive closure algorithm and Floyd's [8] shortest path algorithm. Algorithm 5.5 needs only one iteration of the equivalent of lines 4–10 because they require that · be distributive over + (& in our case) whereas here there is no guarantee that composition is distributive over intersection of binary matrices.

PC-1 is correct but it consumes more time and space than it need. In pursuing this thought it is profitable to see that PC-1 is a generalization of AC-1. PC-1 essentially becomes AC-1 if we substitute

$$8 \quad Y^k_{ii} \leftarrow Y^{k-1}_{ii} \,\&\, Y^{k-1}_{ik} \cdot Y^{k-1}_{kk} \cdot Y^{k-1}_{ki}$$

for lines 8–9 of PC-1. (See Section 7.3.1.2 if this is not clear.)

Pursuing the comparison with AC-1, we ask if it is necessary to keep $n+2$ copies of the network of relations: R, Y^0 and $Y^k\,(1 \leqslant k \leqslant n)$, each of which will be very large even for moderate n. R is clearly unnecessary. To avoid keeping Y^0 use a flag which is set to *true* when any Y_{ij} is changed. Line 9 requires that one use Y^{k-1}_{ik}, Y^{k-1}_{kk} and Y^{k-1}_{kj} even though one or more of the updated versions Y^k_{ik}, Y^k_{kk} and Y^k_{kj} may already have been computed. Clearly the only possible effect of using the updated versions of those relations is to speed convergence. The outcome is then that only a single copy of Y which is continually updated need be used.

Secondly, some computations predictably have a null effect (e.g., $Y^k_{kk} = Y^{k-1}_{kk}$) so need not be done. Third, since $Y_{ji} = Y^T_{ij}$ almost half the computation can be avoided.

But these improvements are matters of detail not substance. A substantial improvement can however be effected by pursuing further the analogy with AC-1. There we noted that whenever an arc was made consistent by deleting values from the node at its tail rather than require another complete iteration through the entire set of arcs one could specify just which arcs might be affected and put them on a queue either to be dealt with when the current set of arcs was exhausted (AC-2) or whenever was convenient (AC-3). Here we can see that we are considering the entire set of paths of arc length 2. If a path is not consistent we make it so by changing the necessary 1's to 0's in the binary matrix relating the two terminal nodes of the path. When we do so every path of length 2 that has as one of its component arcs the arc between the terminal nodes of the path just made consistent must be (re)checked for consistency. However, some of these paths may already be waiting in the queue to be considered. As in the case of arc consistency we define a procedure REVISE which checks a path of length 2 from node i through node k to node j for consistency. If it must be made consistent by modifying Y_{ij} REVISE returns *true* otherwise *false*.

```
procedure REVISE ((i, k, j))
begin
  Z ← Y_ij & Y_ik · Y_kk · Y_kj
  if Z = Y_ij then return false
    else Y_ij ← Z; return true
end
```

We also need a procedure RELATED PATHS((i, k, j)) that returns a set of length 2 paths that need to be REVISEd if REVISE((i, k, j)) returns *true*. Since $Y_{ij} = Y_{ji}^T$ we need only compute Y_{ij} if $i \leqslant j$ so RELATED PATHS has two cases to consider: (a) $i < j$ and (b) $i = j$.

(a) $i < j$. i and j are distinct nodes so we want the set of all paths of length 2 that have arc (i, j) or arc (j, i) as one of their arcs. Also, we want to exclude paths (i, j, j) and (i, i, j) because on both REVISE will predictably return *false*.

In this case, the set of paths to be returned is

$$\begin{aligned} S_a = \; & \{(i, j, m) \mid (i \leqslant m \leqslant n), (m \neq j)\} \\ & \cup \{(m, i, j) \mid (1 \leqslant m \leqslant j), (m \neq i)\} \\ & \cup \{(j, i, m) \mid j < m \leqslant n\} \\ & \cup \{(m, j, i) \mid 1 \leqslant m < i\} \end{aligned}$$

S_a has $2n-2$ members.

(b) $i = j$. In this case Y_{ii} has changed so every path of length 2 that uses i as its intermediate node must be checked with the exception of paths (i, i, i) and (k, i, k). The set of paths to be returned is $S_b = \{(p, i, m) \mid (1 \leqslant p \leqslant m), (1 \leqslant m \leqslant n), \neg(p = i = m), \neg(p = m = k)\}$ S_b has $n(n+1)/2-2$ members. The paths (i, i, i) and (k, i, k) are excluded because they would result in REVISE returning *false*.

Note that the exclusion of (k, i, k) from the set of paths related to (i, k, i) corresponds exactly to the exclusion of arc (m, k) when REVISE((k, m)) was predictably *false* there as REVISE((k, i, k)) is predictably *false* here.

Finally,

procedure RELATED PATHS((i, k, j)):
if $i < j$ *then return* S_a *else return* S_b

Now we have the components for a more efficient path consistency algorithm, PC-2.

```
begin
  Q ← {(i, k, j) | (i ≤ j), ¬(i = k = j)}
  while Q is not empty do
    begin
      select and delete a path (i, k ,j) from Q;
      if REVISE((i, k, j)) then Q ← Q ∪ RELATED PATHS((i, k, j))
    end
end
```

PC-2: the second path consistency algorithm

The order of path selection from Q does not affect the outcome of the algorithm but it may affect its efficiency. In particular if Q is ordered on the value of k then the initial set of paths is processed in essentially the same order as in PC-1. If the relations are such that composition does distribute over intersection then we are guaranteed that the value of Y^n after the first iteration of PC-1 lines 4–10 will be its final value, Y: on the second iteration there will be no further change. (This is so because in that case the task is that of Aho, Hopcroft and Ullman's [1] Algorithm 5.5. See that reference for a precise specification of a set of conditions sufficient to ensure that only one iteration of PC-1 is necessary.) Thus, if Q is so ordered in PC-2 then only on the original set of paths in Q (of which there are $(n^3+n^2-n)/2$) will REVISE return *true* and hence possibly increase the length of Q. Any other ordering may not have that effect.

8. The Use of Consistency Methods in Problem Solving

The consistency methods discussed were initially motivated here by reference to three situations that caused pathological thrashing behavior in a backtracking problem solver. How then are these consistency algorithms to be used? Clearly, applying PC-2 before backtracking will ensure that none of the thrashing behaviors discussed in Section 3 will occur; however, it is possible to do better. As Fikes showed in REF-ARF alternating constraint manipulation and instantiation of a variable is a good strategy for Boolean constraint problems. Burstall [3] in a program for solving cryptarithmetic puzzles alternated constraint manipulation and the bisection of variable domains. A formulation that includes these two approaches as special cases is the alternation of constraint manipulation and case analysis. By case analysis is meant the creation of p subproblems by adding to each of p copies of the network an additional case constraint where the p case constraints OR'ed together constitute a tautology. (The additional tautological constraint may involve more than one variable.) The resultant OR graph may be searched in any of the usual ways [16]; a solved subproblem has a unique instantiation of the variables after PC-2 has been applied (i.e., each Y_{ii} has exactly one 1 on the diagonal) whereas an unsolvable subproblem has some Y_{ij} with all entries 0 (in fact in that case all Y_{ij} will have all entries zero after PC-2 has been applied.)

9. Applications

9.1. Finite, discrete state space problems

9.1.1. *Puzzles*

The most obvious applications of these techniques are to the traditional puzzle-solving problems. Gaschnig [10], for example, has used an iteration of a modification of AC-3 and instantiation to solve Instant Insanity and cryptarithmetic puzzles and has shown how the search space is drastically reduced. That version of AC-3 does not, however, distinguish between the arc (i, j) and the arc (j, i) so that the equivalent of REVISE((i, j)) must check every value of D_i and find a corresponding value in D_j and also must similarly check every value of D_j for the existence of a compatible value in D_i, although as shown in Section 6 when REVISE is called on a pair of adjacent nodes it is known which of the two arcs is possibly inconsistent.

Other puzzles to which these methods apply are magic square problems and the n-queens problem. The list could be longer.

9.1.2. *Other combinatorial problems*

It remains to be seen whether the approach suggested will lead to more effective algorithms for such traditional combinatorial tasks as computing the chromatic number of a graph and the graph isomorphism problem although it is clear that Unger's [23] approach to graph isomorphism contains some of the seeds of this approach. In a similar vein Suzman and Barrow [21] have been applying an arc consistency algorithm to clique detection.

9.2. Continuous variable domains

The requirement that the relations between variables be explicitly represented does not lead of necessity to the Boolean matrix representation. As Montanari points out, any representation of the relations that allow composition and intersection is sufficient. For example, using as the domains subsets of R^n allows one to treat space planning [5] and n-dimensional space packing problems such as cloth cutting [11] and the FINDSPACE problem [20].

9.3. Vision

In the Waltz filtering algorithm the variables are picture junctions whose values are their possible interpretations as corners. The initial variable domains arise from the shape of the junctions; the unary predicates arise from lighting inferences while the binary predicates simply require each edge to have the same interpretation at both of its ends. An interesting question to pursue is to ask how the processing time depends on the complexity of the picture. From the available results [24], the dependence could well be linear. Waltz suggests that this is so because when each new junction is introduced the propagation of arc revision is restricted for the most part to that set of lines forming the image of a single body of which that junction is a part. The effect is so restricted because T junctions do not transmit constraining action from the stem to the crossbar or vice versa. Unless this decoupling effect obtains in other domains there is no reason to expect linear behavior from AC-2 or AC-3. Moreover, in this domain, the interpretation of pictures of more and more complex individual polyhedra rather than of more and more polyhedra of fixed complexity would not presumably display linear behavior. Worst case analysis of AC-1 suggests that the processing time is $O(a^2)$ where a is the number of arcs in in the graph. Turner [22] has generalized the Waltz' algorithm to apply to certain curved objects.

The author has previously proposed [12] the use of arc consistency algorithms in the task of interpreting pictures of polyhedral scenes. In that application, the variables are the regions whose values are the positions and orientations of their possible interpretations as surfaces. The unary and binary predicates arise both from

(a) Constraints on the surface positions and orientations taken individually and pair-wise together, if they intersect in an edge, imposed by the geometry of the picture formation process. (These are the constraints exploited by the author's earlier program, POLY [13].)

And

(b) Constraints on surface size, shape and pairwise connectivity imposed by a priori knowledge of the objects that can appear in the world.

Barrow and Tenenbaum [17] have an application of arc consistency in which the variables are picture regions and the values are the names of their interpretations as surfaces (such as, "door", "wall" and "picture"). Rather than just satisfy the constraints they seek an assignment of values to variables that will maximize the likelihood of the region interpretations being correct. In a related study, Rosenfeld, Hummel and Zucker [18] investigate various probabilistic models using AC-1.

Finally, Montanari [14] suggested that the variables be distinctive, recognizable subpictures of the picture one is interpreting. If the values are the pictorial location of these subpictures then one could use the consistency algorithms and subpictures already located to constrain the search area for an as yet unlocated subpicture.

9.4. AI programming languages

Consistency methods could well solve some of the problems of retrieval from a data base that essentially takes the form of a semantic network. The criticisms that Sussman and McDermott [19] leveled at the crucial position occupied by automatic backtrack control in PLANNER were well founded and yet it is also clear that, unless we are to abandon completely the goal of a high-level programming language for AI, default search and data base retrieval mechanisms should be available to the user. (And yet again, these should not be forced upon the user. If he wants to program his own, the primitives should be available as they are in Conniver.)

The consistency methods advocated here are clearly more effective than automatic backtracking and so deserve to be considered as a default database retrieval mechanism.

As an example, "Find a large rectangle which is touching a triangle and inside a circle" could appear in MICRO-PLANNER as

```
(THPROG (X Y Z)
  (THGOAL (OBJ $?X RECTANGLE))
  (THGOAL (SIZE $?X BIG))
  (THGOAL (TOUCHING $?Y $?X))
  (THGOAL (OBJ $?Y TRIANGLE))
  (THGOAL (OBJ $?Z CIRCLE))
  (THGOAL (INSIDE $?X $?Z))
  (THRETURN $?X))
```

or in network form as in Fig. 5. One need not enumerate again all the thrashing problems that the execution of that MICRO-PLANNER code would encounter in various configurations of the world. As a simple example, just consider a situation in which there are a large number of rectangles only one of which is inside the only circle. Backtracking could thrash for a very long time before discovering the right rectangle whereas a "truly smart" procedure would take the circle, find out what is inside it, ... The effect of that smart procedure would be achieved by the consistency algorithms described here.

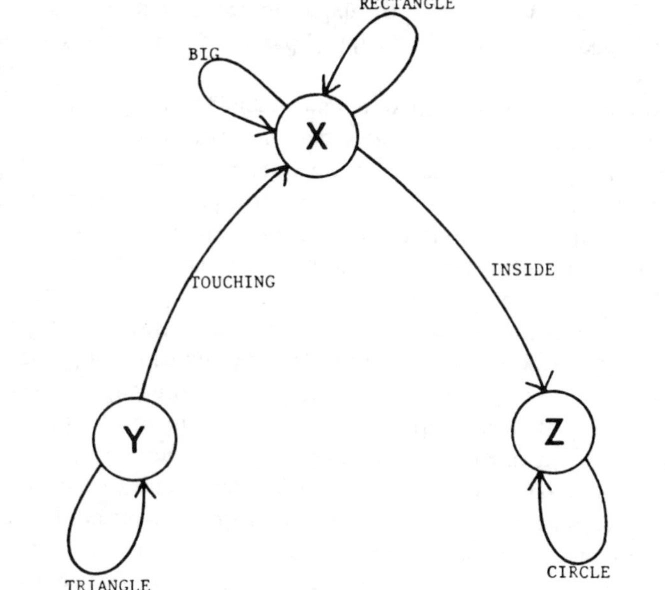

FIG. 5. A network representation of a retrieval task.

10. Conclusion

In this paper, we have been concerned with a class of algorithm, which could be named network consistency algorithms, designed to aid in the discovery of a situation that satisfies a set of simultaneous constraints that has been imposed on any candidate solution.

By being presented and extended in a uniform framework these algorithms will perhaps become more accessible to others as will the pursuit of their development in the context of a variety of applications many of which have been discussed here.

ACKNOWLEDGMENTS

I am indebted to F. O'Gorman for some initial conversations on this topic. The support of the National Research Council of Canada, under Grant A9281, is gratefully acknowledged.

REFERENCES

1. Aho, A. V., Hopcroft, J. E. and Ullman, J. D., *The Design and Analysis of Computer Algorithms*, Addison-Wesley, Reading, Mass., 1974.
2. Bobrow, D. G. and Raphael, B., New programming languages for AI research, *Comput. Surv.* **6** (1974), 153–174.
3. Burstall, R. M., A program for solving word sum puzzles, *Comp. J.* **12** (1969) 48–51.
4. Dahl, O. J., Djikstra, E. W. and Hoare, C. A. R. *Structured Programming*, Academic Press, 1972.
5. Eastman, C. M. Automated space planning, *Artificial Intelligence*, **4** (1973), 41–64.
6. Fikes, R. E. REF–ARF: A system for solving problems stated as procedures, *Artificial Intelligence*, **1** (1970), 27–120.
7. Floyd. R. W., Nondeterministic algorithms, *J. Assoc. Comput. Mach.* **14** (1967), 636–644.
8. Floyd, R. W. Algorithm 97: shortest path, *Comm. ACM* **5** (1962), 345.
9. Garey, M. R., Johnson, D. S. and Stockmeyer, L. Some simplified NP-complete problems. *Proc. 6th Annu. ACM Symp. Theory Comput.*, Seattle, Wash. (1974), pp. 47–63.
10. Gaschnig, J. A. Constraint satisfaction method for inference making, *Proc. 12th Annu. Allerton Conf. Circuit System Theory*, U. Ill., Urbana-Champaign (1974).
11. Haims, M., On the optimum two-dimensional allocation problem, Ph.D. Thesis, Dept. of Electrical Engineering, New York University, New York (1966).
12. Mackworth, A. K. Using models to see. *Proc. Artificial Intelligence and the Simulation of Behaviour Summer Conf.*, University of Sussex (1974), pp. 127–137.
13. Mackworth, A. K. Interpreting pictures of polyhedral scenes, *Artificial Intelligence*, **4** (1973), 121–137.
14. Montanari, U. Networks of constraints: fundamental properties and applications to picture processing, *Inform. Sci.* **7** (1974), 95–132.
15. Montanari, U. Optimization methods in image processing. *Proc. IFIP Congress*, North-Holland, 1974, pp. 727–732.
16. Nilsson, N. J. *Problem-solving Methods in Artificial Intelligence*, McGraw-Hill, 1971.
17. Nilsson, N. (Ed.), Artificial intelligence—research and applications, progress report, Stanford Research Institute (1975).
18. Rosenfeld, A., Hummel, A. and Zucker, S. W. Scene labelling by relaxation operations, Computer Science TR-379, University of Maryland (1975).
19. Sussman, G. J. and McDermott, D. V., Why conniving is better than planning, Artificial Intelligence Memo. No. 255A, MIT (1972).
20. Sussman, G. J. The FINDSPACE problem, Artificial Intelligence Memo. No. 286, MIT (1973).
21. Suzman, P. and Barrow, H. G. Private communication, 1975.
22. Turner, K. J. Computer perception of curved objects using a television camera, Ph.D. Thesis, Dept. of Machine Intelligence, School of Artificial Intelligence, University of Edinburgh (1974).
23. Unger, S. H., GIT—a heuristic program for testing pairs of directed line graphs for isomorphism, *Comm. ACM*, **7** (1964), 26–34.
24. Waltz, D. L., Generating semantic descriptions from drawings of scenes with shadows, MAC AI-TR-271, MIT (1972).
25. Warshall, S. A theorem on Boolean matrices, *J. Assoc. Comput. Mach.* **9** (1962), 11-12.

The B* Tree Search Algorithm: A Best-First Proof Procedure†

Hans Berliner

Computer Science Department, Carnegie–Mellon University, Pittsburgh, PA 15213, U.S.A.

ABSTRACT

In this paper we present a new algorithm for searching trees. The algorithm, which we have named **B***, *finds a proof that an arc at the root of a search tree is better than any other. It does this by attempting to find both the best arc at the root and the simplest proof, in best-first fashion. This strategy determines the order of node expansion. Any node that is expanded is assigned two values: an upper (or optimistic) bound and a lower (or pessimistic) bound. During the course of a search, these bounds at a node tend to converge, producing natural termination of the search. As long as all nodal bounds in a sub-tree are valid,* **B*** *will select the best arc at the root of that sub-tree. We present experimental and analytic evidence that* **B*** *is much more effective than present methods of searching adversary trees.*

The **B*** *method assigns a greater responsibility for guiding the search to the evaluation functions that compute the bounds than has been done before. In this way knowledge, rather than a set of arbitrary predefined limits can be used to terminate the search itself. It is interesting to note that the evaluation functions may measure any properties of the domain, thus resulting in selecting the arc that leads to the greatest quantity of whatever is being measured. We conjecture that this method is that used by chess masters in analyzing chess trees.*

1. Introduction

Tree searching permeates all of Artificial Intelligence and much of what is computation. Searches are conducted whenever selection cannot be done effectively by computing a function of some state description of the competing alternatives. The problem with tree searching is that the search space grows as B^D, where B (branching factor) is the average breadth of alternatives and D the depth to which the search must penetrate.

† This research was sponsored by the Defense Advanced Research Projects Agency (DOD), ARPA Order No. 3597, monitored by the Air Force Avionics Laboratory Under Contract F33615–78–C–1551.

We find it useful to distinguish between searches that continue until they have reached a goal, and those that can stop short of a goal. When a goal reaching search has been completed, there should be no further secrets in the problem presented. The path to the goal (and presumably alternate paths in the case where an opponent exists and has choices) are known. Thus, once a step down the solution path is taken, all future steps are also known.

The case is quite different when no goal is reached. Here, an evaluation function is required to produce some measure of the nearness of the goal. Since a given search usually does not encounter a goal, it will have to be repeated after the action associated with the "solution" has been taken. Thus, the ultimate solution to the problem proceeds in steps, where new problems are along what is believed to be the path to the goal. We will call this type of search *iterative*.[1] Searches that look for a goal must either succeed or fail. However, searches that work by iteration are expected to produce a meaningful answer at each iteration, for better or for worse.

If a problem has a very large search space and can be solved by iteration (unlike problems such as theorem proving where the search must continue until a proof is found), there is usually no alternative to using the iterative approach. Here, there is a serious problem in bounding the effort so that the search is tractable. For this reason, the search is usually limited in some way (e.g., number of nodes to be expanded, or maximum depth to which it may go). Since it is not expected that a goal node will be encountered, an evaluation function must be invoked to decide the approximate closeness to the goal of a given node at the periphery of the search. This or a similar function can also be used for deciding which tip node to sprout from next in a best-first search. Thus evaluation functions and effort limits appear to be necessary for finding a solution by iteration. However, such conditions on the search appear to cause other problems such as the horizon effect [2].

It is desirable to have a search proceed in best-first fashion for several reasons. If we can specify a certain degree of closeness to a goal as a terminating condition, and achieve this condition, then this reduces the degree of arbitrariness in stopping when no goal is encountered. Therefore, Harris [7] advanced the notion of a bandwidth. A goal together with a bandwidth condition around the value of the goal would guarantee a solution of value no worse than the bandwidth away from the goal, providing the search terminated. However, selecting goals (or sub-goals in case the goal is deemed too remote) and bandwidths that give the search a chance to terminate in a reasonable fashion is extremely difficult. Further, while the bandwidth condition does produce a certain degree of discipline in stopping, it adds further arbitrariness to the search process.

Best-first searches tend to put the searching effort into those sub-trees that seem most promising (i.e. have the most likelihood of containing the solution). However,

[1] We want to assure that this definition of iteration is not confused with *iterative deepening* [15], a method now in popular use for controlling the depth of a depth-first search.

best–first searches require a great deal of bookkeeping for keeping track of all competing nodes, contrary to the great efficiencies possible in depth–first searches.

Depth–first searches, on the other hand, tend to be forced to stop at inappropriate moments thus giving rise to the horizon effect. They also tend to investigate huge trees, large parts of which have nothing to do with any solution (since every potential arc of the losing side must be refuted). However, these large trees sometimes turn up something that the evaluation functions would not have found were they guiding the search. This method of discovery has become quite popular of late, since new efficiencies in managing the search have been found [15]. At the moment the efficiencies and discovery potential of the depth–first methods appear to outweight what best–first methods have to offer. However, both methods have some glaring deficiencies.

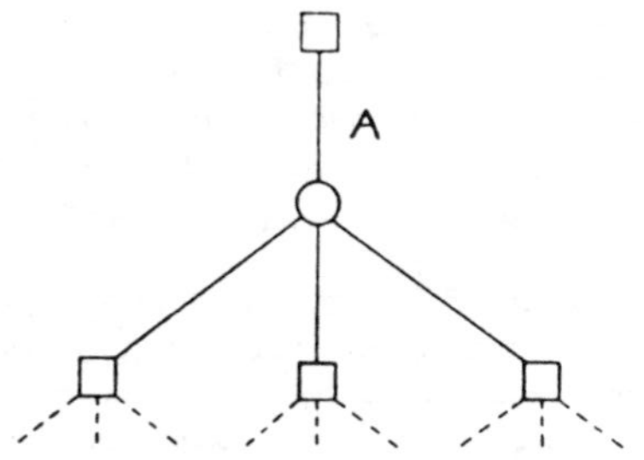

FIG. 1.

In the situation of Fig. 1, both best–first and depth–first searches will expend their allotted effort and come to the conclusion that the arc labelled *A* is best. Clearly, no search is required for this conclusion, since it is the only arc from the root. To overcome this waste of effort, the developers of performance programs (notably chess programs) test for this condition before embarking on any search.

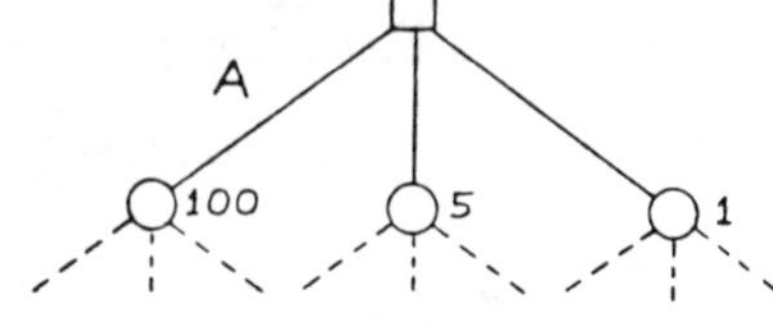

FIG. 2.

In Fig. 2 the situation is different as there are three legal successors to the root node. Numbers at the descendant nodes are intended to show how an evaluation function would appraise the relative merits of the three nodes. Here the depth–first search has no recourse but to do its search, and (if the initial evaluation is reasonably correct) eventually report that arc *A* should be chosen. A best–first search on the other hand, would probably expend its entire effort in the sub-tree of arc *A*, and eventually come to the conclusion that it was best. These incongruities require no further explanation.

2. The B* Algorithm

In present methods for doing iterative searches, there is no natural way to stop the search. Further, for any given effort limit, the algorithm's idea of what is the best arc at the root, may change so that each new effort increment could produce a radical change in the algorithm's idea of what is correct. To prevent this and to provide for natural termination, the B* search provides that each node has two evaluations: an optimistic one and a pessimistic one. Together, these provide a range on the values that are (likely) to be found in the node's sub-tree. Intuitively, these bounds delimit the area of uncertainty in the evaluation. If the evaluations are valid bounds, the values in a given sub-tree will be within the range specified at the root of the sub-tree. As new nodes in a given sub-tree are expanded and this information is backed up, the range of the root node of that sub-tree will be gradually reduced until, if necessary, it converges on a single value. This feature of our method augurs well for the tractability of searches. In fact, a simple best–first search in the two valued system would converge if all bounds are valid. However, as we shall show, a B* search converges more rapidly.

The domain of B* is both 1-person searches and 2-person (adversary) searches. We shall explain the B* algorithm using adversary searches, where one player tries to maximize a given function while the other tries to minimize it. In the canonical case where nodes have a single value [11, pp. 137–140], MAX is assumed to be on move at the root, and the arc chosen at the root has a backed-up minimax value that is no worse than that of any other arc at the root. In the two valued system that we introduced above, this condition is slightly relaxed: MAX need only show that the *pessimistic value of an arc at the root is no worse than the optimistic value of any of the other arcs at the root*. This is the terminal condition for finding the best arc.

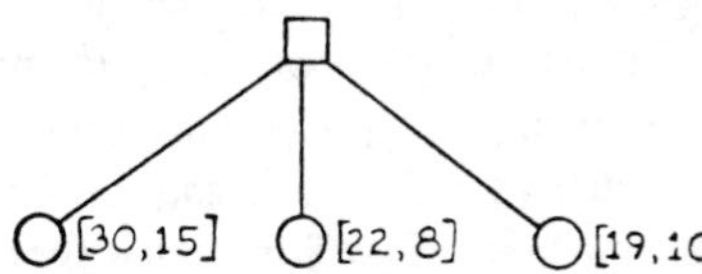

FIG. 3. Start of a B* search.

We show the basic situation at the start of a 2-person ternary search tree in Fig. 3. The optimistic and pessimistic values associated with any node are shown next to it in brackets, the optimistic value being the leftmost of the pair. These values will be updated as the search progresses. In Fig. 3, it appears that the leftmost arc has the greatest potential for being the best. It should be noted that if this search were with single valued nodes and this were maximum depth, the search would terminate here without exploring the question of the uncertainty in the evaluation. In the case of B*, there are no terminating conditions other than the one previously enunciated. When at the root, the B* search may pursue one of two strategies:

(1) It may try to raise the lower bound of the leftmost (most optimistic) node so that it is not worse than the upper bound of any of its sibling nodes. We will call this the PROVEBEST strategy.

(2) It may try to lower the upper bounds of all the other nodes at depth 1, so that none are better than the lower bound of the leftmost node. We will call this the DISPROVEREST strategy.

In either case, the strategy will have to create a proof tree to demonstrate that it has succeeded. We show the simplest cases of the alternate strategies in Figs. 4 and 5. In the figures, the numbers inside the node symbols indicate the order of node expansion, and backed up values are shown above the bracketed value they replace.

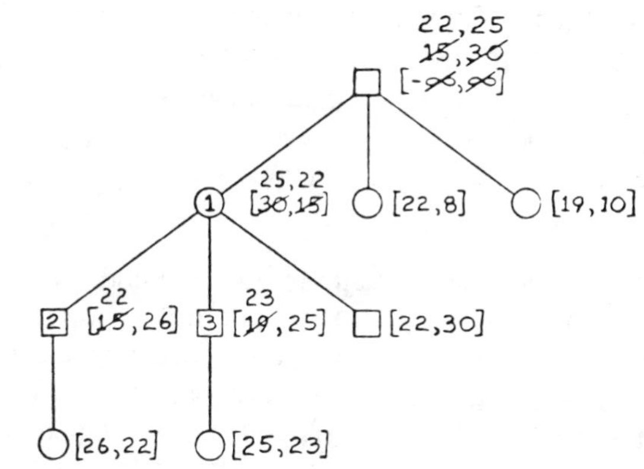

FIG. 4. The PROVEBEST strategy.

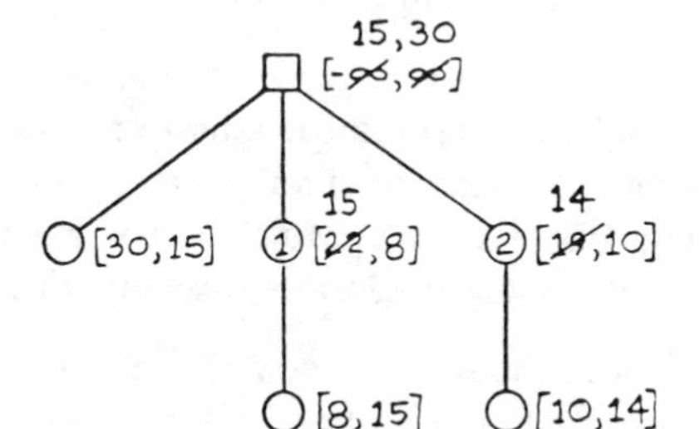

FIG. 5. The DISPROVEREST strategy.

From Figs. 4 and 5 it can be seen that, if conditions are right, the seemingly more cumbersone DISPROVEREST strategy can involve less effort than the PROVEBEST strategy. Further, there is no guarantee that the node with the original best optimistic value will be the ultimate best node. Thus it can be seen that the selection of a *method* to establish which arc is best at the root is not a trivial problem.

The B* algorithm addresses itself to this task by doing a best–first proving search. The search decides on a strategy whenever it is at the root. Then it pursues the strategy by always selecting the best branch in the chosen sub-tree until it reaches a leaf node. That node is then expanded. Backing up of the search will occur whenever the expansion of a node produces a value that changes the bounds of its parent node. This change is rippled back until no further changes take place; whereupon the forward search is resumed. The search terminates when the pessimistic value of the best node at the root is no worse than the optimistic value of all its siblings.

Since new values are always backed up, any value which survives back to the root will cause a re-examination of the strategy. This assures that the search will not continue searching a branch the *value of which is already sufficient for the proof that is being attempted.* A small economy is also possible in the generation of descendants. Since any descendant may provide a sufficient condition for causing backup, they may be generated and tested, one at a time, thus saving the cost of doing a complete successor generation at leaf nodes. It should be noted that backing up from a node in no way implies that the search will not go back to this node later, as is typical in best–first searches.

When the search backs up, the best optimistic value of the set of descendants of a node becomes its pessimistic value, and the best pessimistic value of the set of descendants becomes its optimistic value. For MAX, optimistic values are larger than pessimistic, while for MIN optimistic values are smaller than pessimistic. Backing up is applied iteratively as long as there are new values to back up. As backed up values become available, it may be that certain nodes will become logically eliminated from the search. These may be deleted or ignored; it is only a matter of convenience in bookkeeping, as they can not influence the result. When backing up, the search resumes from the last node the values of which were changed. If this node is an immediate descendant of the root, then the question of what strategy to pursue is re-examined.

Two features distinguish a B* search from a simple best–first search:

(1) A best–first search is intent on finding a goal and thus only backs up to always sprout from the best minimaxed node. However, since the B* search is only interested in finding the best first step toward a goal, it will only continue this finding of the best minimaxed node as long as the proof is not complete. There is a

subtle point involved here. It is senseless to extend a branch, the value of which is sufficient for a proof; *improving its value will not change the status of the proof.* However, a pure best-first search would not understand this.

(2) The B∗ search can choose a strategy whenever it is at the root of the tree. This allows directing the search effort in such a way that the most meaningful contribution to the proof of which arc is best can be made in the most inexpensive way. Later in the paper, we discuss criteria that have been applied experimentally for making the strategy selection.

We now present the B∗ algorithm. It utilizes the variable CURNODE to keep track of the current node, DEPTH to remember the distance of CURNODE from the root, OPTIM and PESSIM at each node to remember the bounds, PARENT to point to the name of the node's parent, MAXOPTIM to keep track of the most optimistic value of all successors to CURNODE, and MAXPESS to keep track of the best pessimistic value of all successors to CURNODE. There are two tests in Step 4 of the algorithm which are presented from MAX's point of view. We introduce the operator " ' " to indicate that the sense of a test should be complemented to get MIN's point of view at alternate level of the tree; i.e. >' becomes <, and <' becomes >.

```
(1) DEPTH ← ∅; CURNODE ← ∅; OPTIM[∅] ← −∞; PESSIM[∅] ← ∞;
(2) if CURNODE has not been expanded yet then generate and evaluate
    successors, giving each a name and a pointer to CURNODE.
(3) BESTNODE ← name of successor of CURNODE with best OPTIM value;
    ALTERN ← name of successor with second best OPTIM value;
    MAXOPTIM ← OPTIM[BESTNODE];
    MAXPESS ← Value of the best PESSIM value of all successors;
(4) if (MAXOPTIM <' PESSIM[CURNODE])
      or (MAXPESS >' OPTIM[CURNODE]) then
    begin                                   ! Back-up (values and search)
        PESSIM[CURNODE] ← MAXOPTIM;
        OPTIM[CURNODE] ← MAXPESS;
        if DEPTH > ∅ then
        begin
          CURNODE ← PARENT[CURNODE];
          DEPTH ← DEPTH−1;
          go to 3;
        end
        else if DEPTH = ∅ then              ! Check for termination
              if PESSIM[BESTNODE] ⩾ OPTIM[ALTERN] then
                exit with ANSWER = BESTNODE;
    end;
(5) if DEPTH = ∅ then
    begin
      decide STRATEGY;
      if STRATEGY = DISPROVEREST then CURNODE ← ALTERN
      else if STRATEGY = PROVEBEST then CURNODE ← BESTNODE;
    end;
(6) if (DEPTH ≠ ∅) then CURNODE ← BESTNODE;
(7) DEPTH ← DEPTH+1; go to 2.                ! Go forward
```

It should be noted that there is never any point to invoking the DISPROVEREST strategy unless PESSIM[BESTNODE] = MAXPESS. This is because there will be at least one node in the alternative set, the value of which cannot be lowered below MAXPESS. As long as this value is greater than PESSIM[BESTNODE], then this proof cannot succeed. In the presented algorithm, if two or more successors are tied for the best OPTIM value, BESTNODE is the one with the smallest range.

The observant reader may have noted that since each proof tree is an AND/OR tree, *all* arcs must be searched at alternate levels of the tree corresponding to the side against whom the proof is directed. At such a point, it is not always optimal to search the "best" arc first as indicated in Step 6 above. There are cases where it is superior to search the branch involving the most difficult proof first, since if that fails, then the whole proof at this juncture will fail, and the search can be redirected to another sub-tree. Reasoning along similar lines is presented in Harris [8, p. 160]. We are at present working on a general method to define when the best node should be searched next and when the one with the greatest pessimistic value, for all levels of the tree.

3. Tests of the B∗ Algorithm

We have simulated the conduct of searches with several versions of the B∗ algorithm. In the simulation, adversary trees of constant width were generated, with the range of admissible values at the root and the width of the tree varying over sets of runs. As explained in Appendix I, it is possible to generate such trees so that any node in the tree will have its initial bounds determined as a function of its position in the tree and the run number, regardless of when the node is searched. This guarantees that each algorithm searches the same trees.

In assigning each descendant its bounds, we invoked the proviso that at least one descendant must have an optimistic value equal to that of the parent, and one must have a pessimistic value equal to that of the parent. It was possible in this process, for a descendant to have the same value as its parent.

Searches were performed according to the following scheme. A run consisted of 1600 tree searches. In these there were two principal variables, the range and the width of the tree.

(1) The range (the number of discrete values) of the evaluation function was varied from 100 to 6400 by factors of four.

(2) The width of branching was varied from 3 to 10 in increments of 1.

Thus there are 32 basic conditions, and 50 tree searches were performed for each condition. For each such run a different search algorithm was tested. Any search that penetrated beyond depth 100, or which put more than 30,000 nodes into its nodes dictionary was declared intractable and aborted.

Several observations could be made about the test data. In general, tree size grew with width. Range, on the other hand, turned out to be a non-monotonic function. Searches with the smallest and largest ranges required the least effort in general. Searches of range 400 were hardly ever the largest for any given width and algorithm, while searches of range 1600 were hardly ever the smallest for any given width and algorithm. We cannot interpret this result beyond it indicating that there seems to be a range value for which searches will require most effort and that ranges above and below this will require less.

We tested several distinct variations of the B* algorithm. These related to the criteria for selecting the strategy at the root. The variations are explained below; although we did not test all combinations of these conditions.

(1) Number of alternatives considered when making strategy decision at root.

2 — Best plus one alternative.
3 — Best plus two alternatives.
A — All alternatives.

(2) Criterion applied to decide strategy.

D — If the sum of the squares of the depths from which the optimistic bounds of the alternatives had been backed up was less than the square of the depth from which the value of the best arc had been backed up, then the best alternative was chosen, else the best arc. This favors exploring sub-trees which have not yet been explored deeply.

R — Criterion information ("D" above or unity) was divided by the range of the node (thus favoring the searching of nodes with larger ranges).

These alpha-numeric keys are used to label column headings in Table 1 to show which algorithm is being tested. BF indicates the results of running a best-first search on the same data, and these are used as a base for comparison.

The categories on the left are based upon how the best-first search did on a given tree. A given tree is in the intractable category, if any of the algorithms tested found it intractable. The entries in the table indicate the ratio of effort, in terms of nodes visited, compared to how the best-first search did on the set; e.g. 0.50 means that half the effort was required. All but the last row indicate the effort ratio; the last row indicates the number of intractable searches for each version.

TABLE 1. Effort compared to best-first for various implementations of B*

Size/Alg	BF	2D	2DR	3D	AD	2DRX
≤ 50	1.00	0.82	0.81	0.83	0.84	0.84
≤ 200	1.00	0.65	0.62	0.62	0.64	0.71
≤ 1000	1.00	0.61	0.56	0.48	0.47	0.64
>1000	1.00	0.51	0.48	0.35	0.32	0.56
Intractable	1.00	0.70	0.64	0.59	0.52	0.69
No. Intractable	226	100	76	83	71	81

The data support several conclusions:

(1) The greater the number of parameters considered when making the strategy decision between PROVEBEST and DISPROVEREST, the better the result.

(2) In general, the larger the tree, the more pronounced the effect of a good algorithm.

(3) The right-most column headed "2DRX" is a test of what would happen if the nodal bounds were not valid. Here we used algorithm "2DR" but allowed 5% of all nodes to have their successors have a range which was 50% larger than the parent; i.e. 25% on either side. The net effect of this appears to be a 5–10% increase in the amount of effort.

Thus it is quite likely that changing Step 4 of the algorithm to allow the backing up of values outside the expected range as well as those within the range is quite acceptable. This will result in the search changing its mind about what is going on more often, but will allow new data to have an impact on the search. The degree to which the search will vacillate would appear to depend upon how often an out-of-bounds datum was discovered; however, with a moderate rate of such occurrences, this effect would appear minimal.

Using the largest amount of data for strategy selection appears to produce the best results. Further, it seems to us that with additional effort on improving the strategy selection criterion, the best algorithm could become twice as good as the "AD" algorithm. Since the method of selecting strategies and assigning limits in this experiment is essentially syntactic (there is no use made of the semantics of the domain being searched), it seems reasonable to suppose that the availability of semantic information would allow even better decisions with consequent improvement in the search effort required.

We examined many of the cases where intractable searches occurred. These are due to the stringent way that values are assigned to descendants. When the range of a node gets rather small, and there are a relatively large number of descendants, the probability that at least one will have the same limits as its parent is extremely high. This prevents any progress toward a solution at such a node, and if the probability of this occurring is high enough, the probability of a string of such occurrences can be quite high too. This was borne out when we did a run of the best algorithm with the additional proviso that any node for which the range was reduced to 2 or less, arbitrarily received a value equal to the mean of its optimistic and pessimistic value. For this change, the number of intractable searches went from 71 to 4, and each of these was due to overflow of the nodes dictionary rather than exceeding the maximum depth. This method is somewhat reminiscent of Samuel's idea [12] of terminating search at a node when Alpha and Beta are very close together.

To get another benchmark for comparing B*, we ran a depth–first alpha–beta search on the same data. Here, we allowed the forward prune paradigm, since the bounds on any node were assumed valid. In a search without the two-value system, each node expansion could produce a value any distance from the value of its parent. Since this cannot happen under the two-value scheme, it is logical to not search any node the range of which indicates it cannot influence the solution; thus the use of the forward prune paradigm. In order to prevent the search from running away in depth, we used the iterative deepening approach [15] which goes to depth N, then to depth $N+1$, etc., until it finds a solution or becomes intractable. Searches were started with $N = 1$. The results showed that depth–first typically expands three to seven times as many nodes as the BF algorithm. Although it did manage to do a few problems in fewer nodes than the best B* algorithm, it was unable to solve any problem of depth greater than 19, and became intractable on almost twice as many searches as the BF algorithm. In contrast, the best B* algorithm solved some problems as deep as 94 ply, although it is conceivable that shallower solutions existed.

4. Considerations that Led to the Discovery of the Algorithm

In the course of working on computer chess, we have had occasion to examine the standard methods for searching adversary trees. The behavior of these algorithms appeared more cumbersome than the searches which I, as a chess master, believed myself capable of performing. The real issue was whether a well defined algorithm existed for doing such searches.

(1) Our initial motivation came from the fact that all searches that were not expected to reach a goal required effort limits. Such effort limits, in turn, appeared to bring on undesirable consequences such as the horizon effect. While there are patches to ameliorate such idiosyncracies of the search, the feeling that these were not "natural" algorithms persisted.

(2) There are two meaningful proposals to overcome the effort limit problem. Harris [7] proposed a bandwidth condition for terminating the search. However, this shifts the limiting quantity from a physical search effort limit, to a distance from the goal limit which, as indicated earlier, has other problems. Another attempt to avoid these problems was to use a set of maximum depths in a depth–first search for terminating searches which qualified moves for other searches in the chess program KAISSA (see [1]). For a set of maximum depths, first all moves, then all material threatening moves plus captures, then all captures and checks, and finally only captures were considered. With an effort limit for each category of moves, it was hoped that everything of importance would somehow be covered. There are no reports of how this approach worked out, but it would appear to have the same essential limitations as all the other effort limited searches. This is borne out by the fact that the authors have now implemented another method of searching for their program. In none of the existing tractable search procedures is there a natural terminating condition without any parameters which specify under what conditions to halt.

(3) We have noted that standard searches may at times investigate a very large number of nodes that have no apparent relevance to a solution. Consider the following situation: If there is only one legal successor to the root node, any iterative solution technique can easily check for this condition and indicate this is the best successor without further analysis. However, if there is only one *sensible* arc, a depth–first program will still insist on refuting all other arcs at the root to the prescribed depth, while a best–first program may investigate the one good arc *ad infinitum*. We have demonstrated these cases in Section 1. Usually, it is possible to determine that the one sensible arc is best without going at all deep in the search. It appears that some essential ingredient is missing. We have felt for some time that the notion of level of aspiration (as first put forward by Newell in [10]) was the key to the proper construction. The alpha–beta search procedure appears to have such a level of aspiration scheme. However, this scheme has an aspiration level for each side, and that only serves to bound those branches that can be a part of the solution. The correct level of aspiration specifies the value required for a "solution". We attempted such a construction in the search scheme of CAPS–II (see [3]), which relied heavily on notions of optimism, pessimism and aspiration. However, we performed depth limited depth–first searches in CAPS. Without the best–first requirement there was no need to keep track of alternatives, nor to maintain the optimistic and pessimistic values at each node.

(4) We have always liked the way the search could be terminated at the root node, when the backed up (sure) value of one alternative is better than the optimistic (static) values of all the other alternatives. This is the forward prune paradigm, and while it can be used to keep the search from investigating branches that appear useless at any depth, it only terminates the search if applicable at the root. In B*, the forward prune of all remaining alternatives at the root (when PESSIM[CURNODE] $\geqslant$ OPTIM[ALTERN]) not only terminates the search, but it provides a logic for all actions taken in the search. Thus, when the final test succeeds, a massive forward prune of all of the tree not connected with the solution is effected.

(5) Protocols collected by De Groot [6] of chess masters analyzing chess positions show a phenomenon known as progressive deepening. Roughly, this appears to be the investigating of a line of play, abandonment of the investigation of this line, and the subsequent return to the investigation of the line but with the analysis being followed to a greater depth in the tree. The deepening process may occur several times during the analysis. Since humans investigate very sparse trees and chess masters play chess very well, it was thought that this procedure (whatever it consisted of) should be an effective way of managing the search. The real question was whether there was an actual search algorithm, or whether the deepening was the result of ad hoc procedures. I have held to the former view.

In fact, De Groot came very close to discovering our algorithm. In "Thought and Choice in Chess" [6, pp. 28–32], he outlines a proof procedure involving the basic strategies for demonstrating that a move is better than its nearest competitor, and shows that this seems to be at the core of many of the protocols he collected. However, he fails to relate it to a tree searching procedure, or to any notion of optimistic and pessimistic limits.

Some of the protocols (particularly pp. 213–217) appear to us to support the B∗ paradigm very strongly. What is being called progressive deepening, is really nothing other than the retracing of a branch of the search which may have been abandoned for any of the several reasons that exist for backing up. At the level of the protocol, only the jumping around is noticed. This is then interpreted as a best–first search with progressive deepening since the underlying logic is not readily apparent.

5. Evaluation Functions and Meaningful Bounds

Most existing search algorithms rely on assigning a single value to a node, under the assumption that each node expansion will bring in new and useful information that can be backed up and used to produce a more informed opinion about the node's sub-tree. However, this ignores the variability about the estimate that is made by the terminal evaluation function. It is precisely for this reason that chess programs indulge in quiescence searches when the variability at a terminal node is considered too high. Our method can thus be considered to carry a specification of variability of the evaluation for every node in the tree. Thus any posed issue (as represented by its variability) cannot be abandoned until it can be shown to be irrelevant to determining the solution.

Because of this, evaluation functions are very important. The B∗ search transfers the responsibility for determining how much effort to spend (which has previously been the responsibility of search parameters such as depth limit, effort limit, bandwidth, etc.) to the evaluation functions which now determine the effort limit due to their crispness and ability to narrow the range between optimistic and pessimistic. In the final analysis, the B∗ search is a conversation between an evaluation function and a control procedure which terminates when enough has been discovered in the search to justify a selection at the root.

In the course of our investigations, we have attempted to apply the B∗ algorithm to some optimization problems, notably the 8-puzzle [11]. During this effort, we succeeded in creating lower bounding functions which were monotonic and several times more sensitive than any previously published for this particular problem. However, we could not devise a really useful upper bounding function. Such a function should form a reasonable range together with the lower bounding function and should also be monotonic. The most difficult 8-puzzle configurations can be solved in 30 steps [14]. Our best upper bounding function "grabbed" at about 8 ply from a solution. Thus problems of depth 12 or so could be solved easily by B∗, but for deeper problems the upper bounding function was not able to contribute to the solution during the early stages of the search.

We also spent some time on the travelling salesman problem. In both these problems the function to be optimized is the cost of the solution path. In both, we found that the greatest difficulty was in getting good upper bounding functions. This appears to be due to the fact that a maximum path length turns out to not be a good upper bound, while refined estimates of minimum path length are quite reasonable lower bounds. However, for relatively short paths (or nearby sub-goals) it was possible to construct useful upper bounding functions. The guiding principle here was to use a pattern-based approach; i.e. a certain pattern was recognized as being embedded at a node and requiring at most N steps for a solution. We feel that this distinction in the way effective bounding functions can be constructed is extremely important, and could very well account for why humans do such a good job at sub-optimizing tasks.

Optimality searches require that the search determine the minimum cost for reaching a goal. Since an iterative procedure could stop short of a goal, it would need extremely tight bounding functions to be able to "see" the goal from a great enough distance to be useful in most cases. Thus it seems that optimality tasks are just not well suited to B∗'s capabilities. Finding an optimal path is approximately equivalent to finding the shortest mate in a game of chess, and this is seldom relevant to making the best move, if one considers only tractable searches. An iterative algorithm prefers to find a good start on a path, which may be optimal, but in any case meets a satisficing criterion, and can be found with a reasonable effort (few nodes). Optimization problems just do not fit well into such a mold.

On the other hand, satisficing searches appear very well suited to B∗'s capabilities. With knowledgable bounding functions to guide the process, we feel convinced that B∗ would produce satisficing solutions to 8-puzzle problems very much as humans do; with few nodes expanded and solution paths of somewhat greater than optimal length. Further, adversary situations appear still easier to handle than one person situations, since one adversary's optimistic function is the other's pessimistic one. It should be noted that good B∗ bounding functions will in all likelihood not measure what an optimality function would measure. Thus for chess, a good function might measure attack potential rather than distance to a mate, and for a graph traversal problem, ease of traversing a local sub-graph rather than total path length. This tends to partition the total task into small segments which (hopefully) would be bounded by what is being measured. Thus, in the chess example the search would terminate when the attack issue is resolved (rather than continuing the analysis into the endgame), and in the path example the search would terminate once a local graph had been resolved with a convenient connection to another part of the total graph. In this way the evaluation functions can keep measuring the next thing to be optimized, and thus lead the process through a series of sub-optimal paths on the way to what is hoped to be the best ultimate goal. If new issues arise during a particular search, and De Groot presents some evidence that they do in chess searches, humans change their aspiration level (which could mean changing the evaluation function). We present analytic evidence for such changes in [4].

We have constructed reasonable bounding functions for chess tactics, although we did not then know of the B* algorithm [3]. The key for such constructions, is that one side's optimism is the other's pessimism. For instance, our evaluation function calculates the optimistic value of a tactical move to be the current material balance plus the sum of all our recognized threats against material. The pessimistic value is the material balance minus the sum of all the opponent's recognized threats.

When evaluation function estimates do not validly bound the actual value of a node, errors in arc selection can occur. However, there is no reason why these should be more severe than errors produced by any other search technique using an estimating function which is applied at leaf nodes that are not terminal in the domain *per se*. Thus, if an arc at the root is chosen because an estimate was in error somewhere in the tree, this would be no different than in searches with a single evaluation function. If the error was detected prior to termination, data from our simulations seem to indicate that small and infrequent intrusions of this type (which would happen when relatively good bounding functions do exist) have little effect on the magnitude of the search effort.

The issue of when a B* search fails to terminate is more serious and could still stand further investigation. In cases where the range of the best node at the root remains overlapped with the ranges of at least one of its sibling nodes even after a considerable search, several options are possible. One could select the arc with the greatest average value, or temper this with some function of the depth of investigation of each competing arc. Such contingencies probably arise in human searches ard are resolved by humans in such situations by various means that we have yet to understand. I am particularly struck by a quote from former World Chess Champion Alexander Alekhin in [6, p. 409]: "Well, in case of time pressure I would play 1. B×N/5". A clear case of using an external criterion to resolve some small remaining uncertainty.

Unfortunately, very little appears to have been done toward making a science of the construction of sensitive evaluation functions, since the highly significant work of Samuels [12, 13]. We have been investigating how such evaluation functions can be constructed of many layers of increasingly more complex primitives in connection with the 8-puzzle and backgammon [5]. In the latter great amounts of knowledge need to be brought to bear, since search is not practical because of a very large branching factor.

6. Comparison to other Search Algorithms

It is interesting to compare the basic features of B* with those of well-known search algorithms. Consider the A* search algorithm [11]. It could easily operate under the two value system in a mode that is satisfied to find the best arc at the root, and the cost of the path without finding the complete path itself. This algorithm would be equivalent to B* using only the PROVEBEST strategy, and being able to halt search on a branch only when a goal was reached or if the upper and lower bounds on the branch became equal; i.e. the cost of the path is known. Another step in the direction of iteration would be to only use the PROVEBEST strategy and allow the search to halt when a best node at the root had been identified. In this mode the exact cost of the path would not be known. This produces the best–first algorithm used for the column headed BF in Table 1. Finally, the full-fledged B* algorithm working with both strategies discovers the best node without the exact cost of the path. However, it does enough shallow searching so that it explores considerably fewer nodes than any of the algorithms described above.

Having the two strategies without the two value system has no meaning at all, since there is no way of pronouncing one node at the root better than any other without having an effort limit. Just using a depth–first iterative deepening procedure, although it spreads the search over the shallower portions of the search tree, investigates too many non-pertinent nodes.

Finally, it should be noted that the optimistic and pessimistic values at a node correspond exactly to alpha and beta in an alpha–beta minimax search. That is they delimit the range of acceptable values that can be returned from their sub-tree.

7. Summary

There are two things that distinguish the B* algorithm from other known tree search procedures:

(1) The optimistic and pessimistic value system allows for termination of a search without encountering a goal node, and without any effort limit.

(2) The option to exercise either of two search strategies allows the search to spread its effort through the shallowest portion of a tree where it is least expensive, instead of being forced to pursue the best alternative to great depths, or pursue all alternatives to the same depth.

In selecting a strategy, it is good to consider the present range of a node, and the depth from which its current bounds have come. This allows some gauging of the cost of employing a particular strategy. Further, domain-dependent knowledge associated with an evaluation (not merely its magnitude), would no doubt also aid in strategy selection.

I have had a number of discussion with colleagues about whether B* is a Branch and Bound (BB) algorithm. The view that it is has support in that some BB algorithms do employ best–first methods and some do use upper and lower bounds to produce their effects. The BB technique derives its main effect by eliminating the search of branches that can not contain the solution. B* will never knowingly visit such branches either. In B*, superceded nodes can be (and are in our implementation) permanently eliminated from the search as a matter of course.

However, in our view, B* is definitely not a BB algorithm. The main strength of the B* algorithm is the ability to pursue branches that are known to *not be best*, and no other algorithm that we know of can opt for such a strategy. Therefore, we assert B* is quite different from the class referred to as BB algorithms. The reader may wish to judge for himself by perusing a comprehensive reference such as [9].

There are a number of issues left for investigation: (1) it is important to discover how to construct good bounding functions; (2) more light should be shed on the question of how much of an effect is caused when the value of a new node is not within the bounds of its parent; (3) there seems to be a more optimal strategy than always pursuing the best branch lower in the tree.

Given the fact that all search techniques are limited by the accuracy of the evaluations of leaf nodes, B* appears to expand fewer nodes than any other technique available for doing iterative searches. B* achieves its results because it is continually aware of the status of alternatives and exactly what is required to prove one alternative better than the rest. In this it seems very similar to the underlying method that humans exibit in doing game tree searches, and we conjecture that it is indeed this method that the B* algorithm captures.

Appendix I. How to Generate Canonical Trees of Uniform Width

We here show how to generate canonical trees which are independent of the order of search. We note that a tree can receive a unique name by specifying the range of values at its root, the width (number of immediate successors at each node), and the iteration number for a tree of this type. To find a unique name for each node in such a tree, we note that if we assign the name "0" to the root, and have the immediate descendants of any node be named

(parentname * width + 1),(parentname * width + 2),—(parentname * width + width)

then this provides a unique naming scheme. Now it is self-evident that the bounds on a node that has not yet been sprouted from must be a function of its position in the tree (name) and the name of the tree. Thus, if we initialize the random number generator that assigns values to the immediate descendants of a node as a function of its original bounds, its name, the width, and the iteration number, then the descendants of node "X" will look the same for all trees with the same initial parameters, regardless of the order of search or whether a node is actually ever expanded. The actual function we use to initialize the random number generator is (parentname + width) * (iterationnumber + range). This avoids initializing at zero since width and range are never zero. The bounds of the parent node serve as bounds on the range of values that the random number generator is allowed to produce.

ACKNOWLEDGMENT

The author wishes to acknowledge the help of the following persons who provided assistance in discussing the properties of the algorithm, improvement in its formulation, and improvement in the readability of this paper: Allen Newell, Herbert Simon, Charles Leiserson, Andrew Palay, John Gaschnig, Jon Bentley, and the referees, whose comments were most helpful.

REFERENCES

1. Adelson-Velskiy, G. M., Arlasarov, V. L. and Donskoy, M. V., Some methods of controlling the tree search in chess programs, *Artificial Intelligence* **6**(4) (1975).
2. Berliner, H. J., Some necessary conditions for a master chess program, *Proceedings of the 3rd International Joint Conference on Artificial Intelligence* (August 1973) 77–85.
3. Berliner, H. J., Chess as problem solving: The development of a tactics analyzer, Dissertation, Comput. Sci. Dept., Carnegie–Mellon University (March 1974).
4. Berliner, H. J., On the use of domain-dependent descriptions in tree searching, in: Jones, A. K. (Ed.), *Perspectives on Computer Science* (Academic Press, New York, 1977).
5. Berliner, H. J., BKG — A program that plays backgammon, Comput. Sci. Dept., Carnegie–Mellon University (1977).
6. De Groot, A. D., *Thought and Choice in Chess* (Mouton and Co., Der Haag, 1965).
7. Harris, L., The heuristic search under conditions of error, *Artificial Intelligence*, **5** (1974) 217–234.
8. Harris, L. R., The heuristic search: An alternative to the alpha–beta minimax procedure, in: Frey, P. (Ed.), *Chess Skill in Man and Machine* (Springer-Verlag, Berlin, 1977).
9. Lawler, E. L. and Wood, D. E., Branch-and-bounds methods: A survey, *Operations Res.* **14** (1966) 699–719.
10. Newell, A., The chess machine: An example of dealing with a complex task by adaptation, *Proceedings Western Joint Computer Conference* (1955) 101–108.
11. Nilsson, N. J., *Problem-Solving Methods in Artificial Intelligence* (McGraw-Hill, New York, 1971).
12. Samuel, A. L., Some studies in machine learning using the game of checkers, *IBM J. Res. Develop.* **3** (1959) 210–229.
13. Samuel, A. L., Some studies in machine learning using the game of checkers, II — Recent Progress, *IBM J. Res. Develop.* (1967) 601–617.
14. Schofield, P. D. A., Complete solution of the 'Eight-puzzle', in: Collins, N. L. and Michie, D. (Eds.), *Machine Intelligence* **1** (American Elsevier Publishing Co., New York, 1967).
15. Slate, D. J. and Atkin, L. R., CHESS 4.5 — The Northwestern University Chess Program, in: Frey, P. (Ed.), *Chess Skill in Man and Machine* (Springer-Verlag, Berlin, 1977).

2 / Deduction

The use of predicate logic is now firmly established in AI as a useful way to represent declarative knowledge. Logical deduction (or "theorem-proving") is the process of generating conclusions that are not explicitly represented as logical statements themselves, but that are implied by the knowledge that is explicitly represented. Deductive methods are quite important in AI approaches to database question-answering, to automatic planning, to program synthesis and verification, and to natural-language processing.

Uniform procedures using resolution refutation have been studied extensively in AI as a basis for mechanizing deduction. In reaction to the inefficiency of such uniform approaches, several researchers renewed work on nonresolution methods based on techniques such as "natural deduction." On close inspection, many of the "nonresolution" methods are simply variations of the basic techniques used in resolution—variations in which efficient, domain-dependent control information can be more easily marshaled. Bledsoe's paper gives a good description of some efficient alternatives to uniform resolution.

Chang and Slagle's paper addresses the problem of making theorem-proving more efficient by "precompiling" potential matches between clauses. These matches are stored in structures called "connection graphs" that play a useful role in theorem-proving. They are similar to other precompiled deduction structures, such as the inference networks used in the expert system PROSPECTOR (see the paper by Duda, Gaschnig and Hart in Chapter 4 of this volume).

In looking at the use of theorem-proving or of rule-based deduction systems in question-answering, one has to consider the problem of getting not just single answers to questions of "who," "what," "where," and "when," questions, but of getting all the possible answers that are explicit or deducible from the data base. This problem is made easier if one assumes that the data base contains *all* the positive things that are to be known. Reiter's paper explores some of the important consequences of this so-called "closed world" assumption.

The relation between computation and deduction is explored in Manna and Waldinger's paper. They generalize the resolution inference rule to a form that allows the synthesis of programs with conditional branching and recursion.

There is continuing inherent conflict in AI between the goals of performing a task efficiently (using *procedural* methods) and reasoning about that task (using *declarative* methods). Most systems that perform a task procedurally cannot be asked questions about it; systems that are able to reason about a task usually perform it inefficiently. Weyhrauch's paper shows (among other things) how to combine procedural and declarative methods in systems that acquit themselves well in both performance and reasoning.

The problem of reasoning from incomplete or uncertain evidence is not a new one for artificial intelligence, but it is one that continues to challenge many researchers and to spawn a wide range of strategies for dealing with it. In their paper on rule-based inference systems, Duda, Hart, and Nilsson attack this problem by combining formal Bayesian and logical methods with informal intuitions.

Non-resolution Theorem Proving[1]

W. W. Bledsoe

Department of Mathematics, The University of Texas at Austin, 78712, U.S.A.

ABSTRACT

This talk reviews those efforts in automatic theorem proving, during the past few years, which have emphasized techniques other than resolution. These include: knowledge bases, natural deduction, reduction, (rewrite rules), typing, procedures, advice, controlled forward chaining, algebraic simplification, built-in associativity and commutativity, models, analogy, and man–machine systems. Examples are given and suggestions are made for future work.

1. Introduction

Automatic theorem proving was born in the early 1930s with the work of Herbrand, but did not get much interest until high speed digital computers were developed. Earlier work by Newell, Simon, Shaw, and Gelernter in the middle and late 1950s emphasized the heuristic approach, but the weight soon shifted to various syntactic methods culminating in a large effort on resolution type systems in the last half of the 1960s. It was about 1970 when considerable interest was revived in heuristic methods and the use of human supplied, domain dependent, knowledge.

It is not my intention here to slight the great names in automatic theorem proving, and their contributions to all we do, but rather to show another side of it. For recent books on automatic theorem proving see Chang and Lee [19], Loveland [44], and Hayes [31]. Also see Nilsson's recent review article [61].

The word "resolution" has come to be associated with general purpose types of theorem provers which use very little domain dependent information and few if any special heuristics besides those of a syntactic nature. It has also connoted the use of clauses and refutation proofs.

There was much hope in the late 60's that such systems, especially with various exciting improvements, such as set of support, model elimination, etc., would be powerful provers. But by the early 70's there was emerging a belief that resolution type systems could never really "hack" it, could not prove really hard mathematical theorems, without some extensive changes in philosophy.

This report is about this other non-resolution effort. But we do not just want to emphasize non-*resolution*, but rather to emphasize the efforts that are less syntactic in nature, that use heuristics and user supplied knowledge, which is often domain dependent. Our belief is that other purely syntactic methods such as Gentzen systems will fare only about as well as resolution systems, unless they employ some of the kinds of concepts we mention below. Also much improvement in resolution systems can be gained by using such concepts, and this has been done in many cases.

The author was one of the researchers working on resolution type systems who "made the switch". It was in trying to prove a rather simple theorem in set theory[2] by paramodulation and resolution, where the program was experiencing a great deal of difficulty, that we became convinced that we were on the wrong track. The addition of a few semantically oriented rewrite rules and subgoaling procedures [7] made the proof of this theorem, as well as similar theorems in elementary set theory, very easy for the computer. Put simply: the computer was not doing what the human would do in proving this theorem. When we instructed it to proceed in a "human-like" way, it easily succeeded. Other researchers were having similar experiences.

This is not really a general review in any fair sense. Rather it is a list of things I feel are important, with a real bias toward my work and that of my students and friends.

A list of references is given at the end of the paper.

2. Concepts

We will now list some of the concepts and techniques that we have in mind, that seem to hold promise in automatic theorem proving, and briefly discuss them. Of course no such list could be complete and we apologize for glaring omissions. Also these concepts are not mutually exclusive, some being special cases of others.

The word "knowledge" is a key to much of this modern theorem proving. Somehow we want to use the knowledge accumulated by humans over the last few thousand years, to help direct the *search* for proofs. Once a proof has been found it is a relatively simple matter to verify its validity by purely syntactic

KNOWLEDGE
- Build-in man's knowledge
- Often Domain-specific
- Contextual and Permanent

AVOID LISTING OF AXIOMS
- Clogs up the system

EASY TO USE and CHANGE

FIG. 1. Basic concepts.

[1] This is an edited version of an invited lecture at the 4th International Joint Conference on Artificial Intelligence, held in Tbilisi, Georgia, U.S.S.R., September 1975.

[2] The family of subsets of $(A \cap B)$ is the same as the intersection of the family of subsets of A and the family of subsets of B. This example is treated later.

procedures. So in a sense all of our concepts have to do with the storage and manipulation of knowledge of one sort or another. See Fig. 1.

The use of knowledge and built-in procedures partially eliminates the need for long lists of axioms, which tend to slow up proofs and use excessive amounts of memory. Such knowledge must be organized in a way that is easy to use and change.

Fig. 2 shows the 13 concepts we will discuss in the succeeding pages.

1. Knowledge Base
2. Reductions (rewrite rules)
3. Algebraic Simplification
4. Built-in Inequalities (and total ordering)
5. Natural Systems
6. Forward Chaining
7. Overdirector
8. Types
9. Advice
10. Procedures (and Built-in Concepts)
11. Models (and counterexamples)
12. Analogy
13. Man–machine

FIG. 2. Concepts.

2.1. Knowledge base

We store information in a knowledge base (or data base), process that information to obtain other information (by procedural forward chaining, etc.), and interrogate the data base when necessary to answer questions. A central idea here is, that facts are stored about "objects" rather than "predicates". For example the hypothesis Open(A_0) would be stored with "Open" as a property of "A_0" rather than with "A_0" as a property of "Open". (Objects are the skolem constants arising in a proof.) Also knowledge is stored about concepts. This knowledge can be stored in procedures or in lists or other structures.

The planner—QA4 type systems are ideally suited for using these concepts. See for example Winograd's Thesis [84], especially Sections 3.1.3–3.3.1 for an excellent description of some of these concepts.

Some concepts associated with a knowledge base are shown in Fig. 3. Demons are routines that watch the knowledge base and only act whenever certain properties become true of the data base. Languages like Microplanner, Conniver, and QA4 greatly facilitate the use of demons.

Some parts of the base remains static (as for example, properties of continuous functions) while other parts such as information about objects in the proof are dynamic and should be carried in a contextual data base.

Contains FACTS about Concepts and Objects
Facts are manipulated during proof to obtain new facts (contextual)
Procedural forward chaining
Static Information
Look up Answers
Object oriented: Open (A_0)
  Property list A_0 ≀ open
Demons
Examples
  Partial Sets }
  Monads } See later
  Reduction Rules }
"Graph" Provers
MODELS
FRAMES

FIG. 3. Knowledge base.

The "graph" provers of Bundy [17], Ballantyne and Bennett [4] use such a data base, as do the provers of Winograd [84], Goldstein [28], and others. Minsky's frames [55] appear to offer good advice for organizing data for a knowledge base.

Shortly we will show an example from analysis [5] which utilizes a data base with many of the concepts we have discussed in this paper.

2.2. Reduction

A reduction is a rewrite rule,

$$A \dashrightarrow B.$$

For example, the rule

$$t \in (A \cap B) \dashrightarrow t \in A \wedge t \in B$$

requires that we change all subformulas of the form $t \in (A \cap B)$ into the form $(t \in A \wedge t \in B)$, (but never rewrite the latter into the former). Such rules are

IN	OUT
$t \in (A \cap B)$	$t \in A \wedge t \in B$
$t \in (A \cup B)$	$t \in A \vee t \in B$
$t \in \{x : P(x)\}$	$P(t)$
$t \in$ subsets (A)	$t \subseteq A$
$t \subseteq A \cap B$	$t \subseteq A \wedge t \subseteq B$
$t \in \bigcup_{\alpha \in F} g(\alpha)$	$\exists\alpha(\alpha \in F \wedge t \in g(\alpha))$
.	
.	
.	

FIG. 4. Some REDUCE rules (rewrite rules).

semantic; their inclusion, and their use is not based upon their syntactic structure but on their meaning. The user supplies these rules. Fig. 4 lists some such rules, and Fig. 5 gives some definitions.

$A = B$	$A \subseteq B \wedge B \subseteq A$	(set equality)
$A \subseteq B$	$\forall x(x \in A \rightarrow x \in B)$	
	skolem form	
	$(x_0 \in A \rightarrow x_0 \in B)$	in "conclusion"
	$(x \in A \rightarrow x \in B)$	in "hypothesis"
Subsets (A)	$\{B : B \subseteq A\}$	
sb(A)	Subsets (A)	

FIG. 5. Some definitions.

The use of REDUCTIONS is best illustrated by an example from [7]. See Fig. 6. Here the formula "subsets(A)" means the set of all subsets of A; we have shortened it to "sb(A)" for this proof.

THEOREM. $\forall A \forall B$ (subsets $(A \cap B)$ = subsets $(A) \cap$ subsets (B))

PROOF. $\text{sb}(A \cap B) = \text{sb}(A) \cap \text{sb}(B)$	THE GOAL	(1)
$[\text{sb}(A \cap B) \subseteq \text{sb}(A) \cap \text{sb}(B)] \wedge [\ldots \supseteq \ldots]$,	defn of = SUBGOAL 1	
$[\text{sb}(A \cap B) \subseteq \text{sb}(A) \cap \text{sb}(B)]$		(11)
$[t_0 \in \text{sb}(A \cap B) \Rightarrow t_0 \in (\text{sb}(A) \cap \text{sb}(B))]$,	defn of $\subseteq$	
$[t_0 \subseteq (A \cap B) \Rightarrow t_0 \in \text{sb}(A) \wedge t_0 \in \text{sb}(B)]$	Reduce	
$[t_0 \subseteq A \wedge t_0 \subseteq B \Rightarrow t_0 \subseteq A \wedge t_0 \subseteq B]$	Reduce	
"T"		
$[\text{sb}(A) \cap \text{sb}(B) \subseteq \text{sb}(A \cap B)]$	SUBGOAL 2	(12)
"T" Similarly		

FIG. 6. An example of a proof.

IN	OUT
$\emptyset \subseteq A$	"T"
$A \subseteq A$	"T"
$\emptyset \in \omega$	"T"
$A \in \emptyset$	"False"
$0 \leqslant 1$	"T"
Open $\emptyset$	"T"
$A \subseteq \bar{A}$	"T"
.	
.	
.	
We would not include	
$P(y) \wedge \forall x\,(P(x) \rightarrow Q(x)) \rightarrow Q(y)$	"T"
because it is too complex.	

FIG. 7. Storing unit facts as reductions.

The reduction rules and definitions given in Fig. 4 and 5 are used in the proof. Notice how easy and "human-like" the proof proceeds when reductions are used. A corresponding resolution proof (without built-in partial ordering) required 14 clauses and a lengthy deduction.

Reductions also offer a convenient way for storing unit facts that can be easily used during proofs. See Fig. 7.

We are concerned with the four types of REDUCTION shown in Fig. 8.

REDUCTION (Rewrite Rules)
Conditional Reduction
Controlled Definition Instantiation
Complete Sets of Reductions

FIG. 8. Four kinds of REDUCTION.

2.2.1. Controlled definition instantiation

In this example we did *not* instantiate all definitions possible, but rather followed the rule: when all other strategies fail, instantiate the definition of the main connective of the conclusion. See Fig. 9.

EXAMPLES. Do not expand definitions in:

$$(A \subseteq B \wedge x \in A \wedge \text{Open } A \Rightarrow \text{Open } A).$$

Do expand the definition of "OCCLFR" in

$$(\text{Regular } (\mathcal{T}) \wedge \text{OCLFR}(\mathcal{T}) \Rightarrow \text{OCCLFR}(\mathcal{T}))$$

if other attempts fail.

FIG. 9. Controlled definition instantiation.

Instantiating all definitions can badly clutter up the proof and is often not needed. In general, definition instantiation should be carefully controlled.

2.2.2. Conditional reduction

This is a slight generalization of the reduction concept, whereby the program will perform the reduction only if a given stated condition is true in the *data base*. We do *not* want a large effort expended to determine whether the condition is true, because reductions are supposed to be performed quickly, so we verify the condition in the data base (rather than call the prover itself for this purpose). See Fig. 10 for a simple example.

2.2.3. Complete sets of reductions (written by D. Lankford).

Instead of using a reduction (A ---> B) one could get the same effect by adding the formula ($A = B$) as another hypothesis. But computational experience [5, 9, 30, 37, 39A, 40, 42, 56] has shown it is desirable to use equations as rewrite rules or to incorporate them into a normal form algorithm, in order to reduce the computation time and storage space needed. To what extent this can be done has

IN	CONDITION	OUT
INTERIOR (A)	OPEN (A)	A
CLOSURE (A)	CLOSED (A)	A
$\|A\|$	$A \geqslant 0$	A
$\|A\|$	$A < 0$	$-A$

EXAMPLE THEOREM. $2 \leqslant I \wedge 4 \leqslant J \leqslant 9 \wedge (0 \leqslant K \wedge L \leqslant 10 \rightarrow P(K, L)) \rightarrow P(I, |J|)$.

PROOF. The hypothesis $2 \leqslant I$ and $4 \leqslant J \leqslant 9$ are stored in the data base on the property lists of I and J. The term $|J|$ is reduced (rewritten) to J after a check in the data base verifies the condition $J \geqslant 0$.

Backchaining on the third hypotheses now gives the subgoal ($0 \leqslant I$ and $J \leqslant 10$) which is easily verified by the data base.

FIG. 10. Conditional reductions and an example.

been the object of considerable research. Fig. 11 lists some of the principal workers in this area with brief descriptions of their contributions. The pioneering works of Knuth and Bendix [40] and Slagle [73] focused on certain sets of rewrite rules for special study, those which determine normal forms for the corresponding equational theories. These decision procedures, called *complete sets of reductions* by Knuth and Bendix [40] and *sets of simplifiers* by Slagle [73], are defined by two properties: the finite termination property—no term can be infinitely reduced, and the unique termination property—any two sequences of immediate reductions, starting with the same term and terminating in irreducible terms, terminate with identical terms. Knuth and Bendix [40] developed an effective procedure which often derives a complete set of reductions from a given set of equations. Fig. 12 shows the end result of their derivation of a complete set of reductions for group theory beginning with the three left minimal axioms. Slagle [73] initiated the study of refutation complete methods for combining complete sets of reductions with resolution and paramodulation. Lankford [41, 42] generalizes a synthesis of their methods. Fig. 13 gives a proof in group theory using the Knuth–Bendix reductions.

Unfortunately, complete sets of reductions fail to exist for some equational theories, such as commutative group theory and ring theory, for the simple reason that some equations, such as commutative equations, cannot be expressed as rewrite rules with the finite termination property. For example, in proving a theorem in group theory like that in Fig. 14, when the hypothesis $(x+(x+x) = 0)$ is added to the axioms of group theory, the whole set can no longer be converted to a complete set of reductions. The existence of undecidable word problems, such as the theory defined by four equations found by Matijasevic [49A], shows that this limitation cannot be entirely overcome by a modification of the notion of complete sets of reductions. In addition, many important theories contain

Ballantyne and Bledsoe [5]: Metatheoretical concepts of non-standard analysis encoded as rewrite rules.

Bledsoe, et al. [9]: Ring theory normal form generator.

Guard, et al. [30]: Semi-automatic proof of SAM's lemma.

Knuth [39A]: Automatic proof of a conjecture from central groupoid theory.

Knuth and Bendix [40]: Complete sets of reductions; A class of finite termination tests; a test dependent unique termination algorithm.

Lankford [41, 42]: A test independent unique termination algorithm; an enlarged class of finite termination tests; refutation completeness results for complete and incomplete sets of reductions.

Nevins [56]: An experimental anticipation of many of the concepts related to complete sets of reductions.

Plotkin [63]: Refutation completeness results for theories having normal forms by specialization of the unification algorithm.

Slagle [73]: Complete sets of reductions; refutation completeness results for complete sets of reductions for fully narrowed input sets.

Winker [83]: Dynamic demodulation; a class of finite termination tests.

FIG. 11. Workers in the area of complete sets of reductions.

KB1	$x+0 \rightarrow x$
KB2	$0+x \rightarrow x$
KB3	$x+(-x) \rightarrow 0$
KB4	$(-x)+x \rightarrow 0$
KB5	$(x+y)+z \rightarrow x+(y+z)$
KB6	$-0 \rightarrow 0$
KB7	$-(-x) \rightarrow x$
KB8	$-(x+y) \rightarrow (-y)+(-x)$
KB9	$x+((-x)+y)) \rightarrow y$
KB10	$(-x)+(x+y) \rightarrow y$

FIG. 12. Knuth and Bendix's complete sets of reductions for a group.

THEOREM. $\cdot[(D+(C+(-C)))+(-(0+(-A)))] \in H \rightarrow (D+A) \in H$

Proof.

$\cdot[(D+(C+(-C)))+(-(-A))] \in H \rightarrow (D+A) \in H$	KB2
$\cdot[(D+0)+(-(-A))] \in H \rightarrow (D+A) \in H$	KB3
$\cdot[D+(-(-A))] \in H \rightarrow (D+A) \in H$	KB1
$\cdot[D+A] \in H \rightarrow (D+A) \in H$	KB7
TRUE	MATCH

FIG. 13. A proof in group theory using complete sets of reductions.

equations that occur in non-unit clauses. And the well-known result of Birkhoff on equational definability shows that this situation cannot be avoided. Nevertheless, we believe that modifications and adaptations of the concept of complete sets of reductions [41, 42, 63, 73] will lead to significant improvement in the treatment of equality when combined with heuristic methods and built-in procedures [5, 9, 56, 63, 76].

For example, consider the theorem that in a group with $x+x+x=0$, $h(h(x,y),y)=0$ where $h(x,y)=x+y+(-x)+(-y)$. This theorem has received repeated attention in the literature [61A, 67A] as a difficult theorem for mechanical (and human!) theorem provers, and was only recently proved fully automatically without hints by Nevins [56]. Lankford's methods [42] in Fig. 14 and 15 were implemented by Ballantyne and Lankford [5A] and show considerable improvement over Nevin's methods, primarily because of Nevin's treating associativity by unification rather than as a rewrite rule.

THEOREM. $x+(x+x)=0 \to h(h(a,b),a)=0$.

Proof. The conclusion is reduced to

$a+b+(-a)+b+a+(-b)+(-a)+(-b)=0$ (associate to the right).

The hypothesis $(x+(x+x)\to 0)$ is added as another rewrite rule.

11 $x+(x+x)\to 0$ added.

In the first round, three new reductions are generated, and one equality:

N1 $x+x+x+y\to y$ 11, KB5

N2 $x+y+x+y+x+y\to 0$ 11, KB5

N3 $-x\to x+x$ 11, KB10

E1 $x+y+x+y=y+y+x+x$ N3, KB8
(this cannot be made a reduction).

N1-3 Act upon KB1-10, 11 and eliminate all of KB1-10, 11 except

KB1 $x+0\to x$

KB2 $0+x\to x$

KB5 $(x+y)+z\to x+(y+z)$

11 $x+x+x\to 0$.

FIG. 14. First round of the proof using Lankford's method (using Fig. 12).

In the second round, three new reductions are generated, and no new equations:

N4 $x+y+x+y+x+y+z\to 0$

N5 $x+y+z+x+y+z+x+y+z\to 0$

N6 $x+y+x+y+x\to y+y$.

The Goal:

$$a+b+(-a)+b+a+(-b)+(-a)+(-b)=0$$

is proved in this round by applying N3, E1, N1, N6 and 11.

Steps: 2.

Formulas saved: 7.

Time: 30 seconds.

FIG. 15. Second round of the proof.

Fig. 16 gives a challenging problem for automatic provers from ring theory which seems beyond present methods.

THEOREM. *In a RING*

$$x^3=x\to ab=ba.$$

(*Recall that a ring is +commutative.*)

FIG. 16. A challenging problem for automatic provers.

2.3. Algebraic simplification

There is a strong need to avoid adding the field axioms for the real numbers as hypotheses to a theorem being proved, because this greatly slows proofs. The associativity and commutativity axioms for + and · are especially troublesome, so several efforts have been made to "build these in".

Some references to this work are: Slagle and Norton [74, 75]; QA4; QLISP [65, 68]; Plotkin [63]; Frönig [25]; Stickel [77]; Bledsoe, et al. [9, 12].

Of course much is learned from the researchers working in the field of symbol manipulation and algebraic simplification, where these methods have been applied to other problems in physics and mathematics. However, automatic theorem proving presents difficulties not covered by that work.

For example, the theorem

$$P(a+b+c)\to P(b+a+c)$$

is easily handled by using a canonical form, but the theorem

$$P(k+2)\to P(b+5)$$

where k is a variable and b is a constant, presents more difficulty. An ordinary unification algorithm

$$\text{UNIFY}(k+2,\ b+5)$$

would put b for k, b/k, and fail. An "Algebraic Unifier", could write the equation

$$k+2=b+5,$$

and "solve for" k, getting $k=b+3$, and return $(b+3)$ for k, to successfully complete the proof.

A similar approach works on the example

$$\text{UNIFY}(B[k+1]=\text{Amax}(B,j,k+1),\quad A_0[i_0]=\text{Amax}(A_0,1,i_0))$$

where B, j, k are variables, and A_0, i_0 are constants. This example is from the field of program verification (see [13], pp. 27–28).

Data types such as sets, bags, and triples [68, 65] handle some of these problems.

2.4. Built-in inequalities (and total orderings)

Again we must avoid the explicit use of such axioms as the transitivity axiom

$$(x \leqslant y \wedge y \leqslant z \rightarrow x \leqslant z).$$

Bledsoe et al. [8, 9, 13, 29] employ "interval types" for dealing with certain inequalities, and Slagle and Norton [75] have built-in axioms for handling total and partial ordering (including inequalities). See Fig. 17.

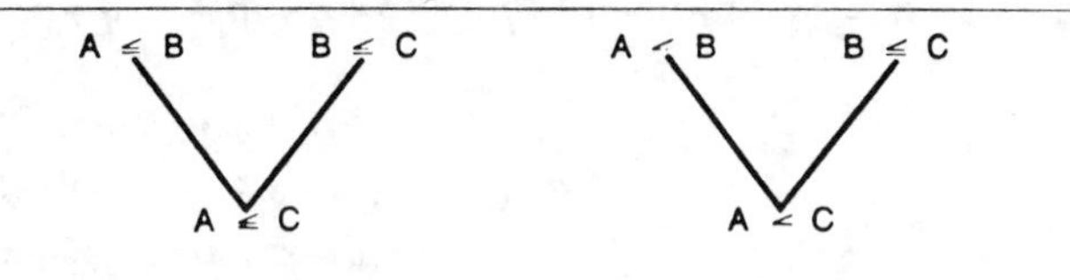

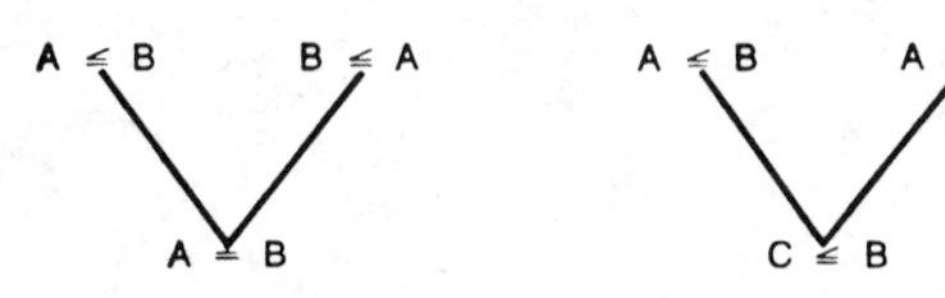

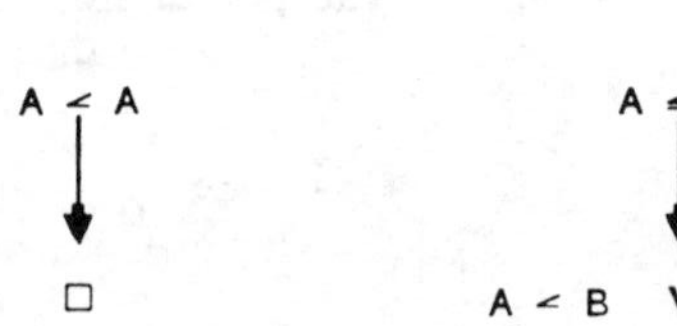

ALLOW UNIFICATION IN ALL OF THESE CASES

FIG. 17. Slagle and Norton's build-in partial and total ordering.

The following is a theorem from program verification which was proved by Slagle and Norton's program. This theorem, which is a verification condition from Hoare's FIND program, and others like it have been proved by the "interval type" methods of Bledsoe and Tyson [8, 13], and by others.

THEOREM.

$$\begin{aligned} & j < i \\ & \wedge\ m \leqslant p \leqslant q \leqslant n \\ & \wedge\ \forall x \forall y (m \leqslant x < i \wedge j < y \leqslant n \rightarrow A[x] \leqslant A[y]) \\ & \wedge\ \forall x \forall y (m \leqslant x \leqslant y \leqslant j \rightarrow A[x] \leqslant A[y]) \\ & \wedge\ \forall x \forall y (i \leqslant x \leqslant y \leqslant n \rightarrow A[x] \leqslant A[y]) \\ & \quad \rightarrow A[p] \leqslant A[q]. \end{aligned}$$

Also Slagle and Norton have built-in partial ordering for handling some problems in set theory.

2.5. Natural systems

We have chosen to emphasize the so called "natural" systems in this report. I would not like to define the term, but will only give examples. In general we are not talking about refutation systems such as resolution, though we sometimes do proofs by contradiction [66]. They are sometimes called goal oriented systems, or Gentzen type systems.

We are given a goal G and a hypothesis H and wish to show that G follows from H,

$$(H \rightarrow G)$$

or more generally to find a substitution θ for which

$$(H\theta \rightarrow G\theta)$$

is a propositionally valid formula. A set of rules is given for manipulating H and G to obtain the desired θ. For example, $(P(a) \wedge (P(x) \rightarrow Q(x)) \Rightarrow Q(a))$ has the solution $\theta \equiv a/x$.[3] The Rules in Fig. 18 and 19 are from the IMPLY System described in [9, 12]. They are given more precisely and completely in [12]. See Fig. 20 for a simple example.

I4. $(H \Rightarrow A \wedge B)$ "SPLIT"
    If $(H \Rightarrow A)$ returns θ
    and $(H \Rightarrow B\theta)$ returns λ
    then return $\theta \circ \lambda$.

I3. $(H_1 \vee H_2 \Rightarrow C)$ "CASES"
    If $(H_1 \Rightarrow C)$ returns θ
    and $(H_2\theta \Rightarrow C)$ returns λ
    then return $\theta \circ \lambda$.

I5. $(H \Rightarrow C)$
    Put C': = REDUCE(C): H': = REDUCE(H)
    Call $(H' \Rightarrow C')$.

I7. $(H \Rightarrow (A \rightarrow B))$ "PROMOTE"
    Call $(H \wedge A \Rightarrow B)$.

I13. $(H \Rightarrow C)$
    Put C': = DEFINE(C)
    Call $(H \Rightarrow C')$.
    (See [12] for the ordering of these rules)

FIG. 18. IMPLY rules. A partial set from [12].

[3] Sometimes θ must be more complicated, (see App. 3 of [12]) as in the example $(P(x) \rightarrow P(a) \wedge P(b))$ which has the solution $\theta \equiv a/x \vee b/x$.

H2. $(H \Rightarrow C)$ "MATCH"
If $H\theta \equiv C\theta$, return θ,

H6. $(A \wedge B \Rightarrow C)$ "OR–FORK"
If $(A \Rightarrow C)$ returns θ (not NIL), return θ,
Else Call $(B \Rightarrow C)$

H7. $H \wedge (A \rightarrow D) \Rightarrow C$ "BACK-CHAIN"
If $(D \Rightarrow C)$ returns θ,
and $(H \Rightarrow A\theta)$ returns λ,
then return $\theta \circ \lambda$

H9. $H \wedge (a = b) \Rightarrow C$ "SUB="
Put $a' := \text{CHOOSE}(a, b)$, $b' := \text{OTHER}(a, b)$
Call $(H(a'/b') \Rightarrow C(a'/b'))$.

FIG. 19. IMPLY rules (contd.).

THEOREM. $(P(a) \wedge \forall x(P(x) \rightarrow Q(x)) \rightarrow Q(a))$.

$P(a) \wedge (P(x) \rightarrow Q(x)) \Rightarrow Q(a))$	
$(P(a) \Rightarrow (Q(a))$	H6
FAILS	
$(P(x) \rightarrow Q(x)) \Rightarrow Q(a))$	
$(Q(x) \Rightarrow Q(a))$	H7
Return $\theta \equiv a \mid x$	H2
$(P(a) \Rightarrow P(x)(a \mid x))$	
Return TRUE.	
Returns $a \mid x$.	

FIG. 20. An example proved by IMPLY.

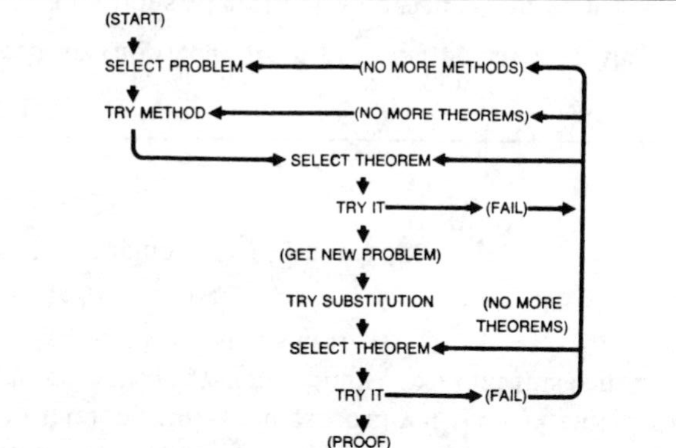

FIG. 21. General flow diagrams of the LOGIC THEORIST [59].

Newell, Simon, and Shaw's logic theorist [59, 60], and Gelernter's geometry machine [26], were natural (or goal directed) systems, although we see that they included various other features. See Fig. 21 and 22. Reiter's MATH–HACK

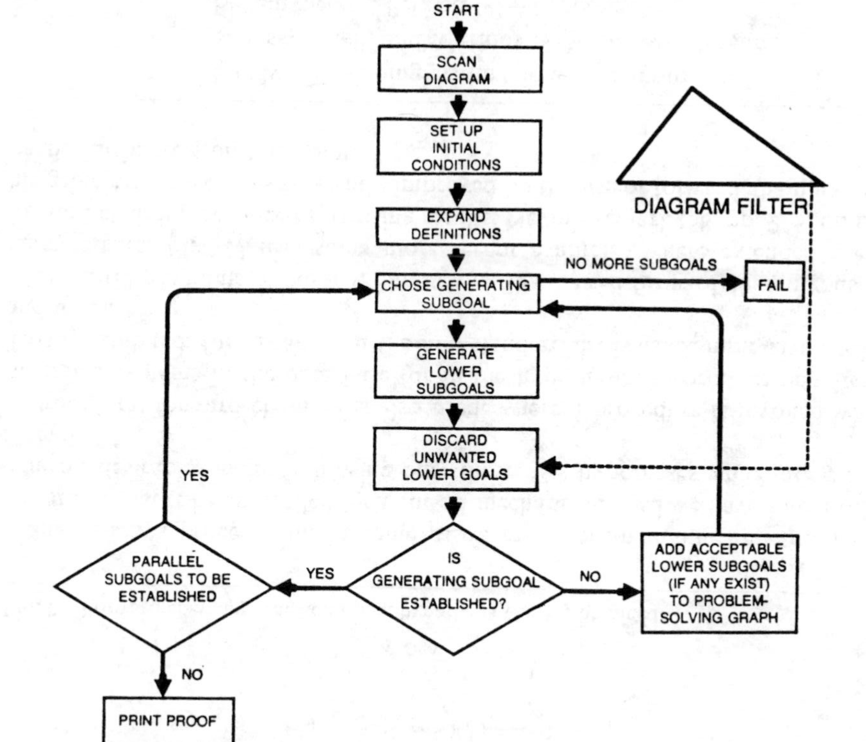

FIG. 22. Simplified flow chart for the geometry–theorem proving machine (Fig. 3 of [26]).

NSS—Logic Theorist [60]
Gelernter's Geometry machine [26]
Reiter's math–hac [66]—much like [12] but more
Maslov [48]
Bibel [6]
Ernst [23]
Boyer–Moore [14]
Nevins [56–58]
Planner [34, 78]
Conniver [52]
QA4, QLISP [68, 65]
Goldstein [28]
Ullman [80]

FIG. 23. Other natural systems.

system [66] is much like that of [12] but has the important addition of models which we will mention later, and other features.

Other natural systems include the Planner–Conniver–QA4 group, and those of Maslov, Goldstein, Nevins, Bibel, Boyer-Moore, Ernst, [48, 49, 28, 34, 78, 52, 68, 65, 6, 14, 23, 46, 15, 30] and others. See Fig. 23.

What are the advantages (if any) of the natural systems? There may be none—especially in the long run—and especially if the techniques we emphasize here are built into the resolution systems. But we feel that this is not easy to do. Specifically we feel that the natural systems are:

- Easier for human use.
- Easier for machine use of knowledge.

See Fig. 24 and 25.

HUMAN USE

Bring to bear knowledge from pure mathematics in the same form used there.

Recognize situations where such knowledge can be used.

Professional mathematician will want to participate.

Easier to design, augment, work upon.

Essential for man–machine interaction (where the man is a trained mathematician).

FIG. 24. Advantages of natural systems.

MACHINE USE

Automatically limits the search. Does not start all proofs of the theorem. (Syntactic search strategy.)

A natural vehicle to hang on heuristics, knowledge, semantics. (Semantic search strategies.)

Easier to combine procedures with deduction.

Contextual data base problem. (One data base would be needed for each clause.)

New Languages (PLANNER, QA4). Ease the implementation.

FIG. 25. Advantages of natural systems (contd.).

We include here two quotes regarding the advantages of natural systems.

"There is a naturalness with which systems of natural deduction admit a semantic component with the result that a great deal of control is gained over the search for a proof. It is precisely for this reason that we argue in favour of their use in automatic theorem-proving, in opposition to the usual resolution-based systems, which appear to lack any kind of reasonable control over dead-end searches." Raymond Reiter [66].

"A point worthy of stress is that a deductive system is not "simpler" merely because it employs fewer rules of inference. A more meaningful measure of simplicity is the ease with which heuristic considerations can be absorbed into the system." Arthur Nevins [56].

2.6. Forward chaining

Forward chaining is accomplished when one hypothesis is applied to another to obtain an additional hypothesis. See the example in Fig. 26.

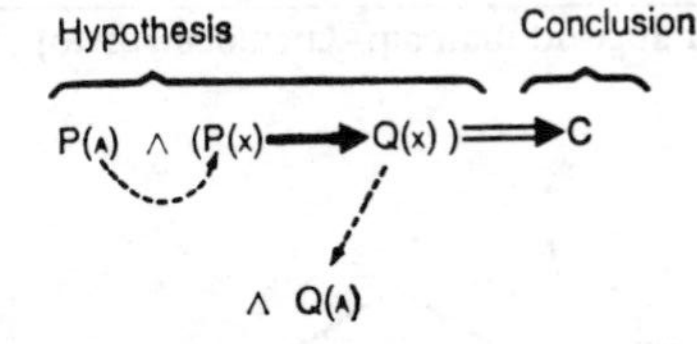

FIG. 26. Forward chaining. The additional hypothesis $Q(A)$ is obtained.

Since such a process can, in some cases, result in an infinite repetition it is important that it be controlled by a cut-off mechanism. Also we have found other controls desirable, such as allowing only those new hypotheses which are *ground* formulas.

Procedural forward chaining is also used, where a procedure is invoked which manipulates items in the data base (or in the hypothesis) to produce new items. This is exhibited, for instance, in the non-standard analysis example given below and in [5].

The early programs of Newell, Simon and Shaw, used forward chaining, as did many others. Fig. 27 lists some more recent examples where extended use of forward chaining produced surprising results. Nevin's remark [58, pp. 2, 3] on how his geometry prover was so greatly improved by the use of forward chaining, is of particular interest on this point.

Bundy [17]—Doing arithmetic with diagrams.
Siklossy, Rich, and Marinov [71]—British Museum.
Ballantyne and Bennett [4]—Topology.
Nevins [58]—Plane Geometry.
Ballantyne—Non-Standard-Analysis [5].

FIG. 27. Extensive use of forward chaining.

2.7. Overdirector

Every prover has a control routine which directs the search tree. See Newell, Simon, and Shaw's control structure was shown in Fig. 21.

This overdirector can bring to bear strategies or experts (see [28]), heuristics, and advice tables, controlled backup, etc. as it sees fit.

It is important that such an overdirector have the flexibility to switch from one line of attack to another, and back again, as the proof proceeds, thus providing a parallel search capability. This of course, requires a (controlled) back-up mechanism such as that possessed by Conniver. Unrestricted back-up is intolerable. A contextual data base, which can be consulted by the overdirector to help it decide whether and how much to back-up, or what other line of attach to take, is an indispensable part of the prover we have in mind. The concepts of Conniver [52] and QA4 [68, 65] apply here.

EXAMPLE. (From Non-Standard Analysis.) The following example is given here to exhibit the use of some of the concepts we have described above. These techniques have been used by Mike Ballantyne to prove by computer (not interactively) several difficult theorems in intermediate analysis. See [5] for a complete description of this work.

The reader need not be conversant with non-standard analysis (or even intermediate analysis) to follow the example given in Fig. 28 and 29.

Notice that the proof follows the general procedure described by the rules of Figs 18–19. First, the fact that f is continuous, is noted in the data base and the hypothesis Cont(f, S_0) is dropped. Next the term "Compact" is defined (in non-standard terms), and the formula $x_0 \in f(S_0)$ is "promoted" to the hypothesis by Rule I7 of Fig. 18, and then reduced to produce the new hypothesis.

$$V_0 \in S_0 \wedge x_0 = f(V_0).$$

Forward chaining then gives the additional hypothesis: $\mathrm{st}(V_0) \in S_0$.

At this point we leave the rules of Fig. 18 and 19, and work with the data base. See [5] for details.

Various routines such as EL, STANDARD, FINITE, CONTINUOUS, are used to put items into the data base and to manipulate them to obtain others. This is called procedural forward chaining. For example the program detects $(V_0 \in S_0)$ and $(\mathrm{st}(V_0) \in S_0)$ in the hypothesis and calls EL which builds a set S_0' in the data base with the elements V_0, and $\mathrm{st}(V_0)$, and drops $(V_0 \in S_0)$ and $(\mathrm{st}(V_0) \in S_0)$ from the hypothesis. This set S_0' with only two elements represents the set S_0 which may be infinite.

Similarly the monad M_1:$(\mathrm{st}(V_0), V_0)$ is built in the data base. The reader needs only to understand that continuous functions map monads into monads, (and not what a monad is) and hence that the monad M_1 is mapped into the monad M_2:$(f(\mathrm{st}(V_0)), f(V_0))$.

The hypothesis $(x_0 = f(V_0))$ is used to generate the reduce rule R_1 and another hypothesis generates R_2. Thus the goal $\mathrm{st}(x_0) \in f(S_0)$ is easily converted to the new

5.2. THEOREM. *If f is continuous on a compact set S, then $f(S)$ is compact.*

Proof.

- $\mathrm{Cont}(f, S_0) \wedge \mathrm{Compact}(S_0) \Rightarrow \mathrm{Compact}(f(S_0))$

  Note: f is continuous on S_0. (In Data Base)

- $\mathrm{Compact}(S_0) \Rightarrow \mathrm{Compact}(f(S_0))$
  ↘ ↘
- $(x \in S_0 \to \mathrm{st}(x) \in S_0) \Rightarrow (x_0 \in f(S_0) \to \mathrm{st}(x_0) \in f(S_0))$
  definition
- $(x \in S_0 \to \mathrm{st}(x) \in S_0) \wedge x_0 \in f(S_0) \Rightarrow \mathrm{st}(x_0) \in f(S_0)$
  ↘ promote (See Fig 18).
- $(x \in S_0 \to \mathrm{st}(x) \in S_0) \wedge (V_0 \in S_0 \wedge x_0 = f(V_0) \Rightarrow \mathrm{st}(x_0) \in f(S_0)$
  reduce

  $(x \in S_0 \to \mathrm{st}(x) \in S_0) \wedge (V_0 \in S_0 \wedge x_0 = f(V_0)$
  $\wedge\ \underline{\mathrm{st}(V_0) \in S_0} \Rightarrow \mathrm{st}(x_0) \in f(S_0)$
  forward chain

FIG. 28. An example of a proof by Ballantyne's prover.

DATA BASE	AGENT
• S_0': $(\mathrm{st}(V_0), V_0)$	EL
Type: $\mathrm{st}(V_0)$, Standard	Standard
Type: $\mathrm{st}(V_0)$, Finite	Standard
V_0., Finite	
M_1: $(\mathrm{st}(V_0), V_0)$	Finite
R_1: x_0 ---> $f(V_0)$	Equals
• M_2: $(f(\mathrm{st}(V_0)), f(V_0))$	Continuous
• R_2: $\mathrm{st}(f(V_0))$ ---> $f(\mathrm{st}(V_0))$	Continuous
$f(S_0)'$: $(f(\mathrm{st}(V_0)), f(x_0))$	Continuous
• $(x \in S_0 \to \mathrm{st}(x) \in S_0) \Rightarrow \mathrm{st}(x_0) \in f(S_0)$	
• $(x \in S_0 \to \mathrm{st}(x) \in S_0) \Rightarrow \mathrm{st}(f(V_0)) \in f(S_0)$	R_1
• $(x \in S_0 \to \mathrm{st}(x) \in S_0) \Rightarrow f(\mathrm{st}(V_0)) \in f(S_0)$	R_2
• TRUE	$f(S_0)'$

FIG. 29. Proof (contd.).

goal $f(\mathrm{st}(V_0)) \in f(S_0)$, which is readily verified *by inspection*; i.e., the program notes that the set $f(S_0)'$ in the data base, contains the item $f(\mathrm{st}(V_0))$.

In summary, one sees the manipulation of a data base and the execution of a few logical operations, to produce the proof of this theorem.

2.8. Types

The concept of typing plays a fundamental role in mathematics and computer science. Using a letter e for the identity element of a group, lower case letters x, y, z, for members of the group, and capital letters G, H, for groups and subgroups, is immensely helpful to humans in proving theorems.

Similar typing is helpful in automatic provers. Other data types such as integer, real, negative, complex, bags, sets, types, interval types, infinitesimals, infinitely large, etc., can be advantageous in certain applications. See Fig. 30.

e	identity in a group
x, y, z	members of a group
G, H	groups, subgroups
x, y, z	points
A, B, C	sets
F, G, H	Families
$\mathscr{T}$	topology
P, Q	predicates
x, y	reals
z	complex
I, J, K	Integers
ε, δ	Infinitesimals
r, s, t	standard reals
x, y, z	non-standard reals
ω	infinitely large integers

Bags, sets, types
Interval types

FIG. 30. Some examples of types.

2.9. Advice

One of the most powerful things a human can do to aid the prover is to provide "advice" for the use of a theorem or lemma. Carl Hewitt's PLANNER [34] exploits this idea.

For example in Fig. 31 we see an example of Winograd's [84] where, to determine that a thing x is a thesis we are "advised" to either verify that it is long, or that it contains a persuasive argument. This is given in Micro-planner language in Fig. 32.

Another such advice lemma is given in Fig. 33, and this is used in Fig. 34 to prove a theorem. This proof also clearly emphasizes the need for simplification routines and eqation solving routines in proofs in analysis.

GOAL	VERIFY
(Thesis x)	(Long x) (Use: contents—check, count pages)
	or
	(x contains y)
	and
	(argument y)
	and
	(persuasive y)

FIG. 31. Winograd's example.

```
(DEFINE THEOREM EVALUATE
                                                  ;EVALUATE is the name we are
                                                  ;giving to the theorem
 (THCONSE(X Y)
                                                  ;this indicates the type of
                                                  ;theorem and names its
                                                  ;variables
  (THGOAL(# THESIS $?X))
                                                  ;show that X is a thesis
                                                  ;the " $?" indicates a variable
  (THOR
                                                  ;THOR is like "or", trying things
                                                  ;in the order given until one works
   (THGOAL(# LONG $?X)(THUSE CONTENTS-CHECK COUNTPAGES))
                                                  ;THUSE says to try the theorem
                                                  ;named CONTENTS-CHECK first,
                                                  ;then if that doesn't work, try
                                                  ;the one named COUNTPAGES
   (THAND
                                                  ;THAND is like "and"
    (THGOAL(# CONTAINS $?X $?Y))
                                                  ;find something Y which is
                                                  ;contained in X
    (THGOAL(# ARGUMENT $?Y))
                                                  ;show that it is an argument
    (THGOAL(# PERSUASIVE $?Y)(THTBF THTRUE))))))
                                                  ;prove that it is persuasive, using
                                                  ;any theorems which are applicable
```

FIG. 32. PLANNER Representation of the advice lemma in Fig. 31 (Fig. 53 of [84]).

GOAL	VERIFY	
$(\lvert A\rvert \leqslant \varepsilon)$	$(A = B+C)$	1
	and	
	$(\lvert B\rvert \leqslant \varepsilon_1)$	2
	and	
	$(\lvert C\rvert \leqslant \varepsilon_2)$	3

and
    $(\varepsilon_1+\varepsilon_2 \leqslant \varepsilon)$ 4
or
    (Other advice)
    $(A = B \cdot C)$ 1
and
    $(|B| \leqslant \varepsilon_1)$ 2
and
    $|C| \leqslant \varepsilon_2)$ 3
and
    $(\varepsilon_1 \cdot \varepsilon_2 \leqslant \varepsilon)$ 4
or
    (Other advice)

FIG. 33. An advice lemma.

THEOREM. $|a| \leqslant E^{\alpha}-1 \wedge |b| \leqslant E^{\beta}-1 \wedge 1+c = (a+1)(b+1) \rightarrow |c| \leqslant E^{\alpha+\beta}-1$

Proof. Goal: $|c| \leqslant E^{\alpha+\beta}-1$.

Parts 1–4 of the advice lemma (Fig 33) are used to convert this to subgoals (1)–(4) below.

(1) $c = B+C$

To solve this, convert the hypothesis $1+c = (a+1)(b+1)$ to $c = a\cdot b+a+b$ and substitute $a \cdot b/B$, $a+c/C$ (i.e. substitute $a \cdot b$ for B and $a+b$ for C)

(2)	$\lvert a \cdot b\rvert \leqslant \varepsilon_1$	use parts 1′–4′ of the advice lemma.
(21)	$a \cdot b = B \cdot C$	$a/B, b/C$
(22)	$\lvert a\rvert \leqslant \varepsilon_{11}$	$E^{\alpha}-1/\varepsilon_{11}$
(23)	$\lvert b\rvert \leqslant \varepsilon_{12}$	$E^{\beta}-1/\varepsilon_{12}$
(24)	$(E^{\alpha}-1)\cdot(E^{\beta}-1) \leqslant \varepsilon_1$	$(\ )\cdot(\ )/\varepsilon_1$
(3)	$\lvert a+b\rvert \leqslant \varepsilon_2$	use parts 1–4 of the advice Lemma (again).
(32)	$\lvert a\rvert \leqslant \varepsilon_{21}$	$E^{\alpha}-1/\varepsilon_{21}$
(33)	$\lvert b\rvert \leqslant \varepsilon_{22}$	$E^{\beta}-1/\varepsilon_{22}$
(34)	$(E^{\alpha}-1)+(E^{\beta}-1) \leqslant \epsilon_2$	$(E^{\alpha}-1)+(E^{\beta}-1)/\varepsilon_2$
(4)	$(E^{\alpha}-1)\cdot(E^{\beta}-1)+((E^{\alpha}-1)+(E^{\beta}-1)) \leqslant E^{\alpha+\beta}-1$	use simplification.
	$E^{\alpha+\beta}-1 \leqslant E^{\alpha+\beta}-1$	TRUE

FIG. 34. The proof of an example (due to Overbeek) using the advice lemma of Fig. 33.

The concept depicted in Fig. 33, might be generalized in a manner shown in Fig. 35. Then perhaps an instantiation of it (like Fig. 33) could be saved by the program for future use.

GOAL	VERIFY
$P(C)$	Find $P(A)$ in Hypothesis
	and
	Express C in terms of A, $C = f(A, B)$
	and
	Find $P(\alpha) \wedge P(\beta) \rightarrow P(f(\alpha, \beta))$
	and
	Goal $P(B)$
	or
	(Other Advice)

FIG. 35. A more general advice lemma.

2.10. Procedures (and built-in concepts)

These have been discussed already, especially in the non-standard analysis example given in Section 7.

Fig. 36 lists some of these concepts and examples. An "expert" is a set of procedures for solving one type of problem. See Goldstein [28].

Strategies
Heuristics
  Syntactic
  Semantic (domain dependent)
Experts
EXAMPLES:
  Induction
  Built-in partial and total ordering, inequality, associativity, etc.
  "Solvers"
  Goldstein's geometry prover
  Limit heuristic
  PAIRS heuristic
CONCEPTS:
  Follow a plan rather than search.
  Calculate an answer rather than prove a formula.

FIG. 36. Some procedures.

In Fig. 37 we see an INDUCTION heuristic being applied [7]. In general when a heuristic is to be applied, the program detects a pattern and consults a list of recommendations. In this example it detects the presence of ω in the theorem being proved and proceeds as shown. Details of this proof are omitted.

THEOREM. $\omega = \bigcup_{\alpha \in \omega} \alpha$

(1) $(\omega \subseteq \bigcup_{\alpha\in\omega} \alpha) \wedge (\bigcup_{\alpha\in\omega} \alpha \subseteq \omega)$. *Defn of = SUBGOAL 1*

SUBGOAL 1

(11) $(\omega \subseteq \bigcup_{\alpha\in\omega} \alpha)$ *EASY*

SUBGOAL 2

(12) $(\bigcup_{\alpha\in\omega} \alpha \subseteq \omega)$

$(t_0 \in \bigcup_{\alpha\in\omega} \alpha \rightarrow t_0 \in \omega)$. *Defn of* $\subseteq$

$(\alpha_0 \in \omega \wedge t_0 \in \alpha_0 \rightarrow t_0 \in \omega)$. *REDUCE*

The proof fails by the normal procedures. It detects the presence of ω, and decides to try INDUCTION. Pre-INDUCTION converts it to the form:

$$\underbrace{(\alpha_0 \in \omega \rightarrow (t_0 \in \alpha_0 \rightarrow t_0 \in \omega))}_{P(\alpha_0)}.$$

It now trys:

$$\underset{\cdot 1}{P(0)} \text{ and } \underset{\cdot 2}{(P(\alpha_0) \rightarrow P(\alpha_0+1))}.$$

(12.1) $(t_0 \in 0 \rightarrow t_0 \in \omega)$ SUCCEEDS

(12.1) $(\alpha_0 \in \omega \wedge (t_0 \in \alpha_0 \rightarrow t_0 \in \omega) \rightarrow (\underbrace{t_0 \in (\alpha_0+1)}_{t_0 = \alpha_0 \vee t_0 \in \alpha_0} \rightarrow t_0 \in \omega))$.
SUCCEEDS

FIG. 37. The use of an INDUCTION heuristic to prove a theorem.

Fig. 39 shows some strategies from Goldstein's geometry prover [28], and Fig. 40 shows an example where the PAIRS heuristic [10] is being applied. In this example a *partial match* was obtained between the two formulas

$$\text{Cover}(G_0) \text{ and } \text{Cover}(\bar{\bar{G}}_0),$$

which triggered the program to consult the PAIRS table (see Fig. 41) for advice. The first advice given from the PAIRS table, namely $(G_0 \subseteq \bar{\bar{G}}_0)$, failed, but the second one, $(G_0 \subseteq\subseteq \bar{\bar{G}}_0)$, succeeded.

STRATEGY EQTR13
TO-PROVE: Triangle XYZ = Triangle UVW
ESTABLISH: 10 seq XZ = seq VW
20 angle XYZ = angle UVW
30 angle YZX = angle VWU
REASON: congruence by asa
(This is like backchaining)

CONVERSION ANGLE-BISECTOR
GIVEN: seq DB bisects angle ABC
ASSERT: angle ABD = angle CDB
FORGET: given
(This is like reduce)

COROLLARY EQTRI-2
GIVEN: Triangle XYZ = Triangle UVW
ASSERT: Angle XYZ = angle UVW
angle YZX = angle VWU
angle ZXY = angle WUV

FIG. 39. Some strategies from Goldstein's Prover.

THEOREM. $\forall G\,(Cover\,(G) \rightarrow Cover\,(\bar{\bar{G}}))$

(1) $Cover\,(G_0) \rightarrow Cover\,(\bar{\bar{G}}_0)$

No Match

Partial Match: Use PAIRS heuristic
Consult PAIRS table under "Cover"

(1.1) *Try* $(G_0 \subseteq \bar{\bar{G}}_0)$ *Fails*

(1.2) *Try* $(G_0 \subseteq\subseteq \bar{\bar{G}}_0)$ "T" *by REDUCE*

or

$(A_0 \in G_0 \Rightarrow \underbrace{C \in \bar{\bar{G}}_0}_{} \wedge A_0 \subseteq C)$ *defn of* $\subseteq\subseteq$

$(A_0 \in G_0 \Rightarrow B \in G_0 \wedge C = \bar{B} \wedge A_0 \subseteq C)$

$(A_0 \in G_0 \Rightarrow B \in G_0 \wedge A_0 \subseteq \bar{B})$ *sub* =

SUBGOAL 1

(1.21) $(A_0 \in G_0 \Rightarrow B \in G_0)$ A_0/B

SUBGOAL 2

(1.22) $(A_0 \in G_0 \Rightarrow A_0 \subseteq \bar{A}_0)$ "T" *by REDUCE*

QED.

FIG. 40. An example using Bledsoe's PAIRS heuristic.

PAIRS table—

IN	*Pattern*	*Recommendations*
Cover	(Cover $(G) \to$ Cover (F))	$[(G \subseteq F)(G \subseteq\subseteq F) \ldots]$ .1 .2
Countable	(Countable $A \to$ Countable B)	$[(B \subseteq A)$ .1
	$(\exists f\,(f$ is a function $\wedge$ domain $f \subseteq A \wedge B \subseteq$ range $f)) \ldots]$ .2	

·
·
·

DEFINITION table—
$\bar{A} \equiv$ The Closure of A. (note: $A \subseteq \bar{A}$).
$\bar{\bar{G}} \equiv \{\bar{A} : A \in G\}$
cover $(G, X) \equiv X \subseteq \bigcup_{\alpha \in G} \alpha$
$G \subseteq\subseteq F$ (G is a refinement of F)
$\equiv \forall A \in G\, \exists C \in F\, (A \subseteq C)$

REDUCE TABLE (single entry)

IN	*OUT*
$A \subseteq \bar{A}$	"T"
$G \subseteq\subseteq \bar{\bar{G}}$	"T"

·
·
·

FIG. 41. A PAIRS table, definitions, and reductions, used in Fig. 40.

2.11. Models

In Fig. 22, we saw the flow chart of Gelernter's geometry prover, with its famous "diagram filter", being used to discard unwanted subgoals. This is an excellent example of a MODEL or counterexample being used to help with a proof. Since models and counterexamples play such crucial roles in mathematics it is not surprising that they have been found useful in automatic provers. We expect their role to be expanded.

Fig. 42 shows Reiter's Rule 4 (see [66]) and an explanation of how the model M is used in the execution of this rule; and Fig. 43 gives an example of a theorem being proved by his system. In this example the Model M might be, for example, the Klein–four Group (Fig. 44) in which the goal (122), $BB^{-1} = B^{-1}$ clearly fails. More complicated models are needed for other proofs, especially where commutativity is *not* assumed.

4. $\psi \vdash A \wedge B$
If $\psi \vdash A$ returns σ_1, $M \vDash_E B\sigma_1$,
and $\psi \vdash B\sigma$, returns σ_2

$$\sigma_1\sigma_2$$

Suppose that, during an attempted proof of A, x is instantiated by the term t. At this point, make the semantic test $M \vDash_E B(t)$. If successful, proceed with the proof of A. Otherwise, A's proof has obviously gone astray and must be redirected. Thus, rather than patiently waiting for A to deliver a (possibly wrong) σ_1, the wff B should be continuously semantically monitoring the proof of A, thereby minimizing the risk of receiving an incorrect σ_1. We believe that this kind of parallel processing of dependent subgoals will considerably alleviate the problem of back-up encountered by purely syntactic theorem-provers.

FIG. 42. Reiter's rule 4 in MATH-HACK for the use of models, and his accompanying comment.

THEOREM. *If S is a subset of a group such that $xy^{-1} \in S$ whenever x and $y \in S$, then $x^{-1} \in S$ whenever $x \in S$.*

Proof. $ex = x \wedge xe = x \wedge xx^{-1} = e \wedge x^{-1}x = e \wedge b \in S$

$$\underbrace{\wedge\,(x \in S \wedge y \in S \wedge xy^{-1} = z \to z \in S)}_{\alpha} \vdash b^{-1} \in S.$$

Backchain on α to get the subgoal

(1) $\vdash x \in S \wedge y \in S \wedge xy^{-1} = b^{-1}$
(11) $\vdash x \in S$ $\quad b/x$
(12) $\vdash y \in S \wedge by^{-1} = b^{-1}$
(121) $\vdash y \in S$ $\quad b/y$
(122) $\vdash bb^{-1} = b$

Fails in the model, so back up to (1). Reorder subgoals.

(11) $\vdash xy^{-1} = b^{-1}$ $\quad e/x, b/y$
(12) $\vdash e \in S \wedge b \in S$

Easily proved.

FIG. 43. An example proved by Reiter's system.

For Reiter example

	e	*a*	*b*	*c*
e	*e*	*a*	*b*	*c*
a	*a*	*e*	*c*	*b*
b	*b*	*c*	*e*	*a*
c	*c*	*b*	*a*	*e*

FIG. 44. The Klein-four group.

Some others using models and counterexamples in automatic proofs are:

Gelernter [26]—Geometry.
Slagle [72]—Resolution.
Reiter [66]—Groups.
Nevins [58]—Geometry.
Siklossy [70]—Robots (DISPROVER).
Winograd [84]—Block's world.
Ballantyne [3]—Topology.
Henschen [33]—Groups.

2.12. Analogy

Perhaps the biggest error made by researchers in automatic theorem proving has been in essentially ignoring the concept of *analogy* in proof discovery. It is the very heart of most mathematical activity and yet only Kling [39] has used it in an automatic prover. His paper showed how, with the use of knowledge, a proof in group theory could be used to help obtain a similar proof in ring theory.

We strongly urge that other workers in this field familiarize themselves with Kling's work and extend and apply them more effectively.

2.13. Man-machine

One of the most irksome things about current automatic theorem provers is the apparent need for the human user to prove the theorem himself before he gives it to the computer to prove. This is necessary because he must determine (for the computer) what axioms, or supporting theorems, are needed in the proof, and if he puts in too many, the proof will bog down. See [12, p. 45].

This problem is partially eliminated by the use of the various concepts mentioned above, such as procedures and REDUCTION tables, which effectively carry the information needed from some of these reference theorems, and are able to give this information when needed without slowing the system down. The remainder of the difficulty can be eliminated by having the human user insert reference theorems only when they are needed. See Fig. 45.

Also present systems cannot prove very hard theorems, so they don't get involved in interesting mathematics. We take as a maxim:

> Automatic provers will not compete successfully with humans for the next 100 years. Therefore the most effective systems will be those in which the computer acts as an *assistant* to the human user.

Thus it is imperative that this work attracts researchers from pure mathematics, and therefore, that interactive programs be made convenient for the *user*, not the programmer.

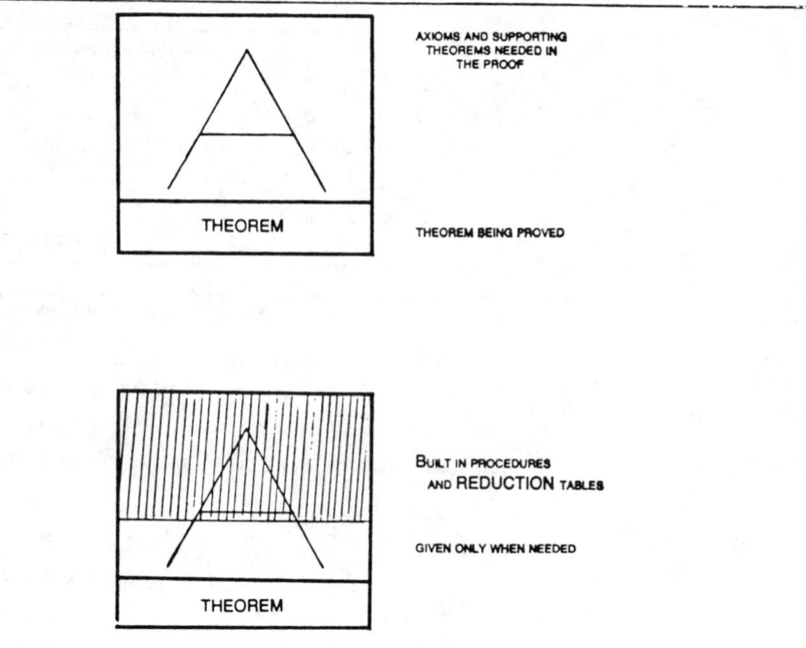

FIG. 45.

Some of the needs of the user mathematician are listed on Fig. 46. Point 3 Fig. 46 is important because a mathematician will not long use a system which repeatedly requires him to give trivial information to the system.

1. READ and easily COMPREHEND the scope.
2. FOLLOW the PROOF.
3. HELP COMPUTER *only* when needed.
4. Axioms and Reference theorems:
   (i) Built-in (some),
   (ii) Others added only when needed.
5. Convenient Commands.

FIG. 46. Some needs of a mathematician interacting with a mechanical prover.

We feel that a well-built system can be exercised on a *large* number of examples, thereby obtaining much valuable information on the utility of concepts in the program.

By running a large number of examples, the user can learn by experience, those places where he needs to improve the automatic part of the system, places where a little extra programming can greatly reduce the load on the human user.

This objective has been partly attained in an interactive program verification system [29, 13] which has been running for the last year in Ralph London's laboratory of the Information Science Institute, Los Angeles, and is now also running at the University of Texas. Peter Bruell, Mabry Tyson, and Larry Fagan were instrumental in developing this system. Much more needs to be done on it to make it truly effective.

Others who have (earlier) worked on interactive systems include: Guard, et al. [30]; Allen and Luckham [2]; Huet [37] and others.

3. Programming Languages

The new programming languages, such as PLANNER [34], MICRO-PLANNER [78], QA-4 [68], Q-LISP [65], and PLASMA [35], which have been proposed and/or implemented during the last few years have much to offer automatic theorem proving. Especially are they rich in concepts such as: Knowledge, data base, procedures, goal oriented, automatic backup, pattern directed invocation, demons, data types.

Also these languages have built-in structures and controls to handle the kinds of things we propose.

However, we do not believe that the lack of use of these programming languages in current automatic prover has hurt their performance. No proof of a hard theorem has been omitted because the user did not use one of these. This may not remain to be the case as automatic provers get more sophisticated, and as these languages get more powerful and efficient. Many of their features are ready-made for provers, and we should move toward adopting them, with needed modifications, for our use.

4. Comments

The reader should not get the idea that we have found the secret to automatic theorem proving. We believe in these concepts but are certain that others will evolve.

We have *talked* a lot and proved very *few* hard theorems (by computer) during the last several years. It is time to *do*, to show that our concepts are good. It is time to get a lot more *experience* with our provers. This will allow us to eliminate some of our "good" ideas.

It is *not* the time to give up on automatic theorem proving. How can that be advisable at a time when so little has been done to develop and apply the ideas we already have? For example, why doesn't someone else use analogy in automatic proofs?

One thing that would help push this field ahead, would be for authors to follow the practice of publishing the proof of at least one *hard theorem* in each new methods paper. We do not believe this field will remain vital unless we develop truly powerful provers, and not just theories.

Completeness in itself is not a bad concept, if handled correctly. For example, a complete unification system with built-in associativity and commutativity, such as [77], needs to be reworked in a way that will make it a useful part of a practical prover. It is believed that a properly constructed *overdirector* (see II.7) can so direct the search that one can have both efficiency and (essential) completeness. At least we can try for this.

"Trapping" remains a serious problem, whereby a substitution a/x that satisfies a goal $P(x)$ may fail on $Q(x)$, and hence on

$$(P(x) \wedge Q(x)).$$

Backing-up theoretically solves this but can be very time consuming. Huet's "delaying" as used for matching in higher order logic [36] might be a good idea here.

Another worry is the "learning" problem. During the last decade most researchers in A.I. have avoided machine learning, because of such poor results from earlier experiments, and have favored the use of Man's "knowledge" in A.I. programs or human imposed learning such as used by Winston [85]. However, eventually that barrier must be removed if the automatic prover is to be very effective. Figs 35 and 33 and accompanying comments provide an example of the kind of controlled learning that might be useful.

Other work such as studies on induction (by Meltzer [53] and others) might be important to our efforts.

One should also not ignore proof checking as a potential use for automatic theorem proving [1, 11, 51], and also computer aided teaching of mathematics [47].

Another recent effort which may have a far reaching effect on automatic theorem proving is the work of Lenat [42A] which automatically discovers concepts in mathematics.

5. Challenges

Let me close by suggesting a few theorems, from various fields of mathematics, whose proofs by automatic means would be impressive at this time or in the near future. See Table 1.

In our efforts to mold our experience into an effective theorem prover, we are reminded of a 1918 statement by Albert Einstein [62]:

> Man tries to make for himself in the fashion that suits him best a simplified and intelligible picture of the world. He then tries to some extent to substitute this cosmos of his for the world of experience, and thus to overcome it . . . .
> The supreme task . . . is to arrive at those universal elementary laws from which the cosmos can be built up by pure deduction. There is no logical path to these laws; only intuition, resting on sympathetic understanding of experience, can reach them . . . .

TABLE 1. Some challenging theorems for automatic provers

Field	Theorems Proved	Challenge
Set theory	Elementary set theory $\omega = \omega \cap \text{Subsets}(\omega)$ $\omega = \bigcup_{\alpha \in \omega} \alpha$	Schoeder–Bernstein Theorem
Calculus	Limit Theorems (with Limit Heuristic)	Limit Theorems (ω/o Limit Heuristic) Rolle's Theorem $\int f\,dx$ exists for f continuous
Analysis	Bolzano Weierstrass Theorem Cont. *fcn* on a Compact set is Uniformly Cont. (Using Non-Standard Anal.)	Bolzano Weierstrass Theorem (ω/o Non-Standard Analysis) Cont. *fcn* on a Compact Set is Uniformly Cont. (ω/o Non-Standard Analysis) Heine Borel Theorem Hahn Banach Theorem
Geometry	Gelernter's	Pythagorean Theorem
Topology	Open $(A) \wedge$ Open (B) $\rightarrow$ Open $(A \cup B)$	A separable, normal space is metrizable Tichenoff Theorem
Algebra	Group Right Identity $x+(x+x) = 0 \rightarrow a+b+(-a)+b+a+(-b)+(-a)+(-b) = 0$	Ring $x^3 = x$ for $x \neq 0$ $\rightarrow a \cdot b = b \cdot a$

REFERENCES

1. Abrahams, P. W., in: *The Programming Language* LISP: *Its Operation and Applications*, Application of LISP to checking mathematical proofs (The M.I.T. Press, Cambridge, MA, 1966) 137–160.
2. Allen, J. and Luckham, D., An interactive theorem-proving program, *Machine Intelligence* **5** (1970) 321–336.
3. Ballantyne, M., Computer generation of counterexamples in topology, The University of Texas at Austin Math. Dept. Memo ATP-24 (1975).
4. Ballantyne, M. and Bennett, W., Graphing methods for topological proofs, The University of Texas at Austin Math. Dept. Memo ATP-7 (1973).
5. Ballantyne, A. M. and Bledsoe, W. W., Automatic proofs of theorems in analysis using non-standard techniques, The University of Texas at Austin Math. Dept. Memo ATP-23 (July 1975); *J. ACM*, to appear, July 1977.

5A. Ballantyne, A. M. and Lankford, D.S., An implementation of derived reduction, Local Memo ATP Project, Dept. of Math. and Comput. Sci., University of Texas, Austin, TX (August 1975).

6. Bibel, W. and Schreiber, J., Proof search in a Gentzen-like system of first order logic, Bericht Nr. 7412, Technische Universität (1974).
7. Bledsoe, W. W., Splitting and reduction heuristics in automatic theorem proving, *Artificial Intelligence* **2** (1971) 55–77.
8. Bledsoe, W. W., The sup-inf method in Presburger arithmetic, Dept. of Math., The University of Texas at Austin, Memo ATP-18 (December 1974); essentially the same as: A new method for proving certain Presburger formulas, *Fourth Int. Joint Conf. Artificial Intelligence*, Tbilisi, U.S.S.R., September 3–8 (1975).
9. Bledsoe, W. W., Boyer, R. S. and Henneman, W. H., Computer proofs of limit theorems, *Artificial Intelligence* **3** (1972) 27–60.
10. Bledsoe, W. W. and Bruell, P., A man–machine theorem-proving system, in: *Adv. Papers 3rd Int. Joint Conf. Artificial Intelligence* (1973) 55–65; also *Artificial Intelligence* **5** (1974) 51–72.
11. Bledsoe, W. W. and Gilbert, E. J., Automatic theorem proof-checking in set theory, Sandia Corp. Research Report, SC-RR-67-525 (July 1967).
12. Bledsoe, W. W. and Tyson, M. The UT interactive theorem prover, The University of Texas at Austin Math. Dept. Memo ATP-17 (May 1975).
13. Bledsoe, W. W. and Tyson, M., Typing and proof by cases in program verification, The University of Texas at Austin Math. Dept. Memo ATP-15 (May 1975). In MI 8.
14. Boyer, R. S. and Moore, J. S., Proving theorems about Lisp functions, *J. ACM*, **22** (1975) 129–144.
15. Brown, F., Unfinished Ph.D. thesis on automatic theorem proving, University of Edinburgh (1975).
16. Bruell, P., A description of the functions of the man–machine topology theorem prover, The University of Texas at Austin Math. Dept. Memo ATP-8 (1973).
17. Bundy, A., Doing arithmetic with diagrams, *Adv. Papers 3rd Int. Joint Conf. Artificial Intelligence* (1973) 130–138.
18. de Carvalho, R. L., Some results in automatic theorem-proving with applications in elementary set theory and topology, Ph.D. Thesis, Dept. of C.S., University of Toronto, Canada; Tech. Report No. 71 (November 1974).
19. Chang, C., and Lee, R. C., *Symbolic Logic and Mechanical Theorem Proving* (Academic Press, New York, 1973).
20. Cooper, D. C., Theorem proving in computers, in: Fox, L. (Ed.), *Advances in Programming and Non-numeric Computation* (Pergamon, NY, 1966) 155–182.
21. Darlington, J. L., Automatic theorem proving with equality substitution and mathematical induction, *Machine Intelligence* **3** (1968) 113–127.
22. Deutsch, L. P., An interactive program verifier, Ph.D. Thesis, University of California, Berkeley (1973); also Xerox Palo Alto Research Center Report CSL-73-1 (May 1973).
23. Ernst, G. W., The utility of independent subgoals in theorem proving, *Information and Control* (April, 1971); A definition-driven theorem prover, *Int. Joint Conf. Artificial Intelligence*, Stanford, CA (August 1973) 51–55.
24. Fishman, D. H., Experiments with a resolution-based deductive question–answering system and a proposed clause representation for parallel search, Ph.D. Thesis, Dept. of Comp. Sci., University of Maryland (1973).
25. Fronig, X., private communication, Institut fur informatik, Universität Bonn (1975).
26. Gelernter, H., Realization of a geometry theorem-proving machine, *Proc. Int. Conf. Information Processing*, Paris UNESCO House (1959) 273–282.
27. Gentzen, G., Untersuchungen über das logische Schliessen I, *Math. Zeitschrift* **39** (1935) 176–210.
28. Goldstein, I., Elementary geometry theorem proving, M.I.T.-AI Lab Memo 280 (April 1973).
29. Good, D. I., London, R. L. and Bledsoe, W. W., An interactive verification system, *Proc. Int. Conf. Reliable Software*, Los Angeles (April 1975) 482–492; *IEEE Trans. on Software Engineering* **1** (1975) 59–67.
30. Guard, J. R., Oglesby, F. C., Bennett, J. H. and Settle, L. G., Semi-automated mathematics, *J. ACM* **16** (1969) 49–62.

31. Hayes, P., Forthcoming book on automatic theorem proving, University of Essex.
32. Hearn, A. C., Reduce 2: A system and language for algebraic manipulation, *Proc. ACM 2nd Symp. Symbolic and Algebraic Manipulation* (1971) 128–133; also Reduce 2 User's Manual, 2nd ed. (University of Utah, Salt Lake City, UCP-19, 1974).
33. Henschen, L. J., Semantic resolution of horn sets, *Adv. Papers Int. Joint Conf. Artificial Intelligence*, Tbilisi, U.S.S.R. (September 1975).
34. Hewitt, C., Description and theoretical analysis (using schemata) of PLANNER: a language for proving theorems and manipulating models in a robot, Ph.D. Thesis (June, 1971); AI-TR-258 M.I.T.–AI-Lab. (April 1972).
35. Hewitt, C., How to use what you know, M.I.T.-AI Lab. working paper 93, (May 1975).
36. Huet, G. P., Constrained resolution: a complete method for higher order logic, Ph.D. thesis, Report 1117, Jennings Computing Center, Case Western Reserve University.
37. Huet, G. P., Experiments with an interactive prover for logic with equality, Report 1106, Jennings Computing Center, Case Western Reserve University.
38. King, J. C., A program verifier, Ph.D. dissertation, Carnegie-Mellon University, Pittsburgh, PA (1969).
39. Kling, R. E., A paradigm for reasoning by analogy, *Artificial Intelligence* **2** (1971) 147–178.
39A. Knuth, D. E., Notes on central groupoids, *J. Combinatorial Theory* **8** (1970) 376–390.
40. Knuth, D. E. and Bendix, P. B., Simple word problems in universal algebras, in: Leech, J. (Ed.), *Computational Problems in Abstract Algebra* (Pergamon Press, Oxford, 1970) 263–297.
41. Lankford, D. S., Complete sets of reductions for computational logic, The University of Texas at Austin Math. Dept. Memo ATP-21 (January 1975).
42. Lankford, D. S., Canonical algebraic simplification in computational logic, The University of Texas at Austin Math. Dept. Memo ATP-25 (1975).
42A. Lenat, D. B., AM: An artificial intelligence approach to discovery in mathematics as heuristic search, Stanford AI Lab. Memo AIM-286 (July 1976).
43. Lifsic, V. A., Specialization of the form of deduction in the predicate calculus with equality and function symbols, *Proc.* steklov *Inst. Math.* **98** (1968) 1–23.
44. Loveland, D. W., *Automatic Theorem Proving: A Logical Basis* (North-Holland, Amsterdam, 1977).
45. Loveland, D. W. and Stickel, M. E., A hole in goal trees: some guidance from resolution theory, *Proc. Third Int. Joint Conf. Artificial Intelligence*, Stanford, CA (1973) 153–161.
46. Luya, B., Un systeme complet de deduction naturelle, Thesis, University of Paris VII (January 1975).
47. Marinov, V., An interactive system for teaching set theory by computer at IMSSS, Ventura Hall, Stanford, private communication.
48. Ju Maslov, S., Proof-search strategies for methods of the resolution type, *Machine Intelligence* **6** (1971) 77–90.
49. Maslov, Ju S., An inverse method of establishing deducibility in classical predicate calculus, *Dokl. Nauk SSSR* **159** (1964) 17–20.
49A. Matijasevic, J. V., Simple examples of undecidable associative calculi, *Soviet Math. Dokl.* **8** (1967) 555–557.
50. McCarthy, J., Programs with common sense. (The advice taker), in: Minsky, M. (Ed.), *Semantic Information Processing*, 403–418.
51. McCarthy, J., Computer programs for checking mathematical proofs, *Proc. Amer. Math. Soc. Recursive Function Theory*, New York (April 1961).
52. McDermott, D. V. and Sussman, G. J., The CONNIVER reference manual, AI Memo 259, M.I.T.-AI-Lab (May 1972); revised (July 1973).
53. Meltzer, B., The programming of deduction and induction, University of Edinburgh, Dept. of Art. Int., DCL Memo 45 (1971); also *Artificial Intelligence* **1** (1970) 189–192.
54. Minker, J., Fishman, D. H. and McSkimin, J. R., The Q* algorithm—A search strategy for a deductive question-answering system, *Artificial Intelligence* **4** (1973) 225–243.
55. Minsky, M., A framework for representing knowledge, in: Winston, P. (Ed.), *The Psychology of Computer Vision* (McGraw-Hill, New York, 1974).
55A. Moore, R. C., Reasoning from incomplete knowledge in a procedural deduction system, M.I.T.-AI Lab Memo AI-TR-347 (December 1975).
56. Nevins, A. J., A human oriented logic for automatic theorem proving, M.I.T.-AI-Lab Memo 268 (October 1972); *J. ACM* **21** (1974) 606–621.
57. Nevins, A. J., A relaxation approach to splitting in an automatic theorem prover, M.I.T.-AI-Lab. Memo 302 (January 1974); *Artificial Intelligence*, **6** (1975) 25–39.
58. Nevins, A. J., Plane geometry theorem proving using forward chaining, M.I.T.-AI-Lab. Memo 303 (January 1974). *Artificial Intelligence*, **6** (1975) 1–23.
59. Newell, A., Shaw, J. C. and Simon, H. A., Empirical explorations of the logic theory machine: a case in heuristics, RAND Corp. Memo P-951 (28 February 1957); *Proc. Western Joint Computer Conf.* (1956) 218–239; also in: Feigenbaum and Feldman (Eds.) *Computers and Thought*, 134–152.
60. Newell, A., Shaw, J. C. and Simon, H. A., Report on a general problem-solving program, RAND Corp. Memo P-1584 (30 December 1958).
61. Nilsson, N., Artificial Intelligence (including a review of automatic theorem proving) IFIP, Stockholm, Sweden (1974).
61A. Overbeek, R. A., A new class of automatic theorem proving algorithms, *J. ACM* **21** (1974) 191–200.
62. Pirsig, R. M., *Zen and the Art of Motorcycle Maintenance*, 106–107.
63. Plotkin, G. D., Building equational theories, *Machine Intelligence* **7** (1972) 73–89.
64. Prawitz, D., An improved proof procedure, *Theoria* **25** (1960) 102–139.
65. Reboh, R. and Sacerdoti, E., A preliminary QLISP manual, Stanford Research Inst., AI Center Tech. Note 81 (August 1973).
66. Reiter, R., A semantically guided deductive system for automatic theorem proving, *Proc. Third Int. Joint Conf. Artificial Intelligence* (1973) 41–46; *IEEE Trans. on Elec. Computing* C-**25** (1976) 328–334.
67. Reiter, R., A paradigm for automated formal inference, *IEEE Theorem Proving Workshop*, Argonne Nat. Lab., IL (3-5 June 1975).
67A. Robinson, G. and Wos, L., Paramodulation and theorem-proving in first-order theories with equality, *Proc. IRIA Symposium on Automatic Demonstration*, Versailles, France (1968); (Springer-Verlag, Berlin, 1970) 276–310.
68. Rulifson, J. R., Derksen, J. A. and Waldinger, R. J., QA4: a procedural calculus for intuitive reasoning, Stanford Research Inst. AI Center, Stanford, CA Tech. Note 13 (November 1972).
69. Shostak, R. S., On the completeness of the sup-inf method, Stanford Research Institute, Report (1975).
70. Siklossy, L. and Roach, J., Proving the impossible is impossible is possible: disproofs based on hereditary partitions, *Int. Joint Conf. Artificial Intelligence* (1973) 383–387.
71. Siklossy, L., Rich, A. and Marinov, V., Breadth-first search: some surprising results, *Artificial Intelligence* **4** (1973) 1–28.
72. Slagle, J. R., Automatic theorem proving with renamable and semantic resolution, *J. ACM* **14** (1967) 687–697.
73. Slagle, J. R., Automated theorem-proving for theories with simplifiers, commutativity and associativity, *J. ACM* **21** (1974) 622–642.
74. Slagle, J. R., Automatic theorem proving with built-in theories of equality, partial order and sets, *J. ACM* **19** (1972) 120–135.
75. Slagle, J. R. and Norton, L., Experiments with an automatic theorem prover having partial ordering rules, *Commun. ACM* **16** (1973) 682–688.
76. Norton, L. M., Experiments with a heuristic theorem-proving program for the predicate calculus with equality, *Artificial Intelligence* **2** (1971) 261–284.

77. Stickel, M., A complete unification algorithm for associative-commutative functions, *Adv. Papers, Int. Joint Conf. Artificial Intelligence*, Tbilisi, U.S.S.R (September 1975) 71–76.
78. Sussman, G. J., Winograd, T. and Charniak, E., Micro-planner manual, M.I.T.-AI Lab. Memo 203A (December 1971).
79. Suzuki, N., Verifying programs by algebraic and logical reduction, *Proc. Int. Conf. Reliable Software* (1975) 473–481.
80. Ullman, S., Model-Driven Geometry Theorem Prover, M.I.T.-AI Lab Memo 321 (May 1975).
81. Waldinger, R. J. and Levitt, K. N., Reasoning about programs, *Artificial Intelligence* **5** (1974) 235–316.
82. Wang, H., Toward mechanical mathematics, *IBM J. Res. Dev.* **4** (1960) 224–268.
83. Winker, S. K., Complete demodulations in automatic theorem proving, University of Northern Illinois, Computer Science Department (July 1975).
84. Winograd, T., Procedures as a representation for data in a computer program for understanding natural language, Ph.D. Thesis, M.I.T. MAC-TR-84 (February 1971).
85. Winston, P. H., Learning structural descriptions from examples, in: Winston, P. H. (Ed.), *The Psychology of Computer Vision* (McGraw-Hill, New York, 1974).

Using Rewriting Rules for Connection Graphs to Prove Theorems

C. L. Chang

IBM Research Laboratory, San Jose, CA 95193, U.S.A.

J. R. Slagle

Naval Research Laboratory, Washington, DC 20375, U.S.A.

ABSTRACT

Essentially, a connection graph is merely a data structure for a set of clauses indicating possible refutations. The graph itself is not an inference system. To use the graph, one has to introduce operations on the graph. In this paper, we shall describe a method to obtain rewriting rules from the graph, and then to show that these rewriting rules can be used to generate a refutation plan that may correspond to a large number of linear resolution refutations. Using this method, many redundant resolution steps can be avoided.

1. Introduction

The oldest technique used in mechanical theorem proving is Herbrand's method. Since this method requires to generate a very large number of ground clauses, it was abandoned in favor of two alternative approaches. One of these approaches is Robinson's resolution principle [21]. The other is to use the idea proposed by Prawitz [19, 20]. For the last decade, the resolution principle has got most of the attention of researchers, and has been playing a dominant role in the field. Many useful strategies [5] for resolution have been proposed. Recently, the attention seems to be shifted to Prawitz's idea. Compared to resolution, Prawitz's idea is relatively unexplored. There is some hope that his idea might be developed into an efficient theorem proving system.

Given a set S of clauses, Prawitz's idea is that, instead of generating the ground instances of clauses of S in some arbitrarily defined order, one should find by calculations the values that, when substituted for variables in S, give an unsatisfiable set of ground instances. Essentially, Prawitz's idea is based upon the observation that a set of clauses is unsatisfiable if and only if there is a set M of copies (variants) of clauses in S and a ground substitution θ such that $M\theta$ is truth-functionally unsatisfiable. We call θ a solution of M. This observation is actually Herbrand's theorem in a different form. Many methods [1, 3, 4, 8–10, 19, 20, 25] have been proposed to find such M and θ. In this paper, we shall propose another method for finding such M and θ. The approach we take is as follows:

(a) First, find a connection graph for a set S of clauses;

(b) Change the connection graph to a directed graph;

(c) from the directed graph, obtain a set of rewriting rules;

(d) use the rewriting rules to generate a refutation plan;

(e) Finally, use a unification algorithm to check whether the plan is acceptable or not. We note that the main difference between our method and the others is that we want to generate a plan, and then perform unification at *the last step* of a proof. In the sequel, we shall describe our method in detail.

2. Connection Graphs

The concept of a connection graph has been considered by many authors [1, 12, 13, 24, 25, 29]. Essentially, a connection graph is merely a data structure for a set of clauses indicating possible refutations. The graph itself is not an inference system. To use the graph, one has to introduce operations on the graph. For example, Andrews [1] and Shostak [24] define a criterion in terms of a connection graph for a truth-functionally unsatisfiable set of clauses; Kowalski [13] uses it for performing resolution; Sickel [25] uses it for graph-walking and graph-unrolling; and Yate et al. [29] use it for proving the completeness of linear resolution. Different operations on connection graphs lead to different theorem proving systems. In this paper, we shall use a connection graph to obtain rewriting rules. Then, finding a solution of M can be directly solved by using the rewriting rules.

In the sequel, we let S be a set of input clauses. By a copy of clause C in S, we mean that it is C itself, or a clause obtained from C by renaming variables in C. Let M be a set of zero or more copies of each clause in S. Without loss of generality, we assume that no two clauses in M have variables in common. A substitution θ is called a *solution* of M if $M\theta$ is truth-functionally unsatisfiable. A pair of literals $L1$ and $L2$ are called *potentially complementary* if $L1$ and $L2$ can be made complementary by applying some substitution, after renaming variables so that $L1$ and $L2$ share no variables.

A connection graph for a set S of clauses is constructed as follows: (This is called a clause interconnectivity graph by Sickel [25], p. 825).

(1) Exactly one copy of each clause of S is allowed to appear in the graph.

(2) For every clause, $L1 \vee \ldots \vee Lr$, in S, where $L1, \ldots, Lr$ are literals, it is represented in the graph as

Ll ••• Lr

FIG. 1.

(3) For every pair of potentially complementary literals, draw an edge connecting the literals. Label each such edge by a distinct name representing the most general unifier which makes the literals complementary, after variables in the literals are properly renamed. (In the subsequent section, a procedure will be given to rename variables.)

Example 1. Fig. 2 is a connection graph for the set,

$$\{P(x) \vee Q(y), \sim P(a), \sim Q(b)\}.$$

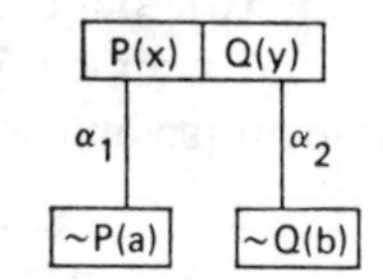

FIG. 2.

Example 2. Fig. 3 is a connection graph for the set,

$$\{\sim P(x) \vee P(f(x)), P(a), \sim P(f(f(a)))\}.$$

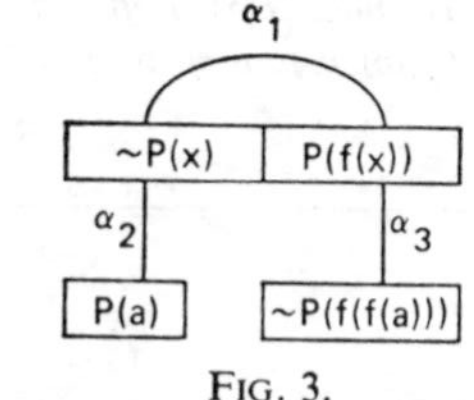

FIG. 3.

3. Combinations of Substitutions

In finding a solution of a set of clauses, it is often necessary to test whether or not we can combine substitutions. For example, $\{a/x\}$ and $\{b/y\}$ can be combined, while $\{a/x\}$ and $\{b/x\}$ can not be combined. For this purpose, we give the following definition and examples which are taken from [4] and Chapter 9 of [5].

Definition. Let $\theta_1 = \{t_{11}/v_{11}, \ldots, t_{1n_1}/v_{1n_1}\}, \ldots, \quad \theta_r = \{t_{r_1}/v_{r_1}, \ldots, t_{rn_r}/v_{rn_r}\}$ be substitutions, $r \geqslant 2$. From $\theta_1, \ldots, \theta_r$ we define two expressions,

$$\text{E1} = (v_{11}, \ldots, v_{1n_1}, \ldots, v_{r1}, \ldots, v_{rn_r}), \text{ and}$$

$$\text{E2} = (t_{11}, \ldots, t_{1n_1}, \ldots, t_{r1}, \ldots, t_{rn_r}).$$

Then, $\theta_1, \ldots, \theta_r$ are said to be *consistent* if and only if E1 and E2 are unifiable. A most general unifier for {E1, E2}, denoted as $\theta_1 \cdots \theta_r$, is called a combination of $\theta_1, \ldots, \theta_r$. The substitutions $\theta_1, \ldots, \theta_r$ are said to be *inconsistent* if and only if they are not consistent.

Example 3. Consider $\theta_1 = \{a/x\}$ and $\theta_2 = \{f(a)/x\}$. For this case, we have E1 $= (x, x)$ and E2 $= (a, f(a))$. Since E1 and E2 are not unifiable, θ_1 and θ_2 are inconsistent.

Example 4. Let $\theta_1 = \{g(y)/x\}$ and $\theta_2 = \{f(x)/y\}$. For this case, we have E1 $= (x,y)$ and E2 $= (g(y), f(x))$. Since E1 and E2 are not unifiable, θ_1 and θ_2 are inconsistent.

Example 5. Let $\theta_1 = \{f(g(x1))/x3, f(x2)/x4\}$ and $\theta_2 = \{x4/x3, g(x1)/x2\}$. For this case, E1 $= (x3, x4, x3, x2)$ and E2 $= (f(g(x1)), f(x2), x4, g(x1))$. Since E1 and E2 are unifiable, θ_1 and θ_2 are consistent. The combination $\theta_1\theta_2$ is $\{f(g(x1))/x3, f(g(x1))/x4, g(x1)/x2\}$.

We note that the combination operation is associative and commutative, while the composition operation on substitutions is associative, but not commutative. In the sequel, if θ is a substitution and W is a set of substitutions, then θW is defined as

$$\theta W = \{\theta\lambda \mid \lambda \in W\}.$$

More generally, $W_1, \ldots, W_m$ are sets of substitutions, we define $W_1 \cdots W_m$ as

$$W_1 \cdots W_m = \{\lambda_1 \cdots \lambda_m \mid \lambda_1 \in W_1, \ldots, \lambda_m \in W_m\}.$$

The above concepts will be useful for giving a meaning to rewriting rules to be described in the next section. For simplicity, we shall write $\{\theta_1 \cdots \theta_n\}$, a set consisting of a combination, as $\theta_1 \cdots \theta_n$.

4. Obtaining rewriting Rules from a Connection Graph

In order to obtain rewriting rules, we first have to change an undirected connection graph into a directed one. This is done as follows:

Step 1. Choose a clause in the connection graph as a start clause. Every literal in the start clause will be labeled as a *goal* literal. (Note that a start clause is the same as a top clause in linear resolution [5].)

Step 2. For every goal literal L and every clause C in the graph, if there is an edge E connecting literal L and a literal L' of clause C, change edge E to a directed edge by pointing from literal L' to literal L. Label all the remaining literals in C as goal literals. Literal L' will be called a *premise* literal. (Note that edges within a clause are allowed.)

Step 3. Repeat Step (2) until every goal literal has been considered.

Example 6. Consider the connection graph shown in Fig. 4, which is taken from [25]. If we choose the clause consisting of literals 9 and 8 as a start clause, we obtain a directed connection graph shown in Fig. 5. However, if we choose the clause consisting of literals 1 and 2 as a start clause, we obtain a directed connection graph shown in Fig. 6. We note that edges α_1, α_2 and α_3 are bi-directional edges. This means that a literal can be a goal literal as well as a premise literal.

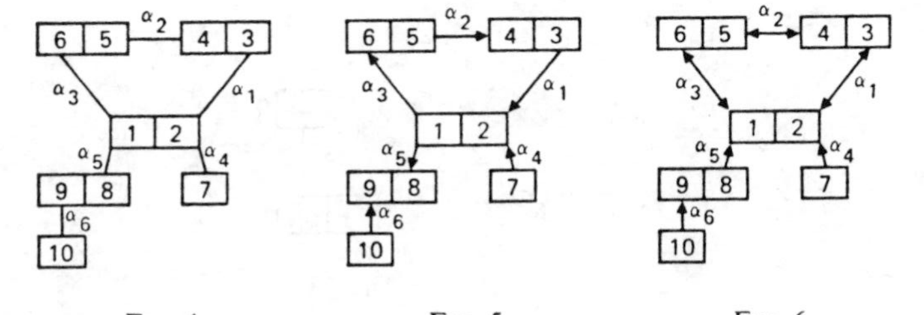

FIG. 4. FIG. 5. FIG. 6.

From a directed connection graph, we can obtain rewriting rules. In the following, if L is a literal in the connection graph, we shall use $W(L)$ to denote a set of substitutions obtained from proving L. Now, we obtain rewriting rules as follows:

(1) For each goal literal n, if $m_1, \ldots, m_r$ are all premise literals of n shown in Fig. 7, where $\alpha_1, \ldots, \alpha_r$ are substitutions, then we obtain a rewriting rule as

(R1) $\quad W(n) = \alpha_1 W(m_1) \cup \cdots \cup \alpha_r W(m_r),$

where $\alpha_i W(m_i)$ is a combination of α_i and $W(m_i)$, $i = 1, \ldots, r$. The meaning of this rule is: If we know that $W(m_1), \ldots, W(m_r)$ are sets of substitutions obtained from proving literals $m_1, \ldots, m_r$, respectively, then a set of substitutions for proving literal n can be recursively described by the rule.

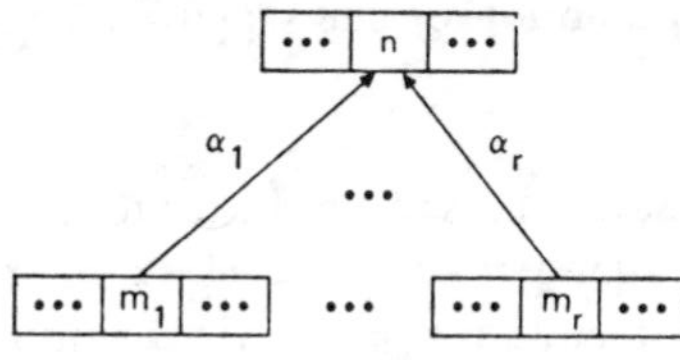

FIG. 7.

(2) For each clause of the graph shown in Fig. 8, where m_i is a premise literal, and $m_1, \ldots, m_{i-1}, m_{i+1}, \ldots, m_r$, $r \geqslant 2$, are all the remaining literals in the clause, we obtain a rewriting rule as

(R2) $\quad W(m_i) = W(m_1) \cdots W(m_{i-1}) W(m_{i+1}) \cdots W(m_r).$

The meaning of this rule is: If we want to use m_i as a premise literal, then all the other literals $m_1, \ldots, m_{i-1}, m_{i+1}, \ldots, m_r$ have to be proved first. Suppose that $W(m_k)$, $k = 1, \ldots, i-1, i+1, \ldots, r$, are sets of substitutions obtained from proving m_k independently. To make sure that the substitutions are consistent, we take a combination of them as shown in the rule.

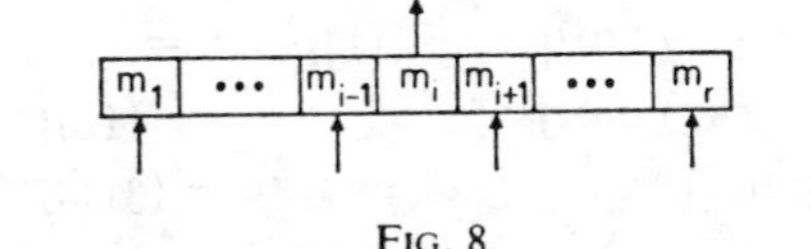

FIG. 8.

(3) For each unit clause, if literal m in the clause is used as a premise literal as shown in Fig. 9, we obtain a rewriting rule

(R3) $\quad W(m) = \{\varepsilon\},$

where ε is the empty substitution. The meaning of this rule is: Since a unit clause by itself can be used as a premise literal, we do not need to check consistency.

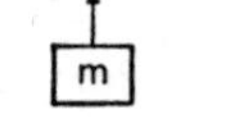

FIG. 9.

(4) For a start clause as shown in Fig. 10, we obtain a rewriting rule as

(R4) $\quad T = W(m_1) \cdots W(m_r).$

The meaning of this rule is: T is considered as a set of substitutions obtained for proving the start clause. Now, if $W(m_k)$, $k = 1, \ldots, r$ are sets of substitutions obtained independently from proving m_k, respectively, then a consistent combination of these substitutions is T, that is, a set of substitutions for proving the start clause. We note that the rewriting rules cast in a tree representation are also independently described in [25].

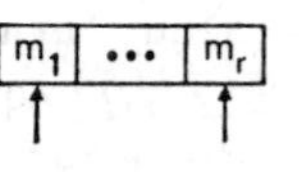

FIG. 10.

Example 7. Consider the directed connection graph shown in Fig. 5. From the edges, we obtain the rewriting rules

(1) $\quad W(9) = \alpha_6 W(10)$

(2) $\quad W(8) = \alpha_5 W(1)$

(3) $\quad W(6) = \alpha_3 W(1)$

(4) $\quad W(4) = \alpha_2 W(5)$

(5) $\quad W(2) = \alpha_1 W(3) \cup \alpha_4 W(7)$

From the clauses, we obtain the rewriting rules

(6) $\quad W(1) = W(2)$

(7) $\quad W(5) = W(6)$

(8) $\quad W(3) = W(4)$

(9) $\quad W(7) = \{\varepsilon\}$

(10) $\quad W(10) = \{\varepsilon\}$

(11) $\quad T = W(9) W(8)$

Rules (1) through (11) can be simplified as follows:

(12)	$W(9) = \alpha_6 W(10) = \alpha_6\{\varepsilon\} = \alpha_6$	from (1) and (10)
(13)	$W(8) = \alpha_5 W(1)$	from (2)
(14)	$T = W(9)W(8) = \alpha_6\alpha_5 W(1)$	from (11), (12) and (13)
(15)	$W(1) = W(2)$	from (6)
	$= \alpha_1 W(3) \cup \alpha_4 W(7)$	from (5)
	$= \alpha_1 W(4) \cup \alpha_4\{\varepsilon\}$	from (8) and (9)
	$= \alpha_1\alpha_2 W(5) \cup \alpha_4$	from (4)
	$= \alpha_1\alpha_2 W(6) \cup \alpha_4$	from (7)
	$= \alpha_1\alpha_2\alpha_3 W(1) \cup \alpha_4$	from (3)

Therefore, we have to keep only these two rules:

(16) $T = \alpha_6\alpha_5 W(1)$

(17) $W(1) = \alpha_1\alpha_2\alpha_3 W(1) \cup \alpha_4$

where α_1, α_2, α_3, α_4, α_5 and α_6 are treated as terminal symbols, and T and $W(1)$ as nonterminal symbols in a context-free grammar. (The non-terminal symbol T is the symbol for a sentence in the grammar.) Using these rules, we can generate the following sentences: $\alpha_6\alpha_5\alpha_4$, $\alpha_6\alpha_5\alpha_1\alpha_2\alpha_3\alpha_4$, ... Each of these sentences will be called a *plan*. In the next section, we shall describe how to check whether a plan is acceptable or not.

5. Renaming Variables and Performing Unifications

When we check the acceptability of a plan, we have to make sure that variables are properly renamed. That is, variables should be renamed (standardized apart) so that no two copies of clauses in the plan have variables in common. In the following, we shall give a method for standardizing apart variables in a plan. To do this, we shall label a clause by a distinct name and then refer to a literal in the clause by its position in the clause. That is, if C is a clause, then Cn is the nth literal (counting from the left) of clause C, where n is an integer. Once we have this naming scheme for literals, we can build a table for substitutions. For example, we redraw the connection graph of Fig. 4 into Fig. 11 by giving names to the clauses. From Fig. 11, we can build Table 1 for the substitutions $\alpha_1, \ldots, \alpha_6$ in the graph.

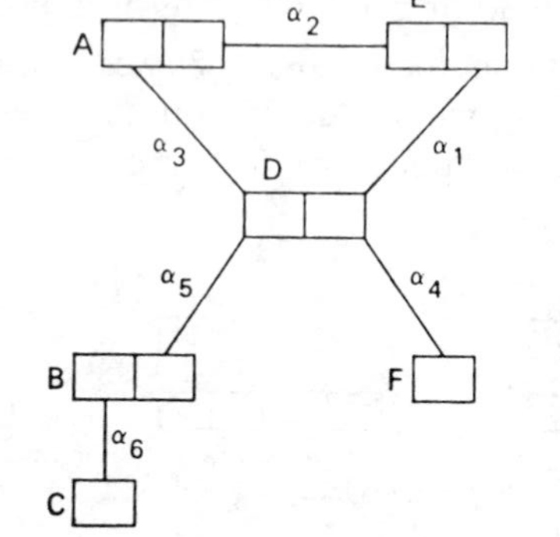

FIG. 11.

TABLE 1.

α_1	$D2$	$E2$
α_2	$A2$	$E1$
α_3	$A1$	$D1$
α_4	$D2$	$F1$
α_5	$D1$	$B2$
α_6	$B1$	$C1$

In Table 1, the first row (α_1, $D2$, $E2$) indicates that α_1 is the most general unifier that makes the 2nd literal of clause D (i.e., $D2$) and the 2nd literal of clause E (i.e., $E2$) complementary (after variables are renamed). The second row (α_2, $A2$, $E1$) indicates that α_2 is the most general unifier that makes the 2nd literal of clause A(i.e., $A2$) and the 1st literal of clause E (i.e., $E1$) complementary, and so on. Using Table 1, we can replace $\alpha_1, \ldots, \alpha_6$ in a plan by their corresponding pairs of literals. That is, we can replace α_1 by ($D2$, $E2$), α_2 by ($A2$, $E1$), and so on. For example, we know that $\alpha_6\alpha_5\alpha_4$ is a plan. This plan can be expressed as

$$(B1, C1) \quad (D1, B2) \quad (D2, F1)$$

by replacing α_6, α_5 and α_4 by ($B1$, $C1$), ($D1$, $B2$) and ($D2$, $F1$), respectively. We see that there are four clauses participating in the plan. That is, $C1$ belongs to a copy of clause C, $B1$ and $B2$ to a copy of B, $D1$ and $D2$ to a copy of D, and $F1$ to a copy of F. Once we identify which literal in the plan belongs to which copy of which clause, we then rename variables in these copies of the clauses so that they share no variables in common. After the variables are renamed, we then try to find the most general unifier θ such that $(C1, B1)\theta$, $(B2, D1)\theta$ and $(D2, F1)\theta$ are all complementary pairs of literals. If such θ can be found, then θ is a solution, and the plan is acceptable. We note that if $|L|$ denotes the atomic formula in a literal L, that is, if $|L|$ is obtained from L by deleting the negation sign (if any) from L, then θ can be obtained by unifying the two expressions, $(|B1|, |D1|, |D2|)$ and $(|C1|, |B2|, |F1|)$.

In general, if $(L1, M1)(L2, M2)\cdots(Lr, Mr)$ is a plan, a solution may be attempted by finding the most general unifier of two expressions,

$$(|L1|, |L2|, \ldots, |Lr|) \text{ and } (|M1|, |M2|, \ldots, |Mr|).$$

The plan, $(B1, C1)(D1, B2)(D2, F1)$, considered above needs only one copy of each of clauses C, B, D and F. In general, if the same literal of a clause appears in a plan n times, then n copies of the clause may be required. For instance, in

Example 7, we know that $\alpha_6\alpha_5\alpha_1\alpha_2\alpha_3\alpha_4$ is also a plan. Expressing this plan by replacing the substitutions by the pairs of literals, we obtain

$$(B1, C1) \quad (D1, B2) \quad (D2, E2) \quad (A2, E1) \quad (A1, D1) \quad (D2, F1).$$

In this plan, since literal $D1$ occurs twice, two copies of clause D may be needed. Actually, we note that the first $D1$ and $D2$ encountered in the plan come from one copy of clause D, and $D1$ and $D2$ encountered afterwards come from another copy of clause D. Thus, the plan may look like

$$(B1, C1) \quad (D1, B2) \quad (D2, E2) \quad (A2, E1) \quad (A1, D1) \quad (D2, F1).$$

where literals belong to the same copy of a clause are linked together. Once we know where literals of each copy of a clause are, we can then standardize variables apart. In the following, we shall use the criterion given by Andrews [1] and Shostak [24] to link literals into copies of clauses.

In [1], Andrews defines that a connection graph is acceptable if it satisfies each of the following conditions:

(a) Every literal in the connection graph is linked to a complementary literal:

(b) Every cycle contains a merge.

He and Shostak [24] independently prove the following theorem:

Theorem 1. *A set S of clauses is unsatisfiable iff there is an acceptable connection graph for a nonempty finite set of copies of clauses in S.*

To use the above theorem, we have to state it in terms of a plan, instead of a connection graph as follows: in a plan, for each pair of literals within a pair of parentheses, draw an edge. For all literals that belong to a copy of a clause, we draw edges from the literals to a common dot. For example, the above plan can be represented as

$$(B1—C1) \quad (D1—B2) \quad (D2—E2) \quad (A2—E1) \quad (A1—D1) \quad (D2—F1)$$

Let us call this a *linked plan*.

If we consider a literal or a dot as a node, clearly a linked plan can be considered as a graph. Therefore, we can conveniently talk about a cycle in a linked plan. We said that a cycle in a linked plan has a *merge* iff it contains a literal which appears in two pairs of literals in the cycle. For example, the following is a cycle

$$(A1—B1) \quad (A1—E2)$$

This cycle has a merge because literal $A1$ appears in the two pairs of literals, namely, $(A1—B1)$ and $(A1—B2)$.

Definition. A linked plan for a set S of clauses *is acceptable* iff it satisfies each of the following conditions:

(a) There is a substitution θ which simultaneously makes every pair of literals within a pair of parentheses complementary, after variables are standardized apart.

(b) Every cycle in the linked plan has a merge.

(c) Every bag of literals connected to a dot is a bag of all literals in one or more copies of a clause in S. For example, if $A1 \vee A2$ is a clause, the bag $(A1, A2, A1, A2)$ is such a bag, while the bag $(A1, A2, A1)$ is not. (Note that a bag is an unordered collection of elements, where the elements may be duplicated.)

Now, Theorem 1 can be stated as follows:

Theorem 2. A set of clauses *is unsatisfiable* iff there is an acceptable linked plan for S.

Example 8. Consider Fig. 12 and Table 2 for the substitutions in Fig. 12. Note that the clause $P(a)$ is the start clause. Now, from Fig. 12, we obtain the following rules:

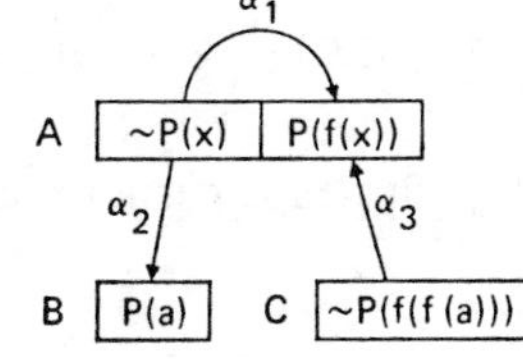

FIG. 12.

TABLE 2.

α_1	$A2$	$A1$
α_2	$B1$	$A1$
α_3	$A2$	$C1$

$$W(B1) = \alpha_2 W(A1) \quad (1)$$
$$W(A2) = \alpha_1 W(A1) \cup \alpha_3 W(C1) \quad (2)$$
$$W(A1) = W(A2) \quad (3)$$
$$W(C1) = \{\varepsilon\} \quad (4)$$
$$T = W(B1) \quad (5)$$

Then, a plan P can be generated as follows:

$$P = T$$
$$= W(B1) \qquad \text{from (5)}$$

$$
\begin{aligned}
&= \alpha_2 W(A1) && \text{from (1)}\\
&= \alpha_2 W(A2) && \text{from (3)}\\
&= \alpha_2\alpha_1 W(A1) && \text{from (2)}\\
&= \alpha_2\alpha_1 W(A2) && \text{from (3)}\\
&= \alpha_2\alpha_1\alpha_3 W(C1) && \text{from (2)}\\
&= \alpha_2\alpha_1\alpha_3\{\varepsilon\} && \text{from (4)}\\
&= \alpha_2\alpha_1\alpha_3 &&\\
&= (B1, A1)\quad (A2, A1)\quad (A2, C1) && \text{using Table 2.}
\end{aligned}
$$

From plan P, we can obtain the following linked plan

$$(B1—A1)\quad (A2—A1)\quad (A2—C1)$$

However, this linked plan is not acceptable because it has the following cycle which does not have a merge and violates Theorem 2:

$$(A2—A1)$$

Therefore, we obtain another linked plan from plan P as follows:

$$(B1—A1)\quad (A2—A1)\quad (A2—C1)$$

This linked plan does not have a cycle. Now, substituting actual literals for $A1$, $A2$, $B1$ and $C1$ in the above linked plan, we obtain

$$(P(a), \sim P(x))\quad (P(f(x)), \sim P(x))\quad (P(f(x)), \sim P(f(f(a)))).$$

Renaming the variable so that the different copies of the clause have no variables in common, we obtain

$$(P(a), \sim P(x))\quad (P(f(x)), \sim P(y))\quad (P(f(y)), \sim P(f(f(a)))).$$

From the above plan, a solution can be attempted by trying to unify the two expressions, $(P(a), P(f(x)), P(f(y)))$ and $(P(x), P(y), P(f(f(a))))$. Since $\{a/x, f(a)/y\}$ is the most general unifier of these two expressions, $\{a/x, f(a)/y\}$ is a solution for the set of the following clauses:

$$
\left\{
\begin{array}{l}
P(a)\\
\sim P(x) \vee P(f(x))\\
\sim P(y) \vee P(f(y))\\
\sim P(f(f(a))).
\end{array}
\right.
$$

6. Cyclic Rewriting Rules

In Section 4, we describe how to obtain a set of rewriting rules from a connection graph. We note that this set of rewriting rules represents a context-free grammar. We have shown that the rewriting rules can be used to generate sentences, and we call them (refutation) plans. However, in some cases, we may not be able to generate sentences, because we may not have rules which rewrite a non-terminal symbol (e.g., $W(n)$) into only terminal symbol (e.g., α_2). This is especially true when there is no unit clause in a set S of clauses. For example, consider the set of clauses, $S = \{P(x) \vee P(y), \sim P(u) \vee \sim P(v)\}$. Suppose we choose $P(x) \vee P(y)$ as the start clause. Then, we obtain a directed connection graph shown in Fig. 13.

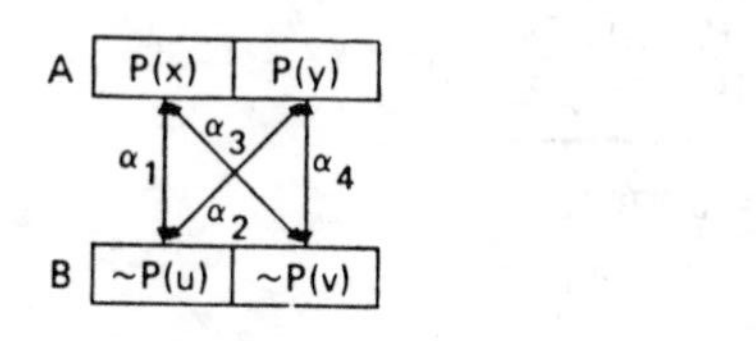

FIG. 13.

TABLE 3.

α_1	$A1$	$B1$
α_2	$A2$	$B1$
α_3	$A1$	$B2$
α_4	$A2$	$B2$

Table 3 is a table for substitutions. From Fig. 13, we can obtain the following rewriting rules:

(1) $W(A1) = \alpha_1 W(B1) \cup \alpha_3 W(B2)$,

(2) $W(B1) = \alpha_1 W(A1) \cup \alpha_2 W(A2)$,

(3) $W(A2) = \alpha_2 W(B1) \cup \alpha_4 W(B2)$,

(4) $W(B2) = \alpha_3 W(A1) \cup \alpha_4 W(A2)$,

(5) $W(A1) = W(A2)$,

(6) $W(B1) = W(B2)$,

(7) $T = W(A1)W(A2)$.

Now, we can obtain

$$
\begin{aligned}
(8)\quad W(A1) &= \alpha_1 W(B1), && \text{from (1)}\\
&= \alpha_1 W(B2), && \text{from (6)}\\
&= \alpha_1\alpha_3 W(A1), && \text{from (4)}\\
(9)\quad W(A2) &= \alpha_2 W(B1), && \text{from (3)}\\
&= \alpha_2 W(B2), && \text{from (6)}\\
&= \alpha_2\alpha_4 W(A2). && \text{from (4)}
\end{aligned}
$$

Clearly, $W(A1)$ and $W(A2)$ can not be rewritten into strings of terminal symbols.

In cases like this, we modify rules as follows: If we can generate

$$W(n) = \alpha_1 \cdots \alpha_r W(n),$$

then we check whether or not $\alpha_1 \cdots \alpha_r$ corresponds to a cycle which has a merge. If yes, the rule is changed to

$$W(n) = \alpha_1 \cdots \alpha_r W(n) \cup \alpha_1 \cdots \alpha_r.$$

Now, consider Rule (8), that is,

$$W(A1) = \alpha_1 \alpha_3 W(A1).$$

Using Table 3, we can express $\alpha_1\alpha_3$ as

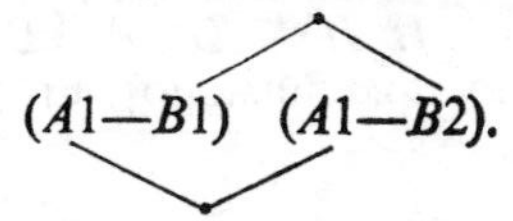

$$(A1\text{—}B1) \quad (A1\text{—}B2).$$

Clearly, the above graph is a cycle which has a merge $A1$. Therefore, Rule (8) is changed to

(8′) $\quad W(A1) = \alpha_1\alpha_3 W(A1) \cup \alpha_1\alpha_3.$

Similarly, using Table 3, we can express $\alpha_2\alpha_4$ as

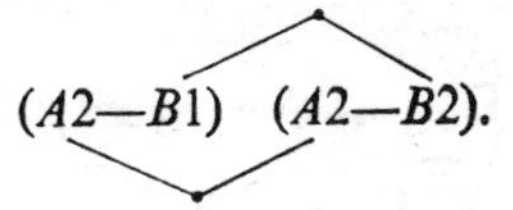

$$(A2\text{—}B1) \quad (A2\text{—}B2).$$

The above graph is a cycle which has a merge $A2$. Therefore, Rule (9) is changed to

(9′) $\quad W(A2) = \alpha_2\alpha_4 W(A2) \cup \alpha_2\alpha_4.$

Now, we can generate a plan P as follows:

$$\begin{aligned} P &= T \\ &= W(A1)W(A2) && \text{from (7)} \\ &= \alpha_1\alpha_3\alpha_2\alpha_4 && \text{from (8′) and (9′)} \end{aligned}$$

From P, we can obtain a linked plan

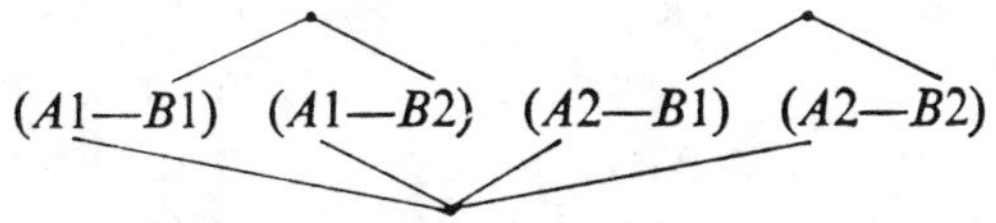

$$(A1\text{—}B1) \quad (A1\text{—}B2) \quad (A2\text{—}B1) \quad (A2\text{—}B2)$$

The above linked plan satisfies conditions (b) and (c) in the definition of an acceptable linked plan. To check condition (a), we substitute real literals for $A1$, $A2$, $B1$ and $B2$, and obtain

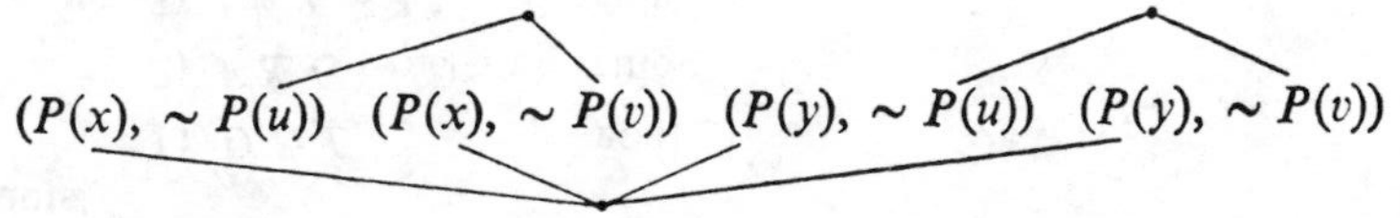

$$(P(x), \sim P(u)) \quad (P(x), \sim P(v)) \quad (P(y), \sim P(u)) \quad (P(y), \sim P(v))$$

Renaming the variables, we obtain

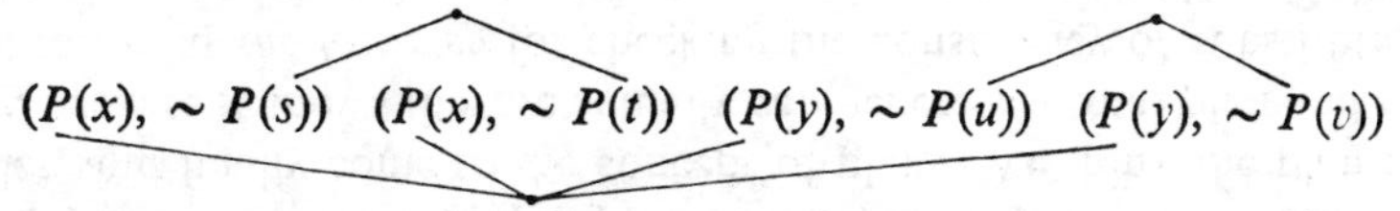

$$(P(x), \sim P(s)) \quad (P(x), \sim P(t)) \quad (P(y), \sim P(u)) \quad (P(y), \sim P(v))$$

Unifying the two expressions,

$$(P(x), P(x), P(y), P(y)) \text{ and}$$
$$(P(s), P(t), P(u), P(v)),$$

we obtain a substitution

$$\theta = \{x/s, x/t, y/u, y/v\}.$$

This substitution is a solution of the set M of the following clauses,

$$\begin{cases} P(x) \vee P(y) \\ \sim P(s) \vee \sim P(t) \\ \sim P(u) \vee \sim P(v), \end{cases}$$

because $M\theta$ is

$$\begin{cases} P(x) \vee P(y) \\ \sim P(x) \\ \sim P(y), \end{cases}$$

and is truth-functionally unsatisfiable.

7. Relationship with Existing AI work

This section was suggested by Nilsson [17], and the material in 7.1 and 7.2. are mostly contributed by him. Some people may be more familiar with other work such as AND/OR tree type problem solving systems in artificial intelligence than they are with the resolution systems. Therefore, it would be a good idea to adapt or apply our method to the existing AI work.

7.1. Use of plans in AND/OR tree type problem solving systems

For illustration purposes, we shall consider only problem solving systems which use rules of the form

$$A1 \;\&\; A2 \;\&\; \cdots \;\&\; AN \rightarrow B,$$

where the Ai (the antecedents) and B (the consequent) are positive literals (with variables). Such rules are called *Horn* clauses. (An extension to non-Horn clauses is given in [16].) Given a goal $G1 \;\&\; G2 \;\&\; \cdots \;\&\; GM$, an AND/OR problem solving tree can be generated by splitting the Gi into AND nodes, unifying each with a rule consequent, and then splitting the (subgoal) antecedents, etc. A proof is obtained when all of the AND subgoals unify with elements of a set of fact literals say $F1, \ldots, FK$.

A simple example is shown below: Suppose we are given the following goal, rules and facts,

1) $D \& E$	goal
2) $F \& G \rightarrow D'$	rule
3) $I \& J \rightarrow E''$	rule
4) $H \rightarrow D''$	rule
5) E'	fact
6) F'	fact
7) G'	fact
8) G''	fact
9) H'	fact
10) I'	fact
11) J'	fact

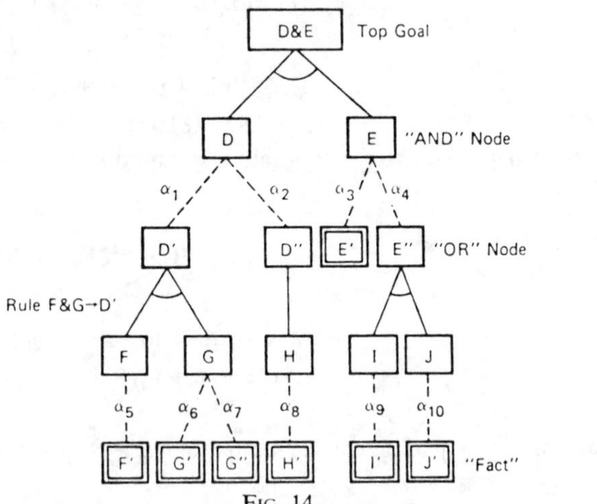

FIG. 14.

Assume only the following pairs of literals are unifiable: (D, D'), (D, D''), (E, E'), (F, F'), (G, G'), (G, G''), (H, H'), (I, I') and (J, J'). Then, starting with the goal $D \& E$, we can grow an AND/OR problem solving tree as shown in Fig. 14, where "boxed" nodes are facts, and dotted edges indicate unifiable pairs of literals. Now, to check for consistency of substitutions, we could read the following plans directly from Fig. 14:

1) $(D, D')(F, F')(G, G')(E, E')$
2) $(D, D')(F, F')(G, G'')(E, E')$
3) $(D, D'')(H, H')(E, E')$

etc.

Each plan corresponds to a possible solution tree for Fig. 14, and we must next choose a plan, rename variables in literals of the plan, and find a simultaneous unifier for all the pairs of literals in the plan.

Now, after seeing the above example, for rewriting rules R1, R2, R3 and R4 in Section 4, we can state the following analogy with AND/OR trees: R1 corresponds to OR node generation; R2 corresponds to AND node generation; R3 corresponds to "terminal nodes"; and R4 corresponds to the top AND node split.

7.2. Connection with PROLOG

The plan idea given in this paper may be also useful for PROLOG [27]. The PROLOG programming language involves an interpreter that essentially searches AND/OR trees of the type described above. The idea is this: A PROLOG program would first be converted into an AND/OR tree. Then plans would be computed. Then, these plans would be checked for consistency of substitutions. When a consistent one was found, it would be used on the "calling clauses" to produce the solution.

7.3. Applications in query transformation

A relational data base consists of a finite number of relations, each of which can be viewed as a table with a finite number of columns and rows. These relations which are explicitly stored are called *base relations*. Clearly, we can consider each row of a table a "fact" literal. Besides the base relations, there are *virtual relations* which are defined in terms of base and virtual relations. In [6, 7], virtual relations are defined by Horn clauses. For example, we may have a base relation, FATHER(x, y). Then, a virtual relation CHILD(y, x) can be defined by

$$\text{FATHER}(x, y) \rightarrow \text{CHILD}(y, x).$$

Once virtual relations are defined, a user can ask a query against base and virtual relations. In [6, 7], a query language called DEDUCE is proposed. Essentially, a DEDUCE query is similar to a formula in first order logic. A DEDUCE query may contain virtual relations. To evaluate the query, it has to be transformed into a query containing only base relations and then the transformed query is evaluated by a relational data base management system. In [7], it is shown that the rewriting rule method given in this paper can be used to transform DEDUCE queries. For detail, the reader is referred to [7].

7.4. Relationship with existing theorem proving techniques

Starting with Prawitz's idea [19, 20], we first use the concept of consistency of substitutions [4] and connection graphs [1, 12, 13, 24, 25, 29]. Then, we introduce rewriting rules, and finally come to the concept of plans. We think the plan idea is interesting, because it shows that we actually can generate a total plan and then perform unification at *the last step* for checking the consistency of substitutions. In [12], Klahr also uses plans based upon only predicate symbols. We shall now try to relate our results to other theorem proving techniques in terms of the plan concept. For example, binary resolution involves a partial plan which uses only two literals, because only the two literals are unified. Hyper-resolution involves a partial plan using one or more pairs of literals. Davis' linked conjunct [8, 9] also involves partial plans. We think our total plan approach is better than partial plan approaches, because it eliminates redundancies. For example, suppose a solution involves the following total plan

$$(A, A') \quad (B, B') \quad (C, C').$$

Using our approach, we need only to check the consistency of substitutions for this plan. However, if we use a partial plan approach, first, we may generate the three partial plans. (A, A'), (B, B') and (C, C'). After checking the consistencies of these three partial plans, each of them may be combined with other pairs of literals to make other partial plans. For example, combining (A, A') with (B, B') and (C, C') respectively, we obtain the two partial plans,

$$(A, A')\,(B, B'),$$
$$(A, A')\,(C, C').$$

We can continue this process by testing consistencies of these partial plans and adding other pairs of literals to them. If we use the breadth-first method, eventually we may generate the following total plans:

$$(A, A')\,(B, B')\,(C, C'),$$
$$(A, A')\,(C, C')\,(B, B'),$$
$$(B, B')\,(A, A')\,(C, C'),$$
$$(B, B')\,(C, C')\,(A, A'),$$
$$(C, C')\,(A, A')\,(B, B'),$$
$$(C, C')\,(B, B')\,(A, A').$$

All of these plans are different only in their orderings of pairs of literals. For binary resolution, it is even worse, because even the ordering of literals within a pair of parentheses may make a difference. For example, some resolution strategies may consider these two partial plans (A, A') and (A', A) differently. In our total plan approach, we regard all these orderings as immaterial. Therefore, we think our approach is more efficient because it eliminates many redundant (total or partial) plans.

Of course, one may organize the generation of plans as a tree searching problem as shown in Section 7.1. As an AND/OR tree is growing, unification can be applied to partial plans so far generated. As soon as inconsistencies are detected, the partial plans could be eliminated. This tree growing method is similar to Sickel's unrolling technique [25] that checks for consistency. However, using inconsistency for pruning the tree can not eliminate the redundancies described above. That is, for the above example, no partial plans will be eliminated, because we assume that any combinations of (A, A'), (B, B') and (C, C') are consistent.

As we know, renaming of variables is a very important operation, because it is closely related to the number of copies of each clause needed in a proof. In this paper, based upon a variant of the theorem given by Andrews [1] and Shostak [24], we painstakingly describe a method for renaming variables in a plan. However, if we organize plan generation as tree growing, sometimes the variable-renaming operation can not be easily incorporated into the tree-growing process. For cases involving only Horn clauses as shown in Section 7.1, we may just use new variables for a rule (Horn clause) as soon as it is introduced for node expansion. However, for cases involving non-Horn clauses, it is not so easy, because we essentially generate an AND/OR graph, instead of an AND/OR tree. The reader may try to grow an AND/OR tree for the example in Section 6 just to convince himself that it is not obvious how variables should be *exactly* renamed. For this reason, we would prefer using rewriting rules. (A method based on formal grammars is also independently proposed in [26]. However, the concept and notation of plans, and explicit algorithms for performing the variable-renaming operation are not discussed.)

Finally, we think that the rewriting rule approach is better than the connection (AND/OR) graph approach [25], because it uses simplified rewriting rules (e.g., (16) and (17) in Example 7 of Section 4) and cyclic rewriting rules (see Section 6) to segment out the necessary subgraphs from a connection graph for possible uses in a proof.

8. Summary

We have given a method for proving theorems in first-order logic. Given a set S of clauses, our method can be described as follows:

(a) First, find a connection graph for S;

(b) Change the connection graph to a directed graph;

(c) From the directed graph, obtain a set of rewriting rules;

(d) Use the rewriting rules to generate a refutation plan;

(e) Check whether or not the plan is acceptable. If yes, we obtain a solution. Otherwise, go to Step (d) again to generate another plan.

To check a plan P, we use Theorem 2. That is, we first try to obtain a linked plan P^* from P such that every cycle (if any) in P^* has a merge; then we rename variables if necessary so that no copies of clauses share variables in common; finally, we perform unification as the last step. If a unifier can be obtained, then plan P is acceptable, and the unifier is a solution. Otherwise, it is not acceptable.

In reviewing the steps of our method, we see that Steps (a), (b) and (c) are straightforward. Step (e) is well-defined. Besides, many efficient unification algorithms [2, 11, 14, 15, 18, 22, 23] have been recently proposed. Some are in linear time and space. Therefore, Step (e) should be manageable. Step (d) is non-deterministic. In general, many plans can be generated. Which one is to be preferred, and how to organize the generation of plans must be studied in the future. Also, there is a question whether to separate Steps (d) and (e), or combine then One may argue that in Step (e) if a plan is found to be unacceptable, computational results for some partial plans should be saved because they may be useful for other plans. However, we would think that Step (e) may be so fast that it would be more advantageous to recompute than to save them. In addition, if we separate Steps (d) and (e), then parallel processing can be applied easily because plans are independently treated, and each of them can be processed independently.

REFERENCES

1. Andrews, P., Refutations by matings, *IEEE Transactions on Computers* C-25 (1976) 801–806.
2. Baxter, L. D., An efficient unification algorithm, University of Waterloo, Waterloo, Ontario, Canada (1973).
3. Chang, C. L., Theorem proving by generation of peudosemantic trees, Div. of Computer Research and Technology, National Institutes of Health, Bethesda, Maryland (1971).
4. Chang, C. L.,Theorem proving with variable-constrained resolution, *Information Sci.* **4** (1972) 217–231.
5. Chang, C. L. and Lee, R. C. T., *Symbolic Logic and Mechanical Theorem Proving* (Academic Press, New York, 1973).
6. Chang, C. L., DEDUCE—A deductive query language for relational data bases, in: C. H. Chen (Ed.) *Pattern Recognition and Artificial Intelligence* (Academic Press, N.Y., 1976).
7. Chang, C. L., DEDUCE 2—Further investigations of deduction in relational data bases, IBM Research Report RJ2147, San José, California, 1978.
8. Chinlund, T. J., Davis, M., Hineman, P. G. and McIlroy, M. D., Theorem proving by matching, Bell Laboratory (1964).
9. Davis, M., Eliminating the irrelevant from mechanical proofs, *Proc. Symp. Appl. Math.* **15** (1963) 15–30.
10. Henschen, L. J. and Evangelist, W. M., Theorem proving by covering expressions, *Proc. 5th International Joint Conference on Artificial Intelligence*, MIT, Massachusetts (1977).
11. Huet, G., Algebraic aspects of unification, Presented at Automatic Theorem Proving Workshop, Oberwolfach, West Germany, 1976.
12. Klahr, P., Planning techniques for rule selection in deductive question-answering, in: Waterman and Hayes-Roth (eds.) *Pattern-Directed Inference Systems* (Academic Press, NY, 1977).
13. Kowalski, R., A proof procedure using connection graphs, *JACM* **22**(4) (October 1975) 572–595.
14. Martelli, A. and Montanari, U., Unification in linear time and space: A structured presentation, Istituto Di Elaborazione Della Informazione, Consiglio Nazionale Delle Ricerche, Pisa, Italy (1976).
15. Martelli, A. and Montanari, U., Theorem proving with structure sharing and efficient unification, Istituto Di Scienze Dell'Informazione, Università Degli Studi Di Pisa, Italy (1977).
16. Nilsson, N. J., A production system for automatic deduction, Technical Note 148, Stanford Research Institute, Menolo Park, California, July 1977.
17. Nilsson, N. J. (1978): Private communications.
18. Patterson, M. S. and Wegman, M. N., Linear Unification, RC5904 (#25518), IBM Thomas J. Watson Research Center, Yorktown Heights, NY (1976).
19. Prawitz, D., An improved proof procedure, *Theoria* **26** (1960) 102–139.
20. Prawitz, D., Advances and problems in mechanical proof procedures, in: Meltzer, B. and Michie, D. (Eds.), *Machine Intelligence* **4** (American Elsevier, New York, 1969) 59–71.
21. Robinson, J. A., A Machine-oriented logic based on the resolution principle, *JACM* **12**(1) (1965) 23–41.
22. Robinson, J. A., Computational logic: the unification computation, in: Meltzer, B. and Michie, D. (Eds.), *Machine Intelligence* (Edinburgh University Press, 1971) **6** 63–72.
23. Robinson, J. A., Fast unification, Presented at Automatic Theorem Proving Workshop, Oberwolfach, West Germany, 1976.
24. Shostak, R., Refutation graphs, *Artificial Intelligence* **7** (1976) 51–64.
25. Sickel, S., A search technique for clause interconnectivity graphs, *IEEE Transactions on Computers* C-25 (1976) 823–834.
26. Sickel, S., Formal grammars as models of logic derivations, Proc. of IJCAI-77 (1977) 544–551.
27. Warren, D. H. and Pereira, L. M., . ROLOG: The language and its implementation compared with LISP, Proc. ACM Symp. on Artificial Intelligence and Programming, University of Rochester, Rochester, NY, August 15–17, 1977 (1977) 109–115.
28. Yarmush, D. L., The linear conjunct and other algorithms for mechanical theorem proving, IMM 412, Courant Institute of Mathematic Sciences, New York University, New York, NY (July 1976).
29. Yates, R., Raphael, B. and Hart, T., Resolution graphs, *Artificial Intelligence* **1**(4) (1970) 257–290.

ON CLOSED WORLD DATA BASES

Raymond Reiter

The University of British Columbia

Vancouver, British Columbia

ABSTRACT

Deductive question-answering systems generally evaluate queries under one of two possible assumptions which we in this paper refer to as the open and closed world assumptions. The open world assumption corresponds to the usual first order approach to query evaluation: Given a data base DB and a query Q, the only answers to Q are those which obtain from proofs of Q given DB as hypotheses. Under the closed world assumption, certain answers are admitted as a result of failure to find a proof. More specifically, if no proof of a positive ground literal exists, then the negation of that literal is assumed true.

In this paper, we show that closed world evaluation of an arbitrary query may be reduced to open world evaluation of so-called atomic queries. We then show that the closed world assumption can lead to inconsistencies, but for Horn data bases no such inconsistencies can arise. Finally, we show how for Horn data bases under the closed world assumption purely negative clauses are irrelevant for deductive retrieval and function instead as integrity constraints.

INTRODUCTION

Deductive question-answering systems generally evaluate queries under one of two possible assumptions which we in this paper refer to as the open and closed world assumptions. The open world assumption corresponds to the usual first order approach to query evaluation: Given a data base DB and a query Q, the only answers to Q are those which obtain from proofs of Q given DB as hypotheses. Under the closed world assumption, certain answers are admitted as a result of failure to find a proof. More specifically, if no proof of a positive ground literal exists, then the negation of that literal is assumed true. This can be viewed as equivalent to implicitly augmenting the given data base with all such negated literals.

For many domains of application, closed world query evaluation is appropriate since, in such domains, it is natural to explicitly represent only positive knowledge and to assume the truth of negative facts by default. For example, in an airline data base, all flights and the cities which they connect will be explicitly represented. Failure to find an entry indicating that Air Canada flight 103 connects Vancouver with Toulouse permits one to conclude that it does not.

This paper is concerned with closed world query evaluation and its relationship to open world evaluation. In the section, Data Bases and Queries, we define a query language and the notion of an open world answer to a query. The section called The Closed World Assumption formally defines the notion of a closed world answer. The section, Query Evaluation Under the CWA, shows how closed world query evaluation may be decomposed into open world evaluation of so-called "atomic queries" in conjunction with the set operations of intersection, union and difference, and the relational algebra operation of projection. In the section, On Data Bases Consistent with the CWA, we show that the closed world assumption can lead to inconsistencies. We prove, moreover, that for Horn data bases no such inconsistencies can arise. Also, for Horn data bases, the occurrence of purely negative clauses is irrelevant to closed world query evaluation. By removing such negative clauses one is left with so-called definite data bases which are then consistent under both the open and closed world assumptions. Finally, in the section, The CWA and Data Base Integrity, we show that these purely negative clauses, although irrelevant to deductive retrieval, have a function in maintaining data base integrity.

In order to preserve continuity we have relegated all proofs of the results in the main body of this paper to an appendix.

DATA BASES AND QUERIES

The query language of this paper is set oriented, i.e. we seek all objects (or tuples of objects) having a given property. For example, in an airline data base the request "Give all flights and their carriers which fly from Boston to England" might be represented in our query language by:

$$< x/\text{Flight},\ y/\text{Airline} \mid (Ez/\text{City})\text{Connect } x,\text{Boston},z \wedge \text{Owns } y,x \wedge \text{City-of } z,\text{England} >$$

which denotes the set of all ordered pairs (x,y) such that x is a flight, y is an airline and

$$(Ez/\text{City})\text{Connect } x,\text{Boston},z \wedge \text{Owns } y,x \wedge \text{City-of } z,\text{England}$$

is true. The syntactic objects Flight, Airline and City are called types and serve to restrict the variables associated with them to range over objects of that type. Thus, (Ez/City) may be read as "There is a z which is a city".

Formally, all queries have the form

$$< x_1/\tau_1,\ldots,x_n/\tau_n \mid (Ey_1/\theta_1)\ldots(Ey_m/\theta_m)W(x_1,\ldots,x_n,y_1,\ldots,y_m) >$$

where $W(x_1,\ldots,x_n,y_1,\ldots,y_m)$ is a quantifier-free formula with free variables $x_1,\ldots,x_n,y_1,\ldots,y_m$ and moreover W contains no function signs. For brevity we shall often denote a typical such query by $< \vec{x}/\vec{\tau} \mid (E\vec{y}/\vec{\theta})W >$. The τ's and θ's are called <u>types</u>. We assume that with each type τ is associated a set of constant signs which we denote by $|\tau|$. For example, in an airline data base, |City| might be {Toronto, Boston, Paris,...,}. If $\vec{\tau} = \tau_1,\ldots,\tau_n$ is a sequence of types we denote by $|\vec{\tau}|$the set $|\tau_1| \times\ldots\times |\tau_n|$.

A <u>data base</u> (DB) is a set of clauses containing no function signs. For an airline data base, DB might contain such information as:

"Air Canada flight 203 connects Toronto and Vancouver."

Connect AC203, Toronto, Vancouver

"All flights from Boston to Los Angeles serve meals."

(x/Flight)Connect x,Boston,LA ⊃Meal-serve x

Let $Q = < \vec{x}/\vec{\tau} \mid (E\vec{y}/\vec{\theta})W(\vec{x},\vec{y}) >$ and let DB be a data base. A set of n-tuples of constant signs $\{\vec{c}^{(1)},\ldots,\vec{c}^{(r)}\}$ is an <u>answer</u> to Q (with respect to DB) iff

1. $\vec{c}^{(i)} \in |\vec{\tau}| \quad i = 1,\ldots,r$ and
2. $DB \vdash \bigvee_{i\le r} (E\vec{y}/\vec{\theta})W(\vec{c}^{(i)},\vec{y})$

Notice that if $\{\vec{c}^{(1)},\ldots,\vec{c}^{(r)}\}$ is an answer to Q, and $\vec{c}$ is any n-tuple of constant signs satisfying 1. then so also is $\{\vec{c}^{(1)},\ldots,\vec{c}^{(r)},\vec{c}\}$ an answer to Q. This suggests the need for the following definitions:

An answer A to Q is <u>minimal</u> iff no proper subset of A is an answer to Q. If A is a minimal answer to Q, then if A consists of a single n-tuple, A is a <u>definite</u> answer to Q. Otherwise, A is an <u>indefinite</u> answer to Q. Finally define $\|Q\|_{OWA}$ to be the set of minimal answers to Q. (For reasons which will become apparent later, the subscript OWA stands for "Open World Assumption".) Notice the interpretation assigned to an indefinite answer $\{\vec{c}^{(1)},\ldots,\vec{c}^{(r)}\}$ to Q: $\vec{x}$ is either $\vec{c}^{(1)}$ or $\vec{c}^{(2)}$ or...or $\vec{c}^{(r)}$ but there is no way, given the information in DB, of determining which. Instead of denoting an answer as a set of tuples $\{\vec{c}^{(1)},\ldots,\vec{c}^{(r)}\}$ we prefer the more suggestive notation $\vec{c}^{(1)}+\ldots+\vec{c}^{(r)}$, a notation we shall use in the remainder of this paper.

<u>Example 1.</u>

Suppose DB knows of 4 humans and 2 cities:

$|\text{Human}| = \{a,b,c,d\} \quad |\text{City}| = \{B,V\}$

Suppose further that everyone is either in B or in V:

(x/Human)Loc x,B ∨ Loc x,V

and moreover, a is in B and b is in V:

Loc a,B   Loc b,V

Then for the query "Where is everybody?"

$Q = <x/\text{Human}, y/\text{City} \mid \text{Loc } x,y>$

we have

$\|Q\|_{OWA} = \{(a,B),(b,V),(c,B)+(c,V),(d,B)+(d,V)\}$

i.e. a is in B, b is in V, c is either in B or V and d is either in B or V.

Since it is beyond the scope of this paper, the reader is referred to Reiter [1977] or Reiter [1978] for an approach to query evaluation which returns $\|Q\|_{OWA}$ given any query Q.

THE CLOSED WORLD ASSUMPTION

In order to illustrate the central concept of this paper, we consider the following purely <u>extensional</u> data base (i.e., a data base consisting of ground literals only):

$$|Teacher| = \{a,b,c,d\}$$

$$|Student| = \{A,B,C\}$$

Teach	
a	A
b	B
c	C
a	B

Now consider the query: Who does not teach B?

$$Q = \langle x/Teacher \mid \overline{Teach}\ x,B \rangle$$

By the definition of the previous section, we conclude, counter-intuitively, that

$$||Q||_{OWA} = \phi \ .$$

Intuitively, we want $\{c,d\}$ i.e. $|Teacher| - || \langle x/Teacher | Teach\ x,B \rangle ||_{OWA}$. The reason for the counterintuitive result is that first order logic interprets the DB literally; all the logic knows for certain is what is explicitly represented in the DB. Just because $\overline{Teach}$ c,B is not present in the DB is no reason to conclude that $\overline{Teach}$ c,B is true. Rather, as far as the logic is concerned, the truth of Teach c,B is unknown! Thus, we would also have to include the following facts about Teach:

$\overline{Teach}$	
a	C
b	A
b	C
c	A
c	B
d	A
d	B
d	C

Unfortunately, the number of negative facts about a given domain will, in general, far exceed the number of positive ones so that the requirement that all facts, both positive and negative, be explicitly represented may well be unfeasible. In the case of purely extensional data bases there is a ready solution to this problem. Merely *explicitly* represent *positive* facts. A negative fact is *implicitly* present provided its positive counterpart is *not explicitly* present. Notice, however, that by adopting this convention, we are making an assumption about our knowledge about the domain, namely, that we know everything about each predicate of the domain. There are no gaps in our knowledge. For example, if we were ignorant as to whether or not a teaches C, we could not permit the above implicit representation of negative facts. This is an important point. *The implicit representation of negative facts presumes total knolwedge about the domain being represented.* Fortunately, in most applications, such an assumption is warranted. We shall refer to this as the *closed world assumption* (CWA). Its opposite, the *open world assumption* (OWA), assumes only the information given in the data base and hence requires all facts, both positive and negative, to be explicitly represented. Under the OWA, "gaps" in one's knowledge about the domain are permitted.

Formally, we can define the notion of an answer to a query under the CWA as follows:

Let DB be an extensional data base and let $\overline{EDB} = \{\overline{P\vec{c}} \mid P$ is a predicate sign, $\vec{c}$ a tuple of constant signs and $P\vec{c} \notin DB\}$
Then $\vec{c}$ is a *CWA answer* to $< \vec{x}/\vec{\tau} \mid (E\vec{y}/\vec{\theta})W(\vec{x},\vec{y}) >$ (with respect to DB) iff

1. $\vec{c} \in |\vec{\tau}|$ and

2, $DB \cup \overline{EDB} \vdash (E\vec{y}/\vec{\theta})W(\vec{c},\vec{y})$

For purely extensional data bases, the CWA poses no difficulties. One merely imagines the DB to contain all negative facts each of which has no positive version in the DB. This conceptual view of the DB fails in the presence of non ground clauses. For if $P\vec{c} \notin DB$, it may nevertheless be possible to infer $P\vec{c}$ from the DB, so that we cannot, with impunity, imagine $\overline{P\vec{c}} \in DB$. The obvious generalization is to assume that the DB implicitly contains $\overline{P\vec{c}}$ whenever it is not the case that $DB \vdash P\vec{c}$.

Formally, we can define the notion of an answer to a query under the CWA for an arbitrary data base DB as follows:

Let

$\overline{EDB} = \{\overline{P\vec{c}} \mid P$ is a predicate sign, $\vec{c}$ a tuple of constant signs and $DB \nvdash P\vec{c}\,\}$

Then $\vec{c}^{(1)} + \ldots + \vec{c}^{(r)}$ is a *CWA answer* to

$< \vec{x}/\vec{\tau} \mid (E\vec{y}/\vec{\theta})W(\vec{x},\vec{y}) >$ (with respect to DB) iff

1. $\vec{c}^{(i)} \in |\vec{\tau}|$ i=1,...,r and

2. $DB \cup \overline{EDB} \vdash \bigvee_{i \leq r} (E\vec{y}/\vec{\theta})W(\vec{c}^{(i)},\vec{y})$

This definition should be compared with the definition of an answer in the previous section. We shall refer to this latter notion as an OWA answer. As under the OWA, we shall require the notions of minimal, indefinite and definite CWA answers. If Q is a query, we shall denote the set of minimal CWA answers to Q by $||Q||_{CWA}$.

Example 2.

We consider a fragment of an inventory data base.

1. Every supplier of a part supplies all its subparts.

   (x/Supplier)(yz/Part)Supplies x,y ∧ Subpart z,y ⊃ Supplies x,z

2. Foobar Inc. supplies all widgets.

   (x/Widget)Supplies Foobar,x

3. The subpart relation is transitive.

   (xyz/Part)Subpart z,y ∧ Subpart y,x ⊃ Subpart z,x

Assume the following type extensions:

$|Supplier| = \{Acme, Foobar, AAA\}$

$|Widget| = \{w_1, w_2, w_3, w_4\}$

$|Part| = \{p_1, p_2, p_3, w_1, w_2, w_3, w_4\}$

Finally, assume the following extensional data base:

Supplies	x	y
	Acme	p_1
	AAA	w_3
	AAA	w_4

Subpart	x	y
	p_2	p_1
	p_3	p_2
	w_1	p_1
	w_2	w_1

Then $\overline{EDB}$ is:

Supplies	x	y
	Acme	w_3
	Acme	w_4
	AAA	p_1
	AAA	p_2
	AAA	p_3
	AAA	w_1
	AAA	w_2
	Foobar	p_1
	Foobar	p_2
	Foobar	p_3
	p_1	Acme
	p_1	AAA
	p_1	Foobar
	p_1	p_1
	p_1	p_2
	p_1	p_3
	p_1	w_1
	etc.	

Subpart	x	y
	p_1	p_1
	p_1	p_2
	p_1	p_3
	p_1	w_1
	p_1	w_2
	p_1	w_3
	p_1	w_4
	p_2	p_2
	p_2	p_3
	p_2	w_1
	p_2	w_2
	p_2	w_3
	p_2	w_4
	p_3	p_3
	p_3	w_1
	p_3	w_2
	p_3	w_3
	p_3	w_4
	etc.	

The notion of a CWA answer is obviously intimately related to the negation operators of PLANNER (Hewitt [1972]) and PROLOG (Roussel [1975]) since in these languages, negation means "not provable" and the definition of $\overline{EDB}$ critically depends upon this notion. Clark [1978] investigates the relation between this notion of negation as failure and its truth functional semantics. The need for the CWA in deductive question-answering systems has been articulated in Nicolas and Syre [1974].

Notice that under the CWA, there can be no "gaps" in our knowledge about the domain. More formally, for each predicate sign P and each tuple of constant signs $\vec{c}$, either $DB \vdash P\vec{c}$ or $\overline{EDB} \vdash \overline{P\vec{c}}$ and since, under the CWA the data base is taken to be $DB \cup \overline{EDB}$, we can always infer either $P\vec{c}$ or $\overline{P\vec{c}}$ from $DB \cup \overline{EDB}$. Since there are no "knowledge gaps" under the CWA, it should be intuitively clear that indefinite CWA answers cannot arise, i.e. each minimal CWA answer to a query is of the form $\vec{c}$. The following result confirms this intuition.

Theorem 1.

Let $Q = \langle \vec{x}/\vec{\tau} \mid (E\vec{y}/\vec{\theta})W(\vec{x},\vec{y})\rangle$. Then every minimal CWA answer to Q is definite.

There is one obvious difficulty in directly applying the definition of a CWA answer to the evaluation of queries. The definition requires that we explicitly know $\overline{EDB}$ and, as Example 2 demonstrates, the determination of $\overline{EDB}$ is generally non trivial.

In any event, for non toy domains, $\overline{EDB}$ would be so large that its explicit representation would be totally unfeasible. Fortunately, as we shall see in the next section, there is no need to know the elements of $\overline{EDB}$ i.e. it is possible to determine the set of closed world answers to an arbitrary query Q by appealing only to the given data base DB.

QUERY EVALUATION UNDER THE CWA

It turns out that the CWA admits a number of significant simplifications in the query evaluation process. The simplest of these permits the elimination of the logical connectives $\wedge$ and $\vee$ in favour of set intersection and union respectively, as follows:

Theorem 2.

1. $\| < \vec{x}/\vec{\tau} \mid (E\vec{y}/\vec{\theta})(W_1 \vee W_2)> \|_{CWA} = \| < \vec{x}/\vec{\tau} \mid (E\vec{y}/\vec{\theta})W_1> \|_{CWA} \cup$
$\| < \vec{x}/\vec{\tau} \mid (E\vec{y}/\vec{\theta})W_2> \|_{CWA}$

2. $\| < \vec{x}/\vec{\tau} \mid W_1 \wedge W_2 > \|_{CWA} = \| < \vec{x}/\vec{\tau} \mid W_1 > \|_{CWA} \cap \| < \vec{x}/\vec{\tau} \mid W_2 > \|_{CWA}$

Notice that in the identity 2, the query must be quantifier free. Notice also that the identities of Theorem 2 fail under the OWA. To see why, consider the following:

Example 3

$|\tau| = \{a\}$

DB: Pa $\vee$ Ra

$Q = < x/\tau \mid Px \vee Rx >$

$\|Q\|_{OWA} = \{a\}$

but

$\| < x/\tau \mid Px > \|_{OWA} = \| < x/\tau \mid Rx > \|_{OWA} = \phi$

Example 4

$|\tau| = \{a,b\}$

DB: Pa $\vee$ Pb, Ra, Rb

$Q = < x/\tau \mid Px \wedge Rx >$

$$\|Q\|_{OWA} = \{a+b\}$$

but

$$\|< x/\tau \mid Px >\|_{OWA} = \{a+b\}$$

$$\|< x/\tau \mid Rx >\|_{OWA} = \{a,b\}$$

One might also expect that all occurrences of negation can be eliminated in favour of set difference for CWA query evaluation. This is indeed the case, but only for quantifier free queries and then only when DB $\cup$ $\overline{EDB}$ is consistent.

Theorem 3.

If W, W_1 and W_2 are quantifier free, and DB $\cup$ $\overline{EDB}$ is consistent, then

1. $\| < \vec{x}/\vec{\tau} \mid \overline{W} > \|_{CWA} = |\vec{\tau}| - \| < \vec{x}/\vec{\tau} \mid W > \|_{CWA}$
2. $\| < \vec{x}/\vec{\tau} \mid W_1 \wedge \overline{W}_2 > \|_{CWA} = \|< \vec{x}/\vec{\tau} \mid W_1 >\|_{CWA} - \|< \vec{x}/\vec{\tau} \mid W_2 >\|_{CWA}$

To see why Theorem 3 fails for quantified queries, consider the following:

Example 5

$|\tau| = \{a,b\}$

DB: Pa,a

Then $\overline{EDB} = \{\overline{P}a,b,\ \overline{P}b,a,\ \overline{P}b,b\}$

Let $Q(P) = < x/\tau \mid (Ey/\tau)Px,y >$

$Q(\overline{P}) = < x/\tau \mid (Ey/\tau)\overline{P}x,y >$

Then $\| Q(P)\|_{CWA} = \{a\}$

$\| Q(\overline{P})\|_{CWA} = \{a,b\} \neq |\tau| - \|Q(P)\|_{CWA}$

Notice also that Theorem 3 fails under the OWA.

By an atomic query we mean any query of the form $< \vec{x}/\vec{\tau} \mid (E\vec{y}/\vec{\theta})Pt_1,\ldots,t_n >$ where P is a predicate sign and each t is a constant sign, an x, or a y.

Theorems 2 and 3 assure us that for quantifier free queries, CWA query evaluation can be reduced to the Boolean operations of set intersection union and difference applied to atomic queries. However, we can deal with quantified queries by introducing the following <u>projection operator</u> (Codd [1972]):

Let $Q = < \vec{x}/\vec{\tau}, z/\psi | W >$ where W is a possibly existentially quantified formula, and $\vec{x}$ is the n-tuple $x_1, \ldots, x_n$. Then $\|Q\|_{CWA}$ is a set of (n+1)-tuples, and the <u>projection of</u> $\|Q\|_{CWA}$ <u>with respect to z</u>, $\pi_z \|Q\|_{CWA}$, is the set of n-tuples obtained from $\|Q\|_{CWA}$ by deleting the (n+1)st component from each (n+1)-tuple of $\|Q\|_{CWA}$. For example, if $Q = < x_1/\tau_1, x_2/\tau_2, z/\psi | W >$ and if

$$\|Q\|_{CWA} = \{(a,b,c),(a,b,d),(c,a,b)\}$$

then

$$\pi_z \|Q\|_{CWA} = \{(a,b),(c,a)\}$$

<u>Theorem 4.</u>

$$\|< \vec{x}/\vec{\tau} | (E\vec{y}/\vec{\theta})W >\|_{CWA} = \pi_{\vec{y}} \|< \vec{x}/\vec{\tau}, \vec{y}/\vec{\theta} | W >\|_{CWA}$$

where $\pi_{\vec{y}}$ denotes $\pi_{y_1} \pi_{y_2} \cdots \pi_{y_m}$

<u>Corollary 4.1</u>

1. $\|< \vec{x}/\vec{\tau} | (E\vec{y}/\vec{\theta})\overline{W} >\|_{CWA} = \pi_{\vec{y}} \|< \vec{x}/\vec{\tau}, \vec{y}/\vec{\theta} | \overline{W} >\|_{CWA}$
$= \pi_{\vec{y}}(|\vec{\tau}| \times |\vec{\theta}| - \|< \vec{x}/\vec{\tau}, \vec{y}/\vec{\theta} | W >\|_{CWA})$

2. $\|< \vec{x}/\vec{\tau} | (E\vec{y}/\vec{\theta})W_1 \wedge W_2 >\|_{CWA} = \pi_{\vec{y}}(\|< \vec{x}/\vec{\tau}, \vec{y}/\vec{\theta} | W_1 >\|_{CWA}$
$\cap \|< \vec{x}/\vec{\tau}, \vec{y}/\vec{\theta} | W_2 >\|_{CWA})$

Thus, in all cases, an existentially quantified query may be decomposed into atomic queries each of which is evaluated under the CWA. The resulting sets of answers are combined under set union, intersection and difference, but only after the projection operator is applied, if necessary.

<u>Example 6.</u>

$$\|< x/\tau | (Ey/\theta)Px,y \vee Qx,y\ Rx,y >\|_{CWA}$$

$$= \|< x/\tau | (Ey/\theta)Px,y\|_{CWA} \cup \pi_y(\|< x/\tau, y/\theta | Qx,y >\|_{CWA}$$

$$\cap \|< x/\tau, y/\theta | Rx,y >\|_{CWA})$$

$$\| < x/\tau \mid PxQx \vee \overline{R}x > \|_{CWA} = \| < x/\tau \mid Px > \|_{CWA}$$
$$\cap \| < x/\tau \mid Qx > \|_{CWA} \cup [\,|\tau| - \| < x/\tau \mid Rx > \|_{CWA}]$$

$$\| < x/\tau \mid (Ey/\theta)Px,y \vee Qx,y\ \overline{R}x,y > \|_{CWA}$$
$$= \| < x/\tau \mid (Ey/\theta)Px,y > \|_{CWA} \cup \pi_y(< x/\tau, y/\theta \mid Qx,y > \|_{CWA}$$
$$- \| < x/\tau, y/\theta \mid Rx,y > \|_{CWA})$$

In view of the above results, we need consider CWA query evaluation only for atomic queries.

We shall say that DB is consistent with the CWA iff DB $\cup$ $\overline{EDB}$ is consistent.

Theorem 5.

Let Q be an atomic query. Then if DB is consistent with the CWA, $\|Q\|_{CWA} = \|Q\|_{OWA}$.

Theorem 5 is the principal result of this section. When coupled with Theorems 2 and 3 and the remarks following Corollary 4.1 it provides us with a complete characterization of the CWA answers to an arbitrary existential query Q in terms of the application of the operations of projection, set union, intersection and difference as applied to the OWA answers to atomic queries. In other words, CWA query evaluation has been reduced to OWA atomic query evaluation. A consequence of this result is that we need never know the elements of $\overline{EDB}$. CWA query evaluation appeals only to the given data base DB.

Example 7.

We consider the inventory data base of Example 2. Suppose the following query:

$$Q = < x/Supplier \mid (Ey/Widget)Supplies\ x,y \wedge Subpart\ y,p_1 \wedge \overline{Supplies}\ x,p_3 >$$

Then

$$\|Q\|_{CWA} = \pi_y(\|Q_1\|_{OWA} \cap \|Q_2\|_{OWA}) \cap (|Supplier| - \|Q_3\|_{OWA})$$

where

$$Q_1 = < x/Supplier,\ y/Widget \mid Supplies\ x,y >$$

$Q_2 = <$ x/Supplier, y/Widget | Subpart y,p_1 $>$

$Q_3 = <$ x/Supplier | Supplies x,p_3 $>$

It is easy to see that

$||Q_1||_{OWA}$ = {(Foobar,w_1), (Foobar,w_2), (Foobar,w_3), (Foobar,w_4), (AAA,w_3), (AAA,w_4), (Acme,w_1), (Acme,w_2)}

$||Q_2||_{OWA}$ = {(Acme,w_1), (Acme,w_2), (AAA,w_1), (AAA,w_2), (Foobar,w_1), (Foobar, w_2)}

$||Q_3||_{OWA}$ = {Acme}

whence

$\pi_y(||Q_1||_{OWA} \cap ||Q_2||_{OWA})$ = {Foobar,Acme}

and

$|Supplier| - ||Q_3||_{OWA}$ = {Foobar,AAA}

Hence

$||Q||_{CWA}$ = {Foobar}.

ON DATA BASES CONSISTENT WITH THE CWA

Not every consistent data base remains consistent under the CWA.

Example 8.

DB: Pa $\vee$ Pb

Then, since DB $\not\vdash$ Pa and Db $\not\vdash$ Pb , $\overline{EDB}$ = {$\overline{P}$a, $\overline{P}$b} so that DB $\cup$ $\overline{EDB}$ is inconsistent.

Given this observation, it is natural to seek a characterization of those data bases which remain consistent under the CWA. Although we know of no such characterization, it is possible to give a sufficient condition for CWA consistency which encompasses a large natural class of data bases, namely the Horn data bases. (A data base is Horn iff every clause is Horn i.e. contains at most one positive literal. The data base of Example 2 is Horn.)

Theorem 6

Suppose DB is Horn, and consistent. Then DB $\cup \overline{EDB}$ is consistent i.e., DB is consistent with the CWA.

Following van Emden [1977] we shall refer to a Horn clause with exactly one positive literal as a definite clause. If DB is Horn, let Δ(DB) be obtained from DB by removing all non definite clauses i.e., all negative clauses. The following Theorem demonstrates the central importance of these concepts:

Theorem 7

If $Q = < \vec{x}/\vec{\tau} \mid (E\vec{y}/\vec{\theta})W >$ and DB is Horn and consistent, then $\|Q\|_{CWA}$ when evaluated with respect to DB yields the same set of answers as when evaluated with respect to Δ(DB). In other words, negative clauses in DB have no influence on CWA query evaluation.

Theorem 7 allows us, when given a consistent Horn DB, to discard all its negative clauses without affecting CWA query evaluation. Theorem 7 fails for non Horn DBs, as the following example demonstrates:

Example 9

DB: $\overline{P}a \vee \overline{R}a$, Ra $\vee$ Sa, Pa

Then DB $\vdash$ Sa

But Δ(DB) = {Ra $\vee$ Sa, Pa} and Δ(DB) $\nvdash$ Sa.

Let us call a data base for which all clauses are definite a definite data base.

Theorem 8

If DB is definite then DB is consistent.

Corollary 8.1

If DB is definite then

(i) DB is consistent

(ii) DB is consistent with the CWA.

Corollary 8.1 is a central result. It guarantees data base and CWA consistency for a large and natural class of data bases. Since the data base of Example 2 is definite we are assured that it is consistent with the CWA.

In van Emden [1977], he addresses, from a semantic point of view, the issues of data base consistency under the CWA. He defines the notion of a "minimal model" for a data base as the intersection of all its models. If this minimal model is itself a model of the data base, then the data base is consistent with the CWA. Van Emden goes on to point out some intriguing connections between minimal models and Scott's minimal fixpoint approach to the theory of computation, results which are elaborated in van Emden and Kowalski [1976].

THE CWA AND DATA BASE INTEGRITY

Theorem 7 has an interesting consequence with respect to data base integrity. In a first order data base, both intensional and extensional facts may serve a dual purpose. They can be used for deductive retrieval, or they can function as integrity constraints. In this latter capacity they are used to detect inconsistencies whenever the data base is modified. For example, if the data base is updated with a new fact then logical consequences of this fact can be derived using the entire data base. If these consequences lead to an inconsistency, the update will be rejected.

In general, it is not clear whether a given fact in a data base functions exclusively as an integrity constraint, or for deductive retrieval, or both (Nicolas and Gallaire [1978]). However, if the data base is both Horn and closed world, Theorem 7 tells us that purely negative clauses can function only as integrity constraints. Thus the CWA induces a partition of a Horn data base into negative and non-negative clauses. The latter are used only for deductive retrieval. Both are used for enforcing integrity.

SUMMARY

We have introduced the notion of the closed world assumption for deductive question-answering. This says, in effect, "Every positive statement that you don't know to be true may be assumed false". We have then shown how query evaluation under the closed world assumption reduces to the usual first order proof theoretic approach to query evaluation as applied to atomic queries. Finally, we have shown that consistent Horn data bases remain consistent under the closed world assumption and that definite data bases are consistent with the closed world assumption.

ACKNOWLEDGMENT

This paper was written with the financial support of the National Research Council of Canada under grant A7642. Much of this research was done while the author was visiting at Bolt, Beranek and Newman, Inc., Cambridge, Mass. I wish to thank Craig Bishop for his careful criticism of an earlier draft of this paper.

APPENDIX

Proofs of Theorems

Theorem 1.

Let $Q = <\vec{x}/\vec{\tau} \mid (E\vec{y}/\vec{\theta})W(\vec{x},\vec{y})>$. Then every minimal CWA to Q is definite.

The proof requires the following two lemmas:

Lemma 1

Let $W_1, \ldots, W_r$ be propositional formulae. Then

$DB \cup \overline{EDB} \vdash W_1 \vee \ldots \vee W_r$

iff $DB \cup \overline{EDB} \vdash W_i$ for some i.

Proof: The "only if" half is immediate.

With no loss in generality, assume that the set of W's is minimal, i.e., for no i do we have

$$DB \cup \overline{EDB} \vdash W_1 \vee \ldots \vee W_{i-1} \vee W_{i+1} \vee \ldots \vee W_r .$$

Suppose W_1 is represented in conjunctive normal form, i.e. as a conjunct of clauses. Let $C = L_1 \vee \ldots \vee L_m$ be a typical such clause. Then $DB \cup \overline{EDB} \vdash L_i$ or $DB \cup \overline{EDB} \vdash \overline{L_i}$, $i=1,\ldots,m$. Suppose the latter is the case for each i, $1 \le i \le m$. Then $DB \cup \overline{EDB} \vdash \overline{C}$ so that $DB \cup \overline{EDB} \vdash \overline{W_1}$. Since also $DB \cup \overline{EDB} \vdash W_1 \vee \ldots \vee W_r$, then $DB \cup \overline{EDB} \vdash W_2 \vee \ldots \vee W_r$ contradicting the assumption that the set of W's is minimal. Hence, for some i, $1 \le i \le m$, $DB \cup \overline{EDB} \vdash L_i$ so that $DB \cup \overline{EDB} \vdash C$. Since C was an arbitrary clause of W_1, $DB \cup \overline{EDB} \vdash W_1$ which establishes the lemma.

Lemma 2

$DB \cup \overline{EDB} \vdash (E\vec{y}/\vec{\theta})W(\vec{y})$ iff there is a tuple $\vec{d} \in |\vec{\theta}|$ such that $DB \cup \overline{EDB} \vdash W(\vec{d})$.

Proof: The "only if" half is immediate.

Since $DB \cup \overline{EDB} \vdash (E\vec{y}/\vec{\theta})W(\vec{y})$ then for tuples $\vec{d}^{(1)}, \ldots, \vec{d}^{(r)} \in |\vec{\theta}|$

$$DB \cup \overline{EDB} \vdash \bigvee_{i \le r} W(\vec{d}^{(i)})$$

The result now follows by Lemma 1.

Proof of Theorem 1:

Suppose, to the contrary, that for $m \geq 2$, $\vec{c}^{(1)}+\ldots+\vec{c}^{(m)}$ is a minimal CWA answer to Q. Then

$$DB \cup \overline{EDB} \vdash \bigvee_{i \leq m} (E\vec{y}/\vec{\theta}) W(\vec{c}^{(i)},\vec{y})$$

i.e.,

$$DB \cup \overline{EDB} \vdash (E\vec{y}/\vec{\theta}) \bigvee_{i \leq m} W(\vec{c}^{(i)},\vec{y})$$

so by Lemma 2 there is a tuple $\vec{d} \in |\vec{\theta}|$ such that

$$DB \cup \overline{EDB} \vdash \bigvee_{i \leq m} W(\vec{c}^{(i)},\vec{d})$$

By Lemma 1, $DB \cup \overline{EDB} \vdash W(\vec{c}^{(i)},\vec{d})$ for some i whence $\vec{c}^{(i)}$ is an answer to Q, contradicting the assumed indefiniteness of $\vec{c}^{(1)}+\ldots+\vec{c}^{(m)}$.

<u>Theorem 2.</u>

1. $\| < \vec{x}/\vec{\tau} \mid (E\vec{y}/\vec{\theta})(W_1 \vee W_2) > \|_{CWA} = \| < \vec{x}/\vec{\tau} \mid (E\vec{y}/\vec{\theta})W_1 > \|_{CWA} \cup \| < \vec{x}/\vec{\tau} \mid (E\vec{y}/\vec{\theta})W_2 > \|_{CWA}$

2. $\| < \vec{x}/\vec{\tau} \mid W_1 \wedge W_2 > \|_{CWA} = \| < \vec{x}/\vec{\tau} \mid W_1 > \|_{CWA} \cap \| < x/\tau \mid W_2 > \|_{CWA}$

Proof: 1. follows from Lemmas 1 and 2 and Theorem 1. The proof of 2. is immediate from Theorem 1.

<u>Theorem 3.</u>

If W, W_1 and W_2 are quantifier free, and $DB \cup \overline{EDB}$ is consistent, then

1. $\| < \vec{x}/\vec{\tau} \mid \overline{W} > \|_{CWA} = |\vec{\tau}| - \| < \vec{x}/\vec{\tau} \mid W > \|_{CWA}$

2. $\| < \vec{x}/\vec{\tau} \mid W_1 \wedge \overline{W}_2 > \|_{CWA} = \| < \vec{x}/\vec{\tau} \mid W_1 > \|_{CWA} - \| < \vec{x}/\vec{\tau} \mid W_2 > \|_{CWA}$

Proof: 1. The proof is by structural induction on W. Denote $\| < \vec{x}/\vec{\tau} \mid W > \|_{CWA}$ by Q(W).

We must prove

$$Q(\overline{W}) = |\vec{\tau}| - Q(W) .$$

Case 1: W is $Pt_1,\ldots,t_m$ where P is a predicate sign and $t_1,\ldots,t_m$ are terms.

Suppose $\vec{c} \in Q(\overline{W})$. Let $\Pi(\vec{c})$ be $Pt_1,\ldots,t_m$ with all occurrences of x_i replaced by c_i. Then $DB \cup \overline{EDB} \vdash \overline{\Pi}(\vec{c})$. Since $DB \cup \overline{EDB}$ is consistent, $DB \cup \overline{EDB} \not\vdash \Pi(\vec{c})$, i.e. $\vec{c} \notin Q(W)$. Since $\vec{c} \in |\vec{\tau}|$, then $\vec{c} \in |\vec{\tau}| - Q(W)$, so that $Q(\overline{W}) \subseteq |\vec{\tau}| - Q(W)$. Now suppose $\vec{c} \in |\vec{\tau}| - Q(W)$. Then $\vec{c} \notin Q(W)$ so $DB \cup \overline{EDB} \not\vdash \Pi(\vec{c})$. But then $DB \cup \overline{EDB} \vdash \overline{\Pi}(\vec{c})$, and since $\vec{c} \in |\vec{\tau}|$, then $\vec{c} \in Q(\overline{W})$, so that $|\vec{\tau}| - Q(W) \subseteq Q(\overline{W})$.

Case 2: W is $U_1 \wedge U_2$.

Assume, for i=1,2 that $Q(\overline{U_i}) = |\vec{\tau}| - Q(U_i)$.

Then
$$\begin{aligned} Q(\overline{W}) &= Q(\overline{U_1 \wedge U_2}) \\ &= Q(\overline{U}_1 \vee \overline{U}_2) \\ &= Q(\overline{U}_1) \cup Q(\overline{U}_2) \quad \text{by Theorem 2} \\ &= [|\vec{\tau}| - Q(U_1)] \cup [|\vec{\tau}| - Q(U_2)] \\ &= |\vec{\tau}| - [Q(U_1) \cap Q(U_2) \\ &= |\vec{\tau}| - Q(U_1 \wedge U_2) \quad \text{by Theorem 2} \\ &= |\vec{\tau}| - Q(W) \end{aligned}$$

Case 3: W is $U_1 \vee U_2$.

The proof is the dual of Case 2.

Case 4: W is $\overline{U}$.

Assume that $Q(\overline{U}) = |\vec{\tau}| - Q(U)$. Since $Q(U) \subseteq |\vec{\tau}|$, it follows that $Q(U) = |\vec{\tau}| - Q(\overline{U})$. i.e. $Q(\overline{W}) = |\vec{\tau}| - Q(W)$.

$$\begin{aligned} Q(W_1 \wedge \overline{W}_2) &= Q(W_1) \cap Q(\overline{W}_2) \quad \text{by Theorem 2} \\ &= Q(W_1) \cap [|\vec{\tau}| - Q(W_2)] \text{ by 1.} \\ &= Q(W_1) - Q(W_2) \quad \text{since } Q(W_1) \subseteq |\vec{\tau}|. \end{aligned}$$

Theorem 4.

$$\| < \vec{x}/\vec{\tau} \,|\, (E\vec{y}/\vec{\theta})W(\vec{x},\vec{y}) > \|_{CWA} = \pi_{\vec{y}} \| < \vec{x}/\vec{\tau}, \vec{y}/\vec{\theta} \,|\, W(\vec{x},\vec{y}) > \|_{CWA}$$

where $\pi_{\vec{y}}$ denotes $\pi_{y_1} \pi_{y_2} \ldots \pi_{y_m}$

Proof:

Suppose $\vec{c} \in \| < \vec{x}/\vec{\tau} \,|\, (E\vec{y}/\vec{\theta})W(\vec{x},\vec{y}) > \|_{CWA}$

Then by definition

$DB \cup \overline{EDB} \vdash (E\vec{y}/\vec{\theta})W(\vec{c},\vec{y})$

whence by Lemma 2 there is a tuple $\vec{d} \in |\vec{\theta}|$ such that

$DB \cup \overline{EDB} \vdash W(\vec{c},\vec{d})$

i.e., $\vec{c},\vec{d} \in \| < \vec{x}/\vec{\tau},\vec{y}/\vec{\theta} \,|\, W(\vec{x},\vec{y}) > \|_{CWA}$

i.e., $\vec{c} \in \Pi_{\vec{y}} \| < \vec{x}/\vec{\tau},\vec{y}/\vec{\theta} \,|\, W(\vec{x},\vec{y}) > \|_{CWA}$

Now Suppose $\vec{c} \in \Pi_{\vec{y}} \| < \vec{x}/\vec{\tau},\vec{y}/\vec{\theta} \,|\, W(\vec{x},\vec{y}) > \|_{CWA}$

Then for some tuple $\vec{d} \in |\vec{\theta}|$

$\vec{c},\vec{d} \in \| < \vec{x}/\vec{\tau},\vec{y}/\vec{\theta} \,|\, W(\vec{x},\vec{y}) > \|_{CWA}$

so that $DB \cup \overline{EDB} \vdash W(\vec{c},\vec{d})$

i.e., $DB \cup \overline{EDB} \vdash (E\vec{y}/\vec{\theta})W(\vec{c},\vec{y})$

i.e. $\vec{c} \in \| < \vec{x}/\vec{\tau} \,|\, (E\vec{y}/\vec{\theta})W(\vec{x},\vec{y}) > \|_{CWA}$

<u>Theorem 5.</u>

Let Q be an atomic query. Then if DB is consistent with the CWA, $\|Q\|_{CWA} = \|Q\|_{OWA}$

Proof: The proof requires the following:

<u>Lemma 3</u>

If DB is consistent with the CWA then every atomic query has only definite OWA answers.

Proof:

Let $Q = < \vec{x}/\vec{\tau} \,|\, (E\vec{y}/\vec{\theta})P(\vec{x},\vec{y}) >$ be an atomic query where $P(\vec{x},\vec{y})$ is a positive literal. Suppose, on the contrary, that Q has an indefinite OWA answer $\vec{c}^{(1)} + \ldots + \vec{c}^{(m)}$ for $m \geq 2$. Then

$$DB \vdash \bigvee_{i \leq m} (E\vec{y}/\vec{\theta})P(\vec{c}^{(i)},\vec{y}) \qquad (1)$$

and for no i, $1 \leq i \leq m$, is it the case that $DB \vdash (E\vec{y}/\vec{\theta})P(\vec{c}^{(i)},\vec{y})$.

Hence, for all $\vec{d} \in |\vec{\theta}|$, $DB \nvdash P(\vec{c}^{(i)}, \vec{d})$ $i=1,\ldots,m$.

Thus $\overline{P}(\vec{c}^{(i)}, \vec{d}) \in \overline{EDB}$ for all $\vec{d} \in |\vec{\theta}|$, $i=1,\ldots,m$.

Hence, $DB \cup \overline{EDB} \vdash \overline{P}(\vec{c}^{(i)}, \vec{d})$ for all $\vec{d} \in |\vec{\theta}|$, $i=1,\ldots,m$ and from (1), $DB \cup \overline{EDB} \vdash \bigvee_{i \le m} (E\vec{y}/\vec{\theta})P(\vec{c}^{(i)}, \vec{y})$

i.e. $DB \cup \overline{EDB}$ is inconsistent, contradiction.

Proof of Theorem 5:

Let $Q = < \vec{x}/\vec{\tau} \mid (E\vec{y}/\vec{\theta})P(\vec{x},\vec{y}) >$ where $P(\vec{x},\vec{y})$ is a positive literal. By Lemma 3 $||Q||_{OWA}$ consists only of definite answers. Now

$$\vec{c} \in ||Q||_{OWA} \text{ iff } \vec{c} \in |\vec{\tau}| \text{ and } DB \vdash (E\vec{y}/\vec{\theta})P(\vec{c},\vec{y})$$
$$\vec{c} \in ||Q||_{CWA} \text{ iff } \vec{c} \in |\vec{\tau}| \text{ and } DB \cup \overline{EDB} \vdash (E\vec{y}/\vec{\theta})P(\vec{c},\vec{y})$$

Hence $||Q||_{OWA} \subseteq ||Q||_{CWA}$.

We prove $||Q||_{CWA} \subseteq ||Q||_{OWA}$. To that end, let $\vec{c} \in ||Q||_{CWA}$. Then $DB \cup \overline{EDB} \vdash P(\vec{c},\vec{d})$ for some $\vec{d} \in |\vec{\theta}|$.

If $DB \vdash P(\vec{c},\vec{d})$, then $\vec{c} \in ||Q||_{OWA}$ and we are done.

Otherwise, $DB \nvdash P(\vec{c},\vec{d})$ so that $\overline{P}(\vec{c},\vec{d}) \in \overline{EDB}$

i.e. $DB \cup \overline{EDB} \vdash P(\vec{c},\vec{d})$ and $DB \cup \overline{EDB} \vdash \overline{P}(\vec{c},\vec{d})$

i.e. DB is inconsistent with the CWA, contradiction.

<u>Theorem 6.</u>

Suppose DB is Horn, and consistent. Then $DB \cup \overline{EDB}$ is consistent, i.e. DB is consistent with the CWA.

Proof: Suppose, on the contrary, that $DB \cup \overline{EDB}$ is inconsistent. Now a theorem of Henschen and Wos [1974] assures us that any inconsistent set of Horn clauses has a positive unit refutation by binary resolution in which one parent of each resolution operation is a positive unit. We shall assume this result, without proof, for typed resolution*. Then since $DB \cup \overline{EDB}$ is an inconsistent

---

*Because all variables are typed, the usual unification algorithm (Robinson [1965]) must be modified to enforce consistency of types. Resolvents are then formed using typed unification. For details, see (Reiter [1977]).

Horn set, it has such a (typed) positive unit refutation. Since all clauses of $\overline{EDB}$ are negative units, the only occurrence of a negative unit of $\overline{EDB}$ in this refutation can be as one of the parents in the final resolution operation yielding the empty clause. There must be such an occurrence of some $\overline{U} \in \overline{EDB}$, for otherwise $\overline{EDB}$ does not enter into the refutation in which case DB must be inconsistent. Hence, DB $\cup \{\overline{U}\}$ is unsatisfiable, i.e. DB $\vdash$ U . But then $\overline{U}$ cannot be a member of $\overline{EDB}$, contradiction.

Theorem 7.

If $Q = < \vec{x}/\vec{\tau} \mid (E\vec{y}/\vec{\theta})W >$ and DB is Horn and consistent, then $\|Q\|_{CWA}$ when evaluated with respect to DB yields the same set of answers as when evaluated with respect to Δ(DB). In other words, negative clauses in PB have no influence on CWA query evaluation.

Proof: By Theorems 2, 3, and 4 CWA query evaluation is reducible to OWA evaluation of atomic queries whenever DB is consistent. Hence, with no loss in generality, we can take Q to be an atomic query. Suppose then that $Q = < \vec{x}/\vec{\tau} \mid (E\vec{y}/\vec{\theta})P(\vec{x},\vec{y}) >$, where $P(\vec{x},\vec{y})$ is a positive literal. Denote the value of $\|Q\|_{CWA}$ with respect to DB by $\|Q\|^{DB}_{CWA}$. Similarly, $\|Q\|^{\Delta(DB)}_{CWA}$, $\|Q\|^{DB}_{OWA}$, $\|Q\|^{\Delta(DB)}_{OWA}$. We must prove $\|Q\|^{DB}_{CWA} = \|Q\|^{\Delta(DB)}_{CWA}$. Since DB is consistent and Horn, so also is Δ(DB) so by Theorem 6, both DB and Δ(DB) are consistent with the CWA. Hence, by Theorem 5, it is sufficient to prove $\|Q\|^{DB}_{OWA} = \|Q\|^{\Delta(DB)}_{OWA}$. Clearly $\|Q\|^{\Delta(DB)}_{OWA} \subseteq \|Q\|^{DB}_{OWA}$ since $\Delta(DB) \subseteq DB$. We prove $\|Q\|^{DB}_{OWA} \subseteq \|Q\|^{\Delta(DB)}_{OWA}$. To that end, let $\vec{c} \in \|Q\|^{DB}_{OWA}$. Then $DB \vdash (E\vec{y}/\vec{\theta})P(\vec{c},\vec{y})$. Hence, as in the proof of Theorem 6, there is a (typed) positive unit refutation of DB $\cup \{\overline{P}(\vec{c},\vec{y})\}$. Since DB is Horn and consistent, $\overline{P}(\vec{c},\vec{y})$ enters into this refutation, and then only in the final resolution operation which yields the empty clause. Clearly, no negative clause other than $\overline{P}(\vec{c},\vec{y})$ can take part in this refutation i.e. only definite clauses of DB enter into the refutation. Hence we can construct the same refutation from $\Delta(DB) \cup \{\overline{P}(\vec{x},\vec{y})\}$ so that $\Delta(DB) \vdash P(\vec{c},\vec{y})$ i.e. $\vec{c} \in \|Q\|^{\Delta(DB)}_{OWA}$.

Theorem 8.

If DB is definite, then DB is consistent.

Proof: Every inconsistent set of clauses contains at least one negative clause.

REFERENCES

1. Clark, K.L. [1978] Negation as Failure, In *Logic and Data Bases* (H. Gallaire and J. Minker, Eds.), Plenum Press, New York, N.Y., 1978, 293-322.

2. Codd, E.F. [1972] Relational Completeness of Data Base Sub-languages, In *Data Base Systems* (R. Rustin, Ed.), Prentice-Hall, Englewood Cliffs, N.J., 1972, 65-98.

3. Henschen, L. and Wos, L. [1974] Unit Refutations and Horn Sets, *JACM 21*, 4 (October 1974), 590-605.

4. Hewitt, C. [1972] Description and Theoretical Analysis (Using Schemata) of PLANNER: A Language for Proving Theorems and Manipulating Models in a Robot, *AI Memo No. 251*, MIT Project MAC, Cambridge, Mass., April 1972.

5. Nicolas, J.M. and Gallaire, H. [1978] Data Bases: Theory vs. Interpretation, In *Logic and Data Bases* (H. Gallaire and J. Minker, Eds.), Plenum Press, New York, 1978, 33-54.

6. Nicolas, J. M. and Syre, J.C. [1974] Natural Question Answering and Automatic Deduction in the System Syntex, *Proceedings IFIP Congress 1974*, Stockholm, Sweden, August, 1974.

7. Reiter, R. [1977] An Approach to Deductive Question-Answering, *BBN Report No. 3649*, Bolt, Beranek and Newman, Inc., Cambridge, Mass., Sept. 1977.

8. Reiter, R. [1978] Deductive Question-Answering on Relational Data Bases, In *Logic and Data Bases* (H. Gallaire and J. Minker, Eds.), Plenum Press, New York, N.Y., 1978, 149-177.

9. Robinson, J. A. [1965] A Machine Oriented Logic Based on the Resolution Principle, *JACM 12*, (January 1965), 25-41.

10. Roussel, P. [1975] PROLOG: Manuel de Reference et d'Utilisation, Groupe d'Intelligence Artificielle, U.E.R. de Luminy, Universite d'Aix-Marseille, Sept. 1975.

11. van Emden, M. H. [1977] Computation and Deductive Information Retrieval, Dept. of Computer Science, University of Waterloo, Ont., Research Report CS-77-16, May 1977.

12. van Emden, M.H. and Kowalski, R.A. [1976] The Semantics of Predicate Logic as a Programming Language, *JACM 23*, (Oct. 1976), 733-742.

A Deductive Approach to Program Synthesis

ZOHAR MANNA
Stanford University and Weizmann Institute
and
RICHARD WALDINGER
SRI International

Program synthesis is the systematic derivation of a program from a given specification. A deductive approach to program synthesis is presented for the construction of recursive programs. This approach regards program synthesis as a theorem-proving task and relies on a theorem-proving method that combines the features of transformation rules, unification, and mathematical induction within a single framework.

Key Words and Phrases: mathematical induction, program synthesis, program transformation, resolution, theorem proving
CR Categories: 3.64, 4.20, 5.21, 5.24

MOTIVATION

The early work in program synthesis relied strongly on mechanical theorem-proving techniques. The work of Green [5] and Waldinger and Lee [13], for example, depended on resolution-based theorem proving; however, the difficulty of representing the principle of mathematical induction in a resolution framework hampered these systems in the formation of programs with iterative or recursive loops. More recently, program synthesis and theorem proving have tended to go their separate ways. Newer theorem-proving systems are able to perform proofs by mathematical induction (e.g., Boyer and Moore [2]) but are useless for program synthesis because they have sacrificed the ability to prove theorems involving existential quantifiers. Recent work in program synthesis (e.g., Burstall and Darlington [3] and Manna and Waldinger [7]), on the other hand, has abandoned

This research was supported in part by the National Science Foundation under Grants MCS 76-83655 and MCS 78-02591, in part by the Office of Naval Research under Contracts N00014-76-C-0687 and N00014-75-C-0816, in part by the Defense Advanced Research Projects Agency of the Department of Defense under Contract MDA903-76-C-0206, and in part by the United States–Israel Binational Science Foundation.

Authors' addresses: Z. Manna, Department of Computer Science, Stanford University, Stanford, CA 94305; R. Waldinger, Artificial Intelligence Center, SRI International, 333 Ravenswood Ave., Menlo Park, CA 94025.

the theorem-proving approach and has relied instead on the direct application of transformation or rewriting rules to the program's specification; in choosing this path, these systems have renounced the use of such theorem-proving techniques as unification or induction.

In this paper we describe a framework for program synthesis that again relies on a theorem-proving approach. This approach combines techniques of unification, mathematical induction, and transformation rules within a single deductive system. We outline the logical structure of this system without considering the strategic aspects of how deductions are directed. Although no implementation exists, the approach is machine oriented and ultimately intended for implementation in automatic synthesis systems.

In the next section we give examples of specifications accepted by the system. In the succeeding sections we explain the relation between theorem proving and our approach to program synthesis.

SPECIFICATION

The specification of a program allows us to express the purpose of the desired program, without indicating an algorithm by which that purpose is to be achieved. Specifications may contain high-level constructs that are not computable, but are close to our way of thinking. Typically, specifications involve such constructs as the quantifiers *for all* . . . and *for some* . . . , the set constructor $\{x: \ldots\}$, and the descriptor *find z such that* . . . .

For example, to specify a program to compute the integer square root of a nonnegative integer n, we would write

$$\begin{aligned} &sqrt(n) \Leftarrow \textit{find } z \textit{ such that} \\ &\qquad integer(z) \textit{ and } z^2 \le n < (z+1)^2 \\ &\textit{where } integer(n) \textit{ and } 0 \le n. \end{aligned}$$

Here, the *input condition*

$$integer(n) \textit{ and } 0 \le n$$

expresses the class of legal inputs to which the program is expected to apply. The *output condition*

$$integer(z) \textit{ and } z^2 \le n < (z+1)^2$$

describes the relation the output z is intended to satisfy.

To describe a program to sort a list l, we might write

$$\begin{aligned} &sort(l) \Leftarrow \textit{find } z \textit{ such that} \\ &\qquad ordered(z) \textit{ and } perm(l, z) \\ &\textit{where } islist(l). \end{aligned}$$

Here, *ordered*(z) expresses that the elements of the output list z should be in nondecreasing order; *perm*(l, z) expresses that z should be a permutation of the input l; and *islist*(l) expresses that l can be assumed to be a list.

To describe a program to find the last element of a nonempty list l, we might write

$$\begin{aligned} &last(l) \Leftarrow \textit{find } z \textit{ such that} \\ &\qquad \textit{for some } y,\ l = y <> [z] \\ &\textit{where } islist(l) \textit{ and } l \ne [\,]. \end{aligned}$$

Here, $u<>v$ denotes the result of appending the two lists u and v; $[u]$ denotes the list whose sole element is u; and [] denotes the empty list. (Thus, [A B C]<>[D] yields [A B C D]; therefore, by the above specification, *last*([A B C D]) = D.)

In general, we are considering the synthesis of programs whose specifications have the form

$$f(a) \Leftarrow \textit{find } z \textit{ such that } R(a, z)$$
$$\textit{where } P(a).$$

Here, a denotes the input of the desired program and z denotes its output; the input condition $P(a)$ and the output condition $R(a, z)$ may themselves contain quantifiers and set constructors (but not the *find* descriptor).

The above specification describes an applicative program, one which yields an output but produces no side effects. To derive a program from such a specification, we attempt to prove a theorem of the form

for all a,
if P(a)
then for some z, R(a, z).

The proof of this theorem must be constructive, in the sense that it must tell us how to find an output z satisfying the desired output condition. From such a proof, a program to compute z can be extracted.

The above notation can be extended to describe several related programs at once. For example, to specify the programs $div(i, j)$ and $rem(i, j)$ for finding the integer quotient and remainder, respectively, of dividing a nonnegative integer i by a positive integer j, we write

$$(div(i, j), rem(i, j)) \Leftarrow \textit{find } (y, z) \textit{ such that integer}(y) \textit{ and}$$
$$\textit{integer}(z) \textit{ and } i = y \cdot j + z \textit{ and } 0 \le z \textit{ and } z < j$$
$$\textit{where integer}(i) \textit{ and integer}(j) \textit{ and } 0 \le i \textit{ and } 0 < j.$$

BASIC STRUCTURE

The basic structure employed in our approach is the *sequent*, which consists of two lists of sentences, the *assertions* $A_1, A_2, \ldots, A_m$, and the *goals* $G_1, G_2, \ldots, G_n$. With each assertion or goal there may be associated an entry called the *output expression*. This output entry has no bearing on the proof itself, but records the program segment that has been constructed at each stage of the derivation (cf. the "answer literal" in Green [5]). We denote a sequent by a table with three columns: assertions, goals, and outputs. Each row in the sequent has the form

assertions	*goals*	*outputs*
$A_i(a, x)$		$t_i(a, x)$

or

	$G_j(a, x)$	$t_j(a, x)$

The meaning of a sequent is that if all instances of each of the assertions are true, then some instances of at least one of the goals is true; more precisely, the sequent has the same meaning as its *associated sentence*

if for all x, $A_1(a, x)$ *and*
for all x, $A_2(a, x)$ *and*
.
.
.
for all x, $A_m(a, x)$
then for some x, $G_1(a, x)$ *or*
for some x, $G_2(a, x)$ *or*
.
.
.
for some x, $G_n(a, x)$

where a denotes all the constants of the sequent and x denotes all the free variables. (In general, we denote constants or tuples of constants by $a, b, c, \ldots, n$ and variables or tuples of variables by $u, v, w, \ldots, z$.) If some instance of a goal is true (or some instance of an assertion is false), the corresponding instance of its output expression satisfies the given specification. In other words, if some instance $G_j(a, e)$ is true (or some instance $A_i(a, e)$ is false), then the corresponding instance $t_j(a, e)$(or $t_i(a, e)$) is an acceptable output.

Note that (1) an assertion or goal is not required to have an output entry; (2) an assertion and a goal never occupy the same row of the sequent; (3) the variables in each row are "dummies" that we can systematically rename without changing the meaning of the sequent.

The distinction between assertions and goals is artificial and does not increase the logical power of the deductive system. In fact, if we delete a goal from a sequent and add its negation as a new assertion, we obtain an equivalent sequent; similarly, we can delete an assertion from a sequent and add its negation as a new goal without changing the meaning of the sequent. This property is known as *duality*. Nevertheless, the distinction between assertions and goals makes our deductions easier to understand.

If initially we are given the specification

$$f(a) \Leftarrow \textit{find } z \textit{ such that } R(a, z) \quad \textit{where } P(a),$$

we construct the initial sequent

assertions	*goals*	*outputs* $f(a)$
$P(a)$		
	$R(a, z)$	z

In other words, we assume that the input condition $P(a)$ is true, and we want to prove that for some z, the goal $R(a, z)$ is true; if so, z represents the desired output of the program $f(a)$. The output z is a variable, for which we can make substitutions; the input a is a constant. If we prefer, we may remove quantifiers in $P(a)$ and $R(a, z)$ by the usual skolemization procedure (see, e.g., Nilsson [11]).

The input condition $P(a)$ is not the only assertion in the sequent; typically, simple, basic axioms, such as $u = u$, are represented as assertions that are tacitly present in all sequents. Many properties of the subject domain, however, are represented by other means, as we shall see.

The deductive system we describe operates by causing new assertions and goals, and corresponding new output expressions, to be added to the sequent without changing its meaning. The process terminates if the goal *true* (or the assertion *false*) is produced, whose corresponding output expression consists entirely of primitives from the target programming language; this expression is the desired program. In other words, if we develop a row of form

	true	t

or

false		t

where t is a primitive expression, the desired program is of form

$$f(a) \Leftarrow t.$$

Note that this deductive procedure never requires us to establish new sequents or (except for strategic purposes) to delete an existing assertion or goal. In this sense, the approach more resembles resolution than "natural deduction."

Suppose we are required to construct two related programs $f(a)$ and $g(a)$; i.e., we are given the specification

$$(f(a), g(a)) \Leftarrow \textit{find } (y, z) \textit{ such that } R(a, y, z)$$
$$\textit{where } P(a).$$

Then we construct an initial sequent with two output columns

assertions	*goals*	*outputs* $f(a)$	$g(a)$
$P(a)$			
	$R(a, y, z)$	y	z

If we subsequently succeed in developing a terminal row, say of form

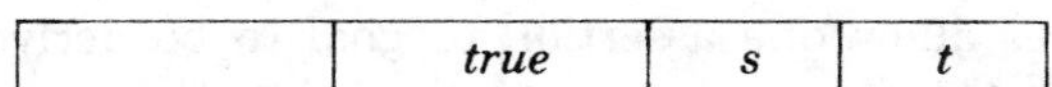

where both s and t are primitive expressions, then the desired programs are

$$f(a) \Leftarrow s$$

and

$$g(a) \Leftarrow t.$$

In the remainder of this paper we outline the deductive rules of our system and their application to program synthesis.

SPLITTING RULES

The splitting rules allow us to decompose an assertion or goal into its logical components. For example, if our sequent contains an assertion of form *F and G*, we can introduce the two assertions F and G into the sequent without changing its meaning. We will call this the *andsplit rule* and express it in the following notation:

assertions	*goals*	*outputs*
F and G		*t*
F		*t*
G		*t*

This means that if rows matching those above the double line are present in the sequent, then the corresponding rows below the double line may be added.

Similarly, we have the *orsplit rule*

assertions	*goals*	*outputs*
	F or G	*t*
	F	*t*
	G	*t*

and the *ifsplit rule*

assertions	*goals*	*outputs*
	if F then G	*t*
F		*t*
	G	*t*

There is no *orsplit rule* or *ifsplit rule* for assertions and no *andsplit rule* for goals. Note that the output entries for the consequents of the splitting rules are exactly the same as the entries for their antecedents.

Although initially only the goal has an output entry, the *ifsplit rule* can introduce an assertion with an output entry. Such assertions are rare in practice, but can arise by the action of such rules.

TRANSFORMATION RULES

Transformation rules allow one assertion or goal to be derived from another. Typically, transformations are expressed as conditional rewriting rules

$$r \Rightarrow s \quad \textit{if } P$$

meaning that in any assertion, goal, or output expression, a subexpression of form r can be replaced by the corresponding expression of form s, provided that the condition P holds. We never write such a rule unless r and s are equal terms or equivalent sentences, whenever condition P holds. For example, the transformation rule

$$u \in v \Rightarrow u = head(v) \textit{ or } u \in tail(v) \quad \textit{if } islist(v) \textit{ and } v \neq []$$

expresses that an element belongs to a nonempty list if it equals the head of the list or belongs to its tail. (Here, *head*(v) denotes the first element of the list v, and *tail*(v) denotes the list of all but the first element.) The rule

$$u \mid 0 \Rightarrow \textit{true} \quad \textit{if } integer(u) \textit{ and } u \neq 0$$

expresses that every nonzero integer divides zero.

If a rule has the vacuous condition *true*, we write it with no condition; for example, the logical rule

$$Q \text{ and true} \Rightarrow Q$$

may be applied to any subexpression that matches its left-hand side.

A transformation rule

$$r \Rightarrow s \quad \text{if } P$$

is not permitted to replace an expression of form s by the corresponding expression of form r when the condition P holds, even though these two expressions have the same values. For that purpose, we would require a second rule

$$s \Rightarrow r \quad \text{if } P.$$

For example, we might include the rule

$$x + 0 \Rightarrow x \quad \text{if } number(x)$$

but not the rule

$$x \Rightarrow x + 0 \quad \text{if } number(x).$$

Assertions and goals are affected differently by transformation rules. Suppose

$$r \Rightarrow s \quad \text{if } P$$

is a transformation rule and F is an assertion containing a subexpression r' which is not within the scope of any quantifier. Suppose also that there exists a *unifier* for r and r', i.e., a substitution θ such that $r\theta$ and $r'\theta$ are identical. Here, $r\theta$ denotes the result of applying the substitution θ to the expression r. We can assume that θ is a "most general" unifier (in the sense of Robinson [12]) of r and r'. We rename the variables of F, if necessary, to ensure that it has no variables in common with the transformation rule. By the rule, we can conclude that if $P\theta$ holds, then $r\theta$ and $s\theta$ are equal terms or equivalent sentences. Therefore, we can add the assertion

$$\text{if } P\theta \text{ then } F\theta[r\theta \leftarrow s\theta]$$

to our sequent. Here, the notation $F\theta[r\theta \leftarrow s\theta]$ indicates that every occurrence of $r\theta$ in $F\theta$ is to be replaced by $s\theta$.

For example, suppose we have the assertion

$$a \in l \text{ and } a \neq 0$$

and we apply the transformation rule

$$u \in v \Rightarrow u = head(v) \text{ or } u \in tail(v) \quad \text{if } islist(v) \text{ and } v \neq [],$$

taking r' to be $a \in l$ and θ to be the substitution $[u \leftarrow a;\ v \leftarrow l]$; then we obtain the new assertion

$$\begin{aligned}&\text{if } islist(l) \text{ and } l \neq [] \\ &\text{then } (a = head(l) \text{ or } a \in tail(l)) \text{ and } a \neq 0.\end{aligned}$$

Note that a and l are constants, while u and v are variables, and indeed, the substitution was made for the variables of the rule but not for the constants of the assertion.

In general, if the given assertion F has an associated output entry t, the new output entry is formed by applying the substitution θ to t. For, suppose some instance of the new assertion "*if* $P\theta$ *then* $F\theta[r\theta \leftarrow s\theta]$" is false; then the corresponding instance of $P\theta$ is true, and the corresponding instance of $F\theta[r\theta \leftarrow s\theta]$ is false. Then, by the transformation rule, the instances of $r\theta$ and $s\theta$ are equal; hence the corresponding instance of $F\theta$ is false. We know that if any instance of F is false, the corresponding instance of t satisfies the given specification. Hence, because some instance of $F\theta$ is false, the corresponding instance of $t\theta$ is the desired output.

In our deduction rule notation, we write

assertions	*goals*	*outputs*
F		t
if $P\theta$ *then* $F\theta[r\theta \leftarrow s\theta]$		$t\theta$

The corresponding dual deduction rule for goals is

assertions	*goals*	*outputs*
	F	t
	$P\theta$ *and* $F\theta[r\theta \leftarrow s\theta]$	$t\theta$

For example, suppose we have the goal

	$a \mid z$ *and* $b \mid z$	$z + 1$

and we apply the transformation rule

$$u \mid 0 \Rightarrow \textit{true} \quad \textit{if integer}(u) \textit{ and } u \neq 0,$$

taking r' to be $a \mid z$ and θ to be the substitution $[z \leftarrow 0;\ u \leftarrow a]$. Then we obtain the goal

	(*integer*(a) *and* $a \neq 0$) *and* (*true and* $b \mid 0$)	$0 + 1$

which can be further transformed to

	integer(a) *and* $a \neq 0$ *and* $b \mid 0$	1

Note that applying the transformation rule caused a substitution to be made for the occurrences of the variable z in the goal and the output entry.

Transformation rules can also be applied to output entries in an analogous manner.

Transformation rules need not be simple rewriting rules; they may represent arbitrary procedures. For example, r could be an equation $f(x) = a$, s could be its solution $x = e$, and P could be the condition under which that solution applies. Another example: the skolemization procedure for removing quantifiers can be represented as a transformation rule. In fact, decision methods for particular subtheories may also be represented as transformation rules (see, e.g., Bledsoe [1] or Nelson and Oppen [9]).

Transformation rules play the role of the "antecedent theorems" and "consequent theorems" of PLANNER (Hewitt [6]). For example, a consequent theorem that we might write as

$$\textit{to prove } f(u) = f(v)$$
$$\textit{prove } u = v$$

can be represented by the transformation rule

$$f(u) = f(v) \Rightarrow \textit{true} \quad \textit{if } u = v.$$

This rule will have the desired effect of reducing the goal $f(a) = f(b)$ to the simpler subgoal $a = b$, and (like the consequent theorem) will not have the pernicious side effect of deriving from the simple assertion $a = b$ the more complex assertion $f(a) = f(b)$. The axiomatic representation of the same fact would have both results. (Incidentally, the transformation rule has the beneficial effect, not shared by the consequent theorem, of deriving from the complex assertion $\textit{not}(f(a) = f(b))$ the simpler assertion $\textit{not}(a = b)$.)

RESOLUTION

The original resolution principle (Robinson [12]) required that sentences be put into conjunctive normal form. As a result, the set of clauses sometimes exploded to an unmanageable size and the proofs lost their intuitive content. The version of resolution we employ does not require the sentences to be in conjunctive normal form.

Assume our sequent contains two assertions F and G, containing subsentences P_1 and P_2, respectively, that are not within the scope of any quantifier. For the time being, let us ignore the output expressions corresponding to these assertions. Suppose there exists a unifier for P_1 and P_2, i.e., a substitution θ such that $P_1\theta$ and $P_2\theta$ are identical. We can take θ to be the most general unifier. The *AA-resolution rule* allows us to deduce the new assertion

$$F\theta[P_1\theta \leftarrow \textit{true}] \textit{ or } G\theta[P_2\theta \leftarrow \textit{false}]$$

and add it to the sequent. Recall that the notation $F\theta[P_1\theta \leftarrow \textit{true}]$ indicates that every instance of the subsentence $P_1\theta$ in $F\theta$ is to be replaced by *true*. (Of course, we may need to do the usual renaming to ensure that F and G have no variables in common.) We will call θ the *unifying substitution* and $P_1\theta(=P_2\theta)$ the *eliminated subexpression*; the deduced assertion is called the *resolvent*. Note that the rule is symmetric, so the roles of F and G may be reversed.

For example, suppose our sequent contains the assertions

$$\textit{if } (P(x) \textit{ and } Q(b)) \textit{ then } R(x)$$

and

$$P(a) \textit{ and } Q(y).$$

The two subsentences "$P(x)$ *and* $Q(b)$" and "$P(a)$ *and* $Q(y)$" can be unified by the substitution

$$\theta = [x \leftarrow a;\ y \leftarrow b].$$

Therefore, the AA-resolution rule allows us to eliminate the subexpression "*P(a) and Q(b)*" and derive the conclusion

$$(\textit{if true then } R(a)) \textit{ or false},$$

which reduces to

$$R(a)$$

by application of the appropriate transformation rules.

The conventional resolution rule may be regarded as a special case of the above AA-resolution rule. The conventional rule allows us to derive from the two assertions

$$(\textit{not } P_1) \textit{ or } Q$$

and

$$P_2 \textit{ or } R$$

the new assertion

$$Q\theta \textit{ or } R\theta,$$

where θ is a most general unifier of P_1 and P_2. From the same two assertions we can use our AA-resolution rule to derive

$$(((\textit{not } P_1 \textit{ or } Q)\theta)[P_1\theta \leftarrow \textit{true}] \textit{ or } (((P_2 \textit{ or } R)\theta)[P_2\theta \leftarrow \textit{false}]$$

i.e.,

$$((\textit{not true}) \textit{ or } Q\theta) \textit{ or } (\textit{false or } R\theta),$$

which reduces to the same conclusion

$$Q\theta \textit{ or } R\theta$$

as the original resolution rule.

The justification for the AA-resolution rule is straightforward: Because F holds, if $P_1\theta$ is true, then $F\theta[P_1\theta \leftarrow \textit{true}]$ holds; on the other hand, because G holds, if $P_1\theta (= P_2\theta)$ is false, $G\theta[P_2\theta \leftarrow \textit{false}]$ holds. In either case, the disjunction

$$F\theta[P_1\theta \leftarrow \textit{true}] \textit{ or } G\theta[P_2\theta \leftarrow \textit{false}]$$

holds.

A "nonclausal" resolution rule similar to ours has been developed by Murray [8]. Other such rules have been proposed by Wilkins [14] and Nilsson [10].

THE RESOLUTION RULES

We have defined the AA-resolution rule to derive conclusions from assertions.

The *AA-resolution rule*

assertions	*goals*
F G	
$F\theta[P_1\theta \leftarrow \textit{true}] \textit{ or } G\theta[P_2\theta \leftarrow \textit{false}]$	

where $P_1\theta = P_2\theta$, and θ is most general.

By duality, we can regard goals as negated assertions; consequently, the following three rules are corollaries of the AA-resolution rule.

The *GG-resolution rule*

assertions	*goals*
	F G
	$F\theta[P_1\theta \leftarrow true]$ *and* $G\theta[P_2\theta \leftarrow false]$

The *GA-resolution rule*

assertions	*goals*
	F
G	
	$F\theta[P_1\theta \leftarrow true]$ *and* *not* $(G\theta[P_2\theta \leftarrow false])$

The *AG-resolution rule*

assertions	*goals*
F	
	G
	not$(F\theta[P_1\theta \leftarrow true])$ *and* $G\theta[P_2\theta \leftarrow false]$

where P_1, P_2, and θ satisfy the same condition as for the AA-resolution rule.

Up to now, we have ignored the output expressions of the assertions and goals. However, if at least one of the sentences to which a resolution rule is applied has a corresponding output expression, the resolvent will also have an output expression. If only one of the sentences has an output expression, say t, then the resolvent will have the output expression $t\theta$. On the other hand, if the two sentences F and G have output expressions t_1 and t_2, respectively, the resolvent will have the output expression

$$\textit{if } P_1\theta \textit{ then } t_1\theta \textit{ else } t_2\theta.$$

(Of course, if $t_1\theta$ and $t_2\theta$ are identical, no conditional expression need be formed; the output expression is simply $t_1\theta$.)

The justification for constructing this conditional as an output expression is as follows. We consider only the GG case: Suppose that the goal

$$F\theta[P_1\theta \leftarrow \textit{true}] \textit{ and } G\theta[P_2\theta \leftarrow \textit{false}]$$

has been obtained by GG-resolution from two goals F and G. We would like to show that if the goal is true, the conditional output expression satisfies the desired specification. We assume that the resolvent is true; therefore both $F\theta[P_1\theta \leftarrow true]$ and $G\theta[P_2\theta \leftarrow false]$ are true. In the case that $P_1\theta$ is true, we have that $F\theta$ is also true. Consequently, the corresponding instance $t_1\theta$ of the output expression t_1 satisfies the specification of the desired program. In the other case, in which $P_1\theta$ is false, $P_2\theta$ is false, and the same reasoning allows us to conclude that $t_2\theta$ satisfies the specification of the desired program. In either case we can conclude that the conditional

$$if\ P_1\theta\ then\ t_1\theta\ else\ t_2\theta$$

satisfies the desired specification. By duality, the same output expression can be derived for the AA-resolution, GA-resolution, and AG-resolution.

For example, let $u \cdot v$ denote the operation of inserting u before the first element of the list v, and suppose we have the goal

assertions	*goals*	*outputs* $f(a, b)$
	$head(z) = a$ *and* $tail(z) = b$	z

and we have the assertion

$head(u \cdot v) = u$		

with no output expression; then by GA-resolution, applying the substitution

$$\theta = [u \leftarrow a;\ z \leftarrow a \cdot v]$$

and eliminating the subsentence

$$head(a \cdot v) = a,$$

we obtain the new goal

	(*true and* $tail(a \cdot v) = b$) *and* (*not false*)	$a \cdot v$

which can be reduced to

	$tail(a \cdot v) = b$	$a \cdot v$

by application of the appropriate transformation rules. Note that we have applied the substitution$[u \leftarrow a;\ z \leftarrow a \cdot v]$ to the original output expression z, obtaining the new output expression $a \cdot v$. Therefore, if we can find v such that $tail(a \cdot v) = b$, the corresponding instance of $a \cdot v$ will satisfy the desired specification.

Another example: Suppose we have derived the two goals

assertions	*goals*	*outputs* $max(l)$
	$max(tail(l)) \geq head(l)$ *and* $tail(l) \neq []$	$max(tail(l))$
	$not(max(tail(l)) \geq head(l))$ *and* $tail(l) \neq []$	$head(l)$

Then by GG-resolution, eliminating the subsentence $max(tail(l)) \geq head(l)$, we can derive the new goal

	(*true and* $tail(l) \neq []$) *and* (*not false*) *and* $tail(l) \neq []$)	*if* $max(tail(l)) \geq head(l)$ *then* $max(tail(l))$ *else* $head(l)$

which can be reduced to

	$tail(l) \neq []$	*if* $max(tail(l)) \geq head(l)$ *then* $max(tail(l))$ *else* $head(l)$

THE POLARITY STRATEGY

Not all applications of the resolution rules will produce valuable conclusions. For example, suppose we are given the goal

assertions	*goals*	*outputs*
	$P(c, x)$ *and* $Q(x, a)$	

and the assertion

if $P(y, d)$ *then* $Q(b, y)$		

Then if we apply GA-resolution, eliminating $Q(b, a)$, we can obtain the resolvent

$(P(c, b)$ *and true*) *and not*(*if* $P(a, d)$ *then false*),

which reduces to the goal

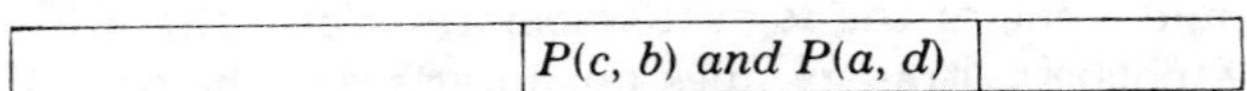

	$P(c, b)$ *and* $P(a, d)$	

However, we can also apply GA-resolution and eliminate $P(c, d)$, yielding the resolvent

(*true and* $Q(d, a)$) *and not*(*if false then* $Q(b, c)$),

which reduces to the trivial goal

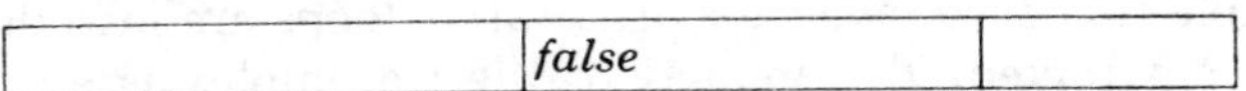

	false	

Finally, we can also apply AG-resolution to the same assertion and goal in two different ways, eliminating $P(c, d)$ and eliminating $Q(b, a)$; both of these applications lead to the same trivial goal *false*.

A *polarity strategy* adapted from Murray [8] restricts the resolution rules to prevent many such fruitless applications. We first assign a *polarity* (either positive or negative) to every subsentence of a given sequent as follows:

(1) each goal is positive;
(2) each assertion is negative;
(3) if a subsentence S has form "*not* α," then its component α has polarity opposite to S;
(4) if a subsentence S has form "α *and* β," "α *or* β," "*for all* x, α," or "*for some* x, β," then its components α and β have the same polarity as S;
(5) if a subsentence S has form "*if* α *then* β," then β has the same polarity as S, but α has the opposite polarity.

For example, the above goal and assertion are annotated with the polarity of each subsentence, as follows:

assertions	*goals*	*outputs*
$(if\ P(y, d)^{+}\ then\ Q(b, y)^{-})^{-}$		
	$(P(c, x)^{+}\ and\ Q(x, a)^{+})^{+}$	

The four resolution rules we have presented replace certain subsentences by *true*, and others by *false*. The polarity strategy, then, permits a subsentence to be replaced by *true* only if it has at least one positive occurrence, and by *false* only if it has at least one negative occurrence. For example, we are permitted to apply GA-resolution to the above goal and assertion, eliminating $Q(b, a)$ because $Q(x, a)$, which is replaced by *true*, occurs positively in the goal, and $Q(b, y)$, which is replaced by *false*, occurs negatively in the assertion. On the other hand, we are not permitted to apply GA-resolution to eliminate $P(c, d)$, because $P(y, d)$, which is replaced by *false*, only occurs positively in the assertion. Similarly, we are not permitted to apply AG-resolution between this assertion and goal, whether we eliminate $P(c, d)$ or $Q(b, a)$. Indeed, the only application of resolution permitted by the polarity strategy is the one that led to a nontrivial conclusion.

The deductive system we have presented so far, including the splitting rules, the resolution rules, and an appropriate set of logical transformation rules, has been proved by Murray to constitute a complete system for first-order logic, in the sense that a derivation exists for every valid sentence. (Actually, only the resolution rules and some of the logical transformation rules are strictly necessary.) The above polarity strategy does not interfere with the completeness of the system.

MATHEMATICAL INDUCTION AND THE FORMATION OF RECURSIVE CALLS

Mathematical induction is of special importance for deductive systems intended for program synthesis because it is only by the application of some form of the induction principle that recursive calls or iterative loops are introduced into the program being constructed. The induction rule we employ is a version of the principle of mathematical induction over a well-founded set, known in the computer science literature as "structural induction."

We may describe this principle as follows: In attempting to prove that a sentence of form $F(a)$ holds for an arbitrary element a of some well-founded set, we may assume inductively that the sentence holds for all u that are strictly less than a in the well-founded ordering $\prec_w$. Thus, in trying to prove $F(a)$, the well-founded induction principle allows us to assume the induction hypothesis

$$for\ all\ u,\ if\ u \prec_w a\ then\ F(u).$$

In the case that the well-founded set is the nonnegative integers under the usual $<$ ordering, well-founded induction reduces to the familiar complete induction principle: To prove that $F(n)$ holds for an arbitrary nonnegative integer n, we may assume inductively that the sentence $F(u)$ holds for all nonnegative integers u such that $u < n$.

In our inference system, the principle of well-founded induction is represented as a deduction rule (rather than, say, an axiom schema). We present only a special case of this rule here.

Suppose we are constructing a program whose specification is of form

$$f(a) \Leftarrow \textit{find } z \textit{ such that } R(a, z)$$
$$\textit{where } P(a).$$

Our initial sequent is thus

assertions	*goals*	*outputs* $f(a)$
$P(a)$		
	$R(a, z)$	z

Then we can always add to our sequent a new assertion, the induction hypothesis

if $u <_w a$ *then if* $P(u)$ *then* $R(u, f(u))$		

Here, f denotes the program we are trying to construct. The well-founded set and the particular well-founded $<_w$ to be employed in the proof have not yet been determined. If the induction hypothesis is used more than once in the proof, it always refers to the same well-founded ordering $<_w$.

Let us paraphrase: We are attempting to construct a program f such that for an arbitrary input a satisfying the input condition $P(a)$, the output $f(a)$ will satisfy the output condition $R(a, f(a))$. By the well-founded induction principle, we can assume inductively that for every u less than a (in some well-founded ordering) such that the input condition $P(u)$ holds, the output $f(u)$ will satisfy the same output condition $R(u, f(u))$. By employing the induction hypothesis in the proof, recursive calls to f can be introduced into the output expression for $f(a)$.

As we shall see in a later section, we can introduce an induction hypothesis corresponding to any subset of the assertions or goals in our sequent, not just the initial assertion and goal; most of these induction hypotheses are not relevant to the final proof, and the proliferation of new assertions obstructs our efforts to find a proof. Therefore, we employ the following *recurrence strategy* for determining when to introduce an induction hypothesis.

Let us restrict our attention to the case where the induction hypothesis is formed from the initial sequent. Suppose that at some point in the derivation a goal is developed of form

	$R(s, z')$	$t(z')$

where s is an arbitrary term. In other words, the new goal is a precise instance of the initial goal $R(a, z)$ obtained by replacing a by s. This recurrence motivates us to add the induction hypothesis

if $u <_w a$ *then if* $P(u)$ *then* $R(u, f(u))$		

The rationale for introducing the induction hypothesis at this point is that now we can perform GA-resolution between the newly developed goal $R(s, z')$ and the induction hypothesis. The resulting goal is then

	true and *not if* $s <_w a$ *then if* $P(s)$ *then false*	$t(f(s))$

This simplifies (by the application of logical transformation rules) to

	$s <_w a$ *and* $P(s)$	$t(f(s))$

Note that a recursive call $f(s)$ has been introduced into the output expression for $f(a)$. By proving the expression $s <_w a$, we ensure that this recursive call will terminate; by proving the expression $P(s)$, we guarantee that the argument s of the recursive call will satisfy the input condition of the program f.

The particular well-founded ordering $<_w$ to be employed by the proof has not yet been determined. We assume the existence of transformation rules of form

$$u <_{w_1} v \Rightarrow true \quad if\ Q(u, v)$$

capable of choosing or combining well-founded orderings applicable to the particular theories under consideration (e.g., numbers, lists, and sets).

Let us look at an example. Suppose we are constructing two programs $div(i, j)$ and $rem(i, j)$ to compute the quotient and remainder, respectively, of dividing a nonnegative integer i by a positive integer j; the specification may be expressed as

$$(div(i, j), rem(i, j)) \Leftarrow find\ (y, z)\ such\ that$$
$$i = y \cdot j + z\ and\ 0 \leq z\ and\ z < j$$
$$where\ 0 \leq i\ and\ 0 < j.$$

(Note that, for simplicity, we have omitted type requirements such as *integer*(i).) Our initial sequent is then

assertions	*goals*	*outputs* $div(i, j)$	$rem(i, j)$
$0 \leq i$ *and* $0 < j$			
	$i = y \cdot j + z$ *and* $0 \leq z$ *and* $z < j$	y	z

Here, the inputs i and j are constants, for which we can make no substitution; y and the output z are variables.

Assume that during the course of the derivation we develop the goal

	$i - j = y_1 \cdot j + z$ *and* $0 \leq z$ *and* $z < j$	$y_1 + 1$	z

This goal is a precise instance of the initial goal

$$i = y \cdot j + z\ and\ 0 \leq z\ and\ z < j$$

obtained by replacing i by $i-j$. Therefore, we add as a new assertion the induction hypothesis.

if $(u_1, u_2) <_w (i, j)$ *then if* $0 \leq u_1$ *and* $0 < u_2$ *then* $u_1 = div(u_1, u_2) \cdot u_2 + rem(u_1, u_2)$ *and* $0 \leq rem(u_1, u_2)$ *and* $rem(u_1, u_2) < u_2$			

Here, $<_w$ is an arbitrary well-founded ordering, defined on pairs because the desired program f has a pair of inputs.

We can now apply GA-resolution between the goal

	$i-j = y_1 \cdot j + z$ *and* $0 \leq z$ *and* $z < j$	y_1+1	z

and the induction hypothesis; the unifying substitution θ is

$$[u_1 \leftarrow i-j;\ u_2 \leftarrow j;\ y_1 \leftarrow div(i-j, j);\ z \leftarrow rem(i-j, j)].$$

The new goal is

	true and *not* (*if* $(i-j, j) <_w (i, j)$ *then if* $0 \leq i-j$ *and* $0 < j$ *then false*)	$div(i-j, j)+1$	$rem(i-j, j)$

which reduces to

	$(i-j, j) <_w (i, j)$ *and* $0 \leq i-j$ *and* $0 < j$	$div(i-j, j)+1$	$rem(i-j, j)$

Note that the recursive calls $div(i-j, j)$ and $rem(i-j, j)$ have been introduced into the output entry.

The particular well-founded ordering $<_w$ to be employed in the proof has not yet been determined. It can be chosen to be the $<$ ordering on the first component of the pairs, by application of the transformation rule

$$(u_1, u_2) <_{N1} (v_1, v_2) \Rightarrow true \quad if\ u_1 < v_1\ and\ 0 \leq u_1\ and\ 0 \leq v_1.$$

A new goal

	$i-j < i$ *and* $0 \leq i-j$ *and* $0 \leq i$ *and true* *and* $0 \leq i-j$ *and* $0 < j$	$div(i-j, j)+1$	$rem(i-j, j)$

is produced; this goal ultimately reduces to

	$j \leq i$	$div(i-j, j)+1$	$rem(i-j, j)$

In other words, in the case that $j \leq i$, the outputs $div(i-j, j)+1$ and $rem(i-j, j)$ satisfy the desired program's specification. In the next section, we give the full derivation of these programs.

In our presentation of the induction rule, several limitations were imposed for simplicity but are not actually essential:

(1) In the example we considered, the only skolem functions in the initial

sequent are the constants corresponding to the program's inputs, and the only variables are those corresponding to the program's outputs; the sequent was of form

assertions	*goals*	*outputs* $f(a)$
$P(a)$		
	$R(a, z)$	z

In forming the induction hypothesis, the skolem constant a is replaced by a variable u and the variable z is replaced by the term $f(u)$; the induction hypothesis was of form

if $u \prec_u a$ *then if* $P(u)$ *then* $R(u, f(u))$		

However, if there are other skolem functions in the initial sequent, they too must be replaced by variables in the induction hypothesis; if there are other variables in the initial sequent, they must be replaced by new skolem functions. For example, suppose the initial sequent is of form

$f(a) \Leftarrow$ *find* z *such that*
for all x_1,
for some x_2,
$R(a, z, x_1, x_2)$
where $P(a)$.

Then the initial sequent is of form

assertions	*goals*	*outputs* $f(a)$
$P(a)$		
	$R(a, z, g_1(z), x_2)$	z

where $g_1(z)$ is the skolem function corresponding to x_1. The induction hypothesis is then of form

if $u \prec_w a$ *then if* $P(u)$ *then* $R(u, f(u), v, g_2(u, v))$		

Here, the skolem function $g_1(z)$ has been replaced by the variable v, and the variable x_2 has been replaced by a new skolem function $g_2(u, v)$.

(2) One limitation to the recurrence strategy was that the induction hypothesis was introduced only when an entire goal is an instance of the initial goal. In fact, the strategy can be extended so that the hypothesis is introduced when some subsentence of a goal is an instance of some subsentence of the initial goal, because the resolution rule can then be applied between the goal and the induction hypothesis. This extension is straightforward.

(3) A final observation: The induction hypothesis was always formed directly from the initial sequent; thus, the theorem itself was proved by induction. In later sections we extend the rule so that induction can be applied to lemmas that are stronger or more general than the theorem itself. This extension also accounts for the formation of auxiliary procedures in the program being constructed.

Some early efforts toward incorporating mathematical induction in a resolution framework were made by Darlington [4]. His system treated the induction principle as a second-order axiom schema rather than as a deduction rule; it had a limited ability to perform second-order unifications.

A COMPLETE EXAMPLE: FINDING THE QUOTIENT OF TWO INTEGERS

In this section, we present a complete example that exploits most of the features of the deductive synthesis approach. Our task is to construct programs *div*(i, j) and *rem*(i, j) for finding the integer quotient of dividing a nonnegative integer i by a positive integer j. Portions of this synthesis have been used to illustrate the induction principle in the previous section.

Our specification is expressed as

$$(\mathit{div}(i,j), \mathit{rem}(i,j)) \Leftarrow \mathit{find}\ (y, z)\ \mathit{such\ that}\ i = y \cdot j + z\ \mathit{and}\ 0 \leq z\ \mathit{and}\ z < j$$
$$\mathit{where}\ 0 \leq i\ \mathit{and}\ 0 < j.$$

(For simplicity, we again omit type conditions, such as *integer*(i), from this discussion.) Our initial sequent is therefore

assertions	*goals*	*outputs* *div*(i,j)	*rem*(i,j)
1. $0 \leq i$ *and* $0 < j$			
	2. $i = y \cdot j + z$ *and* $0 \leq z$ *and* $z < j$	y	z

(Note that we are enumerating the assertions and goals.)

In presenting the derivation we sometimes apply simple logical and algebraic transformation rules without mentioning them explicitly. We assume that our background knowledge includes the two assertions

3. $u = u$			
4. $u \leq v$ *or* $v < u$			

Applying the *andsplit rule* to assertion 1 yields the new assertions

5. $0 \leq i$			
6. $0 < j$			

Assume we have the following transformation rules that define integer multiplication:

$$0 \cdot v \Rightarrow 0$$

$$(u + 1) \cdot v \Rightarrow u \cdot v + v.$$

Applying the first of these rules to the subexpression $y \cdot j$ in goal 2 yields

	7. $i = 0 + z$ *and* $0 \leq z$ *and* $z < j$	0	z

The unifying substitution in deriving goal 7 is

$$\theta = [y \leftarrow 0;\ v \leftarrow j];$$

applying this substitution to the output entry y produced the new output 0.

Applying the numerical transformation rule

$$0 + v \Rightarrow v$$

yields

	8. $i = z$ *and* $0 \leq z$ *and* $z < j$	0	z

The GA-resolution rule can now be applied between goal 8 and the equality assertion 3, $u = u$. The unifying substitution is

$$\theta = [u \leftarrow i;\ z \leftarrow i]$$

and the eliminated subexpression is $i = i$; we obtain

	9. $0 \leq i$ *and* $i < j$	0	i

By applying GA-resolution again, against assertion 5, $0 \leq i$, we obtain

	10. $i < j$	0	i

In other words, we have found that in the case that $i < j$, the output 0 will satisfy the specification for the quotient program and the output i will satisfy the specification for the remainder program.

Let us return our attention to the initial goal 2,

$$i = y \cdot j + z \text{ and } 0 \leq z \text{ and } z < j.$$

Recall that we have a second transformation rule

$$(u + 1) \cdot v \Rightarrow u \cdot v + v$$

for the multiplication function. Applying this rule to goal 2 yields

	11. $i = y_1 \cdot j + j + z$ *and* $0 \leq z$ *and* $z < j$	$y_1 + 1$	z

where y_1 is a new variable. Here, the unifying substitution is

$$\theta = [y \leftarrow y_1{+}1;\ u \leftarrow y_1;\ v \leftarrow j];$$

applying this substitution to the output entry y produced the new output $y_1{+}1$ in the *div* program.

The transformation rule

$$u = v + w \Rightarrow u - v = w$$

applied to goal 11 yields

	12. $i-j = y_1 \cdot j + z$ *and* $0 \le z$ *and* $z < j$	$y_1 + 1$	z

Goal 12 is a precise instance of the initial goal 2,

$$i = y \cdot j + z \textit{ and } 0 \le z \textit{ and } z < j,$$

obtained by replacing the input i by $i-j$. (Again, the replacement of the dummy variable y by y_1 is not significant.) Therefore, the following induction hypothesis is formed:

13. *if* $(u_1, u_2) \prec_u (i, j)$ *then if* $0 \le u_1$ *and* $0 < u_2$ *then* $u_1 = div(u_1, u_2) \cdot u_2 + rem(u_1, u_2)$ *and* $0 \le rem(u_1, u_2)$ *and* $rem(u_1, u_2) < u_2$			

Here, $\prec_u$ is an arbitrary well-founded ordering.

By applying GA-resolution between goal 12 and the induction hypothesis, we obtain the goal

	14. *true and not* (*if* $(i-j, j) \prec_u (i, j)$ *then if* $0 \le i-j$ *and* $0 < j$ *then false*)	$div(i-j, j) + 1$	$rem(i-j, j)$

Here, the unifying substitution is

$$\theta = [u_1 \leftarrow i-j;\ u_2 \leftarrow j;\ y_1 \leftarrow div(i-j, j);\ z \leftarrow rem(i-j, j)]$$

and the eliminated subexpression is

$$i-j = div(i-j, j) \cdot j + rem(i-j, j) \textit{ and } 0 \le rem(i-j, j) \textit{ and } rem(i-j, j) < j.$$

Note that the substitution to the variable y_1 has caused the output entry $y_1 + 1$ to be changed to $div(i-j, j) + 1$ and the output entry z to be replaced by $rem(i-j, j)$. The use of the induction hypothesis has introduced the recursive calls $div(i-j, j)$ and $rem(i-j, j)$ into the output.

Goal 14 reduces to

	15. $(i-j, j) \prec_u (i, j)$ *and* $0 \le i-j$ *and* $0 < j$	$div(i-j, j) + 1$	$rem(i-j, j)$

The particular ordering $\prec_u$ has not yet been determined; however, it is chosen to be the $<$ ordering on the first component of the pairs, by application of the transformation rule

$$(u_1, u_2) \prec_{N1} (v_1, v_2) \Rightarrow \textit{true} \quad \textit{if } u_1 < v_1 \textit{ and } 0 \le u_1 \textit{ and } 0 \le v_1.$$

A new goal is produced:

	16. $i-j < i$ *and* $0 \le i-j$ *and* $0 \le i$ *and* $0 \le i-j$ *and* $0 < j$	$div(i-j, j) + 1$	$rem(i-j, j)$

Note that the conditions of the transformation rule caused new conjuncts to be added to the goal.

By application of algebraic and logical transformation rules, and GA-resolution with the assertion 5, $0 \leq i$, and assertion 6, $0 < j$, goal 16 is reduced to

	17. $j \leq i$	$div(i-j, j) + 1$	$rem(i-j, j)$

In other words, we have learned that in the case that $j \leq i$, the outputs $div(i-j, j) + 1$ and $rem(i-j, j)$ satisfy the specification of the *div* program. On the other hand, in deriving goal 10 we learned that in the case that $i < j$, 0 and i are satisfactory outputs. Assuming we have the assertion 4

$$u \leq v \text{ or } v < u,$$

we can obtain the goal

	18. $not(i < j)$	$div(i-j, j) + 1$	$rem(i-j, j)$

by GA-resolution.

The final goal

	19. *true*	*if* $i < j$ *then* 0 *else* $div(i-j, j) + 1$	*if* $i < j$ *then* i *else* $rem(i-j, j)$

can then be obtained by GG-resolution between goals 10 and 18. The conditional expressions have been formed because both goals have a corresponding output entry. Because we have developed the goal *true* and a corresponding primitive output entry, the derivation is complete. The final programs

$$div(i, j) \Leftarrow \text{if } i < j \text{ then } 0 \text{ else } div(i-j, j) + 1$$

and

$$rem(i, j) \Leftarrow \text{if } i < j \text{ then } i \text{ else } rem(i-j, j)$$

are obtained directly from the final output entries.

THE FORMATION OF AUXILIARY PROCEDURES

We have remarked that mathematical induction need not be restricted to apply only to the initial assertion and goal but may legitimately be applied to any subset of the assertions and goals in the sequent. In fact, when induction is applied in this more general setting, *auxiliary procedures* may be introduced into the program being constructed. For example, in constructing a program *sort* to order a list, we might introduce an auxiliary procedure *merge* to insert a number in its place in an ordered list of numbers. In this section we develop the extended form of the induction principle that accounts for the formation of auxiliary procedures. We begin with a description of the recurrence strategy that applies to this extended induction.

Assume that we are in the process of constructing a program $f(a)$ whose specification is of form

$$f(a) \Leftarrow \textit{find } z \textit{ such that } R(a, z)$$
$$\textit{where } P(a).$$

Then our initial sequent is of form

assertions	*goals*	*outputs* $f(a)$
$P(a)$		
	$R(a, z)$	z

Let goal A be any goal obtained during the derivation of $f(a)$, and assume that goal A is of form

A:		$R'(a, z')$	$t'(z')$

Suppose that by applying deduction rules successively to goal A and to the assertions $P'_1(a), P'_2(a), \ldots, P'_k(a)$ of the sequent, we obtain a goal B of form

B:		$R'(s, z'')$	$t''(z'')$

where s is an arbitrary term. (For simplicity, we assume that no goals are required other than those derived from goal A, and that none of the k required assertions have associated output entries.)

In summation, we have developed a new goal (goal B) that is a precise instance of the earlier goal (goal A), obtained by replacing the input a by the term s. This recurrence motivates us to define an auxiliary procedure *fnew*(a) whose output condition is goal A; we then hope to achieve goal B by a recursive call to the new procedure.

Let us be more precise. The specification for *fnew*(a') is

$$\textit{fnew}(a') \Leftarrow \textit{find } z' \textit{ such that } R'(a', z')$$
$$\textit{where } P'(a').$$

Here, the input condition $P'(a')$ is $P'_1(a')$ *and* $P'_2(a')$ *and* $\cdots$ *and* $P'_k(a')$. If we succeed in constructing a program that meets this specification, we can employ it as an auxiliary procedure of the main program $f(a)$.

Consequently, at this point we add a new output column for *fnew*(a') to the sequent, and we introduce the new rows

	assertions	*goals*	*outputs* $f(a)$	*fnew*(a')
	$P'(a')$			
A′:		$R'(a', z')$	$t'(\textit{fnew}(a))$	z'

Note that in these rows we have replaced the input constant a by a new constant a'. This step is logically necessary; adding the induction hypothesis without renaming the constant can lead to false results. The second row (goal A′) indicates that if we succeed in constructing *fnew*(a') to satisfy the above specification, then $f(a)$ may be computed by a call $t'(\textit{fnew}(a))$ to the new procedure.

By introducing the procedure *fnew*(a') we are able to call it recursively. In other words, we are now able to form an induction hypothesis from the assertion $P'(a')$ and the goal $R'(a', z')$, namely,

if $u' \prec_{w'} a'$ *then if* $P'(u')$ *then* $R'(u', fnew(u'))$			

If this assertion is employed during a proof, a recursive call to *fnew* can be introduced into the output column for *fnew*(a'). The well-founded ordering $\prec_{w'}$, corresponding to *fnew*(a') may be distinct from the ordering $\prec_w$ corresponding to $f(a)$.

Note that we do not begin a new sequent for the derivation of the auxiliary procedure *fnew*; the synthesis of the main program $f(a)$ and the auxiliary procedure *fnew*(a') are both conducted by applying derivation rules to the same sequent. Those rows with output entries for *fnew*(a') always have the expression $t'(fnew(a))$ as the output entry for $f(a)$.

Suppose we ultimately succeed in obtaining the goal *true* with primitive output entries t and t':

assertions	*goals*	*outputs* $f(a)$	*fnew*(a')
	true	t	t'

Then the final program is

$$f(a) \Leftarrow t$$

and

$$fnew(a') \Leftarrow t'.$$

Note that although the portion of the derivation leading from goal A to goal B serves to motivate the formation of the auxiliary procedure, it may actually have no part in the derivation of the final program; its role has been taken over by the derivation of goal B′ from goal A′.

It is possible to introduce many auxiliary procedures for the same main program, each adding a new output column to the sequent. An auxiliary procedure may have its own set of auxiliary procedures. An auxiliary procedure may call the main program or any of the other procedures; in other words, the system of procedures can be "mutually recursive."

If we fail to complete the derivation of an auxiliary procedure *fnew*(a'), we may still succeed in finding some other way of completing the derivation of $f(a)$ without using *fnew*, by applying deduction rules to rows that have no output entry for *fnew*(a').

To illustrate the formation of auxiliary procedures, we consider the synthesis of a program *cart*(s, t) to compute the cartesian product of two (finite) sets s and t, i.e., the set of all pairs whose first component belongs to s and whose second component belongs to t. The specification for this program is

$$cart(s, t) \Leftarrow find\ z\ such\ that$$
$$z = \{(a, b): a \in s\ and\ b \in t\}.$$

The initial sequent is then

assertions	goals	outputs $cart(s, t)$
	$z = \{(a, b): a \in s\ and\ b \in t\}$	z

(Note that this specification has no input condition, except for the type condition $isset(s)$ and $isset(t)$, which we omit for simplicity.)

We denote the empty set by $\{\}$. If u is a nonempty set, then $choice(u)$ denotes some particular element of u, and $rest(u)$ denotes the set of all other elements. We assume that the transformation rules concerning finite sets include:

$$u \in v \Rightarrow false \quad if\ v = \{\}$$
$$u \in v \Rightarrow u = choice(v)\ or\ u \in rest(v) \quad if\ v \neq \{\}$$
$$\{u: false\} \Rightarrow \{\}$$
$$\{u: P\ or\ Q\} \Rightarrow \{u: P\} \cup \{u: Q\}$$
$$rest(u) <_{s_1} u \Rightarrow true \quad if\ u \neq \{\}$$
$$\{u: u = v\} \Rightarrow \{v\} \quad \text{(where } u \text{ does not occur in } v\text{)}$$

We will not reproduce the complete derivation, but only those portions that concern the formation of auxiliary procedures.

By application of deduction rules to the initial sequent, we obtain the goal

A:		$z' = \{(a, b): a = choice(s)\ and\ b \in t\}$	*if* $s = \{\}$ *then* $\{\}$ *else* $z' \cup cart(rest(s), t)$

By applying several deductive rules to this goal alone, we obtain the new goal

B:		$z'' = \{(a, b): a = choice(s)\ and\ b \in rest(t)\}$	*if* $t = \{\}$ *then* $\{\}$ *else if* $s = \{\}$ *then* $\{\}$ *else* $(choice(s), choice(t)) \cup$ $cart(rest(s), t) \cup z''$

This goal is a precise instance of the earlier goal; consequently, our recurrence strategy motivates us to form an auxiliary procedure $cartnew(s, t)$ having the earlier goal as its output specification, i.e.,

$$cartnew(s', t') \Leftarrow \{(a, b): a = choice(s')\ and\ b \in t'\}.$$

We therefore introduce an additional output column corresponding to the new procedure, and we add to the sequent the row

	assertions	goals	outputs $cart(s, t)$	outputs $cartnew(s', t')$
A′:		$z' = \{(a, b)$: $a = choice(s')$ *and* $b \in t')$	*if* $s = \{\}$ *then* $\{\}$ *else* $cartnew(s, t) \cup cart(rest(s), t)$	z'

The induction hypothesis corresponding to this goal is then

if $(u', v') \prec_{w'} (s', t')$ *then* $cartnew(u', v') = \{(a, b)$: $a = choice(u')$ *and* $b \in v'\}$			

By applying deduction rules to the new goal, we obtain the goal

B′:		$z'' = \{(a, b)$: $a = choice(s')$ *and* $b \in rest(t')\}$	*if* $s = \{\}$ *then* $\{\}$ *else* $cartnew(s, t) \cup cart(rest(s), t)$	*if* $t' = \{\}$ *then* $\{\}$ *else* $(choice(s'), choice(t')) \cup z''$

Applying GA-resolution between this goal and the induction hypothesis, and simplying by transformation rules, we obtain the goal

	$(s', rest(t')) \prec_{w'} (s', t')$	*if* $s = \{\}$ *then* $\{\}$ *else* $cartnew(s, t) \cup cart(rest(s), t)$	*if* $t' = \{\}$ *then* $\{\}$ *else* $(choice(s'), choice(t')) \cup cartnew(s', rest(t'))$

Note that a recursive call has now appeared in the output entry for the auxiliary procedure *cartnew*. By further transformation, the well-founded ordering $\prec_{w'}$ is chosen to be $\prec_{s_2}$, defined by

$$(u_1, u_2) \prec_{s_2} (v_1, v_2) \quad \text{if } u_2 \text{ is a proper subset of } v_2.$$

The final program obtained from this derivation is

$cart(s, t) \Leftarrow$ *if* $s = \{\}$
then $\{\}$
else $cartnew(s, t) \cup$
$cart(rest(s), t)$

$cartnew(s', t') \Leftarrow$ *if* $t' = \{\}$
then $\{\}$
else $(choice(s'), choice(t')) \cup$
$cartnew(s', rest(t'))$.

There are a few extensions to the method for forming auxiliary procedures that we will not describe in detail:

(1) We have been led to introduce an auxiliary procedure when an entire goal was found to be an instance of a previous goal. As we remarked in the section on

mathematical induction, we can actually introduce an auxiliary procedure when some subsentence of a goal is an instance of some subsentence of a previous goal.

(2) Special treatment is required if the assertions and goal incorporated into the induction hypothesis contain more than one occurrence of the same skolem function. We do not describe the formation of such an induction hypothesis here.

(3) To complete the derivation of the auxiliary procedure, we may be forced to weaken or strengthen its specification by adding input or output conditions incrementally. We do not present here the extension of the procedure-formation principle that permits this flexibility.

GENERALIZATION

In performing a proof by mathematical induction, it is often necessary to generalize the theorem to be proved, so as to have the advantage of a stronger induction hypothesis in proving the inductive step. Paradoxically, the more general statement may be easier to prove. If the proof is part of the synthesis of a program, generalizing the theorem can result in the construction of a more general procedure, so that recursive calls to the procedure will be able to achieve the desired subgoals. The recurrence strategy we have outlined earlier provides a strong clue as to how the theorem is to be generalized.

We have formed an auxiliary procedure when a goal is found to be a precise instance of a previous goal. However, in some derivations it is found that the new goal is not a precise instance of the earlier goal, but that both are instances of some more general expression. This situation suggests introducing a new auxiliary procedure whose output condition is the more general expression, in the hope that both goals may be achieved by calls to this procedure.

Let us be more precise. Suppose we are in the midst of a derivation and that we have already developed a goal A, of form

	assertions	*goals*	*outputs* $f(a)$
A:		$R'(a, s_1, z_1)$	$t_1(z_1)$

where s_1 is an arbitrary term. Assume that by applying deduction rules only to goal A and some assertions $P'_1(a), P'_2(a), \ldots, P'_k(a)$, we obtain a goal B, of form

B:		$R'(a, s_2, z_2)$	$t_2(z_2)$

where s_2 is a term that does not match s_1. Thus, the new goal (goal B) is not a precise instance of the earlier goal (goal A). Hence, if an induction hypothesis is formed for goal A itself, the resolution rule cannot be applied between goal B and the induction hypothesis.

However, both goals A and B may be regarded as instances of the more general expression $R'(a, b', z')$, where b' is a new constant: goal A is obtained by replacing b' by s_1, and goal B is obtained by replacing b' by s_2. This suggests that we attempt to establish a more general expression (goal A′) hoping that the proof of goal A′ will contain a subgoal (goal B′) corresponding to the original goal B, so that the induction hypothesis resulting from goal A′ will be strong enough to establish goal B′.

The new goal A′ constitutes the output condition for an auxiliary procedure, whose specification is

$$fnew(a', b') \Leftarrow \textit{find } z' \textit{ such that } R'(a', b', z') \quad \textit{where } P'(a').$$

(Here, $P'(a')$ is the conjunction $P'_1(a')$ *and* $P'_2(a')$ ··· *and* $P'_k(a')$.) Consequently, we introduce a new output column to the sequent, and we add the new assertion

assertions	*goals*	*outputs* $f(a)$	$fnew(a', b')$
$P'(a')$			

and the new goal

	assertions	*goals*	*outputs*
A′:		$R'(a', b', z')t_1(fnew(a, s_1))$	z'

(Note again that it is logically necessary to replace the input constant a by a new constant a'.) Corresponding to this assertion and goal we have the induction hypothesis

assertions	*goals*	*outputs*	
if $(u', v') \prec_{w'} (a', b')$ *then if* $P'(u')$ *then* $R(u', v', fnew(u', v'))$			

There is no guarantee that we will be able to develop from goal A′ a goal B′ such that the resolution rule can be applied between goal B′ and the induction hypothesis. Nor can we be sure that we will conclude the derivation of *fnew* successfully. If we fail to derive *fnew*, we may still complete the derivation of f in some other way.

We illustrate the generalization process with an example that also serves to show how program-synthesis techniques can be applied as well to *program transformation* (see, e.g., Burstall and Darlington [3]). In this application we are given a clear and concise program, which may be inefficient; we attempt to derive an equivalent program that is more efficient, even though it may be neither clear nor concise.

We are given the program

$$reverse(l) \Leftarrow \textit{if } l = [\,] \textit{ then } [\,] \textit{ else } reverse(tail(l)) <> [head(l)]$$

for reversing the order of the elements of a list l. Here, *head*(l) is the first element of a nonempty list l and *tail*(l) is the list of all but the first element of l. Recall that $u <> v$ is the result of appending two lists u and v, [] denotes the empty list, and $[w]$ is the list whose sole element is w. As usual, we omit type conditions, such as *islist*(l), from our discussion.

This *reverse* program is inefficient, for it requires many recursive calls to *reverse* and to the append procedure <>. We attempt to transform it to a more efficient version. The specification for the transformed program *rev*(l) is

$$rev(l) \Leftarrow \textit{find } z_1 \textit{ such that } z_1 = reverse(l).$$

The initial sequent is thus

	assertions	*goals*	*outputs* $rev(l)$
A:		$z_1 = reverse(l)$	z_1

The given *reverse* program is not considered to be a primitive. However, we admit the transformation rules

$$reverse(u) \Rightarrow [] \quad if\ u = []$$

and

$$reverse(u) \Rightarrow reverse(tail(u)) <> [head(u)] \quad if\ u \neq [];$$

obtained directly from the *reverse* program.

We assume that the transformation rules we have concerning lists include:

$$head(u \cdot v) \Rightarrow u$$

$$tail(u \cdot v) \Rightarrow v$$

$$[u] \Rightarrow u \cdot []$$

$$(u \cdot v = []) \Rightarrow false$$

(where $u \cdot v$ is the result of inserting u before the first element of the list v; it is the Lisp *cons* function)

$$u <> v \Rightarrow v \quad if\ u = []$$

$$u <> v \Rightarrow u \quad if\ v = []$$

$$u <> v \Rightarrow head(u) \cdot (tail(u) <> v) \quad if\ u \neq []$$

$$(u <> v) <> w \Rightarrow u <> (v <> w)$$

$$tail(l) <_L l \Rightarrow true \quad if\ l \neq []$$

Applying transformation rules to the initial goal, we obtain a subgoal

B:		$z_2 = reverse(tail(l)) <> [head(l)]$	*if* $l = []$ *then* $[]$ *else* z_2

This goal is not a precise instance of goal A. However, both goals may be regarded as instances of the more general expression

$$z' = reverse(l') <> m'.$$

Goal A is obtained by replacing l' by $tail(l)$ and m' by $[]$ (because $u <> [] = u$), and goal B is obtained by replacing l' by $tail(l)$ and m' by $[head(l)]$. This suggests that we attempt to construct an auxiliary procedure having the more general expression as an output condition; the specification for this procedure is

$$revnew(l', m') \Leftarrow find\ z'\ such\ that\ z' = reverse(l') <> m'.$$

Consequently, we introduce a new output column to the sequent, and we add the new goal

	assertions	goals	outputs	
			rev(l)	*revnew(l′, m′)*
A′:		$z' = reverse(l') <> m'$	$revnew(l, [\,])$	z'

The induction hypothesis corresponding to this goal is then

if $(u', v') \prec_{w'} (l', m')$ *then* $revnew(u', v') = reverse(u') <> v'$		

By applying deduction rules to the goal A′, we eventually obtain

	assertions	goals	outputs	
			rev(l)	*revnew(l′, m′)*
B′:		$z'' = reverse(tail(l')) <> (head(l') \cdot m')$	$revnew(l, [\,])$	*if* $l' = [\,]$ *then* m' *else* z''

We succeed in applying the resolution rule between this goal and the induction hypothesis.

Ultimately, we obtain the final program

$$\begin{aligned} rev(l) &\Leftarrow revnew(l, [\,]) \\ revnew(l', m') &\Leftarrow \; if\ l' = [\,] \\ &\qquad then\ m' \\ &\qquad else\ revnew(tail(l'), head(l') \cdot m'). \end{aligned}$$

This program turns out to be more efficient than the given program *reverse(l)*; it is essentially iterative and employs the insertion operation $\cdot$ instead of the expensive append operation $<>$. In general, however, we have no guarantee that the program produced by this approach will be more efficient than the given program. A possible remedy is to include efficiency criteria explicitly in the specification of the program. For example, we might require that the *rev* program should run in time linear to the length of *l*. In proving the theorem obtained from such a specification, we would be ensuring that the program constructed would operate within the specified limitations. Of course, the difficulty of the theorem-proving task would be compounded by such measures.

Some generalizations are quite straightforward to discover. For example, if goal A is of form $R'(a, 0, z_1)$ and goal B is of form $R'(a, 1, z_2)$, this immediately suggests that we employ the general expression $R'(a, b', z')$. Other generalizations may require more ingenuity to discover. In the *reverse* example, for instance, it is not immediately obvious that $z_1 = reverse(l)$ and $z_2 = reverse(tail(l)) <> [head(l)]$ should both be regarded as instances of the more general expression $z' = reverse(l') <> m'$.

Our strategy for determining how to generalize an induction hypothesis is distinct from that of Boyer and Moore [2]. Their system predicts how to generalize a goal before developing any subgoals in our approach, recurrences between a goal and its subgoals suggest how the goal is to be generalized.

COMPARISON WITH THE PURE TRANSFORMATION-RULE APPROACH

Recent work (e.g., Manna and Waldinger [7], as well as Burstall and Darlington [3]) does not regard program synthesis as a theorem-proving task, but instead adopts the basic approach of applying transformation rules directly to the given specification. What advantage do we obtain by shifting to a theorem-proving approach, when that approach has already been attempted and abandoned?

The structure we outline here is considerably simpler than, say, our implemented synthesis system DEDALUS, but retains the full power of that system. DEDALUS required special mechanisms for the formation of conditional expressions and recursive calls, and for the satisfaction of "conjunctive goals" (of form "*find z such that* $R_1(z)$ *and* $R_2(z)$"). It could not treat specifications involving quantifiers. It relied on a backtracking control structure, which required it to explore one goal completely before attention could be passed to another goal. In the present system, these constructs are handled as a natural outgrowth of the theorem-proving process. In addition, the foundation is laid for the application of more sophisticated search strategies, in which attention is passed back and forth freely between several competing assertions and goals. The present framework can take advantage of parallel hardware.

Furthermore, the task of program synthesis always involves a theorem-proving component, which is needed, say, to prove the termination of the program being constructed, or to establish the input condition for recursive calls. (The Burstall-Darlington system is interactive and relies on the user to prove these theorems; DEDALUS incorporates a separate theorem prover.) If we retain the artificial distinction between program synthesis and theorem proving, each component must duplicate the efforts of the other. The mechanism for forming recursive calls will be separate from the induction principle; the facility for handling specifications of the form

find z such that $R_1(z)$ *and* $R_2(z)$

will be distinct from the facility for proving theorems of form

for some z, $R_1(z)$ *and* $R_2(z)$;

and so forth. By adopting a theorem-proving approach, we can unify these two components.

Theorem proving was abandoned as an approach to program synthesis when the development of sufficiently powerful automatic theorem provers appeared to flounder. However, theorem provers have been exhibiting a steady increase in their effectiveness, and program synthesis is one of the most natural applications of these systems.

ACKNOWLEDGMENTS

We would like to thank John Darlington, Chris Goad, Jim King, Neil Murray, Nils Nilsson, and Earl Sacerdoti for valuable discussions and comments. Thanks are due also to Patte Wood for aid in the preparation of this manuscript.

REFERENCES

1. BLEDSOE, W.W. Non-resolution theorem proving. *Artif. Intell. J. 9*, (1977), 1–35.
2. BOYER, R.S., AND MOORE, JS. Proving theorems about LISP functions *J. ACM 22*, 1 (Jan. 1975), 129–144.
3. BURSTALL, R.M., AND DARLINGTON, J. A transformation system for developing recursive programs. *J. ACM 24*, 1 (Jan. 1977), 44–67.
4. DARLINGTON, J.L. Automatic theorem proving with equality substitutions and mathematical induction. *Machine Intell. 3* (Edinburgh, Scotland) (1968), 113–127.
5. GREEN, C.C. Application of theorem proving to problem solving. In *Proc. Int. Joint Conf. on Artificial Intelligence* (Washington D.C., May 1969), 219–239.
6. HEWITT, C. Description and theoretical analysis (using schemata) of PLANNER: A language for proving theorems and manipulating models in a robot. Ph.D. Diss., M.I.T., Cambridge, Mass., 1971.
7. MANNA, Z., AND WALDINGER, R. Synthesis: dreams ⇒ programs. *IEEE Trans. Softw. Eng. SE-5*, 4 (July 1979), 294–328.
8. MURRAY, N. A proof procedure for non-clausal first-order logic. Tech. Rep. Syracuse Univ., Syracuse, N.Y., 1978.
9. NELSON, G., AND OPPEN, D.C. A simplifier based on efficient decision algorithms. In *Proc. 5th ACM Symp. Principles of Programming Languages* (Tucson, Ariz., Jan. 1978), pp. 141–150.
10. NILSSON, N.J. A production system for automatic deduction. *Machine Intell. 9*, Ellis Horwood, Chichester, England, 1979.
11. NILSSON, N.J. *Problem-solving methods in artificial intelligence*. McGraw-Hill, New York, 1971, pp. 165–168.
12. ROBINSON, J.A. A machine-oriented logic based on the resolution principle. *J.ACM 12*, 1 (Jan. 1965), 23–41.
13. WALDINGER, R.J., AND LEE, R.C.T. PROW: A step toward automatic program writing. In *Proc. Int. Joint Conf. on Artificial Intelligence* (Washington D.C., May 1969), pp. 241–252.
14. WILKINS, D. QUEST—A non-clausal theorem proving system. M.Sc. Th., Univ. of Essex, England, 1973.

Prolegomena to a Theory of Mechanized Formal Reasoning

Richard W. Weyhrauch

Stanford University, Stanford, CA, U.S.A.

ABSTRACT

This is an informal description of my ideas about using formal logic as a tool for reasoning systems using computers. The theoretical ideas are illustrated by the features of FOL. *All of the examples presented have actually run using the* FOL *system.*

1. Introduction

The title of this paper contains both the words '*mechanized*' and '*theory*'. I want to make the point that the ideas presented here are not only of interest to theoreticians. I believe that any theory of interest to artificial intelligence must be realizable on a computer.

I am going to describe a working computer program, FOL, that embodies the mechanization of the ideas of logicians *about* theories of reasoning. This system converses with users in some first order language. I will also explain how to build a new structure in which theory and metatheory interact in a particularly natural way. This structure has the additional property that it can be designed to reason about itself. This kind of self reflexive logical structure is new and a discussion of the full extent of its power will appear in another paper.

The purpose of this paper is to set down the main ideas underlying the system. Each example in this paper was chosen to illustrate an *idea* and each idea is developed by showing how the corresponding FOL feature works. I will not present difficult examples. More extensive examples and discussions of the limits of these features will be described in other places. The real power of this theory (and FOL) comes from an understanding of the interaction of these separate features. This means that after this paper is read it still requires some work to see how all of these features can be used. Complex examples will only confuse the issues at this point. Before these can be explained the logical system must be fully understood.

The FOL project can be thought of in several different ways:

(1) Most important, FOL is an environment for studying epistemological questions. I look on logic as an empirical, applied science. It is like physics. The data we have is the actual reasoning activity of people. We try to build a theory of what that's like. I try to look at the traditional work on logic from this point of view. The important question is: in what way does logic adequately represent the actual practice of reasoning? In addition, its usefulness to artificial intelligence requires a stronger form of adequacy. Such a theory must be *mechanizable*. My notion of mechanizable is informal. I hope by the end of this note it will be clearer. Below, I outline the mechanizable analogues of the usual notions of model, interpretation, satisfaction, theory, and reflection principle.

(2) FOL is a conversational machine. We use it by having a conversation with it. The importance of this idea cannot be overestimated. One of the recurring themes of this paper is the question: what is the nature of the conversation we wish to have with an expert in reasoning? In AI we talk about *expert systems*. FOL can be thought of as a system whose expertise is reasoning. We have tried to explore the question: what properties does an expert conversational reasoning machine have to have, independent of its domain of expertise? I believe that we will begin to call machines intelligent when we can have the kinds of discussions with them that we have with our friends. Let me elaborate on this a little. Humans are not ever likely to come to depend on the advice of a computer which has a simplistic one bit output. Imagine that you are asking it to make decisions about what stocks you should buy. Suppose it says "I have reviewed all the data you gave me. Sell everything you own and buy stock in FOL Incorporated." Most reasonable people would like to ask some additional questions! Why did you make that choice? What theory of price behavior did you use? Why is that better than using a dartboard? And so forth. These questions require a system that knows about more things than the stock market. For example, it needs to know how to reason about its *theories* of price movement. In FOL we have begged the question of *natural* language. The only important thing is having a sufficiently rich language for carrying out the above kinds of conversations. This paper should be looked at from this point of view.

This work has direct application in several areas. The details are referenced below.

(1) *Artificial Intelligence*. I propose that the *language/simulation structure* pairs described below are important building blocks in a viable and mechanizable theory of knowledge representation for AI. The central idea is that FOL makes systematic use of the distinction between a language and the objects that this language describes. This distinction allows us to deal with the questions of how to manipulate theories of theory building, how to deal with modalities, how to reason about possibly inconsistent theories, how to treat 'non-monotonic' reasoning and how

to build a mechanizable theory of perception. By perception I mean the question of how it is possible for us to go from sense impressions to theories about what our exterior is like.

(2) *Mathematical Theory of Computation.* FOL is an environment that can deal effectively both with a theory and its metatheory. Many aspects of program semantics are nicely expressable when this is viewed as a reasoning *system.* For a long time I have wanted to have a system in which I could develop the theory of LISP, following the ideas of Kleene (1952) when he developed recursion theory. The recent work of Cartwright (1977) and McCarthy (1978) have made this even more practicable. One main feature of this system is that it can incorporate both computation induction and the inductive assertion method in the same system. We can do this because both of these methodologies can be expressed as theorems of the metatheory. This is an example of the expressive power of the FOL system. If as above we claim that we want to be able to have discussions with FOL about anything, then programs are an interesting subject. We are currently building an 'expert' system for discussing LISP programs.

(3) *Logic.* The FOL system is not a formal system in the popular sense of the word. Logicians have used formal systems mainly to describe the sentences that are used in mathematical reasoning. I have tried on the other hand to build a structure which embodies the logicians theories of these theories and thus have a system capable of reasoning about theory building. There are several novel things about the logic of FOL that may be of interest to logicians and workers in AI. First is the way in which many sorted logic is treated. Second is the notion that simulation structures (i.e. partial models) should be represented explicitly. Third is the idea of the general purpose evaluator described below. Fourth is the use of reflection principles to connect a theory with its metatheory. Fifth is to notice that reflection and evaluation with respect to the metatheory is the technical realization of the procedural/declarative discussions which appear in the AI literature. Sixth is the discovery of META, a self reflective structure with a 'locally' Tarskian semantics. This theory META is new and it has already produced some insight into the nature of meta reasoning that I will write about elsewhere.

As I reread this introduction it seems to contain a lot of promises. If they seem exaggerated to you then imagine me as a hopeless romantic, but at least read the rest of this paper. The things I describe here already exist.

2. FOL as a Conversational Program

FOL has previously been advertised as a proof-checker. This sometimes brings to mind the idea that the way you use it is to type out a complicated formal proof, then FOL reads it and says yes or no. This picture is all wrong, and is founded on the theorem proving idea that simply stating a problem is all that a reasoning system should need to know. What FOL actually does is to have a dialogue with a user about some subject. The first step in this conversation is to establish what language we will speak to each other by establishing what words we will use for what parts of speech. In FOL the establishment of this agreement about language is done by making *declarations.* This will be described below.

We can then discuss (in the agreed upon language) what facts (axioms) are to be considered true, and then finally we can chat about the consequences of these facts.

Let me illustrate this by giving a simple FOL proof. We will begin where logic began, with Aristotle (–335). Even a person who has never had a course in formal logic understands the syllogism:

Socrates is a man
  and
All men are mortal
  thus
Socrates is mortal

Before we actually give a dialogue with FOL we need to think informally about how we express these assertions as well formed formulas, WFFs of first order logic. For this purpose we need an individual constant (INDCONST), Socrates, two predicate constants (PREDCONSTs), MAN and MORTAL, each of one argument, and an individual variable (INDVAR), x, to express the all men part of the second line. The usual rules for forming WFFs apply (see Kleene (1967), pp. 7, 78). The three statements above are represented as

$$\text{MAN (Socrates)}$$
$$\forall x.(\text{MAN}(x) \supset \text{MORTAL}(x))$$
$$\text{MORTAL(Socrates)}$$

Our goal is to prove

$$(\text{MAN(Socrates)} \wedge \forall x.(\text{MAN}(x) \supset \text{MORTAL}(x))) \supset \text{MORTAL(Socrates)}$$

As explained above the first thing we do when initiating a discussion with FOL is to make an agreement about language we will use. We do this by making declarations. These have the form

```
*****DECLARE INDCONST Socrates;
*****DECLARE PREDCONST MORTAL MAN 1;
*****DECLARE INDVAR x;
```

The FOL program types out five stars when it expects input. The above lines are exactly what you would type to the FOL system.

FOL knows all of the natural deduction rules of inference (Prawitz (1965)) and many more. In the usual natural deduction style proofs are trees and the leaves of these trees are called assumptions. The assume command looks like

```
*****ASSUME MAN(Socrates) ∧ ∀x.(MAN(x) ⊃ MORTAL(x));
1 MAN(Socrates) ∧ ∀x.(MAN(x) ⊃ MORTAL(x))   (1)
```

The first line above is typed by the user the second is typed by FOL. For each node in the proof tree there is a set of open assumptions. These are printed in parentheses after the proofstep. Notice that assumptions depend on themselves.

We want to instantiate the second half of line one to the particular MAN, Socrates. First we must get this WFF onto a line of its own. FOL can be used to decide tautologies. We type TAUT followed by the WFF we want, and then the line numbers of those lines from which we think it follows.

*****TAUT $\forall x.(\mathrm{MAN}(x) \supset \mathrm{MORTAL}(x))$ 1;

2 $\forall x.(\mathrm{MAN}(x) \supset \mathrm{MORTAL}(x))$ (1)

This line also has the open assumption of line 1. We then use the ∀-elimination rule to conclude

*****∀E 2 Socrates;

3 MAN(Socrates) ⊃ MORTAL(Socrates) (1)

It now follows, tautologically, from lines one and three, that Socrates must be MORTAL. Using the TAUT command again gets this result. More than one line can be given in the reason part of the TAUT command.

*****TAUT MORTAL(Socrates) 1,3;

4 MORTAL(Socrates) (1)

This is almost the desired result, but we are not finished yet; this line still depends upon the original assumption. We close this assumption by creating an implication of the first line implying the fourth. This is done using the deduction theorem. In the natural deduction terminology this is called *implication* (⊃) *introduction.*

*****⊃I 1 ⊃ 4;

5 $(\mathrm{MAN}(\mathrm{Socrates}) \wedge \forall x.(\mathrm{MAN}(x) \supset \mathrm{MORTAL}(x)))$
$\supset \mathrm{MORTAL}(\mathrm{Socrates})$

This is the WFF we wanted to prove. Since it has no dependencies, it is a theorem. It is roughly equivalent to the English sentence, If Socrates is a man, and for all x if x is a man, then x is mortal, then Socrates is mortal.

This example was also used in Filman and Weyhrauch (1976) and illustrates the sense in which FOL is an interactive proof constructor, not simply a proof checker.

3. The Logic Used by FOL

The logic used by FOL is an extension of the system of first order predicate calculus described in Prawitz (1965). The most important change is that FOL languages contain equality and allow for sorted variables where there is a partial order on the sorts. This latter facility is extremely important for making discussions with FOL more natural. The properties of this extension of ordinary logic together with detailed examples appear in Weyhrauch (1979). In addition there are several features which are primarily syntactic improvements. A somewhat old description of how to use FOL is found in Weyhrauch (1977).

Prawitz distinguishes between individual variables and individual parameters. In FOL individual variables may appear both free and bound in WFFs. As in Prawitz individual parameters must always appear free. Natural numbers are automatically declared individual constants of sort NATNUM. This is one of the few defaults in FOL. The only kind of numbers understood by FOL are natural numbers, i.e. non-negative integers. -3 should be thought of not as an individual constant, but rather as the prefix operator $-$ applied to the individual constant 3.

A user may specify that binary predicate and operation symbols are to be used as infixes. The declaration of a unary application symbol to be prefix makes the parentheses around its argument optional. The number of arguments of an application term is called its *arity.*

FOL always considers two WFFs to be equal if they can both be changed into the same WFF by making allowable changes of bound variables. Thus, for example, the TAUT rule will accept $\forall x.\mathrm{P}(x) \supset \forall y.\mathrm{P}(y)$ as a tautology if x and y are of the same sort.

We have also introduced the use of conditional expressions for both WFFs and TERMs. These expressions are not used in standard descriptions of predicate calculus because they complicate the definition of satisfaction by making the value of a TERM and the truth value of a WFF mutually recursive. Hilbert and Bernays (1934) proved that these additions were a conservative extension of ordinary predicate calculus so, in some sense, they are not needed. McCarthy (1963) stressed, however, that the increased naturalness when using conditional expressions to describe functions, is more than adequate compensation for the additional complexity.

Simple derivations in FOL are generated by using the natural deduction rules described in Prawitz (1965) together with some well-known decision procedures. These include TAUT for deciding tautologies, TAUTEQ for deciding the propositional theory of equality and MONADIC which decides formulas of the monadic predicate calculus. In actual fact MONADIC decides the case of ∀∃ formulas. These features are not explained in this paper. This is probably is a good place to mention that the first two decision procedures were designed and coded by Ashok Chandra and the last by William Glassmire. The important additions to the deductive mechanisms of first order logic are the syntactic and semantic simplification routines, the convenient use of metatheory and a not yet completed goal structure (Juan Bulnes (1979)). It is these later features that are described below.

4. Simulation Structures and Semantic Attachment

Here I introduce one of the most important ideas in this paper, i.e. *simulation structures.* Simulation structures are intended to be the *mechanizable* analogue of the notion of model. We can intuitively understand them as the computable part of some model. It has been suggested that I call them *effective partial interpretations*, but I have reserved that slogan for a somewhat more general notion. A full mathematical description of these ideas is beyond the scope of this paper but appears in Weyhrauch [Note 15]. In this paper I will give an operational description, mostly by means of some examples.

Consider the first order language L, and a model M.

L = (P,F,C)
M = (D,P,F,C)

As usual, L is determined by a collection, P, of predicate symbols, a collection, F, of function symbols, and a collection, C, of constant symbols (Kleene (1952, pp. 83–93)). M is a structure which contains a domain D, and the predicates, functions and objects which correspond to the symbols in L.

S = (*D*,*P*,*F*,*C*)

Loosely speaking, a simulation structure, S, also has a domain, *D*, a set of 'predicates', *P*, a set of 'functions', *F*, and a distinguished subset, *C*, of its domain. However, they have strong restrictions. Since we are imagining simulation structures as the mechanizable analogues of models we want to be able to actually implement them on a computer. To facilitate this we imagine that we intend to use a computer language in which there is some reasonable collection of data structures. In FOL we use LISP. The domain of a simulation structure is presented as an algorithm that acts as the characteristic function of some subset of the data structures. For example, if we want to construct a simulation structure for Peano arithmetic the domain is specified by a LISP function which returns T (for true) on natural numbers and NIL (for false) on all other s-expressions. Each 'predicate' is represented by an algorithm that decides for each collection of arguments if the predicate is true or false or if it doesn't know. This algorithm is also total. Notice that it can tell you what is false as well as what true. Each 'function' is an algorithm that computes for each set of arguments either a value or returns the fact that it doesn't know the answer. It too is total. The distinguished subset of the domain must also be given by its characteristic function. These restrictions are best illustrated by an example. A possible simulation structure for Peano arithmetic together with a relation symbol for 'less than' is

S = (natural numbers, ⟨{$2 < 3, \neg\, 5 < 2$}⟩, ⟨plus⟩, {2,3})

I have not presented this simulation structure by actually giving algorithms but they can easily be supplied. This simulation structure contains only two facts about 'less than'—two is less than three, and it's false that five is less than two. As mentioned above, since this discussion is informal {$2 < 3, \neg\, 5 < 2$} should be taken as the description of an algorithm that answers correctly the two questions it knows about and in all other cases returns the fact that it cannot decide 'plus' is the name of an algorithm that computes the sum of two natural numbers. The only numerals that have interpretations are two and three. These have their usual meaning.

Intuitively, if we ask is '2 < 3' (where here '2' and '3' are numerals in L) we get the answer yes. If we ask is '5 < 2' it says, "I don't know"! This is because there is no interpretation in the simulation structure of the numeral '5'. Curiously, if you ask is '2+3 < 2' it will say false. The reason is that the simulation structure has an interpretation of '+' as the algorithm 'plus' and 5 is in the domain even though it is not known to be the interpretation of any numeral in L.

A more reasonable simulation structure for Peano arithmetic might be

S = ⟨natural numbers, ⟨lessthan⟩, ⟨suc,pred,plus,times⟩,
natural numbers⟩

Simulation structures are not models. One difference is that there are no closure conditions required of the function fragments. Thus we could know that three times two is six without knowing about the multiplicative properties of two and six.

Just as in the case of a model, we get a natural interpretation of a language with respect to a simulation structure. This allows us to introduce the idea of a sentence of L being satisfiable with respect to a simulation structure. Because of the lack of closure conditions and the partialness of the 'predicates', etc. (unlike ordinary satisfaction) this routine will sometimes return 'I don't know'. There are several reasons for this. Our mechanized satisfaction cannot compute the truth or falsity of quantified formulas. This in general requires an infinite amount of computing. It should be remarked that this is exactly why we have logic at all. It facilitates our reasoning about the result of an infinite amount of computation with a single sentence.

It is also important to understand that we are not introducing a three valued logic or partial functions. We simply acknowledge that, with respect to some simulation structures, we don't have any information about certain expressions in our language.

Below is an example of the FOL commands that would define this language, assert some axioms and build this simulation structure. As mentioned above, in the FOL system one of the few defaults is that numerals automatically come declared as individual constants and are attached to the expected integers. Thus the following axiomatization includes the numerals and their attachments by default.

The first group of commands creates the language. The second group are Robinson's axioms Q without the equality axioms (Robinson (1950)). The next is the induction axiom. The fourth group makes the semantic attachments that build the simulation structure. The expressions containing the word 'LAMBDA' are LISP programs. I will not explain the REPRESENT command as it is unimportant here. The parts of the declarations in square brackets specify binding power information to the FOL parser.

```
DECLARE INDVAR n m p q ∈ NATNUM;
DECLARE OPCONST suc pred (NATNUM) = NATNUM;
DECLARE OPCONST+(NATNUM, NATNUM) = NATNUM [R← 458, L← 455];
DECLARE OPCONST * (NATNUM, NATNUM = NATNUM [R← 558, L← 555];
DECLARE PREDCONST↔ (NATNUM, NATNUM) [INF];
DECLARE PREDPAR P (NATNUM);

AXIOM  Q:
AXIOM  ONEONE: ∀n m.(suc(n) = suc(m) ⊃ n = m);
       SUCC1:  ∀n.¬ (∅ = suc(n));
       SUCC2:  ∀n.(¬ ∅ = n ⊃ ∃m.(n = suc(m));
       PLUS:   ∀n.n+∅ = n
               ∀n m.n+suc(m) = suc(n+m);
       TIMES:  ∀n.n*∅ = ∅
               ∀n m.n*suc(m) = (n*m)+m;;;

AXIOM  INDUCT: P(∅) ∧ ∀n.(P(n) ⊃ P(suc(n))) ⊃ ∀n.P(n);;

REPRESENT {NATNUM} AS NATNUMREP;
ATTACH suc  ↔ (LAMBDA (X)(ADD1 X));
ATTACH pred ↔ (LAMBDA (X)(COND ((GREATERP X ∅) (SUB1 X)) (T ∅)));
ATTACH+     ↔ (LAMBDA (X Y)(PLUS X Y));
ATTACH *    ↔ (LAMBDA (X Y)(TIMES X Y));
ATTACH <    ↔ (LAMBDA (X Y)(LESSP X Y));
```

Using these commands we can ask questions like

```
*****SIMPLIFY 2+3 < pred(7);
*****SIMPLIFY 4*suc(2)+pred(3) < pred(pred(8));
```

Of course semantic simplification only works on ground terms, i.e. only on those quantifier free expressions whose only individual symbols are individual constants. Furthermore, such an expression will not evaluate unless all the constants have attachments, and there is a constant in the language for value of the expression. Thus a command like

```
*****SIMPLIFY n*∅ < 3;
```

where n is a variable, will not simplify.

This facility may seem weak as we usually don't have ground expressions to evaluate. Below I will show that when we use the metatheory and the meta-metatheory we frequently do have ground terms to evaluate, thus making this a very useful tool.

5. Syntactic Simplifier

FOL also contains a syntactic simplifier, called REWRITE. This facility allows a user to specify a particular set of universally quantified equations or equivalences as rewriting rules. We call such a collection a *simplification set*. The simplifier uses them by replacing the left hand side of an equation by its right hand side after making the appropriate substitutions for the universal variables.

For example, $\forall x\ y.\mathrm{car}(\mathrm{cons}(x,y)) = x$ will rewrite any expression of the form $\mathrm{car}(\mathrm{cons}(t_1, t_2))$ to t_1, where t_1 and t_2 are arbitrary terms.

When given an expression to simplify, REWRITE uses its entire collection of rewrite rules over and over again until it is no longer possible to apply any. Unfortunately, if you give it a rule like

$$\forall x\ y.x+y = y+x$$

it will simply go on switching the two arguments to '+' forever. This is because the rewritten term again matches the rule. This is actually a desired property of this system. First, it is impossible in general to decide if a given collection of rewrite rules will lead to a non-terminating sequence of replacements. Second any simple way of guaranteeing termination will exclude a lot of things that you really want to use. For example, suppose you had the restriction that no sub-expression of the right hand side should match the left hand side of a rewrite rule. Then you could not include the definition of a recursive function even if you know that it will not rewrite itself forever in the particular case you are considering. This case occurs quite frequently.

This simplifier is quite complicated and I will not describe its details here. There are three distinct subparts.

(1) *A matching part.* This determines when a left hand side matches a particular formula.

(2) *An action part.* This determines what action to take when a match is found. At present the only thing that the simplifier can do under the control of a user is the replacement of the matched expression by its right hand side.

(3) *The threading part.* That is, given an expression in what order should the sub-expressions be matched.

The details of these parts are found in Weyhrauch [Note 6]. This simplifier behaves much like a PROLOG interpreter (Warren (1977)), but treates a more extensive collection of sentences. I will say more about first order logic as a programming language (Kowalski (1974)) below.

In Appendix E here is a detailed example which illustrates the control structure of the simplifier.

6. A General First Order Logic Expression Evaluator

Unfortunately, neither of the above simplifiers will do enough for our purposes. This section describes an evaluator for arbitrary first order expressions which is adequate for our needs. I believe that the evaluator presented below is the only natural way of considering first order logic as a programming language.

Consider adding the definition of the factorial function to the axioms above.

```
DECLARE OPCONST fact(NATNUM) = NATNUM;
AXIOM FACT: ∀n.fact(n) = IF n = ∅ THEN 1 ELSE n*fact(pred(n));;
```

Suppose we ask the semantic simplifier to

```
*****SIMPLIFY fact(3);
```

Quite justifiably it will say, "no simplifications". There is no semantic attachment to fact.

Now consider what the syntactic simplifier will do to fact(3) just given the definition of factorial.

```
fact (3) = IF 3 = ∅ THEN 1 ELSE 3*fact(pred(3))
         = IF 3 = ∅ THEN 1
                ELSE 3*(IF pred(3) = ∅ THEN 1 ELSE pred(3)*fact(pred(pred(3))))
```

The rewriting will never terminate because the syntactic simplifier doesn't know anything about $3 = \emptyset$ or pred $(3) = \emptyset$, etc. Thus it will blindly replace fact by its definition forever.

The above computation could be made to stop in several ways. For example, it would stop if

$$(3 = 0) \equiv \text{FALSE}$$
$$\forall X\, Y.(\text{IF FALSE THEN } X \text{ ELSE } Y) = Y$$
$$\text{pred}(3) = 2$$
$$\text{fact}(2) = 2$$
$$3*2 = 6$$

were all in the simplification set.

Or if we stopped after the first step and the semantic attachment mechanism knew about = on integers and pred then we would get

```
syn   fact(3) = IF 3 = ∅ THEN 1 ELSE 3*fact(pred(3))
sem           = 3*fact(2)
syn           = 3*(IF 2 = ∅ THEN 1 ELSE 2*fact(pred(2)))
sem           = 3*(2*fact(1))
syn           = 3*(2*(IF 1 = ∅ THEN 1 ELSE 1*fact(pred(1))))
sem           = 3*(2*(1*fact(∅)))
syn           = 3*(2*(1*(IF ∅ = ∅ THEN 1 ELSE ∅*fact(pred(∅)))))
sem           = 3*(2*(1*1))
                halt
```

This 'looks better'. The interesting thing to note is that if we had a semantic attachment to * this would have computed fully. On the other hand if we had added the definition of * in terms of + then it would have reduced to some expression in terms of addition. In this case if we didn't have a semantic attachment to * but only to + this expression would have also 'computed' 6.

Notice that this combination of semantic plus syntactic simplification acts very much like an ordinary interpreter. We have implemented such an interpreter and it has the following properties.

(1) It will compute any function whose definition is hereditarily built up, in a quantifier free way, out of functions that have attachments, on domains that have attachments.

(2) Every step is a logical consequence of the function definitions and the semantic attachments. This implies that as a programming system this evaluator cannot produce an incorrect result. Thus the correctness of the expression as a 'program' is free.

This evaluator will be used extensively below. I would like to remark that this evaluator is completely general in that it takes an arbitrary set of first order sentences and an arbitrary simulation structure and does both semantic evaluation and syntactic evaluation until it no longer knows what to do. You should observe that the expressions you give it are any first order sentences you like. In this sense it is a substantial extension of PROLOG (Warren (1977)) that is not tied down to clause form and skolemization. In the examples below those familiar with PROLOG can see the naturalness that this kind of evaluation of first order sentences allows. Just look at the above definition of factorial. We allow for functions to have their natural definitions as terms. The introduction of semantic simplifications also gives arbitrary interpretations to particular predicates and functions.

7. Systems of Languages and Simulation Structures

As mentioned in the introduction, one of the important things about the FOL system is its ability to deal with metatheory. In order to do this effectively we need to conceptualize on what *objects* FOL is manipulating. As I have described it above, FOL can be thought of as always having its attention directed at a object consisting of a language, L, a simulation structure, SS, attachments between the two, and a set of facts, F, i.e. the finite set of facts that have asserted or proved.

We can view this as shown in Fig. 1.

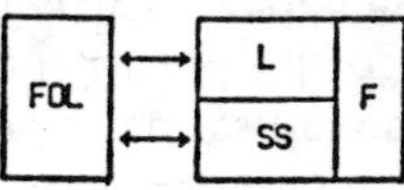

FIG. 1.

Below I will sometimes represent these 3-tuples schematically as

$$\langle L, SS, F \rangle$$

I will abuse language in two ways. Most of the time I will call these structures *LS pairs*, to emphasize the importance of having explicit representations as data structures for languages, the objects mentioned and the correspondence between the two. At other times I will call this kind of structure a *theory*.

The importance of LS pairs cannot be overestimated. I believe they fill a gap in the kinds of structures that have previously used to formalize reasoning.

Informally their introduction corresponds to the recognition that we reason about objects, and that our reasoning makes use of our understanding of the things we reason about.

Let me give a mathematical example and a more traditional AI example.

Consider the following theorem of real analysis (Royden (1963)).

Theorem. *Let $\langle F_n \rangle$ be a sequence of nonempty closed intervals on the real line with $F_{n+1} \subset F_n$, then, if one of the F_n is bounded, the intersection of the F_n is nonempty.*

The goal I would like you to consider is: Give an example to show that this conclusion may be false if we do not require one of these sets to be bounded.

The usual counterexample expected is the set of closed intervals $[n,\infty]$ of real numbers. Clearly none of these are bounded and their intersection is empty. The idea of describing a counterexample simply cannot be made sense of if we do not have some knowledge of the models of our theories. That is, we need some idea of what objects we are reasoning about. The actualization of objects in the form of simulation structures is aimed in part at this kind of question.

As an AI example I will have to use the missionaries and cannibals puzzle. As the problem is usually posed we are asked to imagine three missionaries, three cannibals, a river, its two banks and a boat. We then build a theory about those objects. The point here is that we have explicitly distinguished between the objects mentioned and our theory of these objects. That is, we have (in our minds, so to speak) an explicit image of the objects we are reasoning about. This is a simulation structure as defined above.

One could argue that simulation structures are just linguistic objects anyway and we should think of them as part of the theory. I believe this is fundamentally wrong. In the examples below we make essential use of this distinction between an object and the words we use to mention it.

In addition to the practical usefulness that simulation structures have, they allow us, in a mechanized way, to make sense out of the traditional philosophic questions of sense and denotation. That is, they allow us to mention in a completely formal and natural way the relation between the objects we are reasoning about and the words we are using to mention them. This basic distinction is exactly what we have realized by making models of a language into explicit data structures.

One way of describing what we have done is that we have built a data structure that embodies the idea that when we reason we need a language to carry out our discussions, some information about the object this language talks about, and some facts about the objects expressed in the language. This structure can be thought of as a mechanizable analogue of a theory. Since it is a data structure like any other we can reason about this theory by considering it as an object described by some other theory. Thus we give up the idea of a 'universal' language about all objects to gain the ability to formally discuss our various theories of these objects.

Currently FOL has the facility to simultaneously handle as many LS pairs as you want. It also provides a facility for changing one's attention from one pair to another. We use this feature for changing attention from theory to metatheory as explained below.

8. Metatheory

I have already used the word 'metatheory' many times and since it is an important part of what follows I want to be a little more careful about what I mean by it. In this note I am not concerned with the philosophical questions logicians raise in discussions of consistency, etc. I am interested in how metatheory can be used to facilitate reasoning using computers. One of the main contributions of this paper is the way in which I use *reflection principles* (Feferman (1962)) to connect theories and metatheories. Reflection principles are described in the next section.

In this section I do not want to justify the use of metatheory. In ordinary reasoning it is used all the time. Some common examples of metatheory are presented in the next section. Here I will present examples taken from logic itself, as they require no additional explanation.

In its simplest form metatheory is used in the following way. Imagine that you want to prove some theorem of the theory, i.e. to extend the facts part, f, of some LS to F. One way of doing this is by using FOL in the ordinary theorem constructing way to generate a new fact about the objects mentioned by the theory. An alternative way of doing it may be to use some metatheorem which 'shortens' the proof by stating that the *result* of some complicated theorem generation scheme is valid. Such shortcuts are sometimes called *subsidiary deduction rules* (Kleene (1952), p. 86).

We represent this schematically by the following diagram.

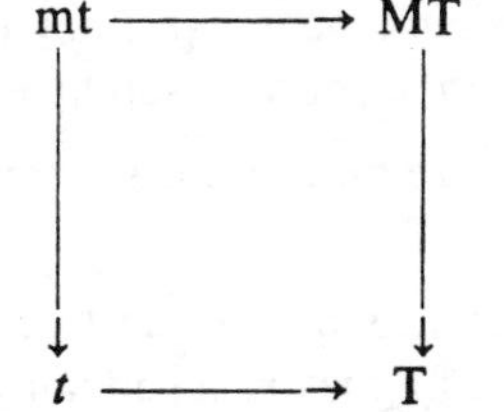

Consider the metatheorem: if you have a propositional WFF whose only sentential connective is the equivalence sign, then the WFF is a theorem if each sentential symbol occurs an even number of times. In FOL this could be expressed by the metatheory sentence

$$\forall w.(\text{PROPWFF}(w) \wedge \text{CONTAINS\_ONLY\_EQUIVALENCES}(w) \supset (\forall s.(\text{SENTSYM}(s) \wedge \text{OCCURS}(s,w) \supset \text{EVEN}(\text{count}(s,w))) \supset \text{THEOREM}(w)))$$

The idea of this theorem is that since it is easier to count than to construct the proofs of complicated theorems, this metatheorem can save you the work of generating a proof. In FOLs metatheory this theorem can be either be proved or simply asserted as axiom.

We use this theorem by directing our attention to the metatheory and instantiating it to some WFF and proving that THEOREM(w). Since we are assuming that our axiomatization of the metatheory is sound, we are then justified in asserting w in the theory. The reflection principles stated below should be looked at as the *reason* that we are justified in asserting w. More detailed examples will be given in the next section.

In FOL we introduce a special LS pair META. It is intended that META is a general theory of LS pairs. When we start, it contains facts about only those things that are common to all LS pairs. Since META behaves like any other first order LS pair additional axioms, etc., can be added to it. This allows a user to assert many other things about a particular theory. Several examples will be given below.

An example of how we axiomatize the notion of well formed

$$\forall \text{Is expr}.(\text{WFF}(\text{expr},\text{Is}) \equiv \text{PROPWFF}(\text{expr},\text{Is}) \lor \text{QUANTWFF}(\text{expr},\text{Is}))$$

An expression is a WFF (relative to a particular LS pair) if it is either a propositional WFF or a quantifier WFF.

$$\forall \text{Is expr}.(\text{PROPWFF}(\text{expr},\text{Is}) \equiv \text{APPLPWFF}(\text{expr},\text{Is}) \lor \text{AWFF}(\text{expr},\text{Is}))$$

A propositional WFF is either an application propositional WFF or an atomic WFF.

$$\forall \text{Is expr}.(\text{APPLPWFF}(\text{expr},\text{Is}) \equiv \text{PROPCONN}(\text{mainsym}(\text{expr})) \land \forall \text{n}.(\emptyset < \text{n} \land \text{n} \leqslant \text{arity}(\text{mainsym}(\text{expr}),\text{Is}) \supset \text{WFF}(\text{arg}(\text{n},\text{expr}),\text{Is})))$$

An application propositional WFF is an expression whose main symbol is a propositional connective, and if n is between 0 and the arity of the propositional connective then the n-th argument of the expression must be a WFF. Notice that this definition is mutually recursive with that of PROPWFF and WFF.

$$\forall \text{Is expr}.(\text{QUANTWFF}(\text{expr},\text{Is}) \equiv \text{QUANT}(\text{mainsym}(\text{expr})) \land \text{INDVAR}(\text{bvar}(\text{expr}),\text{Is}) \land \text{WFF}(\text{matrix}(\text{expr}),\text{Is})$$

A quantifier WFF is an expression whose main symbol is a quantifier, whose bound variable is an individual variable and whose matrix is a WFF.

$$\forall \text{Is expr}.(\text{AWFF}(\text{expr},\text{Is}) \equiv \text{SENTSYM}(\text{expr},\text{Is}) \lor \text{APPLAWFF}(\text{expr},\text{Is}))$$

An atomic WFF is either a sentential symbol or an application atomic WFF.

$$\forall \text{Is expr}.(\text{APPLAWFF}(\text{expr},\text{Is}) \equiv \text{PREDSYM}(\text{mainsym}(\text{expr}),\text{Is}) \land \forall \text{n}.(\emptyset < \text{n} \land \text{n} \leqslant \text{arity}(\text{mainsym}(\text{expr}),\text{Is}) \supset \text{TERM}(\text{arg}(\text{n},\text{e}),\text{Is})))$$

An atomic application WFF is an expression whose main symbol is a predicate symbol and each argument of this expression in the appropraite range is a TERM.

$$\forall \text{Is expr}.(\text{TERM}(\text{expr},\text{Is}) \equiv \text{INDSYM}(\text{expr},\text{Is}) \lor \text{APPLTERM}(\text{expr},\text{Is}))$$

$$\forall \text{Is expr}.(\text{APPLTERM}(\text{expr},\text{Is}) \equiv \text{OPSYM}(\text{mainsym}(\text{expr}),\text{Is}) \land \forall \text{n}.(\emptyset < \text{n} \land \text{n} \leqslant \text{arity}(\text{mainsym}(\text{expr},\text{Is})) \supset \text{TERM}(\text{arg}(\text{n},\text{expr}),\text{Is})))$$

A TERM is either an individual symbol or an application TERM, etc.

This is by no means a complete description of LS pairs but it does give some idea of what sentences in META look like. These axioms are collected together in appendix C. The extent of META isn't critical and this paper is not an appropriate place to discuss its details as implemented in FOL. Of course, in addition to the descriptions of the objects contained in the LS pair, it also has axioms about what it means to be a 'theorem', etc.

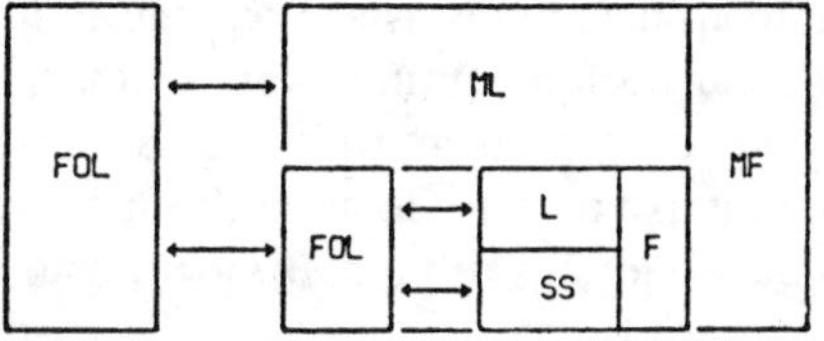

FIG. 2.

Thus META contains the proof theory and some of the model theory of an LS pair. As with any first order theory its language is built up of predicate constants, function symbols and individual constant symbols. What are these? There are constants for WFFs, TERMs, derivations, simulation structures, models, etc. It contains functions for doing 'and introductions', for substituting TERMs into WFFs, constructors and selectors on data structures. It has predicates 'is a well formed formula', 'is a term', 'equality of expressions except for change of bound variables', 'is a model', 'is a simulation structure', 'is a proof', etc.

Suppose that we are considering the metatheory of some particular LS pair, LSO = ⟨L,SS,F⟩. At this point we need to ask a critical question.

What is the *natural* simulation structure for META?

The answer is: (1) we actually have in hand the object we are trying to axiomatize, LSO, and (2) the code of FOL itself contains algorithms for the predicates and functions mentioned above.

This leads to the picture of Fig. 2.It is this picture that leads to the first hint of how to construct a system of logic that can *look* at itself. The trick is that when we carry out the above construction on a computer, the two boxes labeled FOL are physically the same object. I will expand on this in the section on self reflection.

9. Reflection

A *reflection principle* is a statement of a relation between a theory and its metatheory. Although logicians use considerably stronger principles (see Feferman (1962)), we will only use some simple examples, i.e., statements of the soundness of the axiomatization in the metatheory of the theory. An example of a reflection principle is

(in T) \|/
w

(in MT) Prf("\|/","w")

In natural deduction formulations of logic proofs are represented as trees. In the above diagram let '\|/' be a proof and '*w*' be the well formed formula which it proves. Let Prf be a predicate constant in the metatheory, with Prf(p,x) true if and only if p is a proof, x is a wff, and p is a proof of x. Also, let "\|/" and "*w*" be the individual constants in the metatheory that are the names of '\|/' and '*w*', respectively. Then the above reflection principle can be read as: if '\|/' is a proof of '*w*' in the theory we are allowed to assert Prf("\|/","*w*") in the metatheory and vice versa.

A special case of this rule is '*w*' has no dependencies, i.e. it is a theorem.

(in T) *w* with no dependencies
(in META) THEOREM("*w*")

A simpler example is

(in T) an individual variable x
(in META) INDVAR("x")

Suppose we have the metatheorem

ANDI: ∀thm1 thm2.THEOREM(mkand(wffof(thm1),wffof(thm2)))

This (meta)theorem says that if we have any two theorems of the theory, then we get a theorem by taking the conjunction of the two wffs associated with these theorems. I need to remark about what I mean by the WFF associated with a theorem. Theorems should be thought of as particular kinds of facts. Facts are more complicated objects than only sentences. They also contain other information. For example, they include the reason we are willing to assert them and what other facts their assertion depends on. Facts also have names. Thus the above line is an incomplete representation of the metatheoretic fact whose name is ANDI. The WFF associated with this fact is just

∀thm1 thm2.THEOREM(mkand(wffof(thm1),wffof(thm2)))

Remember the reflection principle assocaited with THEOREM is

(in T) *w* with no dependencies
(in META) THEOREM("*w*")

Thus we can imagine the following scenario.

Suppose we have two theorems called T1 and T2 in the theory. These facts are represented as FOL data structures. Now suppose we want to assert the conjunction of these two in the theory. One way to do this is to use the *and introduction* rule of FOL. This example, however, is going to do it the hard way. First we switch to the metatheory carrying with us the data structures for T1 and T2. We then declare some individual constants t1 and t2 to be of sort theorem in the metatheory, and use the semantic attachment mechanism at the metatheory level to attach the data structures for T1 and T2 to the individual constants t_1 and t_2 respectively. We then instantiate the metatheorem ANDI to t1 and t2. Note that the resulting formula is a ground instance of a sentence without quantifiers. This means that if we have attachments to all the symbols in the formula we can evaluate this formula. In this theorem we have the predicate constant THEOREM. In META it is the only constant in this sentence that is not likely to have an attachment. This is because being a theorem is not in general decidable. Fortunately, we can still use the reflection principle, because we understand the intended interpretation of the metatheory. So if we use the evaluator on

mkand(wffof(t1),wffof(t2)),

we can pick up the data structure computed in the model, instead of the term. Then since we know that it is a theorem we can make it into one in the theory.

This idea has been implemented in a very nice way. In FOL we have the following command.

```
*****REFLECT ANDI T1,T2;
```

The reflect command understands some fixed list of reflection principles, which includes those above. When FOL sees the word 'REFLECT' it expects the next thing in the input stream to be the name of a fact in the metatheory of the current theory. So it switches to the metatheory and scans for a fact. It then finds that this fact is universally quantified with two variables ranging over facts in the theory. It switches back to the theory and scans for two facts in the theory. It holds on to the data structures that it gets in that way and switches back to the metatheory. Once there it makes the attachments of these structures to two newly created individual constants, first checking whether or not it already has an attachment for either of these structures. We then instantiate the theorem to the relevant constants and evaluate the result. When we look at the result we notice that it will probably simply evaluate to

THEOREM(mkand(wffof(t1),wffof(t2)))

This is because we don't have an attachment to THEOREM and we also don't have an individual constant which names mkand(wffof(t1),wffof(t2)). But what we do notice is that we have reduced the theorem to the form THEOREM(-), and we know about reflection principles involving THEOREM. Thus we go back and evaluate its argument, mkand(wffof(t1),wffof(t2)), and see if it has a value in the model. In this case since it does we can reflect it back into the theory, by returning to the theory and constructing the appropriate theorem.

This example is a particularly simple one, but the feature described is very general. I will give some more examples below. One thing I want to emphasise here is that what we have done is *to change theorem proving in the theory into evaluation in the metatheory*. I claim that this idea of using reflection with evaluation is the most general case of this and that this feature is not only an extremely useful operation but a fundamental one as well. It is the correct technical realization of how we can *use* declarative information. That is, the only thing you expect a sentence to do is to take its intended interpretation seriously.

The metatheorem we use in reflection does not need to be of the form THEOREM(-). This is the reason for needing the evaluater rather than simply either the syntactic or the semantic simplification mechanisms alone. Consider the following general metatheorems *about* the theory of natural numbers. If you find it hard to read it is explained in detail in the next subsection.

$\forall \text{vl}\ x.(\text{LINEAREQ}(\text{wffof}(\text{vl}),x) \supset \text{THEOREM}(\text{mkequal}(x,\text{solve}(\text{wffof}(\text{vl}),x))));$

$\forall w\ x.(\text{LINEAREQ}(w,x) \equiv$
$\quad \text{mainsym}(w) = \text{Equal} \wedge$
$\quad (\text{mainsym}(\text{lhs}(w)) = \text{Sum} \vee \text{mainsym}(\text{lhs}(w)) = \text{Diff}) \wedge$
$\quad \text{larg}(\text{lhs}(w)) = x \wedge$
$\quad \text{NUMERAL}(\text{rarg}(\text{lhs}(w))) \wedge$
$\quad \text{NUMERAL}(\text{rhs}(w))) \wedge$
$\quad (\text{mainsym}(\text{lhs}(w)) = \text{Sum} \supset \text{mknum}(\text{rhs}(w)) < \text{mknum}(\text{rarg}(\text{lhs}(w))));$

$\forall w\ x.(\text{solve}(w,x) = \text{IF mainsym}(\text{lhs}(w)) = \text{Sum}$
$\quad \text{THEN mknumeral}(\text{mknum}(\text{rhs}(w)) - \text{mknum}(\text{rarg}(\text{lhs}(w))))$
$\quad \text{ELSE mknumeral}(\text{mknum}(\text{rhs}(w)) +$
$\qquad \text{mknum}(\text{rarg}(\text{lhs}(w)))));;$

These axioms together with the reflection mechanism extend FOL, so that it can solve equations of the form $x+a = b$ or $x-a = b$, when there is a solution in natural numbers. We could have given a solution in integers or for n simultaneous equations in n unknowns. Each of these requires a different collection of theorems in the metatheory.

This axiomatization may look inefficient but let me point out that solve is exactly the same amount of writing that you would need to write code to solve the same equation. The definition of LINEAREQ is divided into two parts. The first five conjunctions are to do type checking, the sixth conjunct checks for the existence of a solution before you try to use solve to find it. The above example actually does a lot. It type checks the argument, guarantees a solution and then finds it.

9.1. Can a program learn?

In this section I want to digress from the stated intent of the paper and speak a little more generally about AI. It is my feeling that it is the task of AI to explain how it might be possible to build a computer individual that we can interact with as a partner in some problem solving area. This leads to the question of what kinds of conversations we want to have with such an individual and what the nature of our interactions with him should be.

Below I describe a conversation with FOL about solving linear equations. As an example it has two purposes. First it is to illustrate the sense in which FOL is a conversational machine that can have rich discussions (even if not in natural language). And second to explore my ideas of what kinds of dialogues we can have with machines that might be construed as the computer individual learning. I believe that after the discussion presented below we could reasonably say that FOL had learned to solve linear equations. That is, by having this conversation with FOL we have taught FOL some elementary algebra.

Imagine that we have told FOL about Peano arithmetic. We could do this by reading in the axioms presented in Appendix B. We can then have a discussion about *numbers*. For example, we might say

*****ASSUME $n+2 = 7$;

1 $(n+2) = 7$ (1)

and we might want to know what is the value of n. Since we are talking about numbers in the language of Peano arithmetic the *only* way we have of discussing this problem is by using facts about numbers. Suppose that we already know the theorems

THM1: $\forall p\ q\ m.(p = q \supset p-m = q-m)$
THM2: $\forall p\ q\ m.(p+q)-r = p+(q-r)$
THM3: $\forall p.(p+\emptyset) = p$

Then we can prove that $n = 5$

*****∀E THM1 n+2,7,2;

2 $(n+2) = 7 \supset ((n+2)-2) = (7-2)$

*****EVAL BY {THM2,THM3};

3 $(n+2) = 7 \supset n = 5$

***** ⊃ E 1,3;

4 $n = 5$ (1)

In this case what we have done is proved that $n = 5$ by using facts about *arithmetic*. To put it in the perspective of *conversation*, we are having a discussion about numbers.

If we were expecting to discuss with FOL many such facts, rather than repeating the above conversation many times we might choose to have a single discussion about *algebra*. This would be carried out by introducing the notion of *equation* and a description of how to *solve* them. What is an equation? Well, it simply turns out to be a special kind of *atomic formula* of the theory of arithmetic. That is, we can discuss the solution to equantions by using metatheory.

In FOL we switch to the metatheory. We make some declarations and then define what it means to be a linear equation with a solution by stating the axiom

```
∀w x.(LINEAREQ(w,x) ≡
        mainsym(w) = Equal ∧
        (mainsym(lhs(w)) = Sum ∨ mainsym(lhs(w)) = Diff) ∧
        larg(lhs(w)) = x ∧
        NUMERAL(rarg(lhs(w))) ∧
        NUMERAL(rhs(w)) ∧
        (mainsym(lhs(w)) = Sum ⊃ mknum(rhs(w)) > mknum(rarg(lhs(w))))
```

Here w is a (meta)variable ranging over WFFs, and x is a (meta)variable ranging over individual variables. Spelled out in English this sentence says that a well formed formula is a linear equation if and only if:

(i) it is an equality,

(ii) its left hand side is either a sum or a difference,

(iii) the left hand argument of the left hand side of the equality is x,

(iv) then right hand argument of the left hand side of the equality is a numeral,

(v) the right hand side of the equality is a numeral and

(vi) if the left hand side is a sum then the number denoted by the numeral on the right hand side is greater than the number denoted by the numeral appearing in the left hand side.

In more mathematical terminology it is: that the well formed formula must be either of the form $x+a = b$ or $x-a = b$ where a and b are numerals and x is an individual variable. Since here we are only interested in the natural numbers, the last restriction in the definition of LINEAREQ is needed to guarantee the existence of a solution.

We also describe how to find out what is the *solution* to an equation.

```
∀w x.(solve(w,x) = IF mainsym(lhs(w)) = Sum
                   THEN mknumeral(mknum(rhs(w))−
                                  mkum(rarg(lhs(w))))
                   ELSE mknumeral(mknum(rhs(w))+
                                  mknum(rarg(lhs(w)))) );;
```

This is a function definition in the meta theory. Finally we assert that if we have an equation in the theory then the numeral constructed by the solver can be asserted to be the answer.

```
∀vl x.(LINEAREQ(wffof(vl),x) ⊃ THEOREM(mkequal(x,solve(wffof(vl),x))));
```

We then tell FOL to remember these facts in a way that is convenient to be used by FOL's evaluator.

This then is the conversation we have with FOL about equations. Now we are ready to see how FOL can use that information, so we switch FOL's attention back to the theory. Now, whenever we want to solve a linear equation, we simply remark, using the reflect command, that he should remember our discussion about solving equations.

We can now get the effect of the small proof above by saying

```
*****REFLECT SOLVE 1;
5 n = 5   (1)
```

In effect FOL has learned to solve simple linear equations.

We could go on to ask FOL to prove that the function solve actually provides a solution to the equation, rather than our just telling FOL that it does, but this is simply a matter of sophistication. It has to do with the question of what you are willing to accept as a justification.

One reasonable justification is that the teacher told me. This is exactly the state we are in above. On the other hand if that is not satisfactory then it is possible to discuss with FOL the justification of the solution. This could be accomplished by explaining to FOL (in the metatheory) not to assert the solution of the equations in the theory, but rather to construct a proof of the correctness of the solution as we did when we started. Clearly this can be done using same machinery that was used here. This is important because it means that our reasoning system does not need to be expanded. We only have to tell it more information.

A much more reasonable alternative is to tell FOL (again in the metatheory) two things. One is what we have above, i.e., to assert the solution of the equation. Second is that if asked to justify the solution, then to produce that proof. This combines the advantages each of the above possibilities. I want to point out that this is very close to the kinds of discussions that you want to be able to have with people about simple algebra.

Informally we always speak about solving *equations*. That is, we think of them as syntactic and learn how to manipulate them. This is not thinking about them as relations, which is their usual first order interpretation. In this sense going to the metatheory and treating them as syntactic objects is very close to our informal use of these notions.

I believe that this is exactly what we want in an AI system dealing with the question of *teaching*. Notice that we have the best of both worlds. On the one hand, at the theory level, we can 'execute' this learning, i.e. use it, and on the other hand, at the metatheory level, we can reason about what we have learned about manipulating equations. In addition the correct distinction between equations as facts and equations as syntactic objects has been maintained. The division between theory and metatheory has allowed us to view the same object in both these ways without contradiction or the possibility of confusion.

As is evident from the above description, one of the things we have here is a very general purpose programming system. In addition it is extendable. Above we have showed how to introduce any new subsidiary deduction rule that you chose, 'simply' by telling FOL what you would like it to do. This satisfies the desires of Davis and Schwartz (1977) but in a setting not restricted to the theory of hereditarily finite sets. As I said above: we are using first order logic in what I believe is its most general and natural setting.

There are hundreds of examples of this kind where their natural description is in the metatheory. In a later paper I will discuss just how much of the intent of natural language can only be understood if you realize that a lot of what we say is about our use of language, not about objects in the world. This kind of conversation is most naturally carried out in the metatheory with the use of the kind of self-reflective structures hinted about below.

9.2. Using metametatheory

We can take another leap by allowing ourselves to iterate the above procedure and using metametatheory. This section is quite sketchy but would require a full paper to write out the details.

We can use the metametatheory to describe declaratively what we generally call heuristics. Consider an idealized version of the Boyer and Moore (1979) theorem prover for recursive functions. This prover looks at a function definition and tries to decide whether or not to try to prove some property of the function using either CAR-induction or CDR-induction, depending on the form of the function definition.

CAR and CDR inductions are axiom schemas, which depend on the form of the function definition and the WFF being proved. Imagine that these had already told to FOL in the metatheory. Suppose we had called them CARIND and CDRIND. Then using the facilities described above we could use these facts by reflection. For example,

*****ASSUME ∀*u*.counta(*u*) = if atom(*u*) then *u* else counta(car(*u*));

1 ∀*u*.counta(*u*) = if atom(*u*) then *u* else counta(car(*u*)) (1)

*****REFLECT CARIND 1 ∀*u*.ATOM(counta(*u*));

2 ∀*u*.ATOM(counta(*u*)) (1)

*****ASSUME ∀*u*.countd(*u*) = if null(*u*) then 'NIL else countd(cdr(*u*));

3 ∀*u*.countd(*u*) = if null(*u*) then 'NIL else countd(cdr(*u*)) (3)

*****REFLECT CDRIND 3 ∀*u*.countd(*u*) = 'NIL;

4 ∀*u*.countd(*u*) = 'NIL (3)

The use of this kind of command can be discussed in the metametatheory. We introduce a function, T_reflect, in the metametatheory, which we attach using semantic attachment to the FOL code that implements the above reflect command. Thus T_reflect takes a fact, ∨I and a list of arguments, and if it succeeds returns a new proof whose last step is the newly asserted fact and if it fails returns some error. Suppose also that Carind and Cdrind are the metametatheory's name for CARIND and CDRIND respectively. Then suppose in the metametatheory we let

WFF1 = mkforall(T_*u*,mkapplw1(T_ATOM,
(mkapplt1(T_counta,T_*u*))))

WFF2 = mkforall(T_*u*,mkequal(mkapplt1(T_countd,T_*u*),
mksexp('NIL)))

that is, A*u*.ATOM(counta(*u*)) and ∀*u*.countd(*u*) = 'NIL, respectively. We prefix things refering to the theory by "T_". The effect of the above commands (without actually asserting anything) is gotten by using the FOL evaluator on

T_reflect(Cdrind, < T_fact(1),WFF1 ⟩)
T_reflect(Cdrind, < T_fact(3),WFF1 ⟩).

Now suppose that ∨I ranges over facts in the theory, *f* ranges over function symbols, and *w* ranges over WFFs. The micro Boyer and Moore theorem prover can be expressed by

```
∀∨I f w.
  (IS_T_FUNDEF(∨I,f) ⊃
     (CONTAINS_ONLY_CAR_RECURSION(∨I,f) ∧
        NOERROR(T_REFLECT(Carind,⟨∨I,w⟩)) ⊃
        T_THEOREM(last_T_step(T_REFLECT(Carind,⟨∨I,w⟩)))) ∧
     (CONTAINS_ONLY_CDR_RECURSION(∨I,f) ∧
        NOERROR(T_REFLECT(Cdrind,⟨∨I,w⟩)) ⊃
        T_THEOREM(last_T_step(T_REFLECT(Cdrind,⟨∨I,w⟩)))) )
```

In the metametatheory we call this fact BOYER_and_MOORE. It is read as follows: if in the theory, ∨I is a function definition of the function symbol *f*, then if this function definition only contains recursions on car, and if when you apply reflection from the theory level to the metatheorem called Carind you don't get an error, then the result of this reflection is a theorem at the theory level, similarly for cdr induction.

As explained in the previous sections, asserting this in the metametatheory allows it to be used at the theory level by using the same reflection device as before.

When our attention is directed to the theory we can say

*****MREFLECT BOYER_and_MOORE 1,counta,∀*u*.ATOM(counta(*u*));

5 ∀*u*.ATOM(counta(*u*)) (1)

*****MREFLECT BOYER_and_MOORE 3,countd,∀*u*.countd(*u*) = 'NIL;

6 ∀*u*.countd(*u*) = 'NIL (3)

Here MREFLECT simply means reflect into the metametatheory.

This example shows how the metametatheory, together with reflection, can be used to drive the proof checker itself. Thus we have the ability to declaratively state heuristics and have them effectively used. The ability to reason about heuristics and prove additional theorems about them provides us with an enormous extra power. Notice that we have once again changed theorem proving at the theory level into computation at the metametatheory level. This is part of the leverage that we get by having all of this machinery around simultaneously.

This example, as it is described above, has not yet been run in FOL. It is the only example in this paper which has not actually been done using the FOL system, but it is clear that it will work simply given the current features.

A good way of looking at all of this is that the same *kind* of language that we use to carry on ordinary conversations with FOL can be used to discuss the control structures of FOL itself. Thus it can be used to discuss its own actions.

10. Self Reflection

In the traditional view of metatheory we start with a theory and we axiomatize that theory. This gives us metatheory. Later we may axiomatize that theory. That gives us metametatheory. If you believe that most reasoning is at some level (as I do) then this view of towers of metatheories leads to many questions. For example, how is it that human memory space doesn't overflow. Each theory in the tower seems to contain a complete description of the theory below thus exponentiating the amount of space needed!

In the section on metatheory, I introduced the LS pair, META. Since it is a first order theory just like any other, FOL can deal with it just like any other. Since META is the general theory of LS pairs and META is an LS pair this might suggest that META is also a theory that contains facts about itself. That is, by introducing the individual constant Meta into the theory META and by using semantic attachment to attach the theory (i.e., the actual machine data structure) META to Meta we can give META its own name. The rest of this section is somewhat vague. We have just begun to work out the consequences of this observation.

FOL handles many LS pairs simultaneously. I have showed how given any LS pair we can direct FOL's attention to META using reflection. Once META has an individual constant which is a name for itself and we have attached META to this constant, then META is FOL's theory of itself. Notice several things:

(1) If META has names for all of the LS pairs known to FOL then it has the entire FOL system as its simulation structure;

(2) Since META is a theory about any LS pair, we can use it to reason about itself.

We can illustrate this in FOL by switching to META and executing the following command.

*****REFLECT ANDI ANDI ANDI;

1 ∀thm1 thm2.THEOREM(mkand(wffof(thm1),wffof(thm2))) ∧
∀thm1 thm2.THEOREM(mkand(wffof(thm1),wffof(thm2)))

The effect we have achieved is that when FOL's attention is directed at itself, then when we reflect into its own metatheory we have a system that is capable of reasoning about itself.

When looking at human reasoning I am struck by two facts. First, we seem to be able to apply the Meta facts that we know to any problems that we are trying to solve, and second, even though it is possible to construct simple examples of use/mention conflicts, most people arrive at correct answers to questions without even knowing there is a problem. Namely, although natural language is filled with apparent puns that arise out of use/mention confusions, the people speaking do not confuse the names of things with the things. That is, the *meaning* is clear to them.

The above command suggests one possible technical way in which both of these problems can be addressed. The structure of FOL *knew* that the first occurrence of ANDI in the above command was a 'use' and that the second and third were 'mentions'. Furthermore, the same routines that dealt effectively with the ordinary non self reflective way of looking at theory/metatheory relations also dealt with this case of self reflection without difficulty.

Notice that I said, 'this case'. It is possible with the structure that I have described above to ask META embarrassing questions. For example, if you ask META twice in a row what the largest step number in its proof is you will get two different answers. This would seem to lead to a contradiction.

The source of this problem is in what I believe is in our traditional idea of what it means to be a *rule of inference*. Self reflective systems have properties that are different from ordinary systems. In particular, whenever you 'apply a rule of inference' to the facts of this system you change the structure of META itself and as a result you change the attachment to Meta. This process of having a rule of inference changes the models of a theory as well as the already proven facts simply does not happen in traditional logics. This change of point of view requires a new idea of what is a valid rule of inference for such systems.

The extent of the soundness of the structure that I propose here is well beyond the scope of this elementary paper. Also FOL was built largely before I understood anything about this more general idea of rule of inference, thus the current FOL code cannot adequately implement these ideas. One of many main current research interests is in working out the consequences of these self reflective structures.

META has many strange properties which I have just begun to appreciate and is a large topic for further research.

11. Conclusion

11.1. Summary of important results

I want to review what I consider to be the important results of this paper.

One is the observation that, when we reason, we use representations of the objects we are reasoning about as well as a representation of the facts about these objects. This is technically realized by FOL's manipulation of LS pairs using semantic attachment. It is incorrect to view this as a procedural representation of facts. Instead we should look at it as an ability to explicitly represent procedures. That is, simulation structures give us an opportunity to have a machine representation of the objects we want to reason about as well as the sentences we use to mention them.

Second, the evaluator I described above is an important object. When used by itself it represents a mathematical way of describing algorithms together with the assurance that they are correctly implemented. This is a consequence of the fact that the evaluator only performs logically valid transformations on the function definitions. In this way we could use the evaluator to actually generate a proof that the computed answer is correct. In these cases evaluation and deduction become the same thing. This is similar in spirit to the work of Kowalski (1974), but does not rely on any normalization of formulas. It considers the usual logical function definitions and takes their intended interpretation seriously. This evaluator works on any expression with respect to any LS pair and its implementation has proved to be only two to three times slower than a lisp interpreter.

Third is the observation that the FOL proof checker is itself the natural simulation structure for the theory META of LS pairs. This gives us a clean way of saying what the intended interpretation of META is. This observation makes evaluation in META a very powerful tool. It is also the seed of a theory of self reflective logic structures that, like humans, can reason about themselves.

Fourth is the use of reflection principles to connect an LS pair with META. This, together with the REFLECT command, is a technical explanation of what has been called the declarative/procedural controversy. Consider the META theorem ANDI described above. When we use the REFLECT command to point at it from some LS pair, ANDI is viewed procedurally. We want it to do an *and introduction*. On the other hand when we are reasoning in META, it is a sentence like any other. Whether a sentence is looked at declaratively or procedurally depends on your point of view, that is, it depends where you are standing when you look at it.

I have presented here a general description of a working reasoning system that includes not only theories but also metatheories of arbitrarily high level. I have given several examples of how these features, together with reflection can be used to dynamically extend the reasoning power of the working FOL system. I have made some references to the way in which one can use the self reflective parts of this system. I have given examples of how heuristics for using subsidiary deduction rules can be described using these structures. In addition, since everything you type to FOL refers to some LS pair, all of the above things can be reasoned about using the same machinery.

11.2. Concluding remarks, history and thanks

I have tried in this paper to give a summary of the ideas which motivate the current FOL system. Unfortunately this leaves little room for complex examples so I should say a little about history, the kinds of things that have been done and what is being done now.

FOL was started in 1972 and the basic ideas for this system were already known in the summer of 1973. Many of the ideas of this system come directly out of taking seriously John McCarthy's idea that before we can ever expect to do interesting problem solving we need a device that can represent the ideas involved in the problem. I started by attempting to use ordinary first order logic and set theory to represent the ideas of mathematics. My discovery of the explicit use of computable partial models (i.e. simulation structures) came out of thinking about a general form for what McCarthy (1973) called a 'computation rule' for logic, together with thinking about problems like the one about real numbers mentioned above. The first implementation of semantic evaluation was in 1974 by me. Since then it has been worked on by Arthur Thomas, Chris Goad, Juan Bulnes and most recently by Andrew Robinson. The first aggressive use of semantic attachment was by Bob Filman (1978) in his thesis.

This idea of attaching algorithms to function and predicate letters is not new to AI. It appears first in Green (1969) I believe, but since then in too many places to cite them all. What is new here is that we have done it uniformly, in such a way that the process can be reasoned about. We have also arranged it so that there can be no confusion between what parts of our data structure is code and what parts are sentences of logic.

The real push for metatheory came from several directions. One was the realization that most of mathematical reasoning in practice was metatheoretic. This conflicted with most current theorem proving ideas of carrying out the reasoning in the theory itself. Second was my desire to be able to do the proofs in Kleene (1952) about the correctness of programs. In the near future we are planning to carry out this dream. Carolyn Talcott and I plan to completely formalize LISP using all the power of the FOL system described above. In addition there will be people working on program transformations in the style of Burstall and Darlington

(1977). The third push for metatheory was a desire to address the question of common sense reasoning. This more than anything needs the ability to be able to reason about our theories of the world. One step in this direction has been taken by Carolyn Talcott and myself. We have worked out D. Michie's Keys and boxes problem using this way of thinking and are currently writing it up.

The desire to deal with metatheory led to the invention of the FOL reflection command. Metatheory is pretty useless without a way of connecting it to the theory. I believe that I am the first to use reflection in this way.

All of the above ideas were presented at the informal session at IJCAI 1973. This panel was composed of Carl Hewitt, Allen Newell, Alan Kay and myself.

The idea of self reflection grew out of thinking about the picture in the section on metatheory.

It has taken several years to make these routines all work together. They first all worked in June 1977 when Dan Blom finished the coding of the evaluator. I gave some informal demos of the examples in this paper at IJCAI 1977.

I suppose that here is as good a place as any to thank all the people that helped this effort. Particularly John McCarthy for his vision and for supporting FOL all these years. I would not have had as much fun doing it alone. Thanks.

I hope to write detailed papers on each of these features with substantial examples. In the meantime I hope this gives a reasonable idea of how FOL works.

Appendices

A. An axiomatization of natural numbers

The commands below repeat those given in Section 4. They will be used in the examples below. One should keep in mind that this is an axiomatization of the natural numbers (including 0), not an axiomatization of the integers.

```
DECLARE INDVAR n m p q ∈ NATNUM;
DECLARE OPCONST suc pred(NATNUM) = NATNUM;
DECLARE OPCONST+(NATNUM, NATNUM) = NATNUM [R← 458,L← 455];
DECLARE OPCONST *(NATNUM, NATNUM) = NATNUM [R← 558,L← 5551;
DECLARE PREDCONST < (NATNUM, NATNUM) [INF];
DECLARE PREDPAR P(NATNUM);
AXIOM  Q:
        ONEONE: ∀n m.(suc(n) = suc(m) ⊃ n = m);
        SUCC1:  ∀n.¬ (0 = suc(n));
        SUCC2:  ∀n.(¬ 0 = n ⊃ ∃m.(n = suc(m)));
        PLUS:   ∀n.n+0 = n
                ∀n m.n+suc(m) = suc(n+m);
        TIMES:  ∀n.n*0 = 0
                ∀n m.n*suc(m) = (n*m)+m; ;;
AXIOM  INDUCT:  P(0)∧ ∀n.(P(n) ⊃ P(suc(n))) ⊃ ∀n.P(n); ;
REPRESENT {NATNUM} AS NATNUMREP;
ATTACH suc  ↔ (LAMBDA (X) (ADD1 X));
ATTACH pred ↔ (LAMBDA (X) (COND ((GREATERP X 0) (SUB1 X)) (T 0)));
ATTACH+     ↔ (LAMBDA (X Y) (PLUS X Y));
ATTACH*     ↔ (LAMBDA (X Y) (TIMES X Y));
ATTACH <    ↔ (LAMBDA (X Y) (LESSP X Y));
```

B. An axiomatization of s-expressions

These commands describe to FOL a simple theory of s-expressions. In addition it contains the definitions on the functions @, for appending two lists, and rev, for reversing a list.

```
DECLARE INDVAR x y z ∈ Sexp;
DECLARE INDVAR u v w ∈ List;
DECLARE INDCONST nil ∈ Null;

DECLARE OPCONST car cdr 1;
DECLARE OPCONST cons(Sexp,List) = List;
DECLARE OPCONST rev 1;
DECLARE OPCONST @ 2 [inf];

DECLARE SIMPSET Basic;
DECLARE SIMPSET Funs;

MOREGENERAL Sexp ≥ {List, Atom, Null};
MOREGENERAL List ≥ {Null};

REPRESENT {Sexp} AS SEXPREP;

AXIOM CAR: ∀x y.car(cons(x,y)) = x;;
AXIOM CDR: ∀x y.cdr(cons(x,y)) = y;;
AXIOM CONS: ∀x y.¬ Null(cons(x,y));;

Basic← {CAR,COR,CONS};

AXIOM REV: ∀u.(rev(u) = IF Null (u) THEN u ELSE rev(cdr(u)) @ cons(car(u),nil));;
AXIOM APPEND: ∀u v.(u@v = IF Null(u) THEN  v ELSE cons(car(u),cdr(u)@v);;

Funs← {REV,APPEND};
```

C. An axiomatization of well formed formulas

This is an example of how WFFs are axiomatized in META. It simply collects together the formulas of Section 8

```
∀Is expr.(WFF(expr,Is) ≡ PROPWFF(expr,Is) ∨
                              QUANTWFF(expr,Is))
∀Is expr.(PROPWFF(expr,Is) ≡ APPLPWFF(expr,Is) ∨
                                       AWFF(expr,Is))
∀Is expr.(APPLPWFF(expr,Is) ≡ PROPCONN(mainsym(expr)) ∧
      ∀n.(0 < n ∧ n ≤ arity(mainsym(expr),Is) ⊃
                                   WFF(arg(n,expr),Is)))
∀Is expr.(QUANTWFF(expr,Is) ≡
      QUANT(mainsym(expr)) ∧ INDVAR(bvar(expr),Is ∧
                                   WFF(matrix(expr),Is)
∀Is expr.(AWFF(expr,Is) ≡ SENTSYM(expr,Is) ∨
                              APPLAWFF(expr,Is)
∀Is expr.(APPLAWFF(expr,Is) ≡ PREDSYM(mainsym(expr),Is) ∧
      ∀n.(0 < n ∧ n ≤ arity(mainsym(expr),Is) ⊃
                              TERM(arg(n,e),Is)))
∀Is expr.(TERM(expr,Is) ≡ INDSYM(expr,Is) ∨ APPLTERM(expr,Is))
∀Is expr.(APPLTERM(expr,Is) ≡ OPSYM(mainsym(expr),Is) ∧
      ∀n.(0 < n ∧ n ≤ arity(mainsym(expr,Is)) ⊃
                              TERM(arg(n.expr).Is)))
```

D. Examples of semantic evaluations

We give two sets of examples of semantic evaluation.

In the theory of s-expressions

```
*****DECLARE OPCONST length(Sexp) = Sexp;
*****ATTACH length ↔ LENGTH;
length attached to LENGTH
*****SIMPLIFY length('(A B));
1 length ('(A B)) = '2
*****SIMPLIFY length ('(A B)) = 2;
2 length ('(A B)) = 2 ≡ '2 = 2
*****SIMPLIFY '2 = 2;
Can't simplify
*****SIMPLIFY '2 = '4;
3¬ ('2 = '4)
```

In the theory of natural numbers

```
%6*****SIMPLIFY 2+3 < pred(7);
1 2+3 < pred(7)
*****SIMPLIFY 4*suc(2)+pred(3) < pred(pred(8));
2¬ 4*suc(2)+pred(3) < pred(pred(8))
*****SIMPLIFY n*0 < 3;
no simplifications
```

E. An example of syntactic simplification

After

*****simplify Null(nil);

1 Null(nil)

the command

REWRITE rev cons(x,nil) BY Basic ∪ Funs ∪ {1} ∪ LOGICTREE;

produces the result

2 rev(cons(x,nil)) = cons(x,nil)

by a single syntactic simplification. The exact details of what the simplifier did are recorded below. The numbers on the left refer to notes below the example.

```
   Trying to simplify
   |    rev(cons(x,nil))
   |
   succeeded using REV yielding
   |    IF Null(cons(x,nil))
   |       THEN cons(x,nil)
   |       ELSE (rev(cdr(cons(x,nil)))*cons(car(cons(x,nil)),nil))
   |
   Trying to simplify
   |    IF Null(cons(x,nil))
   |       THEN cons(x,nil)
   |       ELSE (rev(cdr(cons(x,nil)))*cons(car(cons(x,nil)),nil))
   |
   failed
   →→→Trying to simplify the condition
        | Null(cons(x,nil))
        |
        succeeded using CONS yielding
        | FALSE
        |
   popping up
   Trying to simplify
   |    IF FALSE
   |       THEN cons(x,nil)
   |       ELSE (rev(cdr(cons(x,nil)))*cons(car(cons(x,nil)),nil))
   |
   succeeded using LOGICTREE yielding
   |    (rev(cdr(cons(x,nil)))*cons(car(cons(x,nil)),nil))
   |
   Trying to simplify
   |    (rev(cdr(cons(x,nil)))*cons(car(cons(x,nil)),nil))
   |
1  |while trying to match *, SORT scruples do not permit me to bind u
   |    to rev(cdr(cons(x,nil)))
   |
   →→→Trying to simplify argument 1
        |       rev(cdr(cons(x,nil)))
        |
        |while trying to match rev, SORT scruples do not permit me to bind u
        |       to cdr(cons(x,nil))
        |
        →→→Trying argument 1
             | cdr(cons(x,nil))
             |
             | nil
             |
        popping up
        Trying to simplfy
2       |       rev(nil)
        |
        succeeded using REV yielding
        |       IF Null(nil) THEN nil ELSE (rev(cdr(nil))*cons(car(nil),nil))
        |
   popping up
   Trying to simplify
   |    (IF Null(nil) THEN nil ELSE (rev(cdr(nil))*cons(car(nil),nil))*
   |         cons(car(cons(x,nil),nil)))
   |
3  |while trying to match *, SORT scruples do not permit me to bind u
   |    to IF Null(nil) THEN nil ELSE rev(cdr(nil)*cons(car(nil),nil)
   |
   →→→Trying to simplify argument 1
```

```
        |     IF Null(nil THEN nil ELSE rev(cdr(nil)*cons(car(nil),nil)
        |
        failed
        →→→Trying to simplify condition
              | Null(nil)
              |
              succeeded using line 1 uielding
              | TRUE
              |
        popping up
        Trying to simplify
        |     IF TRUE THEN nil ELSE rev(cdr(nil)*cons(car(nil),nil)
        |
        succeeded using LOGICTREE yielding
        |     nil
  popping up
  Trying to simplify
  |     nil*cons(car(cons(x,nil)),nil)
  |
4 |while trying to match *, SORT scruples do not permit me to bind v
  |     to cons(car(cons(x,nil)),nil)
  |
  →→→Trying to simplify argument 1
        | nil
        |
5       failed but we are at a leaf: argument 1 completely simplified
  popping up
  →→→Trying to simplify argument 2
        |     cons(car(cons(x,nil)),nil)
        |
        failed
        →→→Trying to simplify argument 1
              | car(cons(x,nil))
              |
              succeeded using CAR yielding
              | x
              |
        popping up
        Trying to simplify
        |     cons(x,nil)
        |
        failed
        →→→Trying to simplify argument 1
              | x
              |
              failed but we are at a leaf: argument 1 completely simplified
        popping up
        →→→Trying to simplify argument 2
              | nil
              |
              failed but we are at a leaf: argument 2 completely simplified
        popping up
        argument 2 completely simplified
        popping up
        Trying to simplify
  |     nil*cons(x,nil)
  |
  succeeded using APPEND yielding
  |     IF Null(nil) THEN cons(x,nil) ELSE cons(car(nil),(cdr(nil)*cons(x,nil)))
  |
  Trying to simplify
  |     IF Null(nil) THEN cons(x,nil) ELSE cons(car(nil)*cons(x,nil)))
  |
  failed
  →→→Trying to simplify condition
        |     Null(nil)
        |
        succeeded using line 1 yielding
        |     TRUE
        |
  popping up
  Trying to simplify
  |     IF TRUE THEN cons(x,nil) ELSE cons(car(nil),(cdr(nil)*cons(x,nil)))
  |
  succeeded using LOGICTREE yielding
  |     cons(x,nil)
  |
  Trying to simplify
  |     cons(x,nil)
  |
6 this node already maximally simplified
  return cons(x,nil)
  11 substitutions were made
  26 calls were made to SIMPLIFY
```

Note 1. This is the FOL sort checking mechanism at work. FOL knows that x is an Sexp (by declaration) and that nil is a List because nil is of sort Null and Lists are more general than Nulls. This means that it knows by declaration that cons(x,nil) is a List. Unfortunately, it knows nothing about the cdr of a List. Thus since the definition of rev requires that u be instantiated to a Lists, this attempted replacement fails, and we try to simplify its arguments.

Note 2. Notice that the argument to rev actually simplifies to something that FOL can recognize as a List. This means that sort scruples do not prohibit the instantiation of the definition of rev.

Note 3. Unfortunately we have the same problem as in Note 1.

Note 4. This time the first argument to * is ok, but the second is not. Again we try to simplify the arguments.

Note 5. This time when we try to simplify nil nothing happens. In this case as a subterm it is completely simplified and gets marked in such a way that the simplifier never tries to do this again.

Note 6. It is very clever and remembers that it saw this before and since it is at the top level with a maximally simplified formula it stops.

F. An example of evaluation

This is an abbreviated trace of the evaluation of fact (2).

```
eval
|       fact (2)

interpreting
|       fact
fails

→→→Syntactic simplification succeeds, yielding
    |  IF    2 = ∅ THEN 1 ELSE 2*fact(pred(2))
    |
    eval
    |  IF    2 = ∅ THEN 1 ELSE 2*fact(pred(2))
    |
    →→→eval
        | 2 = ∅
        semantic evaluation succeeds, yielding
        | FALSE
    popping up
    semantic evaluation succeeds, yielding
    |  2*fact(pred(2))
    |
    interpreting
    | *
    succeeds evaluating args
      1   eval
          | 2
          semantic evaluation succeeds, yielding
          | 2
          |
      2   eval
          |  fact(pred(2))
          |
          interpreting
          |  fact
          fails
          |
          Syntactic simplification succeeds, yielding
          |  IF pred(2) = ∅ THEN 1 ELSE pred(2)*fact(pred(pred(2)))
          |
          →→→eval
                |IF pred(2) = ∅
                semantic evaluation succeeds, yielding
                |  FALSE
              popping up
              semantic simplification succeeds, yielding
              |  pred(2)*fact(pred(pred(2)))
              |
              eval
              | pred(2)*fact(pred(pred(2)))
              |
              interpreting
              | *
              succeeds evaluating args
                1   eval
                    |  pred(2)
                    semantic simplification succeeds, yielding
                    | 1
                    |
                2   eval
                    |  fact(pred(pred(2)))
                    |
                    interpreting
                    |  fact
                    fails
                    |
                    Syntactic simplification succeeds, yielding
                    |  IF pred(pred(2)) = ∅
                    |     THEN 1 ELSE pred(pred(2))*fact(pred(pred(pred(2))))
                    |
                    eval
                    |  IF pred(pred(2)) = ∅
                    |   THEN 1 ELSE pred(pred(2))*fact(pred(pred(pred(2))))
                    |
                    eval
                    |  pred(pred(2)) = ∅
                    semantic evaluating succeeds, yielding
                    |  TRUE
                    |
                    semantic evaluation succeeds, yielding
                    |  1
                    |
                  Evaluating 1 gives 1
                Evaluating IF pred(pred(2)) = ∅ THEN 1 ELSE pred(pred(2))*fact(pred(pred
                                                                    (pred(2)))) gives 1
              Evaluating fact(pred(pred(2))) gives 1
            Evaluating pred(2)*fact(pred(pred(2))) gives 1
          Evaluating IF pred(2) = ∅ THEN 1 ELSE pred(2)*fact(pred(pred(2))) gives 1
        Evaluating fact(pred(2)) gives 1
      Evaluating 2*fact(pred(2)) gives 2
    Evaluating IF 2 = ∅ THEN 1 ELSE 2*fact(pred(2)) gives 2
Evaluating fact(2) gives 2
1 fact(2) = 2
```

REFERENCES

1. Aristotle (–350) Organan.
2. Boyer, R. S. and Moore, J. S. (1979), *A Computational Logic*. To be published in the ACM Monograph Series (Academic Press).
3. Bulnes, J. (1978), GOAL: A goal oriented command language for interactive proof construction forthcoming Ph.D. thesis, Stanford University, Stanford.
4. Burstall, R. M. and Darlington, J. (1977), A transformation system for developing recursive programs, *JACM* **24** (1), 44–67.
5. Cartwright, R. (1977), Practical formal semantic definition and verification systems, Ph.D. thesis, Stanford University, Stanford.
6. Davis, M. and Schwartz, J. T. (1977), Correct-program technology/extensibility of verifiers–Two papers on program verification, Courant Computer Science Report #12, New York University.
7. Diffie, W. (1973), PCHECK: operation of the proof checker, unpublished.
8. Feferman, S. (1962), Transfinite recursive progressions of axiomatic theories, *J. Symbolic Logic* **27**, 259–316.
9. Filman, R. E. and Weyhrauch, R. W. (1976), A FOL Primer, Stanford Artificial Intelligence Laboratory Memo AIM–228, Stanford University, Stanford.
10. Filman, R. E. (1978), The interaction of observation and inference, forthcoming Ph.D. thesis, Stanford University, Stanford.
11. Green, C. (1969), The application of theorem proving to question-answering systems, Ph.D. thesis, Stanford University, Stanford.
12. Kelley, J. L. (1955), *General topology* (Van Nostrand, Princeton, NJ.) 298 pp.
13. Kleene, S. C. (1952), *Introduction to Metamathematics* (Van Nostrand, Princeton, NJ.) 550 pp.
14. Kleene, S. C. (1967), *Mathematical Logic* (Wiley, New York) 398 pp.
15. Kowalski, R. (1974), Predicate logic as a programming language, *Proc. IFIP Congress* **1974**.
16. Kreisel, G. (1971a), Five notes on the application of proof theory to computer science, Stanford University: IMSSS Technical Report 182, Stanford.
17. Kreisel, G. (1971b), A survey of proof theory, II in: Fenstad, J. E. (Ed.), *Proc. the Second Scandinavian Logic Symposium* (North-Holland, Amsterdam).
18. McCarthy, J. (1963), A basis for a mathematical theory of computation, in: Computer Programming and Formal Systems (North-Holland, Amsterdam).
19. McCarthy, J. and Hayes, P. J. (1969), Some philosophical problems from the viewpoint of Artificial Intelligence, in: Michie, D. (Ed.), *Machine Intelligence* **7** (Edinburgh U.P., Edinburgh).
20. McCarthy, J. (1973), appendix to: Diffie. W., PCHECK: Operation of the proof checker. Unpublished.
21. McCarthy, J. (1978), Representation of recursive programs in first order logic, in: *Proc. International Conference on Mathematical Studies of Information Processing, Kyoto, Japan.*
22. Prawitz, D. (1965), *Natural Deduction—a proof-theoretical study* (Almqvist & Wiksell, Stockholm).
23. Robinson, R. M. (1950), An essentially undecidable axiom system, in: *Proc. Int. Cong. Math.* **1**, 729–730.
24. Royden, H. L. (1963), *Real Analysis* (Macmillan, New York).
25. Warren, D. (1977), *Implementing PROLOG—compiling predicate logic programs*, Vol. 1 and Vol. 2, DAI Research Reports Nos. 39 and 40, Edinburgh.
26. Weyhrauch, Richard W. (1977), FOL: A proof checker for first-order logic, Stanford Artificial Intelligence Laboratory Memo AIM–235.1, Stanford University, Stanford.
27. Weyhrauch, Richard W. (1978), Lecture notes on the use of logic in artificial intelligence and mathematical theory of computation, Summer school on the foundations of artificial intelligence and computer science (FAICS), Pisa.

The following series of notes refers to my working papers which are sometimes available from me.

[Note 6]. Weyhrauch, Richard W., FOL: a reasoning system, Informal Note 6. Unpublished.
[Note 15]. Weyhrauch, Richard W., The logic of FOL, Informal Note 15. Unpublished.

Subjective Bayesian methods for rule-based inference systems*

by RICHARD O. DUDA, PETER E. HART and NILS J. NILSSON
Stanford Research Institute
Menlo Park, California

ABSTRACT

The general problem of drawing inferences from uncertain or incomplete evidence has invited a variety of technical approaches, some mathematically rigorous and some largely informal and intuitive. Most current inference systems in artificial intelligence have emphasized intuitive methods, because the absence of adequate statistical samples forces a reliance on the subjective judgment of human experts. We describe in this paper a subjective Bayesian inference method that realizes some of the advantages of both formal and informal approaches. Of particular interest are the modifications needed to deal with the inconsistencies usually found in collections of subjective statements.

INTRODUCTION

One of the characteristics of human reasoning is the ability to form useful judgments from uncertain and incomplete evidence. This ability is not only needed for everyday activities, which people would normally never formalize, but also for tasks such as medical diagnosis or securities analysis, which have been subjected to formal treatment.

Because the general need to form judgments from incomplete data is so widespread, many techniques have been developed to aid or supplant people in this task. Probability theory and statistics provide a powerful framework for dealing with many inference problems.[1,2] In standard approaches, the link between alternative hypotheses and relevant evidence is represented by conditional or joint probabilities that are estimated from statistical samples. If the number of alternative hypotheses and the amount of relevant evidence are not too great, and if the available sample is sufficiently large, then probability and statistics furnish the preferred analytical tools. However, when many kinds of evidence simultaneously bear on an hypothesis, traditional statistical approaches become inappropriate because estimation problems become unmanageable.

Recent work in artificial intelligence has suggested other approaches to the problem of resolving hypotheses on the basis of a mass of uncertain evidence. Among the most attractive are *rule-based systems,* which use a large body of *inference rules,* supplied by experts, to provide the knowledge needed to distinguish among competing hypotheses.[3-6] Each inference rule defines the role of a particular set of evidence in resolving a particular hypothesis. Typically, an ad hoc scoring function is used to combine the effects of collections of uncertain evidence acting through several inference rules on the same hypothesis. Thus, rule-based systems attempt to substitute judgments distilled from long experience for joint probabilities estimated from prohibitively large samples.

Our purpose in this paper is to describe a subjective Bayesian technique that can be used in place of ad hoc scoring functions in rule-based inference systems. Our intent is to retain insofar as possible the well-understood methods of probability theory, introducing only those modifications needed because we are dealing with networks of subjective inference rules. The scope of the paper is limited; we shall not discuss here the more general issues of representation and control that must be faced when designing a complete rule-based inference system.

FUNDAMENTALS

In a rule-based inference system, the rules are typically of the form

$$\textit{If } E_1 \textit{ and } E_2 \textit{ and } \ldots \textit{ and } E_n \quad \textit{then } H$$

where E_i $(i=1 \ldots n)$ is the ith piece of evidence and H is an hypothesis suggested by the evidence. Each inference rule has a certain *strength* measured by parameters that will be defined later. For now it suffices to say that the greater the strength, the greater is the power of the evidence to confirm the hypothesis. In most applications, the rules and their strengths are provided by carefully interviewing experts.

The individual pieces of evidence (the E_i) and the hypothesis (H) of a rule are propositional statements. Instead of being either absolutely true or false, the truth values of these propositional statements may be

* The work reported herein was supported by the Advanced Research Projects Agency of the Department of Defense under Contract DAHC04-75-C-0005.

uncertain. In this paper we shall represent these uncertainties by probabilities, so that associated with each propositional statement is a corresponding probability value.

To simplify matters, we shall assume (without loss of generality) that each rule has only a single propositional statement as evidence on its left-hand side. To reduce a conjunction to a single statement, we need a method for computing the joint probability, $P(E_1, \ldots, E_n)$ from the individual probabilities $P(E_i)$. Two simple alternatives are to assume independence of the E_i or to use the fuzzy set computation $P(E_1, \ldots, E_n) = \min P(E_i)$. More generally, the left-hand side of a rule could contain an arbitrary logical expression, E. The results of this paper do not depend on how the probability of E is computed.

We represent a rule of the form "*if* E *then* H" graphically by the following structure:

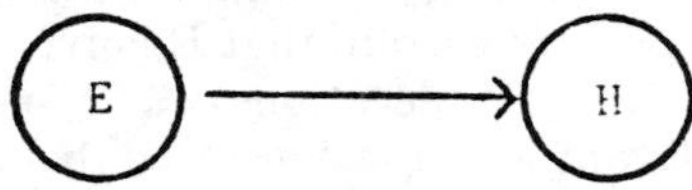

Here a propositional statement is being represented as a node, and an inference rule is being represented as an arc. A collection of rules about some specific subject area invariably uses the same pieces of evidence to imply several different hypotheses. It also frequently happens that several alternative pieces of evidence imply the same hypothesis. Furthermore, there are often chains of evidences and hypotheses. For these reasons it is natural to represent a collection of rules as a graph structure or *inference net*.

An example of an inference net is shown in Figure 1.

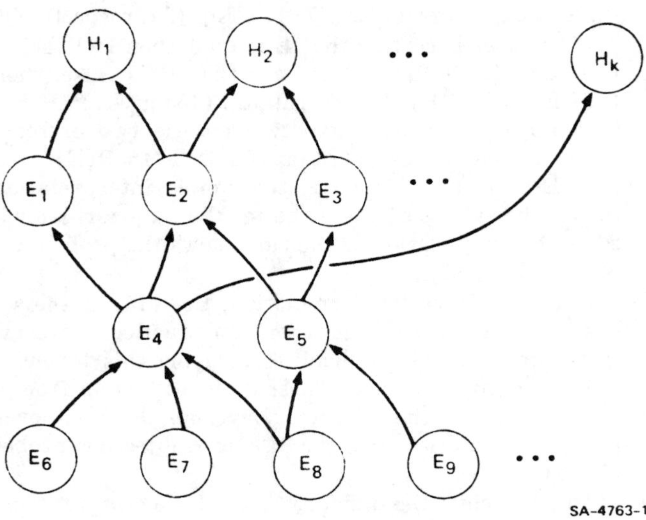

Figure 1—A simple inference net

The H_i at the top of the net are alternative hypotheses to be resolved. Each arc entering a node represents an inference rule and has associated with it a strength. Notice that a typical intermediate node like E_5 can play two roles: it provides supporting evidence for the nodes above it (E_2 and E_3), and it acts as an hypothesis to be resolved by evidence below it (E_8 and E_9).

The main problem to be considered in this paper concerns the propagation of probabilities through the net. Suppose for example, that a user of the net provides evidence by deciding that the probability of a node, say E_6, should be changed from its prior value to some new value. Obviously this should require updating of the probability of E_4 and, in turn, E_1, E_2, and H_k, and so on. Any mechanism used for propagating probabilities must be able to cope with a number of problems. The rules have uncertainty associated with them, and the evidence provided by a user may be uncertain. These two different kinds of uncertainty must somehow be combined. Multiple evidence typically bears on a single hypothesis, so that some form of independence must usually be assumed. Finally, the rules are provided subjectively by experts, so certain kinds of inconsistencies arise that can seriously jeopardize success. In the following sections we suggest a Bayesian updating scheme that addresses these concerns.

SUBJECTIVE BAYESIAN UPDATING

Suppose we are given a rule *if* E, *then* H. Let us begin with the simplified problem of updating the probability of H given its prior value and given that E is observed to be true. By Bayes rule, we have

$$P(H|E) = \frac{P(E|H)P(H)}{P(E)}. \tag{1}$$

For our purposes, a more convenient form of Bayes rule is arrived at by writing the complementary form for the negation of H

$$P(\bar{H}|E) = \frac{P(E|\bar{H})P(\bar{H})}{P(E)}, \tag{2}$$

and dividing Eq. (1) by Eq. (2), to obtain

$$\frac{P(H|E)}{P(\bar{H}|E)} = \frac{P(E|H)}{P(E|\bar{H})}\frac{P(H)}{P(\bar{H})}. \tag{3}$$

Each of the three terms in this equation has a traditional interpretation. We define the *prior odds* on H to be

$$O(H) = \frac{P(H)}{P(\bar{H})} = \frac{P(H)}{1-P(H)} \tag{4}$$

and the *posterior odds* to be

$$O(H|E) = \frac{P(H|E)}{P(\bar{H}|E)} = \frac{P(H|E)}{1-P(H|E)}. \tag{5}$$

Now the *likelihood ratio* is defined by

$$\lambda = \frac{P(E|H)}{P(E|\bar{H})}, \tag{6}$$

so Eq. 3 becomes the *odds-likelihood* formulation of Bayes rule:

$$O(H|E) = \lambda O(H). \tag{7}$$

This equation tells us how to update the odds on H given the observation of E. For rule-based inference systems, we assume that a human expert has given the rule and has provided the likelihood ratio λ to indicate the "strength" of the rule. A high value of $\lambda (\lambda \gg 1)$ represents, roughly speaking, the fact that E is sufficient for H, since the observation that E is true will transform indifferent prior odds on H into heavy posterior odds in favor of H. Notice, incidentally, that the underlying probabilities can be recovered from their odds by the simple formula

$$P = \frac{O}{O+1}, \tag{8}$$

so that the odds and the probabilities give exactly the same information.

Suppose now that we wish to update the odds on H given that E is observed to be false. In a strictly analogous fashion, we write.

$$O(H|\bar{E}) = \bar{\lambda} O(H), \tag{9}$$

where we define λ by

$$\lambda = \frac{P(\bar{E}|H)}{P(\bar{E}|H)} = \frac{1-P(E|H)}{1-P(E|\bar{H})}. \tag{10}$$

Notice that $\bar{\lambda}$ must also be provided by the human expert; it cannot be derived from λ. A low value of $\bar{\lambda}$, $(O \leq \bar{\lambda} \ll 1)$ represents, roughly speaking, the fact that E is necessary for H, since the observation that E is false will by Eq. 9 transform indifferent prior odds on H into odds heavily against H. Curiously, although λ and $\bar{\lambda}$ must be separately provided by the expert, they are not completely independent of each other. In particular, Eqs. (6) and (10) yield

$$\bar{\lambda} = \frac{1-\lambda P(E|\bar{H})}{1-P(E|\bar{H})}, \tag{11}$$

so that, if we exclude the extreme cases of $P(E|\bar{H})$ being either 0 or 1, we see that $\lambda > 1$ implies $\bar{\lambda} < 1$, and $\lambda < 1$ implies $\bar{\lambda} > 1$. Further, we have $\lambda = 1$ if and only if $\bar{\lambda} = 1$. This means that if the expert gives a rule such that the presence of E enhances the odds on H (i.e., $\lambda > 1$), he should also tell us that the absence of E depresses the odds on H (i.e., $\bar{\lambda} < 1$). To some extent, this mathematical requirement does violence to intuition. People who work with rule-based inference systems are commonly told by experts that "The presence of E enhances the odds on H, but the absence of E has no significance." In other words, the expert says that $\lambda > 1$, but $\bar{\lambda} = 1$. Subsequently, we shall suggest some modifications that address this and other problems of inconsistency.

We note in passing that knowledge of both λ and $\bar{\lambda}$ is equivalent to knowledge of both $P(E|H)$ and $P(E|\bar{H})$. Indeed, it follows at once from Eqs. (6) and (10) that

$$P(E|H) = \lambda \frac{1-\bar{\lambda}}{\lambda-\bar{\lambda}} \tag{12}$$

and

$$P(E|\bar{H}) = \frac{1-\bar{\lambda}}{\lambda-\bar{\lambda}} \tag{13}$$

Thus, whether the expert should be asked to provide λ and λ, $P(E|H)$ and $P(E|H)$, or, indeed, some other equivalent information is a psychological rather than a mathematical question.[7]

UNCERTAIN EVIDENCE AND THE PROBLEM OF PRIOR PROBABILITIES

Having seen how to update the probability of an hypothesis when the evidence is known to be either certainly true or certainly false, let us consider now how updating should proceed when the user of the system is uncertain. We begin by assuming that when a user says "I am 70 percent certain that E is true," he means that $P(E|$ relevant observations$) = .7$. We designate by E' the relevant observations that he makes, and simply write $P(E|E')$ for the user's response.

We now need to obtain an expression for $P(H|E')$. Formally,

$$\begin{aligned} P(H|E') &= P(H,E|E') + P(H,\bar{E}|E') \\ &= P(H|E,E')P(E|E') \\ &\quad + P(H|\bar{E},E')P(\bar{E}|E'). \end{aligned} \tag{14}$$

We make the reasonable assumption that if we *know* E to be true (or false), then the observations E' relevant to E provide no further information about H. With this assumption, Eq. (14) becomes

$$P(H|E') = P(H|E)P(E|E') + P(H|\bar{E})P(\bar{E}|E'). \tag{15}$$

Here $P(H|E)$ and $P(H|\bar{E})$ are obtained directly from Bayes rule, i.e., from Eq. (7) and Eq. (9), respectively.

If the user is certain that E is true, then $P(H|E') = P(H|E)$. If the user is certain that E is false, then $P(H|E') = P(H|\bar{E})$. In general, Eq. (15) gives $P(H|E')$ as a linear interpolation between these two extreme cases. In particular, note that if $P(E|E') = P(E)$ then $P(H|E') = P(H)$. This has the simple interpretation that if the evidence E' is no better than a priori knowledge, then application of the rule leaves the probability of H unchanged.

In a pure Bayesian formulation, Eq. (15) is the solution to the updating question. In practice, however, there are significant difficulties in using this formulation in an inference net. These difficulties stem from a combination of the classical Bayesian dilemma over prior probabilities and the use of subjective probabilities.

To appreciate the difficulty, consider again a typical pair of nodes E and H embedded in an inference net. It is apparent from Eqs. (7) and (9) that the updating procedure depends on the availability of the prior odds

O(H). Thus, although we have not emphasized the point until now, we see that the expert must be depended upon to provide the prior odds as well as λ and $\bar{\lambda}$ when the inference rule is given. On the other hand, recall our earlier observation that E also acts as an hypothesis to be resolved by the nodes below it in the net. Thus, the expert must also provide prior odds on E. If all of these quantities were specified consistently, then the situation would be as represented in Figure 2. The straight line plotted is simply Eq. (15), and shows the interpolation noted above. In particular, note that if the user asserts that $P(E|E') = P(E)$, then the updated probability is $P(H|E') = P(H)$. In other words, if the user provides no new evidence, then the probability of H remains unchanged.

In the practical case, unfortunately, the subjectively obtained prior probabilities are virtually certain to be inconsistent, and the situation becomes as shown in Figure 3. Note that P(E), the prior probability provided by the expert, is different from $P_c(E)$, the probability consistent with P(H). Here, if the user provides no new evidence—i.e., if $P(E|E') = P(E)$—then the formal Bayesian updating scheme will substantially change the probability of H from its prior value P(H). Furthermore, for the case shown in Figure 3, if the user asserts that E is true with a probability $P(E|E')$ lying in the interval between P(E) and $P_c(E)$, then the updated probability $P(H|E')$ will be less than P(H). Thus, we have here an example of a rule intended to increase the probability of H if E is found to be true, but which turns out to have the opposite effect. This type of error can be compounded as probabilities are propagated through the net.

Several measures can be taken to correct the unfortunate effects of priors that are inconsistent with inference rules. Since the problem can be thought of as one of overspecification, one approach would be to relax

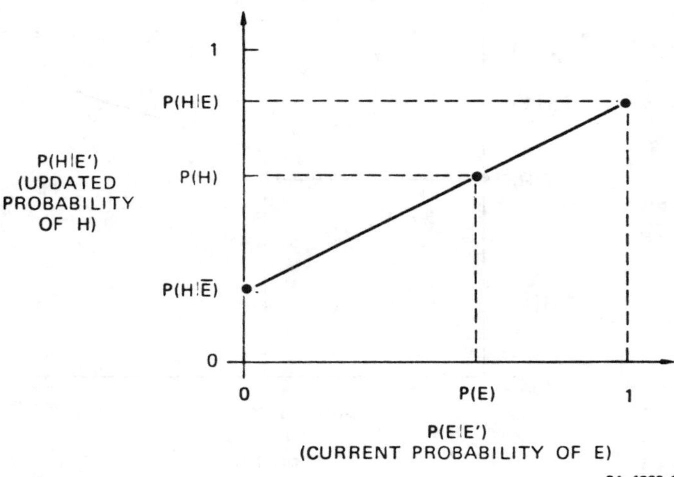

Figure 2—Idealized updating of $P(H|E')$

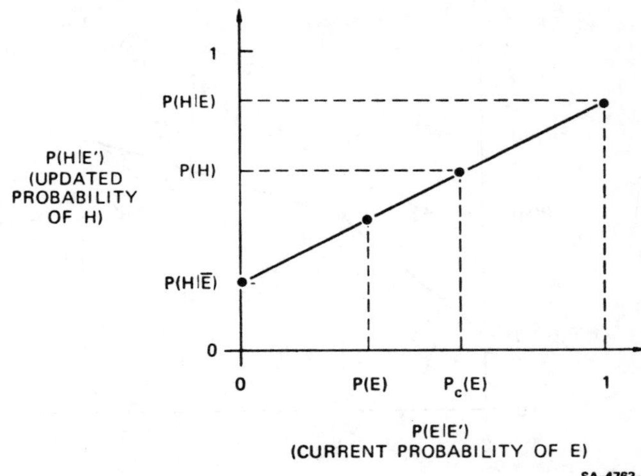

Figure 3—Inconsistent priors

the specification of whatever quantities are subjectively least certain. For example, if the subjective specification of P(E) were least certain (in the expert's opinion), then we might set $P(E) = P_c(E)$. This approach leads to difficulties because the pair of nodes E and H under consideration are embedded in a large net. For example, in Figure 1, we might be considering node E_2 as the hypothesis H, and node E_5 as the evidence E. If we were to establish a prior probability $P(E_5)$ to be consistent with $P(E_2)$, we would simultaneously make $P(E_5)$ inconsistent with the priors on E_8 and E_9, which provide supporting evidence for E_5. Prior probabilities can therefore not be forced into consistency on the basis of the local structure of the inference net; apparently, a more global process—perhaps a relaxation process—would be required.

A second alternative for achieving consistency would be to adjust the linear interpolation function shown in Figure 3. There are several possibilities, one of which is illustrated in Figure 4a. The linear function has been broken into a piecewise linear function at the coordinates of the prior probabilities, forcing consistent updating of the probability of H given E'. Two other possibilities are shown in Figures 4b and 4c. In Figure 4b we have introduced a dead zone over the interval between the specified prior probability P(E) and the consistent prior $P_c(E)$. Intuitively, the argument in support of this consistent interpolation function is that if the user cannot give a response outside this interval, then he is not sufficiently certain of his response to warrant any change in the probability of H. Figure 4c shows another possibility, motivated by the earlier observation that experts often give rules of the form "The presence of E enhances the odds on H, but the absence of E has no significance." By keeping $P(H|E')$ equal to P(H) when $P(E|E')$ is less than P(E) we are

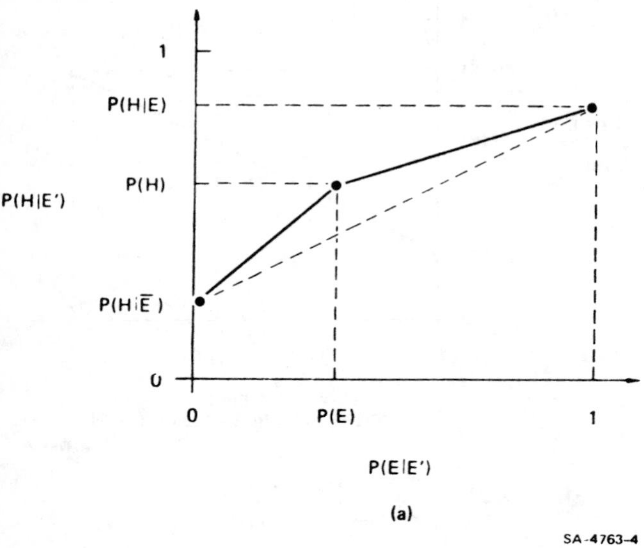

Figure 4(a)—Consistent interpolation functions

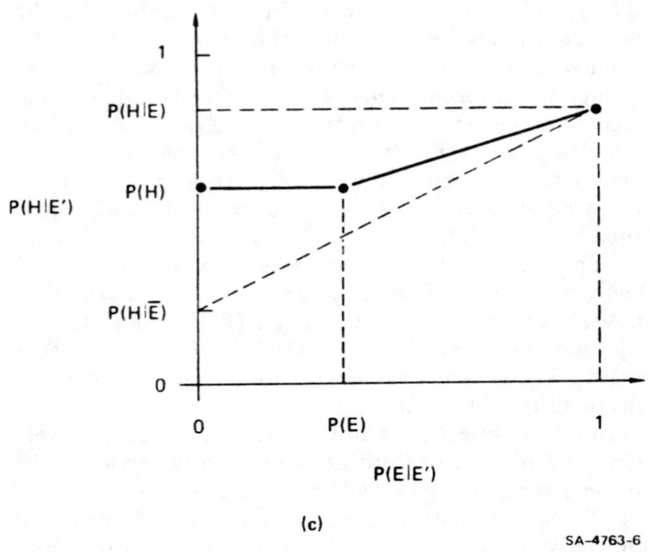

Figure 4(c)—Consistent interpolation functions (concluded)

effectively allowing the forbidden situation where $\lambda > 1$ and $\bar{\lambda} = 1$. In effect, this is equivalent to the method illustrated in Figure 4a under the assumption that $P(H|\bar{E}) = P(H)$.

It is interesting to compare these modifications with the procedure used by Shortliffe to handle uncertain evidence in the MYCIN system.[4,5] While the nonlinear equations that result from use of Shortliffe's version of confirmation theory prevent a general comparison, it is possible to express his procedure in our terms for the special case of a single rule. The result for the case in which the presence of E supports H is shown in Figure 5. Clearly, the solution is identical to that of Figure 4c except for the interval from P(E) to $P_t(E)$ within which Shortliffe's solution maintains $P(H|E')$ at the a priori value P(H).

The graphical representations in Figures 2 through 4 provide a nice vehicle for visualizing the discrepancies between formal and subjective Bayesian updating, and make it easy to invent other alternatives for reconciling inconsistencies. For completeness, the Appendix contains the easily computable algebraic representa-

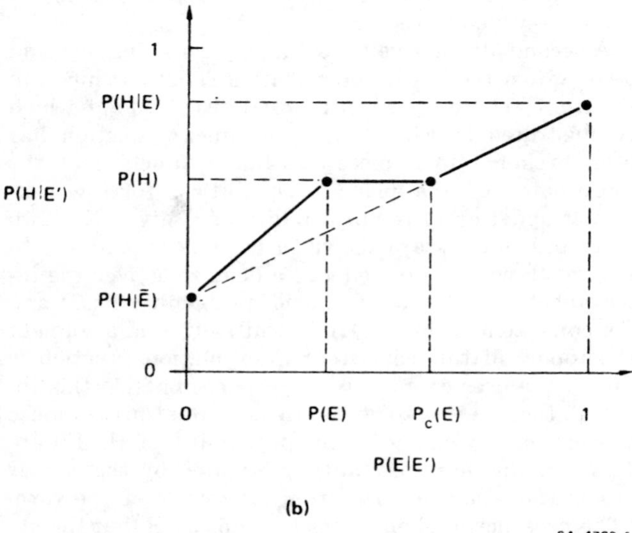

Figure 4(b)—Consistent interpolation functions (continued)

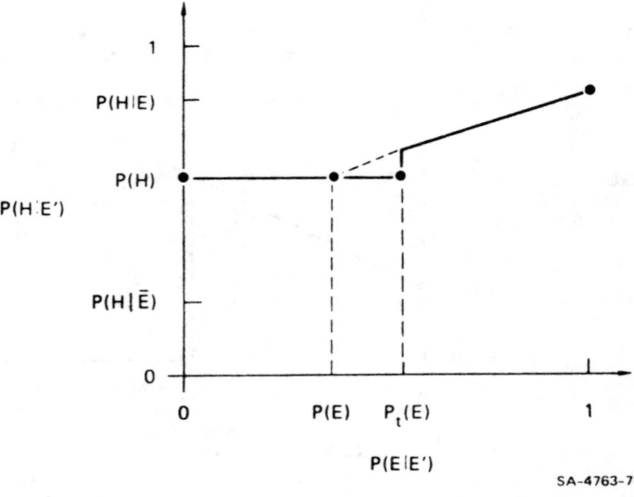

Figure 5—The interpolation function used in the mycin system $P_t(E) = P(E) + t[1 - P(E)]$. Typically, $t = 0.2$.

tions of these functions, and also treats the complementary case in which the straight line given by Eq. (15) has a negative slope (the case in which $\lambda<\bar{\lambda}$). In a small experimental system, the function shown in Figure 4a has given satisfactory preliminary results.[8]

THE USE OF MULTIPLE EVIDENCE

We turn now to the more general updating problem in which several rules of the form $E_1 \rightarrow H, \ldots, E_n \rightarrow H$ all concern the same hypothesis H.* Since most nodes in actual inference nets have several incoming arcs, this is the case of greatest practical interest. In order to gain some insight about how multiple evidence should be used to update H when the evidence is uncertain and the priors are inconsistent, let us first consider briefly how updating would formally proceed in simpler cases.

Suppose the ith inference rule has associated with it the usual two quantities λ_i and $\bar{\lambda}_i$. For a first simple case, how should H be updated when all the E_i have been observed to be certainly true? This case is analogous to the case summarized by Eq. (7). Under the assumption that the pieces of evidence are conditionally independent (i.e., that $P(E_1, \ldots, E_n|H) = \prod_{i=1}^{n} P(E_i|H)$ and that $P(E_1, \ldots, E_n|\bar{H}) = \prod_{i=1}^{n} P(E_i|\bar{H})$), it is not difficult to reach an analogous answer. Specifically, the odds on H are updated by the expression

$$O(H|E_1, \ldots, E_n) = \left[\prod_{i=1}^{n} \lambda_i\right] O(H), \tag{16}$$

where

$$\lambda_i = \frac{P(E_i|H)}{P(E_i|\bar{H})}. \tag{17}$$

Similarly, if all the evidence is observed to be certainly false, we can under conditional independence assumptions again factor the joint likelihood ratio to obtain

$$O(H|\bar{E}_1, \ldots, \bar{E}_n) = \left[\prod_{i=1}^{n} \bar{\lambda}_i\right] O(H). \tag{18}$$

Now let us consider the general case of uncertain evidence and inconsistent prior probabilities. We already know that the posterior odds $O(H|E_i')$ given a single observation E_i' can be computed using updating functions like the ones shown in Figure 4. We can therefore define, for a single inference rule, an effective likelihood ratio λ_i' by

$$\lambda_i' \stackrel{\Delta}{=} \frac{O(H|E_i')}{O(H)}. \tag{19}$$

* This should not be confused with the conjunctive premise mentioned earlier.

By making the assumption now that the E_i' are independent, we can obtain for the general case an expression similar to the simple updating formulas given by Eqs. (16) and (18):

$$O(H|E_1', \ldots, E_n') = \left[\prod_{i=1}^{n} \lambda_i'\right] O(H). \tag{20}$$

To use this expression in an inference net system, we simply store with each node its prior odds (or probability), and store with each incoming arc an effective likelihood ratio λ_i'. Whenever a piece of evidence provided by the user causes $P(E_i|E_i')$ to be updated, a new effective likelihood ratio is computed and the posterior odds in favor of H is computed using Eq. (20). This procedure has the following consequences:

(1) If no evidence is obtained for a rule, then it will retain an initial effective likelihood ratio of unity, since prior and "posterior" odds are the same.
(2) The order in which evidence is obtained and rules are applied does not affect the final posterior probabilities.
(3) The same rule can be used repeatedly, with the same or different values for the probability of the evidence. In particular, if a user changes his mind and modifies an earlier assertion, the new assertion will correctly "undo" any effects of earlier statements.

CONCLUSIONS

The probability updating procedure presented here has several points to recommend it. It accepts subjective information that can readily be obtained from experts. The two conditional probabilities, $P(E|H)$ and $P(E|\bar{H})$, that determine the strength of an inference rule typically are intuitively meaningful measures, and the procedure is tolerant of the inevitable inconsistencies in subjective expert information. The basis in probability theory of our procedure provides a useful theoretical foundation for calculating the effects of uncertain evidence. One value of theory is that it makes us explicitly aware of certain underlying assumptions about such matters as conditional independence, prior probabilities, and inconsistent information. Finally, our procedure is straightforward computationally and can be readily implemented in inference net systems.

There are, however, some questions that remain to be dealt with. If the network contains multiple paths linking a given piece of evidence to the same hypothesis, the independence assumption is obviously violated. It is important to settle on a reasonable (if ad hoc) modification of our basic procedure that behaves appropriately in such situations. (A more extreme complication would involve being able to avoid the circular reasoning implied by inference nets with loops.)

There are sometimes cases where some of the nodes in an inference net are related by a constraint not expressed in any given rule. For example, a subset of hypotheses may be mutually exclusive and exhaustive, in which case their probabilities must always sum to one, regardless of their individual values. Such a constraint may be inconsistent with the associated rule strengths given us by the experts. Perhaps a simple expedient, such as renormalization of probability values, can be justified in this case.

We have not addressed here at all issues of inference net control strategy: for example, which hypotheses should be pursued and which evidence should be sought at any step. The answers to these sorts of questions may be heavily dependent on the particular application. Another global question concerns rules containing logical statements that may include quantifiers and variables. But in whatever way these questions are answered, the basic updating procedure presented here would appear to be a useful component of rule-based inference systems.

ACKNOWLEDGMENTS

We have benefited from the comments of many of our colleagues, but would like particularly to acknowledge the contributions of Georgia Sutherland at SRI, and the stimulating and helpful discussions with E. H. Shortliffe, Bruce Buchanan, Randall Davis, and Dana Ludwig at Stanford University. This work was supported by the Advanced Projects Research Agency under Contract DAHCO4-75-C-0005.

REFERENCES

1. Hadley, G., *Introduction to Probability and Statistical Decision Theory,* Holden-Day, San Francisco, California, 1967.
2. Raiffa, H., *Decision Analysis,* Addison-Wesley, New York, New York, 1968.
3. Waterman, D. A., "Generalization Learning Techniques for Automating the Learning of Heuristics," *Artificial Intelligence,* Vol. 1, pp. 121-170, Spring 1970.
4. Shortliffe, E. H., *MYCIN: A Rule-Based Computer Program for Advising Physicians Regarding Antimicrobial Therapy Selection,* Stanford Artificial Intelligence Laboratory Memo AIM-251, Stanford University, Stanford, California, October 1974.
5. Shortliffe, E. H. and B. G. Buchanan, "A Model of Inexact Reasoning in Medicine," *Mathematical Biosciences,* Vol. 23, pp. 351-379, 1975.
6. Davis, R. and J. King, "An Overview of Production Systems," in *Machine Representations of Knowledge,* D. Reidel Publishing Co.; forthcoming.
7. Gustafson, D. H., et al., "Wisconsin Computer Aided Medical Diagnosis Project—Progress Report," in *Computer Diagnosis and Diagnostic Methods,* pp. 255-278, J. A. Jacquez, ed., Charles C. Thomas, Springfield, Illinois, 1972.
8. Sutherland, G., *Implementation of Inference Nets—II,* Technical Note 122, Artificial Intelligence Center, Stanford Research Institute, Menlo Park, California, January 1976.

APPENDIX

Complete analytical expressions giving $P(H|E')$ as a piecewise linear function of $P(E|E')$ are given in this Appendix. These expressions correspond to the three graphical representations illustrated in Figure 4. The simplest expression corresponds to Figure 4a:

$$P(H|E') = \begin{cases} P(H|\bar{E}) + \dfrac{P(E|E')}{P(E)}[P(H) - P(H|\bar{E})] & 0 \leq P(E|E') \leq P(E) \\ \dfrac{P(H) - P(H|E)P(E)}{1-P(E)} + P(E|E')\dfrac{P(H|E) - P(H)}{1-P(E)} & P(E) \leq P(E|E') \leq 1 \end{cases} \tag{A1}$$

Here it is important to note that the four quantities $P(H)$, $P(E)$, $P(H|E)$, and $P(H|\bar{E})$ are assumed to be estimates obtained from experts. Were the true probabilities to be used in this formula, it would reduce at once to the linear expression given by Eq. (15). The estimates of $P(H|E)$ and $P(H|\bar{E})$ might be obtained directly from an expert, but would more often be obtained through Bayes rule [Eqs. (7) and (9), respectively]. To be explicit,

$$P(H|E) = \frac{P(E|H)P(H)}{[P(E|H) - P(E|\bar{H})]P(H) + P(E|\bar{H})} = \frac{\lambda P(H)}{(\lambda-1)P(H)+1} \tag{A2}$$

and

$$P(H|\bar{E}) = \frac{[1-P(E|H)]P(H)}{[P(E|\bar{H}) - P(E|H)]P(H) + 1 - P(E|\bar{H})} = \frac{\bar{\lambda} P(H)}{(\lambda-1)P(H)+1} \tag{A3}$$

To obtain the equations for Figure 4b, we define $P_c(E)$ by

$$P_c(E) = \frac{P(H) - P(H|\bar{E})}{P(H|E) - P(H|\bar{E})} \tag{A4}$$

In general, this quantity will differ from the $P(E)$ value supplied by the expert. For Figure 4b we must distinguish between the two cases $P(E) \leq P_c(E)$ and $P(E) > P_c(E)$. The equations are as follows:

Case 1: $P(E) \leq P_c(E)$

$$P(H|E) = \begin{cases} P(H|\bar{E}) + \dfrac{P(E|E')}{P(E)}[P(H) - P(H|\bar{E})] & 0 \leq P(E|E') \leq P(E) \\ P(H) & P(E) \leq P(E|E') \leq P_c(E) \\ P(H|\bar{E}) + P(E|E')[P(H|E) - P(H|\bar{E})] & P_c(E) \leq P(E|E') \leq 1 \end{cases} \tag{A5}$$

Case 2: $P(E) > P_c(E)$

$$P(H|E') = \begin{cases} P(H|\bar{E}) + P(E|E')[P(H|E) - P(H|\bar{E})] & 0 \leq P(E|E') \leq P_c(E) \\ P(H) & P_c(E) \leq P(E|E') \leq P(E) \\ \dfrac{P(H) - P(H|E)P(E)}{1 - P(E)} + P(E|E')\dfrac{P(H|E) - P(H)}{1 - P(E)} & P(E) \leq P(E|E') \leq 1 \end{cases} \tag{A6}$$

Finally, there are also two cases to be distinguished for Figure 4c. The first case corresponds to assuming that $P(H|\bar{E}) \approx P(H)$, so that $P_c(E) \approx 0$. The second case corresponds to assuming that $P(H|E) \approx P(H)$, so that $P_c(E) \approx 1$. In effect, these cases correspond to the rules $E \xrightarrow{\lambda} H$ and $\bar{E} \xrightarrow{\bar{\lambda}} H$ taken separately. The corresponding equations are special cases of Eqs. (A5) and (A6):

Case 1: $E \xrightarrow{\lambda} H$

$$P(H|E') = \begin{cases} P(H) & 0 \leq P(E|E') \leq P(E) \\ \dfrac{P(H) - P(H|E)P(E)}{1 - P(E)} + P(E|E')\dfrac{P(H|E) - P(H)}{1 - P(E)} & P(E) \leq P(E|E') \leq 1 \end{cases} \tag{A7}$$

Case 2: $\bar{E} \xrightarrow{\bar{\lambda}} H$

$$P(H|E') = \begin{cases} P(H|\bar{E}) + \dfrac{P(E|E')}{P(E)}[P(H) - P(H|\bar{E})] & 0 \leq P(E|E') \leq P(E) \\ P(H) & P(E) \leq P(E|E') \leq 1 \end{cases} \tag{A8}$$

Ordinarily one would view this as a simplified approximation that is useful when one of the two likelihood ratios is dominant. However, it is interesting to observe that if both λ and $\bar{\lambda}$ are significant and if the two separate rules $E \xrightarrow{\lambda} H$ and $\bar{E} \xrightarrow{\bar{\lambda}} H$ are treated as if E and $\bar{E}$ were statistically independent, then Eqs. (A7) and (A8) yield the same result as Eq. (A1). This follows from the fact that when $P(H|E') = P(H)$ we have $O(H|E') = O(H)$, so that Eq. (19) yields $\lambda' = 1$. Thus, if $0 \leq P(E|E') \leq P(E)$ only the rule $\bar{E} \xrightarrow{\bar{\lambda}} H$ contributes to $P(H|E')$, while if $P(E) \leq P(E|E') \leq 1$ only the rule $E \xrightarrow{\lambda} H$ contributes to $P(H|E')$, the contributions being exactly those given in Eq. (A1).

3 / Problem-Solving and Planning

In AI research, *planning* denotes the task of composing a sequence of actions to accomplish a stated goal. The action sequence itself is called a *plan*. Many of the AI planning techniques were developed and tested by considering how best to achieve certain arrangements of toy blocks with a robot arm.

Green's paper shows how a purely deductive approach based on first-order logic can be used to generate robot plans in "the blocks world." Green's work built upon earlier ideas of McCarthy. Green employed a "situation term" in each predicate to denote different states of the blocks world. Each potential robot action was defined in terms of its projected effect upon situations.

One difficulty faced by all planning systems is that the consequences of actions can be quite complicated. Green's approach to robot planning left open the possibility that arbitrary predicates satisfied by a situation prior to the actual performance of an action might not be satisfied post factum. Hayes's paper discusses this so-called *frame problem* of how to specify the effects of actions in an economical way.

The paper by Fikes, Hart, and Nilsson describes a planning system, STRIPS, in which an action is regarded as affecting only those predicates specifically named in the action description. The paper describes techniques for monitoring the execution of plans generated by STRIPS and for utilizing previously generated plans.

Waldinger's paper examines the problem of achieving multiple goals simultaneously. His technique is "goal regression," a method similar to passing a condition back over an operation in program verification. Achieving simultaneous goals posed difficulties for STRIPS and other problem solvers.

Reasoning about reasoning methods, or *metareasoning*, has applications in tasks where knowledge is uncertain or incomplete, where resources are limited, or where control knowledge can be stated declaratively. The paper by Weyhrauch in Chapter 2 of this book discusses metareasoning from a theoretical point of view. Stefik's paper is valuable in that it illustrates metareasoning applied to the practical problem of procedure design. In particular, Stefik applies metareasoning to the problem of deciding what part of a design task the system can optimally work on next.

APPLICATION OF THEOREM PROVING TO PROBLEM SOLVING*†

Cordell Green
Stanford Research Institute
Menlo Park, California

Abstract

This paper shows how an extension of the resolution proof procedure can be used to construct problem solutions. The extended proof procedure can solve problems involving state transformations. The paper explores several alternate problem representations and provides a discussion of solutions to sample problems including the "Monkey and Bananas" puzzle and the "Tower of Hanoi" puzzle. The paper exhibits solutions to these problems obtained by QA3, a computer program based on these theorem-proving methods. In addition, the paper shows how QA3 can write simple computer programs and can solve practical problems for a simple robot.

Key Words: Theorem proving, resolution, problem solving, automatic programming, program writing, robots, state transformations, question answering.

Automatic theorem proving by the resolution proof procedure[1]§ represents perhaps the most powerful known method for automatically determining the validity of a statement of first-order logic. In an earlier paper Green and Raphael[2] illustrated how an extended resolution procedure can be used as a question answerer--e.g., if the statement $(\exists x)P(x)$ can be shown to follow from a set of axioms by the resolution proof procedure, then the extended proof procedure will find or construct an x that satisfies P(x). This earlier paper (1) showed how one can axiomatize simple question-answering subjects, (2) described a question-answering program called QA2 based on this procedure, and (3) presented examples of simple question-answering dialogues with QA2. In a more recent paper[3] the author (1) presents the answer construction method in detail and proves its correctness, (2) describes the latest version of the program, QA3, and (3) introduces state-transformation methods into the constructive proof formalism. In addition to the question-answering applications illustrated in these earlier papers, QA3 has been used as an SRI robot[4] problem solver and as an automatic program writer. The purpose of this paper is twofold: (1) to explore the question of predicate calculus representation for state-transformation problems in general, and (2) to elaborate upon robot and program-writing applications of this approach and the mechanisms underlying them.

Exactly how one can use logic and theorem proving for problem solving requires careful thought on the part of the user. Judging from my experience, and that of others using QA2 and QA3, one of the first difficulties encountered is the representation of problems, especially state-transformation problems, by statements in formal logic. Interest has been shown in seeing several detailed examples that illustrate alternate methods of axiomatizing such problems--i.e., techniques for "programming" in first-order logic. This paper provides detailed examples of various methods of representation. After presenting methods in Secs. I and II, a solution to the classic "Monkey and Bananas" problem is provided in Sec. III. Next, Sec. IV compares several alternate representations for the "Tower of Hanoi" puzzle. Two applications, robot problem solving and automatic programming, are discussed in Secs. V and VI, respectively.

I. An Introduction to State-Transformation Methods

The concepts of states and state transformations have of course been in existence for a long time, and the usefulness of these concepts for problem solving is well known. The purpose of this paper is not to discuss states and state transformations as such, but instead to show how these concepts can be used by an automatic resolution theorem prover. In practice, the employment of these methods has greatly extended the problem-solving capacity of QA2 and QA3. McCarthy and Hayes[5] present a relevant discussion of philosophical problems involved in attempting such formalizations.

First we will present a simple example. We begin by considering how a particular universe of discourse might be described in logic.

Facts describing the universe of discourse are expressed in the form of statements of mathematical logic. Questions or problems are stated as conjectures to be proved. If a theorem is proved, then the nature of our extended theorem prover is such that the proof is "constructive"--i.e., if the theorem asserts the existence of an object then the proof finds or constructs such an object.

At any given moment the universe under consideration may be said to be in a given state.

* This research is a part of Project Defender and was supported by the Advanced Research Projects Agency of the Department of Defense and was monitored by Rome Air Development Center under Contracts AF 30(602)-4147 and F30602-69-C-0056.

† This preprint is a preliminary version and is subject to modification prior to publication.

§ References are listed at the end of this paper.

We will represent a particular state by a subscripted s--e.g., s_{17}. The letter s, with no subscript, will be a variable, ranging over states. A state is described by means of predicates. For example, if the predicate $AT(object_1,b,s_1)$ is true, then in state s_1 the object, $object_1$, is at position b. Let this predicate be axiom A1:

A1. $AT(object_1,b,s_1)$.

The question "Where is $object_1$ in state s_1?" can be expressed in logic as the theorem $(\exists x)AT(object_1,x,s_1)$. The answer found by using system QA3 to prove this theorem is "yes, x = b."

Changes in states are brought about by performing actions and sequences of actions. An action can be represented by an action function that maps states into new states (achieved by executing the action). An axiom describing the effect of an action is typically of the form

$$(\forall s)[P(s) \supset Q(f(s))]$$

where s is a state variable
- P is a predicate describing a state
- f is an action function (corresponding to some action) that maps a state into a new state (achieved by executing the action)
- Q is a predicate describing the new state.

(Entities such as P and f are termed "situational fluents" by McCarthy.)

As an example, consider an axiom describing the fact that $object_1$ can be pushed from point b to point c. The axiom is

A2. $(\forall s)[AT(object_1,b,s) \supset AT(object_1,c,push(object_1,b,c,s))]$.

The function $push(object_1,b,c,s)$ corresponds to the action of pushing $object_1$ from b to c. (Assume, for example, that a robot is the executor of these actions.)

Now consider the question, "Does there exist a sequence of actions such that $object_1$ is at point c?" Equivalently, one may ask, "Does there exist a state, possibly resulting from applying action functions to an initial state s_1, such that $object_1$ is at point c?" This question, in logic, is $(\exists s)AT(object_1,c,s)$, and the answer, provided by the theorem-proving program applied to axioms A1 and A2, is "yes, $s = push(object_1,b,c,s_1)$."

Suppose a third axiom indicates that $object_1$ can be pushed from c to d:

A3. $(\forall s)[AT(object_1,c,s) \supset AT(object_1,d,push(object_1,c,d,s))]$.

Together, these three axioms imply that starting in state s_1, $object_1$ can be pushed from b to c and then from c to d. This sequence of actions (a program for our robot) can be expressed by the composition of the two push functions, $push(object_1,c,d,push(object_1,b,c,s_1))$. The normal order of function evaluation, from the innermost function to the outermost, gives the correct sequence in which to perform the actions.

To find this solution to the problem of getting $object_1$ to position d, the following conjecture is posed to the theorem prover: "Does there exist a state such that $object_1$ is at position d?" or, stated in logic, $(\exists s)AT(object_1,d,s)$. The answer returned is "yes, $s = push(object_1,c,d,push(object_1,b,c,s_1))$."

The proof by resolution, given below, demonstrates how the desired answer is formed as a composition of action functions, thus describing a sequence of necessary actions. The mechanism for finding this answer is a special literal,* the "answer literal." This method of finding an answer is explained in detail in Ref. 3. For our purposes here, we will just show how it works by example. In the proof below, each answer literal is displayed beneath the clause containing it. At each step in the proof the answer literal will contain the current value of the object being constructed by the theorem prover. In this example the object being constructed is the sequence of actions s. So initially the answer literal <u>ANSWER</u>(s) is added to the clause representing the negation of the question. (One can interpret this clause, Clause 1, as "either $object_1$ is not at d in state s, or s is an answer.") The state variable s, inside the answer literal, is the "place holder" where the solution sequence is constructed. The construction process in this proof consists of successive instantiations of s. An instantiation of s can occur whenever a literal containing s is instantiated in the creation of a resolvent. Each instantiation* of s fills in a new action or an argument of an action function. In general, a particular inference step in the proof (either by factoring* or resolving*) need not necessarily further instantiate s. For example, the step might be an inference that verifies that some particular property holds for the current answer at that step in the proof. The final step in the proof yields Clause 7, "an answer is $push(object_1,c,d,push(object_1,b,c,s_1))$," which terminates the proof.

---

* We assume the reader is familiar with the vocabulary of the field of theorem proving by resolution as described in Refs. 1, 7, and 8.

Proof

1. $\sim$AT(object$_1$,d,s) — Negation of theorem

ANSWER(s)

2. $\sim$AT(object$_1$,c,s) ∨ AT(object$_1$,d,push(object$_1$,c,d,s)) — Axiom A3

3. $\sim$AT(object$_1$,c,s) — Resolve 1,2

ANSWER(push(object$_1$,c,d,s))

4. $\sim$AT(object$_1$,b,s) ∨ AT(object$_1$,c,push(object$_1$,b,c,s)) — Axiom A2

5. $\sim$AT(object$_1$,b,s) — Resolve 3,4

ANSWER(push(object$_1$,c,d, push(object$_1$,b,c,s)))

6. AT(object$_1$,b,s_1) — Axiom A1

7. Contradiction — Resolve 5,6

ANSWER(push(object$_1$,c,d, push(object$_1$,b,c,s_1)))

For the particular proof exhibited here, the order of generating the solution sequence during the search for the proof happens to be the same order in which the printout of the proof indicates s is instantiated. This order consists of working backward from the goal by filling in the last action, then the next-to-last action, etc. In general, the order in which the solution sequence is generated depends upon the proof strategy, since the proof strategy determines the order in which clauses are resolved or factored. The proof that this method always produces correct answers, given in Ref. 4, shows that the answers are correct regardless of the proof strategy used.

II. Refinements of the Method

The purpose of this section is to discuss variations of the formulation presented in the previous section and to show how other considerations such as time and conditional operations can be brought into the formalism. The reader who is interested in applications rather than additional material on representation may omit Secs. II, III, and IV, and read Secs. V and VI.

A. An Alternate Formulation

The first subject we shall discuss is an alternate to the previously given formulation. We shall refer to the original, presented in Sec. I, as formulation I, and this alternate as formulation II. Formulation II corresponds to a system-theoretic notion of state transformations. The state transformation function for a system gives the mapping of an action and a state into a new state. Let f represent the state transformation function, whose arguments are an action and a state and whose value is the new state obtained by applying the action to the state. Let $\{a_i\}$ be the actions, and nil be the null action. Let g be a function that maps two actions into a single composite action whose effect is the same as that of the argument actions applied sequentially. For example, axioms of the following form would partially define the state transformation function f:

B1. $(\forall s)[P(s) \supset Q(f(a_1,s))]$

B2. $(\forall s)[f(nil,s) = s]$

B3. $(\forall s,a_i,a_j)[f(a_j,f(a_i,s)) = f(g(a_i,a_j),s)]$.

The predicates P and Q represent descriptors of states. Axiom B1 describes the result of an action a_1 applied to the class of states that are equivalent in that they all have the property P(s). The resulting states are thus equivalent in that they have property Q(s). Axiom B2 indicates that the null action has no effect. The equation in B3 says that the effect of the composite action sequence $g(a_i,a_j)$ is the same as that of actions a_i and a_j applied sequentially. The question posed in this formulation can include an initial state--e.g., a question might be $(\exists x)Q(f(x,s_0))$, meaning "Does there exist a sequence of actions x that maps state s_0 into a state satisfying the predicate Q?" Observe that we are not insisting on finding a particular sequence of actions, but any sequence that leads us to a satisfactory state within the target class of states.

This representation is more complex, but has the advantage over the previous representation that both the starting state of a transformation and the sequence of actions are explicitly given as the arguments of the state-transformation function. Thus, one can quantify over, or specify in particular, either the starting state or the sequence, or both.

Next we shall show how other considerations can be brought into a state-transformation formalism. Both the original formulation (I) and the alternate (II) will be used as needed.

B. No Change of State

This kind of statement represents an implication that holds for a fixed state. An axiom typical of this class might describe the relationship between movable objects; e.g., if x is to the left of y and y is to the left of z, then x is to the left of z.

$$(\forall x,y,z,s)[LEFT(x,y,s) \wedge LEFT(y,z,s) \supset LEFT(x,z,s)]$$

C. Time

Time can be a function of a state, to express the timing of actions and states. For example, if the function time(s) gives the time of an instantaneous state, in the axiom

$$(\forall s)[P(s) \supset [Q(f(s)) \wedge \text{EQUAL}(\text{difference}(\text{time}(f(s)),\text{time}(s)),\tau)]],$$

where P(s) describes the initial state and Q(s) describes the final state, the state transformation takes τ seconds to complete.

D. State-Independent Truths

An example is

$$(\forall x,y,z)[\text{EQUAL}(\text{plus}(x,17),z) \supset \text{EQUAL}(\text{difference}(z,x),17)]$$

illustrating how functions and predicates are explicitly made state independent by not taking states as arguments.

E. Descriptors of Transformations

A descriptor or modifier of an action may be added in the form of a predicate that takes as an argument the state transformation that is to be described. For example,

WISHED-FOR(f(action,state),person)

might indicate a wished-for occurrence of an action;

LOCATION(f(action,state),place)

indicates that an action occurred at a certain place.

F. Disjunctive Answers

Consider a case in which an action results in one of two possibilities. As an example, consider an automaton that is to move from a to d.

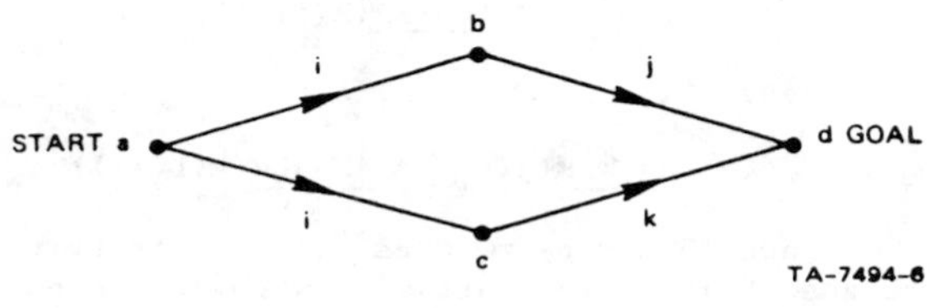

The above figure shows that action i leads to either b or c from a. The function f is single-valued but we don't know its value. The goal d can be reached from b by action j, or from c by action k. In the formalization given below it is possible to prove that the goal is reachable although a correct sequence of actions necessary to reach the goal is not generated. Instead, the answer produced is a disjunction of two sequences-- $j(i(s_0))$ or $k(i(s_0))$.

We use formulation I. Axiom M1 specifies the starting state s_0 and starting position a. Axioms M2, M3, and M4 specify positions resulting from the allowed moves.

M1. $AT(a,s_0)$

M2. $(\forall s)[AT(a,s) \supset AT(b,i(s)) \vee AT(c,i(s))]$

M3. $(\forall s)[AT(b,s) \supset AT(d,j(s))]$

M4. $(\forall s)[AT(c,s) \supset AT(d,k(s))]$

To find if the goal d is reachable, we ask the following question:

Question: $(\exists s)AT(d,s)$

to which an answer is:

Answer: Yes, $s = j(i(s_0))$ or $s = k(i(s_0))$.

The proof is:

Proof

1.	$\sim AT(d,s)$ <u>ANSWER</u>(s)	Negation of theorem
2.	$\sim AT(b,s) \vee AT(d,j(s))$	Axiom M3
3.	$\sim AT(b,s)$ <u>ANSWER</u>(j(s))	From 1,2
4.	$\sim AT(c,s) \vee AT(d,k(s))$	Axiom M4
5.	$\sim AT(c,s)$ <u>ANSWER</u>(k(s))	From 1,4
6.	$\sim AT(a,s) \vee AT(b,i(s)) \vee AT(c,i(s))$	Axiom M2
7.	$\sim AT(a,s) \vee AT(b,i(s))$ <u>ANSWER</u>(k(i(s)))	From 5,6
8.	$\sim AT(a,s)$ <u>ANSWER</u>(j(i(s))) ∨ <u>ANSWER</u>(k(i(s)))	From 3,7
9.	$AT(a,s_0)$	Axiom M1
10.	Contradiction <u>ANSWER</u>($j(i(s_0))$) ∨ <u>ANSWER</u>($k(i(s_0))$)	From 8,9

Observe that clause 8 has two answers, one coming from clause 3 corresponding to the action k and one from clause 7 corresponding to the action j. This shows how an "or" answer can arise.

G. Answers with Conditionals

A conditional operation such as "if p then q else r" allows a program to branch to either operation q or r depending upon the outcome of the test condition p. By allowing a conditional operation, a better solution to the above problem is made possible, namely, "beginning in state s_0 take action i; if at b take action j, otherwise take action k."

Consider the problem above that yields disjunctive answers. The information in the above problem formulation, axioms M1 through M4, plus additional information allows the creation of a program with a conditional and a test operation. The following additional information is needed, which we shall furnish in the form of axioms.

The first addition needed is a conditional operation, along with a description of what the operation does. Since our programs are in the form of functions, a conditional function is needed. One such possible function is the LISP conditional function "cond" which will be discussed in Sec. VI. However, another function, a simple "select" function is slightly easier to describe and will be used here. The function select(x,y,z,w) is defined to have the value z if x equals y and w otherwise.

M5. $(\forall x,y,z,w)[x = y \supset \mathrm{select}(x,y,z,w) = z]$

M6. $(\forall x,y,z,w)[x \neq y \supset \mathrm{select}(x,y,z,w) = w]$

The second addition needed is a test operation, along with a description of what it does. Since our programs are in the form of functions, a test function is needed. We shall use "atf", meaning "at-function." The function "atf" applied to a state yields the location in that state, e.g., $\mathrm{atf}(s_0) = a$. The atf function is described by

M7. $(\forall x,s)[\mathrm{AT}(x,s) \equiv (\mathrm{atf}(s) = x)]$.

These axioms lead to the solution

$$s = \mathrm{select}(\mathrm{atf}(i(s_0)),b,j(i(s_0)),k(i(s_0))),$$

meaning "if at b after applying i to s_0, take action j otherwise action k."

Although the new axioms allow the conditional solution, just the addition of these axioms does not guarantee that disjunctive answers will not occur. To prevent the possibility of disjunctive answers, we simply tell the theorem prover not to accept any clauses having two answers that don't unify.

What may be a preferable problem formulation and solution can result from the use of the alternative state formulation, II, exemplified in axioms B1, B2, and B3 above. Recall that f(i,s) is the state transformation function that maps action i and state s into a new state, the function g(i,j) maps the action i and the action j into the sequence of the two actions--i then j. The interrelation of f and g is described by

B3. $(\forall i,j,s)[f(j,f(i,s)) = f(g(i,j),s)]$

Axioms M1 through M4 remain the same but axioms M5, M6, and M7 are replaced. The new select function is described by the two axioms:

M5′. $(\forall i,j,s,p,b)[\mathrm{test}(p,s) = b \supset f(\mathrm{select}(p,b,i,j),s) = f(i,s)]$

M6′. $(\forall i,j,s,p,b)[\mathrm{test}(p,s) \neq b \supset f(\mathrm{select}(p,b,i,j),s) = f(j,s)]$,

where the function test applies the test condition p (which will correspond to atf for this problem) to state s. The test condition atf is defined by

M7′. $(\forall x,s)[\mathrm{AT}(x,s) \equiv \mathrm{test}(\mathrm{atf},s) = x]$.

The new solution is

$$s = f(g(i,\mathrm{select}(\mathrm{atf},b,j,k)),s_0).$$

Further discussion of program writing, including recursion, is given in Sec. VI.

Another method of forming conditional answers is possible. This involves inspecting an existence proof such as the one given in Sec. II-F above. First, such a proof is generated in which clauses having multiple answers are allowed. The conditional operation is constructed by observing the two literals which are resolved upon to generate the two-answer clause. For example, in the above proof clauses 3 and 7 resolve to yield 8. This step is repeated below, using the variable s' in 3 to emphasize that s' is different from s in 7.

Clause 3. $\sim\mathrm{AT}(b,s')$

$\underline{\mathrm{ANSWER}}(j(s'))$

Clause 7. $\sim\mathrm{AT}(a,s) \vee \mathrm{AT}(b,(i(s)))$

$\underline{\mathrm{ANSWER}}(k(i(s)))$

Clause 8. $\sim\mathrm{AT}(a,s)$

$\underline{\mathrm{ANSWER}}(j(s)) \vee \underline{\mathrm{ANSWER}}(k(i(s)))$

Clause 3 may be read as "if at b in state s', the answer is to take action j when in state s'." Clause 7 may be read as "if not at b in state i(s) and if at a in state s, the answer is to take action k when in state i(s)." Observing that the resolution binds s' to i(s) in Clause 8, one knows from Clauses 3 and 7 the test condition by which one decides which answer to choose in Clause 8, "if at a in state s the answer depends on i(s); if at b in i(s) take action j; otherwise take action k."

This discussion illustrates that the creation of a clause with two answer literals indicates that a conditional operation is needed to create a single conditional answer. This information provides a useful heuristic for the program-writing applications of QA3: When a clause having two answer literals is about to be generated, let the proof strategy call for the axioms that describe the conditional operation (such as M5 and M6). These axioms are then applied to create a single conditional answer.

Waldinger and Lee[6] have implemented a program-writing program PROW that also uses a resolution theorem prover to create constructive proofs, but by a different method than that of QA3. (The second method for creating conditionals by combining two answers is closely related to a technique used in PROW.) Information about (1) the target program operations, (2) the general relationship of the problem statement and axioms to the allowed target program operations including the test conditions, and (3) the syntax of the target language, is embedded in the PROW program. In QA3 this information is all in the axioms--such as axioms M5, M6, and M7.

H. Acquisition of Information

Another situation that arises in problem solving is one in which at the time the problem is stated and a solution is to be produced, there is insufficient information to completely specify a solution. More precisely, the solution cannot name every action and test condition in advance. As an example, consider a robot that is to move from a to c. The action i leads from a to b but no path to c is known, as illustrated below.

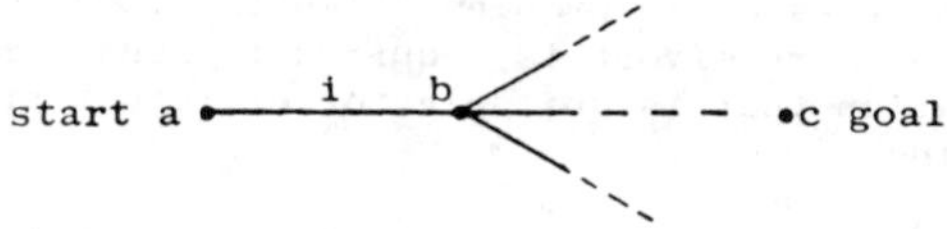

However, once point b is reached, more information can be acquired--for example, a guide to the area lives at b and will provide a path to point c if asked. Or perhaps once point b is reached, the robot might use its sensors to observe or discover paths to c.

To formalize this, assume that the action ask-path(b,c) will result in a proper path to c, when taken at b. For simplicity, assume that the name of the path is equal to the state resulting from asking the question. Using formulation II, one suitable set of axioms is:

N1. $AT(a,s_0) \wedge PATH(a,b,i)$

N2. $(\forall s,x,y,j)[AT(x,s) \wedge PATH(x,y,j) \supset AT(y,f(j,s))]$

N3. $(\forall s)[AT(b,s) \supset PATH(b,c,f(ask\text{-}path(b,c),s)) \wedge AT(b,f(ask\text{-}path(b,c),s))]$

where PATH(a,b,i) means that i is a path from a to b. The question $(\exists s)AT(c,s)$ results in the solution,

"yes, s = f(f(ask-path(b,c),f(i,s)),f(i,s))".

Axiom N3 illustrates an important aspect of this formalism for problem solving: If a condition (such as the robot's) is made state dependent, then we must specify how this condition changes when the state is changed. Thus in axiom N3 we must indicate that the robot's location is not changed by asking for a path. In a pure theorem-proving formalism, this means that if we want to know any condition in a given state, we must prove what that condition is. If a large number of state-dependent conditions need to be known at each state in a solution, then the theorem prover must prove what each condition is at each state in a conjectured solution. In such a case the theorem prover will take a long time to find the solution. McCarthy[5] refers to this problem as the frame problem, where the word "frame" refers to the frame of reference or the set of relevant conditions. Discussion of a method for easing this problem is presented in Sec. V.

I. Assignment Operations

An assignment operation is one that assigns a value to a variable. An example of an assignment is the statement $a \leftarrow h(a)$, meaning that the value of a is to be changed to the value of the function h(a). In our representation, we shall use an assignment function--i.e., assign(a,h(a)). Using Formulation II this function is described by the axiom

$$(\forall a,a_0,s)[VALUE(a,a_0,s) \supset VALUE(a,h(a_0),f(assign(a,h(a)),s))]$$

where the predicate $VALUE(a,a_0,s)$ means that variable a has value a_0 in state s.

III. An Example: The Monkey and The Bananas

To illustrate the methods described earlier, we present an axiomatization of McCarthy's "Monkey and Bananas" problem.

The monkey is faced with the problem of getting a bunch of bananas hanging from the ceiling just beyond his reach. To solve the problem, the monkey must push a box to an empty place under the bananas, climb on top of the box, and then reach them.

The constants are monkey, box, bananas, and under-bananas. The functions are reach, climb, and move, meaning the following:

reach(m,z,s)	The state resulting from the action of m reaching z, starting from state s
climb(m,b,s)	The state resulting from the action of m climbing b, starting from state s
move(m,b,u,s)	The state resulting from the action of m moving b to place u, starting from state s.

The predicates are:

MOVABLE(b)	b is movable
AT(m,u,s)	m is at place u in state s
ON(m,b,s)	m is on b in state s
HAS(m,z,s)	m has z in state s
CLIMBABLE(m,b,s)	m can climb b in state s
REACHABLE(m,b,s)	m can reach b in state s.

The axioms* are:

MB1. MOVABLE(box)

MB2. $AT(box,place_b,s_0)$

MB3. $(\forall x) \sim AT(x,under\text{-}bananas,s_0)$

MB4. $(\forall b,p_1,p_2,s)[[AT(b,p_1,s) \land MOVABLE(b) \land (\forall x) \sim AT(x,p_2,s)] \supset [AT(b,p_2,move(monkey,b,p_2,s)) \land AT(monkey,p_2,move(monkey,b,p_2,s))]]$

MB5. $(\forall s)CLIMBABLE(monkey,box,s)$

MB6. $(\forall m,p,b,s)[[AT(b,p,s) \land CLIMBABLE(m,b,s)] \supset [AT(b,p,climb(m,b,s)) \land ON(m,b,climb(m,b,s))]]$

MB7. $(\forall s)[[AT(box,under\text{-}bananas,s) \land ON(monkey,box,s)] \supset REACHABLE(monkey,bananas,s)]$

* The astute reader will notice that the axioms leave much to be desired. In keeping with the "toy problem" tradition we present an unrealistic axiomatization of this unrealistic problem. The problem's value lies in the fact that it is a reasonably interesting problem that may be familiar to the reader.

MB8. $(\forall m,z,s)[REACHABLE(m,z,s) \supset HAS(m,z,reach(m,z,s))]$.

The question is "Does there exist a state s (sequence of actions) in which the monkey has the bananas?"

QUESTION: $(\exists s)HAS(monkey,bananas,s)$.

The answer is yes,

$$s = reach(monkey,bananas,climb(monkey,box,move(monkey,box,under\text{-}bananas,s_0)))\,.$$

By executing this function, the monkey gets the bananas. The monkey must, of course, execute the functions in the usual order, starting with the innermost and working outward. Thus he first moves the box under the bananas, then climbs on the box, and then reaches the bananas.

The printout of the proof is given in the appendix.

IV. Formalizations for the Tower of Hanoi Puzzle

The first applications of our question-answering programs were to "question-answering" examples. Commonly used question-answering examples have short proofs, and usually there are a few obvious formulations for a given subject area. (The major difficulty in question-answering problems usually is searching a large data base, rather than finding a long and difficult proof.) Typically any reasonable formulation works well. As one goes on to problems like the Tower of Hanoi puzzle, more effort is required to find a representation that is suitable for efficient problem solving.

This puzzle has proved to be an interesting study of representation. Several people using QA3 have set up axiom systems for the puzzle. Apparently, a "good" axiomatization--one leading to quick solutions--is not entirely obvious, since many axiomatizations did not result in solutions. In this section we will present and compare several alternate representations, including ones that lead to a solution.

There are three pegs--peg_1, peg_2, and peg_3. There are a number of discs each of whose diameter is different from that of all the other discs. Initially all discs are stacked on peg_1, in order of descending size. The three-disc version is illustrated below.

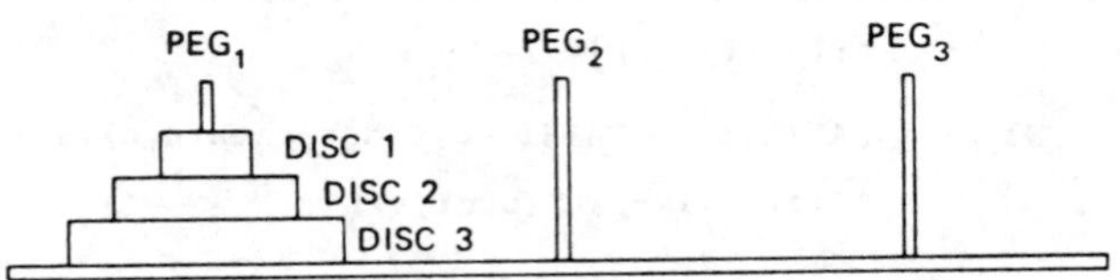

The object of the puzzle is to find a sequence of moves that will transfer all the discs from peg_1 to peg_3. The allowed moves consist of taking the top disc from any peg and placing it on another peg, but a disc can never be placed on top of a smaller disc.

In order to correctly specify the problem, any formalization must: (1) specify the positions of the discs for each state; (2) specify how actions change the position of the discs; and (3) specify the rules of the game, i.e., what is legal.

Let the predicate ON specify disc positions. In the simplest representation the predicate ON specifies the position of one disc--e.g., $ON(disc_1, peg_1, s)$ says that in state s $disc_1$ is on peg_1. This representation requires one predicate to specify the position of each disc. The relative position of each disc either must be specified by another statement, or else if two discs are on the same peg it must be implicitly understood that they are in the proper order. Perhaps the simplest extension is to allow the predicate another argument that specifies the position of the disc--i.e., $ON(disc_1, peg_1, position_2, s)$. Again, this requires many statements to specify a complete configuration.

Since various moves are constructing stacks of discs, and since stacks can be represented as lists, consider as an alternative representation a list to represent a stack of discs. Let the function $\ell(x,y)$ represent the list that has x as its first element (representing the top disc in the stack) and y as the rest of the list (representing the rest of the discs in the stack). This function ℓ corresponds to the "cons" function in LISP. Let nil be the empty list. The statement $ON(\ell(disc_1, \ell(disc_2, nil)), peg_1, s)$ asserts that the stack having top disc, $disc_1$, and second disc, $disc_2$, is on peg_1. This representation illustrates a useful technique in logic--namely, the use of functions as the construction (and selection) operators. This notion is consistent with the use of action functions as constructors of sequences.

Next, consider how to express possible changes in states. Perhaps the simplest idea is to say that a given state implies that certain moves are legal. One must then have other statements indicating the result of each move. This method is a bit lengthy. It is easier to express in one statement the fact that given some state, a new state is the result of a move. Thus one such move to a new state is described by $(\forall s)[ON(\ell(disc_1, nil), peg_1, s) \wedge ON(nil, peg_2, s) \wedge ON(\ell(disc_2, \ell(disc_3, nil)), peg_3, s) \supset ON(nil, peg_1, move(disc_1, peg_1, peg_2, s)) \wedge ON(\ell(disc_1, nil), peg_2, move(disc_1, peg_1, peg_2, s)) \wedge ON(\ell(disc_2, \ell(disc_3, nil)), peg_3, move(disc_1, peg_1, peg_2, s))]$.

With this method it is possible to enumerate all possible moves and configuration combinations. However, it is still easier to use variables to represent whole classes of states and moves. Thus $(\forall s, x, y, z, p_i, p_j, p_k, d)[ON(\ell(d,x), p_i, s) \wedge ON(y, p_j, s) \wedge ON(z, p_k, s) \supset ON(x, p_i, move(d, p_i, p_j, s)) \wedge ON(\ell(d,y), p_j, move(d, p_i, p_j, s)) \wedge ON(z, p_k, move(d, p_i, p_j, s))]$ specifies a whole class of moves. The problem here is that additional restrictions must be added so that illegal states cannot be part of a solution. In the previous formalism, one could let the axioms enumerate just the legal moves and states, thus preventing incorrect solutions.

The first method for adding restrictions is to have a predicate that restricts moves to just the legitimate states. Since the starting state is legal, one might think that only legal states can be reached. However, the resolution process (set-of-support strategy[7]) typically works backward from the goal state toward states that can reach the goal state--such states are sometimes called "forcing states." Thus illegal but forcing states can be reached by working backward from the goal state. This does not allow for incorrect solutions, since the only forcing states that can appear in the solution must be those reached from the starting state (which is a legal state). The restriction of moving only to new legal states thus prevents an error. But the search is unnecessarily large, since the theorem prover is considering illegal states that cannot lead to a solution. So a better solution is to eliminate these illegal forcing states by allowing moves only from legal states to legal states. This is perhaps the best specification, in a sense. Such an axiom is $(\forall s, x, y, z, p_i, p_j, p_k, d)[ON(\ell(d,x), p_i, s) \wedge ON(y, p_j, s) \wedge ON(z, p_k, s) \wedge LEGAL(\ell(d,x)) \wedge LEGAL(\ell(d,y)) \wedge DISTINCT(p_i, p_j, p_k) \supset ON(x, p_i, move(d, p_i, p_j, s)) \wedge ON(\ell(d,y), p_j, move(d, p_i, p_j, s)) \wedge ON(z, p_k, move(d, p_i, p_j, s))]$. The predicate LEGAL(x) is true if and only if the discs are listed in order of increasing size. (One can "cheat" and have a simpler axiom by omitting the predicate that requires that the state resulting from a move have a legal stack of discs. Since the set-of-support strategy forces the theorem prover to work backward starting from a legal final state, it will only consider legal states. However, one is then using an axiomatization that, by itself, is incorrect.) The additional LEGAL predicate is a typical example of how additional information in the axioms results in a quicker solution. The predicate $DISTINCT(p_i, p_j, p_k)$ means no two pegs are equal.

The clauses generated during the search that are concerned with illegal states are subsumed[8] by ~LEGAL predicates such as $(\forall s)\sim LEGAL(\ell(disc_2, (disc_1, x)))$. The stacks are formed by placing one new disc on top of a legal stack. If the new top disc is smaller than the old top disc then it is of course smaller than all the others on the stack. Thus the legal stack axioms need only to specify that the top disc is smaller than the second disc for a stack to be legal. This blocks the construction of incorrect stacks.

One complete axiomatization is as follows:

AX1. $(\forall x,y,z,m,n,p_i,p_j,p_k)[\mathrm{ON}(\ell(d(m),x),p_i,s) \wedge$
$\mathrm{ON}(y,p_j,s) \wedge \mathrm{ON}(z,p_k,s) \wedge$
$\mathrm{DISTINCT}(p_i,p_j,p_k) \wedge \mathrm{LEGAL}(\ell(d(m),x)) \wedge$
$\mathrm{LEGAL}(\ell(d(n),y)) \supset$
$\mathrm{ON}(x,p_i,\mathrm{move}(d(m),p_i,p_j,s)) \wedge$
$\mathrm{ON}(\ell(d(m),y),p_j,\mathrm{move}(d(m),p_i,p_j,s)) \wedge$
$\mathrm{ON}(z,p_k,\mathrm{move}(d(m),p_i,p_j,s))]$

AX2. $(\forall m \quad x)[\mathrm{LEGAL}(\ell(d(m),\ell(d(n),x))) \equiv$
$\mathrm{LESS}(m,n)] \wedge (\forall n)\mathrm{LEGAL}(\ell(d(n),\mathrm{nil})) \wedge$
$\mathrm{LEGAL}(\mathrm{nil})$

Instead of naming each disc, the disc number n is an argument of the function d(n) that represents the nth disc. This representation illustrates how the proof procedure can be shortened by solving frequent decidable subproblems with special available tools--namely, the LISP programming language. The theorem prover uses LISP (the "lessp" function) to evaluate the LESS(n,m) predicate--a very quick step. This mechanism has the effect of generating, wherever needed, such axioms as ~LESS(3,2) or LESS(2,3) to resolve against or subsume literals in generated clauses. Similarly, LISP evaluates the DISTINCT predicate.

Note that the move axiom, AX1, breaks up into three clauses, each clause specifying the change in the task for one particular peg. The process of making one move requires nine binary resolutions, and two binary factorings of clauses.

Still other solutions are possible by using special term-matching capabilities in QA3 that extend the unification and subsumption algorithms to include list terms, set terms, and certain types of symmetries.

In another axiomatization, the complete configuration of the puzzle in a given state is specified by the predicate ON. ON(x,y,z,s) means that in state s, stack x in on peg_1, stack y is on peg_2, and stack z is on peg_3. Thus if the predicate $\mathrm{ON}(\ell(d_1,\ell(d_2,\mathrm{nil}))),\mathrm{nil},\ell(d_3,\mathrm{nil}),s_k)$ holds, the stack $d_1 - d_2$ is on peg_1 and d_3 is on peg_3. The predicate LEGAL again indicates that a given stack of discs is allowed.

Two kinds of axioms are required--move axioms and legal stack axioms. One legal stack axiom is $\mathrm{LEGAL}(\ell(d_1,\ell(d_2,\mathrm{nil})))$. One move axiom is $(\forall d,x,y,z,s)[\mathrm{ON}(\ell(d,x),y,z,s) \wedge \mathrm{LEGAL}(\ell(d,x)) \wedge \mathrm{LEGAL}(\ell(d,y)) \supset \mathrm{ON}(x,\ell(d,y),z,\mathrm{move}(d,p_1,p_2,s))]$. This axiom states that disc d can be moved from peg_1 to peg_2 if the initial stack on peg_1 is legal and the resultant stack on peg_2 is legal.

In this last-mentioned formalization, using 13 axioms to specify the problem, QA3 easily solved this problem for the three-disc puzzle. During the search for a proof, 98 clauses were generated buy only 25 of the clauses were accepted. Of the 25, 12 were not in the proof. The solution entails seven moves, thus passing through eight states (counting the initial and final states). The 12 clauses not in the proof correspond to searching through 5 states that are not used in the solution. Thus the solution is found rather easily. Of course, if a sufficiently poor axiomatization is chosen--one requiring an enumeration of enough correct and incorrect disc positions--the system becomes saturated and fails to obtain a solution within time and space constraints. An important factor in the proof search is the elimination of extra clauses corresponding to alternate paths that reach a given state. In the above problem it happens that the subsumption heuristic[8] eliminates 73 of these redundant clauses. However, this particular use of subsumption is problem dependent, thus one must examine any given problem formulation to determine whether or not subsumption will eliminate alternate paths to equivalent states.

The four-disc version of the puzzle can be much more difficult than the three-disc puzzle in terms of search. At about this level of difficulty one must be somewhat more careful to obtain a low-cost solution.

Ernst[9] formalizes the notion of "difference" used by GPS and shows what properties these differences must possess for GPS to succeed on a problem. He then presents a "good" set of differences for the Tower of Hanoi problem. Utilizing this information, GPS solves the problem for four discs, considering no incorrect states in its search. Thus Ernst has chosen a set of differences that guide GPS directly to the solution.

Another method of solution is possible. First, solve the three-disc puzzle. Save the solution to the three-disc puzzle (using the answer statement[4]). Then ask for a solution to the four-disc puzzle. The solution then is: Move the top three discs from peg_1 to peg_2; move $disc_4$ from peg_1 to peg_3; move the three discs on peg_2 to peg_3. This method produces a much easier solution. But this can be considered as cheating, since the machine is "guided" to a solution by being told which subproblem to first solve and store away. The use of the differences by GPS similarly lets the problem solver be "guided" toward a solution.

There is another possibly more desirable solution. The four-disc puzzle can be posed as the problem, with no three-disc solution. If the solution of the three-disc puzzle occurs during the search for a solution to the four-disc puzzle, and if it is automatically recognized and saved as a lemma, then the four-disc solution should follow easily.

Finally, if an induction axiom is provided, the axioms imply a solution in the form of a recursive program that solves the puzzle for an arbitrary number of discs. Aiko Hormann[10] discusses the related solutions of the four-disc problem by the program GAKU (not an automatic theorem-proving program). The solutions by lemma finding, induction, and search guided by differences have not been run on QA3.

V. Applications to the Robot Project

A. Introduction to Robot Problem Solving

In this section we discuss how theorem-proving methods are being tested for several applications in the Stanford Research Institute Artificial Intelligence Group's Automaton (robot). We emphasize that this section describes work that is now in progress, rather than work that is completed. These methods represent explorations in problem solving, rather than final decisions about how the robot is to do problem solving. An overview of the current status of the entire SRI robot project is provided by Nilsson[4]. Coles[11] has developed an English-to-logic translator that is part of the robot.

We use theorem-proving methods for three purposes, the simplest being the use of QA3 as a central information storage and retrieval system that is accessible to various parts of the system as well as the human users. The data base of QA3 is thus one of the robot's models of its world, including itself.

A second use is as an experimental tool to test out a particular problem formulation. When a suitable formulation is found, it may then be desirable to write a faster or more efficient specific program that implements this formulation, perhaps involving little or no search. If the special program is not as general as the axiom system is, so that the special program fails in certain cases, the axioms can be retained to be used in the troublesome cases. Both solutions can be made available by storing, as the first axiom to be tried, a special axiom that describes the special solution. The predicate-evaluation mechanism can then call LISP to run the special solution. If it fails, the other axioms will then be used.

The third use is as a real-time problem solver. In the implementation we are now using, statements of logic--clauses--are the basic units of information. Statements are derived from several sources: teletype entries, axioms stored in memory, clauses or statements generated by the theorem prover, and statements evaluated by programs--subroutines in LISP, FORTRAN, or machine language. These programs can use robot sensors and sensory data to verify, disprove, or generate statements of logic.

The SRI robot is a cart on wheels, having a TV camera and a range-finder mounted on the cart. There are bumpers on the cart, but no arms or grasping agents, so the only way the robot can manipulate its environment is by simple pushing actions. Given this rather severe restriction of no grasping, the robot must be clever to effectively solve problems involving modifying its world. We present below some axioms for robot problem solving.

The first axiom describes the move routines of the robot:

R1. $(\forall s,p_1,p_2,path_{12})[AT(robot,p_1,s) \wedge PATH(p_1,p_2,path_{12},s) \supset AT(robot,p_2,move(robot,path_{12},s))]$.

This axiom says that if the robot is at p_1 and there is a path to p_2, the robot will be at p_2 after moving along the path. The predicate PATH indicates there exists a robot-path, $path_{12}$, from place p_1 to place p_2. A robot-path is a path adequate for the robot's movement. The terms p_1 and p_2 describe the position of the robot.

In general, it may be very inefficient to use the theorem prover to find the $path_{12}$ such that $PATH(p_1,p_2,path_{12})$ is true. Several existing FORTRAN subroutines, having sophisticated problem-solving capabilities of their own, may be used to determine a good path through obstacles on level ground. We will show later a case where the theorem prover may be used to find a more obscure kind of path. For the less obscure paths, the axiom R1 is merely a description of the semantics of these FORTRAN programs, so that new and meaningful programs can be generated by QA3 by using the efficient path-generating programs as subprograms. The "predicate-evaluation" mechanism is used to call the FORTRAN path-finding routines. The effect of this evaluation mechanism is the same as if the family of axioms of the form $PATH(p_1,p_2,path_{12})$ for all p_1 and p_2 such that $path_{12}$ exists, were all stored in memory and available to the theorem prover.

The second axiom is a push axiom that describes the effect of pushing an object. The robot has no arm or graspers, just a bumper. Its world consists of large objects such as boxes, wedges, cubes, etc. These objects are roughly the same size as the robot itself.

The basic predicate that specifies the position of an object is ATO, meaning at-object. The predicate

$$ATO(object_1,description_1,position_1,s_1)$$

indicates that $object_1$, having structural description "$description_1$", is in position "$position_1$", in state "s_1". At the time of this writing, a particular set of "standard" structure descriptions has not yet been selected. So far several have been used. The simplest description is a point whose position is at the estimated center of gravity of the object. This description is used for the FORTRAN "push in a straight line" routine. Since all the objects in the robot's world are polyhedrons, reasonably simple complete structural de iptions are possible. For example, one structural description consists of the set of polygons that form the surface of the polyhedron. In turn, the structure of the polygons is given by the set of vertices in its boundary. Connectivity of structures can be stated explicitly or else implied by common boundaries. The position of an object is given by a mapping of the topologically-described structure into the robot's coordinate system. Such structural descriptions may be given as axioms or supplied by the scene-analysis programs used by the robot.

A basic axiom describing the robot's manipulation of an object is

R2.

$$(\forall s,obj_1,desc_1,pos_1,pos_2)[ATO(obj_1,desc_1,pos_1,s) \wedge MOVABLE(obj_1) \wedge ROTATE\text{-}TRANSLATE\text{-}ABLE(desc_1, pos_1,pos_2) \wedge OBJECT\text{-}PATH(desc_1,pos_1,pos_2, path_{12},s) \supset ATO(obj_1,desc_1,pos_2,push(obj_1, path_{12},s))]$$

This axiom says that if object 1, described by description 1, is at position 1, and object 1 is movable, and object 1 can be theoretically rotated and translated to the new position 2, and there is an object-path from 1 to 2, then object 1 will be at position 2 as a result of pushing it along the path. The predicate ROTATE-TRANSLATABLE($desc_1$,pos_1,pos_2) checks the necessary condition that the object can be theoretically rotated and translated into the new position. The predicate OBJECT-PATH($desc_1$,pos_1,pos_2,$path_{12}$) means that pos_2 is the estimated new position resulting from pushing along push-path, $path_{12}$.

Let us now return to the frame problem. More specifically, in a state resulting from pushing an object, how can we indicate the location of objects which were not pushed? One such axiom is

R3. $$(\forall obj_1,obj_2,desc_1,pos_1,path_{12},s)[ATO(obj_1, desc_1,pos_1,s) \wedge \sim SAME(obj_1,obj_2) \supset ATO(obj_1,desc_1,pos_1,push(obj_2,path_{12},s))].$$

This axiom says that all objects that are not the same as the pushed object are unmoved. The predicate evaluation mechanism is used to evaluate SAME and speed up the proof. One can use this predicate evaluation mechanism, and perhaps other fast methods for handling classes of deductions (such as special representations of state-dependent information and special programs for updating this information--which is done in the robot), but another problem remains. Observe that axiom R3 assumes that only the objects directly pushed by the robot move. This is not always the case, since an object being pushed might accidentally strike another object and move it. This leads to the question of dealing with the real world and using axioms to approximate the real world.

B. Real-World Problem Solving: Feedback

Our descriptions of the real world, axiomatic or otherwise, are at best only approximations. For example, the new position of an object moved by the robot will not necessarily be accurately predicted, even if one goes to great extremes to calculate a predicted new position. The robot does not have a grasp on the object so that some slippage may occur. The floor surface is not uniform and smooth. The weight distribution of objects is not known. There is only rudimentary kinesthetic sensing feedback--namely, whether or not the bumper is still in contact with the object. Thus it appears that a large feedback loop iterating toward a solution, is necessary: Form a plan for pushing the object (possibl· ·sing the push axiom), push according to the pla.., back up, take a look, see where the object is, compare the position to the desired position, start over again. The new position (to some level of accuracy) is provided by the sensors of the robot. This new position is compared to the position predicted by the axiom. If the move is not successful, the predicate (provided by sensors in the new state) that reasonably accurately gives the object's position in the new state must be used as the description of the initial state for the next attempt.

This feedback method can be extended to sequences of actions. Consider the problem: Find s_f such that $P_3(s_f)$ is true. Suppose the starting state is s_0, with property $P_0(s_0)$. Suppose the axioms are as follows:

$$P_0(s_0)$$

$$(\forall s)[P_0(s) \supset P_1(f_1(s))]$$

$$(\forall s)[P_1(s) \supset P_2(f_2(s))]$$

$$(\forall s)[P_2(s) \supset P_3(f_3(s))].$$

The sequence of actions $f_3(f_2(f_1(s_0)))$ transforms state s_0 with property $P_0(s_0)$ into state s_f having property $P_3(s_f)$.

The solution is thus $s_f = f_3(f_2(f_1(s_0)))$.

Corresponding to each "theoretical" predicate $P_i(s)$ is a corresponding "real-word" predicate $P_i'(s)$. The truth value of $P_i'(s)$ is determined by sensors and the robot's internal model of the world. It has built-in bounds on how close its measurements must be to the correct values in order to assert that it is true.* The proof implies the following description of the result after each step of execution of $f_3(f_2(f_1(s_0)))$:

* At this time, a many-valued logic having degrees of truth is not used, although this is an interesting possibility.

Actions and Successive States	Predicted Theoretical Results	Predicted Real-World Results
s_0	$P_0(s_0)$	$P'_0(s_0)$
$s_1 = f_1(s_0)$	$P_1(s_1)$	$P'_1(s_1)$
$s_2 = f_2(s_1)$	$P_2(s_2)$	$P'_2(s_2)$
$s_f = f_3(s_2)$	$P_3(s_3)$	$P'_3(s_f)$

To measure progress after, say, the ith step, one checks that $P'_i(s_i)$ is true. If not, then some other condition $P''_i(s_i)$ holds and a new problem is generated, given $P''_i(s_i)$ as the starting point. If new information is present, such as is the case when the robot hits an obstacle that is not in its model, the model is updated before a new solution is attempted. The position of this new object of course invalidates the previous plan--i.e., had the new object's position been known, the previous plan would not have been generated.

The new solution may still be able to use that part of the old solution that is not invalidated by any new information. For example, if $P''_i(s_i)$ holds, it may still be possible to reach the jth intermediate state and then continue the planned sequence of actions from the jth state. However, the object-pushing axiom is an example of an axiom that probably will incorrectly predict results and yet no further information, except for the new position, will be available. For this case, the best approach is probably to iterate toward the target state by repeated use of the push axiom to generate a new plan. Hopefully, the process converges.

For a given axiomatization feedback does not necessarily make it any easier to find a proof. However, knowing that the system uses feedback allows us to choose a simpler and less accurate axiom system. Simple axiom systems can then lead to shorter proofs.

One can envision formalizing this entire problem-solving process, including the notion of feedback, verifying whether or not a given condition is met, updating the model, recursively calling the theorem prover, etc. The author has not attempted such a formalization, although he has written a first-order formalization of the theorem prover's own problem-solving strategy. This raises the very interesting possibility of self-modification of strategy; however, in practice such problems lie well beyond the current theorem-proving capacity of the program.

C. A Simple Robot Problem

Now let us consider a problem requiring the use of a ramp to roll onto a platform, as illustrated below.

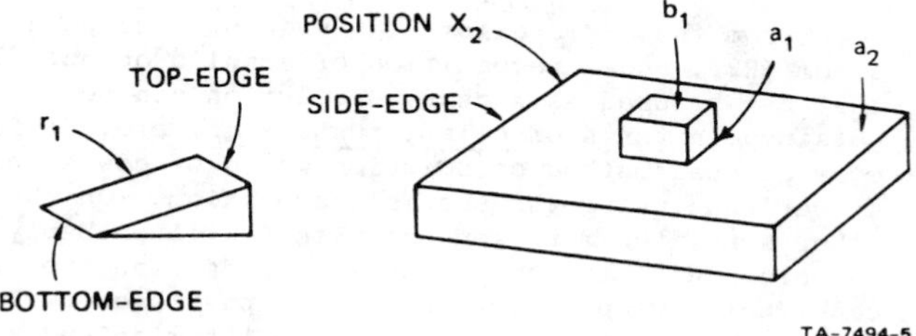

The goal is to push the box b_1 from position x_1 to x_2. To get onto the platform, the robot must push the ramp r_1 to the platform, and then roll up the ramp onto the platform.

A simple problem formulation can use a special ramp-using axiom such as

R4. $(\forall x_1, x_2, s, \text{top-edge}, \text{bottom-edge}, \text{ramp}_1)$
$[\text{AT-RAMP}(\text{ramp}_1, \text{top-edge}, x_2, \text{bottom-edge}, x_1, s) \wedge \text{AT-PLATFORM}(\text{side-edge}, x_2, s) \supset \text{AT}(\text{robot}, x_2, \text{climb}(\text{ramp}_1, x_1, s))]$

with the obvious meaning. Such a solution is quick but leaves much to be desired in terms of generality.

A more general problem statement is one in which the robot has a description of its own capabilities, and a translation of this statement of its abilities into the basic terms that describe its sensory and human-given model of the world. It then learns from a fundamental level to deal with the world. Such a knowledge doesn't make for the quickest solution to a frequently-encountered problem, but certainly does lend itself to learning, greater degrees of problem-solving, and self-reliance in a new problem situation.

Closer to this extreme of greatest generality is the following axiomatization.

R5. $(\forall x_1, x_2, r)[\text{RECTANGLE}(r, x_1, x_2) \wedge \text{LESSP}(\text{maxslope}(r), k_0) \wedge \text{LESSP}(r_0, \text{width}(r)) \wedge \text{CLEAR}(\text{space}(r, h_0), s) \wedge \text{SOLID}(r) \supset \text{PATH}(x_1, x_2, r)]$.

This axiom says that r describes a rectangle having ends x_1 and x_2. The maximum slope is less than a constant k_0, the width of r is greater than the robot's width w_0, the space above r to the robot's height h_0 is clear, and the rectangle r has a solid surface.

Two paths can be joined as follows:

R6. $(\forall x_1,x_2,x_3,r_1,r_2)[\mathrm{PATH}(x_1,x_2,r_1) \wedge \mathrm{PATH}(x_2,x_3,r_2) \supset \mathrm{PATH}(x_1,x_3,\mathrm{join}(r_1,r_2))]$.

From these two axioms (R5 and R6), the push axiom (R2), and a recognition of a solid object that can be used as a ramp, a solution can be obtained in terms of climb, push, join, etc. This more general method of solution would of course be slower than using the special ramp axiom. On the other hand, the more general method will probably be more useful if the robot will be required to construct a ramp, or recognize and push over a potential ramp that is standing on its wide end.

The danger in trying the more general methods is that one may be asking the theorem prover to rederive some significant portion of math or physics, in order to solve some simple problem.

VI. Automatic Programming

A. Introduction

The automatic writing, checking, and debugging of computer programs are problems of great interest both for their independent importance and as useful tools for intelligent machines. This section shows how a theorem prover can be used to solve certain automatic programming problems. The formalization given here will be used to precisely state and solve the problem of automatic generation of programs, including recursive programs, along with concurrent generation of proofs of the correctness of these programs. Thus any programs automatically written by this method have no errors.

We shall take LISP[12,13] as our example of a programming language. In the LISP language, a function is described by two entities: (1) its value, and (2) its side effect. Side effects can be described in terms of their effect upon the state of the program. Methods for describing state-transformation operations, as well as methods for the automatic writing of programs in a state-transformation language, were presented in Secs. I and II. For simplicity, in this section we shall discuss "pure" LISP, in which a LISP function corresponds to the standard notion of a function--i.e., it has a value but no side effect.

Thus we shall use pure LISP 1.5 without the program feature, which is essentially the lambda calculus. In this restricted system, a LISP program is merely a function. For example, the LISP function car applied to a list returns the first element of the list. Thus if the variable x has as value the list (a b c), then car(x) = a. The LISP function cdr yields the remainder of the list, thus CDR(x) = (b c), and car(cdr(x)) = b. There are several approaches one may take in formalizing LISP; the one given here is a simple mapping from LISP's lambda calculus to the predicate calculus. LISP programs are represented by functions. The syntax of pure LISP 1.5, is normal function composition, and the corresponding syntax for the formalization is also function composition. LISP "predicates" are represented in LISP--and in this formalization--as functions having either the value NIL (false) or else a value not equal to NIL (true). The semantics are given by axioms relating LISP functions to list structures, e.g., $(\forall x,y)\mathrm{car}(\mathrm{cons}(x,y)) = x$, where cons(x,y) is the list whose first element is x and whose remainder is y.

In our formulation of programming problems, we emphasize the distinction between the program (represented as a function in LISP), that solves a problem and a test for the validity of a solution to a problem (represented as a predicate in logic). It is often much easier to construct the predicate than it is to construct the function. Indeed, one may say that a problem is not well defined until an effective test for its solution is provided.

For example, suppose we wish to write a program that sorts a list. This problem is not fully specified until the meaning of "sort" is explained; and the method of explanation we choose is to provide a predicate R(x,y) that is true if list y is a sorted version of list x and false otherwise. (The precise method of defining this relation R will be given later.)

In general, our approach to using a theorem prover to solve programming problems in LISP requires that we give the theorem prover two sets of initial axioms:

(1) Axioms defining the functions and constructs of the subset of LISP to be used

(2) Axioms defining an input-output relation such as the relation R(x,y), which is to be true if and only if x is any input of the appropriate form for some LISP program and y is the corresponding output to be produced by such a program.

Given this relation R, and the LISP axioms, by having the theorem prover prove (or disprove) the appropriate question we can formulate the following four kinds of programming problems: checking, simulation, verifying (debugging), and program writing. These problems may be explained using the sort program as an example as follows:

(1) Checking: The form of the question is R(a,b) where a and b are two given lists. By proving R(a,b) true or false, b is checked to be either a sorted version of a or not. The desired answer is accordingly either yes or no.

(2) Simulation: The form of the question is $(\exists x)R(a,x)$, where a is a given input list. If the question $(\exists x)R(a,x)$ is answered yes, then a sorted version of x exists and a sorted version is constructed by the theorem prover. Thus the theorem prover acts as a sort program. If the answer is no, then it has proved that a sorted version of x does not exist (an impossible answer if a is a proper list).

(3) Verifying: The form of the question is $(\forall x)R(x,g(x))$, where g(x) is a program written

by the user. This mode is known as verifying, debugging, proving a program correct, or proving a program incorrect. If the answer to $(\forall x)R(x,g(x))$ is yes, then g(x) sorts every proper input list and the program is correct. If the answer is no, a counterexample list c, that the program will not sort, must be constructed by the theorem prover. This mode requires induction axioms to prove that looping or recursive programs converge.

(4) Program Writing: The form of the question is $(\forall x)(\exists y)R(x,y)$. In this synthesis mode the program is to be constructed or else proved impossible to construct. If the answer is yes, then a program, say f(x), must be constructed that will sort all proper input lists. If the answer is no, an unsortable list (impossible, in this case) must be produced. This mode also requires induction axioms. The form of the problem statement shown here is oversimplified for the sake of clarity. The exact form will be shown later.

In addition to the possibility of "yes" answer and the "no" answer, there is always the possibility of a "no proof found" answer if the search is halted by some time or space bound. The elimination of disjunctive answers, which is assumed in this section, was explained in Sec. B.

These methods are summarized in the following table. The reader may view R(x,y) as representing some general desired input-output relationship.

	Programming Problem	Form of Question	Desired Answer
(1)	Checking	R(a,b)	yes or no
(2)	Simulation	$(\exists x)R(a,x)$	yes, x = b or no
(3)	Verifying	$(\forall x)R(x,g(x))$	yes or no, x = c
(4)	Program Writing	$(\forall x)(\exists y)R(x,y)$	yes, y = f(x) or no, x = c

We now present an axiomatization of LISP followed by two axiomatizations of the sort relation R (one for a special case and one more general).

B. Axiomatization of a Subset of LISP

All LISP functions and predicates will be written in small letters. The functions "equal(x,y)," "at(x)," and "null(x)" evaluate to "nil" if false and something not equal to "nil," say "T," if true. The predicates of first-order logic that are used to describe LISP are written in capital letters. These, of course, have truth values.

The version of LISP described here does not distinguish between an S-expression and a copy of that S-expression. There is some redundancy in the following formulation, in that certain functions and predicates could have been defined in terms of others; however, the redundancy allows us to state the problem more concisely. Also, some axioms could have been eliminated since they are derivable from others, but are included for clarity. The variables x, y, and z are bound by universal quantifiers, but the quantifiers are omitted for the sake of readability wherever possible. The formulation is given below:

Predicates	Meaning
NULL(x)	x = nil
LIST(x)	x is a list
ATOM(x)	x is an atom
x = y	x is equal to y

Functions	Meaning
car(x)	The first element of the list x.
cdr(x)	The rest of the list x.
cons(x,y)	If y is a list then the value of cons(x,y) is a new list that has x as its first element and y as the rest of the list, e.g., cons(1,(2 3)) = (1 2 3). If y is an atom instead of a list, cons(x,y) has as value a "dotted pair," e.g., cons(1,2) = (1·2).
cond(x,y,z)	The conditional statement, if x = nil then y else z. Note that the syntax of this function is slightly different than the usual LISP syntax.
nil	The null (empty) list containing no elements.
equal(x,y)	Equality test, whose value is "nil" if x does not equal y.
atom(x)	Atom test, whose value is "nil" if x is not an atom.
null(x)	Null test, whose value is "nil" if x is not equal to nil.

Axioms

L1: x = car(cons(x,y))

L2: y = cdr(cons(x,y))

L3: $\sim$ATOM(x) $\supset$ x = cons(car(x),cdr(x))

L4: $\sim$ATOM(cons(x,y))

L5: ATOM(nil)

L6: x = nil $\supset$ cond(x,y,z) = z

L7: x $\neq$ nil $\supset$ cond(x,y,z) = y

L8: x = y $\equiv$ equal(x,y) $\neq$ nil

L9: ATOM(x) $\equiv$ atom(x) $\neq$ nil

L10: NULL(x) $\equiv$ null(x) $\neq$ nil

C. A Simplified Sort Problem

Before examining a more general sort problem, consider the following very simple special case.

Instead of a list-sorting program, consider a program that "sorts" a dotted pair of two distinct numbers; i.e., given an input pair the program returns as an output pair the same two numbers, but the first number of the output pair must be smaller than the second. To specify such a program, we must define the simple version of R, $R_0(x,y)$. Let us say that a dotted pair of numbers is "sorted" if the first number is less than the second. Thus $R_0(x,y)$ is true if and only if y equals x when x is sorted and y is the reverse of x when x is not sorted. Stated more precisely, we have

R1. $(\forall x,y)\{R_0(x,y) \equiv [[\text{car}(x) < \text{cdr}(x) \supset y = x] \wedge [\text{car}(x) \nless \text{cdr}(x) \supset \text{car}(y) = \text{cdr}(x) \wedge \text{cdr}(y) = \text{car}(x)]]\}$.

The correspondence of the LISP "lessp" function to the "less-than" relation is provided in the following axiom:

R2. $(\forall x,y)[\text{lessp}(x,y) \neq \text{nil} \equiv x < y]$.

Using the predicate R_0 we will give examples of four programming problems and their solutions:

(1) Checking:

Q: $R_0(\text{cons}(2,1),\text{cons}(1,2))$

A: yes

(2) Simulation:

Q: $(\exists x)R_0(\text{cons}(2,1),x)$

A: yes, x = cons(1,2)

(3) Verifying:

Q: $(\forall x)R_0(x,\text{cond}(\text{lessp}(\text{car}(x),\text{cdr}(x)),x,\text{cons}(\text{cdr}(x),\text{car}(x)))$

A: yes

Thus the program supplied by the user is correct.

(4) Program writing:

Q: $(\forall x)(\exists x)R_0(x,y)$

A: yes, y = cond(lessp(car(x),cdr(x)), x,cons(cdr(x),car(x)))

Translated into a more readable form, the program is:

<u>if</u> car(x) < cdr(x) <u>then</u> x <u>else</u>
cons(cdr(x),car(x)).

Given only the necessary axioms--L1, L2, L6, L7, R1, and R2--QA3 found a proof that constructed the sort program shown above. The paramodulation[14,15] rule of inference was used to handle equality.

We now turn to a more difficult problem.

D. The Sort Axioms

The definition of the predicate R is in terms of the predicates ON and SD. The meaning of these predicates is given below:

R(x,y) A predicate stating that if x is a list of numbers with no number occurring more than once in the list, then y is a list containing the same elements as x, and y is sorted, i.e., the numbers are arranged in order of increasing size.

ON(x,y) A predicate stating that x is an element on the list y.

SD(x) A predicate stating that the list x is sorted.

First we define R(x,y), that y is a sorted version of x, as follows:

S1. $(\forall x,y)\{R(x,y) \equiv [(\forall z)[\text{ON}(z,x) \equiv \text{ON}(z,y)] \wedge \text{SD}(y)]$

Thus a sorted version y of list x contains the same elements as x and is sorted.

Next we define, recursively, the predicate ON(x,y):

S2. $(\forall x,y)\{\text{ON}(x,y) \equiv [\sim\text{ATOM}(y) \wedge [x = \text{car}(y) \vee \text{ON}(x,\text{cdr}(y))]]\}$

This axiom states that x is on y if and only if x is the first element of y or if x is on the rest of y.

Next we define the meaning of a sorted list:

S3. $(\forall x)\{\text{SD}(x) \equiv [\text{NULL}(x) \vee [\sim\text{ATOM}(x) \wedge \text{NULL}(\text{cdr}(x))] \vee [\sim\text{ATOM}(x) \wedge \sim\text{NULL}(\text{cdr}(x)) \wedge \text{car}(x) \leq \text{car}(\text{cdr}(x)) \wedge \text{SD}(\text{cdr}(x))]]\}$.

This axiom states that x is sorted if and only if x is empty, or x contains only one element, or the first element of x is less than the second element and the rest of x is sorted.

To simplify the problem statement we assume that the arguments of the predicates and functions range only over the proper type of objects--i.e., either numbers or lists. In effect, we are assuming that the input list will indeed be a properly formed list of numbers. (The problem statement could be modified to specify correct types by using predicates such as NUMBERP(x)--true only if x is, say, a real number).

The problem is made simpler by using a "merge" function. This function, and a predicate P describing the merge function are named and described as follows:

sort(x) A LISP sort function (to be constructed) giving as its value a sorted version of x.

merge(x,u) A LISP merge function merging x into the sorted list u, such that the list returned contains the elements of u, and also contains x, and this list is sorted.

P(x,u,y) A predicate stating that y is the result of merging x into the sorted list u.

We define P(x,u,y), that y is u with x merged into it:

S4. $(\forall x,u,y)\{P(x,u,y) \equiv [SD(u) \supset [SD(y) \wedge (\forall z)(ON(z,y) \equiv (ON(z,u) \vee z = x))]]\}$.

Thus P(x,u,y) holds if and only if the fact that u is sorted implies that y contains x in addition to the elements of u, and y is sorted. One such merge function is merge(x,u) = cond(null(u),cons(x,u), cond(lessp(x,car(u)),cons(x,u),cons(car(u),merge(x, cdr(u))))).

The axiom required to describe the merge function is:

S5. $(\forall x,u)P(x,u,merge(x,u))$.

This completes a description of the predicates ON, SD, R, and P. Together, these specify the input-output relation for a sort function and a merge function. Before posing the problems to the theorem prover, we need to introduce axioms that describe the convergence of recursive functions.

E. Induction Axioms

In order to prove that a recursive function converges to the proper value, the theorem prover requires an induction axiom. An example of an induction principle is that if one keeps taking "cdr" of a finite list, one will reach the end of the list in a finite number of steps. This is analogous to an induction principle on the non-negative integers, i.e., let "P" be a predicate, and "h" a function. Then for finite lists,

$$[P(h(nil)) \wedge (\forall x)\ [\sim ATOM(x) \wedge P(h(cdr(x))) \supset P(h(x))]] \supset (\forall z)P(h(z))$$

is analogous to

$$[P(h(0)) \wedge (\forall n)[n \not< 0 \wedge P(h(n-1)) \supset P(h(n))]] \supset (\forall m)P(h(m))$$

for nonnegative integers.

There are other kinds of induction criteria besides the one given above. Unfortunately, for each recursive function that is to be shown to converge, the appropriate induction axiom must be carefully formulated by the user. The induction axiom also serves the purpose of introducing the name of the function to be written. We will now give the problem statement for the sort program, introducing appropriate induction information where necessary.

F. The Sort Problem

Examples illustrating the four kinds of problems are shown below.

(1) Checking:

Q: R(cons(2,cons(1,nil)),cons(1,cons(2,nil)))

A: yes

(2) Simulation:

Q: $(\exists x)$R(cons(2,cons(1,nil)),x)

A: yes, x = cons(1,cons(2,nil))

(3) Verifying: Now consider the verifying or debugging problem. Suppose we are given a proposed definition of a sort function and we want to know if it is correct. Suppose the proposed definition is

S6. $(\forall x)[sort(x) \equiv cond(null(x),nil,merge(car(x), sort(cdr(x))))]$.

Thus sort is defined in terms of car, cdr, cond, null, merge, and sort. Each of these functions except sort is already described by previously given axioms. We also need the appropriate induction axiom in terms of sort. Of course, the particular induction axiom needed depends on the definition of the particular sort function given. For this sort function the particular induction axiom needed is

S7. $[R(nil,sort(nil)) \wedge (\forall x)[\sim ATOM(x) \wedge R(cdr(x),sort(cdr(x))) \supset R(x,sort(x))]] \supset (\forall y)R(y,sort(y))$.

The following conjecture can then be posed to the theorem prover:

Q: $(\forall x)$R(x,sort(x))

A: yes

(4) Program writing: The next problem is that of synthesizing or writing a sort function. We assume, of course, that no definition such as S6 is provided. Certain information needed for this particular problem might be considered to be a part of this particular problem statement rather than a part of the data base. We shall phrase the question so that in addition to s primary purpose of asking for a solution, the question provides three more pieces of information: (a) The question assigns a name to the function that is to be constructed. A recursive function is defined in terms of itself, so to construct this definition the name of the function must be known (or else created internally). (b) The question specifies the number of arguments of the function that is to be considered.

(c) The question (rather than an induction axiom) gives the particular inductive hypothesis to be used in constructing the function.

In this form, the question and answer are

$$Q: (\forall x)(\exists y)\{R(nil,y) \wedge [[\sim ATOM(x) \wedge R(cdr(x),sort(cdr(x)))] \supset R(x,y)]\}$$

$$A: yes, y = cond(equal(x,nil),nil,merge(car(x),sort(cdr(x)))).$$

Thus the question names the function to be "sort" and specifies that it is a function of one argument. The question gives the inductive hypothesis--that the function sorts cdr(x)--and then asks for a function that sorts x. When the answer y is found, y is labeled to be the function sort(x).

Using this formulation QA3 was unable to write the sort program in a reasonable amount of time, although the author did find a correct proof within the resolution formalism*. The creation of the merge function can also be posed to the theorem prover by the same methods.

G. Discussion of Automatic Programming Problems

The axioms and conjectures given here illustrate the fundamental ideas of automatic programming. However, this work as well as earlier work by Simon,[16] Slagle,[17] Floyd,[18] Manna,[19] and others provides merely a small part of what needs to be done. Below we present discussion of issues that might profit from futher investigation.

Loops. One obvious extension of this method is to create programs that have loops rather than recursion. A simple technique exists for carrying out this operation. First, one writes just recursive functions. Many recursive functions can then be converted into iteration--i.e., faster-running loops that do not use a stack. McCarthy[20] gives criteria that determine how to convert recursion to iteration. An algorithm for determining cases in which recursion can be converted to iteration, and then performing the conversion process is embedded in modern LISP compilers. This algorithm could be applied to recursive functions written by the theorem-proving program.

Separation of Aspects of Problem Solving. Let us divide information into three types: (1) Information concerning the problem description and semantics. An example of such information is given in the axiom AT(a,s_0), or axiom S1 that defines a sorted list. (2) Information concerning the target programming language, such as the axiom [x = nil ⊃ cond(x,y,z) = z]. (3) Information concerning the interrelation of the problem and the target language, such as [LESS(x,y) ≡ lessp(x,y) ≠ nil].

* After this paper was written the problem was reformulated using a different set of axioms. In the new formulation QA3 created the sort program "sort(x) = cond(x,merge(car(x),sort(cdr(x))),nil).

These kinds of information are not, of course, mutually exclusive.

In the axiom systems presented, no distinction is made between such classes of information. Consequently, during the search for a proof the theorem prover might attempt to use axioms of type 1 for purposes where it needs information of type 2. Such attempts lead nowhere and generate useless clauses. However, as discussed in Sec. II-G, we can place in the proof strategy our knowledge of when such information is to be used, thus leading to more efficient proofs. One such method--calling for the conditional axioms at the right time, as discussed in Sec. II-G--has been implemented in QA3.

The PROW program of Waldinger and Lee[6] provides a very promising method of separating the problem of proof construction from the problem of program construction. In their system, the only axioms used are those that describe the subject--i.e., state the problem. Their proof that a solution exists does not directly construct the program. Instead, information about the target programming language, as well as information about the relationship of the target-programming language to the problem-statement language, is in another part of the PROW program--the "post-processor." The post-processor then uses this information to convert the completed proof into a program. The post-processor also converts recursion into loops and allows several target programming languages.

If our goal is to do automatic programming involving complex programs, we will probably wish to do some optimization or problem solving on the target language itself. For this reason we might want to have axioms that give the semantics of the target language, and also allow the intercommunication of information in the problem-statement language with information in the target language. Two possibilities for how to do this efficiently suggest themselves: (a) Use the methods presented here in which all information is in first-order logic. To gain efficiency, use special problem-solving strategies that minimize unnecessary interaction; (b) Use a higher-order logic system, in which the program construction is separated from the proof construction, possibly by being at another level. The program construction process might then be described in terms of the first-order existence proof.

Problem Formulation. The axiomatization given here has considerable room for improvement: Missing portions of LISP include the program features and the use of lambda to bind variables. The functions to be written must be named by the user, and the number of arguments must also be specified by the user.

Heuristics for Program-Writing Problems. Two heuristics have been considered so far. The first consists of examining the program as it is constructed (by looking inside the answer literal). Even though the syntax is guaranteed correct, the answer literal may contain various nonsense or undefined constructions (such as car(nil)). Any clause containing such constructed answers should be eliminated. Another heuristic is to actually run the partial program by a pseudo-LISP interpreter on a sample problem. The theorem prover knows the correct performance on these sample problems because they have either been solutions or else counterexamples to program-simulation questions that were stored in memory, or else they have been provided by the user. If the pseudo-LISP interpreter can produce a partial output that is incorrect, the partial program can be eliminated. If done properly, such a method might be valuable, but in our limited experience, its usefulness is not yet clear.

Higher-Level Programming Concepts. A necessary requirement for practical program writing is the development of higher-level concepts (such as the LISP "map" function) that describe the use of frequently employed constructs (functions) or partial constructs.

Induction. The various methods of proof by induction should be studied further and related to the kinds of problems in which they are useful. The automatic selection or generation of appropriate induction axioms would be most helpful.

Program Segmentation. Another interesting problem is that of automatically generating the specifications for the subfunctions to be called before writing these functions. For example, in our system, the sort problem was divided into two problems: First, specify and create a merge function, next specify a sort function and then construct this function in terms of the merge function. The segmentation into two problems and the specification of each problem was provided by the user.

VII. Discussion

The theorem prover may be considered an "interpreter" for a high-level assertional or declarative language--logic. As in the case with most high-level programming languages the user may be somewhat distant from the efficiency of "logic" programs unless he knows something about the strategies of the system.

The first applications of QA2 and QA3 were to "question answering." Typical question-answering applications are usually easy for a resolution-type theorem prover. Examples of such easy problem sets given QA3 include the questions done by Raphael's SIR,[21] Slagle's DEDUCOM,[17] and Cooper's chemistry question-answering program.[22] Usually there are a few obvious formulations for some subject area, and any reasonable formulation works well. As one goes to harder problems e the Tower of Hanoi puzzle, and program-writing problems, good and reasonably well-thought-out representations are necessary for efficient problem solving.

Some representations are better than others only because of the particular strategy used to search for a proof. It would be desirable if the theorem prover could adopt the best strategy for a given problem and representation, or even change the representation. I don't believe these goals are impossible, but at present it is not done. However, a library of strategy programs and a strategy language is slowly evolving in QA3. To change strategies in the present version the user must know about set-of-support and other program parameters such as level bound[1] and term-depth bound. To radically change the strategy, the user presently has to know the LISP language and must be able to modify certain strategy sections of the program. In practice, several individuals who have used the system have modified the search strategies to suit their needs. To add and debug a new heuristic or to modify a search strategy where reprogramming is required seems to take from a few minutes to several days, perhaps averaging one day. Ultimately it is intended that the system will be able to write simple strategy programs itself, and "understand" the semantics of its strategies.

Experience with the robot applications and the automatic programming applications emphasize the need for a very versatile logical system. A suitable higher-order logic system seems to be one of the best candidates. Several recent papers are relevant to this topic. A promising higher order system has been proposed by Robinson.[23] Banerji[24] discusses a higher order language. One crucial factor in an inference system is a suitable method for the treatment of the equality relation. Discussion of methods for the treatment of equality is provided by Wos and Robinson,[14] and Robinson and Wos,[15] and Kowalski.[25] McCarthy and Hayes[5] include a discussion of modal logics.

The theorem-proving program can be used as an experimental tool in the testing of problem formulations. In exploring difficult problems it can be useful to write a computer program to test a problem formulation and solution technique, since the machine tends to sharpen one's understanding of the problem. I believe that in some problem-solving applications the "high-level language" of logic along with a theorem-proving program can be a quick programming method for testing ideas. One reason is that a representation in the form of an axiom system can correspond quite closely to one's conceptualization of a problem. Another reason is that it is sometimes easier to reformulate an axiom system rather than to rewrite a problem-solving program, and this ease of reformulation facilitates exploration.

Resolution theorem-proving methods are shown in this paper to have the potential to serve as a general problem-solving system. A modified theorem-proving program can write simple robot problems, and solve simple puzzles. Much work remains to be done before such a system is capable of solving problems that are difficult by human standards.

Acknowledgment

I would like to acknowledge valuable discussions with Dr. Bertram Raphael and Mr. Robert Yates.

REFERENCES

1. J. A. Robinson, "The Present State of Mechanical Theorem Proving," a paper presented at the Fourth Systems Symposium, Cleveland, Ohio, November 19-20, 1968 (proceedings to be published).

2. C. Green and B. Raphael, "The Use of Theorem-Proving Techniques in Question-Answering Systems," Proc. 23rd Nat'l. Conf. ACM, (Thompson Book Company, Washington, D.C., 1968).

3. C. Green, "Theorem Proving by Resolution as a Basis for Question-Answering Systems," Machine Intelligence 4, D. Michie and B. Meltzer, Eds. (Edinburgh University Press, Edinburgh, Scotland, 1969).

4. N. J. Nilsson, "A Mobile Automaton: An Application of Artificial Intelligence Techniques," a paper presented at the International Joint Conference on Artificial Intelligence, Washington, D.C., May 7-9, 1969 (proceedings to be published).

5. J. McCarthy and P. Hayes, "Some Philosophical Problems from the Standpoint of Artificial Intelligence," Machine Intelligence 4, D. Michie and B. Meltzer, Eds. (Edinburgh University Press, Edinburgh, Scotland, 1969).

6. R. J. Waldinger and R. C. T. Lee, "PROW: A Step Toward Automatic Program Writing," a paper presented at the International Joint Conference on Artificial Intelligence, Washington, D.C., May 7-9, 1969 (proceedings to be published).

7. L. Wos, G. A. Robinson, and D. F. Carson, "Efficiency and Completeness of the Set of Support Strategy in Theorem Proving," J.ACM, Vol. 12, No. 4, pp. 536-541 (October 1965).

8. J. A. Robinson, "A Machine-Oriented Logic Based on the Resolution Principle," J.ACM, Vol. 12, No. 1, pp. 23-41 (January 1965).

9. George Ernst, "Sufficient Conditions for the Success of GPS," Report No. SRC-68-17, Systems Research Center, Case Western Reserve University, Celveland, Ohio (July 1968).

10. A. Hormann, "How a Computer System Can Learn," IEEE Spectrum (July 1964).

11. L. S. Coles, "Talking With a Robot in English," paper submitted at the International Joint Conference on Artificial Intelligence, Washington, D.C., May 7-9, 1969 (proceedings to be published).

12. John McCarthy, Paul W. Abrahams, Daniel J. Edwards, Timothy P. Hart, and Michael I. Levin, LISP 1.5 Programmer's Manual (The MIT Press, Cambridge, Mass., 1962).

13. C. Weissman, LISP 1.5 Primer (Dickenson Publishing Company, Inc., Belmont, Calif., 1967).

14. Lawrence Wos and George Robinson, "Paramodulation and Set of Support," summary of paper presented at the IRIA Symposium on Automatic Demonstration at Versailles, France, December 16-21, 1968 (proceedings to be published).

15. G. Robinson and L. Wos, "Paramodulation and Theorem-Proving in First-Order Theories with Equality," Machine Intelligence 4, B. Meltzer and D. Michie, Eds. (Edinburgh University Press, Edinburgh, Scotland, 1969).

16. H. Simon, "Experiments with a Heuristic Compiler," J.ACM, Vol. 10, pp. 493-506 (October 1963).

17. J. R. Slagle, "Experiments with a Deductive, Question-Answering Program," Comm. ACM, Vol. 8, pp. 792-798 (December 1965).

18. R. W. Floyd, "The Verifying Compiler," Computer Science Research Review, Carnegie Mellon University (December 1967).

19. Z. Manna, "The Correctness of Programs," J. Computer and Systems Sciences, Vol. 3 (1969).

20. J. McCarthy, "Towards a Mathematical Science of Computation," Proceedings ICIP (North Holland Publishing Company, Amsterdam, 1962).

21. B. Raphael, "A Computer Program Which 'Understands'," Proc. FJCC, pp. 577-589 (1964).

22. W. S. Cooper, "Fact Retrieval and Deductive Question Answering Information Retrieval Systems," J.ACM, Vol. 11, pp. 117-137 (April 1964).

23. J. A. Robinson, "Mechanizing Higher Order Logic," Machine Intelligence 4, D. Michie and B. Meltzer, Eds. (Edinburgh University Press, Edinburgh, Scotland, 1969).

24. R. B. Banerji, "A Language for Pattern Recognition," Pattern Recognition, Vol. 1, No. 1, pp. 63-74 (1968).

25. R. Kowalski, "The Case for Using Equality Axioms in Automatic Demonstration," paper presented at the IRIA Symposium on Automatic Demonstration at Versailles, France, December 16-21, 1968 (proceedings to be published).

APPENDIX

The axioms for the Monkey and Bananas problem are listed below, followed by the proof. The term SK24(S,P2,P1,B) that first appears in clause 16 of the proof is a Skolem function generated by the elimination of (∀x) in the conversion of axiom MB4 to quantifier-free clause form. (One may think of it as the object that is not at place P2 in state S.)

```
LIST MONKEY
MB1  (MOVABLE BOX)
MB2  (FA(X)(NOT(AT X UNDER-BANANAS SØ)))
MB3  (AT BOX PLACEB SØ)
MB4  (FA(B P1 P2 S)(IF(AND(AT B P1 S)(MOVABLE B)(FA(X)(NOT(AT X P2 S))))(AND(AT MONKEY P2
     (MOVE(MONKEY B P2 S))(AT B P2(MOVE MONKEY B P2 S)))))
MB5  (FA(S)(CLIMBABLE MONKEY BOX S))
MB6  (FA(M P B S)(IF(AND(AT B P S)(CLIMBABLE M B S))(AND(AT B P(CLIMB M B S))(ON M B
     (CLIMB M B S)))))
MB7  (FA(S)(IF(AND(AT BOX UNDER-BANANAS S)(ON MONKEY BOX S))(REACHABLE MONKEY BANANAS S)))
MB8  (FA(M B S)(IF(REACHABLE M B S)(HAS M B(REACH M B S))))
DONE

Q    (EX(S)(HAS MONKEY BANANAS S))
A    YES, S = REACH(MONKEY,BANANAS,CLIMB(MONKEY,BOX,MOVE(MONKEY,BOX,UNDER-BANANAS,SØ)))

PROOF
 1   -AT(X,UNDER-BANANAS,SØ)                                                      AXIOM
 2   AT(BOX,PLACEB,SØ)                                                            AXIOM
 3   CLIMBABLE(MONKEY,BOX,S)                                                      AXIOM
 4   -HAS(MONKEY,BANANAS,S)                                                       NEG OF THM
         ANSWER(S)
 5   HAS(M,B,REACH(M,B,S))  -REACHABLE(M,B,S)                                     AXIOM
 6   -REACHABLE(MONKEY,BANANAS,S)                                                 FROM 4,5
         ANSWER(REACH(MONKEY,BANANAS,S))
 7   REACHABLE(MONKEY,BANANAS,S)  -AT(BOX,UNDER-BANANAS,S)  -ON(MONKEY,BOX,S)     AXIOM
 8   -AT(BOX,UNDER-BANANAS,S)  -ON(MONKEY,BOX,S)                                  FROM 6,7
         ANSWER(REACH(MONKEY,BANANAS,S))
 9   ON(M,B,CLIMB(M,B,S))  -AT(B,P,S)  -CLIMBABLE(M,B,S)                          AXIOM
10   -AT(BOX,UNDER-BANANAS,CLIMB(MONKEY,BOX,S))  -AT(BOX,P,S)  -CLIMBABLE(MONKEY,BOX,S)   FROM 8,9
         ANSWER(REACH(MONKEY,BANANAS,CLIMB(MONKEY,BOX,S)))
11   -AT(BOX,UNDER-BANANAS,CLIMB(MONKEY,BOX,S))  -AT(BOX,P,S)                     FROM 3,10
         ANSWER(REACH(MONKEY,BANANAS,CLIMB(MONKEY,BOX,S)))
12   AT(B,P,CLIMB(M,B,S))  -AT(B,P,S)  -CLIMBABLE(M,B,S)                          AXIOM
13   -AT(BOX,XX1,S)  -AT(BOX,UNDER-BANANAS,S)  -CLIMBABLE(MONKEY,BOX,S)           FROM 11,12
         ANSWER(REACH(MONKEY,BANANAS,CLIMB(MONKEY,BOX,S)))
14   -AT(BOX,XX1,S)  -AT(BOX,UNDER-BANANAS,S)                                     FROM 3,13
         ANSWER(REACH(MONKEY,BANANAS,CLIMB(MONKEY,BOX,S)))
15   -AT(BOX,UNDER-BANANAS,X)                                                     FACTOR 14
         ANSWER(REACH(MONKEY,BANANAS,CLIMB(MONKEY,BOX,S)))
16   AT(B,P2,MOVE(MONKEY,B,P2,S))  -MOVABLE(B)  -AT(B,P1,S)  AT(SK24(S,P2,P1,B),P2,S)    AXIOM
```

```
17   -MOVABLE(BOX)   -AT(BOX,P1,S)   AT(SK24(S,UNDER-BANANAS,P1,BOX),UNDER-BANANAS,S)       FROM 15,16
         ANSWER(REACH(MONKEY,BANANAS,CLIMB(MONKEY,BOX,MOVE(MONKEY,BOX,UNDER-BANANAS,S))))
18   -MOVABLE(BOX)   AT(SK24(SØ,UNDER-BANANAS,PLACEB,BOX),UNDER-BANANAS,SØ)                 FROM 2,17
         ANSWER(REACH(MONKEY,BANANAS,CLIMB(MONKEY,BOX,MOVE(MONKEY,BOX,UNDER-BANANAS,SØ))))
19   -MOVABLE(BOX)                                                                          FROM 1,18
         ANSWER(REACH(MONKEY,BANANAS,CLIMB(MONKEY,BOX,MOVE(MONKEY,BOX,UNDER-BANANAS,SØ))))
20   MOVABLE(BOX)                                                                           AXIOM
21   CONTRADICTION                                                                          FROM 19,20
         ANSWER(REACH(MONKEY,BANANAS,CLIMB(MONKEY,BOX,MOVE(MONKEY,BOX,UNDER-BANANAS,SØ))))
11 CLAUSES LEFT
28 CLAUSES GENERATED
22 CLAUSES ENTERED
```

PATRICK J. HAYES*

The Frame Problem and Related Problems in Artificial Intelligence

Summary

The frame problem arises in attempts to formalise problem–solving processes involving interactions with a complex world. It concerns the difficulty of keeping track of the consequences of the performance of an action in, or more generally of the making of some alteration to, a representation of the world. The paper contains a survey of the problem, showing how it arises in several contexts and relating it to some traditional problems in philosophical logic. In the second part of the paper several suggested partial solutions to the problem are outlined and compared. This comparison necessitates an analysis of what is meant by a representation of a robot's environment. Different notions of representation give rise to different proposed solutions. It is argued that a theory of causal relationships is a necessity for any general solution. The significance of this, and the problem in general, for natural (human and animal) problem solving is discussed, and several desiderata for efficient representational schemes are outlined.

Introduction

We consider some problems which arise in attempting a logical analysis of the structure of a robot's beliefs.

A *robot* is an intelligent system equipped with sensory capabilities, operating in an environment similar to the everyday world inhabited by human robots.

* University of Edinburgh

By *belief* is meant any piece of information which is explicitly stored in the robot's memory. New beliefs are formed by (at least) two distinct processes: *thinking* and *observation*. The former involves operations which are purely internal to the belief system: the latter involves interacting with the *world*, that is, the external environment and, possibly, other aspects of the robot's own structure.

Beliefs will be represented by statements in a formal logical calculus, called the *belief calculus* L_b. The process of inferring new assertions from earlier ones by the *rules of inference* of the calculus will represent thinking (McCarthy, 1959, 1963; McCarthy and Hayes, 1969; Green, 1969; Hayes, 1971).

There are convincing reasons why L_b must *include* L_c – classical first-order logic. It has often been assumed that a moderately adequate belief logic can be obtained merely by adding *axioms* to L_c (a first-order theory); however I believe that it will certainly be necessary to add extra rules of inference to L_c, and extra syntactic richness to handle these extra rules.

One can show that, under very general conditions, logical calculi obey the *extension property*: If $S \vdash p$ and $S \subseteq S'$ then $S' \vdash p$. The importance of this is that if a belief p is added to a set S, then all thinking which was legal before, remains legal, so that the robot need not check it all out again.

Time and Change

For him to think about the real world, the robot's beliefs must handle *time*. This has two distinct but related aspects.

(a) There must be beliefs *about* time. For example, beliefs about causality.

(b) The robot lives *in* time: the world changes about him. His beliefs must accommodate in a rational way to this change.

Of these, the first has been very extensively investigated both in A.I. and philosophical logic, while the second has been largely ignored until very recently: it is more difficult. The first is solely concerned with thinking: the second involves observation.

The standard device for dealing with (a) is the introduction of *situation variables* (McCarthy, 1963; McCarthy and Hayes, 1969) or *possible worlds* (Hintikka, 1967; Kripke, 1963). Symbols prone to change their denotations with the passage of time are enriched with an extra argument place which is filled with a term (often a variable) denoting a *situation* which one can think of intuitively as a time instant; although other readings are possible. In order to make statements about the relationships between situations, and the effects of actions, we also introduce terms denoting *events*, and the function R (read: *result*) which takes events and situations into new situations. Intuitively, "$R(e,s)$" denotes the situation which results when the event e happens in the situation s. By "event" we mean a change in the world: "his switching on the light", "the explosion", "the death of Caesar". This is a minor technical simplification of the notation and terminology used in McCarthy and Hayes (1969) and Hayes (1971). Notice that all the machinery is defined within L_c. The situation calculus is a first-order theory.

Using situations, fairly useful axiomatisations can be obtained for a number of simple problems involving sequences of actions and events in fairly complicated worlds (Green, 1969; McCarthy and Hayes, 1969).

The Frame Problem

Given a certain description of a situation s – that is, a collection of statements of the form $\phi\,[\![s]\!]$, where the fancy brackets mean that *every* situation in ϕ is an occurrence of 's' – we want to be able to infer as much as possible about $R(e,s)$. Of course, what we can infer will depend upon the properties of e. Thus we require assertions of the form:

$$\phi_1[\![s]\!]\ \&\ \psi(e) \supset \phi_2[\![R(e,s)]\!] \qquad (1)$$

Such an assertion will be called a *law of motion*. The frame problem can be briefly stated as the problem of finding adequate collections of laws of motion.

Notice how easily human thinking seems to be able to handle such inferences. Suppose I am describing to a child how to build towers of bricks. I say "You can put the brick on top of this one onto some other one, if that one has not got anything else on it." The child *knows* that the other blocks will stay put during the move. But if I write the corresponding law of motion:

$$(\text{on}\,(b_1,b_2,s)\ \&\ \forall z.\ \neg\text{on}\,(z,b_3,s)) \supset \text{on}(b_1,b_3,R(\text{move}(b_2,b_3),s)) \qquad (2)$$

then nothing follows concerning the other blocks. What assertions could we write down which would capture the knowledge that the child has about the world?

One does not want to be obliged to give a law of motion for *every* aspect of the new situation. For instance, one feels that it is prolix to have a law of motion to the effect that if a block is not *moved*, then it stays where it is. And yet such laws – instances of (1) in which $\phi_1 = \phi_2$ – are necessary in first-order axiomatisations. They are called *frame axioms*. Their only function is to allow the robot to infer that an event does *not* affect an assertion. Such inferences are necessary: but one feels that they should follow from more general considerations than a case-by-case listing of axioms, especially as the number of frame axioms increases rapidly with the complexity of the problem. Raphael (1971) describes the difficulty thoroughly.

This phenomenon is to be expected. Logically, s and $R(e,s)$ are simply different entities. There is no *a priori* justification for inferring any properties of $R(e,s)$ from those of s. If it were usually the case that events made widespread and drastic alterations to the world (explosions, the Second Coming, etc.), then we could hardly expect anything better than the use of frame axioms to describe in detail, for each event, exactly what changes it brings about. Our expectation of a more general solution is based on the fact that the world is, fortunately for robots, fairly stable. Most events – especially those which are likely to be considered in planning – make only small local changes in the world, and are not expected to touch off long chains of cause and effect.

Frame Rules

We introduce some formalism in order to unify the subsequent discussions. Any general solution to the frame problem will be a method for allowing us to transfer properties from a situation s to its successor $R(e,s)$; and we expect such a licence to be sensitive to the form of the assertion, to what is known about the event e, and possibly to other facts.

Consider the rule scheme FR:

$$\chi, \phi[\![s]\!], \psi(e) \vdash \phi[\![R(e,s)]\!] \quad \textit{provided } \aleph(e,\phi,\psi) . \qquad \text{(FR)}$$

where $\aleph$ is some condition on e, ϕ and ψ, expressed of course in the metalanguage. We will call such a rule a *frame rule*. The hope is that frame rules can be used to give a general mechanism for replacing the frame axioms, and also admit an efficient implementation, avoiding the search and relevancy problems which plague systems using axioms (Green, 1969; Raphael, 1971).

One must, when considering a frame rule, be cautious that it does not allow contradictions to be generated. Any addition of an inference rule to L_c, especially if not accompanied by extra syntax, brings the risk of inconsistency, and will, in any case, have dramatic effects on the metatheory of the calculus. For instance, the deduction theorem fails. Thus a careful investigation of each case is needed. In some cases, a frame rule has a sufficiently simple $\aleph$ condition that it may be replaced by an *axiom scheme*, resulting in a more powerful logic in which the deduction theorem holds. This usually makes the metatheory easier and implementation more difficult.

Some Partial Solutions Using Frame Rules

The literature contains at least four suggestions for handling the problem which are describable by frame rules. In each case we need some extra syntactic machinery.

Frames

Following McCarthy and Hayes (1969), one assumes a finite number of monadic second-order predicates P_i. If $\vdash P_i(h)$ for a non-logical symbol h (predicate, function or individual constant) then we say that h is in the ith *block* of the frame. The frame rule is

$$P_{i_1}(h_1), \ldots, P_{i_n}(h_n), \phi[\![s]\!], P_j(e) \vdash \phi[\![R(e,s)]\!] \qquad (3)$$

where $h_1,\ldots,h_n$ are all the non logical symbols which occur *crucially* in ϕ, and $i_k \neq j$, $1 \leqslant k \leqslant n$. Here *crucial* is some syntactic relation between h and ϕ; different relations give different logics, with a stronger or weaker frame rule.

Causal connection

We assume (Hayes 1971) that there is a 3-place predicate $\rightarrow(x,y,s)$ (read: x is connected to y in situation s) which has the intuitive meaning that if x is not connected to y, then any change to y does not affect x. It seems reasonable that $\rightarrow$ should be a partial ordering on its first two arguments (reflexive and transitive). The frame rule is:

$$\phi[\![s]\!], \neg\rightarrow(h_1,e,s), \ldots, \neg\rightarrow(h_n,e,s) \vdash \phi[\![R(e,s)]\!] \qquad (4)$$

where (i) ϕ is an atom or the negation of an atom; (ii) $h_1,\ldots,h_n$ are all the terms which occur *crucially* in ϕ.

If we insisted only that $\neg\rightarrow(h_i,e,s)$ is not provable (rather than $\neg\rightarrow(h_i,e,s)$ *is* provable) then the rule is much stronger but no longer obeys the extension property. This is analogous to PLANNER's method below.

MICRO-PLANNER

The problem solving language MICRO-PLANNER (Sussman and Winograd, 1969) uses a subset of predicate calculus enriched with notations which control the system's search for proofs. We will ignore the latter aspect for the present and describe the underlying formalism. Its chief peculiarity is that it has no negation, and is therefore not troubled by the need for consistency.

Following MICRO-PLANNER we introduce the new unary propositional connective *therase*. Intuitively, *therase* ϕ will mean that ϕ is "erased". We also introduce the notion of a *transition*: an expression $\langle e: \phi_1,\ldots,\phi_n \rangle$. This means intuitively "erase $\phi_1,\ldots,\phi_n$ in passing from s to $R(e,s)$". The frame rule is:

$$\chi, \phi[\![s]\!], \langle e: \phi_1,\ldots,\phi_n \rangle \vdash \phi[\![R(e,s)]\!] \qquad (5)$$

where (i) ϕ is an atom; (ii) ϕ contains no variables (other than s); (iii) χ, *therase* $\phi_1,\ldots,$ *therase* $\phi_n \nvdash$ *therase* $\phi[\![s]\!]$. Notice the negated inference in (iii).

STRIPS

The problem-solving system STRIPS (Fikes and Nilsson, 1971) uses the full predicate calculus enriched with special notations ("operator descriptions") describing events, and ways of declaring certain predicates to be *primitive*. We can use transitions to describe this also. The frame rule is:

$$\phi[\![s]\!], \langle e\colon \phi_1, \ldots, \phi_n \rangle \vdash \phi[\![R(e,s)]\!] \qquad (6)$$

where (i) ϕ is an atom or the negation of an atom; (ii) ϕ contains no variables (other than s); (iii) the predicate symbol in ϕ is *primitive*; (iv) $\phi[\![s]\!]$ is not an instance of any ϕ_i, $1 \leqslant i \leqslant n$. Notice the similarity to (5). *Primitive* can be axiomatised by the use of a monadic second-order predicate, as in (1) above.

These four rules have widely divergent logical properties. Rule (3) is replaceable by an axiom scheme, and is thus rather elementary. It is also very easy to implement efficiently (theorem-proving cognoscenti may be worried by the higher-order expressions, but these are harmless since they contain no variables). Variations are possible, e.g., we might have disjointness axioms for the P_i and require $\neg P_j(h_k)$ rather than $P_{ik}(h_k)$: this would be closely similar to a special case of (4).

Retaining consistency in the presence of (3) requires in non-trivial problems that the P_i classification be rather coarse. (For instance, *no* change in position *ever* affects the colour of things, so predicates of location *could* be classed apart from predicates of colour.) Thus frames, although useful, do not completely solve the problem.

Rule (4) is also replaceable by an axiom scheme, and the restriction to literals can be eliminated, with some resultant complication in the rule. Also, there is a corresponding model theory and a completeness result (Hayes, 1971), so that one can gain an intuition as to what (4) *means*. Retaining consistency with (4) requires some care in making logical definitions.

Rules (5) and (6) have a different character. Notice that (6) is almost a special case of (5): that in which *therase* $\phi \vdash$ *therase* ψ if ψ is not primitive or ψ is an instance of ϕ. The importance of this is that instantiation, and probably primitiveness also, are *decideable*, and conditions (iii) and (iv) in (6) are effectively determined solely by examining the transition, whereas condition (iii) in (5) is in general not decidable and in any case requires an examination of all of χ: in applications, the whole set of beliefs. MICRO-PLANNER uses its ability to control the theorem-proving process to partly compensate for both of these problems, but with a more expressive language they would become harder to handle. Notice also that (5) does not satisfy the extension property, while (6) does, provided we allow at most one transition to be unconditionally asserted for each event.

Maintaining "consistency" with (5) is a matter of the axiom-writer's art. There seem to be no general guidelines. Maintaining consistency with (6) seems to be largely a matter of judicious choice of *primitive* vocabulary. There is no articulated model theory underlying (5) or (6). They are regarded more as syntactic tools – analogous to evaluation rules for a high-level programming language – than as descriptive assertions.

A (Very) Simple Example: Toy Bricks

$$\neg above(x, x, s) \qquad \text{(A1)}$$
$$x = Table \vee above(x, Table, s) \qquad \text{(A2)}$$
$$above(x, y, s) \equiv .\ on(x, y, s) \vee \exists z.on(z, y, s)\ \&\ above(x, z, s) \qquad \text{(A3)}$$
$$free(x, s) \equiv .\forall y \neg on(y, x, s) \qquad \text{(A4)}$$

To enable activity to occur we will have events $move(x,y)$: the brick x is put on top of the brick y. Laws of motion we might consider include:

$$free(x, s)\ \&\ x \neq y.\ \supset on(x, y, R(move(x, y), s)) \qquad \text{(A5)}$$
$$free(x, s)\ \&\ w \neq x\ \&\ on(w, z, s).\ \supset on(w, z, R(move(x, y), s)) \qquad \text{(A6)}$$
$$free(x, s)\ \&\ w \neq x\ \&\ above(w, z, s).\ \supset above(w, z, R(move(x, y), s)) \qquad \text{(A7)}$$
$$free(x, s)\ \&\ w \neq y\ \&\ free(w, s).\ \supset free(w, R(move(x, y), s)) \qquad \text{(A8)}$$

Of these, (A6–A8) are frame axioms. (In fact, (A7) and (A8) are redundant, since they can, with some difficulty, be derived from (A6) and (A3), (A4) respectively.) (A5) assumes somewhat idealistically that there is always enough space on y to put a new brick.

Rule (3) cannot be used in any intuitively satisfactory way to replace A6–A8.

Rule (4) can be used. We need only to specify when bricks are connected to events:

$$\rightarrow (x, move(y, z), s) \equiv .\ x = y \vee above(x, y, s) \qquad (A9)$$

Using (A9) and (A3), (A4), it is not hard to show that

$$free(x, s) \,\&\, w \neq x \,\&\, on(w, z, s). \supset . \neg\rightarrow (w, move(x, y), s) \,\&$$
$$\neg\rightarrow (z, move(x, y), s)$$

and thus, we can infer *on* $\{w, z, R[move(x, y), s]\}$ by rule (7). (A7) and (A8) are similar but simpler. (One should remark also that (A4) is an example of an illegal definition, in the presence of (4), since it suppresses a variable which the rule needs to be aware of. It is easy to fix this up in various ways.)

Rule (5) can also be used, but we must ensure that *therase* does a sufficiently thorough job. Various approaches are possible. The following seems to be most in the spirit of MICRO-PLANNER. In its terms, *on* and *above* statements will be in the data-base, but *free* statements will not. The necessary axioms will be:

$$therase\ free(x, s) \qquad (A10)$$
$$therase\ on(x, y, s) \,\&\, above(y, z, s) \supset therase\ above\ (x, z, s) \qquad (A11)$$
$$free(x, s) \supset \langle move(x, y){:}\ on(x, z, s)\rangle \qquad (A12)$$

To infer statements $free[x, R(e,s)]$, we must first generate enough $on[x, y, R(e,s)]$ statements by rule (5), and then use (A4), since by (A10), rule (5) never makes such an inference directly. (We could omit (A10) and replace (A12) by

$$free(x, s) \supset \langle move(x, y){:}\ on(x, z, s), free(y, s)\rangle\,. \qquad (A13)$$

This would, in MICRO-PLANNER terms, be a decision to keep *free* assertions in the data base.)

Notice that MICRO-PLANNER has no negation and hence no need to *therase* such assertions as $\neg\, on(x,y,s)$. If it had negation we would replace (A12) by

$$free(x, s) \supset \langle move(x, y){:}\ on(x, z, s), \neg on(x, y, s)\rangle \qquad (A14)$$

and add

$$therase\ \neg on(x, y, s) \,\&\, above(y, z, s) \supset therase\ \neg above(x, z, s) \qquad (A15)$$

Notice the close relations between (A3), (A11) and (A15).

Rule (6) can be used similarly to (5), but we are no longer able to use axioms such as (A11) and (A15). The solution which seems closest in spirit to STRIPS is to declare that *on* is primitive but that *above* and *free* are not, and then simply use (A14). The "world model" (Fikes and Nilsson, 1971) would then consist of a collection of atoms *on* (a,b), or their negations, and the system would rederive *above* and *free* assertions when needed. This is very similar to MICRO-PLANNER's "data-base", and we could have used rule (5) in an exactly similar fashion.

Implementing Frame Rules

Some ingenuity with list structures enables one to store assertions in such a way that

(i) Given *s*, one can easily find all assertions $\phi[\![s]\!]$.

(ii) Each symbol denoting a situation is stored only once.

(iii) The relationships between *s* and $R(e,s)$, etc., are stored efficiently and are easily retrieved.

(iv) To apply a frame rule to *s*, one need only:

(a) Create a new cell pointing to *s*.

(b) Move two pointers.

(c) Check each $\phi[\![s]\!]$ for condition $\aleph$: if it holds, move one pointer.

In the case of a rule like (5) or the variation to (4), where $\aleph$ is a *negative* condition ($\not\vdash$), we need only examine those $\phi[\![s]\!]$ for which the condition *fails*, resulting in greater savings.

Space does not permit a description of the method, but MICRO-PLANNER and STRIPS use related ideas. (The authors of these systems seem to confuse to some extent their particular implementations with the logical description of the frame rules, even to the extent of claiming that a logical description is impossible.)

Consistency and Counterfactuals

Frame rules can be efficiently implemented and, in their various ways, allow the replacement of frame axioms by more systematic machinery. But there is a constant danger, in constructing larger axiomatisations, of introducing inconsistency. An alternative approach avoids this by transferring properties ϕ from s to $R(e,s)$ *as long as it is consistent to do so*, rather than according to some fixed-in-advance rule.

Suppose we have a set χ of general laws which are to hold in every situation, and a description of – a set of assertions about – the situation s: $\{\phi_1[\![s]\!],...,\phi_n[\![s]\!]\}$. Using laws of motion we will directly infer certain properties $\psi_1,..., \psi_m$ of $R(e,s)$: the set of these constitutes a partial description of $R(e,s)$. To compute a more adequate one, we add assertions $\phi_i[\![R(e,s)]\!]$ in some order, *checking at each stage for consistency with* χ; if a $\phi_i[\![R(e,s)]\!]$ makes the set inconsistent, it is rejected. This continues until no more ϕ_i can be added. In this way we compute a maximal consistent subset (MCS) of the inconsistent set

$$\chi \cup \{\psi_1, ..., \psi_m, \phi_1[\![R(e,s)]\!], ..., \phi_n[\![R(e,s)]\!]\} .$$

There are two big problems: (1) Consistency is not a decidable or even semi–decidable property. Thus for practicality one has to accept a large restriction on the expressive power of the language. (2) There are in general many different MCSs of an inconsistent set, and so we must have ways of choosing an appropriate one. In terms of the procedure outlined above, we need a good ordering on the ϕ_i.

This procedure is closely similar to one described by Rescher (1964) to provide an analysis of counterfactual reasonings ("If I had struck this match yesterday, it would have lit", when in fact I didn't.). Rescher is aware of the first problem but gives no solution. His major contribution is to the second problem, which he solves by the use of *modal categories*: a hierarchical classification of assertions into grades of law-likeness. One never adds $\phi_i[\![R(e,s)]\!]$ unless every ϕ_j with a lower classification has already been tested. This machinery is especially interesting as in (Simon and Rescher, 1966) it is linked to Simon's theory of causality (Simon, 1953). One puts ϕ_i in a lower category than ϕ_j just in case ϕ_i *causes* ϕ_j (or $\neg\phi_j$), more or less. Space does not permit a complete description of this interesting material which is fully covered in the references cited. In spite of its appeal, the first problem is still unsolved.

In unpublished work at Stanford, Jack Buchanan has independently worked out another version of the procedure. The first problem is handled by accepting a drastic restriction on the language. Every ϕ_i is an atom or the negation of an atom – c.f. frame rules (7), (8) and (9) – and, more seriously, χ contains only assertions of the form $t_1 \neq t_2$ or of the form $P(t_1,...,t,...,t_n)$ and $P(t_1,...,u,...,t_n) \supset t = u$. Under these constraints, consistency is decidable and can even be computed quite efficiently. Moreover, MCSs are unique, so the second problem evaporates. However, it is not clear whether non-trivial problems can be reasonably stated in such a restricted vocabulary.

Conclusions

In the long run, I believe that a mixture of frame rules and consistency-based methods will be required for non-trivial problems, corresponding respectively to the "strategic" and "tactical" aspects of computing descriptions of new situations. In the short term we need to know more about the properties of both procedures.

One outstanding defect of present approaches is the lack of a clear model theory. Formal systems for handling the frame problem are beginning to proliferate, but a clear *semantic* theory is far from sight. Even to begin such a project would seem to require deep insight into our presystematic intuitions about the physical world.

Observations and the Qualification Problem

We have so far been entirely concerned with thinking. The situation calculus is a belief calculus for beliefs *about* time. Observations – interactions with the real world – introduce new problems. We must now consider the second aspect of time (b,p.).

Almost any general belief about the result of his own actions may be contradicted by the robot's observations. He may conclude that he can drive to the airport; only to find a flat tire. A human immediately says, "Ah, now I cannot go". Simply *adding* a new belief ("the tire is flat") renders an earlier conclusion false, though it was a valid conclusion from the earlier set of beliefs, *all of which are still present*. Thus we do *not* assume that the robot had concluded "*If* my tires are OK, *then* I can get to the airport" since there are no end of different things which might go wrong, and he cannot be expected to hedge his conclusions round with thousands of qualifications (McCarthy and Hayes, 1969).

Clearly this implies that the belief logic does not obey the extension property *for observations*: to expect otherwise would be to hope for omnipotence. However, we are little nearer any positive ideas for handling the inferences correctly.

John McCarthy recently pointed out to me that MICRO-PLANNER has a facility (called THNOT) which apparently solves the problem nicely. I will translate this into a slightly different notation.

We introduce a new unary propositional connective *proved*, which is supposed to mean "can be proved from the current collection of beliefs". Then we can write axioms like the following:

$$\mathit{flat}\ (\mathit{tire}) \supset \mathit{kaput}\ (\mathit{car})$$

$$\neg \mathit{proved}\ \mathit{kaput}\ (\mathit{car}) \supset \mathit{at}\{\mathit{robot}, \mathit{airport}, R[\mathit{drive}(\mathit{airport}), s]\} \quad \text{(A17)}$$

from which *at(robot, airport, ...)* should be concluded *until* we add:

$$\mathit{flat}\ (\mathit{tire}) \quad \text{(A18)}$$

at which point the $\neg$*proved...* becomes false. ($\neg$*proved* is PLANNER's THNOT).

To make this work we could try the following rules of inference.

$$\phi \vdash \mathit{proved}\ \phi \quad \text{(P1)}$$

$$\chi \vdash \neg \mathit{proved}\ \phi \quad \text{(P2)}$$

where $\chi \nvdash \phi$.

(P2) fails the extension property, as expected. (It also has the difficulties of effectiveness which worry frame rule (5), but we will ignore these.)

Unfortunately, (P1) and (P2) are *inconsistent*. Suppose $\chi \nvdash \phi$, but that ϕ is consistent with χ. Then by (P2), $\neg$ *proved* ϕ. But if we now add ϕ (an observation: the flat tire), then by (P1) *proved* ϕ: an overt contradiction. MICRO-PLANNER avoids this by denying (P1) and treating "ϕ and $\neg$ *proved* ϕ" as consistent. But this is a counsel of despair, since it clearly is not, according to the intuitive meanings.

The logical answer is to somehow make *proved* refer to the set χ of antecedents. The direct approach to this requires extremely cumbersome notation and a very strong logic which partly contains its own metatheory, thus coming close to Gödel inconsistency. Fortunately we do not need to *describe* sets χ of assertions, but only to *refer* to them, and this can be done with a very weak notation, similar to situation variables.

Assume that every belief is decorated with a constant symbol called the *index*: we will write it as a superscript. Indices denote the robot's internal belief states just as situation terms denote external situations. Observations are analogous to events. Assertions *proved* ϕ now have an extra index which identifies the state of belief at the time the inference was tested. The above rules of inference become:

$$\phi^s \vdash \mathit{proved}^s\ \phi^s \quad \text{(P1')}$$

$$\chi \vdash \neg \mathit{proved}^s\ \phi^s \quad \text{(P2')}$$

where $\chi \nvdash \phi^s$ and every member of χ has index *s*.

In applications we now insist that:

(i) in applying P2′, χ contains *all* beliefs with index *s*;

(ii) whenever an *observation* is added to the beliefs, every index *s* is replaced by a new one *s*′, *except* those on *proved* assertions.

This is just enough to avoid inconsistency; it clearly does not involve any Gödel-ish difficulties; and (ii) can be very efficiently implemented by frame-rule methods (see section Implementing Frame Rules). Indeed, more complex versions of (ii) which allow for direct contradiction between beliefs and observations can be similarly implemented.

The logic of these indices is trivial, but extensions have some interest. For instance, if we identify indices with situation terms, then expressions of the form $\phi[\![s]\!]^s$ become legal, with the intuitive meaning "ϕ is true *now*".

Seen this way, the qualification problem is closely linked with the frame problem, and one expects progress in either area to help with the other.

Acknowledgements

This work was supported in part by the Advanced Research Projects Agency of the Office of the Secretary of Defense (SD–183), and in part by the Science Research Council.

I am also grateful for comment, criticism and contributions from Jack Buchanan, Richard Fikes, Malcolm Newey, Nils Nilsson, John

Rulifson, Richard Waldinger, Richard Weyrauch and from John McCarthy, to whom I am also grateful for the invitation to visit the Stanford Artificial Intelligence Project, where this paper was written. Most of all, I thank my wife, Jackie, for improving my English; controlling my verbosity, and typing innumerable drafts of the manuscript.

Learning and Executing Generalized Robot Plans[1]

Richard E. Fikes, Peter E. Hart and Nils J. Nilsson

Stanford Research Institute, Menlo Park, California 94025

ABSTRACT

In this paper we describe some major new additions to the STRIPS robot problem-solving system. The first addition is a process for generalizing a plan produced by STRIPS so that problem-specific constants appearing in the plan are replaced by problem-independent parameters.

The generalized plan, stored in a convenient format called a triangle table, *has two important functions. The more obvious function is as a single macro action that can be used by STRIPS—either in whole or in part—during the solution of a subsequent problem. Perhaps less obviously, the generalized plan also plays a central part in the process that monitors the real-world execution of a plan, and allows the robot to react "intelligently" to unexpected consequences of actions.*

We conclude with a discussion of experiments with the system on several example problems.

1. Introduction

In this paper we describe a system of computer programs for controlling a mobile robot. This system can conceive and execute plans enabling the robot to accomplish certain tasks such as pushing boxes from one room to another in a simple but real environment. Although these sorts of tasks are commonly thought to demand little skill or intelligence, they pose important conceptual problems and can require quite complex planning and execution strategies.

In previous papers, we described two important components of our robot system, namely, STRIPS [1] and PLANEX [2]. When a task statement is given to the robot, STRIPS produces a plan consisting of a sequence of preprogrammed actions, and PLANEX supervises the execution of this sequence to accomplish the task. In this paper we present a major new addition to the original capabilities of STRIPS and PLANEX that enables the system to generalize and then save a solution to a particular problem. This generalization capability is used in two ways. The more obvious use of a generalized plan is as a "macro action" that can be used as a single component of a new plan to solve a new problem. When used in this fashion, generalization becomes a powerful form of learning that can reduce the planning time for similar tasks as well as allow the formation of much longer plans, previously beyond the combinatoric capabilities of STRIPS.

The second use of generalized plans involves the supervision or monitoring of plan execution. Often, a real-world robot must reexecute a portion of its plan because of some failure that occurred during the first attempt at execution. At such a time, the system has more flexibility if it is not restricted to repeating identically the unsuccessful portion of the plan, but instead can reexecute the offending actions with different arguments.

Before getting into details (and defining just what we mean by *generalize*), we present in outline form a scenario that illustrates some of the capabilities of the system. Suppose we give a robot the task "Close window WIND1 and turn off light LITE1."[2] To accomplish this, let us say that the robot decides to push box BOX1 to window WIND1, climb BOX1 in order to close the window, and then proceed to turn off light LITE1. First, the system generalizes this specific plan to produce a plan that can, under certain specified conditions, close an arbitrary window (not just WIND1) and turn off an arbitrary light. Next, the system applies the appropriate version of this generalized plan to the specific problem at hand, namely, "close WIND1 and turn off LITE1." While executing the appropriate version, let us suppose that the robot fails to push BOX1 to the window because, say, it discovers another box is already under the window. The PLANEX supervisor will recognize that this new box will serve the purpose that BOX1 was to serve, and the plan execution will proceed.

Now let us suppose that, after finishing the first task, the robot is given a new problem, "Close window WIND5 and lock door DOOR1." The system is capable of recognizing that a portion of the old generalized plan can help solve the new task. Thus, the sequence of several component actions needed to close the window can be readily obtained as a single macro action, and the planning time required to solve the new problem thereby reduced.

We shall begin with a brief review of the problem-solving program STRIPS. Then we shall review a novel format for storing plans that conveniently

[1] The research reported herein was supported at SRI by the Advance Research Projects Agency of the Department of Defense, monitored by the U.S. Army Research Office-Durham under Contract DAHC04 72 C 0008.

[2] The scenario is imaginary; our robot cannot actually turn off light switches or close windows.

allows most of the legitimate $2^n - 1$ subsequences of an n-step plan to be extracted as a unit in a subsequent planning activity. We then describe a process by which constants appearing in the plan can be converted to parameters so that each plan can handle a family of different tasks. Thus generalized, the plan can be stored (i.e., learned) for future use. Next, we review the operation of PLANEX and discuss how generalized plans are used during execution to increase the system's capabilities for responding to unplanned-for situations. Finally, we discuss how STRIPS uses stored plans to compose more complex ones and describe some experiments with a sequence of learning tasks.

2. Summary of Strips

2.1. Description

Because STRIPS is basic to our discussion, let us briefly outline its operation. (For a complete discussion and additional examples, see [1].) The primitive actions available to the robot vehicle are precoded in a set of action routines. For example, execution of the routine GOTHRU(D1,R1,R2) causes the robot vehicle actually to go through the doorway D1 from room R1 to room R2. The robot system keeps track of where the robot vehicle is and stores its other knowledge of the world in a model [3] composed of well-formed formulas (wffs) in the predicate calculus. Thus, the system knows that there is a doorway D1 between rooms R1 and R2 by the presence of the wff CONNECTS-ROOMS(D1,R1,R2) in the model.

Tasks are given to the system in the form of predicate calculus wffs. To direct the robot to go to room R2, we pose for it the goal wff INROOM(ROBOT,R2). The planning system, STRIPS, then attempts to find a sequence of primitive actions that would change the world in such a way that the goal wff is true in the correspondingly changed model. In order to generate a plan of actions, STRIPS needs to know about the effects of these actions; that is, STRIPS must have a model of each action. The model actions are called *operators* and, just as the actions change the world, the operators transform one model into another. By applying a sequence of operators to the initial world model, STRIPS can produce a sequence of models (representing hypothetical worlds) ultimately ending in a model in which the goal wff is true. Presumably then, execution of the sequence of actions corresponding to these operators would change the world to accomplish the task.

Each STRIPS operator must be described in some convenient way. We characterize each operator in the repertoire by three entities: an *add list*, a *delete list*, and a *precondition wff*. The meanings of these entities are straightforward. An operator is applicable to a given model only if its precondition wff is satisfied in that model. The effect of applying an (assumed applicable) operator to a given model is to delete from the model all those clauses specified by the delete list and to add to the model all those clauses specified by the add list. Hence, the add and delete lists prescribe how an operator transforms one state into another.

Within this basic framework STRIPS operates in a GPS-like manner [6]. First, it tries to establish that a goal wff is satisfied by a model. (STRIPS uses the QA3 resolution-based theorem prover [3] in its attempts to prove goal wffs.) If the goal wff cannot be proved, STRIPS selects a "relevant" operator that is likely to produce a model in which the goal wff is "more nearly" satisfied. In order to apply a selected operator the precondition wff of that operator must of course be satisfied; this precondition becomes a new subgoal and the process is repeated. At some point we expect to find that the precondition of a relevant operator is already satisfied in the current model. When this happens the operator is *applied*; the initial model is transformed on the basis of the add and delete lists of the operator, and the model thus created is treated in effect as a new initial model of the world.

To complete our review of STRIPS we must indicate how relevant operators are selected. An operator is needed only if a subgoal cannot be proved from the wffs defining a model. In this case the operators are scanned to find one whose effects would allow the proof attempt to continue. Specifically, STRIPS searches for an operator whose add list specifies clauses that would allow the proof to be successfully continued (if not completed). When an add list is found whose clauses do in fact permit an adequate continuation of the proof, then the associated operator is declared relevant; moreover, the substitutions used in the proof continuation serve to instantiate at least partially the arguments of the operator. Typically, more than one relevant operator instance will be found. Thus, the entire STRIPS planning process takes the form of a tree search so that the consequences of considering different relevant operators can be explored. In summary, then, the "inner loop" of STRIPS works as follows:

(1) Select a subgoal and try to establish that it is true in the appropriate model. If it is, go to Step 4. Otherwise:

(2) Choose as a relevant operator one whose add list specifies clauses that allow the incomplete proof of Step 1 to be continued.

(3) The appropriately instantiated precondition wff of the selected operator constitutes a new subgoal. Go to Step 1.

(4) If the subgoal is the main goal, terminate. Otherwise, create a new model by applying the operator whose precondition is the subgoal just established. Go to Step 1.

The final output of STRIPS, then, is a list of instantiated operators whose corresponding actions will achieve the goal.

[3] Our use of the word "model" is consistent with customary terminology in Artificial Intelligence. We hope there will be no confusion between our use of the word and its technical definition in logic, namely an interpretation for a set of formulas.

2.2. An Example

An understanding of STRIPS is greatly aided by an elementary example. The following example considers the simple task of fetching a box from an adjacent room. Let us suppose that the initial state of the world is as shown below:

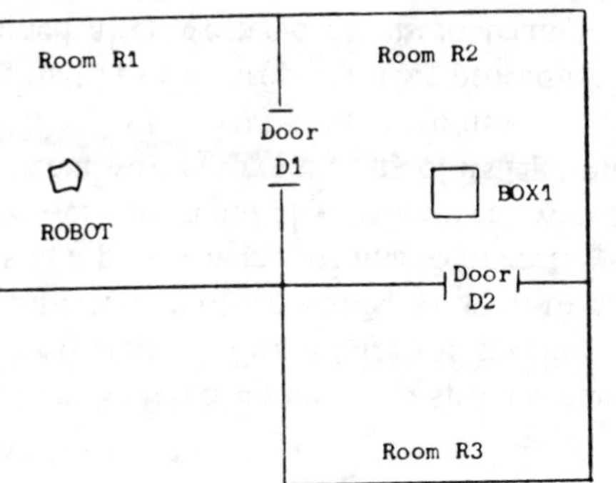

Initial Model

Mo: INROOM(ROBOT,R1)
CONNECTS(D1,R1,R2)
CONNECTS(D2,R2,R3)
BOX(BOX1)
INROOM(BOX1,R2)

.
.
.

$(\forall x\, \forall y\, \forall z)$[CONNECTS$(x,y,z)\Rightarrow$CONNECTS$(x,z,y)$]

Goal wff

Go: $(\exists x)$[BOX(x) $\wedge$ INROOM$(x$,R1)]

We assume for this example that models can be transformed by two operators GOTHRU and PUSHTHRU, having the descriptions given below. Each description specifies an *operator schema* indexed by schema variables. We will call schema variables *parameters*, and denote them by strings beginning with lower-case letters. A particular member of an operator schema is obtained by instantiating all the parameters in its description to constants. It is a straightforward matter to modify a resolution theorem prover to handle wffs containing parameters [1], but for present purposes we need only know that the modification ensures that each parameter can be bound only to one constant; hence, the operator arguments (which may be parameters) can assume unique values. (In all of the following we denote constants by strings beginning with capital letters and quantified variables by x, y or z):

GOTHRU(d,r1,r2)
(Robot goes through Door d from Room r1 into Room r2.)
Precondition wff
INROOM(ROBOT,r1) $\wedge$ CONNECTS(d,r1,r2)
Delete List
INROOM(ROBOT,$)
(Our convention here is to delete any clause containing a predicate of the form INROOM(ROBOT,$) for any value of $.)
Add List
INROOM(ROBOT,r2)

PUSHTHRU(b,d,r1,r2)
(Robot pushes Object *b* through Door d from Room r1 into Room r2.)
Precondition wff
INROOM(b,r1) $\wedge$ INROOM(ROBOT,r1) $\wedge$ CONNECTS(d,r1,r2)
Delete List
INROOM(ROBOT,$)
INROOM(b,$)
Add List
INROOM(ROBOT,r2)
INROOM(b,r2).

When STRIPS is given the problem it first attempts to prove the goal G_0 from the initial model M_0. This proof cannot be completed; however, were the model to contain other clauses, such as INROOM(BOX1,R1), the proof attempt could continue. STRIPS determines that the operator PUSHTHRU can provide the desired clause; in particular, the partial instance PUSHTHRU (BOX1,d,r1,R1) provides the wff INROOM(BOX1,R1).

The precondition G_1 for this instance of PUSHTHRU is

G_1: INROOM(BOX1,r1)
$\wedge$ INROOM(ROBOT,r1)
$\wedge$ CONNECTS(d,r1,R1).

This precondition is set up as a subgoal and STRIPS tries to prove it from M_0.

Although no proof for G_1 can be found, STRIPS determines that if r1 = R2 and d = D1, then the proof of G_1 could continue were the model to contain INROOM(ROBOT,R2). Again STRIPS checks operators for one whose effects could continue the proof and settles on the instance GOTHRU(d,r1,R2). Its precondition is the next subgoal, namely:

G_2: INROOM(ROBOT,r1)
$\wedge$ CONNECTS(d,r1,R2).

STRIPS is able to prove G_2 from M_0, using the substitutions r1 = R1 and d = D1. It therefore applies GOTHRU(D1,R1,R2) to M_0 to yield:

M_1: INROOM(ROBOT,R2)
CONNECTS(D1,R1,R2)
CONNECTS(D2,R2,R3)
BOX(BOX1)
INROOM(BOX1,R2)

.
.
.

$(\forall x \forall y \forall z)$[CONNECTS$(x,y,z)$⇒CONNECTS$(x,z,y)$].

Now STRIPS attempts to prove the subgoal G_1 from the new model M_1. The proof is successful with the instantiations r1 = R2, d = D1. These substitutions yield the operator instance PUSHTHRU(BOX1,D1,R2,R1), which applied to M_1 yields

M_2: INROOM(ROBOT,R1)
CONNECTS(D1,R1,R2)
CONNECTS(D1,R2,R3)
BOX(BOX1)
INROOM(BOX1,R1)

.
.
.

$(\forall x \forall y \forall z)$[CONNECTS$(x,y,z)$⇒CONNECTS$(x,z,y)$].

Next, STRIPS attempts to prove the original goal, G_0, from M_2. This attempt is successful and the final operator sequence is

GOTHRU(D1,R1,R2)
PUSHTHRU(BOX1,D1,R2,R1).

We have just seen how STRIPS computes a specific plan to solve a particular problem. The next step is to generalize the specific plan by replacing constants by new parameters. In other words, we wish to elevate our particular plan to the status of a plan schema, or macro operator, analogous to the primitive operators we were given initially. Moreover, we would like to store a macro operator in such a way as to make any of its legitimate subsequences also available to STRIPS. In the next section we describe a storage format, called a *triangle table*, that has this property. Our procedure for plan generalization will be explained after we have discussed triangle tables and their properties.

3. Triangle Tables

Suppose STRIPS has just computed a plan consisting of the sequence of n operators $OP_1, OP_2, \ldots, OP_n$. In what form should this plan be presented to PLANEX, the system responsible for monitoring the execution of plans? In what form should it be saved? For purposes of monitoring execution, PLANEX needs at every step to be able to answer such questions as

(a) Has the portion of the plan executed so far produced the expected results?

(b) What portion of the plan needs to be executed next so that after its execution the task will be accomplished?

(c) Can this portion be executed in the current state of the world?

Also, for purposes of saving plans so that portions of them can be used in a later planning process, we need to know the preconditions and effects of any portion of the plan.

If we are to have efficient methods for answering Questions (a)–(c), we must store a plan in a way that plainly reveals its internal structure. In particular, we must be able to identify the role of each operator in the overall plan: what its important effects are (as opposed to side effects) and why these effects are needed in the plan. To accomplish this, we decided to store plans in a tabular form called a *triangle table*.[4]

A triangle table is a lower triangular array where rows and columns correspond to the operators of the plan.

An example of a triangle table is shown in Fig. 1. (The reader may temporarily ignore the heavily outlined rectangle.) The columns of the table, with the exception of Column zero, are labelled with the names of the operators of the plan, in this example $OP_1, \ldots, OP_4$. For each Column i, $i = 1, \ldots, 4$, we place in the top cell the add list A_i of operator OP_i. Going down the ith column, we place in consecutive cells the portion of A_i that survives the application of subsequent operators. Thus, $A_{1/2}$ denotes those clauses in A_1 not deleted by OP_2; $A_{1/2,3}$ denotes those clauses in $A_{1/2}$ not deleted by OP_3, and so forth. Thus, the ijth cell of the matrix contains those wffs added by the jth operator that are still true at the time of application of the ith operator.

We can now interpret the contents of the ith row of the table, excluding the left-most column. Since each cell in the ith row (excluding the left-most) contains statements added by one of the first $(i - 1)$ operators but not deleted by any of those operators, we see that the union of the cells in the ith row (excluding the left-most) specifies the add list obtained by applying the $(i - 1)$st *head* of the plain; i.e., by applying in sequence $OP_1, \ldots, OP_{i-1}$. We denote by $A_{1,\ldots,j}$ the add list achieved by the first j operators applied in sequence. The union of the cells in the bottom row of a triangle table evidently specifies the add list of the complete sequence.

The left-most column of the triangle table, which we have thus far ignored, is involved with the preconditions for the stored plan. During the formation

[4] We are indebted to John Munson who prompted us to try a tabular format.

of the plan, STRIPS produced a proof of each operator's preconditions from the model to which the operator was applied. We will define the set of clauses used to prove a formula as the *support* of that formula. We wish to ensure that the *i*th row of a triangle table contains all the wffs in the support of the preconditions for Operator *i*. In general, some clauses in the support for Operator *i* will have been added by the first $i - 1$ operators in the plan and will therefore be included in Row *i*, as described in the previous paragraphs.

	0	1	2	3	4
1	PC_1	OP_1			
2	PC_2	A_1	OP_2		
3	PC_3	$A_{1/2}$	A_2	OP_3	
4	PC_4	$A_{1/2,3}$	$A_{2/3}$	A_3	OP_4
5		$A_{1/2,3,4}$	$A_{2/3,4}$	$A_{3/4}$	A_4

FIG. 1. A triangle table.

The remainder of the support clauses appeared in the initial model and were not deleted by any of the first $i - 1$ operators. These clauses, which we denote by PC_i, are precisely the clauses that are entered into the left-most (Column 0) cell of Row *i*. Hence, we see that Column 0 of a triangle table contains those clauses from the initial model that were used in the precondition proofs for the plan. It is convenient to flag the clauses in each Row *i* that are in the support for Operator *i* and hereafter speak of them as *marked* clauses; by construction, all clauses in Column 0 are marked. Note that in proving the preconditions of operators, STRIPS must save the support clauses so that the triangle table can be constructed.

As an example, we show in Fig. 2 the triangle table for the plan discussed in the previous section. The clauses that are marked by an asterisk "*" were all used in the proofs of preconditions.

We have seen how the marked clauses on Row *i* constitute the support of the preconditions for the *i*th operator. Let us now investigate the preconditions for the *i*th *tail* of the plan—that is, the preconditions for applying the operator sequence $OP_i, OP_{i+1}, \ldots, OP_n$. The key observation here is that the *i*th tail is applicable to a model if the model already contains that portion of the support of each operator in the tail that is not supplied within the tail itself. This observation may be formulated more precisely by introducing the notion of a *kernel* of a triangle table. We define the *i*th kernel of a table to be the unique rectangular subarray containing the lower left-most cell and Row *i*. We assert now that the *i*th tail of a plan applicable to a model if all the marked clauses in the *i*th kernel are true in that model. Let us see by example why this is so.

1	*INROOM(ROBOT,R1) *CONNECTS(D1,R1,R2)	GOTHRU(D1,R1,R2)	
2	*INROOM(BOX1,R2) *CONNECTS(D1,R1,R2) *CONNECTS(x,y,z) ⊃ CONNECTS(x,z,y)	*INROOM(ROBOT,R2)	PUSHTHRU(BOX1,D1,R2,R1)
3			INROOM(ROBOT,R1) INROOM(BOX1,R1)

FIG. 2. Triangle table for example plan.
(A "*" preceding a clause indicates a "marked" clause.)

Consider again Fig. 1, in which we have heavily outlined Kernel 3. Let us assume that all marked clauses in this kernel are true in the current model. (When all the marked clauses in a kernel are true, we shall say that the kernel is true.) Certainly, OP_3 is applicable; the marked clauses in Row 3 are true, and these marked clauses support the proof of the preconditions of OP_3. Suppose now that OP_3 is applied to the current model to produce a new model in which A_3, the set of clauses added by OP_3, is true. Evidently, OP_4 is now applicable, since all the marked clauses in Row 4 are true: those clauses within the outlined kernel were true before applying OP_3 (and by construction of the triangle table are still true), and those outside the kernel (that is, A_3)

are true because they were added by OP_3. Thus, the truth of the marked clauses in Kernel 3 is a sufficient condition for the applicability of the tail of the plan beginning with OP_3.

We have some additional observations to make about triangle tables before moving on to the matter of plan generalization. First, notice that Kernel 1—that is, the left-most column of a triangle table—constitutes a set of sufficient conditions for the applicability of the entire plan. Thus, we can take the conjunction of the clauses in Column 0 to be a precondition formula for the whole plan.

A second observation may help the reader gain a little more insight into the structure of triangle tables. Consider again the table of Fig. 1, and let us suppose this time that Kernel 2 is true. Since Kernel 2 is true, the sequence OP_2, OP_3, OP_4 is applicable. Upon applying OP_2, which is immediately applicable because the marked clauses in Row 2 are true, we effectively add Column 2 to the table. Moreover, we lose interest in Row 2 because OP_2 has already been applied. Thus the application of OP_2 transforms a true Kernel 2 into a true Kernel 3, and the application of the operators in the tail of the plan can continue.

4. Generalizing Plans

4.1. Motivation

The need for plan generalization in a learning system is readily apparent. Consider the specific plan produced in the example of Section 2:

GOTHRU(D1,R1,R2)
PUSHTHRU(BOX1,D1,R2,R1).

While this sequence solves the original task, it probably doesn't warrant being saved for the future unless, of course, we expect that the robot would often need to go from Room R1 through Door D1 to Room R2 to push back the specific box, BOX1, through Door D1 into Room R1. We would like to generalize the plan so that it could be free from the specific constants, D1, R1, R2, and BOX1 and could be used in situations involving arbitrary doors, rooms, and boxes.

In considering possible procedures for generalizing plans we must first reject the naive suggestion of merely replacing each constant in the plan by a parameter. Some of the constants may really need to have specific values in order for the plan to work at all. For example, consider a modification of our box-fetching plan in which the second step of the plan is an operator that *only* pushes objects from room R2 into room R1. The specific plan might then be

GOTHRU(D1,R1,R2)
SPECIALPUSH(BOX1).

When we generalize this plan we cannot replace all constants by parameters, since the plan only works when the third argument of GOTHRU is R2. We would want our procedure to recognize this fact and produce the plan

GOTHRU(d1,r1,R2)
SPECIALPUSH(b1).

Another reason for rejecting the simple replacement of constants by parameters is that there is often more generality readily available in many plans than this simple procedure will extract. For example, the form of our box-pushing plan, GOTHRU followed by PUSHTHRU, does not require that the room in which the robot begins be the same room into which the box is pushed. Hence the plan could be generalized as follows:

GOTHRU(d1,r1,r2)
PUSHTHRU(b,d2,r2,r3)

and be used to go from one room to an adjacent second room and push a box to an adjacent third room.

Our plan-generalization procedure overcomes these difficulties by taking into account the internal structure of the plan and the preconditions of each operator. The remainder of this section is a description of this generalization procedure.

4.2. The Generalization Procedure

The first step in our generalization procedure is to "lift" the triangle table to its most general form as follows: We first replace every occurrence of a constant in the clauses of the left-most column by a new parameter. (Multiple occurrences of the same constant are replaced by distinct parameters.) Then the remainder of the table is filled in with appropriate add clauses assuming completely uninstantiated operators (i.e., as these add clauses appear in the operator descriptions), and assuming the same deletions as occurred in the original table. As an example, Fig. 3 shows the table from Fig. 2 in its most general form.

The lifted table thus obtained is too general; we wish to constrain it so that the marked clauses in each row support the preconditions of the operator on that row, while retaining the property that the lifted table has the original table as an instance. To determine the constraints we redo each operator's precondition proof using the support clauses in the lifted table as axioms and the precondition formulas from the operator descriptions as the theorems to be proved. Each new proof is constructed as an isomorphic image of STRIPS' original preconditions proof by performing at each step resolutions on the same clauses and unifications on the same literals as in the original proof. This proof process ensures that each original proof is an instance of the new

	0	1	2
1	*INROOM(p1,p2) *CONNECTS(p3,p4,p5)	GOTHRU(p11,p12,p13)	
2	*INROOM(p6,p7) *CONNECTS(p8,p9,p10) *CONNECTS(x,y,z) ⊃ CONNECTS(x,z,y)	*INROOM(ROBOT,p13)	PUSHTHRU(p14,p15,p16,p17)
3			INROOM(ROBOT,p17) INROOM(p14,p17)

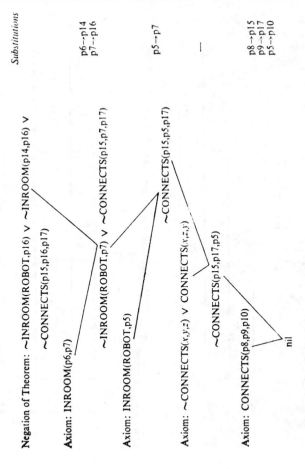

FIG. 3. Triangle table after initial lifting process.

generalized proof and therefore provides the basis for ensuring that the original table is an instance of the lifted table. Any substitutions of parameters for constants or for other parameters in the new proofs act as constraints on the generality of the plan and must be reflected in the lifted table. Hence these parameter substitutions are made throughout the lifted table and the generalized plan. The table resulting from the substitutions determined by the new proofs is constrained in the desired way.

Consider the effects of the new precondition proofs on the example table shown in Fig. 3. The precondition proof for GOTHRU(p11,p12,p13) proceeds as follows:

Substitutions

Negation of Theorem: ~INROOM(ROBOT,p12) ∨ ~CONNECTS(p11,p12,p13).

Axiom: INROOM(p1,p2) — ROBOT→p1, p2→p12

~CONNECTS(p11,p2,p13)

Axiom: CONNECTS(p3,p4,p5) — p3→p11, p2→p4, p5→p13

nil

The substitutions from the proof are made in the table and then the following precondition proof for PUSHTHRU(p14,p15,p16,p17) is performed:

Substitutions

Negation of Theorem: ~INROOM(ROBOT,p16) ∨ ~INROOM(p14,p16) ∨ ~CONNECTS(p15,p16,p17)

Axiom: INROOM(p6,p7) — p6→p14, p7→p16

~INROOM(ROBOT,p7) ∨ ~CONNECTS(p15,p7,p17)

Axiom: INROOM(ROBOT,p5) — p5→p7

~CONNECTS(p15,p5,p17)

Axiom: ~CONNECTS(x,y,z) ∨ CONNECTS(x,z,y) — —

~CONNECTS(p15,p17,p5)

Axiom: CONNECTS(p8,p9,p10) — p8→p15, p9→p17, p5→p10

nil

The substitutions from this proof are then used to produce the triangle table shown in Fig. 4.

The two proofs have constrained the plan so that the room into which the first operator takes the robot is the same room that contains the object to be pushed by the second operator. The robot's initial room and the target room for the push, however, remain distinct parameters constrained only by the precondition requirements that they each be adjacent to the object's initial room.

4.3. Two Refinements

Before a generalized plan is stored, two additional processing steps are carried out—one to improve efficiency and the other to remove possible inconsistencies. The first step eliminates some cases of overgeneralization produced during the lifting process and therefore makes more efficient the use of the plan by STRIPS and PLANEX. Often a clause in a plan's initial model will be in the support set of more than one operator, and therefore will appear more than once in Column 0 of the triangle table. When the table is lifted, each occurrence of the clause will generate new parameters. For example, in Fig. 3, CONNECTS(D1,R1,R2) was lifted to CONNECTS-(p3,p4,p5) and to CONNECTS(p8,p9,p10). In many cases this lifting pro-

1	*INROOM(ROBOT,p2) *CONNECTS(p3,p2,p5)	GOTHRU(p3,p2,p5)	
2	*INROOM(p6,p5) *CONNECTS(p8,p9,p5) *CONNECTS(x,y,z) ⊃ CONNECTS(x,z,y)	*INROOM(ROBOT,p5)	PUSHTHRU(p6,p8,p5,p9)
3			INROOM(ROBOT,p9) INROOM(p6,p9)
	0	1	2

FIG. 4. Final form of triangle table for generalized plan.

cedure enhances the generality of the plan (as it did for the box-fetching plan by allowing the first and third rooms to be distinct), but it also produces cases of over-generalization that, while not incorrect, can lead to inefficiencies. For example, consider a case in which INROOM(BOX1,R1) appears twice in Column 0 of a triangle table. When the table is lifted, the occurrences of the clause in Column 0 might become INROOM(p1,p2) and INROOM(p3, p4). If the precondition proofs cause p1 to be substituted for p3, but do not constrain p2 and p4, then we have a plan whose preconditions include the clauses

INROOM(p1,p2) and
INROOM(p1,p4).

Therefore we have a plan whose preconditions allow Object p1 to be in two distinct rooms at the same time, even though we know that in any semantically correct model Object p1 will be in only one room.

We eliminate most cases of this overgeneralization by recognizing those cases where two parameters are produced from a single occurrence of a constant in a single clause; if both such parameters do not appear as arguments of operators in the plan, then they can be bound together and one substituted for the other throughout the table without effectively inhibiting the generality of the plan. This procedure would substitute p2 for p4 in the INROOM example above, thereby making the two occurrences of the clause identical, but would not generate any constraining substitutions for the CONNECTS clause in the box-fetching example.

The second processing step that is performed before the plan is stored is needed to avoid inconsistencies that can occur in the lifted tables. The difficulty can be illustrated with the following example.

Consider a simple plan, PUSH(BOX1,LOC1), PUSH(BOX2,LOC2), for pushing two boxes to two locations. The unlifted triangle table for this plan might be as shown in Fig. 5a, where for simplicity we have not shown all clauses. When this table is lifted and the precondition proofs redone, no constraints are placed on the lifted table and it has the form shown in Fig. 5b. Suppose now that STRIPS were to use this plan with box1 and box2 instantiated to the same object and loc1 and loc2 instantiated to distinct locations. In that case STRIPS would evidently have a plan for achieving a state in which the same object is simultaneously at two different places!

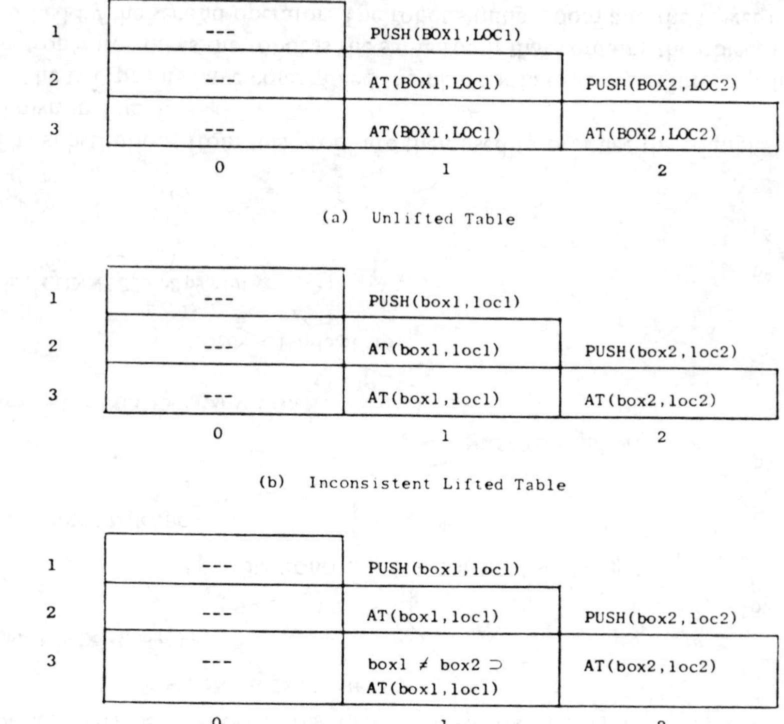

1	---	PUSH(BOX1,LOC1)	
2	---	AT(BOX1,LOC1)	PUSH(BOX2,LOC2)
3	---	AT(BOX1,LOC1)	AT(BOX2,LOC2)
	0	1	2

(a) Unlifted Table

1	---	PUSH(box1,loc1)	
2	---	AT(box1,loc1)	PUSH(box2,loc2)
3	---	AT(box1,loc1)	AT(box2,loc2)
	0	1	2

(b) Inconsistent Lifted Table

1	---	PUSH(box1,loc1)	
2	---	AT(box1,loc1)	PUSH(box2,loc2)
3	---	box1 ≠ box2 ⊃ AT(box1,loc1)	AT(box2,loc2)
	0	1	2

(c) Correct Lifted Table

FIG. 5. Triangle table for box-pushing plan

The source of this embarrassment lies in the assumption made above that the deletions in the lifted table can be the same as in the unlifted table. In our example, the clause AT(box1,loc1) should be deleted by the PUSH(box2, loc2) operator in the case where box1 and box2 are bound to the same object, but not deleted otherwise. Using the deletion algorithm described below, we represent this situation in the lifted table by replacing the clause AT(box1, loc1) in Row 3 by the clause form of

$$box1 \neq box2 \supset AT(box1,loc1)$$

as shown in Fig. 5(c). This implication serves us well since the theorem prover can deduce AT(box1,loc1) as being part of the plan's additions list for exactly those cases in which box1 and box2 are distinct.

We now consider in general how deletions are correctly accounted for in the lifted triangle tables. After all the precondition proofs are redone for the lifted table, the delete list of each operator is considered beginning with the first operator and continuing in sequence through the plan. The delete list of the ith operator is applied to the clauses in Row i of the table to determine which clauses should appear in Row $i + 1$ of the table.[5] Recall that an operator's delete list is specified to STRIPS as a list of literals, and any clause that unifies with one of these literals is deleted. Application of the delete list will cause the lifted table to be modified only when a unification with a delete literal requires that a parameter p1 be replaced by another parameter p2 or by a constant C1. In that case the clause will unify with the delete literal only when p1 and p2 are instantiated to the same constant or when p1 is instantiated to C1. Hence the clause is replaced in the next row of the table by an implication as follows:

$$p1 \neq p2 \supset \text{clause} \quad \text{or}$$
$$p1 \neq C1 \supset \text{clause}.$$

This implication allows the theorem prover to deduce the clause in only those cases where the operator's delete list would not have deleted it from the model.

If the clause that is replaced by the implication in a conditional deletion is part of the support of an operator in the plan (i.e., the clause is marked), then the implication must be accompanied by another addition to the table. In particular, if a clause CL1 is part of the support for the jth operator of the plan and CL1 is replaced in Row j of the table by the implication $p1 \neq p2 \supset CL1$, then $p1 \neq p2$ must be added as a marked clause to Cell $(j, 0)$ of the table. This addition to the table ensures that the jth operator's preconditions can be proved from the marked clauses in Row j of the table. The preconditions proof previously obtained will remain valid with the addition of a preliminary proof step in which clause CL1 is derived from $p1 \neq p2$ and $p1 \neq p2 \supset CL1$.

After these two processing steps are completed, the generalized plan is ready to be stored away as a macro operator, or *MACROP*, for later use by STRIPS and PLANEX.

5. Execution Strategies

5.1. Requirements for the Plan Executor

In this section we shall describe how a program called PLANEX uses triangle tables to monitor the execution of plans. An early version of PLANEX was described by Fikes [2]. It is now being used in conjunction with STRIPS and the MACROP generation procedures to control the SRI robot [4].

One of the novel elements introduced into artificial intelligence research by work on robots is the study of execution strategies and how they interact with planning activities. Since robot plans must ultimately be executed in the real world by a mechanical device, as opposed to being carried out in a mathematical space or by a simulator, consideration must be given by the executor to the possibility that operations in the plan may not accomplish what they were intended to, that data obtained from sensory devices may be inaccurate, and that mechanical tolerances may introduce errors as the plan is executed.

Many of these problems of plan execution would disappear if our system generated a whole new plan after each execution step. Obviously, such a strategy would be too costly, so we instead seek a plan execution scheme with the following properties:

(1) When new information obtained during plan execution implies that some remaining portion of the plan need not be executed, the executor should recognize such information and omit the unneeded plan steps.

(2) When execution of some portion of the plan fails to achieve the intended results, the executor should recognize the failure and either direct reexecution of some portion of the plan or, as a default, call for a replanning activity.

5.2. Preparation of the MACROP for Execution

Rather than working with the specific version of the plan originally produced by STRIPS, PLANEX uses the generalized MACROP to guide execution. The generalized plan allows a modest amount of replanning by the executor should parts of the plan fail in certain ways.

Before a MACROP can be used by PLANEX, its parameters must be partially instantiated using the specific constants of the goal wff. This specializes the MACROP to the specific task at hand while it leaves as general as possible the conditions under which it can be executed. This partial instantiation process is quite simple: We put in the lower left-most cell of the triangle

[5] This characterization of the deletion applications requires that we include in Cell (1, 0) of the table all the clauses that appear anywhere in Column 0. The resulting redundant occurrences of Column 0 clauses can be edited out before the table is stored.

table those clauses from the original model that were used by STRIPS in proving the goal wff. Then we use all of the clauses in the entire last row of the MACROP to prove the goal wff. Those substitutions made during this proof are then made on the entire MACROP. In addition we mark those clauses in the last row of the MACROP that were used to support the goal wff proof. This version of the MACROP is the one used to control execution.[6]

Let us illustrate what we have said about preparing a MACROP for execution by considering our example of fetching a box. In Fig. 4, we have the MACROP for this task. In Section 2, the goal wff for this task was given as

$$(\exists x)[\text{BOX}(x) \wedge \text{INROOM}(x,\text{R1})].$$

In the proof of this goal wff we used the clause BOX(BOX1) from the original model, M_0. Therefore, we insert this clause in Cell (3,0) of the triangle table. We now use the clauses in Row 3 of the MACROP in Fig. 4 (together with BOX(BOX1), just inserted) to prove the goal wff. That is, we use BOX(BOX1), INROOM(ROBOT,p9) and INROOM(p6,p9) to prove $(\exists x)[\text{BOX}(x) \wedge \text{INROOM}(x,\text{R1})]$. The substitutions made in obtaining the proof are BOX1 for p6 and R1 for p9. When these substitutions are applied to the MACROP of Fig. 4 and the support clauses for the new proof are marked, we obtain the execution MACROP shown in Fig. 6.

1	*INROOM(ROBOT,p2) *CONNECTS(p3,p2,p10)	GOTHRU(p3,p2,p10)	
2	*INROOM(BOX1,p10) *CONNECTS(p8,R1,p10) *CONNECTS(x,y,z) ⊃ CONNECTS(x,z,y)	*INROOM(ROBOT,p10)	PUSHTHROUGH(BOX1,p8,p10,R1)
3	*BOX(BOX1)		INROOM(ROBOT,R1) *INROOM(BOX1,R1)

FIG. 6. Execution MACROP for the fetch a box task.

[6] Some increase in generality can be obtained by putting in the lower leftmost cell of the triangle table *generalized* versions of the original model clauses. Some of the parameters in these generalized clauses might remain unbound in the proof of the goal wff, thereby making the table more general. In our implementation we shunned this additional complication.

5.3. The PLANEX Execution Strategy

Our strategy for monitoring the execution of plans makes use of the kernels of the execution MACROP. Recall that the ith kernel of a triangle table for an n-step plan is the unique rectangular subarray containing Row i and Cell $(n+1, 0)$. The importance of the ith kernel stems from the fact that it contains (as marked clauses) the support of the preconditions for the ith tail of the plan—that is, for the operator sequence $\{OP_i, \ldots, OP_n\}$. Thus if at some stage of plan execution the marked clauses in the ith kernel are provable, then we know that the ith tail is an appropriate operator sequence for achieving the goal. At each state of execution we must have at least one true kernel if we are to continue execution of the plan.

At the beginning of execution we know that the first kernel is true, since the initial model was used by STRIPS when the plan was created. But at later stages, unplanned outcomes might place us either unexpectedly close to the goal or throw us off the track completely. Our present implementation adopts a rather optimistic bias. We check each kernel in turn starting with the highest numbered one (which is the last row of the MACROP) and work backwards from the goal until we find a kernel that is true. If the goal kernel (the last row) is true, execution halts; otherwise we determine if the next-to-last kernel is true, and so on, until we find a true kernel k_i and a corresponding tail of the plan $\{OP_i, \ldots, OP_n\}$. The execution strategy then executes the action corresponding to OP_i and checks the outcome, as before, by searching for the highest-numbered true kernel. In an "ideal" world this procedure merely executes in order each operator in the plan. On the other hand, the procedure has the freedom to omit execution of unnecessary operators and to overcome failures by repeating the execution of operators. Replanning by STRIPS is initiated when no kernels are true.[7]

When checking to see if a kernel is true, we check to see if some instance of the conjunction of marked clauses in the kernel can be proved from the present model. Once such an instance is found, we determine the corresponding instance of the first operator in the tail of the plan and execute the action corresponding to that instance. Thus the generality of representation of the execution MACROP allows a great deal of flexibility in plan execution. For example, consider a case where PLANEX is executing a plan that takes the robot from one room through a second room into a third room. If, when the robot attempts to go through the door connecting the second and third rooms, the door is found to be locked, then PLANEX may be able to

[7] Typically, when replanning is necessary it is sufficient to produce a short sequence of operators to "get back onto the track" of the original plan. Since STRIPS has the MACROP for the original plan in its repertoire of operators, the new plan can often be formed by composing a sequence of operators and appending it to an appropriate tail of the MACROP.

reinstantiate parameters so that the first part of the plan can be reexecuted to take the robot from the second room through some new fourth room and then into the target third room.

An interesting by-product of our optimistic strategy of examining kernels in backwards order is that PLANEX sometimes remedies certain blunders made by STRIPS. Occasionally, STRIPS produces a plan containing an entirely superfluous subsequence—for example, a subsequence of the form OP, OP^{-1}, where OP^{-1} precisely negates the effects of OP. (Such a "detour" in a plan would reflect inadequacies in the search heuristics used by STRIPS.) During plan execution, however, PLANEX would effectively recognize that the state following OP^{-1} is the same as the state preceding OP, and would therefore not execute the superfluous subsequence.

5.4. The PLANEX Scanning Algorithm

The triangle table is a compact way of representing the kernels of a MACROP; most cells of the table occur in more than one kernel. We have exploited this economy of representation by designing an efficient algorithm for finding the highest-numbered true kernel. This algorithm, called the *PLANEX scan*, involves a cell-by-cell scan of the triangle table. We give a brief description of it here and refer the reader to Fikes [2] for more details. Each cell examined is evaluated as either *True* (i.e., all the marked clauses are provable from the current model) or *False*. The interest of the algorithm stems from the order in which cells are examined. Let us call a kernel "potentially true" at some stage in the scan if all evaluated cells of the kernel are true. The scan algorithm can then be succinctly stated as: *Among all unevaluated cells in the highest-indexed potentially true kernel, evaluate the left-most. Break "left-most ties" arbitrarily*. The reader can verify that, roughly speaking, this table-scanning rule results in a left-to-right, bottom-to-top scan of the table. However, the table is never scanned to the right of any cell already evaluated as false. An equivalent statement of the algorithm is "Among all unevaluated cells, evaluate the cell common to the largest number of potentially true kernels. Break ties arbitrarily." We conjecture that this scanning algorithm is optimal in the sense that it evaluates, on the average, fewer cells than any other scan guaranteed always to find the highest true kernel. A proof of this conjecture has not been found.

As the cells in the table are scanned we will be making substitutions for the MACROP parameters as dictated by the proofs of the cells' clauses. It is important to note that a substitution made to establish the truth of clauses in a particular cell must be applied to the entire table. When there are alternative choices about which substitutions to make, we keep a tree of possibilities so that backtracking can occur if needed.

6. Planning with MACROPS

In the preceding sections, we described the construction of MACROPS and how they are used to control execution. Now let us consider how a MACROP can be used by STRIPS during a subsequent planning process.

6.1. Extracting a Relevant Operator Sequence from a MACROP

Recall that the $(i + 1)$st row of a triangle table (excluding the first cell) represents the add list, $A_{1,\ldots,i}$, of the ith head of the plan, i.e. of the sequence $OP_1, \ldots, OP_i$. An n-step plan presents STRIPS with n alternative add lists, any one of which can be used to reduce a difference encountered during the normal planning process. STRIPS tests the relevance of each of a MACROP's add lists in the usual fashion, and the add lists that provide the greatest reduction in the difference are selected. Often a given set of relevant clauses will appear in more than one row of the table. In that case only the lowest-numbered row is selected, since this choice results in the shortest operator sequence capable of producing the desired clauses.

Suppose that STRIPS selects the ith add list $A_{1,\ldots,i}$, $i < n$. Since this add list is achieved by applying in sequence $OP_1, \ldots, OP_i$, we will obviously not be interested in the application of $OP_{i+1}, \ldots, OP_n$, and will therefore not be interested in establishing any of the preconditions for these operators. Now in general, some steps of a plan are needed only to establish preconditions for subsequent steps. If we lose interest in a tail of a plan, then the relevant instance of the MACROP need not contain those operators whose sole purpose is to establish preconditions for the tail. Also, STRIPS will, in general, have used only some subset of $A_{1,\ldots,i}$ in establishing the relevance of the ith head of the plan. Any of the first i operators that does not add some clause in this subset or help establish the preconditions for some operator that adds a clause in the subset is not needed in the relevant instance of the MACROP.

Conceptually, then, we can think of a single triangle table as representing a family of generalized operators. Upon the selection by STRIPS of a relevant add list, we must extract from this family an economical parameterized operator achieving the add list. In the following paragraphs, we will explain by means of an example an editing algorithm for accomplishing this task of operator extraction.

6.2. The Editing Algorithm

Consider the illustrative triangle table shown in Fig. 7. Each of the numbers within cells represents a single clause. The circled clauses are "marked" in the sense described earlier; that is, they are used to prove the precondition of the operator whose name appears on the same row. A summary of the structure

	0	1	2	3	4	5	6	7
		OP_1	OP_2	OP_3	OP_4	OP_5	OP_6	OP_7
1	(1,2)							
2	(3)	11, 12, 13						
3	(4,5)	11, 12	14, 15, 16					
4	(6)	(11), 12	15, 16	17, 18, 19, 20				
5	(7)	12	(16)	17, 18, 19, 20	21, 22, 23			
6	(8,9)	12	16	17, 18	21, 22	(24)		
7	(10)		16*	17, (18)	21, 22	24	(25)*	
8				17	21	24		26

TA 8973-13

FIG. 7. MACROP with marked clauses.

of this plan is shown below, where "I" refers to the initial state and "F" to the final state:

OPERATOR	PRECONDITION SUPPORT SUPPLIED BY	PRECONDITION SUPPORT SUPPLIED TO
OP_1	I	OP_4
OP_2	I	OP_5
OP_3	I	OP_7,F
OP_4	I,OP_1	F
OP_5	I,OP_2	OP_6,F
OP_6	I,OP_5	OP_7
OP_7	I,OP_3,OP_6	F

Suppose now that STRIPS selects $A_{1,\ldots,6}$ as the desired add list and, in particular, selects Clause 16 and Clause 25 as the particular members of the add list that are relevant to reducing the difference of immediate interest. These clauses have been indicated on the table by an asterisk (*). The editing algorithm proceeds by examining the table to determine what effects of individual operators are not needed to produce Clauses 16 and 25. First, OP_7 is obviously not needed; we can therefore remove all circle marks from Row 7, since those marks indicate the support of the preconditions of OP_7. We now inspect the columns, beginning with Column 6 and going from right to left, to find the first column with no marks of either kind (circles or asterisks). Column 4 is the first such column. The absence of marked clauses in Column 4 means that the clauses added by OP_4 are not needed to reduce the difference and are not required to prove the pre-condition of any subsequent operator; hence OP_4 will not be in the edited operator sequence and we can unmark all clauses in Row 4. Continuing our right-to-left scan of the columns, we note that Column 3 contains no marked clauses. (Recall that we have already unmarked Clause 18.) We therefore delete OP_3 from the plan and unmark all clauses in Row 3. Continuing the scan, we note that Column 1 contains no marked entries (we have already unmarked Clause 11), and therefore we can delete OP_1 and the marked entries in Row 1.

The result of this editing process is to reduce the original seven-step plan to the compact three-step plan, $\{OP_2, OP_5, OP_6\}$, whose add list specifically includes the relevant clauses. The structure of this plan is shown below.

OPERATOR	PRECONDITION SUPPORT SUPPLIED BY	PRECONDITION SUPPORT SUPPLIED TO
OP_2	I	OP_5,F
OP_5	I,OP_2	OP_6,F
OP_6	I,OP_5	F

6.3. Use of Edited MACROPS as Relevant Operators

Once an edited MACROP has been constructed, we would like STRIPS to use it in the same manner as any other operator. We have some latitude though, in specifying the preconditions of the MACROP. An obvious choice would be to use the conjunction of the clauses in the left-most column, but there is a difficulty with this straightforward choice that can be made clear with the aid of a simple example. Suppose we are currently in a state in which the first kernel of an edited MACROP—that is, its left-most column—is false, but suppose further that, say, the third kernel is true. Since the third kernel is true, the tail of the MACROP beginning with OP_3 is immediately applicable and would produce the desired relevant additions to the model. If STRIPS were to ignore this opportunity and set up the left-most column of the MACROP as a subgoal, it would thereby take the proverbial one step backward to go two steps forward.

This example suggests that we employ a PLANEX scan on the edited table so that all tails of the relevant MACROP will be tested for applicability. If an applicable tail is found, STRIPS applies, in sequence, each operator in this tail to produce a new planning model. Each operator application is performed in the usual manner using the add and delete lists of the individual operators. If the PLANEX scan fails to find a true kernel, then no tail is applicable and the conjunction of the marked clauses in the first kernel is set up as a subgoal to be achieved by STRIPS. Actually, any kernel would constitute a perfectly good subgoal and, in principle, the disjunction of all the kernels would be better still. Unfortunately, this disjunction places excessive demands on both the theorem prover and the STRIPS executive, so we restrict ourselves to consideration of the first kernel.

We have seen that STRIPS uses a MACROP during planning by extracting a relevant subsequence of the MACROP's operators, and then including that subsequence in the new plan being constructed. When the new plan is made into a MACROP it is often the case that it will contain add lists that are subsets of add lists in already existing tables. For example, if an entire existing MACROP is used in the construction of a new plan, and the parameter substitutions in the new MACROP correspond to those in the old MACROP, then each add list in the old MACROP will be a subset of an add list in the new MACROP. To assist STRIPS in its use of MACROPS, we have designed a procedure that will remove redundant add lists from consideration during planning, and in cases where an entire MACROP is contained within another, will delete the contained MACROP from the system.

Our procedure takes the following action: If every instance of the operator sequence that is the *i*th head of some MACROP is also an instance of a sequence occurring anywhere else in the same or some other MACROP, then all the add lists in that head (i.e. Rows 2 through $i + 1$) are disallowed for consideration by STRIPS.[8] For example, consider the following two generalized plans:

Plan A: OPA(p1),OPB(p1,p2),OPC(p3),OPD(p3,C1),OPA(p3),OPB(p4,p5)

Plan B: OPC(p6),OPD(p6,C1),OPA(p7),OPF(p6,p7).

Rows 2 and 3 of Plan A are disallowed for consideration as add lists since every instance of the sequence, OPA(p1),OPB(p1,p2), is also an instance of the sequence, OPA(p3),OPB(p4,p5), that occurs at the end of Plan A. Rows 2 and 3 of Plan B are disallowed because of the sequence, OPC(p3),OPD(p3,C1), that occurs in Plan A. Note that Row 4 of Plan B could not be disallowed for consideration by Plan A since there are instances of the sequence, OPC(p6),OPD(p6,C1),OPA(p7), that are not instances of OPC(p3), OPD(p3,C1),OPA(p3).

This procedure is applied whenever a new MACROP is added to the system. It has proved to be quite effective at minimizing the number of MACROP add lists that STRIPS must consider during planning. (See Section 7, for examples.) A difficulty arises in the use of this procedure when the same operator appears in two MACROPs and the support sets for the precondition proofs of that operator differ markedly in the two triangle tables. This can occur, for example, when the precondition is a disjunction of two wffs and in one case the first disjunct was proven to be true and in the other case the second disjunct was proven to be true. In those situations the two occurrences of the operator should not be considered as instances of the same operator since each occurrence effectively had different preconditions. A refinement of our procedure that would include an appropriate comparison of the support sets could be employed to overcome this difficulty.

[8] Note that the first row of a MACROP contains no add clauses.

7. Experimental Results

The mechanisms we have described for generating and using MACROPS have been implemented as additions and modifications to the existing STRIPS and PLANEX systems. In this section we will describe the results of some of the experiments we have run with the new system. Problems were posed to the system in the SRI robot's current experimental environment of seven rooms, eight doors, and several boxes about two feet high. The robot is a mobile vehicle equipped with touch sensors, a television camera, and a push bar that allows the robot to push the boxes [4]. A typical state of this experimental environment is modeled by STRIPS using about 160 axioms.

7.1. Operator Descriptions

The operator descriptions given to STRIPS for these experiments model the robot's preprogrammed action routines for moving the robot next to a door in a room, next to a box in a room, to a location in a room, or through a door. There are also operators that model action routines for pushing a box next to another box in a room, to a location in a room, or through a door. In addition, we have included operator descriptions that model fictitious action routines for opening and closing doors. These descriptions are as follows:

GOTOB(*bx*) *Go to object bx.*
Preconditions: TYPE(*bx*,OBJECT),(∃*rx*)[INROOM(*bx*,*rx*) ∧ INROOM(ROBOT,*rx*)]
Deletions: AT(ROBOT,$1,$2),NEXTTO(ROBOT,$1)
Additions: *NEXTTO(ROBOT,*bx*)

GOTOD(*dx*) *Go to door dx.*
Preconditions: TYPE(*dx*,DOOR),(∃*rx*)(∃*ry*)[INROOM(ROBOT,*rx*) ∧ CONNECTS(*dx*,*rx*,*ry*)]
Deletions: AT(ROBOT,$1,$2),NEXTTO(ROBOT,$1)
Additions: *NEXTTO(ROBOT,*dx*)

GOTOL(*x*,*y*) *Go to coordinate location (x,y).*
Preconditions: (∃*rx*)[INROOM(ROBOT,*rx*) ∧ LOCINROOM(*x*,*y*,*rx*)]
Deletions: AT(ROBOT,$1,$2),NEXTTO(ROBOT,$1)
Additions: *AT(ROBOT,*x*,*y*)

PUSHB(*bx*,*by*) *Push bx to object by.*
Preconditions: TYPE(*by*,OBJECT),PUSHABLE(*bx*),NEXTTO(ROBOT,*bx*),
(∃*rx*)[INROOM(*bx*,*rx*) ∧ INROOM(*by*,*rx*)]
Deletions: AT(ROBOT,$1,$2),NEXTTO(ROBOT,$1),AT(*bx*,$1,$2),NEXTTO(*bx*,$1),
NEXTTO($1,*bx*)
Additions: *NEXTTO(*bx*,*dx*),NEXTTO(ROBOT,*bx*)

PUSHD(*bx*,*dx*) *Push bx to door dx.*
Preconditions: PUSHABLE(*bx*),TYPE(*dx*,DOOR),NEXTTO(ROBOT,*bx*)
(∃*rx*)(∃*ry*)[INROOM(*bx*,*rx*) ∧ CONNECTS(*dx*,*rx*,*ry*)]
Deletions: AT(ROBOT,$1,$2),NEXTTO(ROBOT,$1),AT(*bx*,$1,$2),NEXTTO(*bx*,$1),
NEXTTO($1,*bx*)
Additions: *NEXTTO(*bx*,*dx*),NEXTTO(ROBOT,*bx*)

PUSHL(*bx*,*x*,*y*) *Push bx to coordinate location (x,y).*
Preconditions: PUSHABLE(*bx*),NEXTTO(ROBOT,*bx*),(∃*rx*)[INROOM(ROBOT,*rx*) ∧
LOCINROOM(*x*,*y*,*rx*)]
Deletions: AT(ROBOT,$1,$2),NEXTTO(ROBOT,$1),AT(*bx*,$1,$2),NEXTTO(*bx*,$1),
NEXTTO($1,*bx*)
Additions: *AT(*bx*,*x*,*y*),NEXTTO(ROBOT,*bx*)

GOTHRUDR(*dx*,*rx*) *Go through door dx into room rx.*
Preconditions: TYPE(*dx*,DOOR),STATUS(*dx*,OPEN),TYPE(*rx*,ROOM),
NEXTTO(ROBOT,*dx*) (∃*ry*)[INROOM(ROBOT,*ry*) ∧ CONNECTS(*dx*,*ry*,*rx*)]
Deletions: AT(ROBOT,$1,$2),NEXTTO(ROBOT,$1),INROOM(ROBOT,$1)
Additions: *INROOM(ROBOT,*rx*)

PUSHTHRUDR(*bx*,*dx*,*rx*) *Push bx through door dx into room rx.*
Preconditions: PUSHABLE(*bx*),TYPE(*dx*,DOOR),STATUS(*dx*,OPEN),TYPE(*rx*,
ROOM),NEXTTO(*bx*,*dx*),NEXTTO(ROBOT,*bx*),(∃*ry*)[INROOM(*bx*,*ry*) ∧
CONNECTS(*dx*,*ry*,*rx*)]
Deletions: AT(ROBOT,$1,$2),NEXTTO(ROBOT,$1),AT(*bx*,$1,$2),NEXTTO(*bx*,$1),
NEXTTO($1,*bx*),INROOM(ROBOT,$1),INROOM(*bx*,$1)
Additions: *INROOM(*bx*,*rx*),INROOM(ROBOT,*rx*),NEXTTO(ROBOT,*bx*)

OPEN(*dx*) *Open door dx.*
Preconditions: NEXTTO(ROBOT,*dx*),TYPE(*dx*,DOOR),STATUS(*dx*,CLOSED)
Deletions: STATUS(*dx*,CLOSED)
Additions: *STATUS(*dx*,OPEN)

CLOSE(*dx*) *Close door dx.*
Preconditions: NEXTTO(ROBOT,*dx*),TYPE(*dx*,DOOR),STATUS(*dx*,OPEN)
Deletions: STATUS(*dx*,OPEN)
Additions: *STATUS(*dx*,CLOSED)

Note: The addition clauses preceded by an asterisk are the *primary additions* of the operator. When STRIPS searches for a relevant operator is considers only these primary addition clauses.

7.2. Example Problems

7.2.1. SUMMARY. A sequence of five problems was designed to illustrate the various ways in which MACROPs are used during planning. We show in the next subsection an annotated trace of the system's behaviour for each problem in the sequence. Each trace is preceded by a diagram of the problem's initial and final states, and includes the sequence of subgoal generations and operator applications actually occurring in the STRIPS solution. STRIPS' attention was directed to the rooms shown in the diagrams by closing the doors connecting all other rooms.

The plan for the first problem in the sequence pushes two boxes together and then takes the robot into an adjacent room. The second problem is similar to the first except that different rooms and different boxes are involved, and the robot begins in a room adjacent to the room containing the boxes. STRIPS uses a tail of MACROP1 to get the robot into the room with the boxes and then uses the entire MACROP1 to complete the plan.

The third problem involves taking the robot from one room through a second room and into a third room, with the added complication that the door connecting the second and third rooms is closed. STRIPS first decides to use MACROP2 with the box-pushing sequence edited out and then finds that the door must be opened; to get the robot next to the closed door, a head of MACROP2 is selected with the box-pushing sequence again edited out. After formation of the plan to go to the door and open it, the PLANEX scan observes that only the final operator of the first relevant instance of MACROP2 is needed to complete the plan.

The fourth problem requires that three boxes be pushed together, with the robot beginning in a room adjacent to the room containing the boxes. A head of MACROP2 is used to get the robot into the room with the boxes and to push two of them together; the box-pushing sequence of MACROP2 is used to complete the plan, again with the assistance of the PLANEX scan.

The fifth problem requires the robot to go from one room into a second room, open a door that leads into a third room, go through the third room into a fourth room, and then push together two pairs of boxes. The plan, which is formed by combining all of MACROP4 with all of MACROP3, is well beyond the range of plans producible by STRIPS without the use of MACROPs. Note that although MACROP4 was created by lifting a plan that pushed three boxes together, it has enough generality to handle this form of a four-box problem. Note also that MACROP1, MACROP3, and MACROP4 have been recognized as redundant and deleted, so that the net result of this learning sequence is to add only MACROP2 and MACROP5 to the system.

In Table I we present a table showing the search tree sizes and running times for the five problems. The problems were run both with and without the use of MACROPs for comparison. Even when MACROPs were not being used for planning we include the MACROP production time since PLANEX needs the MACROP to monitor plan execution. Note that the times and the search tree sizes are all smaller when MACROPS are used and that the MACROPs allow longer plans to be formed without necessarily incurring an exponential increase in planning time.

TABLE I
Statistics for STRIPS behavior

	PROBLEM 1	PROBLEM 2	PROBLEM 3	PROBLEM 4	PROBLEM 5
Without MACROPS					
Total time (minutes)	3 : 05	9 : 42	7 : 03	14 : 09	–
Time to produce MACROP	1 : 00	1 : 28	1 : 11	1 : 43	–
Time to find unlifted plan	2 : 05	8 : 14	5 : 52	12 : 26	–
Total nodes in search tree	10	33	22	51	–
Nodes on solution path	9	13	11	15	–
Operators in plan	4	6	5	7	–
With MACROPS					
Total time (minutes)	3 : 05	3 : 54	6 : 34	4 : 37	9 : 13
Time to produce MACROP	1 : 00	1 : 32	1 : 16	1 : 37	3 : 24
Time to find unlifted plan	2 : 05	2 : 22	5 : 18	3 : 00	5 : 49
Total nodes in search tree	10	9	14	9	14
Nodes on solution path	9	9	9	9	14
Operators in plan	4	6	5	6	11

STRIPS is written in BBN-LISP and runs as compiled code on a PDP-10 computer under the TENEX time-sharing system.

STRIPS could not solve Problem 5 without using MACROPs.

7.2.2. Annotated Trace of System Behavior for Each Example Problem.

Problem 1

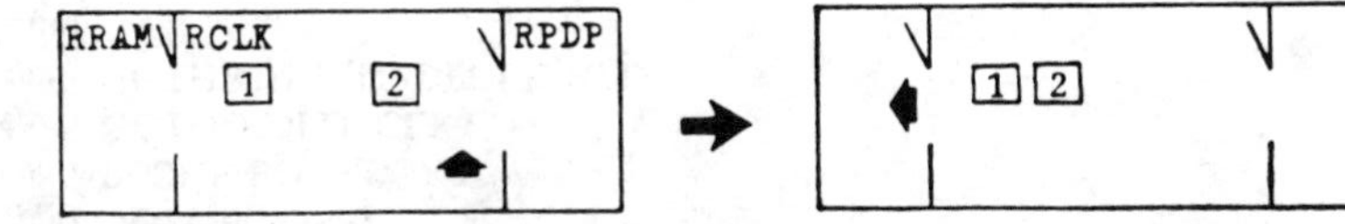

G1: INROOM(ROBOT,RRAM) ∧ NEXTTO(BOX1,BOX2)

*****

G1 is the task statement.

*****

G2: Preconditions for PUSHB(BOX2,BOX1)
G3: Preconditions for GOTOB(BOX2)
Apply GOTOB(BOX2)
Apply PUSHB(BOX2,BOX1)
G4: Preconditions for GOTHRUDR(par18,RRAM)
G6: Preconditions for GOTOD(DRAMCLK)

*****

G5 was the precondition for an operator that did not appear in the completed plan.

*****

Apply GOTOD(DRAMCLK)
Apply GOTHRUDR(DRAMCLK,RRAM)
Solution

Form MACROP1(par29,par37,par45,par54,par33)

*****

The parameter list for a MACROP contains all the parameters that occur in the triangle table.

*****

GOTOB(par29)
PUSHB(par29,par37)
GOTOD(par45)
GOTHRUDR(par45,par54)

*****

The generalized plan pushes two boxes together and takes the robot into an adjacent room, given that the robot and the boxes are initially all in the same room.

*****

Set first additions row of MACROP1 to 3.

*****

STRIPS will consider only rows numbered 3 and higher as add lists during planning. Rows 1 and 2 of a triangle table are never considered as add lists since there are no add clauses in Row 1, and the add clauses in Row 2 are redundant with respect to the operator description of the first operator in the MACROP.

*****

Problem 2

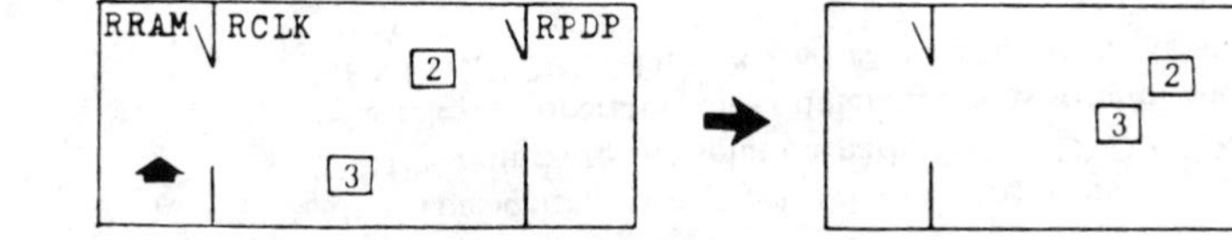

G1: INROOM(ROBOT,RPDP) ∧ NEXTTO(BOX2,BOX3)

*****

G1 is the task statement.

*****

G2: Preconditions for MACROP1:5(BOX3,BOX2,par3,RPDP,par5)

*****

The notation MACROP1:5 means that Row 5 of MACROP1 is selected as a relevant add list. MACROP1 is instantiated so that Row 5 contains the relevant clauses INROOM(ROBOT,RPDP) added by GOTHRUDR(par3,RPDP) and NEXTTO(BOX2,BOX3) added by PUSHB(BOX3,BOX2). All four operators in MACROP1 are needed to produce these relevant clauses. No kernels in the triangle table are satisfied. A difference consisting of the single clause INROOM (ROBOT,RCLK) is extracted from the first kernel.

*****

G3: Preconditions for MACROP1:5(par17,par18,par19,RCLK,par21)

*****

Row 5 of MACROP1 is again selected as a relevant add list. MACROP1 is instantiated so that Row 5 contains the relevant clause INROOM-(ROBOT,RCLK) added by GOTHRUDR(par19,RCLK). Only the last two operators in MACROP1 are needed to produce the relevant clause.

*****

Kernel 3 satisfied

*****

Kernel 3 is the precondition for the last two operators in MACROP1.

*****

Apply GOTOD(DRAMCLK)
Apply GOTHRUDR(DRAMCLK,RCLK)
Kernel 1 satisfied
Apply GOTOB(BOX3)
Apply PUSHB(BOX3,BOX2)
Apply GOTOD(DPDPCLK)
Apply GOTHRUDR(DPDPCLK,RPDP)
Solution

Form MACROP2(par27,par52,par72,par91,par111,par38,par40)
GOTOD(par27)
GOTHRUDR(par27,par40)
GOTOB(par52)
PUSHB(par52,par72)
GOTOD(par91)
GOTHRUDR(par91,par111)

*****

The generalized plan takes the robot from one room into an adjacent room, pushes two boxes together in the second room, and then takes the robot into a third room adjacent to the second.

*****

Erase MACROP1.

*****

MACROP1 is completely contained in MACROP2.

*****

Set first additions row of MACROP2 to 4.

*****

The first two operators of MACROP2 match the last two operators of MACROP2.

*****

Problem 3

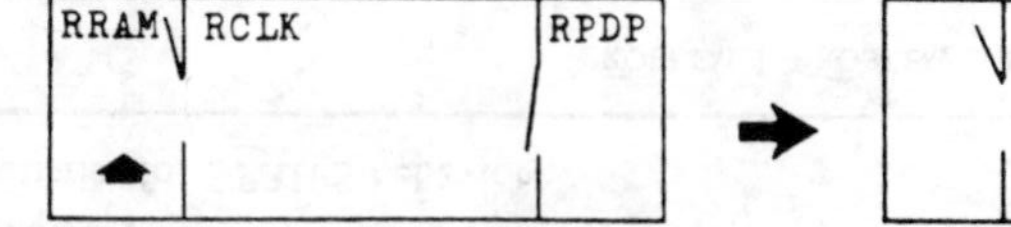

G1: INROOM(ROBOT,RPDP)

*****

G1 is the task statement.

*****

G2: Preconditions for MACROP2:7(par1,par2,par3,par4,RPDP,par6,par7)

*****

Row 7 of MACROP2 is selected as a relevant add list. MACROP2 is instantiated so that Row 7 contains the relevant clause INROOM-(ROBOT,RPDP) added by GOTHRUDR(par4,RPDP). Only the first, second, fifth, and sixth operators are needed to produce this relevant clause. No kernels in the triangle table are satisfied. A difference consisting of the single clause STATUS(DPDPCLK,OPEN) is extracted from the first kernel.

*****

G5: Preconditions for OPEN(DPDPCLK)

*****

After considering two other relevant operators for achieving G1, STRIPS returns to the solution path. OPEN(DPDPCLK) is found to be a relevant operator and a difference consisting of the single clause NEXTTO(ROBOT,DPDPCLK) is extracted from the preconditions.

*****

G9: Preconditions for MACROP2:6(par15,par16,par17,DPDPCLK,par19, par20,par21)

*****

After considering three other relevant operators for achieving G5, STRIPS selects Row 6 of MACROP2 as a relevant add list. MACROP2 is instantiated so that Row 6 contains the relevant clause NEXTTO-(ROBOT,DPDPCLK) added by GOTOD(DPDPCLK). Only the first, second, and fifth operators are needed to produce this relevant clause.

*****

Kernel 1 satisfied.
Apply GOTOD(DRAMCLK)
Apply GOTHRUDR(DRAMCLK,RCLK)
Apply GOTOD(DPDPCLK)
Apply OPEN(DPDPCLK)
Kernel 6 satisfied

*****

A PLANEX scan is used so that all kernels are checked. Kernel 6 is the precondition for the final operator in the relevant instance of MACROP2.

*****

Apply GOTHRUDR(DPDPCLK,RPDP)
Solution

Form MACROP3(par24,par59,par82,par32,par42)
GOTOD(par24)
GOTHRUDR(par24,par42)
GOTOD(par59)
OPEN(par59)
GOTHRUDR(par59,par82)

*****

The generalized plan takes the robot from one room into an adjacent room, then to a closed door in the second room, opens the closed door, and then takes the robot through the opened door into a third room.

*****

Set first additions row of MACROP3 to 4.

*****

The first two operators of MACROP3 match the first two operators of MACROP2.

Problem 4

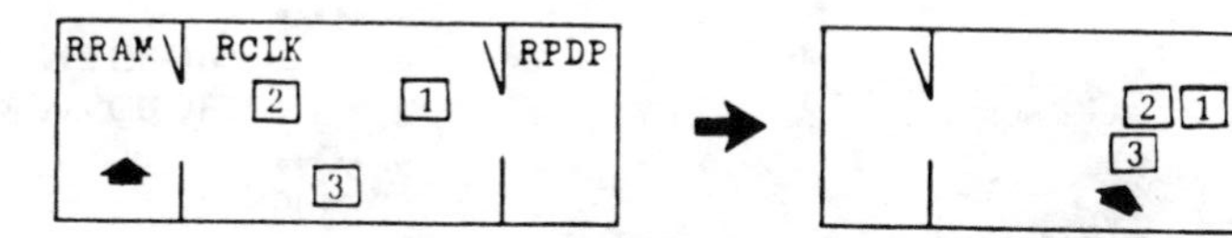

G1: NEXTTO(BOX1,BOX2) ∧ NEXTTO(BOX2,BOX3)

*****

G1 is the task statement.

*****

G2: Preconditions for MACROP2:5(par1,BOX2,BOX1,par4,par5,par6,par7)

*****

Row 5 of MACROP2 is selected as a relevant add list. MACROP2 is instantiated so that Row 5 contains the relevant clause NEXTTO-(BOX1,BOX2) added by PUSHB(BOX2,BOX1). All of the first four operators in MACROP2 are needed to produce this relevant clause.

*****

Kernel 1 satisfied
Apply GOTOD(DRAMCLK)
Apply GOTHRUDR(DRAMCLK,RCLK)
Apply GOTOB(BOX2)
Apply PUSHB(BOX2,BOX1)
G3: Preconditions for MACROP2:5(par19,BOX3,BOX2,par22,par23,par24,par25)

*****

Row 5 of MACROP2 is selected as before. The instantiation is so that Row 5 contains the relevant clause NEXTTO(BOX2,BOX3) added by PUSHB(BOX3,BOX2). Again all of the first four operators are included in the relevant instance of MACROP2.

*****

Kernel 3 satisfied

*****

A PLANEX scan is used so that all kernels are checked. Kernel 3 is the precondition for the third and fourth operators.

*****

Apply GOTOB(BOX3)
Apply PUSHB(BOX3,BOX2)
Solution

Form MACROP4(par37,par80,par102,par123,par134,par57,par59)
GOTOD(par37)
GOTHRUDR(par37,par59)
GOTOB(par80)
PUSHB(par80,par102)
GOTOB(par123)
PUSHB(par123,par134)

*****

The generalized plan takes the robot from one room into an adjacent room, pushes one box to a second box, and then pushes a third box to a fourth box.

*****

Set first additions row of MACROP2 to 6.

*****

The first 4 operators of MACROP2 match the first 4 operators of MACROP4.

*****

Set first additions row of MACROP4 to 4.

*****

The first 2 operators of MACROP4 match the last 2 operators of MACROP2.

*****

Problem 5

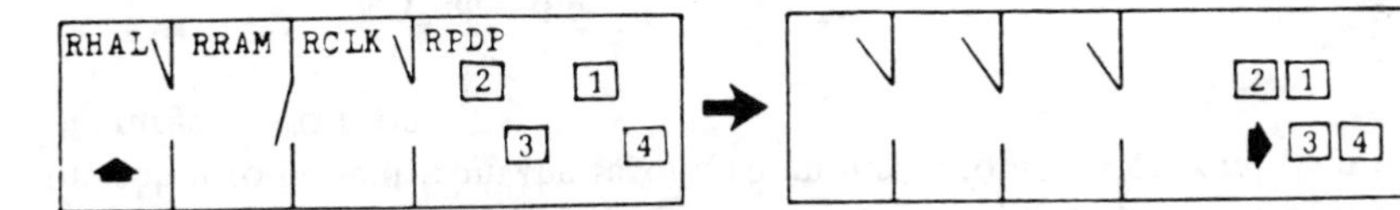

G1: NEXTTO(BOX1,BOX2) ∧ NEXTTO(BOX3,BOX4)

*****

G1 is the task statement.

*****

G2: Preconditions for MACROP4:7(par13,BOX2,BOX1,BOX3,BOX4,par18,par19)

*****

Row 7 of MACROP4 is selected as a relevant add list. MACROP4 is instantiated so that Row 7 contains the relevant clauses NEXTTO (BOX1,BOX2) added by PUSHB(BOX2,BOX1) and NEXTTO (BOX3,BOX4) added by PUSHB(BOX3,BOX4). All six operators in MACROP4 are needed to produce these relevant clauses. No kernels in the triangle table are satisfied. A difference consisting of the single clause INROOM(ROBOT,RCLK) is extracted from the first kernel.

*****

G3: Preconditions for MACROP3:6(par27,par28,RCLK,par30,par31)

*****

Row 6 of MACROP3 is selected as a relevant add list. MACROP3 is instantiated so that Row 6 contains the relevant clause INROOM (ROBOT,RCLK) added by GOTHRUDR(par28,RCLK). All five

```
                operators in MACROP3 are needed to produce this relevant clause.
                *****
    Kernel 1 satisfied
    Apply GOTOD(DRAMHAL)
    Apply GOTHRUDR(DRAMHAL,RRAM)
    Apply GOTOD(DRAMCLK)
    Apply OPEN(DRAMCLK)
    Apply GOTHRUDR(DRAMCLK,RCLK)
  Kernel 1 satisfied
  Apply GOTOD(DPDPCLK)
  Apply GOTHRUDR(DPDPCLK,RPDP)
  Apply GOTOB(BOX2)
  Apply PUSHB(BOX2,BOX1)
  Apply GOTOB(BOX3)
  Apply PUSHB(BOX3,BOX4)
Solution

Form MACROP5(par44,par87,par151,par208,par237,par265,par294,par180,par130,
    par64,par66)
  GOTOD(par44)
  GOTHRUDR(par44,par66)
  GOTOD(par87)
  OPEN(par87)
  GOTHRUDR(par87,par130)
  GOTOD(par151)
  GOTHRUDR(par151,par180)
  GOTOB(par208)
  PUSHB(par208,par237)
  GOTOB(par265)
  PUSHB(par265,par294)
                *****
                The generalized plan takes the robot from one room into a second
                room, opens a door leading to a third room, takes the robot through
                the third room into a fourth room, and then pushes together two pairs
                of boxes.
                *****
Erase MACROP3.
Erase MACROP4.
                *****
                MACROP3 and MACROP4 are completely contained in MACROP5.
                *****
Set first additions row of MACROP5 to 4.
                *****
                The first two operators of MACROP5 match the sixth and seventh
                operators of MACROP5.
                *****
```

7.3. Further Experiments

In another set of experiments that were run with the new system, the primary goal was to produce long plans. We ran a sequence of eight problems in our robot environment that culminated in the production of a 19-operator plan for fetching three boxes from three different rooms and then-pushing the three boxes together. This final MACROP subsumed the seven earlier ones so that only one MACROP was retained by the system. Subsequences of the 19-step MACROP could be used to fetch boxes, push boxes together, move the robot from room to room, etc.

The experiments we have been discussing show the use of MACROPs during planning. We have also run experiments with PLANEX to illustrate the use of MACROPs during plan execution. One such experiment is documented in a report [4] and film [5] that illustrate how PLANEX monitors robot task execution in the seven-room experimental environment. One interesting sequence in this experiment involves the robot attempting to go from one room through a second room into a third room. After entering the second room, the robot discovers that a box is blocking the door that leads into the third room. Since PLANEX is working with a generalized plan, the difficulty can be overcome by finding a different instance of the plan's first kernel that is satisfied. This new instantiation of the plan's parameters causes the robot to be sent from the second room into a fourth room and then into the target third room.

8. Conclusions

We have presented in considerable detail methods by which a problem-solving program can "learn" old solutions and use them both to monitor real-world execution and to aid in the solution of new problems. We view these methods as representing only a preliminary excursion into an area that, in the long run, may hold high potential for the design of "intelligent" robots. Before such potential is realized, however, there are a number of substantial technical problems to be solved; in this final section we briefly point out a few of these.

8.1. Abstracting Preconditions

It is a commonplace observation that successful problem solvers (human or machine) must plan at a level of detail appropriate to the problem at hand. In typical problem-solving programs, the level of detail is set a priori by the experimenter when he carefully selects the representations employed. This situation changes when the problem solver can create its own MACROPS. Now we have the possibility of creating powerful macro operators whose specification is at the same level of detail as each component operator. In terms of our system, we may create a large triangle table whose preconditions (its first kernel) is the conjunction of so many literals that the theorem prover has little hope of success. What we need is a way of appropriately abstracting the preconditions of a MACROP so that only its "main" preconditions remain. A plan would first be attempted using these abstract preconditions; if successful, a subsequent planning process would fill in the details (and perhaps suggest changes to the abstract plan) as needed. As a rough example of the sort of process we have in mind, suppose we have a MACROP that requires the robot to travel through several doors. An abstract precondition for the MACROP might not contain the requirement that the doors be open on the supposition that, should they be closed, the robot could easily open them at the appropriate time. In whatever manner such a scheme is ultimately implemented, it seems clear that a problem solver will be able to increase its power with experience only if it can use this experience at an appropriate level of abstraction.

8.2. Saving MACROPS

We discussed previously a method for discarding a MACROP when it is subsumed by another, more powerful MACROP. In general, any system that learns plans must also either incorporate a mechanism for forgetting old plans or else face the danger of being swamped by an ever-increasing repertoire of stored plans. One straightforward approach to this problem would be to keep some statistics on the frequencies with which the various MACROPS are used, and discard those that fall below some threshold. We have not, however, experimented with any such mechanisms.

8.3. Other Forms of Learning

The generalization scheme discussed in this paper is but one of many possible forms of machine learning. Another form of learning that would be interesting to investigate involves reconciling predicted and observed behavior. Suppose, by way of example, that an operator *OP* is originally thought to add Clause *C* whenever it is applied, but suppose we notice that the action corresponding to *OP* consistently fails to add *C*. We would like the system to remedy this situation by taking one of three steps: drop *C* from the add list of *OP*, restrict the preconditions of *OP* to those (if any) that guarantee that *C* is added by the action, or change the actual action routine so that it does in fact behave as originally advertised. While we offer no algorithms for accomplishing these forms of learning, it is interesting to note that the problem itself arises only when we deal with real, as opposed to simulated, robot systems. It is the occurrence of problems of this sort that persuades us of the continuing interest and importance of robot problem solving.

REFERENCES

1. Fikes, R. E. and Nilsson, N. J. STRIPS: A new approach to the application of theorem proving to problem solving. *Artificial Intelligence* **2** (1971), 189–208.
2. Fikes, R. E. Monitored execution of robot plans produced by STRIPS. *Proc. IFIP Congress* 71, Ljubljana, Yugoslavia (August 23–28, 1971).
3. Garvey, T. D. and Kling, R. E. User's Guide to QA3.5 Question-Answering System. Technical Note 15, Artificial Intelligence Group, Stanford Research Institute, Menlo Park, California (December 1969).
4. Raphael, B. et al. Research and Applications—Artificial Intelligence. Final Report, Contract NASW-2164, Stanford Research Institute, Menlo Park, California (December 1971).
5. Hart, P. E. and Nilsson, N. J. Shakey: Experiments in Robot Planning and Learning. Film produced at Stanford Research Institute, Menlo Park, California (1972).
6. Ernst, G. and Newell, A. *GPS: A Case Study in Generality and Problem Solving*. ACM Monograph Series. Academic Press, New York, New York, 1969.

Achieving Several Goals Simultaneously*

Richard Waldinger

Artificial Intelligence Center
Stanford Research Institute

In the synthesis of a plan or computer program, the problem of achieving several goals simultaneously presents special difficulties, since a plan to achieve one goal may interfere with attaining the others. This paper develops the following strategy: to achieve two goals simultaneously, develop a plan to achieve one of them and then modify that plan to achieve the second as well. A systematic program modification technique is presented to support this strategy. The technique requires the introduction of a special "skeleton model" to represent a changing world that can accommodate modifications in the plan. This skeleton model also provides a novel approach to the "frame problem."

The strategy is illustrated by its application to three examples. Two examples involve synthesizing the following programs: interchanging the values of two variables and sorting three variables. The third entails formulating tricky blocks-world plans. The strategy has been implemented in a simple QLISP program.

It is argued that skeleton modelling is valuable as a planning technique apart from its use in plan modification, particularly because it facilitates the representation of "influential actions" whose effects may be far reaching.

The second part of the paper is a critical survey of contemporary planning literature, which compares our approach with other techniques for facing the same problems. The following is the outline of contents.

CONTENTS

INTRODUCTION

My feet want to dance in the sun
My head wants to rest in the shade
The Lord says "Go out and have fun!"
But the landlord says "Your rent ain't paid!"

E.Y. Harburg, *Finian's Rainbow*

It is often easier to achieve either of two goals than to achieve both at the same time. In the course of achieving the second goal we may undo the effects of achieving the first. Terry Winograd points out in a *Psychology Today* article (Winograd, 1974) that his blocks program

> cannot carry out the command, "Build a stack without touching any pyramids," because it has no way to work on one goal (building a stack) while keeping track of another one (avoiding contact with pyramids).

The reasoning subprograms of his natural language processor "have a sort of one-track mind unsuited to complicated tasks."

In program synthesis, such "simultaneous goal" problems are rampant. A

*The research reported herein was sponsored by the National Science Foundation under Grant GJ-36146.

typical example: the goal of a sort program is to rearrange an array in ascending order while ensuring at the same time that the resulting array is a permutation of the original. Simultaneous goal problems occur in mathematical equation solving, in robot tasks, and in real life as well.

An earlier paper (Manna and Waldinger, 1974) proposes a method for dealing with simultaneous goal problems in program synthesis. The present paper elaborates on the description of the method, reports on its implementation, discusses its application to general planning and robot problem solving, and points out some of its shortcomings and some projected improvements.

The general strategy proposed in (Manna and Waldinger, 1974) is: in order to construct a plan to achieve P and Q, construct a plan to achieve P, and then modify that plan to achieve Q as well. In the course of the modification, the relation P is "protected": no modifications that might make P false are permitted. If no satisfactory modification is found, the same strategy is attempted with the roles of P and Q reversed.

The earlier paper considers the construction of programs with branches and recursive loops; here, the discussion is strictly limited to the construction of straight-line programs. The simultaneous goal strategy can be integrated with the branch and loop formation techniques discussed in our earlier paper; however, this integration has not yet been implemented. Furthermore, the straight-line case is rich enough to be interesting in its own right.

The paper is divided into two main parts. Part 1 describes the simultaneous goal strategy in full detail, the program modification technique, and the modelling structure that the strategy requires. The strategy is illustrated by several examples, including the development of programs to interchange the values of two variables and to sort three variables, and the solution of the "anomaly" blocks-world problem from Sussman's (Sussman, 1973) thesis. These examples are not chosen to be impressive; they have been refined to present no difficulties other than the simultaneous goal problem itself.

Part 2 tries to relate this work to some other problem-solving efforts, and provides a critical survey of the way these systems represent a changing world in terms of the framework developed in Part 1. A summary of Part 2 appears in Section 2.9.

PART 1

SIMULTANEOUS GOALS, PROGRAM MODIFICATION, AND THE REPRESENTATION OF ACTIONS

1.1 A description of our approach

1.1.1 Achieving primitive goals

Below, the boarhound and the boar
Pursue their pattern as before
But reconciled among the stars.

T.S. Eliot, *Four Quartets*

Before we are ready to face multiple simultaneous goals, it may be helpful to say a few words about our approach to simple goals. Our system has a number of built-in techniques and knowledge of the kinds of goal to which each technique applies. When faced with a new goal, the system tries to determine if that goal is already true in its model of the world—if the goal is true it is already achieved. Otherwise, the system retrieves those techniques that seem applicable. Each of these techniques is attempted in turn until one of them is successful.

An important clue to the choice of technique is the form of the given goal. For instance, suppose we are working on blocks-world problems, and we are faced with the goal that block A be directly on top of block B. Assume that we have an arm that can move only one block at a time. Then we may build in the following strategy applicable to all goals of form, "Achieve: x is on y": clear the top of x and the top of y, and then put x on y. That x be clear is a new goal, which may already be true in the model, or which may need to be achieved itself (by moving some other block from the top of x to the table, say). "Put x on y" is a step in the plan we are developing. If we can successfully apply this technique, we have developed a plan to put A directly on top of B. However, for a variety of reasons this technique may fail, and then we will have to try another technique.

An example from the program synthesis domain: suppose our goal is to achieve that a variable X have some value b. One approach to goals of this form is to achieve that some other variable v has value b, and then execute the assignment statement $X \leftarrow v$.* Here again, the relation "v has value b" is a subgoal, which may already be true or which may need to be achieved by inserting some other instructions into the plan. The assignment statement $X \leftarrow v$ is an operation that this technique itself inserts into the plan. (Note that if we are not careful, this technique will be applicable to its own subgoal, perhaps resulting in an infinite computation.) Of course, there may be other techniques to achieve goals of form "X has value b"; if the original technique fails, the others are applied.

The practice of retrieving techniques according to the form of the goal and then trying them each in turn until one is successful is called "pattern-directed function invocation," after Hewitt (Hewitt, 1972). A problem solver organized around these principles can be aware of only one goal at a time: hence the single-mindedness that Winograd complains of. When given multiple simultaneous goals, we would like to be able to apply the techniques applicable to each goal and somehow combine the results into a single coherent plan that achieves all of them at once.

1.1.2 Goal regression

Change lays not her hand upon truth.

A.C. Swinburne, *Poems: Dedication*

---

*We use a lower case "v" but an upper case "X" because here, X is the name of a specific variable while v is a symbol that can be instantiated to represent any variable.

Our approach to simultaneous goals depends heavily on having an effective program modification technique. Our program modification technique in turn depends on knowing how our program instructions interact with the relations we use to specify the program's goals.

Suppose P is a relation and F is an action of program instruction; if P is true, and we execute F, then of course we have no guarantee that P will still be true. However, given P, it is always possible to find a relation P′ such that achieving P′ and then executing F guarantees that P will be true afterwards. For example, in a simple blocks world if P is "block C is clear" (meaning C has no blocks on top of it) and F is "Put block A on block B," then P′ is the relation "C is clear or A is on C": for if C is clear before putting A on B, then C will still be clear afterwards, while if A is on C before being put on B, then the action itself will clear the top of C.*

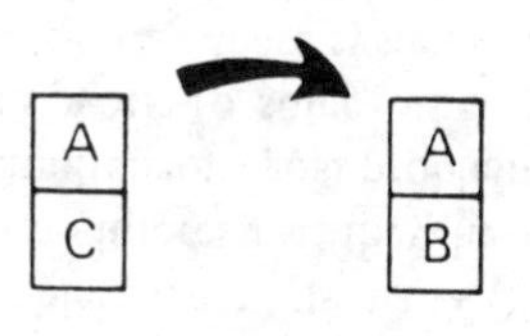

FIGURE 1

We will demand that P′ be the weakest relation that ensures the subsequent truth of P; in other words, if P′ is not true before executing F, P may not be true afterwards. Otherwise, we could always take P′ to be the relation that is always false. We will call P′ the result of passing P back over F, and we will call the operation of passing P back "regression."

Another example: suppose F is an assignment statement "X ← t" where X is a variable and t an expression, and let P be any relation between the values of the variables of our program, written P(X). Then P′ is P(t), the relation obtained by replacing X by t in P(X). For if P(t) is true before executing X ← t, then P(X) will certainly be true afterwards. For instance, if P(X) is "X=A*B," and F is "X ← U*V," then P′=P(U*V) is "U*V=A*B," for if U*V=A*B before executing X ← U*V, then X=A*B afterwards. Furthermore, if U*V=A*B is false before the assignment, then X=A*B will be false afterwards.

Note that if X does not occur in P(X), then P(t) is the same as P(X); the instruction has no effect on the truth of the relation.

Regression will play an important part in our program modification technique and also in the way we construct our models. The use of a static relational description to describe a dynamic program has been variously attributed to (Floyd, 1967), (Naur, 1966), (Turing, 1950), and (Goldstine and von Neumann, 1947), but the observation that it is technically simpler to look at the "weakest preconditions" of a relation (passing it back), as we do, instead of the "strongest postconditions" (passing it forward), appears to be due to (Manna, 1968), (Hoare, 1969), and (King, 1969). The term "weakest precondition" is Dijkstra's (1975); we will not use it because the word "precondition" has a different meaning in the artificial intelligence literature. All these authors apply the idea to proving the correctness of programs; (Manna, 1974) contains a survey of this application. We now go on to show how the idea applies to program modification as well.

*We assume that the blocks are all the same size, so that only one block can fit immediately on top of another.

1.1.3 Plan modification

It is a bad plan that admits of no modification.

Publilius Syrus, *Sententiae*

In order to achieve a goal of form P and Q, we construct a plan F that achieves P, and then modify F so that it achieves Q while still achieving P. The simplest way to modify F is to add new instructions to the end so as to achieve Q. This method is called a "linear theory plan" by Sussman (Sussman, 1973). However, this linear strategy may be flatly inadequate; for instance, executing the plan F may destroy objects or information necessary to achieve Q. Furthermore, even if Q can be achieved by some composite plan ⟨F:G⟩ (execute F, then execute G), how can we be sure that plan G will not cause P to be made false?

However, we may also modify F by adding new instructions to the beginning or middle, or by changing instructions that are already there. Let us assume that F is a linear sequence of instructions $\langle F_1,...,F_n\rangle$. As we have seen, in order to achieve Q after executing F, it suffices to achieve Q′ immediately before executing F_n, where Q′ is the result of passing Q back over F_n. Similarly, it suffices to achieve Q″ immediately before executing F_{n-1}, where Q″ is the result of passing Q′ back over F_{n-1}.

How can we benefit by passing a goal back over steps in the plan? A goal that is difficult or impossible to achieve after F has been executed may be easier to achieve at some earlier point in the plan. Furthermore, if achieving Q after executing F destroys the truth of P, it is possible that planning to achieve Q′ or Q″ earlier will not disturb P at all; a planner should be free to achieve Q in any of these ways.

How is the planner supposed to know how to pass a relation back over a given plan step? First of all, the information can be given explicitly, as one of a set of rules. These "regression rules," which can themselves be expressed as programs, are regarded as part of the definition of the plan step. Alternatively, if a relation is defined in terms of other relations, it may be possible to pass back those defining relations. Furthermore, if the plan step is defined in terms of simpler component plan steps, then knowing how to pass relations back over the components allows one to pass the relation back over the original plan step. Finally, if no information at all exists as to how to pass a relation back over a plan step, it is assumed that the plan step has absolutely no effect on the relation. This assumption makes it unnecessary to state a large number of rules, each saying that a certain action has no effect at all on a certain relation. Thus we avoid the so-called "frame problem" (cf. [McCarthy and Hayes, 1969]).

In modifying a program it is necessary to ensure that it still achieves the purpose for which it was originally intended. This task is performed by the protection mechanism we will now describe.

1.1.4 Protection

> Protection is not a principle, but an expedient.
>
> Disraeli, Speech

Our strategy for achieving two goals P and Q simultaneously requires that after developing a plan F that achieves P we modify F so that it achieves Q while still achieving P. This strategy requires that in the course of modifying F the system should remember that F was originally intended to achieve P and check that it still does. It does this by means of a device called the protection point: we attach P to the end of F as a comment. This comment has imperative force: no modifications are permitted in F that do not preserve the truth of P at the end of the modified plan. We will say that we are protecting P at the end of F. Any action that destroys the truth of P will be said to violate P. Relations may be protected at any point in a plan; if a relation is protected at a certain point, that relation must be true when control passes through that point.*

Protection has purposes other than ensuring that simultaneous goals do not interfere with each other: for instance, if an action requires that a certain conditon be true before it can be applied, we must protect that condition at the point before the action is taken to see that no modification in the plan can violate it.

In order to ensure that a modification cannot violate any of the protected relations, we check each of these relations to see that it is still true after the proposed modification has been made: otherwise, the modification must be retracted.

In the next section we will examine a very simple example involving two simultaneous goals in order to demonstrate the techniques we have described.

1.1.5 A very simple example

Suppose we have three blocks, A, B, and C, sitting on a table.

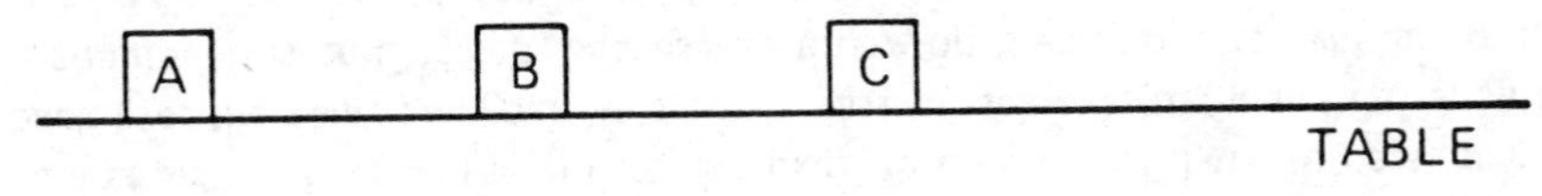

FIGURE 2

*(Sussman, 1973) was the first to use protection in program synthesis, and to apply it to the simultaneous goal problem.

Our goal is to make a tower of the three blocks, with A on top and C on the bottom.

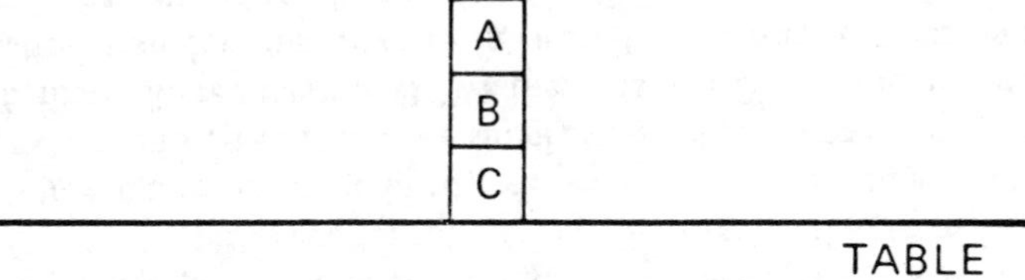

FIGURE 3

We express this goal as a conjunction of two goals. "A is on B" and "B is on C." (We'll forget about saying that C is on the table.) Of course, if we approach these goals in the reverse order we have no problem: we simply put B on top of C and then put A on top of B; no destructive interactions arise. However, if we approach them in the given order we run into a blind alley.

We first attempt to achieve that A is on top of B. In order to do this, we see if A and B are clear (they are), and then we plan to put A on top of B. We have thus planned to achieve our first goal. Because we will now work on another goal to be achieved simultaneously we protect the relation that A is on top of B. We will adopt a notation for representing plans under development in which the left-most column will represent the steps of the plan, the second column will represent the anticipated model or state of the world between the respective plan steps, and the third column will represent any goals that we have yet to achieve, and relations that have already been achieved but must be protected at that point. In this notation our plan so far is as follows:

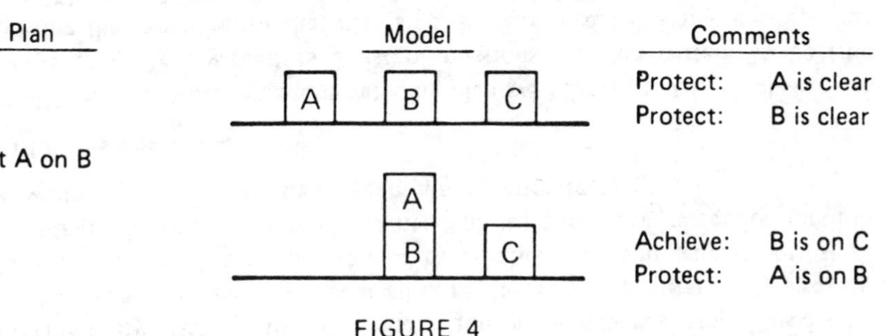

FIGURE 4

In order to put A on top of B we must be sure that A and B are both clear: therefore we have protected these two relations at the point before the action is applied. (Of course, the action itself violates one of the conditions afterwards: we merely want to ensure that the conditions will be true immediately before the action is applied, regardless of what modifications are made to the plan.) We put the goal "Achieve: B is on C" after the plan step and not before because we are initially attempting to achieve the goal by adding steps to the end of the plan and not the beginning.

Now, since our arm can lift only one block at a time, we will be forced to put A back on the table again in order to get B on top of C. This will violate our protected relation (A is on B) so we cannot hope to achieve our second goal by adding instructions to the end of the plan. But we can still try to pass the goal back over the plan. The goal "B is on C" passed back over the plan "Put A on B" is simply "B is on C" itself, because putting A on B will not alter whether or not B is on C. The plan state so far is as follows:

Plan	Comments	
	Achieve:	B is on C
	Protect:	A is clear
	Protect:	B is clear
Put A on B		
	Protect:	A is on B

FIGURE 5

The goal "Achieve: B is on C" now occurs before the plan step.

Our goal "B in on C" can now be achieved by simply putting B on C; the appropriate plan step will be added to the beginning of the plan instead of to the end. The resulting plan state is illustrated in Figure 6.

Plan	Comments	
	Protect:	B is clear
Put B on C	Protect:	C is clear
	Protect:	A is clear
	Protect:	B is clear
	Protect:	B is on C
	Protect:	A is on B

FIGURE 6

Note that the new plan step did not interfere with any of the protected relations: otherwise we would have had to retract the step and find some other solution. As it is, the two-step plan "Put B on C; Put A on B" achieves the desired goal. The method of passing goals back over plan steps has enabled us to avoid backing up and reversing the order in which the goals are approached. This technique will not always prevent such goal reordering; however, we will see that it will allow us to solve some problems that cannot readily be solved, regardless of the order in which the goals are attempted.

The reader may note that the model following the plan step "Put A on B" changes between Figure 5 and Figure 6, because of the insertion of the earlier plan step "Put B on C." It we maintained a model corresponding to each plan step, we would be faced with the task of updating the entire sequence of models following every insertion to reflect the action of the new plan step. This can be an arduous chore if the model is at all large. Instead we maintain only a scanty "skeleton" model that is not affected by an alteration, and generate or "flesh out" other portions of the model as needed, using the same regression method that we introduced earlier as a program modification technique.

1.1.6 Skeleton models

Following each step in the developing plan we have a model, which for our purposes may be regarded as a list of relations that are certain to be true following the execution of that plan step. For instance, following the step "Put A on B" we include in the model the relation "A is on B" and perhaps the relation "A is clear," meaning that no block is on top of A. However, we do not usually include any information about the location of B, for example, because, unless protected, the location of B can be changed by inserting new steps earlier in the plan.

Similarly, after an assignment statement $X \leftarrow t$ we do no generally include the fact that X has value 2 even if we believe that t has value 2 before the statement is executed, because subsequent modifications to the beginning of the program could change the value of t, unless that value is protected. In fact, the model following an assignment statement may be absolutely empty.

In addition to the models that follow each statement in the plan, we have an initial model that describes that situation at the beginning (as given by the problem statement), and we have a global model of the "eternal verities," relations such as x=x, that are unchanged by any action or the passage of time. Information in the global model is implicitly present in all the other models.

The models that follow each action in the plan are incomplete: much knowledge about the situation is not included explicitly. How are we to compensate for this deficiency?

Suppose that we are given a plan $F_1,...,F_n$, and we need to know whether some relation Q is true after execution of step F_i. We first see if Q is explicitly in the model following F_i; in other words, we see if Q is an immediate consequence of the execution of F_1. If not, we simply pass Q back over the plan step F_i, yielding a perhaps altered relation Q'. We then check if Q' is in the preceding model. The justification for this measure is clear: Q' has been defined as the relation that must be true before the execution of F_i in order that Q will be true afterwards.

If we fail to determine if Q' is true, we pass Q' back over F_{i-1} and repeat the process until we have passed Q all the way back to the intitial model. If we are still unable to determine whether Q is true we must give up. Even if we determine that Q is true, we must generally resist the temptation to add it to the model that follows F_i: unless Q is protected, later plan alterations could make Q false, and then the model would be inaccurate.

An example: suppose we are given a model in which block A is on C, but blocks A and B both have a clear top.

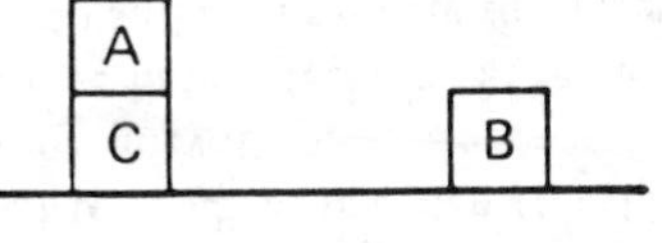

FIGURE 7

We somehow develop the plan step "Put A on B," and we are led to inquire if C is clear. We cannot determine this from the model that follows "Put A on B," because that model only contains the relations "A is on B" and "A is clear." However, we can pass that relation back over the plan step using a regression rule (as described in Section 1.1.2), leading us to ask if "C is clear or A is on C." Since we know "A is on C" initially, we can conclude "C is clear" in the model following the plan step.

The skeleton model is a technique in which the partial plan that has been constructed is regarded as a central part of the model. Important relationships and the plan itself are in the model explicitly; other relationships may be inferred using the regression rules.

It is traditional in problem solving to distinguish between rules that work backwards from the goal and rules that work forwards from the present state of the world. In Hewitt's (Hewitt, 1972) terminology, these rules are called "consequent theorems" and "antecedent theorems" respectively. Regression rules are a special kind of consequent theorem that can refer explicitly to steps in the plan as well as relations in the model. (Kowalski, 1974) and (Warren, 1974) also discuss the application of regression rules as a modelling technique.

The use of skeleton models means that if a relation P is protected at the end of a plan, no modification can be made at any point in the plan that will not leave P true at the end, because, in checking the truth of P after the modification has been made, we will percolate P back up through the plan, and the unfortunate interaction between P and the new plan step will be discovered.

For instance, suppose a plan step $X \leftarrow Y$ achieves a protected relation P(X), and a new instruction $Y \leftarrow Z$ is inserted at the beginning of the plan, where P(Z) is false. We will try to check that the protected relation P(X) is still true at the end of the modified program. Using regression, we will therefore check if P(Y) is true in the middle of the program, and thus that P(Z) is true at the beginning. Since P(Z) is false, we will detect a protection violation and reject the proposed modification.

This mechanism means that it is necessary to protect a relation only at the point at which we need it to be true. In the previous example, we must protect P(X) after the assignment statement $X \leftarrow Y$, but we need not protect P(Y) before the statement; the latter protection is implicit in the former.

A description of how skeleton models can be implemented using the "context" mechanism of the new artificial intelligence programming languages occurs in Section 2.7.

We have concluded the general description of our approach to simultaneous goals. The balance of Part 1 concerns how this technique has been applied to specific subject domains in order to solve the sample problems.

1.2 Interchanging the values of two variables

1.2.1 Relations that refer to variables

So first, your memory I'll jog,
And say: A CAT IS NOT A DOG.

T.S. Eliot, *Old Possum's Book of Practical Cats*

In the next section we will show the synthesis of a more complex program whose specification is represented as a set of simultaneous goals. The subject domain of this program will be variables and their values. However, we must first examine a certain kind of relation more closely: the relation that refers directly to the variable itself, as opposed to its value. For instance, the relation "variable X has value a," written "X:a," refers both to the variable X and its value a. The relations "variable X is identical to variable Y," written "$X \approx Y$," and its negation "variable X is distinct from variable Y," written "$X \not\approx Y$" refer to variables X and Y, but do not refer at all to their values. $X \not\approx Y$ means "X and Y are not identical," and is true regardless of whether X and Y have the same value. Relations such as $\approx$, which do not refer to values at all, are not affected by assignment statements or any program instructions we are going to consider. Relations such as ":" are more complicated. For instance, the relation X:a passed back over the assignment statement $X \leftarrow Y$ yields Y:a, where X and Y are both variables. (A more general rule covers the case in which an arbitrary term plays the role of the variable Y, but we will have no need to consider this case in the following examples.) A more complex situation arises if the variable in the relation is existentially quantified. Such a situation arises if the relation is a goal to find a variable with a certain value. For instance, how do we pass back a goal such as "Find a variable v such that v:a" over the instruction $X \leftarrow Y$? If there is a variable v such that v:a before the assignment statement is executed, and if that variable is distinct from X, then certainly v:a after the execution of $X \leftarrow Y$. Furthermore, if Y:a before the execution, then v can be identical to X as well. Therefore, passing the goal "Find a variable v such that v:a" back over the assignment statement $X \leftarrow Y$ yields

"Find a variable v such that

$v \not\approx X$ and v:a

or $v \approx X$ and Y:a."

We will assume the system knows verities such as $x \approx x$, $X \not\approx Y$, or $X \not\approx Z$. In the example of the next section we will use one additional fact about the relation $\not\approx$: the fact that we can always invent a new variable. In particular, we will assume we can find a variable v such that $v \not\approx X$ by taking v to be the value of a program GENSYM that invents a new symbol every time it is called.

There is, of course, much more to be said about these peculiar relations that refer to variables themselves. They do not follow the usual Floyd-Naur-Manna-King-Hoare rule for the assignment statement. However, the discussion in this section will be enough to carry us through our next example.

1.2.2 The solution to the two variable problem*

But above and beyond there's still one name left over,
And that is the name that you never will guess
The name that no human research can discover–
But THE CAT HIMSELF KNOWS, and will never confess.

T.S. Eliot, *Old Possum's Book of Practical Cats*

The problem of exchanging the values of two variables is a common beginner's programming example. It is difficult because it requires the use of a "temporary" variable for storage. Part of the interest of this synthesis involves the system itself originating the idea of using a generated variable for temporary storage.

We are given two variables X and Y, whose initial values are a and b; in other words, X:a and Y:b. Our goal is to produce a program that achieves X:b and Y:a simultaneously.

Recall that our strategy when faced with a goal P and Q is to try to form a plan to achieve P, and then to modify that plan to achieve Q as well. Thus our first step is to form a plan to achieve X:b.

For a goal of form X:b we have a technique (Section 1.1.1) that tells us to find a variable v such that v:b and then execute the assignment statement $X \leftarrow v$. We have such a v, namely Y. Therefore, we develop a plan, $X \leftarrow Y$, that achieves X:b. We must now modify this plan to achieve Y:a while protecting the relation X:b that the plan was developed to achieve. In our tabular notation:

Plan	Model	Comments
	X:a Y:b	
$X \leftarrow Y$		Achieve: Y:a
	X:b Y:b	Protect: X:b

FIGURE 8

(In our table we record the full model at each stage even though the implementation does not store this model explicitly.

In trying to achieve Y:a we attempt to find a variable v such that v:a. Once we have executed $X \leftarrow Y$, no such variable exists. However, we pass the goal "Find v such that v:a" back over the plan step $X \leftarrow Y$, yielding

Find v such that

$v \not\approx X$ and v:a

or $v \approx X$ and Y:a,

as explained in the preceding section. We now attempt to achieve this goal at the beginning of the plan. In tabular form

Plan	Model	Comments
	X:a Y:b	Achieve: Find v such that $v \not\approx X$ and v:a or $v \approx X$ and Y:a
$X \leftarrow Y$		
	X:b Y:b	Protect: X:b

FIGURE 9

Once the outstanding goal is achieved, we will add an assignment statement $Y \leftarrow v$ to the end of the program, where v is the variable that achieves the goal.

If we work on the goals in the given order, we try to find a v such that $v \not\approx X$. Here we know that GENSYM will give us a new variable name, say G_1, guaranteed to be distinct from X. Our problem is now to achieve the first conjunct, namely G_1:a. But this can easily be achieved by inserting the assignment statement $G_1 \leftarrow X$ at the beginning of the plan, since X:a initially. Inserting this instruction does not disturb our protected relation.

We have been trying to find a v satisfying the disjunction

$v \not\approx X$ and v:a

or $v \approx X$ and Y:a

We have satisfied the first disjunct, and therefore we can ignore the second. (We

*Another way of approaching this problem is discussed in (Green *et al.*, 1974). Green's system has the concept of temporary variable built in. He uses a convention of inserting a comment whenever information is destroyed, so that a patch can be inserted later in case the destroyed information turns out to be important.

will consider later what happens if we reverse the order in which we approach some of the subgoals.)

We have thus managed to find a v such that v:a at the end of the program, namely $v \approx G_1$. Since our ultimate purpose in finding such a v was to achieve Y:a, we append to our program the assignment statement $Y \leftarrow G_1$. This addition violates no protected relations, and achieves the last of the extant goals. The final program is thus

Plan	Model	Comments
	X:a Y:b	
$G_1 \leftarrow X$		
	X:a Y:b G_1:a	
$X \leftarrow Y$		
	X:b Y:b G_1:a	
$Y \leftarrow G_1$		
		Protect: Y:a
	X:b Y:a G_1:a	Protect: X:b

FIGURE 10

The program has "invented" the concept of "temporary variable" by combining two pieces of already existing knowledge: the fact that GENSYM produces a variable distinct from any given variable, and the rule for passing a goal "Find a v such that v:a" back over an assignment statement. Of course, we could have built in the temporary variable concept itself, and then the solution would have been found more easily. But in this case the invention process is of more interest than the task itself.

Notice that at no point in the construction did we violate a protected relation. This is because of the fortunate order in which we have approached our subgoals. For example, if we had chosen to work on the disjunct

$$v \approx X \text{ and } Y{:}a$$

instead of

$$v \not\approx X \text{ and } v{:}a,$$

we would have inserted the assignment statement $Y \leftarrow X$ at the beginning of the program in order to achieve Y:a, and we would have proposed the program

```
Y ← X
X ← Y
Y ← X
```

which violates the protected relation X:b. Other alternative choices in this synthesis are either successful or terminated with equal dispatch.

1.3 Sorting three variables*

1.3.1 Sorting two variables

In our next example we will see how to construct a program to sort the values of three variables. This program will use as a primitive the instruction sort2, which sorts the values of two variables. Before we can proceed with the example, therefore, we must consider how to pass a relation back over the instruction sort2.

Executing sort2(X Y) will leave X and Y unchanged if X is less than or equal to Y ($X \leqslant Y$), but will interchange the values of X and Y otherwise. Let P(X Y) be any relation between the values of X and Y. We must construct a relation P′(X Y) such that if P′(X Y) is true before sorting X and Y, P(X Y) will be true afterwards. Clearly, if $X \leqslant Y$, it suffices to know that P(X Y) itself is true before sorting, because the sorting operation will not change the values. On the other hand, if $Y < X$ it suffices to know P(Y X), the expression derived from P(X Y) by exchanging X and Y, because the values of X and Y will be interchanged by the sorting. Therefore, the relation P′(X Y) is the conjunction

$$\begin{aligned} &\text{if } X \leqslant Y \text{ then } P(X\ Y) \\ \text{and } &\text{if } Y < X \text{ then } P(Y\ X) \end{aligned}$$

A similar argument shows that the above P′ is as weak as possible. The same line of reasoning applies even if X or Y does not actually occur in P. For instance, if X does not occur, P(Y X) is simply P(X Y) with Y replaced by X.

Given the appropriate definition of sort2, it is straightforward to derive the above relation mechanically (e.g., see [Manna, 1974]). However, that would require the system to know about conditional expressions, and we do not wish to discuss those statements here. For our purposes, it suffices to assume that the system knows explicitly how to pass a relation back over a sort2 instruction.

1.3.2 Achieving an implication

We have excluded the use of conditionals in the programs we construct. However, we cannot afford to exclude the goals of form "if P then Q" from the specifications for the program being constructed. For instance, such specifications can be introduced by passing any relation back over a sort2 instruction.

*This problem is also discussed in (Green, *et al.*, 1974). Green allows the use of program branches and the program he derives has the form of a nested conditional statement. Green's use of the case analysis avoids any protection violations in his solution: the interaction between the subgoals plays a much lesser role in Green's formulation of the problem. Some other work in the synthesis of sort programs (see [Green and Barstow, 1975], [Darlington, 1975]) does not consider "in-place" sorts at all; goal interactions are still important, but protection issues of the type we are considering do not arise. However, Darlington's concept of "pushing in" a function is the analogue of regression for programs in which nested functional terms play the role of sequential program instructions.

The form of these specifications suggests that the forbidden conditional expression be used in achieving them. Therefore, for purposes of this example we will introduce a particularly simple-minded strategy: to achieve a goal of form "if P then Q," first test if P is known to be false: if so, the goal is already achieved. Otherwise, assume P is true and attempt to achieve Q.

The strategy is simple-minded because it does not allow the program being constructed to itself test whether P is true; a more sophisticated strategy would produce a conditional expression, and the resulting program would be more efficient. However, the simple strategy will carry us through our next example.

1.3.3 The solution to the three-sort problem

Given three variables, X, Y, and Z, we want to rearrange their values so that $X \leq Y$ and $Y \leq Z$. Either of these goals can be achieved independently, by executing sort2(X Y) or sort2(Y Z) respectively. However, the simple linear strategy of concatenating these two instructions does not work; the program

sort2(X Y)
sort2(Y Z)

will not sort X, Y, and Z if Z is initially the smallest of the three. On the other hand, the simultaneous goal strategy we have introduced does work in a straightforward way.

In order to apply our strategy, we first achieve one of our goals, say $X \leq Y$, using the primitive instruction sort2(X Y). We then try to modify our program to achieve $Y \leq Z$ as well. In modifying the program we protect the relation $X \leq Y$. In tabular form, the situation is as follows:

Plan	Model	Comments
sort2(X Y)		
		Achieve: $Y \leq Z$
	$X \leq Y$	Protect: $X \leq Y$

FIGURE 11

As we have pointed out, simply appending a plan step sort2(Y Z) will violate the protected relation $X \leq Y$. Therefore we pass the goal back to see if we can achieve it at an earlier stage. The regressed relation, as explained in the previous section, is

if $X \leq Y$ then $Y \leq Z$
and if $Y < X$ then $X \leq Z$.

(This relation effectively states that Z is the largest of the three numbers.) Our situation therefore is as follows:

Plan	Model	Comments
		Achieve: if $X \leq Y$ then $Y \leq Z$ and if $Y < X$ then $X \leq Z$
sort2(X Y)		
	$X \leq Y$	Protect: $X \leq Y$

FIGURE 12

We must now try to achieve the remaining goal. This goal is itself a conjunction and is handled by the simultaneous goal strategy. The first conjunct, "if $X \leq Y$ then $Y \leq Z$," is an implication. Therefore we first test to see if $X \leq Y$ might be known to be false, in which case the implication would be true. However, nothing is known about whether $X \leq Y$, so we assume it to be true and resign ourselves to achieving the consequent $Y \leq Z$: this can easily be done using the primitive instruction sort2(Y Z). Inserting this instruction at the beginning of the plan does not interfere with the protected relation $X \leq Y$: the protection point is immediately preceded by the instruction sort2(X Y). Our situation is therefore as follows:

Plan	Model	Comments
sort2(Y Z)		
		Achieve: if $Y < X$ then $X \leq Z$
	$Y \leq Z$	Protect: if $X \leq Y$ then $Y \leq Z$
sort2(X Y)		
	$X \leq Y$	Protect: $X \leq Y$

FIGURE 13

(Notice that we do not reproduce the complete model for this example, but only include the skeleton model.)

We have achieved the goal "if $X \leq Y$ then $Y \leq Z$," which is one of two simultaneous goals. We therefore protect the relation we have just achieved and attempt to modify the program to achieve the remaining goal, "if $Y < X$ then $X \leq Z$." Again, we cannot disprove $Y < X$ and therefore we attempt to achieve the consequent, $X \leq Z$. This goal can be achieved immediately by executing sort2(X Z), but we must check that none of the protected relations is disturbed. Our situation is

Plan	Model	Comments
sort2(Y Z)		
	$Y \leq Z$	
sort2(X Z)		
	$X \leq Z$	Protect: if $X \leq Y$ then $Y \leq Z$
sort2(X Y)		
	$X \leq Y$	Protect: $X \leq Y$

FIGURE 14

The second protected relation $X \leqslant Y$ is still preserved: the first presents us with a bit more difficulty, but is in fact true: a human might notice that Z is the largest of the three numbers at this point. Perhaps it is worth explaining how the system verifies this protected relation, thereby illustrating the use of the skeleton model.

After executing the second instruction sort2(X Z), the only information in skeleton model is that $X \leqslant Z$. This is not enough to establish that the protected relation is undisturbed. The system therefore passes the relation back to an earlier model and tries to prove it there. The regressed relation is

$$\begin{aligned} &\text{if } X \leqslant Z \text{ then (if } X \leqslant Y \text{ then } Y \leqslant Z) \\ \text{and } &\text{if } Z < X \text{ then (if } Z \leqslant Y \text{ then } Y \leqslant X). \end{aligned}$$

The earlier model tells us that $Y \leqslant Z$ [because we have just executed sort2(Y Z)]. The first conjunct is thus easy to prove: the conclusion $Y \leqslant Z$ is known explicitly by the model. The second conjunct follows from transitivity: since we know $Y \leqslant Z$ from the model and $Z < X$ from the hypothesis we can conclude that $Y \leqslant X$. (This sort of reasoning is performed by a mechansim described in [Waldinger and Levitt, 1974]). The program in Figure 14 is therefore correct as it stands (although additional relationships should be protected if the plan is to undergo further modification).

It is pleasing that this last bit of deduction was not noticed by Manna and Waldinger in preparing the 1974 paper, but was an original discovery of the program, which was implemented afterwards. Manna and Waldinger assumed the protected relation would be violated and went through a somewhat longer process to arrive at an equivalent program. This is one of those not-so-rare cases in which a program debugs its programmer.

In order to show how these ideas apply to robot-type problems we discuss one further example, Sussman's "anomaly," in the next section.

1.4 The Sussman "anomaly"

We include this problem because it has received a good deal of attention in the robot planning literature (e.g., [Sussman, 1973; Warren, 1974; Tate, 1974; Hewitt, 1975; Sacerdoti, 1975]). However, for reasons that we will explore in Part 2, the solution does not exercise the capabilities of the system as fully as the previous two examples. We are given three blocks in the following configuration:

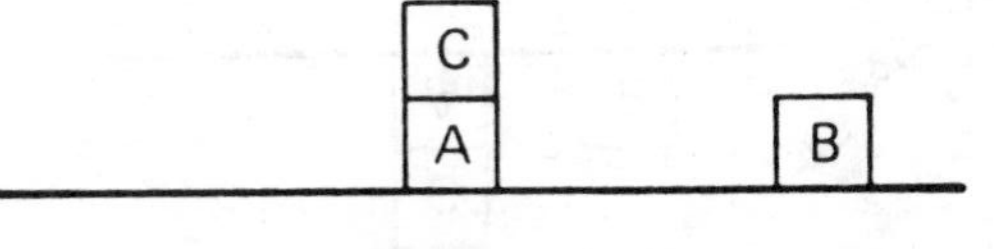

FIGURE 15

We are asked to rearrange them into this configuration:*

FIGURE 16

The goal is thus a simple conjunction "A is on B and B is on C." (We will forget about the table.)

The anomaly is one of the simplest blocks-world problems for which the linear strategy does not work regardless of the order in which we approach the subgoals: if we clear A and put A on B we cannot put B on C without removing A:

FIGURE 17

(Remember the arm can lift only one block at a time.)

On the other hand, if we put B on C first, we have buried A and cannot put it on top of B without disturbing the other blocks:

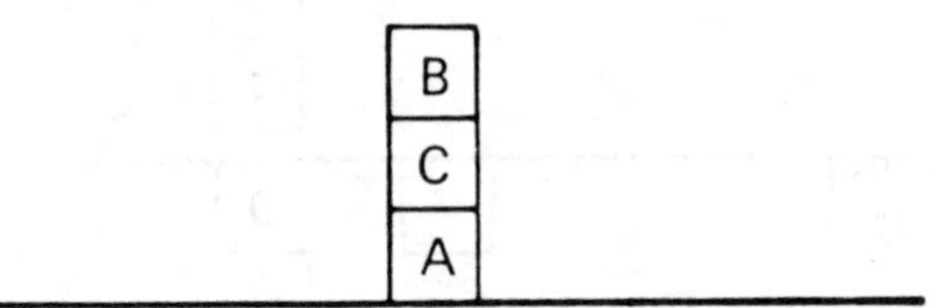

FIGURE 18

Our technique can solve this problem regardless of the order in which it attacks the goals. We will consider just one of these orderings: Assume we attempt to achieve "A is on B." The system will generate subgoals to clear A and B. B is already clear, and A will be cleared by putting C on the table. Then A will be put on B. This much can be done by the elementary strategy for achieving the "on" relationship (Section 1.1.1). Our situation is as follows:

*This problem was proposed by Allan Brown. Perhaps many children thought of it earlier but did not recognize that it was hard.

Plan	Comments
	Protect: C is clear
Put C on TABLE	
	Protect: A is clear Protect: B is clear
Put A on B	
	Achieve: B is on C Protect: A is on B

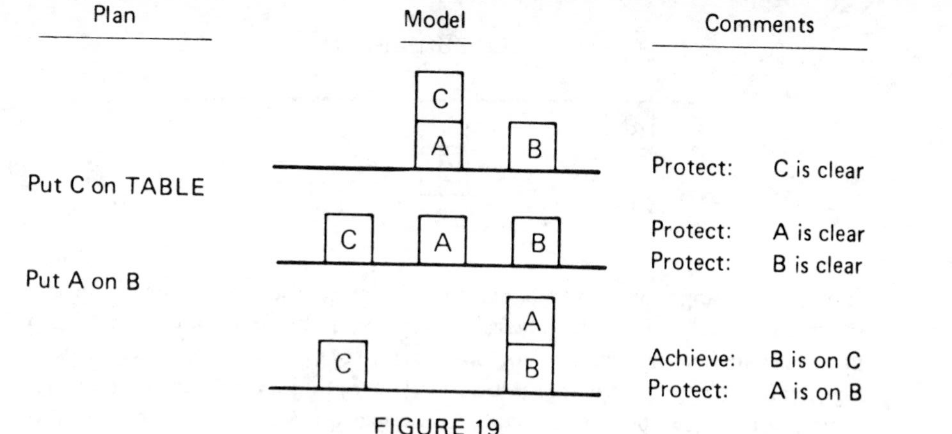

FIGURE 19

We protect "A is on B" because we want to modify the plan to achieve "B is on C" while still achieving "A is on B." We protect "A is clear" and "B is clear" earlier in order to make sure that the operation "Put A on B" will still be legal after the modifications are made.

Now, we have seen that we cannot achieve "B is on C" by adding new steps to the end of the plan without disturbing the protected relation "A is on B." Therefore we again pass the goal back to an earlier stage in the plan, hoping to achieve it before the protected relationship is established.

Passing "B is on C" back over the plan step "Put A on B" yields "B is on C" itself: whether B is on C or not is unaffected by putting A on B. The situation is thus:

Plan	Comments
	Protect: C is clear
Put C on TABLE	
	Achieve: B is on C Protect: A is clear Protect: B is clear
Put A on B	
	Protect: A is on B

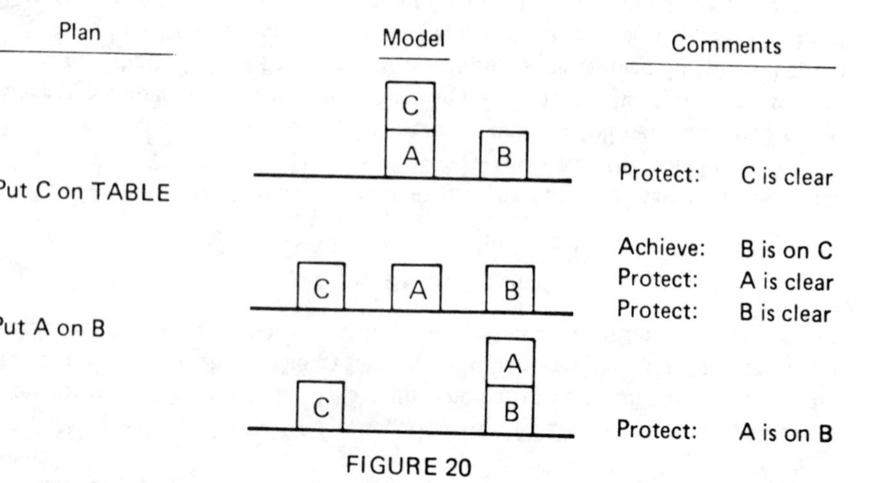

FIGURE 20

The goal "B is on C" can be easily achieved at the earlier stage: B and C are both clear, so we can simply put B on C. Furthermore this operation does not violate any of the protected relations. Since all goals have been achieved, our final plan is as follows:

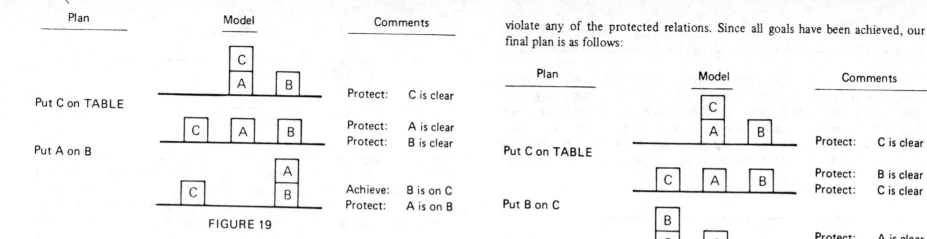

Plan	Model	Comments
	C on A; B	Protect: C is clear
Put C on TABLE		
	C; A; B	Protect: B is clear Protect: C is clear
Put B on C		
	B on C; A	Protect: A is clear Protect: B is clear
Put A on B		
	A on B on C	Protect: A is on B Protect: B is on C

FIGURE 21

The solution is similar if the order in which the goals are attempted is reversed.

This completes the last of our examples. In the next section we discuss some of the limitations of this approach, and consider how they might be transcended.

1.5 Limitations and next steps

> Odin. . .of all powers mightiest far art thou
> Lord over men of Earth, and Gods in heaven,
> Yet even from thee thyself hath been withheld.
> One thing: to undo what thou thyself hast ruled.
>
> Matthew Arnold, *Balder Dead*

The policy maintained by our implementation is to allow no protection violations at all: if a proposed modification causes a violation, that modification is rejected. This policy is a bit rigid and can sometimes inhibit the search for a solution.

For instance, consider the blocks problem in which initially the blocks are as follows:

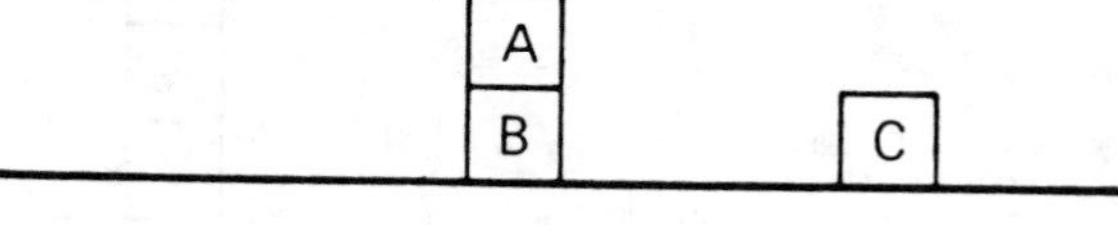

FIGURE 22

and in which the goal is to construct the following stack:

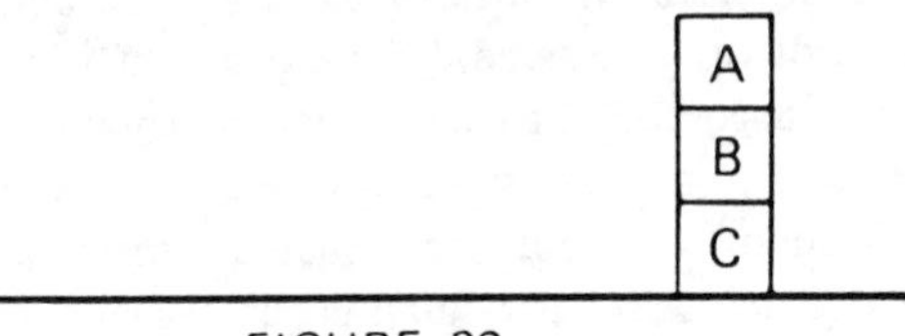

FIGURE 23

The goal may be considered to be the conjunction of two goals, "A is on B" and "B is on C." If these goals are approached in the reverse order, the system has no problem: it clears B by putting A on the table, puts B on C and then puts A on B. However, if the system approaches the goals in the given order, it will attempt to achieve "A is on B" first. This relation is already true, so the system protects it while trying to achieve the goal "B is on C." Here the system is baffled: it cannot put B on C without clearing B, thereby violating the protected relation. Passing the goal backwards into the plan is of no use: there are no plan steps to back it over. Clearly we would like to relax the restriction against protection violation until B is safely on C, and then reachieve the relation "A is on B," but our policy does not permit such a maneuver. The system is forced to reorder the goals in order to find a solution.

The restriction against violating protected relations also lengthens the search in generating the program to sort three variables. If these violations were permitted, a correct program

sort2(X Y)
sort2(Y Z)
sort2(X Y)

could be constructed without the use of regression at all. Why not permit violations, under the condition that a "contract" is maintained to reachieve protected relations that have been violated?

Indeed, such a strategy is quite natural, but we have two objections to it. First, suppose in the course of reachieving one protected relation we violate another. Are we to reachieve that relation later as well, and so on, perhaps ad infinitum? For example, in searching for a plan to reverse the contents of two variables it is possible to generate the infinite sequence of plans

$X \leftarrow Y,$

$Y \leftarrow X$
$X \leftarrow Y,$

$X \leftarrow Y$
$Y \leftarrow X$
$X \leftarrow Y,$

$Y \leftarrow X$
$X \leftarrow Y$
$Y \leftarrow X$
$X \leftarrow Y, \ldots$

Each plan corrects a protection violation perpetrated by the previous plan—but commits an equally heinous violation itself. (This objection is a bit naive: one could invent safeguards against such aberrations, as has been done by Sussman (Sussman, 1973) and Green et al. (Green et al., 1974).

The second objection: allowing temporary protection violations can result in inefficient plans. For example, we could generate the following plan for solving the Sussman anomaly:

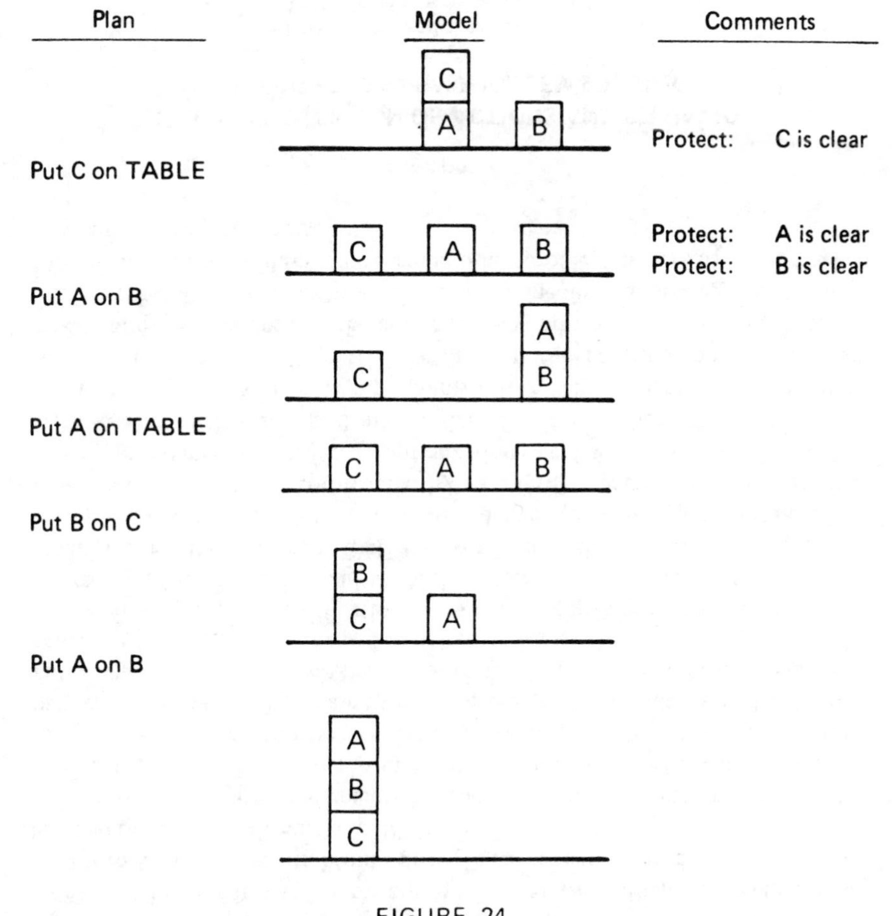

FIGURE 24

This plan is correct but inefficient: We have put A on B only to put A back on the table again because a protection violation was temporarily admitted. In a similar way, Sussman's HACKER produces an equally inefficient plan, approaching the goals in the opposite order. Of course, the plans could later be optimized, but allowing protection violations seems to encourage inefficiency in the plan produced.

Nevertheless, we feel that permitting temporary protection violations in a controlled way is a natural strategy that may be admitted in future versions of the program.

A more serious limitation of our implementation is that the only way it can modify plans is by adding new instructions, never by changing instructions that are already there. For example, suppose we have the initial configuration

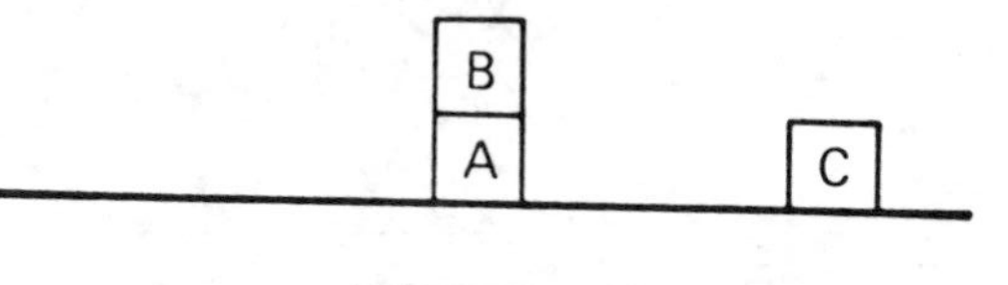

FIGURE 25

and our goal is to construct the stack

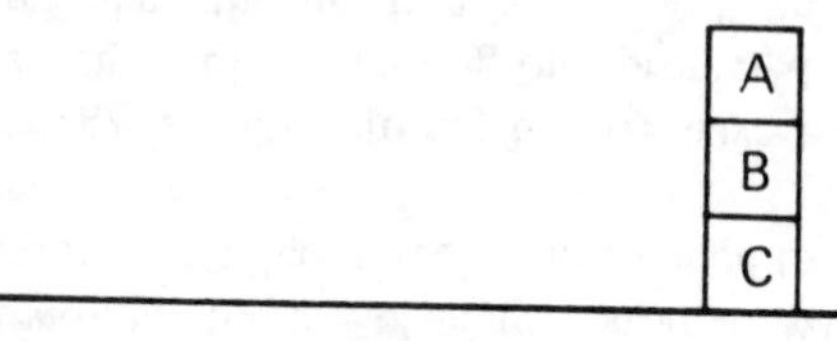

FIGURE 26

Assuming we approach the goal "A is on B" first, we are quite likely to put B on the table and then put A on B. In modifying the plan to achieve "B is on C," it would be clever to plan to put B on C instead of the table, but this sort of modification is beyong the system's capabilities. The "formal object" approach of Sussman (Sussman, 1973) would handle this properly: there, the decision about where to put B (in clearing A) would be deferred until we attempted the second goal "B is on C." However, other sorts of modifications require achieving the same goals in entirely different ways in order to accomodate the demands of the additional specification. Certain protected relations might never be achieved at all in the modified program if the higher level goal that constituted the "purpose" of the protected subgoal could be achieved in some other way. To effect such modifications will require that in the course of modifying a program we retain some of the goal-subgoal hierarchy that caused the original program to be constructed. Such modifications are in the spirit of our approach, but beyond the capabilities of our simple implementation.

The plans we have constructed in our paper are "straight-line" programs; they involve no loops or branches. The system as it exists contains a subsystem for constructing programs with branches and recursive loops (cf. [Manna and Waldinger, 1974]); however, these programs are free of side effects. Since the mechanisms for loop branch construction have not been integrated with the system that constructs structure-altering programs of the sort we have discussed in this paper. Nevertheless, these mechanisms are entirely consistent, and we intend to unite them. Our hand simulations indicate that the system will then be able to construct a variety of array-sorting routines.

The use of goal regression for these more complex programs has been studied by many as a way of proving programs correct. Passing relations back into branches is straightforward (Floyd, 1967, Hoare 1969); passing a relation back into a loop, on the other hand, may require ingenuity to generalize the relation. This problem is discussed by (Katz and Manna, 1973; Wegbreit, 1974; Boyer and Moore, 1973; Moore, 1975) and others, but it is by no means "solved."

All the loops constructed by our synthesizer will initially be recursive: we intend to introduce iteration only during a subsequent optimization phase, following (Darlington and Burstall, 1973).

The way we have implemented skeleton modelling may be remarkably inefficient, particularly if the plan being constructed is to have many steps. It may take a long time to pass a relation back so far, and the transformed relation may grow alarmingly. There are many ways one might consider to make skeleton modelling more efficient. We prefer not to speculate on which of these ways will actually help until we have tried to implement some of them.

We regard program modification as a valuable synthesis technique apart from its role in achieving goals simultaneously. Often we can construct a program by modifying another program that achieves a goal that is somehow similar or analogous. For instance, in (Manna and Waldinger, 1974) we show how a unification algorithm could be constructed by modifying a pattern matcher. Another sort of program modification is optimization: here we try to modify the program to achieve the same goal more efficiently. It is our hope that systems with the ability to modify their own programs will be able to adapt to new situations without needing to be "general." Before that can happen, however, program modification techniques must be developed beyond what has been done here.

This concludes our discussion of the simultaneous goal strategy. In the next part of this paper we discuss how some other problem solvers have approached some of the same problems.

PART 2

THE REPRESENTATION OF ACTIONS AND SITUATIONS IN CONTEMPORARY PROBLEM SOLVING

Time present and time past
Are both perhaps present in time future,
And time future contained in time past.
If all time is eternally present
All time is unredeemable.

T.S. Eliot, *Four Quartets*

In the rest of this paper we will examine a number of problem-solving systems, asking the same question of each system: how are actions and their effects on the world represented? Thus we will not emphasize simultaneous goals in this section, and in discussing a system we will often ignore the very facets that make it unusual. Many of these systems approach problems of far greater complexity than those we have addressed in Part 2, problems involved in manipulating many more objects, and more complex structures. When we compare our approach to theirs, please bear in mind that our implementation has not been extended to handle the problems that our hand simulation dispatches with such ease.

2.1 The classical problem solvers

In the General Problem Solver (GPS) (see [Newell, Shaw, and Simon, 1960]), the various states of the world were completely independent. For each state, GPS had to construct a new model: no information from one state was assumed to carry through to the next automatically, and it was the responsibility of each "operator" (the description of an action) to tell how to construct a new model. The form of the states themselves was not dictated by GPS and varied from one domain to another.

The resolution-based problem solvers (e.g., [Green, 1969; Waldinger and Lee, 1969]) maintained the GPS convention that every action was assumed capable of destroying any relation: in other words it was necessary to state explicitly such observations as that turning on a light switch does not alter the location of any of the objects in a room. To supply a large number of these facts (often called "frame axioms") was tedious, and they tended to distract the problem solver as well. Since most actions leave most of the world unchanged, we want our representation of the world to be biased to expect actions not to affect most existing relations. For a number of reasons we demand that these "obvious" facts be submerged in the representation, so that we (and our system) can focus our attention on the important things, the things that change.

The STRIPS problem solver (Fikes and Nilsson, 1971) was introduced to overcome these obstacles. In order to eliminate the frame axioms, STRIPS adopted the assumption that a given relation is left unchanged by an action unless it is explicitly mentioned in the "addlist" or the "deletelist" of the action: relations in the addlist are always true after the action is performed, while relations in the deletelist are not assumed to be true afterwards even if they were true before. Thus the frame axioms are assumed implictly for every action and relation unless the relation is included in the addlist or deletelist of the action. For instance, a (robot) action "go from A to B" might have "the robot is at B" in its addlist and "the robot is at A" in its deletelist. A relation such as "box C is in room 1" would be assumed to be unaffected by the action because it is not mentioned in either the addlist or the deletelist of the operator.

Henceforth, we shall refer to the belief that an action leaves all the relations in the model unchanged, unless specified otherwise, as the "STRIPS assumption."

A STRIPS model of a world situation, like a STRIPS operator, consists of an addlist and a deletelist: the addlist contains those relations that are true in the corresponding situation but that may not have been true in the initial situation, and the deletelist contains those relations that may not be true in the corresponding situation even though they were true initially. Thus one can determine which relations are true, given the current model and the intial list of relations. Also, given a model and an operator, it is easy to apply the operator to the model and derive a new model. The STRIPS scheme keeps a complete record of all the past states of the system, while allowing the various models to share quite a bit of structure.

STRIPS operators are appealingly simple. In the next section we will examine how the sorts of techniques we have discussed apply if the actions are all STRIPS operators.

2.2 Regression and STRIPS operators

Suppose an action is represented as a STRIPS operator, and that the members of the addlist and the deletelist are all atomic—that is, they contain no logical connectives or quantifiers. It is singularly simple to pass a relation back over such an operator, because the interaction between the operator and the relation are completely specified by the addlist and the deletelist. In order for a relation to be true after the application of such an operator, it must (1) belong to the addlist of the operator, or else (2) be true before application of the operator and not belong to the deletelist of the operator. Thus the rule for passing any relation back over such a STRIPS operator is implicit in the operator description itself.

For instance, an operator such as "move A from B to C" might have addlist "A is on C" and "B is clear" and deletelist "A is on B" and "C is clear." Thus, when passed back over this operator, the relation "A is on C" becomes true, "A is on B" becomes false, and "C is on D" remains the same. The simplicity of regression in this case indicates that we should express our actions in this form whenever possible.

The problem-solver WARPLAN (Warren, 1974) uses precisely the same sort of skeleton model as we do, and uses an identical strategy for handling simultaneous goals, but restricts itself to an atomic add-deletelist representation for operators, thus achieving a marvelous simplicity. Although we imagine that WARPLAN would require extension before it could handle the sort problem or the interchanging of variable values, the principles involved in the WARPLAN design are a special case of those given here.

Thus the clarity of actions expressed in this form makes reasoning about them exceedingly easy. However, many have found the add-deletelist format for representing actions too restrictive. With the advent of the "artificial intelligence programming languages," it became more fashionable to represent actions "procedurally" so that the system designer could describe the effects of the action using the full power of a programming language. We shall examine the impact of the STRIPS assumption on some of these systems in the next section.

2.3 The use of contexts to represent a changing world

What is past, even the fool knows.

Homer, *Iliad*

The new AI languages include PLANNER (Hewitt, 1972), QA4 (Rulifson, *et al.*, 1972). CONNIVER (McDermott and Sussman, 1972) and QLISP (Wilber, 1976), a variant of QA4. A comparative survey of these languages is provided in (Bobrow and Raphael, 1974). Implementers of problem solvers in these languages are fond of saying their systems represent actions "procedurally," as computer programs, rather than "declaratively," as axioms or add-delete lists. Yet in each of these systems the STRIPS assumption is firmly embedded, and the procedures attempt to maintain an updated model by deleting some relations and adding others; which relations an action adds or deletes depends on a computation instead of being explicitly listed beforehand. The STRIPS assumption is expressed not procedurally or declaratively but structurally: it is built into the choice of representation. The more primitive systems (e.g., [Winograd, 1971; Buchanan and Luckham, 1974]), implemented in an early version of PLANNER, maintained a single model which they updated by adding and deleting relations.* This scheme made it impossible for the system to recall any but the most recent world situation without "backtracking," passing control back to an earlier state and effectively undoing any intermediate side effects. The more recent trend† has been to incorporate the assumption by a particular use of the "context" mechanism of the newer implementation languages. We must now describe the context mechanism and its use in building what we will call an "archeological model."

The context mechanism in QA4, CONNIVER, QLISP, AP/1, and HBASE operates roughly as follows: Each of these systems has a data base; assertions can be made and subsequently retrieved. Assertions and queries in these systems are always made with respect to an implicit or explicit context. If T_1 is a context, and we assert that B is on C with respect to T_1, the system will store that fact and answer accordingly to queries made with respect to T_1. There is an operation known as "pushing" a context that produces a new context, an immediate "descendant" of the original "parent" context. We may push T_1 any number of times, each time getting a new immediate descendant of T_1. If T_2 is a descendant of T_1, any assertion made with respect to T_1 will be available to queries made with respect to T_2.

*We do not mean to imply that all these systems were copying STRIPS; Winograd's work was done at the same time.

†See, for example, (Derksen, *et al.*, 1972; Sussman, 1973; Fahlman, 1974; McDermott, 1974; Fikes, 1975). (Balzer, *et al.*, 1974 and Tate, 1974) use the context mechanism of the AP/1 programming system and the HBASE data base system (Barrow, 1974), respectively, in exactly the same way.

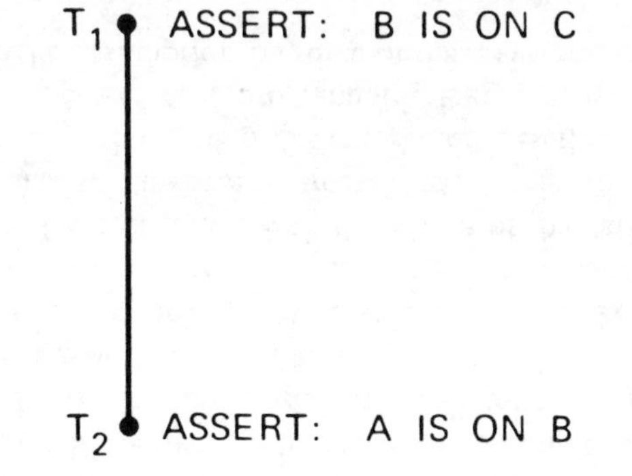

FIGURE 27

Thus if we ask whether B is on C with respect to T_2, we will be told "Yes" (in some fashion). However, assertions made with respect to that descendant are "invisible" to queries made with respect to its parent or any other context aside from its own descendants. For instance, if A is asserted to be on B with respect to T_2, that information will not be available to queries made with respect to T_1 (see Figure 27).

It is also possible to "delete" a relation with respect to a given context. If I delete the fact that B is on C with respect to T_2, the system will be unable to determine whether B is on C with respect to T_2 (on any of its descendants), but it will still know that B is on C with respect to T_1:

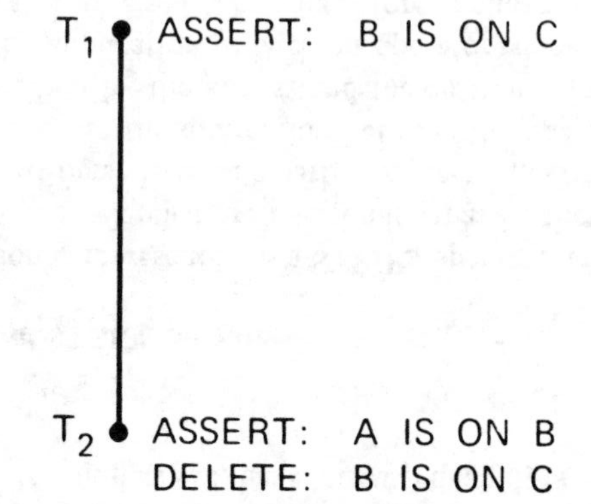

FIGURE 28

The convention taken in planning systems implemented in languages with such a "context-structured data base" has been to equate each situation with a context. Furthermore, if some action occurs in a given situation T_1, resulting in a new situation, the usual practice has been to equate the new situation with an immediate descendant T_2 of the given context T_1. Any relations that are produced by the action are asserted with respect to T_2; any relations that may be disturbed by the action are deleted with respect to T_2. Other relations are still accessible in the new context. Thus if we are in situation T_1 and move block A onto block B from on top of block C, we construct a descendant T_2, asserting that A is on B and deleting that A is on C with respect to T_2. If B was known to be on block D in situation T_1, that information will still be available in situation T_2.

If T_2 is succeeded by another situation T_3, T_3 will be represented by a descendant of T_2, and so on. The structure of the sequence of contexts is represented as

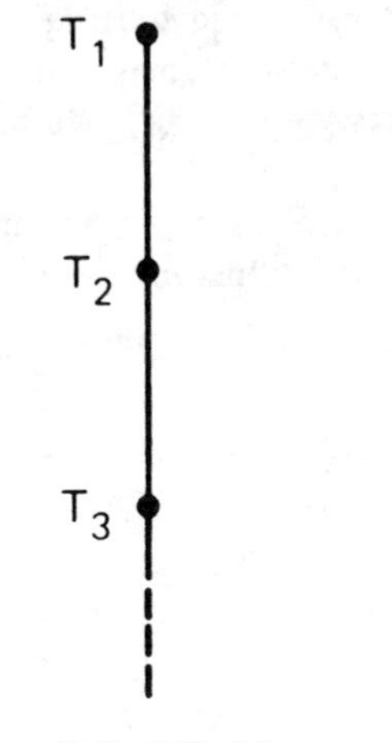

FIGURE 29

Each context is a descendant of the preceding context.

We will call this representation of the world an "archeological" model because it allows us to dig into successive layers of context in order to uncover the past.

In the balance of this paper we will propose that the archeological model is not always ideal. Because any assertion true in a context is automatically true in its descendants (unless specifically deleted), the use of archaeological models implicitly incorporates the STRIPS assumption, and accepts the STRIPS solution to the frame problem. Therefore, most of the planning systems implemented in the new AI languages use representations like that of STRIPS. We have been paying so much attention to the STRIPS assumption for the following reason: we are about to argue that in the future we may not want this assumption so firmly implanted in the structure of our problem solvers; indeed, some researchers have already begun to feel its constriction.

2.4 Influential actions

For want of a nail the shoe was lost,
For want of a shoe the horse was lost,
For want of a horse the rider was lost,
For want of a rider the battle was lost,
For want of a battle the kingdom was lost,
And all for the want of a horseshoe nail.

Nursery Rhyme

The STRIPS assumption, embedded in the archeological model, has been so universally adopted because it banishes the frame axiom nightmare: it is no longer necessary to mention when an action leaves a relation unaffected because every action is assumed to leave every relation unaffected unless explictly stated otherwise. The assumption reflects our intuition about the world, and the archeological model represents the assumption in an efficient way. Having found a mechanism that rids us of the headaches of previous generations of artificial intelligence researchers, shouldn't we swear to honor and cherish it forever?

Indeed, so much can be done within the STRIPS-archeological model framework, and so great are the advantages of staying within its boundaries, that we only abandon it with the greatest reluctance. If we were only modelling robot acts we might still be content to update our models by deleting some relations and adding others. The death blow to this approach is dealt by programming language instructions such as the assignment statement.

Suppose we attempt to express an assignment statement $X \leftarrow Y$ by updating an archeological model. We must delete any relation of form P(X); furthermore, for every relation of form P(Y) in the model we must add a relation of form P(X). In addition, we may need to delete a relation of form "there is a z such that z has value b" even though it does not mention X explicitly. We may need to examine each relation in the model in order to determine whether it depends on X maintaining its old value. The consequences of this instruction on a model are so drastic and far reaching that we cannot afford to delete all the relations that the statement has made false.

How are we to represent the effects of an instruction such as sort2(X Y) on a model? If P(X Y) is the conjunction of everything that is known about X or Y, we might delete P(X Y) and assert $X \leqslant Y$ and (P(X Y) or P(Y X)). This is a massive and unworkable formula if P(X Y) is at all complex; furthermore, it does not express our intuition about the sort, that whether P(X Y) or P(Y X) holds depends on whether or not X was less than or equal to Y before the sort took place. Knowledge of the previous relation between X and Y has been lost.*

Even in the robot domain, for which the STRIPS formalism was orginated, the archeological representation becomes awkward when considering actions with indirect side effects. For example, if a robot is permitted to push more than once box at a time, an operation such as "move box A to point x" can influence the locations of boxes B, C, and D.

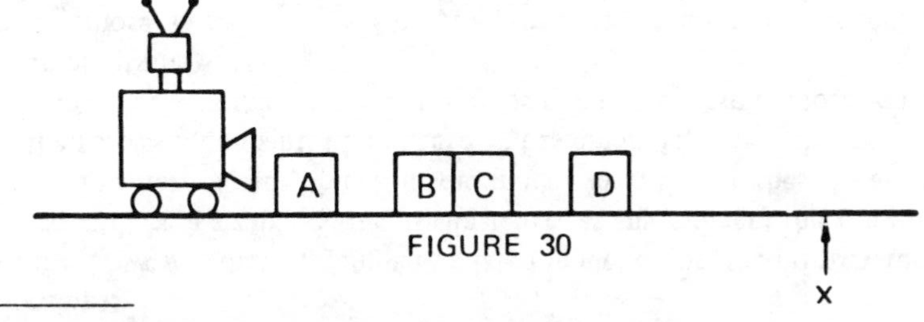

FIGURE 30

*A reply to some of this criticism appears in (Warren, 1976).

This situation becomes worse as the number of elements in the world increases: in moving a complex subassembly of a piece of equipment, we must change the location of every component of the subassembly. If we turn a subassembly upside down, we must replace every relation of form "x is on y" by the relation "y is on x," if x and y are components of the inverted assembly.

These actions are clumsy to model archeologically because so many relations need to be added and deleted from the model, and these relations may involve objects that are not explicitly mentioned by the operator. Furthermore, the operators are insensitive to whether or not these relations are relevant to the problem being solved.

Many of the more recent planning and modelling systems have been attempting to represent these "influential" actions, and we will soon examine how they have overcome the above obstacles. First let us point out that regression provides one technique for modelling these actions; for instance, we need not determine the location of any component indirectly affected by an action until a query concerning that component arises: thus, though many components may be moved, the system need only be concerned with a few of them. When a query about the location does arise, the regression technique will allow the new location to be determined from the original location and from the sequence of actions that has been performed on the subassembly. In particular, if the robot in the previous example (Figure 30) has moved the stack 10 feet to the right in moving box A to point x, the new location of box C will also be several feet to the right of the old location: of course, there is no need to compute the new location of C unless that information is requested.

We have seen that archeological models embed the STRIPS assumption; however, many of the more recent planning systems, while retaining the archeological structure, have been attempting to model actions that must be classified as influential. We will see in the next section how they have resolved the discrepancy.

2.5 Escaping from the STRIPS assumption

Once the archeological model was adopted, the designers of problem solvers devised mechanisms to loosen the STRIPS assumption embedded in their choice of representation.

Fahlman (Fahlman, 1974), using CONNIVER, wanted to simulate a robot that could lift and transport an entire stack or assembly of blocks in one step by carefully raising and moving the bottom block. We characterize this action as "influential" because many blocks will have their location changed when the bottom block is moved. Aware of the difficulty of maintaining a completely updated model, Fahlman distinguishes between "primary" and "secondary" relations. Primary relationships, such as the locations of the blocks, are fundamental to the description of the scene: an updated model is kept of all primary relationships. Secondary relationships, such as whether or not two blocks are touching, are defined in terms of the primary relationships and therefore can be deduced from the model, and added to it, only as needed. The system has thereby avoided deducing large quantities of irrelevant, redundant secondary relationships.

Notice, however, that keeping an updated model of just the primary relationships may still be a sizable chore: for instance, at any moment the system must know the location of every block in the model, even though these locations are often themselves redundant; when a large subassembly is moved, the locations of each of the blocks in the subassembly can be computed from the location of the subassembly itself.

Furthermore, in Fahlman's system if a primary relationship is changed, all the secondary relationships that have been derived from that primary relationship and added to the model must be deleted at once to avoid potential inconsistency.

The modelling system of the SRI Computer Based Consultant (Fikes, 1975), implemented in QLISP, distinguishes between derived and explicitly asserted relations for the same reason that Fahlman distinguishes between primary and secondary data. However, in the SRI system the same relation might be derived in one instance and explictly asserted in another. Thus the location of a component could very well be derived from the location of a subassembly.

Like the Fahlman system, the SRI system deletes all the information derived from an assertion when it deletes the assertion itself.

Note that the SRI system does not behave at all well if the user tries to assert a complex relationship explicitly, say in a problem description. For instance, suppose the user says that block B is between blocks A and C. If the system then moves block A, it will still report that B is between A and C, because that relationship was explicitly asserted and not derived: the system has no way of knowing that it depends on the location of A.

The Fahlman system avoids this difficulty only by forbidding the user to assert any secondary relationships.

Both the Fikes and the Fahlman systems have the following scheme: define actions in terms of the important relationships that they modify, and then define the lesser relationships in terms of the important relationships. This simplifies the description of actions, makes model updating more efficient, and allows the system designer to introduce new relationships without needing to modify the actions' descriptions.

However, it may be impossible to define some lesser relationships in terms of the important ones; we may need to know directly how the lesser relationships are affected by actions. The moving of subassemblies provides a convenient example of this phenomenon.

Consider a row of blocks on a table.

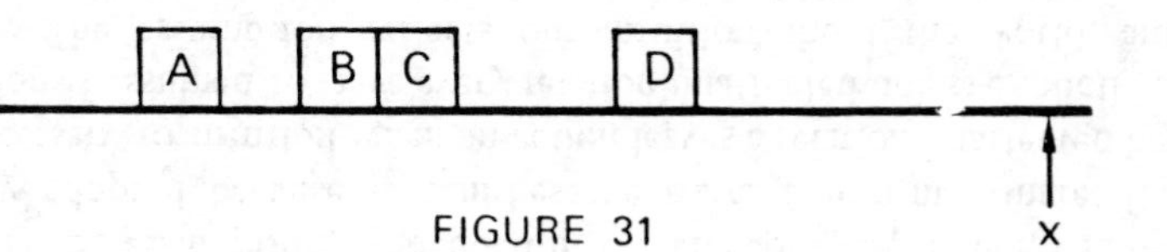

FIGURE 31

We want to move A several feet to the right, to point x. We can either slide A or lift it. If we lift it, blocks B, C, and D will stay where they are, whereas if we slide it, we will inadvertently carry the others along. It is expensive to expect the slide operator to update the model to include the new locations of all the blocks it affects: there may be many of these intermediate blocks and they may not be important to the problem being solved. On the other hand, we cannot expect an archeological system to deduce the new location of B from the new model in case that information turns out to be needed: in order to compute the location of B, the system needs to know whether A has been lifted or slid, and that information is not part of a conventional model. Thus, in an archeological model, locations of intermediate blocks must always be computed at the time the slide is added to the plan.

If skeleton models are adopted, on the other hand, the actions in the plan form an integral part of the model. If A is slid to x, only the new location of A would be explicitly included in the new model. If subsequently we need to determine the location of B, a regression rule sees that A has been slid and asks whether B is in the path of the slide; if not, the location of B after the slide is the same as before; otherwise, the new location of B is somewhere to the right of A.

In both the archeological and the skeletal representations, knowledge about the side effects of sliding must be explicitly expressed. In the skeleton model, the new locations of the intermediate blocks need not be computed until they are needed.

In archeological modelling, the description of an action must be expressed completely in a single operator. For an action with many side effects, the operator is likely to be a rather large and opaque program. Skeleton modelling does not eliminate the need to describe the effects of an action explicitly; however, it does allow the description to be spread over many smaller, and usually clearer programs. Furthermore, one can alter a system to handle new relations merely by adding new regression rules, without changing any previously defined operators. In short, skeleton modelling can sometimes make a system more transparent and modular, as well as more efficient.

Skeleton models do not discard the STRIPS assumption. If this assumption were abandoned, the frame problem would be back upon us at once: for every relation and action it would be necessary to state or deduce a regression rule whether or not the action had any effect at all on the relation. Instead, skeleton models contain a default rule stating that if no other regression rule applies, a given relation is assumed to be left unchanged by a given action. This rule states the STRIPS assumption precisely but does not freeze it into a structure. We have lost in efficiency if actions really do have few side effects, because the archeological model does embed the STRIPS assumption in a structural way and requires no computation if it applies, whereas a skeleton model can only apply the assumption after all the regression rules have failed. The extent to which this modelling technique will be economic depends entirely on the "influence" of actions of the plan—the degree to which they affect the relations in the model.

If skeleton models are adopted, the context mechanism need not be dropped altogether as a way of representing distinct world situations; however, descendent contexts cannot be used to represent successive world states. Our implementation of skeleton models uses contexts in a different way, which we will outline in the next section.

2.6 The use of contexts to implement skeleton models

Recall that we can "push" a given context any number of times, creating a new immediate descendant with every push. These new contexts are independent from each other—none of them is descended from any of the others, and an assertion made with respect to one of them will be invisible to the rest.

In our implementation of skeleton models we represent each situation by a context, but successive situations are all immediate descendents of a single global context T. Thus if situation T_2 results from situation T_1 by performing some act, T_1 and T_2 will both be immediate descendants of T, created by pushing T; T_2 will not be a descendant of T_1. We can represent the skeleton model context structure as follows:

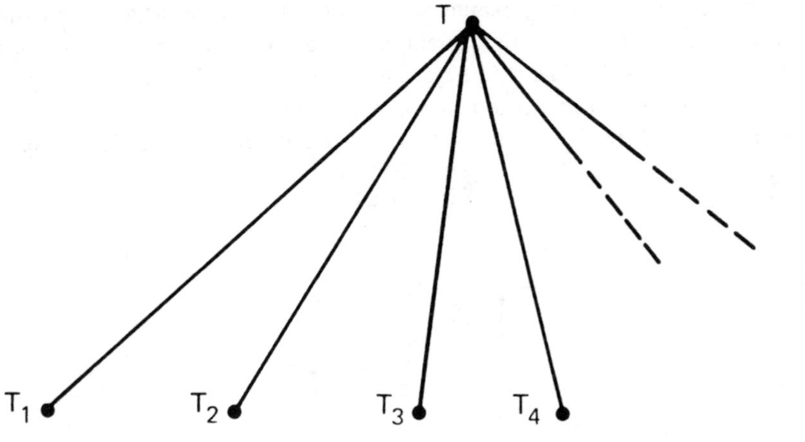

FIGURE 32

Asserting a relation with respect to T_1 does not automatically make it true with respect to T_2, and so on. The only relations asserted in the global context T are the eternal verities.

Since the structure of the skeleton model does not imply any relationship at all between successive states, we represent such knowledge procedurally, by the regression rules for passing a relation back from one state to the preceding one. We suffer a possible loss of efficiency in abandoning the archeological model, but we gain in flexibility and in our ability to represent influential operators efficiently. We do not need to struggle against the assumption incorporated into our representation.

Of course, it is possible to implement skeleton models without using a context mechanism. Problem solvers of the sort advocated by Kowalski (Kowalski, 1974) or implemented by Warren (Warren, 1974) embed a skeleton model representation in a predicate logic formalism in which states of the world are represented by explicit state variables, just as in the early theorem-proving approach. These systems are especially elegant in that the regression rules are indistinguishable from the operator descriptions. They both accept the STRIPS add-deletelist operator representation, but we can envision their incorporating the sort of regression we have employed without requiring any fundamental changes in structure. Hewitt (Hewitt, 1975) has indicated that a version of what we have called skeleton modelling has also been developed independently in the actor formalism, and Sacerdoti (Sacerdoti, 1975) uses another version in conjunction with the procedural net approach.

2.7 Hypothetical worlds

> What might have been is an abstraction
> Remaining a perpetual possibility
> Only in a world of speculation.
> What might have been and what has been
> Point to one end, which is always present.
> Footfalls echo in the memory
> Down the passage which we did not take
> Towards the door we never opened
> Into the rose-garden.
>
> T.S. Eliot, *Four Quartets*

Although so far we have avoided discussing the formation of conditional plans in this paper, it may now be useful to note that using descendent contexts to split into alternate hypothetical worlds (cf. [Rulifson, *et al.*, 1972; McDermott, 1974; Manna and Waldinger, 1974]) is entirely consistent with using independent contexts in skeleton models, but presents something of a problem to archeological models.

In both archeological and skeletal models it is common to represent hypothetical worlds by descendent contexts. For instance, to prepare alternate plans depending on whether or not it is raining in a situation represented by context T_1, two new contexts T_1' and T_1'' are formed, corresponding to the cases in which it is raining and it is not raining, respectively. T_1' and T_1'' are both descendants of T_1, so that any relations known in T_1 will automatically be assumed about T_1' and T_1'' also, as one would have hoped. Furthermore, in T_1' it is asserted to be raining, while in T_1'' it is asserted not to be raining.

The plan for the rainy case would be represented as a sequence of contexts that follows T_1'. In an archeological model these would be successive descendants of T_1' (Figure 33), while in a skeleton model these would be independent contexts linked by regression rules. A similar sequence of contexts beginning with T_1'' would correspond to the plan for the case in which it is not rainy.

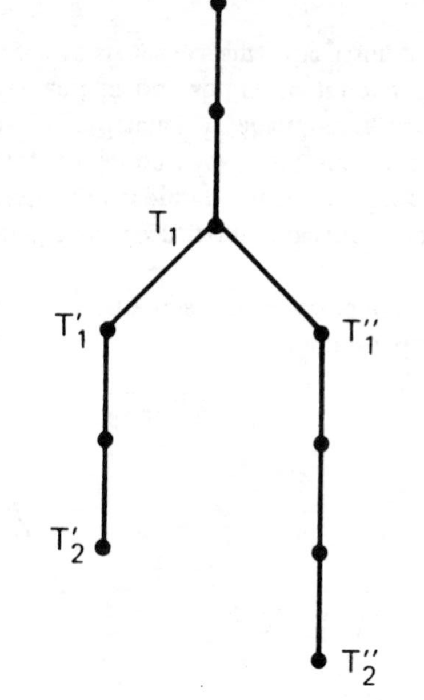

FIGURE 33

Eventually we may reach a situation T_2' and T_2'' in each plan, respectively, after which it becomes irrelevant whether or not it was raining in T_1. In other words our ultimate goal may now be achieved by a single plan that will work in either T_2' or T_2''. Therefore we would like to join our two plans back together into a single plan; we want to form a new context T_2 such that P is true in T_2 if and only if it is true in both T_2' and T_2''. This can be done in a skeleton model by creating an independent context T_2 linked to the previous contexts by the following regression rule: to establish R in T_2, establish R in both T_2' and T_2''.

The situation becomes more difficult if one attempts to maintain an updated archeological model. One could take the following approach: if P and Q are the conjunction of all that is known in T_2' and T_2'', respectively, then assert (P or Q) with respect to T_2. However, (P or Q) is likely to be an unwieldy formula, and we may have lost the information that P corresponds to the rainy situation and Q to the nonrainy one.

We regret that our treatment of hypothetical situations is so terse. A discussion of our own approach, with examples, is given in (Manna and Waldinger, 1974).

2.8 Complexity

> Home is where one starts from. As we grow older
> The world becomes stranger, the pattern more complicated
> Of dead and living.
>
> T.S. Eliot, *Four Quartets*

Perhaps we should say a few words contrasting the work reported here with recent work of Sussman (Sussman, 1973) and Sacerdoti (Sacerdoti, 1975). Although both of these works deal in some of their aspects with simultaneous goals, the principal thrust of their interests is different from ours, and so comparisons are likely to be shallow.

Sussman's main interest is the acquisition of knowledge. Thus he wants his system to learn how to handle simultaneous goals, and is more concerned with learning than with simultaneous goals themselves. We, on the other hand, want our system to know how to handle simultaneous goals from the start, and are not (at present) concerned with learning at all.

The sort of program modification we do is distinct from debugging: the program we are modifying correctly achieves one goal, and we want it to achieve another. We also refrain from actually executing our programs, and ultimately produce programs that are guaranteed correct, whereas Sussman produces programs that may have undiscovered bugs. It is plausible that in tackling more complex problems we will want to introduce bugs and later correct them. We imagine this happening in problems involving serveral levels of detail: a program may work correctly in a crude way, but still contain many minor errors. The problems we have been considering are simple enough so that we have not been forced into using these techniques.

Similarly we view Sacerdoti's procedural nets, like his earlier abstraction hierarchies (Sacerdoti, 1974) as a way of dealing with complexity by submerging detail until a grossly correct plan has been developed. Then the plan is examined in greater depth, and difficulties are ironed out as they emerge. The Sacerdoti formalism can easily represent actions with many subsidiary side effects: these effects are considered only after the initial (approximate) plan has been formulated.

In approaching several simultaneous goals, Sacerdoti develops plans to achieve each of the goals separately; as interactions between the plans are observed, the system will impose orderings on the steps ("Step F_i from plan F must be executed before step G_j from plan G") and even alter the plans themselves to make them impervious to the effects of the other plans. Actions are represented essentially by addlists and deletelists, and the "critics" (cf. [Sussman, 1973]) that recognize the interactions between plans rely strongly on this representation, although the critic principle is more general.

Sacerdoti's approach to simultaneous goals is partially dictated by his application: a consultant system advising a human amateur in a repair task. The user may choose to order the plan steps in any of a number of valid ways; the system cannot force an order except where that order is necessary to avoid harmful interactions; therefore it maintains a highly parallel plan whenever possible until the user himself has selected the order. In a sense, Sacerdoti's system must anticipate all possible plans to achieve a task.

Sacerdoti's idea, deciding what order in which to approach goals only after having done some planning for each of them, is intriguing and avoids a certain amount of goal reordering. However, we believe we will not make best use of hierarchical planning until we are ready to wade into deeper waters of complexity.

2.9 Recapitulation

> You say I am repeating
> Something I have said before. I shall say it again.
>
> T.S. Eliot, *Four Quartets*

In this section we will briefly repeat the main points of the argument in Part 2.

The earliest problem solvers maintained entirely separate models corresponding to each state of the world. In GPS, each operator had the responsibility of constructing a completely new model, whereas in the resolution-based systems the description of the new model created by an action was distributed between several axioms, some describing how relationships were changed by the action, and others (the frame axioms) telling which relationships remained the same.

In an effort to do away with troublesome and obvious frame axioms, later problem solvers adopted what we have called the "STRIPS assumption," that any action will not change most relations, and therefore they described an action by telling which relations it adds and which relations it deletes from the model. The "addlists" and "deletelists" were either given explicitly or computed. Any relation not explicitly added or deleted by an action was assumed to be unaffected.

Systems implemented in artificial intelligence programming languages having a "context" feature tended to incorporate the STRIPS assumption by equating states of the world with contexts, and representing states that occur after a given state by successive descendants of the given context; since any relation asserted with respect to the given context is considered to be true with respect to any of its descendents unless explicitly deleted, the STRIPS assumption is expressed structurally in this "archeological" representation.

Meanwhile, the designers of problem-solving systems entered domains in which the STRIPS assumption began to break down: areas in which the world was modelled in such detail, or in which objects were so highly interrelated, that actions might have many consequences, most of which were irrelevant to the problem at hand. The STRIPS assumption and the archeological structure that expresses it become an obstacle here: it would be cumbersome and inefficient for the description of the action to have to make all these changes in the model. Recent problem solvers have attempted to escape from the STRIPS assumption by distinguishing between the important relations, which are always updated in the model, and the lesser relations, which are defined in terms of the important relations and which are only updated as necessary. These measures are inadequate largely because the designer of the system is prevented from stating explicitly how the lesser relationships are affected by the various actions.

The regression technique advocated here and elsewhere provides a method whereby the actions in the plan become an important part of the model, from which a relational description of the world can be "fleshed out" as necessary. The context mechanism can be used to represent this type of "skeleton model," but successive states are represented as parallel contexts instead of descendants. This latter representation has the additional advantage of being consistent with the use of descendent contexts to represent hypothetical worlds, and with the program modification technique introduced in Part 1.

In my end is my beginning.
T.S. Eliot, *Four Quartets*

ACKNOWLEDGMENTS

This work has been developed through discussions with Zohar Manna and Earl Sacerdoti. The manuscript has benefited from the comments of Rich Fikes, Earl Sacerdoti, and Bert Raphael. The ideas presented here have also been influenced by conversations with Mike Wilber, Bob Boyer, Nachum Dershowitz, Rod Burstall, John Darlington, Gordon Plotkin, Bob Kowalski, Alan Bundy, Bernie Elspas, Nils Nilsson, Peter Hart, Ben Wegbreit, Carl Hewitt, Harry Barrow, Cordell Green, Avra Cohn, Dave Barstow, Doug Lenat, and Lou Steinberg. Mike Wilber has been of special assistance in the use of the QLISP system, which is based on INTERLISP. Our efforts have been encouraged by the environments provided by the Artificial Intelligence Center at SRI, the Department of Artificial Intelligence at the University of Edinburgh, and the Applied Mathematics Department at Weizmann Institute. Linda Katuna and Lorraine Staight prepared many versions of the manuscript.

The National Science Foundation Office of Computing Activities supported this work through Grant GJ-36146.

REFERENCES

Balzer, R.M., N.R. Greenfeld, M.J. Kay, W.C. Mann, W.R. Ryder, D. Wilczynski, and A.L. Zobrist (1974) Domain-independent automatic programming. *Information Processing 74: Proc IFIP 74*, **2**, 326-330.

Barrow, H.G. (1974) HBASE. *POP-2 Library Documentation,* Department of Artificial Intelligence, University of Edinburgh, Edinburgh.

Bobrow, D.G. and B. Raphael (1974) New programming languages for artificial intelligence research. *ACM Computer Surveys,* **6**, 3, 155-174.

Boyer, R.S. and JS Moore (1973) Proving theorems about LISP functions. *Proc IJCAI3,* 486-493, Stanford, CA, also in *JACM,* **22**, 1, 129-144.

Buchanan, J.R. and D.C. Luckham (1974) On automating the construction of programs. *Informal Memo*, Artificial Intelligence Laboratory, Stanford University, Stanford, CA.

Darlington, J. (1975) Application of Program Transformation to Program Synthesis. *Proc Colloques IRIA:* Proving and improving programs, 133-144, Arc et Senans, France.

Darlington, J. and R.M. Burstall (1973) A system which automatically improves programs. *Proc IJCAI3,* 479-485, Stanford, CA.

Derksen, J., J.F. Rulifson and R.J. Waldinger (1972) The QA4 language applied to robot planning. *AFIPS* **41**, Part II, 1181-1187.

Dijkstra, E.W. (1975) Guarded commands, non-determinacy and a calculus for the derivation of programs. *Proceedings, International Conference on Reliable Software* 2-2.13, Los Angeles, CA.

Fahlman, S. (1974) A planning system for robot construction tasks. *Artificial Intelligence,* **5**, 1, 1-49.

Fikes, R.E. (1975) Deductive retrieval mechanisms for state description models. *Technical Note 106*, Artificial Intelligence Center, Stanford Research Institute, Menlo Park, CA.

Fikes, R.E. and N.J. Nilsson (1971) STRIPS: A new approach to the application of theorem proving in problem solving, *Artificial Intelligence,* **2**, 3/4, 189-208.

Floyd, R.W. (1967) Assigning meanings to programs. *Mathematical Aspects of Computer Science*, Proceedings of a Symposium on Applied Mathematics Vol. 19, American Mathematical Society, 19-32.

Goldstine, H.H. and J. von Neumann (1947) Planning and Coding Problems for an Electronic Computer Instrument. *Collected Works of John von Neumann* **5**, 80-235 (Pergamon Press, New York, 1963).

Green, C.C. (1969) Application of theorem proving to problem solving. *Proc IJCAI* 219-239, Washington, DC.

Green, C.C., R.J. Waldinger, D.R. Barstow, R. Elschlager, D.B. Lenat, B.P. McCune, D.E. Shaw and L.I. Steinberg (1974) Progress report on program-understanding systems. *Memo AIM-240*, Stanford Artificial Intelligence Laboratory, Stanford University, Stanford, CA.

Green, C.C. and D. Barstow (1976) A hypothetical dialogue exhibiting a knowledge base for a program-understanding system. *Machine Intelligence* 8, (eds. Elcock, E.W. and Michie, D.), Ellis Horwood Ltd. and John Wiley.

Hewitt, C. (1972) Description and Theoretical Analysis (using Schemata) of PLANNER: A Language for Proving Theorems and Manipulating Models in a Robot. *Ph.D. Thesis* Massachusetts Institute of Technology, Cambridge, Mass.

Hewitt, C. (1975) How to use what you know. *Proc IJCAI4,* 189-198, Tbilisi, Georgia, USSR.

Hoare, C.A.R. (1969) An axiomatic basis for computer programming. *CACM,* **12**, 10, 576-580, 583.

Katz, S.M. and Z. Manna (1976) Logical analysis of programs, *CACM* **19**, 4, 188-206.

King, J.C. (1969) A Program Verifier. *Ph.D. Thesis*, Department of Computer Science, Carnegie-Mellon University, Pittsburgh, PA.

Kowalski, R. (1974) Logic for Problem Solving. *Memo No. 75*, Department of Computational Logic, University of Edinburgh, Edinburgh.

Manna, Z. (1968) Termination of Algorithms. *Ph.D. Thesis* Department of Computer Science, Carnegie-Mellon University, Pittsburgh, PA.

Manna, Z. (1974) *Mathematical Theory of Computation* McGraw Hill, New York.

Manna, Z. and R.J. Waldinger (1974) Knowledge and reasoning in program synthesis. *Artificial Intelligence* **6** 2, 175-208.
CA.

McCarthy, J. and P. Hayes (1969) Some philosophical problems from the standpoint of artificial intelligence, *Machine Intelligence* **4**, (eds. Meltzer, B. and Michie, D.), American Elsevier, New York.

McDermott, D.V. (1974) Assimilation of new information by a natural language-understanding system, *AI Memo 291*, Artificial Intelligence Laboratory, Massachusetts Institute of Technology, Cambridge, MA.

McDermott, D.V. and G.J. Sussman (1972) The Conniver Reference Manual. *AI Memo 259* (revised 1973), Artificial Intelligence Laboratory, Massachusetts Institute of Technology, Cambridge, MA.

Moore, JS (1975) Introducing iteration into the pure LISP theorem prover. *IEEE Transactions on Software Engineering*, **SE-1**, 3, 328-338.

Naur, P. (1966) Proof of algorithms by general snapshots. *BIT* **6**, 4, 310-316.

Newell, A., J.C. Shaw, and H.A. Simon (1960) Report of a General Problem-Solving Program for a Computer. Information Processing. *Proceedings of an International Con-*

ference on Information Processing, 256-264. UNESCO, Paris, France.

Rulifson, J.F., J.A.C. Derksen, and R.J. Waldinger (1972) QA4: A procedural calculus for intuitive reasoning. *Technical Note 73*, Artificial Intelligence Center, Stanford Research Institute, Menlo Park, CA.

Sacerdoti, E.D. (1974) Planning in a Hierarchy of Abstraction Spaces *Artificial Intelligence*, 5, 2, 115-135.

Sacerdoti, E.D. (1975) The non-linear nature of plans. *Proc IJCAI4*, 206-214, Tbilisi, Georgia, USSR.

Sussman, G.J. (1973) A Computational Model of Skill Acquisition. *Ph.D. Thesis*. Massachusetts Institute of Technology, Cambridge, MA.

Tate, A. (1974) INTERPLAN: A plan generation system that can deal with interactions between goals. *Memorandum MIP-R-109*, Machine Intelligence Research Unit, University of Edinburgh, Edinburgh.

Turing, A.M. (1950) Checking a large routine. *Report of a Conference on High Speed Automatic Calculating-Machines*, 66-69. University of Toronto, Toronto.

Waldinger, R.J. and R.C.T. Lee (1969) PROW: A step toward automatic program writing. *Proc IJCAI*, 241-252, Washington, D.C.

Waldinger, R.J. and K.N. Levitt (1974) Reasoning about programs. *Artificial Intelligence*, 5. 3. 235-316.

Warren, D.H.D. (1976) Generating Conditional Plans and Programs. *Proc AISB Summer Conference*, 344-354, Edinburgh.

Wegbreit, B. (1974) The synthesis of loop predicates, *CACM* 17, 2, 102-112.

Wilber, M. A QLISP Reference Manual. *Technical Note 118*, Artificial Intelligence Center, Stanford Research Institute, Menlo Park, CA.

Winograd, T. (1971) Procedures as a Representation for Data in a Computer Program for Understanding Natural Language. *Ph.D. Thesis*, Massachusetts Institute of Technology, Cambridge, MA. also appears as *Understanding Natural Language* Academic Press, New York, NY.

Winograd, T., (1974) Artificial Intelligence–when will computers understand people? *Psychology Today*, 7, 12, 73-79.

Planning and Meta-Planning (MOLGEN: Part 2)

Mark Stefik*

Computer Science Department, Stanford University, Stanford, CA 94305, U.S.A.

ABSTRACT

The selection of what to do next is often the hardest part of resource-limited problem solving. In planning problems, there are typically many goals to be achieved in some order. The goals interact with each other in ways which depend both on the order in which they are achieved and on the particular operators which are used to achieve them. A planning program needs to keep its options open because decisions about one part of a plan are likely to have consequences for another part.

This paper describes an approach to planning which integrates and extends two strategies termed the least-commitment and the heuristic strategies. By integrating these, the approach makes sense of the need for guessing; it resorts to plausible reasoning to compensate for the limitations of its knowledge base. The decision-making knowledge is organized in a layered control structure which separates decisions about the planning problem from decisions about the planning process. The approach, termed meta-planning, exposes and organizes a variety of decisions, which are usually made implicitly and sub-optimally in planning programs with rigid control structures. This is part of a course of research which seeks to enhance the power of a problem solvers by enabling them to reason about their own reasoning processes.

Meta-planning has been implemented and exercised in a knowledge-based program (named MOLGEN) that plans gene cloning experiments in molecular genetics.

1. Introduction

> *Method consists entirely in properly ordering and arranging the things to which we should pay attention.* Descartes, *OEuvres*, vol. X, p. 379; "Rules for the Direction of the Mind," from Polya [17].

> *Verily, as much knowledge is needed to effectively use a fact as there is in the fact,* de Kleer et al. [5].

Problem solvers repeatedly decide what do do. A problem solver has goals and a repetoire of possible actions. It decides when the actions can be applied and how they should be combined. In computational systems, such decisions about actions are called *control* and a framework for organizing these decisions is called a *control structure.*

A sophisticated control structure should provide flexibility for decision-making—so that a problem solver can take advantage of new information, make guesses, and correct mistakes. It should be able to recognize when an approach is succeeding (even by serendipity), and also recognize when it is failing. In substantial planning problems, there are too many possibilities to try everything, so a planner must exercise control by deciding what to try. To plan effectively, a planner must know when to make commitments and when to wait. These capabilities place a premium on flexibility and raise challenges for finding ways to use information effectively.

This paper considers the control of decision making in planning. A computer program, named MOLGEN, has been implemented and used as a vehicle for studying planning. This is the second of two papers about MOLGEN. The first paper [23] considers experiment design as a hierarchical process and characterizes planning decisions in terms of operations on constraints. This paper focusses on the control of those planning decisions.

Experimentation with flexible control structures is of increasing significance in *knowledge-based* problem solvers for which we have an apparent wealth of information in knowledge bases and increased ambitions for intelligent behavior. Almost 20 years ago, Newell [15] surveyed several organizational alternatives for problem solvers. Only a few substantial experiments have been done in the intervening years. The elaboration of the principles for creating effective control structures is hindered by the substantial effort involved in building systems that use them. Most experiments consider only one control structure and a small set of control issues.

This paper describes a control structure, termed *meta*-planning, which enables a planner to reason (to some degree) about its own reasoning process. *Meta*-planning provides a framework for partitioning control knowledge into layers so that flexibility is achieved without the complexity of a large monolithic system. The rationale for this is discussed in Section 2. The implementation of MOLGEN's layered control structure is presented in Section 3. The final sections consider the conceptual ties of this work to other research on layered control and show how additional capabilities not implemented in MOLGEN increase the need for flexible control.

2. The Rationale for Layers

This section presents the rationale for organizing problem solving knowledge as a control hierarchy. It begins with a discussion of the shortcomings of monolithic agenda systems.

* Current address: Xerox Palo Alto Research Center, 3333 Coyote Hill Road, Palo Alto, CA 94304, U.S.A.

2.1. The trouble with agendas

The idea of organizing a problem solver around an *agenda*, that is, around a queue of competing processes, is currently popular as a flexible control structure [2, 8, 13]. The agenda control structure is a generalization of the fetch-execute cycle that is used in the hardware of most digital computers (see Fig. 1). In the fetch-execute cycle, instructions are retrieved by a processor and executed. Execution of the instructions causes changes in memory and (presumably) brings the system closer to the completion of a problem. In agenda systems (see Fig. 2), the tasks are similar to instructions except that they are usually more complicated than machine instructions and the retrieval and selection criteria are richer. Still, the basic organization is the same and the potential for programming the system by altering the tasks and selection criteria is appealing.

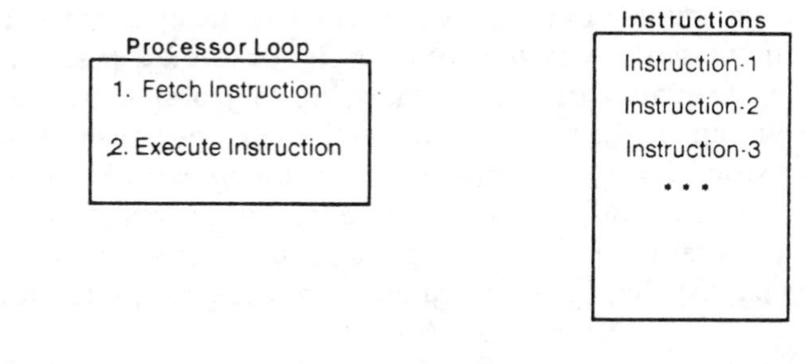

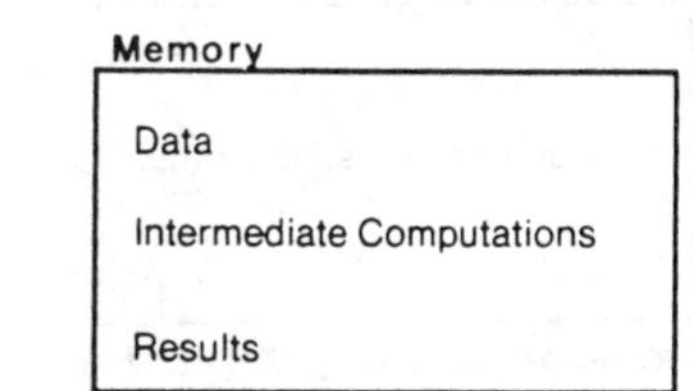

FIG. 1. The Fetch-Execute Cycle. Instructions are retrieved by a processor and executed. Execution of the instructions causes changes in memory and (presumably) brings the system closer to the completion of a problem.

In the basic agenda organization the knowledge for selecting tasks is contained in the interpreter. Hayes [11] has argued that this approach is a return to the 'uniform black-box problem solver':

> We have now come full circle, to a classical problem-solving situation. How can the interpreter decide what order to run the processes in? It doesn't know anything about any particular domain, so it can't decide. So we have to be able to tell it. . . . This is exactly the situation which . . . the proceduralists attacked. In removing the decision to actually *run* from the code and placing it in the interpreter, advocates of [agenda systems] . . . have re-created the uniform black-box problem-solver.

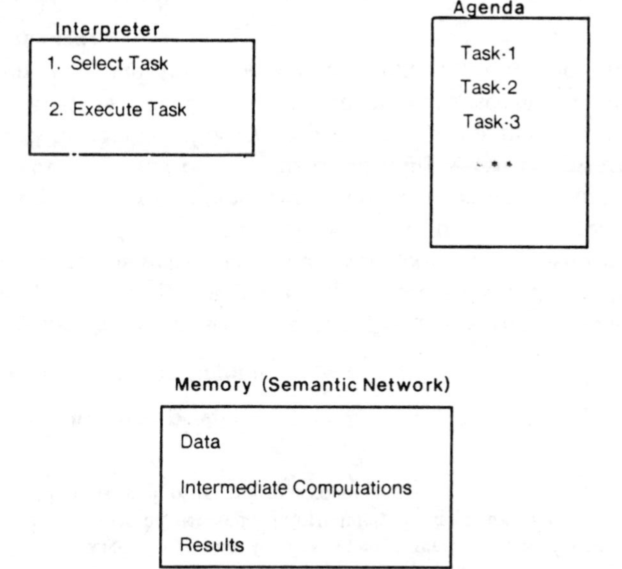

FIG. 2. The agenda control structure. This control structure has essentially the same architecture as a digital computer tasks except that tasks are usually more complicated than machine instructions, and the retrieval and selection criteria are richer. The memory in agenda systems is often structured as a semantic network.

Several modifications in this scheme have been proposed to simplify the interpreter by removing the task selection criteria. One approach is to provide an initial set of tasks and arrange that new tasks are created by earlier tasks as they are run. Tasks are run in a standard order, such as the order in which they were created. This approach limits the amount of scheduling information in the interpreter by the drastic expedient of eliminating it altogether. The priority queue approach (see Fig. 3), which recognizes that some tasks are more important than others, is to assign priorities to tasks and select those with the highest priorities.

Several embellishments are possible on the priority queue approach. One embellishment is to raise or lower priorities to reflect changing conditions. For example, the reasons for running a task may lose validity if other tasks have been executed between the time that a task is created and the time that it

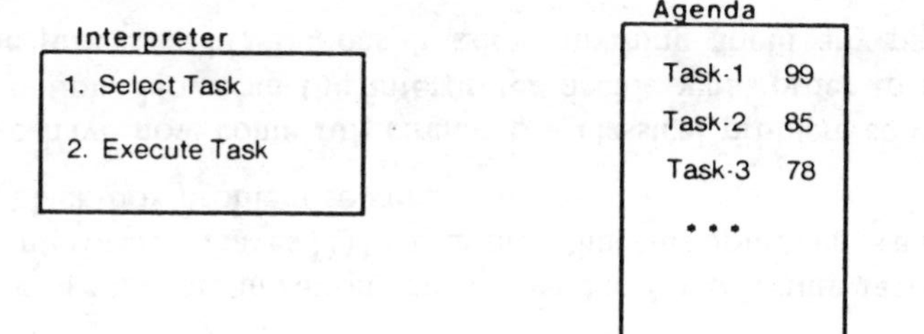

FIG. 3. Priority Queue. The task description in agenda control structures can be augmented to include priority information to represent the idea that some tasks are more important than others. This begs the question of where to put the knowledge for setting the priorities.

reaches the top of the agenda. Some programs distinguish between activation-conditions and pre-conditions to handle this case. In programs like Lenat's AM a task may increase in importance as reasons for running it accumulate.

Task-centered scheduling is an augmentation of the priority queue idea that associates priority-estimating functions with each of the tasks, instead of numeric priorities (see Fig. 4). However, the treatment of complexity is not necessarily much improved. If the problem solver has multiple goals, each priority-estimating function must potentially know about all of them. In the worst case, the priority-estimating functions for each task need to take into account all of the other possible tasks. Unfortunately, the number of possible interactions grows rapidly with the number of tasks. Even if we consider only pairwise interactions, their number is proportional to the square of the number of tasks; if we count interactions between groups of tasks, the number of possible interactions grows exponentially with the number of tasks.

While the worst case does not usually hold in practice, this shows how the control knowledge can become unmanageably complicated in a monolithic organization. The fix for the complexity problem is not simply a choice between a centralized or decentralized organization. In the absense of some other kind of simplifying organization, we have only a choice between (1) maintaining an arbitrarily complex central function, or (2) maintaining a set of interacting task-centered functions.

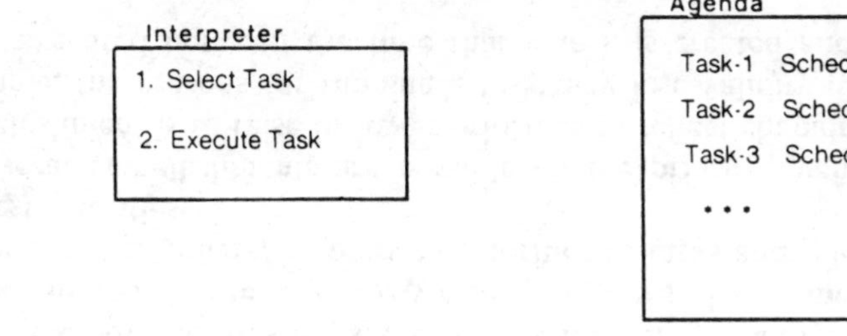

FIG. 4. Task-centered computation of priorities. In some tasks, priorities (or even applicabilities) change as conditions change. To account for this, some systems associate functions with tasks to compute the current priority on demand. Unfortunately, if there are many possible goals, each function must be able to take all of them into account.

2.2. Recognizing the *meta*-problem

Continuing with Hayes's argument:

> A somewhat more sophisticated idea is to allow descriptors for subqueues and allow processes to access these descriptors. . . . But none of these ideas seem very convincing. And we have now moved down another level, to the interpreter of the interpreter-writing language of the representation language.
>
> The only way out of this descending spiral is upwards. We need to be able to describe processing strategies in a language at least as rich as that in which we describe the external domains, and for good engineering, it should be the *same* language.

This argument is supported by the observation that many of the important actions, goals, and constraints can be characterized as being on a *meta*-level. For example, in the classical Missionaries and Cannibals puzzle, a first-level action would be a trip across the river specifying various occupants of the boat. The first-level goal is to get the people across the river safely and the first-level constraints relate to the eating habits of the people. Introspection while trying to solve the puzzle suggests that much of the thought process is actually on a *meta*-level, that is, it is about the process of solving the puzzle. For example, higher level actions would include (1) generating plausible sequences of first-level actions to find a solution, or (2) describing possible intermediate states in the boating plan, or (3) changing the representation of the first-level problem. The meta-level goal is to find a solution to the puzzle; limitations on the availability of computational resources are examples of meta-level constraints. In general, any choices or evaluation criteria which relate to the process of problem solving can be characterized as *meta*-level considerations.

That many planning decisions are about the *meta*-problem explains the source of the combinatorially explosive number interactions in monolithic organizations. If the tasks in the agenda refer only to first-level actions, then the scheduling functions must take into account not only the applicability considerations of the first-order problem, but also the problem-solving considerations of the meta-problem. If the meta-level tasks are not represented explicitly and are not hidden in a 'black box interpreter', then the higher-level considerations will surface in a confusing way as task interactions on the first level. The basic difficulty with all of the monolithic agenda approaches is that they provide no hierarchical framework for complex control. They provide no meta-level concepts or global perspectives to bear on scheduling and arbitration.

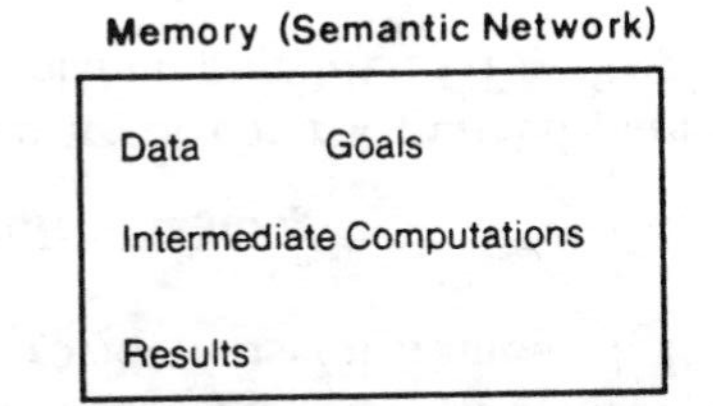

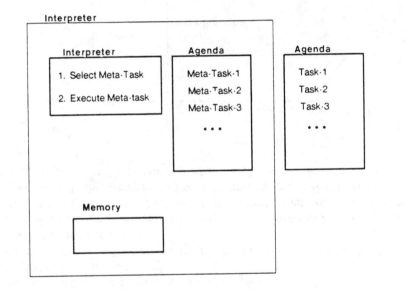

FIG. 5. Layered Agenda Structures. The original interpreter can be replaced by another agenda-based problem solver dedicated to the scheduling problem. The higher problem solver should represent the control concepts necessary for solving the original problem. Tasks in the higher problem solver select and execute tasks in the original problem.

How then might this knowledge be organized? One approach is to extend the agenda idea to a multiple-layered structure with a separate problem solver for the meta-problem. We can replace the complex interpreter in the original agenda structure with a second agenda-based problem solver dedicated to the meta-problem (see Fig. 5). In this *multiple-layered system*, the interpreter of each agenda is essentially another agenda-based system. Tasks in the second layer act collectively as the interpreter of the lower agenda system by creating, ordering, and running the lower tasks.

The layering idea is not limited to two layers; it can be applied recursively. To reduce the apparent complexity of a system, layers can be created until the knowledge remaining in the uppermost interpreter is trivial.

The use of layers has been essential to the creation of computer systems for many years. Most computer programs are built on a succession of layers (or virtual machines)—through hardware, firmware, operating system calls, programming languages, and application software. This practice reduces the amount of expertise that is needed to program a system by providing layers of concepts appropriate for the application. This paper argues for the use of such layers for organizing the control knowledge in a problem solver.

2.3. Advice and control

Many books about problem solving contain advice. For example, the following advice was offered by Polya [18]:

(1) Think on the end before you begin. · · · Let us inquire from what antecedent the desired result could be derived.

(2) Examine your guess. · · · Don't let your suspicion, or guess, or conjecture grow without examination till it becomes ineradicable.

(3) A wise man changes his mind, a fool never does.

(4) Look around when you have got your first mushroom or made your first discovery; they grow in clusters.

It is generally conceded by researchers in AI (artificial intelligence) that there is a considerable gap between advice such as this and its realization in problem solving programs. As Mostow and Hayes-Roth [14] have observed, considerable knowledge is sometimes required in order to interpret such advice. Another part of the difficulty is that there is often no apparent place to put advice in a problem solver. Heuristics like these deal essentially with control concepts, so the absence of an explicit vocabulary of control concepts necessarily impedes the representation of such advice. This research takes some first steps towards defining a vocabulary of control concepts and suggests that layers of control can provide a useful framework for representing them.

3. A Model for Planning

This section presents the layers of control (termed *planning spaces*) that are used to model hierarchical planning in MOLGEN. The main features of the implementation are

(1) a trivial finite-state machine as the top-level interpreter,

(2) the factoring of the knowledge for using plausible and logical reasoning from the planning operations, and

(3) the development of a vocabulary of operators and concepts for hierarchical planning with constraints.

MOLGEN uses three layers and an interpreter as shown in Fig. 6. The three spaces have parallel structure: each space has operators and objects and steps. Each layer controls the creation and scheduling of steps in the layer below it. The spaces are described here starting with the bottom or *domain* space:

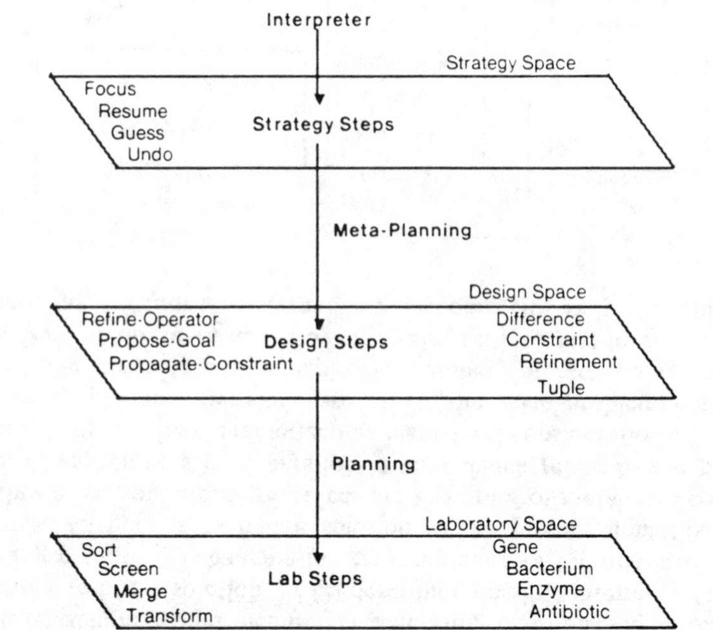

FIG. 6. MOLGEN's planning spaces. The design space *plans* by selecting and executing laboratory steps; the strategy space *meta-plans* by selecting and executing design steps.

(1) ***Laboratory space*** (*or domain* space)—knowledge about the objects and operations of a genetics laboratory. The operators in this space represent actions that can be performed by a laboratory technician; the objects are the things that can be manipulated in the genetics laboratory. (Laboratory space also contains abstractions of these objects and operators.) Steps (i.e., tasks) in laboratory space are executed in order to simulate a real genetics experiment. This bottom space is not a *control* level at all; it represents knowledge about genetics. Laboratory space describes what can be done in the laboratory, but not when to do it in an experiment.

(2) ***Design space***—knowledge about designing plans. This space defines a set of operators for sketching plans abstractly and for propagating constraints around in a laboratory plan as it is refined. These operators model the actions of an *experiment designer*. Steps are executed in design space in order to create and refine the laboratory plan.

(3) ***Strategy space***—knowledge about strategy. This space has two problem-solving approaches: heuristic and least-commitment. Steps are executed in strategy space in order to create and execute the steps in the design space.

(4) The ***Interpreter***—this program is MOLGEN's outermost control loop. It creates and executes steps in the strategy space.

The design operators *plan* by creating and scheduling laboratory steps; the strategy operators '*meta-plan*' by creating and scheduling design steps.

3.1. Control messages

The stratification of control knowledge introduces some organizational requirements:

(1) The operators in a meta-level need to be able to create and schedule first-level tasks.

(2) Meta-level operators should be able to reference and describe first-level entities.

(3) For convenience in a changing knowledge base, an interface between the spaces should isolate the meta-level operators from trivial name changes in the first-level space.

In MOLGEN, the translation of domain-level information into design-level concepts was implemented using an object-centered approach (see Bobrow and Winograd [2]). MOLGEN's operators were represented as 'objects' (called units) that communicated by passing standardized messages. This enabled operators in a *meta*-space to look up information in a lower space and to communicate uniformly with the operators in the lower space. A message passing protocol was implemented using facilities provided by the Units Package representation language [25]. No claim is made that a message-passing protocol is essential for implementing a layered control structure. Indeed, more sophisticated methods for insulating problem solving layers and translating between vocabularies are possible, but were not implemented in MOLGEN.

The following sections discuss the vocabulary and rationale for each of the planning spaces. For concreteness, the operators in each planning space will be described in terms of the *message-passing* protocols that were used. The specific messages will be introduced as needed.

3.2. Laboratory space

Laboratory space is MOLGEN's model of the objects and actions relevant to gene cloning experiments. It was described in the companion paper and will be summarized here briefly. Laboratory space defines the set of possible laboratory experiments by describing the allowable laboratory objects and operators.

The objects in laboratory space represent physical objects that can be manipulated in the genetics laboratory. They include such things as antibiotics, DNA structures, genes, plasmids, enzymes, and organisms. Seventy-four different generic objects are represented in total. The knowledge base includes annotations which indicate which of these objects are available 'off the shelf'.

The operators in laboratory space represent physical processes that can be carried out in the genetics laboratory. They are organized into four groups depending on whether they

(1) combine objects together (***Merge***),
(2) increase the amount of something (***Amplify***),
(3) change the properties of something (***React***), or
(4) separate something into its components (***Sort***).

Collectively, these abstract (or generic) operators are called the **'MARS'** operators. Thirteen specific operators are represented as specializations of these. For example, ***Cleave*** is a ***React*** operator which cuts a DNA molecule with a restriction enzyme; ***Screen*** is a ***Sort*** operator which removes unwanted bacteria from a culture by killing them with an antibiotic.

Steps in laboratory space describe the application of (possibly abstract) genetics operators to genetics objects. When MOLGEN *runs* (i.e., executes) a step in a higher level space, the step is said to have been done and corresponding changes in the plan structure are made. MOLGEN can not actually run the laboratory steps in the sense of doing them in the laboratory; executing the code is interpreted as *simulating* the laboratory step.

Laboratory space does not contain the knowledge about how to effectively plan experiments, that is, how to arrange laboratory steps to achieve experimental goals. This knowledge is organized in the design and strategy spaces.

3.3. Design space

Design space is MOLGEN's first control space. It contains operators for planning, that is, for creating and arranging steps in laboratory space. This section discusses the concepts and operations of meta-planning in enough detail to give a sense of how MOLGEN worked. No claim is advanced that the particular operators described here are universally applicable in problem solving, or that the partitioning of functionality is ideally chosen. Rather, this description is offered as an example of the kinds of operations that can be treated explicitly in problem solving, and it is hoped that the example will provoke the kind of careful thinking that will lead to defining and organizing control information in other systems.

The main idea in organizing MOLGEN's design space is that planning can be viewed as operations on constraints. Three operations on constraints are important: formulation, propagation, and satisfaction. *Constraint formulation* is the dynamic creation of constraints that set limits on the acceptable solutions. Constraints correspond to commitments in planning. By formulating constraints about abstract objects (variables), MOLGEN creates partial descriptions of the objects and postpones complete instantiation until later. *Constraint propagation* performs communication by passing information between nearly independent subproblems. *Constraint satisfaction* refines abstract entities into specific ones. It pools the constraints from the nearly independent problems to work out solutions. The operations on constraints are an important subset of MOLGEN's design operators. These operators provide a repertoire of possible actions that MOLGEN can use to plan hierarchically. Fig. 7 gives an outline of the objects and operators in MOLGEN's design space.

Design-Object
- Constraint
- Difference
- Refinement
- Tuple

Design-Operator
- Comparison
  - Find-Unusual-Features
  - Check-Prediction
- Temporal-Extension
  - Propose-Operator
  - Propose-Goal
  - Predict-Results
- Specialization
  - Refine-Operator
  - Propagate-Constraint
  - Refine-Object

FIG. 7. Outline of the objects and operators in design space.

3.3.1. *Design operators*

MOLGEN has three categories of design operators:

(1) ***Comparison operators*** that compare goals and compute differences,
(2) ***Temporal-extension operators*** that extend a plan forwards or backwards in time, and
(3) ***Specialization operators*** that make an abstract plan more specific.

3.3.1.1. *Comparison operators*
Comparison is a fundamental operation in planning. The results of comparison are represented as *differences.* Differences are represented as objects in MOLGEN's design space. Other design objects include constraints, refinements, and tuples. Examples of these objects are given in the planning trace in the previous paper. Thus, unlike the objects in laboratory space which represent *physical* objects, the objects in design space represent *conceptual* objects.

Typically, MOLGEN chooses laboratory operators that can reduce specific differences. This basic formulation goes back to the Logic Theorist program and has appeared in many planning programs. MOLGEN has two comparison operators: ***Find-Unusual-Features*** and ***Check-Prediction***.

Find-Unusual-Features is a design operator that examines laboratory goals. Sometimes a good way to select abstract operators to synthesize objects in cloning experiments is to find features in which the objects are highly specialized or atypical, and then find operators that act on those features. ***Find-Unusual-Features*** does this by comparing objects (e.g., *Bacterium*-1) with their prototypes (e.g., *Bacterium*). ***Find-Unusual-Features*** searches recursively through units representing the parts of an object and stops when it has found differences at any depth of processing.

Check-Prediction is a design operator that compares the predictions from simulation of a laboratory step with the forward goal for the step. This operator is useful for detecting cases where a plan needs to be adjusted because the predicted results of a laboratory step do not quite match the goals. MOLGEN discovers this mismatch after simulating the laboratory step when the knowledge in its simulation model is more complete than the knowledge that was used for selecting the laboratory operator.

3.3.1.2. *Temporal-extension operators*
A design operator that extends a plan forwards or backwards in time is called a *temporal-extension* operator. MOLGEN has three such operators: ***Propose-Operator***, ***Propose-Goal***, and ***Predict-results***.

Propose-Operator proposes abstract laboratory operators to reduce differences. It is activated when new differences appear in the plan and it creates partially instantiated units to represent laboratory steps. It is responsible for linking the new laboratory steps to the neighboring laboratory steps and goals. ***Propose-Operator*** must determine which of the abstract laboratory operators (i.e., the ***MARS*** operators) are applicable. ***Propose-Operator*** takes advantage of the hierarchical organization of the laboratory operators by considering only the most abstract operators. It sends an *apply?* message to each of the abstract laboratory operators. Each laboratory operator has a procedure for answering the message that determines whether the operator is applicable (given a list of differences and constraints). If more than one laboratory operator is applicable, ***Propose-Operator*** puts the list of candidates in a refinement unit and suspends its operation pending messages from strategy space.

The ***Propose-Goal*** design operator creates goals for laboratory steps. It uses messages to access specialized information for laboratory operators. For example, when it sends a *make-goals* message to the ***Merge*** operator, a local procedure creates goals for each of the parts being put together.

Predict-Results is the design operator for simulating the results of a proposed laboratory step. It activates a simulation model associated with each laboratory operator. In the case that the information in the laboratory step is too incomplete for simulation at this stage of planning, ***Predict-Results*** suspends its execution pending messages from strategy space.

3.3.1.3. *Specialization operators*
A hierarchical planner first makes plans at an abstract level and then adds details to its plans. MOLGEN's specialization operators all add details to partially specified plans. The design operators for this are ***Refine-Operator***, ***Propagate-Constraint***, and ***Refine-Object***.

Refine-Operator is the design operator that replaces abstract domain operators (i.e., the MARS operators) in laboratory steps with specific ones. ***Refine-Operator*** is invoked when there are laboratory steps that have their goals and inputs specified but have abstract specifications of the laboratory operator (i.e., ***Merge***). The inputs to laboratory steps are usually incompletely specified when the operator is chosen. For example, the input may be a 'culture of bacteria' without being precise about the type of bacteria. Because laboratory operators often have specific requirements, the process of refinement is accompanied by the introduction of specific constraints on the input. These constraints make the requirements of the laboratory operator specific, without requiring a full specification of the input at the same time. Like other operators in the design space, ***Refine-Operator*** uses several messages in the design space/laboratory space interface to retrieve information about specific laboratory operators.

Propagate-Constraint creates new constraints from existing constraints in the plan. It is organized around the observation that even long-distance propagations can be decomposed into a series of *one-step* propagations through individual laboratory steps. ***Propagate-Constraint*** is invoked when a new constraint appears in the plan. While constraints can, in principle, be propagated in either a forward or backward direction in a plan, only the backward direction (in time) is implemented in MOLGEN. ***Propagate-Constraint*** is activated whenever new constraints appear in the plan. After trying to propagate a constraint, the design task is suspended for possible reactivation if some new laboratory steps appear in the plan. These tasks are cancelled if a constraint is marked as replaced in the plan.

Refine-Object is MOLGEN's constraint satisfaction operator. It is activated when new constraints appear in the plan. Constraint satisfaction involves a 'buy or build' decision in MOLGEN.[1] MOLGEN first tries to find an available object that satisfies the constraints. If this fails, the constraint is marked as failed and the refinement task is suspended. If the constraint is never replaced by a different constraint and MOLGEN runs out of things to do, it may guess that it should make a subgoal out of building the object—thus making the build decision.

Refine-Object evaluates constraints (**Lambda** expressions) using objects from the knowledge base as arguments. The solutions are pooled with those of other constraints on the same objects in design objects called 'tuples' that keep track of the sets of solutions. Sometimes a new constraint will include objects that are included in disjoint tuples; in such cases ***Refine-Object*** combines the subproblems by integrating the tuples into a new tuple with intersected solutions. When enough constraints have been found to make the solution for any abstract variable unique, that variable is anchored to the solution.

3.3.2. *Interface to laboratory space*

Fig. 8 summarizes the messages that were used in MOLGEN. Each laboratory operator includes a procedure to respond to each kind of message. This

Message	Meaning
APPLY?	Asks a lab operator whether it is applicable to reducing a list of differences given a set of constraints.
REFINE	Instructs a lab operator that it has been chosen as a refinement in the plan. Returns a list of new constraints.
MAKEGOALS?	Asks a lab operator whether it needs to modify the goals of a step.
MAKEGOALS	Instructs a lab operator to modify the goals of a laboratory step as needed.
SIMULATE?	Asks a lab operator whether the input to a lab step is specified precisely enough to do a detailed simulation of the lab step.
SIMULATE	Instructs a lab operator to provide a detailed simulation of laboratory step.
BKWD-PROPAGATE	Instructs a laboratory operator to propagate a constraint backwards (in time) from its forward goals to its input.
FWD-PROPAGATE	Instructs a laboratory operator to propagate a constraint forwards (in time) from its input to its forward goals. (This message was not implemented in MOLGEN.)

FIG. 8. Message-protocol interface to laboratory space. These messages are sent by design space operators to control and retrieve information from laboratory space.

[1] Post-thesis examination of MOLGEN's logic has revealed some gaps and confusions in the implementation of this 'buy or build' decision. Some aspects of this are discussed in Section 5.

approach redundantly represents the knowledge about the laboratory operators, since the queries can be about redundant information and there is a separate attached procedure provided for each kind of query from the design space. A direction for future research is to develop an approach for stating the information declaratively once, and then possibly *compiling* it into the procedures like these.

3.4. Strategy space and its interpreter

The distinction between *least-commitment* and *heuristic* approaches to problem solving is the key to the organization of the knowledge in MOLGEN's strategy space. A least commitment approach requires the ability to defer decisions when they are under-constrained. It relies on a synergistic relationship between subproblems, so that constraints from different parts of a problem can be combined before decisions are made. A heuristic approach utilizes plausible reasoning, to make tentative decisions in situations where information is incomplete.

MOLGEN's strategy space is organized as four strategy operators: ***Focus***, ***Resume***, ***Guess***, and ***Undo*** as described in the next section. Fig. 9 shows how

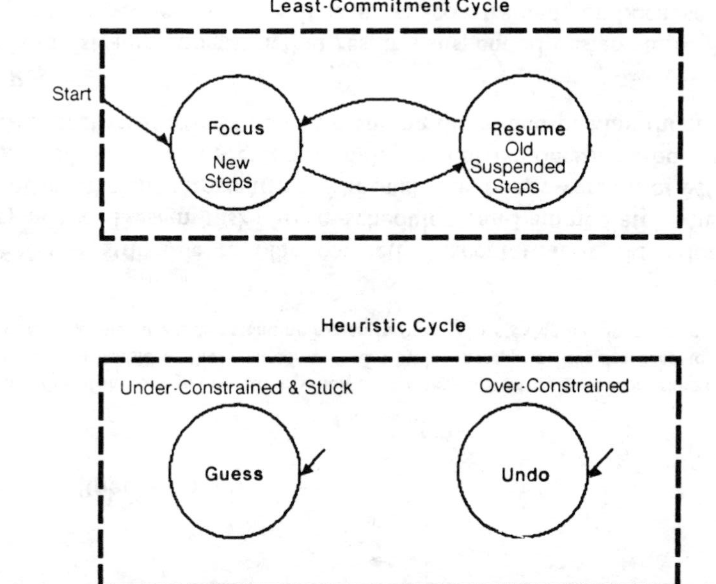

FIG. 9. Least-commitment and heuristic cycles. This diagram shows how the strategy operators are controlled by MOLGEN's interpreter. The least-commitment cycle makes conservative changes in the plan, depending on synergy between subproblems (and constraint propagation) to keep going. When MOLGEN runs out of least-commitment steps, it resorts to guessing using the heuristic cycle.

the strategy operators are controlled by a simple finite state machine, the interpreter, which is composed of two main parts. Section 3.4.2 describes the message-passing protocol that interfaces these operators with the design space. The significance of these ideas is discussed in Section 3.4.3.

3.4.1. *Strategy operators*

The four strategy operators partition the knowledge about logical and plausible reasoning out of the design operators that create the experimental plans. This section describes MOLGEN's strategy operators and how their control of design space is implemented.

3.4.1.1. *Focus*

The ***Focus*** strategy operator is used to create and execute new design tasks. ***Focus*** sends a *find-tasks* message to every design operator. This causes the procedures associated with the design operators to search for work in the current plan and to report back where they can be applied. These procedures mark the places where they have looked in the plan, so that they can avoid redundant checking. The application points are recorded in design steps and the design steps are put into an agenda. In the simplest case, only one design step is ready at any given time. When several design steps are ready simultaneously (usually from different parts of the plan), ***Focus*** has to choose one of them to go first. In MOLGEN, priorities were assigned to the design operators as described in the following paragraphs. These priorities were used by the ***Focus*** and ***Resume*** operators to schedule design steps when several were simultaneously ready.

Focus executes a design task by sending it a *simulate* message. A task may terminate in any of four possible states: done, failed, suspended, or cancelled. ***Focus*** iterates through its agenda. After each execution, it sends out the *find-tasks* message again. As long as steps are successful or are suspended due to being under-constrained, ***Focus*** continues through the agenda. However, if a design-step is over-constrained, ***Focus*** stops processing and returns to the interpreter with the status over-constrained. (This causes the ***Undo*** operator to be invoked.)

The priorities for scheduling competing design tasks are shown in Fig. 10. They reflect a bias towards performing comparison before temporal-extension, and temporal-extension before specialization. This was intended to encourage MOLGEN to look first for differences, then to use them to sketch out an abstract plan, and finally to refine to specific objects and operators. Given such a control scheme, it is interesting to ask whether it was effective or necessary. While no comprehensive set of measurements was done, an experiment was performed accidentally. The original versions of the ***Focus*** and ***Resume*** operators had a bug which caused them to use the priorities precisely backwards, so that the design operators with the lowest priority were tried first. Interestingly,

Operator Class	Design Operator	Priority
Comparison		
	Check-Prediction	9
	Find-Unusual-Features	9
Temporal-Extension		
	Propose-Goal	7
	Propose-Operator	6
	Predict-Results	5
Specialization		
	Refine-Operator	4
	Propagate-Constraints	3
	Refine-Object	2

FIG. 10. Priorities of the design operators. When the strategy operators have more than one design task that seems applicable in the least-commitment cycle, these priorities are used to order the tasks. They reflect a bias towards extending a plan in time before extending it in depth.

MOLGEN was still able to plan correctly, except that it did a lot of unnecessary work. Design tasks were scheduled, and immediately suspended because of insufficient information. Although this buggy version of MOLGEN never completed a plan, it seemed to make the correct decisions, but only after a great deal of fuss; starting tasks, suspending them, and picking them up later.

3.4.1.2. *Resume*

Resume is the strategy operator that restarts suspended design steps. A design step may be suspended because it is under-constrained, or because there is potentially additional work to be found later. ***Resume*** works very much like ***Focus*** in that it creates an agenda and uses priorities to schedule design tasks when more than one is ready. It differs from ***Focus*** in that it does not look for new work to do, only old work to start up again. It sends a *resume?* message to every suspended design-step telling it to indicate if it is ready to run again. ***Resume*** reactivates the design steps that are ready to run by sending them a *resume* message.

Fig. 11 shows an example from a cloning experiment where the ***Resume*** operator was used to activate a design step. The design step in this case is the ***Propagate-Constraint*** step shown in the right center portion of the figure. This step was activated when the constraint (dark box) was added to the plan. The constraint required that the enzyme corresponding to the sticky-ends of the vector should not cut the desired gene (rat-insulin) that it carries. At the time of formulation, there was no place to propagate the constraint, because the ***Cleave*** step in the plan had not yet been added to the plan. Later, other design steps proposed and instantiated the ***Cleave*** step, and the suspended ***Propagate-Constraint*** design step could be resumed.

3.4.1.3. *Guess*

Occasionally during planning, information is not adequate for making any

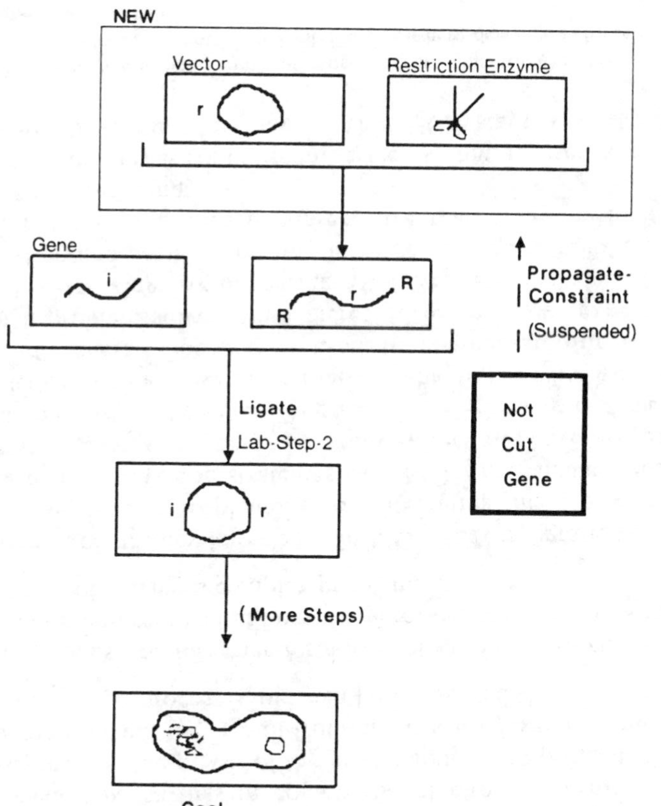

FIG. 11. Example of resuming. The ***Propagate-constraints*** design step was created when the constraint was created, but was suspended until enough of the plan had evolved to create a place for propagating the constraint.

irrevocable decision. When MOLGEN has run out of *least-commitment* changes to a plan, it looks for a plausible commitment that will allow it to continue with the design process. This is recognized by MOLGEN when the ***Focus*** and ***Resume*** strategy operators have nothing to do.

The ***Guess*** operator sends a *guess?* message to the operator of every suspended design step. These design steps represent under-constrained decision points in planning. The *guess?* message causes each suspended step to examine its options and to compute a numerical estimate of the utility of commiting to one of its choices. ***Guess*** then activates the task with the highest rating by sending it a *guess* message. After making a single guess, the ***Guess*** operator returns to the interpreter and another ***Focus*** step is started.

3.4.1.4. ***Undo***

Undo is the strategy operator for backtracking when a plan has become over-constrained. It is the least developed of the strategy operators in this research. Other researchers have developed a more comprehensive approach to dependency-directed backtracking than has been done for MOLGEN; most of the effort in this research has gone towards avoiding backtracking. In Section 3.4.3 it is argued that it is not always feasible to avoid revoking decisions made in planning.

For the record, MOLGEN's (primitive) ***Undo*** operator works as follows. First it picks a candidate design step to undo. It begins by making a list of design steps that were guessed and searches this list for a step whose *output* was the ***input*** of the over-constrained design step. If ***Undo*** finds such a step, it sends it an *undo* message. This tells the design step to remove the effects of its execution from the plan. The design step is then marked as undone. If ***Undo*** finds no candidate, it prints out an apology and quits. ***Undo***, as implemented in MOLGEN, is not capable of tracking down all of the consequences of a decision to be undone and does not check that the undoing actually alleviates the over-constrained situation.

3.4.2. *The interface to design space*

The preceding account of the strategy operators has discussed a number of messages that are sent from the strategy space to the design space. These messages provide an interface to design space that is analogous to the message interface between design space and laboratory space. The interface provides a way for the strategy operators to communicate with the design operators uniformly. They enable strategy operators to invoke design procedures without knowing the names of the procedures. The interface messages in the current implementation are shown in Fig. 12.

Message	Meaning
FIND-TASKS	Instructs the design task to search for new work to do. Returns a list of tasks to do.
SIMULATE	Causes a design task to be executed.
RESUME?	Asks a suspended design task whether it is ready to be re-started.
RESUME	Instructs a suspended design task to resume execution.
GUESS?	Asks a suspended design task whether it can make a plausible guess. Returns a numeric rating of the guess.
GUESS	Instructs a suspended design task to make its best guess.
UNDO	Instructs a finished (guessed) design task to undo the effects of its execution.

FIG. 12. Message-protocol interface from strategy space to design space.

3.4.3. *Significance of the strategy space*

The heuristic and least commitment cycles are reminiscent of two earlier AI programs, HACKER (Sussman [26]) and NOAH (Sacerdoti [20]), respectively. These programs epitomize two points on a spectrum of time of commitment. HACKER epitomizes heuristic early commitment and NOAH epitomizes late (or least) commitment. HACKER guesses its way to a solution using debugging to fix things when the assumptions are bad; NOAH defers decisions and invites the possibility that information will become available later that narrows the possibilities. After NOAH successfully and optimally solved some of the problems that were troublesome for HACKER, Sacerdoti [20] observed that

> HACKER does a lot of wasted work. While the problem solver will eventually produce a correct plan, it does so in many cases by iterating through a cycle of building a wrong plan, then applying all known critics to suggest revisions of the plan, then building a new (still potentially wrong) plan.

The bugs arose, in Sacerdoti's view, from premature and inappropriate decisions by the problem-solver. By delaying judgment, a problem-solver can achieve a considerable savings in computational effort.[2] Sussman and later Goldstein disagreed on the power of the least-commitment principle. Bugs in a design are to be expected; they result from *heuristically justifiable* but incorrect inferences in the design process. Goldstein [10] observed that

> Many bugs are just manifestations of creative thinking—the creation and removal of bugs are ***necessary*** steps in the normal process of solving a complex problem.

The formulation of strategy knowledge in MOLGEN integrates and extends the two earlier approaches to planning. By integrating the least commitment cycle with the heuristic cycle in strategy space, MOLGEN makes sense of the need for guessing: we can guess, but only when we have to. Bugs are inevitable, but only when we guess. The amount of guessing is a measure of missing knowledge; the more we know (and are able to use what we know), the less we need to guess. Guessing is used to compensate for the limited knowledge of a problem solver. With increased expertise we expect reduced guessing and backtracking. By increasing MOLGEN's knowledge about constraint formulation and propagation, we decrease its need to revoke decisions. The least commitment approach is conservative reasoning; the heuristic approach is plausible reasoning.

The appeal of the least commitment cycle is that it uses a monotonic approach towards a solution; as long as MOLGEN stays in this cycle, it is guaranteed to make no wrong moves. The ***Focus*** operator calls on new design operators to make infallible (i.e., irrevocable) changes in the developing plan; the ***Resume*** operator re-starts any suspended design operators which have received additional information. The power of this cycle derives from the ability of the various design tasks to reinforce each other in their decisions. The operators can be suspended when they have insufficient information and restarted when it becomes available. Reinforcement is a consequence of constraint propagation, which passes partial results between subproblems. As long as there are new things to do in the plan or suspended things to restart, MOLGEN stays in the least-commitment cycle. If MOLGEN runs out of things to do (and the plan is incomplete), the plan is said to be *under-constrained* and it calls upon the ***Guess*** operator to make some tentative decision that will enable planning to continue. The ***Guess*** operator calls again upon the design operators to make moves that are plausible, even if they cannot be guaranteed. If MOLGEN discovers at any point that the plan is over-constrained, it calls on the ***Undo*** operator to revoke some of the design decisions, typically undoing a choice that was guessed.

[2] Barstow [1] illustrated this in an example of program refinement when abstraction trees are skinny at the top, and bushy at the bottom. He cited a case where delaying a choice reduced the number of rule applications in half.

4. Relationships to Other Work

This section considers other problem-solving programs with layered control structures. While the idea of layered control was reported as early as 1963, programs which substantially utilize this idea have appeared only recently. Several researchers (e.g., de Kleer et al. [5] and Georgeff [9]) have proposed approaches for controlling inference; this section will consider only approaches that are layered.

4.1. GPS

The idea of layers of control with problem-solving operators was anticipated in 1963 by Simon [22] in his experiments with the heuristic compiler in the GPS framework:

> It should . . . be feasible, by modifying the top-level programs, to bring the Heuristic Compiler into a form which would allow its problem-solving processes to be governed by GPS. . . . That is, GPS would first be applied to the task environment of the General Compiler; applying an operator in this environment would consist in applying GPS to the task environment.

This suggestion anticipates the use of problem-solving operators that are distinct from the domain operators. The idea for the Heuristic Compiler was recursive in that it used an instantiated version of GPS as an operator in the *difference tables* of a higher version of GPS.

4.2. TEIRESIAS

TEIRESIAS (Davis [3, 4]) with its *meta-rules* also used a layered control structure. TEIRESIAS was developed in the context of MYCIN (Shortliffe [21]), a medical-consultation system. MYCIN performs an exhaustive goal-directed search through a diagnostic AND/OR tree. At each stage of the diagnosis, MYCIN retrieves the set of production rules which conclude about a premise of interest. In TEIRESIAS, the system was modified so that object-level production rules could be reordered and pruned according to explicit criteria in *meta-rules*. These criteria were used by TEIRESIAS to shorten or re-order the list of potentially applicable rules considered. The idea of higher order meta-rules (e.g., meta-meta-rules) that would act on other meta-rules was also considered, but the medical domain offered no examples.

4.3. HEARSAY-like systems

Several recent AI programs with layered control structures have been based on ideas from the *unlayered* HEARSAYII program [6] for speech understanding. The architecture of HEARSAY-II incorporated three main ideas which have influenced the design of the later programs:

(1) ***Hierarchical hypothesis structure.*** Each level was more abstract than the level below it. The hypotheses were kept on a global data structure termed the *blackboard.*

(2) ***Knowledge Sources.*** Operators termed *KS*s (for Knowledge Sources) made hypotheses at the different abstraction levels.

(3) ***Focus of attention.*** A centralized control mechanism was used to focus attention on parts of the hypothesis space and to coordinate the KSs.

4.3.1. *SU-X and SU-P*

In 1977, Nii and Feigenbaum [16] described two computer programs, SU-X and SU-P, that did signal interpretation tasks. SU-X interpreted instrument signals in a military context and SU-P (also known as CRYSALIS) interpreted X-ray crystallography data to determine protein structure. These programs extended the HEARSAY-II architecture as follows:

(1) HEARSAY-II's single-layered control structure (the hypothesize and test paradigm) was extended to multiple layers and

(2) HEARSAY-II's blackboard was partitioned into distinct areas.

The control layers in both programs were called *hypothesis-formation*, *hypothesis-activation*, and *strategy*. KSs on the first layer formed hypotheses from the incoming signal. The two operators on the second layer, the *hypothesis-activation layer*, were called the *event-driver* and the *expectation-driver*. They corresponded to data-driven and goal-driven policies for activating KSs on the first layer. The KSs on the third or strategy layer decided (1) how close the system was to a solution and (2) how well the KSs on the second level were performing and (3) when and where to redirect the focus of attention in the data space.

The control layers in MOLGEN are an adaptation of the control layers used in the SU-X and SU-P programs; the differences reflect MOLGEN's more elaborate concern about coordination of subproblems. MOLGEN's explicit management of the communication between nearly independent subproblems led to many more operators on the second level. Thus, the strategy level in SU-X had only to mediate between two analysis operators: goal-driven and event-driven analysis; MOLGEN's strategy operators mediate between eight design operators. Another source of complexity is MOLGEN's ability to save partial results of computations. Operators in SU-X merely succeed or fail without saving partial results; operators in MOLGEN can be suspended with partial results on under-constrained problems and can be restarted with instructions to try again, guess, or undo these steps.

4.3.2. *The Hayes-Roth planning model*

A cognitive model for an errand planning task has been developed by Barbara and Frederick Hayes-Roth [12] that is intended to model the mixture of goal-driven and data-driven behavior observed in human planners. The Hayes-Roths' model proposes pattern-directed invocation and resource allocation as the basic control concepts. Planning knowledge is factored into KSs that suggest decisions about how to approach a problem, what knowledge to use, and what actions to try.

MOLGEN research has paralleled the Hayes-Roths' work and there has been a considerable sharing of ideas. The Hayes-Roths' model evolved from the analysis of human problem-solving behavior in protocols taken from an errand-running task. It characterizes planning as follows:

> Our first assumption is that people plan ***opportunistically***. . . . . [This] implies that the decisions they make can occur at non-adjacent points in the planning space. . . . . A decision at a given level of abstraction specifying action to be taken at a given point in time may precede and influence decisions at either higher or lower levels of abstraction . . . [or] at either earlier or later points in time.

This characterization is consistent with the behavior of MOLGEN using constraint posting.

Like SU-X and SU-P, the Hayes-Roths' model extends the HEARSAYII model by partitioning the blackboard into separate *planes*. In their model, an *executive* plane corresponds roughly to MOLGEN's *strategy* plane; a *meta-plan* plane corresponds to the design plane, and the three remaining planes correspond to the domain plane factored into intermediate states of planning in the errand running task. Resource allocation is governed by procedures in the executive plane. The separation of domain and control knowledge in the Hayes-Roths' model, however, is not rigorously enforced. For example, both domain-level facts and meta-level operations for setting goals appear on the *Knowledge-Base* plane.

Although the authors describe planning behavior as the result of the 'uncoordinated actions' of KSs acting opportunistically, the KSs in their computational model are far from uncoordinated. Specific KSs, such as *middle-management* and *referee*, perform critical control functions by determining focus, setting priorities, and establishing policies. While there is no explicit grouping of productions to make layered interpreters, some productions serve mainly as control functions. Unlike MOLGEN, the operators (production rules) in the model are organized as a monolithic set invoked by pattern invocation. Control is achieved by pattern-directed invocation from records placed in the blackboard planes. Some records represent control information, such as priorities and scheduling policies. The shift in attention from the problem to the meta-problem is controlled by the specification of flags in the planes; these flags are mentioned by the preconditions of the productions and tested by the interpreter. This practice invites the mixing of meta-level and first-level considerations in the rules.

The Hayes-Roths describe two planning paradigms: *hierarchical* and *opportunistic*. The *hierarchical* model is characterized as a systematic top-down exploration of possible plans. This differs from our use of the term *hierarchical planning*. For our purposes, the important feature of hierarchical planning is the use of planning islands, that is, a simplified planning model. While the direction of hierarchical planning is generally top-down, it need not be explored breath-first. Any planning model which makes use of abstractions would be termed hierarchical.

Opportunistic planning in the Hayes-Roth model is described as bi-directional (i.e., top-down and bottom-up) and heterarchical. This allows subplans to be developed independently, possibly at different levels of abstraction, for eventual incorporation into a final plan. The opportunistic idea is manifested in the constraint posting behavior of MOLGEN. Both approaches move the focus of planning activity between fruitful subproblems; both approaches work with constraints and nearly-independent subproblems. For example, the protocols in the Hayes-Roth model reveal time constraints: groceries perish, people get hungry at lunch time, the auto mechanic finishes with the car late in the day. In both cases, success depends on viewing plans as *structured objects* rather than action sequences.

The Hayes-Roths' cite examples of how the bottom-up level observations and decisions can trigger changes in higher-level activity in planning. There is an important distinction to be made here – that has been muddled somewhat in their discussion: the distinction between (1) bottom-up processing and (2) feedback of information to the meta-level. The behavior of a planning program without goals would seem very erratic; similarly a planning program with no event-driven component can have no feedback and can make no advantage of observation. In both cases, it is the *behavior of the planner* that is under scrutiny. This *problem-solving behavior* is controlled by the meta-level, so information relevant to changing problem-solving behavior must be utilized here.

In the Hayes-Roths' model, there seem to be no explicit planning operators for dealing with constraints. Constraints are simply mixed together with other records in the blackboard and somehow it all works. There are also no formal *hierarchical* planning operators and no differentiation of guessing or undoing, as in MOLGEN's heuristic cycle. These differences reflect the different interests of the researchers: the Hayes-Roths want to model human problem-solving as observed in their protocol studies, and are less interested in studying organizations of problem-solving knowledge.

5. Limitations and Further Research

This paper has argued for the use of a multi-layered organization as an antedote for the complexities of a monolithic control structure. Of course, this research has barely scratched the surface in considering the capabilities and organizations of planning systems. Several ideas and issues that go beyond the present work are listed below. This section argues that they expose an even greater need for factoring the knowledge used in a control structure.

(1) ***Guessing and Solution Density.*** When the solution space contains many solutions, almost any plan would probably work. In such situations, it would be reasonable to guess early, before performing all of the bookkeeping entailed in least-commitment approaches. This is related to the allocation of effort to *thinking* versus *thinking about thinking* in that cost/benefit estimates could be associated with the cost of computation and the risk of guessing incorrectly.

MOLGEN's conservative approach is based on a view of genetics experiment planning as a sparse solution space. Random experiments are unlikely to work. In general, the density of solutions varies with the particulars of the problem. It is possible to create additional layers of control to account for this. For example, a second layer of strategy could allow more sophisticated switching between the least-commitment and heuristic cycles. To speed up the planning process, it could recommend, for example, (1) that MOLGEN should play a sufficiently strong hunch instead of waiting until it knows that the problem is under-constrained or (2) that MOLGEN should debug (partially undo) some existing plan if its goals are sufficiently similar to those in the current problem.

(2) ***Incorporating new information.*** Experiments involving real-world feedback push the planning technology in several ways. For example, to do execution-monitoring of experiments, MOLGEN would need to inquire about

the success of laboratory steps. It would need to make judgments about what to observe, and what to do when steps violate expectations. Potentially, it would need to recognize when an unexpected event is a research opportunity and to decide (at a *meta*-level) whether to pursue it (see Feitelson and Stefik [7]). This would provide a setting to study the balance between planning *before* execution and planning *during* execution, that is, between goal-driven and event-driven planning. The ability to defer some of the planning until execution would reduce the burden of planning for all possible contingencies.

(3) ***Reasoning about theories***. MOLGEN has no sense of the scientific method, which guides the creation of experiments to test hypotheses. A full-fledged experiment planner should be able to plan experiments in order to disambiguate and extend a theory. This enterprise would require a system to balance its efforts between proposing, modifying, and testing theories.

(4) ***Reasoning about scenarios.*** There is currently a research opportunity to combine the ideas of 'truth maintenance' and hierarchical reasoning about scenarios. Such a program might reason about a future that depends in part on its own commitments and activities. It would need to consider events caused by its own actions as well as those caused by other actors. The consideration of other actors considerably increases the complexities of planning.

(5) ***Reasoning about failures.*** A geneticist observing MOLGEN would distinguish between the following reasons for not finding a plan to an experiment: (1) conflicting constraints in the problem statement, (2) incompatible constraints introduced during problem solving, (3) incomplete knowledge of the objects and materials available in the laboratory, (4) incomplete knowledge about how to plan an experiment. MOLGEN does not currently distinguish between these possible causes for failure. Knowledge about sources of failure and about the completeness of its knowledge base could be used by MOLGEN to discriminate between these types of failure.

The need for partitioning control knowledge into layers is even more acute in resource-limited problem solvers which must balance these additional issues during computation.

6. Summary

Many of the actions, goals, and constraints that are important in planning can be best understood as belonging on *meta*-levels. That is, some of the decisions and goals refer to the process of problem solving, and not to the particulars of the problem at hand. This paper argues that the organization of a problem solver can be simplified by partitioning problem solving knowledge into layers. Monolithic organizations provide no distinction for meta-level considerations. By factoring out the meta-level considerations, we can reduce the apparent complexity of the interactions between first-level tasks.

MOLGEN is organized into laboratory, design, and strategy spaces. The laboratory space represents MOLGEN's knowledge about objects in the laboratory and operators that can be used to manipulate them to achieve laboratory goals. The design space provides an explicit repertoire of operators for hierarchical planning. The organizational idea behind this space is that hierarchical planning can be understood as operations on constraints. Tasks in the design space are created and executed by the strategy space. The organizational idea behind the strategy space is the distinction between ***least-commitment*** and ***heuristic*** modes of reasoning. MOLGEN's strategy space relies on the synergy between subproblems (via constraint propagation) to stay in the least commitment cycle as long as it can, and to resort to guessing only when it has to. The design operators ***plan*** by creating and scheduling laboratory steps; the strategy operators ***meta-plan*** by creating and scheduling design steps.

ACKNOWLEDGMENT

The research reported here was drawn from my thesis [24]. Special thanks to my advisor, Bruce Buchanan, and the other members of my reading committee: Edward Feigenbaum, Joshua Lederberg, Earl Sacerdoti, and Randall Davis. The idea of *meta*-planning was originally inspired by Davis' research on *meta*-rules in the TEIRESIAS program. Thanks also to the members of the MOLGEN project—Douglas Brutlag, Jerry Feitelson, Peter Friedland, and Lawrence Kedes for their help. At several key points in this research I benefitted from expansive discussions with Frederick and Barbara Hayes-Roth and Stanley Rosenschein. Thanks to Daniel Bobrow, Lewis Creary, and Michael Genesereth for helpful comments on earlier drafts of this paper. Research on MOLGEN was funded by the National Science Foundation grant NSF MCS 78-02777. General support for the planning research was provided by DARPA Contract MDA 903-77-C-0322. Computing support was provided by the SUMEX facility under Biotechnology Resource Grant RR-00785.

REFERENCES

1. Barstow, D., A knowledge-based system for automatic program construction, *Proceedings of the Fifth International Joint Conference on Artificial Intelligence* (1977) 382–388.
2. Bobrow, D.G. and Winograd, T., An overview of KRL, A knowledge representation language, *Cognitive Sci.* **1** (1) (1977) 3–46.
3. Davis, R., Applications of meta level knowledge to the construction, maintenance and use of large knowledge bases, Doctoral Dissertation, Computer Science Department, Stanford University (1976) (Also Stanford Computer Science Department Report No. STAN-CS-76-552.
4. Davis, R., Generalized procedure calling and content-directed invocation, *SIGPLAN Notices* **12** (8) (1977) 45–54.
5. de Kleer, J., Doyle, J., Steele, G.L. and Sussman, G.J., Explict control of reasoning, MIT AI Memo 427 (June 1977).
6. Erman, L.D. and Lesser, V.R., A multi-level organization for problem solving using many, diverse, cooperating sources of knowledge, *Proceedings of the Fourth International Joint Conference on Artificial Intelligence* (1975) 483–490.
7. Feitelson, J. and Stefik, M., A case study of the reasoning in a genetics experiment, Heuristic Programming Project Report 77-18 (working paper), Computer Science Department, Stanford University (April 1977).
8. Fikes, R.E. and Hendrix, G., A network-based knowledge representation and natural deduc-

tion system, *Proceedings of the Fifth International Joint Conference on Artificial Intelligence* (1977) 235–246.

9. Georgeff, M., A framework for control of production systems, *Proceedings of the Sixth International Joint Conference on Artificial Intelligence* (1979) 328–334.
10. Goldstein, I.P. and Miller, M.L., Structured planning and debugging, a linguistic theory of design, MIT AI Memo 387 (December 1976).
11. Hayes, P.J., In defence of logic, *Proceedings of the Fifth International Joint Conference on Artificial Intelligence* (1977) 559–565.
12. Hayes-Roth, B. and Hayes-Roth, F., A cognitive model of planning, *Cognitive Sci.* **3** (1979) 275–310.
13. Lenat, D.B., *AM*: An artificial intelligence approach to discovery in mathematics as heuristic search, Doctoral dissertation, Stanford University, Computer Science Department, 1976. (Also Stanford Computer Science Report AIM-286.)
14. Mostow, J. and Hayes-Roth, F., Operationalizing heuristics: Some AI methods for assisting AI programming, *Proceedings of the Sixth International Joint Conference on Artificial Intelligence* (1979) 601–609.
15. Newell, A., Some problems of basic organization in problem-solving programs, in: Yovits, M.C., Jacobi, G.T. and Goldstein, G.D., Eds., *Proceedings of the Second Conference on Self-Organizing Systems* (Spartan Books, Chicago, Il., 1962).
16. Nii, H.P. and Feigenbaum, E.A., Rule-based understanding of signals, in: Waterman, D.A. and Hayes-Roth, F., Eds., *Pattern-Directed Inference Systems* (Academic Press, New York, 1978).
17. Polya, G., *Mathematical Discovery. 2* (John Wiley and Sons, New York, 1965).
18. Polya, G., *How to solve it* (Doubleday Anchor Books, New York, originally published 1945).
19. Sacerdoti, E.D., Planning in a hierarchy of abstraction spaces, *Artificial Intelligence* **5** (2) (1974) 115–135.
20. Sacerdoti, E.D., *A structure for plans and behavior* (American Elsevier Publishing Company, New York, 1977 (originally published, 1975)).
21. Shortliffe, E.H., *MYCIN*: *Computer-based medical consultations* (American Elsevier, New York, 1976).
22. Simon, H.A., Experiment with a heuristic compiler, *J. Assoc. Comput. Mach.*, **10** (4) (1963) 493–506.
23. Stefik, M.J., Planning with constraints, *Artificial Intelligence* **16**(2) (1981) 111–140 [this issue].
24. Stefik, M.J., *Planning with constraints*, Doctoral Dissertation, Computer Science Department, Stanford University (January 1980). (Also Stanford Computer Science Department Report No. STAN-CS-80-784.)
25. Stefik, M.J., An examination of a frame-structured representation system, *Proceedings of the Sixth International Joint Conference on Artificial Intelligence* (1979) 845–852.
26. Sussman, G.J., *A computer model of skill acquisition* (American Elsevier Publishing Company, New York, 1975 (originally published 1973)).

4 / Expert Systems and AI Applications

The first three chapters of this volume contain papers that address basic AI techniques: search, deduction, and planning. We turn now to papers that describe applications of some of these techniques. The applications range from aids for scientists and physicians to understanding spoken language and playing chess. Many important AI applications involve deductive processes that are based on "production rules." Such rules are useful representations for capturing the knowledge of experts in several domains—hence the term *expert systems*.

Barstow's paper shows how production rules are used in a system for transforming programs from abstract specifications into executable code. These rules encode a great deal of the special knowledge that programmers possess and utilize in deciding exactly how to encode various algorithms.

One of the earliest projects to attact attention as an application of AI ideas to an important problem was the DENDRAL program for inferring the structure of a chemical compound from mass spectrogram and other data. Buchanan and Feigenbaum's paper describes DENDRAL,with particular reference to its contribution as an AI application.

Shortliffe's paper provides a nontechnical overview of the problems an expert system must overcome if it is to find acceptance by its intended (non-computer-oriented) audience. Some of these can be solved by improved technology (e.g., speeding the systems up!), while others require conceptual enhancements to convince users of the reliability of the system's analyses and/or advice.

The paper by Gaschnig, Hart, and Duda describes PROSPECTOR, an expert system that helps a geologist determine the degree to which a collection of geological data constitutes evidence for the presence of a mineral deposit. A particularly attractive feature of the PROSPECTOR approach is its adherence to a well-defined interpretation of uncertainty—in terms of Bayesian analysis—and the clarity of its network type of knowledge representation. (See the paper by Duda, Hart, and Nilsson in Chapter 2 of this volume).

One of the most ambitious applications undertaken by AI researchers in recent years was that of understanding continuous speech. While the effort itself did not culminate in an economically feasible speech-understanding device, it did produce many techniques of both theoretical and practical interest. Woods's "shortfall algorithm" (see Woods's paper in Chapter 1 of this volume) is one such technique; the HEARSAY-II framework for coordinating multiple, independent knowledge sources is another. The paper by Erman et al. describes the HEARSAY architecture and its application to the speech understanding problem. HEARSAY-type designs are also important in other AI applications in which error-contaminated data from several sources must be interpreted.

Wilkins's paper applies rule-based representations of expert knowledge to the problem of chess tactics. His PARADISE system easily solves many complex chess problems that otherwise would have required an impractical amount of search. PARADISE uses production rules to generate chess plans that are then verified by a search process.

The widespread application of expert systems requires further progress in solving two fundamental and complementary problems: how to acquire large knowledge bases of expertise and, once that has been accomplished, how to verify their consistency, coverage, and effects. Davis's paper describes an important initial attempt to deal with these problems. The system he describes, TEIRESIAS, helps an expert in some subject matter, such as medicine, to modify and enlarge a knowledge base on his own (unaided by a computer scientist).

An Experiment in Knowledge-based Automatic Programming

David R. Barstow*

Yale University, New Haven, CT 06520, U.S.A.

ABSTRACT

Human programmers seem to know a lot about programming. This suggests a way to try to build automatic programming systems: encode this knowledge in some machine-usable form. In order to test the viability of this approach, knowledge about elementary symbolic programming has been codified into a set of about four hundred detailed rules, and a system, called PECOS, has been built for applying these rules to the task of implementing abstract algorithms. The implementation techniques covered by the rules include the representation of mappings as tables, sets of pairs, property list markings, and inverted mappings, as well as several techniques for enumerating the elements of a collection. The generality of the rules is suggested by the variety of domains in which PECOS has successfully implemented abstract algorithms, including simple symbolic programming, sorting, graph theory, and even simple number theory. In each case, PECOS's knowledge of different techniques enabled the construction of several alternative implementations. In addition, the rules can be used to explain such programming tricks as the use of property list markings to perform an intersection of two linked lists in linear time. Extrapolating from PECOS's knowledge-based approach and from three other approaches to automatic programming (deductive, transformational, high level language), the future of automatic programming seems to involve a changing role for deduction and a range of positions on the generality-power spectrum.

1. Introduction

1.1 Motivation

The experiment discussed here is based on a simple observation: human programmers seem to know a lot about programming. While it is difficult to state precisely what this knowledge is, several characteristics can be identified. First, human programmers know about a wide variety of concepts. Some of these concepts are rather abstract (e.g., set, node in a graph, sorting, enumeration, pattern matching), while others are relatively concrete (e.g., linked list, integer, conditional, while loop). Second, much of this knowledge deals with specific implementation techniques (e.g., property list markings to represent a set, bucket hashing to represent a mapping, quicksort, binary search). Third, programmers know guidelines or heuristics suggesting when these implementation techniques may be appropriate (e.g., property list markings are inappropriate for sets if the elements are to be enumerated frequently). In addition to these kinds of rather specific knowledge, programmers also seem to know several general strategies or principles (e.g., divide and conquer), which can be applied in a variety of situations. Finally, although programmers often know several different programming languages, much of their knowledge seems to be independent of any particular language.

Is this knowledge precise enough to be used effectively by a machine in performing programming tasks? If not, can it be made precise enough? If so, what might such an automatic programming system be like? The experiment discussed here was designed to shed some light on questions like these. The experimental technique was to select a particular programming domain, elementary symbolic programming, and a particular programming task, the implementation of abstract algorithms, and to try to codify the knowledge needed for the domain and task. For reasons to be discussed later, the form used to express the knowledge was a set of rules, each intended to embody one small fact about elementary symbolic programming. A computer system, called PECOS, was then built for applying such rules to the task of implementing abstract algorithms.

The resulting knowledge base consists of about 400 rules dealing with a variety of symbolic programming concepts. The most abstract concepts are collections[1] and mappings, along with the appropriate operations (e.g., testing for membership in a collection, computing the inverse image of an object under a mapping) and control structures (e.g., enumerating the objects in a collection). The implementation techniques covered by the rules include the representation of collections as linked lists, arrays (both ordered and unordered), and Boolean mappings, the representation of mappings as tables, sets of pairs, property list markings, and inverted mappings (indexed by range element). PECOS writes programs in LISP (specifically, INTERLISP [29]); while some of the rules are specific to LISP, most (about three-fourths) are independent of LISP or any other target language. In addition to the rules concerned with details of the different implementation techniques, PECOS has about a dozen choice-making heuristics dealing with the appropriateness and relative efficiency of the techniques. None of PECOS's rules are concerned with general strategies such as divide and conquer.

The utility of the rules is suggested by the variety of domains in which PECOS

* This research was conducted while the author was affiliated with the Computer Science Department, Stanford University, Stanford, California, 94305. The research was supported by the Advanced Research Projects Agency of the Department of Defense under Contract MDA 903-76-C-0206. The views and conclusions contained in this document are those of the author and should not be interpreted as necessarily representing the official policies, either expressed or implied, of Stanford University, ARPA, or the U.S. Government.

[1] The term "collection" is used since the rules do not distinguish between multisets, which may have repeated elements, and sets, which may not.

was able to implement abstract algorithms, including elementary symbolic programming (simple classification and concept formation algorithms), sorting (several versions of selection and insertion sort), graph theory (a reachability algorithm), and even simple number theory (a prime number algorithm). PECOS's knowledge about different implementation techniques enabled the construction of a variety of alternative implementations of each algorithm, often with significantly different efficiency characteristics.

PECOS has also been used as the Coding Expert of the PSI (Ψ) program synthesis system [13]. Through interaction with the user, Ψ's acquisition phase produces a high level description (in PECOS's specification language) of the desired program. The synthesis phase, consisting of the Coding Expert (PECOS) and the Efficiency Expert (LIBRA [17]), produces an efficient LISP implementation of the user's program. In this process, PECOS can be seen as a "plausible move generator", for which LIBRA acts as an "evaluation function". The nature of the search space produced by PECOS, as well as techniques for choosing a path in that space, will be discussed further in Section 6.1.

1.2. Representations of programming knowledge

Unfortunately, most currently available sources of programming knowledge (e.g., books and articles) lack the precision required for effective use by a machine. The descriptions are often informal, with details omitted and assumptions unstated. Human readers can generally deal with the informality, filling in the details when necessary, and (usually) sharing the same background of assumptions. Before this programming knowledge can be made available to machines, it must be made more precise: the assumptions must be made explicit and the details must be filled in.

Several different machine-usable forms for this knowledge are plausible. Some kind of parameterized templates for standard algorithms is one possibility, and would work well in certain situations, but would probably not be very useful when a problem does not fit precisely the class of problems for which the template was designed. In order to apply the knowledge in different situations, a machine needs some "understanding" of why and how the basic algorithm works. Alternatively, one could imagine some embodiment of general programming principles, which could then be applied in a wider variety of situations. However, such a technique loses much of the power that human programmers gain from their detailed knowledge about dealing with particular situations. The form used in this experiment is something of a middle ground between these two extremes: the knowledge is encoded as a large set of relatively small facts. Each is intended to embody a single specific detail about elementary symbolic programming. Ultimately, of course, automatic programming systems will need knowledge from many places on the power-generality spectrum.

There are still several possible forms for these facts, ranging from explicit formal axioms about the relevant concepts and relations, to explicit but less formal symbolic rules such as those of MYCIN [26], to the implicit form of code embedded within a program designed to perform the task. For this experiment, the form of symbolic rules was selected.[2] Several rules from PECOS's knowledge base are given below (for clarity, English paraphrases of the internal representation are used; the internal representation will be discussed in Section 5.2):

> *A collection may be represented as a mapping of objects to Boolean values; the default range object is* FALSE.
>
> *If the enumeration order is linear with respect to the stored order, the state of an enumeration may be represented as a location in the sequential collection.*
>
> *If a collection is input, its representation may be converted into any other representation before further processing.*
>
> *If a linked list is represented as a* LISP *list without a special header cell, then a retrieval of the first element in the list may be implemented as a call to the function* CAR.
>
> *An association table whose keys are integers from a fixed range may be represented as an array subregion.*

The primary reason for using the symbolic rule representation, as opposed to a mathematical axiomatization of the relevant concepts and relations, is simply that the relevant concepts and relations are not well enough understood (in many cases, not even identified) for an axiomatization to be possible. Ultimately, it may be possible to axiomatize the concepts and relations, but a necessary first step is to identify and understand them. A second reason is that most of the human-oriented sources of programming knowledge are not particularly mathematical in nature, and these sources are the first places to try when looking for programming knowledge. Finally, the development of other rule-based systems has provided considerable knowledge engineering experience that greatly facilitated PECOS's development.

1.3. The value of an explicit rule set

A large part of this experiment involved developing a set of rules about symbolic programming. The rule set itself provides several benefits. First, precision has been added to the human-oriented forms of programming knowledge, in terms of both the unstated assumptions that have been made explicit and the details that have been filled in. For example, the rule given above about representing a collection as a Boolean mapping is a fact that most programmers know; it concerns the characteristic function of a set. Without knowing this rule, or something similar,

[2] Actually, "fact" may be a better term than "rule", but "rule" will be used throughout because of the similarity between PECOS and other "rule-based" systems.

it is almost impossible to understand why a bitstring (or even property list markings) can be used to represent a set. Yet this rule is generally left unstated in discussions of bitstring representations; the author and the reader share this background knowledge, so it need not be stated. As another example, consider the rule given above about representing an association table as an array subregion. The fact that an array is simply a way to represent a mapping of integers to arbitrary values is well known and usually stated explicitly. The detail that the integers must be from a fixed range is usually not stated. Yet if the integers do not satisfy this constraint, an array is the wrong representation, and something like a hash table should be used.

A second major value of PECOS's rule set is the identification of useful programming concepts. Consider, for example, the concept of a sequential collection: a linearly ordered group of locations in which the elements of a collection can be stored. Since there is no constraint on how the linear ordering is implemented, the concept can be seen as an abstraction of both linked lists and arrays. At the same time, the concept is more concrete than that of a collection. One benefit of such intermediate-level concepts is a certain economy of knowledge: much of what programmers know about linked lists and arrays is common to both, and hence can be represented as rules about sequential collections, rather than as one rule set for linked lists and one for arrays. For example, the following two pieces of LISP code are quite similar:

```
(PROG (L)
      (SETQ L C1)
  RPT (COND ((NULL L)
             (RETURN NIL)))
      (RPLACA L (IPLUS (CAR L) 1))
      (SETQ L (CDR L))
      (GO RPT))

(PROG (I)
      (SETQ I 1)
  RPT (COND ((IGREATERP I (ARRAYSIZE C2))
             (RETURN NIL)))
      (SETA C2 I (IPLUS (ELT C2 I) 1))
      (SETQ I (IPLUS I 1))
      (GO RPT))
```

Each adds 1 to every element of a collection. In the first, the collection C1 is represented as a linked list; in the second, the collection C2 is represented as an array. The code is similar because both involve enumerating the objects in a sequential collection. The state of the enumeration is saved as a location in the collection (here, either a pointer L or an integer I). The remaining aspects depend on the representation of the enumeration state: an initial location (here, either C1, a pointer, or 1, an index), a termination test (either (NULL I) or (IGREATERP I (ARRAYSIZE C2))), an incrementation to the next location (either (CDR L) or (IPLUS I 1)), and a way to find the object in a given location (either the CAR of L or the array entry for I in C2). Other than the differences based on the representation of locations, all of the knowledge needed to write these two pieces of code is independent of the way the sequential collection is represented.

This example also illustrates the identification of particular design decisions involved in programming. One of the decisions involved in building an enumerator of the objects in a sequential collection is selecting the order in which they should be enumerated. In both of the above cases, the enumeration order is the "natural" order from first to last in the sequential collection. This decision is often made only implicitly. For example, the use of the LISP function MAPC to enumerate the objects in a list implicitly assumes that the stored order is the right order in which to enumerate them. While this is often correct, there are times when some other order is desired. For example, the selector of a selection sort involves enumerating the objects according to a particular ordering relation.

A final benefit of PECOS's rules is that they provide a certain kind of explanatory power. Consider, for example, the well-known (but little documented) trick for computing the intersection of two linked lists in linear time: map down the first list and put a special mark on the property list of each element; then map down the second collecting only those elements whose property lists contain the special mark. This technique can be explained using the following four of PECOS's rules (in addition to the rules about representing collections as linked lists):

> *The intersection of two collections may be implemented by enumerating the objects in one and collecting those which are members of the other.*
>
> *If a collection is input, its representation may be converted into any other representation before further processing.*
>
> *A collection may be represented as a mapping of objects to Boolean values; the default range object is* FALSE.
>
> *A mapping whose domain objects are atoms may be represented using property list markings.*

Given these rules, it can be seen that the trick works by first converting the representation of one collection from a linked list to property list markings with Boolean values, and then computing the intersection in the standard way, except that a membership test for property list markings involves a call to GETPROP rather than a scan down a linked list.[3]

[3] Since a new property name is created (via GENSYM) each time the conversion routine is executed, there is no need to erase marks after the intersection is computed, except to retrieve the otherwise wasted space.

As another example, consider the use of association lists: lists whose elements are dotted pairs (generally, each CAR in a given list is unique). In some situations such a structure should be viewed simply as a collection represented as a list; in others it should be viewed as a way to represent a mapping. The following rule clarifies the relationship between these two views:

> *A mapping may be represented as a collection whose elements are pairs with a "domain object" part and a "range object" part.*

Thus, in general an association list should be viewed as a mapping, but when implementing particular operations on the mapping, one must implement certain collection operations. For example, retrieving the image of a given domain object involves enumerating the elements of the list, testing the CAR of each pair for equality with the desired domain object. In turn, implementing this search involves rules about sequential collections, enumeration orders, and state-saving schemes such as those mentioned above. Thus, PECOS's rules are sufficient for writing the definition of the LISP function ASSOC.

1.4. Program construction through gradual refinement

PECOS constructs programs through a process of gradual refinement. This process may be simply illustrated as a sequence of program descriptions:

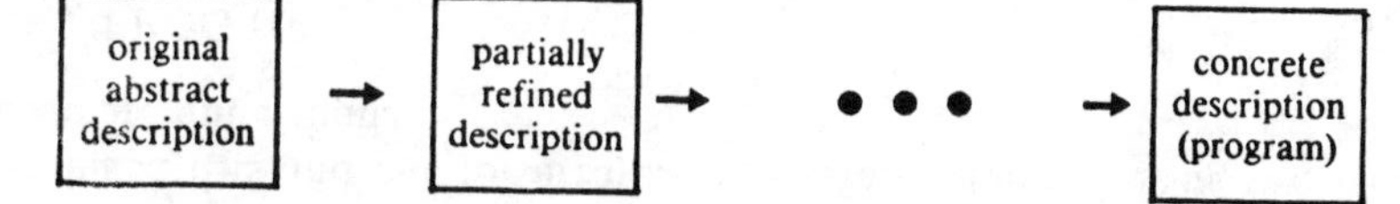

Each description in the sequence is slightly more refined (concrete) than the previous description. The first is the program description in the specification language and the last is the fully implemented program in the target language. Each refinement step is made by applying one of the rules from PECOS's knowledge base, thereby transforming the description slightly. When several rules are relevant in the same situation, PECOS can apply each rule separately. In this way PECOS can construct several different implementations from one specification. This capability for developing different implementations in parallel is used extensively in the interaction between PECOS and LIBRA in Ψ's synthesis phase.

2. Overview of the Knowledge Base

A detailed discussion of PECOS's entire rule set is beyond the scope of this paper and the interested reader is referred elsewhere [3]. Nevertheless, a brief overview may help to clarify what PECOS can and cannot do.

2.1. General rules and LISP rules

The rules can be divided into "general" and "LISP-specific" categories, where the latter deal with such concepts as CONS cells and function calls. Of PECOS's four hundred rules, slightly over one hundred are LISP-specific.[4] Most of the LISP rules are quite straightforward, merely stating that specific actions can be performed by specific LISP functions. Note that knowledge about LISP is associated with the uses to which the LISP constructs can be put. That is, rather than describing the function CAR in terms of axioms or pre- and post-conditions, as is done in most automatic programming and problem solving systems, PECOS has rules dealing with specific uses of CAR, such as returning the item stored in a cell of a "LISP list" or returning the object stored in one of the fields of a record structure represented as a CONS cell. Thus, there is never a necessity of searching through the knowledge base of facts about LISP in order to see whether some function will achieve some desired result; that information is stored with the description of the result. This representation reduces searching significantly, but also lessens the possibilities of "inventing" some new use for a particular LISP function.

The rest of this overview will be concerned only with the "general" rules. Three major categories of implementation techniques are covered by the rules: representation techniques for collections, enumeration techniques for collections, and representation techniques for mappings. The rules also deal with several lower-level aspects of symbolic programming, but they will be omitted completely from this discussion.

2.2. Representation of collections

Conceptually, a collection is a structure consisting of any number of substructures, each an instance of the same generic description. (As noted earlier, PECOS's rules do not distinguish between sets and multisets.) The diagram in Fig. 1 summarizes the representation techniques that PECOS currently employs for collections, as well as several (indicated by dashed lines) that it does not. Each branch in the diagram represents a refinement relationship. For example, a sequential collection may be refined into either a linked list or an array subregion. These refinement relationships are stored in the knowledge base as refinement rules. Of course, the diagram doesn't indicate all of the details that are included in the rules (e.g., that an array subregion includes lower and upper bounds as well as some allocated space).

As can be seen in the diagram of Fig. 1, PECOS knows primarily about the use of Boolean mappings and sequential collections. Both of these general techniques will be illustrated in the derivation of the Reachability Program in Section 4. Although "distributed collection" occurs in a dashed box, PECOS can implement a collection using property list markings by following a path through a Boolean mapping to a distributed mapping. The most significant missing representations

[4] In a preliminary experiment, the LISP-specific rules were replaced by rules for SAIL (an ALGOL-like language [24]), and PECOS wrote a few small SAIL programs [22]. The programs were too simple to justify definite conclusions, but they are an encouraging sign that this distinction between "general" and "language-specific" rules is valid and useful.

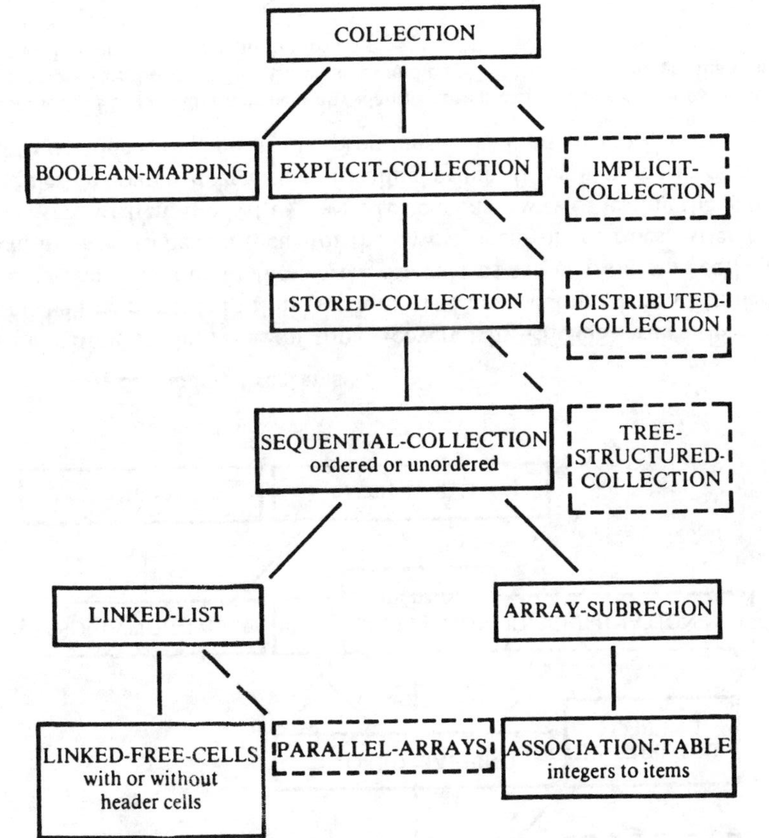

FIG. 1.

are the use of trees (such as AVL trees or 2–3 trees) and implicit collections (such as lower and upper bounds to represent a collection of integers). Codification of knowledge about these techniques would be a valuable extension of PECOS's knowledge base.

Note the extensive use of intermediate-level abstractions. For example, there are four concepts between "collection" and "linked free cells". As noted earlier, such intermediate levels help to economize on the amount of knowledge that must be represented, and also facilitate choice making.

2.3. Enumerations over stored collections

In its most general form, enumerating the elements of a collection may be viewed as an independent process or coroutine. The elements are produced one after another, one element per call. The process must guarantee that every element will be produced on some call and that each will be produced only once. In addition, there must be some wav to indicate that all of the elements have been produced, as well as some way to start up the process initially. The process of constructing an enumerator for a stored collection involves two principal decisions: selecting an appropriate order for enumerating the elements, and selecting a way to save the state of the enumeration.

There are several possible orders in which the elements can be produced. If the enumeration order is constrained to be according to some ordering relation, then clearly that order should be selected. If it is unconstrained, a reasonable choice is to use the stored (first-to-last) order, either from the first cell to the last (for linked lists) or in order of increasing index (for arrays). In some cases, it may be useful to use the opposite (last-to-first) order.

The enumeration state provides a way for the enumerator to remember which elements have been produced and which have not. There are many ways to save such a state. Whenever the enumeration order is first-to-last (or last-to-first), an indicator of the current position is adequate: all elements before (or after, for last-to-first) the current position have been produced and all elements after (before) the position have not. PECOS's rules handle these cases, as well as the case in which the enumeration order is constrained and the collection is kept ordered according to the same constraint, in which case a position indicator is also adequate for saving the state.

The situation is somewhat more complex for nonlinear enumerations (i.e., the enumeration order is not the same as the stored order or its opposite); finding the next element typically involves some kind of search or scan of the entire collection. During such a search, the state must be interrogated somehow to determine whether the element under consideration has already been produced. There are basically two kinds of nonlinear enumeration states, destructive and nondestructive. PECOS's rules deal with one destructive technique, the removal of the element from the collection. A technique not covered by the rules is to overwrite the element. The rules also do not cover any nondestructive techniques.

2.4. Representation of mappings

A mapping is a way of associating objects in one set (range elements) with objects in another set (domain elements).[5] A mapping may (optionally) have a default image: if there is no stored image for a particular domain element, a request to determine its image can return the default image. For example, when a Boolean mapping is used to represent a collection, the default image is FALSE.

The diagram of Fig. 2 summarizes representation techniques for mappings. As with collection representations, there are several intermediate levels of abstraction for mappings. Note that an association list representation is determined by following the path from "mapping" to a "collection" whose elements are domain/range pairs; the refinement path in the collection diagram given earlier then leads to a

[5] PECOS's rules only deal with many-to-one mappings and not with more general correspondences or relations.

linked list of pairs. Property lists give a distributed mapping whose domain is the set of atoms. A plex (or record structure) with several fields would constitute a mapping whose domain is the set of field names. The most significant mapping representations missing from PECOS's rules are implicit mappings (such as function definitions) and discrimination nets. As with the use of trees to represent collections, codifying knowledge about discrimination nets will certainly involve several aspects of graph algorithms. The rules currently deal with only one small aspect of hash tables: the use of INTERLISP's hash arrays. This is clearly another area where further codification would be valuable.

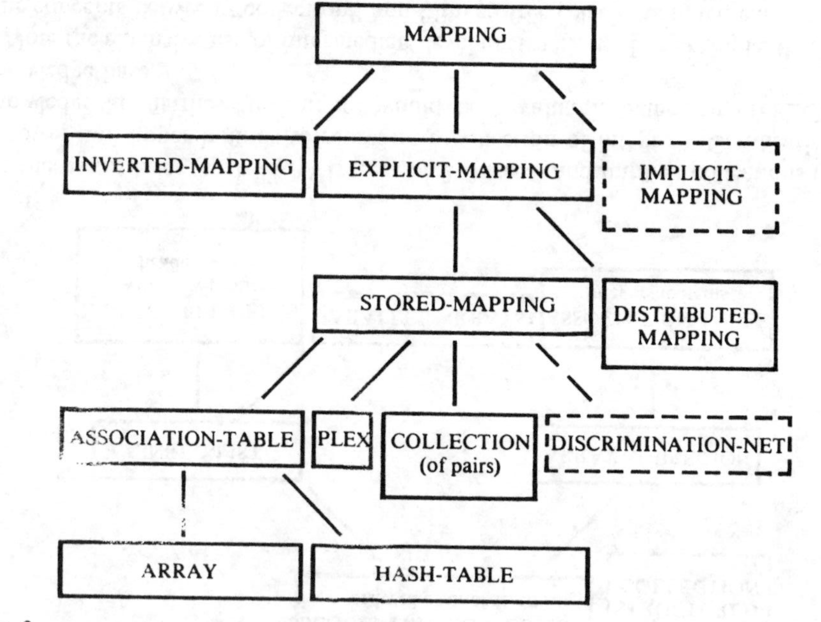

FIG. 2.

3. Sample Programs

As an indication of the rang- of topics covered by PECOS's rules, five sample programs will be presented in this section.[6] The next section gives a detailed look at a sixth. The first four of these were selected as target programs early in the research, in order to have a focus for the development of the rules. After most of the rules were written, the last two were selected as a way of testing the generality of the rules. About a dozen rules (dealing primarily with numeric operations) needed to be added for the last two programs to be constructed.

[6] Theoretically PECOS can implement any algorithm that can be described in its specification language. In practice, however, PECOS cannot handle specifications much longer than "a page" before space limitations become prohibitive.

3.1. Membership test

The variety of implementations that PECOS can produce is illustrated well by a simple membership test. PECOS can implement such a test in about a dozen ways, differing primarily in the way that the collection is represented. If a sequential collection is used, there are several possibilities. In the special case of a linked list, the LISP function MEMBER can be used. In addition, there are various ways of searching that are applicable for either linked lists or arrays. If the collection is ordered, the search can be terminated early when an element larger than the desired element is found. If the collection is unordered, the enumeration must run to completion. A rather strange case is an ordered enumeration of an unordered collection, which gives a membership test whose time requirement is $O(n^2)$. If the collection is represented as a Boolean mapping, a membership test is implemented as the retrieval of the image of the desired element. For each way to represent a mapping, there is a way to retrieve this image. The LISP functions GETHASH, GETPROP, and ELT apply to hash arrays, property list markings, and arrays respectively. In addition, a collection of pairs can be searched for the entry whose CAR is the desired element and the entry's CDR can be returned. PECOS has successfully implemented all of these cases.

3.2. A simple concept classification program

The second target program was a simple classification program called CLASS. CLASS inputs a set (called the concept) and then repeatedly inputs other sets (called scenes) and classifies them on the basis of whether or not the scene fits the concept. A scene fits a concept if every member of the concept is a member of the scene. The specification given to PECOS is paraphrased below[7]:

Data structures

```
CONCEPT    a collection of integers
SCENE      a collection of integers or "QUIT"
```

Algorithm

```
CONCEPT ← input a list of integers;
loop:
    SCENE ← input a list of integers or the string "QUIT";
    if SCENE = "QUIT" then exit the loop;
    if CONCEPT is a subset of SCENE
        then output the message "Fit"
        else output the message "Didn't fit";
    repeat;
```

[7] Integers were used as the elements of the scenes and concept to facilitate the use of ordered collections. A different set of implementations would be possible with different types of elements in the sets.

The major variations in implementations of CLASS involve different representations for SCENE and the role they play in the subset test. The test is refined into an enumeration of the elements of CONCEPT, searching for one that is not a member of SCENE.[8] In the simplest case, the internal representation of SCENE is the same as the input representation, a linked list. The other cases involve converting SCENE into some other representation before performing the subset test. The major motivation for such a conversion is that membership tests for other representations are much faster than for unordered linked lists. One possibility is to sort the list, but the time savings in the membership test may not be sufficient to offset the time required to perform the sorting.[9] Other possibilities include the use of Boolean mappings such as property list markings and hash tables. PECOS has successfully constructed all of these variations.

3.3. A simple formation program

The third target program was TF, a rather simplified version of Winston's concept formation program [32]. TF builds up an internal model of a concept by repeatedly reading in scenes which may or may not be instances of the concept. For each scene, TF determines whether the scene fits the internal model of the concept and verifies the result with the user. The internal model is then updated based on whether or not the result was correct. The internal model consists of a set of relations, each marked as being necessary or possible. A scene fits the model if all of the necessary relations are in the scene. The updating process is divided into four cases: (1) if the model fit the scene and this was correct (indicated by user feedback), all relations in the scene that are not in the model are added to the model and labelled "possible"; (2) if the model fit but this was incorrect, any relation marked "possible" but not in the scene is picked and relabelled as "necessary"; (3) if the model did not fit and this was incorrect, all relations marked "necessary" that are not in the scene are relabelled as "possible"; (4) otherwise, there is no change.

The most interesting variations in the implementation revolve around the representation of the mapping CONCEPT. Inverting this mapping gives two sets to be represented, NECESSARY and POSSIBLE. Since "any" and "all" operations are applied to these sets, a stored collection is appropriate (although for some distributions of input data Boolean mapping representations may be better). Since elements will be added and removed from both sets, linked lists are reasonable representations. The computation of the domain of CONCEPT is fairly interesting as the domain set does not exist explicitly with inverted mappings, but must be computed (in this case by a union of NECESSARY and POSSIBLE). Note, however, that the only operation applied to the domain is a membership test. In such a case, the test can be refined into a disjunction of two membership tests, one on NECESSARY and one on POSSIBLE, and there is no need to explicitly compute the domain of CONCEPT. This is the implementation that PECOS constructed.

[8] For some representations that PECOS cannot handle, other forms for the subset test are appropriate. For example, if CONCEPT and SCENE are both represented as bit vectors, "CONCEPT $\wedge \neg$ SCENE" is zero if and only if CONCEPT is a subset of SCENE.

[9] PECOS cannot currently use the technique of sorting both lists so that they can be scanned in parallel, thereby greatly increasing the savings.

3.4. Sorting

PECOS's development originally began as an investigation into the programming knowledge involved in simple sorting programs [14–16]. PECOS's current rule set is sufficient to synthesize a variety of sorting algorithms within the transfer paradigm, in which sorting is viewed as a process of transferring the elements from the (unordered) input collection one at a time to the (ordered) output collection. Under this view, the part of the program that selects the next element to transfer is simply an enumerator over the elements of the input set. If the enumeration order of this selector is the same as the stored order of the input, the resulting sort program does an insertion sort. If the enumeration order of the selector is the same as (or the opposite of) the sorted order, the program is a selection sort. PECOS has implemented selection and insertion sort programs using both arrays and lists for the input and output collections. Thus, PECOS can carry out (approximately) the reasoning required for what was earlier described as a "hypothetical dialogue" [15].

3.5. Primes

The following problem is taken from Knuth's textbook series [18]:

> 7.1–32. [22] (R. Gale and V. R. Pratt.) The following algorithm can be used to determine all odd prime numbers less than N, making use of sets S and C.
>
> **P1.** [Initialize] Set $j \leftarrow 3$, $C \leftarrow S \leftarrow \{1\}$. (Variable j will run through the odd numbers 3, 5, 7, ... At step P2 we will have
>
> $$C = \{n | n \text{ odd},\ 1 \leqslant n < N,\ n \text{ not prime, and } \operatorname{gpf}(n) \leqslant p(j)\},$$
> $$S = \{n | n \text{ odd},\ 1 \leqslant n < N/p(j), \text{ and } \operatorname{gpf}(n) \leqslant p(j)\},$$
>
> where $p(j)$ is the largest prime less than j and $\operatorname{gpf}(n)$ is the greatest prime factor of n; $\operatorname{gpf}(1) = 1$.)
>
> **P2.** [Done?] If $j \geqslant N/3$, the algorithm terminates (and C contains all the nonprime odd numbers less than N).
>
> **P3.** [Nonprime?] If $j \in C$ then go to step P5.
>
> **P4.** [Update the sets.] For all elements n in S do the following: If $nj < N$ then insert nj into S and into C, otherwise delete n from S. (Repeat this process until all elements n of S have been handled, including those which were just newly inserted.) Then delete j from C.

P5. [Advance j.] Increase j by 2 and return to P2.

Show how to represent the sets in this algorithm so that the total running time to determine all primes $< N$ is $O(N)$. Rewrite the above algorithm at a lower level (i.e., not referring to sets) using your representation.

[Notes: The number of set operations performed in the algorithm is easily seen to be $O(N)$, since each odd number $n < N$ is inserted into S at most once, namely when $j = \text{gpf}(n)$, and deleted from S at most once. Furthermore we are implicitly assuming that the multiplication of n times j in step P4 takes $O(1)$ units of time. Therefore you must simply show how to represent the sets so that each operation needed by the algorithm takes $O(1)$ steps on a random-access computer.]

Since PECOS's rules do not cover enumerations over collections that are being modified during the enumeration, a slightly modified version of the original algorithm was given to PECOS. In this version, the set S has been replaced by two sets $S1$ and $S2$, and the set P is created to output the set of primes (the complement of C).

Data structures

```
C    a set of integers
P    a set of integers
S1   a set of integers
S2   a set of integers
J    an integer
K    an integer
N    an integer
```

Algorithm

```
N← input an integer;
J← 3;
C← {1};
S1← {1};
loop:
  if 3*J > N then exit;
  if J is not a member of C then
    S2← S1;
    S1← { };
    loop until S2 is empty:
      for any X in S2:
        remove X from S2;
        if J*X < N then
          add X to S1;
          add J*X to S2;
          add J*X to C;
```

Algorithm (*continued*)

```
        remove J from C;
    J← J+2;
    repeat;
  K← 3;
  P← { };
  loop:
    if N < K then exit;
    if K is not a member of C
      then add K to P;
    K← K+2;
    repeat;
  output P as a linked list.
```

The only operations being performed on $S2$ are addition, removal, and taking "any" element. The "any" operation suggests that a Boolean mapping may be inappropriate and the frequent destructive operations suggest that an array may be relatively expensive. Thus, an unordered linked list is a reasonable selection. Since the value of $S1$ is assigned to $S2$, a representation conversion can be avoided by using the same representation for both sets. This is especially useful here, since the only operation applied to $S1$, the addition of elements, is relatively simple with unordered linked lists. The only operations applied to C are addition, removal, and two membership tests. Such operations are fairly fast with Boolean mappings. Since the domain elements of the mapping are integers with a relatively high density in their range of possible values, an array of Boolean values is a reasonable representation of C. PECOS has implemented the Primes Program in this way, as well as with a linked list representation for C. To check the relative efficiency of the two implementations, each was timed for various values of N, see Table 1. (Note the approximately linear behaviour of the Boolean array case and the distinctly nonlinear behavior of the linked list case.)

TABLE 1. (Times are given in milliseconds)

N	C as linked list	C as Boolean array
10	0.05	0.04
50	0.28	0.20
100	0.63	0.40
500	6.40	2.02
1000	21.21	4.08

4. A Detailed Example

Perhaps the best way to understand how PECOS works is to see an example of the use of programming rules and the refinement paradigm to construct a particular program. This example also demonstrates that the rules enable PECOS to deal with the program at a very detailed level and that the same rules may be used in several different situations.

In order to focus on the nature of the rules and the refinement process, the example will be presented in English. After a description of the abstract algorithm to be implemented, several specific aspects of it will be discussed in detail. For each of these aspects, the abstract description of that part of the algorithm will be presented, followed by a sequence of rules, together with the refinements they produce in the original description. The result of this sequence of rule applications will be a LISP implementation of the original abstract description.

4.1. The reachability problem

The example is based on a variant of the reachability problem [30]:

Given a directed graph, G, and an initial vertex, v, find the vertices reachable from v by following zero or more arcs.

The problem can be solved with the following algorithm:

Mark v as a boundary vertex and mark the rest of the vertices of G as unexplored. If there are any vertices marked as boundary vertices, select one, mark it as explored, and mark each of its unexplored successors as a boundary vertex. Repeat until there are no more boundary vertices. The set of vertices marked as explored is the desired set of reachable vertices.

Note that the algorithm's major actions involve manipulating a mapping of vertices to markings.

Based on this observation, the algorithm can be expressed at the level of PECOS's specification language. The following is an English paraphrase of the specification given to PECOS when this example was run. (As a notational convenience, $X[Y]$ will be used to denote the image of Y under the mapping X and $X^{-1}[Z]$ will be used to denote the inverse image of Z under X.)

Data structures

VERTICES	a collection of integers
SUCCESSORS	a mapping of integers to collections of integers
START	an integer
MARKS	a mapping of integers to {"EXPLORED", "BOUNDARY", "UNEXPLORED"}

Algorithm

```
VERTICES ← input a list of integers;
SUCCESSORS ← input an association list of ⟨integer, list of integers⟩ pairs;
START ← input an integer;
for all X in VERTICES:
  MARKS[X] ← "UNEXPLORED";
MARKS[START] ← "BOUNDARY";
repeat until MARKS⁻¹["BOUNDARY"] is empty:
  X ← any element of MARKS⁻¹["BOUNDARY"];
  MARKS[X] ← "EXPLORED";
  for all Y in SUCCESSORS[X]:
    if MARKS[Y] = "UNEXPLORED" then MARKS[Y] ← "BOUNDARY";
output MARKS⁻¹["EXPLORED"] as a list of integers.
```


The specification is abstract enough that several significantly different implementations are possible. For example, MARKS could be represented as an association list of ⟨integer, mark⟩ pairs or as an array whose entries are the marks. The relative efficiency of these implementations varies considerably with several factors. For example, if the set of vertices (integers) is relatively sparse in a large range of possible values, then implementing MARKS as an array with a separate index for each possible value would probably require too much space, and an association list would be preferable. On the other hand, if the set of vertices is dense or the range small, an array might allow much faster algorithms because of the random-access capabilities of arrays. For the remainder of this discussion, it will be assumed that the range of possible values for the vertices is small enough that array representations are feasible. Note also that concrete input representations are specified for VERTICES (a linked list), SUCCESSORS (an association list), and START (an integer), and that an output representation is specified for MARKS^{-1}["EXPLORED"] (a linked list). These constrain the input and output but not the internal representation. They are intended to reflect the desires of some hypothetical user and PECOS could handle other input and output representations equally well.

When PECOS was run on the Reachability Algorithm, there were several dozen situations in which more than one rule was applicable. In most of these cases, selecting different rules would result in the construction of different implementations, and PECOS has successfully implemented the algorithm in several different ways. In the following discussion, one particular implementation is synthesized. About two-thirds of the choices made during the synthesis were handled by PECOS's choice-making heuristics, and in the remaining third, a rule was selected interactively in order to construct this particular implementation.

4.2. SUCCESSORS

Under the SUCCESSORS mapping, the image of a vertex is the set of immediate successors of the vertex:

$$\text{SUCCESSORS}[v] = \{x \mid v \rightarrow x \text{ in } G\}$$

SUCCESSORS is constrained to be an association list when it is input, but such a representation may require significant amounts of searching to compute SUCCESSORS[X]. Since this would be done in the inner loop, a significantly faster algorithm can be achieved by using an array representation with the entry at index k being the set of successors of vertex k. In the rest of this section, the derivation of this array representation will be considered in detail.

4.2.1. Representation of SUCCESSORS

SUCCESSORS is a mapping of integers to collections of integers. An English paraphrase of PECOS's internal representation is given below:

SUCCESSORS:
MAPPING (integers → collections of integers)

The selection of an array representation for SUCCESSORS involves four distinct decisions: that each association in the mapping be represented explicitly, that the associations be stored in a single structure, that a tabular structure be used, and that an array be used for the table. These four decisions are made by applying a sequence of four rules (corresponding to the path from "mapping" to "array" in the diagram of mapping representations given earlier). Each rule results in a slight refinement of the abstract description of SUCCESSORS:

A mapping may be represented explicitly.

SUCCESSORS:
EXPLICIT MAPPING (integers → collections of integers)

An explicit mapping may be stored in a single structure.

SUCCESSORS:
STORED MAPPING (integers → collections of integers)

A stored mapping with typical domain element X and typical range element Y may be represented with an association table whose typical key is X and whose typical value is Y.

$\text{SUCCESSORS}_{\text{table}}$:
ASSOCIATION TABLE (integers → collections of integers)

(Subscripts, as in $\text{SUCCESSORS}_{\text{table}}$, are used to distinguish between representations at different refinement levels.)

An association table whose typical key is an integer from a fixed range and whose typical value is Y may be represented as an array with typical entry Y.

$\text{SUCCESSORS}_{\text{array}}$:
ARRAY (collection of integers)

The final step involves selecting a particular data structure in the target language, in this case INTERLISP's array representation:

An array may be represented directly as a LISP *array.*

$\text{SUCCESSORS}_{\text{lisp}}$:
LISP ARRAY (collection of integers)

The objects stored in the array must also be represented. Through a sequence of six rule applications, tracing the path in the collection diagram from "collection" to "linked free cells", followed by a LISP-specific rule, a LISP list representation is developed:

$\text{SUCCESSORS}_{\text{lisp}}$:
LISP ARRAY (*LISP LIST* (integer))

4.2.2. *SUCCESSORS[X]*

Determining the set of successor vertices for a given vertex involves computing the image of that vertex under the SUCCESSORS mapping. The abstract specification of this operation is:

compute the image of *X* under SUCCESSORS

The construction of the program for computing SUCCESSORS[*X*] follows a line parallel to the determination of the representation of SUCCESSORS:

If a mapping is stored as an association table, the image of a domain element X may be computed by retrieving the table entry associated with the key X.

retrieve the entry in $\text{SUCCESSORS}_{\text{table}}$ for the key *X*

If an association table is represented by an array, the entry for a key X may be retrieved by retrieving the array entry whose index is X.

retrieve the entry in $\text{SUCCESSORS}_{\text{array}}$ for the index *X*

If an array is represented as a LISP *array, the entry for an index X may be retrieved by applying the function ELT.*

(ELT $\text{SUCCESSORS}_{\text{lisp}}$ *X*)

4.2.3. *Converting between Representations of SUCCESSORS*

Recall that the input representation for SUCCESSORS is constrained to be an association list of ⟨integer, list of integers⟩ pairs:

$\text{SUCCESSORS}_{\text{input}}$:
LISP LIST (*CONS CELL* (DOMAIN . RANGE))
DOMAIN: integer
RANGE: *LISP LIST* (integer)

Since the input and internal representations differ, a representation conversion must be performed when the association list is input. The description for the input operation is as follows:

```
SUCCESSORS ← input a mapping (as an association list);
```

The following rule introduces the representation conversion:

If a mapping is input, its representation may be converted into any other representation before further processing.

```
SUCCESSORSinput ← input a mapping (as an association list);
SUCCESSORS ← convert SUCCESSORSinput
```

The conversion operation depends on the input representation:

If a mapping is represented as a stored collection of pairs, it may be converted by considering all pairs in the collection and setting the image (under the new mapping) of the "domain object" part of the pair to be the "range object" part.

```
for all X in SUCCESSORSinput:
  set SUCCESSORS[X:DOMAIN] to X:RANGE
```

(Here X:DOMAIN and X:RANGE signify the retrieval of the "domain object" and "range object" parts of the pair X.) Since the pairs in SUCCESSORS$_{input}$ are represented as CONS cells, the X:DOMAIN and X:RANGE operations may be implemented easily through the application of one rule in each case.

If a pair is represented as a CONS cell and part X is stored in the CAR part of the cell, the value of part X may be retrieved by applying the function CAR.

If a pair is represented as a CONS cell and part X is stored in the CDR part of the cell, the value of part X may be retrieved by applying the function CDR.

```
for all X in SUCCESSORSinput:
  set SUCCESSORS[(CAR X)] to (CDR X)
```

The implementation of the "set SUCCESSORS[(CAR X)]" operation is constructed by applying a sequence of rules similar to those used for implementing SUCCESSORS[X] in the previous section, resulting in the following LISP code:

```
for all X in SUCCESSORSinput:
  (SETA SUCCESSORSlisp (CAR X) (CDR X))
```

In constructing the program for the "for all" construct, the first decision is to perform the action one element at a time, rather than in parallel:

An operation of performing some action for all elements of a stored collection may be implemented by a total enumeration of the elements, applying the action to each element as it is enumerated.

```
enumerate X in SUCCESSORSinput:
  (SETA SUCCESSORSlisp (CAR X) (CDR X))
```

Constructing an enumeration involves selecting an enumeration order and a state-saving scheme:

If the enumeration order is unconstrained, the elements of a sequential collection may be enumerated in the order in which they are stored.

If a sequential collection is represented as a linked list and the enumeration order is the stored order, the state of the enumeration may be saved as a pointer to the list cell of the next element.

The derivation now proceeds through several steps based on this particular state-saving scheme, including the determination of the initial state (a pointer to the first cell), a termination test (the LISP function NULL), and an incrementation step (the LISP function CDR):

```
STATE ← SUCCESSORSinput;
loop:
  if (NULL STATE) then exit;
  X ← (CAR STATE);
  (SETA SUCCESSORSlisp (CAR X) (CDR X));
  STATE ← (CDR STATE);
  repeat;
```

The complete LISP code for this part is given below, exactly as produced by PECOS. The variables V0074, V0077, V0071, and V0070 correspond to SUCCESSORS$_{input}$, STATE, X, and SUCCESSORS$_{lisp}$, respectively.

```
(PROG (V0077 V0075 V0074 V0071 V0070)
      (PROGN (PROGN (SETQ V0074 (PROGN (PRIN1 "Links:")
                                        (READ)))
                    (SETQ V0070 (ARRAY 100)))
             (SETQ V0077 V0074))
 G0079
      [PROGN (SETQ V0075 V0077)
             (COND
               ((NULL V0077) (GO L0078)))
             (PROGN (PROGN (SETQ V0071 (CAR V0075))
                           (SETA V0070 (CAR V0071)
                                       (CDR V0071)))
                    (SETQ V0077 (CDR V0077]
      (GO G0079)
 L0078
      (RETURN V0070)))
```

4.3. MARKS

MARKS is the principal data structure involved in the Reachability Algorithm. At each iteration through the main loop it represents what is currently known about the reachability of each of the vertices in the graph:

MARKS[X] = "EXPLORED"
  ⇒ X is reachable and its successors have been noted as reachable
MARKS[X] = "BOUNDARY"
  ⇒ X is reachable and its successors have not been examined
MARKS[X] = "UNEXPLORED"
  ⇒ no path to X has yet been found

In the rest of this section, E, B, and U will denote "EXPLORED", "BOUNDARY", and "UNEXPLORED" respectively.

The abstract description for MARKS is as follows:

MARKS:
  MAPPING (integers → {E, B, U})

Note that the computation of the inverse image of some range element is a common operation on MARKS. In such situations, it is often convenient to use an inverted representation. That is, rather than associating range elements with domain elements, sets of domain elements can be associated with range elements.

A mapping with typical domain element X and typical range element Y may be represented as a mapping with typical domain element Y and typical range element a collection with typical element X.

$MARKS_{inv}$:
  MAPPING ({E, B, U} → collections of integers)

At this point, the same two rules that were applied to SUCCESSORS can be applied to $MARKS_{inv}$:

A mapping may be represented explicitly.
An explicit mapping may be stored in a single structure.

$MARKS_{inv}$:
  STORED MAPPING ({E, B, U} → collections of integers)

When selecting the structure in which to store the mapping, we may take advantage of the fact that the domain is a fixed set (E, B, and U):

A stored mapping whose domain is a fixed set of alternatives and whose typical range element is Y may be represented as a plex with one field for each alternative and with each field being Y.

$MARKS_{plex}$:
  PLEX (UNEXPLORED, BOUNDARY, EXPLORED)
    EXPLORED: collection of integers
    BOUNDARY: collection of integers
    UNEXPLORED: collection of integers

A plex is an abstract record structure consisting of a fixed set of named fields, each with an associated substructure, but without any particular commitment to the way the fields are stored in the plex. In LISP, the obvious way to represent such a structure is with CONS cells:

$MARKS_{lisp}$:
  CONS CELLS (UNEXPLORED BOUNDARY . EXPLORED)
    EXPLORED: collection of integers
    BOUNDARY: collection of integers
    UNEXPLORED: collection of integers

Notice that we are now concerned with three separate collections which need not be represented the same way.

Since MARKS is inverted, the inverse image of an object under MARKS may be computed by retrieving the image of that object under $MARKS_{inv}$. If the domain object (e.g., B) is known at the time the program is constructed, this operation may be further refined into a simple retrieval of a field in the plex:

---

retrieve the BOUNDARY field of $MARKS_{plex}$

Likewise, the image of a domain object may be changed from one value to another (for example, from B to E) by moving the object from one collection to another:

---

remove X from the BOUNDARY field of $MARKS_{plex}$;
add X to the EXPLORED field of $MARKS_{plex}$

4.4. BOUNDARY

BOUNDARY is the set of all vertices that map to B under MARKS. Since MARKS is inverted, this collection exists explicitly and a representation for it must be selected. The abstract description of BOUNDARY is as follows:

BOUNDARY:
  COLLECTION (integer)

The operations that are applied to BOUNDARY include the addition and deletion of elements and the selection of some element from the collection. A linked list is often convenient for such operations. To derive a representation using cells allocated from free storage, we apply a sequence of five rules, which lead from "collection" to "linked free cells" in the collection diagram given earlier:

A collection may be represented explicitly.

An explicit collection may be stored in a single structure.

A stored collection with typical element X may be represented as a sequential arrangement of locations in which instances of X are stored.

A sequential arrangement of locations with typical element X may be represented as a linked list with typical element X.

A linked list may be represented using linked tree cells.

$\text{BOUNDARY}_{\text{cells}}$:
LINKED FREE CELLS (integer)

It is often convenient to use a special header cell with such lists, so that the empty list need not be considered as a special case:

A special header cell may be used with linked free cells.

$\text{BOUNDARY}_{\text{cells}}$:
LINKED FREE CELLS (integer) *with special header cell*

Any use of cells allocated from free storage requires allocation and garbage collection mechanisms. In LISP, both are available with the use of CONS cells:

Linked free cells may be represented using a LISP list of CONS cells.

$\text{BOUNDARY}_{\text{lisp}}$:
LISP LIST (integer) *with special header cell*

4.4.1. *Any Element of MARKS^{-1}["BOUNDARY"]*

The main loop of the Reachability Algorithm is repeated until MARKS^{-1}-["BOUNDARY"] (i.e., the BOUNDARY collection) is empty. At each iteration, one element is selected from the collection:

---

retrieve any element of BOUNDARY

The first refinement step for this operation depends on the earlier decision to represent BOUNDARY as a sequential collection:

If a collection is represented as a sequential collection, the retrieval of any element in the collection may be implemented as the retrieval of the element at any location in the collection.

---

retrieve the element at location *L* of $\text{BOUNDARY}_{\text{seq}}$
L is any location

The next step is then to select the location to be used. The two most useful possibilities for sequential collections are the front and the back. Of these, the front is generally best for linked lists; although the back can also be used, it is usually less efficient:

If a location in a sequential collection is unconstrained, the front may be used.

---

retrieve the element at the front of $\text{BOUNDARY}_{\text{list}}$

The remaining steps are straightforward:

If a linked list is represented using linked free cells with a special header cell, the front location may be computed by retrieving the link from the first cell.

If linked free cells are implemented as a LISP list, the link from the first cell may be computed by using the function CDR.

If linked free cells are implemented as a LISP list, the element at a cell may be computed by using the function CAR.

The result of these three rule applications, when combined with the code for computing $\text{MARKS}_{\text{inv}}[B]$, is the following LISP code for computing "any element of MARKS^{-1}["BOUNDARY"]":

```
(CAR (CDR (CAR (CDR MARKSlisp))))
```

4.4.2. *Remove X from MARKS$_{\text{inv}}$["BOUNDARY"]*

Recall that one of the operations involved in changing the image of *X* from *B* to *E* is the removal of *X* from $\text{MARKS}_{\text{inv}}[B]$:

---

remove *X* from BOUNDARY

The first refinement step is similar to that of the "any element" operation:

If a collection is represented as a sequential collection, an element may be removed by removing the item at the location of the element in the collection.

---

remove the item at location *L* of BOUNDARY
L is the location of X

Normally, determining the location of an element in a sequential collection involves some kind of search for that location. In this case, however, the location is already known, since X was determined by taking the element at the front of BOUNDARY:

> *If an element X was determined by retrieving the element at location L of a sequential collection C, then L is the location of X in C.*

---

remove the item at the front of BOUNDARY

(Testing the condition of this rule involves tracing back over the steps that produce the particular element X and determining that, indeed, the location of X in BOUNDARY is the front.) From this point on, the program construction process is relatively straightforward, and similar to the "any element" derivation. The end result is the following LISP code:

```
(RPLACD (CAR (CDR MARKSlisp))
        (CDR (CDR (CAR (CDR MARKSlisp)))))
```

4.5. UNEXPLORED

The UNEXPLORED collection contains all of those vertices to which no path has yet been found. The initial description of UNEXPLORED is the same as that of BOUNDARY:

UNEXPLORED:
  COLLECTION (integer)

The only operations applied to this collection are membership testing, addition, and deletion. For such operations, it is often convenient to use a different representation than simply storing the elements in a common structure (as was done with the BOUNDARY collection):

> *A collection may be represented as a mapping of objects to Boolean values; the default range object is FALSE.*

UNEXPLORED_{map}:
  MAPPING (integers → {TRUE, FALSE})

Having decided to use a Boolean mapping, all of the rules available for use with general mappings are applicable here. In particular, the same sequence of rules that was applied to derive the representation of SUCCESSORS can be applied with the following result:

UNEXPLORED_{lisp}:
  LISP ARRAY ({TRUE, FALSE})

Thus, UNEXPLORED is represented as an array of Boolean values, where the entry for index k is TRUE if vertex k is in the UNEXPLORED collection and FALSE otherwise.

The implementation of the "change MARKS[Y] from U to B" operation involves removing Y from the UNEXPLORED collection. Since UNEXPLORED is represented differently from BOUNDARY, removing an element must also be done differently. In this case, four rules, together with the LISP representation of FALSE as NIL, give the following LISP code:

```
(SETA UNEXPLOREDlisp Y NIL)
```

4.6. Final program

The other aspects of the implementation of the Reachability Algorithm are similar to those we have seen. The following is a summary of the final program. (Here, $X[Y]$ denotes the Yth entry in the array X and X: Y denotes the Y field of the plex X.)

Reachability Program

```
VERTICES ← input a list of integers;
SUCCESSORSinput ← input an association list of ⟨integer, list of
                                                integers⟩ pairs;
SUCCESSORS ← create an array of size 100;
for all X in the list SUCCESSORSinput;
  SUCCESSORS[X:DOMAIN] ← X:RANGE;
START ← input an integer;
MARKS:UNEXPLORED ← create an array of size 100;
MARKS:BOUNDARY ← create an empty list with header cell;
MARKS:EXPLORED ← create an empty list with header cell;
for all X in the list VERTICES:
  MARKS:UNEXPLORED[X] ← TRUE;
MARKS:UNEXPLORED[START] ← FALSE;
insert START at front of MARKS:BOUNDARY;
loop:
  if MARKS:BOUNDARY is the empty list then exit;
  X ← front element of MARKS:BOUNDARY;
  insert X at front of MARKS:EXPLORED;
  remove front element of MARKS:BOUNDARY;
  for all Y in the list SUCCESSORS[X];
    if MARKS:UNEXPLORED[Y] then
      MARKS:UNEXPLORED[Y] ← FALSE;
      insert Y at front of MARKS:BOUNDARY;
  repeat;
output MARKS:EXPLORED.
```

5. Implementation

There are three important aspects to PECOS's implementation: the representation of program descriptions in a refinement sequence, the representation of programming rules, and the control structure. In this section, each of these will be considered briefly.

5.1. Representation of Program Descriptions

Each program description in a refinement sequence is represented as a collection of nodes, with each node labelled by a particular programming concept. For example, a node labelled IS-ELEMENT represents an operation testing whether a particular item is in a particular collection. Each node also has a set of links or properties related to the node's concept; for example, an IS-ELEMENT node has properties (named ELEMENT and COLLECTION) for its arguments. Although property values may be arbitrary expressions, they are usually links to other nodes (as in the IS-ELEMENT case). Fig. 3 shows part of the internal representation for the expression IS-ELEMENT(X,INVERSE(Y,Z)).[10] Each box is a node. The labels inside the boxes are the concepts and the labeled arrows are property links. The argument links of an operation all point to other operations.

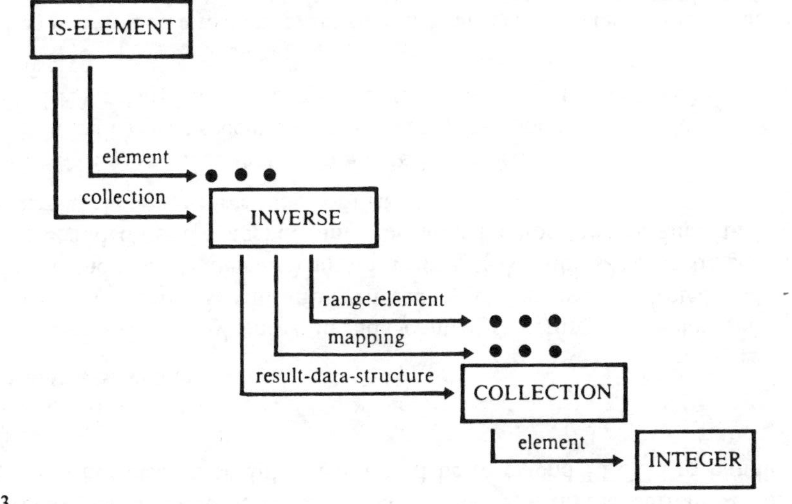

FIG. 3.

For example, the COLLECTION operand of the IS-ELEMENT node is the INVERSE node. The value computed by an operation is indicated by the RESULT-DATA-STRUCTURE property. Thus, the COLLECTION node represents the data structure passed from the INVERSE operation to the IS-ELEMENT operation. (Note that this collection is only implicit in the corresponding English description.) Since refinement rules for an operation have conditions both on the data structure it produces and on the data structures produced by its operands, the refinement of this COLLECTION node enables the refinements of the IS-ELEMENT and INVERSE nodes to be coordinated. Thus, for example, the refined inverse operation does not produce a linked list when the refined membership test expects a Boolean mapping. This explicit representation of every data structure passed from one operation to another is perhaps the most important feature of PECOS's representation of program descriptions.

[10] Read "Is X an element of the inverse image of Y under the mapping Z?".

5.2. Representation of Programming Rules

PECOS's rules all have the form of condition–action pairs, where the conditions are patterns to be matched against subparts of descriptions, and the actions are particular modifications that can be made to program descriptions. Based on the action, the rules are classified into three types:

Refinement rules refine one node pattern into another. The refined node is typically created at the time of rule application. These are the rules which carry out the bulk of the refinement process, and are by far the most common type.

Property rules attach a new property to an already existing node. Property rules are often used to indicate explicit decisions which guide the refinements of distinct but conceptually linked nodes.

Query rules are used to answer queries about a particular description. Such rules are normally called as part of the process of determining the applicability of other rules.

The internal representation of the rules is based on this classification:

(REFINE ⟨*node pattern*⟩⟨*refinement node*⟩)
(PROPERTY ⟨*property name*⟩ ⟨*node pattern*⟩ ⟨*property value*⟩)
(QUERY ⟨*query pattern*⟩ ⟨*query answer*⟩)

where REFINE, PROPERTY, and QUERY are tags indicating rule type. In the REFINE and PROPERTY rules, each ⟨*node pattern*⟩ consists of a ⟨*concept*⟩ and an ⟨*applicability pattern*⟩. For example, the following rule

> *A sequential arrangement of locations with typical element X may be represented as a linked list with typical element X.*

is represented as a refinement rule:

```
(REFINE (SEQUENTIAL-COLLECTION
                   (GET-PROPERTY ELEMENT (BIND X)))
        (NEW-NODE LINKED-LIST
                   (SET-PROPERTY ELEMENT X)))
```

SEQUENTIAL-COLLECTION is the ⟨*concept*⟩ and (GET-PROPERTY ELEMENT (BIND X)) is the ⟨*applicability pattern*⟩.

Several other issues have arisen in the design of the rule base organization, including an indexing scheme for efficient rule retrieval, the design of a pattern matcher, and the breakdown of the condition patterns into separate parts for different uses. Detailed discussions of these issues may be found elsewhere [3]. It should also be noted that several kinds of rules are not easily expressed in the current formalism. For example, more general inferential rules (such as the test constructor used by Manna and Waldinger [23]) and rules about certain kinds of data flow (such as merging an enumeration over a set with the enumeration that constructed it) can not be described conveniently with the current set of rule types. It is not clear how difficult it would be to extend PECOS to handle such cases.

5.3. Control Structure

PECOS uses a relatively simple agenda control structure to develop refinement sequences for a given specification: in each cycle, a task is selected and a rule applied to the task. While working on a given task, subtasks may be generated; these are added to the agenda and considered before the original task is reconsidered. There are three types of tasks:

- (REFINE *n*) specifies that node *n* is to be refined.
- (PROPERTY *p n*) specifies that property *p* of node *n* is to be determined.
- (QUERY rel arg1 arg2 · · ·) specifies that the query (rel arg1 arg2 · · ·) must be answered.

When working on a task, relevant rules are retrieved and tested for applicability. For example, if the task is (REFINE 72) and node 72 is an IS-ELEMENT node, then all rules of the form (REFINE (IS-ELEMENT · · ·) · · ·) will be considered. When testing applicability, it may be necessary to perform a subtask. For example, an argument may need to be refined in order to determine if it is represented as a linked list. This is, in fact, quite common: the refinement of one node is often the critical factor making several rules inapplicable to a task involving another node.

When several rules are applicable, each would result in a different implementation. When a single rule cannot be selected (either by the choice-making heuristics the user, or LIBRA), a refinement sequence can be split, with each rule applied in a different branch. As a result, PECOS creates a tree of descriptions in which the root node is the original specification, each leaf is a program in the target language, and each path from the root to a leaf is a refinement sequence. With the current knowledge base, most refinement sequences lead to complete programs. For the few that do not, the cause is generally that certain operation/data structure combinations do not have any refinement rules. For example, there are no rules for computing the inverse of a distributed mapping, since this might require enumerating a very large set, such as the set of atoms in a LISP core image. If PECOS encounters a situation in which no rules are applicable, the refinement sequence is abandoned.

Further details of the control structure and the context mechanism used for the tree of descriptions may be found elsewhere [3].

6. Discussion

6.1. A Search space of correct programs

The problem of choosing between alternative implementations for the same abstract algorithm is quite important, since the efficiency of the final program can vary considerably with different implementation techniques. Within the framework of Ψ's synthesis phase, this problem has been broken into two components:

(1) constructing a search space whose nodes are implementations (possibly only partial) of the abstract algorithm, and

(2) exploring this space, making choices on the basis of the relative efficiency of the alternatives.

The first is provided by PECOS's rules and refinement paradigm; the second is provided by LIBRA [17], Ψ's Efficiency Expert. PECOS can thus be viewed as a "plausible move generator" for which LIBRA is an "evaluation function".

6.1.1. Refinement trees

The space of alternative implementations generated by PECOS can be seen as a generalization of refinement sequences. Whenever alternative rules can be applied (and hence, alternative implementations produced), a refinement sequence can be split. Thus, we have a refinement tree, as illustrated in Fig. 4. The root of such a tree is the original specification, the leaves are alternative implementations, and each path is a refinement sequence.

Experience, both with PECOS alone and together with LIBRA, has shown that a refinement tree constitutes a fairly "convenient" search space. First, the nodes (program descriptions) all represent "correct" programs.[11] Each node represents a step in a path from the abstract specification to some concrete implementation of it. When paths cannot be completed (as happens occasionally), the cause is generally the absence of rules for dealing with a particular program description, rather than any inherent problem with the description itself. Second, the refinement paradigm provides a sense of direction for the process. Alternatives at a choice point represent reasonable and useful steps toward an implementation. Third, the extensive use of intermediate level abstractions makes the individual refinement steps fairly small and "understandable". For example, the efficiency transformations associated with the rules for use by LIBRA (see Section 6.1.3) are simpler than they would be if the intermediate levels were skipped.

[11] Assuming correctness of the rules, of course; see Section 6.3.

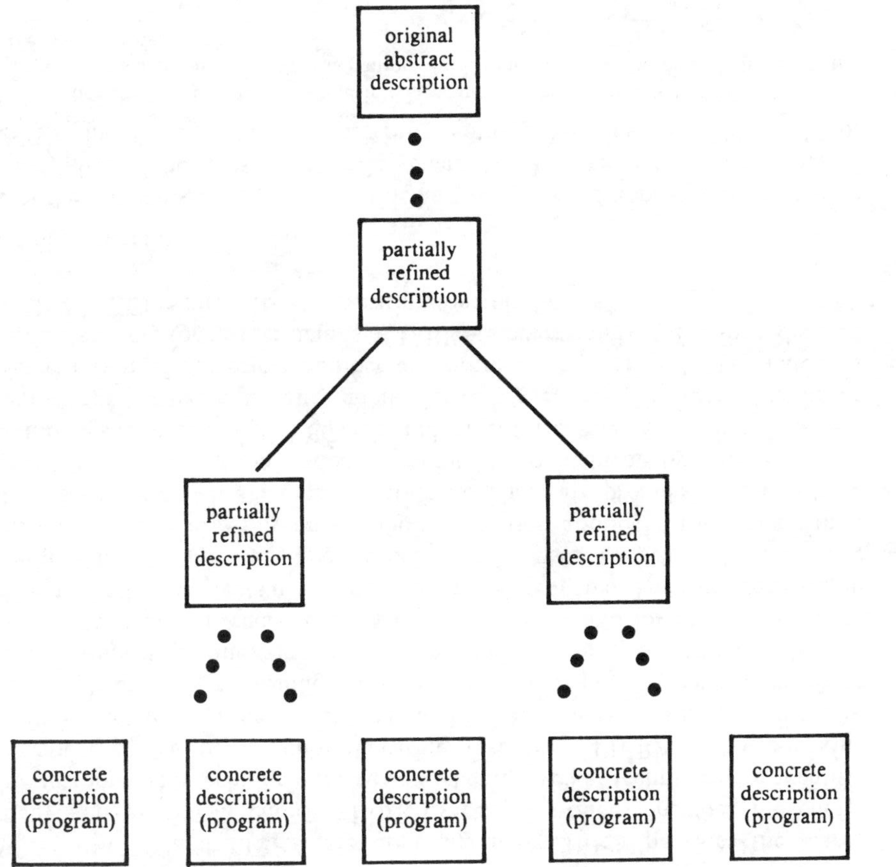

FIG. 4.

6.1.2. Techniques for reducing the space

The size of refinement trees (i.e., the total number of rule applications) may be reduced without eliminating any of the alternative implementations by taking advantage of the fact that many of the steps in a refinement sequence may be reordered without affecting the final implementation: the only absolute ordering requirement is that one task must be achieved first if it is a subtask of another. For example, if a program involves two collections, the refinement steps for each must occur in order, but the two subsequences may be intermingled arbitrarily.

PECOS postpones consideration of all choice points until the only other tasks are those for which some choice point is a subtask.[12] As a result, refinement trees tend to be "skinny" at the top and "bushy" at the bottom. Experience has shown that a considerable reduction in tree size can result. For example, the size of the tree for the four implementations of CLASS (see Section 3) was reduced by about one third by using this technique.

When two choice points are sufficiently independent that a choice for one may be made regardless of what choice is made for the other, a simple extension of the choice point postponement technique permits further pruning. For example, suppose there are two choice points (A and B), each having two applicable rules. The four leaves of the entire tree represent the cross-product of the alternatives for each of the choices. If one (say A) is considered first, then several further refinement steps (for which A had been a subtask) may be made before B needs to be considered. Since A is independent of B, the two paths for A can be carried far enough that a preference for one path over the other can be determined before B is considered. Thus, the alternatives for B along the other path need not be considered at all. In the tree shown below, the branches inside the box need not be explored if A_2 can be selected over A_1 independently of what choice is made for B.

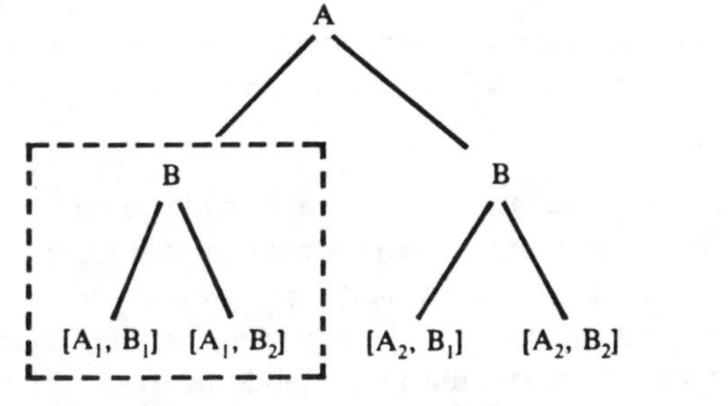

6.1.3. Techniques for making choices

When PECOS is running alone, choices between alternative rules are made either by the user or by a set of about a dozen choice-making heuristics. Some of these heuristics are intended to prune branches that will lead to dead ends (situations in which no rules are applicable). For example, PECOS has no rules for adding an element at the back of a linked list. One of the heuristics (for selecting a position at which an element should be added to a sequential collection) tests whether the sequential collection has been refined into a linked list, and if so rejects "back" as a possibility. One interesting feature of such heuristics is that they embody knowledge about the capabilities of the system itself, and thus should be changed as rules are added and the system's capabilities change.

Other heuristics deal with decisions that can be made on a purely "local" basis, considering only the node being refined and the alternative rules. Sometimes one alternative is known a priori to be better than another; if both are applicable the better alternative should be taken. For example, one of PECOS's heuristics

[12] With the current rule set, choice points are relatively infrequent. In the Reachability Program, for example, there were about three dozen choice points in a refinement sequence that involved about one thousand rule applications.

prefers PROGN to PROG constructs: (PROGN · · ·) is better than (PROG NIL · · ·). In other cases, the cost difference between two alternatives isn't very great, but one is more convenient for most purposes. For example, PECOS has a heuristic that suggests always using special headers for linked free cells, since the extra cost is low (one extra cell) and they are often more easily manipulated.[13]

Experience with programs such as those in Section 3 suggests that PECOS's heuristics are capable of handling a majority of the choice points that arise in refinement sequences. About two-thirds of the three dozen choice points involved in developing the Reachability Program were handled by the heuristics. For example, the front/back heuristic for linked lists handled the selection of the front position of BOUNDARY for the "any" operation. On the other hand, the selection of the array representation for SUCCESSORS was beyond the capabilities of the heuristics, since it involved global considerations, such as the size of the set of integers that might be nodes, the density of nodes within that set, and the cost of conversion.

When PECOS and LIBRA are used together, LIBRA provides the search strategy and makes all choices. LIBRA's search strategy includes the choice point postponement technique described earlier, as well as techniques for identifying critical choice points and allocating resources. LIBRA's choice-making techniques include local heuristics, such as PECOS's, as well as global heuristics. When the heuristics are insufficient, or when a choice point is determined to be especially important, analytic methods are applied. Using cost estimates for the intermediate level constructs, LIBRA computes upper and lower bounds on the efficiency of all refinements of a node in the refinement tree. Then standard search techniques (such as branch and bound) can be used to prune the tree. The efficiency estimates also rely on specific information about the user's algorithm, such as set sizes and branching probabilities. These are provided as part of the original abstract description, and are computed for refinements by efficiency transformations associated with PECOS's refinement rules. PECOS and LIBRA's behavior together has been fairly good. For example, they constructed the linear implementation of the prime number algorithm given by Knuth. The reader is referred elsewhere for further details of LIBRA's operation [17], and for a detailed example of PECOS and LIBRA operating together [4].

6.2. Rule generality

One of the critical issues involved in this knowledge-based approach to automatic programming is the question of rule generality: will many (or even some) of PECOS's rules be useful when other programming domains are codified? If so, there is some hope that a generally useful set of rules can eventually be developed. If not, then the knowledge base required of such a system may be prohibitively large. While it is too early to give a definitive answer, there are several encouraging signs. First, as described in Section 3, PECOS has successfully implemented programs in a variety of domains, ranging from simple symbolic programming to graph theory and even elementary number theory. As mentioned earlier, very few additional rules (about a dozen out of the full 400) needed to be added to the knowledge base in order to write the reachability and prime number programs. Second, the fact that LISP-specific rules could be replaced by SAIL-specific rules, leaving most of the knowledge base unchanged, also suggests a degree of generality in the rules.

In the long run, the question of rule generality can only be resolved by trying to extend the rule set to cover new domains. Work is underway at Yale to codify the programming knowledge needed for elementary graph algorithms [2]. The early signs again suggest the utility of knowledge about sets and mappings. For example, the notion of an enumeration state seems important for enumerating the nodes in a graph, just as it is important for enumerating the elements of a set. The MARKS mapping used in the abstract algorithm in Section 4 encodes the state of the enumeration of the reachable nodes in the graph. As another example, consider the common technique of representing a graph as an adjacency matrix. In order to construct such a representation, only one rule about graphs need be known:

> *A graph may be represented as a pair of sets: a set of vertices (whose elements are primitive objects) and a set of edges (whose elements are pairs of vertices).*

The rest of the necessary knowledge is concerned with sets and mappings and is independent of its application to graphs. For example, in order to derive the bounds on the matrix, one need only know that primitive objects may be represented as integers, that a set of otherwise unconstrained integers may be represented as a sequence of consecutive integers, and that a sequence of consecutive integers may be represented as lower and upper bounds. To derive the representation of the matrix itself, one need only know PECOS's rules about Boolean mappings and association tables, plus the fact that a table whose keys are pairs of integers in fixed ranges may be represented as a two-dimensional matrix.

6.3. Issues of correctness

It seems plausible that access to a large base of programming knowledge would help reduce the search involved in program verification. Consider, for example, the problem of determining the loop invariant in the following program for adding 1 to every entry in an array A:

[13] Note that the heuristic doesn't take into account whether or not the extra cell actually helps in the particular case under consideration. And, indeed, it may be difficult to tell at the time the choice is made.

```
(PROG (I)
        (SETQ I 1)
RPT     (COND ((IGREATERP I N)
               (RETURN NIL)))
        (SETA A I (IPLUS (ELT A I) 1))
        (SETQ I (IPLUS I 1))
        (GO RPT))
```

The invariant, to be attached "between" the RPT label and the COND expression, is as follows:

$$\forall k(1 \leqslant k < \mathrm{I} \supset \mathrm{A}[k] = \mathrm{A}_0[k]+1) \wedge (\mathrm{I} \leqslant k < \mathrm{N} \supset \mathrm{A}[k] = \mathrm{A}_0[k])$$

where $\mathrm{A}[k]$ denotes the current kth entry of A and $\mathrm{A}_0[k]$ denotes the initial kth entry. Knowing the sequence of rule applications that produced this code gives us the invariant almost immediately. The $\forall k$ is suggested by the fact that the loop implements an enumeration over a sequential collection represented as an array subregion. Since the enumeration order is the stored order, and the enumeration state is held by I, we know that the action should have been done for all and only those indices less than I. And since the enumeration is total and the bounds on the subregion are 1 and N, we know the indices of concern are those between 1 and N.

But on another level, we might ask whether PECOS's rules are themselves correct. For refinement rules such as these, a reasonable definition of correctness might be: a rule is correct if, for all programs to which the rule may be applied, all relevant properties of the program are preserved under rule application. Thus, if the original abstract algorithm is correct (i.e., has the properties desired by the user), and if all rules that are applied are correct in this sense, then the final implementation is a correct one. What properties are the relevant ones? Clearly, the same kinds of properties that have been considered in the traditional approaches to program verification: that the value returned by a refined operation be the same as the value returned by the abstract operation under the same conditions, and that the side effects of a refined operation be the same as those of the abstract operation. But note that the question of side effects is complicated by the fact that some of the side effects at a refined level cannot even be discussed at an abstract level. For example, the fact that list cells are being modified when a new object is added to a list doesn't have any relevance at the more abstract level of adding an object to a sequential collection.

Although it would clearly be useful, no formal proofs of PECOS's rules have yet been made. In fact, the relevant properties of the abstract operators have only been specified informally. The goal of this research was rather to lay the groundwork by identifying the useful concepts and relationships, as a necessary precursor to a complete formalization. Nonetheless, some of the issues mentioned above have come up in the process of developing a set of rules that seems at least informally to be correct. As a simple example, consider the operation of inserting a new cell after a given cell in a linked list. PECOS's representation of this operation is approximately (INSERT-AFTER-CELL ⟨cell⟩ ⟨new-object⟩). The obvious refinement rule here indicates that a new cell should be created (for ⟨new-object⟩ and the link from ⟨cell⟩) and that a link to this new cell should be stored in the link field of ⟨cell⟩. Implementing this as a simple macro expansion gives roughly (REPLACE-LINK ⟨cell⟩ (CREATE-CELL ⟨new-object⟩ (GET-LINK ⟨cell⟩))). But notice that, if ⟨cell⟩ is an expression (possibly with side effects), rather than simply the value of a variable, the expression is evaluated twice, which might then violate the correctness criteria discussed above, or at least be somewhat inefficient. Thus, the correct refinement involves storing the value of ⟨cell⟩ before performing the above operations.

7. Approaches to Automatic Programming

The term "automatic programming" is rather difficult to define. In part the problem lies in the long history of the term: it was used over twenty years ago in discussions about early programming languages [1]. Nonetheless, for the sake of this discussion, let us define automatic programming rather loosely as an attempt to automate some part of the programming process. A variety of approaches have been taken in facing this problem, including extending language development to higher level languages [21, 25], formalizing the semantics of programming languages [5, 9], and many attempts involving the application of artificial intelligence techniques [8, 12, 27, 28, 31]. PECOS is an attempt to apply yet another artificial intelligence paradigm, knowledge engineering, to the same goal of automatic programming.

While it is too early to tell how far any of these approaches will lead, insight may be gained by comparing them. In the rest of this section, we will consider four systems, each of which exemplifies a different approach, and compare them with respect to certain fundamental issues of automatic programming. The four systems are DEDALUS [23], based on a *deductive* approach; Darlington and Burstall's system [8], involving a *transformational* approach; Low's system [21], based on *high level languages*; and PECOS, based on a *knowledge-based* approach. Of course, there are aspects of each approach in each of the systems, and, as will become clearer, the differences are less than they might seem at first. But nonetheless, each system will serve to illustrate one approach.

7.1. Summaries of three other automatic programming systems

Before comparing these systems, let us briefly review DEDALUS, Darlington and Burstall's system, and Low's system.

Although DEDALUS employs transformation rules extensively, it is classified as an example of the deductive approach to automatic programming because of the use of deduction in developing the control structure of the target program.

Briefly, DEDALUS takes a program specified non-algorithmically in terms of sets (and lists) of integers, and tries to apply various transformations that introduce primitive constructs in the target language. In the process, conditionals and recursive calls may be introduced when their need is recognized by the deductive system. For example, consider implementing a program to compute $x <$ all(l), that is, whether x is less than every member of l, where x is an integer and l is a list of integers. There are two transformation rules for the all construct. The first transforms P(all(l)) into true if l is the empty list; the second transforms P(all(l)) into P(head(l)) and P(all(tail(l))), if l is not empty. Since l cannot be proved to be either empty or not empty, the original construct is transformed into if empty(l) then true else ($x <$ head(l)) and ($x <$ all(tail(l))). DEDALUS then notices that $x <$ all(tail(l)) is an instance of the original goal $x <$ all(l), suggesting the use of a recursive call to the function being defined. In this way, various control constructs can be introduced into the program by the deductive mechanism. Among the programs which DEDALUS has successfully constructed are programs for computing the maximum element of a list, greatest common divisor, and cartesian product.

Darlington and Burstall developed a system (which we will refer to as DBS) for improving programs by a transformation process. Programs are specified in the form of recursive definitions in the domain of finite sets, and are transformed into an imperative language which includes constructs such as "while" and assignment, as well as recursion. The transformation process goes through four stages: recursion removal, elimination of redundant computation, replacement of procedure calls by their bodies, and causing the program to reuse data cells when they are no longer needed. In addition, DBS could implement the set operations with either bitstring or list representations. Among the programs optimized by DBS are an in-place reverse from its recursive definition and an iterative Fibonacci from its doubly recursive definition. In a later system [6], they incorporated various strategies for developing recursive programs (e.g., a "folding" rule which is similar to Manna and Waldinger's recursion introduction rules).

Low has developed a system (which will be referred to here as LS) for automatically selecting representations for sets. LS accepts programs specified in a subset of SAIL which includes lists and sets as data types, and uses a table of concrete (at the machine code level) implementations for these data types and the associated operations, together with information about the efficiency of the implementations. The available implementation techniques include sorted lists and arrays, balanced trees, bitstrings, hash tables, and attribute bits. LS first partitions the various instances of sets and lists into groups that should be implemented uniformly, then analyzes the frequency of use of the various constructs, both statically and dynamically with sample data, and finally uses a hill-climbing technique to find an optimal implementation. LS has been applied to such programs as insertion sort, merge sort, and transitive closure.

7.2. Techniques of program specification

Programs are specified to the four systems in basically two ways: DEDALUS accepts specifications such as the following:

compute $x <$ all(l)
where x is a number
and l is a list of numbers

This can be seen as simply another way of giving input and output predicates, where the input predicate is the "where" clause and the output predicate is the "compute" clause. The other three systems all accept specifications as abstract algorithms in terms of set operations; PECOS also allows operations on mappings. However, the difference is perhaps less than it might seem, since an abstract operator is simply a shorthand for some implicit input and output predicates. For example, inverse(x, y) is simply another way of saying the following (assuming the domain and range of y are integers):

compute $\{z \mid y(z) = x\}$
where y is a mapping from integers to integers
and x is an integer

The main advantage of the input/output form over the abstract algorithm is increased generality: there may not be a concept whose implied input/output predicates are precisely those desired. On the other hand, the algorithmic form often seems more natural.

There are other specification techniques that one could imagine, such as example input/output pairs, natural language, and even dialogue. In the long run, it seems that a mixture of all of these techniques (and probably more) will be needed—perhaps the prime criterion should be the "naturalness" of the technique to the person specifying the program and the domain under consideration.

7.3. Side effects

The problem of side effects has long been a difficult one for problem-solving and automatic programming systems. HACKER [28], for example, was unable to solve certain kinds of robot problems because the side effects of operations to achieve one goal might interfere with previously achieved goals. Consequently, many automatic programming systems deal with side effects in only limited ways. DBS, for example, only accepts programs specified in an applicative (i.e., without side effects) language, although assignments to variables are allowed in the target language. In addition, the final stage of transformation involves attempting to reuse discarded list cells, instead of calls to CONS. DEDALUS allows only a few target language operations that have side effects (basically, different kinds of assignment), along with specification language constructs like "only z changed", meaning that z is the only variable that may be modified. The problem of interfering goals is faced by labelling certain goals as "protected", and requiring that those which cannot be proved to hold must be re-achieved. LS and PECOS both allow a richer set of specification operators with side effects, such as adding to and removing elements from sets (and, in PECOS's case, operators such as changing the image of an object under a mapping). In each case, the knowledge base (i.e., LS's implementation table and PECOS's rules) include techniques for implementing the specific operators. As mentioned earlier, the nature of side effects sometimes requires that PECOS's rules not be implemented as simple macro expansion: the rule for inserting an object into a list requires that the insertion location be saved, since a call to (REPLACE-LINK ⟨cell⟩ (CREATE-CELL ⟨new-object⟩ (GET-LINK ⟨cell⟩))) would involve computing ⟨cell⟩ twice. In any case, it seems that the problem of side effects is likely to plague automatic programming systems for some time. The problem is, unfortunately, unavoidable, since efficient implementations often require explicit and deliberate use of side effects.

7.4. Abstraction and refinement

Just as abstraction and refinement have become increasingly important in programming methodology [7], and in recent developments in programming languages [20, 33], they have also begun to play a role in automatic programming. In DEDALUS, the role is relatively minor: some of the specification language constructs can be viewed as abstractions. For example, the all construct, as in $x < \text{all}(l)$, is essentially the same as PECOS's abstract control structure FOR-ALL-TRUE, as in (FOR-ALL-TRUE y l (LESS x y)). Abstraction and refinement are much more important in DBS, LS, and PECOS. Each accepts programs specified in abstract terms involving sets (and, in PECOS's case, mappings) and produces a concrete program which is essentially a refinement of the abstract program. For DBS and PECOS the target language is LISP, and for LS the target language is PDP-10 machine code. Perhaps the greatest distinction between the systems is PECOS's use of multiple levels of abstraction. While DBS and LS both refine in one step from the abstract concepts to the target language constructs, PECOS may go through as many as a half dozen levels between the specification level and the target level. This seems to offer several advantages. First, multiple levels contribute to an economy of knowledge. The example noted earlier, sequential collections, illustrates this well: much of the knowledge about linked lists and arrays is common to both and can be stored once as knowledge about sequential collections, rather than once for linked lists and once for arrays (and once for every other kind of sequential collection). Second, multiple levels facilitate the use of different representations in different situations. This was a major problem with LS: the sets to be represented were partitioned into equivalence classes such that all arguments of any operator were in the same equivalence class. The effect, in the case of a transitive closure program, was that all of the sets were represented in the same way. The motivation for this partitioning was that the tables would have to be prohibitively large to allow each of the operators to take different kinds of arguments or to include representation conversions between them. In PECOS, the intermediate levels of abstraction provide convenient hooks for knowledge about converting between representations. For example, the BOUNDARY and UNEXPLORED collections of the Reachability Program are represented differently, while in LS's implementation of transitive closure the corresponding sets were forced to have the same representation. In fact, not only can PECOS avoid the requirement that several related data structures have the same representation, but the same data structure can even have different representations. For example, the SUCCESSORS mapping was input as an association list but converted into a Boolean array, which was more efficient in the inner loop. A third benefit of the muliple levels of abstraction, and perhaps this is the cause of the benefits just described, is that there is room for a rich interplay between the programming concepts involved. The single rule about representing collections as Boolean mappings, for example, leads to a variety of different collection representations because of the knowledge already known about mappings.

7.5. Dealing with alternative implementations

The ultimate goal of an automatic program synthesis system is to produce the best (or at least an adequate) target language program that satisfies the user's specifications. Thus, in a sense, the problem involves search in the space of all legal target programs. This space is obviously too large to be explored exhaustively, so all automatic synthesis systems incorporate (at least implicitly) some way of reducing this space. But notice that there are two aspects of the desired program: it must satisfy the user's requirements, and it should be the best such satisfactory program. Earlier systems (e.g., the Heuristic Compiler [27] and the theorem-prover based systems [12, 31]) basically faced only the first aspect: they were concerned with finding any program that worked. DEDALUS shares this concern: its goal is to find some program in the target language that satisfies the user's specifications. The only sense in which it faces the second aspect is that the user may disable certain rules in the hope that the program found using the remaining rules (if any is found) will be better. DBS, LS, and PECOS all focus on the second aspect, in that there is an explicit space of alternative implementations. DBS allows the user to choose between two alternative implementations of the basic set constructs, lists and bitstrings. LS has its table of seven alternative implementations for set operations, and chooses among them automatically. PECOS's rules deal with about a dozen representations for collections (although not as varied as LS's representations), about a half dozen representations for mappings, and essentially two different enumeration techniques (ordered and unordered). There are several questions that one may ask about such a space of alternative implementations:

Does it include the desired implementation? Are there any dead-end or incorrect paths? How easy is it to explore? LS includes implementation techniques that PECOS does not (e.g., AVL trees). On the other hand, PECOS includes global considerations that LS does not. As noted above, PECOS avoids the restriction that all operands to a set operator must be represented in the same way, and even allows the same set to be represented in different ways in different places in the program. Thus, both LS's and PECOS's spaces include a variety of implementations for a given abstract algorithm, but the spaces seem to differ along slightly different dimensions. With respect to dead-end or incorrect paths, LS clearly has none. As discussed earlier (see Section 6.1), PECOS occasionally has a few dead-ends but no incorrect paths. How easy are the spaces to explore? In LS, after the partitioning restriction is made, the space is searched with a hill-climbing technique that seems both natural and convenient, although the possibility remains that the optimal program may be missed. As discussed in Section 6.1, PECOS's use of intermediate-level abstractions seems to facilitate greatly the process of making choices. PECOS has about a dozen choice-making heuristics that seem able to handle about two-thirds of the cases that arise in practice. LIBRA, Ψ's Efficiency Expert, uses more analytic methods, again taking advantage of the intermediate-level abstractions. In several test cases, LIBRA has performed quite well, although space limitations have prevented PECOS and LIBRA from being applied together to programs as large as the Reachability Algorithm. In the long run, it seems that the problem of choosing among alternative implementations will grow in importance for automatic programming systems, and that better techniques will be required, both for generating spaces that include the desired target programs and are convenient for exploration, and for choosing from among alternatives in such spaces. As far as the choice-making process is concerned, it seems a good guess that heuristic methods will become increasingly important, and that analytic methods (largely because of the cost of using them) will be reserved for cases in which the heuristics are inapplicable.

7.6. The role of deduction

In the earliest attempts to apply AI techniques to automatic programming, deduction (that is, the use of some kind of relatively general purpose theorem prover or problem solver) played a central role. The Heuristic Compiler was based on problem solving within the GPS framework [27]. The work of Green [12] and Waldinger [31] both involved extracting a program directly from a proof of a predicate calculus theorem derived from the input/output specifications of the program. In the more recent systems discussed here, the role of deduction seems less central. In DEDALUS, deduction is used for three purposes. First, some of the transformation rules have conditions associated with them, and these rules cannot be applied unless the conditions have been proven true in the current context. Second, in cases where the conditions have not been proven, a conditional control structure may be introduced in order to provide contexts in which the conditions are provable (and hence, the rule can be applied). Finally, in trying to prove or disprove "protected" conditions, deduction plays an important role in DEDALUS's handling of side effects. In DBS, a simple equality-based theorem prover plays an auxiliary role, similar to the first use of deduction in DEDALUS. Each recursive-to-iterative transformation rule has an associated set of equations over the primitives (e.g., equations satisfied only by associative operators); the rule can only be applied if the equations are satisfied. Deduction plays no role at all in LS. In PECOS, deduction plays a role only in a very limited sense: the QUERY subtasks of a task can be viewed as conditions in the DEDALUS sense described above, and the QUERY rules can be viewed as specialized deduction rules for handling particular situations (as opposed to giving the condition to a more general theorem prover).[14] In the Reachability Program, for example, the "deduction" that the front of BOUNDARY is the location of X was handled by QUERY rules. In the long run, it seems clear that the knowledge-based approach will require access to a more general deductive mechanism than simply a set of QUERY rules. First, it will be impossible to put in rules for all of the kinds of conditions that will need to be tested. For example, consider the following rule:

> *If it is known that an object is larger than all the elements of an ordered sequence, then the object may be added to the sequence by inserting it at the back.*

The "it is known that . . ." should clearly be tested by calling a deductive mechanism. And second, it will also be impossible to put in refinement and transformation rules to handle all possible cases that may arise in program specifications, and a general mechanism may provide the backup capability to handle the extra cases. Nonetheless, the appropriate role for a general deductive mechanism seems to be as an adjunct to the synthesis process, rather than as the driving force behind it.

7.7. Generality vs. power

It has often been stated (e.g., see [10, 11, 19]) that there is a trade-off between generality and power: techniques that are general will not help much in specific complex situations, and techniques that are powerful in particular complex situations will not be applicable in very many. We can see the same trade-off in the four automatic programming systems being discussed here. DEDALUS seems to occupy a point near the "general" end of the spectrum: It is designed to apply a general deductive framework to a wide variety of different problems specified with input/output predicates, but has not yet been successfully applied to very

[14] In fact, the transformation rules of DEDALUS, LS, and PECOS can all be seen as specialized (or perhaps even "compiled") deduction rules; and under this view the control structures serve as special-purpose deductive mechanisms.

complex programs. LS seems to be at the "power" end of the spectrum: it does extremely well at selecting data structure representations for sets, but is inapplicable to other programming problems; even to enable it to choose representations for a machine other than a PDP-10 would require redoing the tables completely. Yet even in these two cases, one can see traces of the other end of the spectrum. DEDALUS includes a large number of specific transformations that increase its power, and LS's control structure, including the partitioning and hill-climbing, could clearly be applied to other situations. DBS and PECOS seem to occupy the middle ground of the spectrum. While DBS's transformations are not universally applicable, they are certainly more general than those of LS. And while PECOS's rules are relatively specific to collections and mappings (and fairly powerful when they can be applied), they seem to possess a degree of generality, as suggested by the different domains in which they have been successfully applied (see Section 3). But note that this "generality" is concerned with a set of rules, rather than with individual rules. This does not necessarily mean that generality can be achieved by incorporating larger and larger numbers of specific rules, but my own belief about the future of automatic programming systems is that, in order to be useful and powerful in a variety of situations, they must necessarily incorporate a large number of rather specific detailed rules (or facts, or frames, or . . .), together with fairly general mechanisms (deductive, analytic, . . .) that can handle the situations in which the rules are inapplicable. And I would suggest that the organization will not be one driven by the general mechanism, with guidance from the rules, but rather one driven by the rules, with the general mechanisms for problem cases.

8. Assessment

The development of PECOS represents the final stage in an experiment investigating a knowledge-based approach to automatic programming. The essence of this approach involves the identification of concepts and decisions involved in the programming process and their codification into individual rules, each dealing with some particular detail of some programming technique. These rules are then represented in a form suitable for use by an automatic programming system.

As seen in Section 4, the process of constructing an implementation for an abstract algorithm involves considering a large number of details. It seems a reasonable conjecture that some kind of ability to reason at a very detailed level will be required if a system is to "understand" what it is doing well enough to perform the complex tasks that will be required of future automatic programming systems. PECOS's ability to deal successfully with such details is based largely on its access to a large store of programming knowledge. Several aspects of PECOS's representation scheme contribute to this ability. The refinement paradigm has proved convenient for coping with some of the complexity and variability that seem inevitable in real-world programs. The use of several levels of abstraction seems particularly important.

One of the critical issues involved in the knowledge-based approach to automatic programming is the question of rule generality: will many (or even some) of PECOS's rules be useful when other programming domains (e.g., graph algorithms) are codified? A definitive answer to this question must wait for other domains to be codified, but PECOS's successful application to the varied algorithms described in Section 3 is an encouraging sign.

In the long run, perhaps the greatest benefit of the knowledge-based approach lies in the rules themselves. Most knowledge about programming is available only informally, couched in unstated assumptions. While such knowledge is usually understandable by people, it lacks the detail necessary for use by a machine. For part of the domain of elementary symbolic programming, PECOS's rules fill in much of the detail and many of the unstated assumptions. Taken together, the rules form a coherent body of knowledge that imposes a structure and taxonomy on part of the programming process.

ACKNOWLEDGEMENTS

Cordell Green, my thesis adviser, and the other members of the Ψ project have been a source of motivation and focus for this work. Interaction with Elaine Kant and her work on LIBRA has been especially beneficial. Juan Ludlow's development of rules for SAIL exposed some of the hidden assumptions in my rules. Brian McCune contributed greatly to the design of the specification language. Randy Davis, Jorge Phillips, Drew McDermott, and Richard Waldinger have provided very helpful comments on drafts of this paper. The referees comments were also quite valuable.

REFERENCES

1. Automatic coding: *Proceedings of a Symposium at the Franklin Institute*, Philadelphia, Pennsylvania, April 1957.
2. Barstow, D. R., *Codification of programming knowledge: graph algorithms* (Yale University, Department of Computer Science, TR 149, December 1978).
3. Barstow, D. R., *Knowledge-based Program Construction* (Elsevier North-Holland, New York, 1979).
4. Barstow, D. R. and Kant, E., Observations on the interaction of coding and efficiency knowledge in the PSI program synthesis system. *Proceedings of the Second International Conference on Software Engineering*, San Francisco, California, October 1976, 19–31.
5. Buchanan, J. and Luckham, D., *On automating the construction of programs* (Stanford University, Computer Science Department, AIM-236, May 1974).
6. Burstall, R. M. and Darlington, J., A transformation system for developing recursive programs. *Journal of the ACM* **24** (January 1977) 44–67.
7. Dahl, O.-J., Dijkstra, E. W. and Hoare, C. A. R., *Structured Programming* (Academic Press, New York, 1972).
8. Darlington, J. and Burstall, R. M., A system which automatically improves programs. *Acta Informatica* **6** (1976) 41–60.
9. Dershowitz, N. and Manna, Z., The evolution of programs: a system for automatic program modification. *IEEE Transactions on Software Engineering* (November 1977) 377–385.
10. Feigenbaum, E. A., The art of artificial intelligence: I. Themes and case studies of knowledge engineering. *Proceedings of the Fifth International Joint Conference on Artificial Intelligence*, Cambridge, Massachusetts, August 1977, 1014–1024.

11. Goldstein, I. and Papert, S., Artificial intelligence, language, and the study of knowledge. *Cognitive Science* **1** (January 1977) 54–123.
12. Green, C. C., *The application of theorem proving to question-answering systems* (Stanford University, Computer Science Department, AIM-96, August 1969).
13. Green, C. C., The design of the PSI program synthesis system. *Proceedings of the Second International Conference on Software Engineering*, San Francisco, California, October 1976, 4–18.
14. Green, C. C. and Barstow, D. R., Some rules for the automatic synthesis of programs. *Advance Papers of the Fourth International Joint Conference on Artificial Intelligence*, Tbilisl, Georgia, USSR, September 1975, 232–239.
15. Green, C. C. and Barstow, D. R., A hypothetical dialogue exhibiting a knowledge base for a program understanding system, in: Elcock, E. W. and Michie, D. (Eds.), *Machine Representations of Knowledge* (Ellis Horwood Ltd. and John Wylie, 1977) 335–359.
16. Green, C. C. and Barstow, D. R., On program synthesis knowledge, *Artificial Intelligence* **10** (November 1978) 241–279.
17. Kant, E., A knowledge based approach to using efficiency estimation in program synthesis. *Sixth International Joint Conference on Artificial Intelligence*, Tokyo, Japan (1979).
18. Knuth, D. E., *The Art of Computer Programming, Combinatorial Algorithms* (Vol. 4) (Addison-Wesley, 1977). (Preprint).
19. Lenat, D. B., The ubiquity of discovery, *Artificial Intelligence* **9** (December 1977) 257–286.
20. Liskov, B., Snyder, A., Atkinson, R. and Schaffert, C., Abstraction mechanisms in CLU. *Commun. ACM*, **20** (August 1977) 564–576.
21. Low, J., *Automatic coding: choice of data structures* (Stanford University, Computer Science Department, AIM-242, August 1974).
22. Ludlow, J., Masters Project (Stanford University, 1977).
23. Manna, Z. and Waldinger, R., Synthesis: dreams ⇒ programs. (SRI International, Technical Note 156, November 1977).
24. Reiser, J. F. (Ed.) SAIL Reference Manual (Stanford University, Computer Science Department, AIM-289, August 1976).
25. Schwartz, J. T., On programming: an interim report on the SETL project (New York University, Courant Institute of Mathematical Sciences, Computer Science Department, June 1975).
26. Shortliffe, E. H., *MYCIN: Computer-Based Medical Consultations* (American Elsevier, New York, 1976).
27. Simon, H. A., Experiments with a heuristic compiler. *Journal of the ACM* **10** (April 1963) 493–506.
28. Sussman, G. J., *A Computer Model of Skill Acquisition* (American Elsevier, New York, 1975).
29. Teitelman, W., INTERLISP Reference Manual (Xerox Palo Alto Research Center, Palo Alto, California, December 1975).
30. Thorelli, L.-E., Marking algorithms. *Behandling Informations-tidskrift for Nodisk* **12** (1972) 555–568.
31. Waldinger, R. J. and Lee, R. C. T., A step toward automatic program writing. *Proceedings of the International Joint Conference on Artificial Intelligence*, Washington, D.C., 1969, 241–252.
32. Winston, P. H., Learning Structural Descriptions from Examples, in: Winston, P. H. (Ed.), *The Psychology of Computer Vision* (McGraw-Hill, 1975).
33. Wulf, W., London, R. and Shaw, M., An introduction to the construction and verification of ALPHARD programs. *IEEE Transactions on Software Engineering* (December 1976) 253–265.

Dendral and Meta-Dendral:

Their Applications Dimension

Bruce G. Buchanan

Computer Science Department, Stanford University, Stanford CA 94305, U.S.A.

Edward A. Feigenbaum

Computer Science Department, Stanford University, Stanford CA 94305, U.S.A.

1. Introduction

The DENDRAL and Meta-DENDRAL programs are products of a large, interdisciplinary group of Stanford University scientists concerned with many and highly varied aspects of the mechanization of scientific reasoning and the formalization of scientific knowledge for this purpose. An early motivation for our work was to explore the power of existing AI methods, such as heuristic search, for reasoning in difficult scientific problems [7]. Another concern has been to exploit the AI methodology to understand better some fundamental questions in the philosophy of science, for example the processes by which explanatory hypotheses are discovered or judged adequate [18]. From the start, the project has had an applications dimension [9, 10, 27]. It has sought to develop "expert level" agents to assist in the solution of problems in their discipline that require complex symbolic reasoning. The applications dimension is the focus of this paper.

In order to achieve high performance, the DENDRAL programs incorporate large amounts of knowledge about the area of science to which they are applied, structure elucidation in organic chemistry. A "smart assistant" for a chemist needs to be able to perform many tasks as well as an expert, but need not necessarily understand the domain at the same theoretical level as the expert. The over-all structure elucidation task is described below (Section 2) followed by a description of the role of the DENDRAL programs within that framework (Section 3). The Meta-DENDRAL programs (Section 4) use a weaker body of knowledge about the domain of mass spectrometry because their task is to formulate rules of mass spectrometry by induction from empirical data. A strong model of the domain would bias the rules unnecessarily.

1.1. Historical perspective

The DENDRAL project began in 1965. Then, as now, we were concerned with the conceptual problems of designing and writing symbol manipulation programs that used substantial bodies of domain-specific scientific knowledge. In contrast, this was a time in the history of AI in which most laboratories were working on general problem solving methods, e.g., in 1965 work on resolution theorem proving was in its prime.

The programs have followed an evolutionary progression. Initial concepts were translated into a working program: the program was tested and improved by confronting simple test cases; and finally a production version of the program including user interaction facilities was released for real applications. This intertwining of short-term pragmatic goals and long-term development of new AI science is an important theme throughout our research. The results presented here have been produced by DENDRAL programs at various stages of development.

2. The General Nature of the Applications Tasks

2.1. Structure elucidation

The application of chemical knowledge to elucidation of molecular structures is fundamental to understanding important problems of biology and medicine. Areas in which we and our collaborators maintain active interest include: (a) identification of natural products isolated from terrestrial or marine sources, particularly those products which demonstrate biological activity or which are key intermediates in biosynthetic pathways; (b) verification of the identity of new synthetic materials; (c) identification of drugs and their metabolites in clinical studies; and (d) detection of metabolic disorders of genetic, developmental, toxic or infectious origins by identification of organic constituents excreted in abnormal quantities in human body fluids.

In most circumstances, especially in the areas of interest summarized above, chemists are faced with structural problems where direct examination of the structure by X-ray crystallography is not possible. In these circumstances they must resort to structure elucidation based on data obtained from a variety of physical, chemical and spectroscopic methods.

This kind of structure elucidation involves a sequence of steps that is roughly approximated by the following scenario. An unknown structure is isolated from some source. The source of the sample and the isolation procedures employed already provide some clues as to the chemical constitution of the compound. A variety of chemical, physical and spectroscopic data are collected on the sample. Interpretation of these data yields structural hypotheses in the form of functional groups or more complex molecular fragments. Assembling these fragments into complete structures provides a set of candidate structures for the unknown. These candidates are examined and experiments are designed to differentiate among them. The experiments, usually collecting additional spectroscopic data and executing sequences of chemical reactions, result in new structural information which serves to reduce the set of candidate structures. Eventually enough information is inferred from experimental data to constrain the candidates to the correct structure.

As long as time permits and the number of unknown structures is small, a manual approach will usually be successful, as it has been in the past. However, the manual approach is amenable to a high degree of computer assistance, which is increasingly necessary for both practical and scientific reasons. One needs only examine current regulatory activities in fields related to chemistry, or the rate at which new compounds are discovered or synthesized to gain a feeling for the practical need for rapid identification of new structures. More important, however, is the contribution such computer assistance can make to scientific creativity in structure elucidation in particular, and chemistry in general, by providing new tools to aid scientists in hypothesis formation. The automated approaches discussed in this paper provide a systematic procedure for verifying hypotheses about chemical structure and ensuring that no plausible alternatives have been overlooked.

2.2. Structure elucidation with constraints from mass spectrometry

The Heuristic DENDRAL Program is designed to help organic chemists determine the molecular structure of unknown compounds. Parts of the program have been highly tuned to work with experimental data from an analytical instrument known as a mass spectrometer. *Mass spectrometry* is a new and still developing analytic technique. It is not ordinarily the only analytic technique used by chemists, but is one of a broad array, including nuclear magnetic resonance (NMR), infrared (IR), ultraviolet (UV), and "wet chemistry" analyses. Mass spectrometry is particularly useful when the quantity of the sample to be identified is very small, for it requires only micrograms of sample.

A mass spectrometer bombards the chemical sample with electrons, causing fragmentations and rearrangements of the molecules. Charged fragments are collected by mass. The data from the instrument, recorded in a histogram known as a mass spectrum, show the masses of charged fragments plotted against the relative abundance of the fragments at a mass. Although the mass spectrum for each molecule may be nearly unique, it is still a difficult task to infer the molecular structure form the 100–300 data points in the mass spectrum. The data are highly redundant because molecules fragment along different pathways. Thus two different masses may or may not include atoms from the same part of the molecules. In short, the theory of mass spectrometry is too incomplete to allow unambiguous reconstruction of the structure from overlapping fragments.

Throughout this paper we will use the following terms to describe the actions of molecules in the mass spectrometer:

(1) Fragmentation—the breaking of a connected graph (molecule) into fragments by breaking one or more edges (bonds) within the graph.

(2) Atom migration—the detachment of nodes (atoms) from one fragment and their reattachment to a second fragment. This process alters the masses of both fragments.

(3) Mass spectral process (or processes)—a fragmentation followed by zero or more atom migrations.

2.3. Structure elucidation with constraints from other data

Other analytic techniques are commonly used in conjunction with, or instead of, mass spectrometry. Some rudimentary capabilities exist in the DENDRAL programs to interpret proton NMR and Carbon 13 (^{13}C) NMR spectra. For the most part, however, interpretation of other spectroscopic and chemical data has been left to the chemist. The programs still need to be able to integrate the chemist's partial knowledge into the generation of structural alternatives.

3. Heuristic DENDRAL as an Intelligent Assistant

3.1. Method

Heuristic DENDRAL is organized as a Plan—Generate—Test sequence. This is not necessarily the same method used by chemists, but it is easily understood by them. It complements their methods by providing such a meticulous search through the space of molecular structures that the chemist is virtually guaranteed that any candidate structure which fails to appear on the final list of plausible structures has been rejected for explicitly stated chemical reasons.

The three main parts of the program are discussed below, starting with the generator because of its fundamental importance.

3.1.1. *The generator*

The heart of a heuristic search program is a generator of the search space. In a chess playing program, for example, the legal move generator completely defines the space of moves and move sequences. In Heuristic DENDRAL the legal move generator is based on the DENDRAL algorithm developed by J. Lederberg [1–4]. This algorithm specifies a systematic enumeration of molecular structures. It treats molecules as planar graphs and generates successively larger graph structures until all chemical atoms are included in graphs in all possible arrangements. Because graphs with cycles presented special problems,[1] initial work was limited to chemical structures without rings (with the exception of [21]).

The number of chemical graphs for molecular formulas of interest to chemists can be extremely large. Thus it is essential to constrain structure generation to only *plausible* molecular structures. The CONGEN program [44],[2] is the DEN-

[1] The symmetries of cyclic graphs prevented prospective avoidance of duplicates during generation. Brown, Hjelmeland and Masinter solved these problems in both theory and practice [31, 36].

[2] Named for constrained generator.

DRAL hypothesis generator now in use. It accepts problem statements of (a) the number of atoms of each type in the molecule and (b) constraints on the correct hypothesis, in order to generate all chemical graphs that fit the stated constraints. These problem statements may come from a chemist interpreting his own experimental data or from a spectrometric data analysis program.

The purpose of CONGEN is to assist the chemist in determining the chemical structure of an unknown compound by (1) allowing him to specify certain types of structural information about the compound which he has determined from any source (e.g., spectoscopy, chemical degradation, method of isolation, etc.) and (2) generating an exhaustive and non-redundant list of structures that are consistent with the information. The generation is a stepwise process, and the program allows interaction at every stage: based upon partial results the chemist may be reminded of additional information which he can specify, thus limiting further the number of structural possibilities.

CONGEN breaks the problem down into several types of subproblems, for example: (i) hydrogen atoms are omitted; (ii) parts of the graph containing no cycles are generated separately from cyclic parts (and combined at the end); (iii) cycles containing only unnamed nodes are generated before labeling the nodes with names of chemical atoms (e.g., carbon or nitrogen); (iv) cycles containing only three-connected (or higher) nodes (e.g., nitrogen or tertiary carbon) are generated before mapping two-connected nodes (e.g., oxygen or secondary carbon) onto the edges. At each step several constraints may be applied to limit the number of emerging chemical graphs [49].

At the heart of CONGEN are two algorithms whose validity has been mathematically proven and whose computer implementation has been well tested. The structure generation algorithm [31, 36, 39, 40] is designed to determine all topologically unique ways of assembling a given set of atoms, each with an associated valence, into molecular structures. The atoms may be chemical atoms with standard chemical valences, or they may be names representing molecular fragments ("superatoms") of any desired complexity, where the valence corresponds to the total number of bonding sites available within the superatom. Because the structure generation algorithm can produce only structures in which the superatoms appear as single nodes (we refer to these as intermediate structures), a second procedure, the imbedding algorithm [36, 44] is needed to expand the superatoms to their full chemical identities.

A substantial amount of effort has been devoted to modifying these two basic procedures, particularly the structure generation algorithm, to accept a variety of other structural information (constraints), using it to prune the list of structural possibilities. Current capabilities include specification of good and bad substructural features, good and bad ring sizes, proton distributions and connectivities of isoprene units [49]. Usually, the chemist has additional information (if only some general rules about chemical stability) of which the program has little knowledge but which can be used to limit the number of structural possibilities. For example, he may know that the chemical procedures used to isolate the compound would change organic acids to esters and thus the program need not consider structures with unchanged acid groups. Also, he is given the facility to impart this knowledge interactively to the program.

To make CONGEN easy to use by research chemists, the program has been provided with an interactive "front end." This interface contains EDITSTRUC, an interactive structure editor, DRAW, a teletype-oriented structure display program [58], and the CONGEN "executive" program which ties together the individual subprograms, such as subprograms for defining superatoms and substructures, creating and editing lists of constraints or superatoms, and saving and restoring superatoms, constraints and structures from secondary storage (disc). The resulting system, for which comprehensive user-level documentation has been prepared, is running on the SUMEX computing facility at Stanford and is available nationwide over the TYMNET network [46]. The use of CONGEN by chemists doing structure elucidation is discussed in Section 3.4.

3.1.2. *The Planning Programs*

Although CONGEN is designed to be useful as a stand-alone package some assistance can also be given with the task of inferring constraints for the generator. This is done by *planning* programs that analyze instrument data and infer constraints (see [10, 22, 28]).

The DENDRAL Planner uses a large amount of knowledge of mass spectrometry to infer constraints. For example, it may infer that the unknown molecule is probably a ketone but definitely not a methylketone. Planning information like this is put on the generator's lists of good and bad structural features. Planning has been limited almost entirely to mass spectrometry, but the same techniques can be used with other data sources as well.

The DENDRAL Planner [28], allows for cooperative (man–machine) problem solving in the interpretation of mass spectra. It uses the chemist's relevant knowledge of mass spectrometry and applies it systematically to the spectrum of an unknown. That is, using the chemist's definitions of the structural skeleton of the molecule and the relevant fragmentation rules, the program does the bookkeeping of associating peaks with fragments and the combinatorics of finding consistent ways of placing substituents around the skeleton.

The output from the DENDRAL Planner is a list of structure descriptions with as much detail filled in as the data and defined fragmentations will allow. Because there are limits to the degree of refinement allowed by mass spectrometry alone, sets of atoms are assigned to sets of skeletal nodes. Thus the task of fleshing out the plan—specifying possible structures assigned to specific skeletal nodes—is left to CONGEN.

3.1.3. *The Testing and Ranking Programs*

The programs MSPRUNE [61] and MSRANK [59] use a large amount of knowledge of mass spectrometry to make testable predictions from each plausible candidate molecule. Predicted data are compared to the data from the unknown compound to throw out some candidates and rank the others [10, 59, 61].

MSPRUNE works with (a) a list of candidate structures from CONGEN, and (b) the mass spectrum of the unknown molecule. It uses a fairly simple theory of mass spectrometry to predict commonly expected fragmentations for each candidate structure. Predictions which deviate greatly from the observed spectrum are considered *prima facie* evidence of incorrectness; the corresponding structures are pruned from the list. MSRANK then uses more subtle rules of mass spectrometry to rank the remaining structures according to the number of predicted peaks found (and not found) in the observed data, weighted by measures of importance of the processes producing those peaks.

3.2. Research Results

The Heuristic DENDRAL effort has shown that it is possible to write a computer program that equals the performance of experts in some limited areas of science. Published papers on the program's analysis of aliphatic ketones, amines, ethers, alcohols, thiols and thioethers [15, 19, 20, 22] make the point that although the program does not know more than an expert (and in fact knows far less), it performs well because of its systematic search through the space of possibilities and its systematic use of what it does know. A paper on the program's analysis of estrogenic steroids makes the point that the program can solve structure elucidation problems for complex organic molecules [28] of current biological interest. Another paper on the analysis of mass spectra of mixtures of estrogenic steroids (without prior separation) establishes the program's ability to do better than experts on some problems [32]. With mixtures, the program succeeds, and people fail, because of the magnitude of the task of correlating data points with each possible fragmentation of each possible component of the mixture. Several articles based on results from CONGEN demonstrate its power and utility for solving current research problems of medical and biochemical importance [42, 48, 50, 53, 62, 58].

3.3. Human Engineering

A successful applications program must demonstrate *competence*, as the previous section emphasized. However, it is also necessary to design the programs to achieve *acceptability*, by the scientists for whom the AI system is written. That is, without proper attention to human engineering, and similar issues, a complex applications program will not be widely used. Besides making the I/O language easy for the user to understand, it is also important to make the scope and limitations of the problem solving methods known to the user as much as possible [60].

The features designed into DENDRAL programs to make them easier and more pleasant to use include graphical drawings of chemical structures [58], a stylized, but easily understood language of expressing and editing chemical constraints [44], on-line help facilities [60], depth-first problem solving to produce some solutions quickly, estimators of problem size and (at any time) amount of work remaining. Documentation and user manuals are written at many levels of detail. And one of our staff is almost always available for consultation by phone or message [46].

3.4. Applications of CONGEN to Chemical Problems

Many persons have used DENDRAL programs (mostly CONGEN) in an experimental mode. Some chemists have used programs on the SUMEX machine, others have requested help by mail, and a few have imported programs to their own computers.

Copies of programs have been distributed to chemists requesting them. However, we have strongly suggested that persons access the local versions by TYMNET to minimize the number of different versions we maintain and to avoid the need for rewriting the INTERLISP code for another machine.

Users do not always tell us about the problems they solve using the DENDRAL programs. To some extent this is one sign of a successful application. The list below thus represents only a sampling of the chemical problems to which the programs have been applied. CONGEN is most used, although other DENDRAL subprograms have been used occasionally.

Since the SUMEX computer is available over the TYMNET network, it is possible for scientists in many parts of the world to access the DENDRAL programs on SUMEX directly. Many scientists interested in using DENDRAL programs in their own work are not located near a network access point, however. These chemists use the mail to send details of their structure elucidation problem to a DENDRAL Project collaborator at Stanford.

DENDRAL programs have been used to aid in structure determination problems of the following kinds:

terpenoid natural products from plant and marine animal sources
marine sterols
organic acids in human urine and other body fluids
photochemical rearrangement products
impurities in manufactured chemicals
conjugates of pesticides with sugars and amino acids
antibiotics
metabolites of microorganisms
insect hormones and pheremones

CONGEN was also applied to published structure elucidation problems by students in Professor Djerassi's class on spectroscopic techniques to check the accuracy and completeness of the published solutions. For several cases, the program found structures which were plausible alternatives to the published structures (based on a problem constraints that appeared in the article). This kind of information thus serves as a valuable check on conclusions drawn from experimental data.

4. Meta-DENDRAL

Because of the difficulty of extracting domain-specific rules from experts for use by DENDRAL, a more efficient means of transferring knowledge into the program was sought. Two alternatives to "handcrafting" each new knowledge base have been explored: interactive knowledge transfer programs and automatic theory formation programs. In this enterprise the separation of domain-specific knowledge from the computer programs themselves has been critical.

One of the stumbling blocks with programs for the interactive transfer of knowledge is that for some areas of chemistry there are no experts with enough specific knowledge to make a high performance problem solving program (see [16]). It is desirable to avoid forcing an expert to focus on original data in order to codify the rules explaining those data because that is such a time-consuming process. For these reasons an effort to build an automatic rule formation program (called Meta-DENDRAL) was initiated.

The DENDRAL programs are structured to read their task-specific knowledge from tables of production rules and execute the rules in new situations, under rather elaborate control structures. The Meta-DENDRAL programs have been constructed to aid in building the knowledge base, i.e., the tables of rules.

4.1. The Task

The present Meta-DENDRAL program [51, 63] interactively helps chemists determine the dependence of mass spectrometric fragmentation on substructural features, under the hypothesis that molecular fragmentations are related to topological graph structural features of molecules. Our goal is to have the program suggest qualitative explanations of the characteristic fragmentations and rearrangements among a set of molecules. We do not now attempt to rationalize all peaks nor find quantitative assessments of the extent to which various processes contribute to peak intensities.

The program emulates many of the reasoning processes of manual approaches to rule discovery. It reasons symbolically, using a modest amount of chemical knowledge. It decides which data points are important and looks for fragmentation processes that will explain them. It attempts to form general rules by correlating plausible fragmentation processes with substructural features of the molecules. Then, as a chemist does, the program tests and modifies the rules.

Each I/O pair for Meta-DENDRAL is: (INPUT) a chemical sample with uniform molecular structure (abbreviated to "a structure"): (OUTPUT) one X–Y point from the histogram of fragment masses and relative abundances of fragments (often referred to as one peak in the mass spectrum).

Since the spectrum of each structure contains 100 to 300 different data points, each structure appears in many I/O pairs. Thus, the program must look for several generating principles, or processes, that operate on a structure to produce many data points. In addition, the data are not guaranteed correct because these are empirical data which may contain noise or contributions from impurities in the original sample. As a result, the program does not attempt to explain every I/O pair. It does, however, choose which data points to explain on the basis of criteria given by the chemist as part of the imposed model of mass-spectrometry.

Rules of mass spectrometry actually used by chemists are often expressed as what AI scientists would call production rules. These rules (when executed by a program) constitute a simulation of the fragmentation and atom migration processes that occur inside the instrument. The left-hand side is a description of the graph structure of some relevant piece of the molecule. The right-hand side is a list of processes which occur: specifically, bond cleavages and atom migrations. For example, one simple rule is

(R1) N—C—C—C → N—C*C—C

where the asterisk indicates breaking the bond at that position and recording the mass of the fragment to the left of the asterisk. (No migration of atoms between fragments is predicted by this rule.)

Although the vocabulary for describing individual atoms in subgraphs is small and the grammar of subgraphs is simple, the size of the subgraph search space is large. In addition to the connectivity of the subgraph, each atom in the subgraph may have up to four (dependent) attributes specified: (a) Atom type (e.g., carbon), (b) Number of connected neighbors (other than hydrogen), (c) Number of hydrogen neighbors, and (d) Number of doubly-bonded neighbors. The size of the space to consider, for example, for subgraphs containing 6 atoms, each with any of (say) 20 attribute-value specifications, is 20^6 possible subgraphs.

The language of processes (right-hand sides of rules) is also simple but can describe many combinations of actions: one or more bonds from the left-hand side may break and zero or more atoms may migrate between fragments.

4.2. Method

The rule formation process for Meta-DENDRAL is a three-stage sequence similar to the plan–generate–test sequence used in Heuristic DENDRAL. In Meta-DENDRAL, the generator (RULEGEN), described in section 4.2.2 below, generates plausible rules within syntactic and semantic constraints and within desired limits of evidential support. The model used to guide the generation of rules is particularly important since the space of rules is very large. The model of mass spectrometry in the program is highly flexible and can be modified by the user to suit his own biases and assumptions about the kinds of rules that are appropriate for the compounds under consideration. The model determines (i) the vocabulary to be used in constructing rules, (ii) the syntax of the rules (as before, the left-hand side of a rule describes a chemical graph, the right-hand side describes a fragmentation and/or rearrangement process to be expected in the mass spectrometer), (iii) some semantic constraints governing the plausibility of rules. For example, the chemist can use a subset of the terms available for describing chemical graphs and can restrict the number of chemical atoms described in the left-hand sides of rules and can restrict the complexity of processes considered in the right-hand sides [63].

The planning part of the program (INTSUM), described in 4.2.1, collects and summarizes the evidential support. The testing part (RULEMOD), described in 4.2.3, looks for counterexamples to rules and makes modifications to the rules in order to increase their generality and simplicity and to decrease the total number of rules. These three major components are discussed briefly in the following subsections.

4.2.1. *Interpret Data as Evidence for Processes*

The INTSUM program [33] (named for data interpretation and summary) interprets spectral data of known compounds in terms of possible fragmentations and atom migrations. For each molecule in a given set, INTSUM first produces the plausible processes which might occur, i.e., breaks and combinations of breaks, with and without atom migrations. These processes are associated with specific bonds in a portion of molecular structure, or skeleton, that is chosen because it is common to the molecules in the given set. Then INTSUM examines the spectra of the molecules looking for evidence (spectral peaks) for each process.

Notice that the association of processes with data points may be ambiguous. For instance, in the molecule CH_3—CH_2—CH_2—NH—CH_2—CH_3 a spectral peak at mass 29 may be attributed to a process which breaks either the second bond from the left or one which breaks the second bond from the right, both producing CH_3—CH_2 fragments.

4.2.2. *Generate Candidate Rules*

After the data have been interpreted by INTSUM, control passes to a heuristic search program known as RULEGEN [51], for rule generation. RULEGEN creates general rules by selecting "important" features of the molecular structure around the site of the fragmentations proposed by INTSUM. These important features are combined to form a subgraph description of the local environment surrounding the broken bonds. Each subgraph considered becomes the left hand side of a candidate rule whose right hand side is INTSUM's proposed process. Essentially RULEGEN searches (within the constraints) through a space of these subgraph descriptions looking for successively more specific subgraphs that are supported by successively "better" sets of evidence.

Conceptually, the program begins with the most general candidate rule, X*X (where X is any unspecified atom and where the asterisk is used to indicate the broken bond, with the detected fragment written to the left of the asterisk). Since the most useful rules lie somewhere between the overly-general candidate, X*X, and the overly-specific complete molecular structure descriptions (with specified bonds breaking), the program generates refined descriptions by successively specifying additional features. This is a coarse search; for efficiency reasons RULEGEN sometimes adds features to several nodes at a time, without considering the intermediate subgraphs.

The program systematically adds features (attribute-value pairs) to subgraphs, starting with the subgraph X*X, and always making each successor more specific than its parent. (Recall that each node can be described with any or all of the following attributes: atom type, number of non-hydrogen neighbors, number of hydrogen neighbors, and number of doubly bonded neighbors.) Working outward, the program assigns one attribute at a time to all atoms that are the same number of atoms away from the breaking bond. Each of the four attributes is considered in turn, and each attribute *value* for which there is supporting evidence generates a new successor. Although different values for the same attribute may be assigned to each atom at a given distance from the breaking bond, the coarseness of the search prevents examination of subgraphs in which this attribute is totally unimportant on *some* of these atoms.

4.2.3. *Refine and Test the Rules*

The last phase of Meta-DENDRAL (called RULEMOD) [51] evaluates the plausible rules generated by RULEGEN and modifies them by making them more general or more specific. In contrast to RULEGEN, RULEMOD considers negative evidence (incorrect predictions) of rules in order to increase the accuracy of the rule's applications within the training set. While RULEGEN performs a coarse search of the rule space for reasons of efficiency, RULEMOD performs a localized, fine search to refine the rules.

RULEMOD will typically output a set of 5 to 10 rules covering substantially the same training data points as the input RULEGEN set of approximately 25 to 100 rules, but with fewer incorrect predictions. This program is written as a set of five tasks, corresponding to the five points below.

Selecting a Subset of Important Rules. The local evaluation in RULEGEN has ignored negative evidence and has not discovered that different RULEGEN pathways may yield rules which are different but explain many of the same data points. Thus there is often a high degree of overlap in those rules and they may make many incorrect predictions. The initial selection removes most of the redundancy in the rule set.

Merging Rules. For any subset of rules which explain many of the same data points, the program attempts to find a slightly more general rule that (a) includes all the evidence covered by the overlapping rules and (b) does not bring in extra negative evidence. If it can find such a rule, the overlapping rules are replaced by the single compact rule.

Deleting Negative Evidence by Making Rules More Specific. RULEMOD tries to add attribute-value specifications to atoms in each rule in order to delete some negative evidence while keeping all of the positive evidence. This involves local search of the possible additions to the subgraph descriptions that were not considered by RULEGEN. Because of the coarseness of RULEGEN's search, some ways of refining rules are not tried, except by RULEMOD.

Making Rules More General. RULEGEN often forms rules that are more specific than they need to be. Thus RULEMOD seeks a more general form that covers the same (and perhaps new) data points without introducing new negative evidence.

Selecting the Final Rule Set. The selection procedure applied at the beginning of RULEMOD is applied again at the very end of RULEMOD in order to remove redundancies that might have been introduced during generalization and specialization.

4.3. Meta-DENDRAL Results

One measure of the proficiency of Meta-DENDRAL is the ability of the corresponding performance program to predict correct spectra of new molecules using the learned rules. One of the DENDRAL performance programs ranks a list of plausible hypotheses (candidate molecules) according to the similarity of their predictions (predicted spectra) to observed data. The rank of the correct hypothesis (i.e. the molecule actually associated with the observed spectrum) provides a quantitative measure of the "discriminatory power" of the rule set.

The Meta-DENDRAL program has successfully rediscovered known, published rules of mass spectrometry for two classes of molecules. More importantly, it has discovered new rules for three closely related families of structures for which rules had not previously been reported. Meta-DENDRAL's rules for these classes have been published in the chemistry literature [51]. Evaluations of all five sets of rules are discussed in that publication.

Recently Meta-DENDRAL has been adapted to a second spectroscopic technique, 13C-nuclear magnetic resonance (13C-NMR) spectroscopy [62, 64]. This new version provides the opportunity to direct the induction machinery of Meta-DENDRAL under a model of 13C-NMR spectroscopy. It generates rules which associate the resonance frequency of a carbon atom in a magnetic field with the local structural environment of the atom. 13C-NMR rules have been generated and used in a candidate molecule ranking program similar to the one described above. 13C-NMR rules formulated by the program for two classes of structures have been successfully used to identify the spectra of additional molecules (of the same classes, but outside the set of training data used in generating the rules).

The quality of rules produced by Meta-DENDRAL has been assessed by

(a) obtaining agreement from mass spectroscopists that they are reasonable explanations of the training data and provide acceptable predictions of new data, and

(b) testing them as discriminators of structures outside the training set.

The question of agreement on previously characterized sets of molecules is relatively easy, since the chemist only needs to compare the program's rules and predictions against published rules and spectra. Agreement has been high on test sets of amines, estrogenic steroids, and aromatic acids. On new data, however, the chemist is forced into spot checks. For example, analyses of some individual androstane spectra from the literature were used as spot checks on the program's analysis of the collections of androstane spectra.

The discrimination test is to determine how well a set of rules allows discrimination of known structures from alternatives on the basis of comparing predicted and actual spectra. For example, given a list of structures (S1, . . ., S*n*) and the mass spectrum for structure S1, can the rules *predict* a spectrum for S1 which matches the *given* spectrum (for S1) better than spectra *predicted* for S2–S*n* match the given spectrum. When this test is repeated for each available spectrum for structures S1–S*n*, the discriminatory power of the rules is determined. The program has found rules with high discriminatory power [51], but much work remains before we standardize on what we consider an optimum mix of generality and discriminatory power in rules.

4.3.1. *Transfer to Applications Problems*

The INTSUM program has begun to receive attention from chemists outside the Stanford community, but so far there have been only inquiries about outside use of the rest of Meta-DENDRAL. INTSUM provides careful assistance in associating plausible explanations with data points, within the chemist's own definition of "plausible". This can save a person many hours, even weeks, of looking at the data under various assumptions about fragmentation patterns.

The uses of INTSUM have been to investigate the mass spectral fragmentations of progesterones [54, 55], marine sterols and antibiotics [in progress].

5. Problems

The science of AI suffers from the absence of satellite engineering firms that can map research programs into marketable products. We have sought alternatives to developing CONGEN ourselves into a program that is widely available and have concluded that the time is not yet ripe for a transfer of responsibility. In the future we hope for two major developments to facilitate dissemination of large

AI programs: (a) off-the-shelf, small (and preferably cheap) computers that run advanced symbol manipulating languages, especially INTERLISP, and (b) software firms that specialize in rewriting AI applications programs to industrial specifications.

While the software is almost too complex to export, our research-oriented computer facility has too little capacity for import. Support of an extensive body of outside users means that resources (people as well as computers) must be diverted from the research goals of the project.

At considerable cost in money and talent, it has been possible to export the programs to Edinburgh.[3] But such extensive and expensive collaborations for technology transfer are almost never done in AI. Even when the software is rewritten for export, there are too few "computational chemists" trained to manage and maintain the programs at local sites.

6. Computers and Languages

The DENDRAL programs are coded largely in INTERLISP and run on the DEC KI-10 system under the TENEX operating system at the SUMEX computer resource at Stanford. Parts of CONGEN are written in FORTRAN and SAIL including some I/O packages and graph manipulation packages. We are currently studying the question of rewriting CONGEN in a less flexible language in order to run the program on a variety of machines with less power and memory. Peripheral programs for data acquisition, data filtering, library search and plotting exist for chemists to use on a DEC PDP 11/45 system, but are coupled to the AI programs only by file transfer.

7. Conclusion

CONGEN has attracted a moderately large following of chemists who consult it for help with structure elucidation problems. INTSUM, too, is used occasionally by persons collecting and codifying a large number of mass spectra.

With the exceptions just noted, the DENDRAL and Meta-DENDRAL programs are not used outside the Stanford University community and thus they represent only a successful *demonstration* of scientific capability. These programs are among the first AI programs to do even this. The achievement is significant in that the task domain was not "smoothed" or "tailored" to fit existing AI techniques. On the contrary, the intrinsic complexity of structure elucidation problems guided the AI research to problems of knowledge acquisition and management that might otherwise have been ignored.

The DENDRAL publications in major chemical journals have introduced to chemists the term "artificial intelligence" along with AI concepts and methods.

[3] R. Carhart is working with Professor Donald Michie's group to bring up a version of CONGEN there.

The large number of publications in the chemistry literature also indicates substantial and continued interest in DENDRAL programs and applications.

ACKNOWLEDGMENTS

The individuals who, in addition to the authors, are collectively responsible for most of the AI concepts and code are:

Raymond Carhart, Carl Djerassi, Joshua Lederberg and Dennis Smith.
Harold Brown, Allan Delfino, Geoff Dromey, Alan Duffield, Larry Masinter, Tom Mitchell, James Nourse, N. S. Sridharan, Georgia Sutherland, Tomas Varkony, and William White.

Other contributors to the DENDRAL project have been:

M. Achenbach, C. Van Antwerp, A. Buchs, L. Creary, L. Dunham, H. Eggert, R. Engelmore, F. Fisher, N. Gray, R. Gritter, S. Hammerum, L. Hjelmeland, S. Johnson, J. Konopelski, K. Morrill, T. Rindfleisch, A. Robertson, G. Schroll, G. Schwenzer, Y. Sheikh, M. Stefik, A. Wegmann, W. Yeager, and A. Yeo.

A large number of individuals have worked on programs for data collection and filtering from the mass spectrometer, as well as on operation and maintenance of the instruments themselves. We are particularly indebted to Tom Rindfleisch for overseeing this necessary part of the DENDRAL project.

In its early years DENDRAL research was sponsored by NASA and ARPA. More recently DENDRAL has been sponsored by the NIH (Grant RR-00612). The project depends upon the SUMEX computing facility located at Stanford University for computing support. SUMEX is sponsored by the NIH (Grant RR-00785) as a national resource for applications of artificial intelligence to medicine and biology.

SELECTED REFERENCES IN CHRONOLOGICAL ORDER

Included below are publications written for chemists, as well as selected papers for computer scientists. For this article, in which applications of AI are stressed, the most noteworthy publications are the 25 papers in the series "Applications of Artificial Intelligence for Chemical Inference." (Reference [14] is the first paper in that series.)

1. Lederberg, J., DENDRAL-64—a system for computer construction, enumeration and notation of organic molecules as tree structures and cyclic graphs (technical reports to NASA, also available from the author and summarized in [12]). (1a) Part I. Notational algorithm for tree structures (1964), CR.57029; (1b) Part II. Topology of cyclic graphs (1965), CR.68898; (1c) Part III. Complete chemical graphs; embedding rings in trees (1969).
2. Lederberg, J., *Computation of Molecular Formulas for Mass Spectrometry*, Holden-Day, Inc. (1964).
3. Lederberg, J., Topological mapping of organic Molecules, *Proc. Nat. Acad. Sci.* **53** 1 (1965).
4. Lederberg, J., Systematics of organic molecules, graph topology and Hamilton circuits. A general outline of the DENDRAL system. NASA CR-48899 (1965).
5. Lederberg, J., Hamilton circuits of convex trivalent polyhedra (up to 18 vertices), *Am. Math. Monthly* **74** 5 (1967).
6. Sutherland, G. L., DENDRAL—A computer program for generating and filtering chemical structures, Stanford Heuristic Programming Project Memo HPP–67–1 (February 1967).
7. Lederberg, J., and Feigenbaum, E. A., Mechanization of inductive inference in organic chemistry, in Kleinmuntz, B. (Ed.), *Formal Representations for Human Judgment*, New York: Wiley (1968).

8. Lederberg, J., Online computation of molecular formulas from mass number, NASA CR–94977 (1968).
9. Feigenbaum, E. A. and Buchanan, B. G., Heuristic DENDRAL: a program for generating explanatory hypotheses in organic chemistry, in Kinariwala, B. J., and Kuo, F. F. (Eds.), *Proceedings, Hawaii International Conference on System Sciences*, University of Hawaii Press (1968).
10. Buchanan, B. G., Sutherland, G. L. and Feigenbaum, E. A., Heuristic DENDRAL: a program for generating explanatory hypotheses in organic chemistry, in Meltzer, B. and Michie, D. (Eds), *Machine Intelligence* **4**, Edinburgh: Edinburgh University Press (1969).
11. Feigenbaum, E. A., Artificial intelligence: themes in the second decade, in *Final Supplement to Proceedings of the IFIP68 International Congress*, Edinburgh (August 1968).
12. Lederberg, J., Topology of Molecules, in *The Mathematical Sciences—A Collection of Essays*, Edited by the National Research Council's Committee on Support of Research in the Mathematical Sciences (COSRIMS), Cambridge, Mass.: The M.I.T. Press (1969).
13. Sutherland, G., Heuristic DENDRAL: a family of LISP programs, Stanford Heuristic Programming Project Memo HPP–69–1 (March 1969).
14. Lederberg, J., Sutherland, G. L., Buchanan, B. G., Feigenbaum, E. A., Robertson, A. V., Duffield, A. M. and Djerassi, C., Applications of artificial intelligence for chemical inference I. The number of possible organic compounds: acyclic structures containing C, H, O and N., *Journal of the American Chemical Society* **91** (1969) 2973.
15. Duffield, A. M., Robertson, A. V., Djerassi, C., Buchanan, B. G., Sutherland, G. L., Feigenbaum, E. A. and Lederberg, J., Application of artificial intelligence for chemical inference. II. Interpretation of low resolution mass spectra of ketones, *Journal of the American Chemical Society* **91** (1969) 11.
16. Buchanan, B. G., Sutherland, G. L. and Feigenbaum, E. A., Toward an understanding of information processes of scientific inference in the context of organic chemistry, in Meltzer, B. and Michie, D. (Eds), *Machine Intelligence* **5** Edinburgh: Edinburgh University Press (1970).
17. Lederberg, J., Sutherland, G. L., Buchanan, B. G. and Feigenbaum, E. A., A heuristic program for solving a scientific inference problem: summary of motivation and implementation, in Banerji, R. and Mesarovic, M. D. (Eds.), *Theoretical Approaches to Non-Numerical Problem Solving*, New York: Springer-Verlag (1970).
18. Churchman, C. W. and Buchanan, B. G., On the design of inductive systems: some philosophical problems, *British Journal for the Philosophy of Science* **20** (1969) 311.
19. Schroll, G., Duffield, A. M., Djerassi, C., Buchanan, B. G., Sutherland, G. L., Feigenbaum, E. A. and Lederberg, J., Application of artificial intelligence for chemical inference. III. Aliphatic ethers diagnosed by their low resolution mass spectra and NMR data, *Journal of the American Chemical Society* **91** (1969) 7440.
20. Buchs, A., Duffield, A. M., Schroll, G., Djerassi, C., Delfino, A. B., Buchanan, B. G., Sutherland, G. L., Feigenbaum, E. A. and Lederberg, J., Applications of artificial intelligence for chemical inference. IV. Saturated amines diagnosed by their low resolution mass spectra and nuclear magnetic resonance spectra, *Journal of the American Chemical Society* **92** (1970) 6831.
21. Sheikh, Y. M., Buchs, A., Delfino, A. B., Schroll, G., Duffield, A. M., Djerassi, C., Buchanan, B. G., Sutherland, G. L., Feigenbaum, E. A. and Lederberg, J., Applications of artificial intelligence for chemical inference. V. An approach to the computer generation of cyclic structures. Differentiation between all the possible isomeric ketones of composition C6H10O, *Organic Mass Spectrometry* **4** (1970) 493.
22. Buchs, A., Delfino, A. B., Duffield, A. M., Djerassi, C., Buchanan, B. G., Fe'genbaum, E. A. and Lederberg, J., Applications of artificial intelligence for chemical inference. VI. Approach to a general method of interpreting low resolution mass spectra with a computer, *Helvetica Chimica Acta* **53** (1970) 1394.
23. Feigenbaum, E. A., Buchanan, B. G. and Lederberg, J., On generality and problem solving: A case study using the DENDRAL program, in Meltzer, B. and Michie, D. (Eds.), *Machine Intelligence* **6** Edinburgh: Edinburgh University Press (1971).
24. Buchs, A., Delfino, A. B., Djerassi, C., Duffield, A. M., Buchanan, B. G., Feigenbaum, E. A., Lederberg, J., Schroll, G. and Sutherland, G. L., The application of artificial intelligence in the interpretation of low-resolution mass spectra, *Advances in Mass Spectrometry* **5** (1971) 314.
25. Buchanan, B. G. and Lederberg, J., The heuristic DENDRAL program for explaining empirical data, in *Proceedings of the IFIP Congress* **71** Ljubljana, Yugoslavia (1971).
26. Buchanan, B. G., Feigenbaum, E. A. and Lederberg, J., A heuristic programming study of theory formation in science, in *Proceedings of the Second International Joint Conference on Artificial Intelligence*, Imperial College, London (September 1971).
27. Buchanan, B. G., Duffield, A. M. and Robertson, A. V., An application of artificial intelligence to the interpretation of mass spectra, *Mass Spectrometry Techniques and Applications*, in Milne, G. W. A. (Ed.), New York: Wiley (1971) p. 121.
28. Smith, D. H., Buchanan, B. G., Engelmore, R. S., Duffield, A. M., Yeo, A., Feigenbaum, E. A., Lederberg, J. and Djerassi, C., Applications of artificial intelligence for chemical inference VIII. An approach to the computer interpretation of the high resolution mass spectra of complex molecules. Structure elucidation of estrogencic steroids, *Journal of the American Chemical Society* **94** (1972) 5962.
29. Buchanan, B. G., Feigenbaum, E. A. and Sridharan, N. S., Heuristic theory formation: data interpretation and rule formation, in Meltzer, B. and Michie, D. (Eds.), *Machine Intelligence* **7** Edinburgh: Edinburgh University Press (1972).
30. Lederberg, J., Rapid calculation of molecular formulas from mass values, *Journal of Chemical Education* **49** (1972) 613.
31. Brown, H., Masinter, L. and Hjelmeland, L., Constructive graph labeling using double cosets, *Discrete Mathematics* **7** (1974) 1.
32. Smith, D. H., Buchanan, B. G., Engelmore, R. S., Adlercreutz, H. and Djerassi, C., Applications of artificial intelligence for chemical inference. IX. Analysis of mixtures without prior separation as illustrated for estrogens, *Journal of the American Chemical Society* **95** (1973) 6078.
33. Smith, D. H., Buchanan, B. G., White, W. C., Feigenbaum, E. A., Djerassi, C. and Lederberg, J., Applications of artificial intelligence for chemical inference. X. Intsum: a data interpretation program as applied to the collected mass spectra of estrogenic steroids, *Tetrahedron* **29** (1973) 3117.
34. Buchanan, B. G. and Sridharan, N. S., Rule formation on non-homogeneous classes of objects, in *Proceedings of the Third International Joint Conference on Artificial Intelligence*, Stanford, California (August 1973).
35. Michie, D. and Buchanan, B. G., Current status of the heuristic DENDRAL program for applying artificial intelligence to the interpretation of mass spectra, in Carrington, R. A. G. (Ed.), *Computers for Spectroscopy*, London: Adam Hilger (1973).
36. Brown, H. and Masinter, L., An algorithm for the construction of the graphs of organic molecules, *Discrete Mathematics*, **8** (1974) 227.
37. Smith, D. H., Masinter, L. M. and Sridharan, N. S., Heuristic DENDRAL: analysis of molecular structure, in Wipke, W. T., Heller, S., Feldmann, R. and Hyde, E. (Eds.), *Computer Representation and Manipulation of Chemical Information*, New York: Wiley (1974), p. 287.
38. Carhart, R. and Djerassi, C., Applications of artificial intelligence for chemical inference. XI. The analysis of C13 NMR data for structure elucidation of acyclic amines, *Journal of the Chemical Society (Perkin II)* (1973) 1753.
39. Masinter, L., Sridharan, N. S., Carhart, R. and Smith, D. H., Application of artificial intelligence for chemical inference XII: exhaustive generation of cyclic and acyclic isomers, *Journal of the American Chemical Society* **96** (1974) 7702.

40. Masinter, L., Sridharan, N. S., Carhart, R. and Smith, D. H., Applications of artificial intelligence for chemical inference. XIII. Labeling of objects having symmetry, *Journal of the American Chemical Society* **96** (1974) 7714.
41. Dromey, R. G., Buchanan, B. G., Lederberg, J. and Djerassi, C., Applications of artificial intelligence for chemical inference. XIV. A general method for predicting molecular ions in mass spectra, *Journal of Organic Chemistry* **40** (1975) 770.
42. Smith, D. H., Applications of artificial intelligence for chemical inference. XV. Constructive graph labeling applied to chemical problems. Chlorinated hydrocarbons, *Analytical Chemistry* **47** (1975) 1176.
43. Carhart, R. E., Smith, D. H., Brown, H. and Sridharan, N. S., Applications of artificial intelligence for chemical inference. XVI. Computer generation of vertex graphs and ring systems, *Journal of Chemical Information and Computer Science* **15** (1975), 124.
44. Carhart, R. E., Smith, D. H., Brown, H. and Djerassi, C., Applications of artificial intelligence for chemical inference. XVII. An approach to computer-assisted elucidation of molecular structure, *Journal of the American Chemical Society* **97** (1975) 5755.
45. Buchanan, B. G., Applications of artificial intelligence to scientific reasoning, in *Proceedings of Second USA–Japan Computer Conference*, American Federation of Information Processing Societies Press, (1975).
46. Carhart, R. E., Johnson, S. M., Smith, D. H., Buchanan, B. G., Dromey, R. G. and Lederberg, J., Networking and a collaborative research community: a case study using the DENDRAL program, in Lykos, P. (Ed.), *Computer Networking and Chemistry*, Washington, D.C.: American Chemical Society (1975), p. 192.
47. Smith, D. H., Applications of artificial intelligence for chemical inference. XVII. The scope of structural isomerism, *Journal of Chemical Information and Computer Science* **15** (1975) 203.
48. Smith, D. H., Konopelski, J. P. and Djerassi, C., Applications of artificial intelligence for chemical inference. XIX. Computer generation of ion structures, *Organic Mass Spectrometry* **11** (1976) 86.
49. Carhart, R. E. and Smith, D. H., Applications of artificial intelligence for chemical inference. XX. "intelligent" use of constraints in computer-assisted structure elucidation, *Computers and Chemistry* **1** (1976) 79.
50. Cheer, C., Smith, D. H., Djerassi, C., Tursch, B., Braekman, J. C. and Daloze, D., Applications of artificial intelligence for chemical inference. XXI. Chemical studies of marine invertebrates. XVII. The computer-assisted identification of [+]-palustrol in the marine organism cespitularia sp., aff. subvirdis, *Tetrahedron* **32** (1976) 1807.
51. Buchanan, B. G., Smith, D. H., White, W. C., Gritter, R., Feigenbaum, E. A., Lederberg, J. and Djerassi, C., Applications of artificial intelligence for chemical inference. XXII. Automatic rule formation in mass spectrometry by means of the meta-DENDRAL program, *Journal of the American Chemical Society* **96** (1976) 6168.
52. Varkony, T. H., Carhart, R. E. and Smith, D. H., Computer-assisted structure elucidation. Modelling chemical reaction sequences used in molecular structure problems, in Wipke, W. T. (Ed.), *Computer-Assisted Organic Synthesis*, Washington, D.C.: American Chemical Society (1977).
53. Smith, D. H. and Carhart, R. E., Applications of artificial intelligence for chemical inference. XXIV. Structural isomerism of mono- and sesquiterpenoid skeletons, *Tetrahedron* **32** (1976) 2513.
54. Hammerum, S. and Djerassi, C., Mass spectrometry in structural and stereochemical problems. CCXLV. The electron impact induced fragmentation reactions of 17-oxygenated progesterones, *Steroids* **25** (1975) 817.
55. Hammerum, S. and Djerassi, C., Mass spectrometry in structural and stereochemical problems. CCXLIV. The influence of substituents and stereochemistry on the mass spectral fragmentation of progesterone, *Tetrahedron*, **31** (1975) 2391.
56. Dunham, L. L., Henrick, C. A., Smith, D. H. and Djerassi, C., Mass spectrometry in structural and stereochemical problems. CCXLVI. Electron impact induced fragmentation of juvenile hormone analogs, *Organic Mass Spectrometry* **11** (1976) 1120.
57. Dromey, R. G., Stefik, M. J., Rindfleisch, T. and Duffield, A. M., Extraction of mass spectra free of background and neighboring component contributions from gas chromatography/mass spectrometry data, *Analytical Chemistry* **48** (1976) 1368.
58. Carhart, R. E., A model-based approach to the teletype printing of chemical structures, in *Journal of Chemical Information and Computer Sciences* **16** (1976) 82.
59. Varkony, T. H., Carhart, R. E. and Smith, D. H., Computer assisted structure elucidation, ranking of candidate structures, based on comparison between predicted and observed mass spectra, in *Proceedings of the ASMS Meeting*, Washington, D.C. (1977).
60. Buchanan, B. G. and Smith, D. H., Computer assisted chemical reasoning, in Ludena, E. V., Sabelli, N. H. and Wahl A. C. (Eds.), *Computers in Chemical Education and Research*, New York: Plenum Publishing (1977), p. 388.
61. Smith, D. H. and Carhart, R. E., Structure elucidation based on computer analysis of high and low resolution mass spectral data, in Gross, M. L. (Ed.), *Proceedings of the Symposium on Chemical Applications of High Performance Spectrometry*, Washington, D.C.: American Chemical Society (in press).
62. Mitchell, T. M. and Schwenzer, G. M., Applications of artificial intelligence for chemical inference. XXV. A computer program for automated empirical 13C NMR rule formation, *Organic Magnetic Resonance* (forthcoming).
63. Buchanan, B. G. and Mitchell, T. M., Model-directed learning of production rules, in Waterman, D. A. and Hayes-Roth, F. (Eds.), *Pattern-Directed Inference Systems*, New York: Academic Press (forthcoming).
64. Schwenzer, G. M., Computer assisted structure elucidation using automatically acquired 13C NMR rules, in Smith, D. (Ed.), *Computer Assisted structure Elucidation*, ACS Symposium Series, vol. 54:58 (1977).
65. Varkony, T. H., Smith, D. H. and Djerassi, C., Computer-assisted structure manipulation: studies in the biosynthesis of natural products, *Tetrahedron* (in press).

CONSULTATION SYSTEMS FOR PHYSICIANS: The Role of Artificial Intelligence Techniques

Edward H. Shortliffe

Departments of Medicine and Computer Science
Heuristic Programming Project
Stanford University School of Medicine
Stanford, California 94305

ABSTRACT

Computer systems for use by physicians have had limited impact on clinical medicine. When one examines the most common reasons for poor acceptance of medical computing systems, the potential relevance of artificial intelligence techniques becomes evident. This paper proposes design criteria for clinical computing systems and demonstrates their relationship to current research in knowledge engineering. The MYCIN System is used to illustrate the ways in which our research group has attempted to respond to the design criteria cited.

1. INTRODUCTION

Although computers have had an increasing impact on the practice of medicine, the successful applications have tended to be in domains where physicians have not been asked to interact at the terminal. Few potential user populations are as demanding of computer-based decision aids. This is due to a variety of factors which include their traditional independence as lone decision makers, the seriousness with which they view actions that may have life and death significance, and the overwhelming time demands that tend to make them impatient with any innovation that breaks up the flow of their daily routine.

This paper examines some of the issues that have limited the acceptance of programs for use by physicians, particularly programs intended to give advice in clinical settings. My goal is to present design criteria which may encourage the use of computer programs by physicians, and to show that AI offers some particularly pertinent methods for responding to the design criteria outlined. Although the emphasis is medical throughout, many of the issues occur in other user communities where the introduction of computer methods must confront similar barriers. After presenting the design considerations and their relationship to AI research, I will use our work with MYCIN to illustrate some of the ways in which we have attempted to respond to the acceptability criteria I have outlined.

1.1. The Nature Of Medical Reasoning

It is frequently observed that clinical medicine is more an "art" than a "science". This statement reflects the varied factors that are typically considered in medical decision making; any practitioner knows that well-trained experts with considerable specialized experience may still reach very different conclusions about how to treat a patient or proceed with a diagnostic workup.

One factor which may contribute to observed discrepancies, even among experts, is the tendency of medical education to emphasize the teaching of facts, with little formal advice regarding the reasoning processes that are most appropriate for decision making. There has been a traditional assumption that future physicians should learn to make decisions by observing other doctors in action and by acquiring as much basic knowledge as possible. More recently, however, there has been interest in studying the ways in which expert physicians reach decisions in hopes that a more structured approach to the teaching of medical decision making can be developed [Kassirer 1978, Elstein 1978].

---

[1]This article is based on a longer paper to be published as a book chapter by Academic Press [Shortliffe 1980].

[2]Dr. Shortliffe is recipient of research career development award LM00048 from the National Library of Medicine.

Computer programs for assisting with medical decision making have tended not to emphasize models of clinical reasoning. Instead they have commonly assigned structure to a domain using statistical techniques such as Bayes' Theorem [deDombal 1972] or formal decision analysis [Gorry 1973]. More recently a number of programs have attempted to draw lessons from analyses of actual human reasoning in clinical settings [Wortman 1972, Pauker 1976]. Although the other methodologies may lead to excellent decisions in the clinical areas to which they have been applied, many believe that programs with greater dependence on models of expert clinical reasoning will have heightened acceptance by the physicians for whom they are designed.

1.2. The Consultation Process

Accelerated growth in medical knowledge has necessitated greater subspecialization and more dependence upon assistance from others when a patient presents with a complex problem outside one's own area of expertise. Such consultations are acceptable to doctors in part because they maintain the primary physician's role as ultimate decision maker. The consultation generally involves a dialog between the two physicians, with the expert explaining the basis for advice that is given and the nonexpert seeking justification of points found puzzling or questionable. Consultants who offered dogmatic advice they were unwilling to discuss or defend would find that their opinions were seldom sought. After a recommendation is given, the primary physician generally makes the decision whether to follow the consultant's advice, seek a second opinion, or proceed in some other fashion. When the consultant's advice is followed, it is frequently because the patient's doctor has been genuinely educated about the particular complex problem for which assistance was sought.

Since such consultations are accepted largely because they allow the primary physician to make the final management decision, it can be argued that medical consultation programs must mimic this human process. Computer-based decision aids have typically emphasized only the accumulation of patient data and the generation of advice [Shortliffe 1979]. On the other hand, an ability to explain decisions may be incorporated into computer-based decision aids if the system is given an adequate internal model of the logic that it uses and can convey this intelligibly to the physician-user. The addition of explanation capabilities may be an important step towards effectively encouraging a system's use.

2. ACCEPTABILITY ISSUES

Studies have shown that many physicians are inherently reluctant to use computers in their practice [Startsman 1972]. Some researchers fear that the psychological barriers are insurmountable, but we are beginning to see systems that have had considerable success in encouraging terminal use by physicians [Watson 1974]. The key seems to be to provide adequate benefits while creating an environment in which the physician can feel comfortable and efficient.

Physicians tend to ask at least seven questions when a new system is presented to them:

(1) Is its performance reliable?

(2) Do I need this system?

(3) Is it fast and easy to use?

(4) Does it help me without being dogmatic?

(5) Does it justify its recommendations so that I can decide for myself what to do?

(6) Does use of the system fit naturally into my daily routine?

(7) Is it designed to make me feel comfortable when I use it?

Experience has shown that reliability alone may not be enough to insure system acceptance [Shortliffe 1979]; the additional issues cited here are also central to the question of how to design consultation systems that doctors will be willing to use.

3. DESIGN CRITERIA

The design considerations for systems to be used by physicians can be divided into three main categories: mechanical, epistemological, and psychological.

3.1. Mechanical Issues

It is clear that the best of systems will eventually fail if the process for getting information in or out of the machine is too arduous, frustrating, or complicated. Someday physician-computer interaction may involve voice communication by telephone or microphone, but technology is likely to require manual interaction for years to come. Thus, careful attention to the mechanics of the interaction, the simplicity of the displays, response time, accessibility of terminals, and self-documentation, are all essential for the successful implementation of clinical computing systems.

3.2. Epistemological Issues

As has been discussed, the quality of a program's performance at its decision making task is a basic acceptability criterion. A variety of approaches to automated advice systems have been developed, and many perform admirably [Shortliffe 1979]. Thus the capturing of knowledge and data, plus a system for using them in a coherent and consistent manner, are the design considerations that have traditionally received the most attention.

Other potential uses of system knowledge must also be recognized, however. As has been noted, physicians often expect to be educated when they request a human consultation, and a computer-based consultant should also be an effective teaching tool. On the other hand, physicians would quickly reject a pedantic program that attempted to convey every pertinent fact in its knowledge base. Thus it is appropriate to design programs that convey knowledge as well as advice, but which serve this educational function only when asked to do so by the physician-user.

As has been mentioned, physicians also prefer to understand the basis for a consultant's advice so that they can decide for themselves whether to follow the recommendation. Hence the educational role of the consultation program can also be seen as providing an explanation or justification capability. When asked to do so, the system should be able to retrieve and display any relevant fact or reasoning step that was brought to bear in considering a given case. It is also important that such explanations be expressed in terms that are easily comprehensible to the physician.

Since it would be unacceptable for a consultation program to explain <u>every</u> relevant reasoning step or fact, it is important that the user be able to request justification for points found to be puzzling. Yet an ability to ask for explanations generally requires that the program be able to understand free-form queries entered by the user. A reasonable design consideration, then, is to attempt to develop an interface whereby simple questions expressed in English can be understood by the system and appropriately answered.

It is perhaps inevitable that consultation programs dealing with complex clinical problems will occasionally reveal errors or knowledge gaps, even after they have been implemented for ongoing use. A common source of frustration is the inability to correct such errors quickly so that they will not recur in subsequent consultation sessions. There is often a lapse of several months between "releases" of a system, with an annoying error recurring persistently in the meantime. It is therefore ideal to design systems in which knowledge is easily modified and integrated; then errors can be rapidly rectified once the missing or erroneous knowledge is identified. This requires a flexible knowledge representation and powerful methods for assessing the interactions of new knowledge with other facts already in the system.

Finally, the acquisition of knowledge can be an arduous task for system developers. In some applications the knowledge may be based largely on statistical data, but in others it may be necessary to extract judgmental information from the minds of experts. Thus another design consideration is the development of interactive techniques to permit acquisition of knowledge from primary data or directly from an expert without requiring that a computer programmer function as an intermediary.

3.3. Psychological Issues

The most difficult problems in designing consultation programs may be the frequently encountered psychological barriers to the use of computers among physicians [Startsman 1972, Croft 1972]. Many of these barriers are reflected in the mechanical and epistemological design criteria mentioned above. However, there are several other pertinent observations:

(1) It is probably a mistake to expect the physician to adapt to changes imposed by a consultation system.

(2) A system's acceptance may be greatly heightened if ways are identified to permit physicians to perform tasks that they have wanted to do but had previously been unable to do [Mesel 1976, Watson 1974].

(3) It is important to avoid premature introduction of a system while it is still "experimental".

(4) System acceptance may be heightened if physicians know that a human expert is available to back up the program when problems arise.

(5) Physicians are used to assessing research and new techniques on the basis of rigorous evaluations; hence novel approaches to assessing both the performance and the clinical impact of medical systems are required.

4. KNOWLEDGE ENGINEERING

In recent years the terms "expert systems" and "knowledge-based systems" have been coined to describe AI programs that contain large amounts of specialized expertise that they convey to system users in the form of consultative advice. The phrase "knowledge engineering" has been devised [Michie 1973] to describe the basic AI problem areas that support the development of expert systems. There are several associated research themes:

(1) Representation of Knowledge. A variety of methods for computer-based representation of human knowledge have been devised, each of which is directed at facilitating the associated symbolic reasoning and at permitting the codification and application of "common sense" as well as expert knowledge of the domain.

(2) Acquisition of Knowledge. Obtaining the knowledge needed by an expert program is often a complex task. In certain domains programs may be able to "learn" through experience or from examples, but typically the system designers and the experts being modelled must work closely together to identify and verify the knowledge of the domain. Recently there has been some early experience devising programs that actually bring the expert to the computer terminal where a "teaching session" can result in direct transfer of knowledge from the expert to the system itself [Davis 1979].

(3) Methods of Inference. Closely linked to the issue of knowledge representation is the mechanism for devising a line of reasoning for a given consultation. Techniques for hypothesis generation and testing are required, as are focusing techniques. A particularly challenging associated problem is the development of techniques for quantitating and manipulating uncertainty. Although inferences can sometimes be based on established techniques such as Bayes' Theorem or decision analysis, utilization of expert judgmental knowledge typically leads to the development of alternate methods for symbolically manipulating inexact knowledge [Shortliffe 1975].

(4) Explanation Capabilities. For reasons I have explained in the medical context above, knowledge engineering has come to include the development of techniques for making explicit the basis for recommendations or decisions. This requirement tends to constrain the methods of inference and the knowledge representation that is used by a complex reasoning program.

(5) The Knowledge Interface. There are a variety of issues that fall in this general category. One is the mechanical interface between the expert program and the individual who is using it; this problem has been mentioned for the medical user, and many of the observations there can be applied directly to the users in other knowledge engineering application domains. Researchers on these systems also are looking for ways to combine AI techniques with more traditional numerical approaches to produce enhanced system performance. There is growing recognition that the greatest power in knowledge-based expert systems may lie in the melding of AI techniques and other computer science methodologies [Shortliffe 1979].

Thus it should be clear that artificial intelligence, and specifically knowledge engineering, are inherently involved with several of the design considerations that have been suggested for medical consultation systems. In the next section I will discuss how our medical AI program has attempted to respond to the design criteria that have been cited.

5. AN EXAMPLE: THE MYCIN SYSTEM

Since 1972 our research group at Stanford University[1] has been involved with the development of computer-based consultation systems. The first was designed to assist physicians with the selection of antibiotics for patients with

---

[1]Several computer scientists, physicians, and a pharmacist have been involved in the development of the MYCIN System. These include J. Aikins, S. Axline, J. Bennett, A. Bonnet, B. Buchanan, W. Clancey, S. Cohen, R. Davis, L. Fagan, F. Rhame, C. Scott, W. vanMelle, S. Wraith, and V. Yu.

serious infections. That program has been termed MYCIN after the suffix utilized in the names of many common antimicrobial agents. MYCIN is still a research tool, but it has been designed largely in response to issues such as those I have described. The details of the system have been discussed in several publications [Shortliffe 1976, Davis 1977, Scott 1977] and may already be well known to many readers. Technical details will therefore be omitted here, but I will briefly describe the program to illustrate the ways in which its structure reflects the design considerations outlined above.

5.1. Knowledge Representation and Acquisition

All infectious disease knowledge in MYCIN is contained in packets of inferential knowledge represented as production rules [Davis 1976]. These rules were acquired from collaborating clinical experts during detailed discussions of specific complex cases on the wards at Stanford Hospital. More recently the system has been given the capability to acquire such rules directly through interaction with the clinical expert[1].

MYCIN currently contains some 600 rules that deal with the diagnosis and treatment of bacteremia (bacteria in the blood) and meningitis (bacteria in the cerebrospinal fluid). These rules are coded in INTERLISP [Teitelman 1978], but routines have been written to translate them into simple English so that they can be displayed and understood by the user. For example, one simple rule which relates a patient's clinical situation with the likely bacteria causing the illness is shown in Fig. 1. The strengths with which the specified inferences can be drawn are indicated by numerical weights, or certainty factors, that are described further below.

RULE300
[This rule applies to all cultures and suspected infections, and is tried in order to find out about the organisms (other than those seen on cultures or smears) which might be causing the infection]

If: 1) The infection which requires therapy is meningitis, and
2) The patient does have evidence of serious skin or soft tissue infection, and
3) Organisms were not seen on the stain of the culture, and
4) The type of the infection is bacterial

Then: There is evidence that the organism (other than those seen on cultures or smears) which might be causing the infection is staphylococcus-coag-pos (.75) streptococcus-group-a (.5)

Figure 1 - A Sample MYCIN Rule

5.2. Inference Methods

5.2.1. Reasoning Model

Production rules provide powerful mechanisms for selecting those that apply to a given consultation. In MYCIN's case the rules are only loosely related to one another before a consultation begins; the program selects the relevant rules and chains them together as it considers a particular patient. Two rules chain together if the action portion of one helps determine the truth value of a condition in the premise of the other. The resulting reasoning network, then, is created dynamically and can be seen as a model of one approach to the patient's problem.

MYCIN's strategy in rule selection is goal-oriented. The program "reasons backwards" from its recognized goal of determining therapy for a patient. It therefore starts by considering rules for therapy selection, but the premise portion of each of those rules in turn sets up new questions or subgoals. These new goals then cause new rules to be invoked and a reasoning network is thereby developed. When the truth of a premise condition is best determined by asking the physician rather than by applying rules (e.g., to determine the value of a laboratory test), a question is displayed. The physician enters the appropriate response and the program continues to select additional rules. Once information on the patient is obtained, some rules will fail to be applicable; in this way the invoked applicable rules will provide a customized patient-specific reasoning network for the case under consideration.

Portions of a sample consultation session are shown in Fig. 2. The physician's responses are in capital letters and follow a double asterisk.

---

[1] This capability was implemented in rudimentary form in early versions of the system [Shortliffe 1976] but was substantially broadened and strengthened by Davis in his Teiresias program [Davis 1979].

Note that the physician can indicate that he does not know the answer to a question (Question 13) and MYCIN will proceed to do the best it can on the basis of the data available. Typographical or spelling errors are automatically corrected (Question 12) with the presumed meaning printed at the left margin so that the physician knows what assumption has been made. Note also that the physician's responses are generally single words.

In Fig. 3 the form of MYCIN's final conclusions and therapy recommendations are demonstrated. Note that the program specifies what organisms are likely to be causing the patient's infection and then suggests a therapeutic regimen appropriate for them. There are also specialized routines to calculate recommended drug doses depending upon the patient's size and kidney function.

```
   --------PATIENT-538--------
   1) Patient's name:
   ** PT538
   2) Age:
   ** 45
   3) Sex:
   ** MALE
   4) Race:
   ** CAUC
=CAUCASIAN
   5) Are there any cultures for Pt538
      which may be related to the present
      illness, and from which organisms
      have been grown successfully in
      the microbiology laboratory?
   ** NO
   6) Are there any pending cultures?
   ** YES

      --------CULTURE-1--------
      7) From what site was the specimen
         for CULTURE-1 taken?
      ** CSF
      8) Please give the date and time
         when the pending csf culture
         (CULTURE-1) was obtained.
      ** 11/28/78
      9) Was a smear examined at the time
         that the specimen for the pending
         csf culture (CULTURE-1) was
         obtained?
      ** YES
      10) Were any organisms seen on the
         smear of the specimen submitted
         as the pending csf culture
         (CULTURE-1)?
      ** YES

         --------ORGANISM-1--------
         11) The stain (Gram, India ink,
            or Ziehl-Neelsen acid-fast) of
            ORGANISM-1:
         ** GRAMNEG
         12) Is ORGANISM-1 a rod or coccus
            (etc.):
         ** ROOD
=ROD
         13) What is the form of the
            individual organisms (e.g.
            Lancet-shaped for cocci,
            fusiform for rods, etc.)?
         ** ??
         Expected responses are: FUSIFORM,
         PLUMP or DUMBBELL-SHAPED
         Enter HELP for list of options.
         ** UNKNOWN
      14) Any other organisms noted on the
         smear?
      ** NO
```

Figure 2
The Beginning Of A Sample Consultation

```
   My therapy recommendations will be
designed to treat for organisms that
either are very likely or, although less
likely, would have a significant effect
on therapy selection if they were
present. It is important to cover for
the following probable infection(s) and
associated organism(s):

INFECTION-1 is MENINGITIS

   + <ITEM-1>  E.COLI
   + <ITEM-2>  PSEUDOMONAS-AERUGINOSA
   + <ITEM-3>  KLEBSIELLA-PNEUMONIAE
   + <ITEM-4>  DIPLOCOCCUS-PNEUMONIAE

   41) Does Pt538 have a clinically
      significant allergic reaction to
      any antimicrobial agent?
   ** NO
   42) Do you have reason to suspect that
      Pt538 may have impaired renal
      function?
   ** NO
   43) Pt538's weight in kilograms:
   ** 70

[REC-1] My preferred therapy
        recommendation is:
   In order to cover for Items <1 2 3 4>:
        Give the following in combination:
        1) AMPICILLIN
        Dose: 3.5g (28.0 ml) q4h IV
              [calculated on basis of 50
              mg/kg]
        2) GENTAMICIN
        Dose: 119 mg (3.0 ml, 80mg/2ml
              ampule) q8h IV [calculated
              on basis of 1.7 mg/kg] plus
              consider giving 5 mg q24h
              intrathecally

Since high concentrations of penicillins
can inactivate aminoglycosides, do not mix
these two antibiotics in the same bottle.
```

Figure 3
Example of MYCIN's Recommendations

5.2.2. Management of Uncertainty

The knowledge expressed in a MYCIN rule is seldom definite but tends to include "suggestive" or "strongly suggestive" evidence in favor of a given conclusion. In order to combine evidence regarding a single hypothesis but derived from a number of different rules, it has been necessary to devise a numeric system for capturing and representing an expert's measure of belief regarding the inference stated in a rule. Although this problem may at first seem amenable to the use of conditional probabilities and Bayes' Theorem, a probabilistic model fails to be adequate for a number of reasons we have detailed elsewhere [Shortliffe 1975]. Instead we use a model that has been influenced by the theory of confirmation, and have devised a system of belief measures known as certainty factors. These numbers lie on a -1 to +1 scale with -1 indicating absolute disproof of an hypothesis, +1 indicating its proof, and 0 indicating the absence of evidence for or against the hypothesis (or equally weighted evidence in both directions). The relationship of the model to formal probability theory and the methods for combining evidence from diverse sources (rules and user estimates) have been described [Shortliffe 1975]. Although the system has served us well to date, it does have several recognized inadequacies [Adams 1976] and can only be seen as a first step towards the development of a coherent theory for the management of uncertainty in complex reasoning domains.

5.3. Explanation

Perhaps the greatest advantage of the rules used in MYCIN is the way in which they facilitate the development of mechanisms for explaining and justifying system performance. These capabilities also contribute greatly to MYCIN's educational role [Clancey 1979]. The explanation program has two options, one of which is limited in scope but fast and easy to use. This option is used during a consultation session and allows examination of the reasoning steps that have generated a specific question. The second option is more powerful but it involves language processing and is therefore less reliable and more time consuming. This question-answering capability is designed to allow full access to all system knowledge, both static (i.e., facts and rules obtained from experts) and dynamic (i.e., conclusions reached by the program for the specific consultation session). Each system is briefly described below.

5.3.1. Answers To Questions About The Reasoning Status

During the consultation, MYCIN may ask questions which the physician finds puzzling, either because they appear irrelevant or because the details of their applicability are unclear. When this occurs, the physician can digress momentarily and seek an explanation of the question[1]. Instead of answering the question MYCIN has asked, the user enters the word "WHY" and the program responds with a translation of the rule which

```
35) Is this a hospital-acquired
    infection?
** WHY

[i.e. WHY is it important to determine
whether the infection was acquired while
the patient was hospitalized?]

[2.0] This will aid in determining the
organisms (other than those seen on
cultures or smears) which might be causing
the infection.
   It has already been established that
        [2.1] the infection which requires
              therapy is meningitis, and
        [2.2] organisms were not seen on
              the stain of this pending
              csf culture, and
        [2.3] the type of the infection is
              bacterial, and
        [2.4] neurosurgery is not one of
              the relevant items from the
              history of pt538, and
        [2.5] the age of pt538 is greater
              than 10 days
    Therefore, if
        [2.6] the infection was acquired
              while the patient was
              hospitalized
    then:
           there is evidence that the
           organism (other than those
           seen on cultures or smears)
           which might be causing the
           infection is e.coli (.75)
           staphylococcus-coag-pos (.3)
           pseudomonas-aeruginosa (.3)
           klebsiella-pneumoniae (.5)

  [back to question 35...]
  **
```

Figure 4
Example of the WHY Command

---

[1]The mechanisms for examining the reasoning status using "WHY" and "HOW" commands were largely the work of Davis in his Teiresias program [Davis 1979]. The techniques he developed are general in their applicability and have been implemented in nonmedical domains as well.

generated the question. An example of this feature is shown in Fig. 4. Note that MYCIN begins its response by phrasing in English its understanding of the "WHY question" asked by the physician. It then displays the relevant rule, specifying which conditions in the premise are already known to be true and which conditions remain to be investigated. In many cases this single rule displayed is an adequate explanation of the current line of reasoning and the physician can then proceed with the consultation by answering the question.

The user can alternatively continue to investigate the current reasoning by repeating the "WHY" command several times. Each additional "WHY" is interpreted by MYCIN as a request for display of the next rule in the current reasoning chain. For example, in Fig. 4 another "WHY" would be equivalent to asking "Well then, why are you trying to determine the organisms which might be causing the infection?" After responding to each "WHY", MYCIN returns to the current question and awaits the physician's response.

The "HOW" command is used in conjunction with the "WHY" command. Note that MYCIN places a unique number before each condition in the premise of a displayed rule (Fig. 4). If the user does not understand how a specified condition was met (or will be met), the "HOW" command, followed by the identifying number of the premise clause in question, can be used. Hence "HOW" requires an argument as shown in Fig. 5. This example follows immediately on the "WHY" example in Fig. 4; thus the argument "2.3" refers to the third condition in the premise of RULE545 in Fig. 4 and "2.5" refers to the fifth. MYCIN's responses to "HOW" commands are self-explanatory. Note also that components of all explanations are given identifiers so that, in Fig. 5, the command "HOW 3.1" would have resulted in a display of RULE526.

Other features of the capability to assess the reasoning status during a consultation are described elsewhere [Davis 1977, Scott 1977, Davis 1979]. Two points require emphasis here, however. First, these features require no English language processing since the user gives simple single-word commands; hence the capability is fast, efficient, and reliable. On the other hand, questions are limited to the immediate reasoning environment surrounding the question asked by MYCIN. Hence general access to other system knowledge or other conclusions previously made by the program is not possible. To provide a more general explanation capability, MYCIN must be able to respond to questions expressed in simple English as described below.

```
   [back to question 35...]
   ** HOW 2.3

[i.e. HOW was it established that the type
      of the infection is bacterial?]

The following rules concluded about the
      likelihood that the type of the
      infection is bacterial:

                Rule           Certainty
      [2.7]     RULE148          (.19)
      [2.8]     RULE500          (.51)
      [2.9]     RULE501          (.95)
      [3.0]     RULE502          (.97)
      [3.1]     RULE526          (.98)
      [3.2]     RULE504          (.97)
      [3.3]     RULE524          (.98)

Thus, it has been established that the
      type of the infection is bacterial.

   [back to question 35...]
   ** HOW 2.5

[i.e. HOW was it established that the age
      of pt538 is greater than 10 days?]

In answer to question 2 you said that the
      age of pt538 is 34 years. Thus, it
      has been established that the age of
      pt538 is greater than 10 days.

   [back to question 35...]
   **
```

Figure 5
Examples of the HOW Command

5.3.2. Answers To Questions About The Consultation And Knowledge Base

MYCIN's general question-answering feature is automatically made available to the user at the end of each consultation session. After a therapy recommendation has been given, the physician may still have several questions regarding details of the consultation and the basis for diagnostic and therapeutic advice. Fig. 6 shows an example of a simple English question which MYCIN understands and attempts to answer. Our approach to natural language understanding is very simplistic [Scott 1977] but often adequate if questions are kept short without subordinate clauses. In many cases questions are best answered simply by retrieving relevant rules and displaying them in a format suitable for the question being asked. In Fig. 6 MYCIN offers a detailed explanation of how it had decided that the patient might be infected with an *E. coli*. All rules are specified by number so that the physician can have them displayed if full details are desired.

```
** WHY DID YOU TREAT E.COLI?

ITEM-1 is E.coli associated with
meningitis.  I decided to treat ITEM-1 on
the basis of clinical evidence only.

The following rules concluded about:
the likelihood that e.coli is one of the
organisms (other than those seen on
cultures or smears) which might be causing
the infection

RULE545 was used to conclude that e.coli
     is one of the organisms (other than
     those seen on cultures or smears)
     which might be causing the infection
     (.74).
RULE557 was used to conclude that e.coli
     is one of the organisms (other than
     those seen on cultures or smears)
     which might be causing the infection
     (.93).

The parameters most frequently used in
these rules:
   the infection which requires therapy
   whether a smear of the culture was
         examined
   whether organisms were seen
   the type of the infection
```

Figure 6
Response To A Free Text Question

Fig. 7 demonstrates the way in which a physician can ask general questions of the knowledge base (static knowledge); neither the questions nor MYCIN's responses refer to any specific consultation session. Note that MYCIN has a sense of its limitations and makes it clear that it has no knowledge specific to pneumonia. Also, a large dictionary includes synonyms and hence permits MYCIN to recognize that "pneumococcal" refers to "pneumococcus", which in turn is the same as "diplococcus-pneumoniae".

Despite their utility, the language understanding features demonstrated in Figs. 6 and 7 have significant limitations. The associated computer code is large, complex, and very slow. Furthermore, we have found that it takes novice users several sessions before they learn the best ways to phra .e questions so that MYCIN will interpret them properly.

5.4. Evaluating MYCIN

As work on MYCIN has progressed, we have begun to devise techniques for analyzing formally the system's

```
** HOW DO YOU DECIDE THAT AN ORGANISM IS
   AN E.COLI?
The following rules conclude about:
   the likelihood that the identity of the
   organism is E.coli
555, 304, 243, 3
Which of the rules do you wish to see?
      ** NONE

** WHAT IS THE TREATMENT FOR
   PNEUMOCOCCAL PNEUMONIA?
The MYCIN system currently can treat the
following infections:  BACTEREMIA
MENINGITIS CYSTITIS. Because the knowledge
base is incomplete, all other infections
will be treated like bacteremia.

   For treatment of DIPLOCOCCUS-PNEUMONIAE
in BACTEREMIA, the drugs of choice (ranked
by relative efficacy, assuming
sensitivity) are:
     1st choice:
         PENICILLIN or AMPICILLIN
     2nd choice:
         NAFCILLIN, CEPHALOTHIN,
         ERYTHROMYCIN, or CLINDAMYCIN
     3rd choice:
         TETRACYCLINE, CHLORAMPHENICOL, or
         VANCOMYCIN

** WHAT DOSE OF ERYTHROMYCIN DO YOU
   RECOMMEND?
When ERYTHROMYCIN is given for BACTEREMIA,
the recommended dosage is:
if age is > 12 yrs then 12 mg/kg q6h IV
else if age > .08 yrs then 5 mg/kg q6h IV
else if age > .02 yrs then 5 mg/kg q12h IV
```

Figure 7
Requests For MYCIN's General Knowledge

performance. It must be emphasized, however, that the decision making performance is only one aspect of overall system acceptability; as I have discussed, many of the most significant problems occur when attempts are made to encourage physicians to use a program, even after it has been shown to reach good decisions.

The details of the evaluation studies will not be presented here[1], but a number of specific points are of interest. First any evaluation is difficult because there is so much difference of opinion in this domain, even among experts. Hence, it is unclear how to select a "gold standard" by which to measure the system's performance.

---

[1]See [Yu 1979a] for the details of the bacteremia evaluation, and [Yu 1979b] for the data on MYCIN's performance selecting therapy for patients with meningitis.

Actual clinical outcome cannot be used because each patient of course is treated in only one way and because a poor outcome in a gravely ill patient cannot necessarily be blamed on the therapy that had been selected.

Second, although MYCIN performed at or near expert level in almost all cases, the evaluating experts in one study [Yu 1979a] had serious reservations about the clinical utility of the program. It is difficult to assess how much of this opinion is due to actual inadequacies in system knowledge or design and how much is related to inherent bias against *any* computer-based consultation aid. In a subsequent study we attempted to eliminate this bias from the study by having the evaluators unaware of which recommendations were MYCIN's and which came from actual physicians [Yu 1979b]. In that setting MYCIN's recommendations were uniformly judged preferable to, or equivalent to, those of five infectious disease experts who recommended therapy for the same patients.

Finally, those cases in which MYCIN has tended to do least well are those in which serious infections have been simultaneously present at sites in the body about which the program has been given no rules. It is reasonable, of course, that the program should fail in areas where it has no knowledge. However, a useful antimicrobial consultation system must know about a broad range of infectious diseases, just as its human counterpart does. Even with excellent performance managing isolated bacteremias and meningitis, the program is therefore not ready for clinical implementation.

There will eventually be several important questions regarding the clinical impact of MYCIN and systems like it. Are they used? If so, do the physicians follow the program's advice? If so, does patient welfare improve? Is the system cost effective when no longer in an experimental form? What are the legal implications in the use of, or failure to use, such systems? The answers to all these questions are years away for most consultation systems, but it must be recognized that all these issues are ultimately just as important as whether the decision making methodology manages to lead the computer to accurate and reliable advice.

6. CONCLUSION

Although I have asserted that AI research potentially offers solutions to many of the important problems confronting researchers in computer-based clinical decision making, the field is not without its serious limitations. However, AI has reached a level of development where it is both appropriate and productive to begin applying the techniques to important real world problems rather than purely theoretical issues. The difficulty lies in the fact that such efforts must still dwell largely in research environments where short term development of systems for service use is not likely to occur.

It is also important to recognize that other computational techniques may meld very naturally with AI approaches as the fields mature. Thus we may see, for example, direct links between AI methods and statistical procedures, decision analysis, pattern recognition techniques, and large databanks. As researchers in other areas become more familiar with AI, it may gradually be brought into fruitful combination with these alternate methodologies. The need for physician acceptance of medical consultation programs is likely to make AI approaches particularly attractive, at least in those settings where hands-on computer use by physicians is desired or necessary. This paper has attempted to explain why the wedding of AI and medical consultation systems is a natural one and to show, in the setting of the MYCIN system, how one early application has responded to design criteria identified for a user community of physicians.

REFERENCES

Adams, J. B. "A probability model of medical reasoning and the MYCIN model." *Math. Biosci.* 32,177-186 (1976).

Clancey, W.J. *Transfer of Rule-Based Expertise Through a Tutorial Dialogue.* Dictoral dissertation, Stanford University, September 1979. Technical memo STAN-CS-79-769.

Croft, D. J. "Is computerized diagnosis possible?" *Comp. Biomed. Res.* 5,351-367 (1972).

Davis, R. and King, J. "An overview of production systems." In *Machine Representation of Knowledge* (E. W. Elcock and D. Michie, eds.), New York: Wiley, 1976.

Davis, R., Buchanan, B. G., and Shortliffe, E. H. "Production rules as a representation for a knowledge-based consultation system." *Artificial Intelligence* 8,15-45 (1977).

Davis, R., "Interactive transfer of expertise: acquisition of new inference rules." Artificial Intelligence, 12,121-157 (1979).

deDombal, F. T., Leaper, D. J., Staniland, J. R., et al. "Computer-aided diagnosis of acute abdominal pain." Brit. Med. J. 2,9-13 (1972).

Elstein, A. S., Shulman, L. S., and Sprafka, S. A. Medical Problem Solving: An Analysis of Clinical Reasoning. Cambridge, Mass.: Harvard Univ. Press, 1978.

Gorry, G. A., Kassirer, J. P., Essig, A., and Schwartz, W. B. "Decision analysis as the basis for computer-aided management of acute renal failure." Amer. J. Med 55,473-484 (1973).

Kassirer, J. P. and Gorry, G. A. "Clinical problem solving: a behavioral analysis." Anns. Int. Med. 89,245-255 (1978).

Mesel, E., Wirtschafter, D. D., Carpenter, J. T., et al. "Clinical algorithms for cancer chemotherapy - systems for community-based consultant-extenders and oncology centers." Meth. Inform. Med. 15,168-173 (1976).

Michie, D. "Knowledge engineering." Cybernetics 2,197-200 (1973).

Pauker, S. G., Gorry, G. A., Kassirer, J. P., and Schwartz, W. B. "Towards the simulation of clinical cognition: taking a present illness by computer." Amer. J. Med. 60:981-996 (1976).

Scott, A. C., Clancey, W., Davis, R., and Shortliffe, E. H. "Explanation capabilities of knowledge-based production systems." Amer. J. Computational Linguistics, Microfiche 62, 1977.

Shortliffe, E. H. and Buchanan, B. G. "A model of inexact reasoning in medicine." Math. Biosci. 23,351-379 (1975).

Shortliffe, E. H. Computer-Based Medical Consultations: MYCIN, New York: Elsevier/North Holland, 1976.

Shortliffe, E. H. Buchanan, B. G. and Feigenbaum, E. A. "Knowledge engineering for medical decision making: a review of computer-based clinical decision aids." PROCEEDINGS of the IEEE, 67,1207-1224 (1979).

Shortliffe, E.H. "Medical consultation systems: designing for doctors." In Communication With Computers (M. Sime and M. Fitter, eds.), Academic Press, London, 1980 (in press).

Startsman, T. S. and Robinson, R. E. "The attitudes of medical and paramedical personnel towards computers." Comp. Biomed. Res. 5,218-227 (1972).

Teitelman, W. INTERLISP Reference Manual, XEROX Corporation, Palo Alto, Calif. and Bolt Beranek and Newman, Cambridge, Mass., October 1978.

Watson, R. J. "Medical staff response to a medical information system with direct physician-computer interface." MEDINFO 74, pp. 299-302, Amsterdam: North-Holland Publishing Company, 1974.

Wortman, P. M. "Medical diagnosis: an information processing approach." Comput. Biomed. Res. 5,315-328 (1972).

Yu, V. L. Buchanan, B. G. Shortliffe, E. H. et al. "Evaluating the performance of a computer-based consultant." Comput. Prog. Biomed. 9,95-102 (1979a).

Yu, V. L. Fagan, L. M. Wraith, S. M. et al. "Computerized consultation in antimicrobial selection - a blinded evaluation by experts." J. Amer. Med. Assoc. 242,1279-1282 (1979b).

MODEL DESIGN IN THE PROSPECTOR CONSULTANT SYSTEM FOR MINERAL EXPLORATION*

Richard Duda, John Gaschnig and Peter Hart

ABSTRACT

Prospector is a computer consultant system intended to aid geologists in evaluating the favorability of an exploration site or region for occurrences of ore deposits of particular types. Knowledge about a particular type of ore deposit is encoded in a computational model representing observable geological features and the relative significance thereof. We describe the form of models in Prospector, focussing on inference networks of geological assertions and the Bayesian propagation formalism used to represent the judgmental reasoning process of the economic geologist who serves as model designer. Following the initial design of a model, simple performance evaluation techniques are used to assess the extent to which the performance of the model reflects faithfully the intent of the model designer. These results identify specific portions of the model that might benefit from "fine tuning", and establish priorities for such revisions. This description of the Prospector system and the model design process serves to illustrate the process of transferring human expertise about a subjective domain into a mechanical realization.

I. INTRODUCTION

In an increasingly complex and specialized world, human expertise about diverse subjects spanning scientific, economic, social, and political issues plays an increasingly important role in the functioning of all kinds of organizations. Although computers have become indispensable tools in many endeavors, we continue to rely heavily on the human expert's ability to identify and synthesize diverse factors, to form judgments, evaluate alternatives, and make decisions – in sum, to apply his or her years of experience to the problem at hand. This is especially valid with regard to domains that are not easily amenable to precise scientific formulations, i.e., to domains in which experience and subjective judgment plays a major role.

The precious resource of human expertise is also a fragile and transient one: the departure of a crucial expert from an organization may cause serious dislocations; senior people impart their knowledge to younger colleagues, but the demand for their talents may not leave sufficient time for such educational efforts.

---

* This work was supported in part by the Office of Resource Analysis of the U.S. Geological Survey under Contract No. 14-08-0001-15985, and in part by the Nonrenewable Resources Section of the National Science Foundation under Grant AER77-04499. Any opinions, findings, conclusions, or recommendations expressed in this publication are those of the authors, and do not necessarily reflect the views of either the U.S. Geological Survey or the National Science Foundation.

During recent years research in the field of artificial intelligence has produced effective new techniques for representing empirical judgmental knowledge and using this knowledge in performing plausible reasoning. The best known application of these techniques has been in the area of medical diagnosis, where computer programs have achieved high levels of performance (Pople et al., 1975; Shortliffe, 1976; Weiss et al., 1977; Yu, 1978; Szolovits, 1976). Other applications include planning experiments in molecular genetics (Martin 1977) and monitoring instruments in intensive care units (Fagan 1978). This paper concerns a similar computer program, called Prospector, that is being developed to help geologists in exploring for hard-rock mineral deposits. The characteristic of plausible reasoning shared by the domains of medical diagnosis and mineral exploration is common, to some degree, to many other diverse evaluation tasks as well. Hence the purpose of this paper is to illustrate, by a case study for the domain of mineral exploration, the general process of capturing and encoding human expertise into a mechanical realization.

II. OVERVIEW OF THE PROSPECTOR SYSTEM

The Prospector system is intended to emulate the reasoning process of an experienced exploration geologist in assessing a given prospect site or region for its likelihood of containing an ore deposit of the type represented by the model he or she designed. Here we use the term "model" to refer to a body of knowledge about a particular domain of expertise that is encoded into the system and on which the system can act. The empirical knowledge contained in Prospector consists of a number of such specially encoded models of certain classes of ore deposits. These models are intended to represent the most authoritative and up-to-date information available about each deposit class.

In Prospector's normal interactive consultation mode, the user is assumed to have obtained some promising field data and is assumed to desire assistance in evaluating the prospect. Thus, the user begins by providing the program with a list of rocks and minerals observed, and by inputting other observations expressed in simple English sentences. The program matches these data against its models, requests additional information of potential value for arriving at more definite conclusions, and provides a summary of the findings. The user can ask at any time for an elaboration of the intent of a question, or for the geological rationale for including a question in the model, or for an ongoing trace of the effects of his answers on Prospector's conclusions. The intent is to provide the user with many of the services that could be provided by giving him telephone access to a panel of senior economic geologists, each an authority on a particular class of ore deposits.

The performance of Prospector depends on the number of models it contains, the types of deposits modeled, and the quality and completeness of each model. Because the Prospector program is primarily a research project, its coverage is still incomplete. It currently contains five prospect-scale models, one regional-scale model, and one drilling site selection model. The prospect-scale models consist of a Kuroko-type massive sulfide model contributed by Charles F. Park, Jr., a Mississippi-Valley-type carbonate lead/zinc model contributed by Neil Campbell, a near-continental-margin porphyry copper model contributed by Marco T. Einaudi, a Komatiitic nickel sulfide model contributed by Anthony J. Naldrett, and a Western-states sandstone uranium model contributed by Ruffin I. Rackley. The regional scale model is a variation of Mr. Rackley's model. The drilling site selection model, for porphyry copper deposits, was contributed by Mr. Victor Hollister, and differs somewhat from the other models: it derives its inputs from digitized maps of geological characteristics, and produces as output a color-coded graphical display of the favorability of each cell on a grid corresponding to the input map. These models were selected for a variety of reasons, including their economic significance, the extent to which they are well understood scientifically, the availability of expert geologists who could collaborate with us in the model development, and the new research issues that their implementation would raise.

Each model is encoded as a separate data structure, independent of the Prospector system per se. Thus, the Prospector program should not be confused with its models. Rather, Prospector should be thought of as a general mechanism for delivering relevant expert information about ore deposits to a user who can supply it with data about a particular prospect or region.

This paper describes briefly the process of developing and encoding such models for Prospector. General overviews of the technical principles are given in Hart, Duda and Einaudi (1978), mathematical aspects in Duda et al. (1976, 1978a), and detailed expositions in Duda et al. (1977, 1978b) and Hart, Duda and Konolige (1978).

III. FORMALISM FOR ENCODING EXPLORATION MODELS

A. Inference Networks of Assertions

For use in Prospector an ore deposit model must be encoded as a so-called inference network, a network of connections or relations between field evidence and important geological hypotheses. Since we sometimes do not wish to distinguish between evidence and hypotheses, we shall refer to either one as an assertion. To illustrate these ideas, we shall draw upon examples taken from M.T. Einaudi's porphyry copper model, which we shall denote by PCDA. Typical assertions in PCDA are "Hornblende has been pervasively altered to biotite" and "The alteration suggests the potassic zone of a porphyry copper deposit." The former would normally be thought of as field evidence, the latter as a geological hypothesis. A small portion of the PCDA inference network is shown in Figure 1. Here the terminal or "leaf" nodes correspond to field evidence asked of the user, while the other nodes represent hypotheses. The text in the boxes in Figure 1 is concise for reasons of graphical display; the actual questions asked of the user are more definitive.

Although assertions are statement that should be either true or false, in a given situation there is usually uncertainty as to whether they are true or false. Initially, the state of each assertion is simply unknown. As evidence is gathered, some assertions may be definitely established, whereas others may become only more

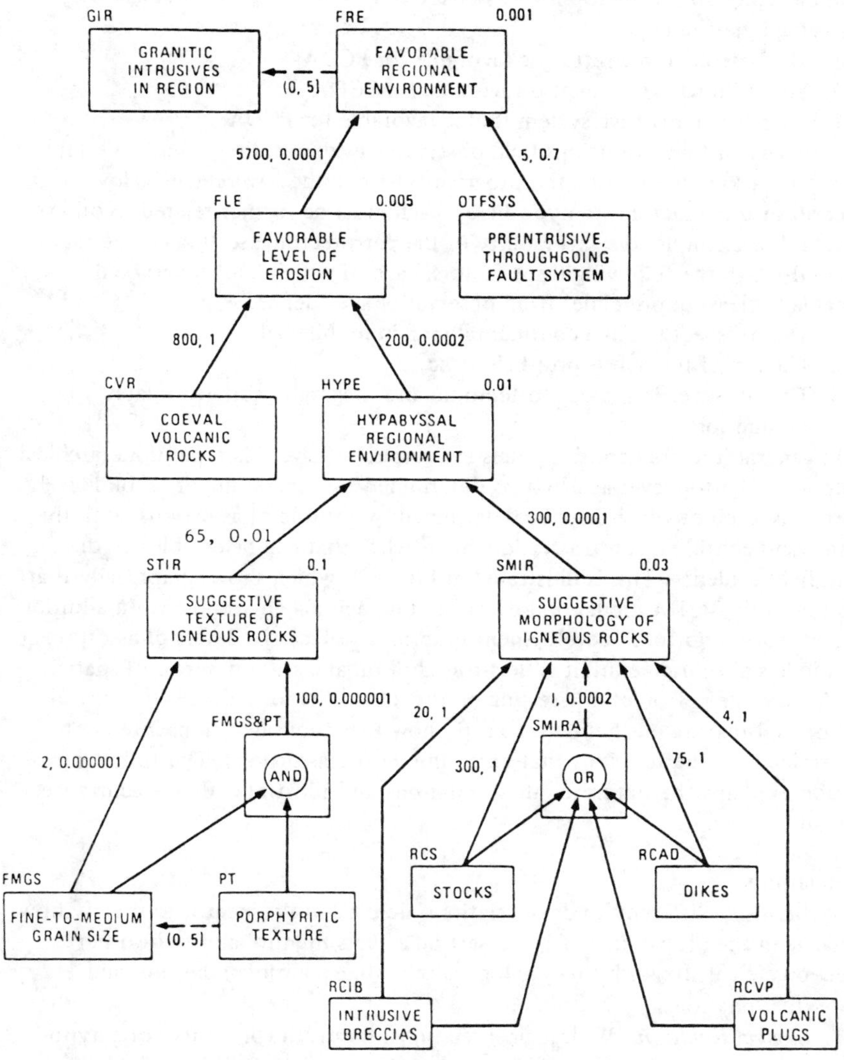

Figure 1. Portion of a Prospector model for porphyry copper deposits. See text for interpretation

or less likely. In general, we associate a probability value with every assertion. The "connections" in the inference network determine how a change in the probability of one assertion will affect those of other assertions.

The principal or top-level assertion in an inference network for a model is the assertion that the available evidence matches that particular model. To establish this assertion, it is usually necessary to establish several major factors. For example, to establish the top-level assertion in PCDA, we must establish the following hypotheses:

1. The petrotectonic setting is favorable for PCDA;
2. The regional evironment is favorable for PCDA;
3. There is an intrusive system that is favorable for PCDA.

Were any of these assertions field-observable evidence, they could be established merely by asking the user of the program whether they were true. However, since all of these factors are hypotheses, each must be further related to other factors. For example, the favorability of the petrotectonic setting can be established through the following three factors, each of which happens to be determinable (at least in principle) from observational evidence:

1. The prospect lies in a continental margin mobile belt;
2. The age of the belt is post-Paleozoic;
3. The prospect is subject to tectonic and magmatic activity related to subduction.

In general, the ore deposit models in Prospector have this type of hierarchical structure. The top-level assertion is determined by several major second-level assertions, each of which may be determined by third-level assertions, with this refinement continuing until assertions are reached that can be established directly from field evidence. This is illustrated in Figure 1, which shows graphically that portion of the PCDA model that describes the regional environment. In addition to this "top-to-bottom" development in terms of successive levels of assertions, the models also often exhibit a "left-to-right" organization in terms of spatial scale, from the petrotectonic setting on the left to the local details of mineralization and texture on the right. Exactly how these considerations interact is determined by the relations that exist among the assertions. The following section explains the nature of these relations and illustrates their occurrence in Figure 1.

B. Relations

Three basically different kinds of relations are used in Prospector to specify how a change in the probability of one assertion affects the probability of other assertions. We distinguish these as logical relations, plausible relations, and contextual relations.

1. *Logical Relations*. With logical relations, the truth (or falsity) of a hypothesis is completely determined by the truth (or falsity) of the assertions that define it. Such relations are composed out of the primitive operations of conjunction (AND), disjunction (OR), and negation (NOT). When several assertions must all be true for a hypothesis to be true, the hypothesis is the conjunction of the assertions. When the hypothesis is true if any of the assertions is true, the hypothesis is the disjunction of the assertions. Negation merely complements an assertion, interchanging truth and falsity. As an example of a logical relation, the PCDA model says that alteration of plagioclase is indicative of the barren-core zone if

1. Plagioclase has been altered to
    a. albite
    or
    b. minor sericite (or both)

and

2. Plagioclase has not been altered to major epidote.

Other examples of logical relations are shown in Figure 1.

Of course, in general we do not know whether the assertions are true, but can only estimate a probability or degree of belief that they are true. With logical relations, to compute the probability of a hypothesis from the probability of its component assertions we employ the fuzzy-set formulas of Zadeh (1965). Using these formulas, the probability of a hypothesis that is defined as the logical conjunction (AND) of several pieces of evidence equals the minimum of the probability values corresponding to the evidence. Similarly, a hypothesis defined as the logical disjunction (OR) of its evidence spaces is assigned a probability value equal to the maximum of those values assigned to the evidence spaces. One property of this procedure is that it often gives no "partial credit." In particular, if all but one of the assertions have been established, but the user can not even guess about the last, then the probability of their conjunction often remains at the value it had when the states of none of the assertions were known. This may be the appropriate conclusion. When it is not, one has the option of using plausible relations.

2. *Plausible Relations.* With plausible relations, each assertion contributes "votes" for or against the truth of the hypothesis. This would be expressed by relating the assertions to the hypothesis through a set of plausible inference rules. Each rule has an associated rule strength that measures the degree to which a change in the probability of the evidence assertion changes the probability of the hypothesis. This change can be positive or negative, since as assertion can be either favorable or unfavorable for a hypothesis. As with all parts of a model, these rule strengths are obtained by interviewing an authority on the corresponding class of ore deposits. Initially he may express the strengths in verbal terms, such as "rather discouraging" or "very encouraging." This is ultimately translated into numerical terms (as shown in Figure 1), the changes in probability being computed in accordance with the rules of Bayesian probability theory, as outlined below and described in detail in Duda et al. (1977).

Prospector's plausible reasoning scheme is based on Bayesian decision theory (Raiffa, 1968), exploiting an elementary theorem of probability known as Bayes' rule. For our purposes, the so-called "odds-likelihood" form of the rule is most convenient. This form relates three quantities involving an evidence assertion E and a hypothesis assertion H: the prior odds O(H) on the hypothesis, the posterior odds O(H | E) on the hypothesis, given that E is observed to be present, and a measure of sufficiency LS. Then Bayes' rule can be stated as

$$O(H \mid E) = LS * O(H) \tag{1}$$

Odds and probabilities are freely interchangeable through the simple relation $O = P / (1 - P)$, where P denotes probability, and hence $P = O / (1 + O)$. The sufficiency measure LS is a standard quantity in statistics called the likelihood ratio, and is defined by

$$LS = \frac{P(E|H)}{P(E|\sim H)} \tag{2}$$

where ~H means "not H."

Equation (1) prescribes a means for updating the probability (or odds) on H, given that the evidence E is observed to be present. An inference rule for which LS is large means that the observation of E is encouraging for H – in the extreme case of LS approaching infinity, E is sufficient to establish H in a strict logical sense. On the other hand, if LS is much less than unity, then the observation of E is discouraging for H, inasmuch as the observation of E diminishes the odds on H.

A complementary set of equations describes the case in which E is known to be absent, that is, when ~E is true. In this case, we can use Bayes' rule to write

$$O(H \mid \sim E) = LN * O(H) \tag{3}$$

where

$$LN = \frac{P(\sim E \mid H)}{P(\sim E \mid \sim H)} \tag{4}$$

The quantity LN is called the necessity measure. If LN is much less than unity, the known absence of E transforms neutral prior odds on H into very small posterior odds in favor of H. In the extreme case of LN approaching zero, E is logically necessary for H. On the other hand, if LN is large, then the absence of E is encouraging for H.

Hence to define an inference rule

IF E
THEN (to degree LS, LN) H,

the model designer must articulate E and H, and must supply numerical values for LS, LN, and O(H).

In general, the user may not be able to state that E is either definitely present or definitely absent. In this case, the updating formulas (1) and (3) cannot be applied directly, but can be extended to accommodate the uncertainty in the evidence. The extension used in Prospector involves a linear interpolation between the extremes of E's being definitely present or definitely absent. See Duda (1976, 1977) for details. The user expresses his certainty about E on an arbitrary –5 to 5 scale, where 5 denotes that the evidence is definitely present, –5 denotes that it is definitely absent, 0 indicates no information, and intermediate values denote degrees of certainty.

We illustrate this plausible inference scheme with examples taken from Figure 1. The two numbers associated with each inference rule in Figure 1 are its LS and LN values, respectively. The number appearing above each box representing a nonterminal node is the prior probability of that assertion's being true. For example, the figure indicates that the existence of stocks is a more highly sufficient indicator of "suggestive morphology of igneous rocks" (i.e., LS = 300) than is the existence of either dikes, intrusive breccias, or volcanic plugs (i.e., LS = 75, 20, and 4, respectively). Similarly, "favorable level of erosion" (FLE) is a highly sufficient and highly necessary factor for establishing "favorable regional environment" (i.e., LS = 5700 and LN = 0.0001), whereas the existence of a "preintrusive throughgoing fault system" (OTFSYS) is only mildly sufficient and mildly necessary for establishing "favorable regional environment." Hence the positive (LS) or negative (LN) votes of FLE are weighted much more heavily than those of OTFSYS.

The section of the model concerned with establishing "suggestive morphology of igneous rocks" (SMIR) illustrates how logical and plausible relations can be combined as building blocks to accomplish the intent of the economic geologist designing the model. This section of the PCDA model can be described as follows. "There are four positive indicators for establishing a suggestive morphology for igneous rocks (SMIR), namely intrusive breccias, stocks, dikes, and volcanic plugs. Each of these factors contributes independently to establishing SMIR, although to differing degrees. The absence of any one of these four factors individually is unimportant [i.e., LN = 1 for those rules]. However, if it is known that none of these factors is present [implying that the disjunction node SMIRA is false], then the probability of a suggestive morphology of igneous rocks is essentially zero [LN = 0.0002 for SMIRA]." In defining an inference network for a model, the object is to induce the model designer to articulate such statements, and then to translate the statements into network constructions.

To see how the effect of a piece of evidence propagates upward through the model, suppose that the user has indicated only that intrusive breccias are present, but this is definite. This fact multiplies the odds of SMIR by a factor of 20, hence raising its probability from 0.03 to 0.382. (The prior odds on SMIR are 0.03 / (1 – 0.03) = 0.030927, giving posterior odds on SMIR equal to 20 * 0.030927 = .61855, which corresponds to a probability of 0.61855 / (1+0.61855) = 0.382.) This in turn increase the odds on HYPE by a factor of 300 weighted by the degree to which SMIR has increased from its prior probability, i.e, by the factor 300 * (0.382–0.03) / (1–0.03) = 108.866. Hence the posterior probability of HYPE is 0.52373, which in turn increases the odds of FLE by a factor of 200 * (0.52373–0.01) / (1–0.01) = 103.78, giving a posterior probability for FLE of 0.34276. The propagation continues in this manner upward through the network.

It should be noted that Prospector expresses its conclusions to the user on the same –5 to 5 certainty scale that the user employs to express his certainty about evidence requested by the system. Prospector maps internal probability values to external certainty scores in a piecewise linear fashion, such that the posterior certainty is proportional to the difference between the posterior probability and the prior probability. For example, since the prior probability of

FLE is 0.005, a posterior probability of 0.34276 corresponds to a posterior certainty of 5 * (0.34276–0.005) / (1–0.005) = 1.697. Similarly, a posterior probability of 0.001 corresponds in this case to a posterior certainty of 5 * (0.001 – 0.005) / 0.005 = –4. See Shortliffe (1975) for a description of the subjective certainty scale used in the MYCIN medical diagnosis system.

3. *Contextual Relations*. It sometimes happens that assertions cannot be considered in an arbitrary order, but must be considered in a particular sequence. For example, one should determine that there is a relevant continental margin mobile belt before considering its age. This is more than a matter of preference, since it would be meaningless for the program to ask about the age of a non-existent belt.

To treat such situations we employ the third class of relations, contextual relations. In general, we use contexts to express a condition that must be established before an assertion can be used in the reasoning process. In the above example, the existence of a continental margin mobile belt would be specified as a context for asking about the age of the belt. Thus, before inquiring about the age, the system would employ all its resources to establish the existence of the belt, and would not ask about its age unless the probability of the belt were greater than its initial value.

Contextual relations are also used when one assertion is geologically significant only if another assertion has already been established. In such instances it would not be nonsensical to ask the former question without first establishing the latter, but it is the case that the former evidence is geologically irrelevant without the latter to establishing a match to the model. Two such instances are depicted by dashed arrows in Figure 1. In one of these instances, the entire "favorable regional environment" section of PCDA model will not be pursued unless it has first been determined that there are granitic intrusives in the region.

IV. OVERVIEW OF THE MODEL DEVELOPMENT PROCESS

Although the development and encoding of a model for Prospector is not a routine process, it does progress through several distinct phases whose general nature can be described. The four most important phases are summarized below.

A. Initial Preparation

Model development is a cooperative enterprise involving an exploration geologist, who is an authority on the type of deposit being modeled, and a computer scientist who understands the operation of the Prospector system. The first step in developing a model is one of introducing the exploration geologist (model designer) to the inference network formalism, and introducing the computer scientist (model implementor) to the general nature of the class of deposits being modeled. In particular, this includes the identification of several known deposits that should fit the model well, and several known deposits that may fit partially, but that lack certain important characteristics. These specific cases help to establish the various factors that must be taken into account.

B. Initial Design

The initial design of the inference network is the most creative phase of the process. It requires the identification of the various assertions, the organization of the assertions into a hierarchical structure (as illustrated in Figure 1), the determination of the types of relations (logical, plausible, and contextual) that exist among assertions, and the estimation of values for the parameters (the voting strengths and initial probabilities). The magnitude of this task depends upon the size and complexity of the model being developed; as a point of reference, the smallest model currently in Prospector contains 28 assertions and 20 inference rules, while the largest contains 212 assertions and 133 inference rules. The initial design is usually facilitated by considering factors in the "top-down" and "left-to-right" sequence described earlier. Delicate refinement is best avoided at this time, since subsequent revision often causes significant sections of the model to be reorganized, enlarged, or otherwise modified.

In addition to the connections between assertions exhibited directly by the inference network, there are connections that exist because of the geological meaning of the assertions. For example, the statement that there are sulfide minerals is obviously related to the statement that there is pyrite in quartz veins; assertion of the latter implies the former, and denial of the former denies the latter. Recognition of such connections within a model avoids redundant or foolish questioning; recognition of such connections between different models allows the program to consider more than one deposit class at a time. Prospector can automatically recognize many of these assertions if each assertion is properly articulated. This articulation, which is described in more detail in Duda (1978b), should also be completed during the initial design.

C. Installation and Debugging of the Model

At the end of Phase B, the model exists in a "pencil-and-paper" form. To be incorporated into the program, the encoding must be given a formal description. This is done through the use of a model description language (see Duda, 1978b). The details of this language are not particularly important here. However, the task itself is important; upon its completion the program can be run, and accidental blunders or bugs can be corrected. In addition, the program can produce a questionnaire for the model that is useful in gathering data for subsequent testing and revision.

D. Performance Evaluation and Model Revision

Given the questionnaire data for a number of actual deposits, it is possible to make a serious quantitative evaluation of how well particular deposits match the model. In our experience, this evaluation inevitably exposes various shortcomings of the model as encoded, requiring revision of the work done in Phases B and C. Some care must be exercised here to avoid "overfitting" the model to the data. In general, the goal is to produce a model that can discriminate different types of deposits without losing the ability to generalize, so as to allow for the variations one would expect in new situations. Achievement of that goal currently remains as much an art as a science. The following section describes in some detail the use of simple performance evaluation techniques as an aid to refining a model.

V. USE OF PERFORMANCE EVALUATION IN REFINING A MODEL

To demonstrate that the performance of an expert knowledge-based system is (or is not) comparable to that of the experts it emulates, it is useful to subject the system to an appropriate objective evaluation. The simple performance evaluation experiments reported in this section serve several purposes: (1) to provide an objective, detailed, quantitative measure of the current performance of a model; (2) to pinpoint those sections of the model that are not performing exactly as intended, thereby establishing priorities for future revisions; (3) to assess consistency of performance across different exploration sites.

We now evaluate a model for a class of porphyry copper deposits (PCDA) designed by Prof. Marco Einaudi of Stanford University. Input data were available for three test cases, namely, the known deposits called Yerington (Nevada), Bingham (Utah), and Kalamazoo (Arizona), each of which is considered an exemplar of the PCDA model.[2] On the –5 to 5 certainty scale described earlier, the overall certainty scores computed by Prospector are 4.769 for the Yerington deposit, 4.721 for Bingham, and 4.756 for Kalamazoo, indicating a good match of these sites to the PCDA model.

To show performance in detail, we give below the hierarchical structure of the major sections of the PCDA model. Included at the right in this enumeration is the total number of questions that may be asked by Prospector for each of the major sections of the model, thus showing the relative distribution of these questions. (The questions in the FAMR section may be asked several times during a consultation session, once for each geographically distinct zone within the prospect area. Each such zone has relatively homogeneous geological characteristics, as determined by the user.)

Section	Total Number of Questions Defined in PCDA Model (Version 2)
Porphyry Copper deposit, type A (PCDA)	81
Favorable petrotectonic setting (FPTS)	4
Favorable regional environment (FRE)	9
Favorable PCDA intrusive system (FPCDAIS)	68
Favorable composition in differentiated sequence (FCDS)	4
Favorable intrusive system (FIS)	9
Favorable alteration and mineralization relations (FAMR)	56

[2]The questionnaire input data used in the present tests are reported in Duda et al., 1978b, pp.185-93.

As a calibration exercise, Prof. Einaudi offered a target value for the certainty score that should be assigned to each of the three deposits for each of the major components of the model listed above, based on the values in the input data set for each prospect site. The target values are given either in the form of a single number (on a –5 to 5 scale), or as two numbers establishing an upper and lower bound on a certainty interval. The estimates are listed in Table 1 on the left for each site in turn, with the scores as determined by execution of Prospector recorded on the right. (We informed Prof. Einaudi of the values on the right only after he had given us those on the left.)

Yerington Deposit

Name of Model Node	Einaudi's Estimate	Prospector Score
PCDA	4.5 to 5.0	4.769
FPTS	4.5 to 5.0	4.528
FRE	4.5	4.540
FPCDAIS	4.5 to 5.0	4.787
FCDS	5	4.524
FIS	5	4.744
FAMR	4.5 to 5.0	4.225

Bingham Deposit

Name of Model Node	Einaudi's Estimate	Prospector Score
PCDA	4.5	4.721
FPTS	3.5 to 4.0	4.449
FRE	4.0 to 4.5	4.829
FPCDAIS	4.5 to 5.0	4.729
FCDS	5	2.407
FIS	5	4.744
FAMR	4.0	4.225

Kalamazoo Deposit

Name of Model Node	Einaudi's Estimate	Prospector Score
PCDA	4.0 to 4.5	4.756
FPTS	4.0 to 4.5	4.449
FRE	3.5	1.784
FPCDAIS	4.5 to 5.0	4.791
FCDS	5	4.722
FIS	5	4.744
FAMR	4.0	4.225

Table 1. Prospector Scores for Several Levels of the PCDA Model (Version 2)

The data in Table 1 show that Prospector scores each of these sections of the model with high certainty for each site, with the exception that model node FCDS for the Bingham deposit and model node FRE for the Kalamazoo deposit are scored somewhat lower. In most cases shown in Table 1 Prospector agrees very closely with Prof. Einaudi's estimate. These conclusions can be expressed quantitatively by first identifying the values in Table 1 with a concise notation, then defining a simple formula for the relative error of Prospector in predicting Prof. Einaudi's estimates. Thus:

Let C(X, Y, Z) = Certainty score given to model node Z by agent X for site Y,

where X denotes either Prospector or Einaudi

For example, C(Prospector, Yerington, FPCDAIS) = 4.787. When Einaudi gave an interval of certainty values instead of a single value, we use the mid-point of the interval as the value of C. Then an error measure is given by

$$E(Y, Z) = \frac{C(\text{Einaudi}, Y, Z) - C(\text{Prospector}, Y, Z)}{C(\text{Einaudi}, Y, Z)}$$

For example, E(Yerington, FPCDAIS) = (4.75 – 4.787) / 4.75 = –0.008, meaning that Prospector's prediction is accurate to within 0.8% in this case. Since Table 1 gives values for seven nodes of the model for each of three known deposits, we can compute the value of E for 21 different instances. For 5 of the 21 data points Prospector predicted Einaudi's estimate to within 1%, while 15 of the 21 data points show agreement to within 10%. The grand average over the 21 data points is 10.3%. For convenience, we list these 21 values of E in Table 2, expressed as percentages.

	Yerington	Bingham	Kalamazoo	Average of Absolute Values
PCDA	–.3 %	–4.9 %	–11.9 %	5.7 %
FPTS	4.7	–18.6	–4.7	9.3
FRE	–.9	–13.6	49.0	21.2
FPCDAIS	–.8	.4	–.9	.7
FCDS	9.5	51.9	5.6	22.3
FIS	5.1	5.1	5.1	5.1
FAMR	11.1	5.6	5.6	7.6
Average of Absolute values:	4.1	14.3	11.8	10.3

Table 2. Relative Error (E) of Prospector Scores as Predictors of Einaudi's Estimates (derived from data in Table 1)

Inspection of Table 2 indicates that efforts to revise the PCDA model should focus on the FRE and FCDS sections. When such revisions are completed, an updated version of Table 2 will indicate the extent to which the revisions achieved the objectives that motivated them.

The small number of cases tested, and the fact that all the present test cases are exemplars of the PCDA model, and the fact that the model designer himself supplied the input data concerning the test cases, are limitations; the present tests are more necessary than sufficient conditions for good performance. Despite these limitations, the preliminary results reported here have proved useful in the ongoing model refinement process. More extensive performance evaluation results are reported in Duda et al. (1978b).

VI. REMARKS

This paper has outlined the typical procedures used to develop an exploration model for the Prospector system. We have described the inference network and Bayesian propagation scheme underlying Prospector models, and we have illustrated the use of simple performance evaluation techniques in "fine-tuning" a model systematically. Our experience indicates that the model design process inherently requires feedback. Although different problem solving domains differ in many details, we believe the process of constructing Prospector-like plausible reasoning systems follows certain general patterns and stages of development such as are described here. Hence we have presented a concrete case study, in the domain of mineral exploration, that may credibly suggest what might be expected in attempts to apply a similar methodology to other domains of expertise.

Besides the running program, there appear to be several other benefits to this type of expert system approach. The model design process challenges the model designer to articulate, organize, and quantify his expertise. Without exception, the economic geologists who have designed Prospector models have reported that the experience aided and sharpened their own thinking on the subject matter of the model. In addition, most of the geologists we know who have had experience with Prospector have remarked about its potential value as an educational tool. In this regard, the models in the system contain explicit, detailed information synthesized from the literature and the experience of expert explorationists, together with explanatory text that can be obtained upon request. Furthermore, a typical consultation session with Prospector costs only about $10 at current commercial computer rates.

VII. ACKNOWLEDGEMENTS

Prospector would not exist without the talents and efforts contributed by many economic geologists and computer scientists. Among these, we are particularly indebted to the economic geologists Alan N. Campbell, Neil Campbell, Marco T. Einaudi, Victor F. Hollister, Anthony J. Naldrett, Charles F. Park, Jr., and Ruffin I.Rackley, and to the computer scientists Phyllis Barrett, Kurt Konolige, Nils J.Nilsson, Rene Reboh, Jonathan Slocum, and B.Michael Wilber.

REFERENCES

Duda, R.O., P.E. Hart and N.J. Nilsson (1976), 'Subjective Bayesian methods for rule-based inference systems,' *Proc. National Computer Conference,* (AFIPS Conference Proceedings, Vol. 45), pp. 1075-1082, 1976.

Duda, R.O., P.E. Hart, N.J. Nilsson, R. Reboh, J. Slocum and G.L. Sutherland (1977), 'Development of a computer-based consultant for mineral exploration,' Annual Report, SRI Projects 5821 and 6415, SRI International, Menlo Park, California, October 1977.

Duda, R.O., P.E. Hart, N.J. Nilsson, and G.L. Sutherland (1978a), 'Semantic network representations in rule-based inference systems,' in *Pattern Directed Inference Systems,* D.A. Waterman and F. Hayes-Roth (Eds.), pp. 203-221, Academic Press, New York, 1978.

Duda, R.O., P.E.Hart, P.Barrett, J.Gaschnig, K.Konolige, R.Reboh and J.Slocum (1978b), "Development of the Prospector system for mineral exploration," Final Report, SRI Projects 5821 and 6415, SRI International, Menlo Park, California, October 1978.

Fagan, L.M. (1978), "Ventilator Manager: A program to provide on-line consultative advice in the intensive care unit." Heuristic Programming Project Memo HPP-78-16, Dept. of Computer Science, Stanford University, September 1978.

Hart, P.E., R.O. Duda, and K. Konolige (1978), "A computer-based consultant for mineral exploration," Second Semiannual Report, SRI Project 6415, SRI International, Menlo Park, California, April 1978.

Hart, P.E., R.O. Duda, and M.T. Einaudi (1978), "A computer-based consultation system for mineral exploration," to appear in *Computer Methods for the 80's*, Society of Mining Engineers of the AIME, 1978.

Martin, N., P. Friedland, J. King, and M. Stefik (1977), "Knowledge Base Management for Experiment Planning in Molecular Genetics," *Proc. of 5th International Joint Conference on Artificial Intelligence*, pp. 882-887, Cambridge, Mass., August 1977.

Pople, H.E., Jr., J.D. Myers, and R.A. Miller (1975), "DIALOG: A model of diagnostic logic for internal medicine," *Proc. of 4th International Joint Conference on Artificial Intelligence*. pp. 848-855, Tbilisi, Georgia, USSR, 1975.

Raiffa, H. (1968), *Decision Analysis*, Addison-Wesley Publishing Co., New York, 1968.

Shortliffe, E.H. (1976), *Computer-Based Medical Consultations: MYCIN*, American Elsevier Publishing Co., New York, 1976.

Shortliffe, E.H., and B.G. Buchanan (1975), "A model of inexact reasoning in medicine," *Math. Biosci.*, Vol. 23, pp. 351-379, 1975.

Szolovits, P., and S.G. Pauker (1976), "Research on a medical consultation system for taking the present illness," *Proc. of 3rd Illinois Conference on Medical Information Systems*, pp. 299-320, University of Illinois at Chicago Circle, November 1976.

Weiss, S.M., C.A. Kulikowski, and A. Safir (1977), "A model-based consultation system for the long-term management of glaucoma," *Proc. of 5th International Joint Conference on Artificial Intelligence*, pp. 826-833, MIT, Cambridge, Massachusetts, 1977.

Yu, V.L., et al. (1978), "Evaluating the performance of a computer-based consultant," Heuristic Programming Project Memo HPP-78-17, Dept. of Computer Science, Stanford University, September 1978.

Zadeh, L.A. (1965), "Fuzzy sets." *Information and Control*, Vol. 8, pp. 338-353, 1965.

The Hearsay-II Speech-Understanding System: Integrating Knowledge to Resolve Uncertainty

LEE D. ERMAN

USC/Information Sciences Institute, Marina del Rey, California 90291

FREDERICK HAYES-ROTH

The Rand Corporation, Santa Monica, California 90406

VICTOR R. LESSER

University of Massachusetts, Amherst, Massachusetts 01003

D. RAJ REDDY

Carnegie-Mellon University, Pittsburgh, Pennsylvania 15213

The Hearsay-II system, developed during the DARPA-sponsored five-year speech-understanding research program, represents both a specific solution to the speech-understanding problem and a general framework for coordinating independent processes to achieve cooperative problem-solving behavior. As a computational problem, speech understanding reflects a large number of intrinsically interesting issues. Spoken sounds are achieved by a long chain of successive transformations, from intentions, through semantic and syntactic structuring, to the eventually resulting audible acoustic waves. As a consequence, interpreting speech means effectively inverting these transformations to recover the speaker's intention from the sound. At each step in the interpretive process, ambiguity and uncertainty arise.

The Hearsay-II problem-solving framework reconstructs an intention from hypothetical interpretations formulated at various levels of abstraction. In addition, it allocates limited processing resources first to the most promising incremental actions. The final configuration of the Hearsay-II system comprises problem-solving components to generate and evaluate speech hypotheses, and a focus-of-control mechanism to identify potential actions of greatest value. Many of these specific procedures reveal novel approaches to speech problems. Most important, the system successfully integrates and coordinates all of these independent activities to resolve uncertainty and control combinatorics. Several adaptations of the Hearsay-II framework have already been undertaken in other problem domains, and it is anticipated that this trend will continue; many future systems necessarily will integrate diverse sources of knowledge to solve complex problems cooperatively.

Discussed in this paper are the characteristics of the speech problem in particular, the special kinds of problem-solving uncertainty in that domain, the structure of the Hearsay-II system developed to cope with that uncertainty, and the relationship between Hearsay-II's structure and those of other speech-understanding systems. The paper is intended for the general computer science audience and presupposes no speech or artificial intelligence background.

Keywords and Phrases: artificial intelligence, blackboard, focus of control, knowledge-based system, multiple diverse knowledge sources, multiple levels of abstraction, problem-solving system, speech-understanding systems, uncertainty resolving

CONTENTS

INTRODUCTION

The Hearsay-II speech-understanding system (SUS) developed at Carnegie-Mellon University recognizes connected speech in a 1000-word vocabulary with correct interpretations for 90 percent of test sentences. Its basic methodology involves the application of symbolic reasoning as an aid to signal processing. A marriage of general artificial intelligence techniques with specific acoustic and linguistic knowledge was needed to accomplish satisfactory speech-understanding performance. Because the various techniques and heuristics employed were embedded within a general problem-solving framework, the Hearsay-II system embodies several design characteristics that are adaptable to other domains as well. Its structure has been applied to such tasks as multisensor interpretation [NII78], protein-crystallographic analysis [ENGE77], image understanding [HANS76], a model of human reading [RUME76], and dialogue comprehension [MANN79]. This paper discusses the characteristics of the speech problem in particular, the special kinds of problem-solving uncertainty in that domain, the structure of the Hearsay-II system developed to cope with that uncertainty, and the relationship between Hearsay-II's structure and the structures of other SUSs.

Uncertainty arises in a problem-solving system if the system's knowledge is inadequate to produce a solution directly. The fundamental method for handling uncertainty is to create a space of candidate solutions and search that space for a solution. "Almost all the basic methods used by intelligent systems can be seen as some variation of search, responsive to the particular knowledge available" [NEWE77, p. 13]. In a difficult problem, i.e., one with a large search space, a problem solver can be effective only if it can search efficiently. To do so, it must apply knowledge to guide the search so that relatively few points in the space need be examined before a solution is found. A key way of accomplishing this is by augmenting the space of candidate solutions with candidate *partial* solutions and then constructing a complete solution by extending and combining partial candidates. A candidate partial solution represents all complete candidates that contain it. By considering partial solution candidates, we can often eliminate whole subspaces from further consideration and simultaneously focus the search on more promising subspaces.

To solve a problem as difficult as speech understanding, a problem solver requires several kinds of capabilities in order to search effectively: It must collect and analyze data, set goals to guide the inferential search processes, produce and retain appro-

This research was supported chiefly by Defense Advanced Research Projects Agency contract F44620-73-C-0074 to Carnegie-Mellon University. In addition, support for the preparation of this paper was provided by USC/ISI, Rand, and the University of Massachusetts. We gratefully acknowledge their support. Views and conclusions contained in this document are those of the authors and should not be interpreted as representing the official opinion or policy of DARPA, the U.S. government, or any other person or agency connected with them.

priate inferences, and decide when to stop working for a possibly better solution. Years ago, when AI problem solvers first emerged, they attempted to provide these capabilities through quite general domain-independent methods, the so-called *weak* methods [NEWE69]. A prime example of such a problem solver is GPS [ERNS69]. More recently, several major problem-solving accomplishments, such as Dendral [FEIG71] and Mycin [SHOR76], have reflected a different philosophy: Powerful problem solvers depend on extensive amounts of knowledge about both the problem domain and the problem-solving strategies effective in that domain [FEIG77]. Much of what we view as expertise consists of these two types of knowledge; without capturing and implementing this knowledge, we could not create effective computer problem solvers. Because knowledge plays a crucial role in these kinds of tasks, many people call the corresponding problem solvers *knowledge-based systems* [BARN77]. The design of Hearsay-II is responsive to both concerns. While formulated as a general system-building framework that would structure and control problem-solving behavior involving multiple, diverse, and error-full sources of knowledge, the current Hearsay-II system consists of a particular collection of programs embedding speech knowledge that are capable of solving the understanding problem.[1]

The difficulty of the speech-understanding problem, and hence the need for powerful problem-solving methods, derives from two inherent sources of uncertainty or error. The first includes ordinary variability and noise in the speech waveform, and the second includes the ambiguous and inaccurate judgments arising from an application of incomplete and imprecise theories of speech. Because we cannot resolve these uncertainties directly, we structure the speech-understanding problem as a space in which our problem solver searches for a solution. The space is the set of (partial and complete) *interpretations* of the input acoustic signal, i.e., the (partial and complete) mappings from the signal to the possible messages. The goal of our problem-solving system is to find a complete interpretation (i.e., a message and mapping) which maximizes some evaluation function based on knowledge about such things as acoustic-phonetics, vocabulary, grammar, semantics, and discourse. This resolution of the combined sources of uncertainty requires the generation, evaluation, and integration of numerous partial interpretations. The need to consider many alternative interpretations without spawning an explosive combinatorial search thus becomes a principal design objective. Each of these issues is discussed in more detail in the following section.

Dimensions of the Problem: Uncertainty and Hypothetical Interpretations

The first source of difficulty in the speech problem arises from the speaking process itself. In the translation from intention to sound, a speaker transforms concepts into speech through processes that introduce variability and noise (see Figure 1). If, for

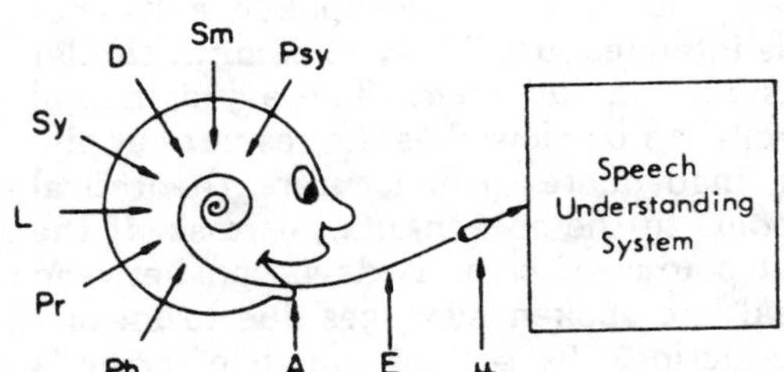

FIGURE 1. Some of the mechanisms that affect the message: psychology of the speaker, semantics, rules of discourse, syntax, lexicon, prosodic system, phonemic system, speaker's articulatory apparatus, ambient environmental noise, and microphone and system. [After NEWE75.]

example, we consider the semantic, syntactic, lexical, and phonemic stages, the types of variance introduced from one level to the next would correspond to errors or peculiarities of conceptualization, grammar, word choice, and articulation. In addition

[1] The problem of speech understanding has been actively pursued recently [REDD75, REDD76, CMU77, BERN76, WALK78, WOOD76, KLAT77, MEDR78, LEA80]. With the exception of HARPY [LOWE80], however, none of the other efforts has been presented as a structure for problem solving in other domains.

to these sources of variability, speech is often affected by pauses, extraneous sounds, or unnecessary phrase repetitions. The effect of these factors upon the physical sound signal is to distort it significantly from the *ideal message*, that is, from the message that would be produced if the production mechanisms did not introduce variability and noise. Accordingly, we speak of the disparity between the ideal and actual signals as *error*, and of the variety of factors that contribute to such distortion as *sources of error*. Thus the first source of error is inherent in the speaker and his environment.

The second source of error in the understanding process is intrinsic to the listener. Just as the speaker must transform his intention through successive intermediate levels of representation, so we presume the listener must accomplish the inverse of those transformations; from the physical signal the listener must detect acoustic-phonetic elements, syllables, words, and syntactic and conceptual structures corresponding to the speaker's intentions. At each step in this reconstruction the listener may introduce new errors corresponding to incorrect perceptual or interpretive judgments.[2] Because a machine speech-understanding system must also develop interpretations of what was spoken and what was intended, it is likely to commit similar mistakes in judgment. These judgmental errors can be viewed as the result of applying inadequate or inaccurate theoretical models to the speech-analysis task. If the first source of error is deviation between ideal and spoken messages due to inexact production, the second source of error is deviation between spoken and interpreted messages due to imprecise rules of comprehension.

To comprehend an utterance in the context of such errors, a speech-understanding system must formulate and evaluate numerous candidate interpretations of speech fragments. Understanding a message requires us to isolate and recognize its individual words and parse their syntactic and conceptual relationships. Each intermediate state of this process can be viewed as either the generation or evaluation of symbolic interpretations for portions of the spoken utterance. We use the term ***hypothesis*** to refer to a partial interpretation actually constructed. During the process of speech interpretation, hypotheses may vary from highly confident identification of particular words to great confusion concerning particular portions of the utterance. Between these two extremes, the listener may entertain simultaneously several competing hypotheses for what was said. Competing alternatives might occur at any of several levels of abstraction. For example, at the word level the listener may struggle to distinguish whether "till" or "tell" was spoken in one portion of the utterance while simultaneously attempting to differentiate the words "brings" and "rings" in another interval. These uncertainties derive from comparable uncertainties at lower levels of interpretation, such as syllabic and acoustic, where multiple competing hypotheses can also exist simultaneously. Similarly, uncertainty among word hypotheses at the lexical level engenders uncertainty at higher levels of interpretation. Thus the previously discussed inability to distinguish between alternative words may be the underlying cause of an inability to distinguish between the four hypothetical phrase interpretations:

till Bob rings
tell Bob rings
till Bob brings
tell Bob brings

Just as this example suggests, higher level interpretations incorporate lower level ones. A phrase-level hypothesis consists of a selection of word hypotheses from each interval of time spanned by the higher level hypothesis. Only one lower level hypothesis in any time interval can be incorporated into the higher level interpretation. Thus a phrase consists of a sequence of words, a word consists of a sequence of syllables, a syllable consists of a sequence of acoustic-phonetic segments, and so on. An overall interpretation of an entire utterance would consist of a syntactic or semantic analysis that recursively incorporated one hypoth-

[2] Though the levels of representation appear to be linearly ordered, the encoding and decoding processes do not necessarily operate sequentially through this ordering.

esis from each level of interpretation for each temporal interval of the utterance.

A fundamental assumption underlying the understanding problem is that a correct interpretation of an utterance should minimize the difference between those properties of the speech that the hypothetical interpretation would predict and those that are observed. This gives rise to the notion of the *consistency* between an interpretation and its supporting data. Thus certain parameter values derived from an acoustic waveform are more or less consistent with various phonetic classifications, particular sequences of phones are more or less consistent with various monosyllabic categorizations, and various syllable sequences are more or less consistent with particular lexical and phrase interpretations. The concept of consistency between two adjacent levels of interpretation can be generalized to permit consideration of the consistency between hypotheses at any two levels and, in particular, the consistency between an overall interpretation of the utterance and its supporting hypotheses at the lowest, acoustic-parametric level. A central assumption is that the greater the consistency between the overall interpretation and the acoustic data, the more likely the interpretation is to be correct.

We refer to the likelihood that some hypothesis is correct as its *credibility*. As the preceding suggests, the credibility of each hypothesis is a measure of consistency between the data generating the hypothesis and the expectations it engenders. A credibility calculation involves a judgment about the knowledge used in creating the hypothesis and therefore is itself subject to uncertainty.

To assess the credibility of a hypothesis, we need basically to evaluate two things: all plausible alternatives to this hypothesis and the degree of support each receives from data. Consider, for example, the evaluation of word hypotheses. Initially, nearly all words in the language are plausible candidates for occurring within any time interval. As a consequence, our uncertainty at the outset, as approximated by the number of equally plausible alternatives, is maximal. Over time we accrue evidence to eliminate some of these alternatives. Moreover, by eliminating one particular hypothesis, we may logically exclude others that are in temporally adjacent regions and that depend directly on that hypothesis. For example, if we have ruled out all possible adjectives and nouns in a particular location, we can also rule out adjectives in the preceding interval. Conversely, if we can identify a particular word as an adjective, we can increase our belief that the following word will be an adjective or noun. In general, each individual hypothesis is strengthened by its apparent combinability with others. Thus we say uncertainty is reduced by detecting mutually supporting hypotheses that are consistent with the acoustic data. Equivalently, the credibility of hypotheses increases as a function of their involvement in such mutually supportive clusters.

This technique for reducing uncertainty leads to the following incremental problem-solving method: The goal of the problem solver is to construct the most credible overall interpretation. The fundamental operations in the construction are hypothesis generation, hypothesis combination, and hypothesis evaluation. At each step in the construction, sources of knowledge use these operations to build larger partial interpretations, adding their constraints to the interpretation. The accrual of constraints reduces the uncertainty inherent in the data and in the knowledge sources themselves.

Three requirements must be met for such a problem solver to be effective:

(1) At least one possible sequence of knowledge-based operations must lead to a correct overall interpretation.
(2) The evaluation procedure should assess the correct overall interpretation as maximally credible among all overall interpretations generated.
(3) The cost of problem solving must satisfy some externally specified limit. Usually this limit restricts the time or space available for computing. As a consequence, it leads to restrictions on the number of alternative partial interpretations that can be considered. Alternative partial solutions must be considered in order to ensure that a correct

one is included. The greater the uncertainty in the knowledge used to generate and evaluate hypotheses, the greater the number of alternatives that must be considered, leading to a possible combinatorial explosion.

As we have seen, the speech-understanding problem is characterized by the need for highly diverse kinds of knowledge for its solution and by large amounts of uncertainty and variability in input data and knowledge. The diversity of knowledge leads to a search space of multilevel partial solutions. The uncertainty and variability mean that the operators used for searching the space are themselves error-prone; therefore many competing alternative hypotheses must be generated. To avoid a combinatorial explosion, a powerful control scheme is needed to exploit selectively the most promising combinations of alternatives. As systems tackle more such difficult real-world problems, such multilevel representations and powerful control schemes will become increasingly important [HAYE78a]. The next section discusses how the Hearsay-II system copes with these representation and control problems.

Hearsay-II Problem-Solving Model

The key functions of generating, combining, and evaluating hypothetical interpretations are performed by diverse and independent programs called *knowledge sources* (KSs). The necessity for diverse KSs derives from the diversity of transformations used by the speaker in creating the acoustic signal and the corresponding inverse transformations needed by the listener for interpreting it. Each KS can be schematized as a condition–action pair. The condition component prescribes the situations in which the KS may contribute to the problem-solving activity, and the action component specifies what that contribution is and how to integrate it into the current situation.[3] According to the original conception of the diverse stages and processes involved in speech understanding, KSs have been developed to perform a variety of functions. These include extracting acoustic parameters, classifying acoustic segments into phonetic classes, recognizing words, parsing phrases, and generating and evaluating predictions for undetected words or syllables. Figure 2 presents a schematic view of the KSs in the September 1976 configuration of the Hearsay-II speech-understanding system. Figure 3 gives a brief functional description of these KSs.

Because each KS is an *independent* condition–action module, KSs communicate through a global database called the *blackboard*. The blackboard records the hypotheses generated by KSs. Any KS can generate a hypothesis (record it on the blackboard) or modify an existing one. These actions in turn may produce structures that satisfy the applicability conditions of other KSs. In this framework the blackboard serves in two roles: It represents intermediate states of problem-solving activity, and it communicates messages (hypotheses) from one KS that activate other KSs.

The blackboard is subdivided into a set of information levels corresponding to the intermediate representation levels of the decoding processes (phrase, word, syllable, etc.). Each hypothesis resides on the blackboard at one of the levels and bears a defining label chosen from a set appropriate to that level (e.g., the word FLYING, the syllable ING, or the phone NG). The hypothesis contains additional information, including its time coordinates within the spoken utterance and a credibility rating. The sequence of levels on the blackboard forms a loose hierarchical structure: hypotheses at each level aggregate or abstract elements at the adjacent lower level. The possible hypotheses at a level form a search space for KSs operating at that level. A partial

[3] The condition and action components of a KS are realized as arbitrary programs. To minimize reevaluating the condition programs continuously, each condition program declares to the system the primitive kinds of situations in which it is interested. The condition program is triggered only when there occur changes that create such situations (and is then given pointers to all of them). This changes a polling action into an interrupt-driven one and is more efficient, especially for a large number of KSs. When executed, the condition program can search among the set of existing hypothetical interpretations for arbitrarily complex configurations of interest to its KS.

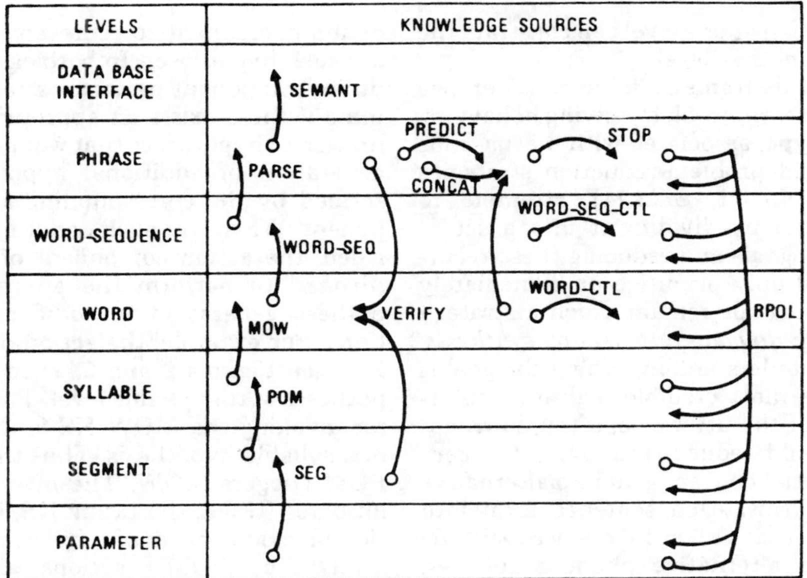

FIGURE 2. The levels and knowledge sources of September 1976. KSs are indicated by vertical arcs with the circled ends indicating the input level and the pointed ends indicating output level.

FIGURE 3. Functional description of the speech-understanding KSs.

Signal Acquisition, Parameter Extraction, Segmentation, and Labeling:
- SEG: Digitizes the signal, measures parameters, and produces a labeled segmentation.

Word Spotting:
- POM: Creates syllable-class hypotheses from segments.
- MOW: Creates word hypotheses from syllable classes.
- WORD-CTL: Controls the number of word hypotheses that MOW creates.

Phrase-Island Generation:
- WORD-SEQ: Creates word-sequence hypotheses that represent potential phrases from word hypotheses and weak grammatical knowledge.
- WORD-SEQ-CTL: Controls the number of hypotheses that WORD-SEQ creates.
- PARSE: Attempts to parse a word sequence and, if successful, creates a phrase hypothesis from it.

Phrase Extending:
- PREDICT: Predicts all possible words that might syntactically precede or follow a given phrase.
- VERIFY: Rates the consistency between segment hypotheses and a contiguous word–phrase pair.
- CONCAT: Creates a phrase hypothesis from a verified contiguous word–phrase pair.

Rating, Halting, and Interpretation:
- RPOL: Rates the credibility of each new or modified hypothesis, using information placed on the hypothesis by other KSs.
- STOP: Decides to halt processing (detects a complete sentence with a sufficiently high rating, or notes the system has exhausted its available resources) and selects the best phrase hypothesis or set of complementary phrase hypotheses as the output.
- SEMANT: Generates an unambiguous interpretation for the information-retrieval system which the user has queried.

interpretation at one level can constrain the search at another level.

Within this framework we consider two general types of problem-solving behaviors. The first type, associated with means–ends analysis and problem-reduction strategies [ERNS69, NILS71, SACE74], attempts to reach a goal by dividing it into a set of simpler subgoals and reducing these recursively until only primitive or immediately solvable subgoals remain. Such a strategy is called *top-down* or *analysis-by-synthesis*. In speech understanding, where the goal is to find the most credible high-level interpretation of the utterance, a top-down approach would reduce recursively the general sentential concept goal into alternative sentence forms, each sentence form into specific alternative word sequences, specific words into alternative phone sequences, and so forth, until the one alternative overall interpretation most consistent with the observed acoustic parameters is identified. The second, or *bottom-up*, method attempts to synthesize interpretations directly from characteristics of the data provided. One type of bottom-up method would employ procedures to classify acoustic segments within phonetic categories by comparing their observed parameters with the ideal parameter values of each phonetic category. Other bottom-up procedures might generate syllable or word hypotheses directly from sequences of phone hypotheses, or might combine temporally adjacent word hypotheses into syntactic or conceptual units. For a hypothesis generated in either the top-down or bottom-up mode, we would like to represent explicitly its relationship to the preexisting hypotheses that suggested it. *Links* are constructed between hypotheses for this purpose.

Both types of problem-solving behaviors can be accommodated simultaneously by the condition–action schema of a Hearsay-II KS. Top-down behaviors represent the reduction of the higher level goal as the condition to be satisfied and the generation of appropriate subgoals as the associated action. Bottom-up behaviors employ the condition component to represent the lower level hypothesis configurations justifying higher level interpretations, and employ the action component to represent and generate such hypotheses. In both cases the condition component performs a test to determine if there exists an appropriate configuration of hypotheses that would justify the generation of additional hypotheses prescribed by the corresponding action component. Whenever such conditions are satisfied, the action component of the KS is *invoked* to perform the appropriate hypothesis generation or modification operations. For example, the action of the POM KS (see Figures 2 and 3) is to create hypotheses at the syllable level. The condition for invoking the MOW KS is the creation of a syllable hypothesis. Thus the action of POM triggers MOW. The invocation condition of RPOL, the rating KS, is the creation or modification of a hypothesis at any level; thus POM's actions also trigger RPOL. In short, control of KS activation is determined by the blackboard actions of other KSs, rather than explicit calls from other KSs or some central sequencing mechanism. This *data-directed* control regime permits a more flexible scheduling of KS actions in response to changing conditions on the blackboard. We refer to such an ability of a system to exploit its best data and most promising methods as *opportunistic* problem solving [NII78, HAYE79a].

While it is true that each condition–action knowledge source is logically independent of the others, effective problem-solving activity depends ultimately on the capability of the individual KS actions to construct cooperatively an overall interpretation of the utterance. This high-level hypothesis and its recursive supports represent the *solution* to the understanding *problem*. Since each KS action simply generates or modifies hypotheses and links based on related information, a large number of individual KS invocations may be needed to construct an overall interpretation.

Any hypothesis that is included in the solution is *cooperative* with the others. Conversely, any hypothesis that is unincorporated into the solution is *competitive*. In a similar way, KS invocations can be considered cooperative or competitive depending on whether their potential actions would or would not contribute to the same solution. Because of the inherent uncertainty in the speech-understanding task, there are inevitably large numbers of plausible alternative actions in each time interval of the utterance. Before the correct interpretation has been found, we cannot evaluate with certainty the prospective value of any potential action. Actions appear cooperative to the extent to which they contribute to the formation and support of increasingly comprehensive interpretations. Conversely, any hypothesis occupying the same time interval as another hypothesis but not part of its support set must be considered competitive. That is, two hypotheses compete if they represent incompatible interpretations of the same portion of the utterance. As a result, KS invocations can be viewed as competitive if their likely actions would generate inconsistent hypotheses, and they can be viewed as cooperative if their actions would combine to form more comprehensive or more strongly supported hypotheses.

The major impediment to discovery of the best overall interpretation in this scheme is the combinatorial explosion of KS invocations that can occur. From the outset, numerous alternative actions are warranted. A purely top-down approach would generate a vast number of possible actions, if unrestrained. Because certainty of recognition is practically never possible and substantial numbers of competing hypotheses must be entertained at each time interval of analysis, any bottom-up approach generates a similarly huge number of competing possible actions. Thus additional constraints on the problem-solving activity must be enforced. This is accomplished by selecting for execution only a limited subset of the invoked KSs.

The objective of *selective attention* is to allocate limited computing resources (processing cycles) to the most important and most promising actions. This selectivity involves three components. First, the probable effects of a potential KS action must be estimated before it is performed. Second, the global significance of an isolated action must be deduced from analysis of its cooperative and competitive relationships with existing hypotheses; *globally significant actions* are those that contribute to the detection, formation, or extension of combinations of redundant hypotheses. Third, the desirability of an action must be assessed in comparison with other potential actions. While the inherent uncertainty of the speech task precludes error-free performance of these component tasks, there have been devised some approximate methods that effectively control the combinatorics and make the speech-understanding problem tractable.

Selective attention is accomplished in the Hearsay-II system by a heuristic scheduler which calculates a priority for each action and executes, at each time, the waiting action with the highest priority [Haye77a]. The priority calculation attempts to estimate the usefulness of the action in fulfilling the overall system goal of recognizing the utterance. The calculation is based on information provided when the condition part of a KS is satisfied. This information includes the *stimulus frame*, which is the set of hypotheses that satisfied the condition, and the *response frame*, a stylized description of the blackboard modifications that the KS action is likely to perform. For example, consider a syllable-based word hypothesizer KS (such as MOW); its stimulus frame would include the specific syllable hypothesis which matched its condition, and its response frame would specify the expected action of generating word hypotheses in a time interval spanning that of the stimulus frame. In addition to this action-specific information, the scheduler uses global state information in its calculations and considers especially the credibility and duration of the best hypotheses in each level and time region and the amount of processing required from the time the current best hypotheses were generated. The latter information allows the system to reappraise its confidence in its current best hypotheses if they are not quickly incorporated into more comprehensive hypotheses.

Hearsay-II Architecture

Figure 4 illustrates the primary architectural features of the Hearsay-II system. At the start of each cycle, the scheduler, in

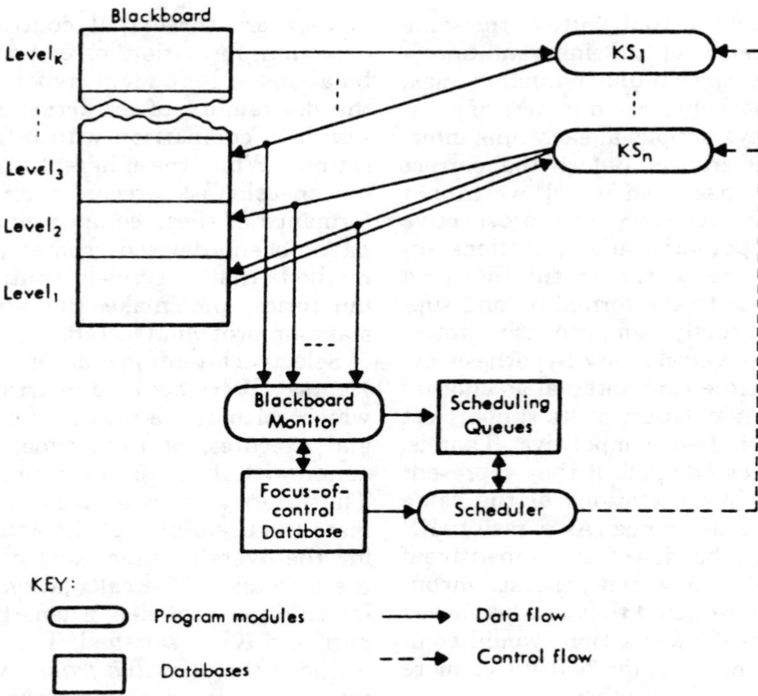

FIGURE 4. Schematic of the Hearsay-II architecture.

accordance with the global state information, calculates a priority for each activity (KS condition program or action program) in the scheduling queues. The highest priority activity is removed from the queues and executed. If the activity is a KS condition program, it may insert new instances of KS action programs into the scheduling queues. If the activity is a KS action program, the blackboard monitor notices the blackboard changes it makes. Whenever a change occurs that would be of interest to a KS condition program, the monitor creates an activity in the scheduling queues for that program. The monitor also updates the global state information to reflect the blackboard modifications.

1. AN EXAMPLE OF RECOGNITION

In this section we present a detailed description of the Hearsay-II speech system understanding one utterance. The task for the system is to answer questions about and retrieve documents from a collection of computer science abstracts (in the area of artificial intelligence). Example sentences:

"Which abstracts refer to theory of computation?"

"List those articles."

"What has McCarthy written since nineteen seventy-four?"

The vocabulary contains 1011 words (in which each extended form of a root, e.g., the plural of a noun, is counted separately if it appears). The grammar defining the legal sentences is context-free and includes recursion. The style of the grammar is such that there are many more nonterminals than in conventional syntactic grammars; the information contained in the greater number of nodes imbeds semantic and pragmatic constraint directly within the grammatical structure. For example, in place of 'Noun' in a conventional grammar, this grammar includes such nonterminals as 'Topic', 'Author', 'Year', and 'Publisher'. Because of its emphasis on semantic categories, this type of grammar is called a *semantic template grammar* or simply a *semantic grammar* [HAYE75, BURT76,

HAYE80]. The grammar allows each word to be followed, on the average, by 17 other words of the vocabulary.[4] The standard deviation of this measure is very high (about 51), since some words (e.g., "about" or "on") can be followed by many others (up to 300 in several cases).

1.1 Introduction to the Example

We will describe how Hearsay-II understood the utterance "ARE ANY BY FEIGENBAUM AND FELDMAN?"[5] Each major *step* of the processing is shown; a step usually corresponds to the action of a knowledge source. Executions of the condition programs of the KSs are not shown explicitly, nor do we list those potential knowledge-source actions which are never chosen by the scheduler for execution. Executions of RPOL are also omitted; in order to calculate credibility ratings for hypotheses, RPOL runs in high priority immediately after any KS action that creates or modifies a hypothesis.

The waveform of the spoken utterance is shown in Figure 5a. The "correct" word boundaries (determined by human inspection) are shown in Figure 5b for reference. The remaining sections of Figure 5 contain all the hypotheses created by the KSs. Each hypothesis is represented by a box; the box's horizontal position indicates the location of the hypothesis within the utterance. The hypotheses are grouped by level: segment, syllable, word, word sequence, and phrase. Links between hypotheses are not shown. The processing will be described in terms of a sequence of *time steps*, where each step corresponds approximately to KS execution governed by one scheduling decision. Within each hypothesis, the number preceding the colon indicates the time step during which the hypothesis was created. The symbol following the colon names the hypothesis. At the word level and above, an asterisk (*) following the symbol indicates that the hypothesis is correct. The trailing number within each hypothesis is the credibility rating on an arbitrary scale ranging from 0 to 100.

In the step-by-step description, the name of the KS executed at each step follows the step number. An asterisk following the KS name indicates that the hypotheses in the stimulus frame of this KS instantiation are all correct. Single numbers in parentheses after hypotheses are their credibility ratings. All times given are in centisecond units; thus the duration of the whole utterance, which was 2.25 seconds, is marked as 225. When begin- and end-times of hypotheses are given, they appear as two numbers separated by a colon (e.g., 52:82). As in the figure, correct hypotheses are marked with an asterisk.

1.2 The Example

The utterance is recorded by a medium-quality Electro-Voice RE-51 close-speaking headset microphone in a moderately noisy environment (>65 dB). The audio signal is low-pass filtered and 9-bit sampled at 10 kHz. All subsequent processing, including the control of the A/D converter, is performed digitally on a time-shared PDP-10 computer. Four acoustic parameters (called ZAPDASH) are derived by simple algorithms operating directly on the sampled signal [GOLD77]. These parameters are extracted in real time and are used initially to detect the beginning and end of the utterance.

Step 1. KS: SEG.
Stimulus: Creation of ZAPDASH parameters for the utterance.
Action: Create segment hypotheses.

The ZAPDASH parameters are used by the *SEG* knowledge source as the basis for an acoustic segmentation and classification of the utterance [GILL78]. This segmentation is accomplished by an iterative refinement technique: First, silence is separated from nonsilence; then the nonsilence is broken down into the sonorant and nonsonorant regions, and so on. Eventually five

[4] Actually, a family of grammars, varying in the number of words (terminals) and in the number and complexity of sentences allowed, was generated. The grammar described here and used in most of the testing is called X05.

[5] To improve clarity, the description differs from the actual computer execution of Hearsay-II in a few minor details.

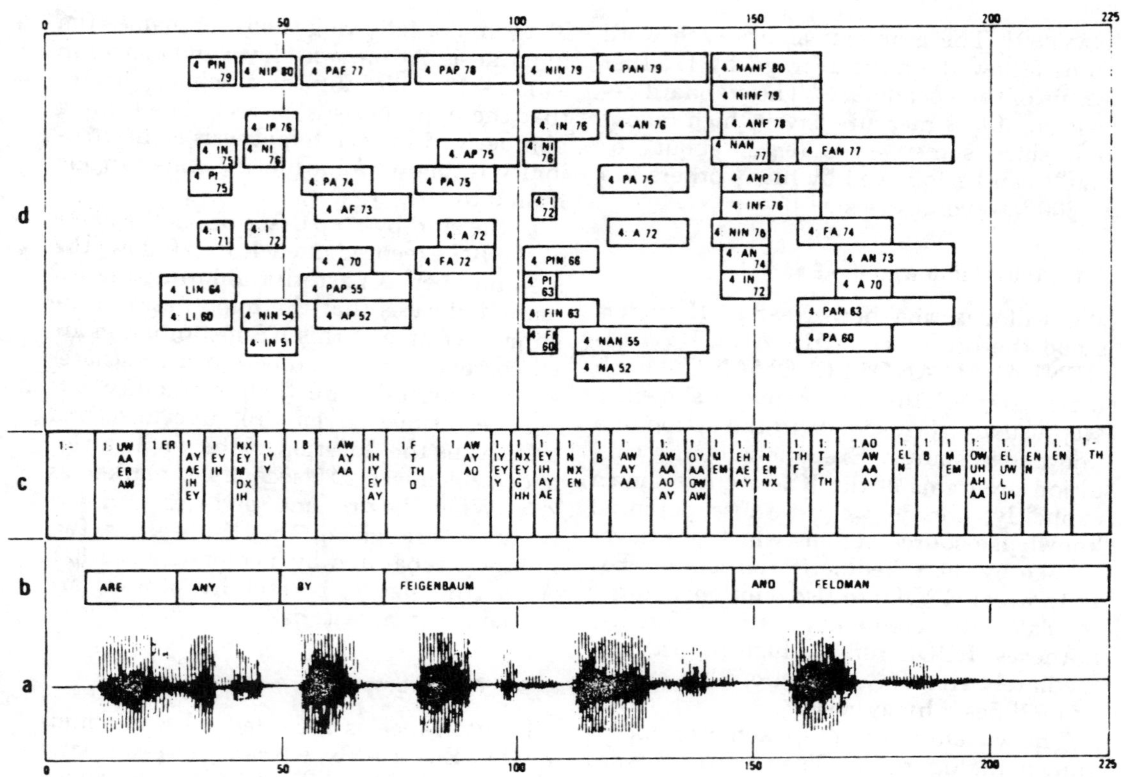

FIGURE 5. The example utterance: (a) the waveform of "Are any by Feigenbaum and Feldman?"; (b) the correct words (for reference); (c) segments; (d) syllable classes; (e) words (created by MOW); (f) words (created by VERIFY); (g) word sequences; (h) phrases. (See facing page for Figure 5e–h.)

classes of segments are produced: silence, sonorant peak, sonorant nonpeak, fricative, and flap. Associated with each classified segment is its duration, absolute amplitude, and amplitude relative to its neighboring segments (i.e., local peak, local valley, or plateau). The segments are contiguous and nonoverlapping, with one class designation for each.

SEG also does a finer labeling of each segment, using a repertory of 98 phonelike labels. Each of the labels is characterized by a vector of autocorrelation coefficients [ITAK75]. These template vectors were generalized from manually labeled speaker-specific training data. The labeling process matches the central portion of each segment against each of the templates using the Itakura metric and produces a vector of 98 numbers. The ith number is an estimate of the (negative log) probability that the segment represents an occurrence of the ith allophone in the label set. For each segment, SEG creates a hypothesis at the segment level and associates with it the vector of estimated allophone probabilities. The several highest rated labels of each segment are shown in Figure 5c.

Step 2. KS: WORD-CTL.
Stimulus: Start of processing.
Action: Create goal hypotheses at the word level. These will control the amount of hypothesization that MOW will do. (The goal hypotheses are not shown in Figure 5.)

Step 3. KS: WORD-SEQ-CTL.
Stimulus: Start of processing.
Action: Create goal hypotheses at the word-sequence le' These will control the amount of hypothesization that WORD-SEQ will do.

Step 4. KS: POM.
Stimulus: New segment hypotheses.
Action: Create syllable-class hypotheses.

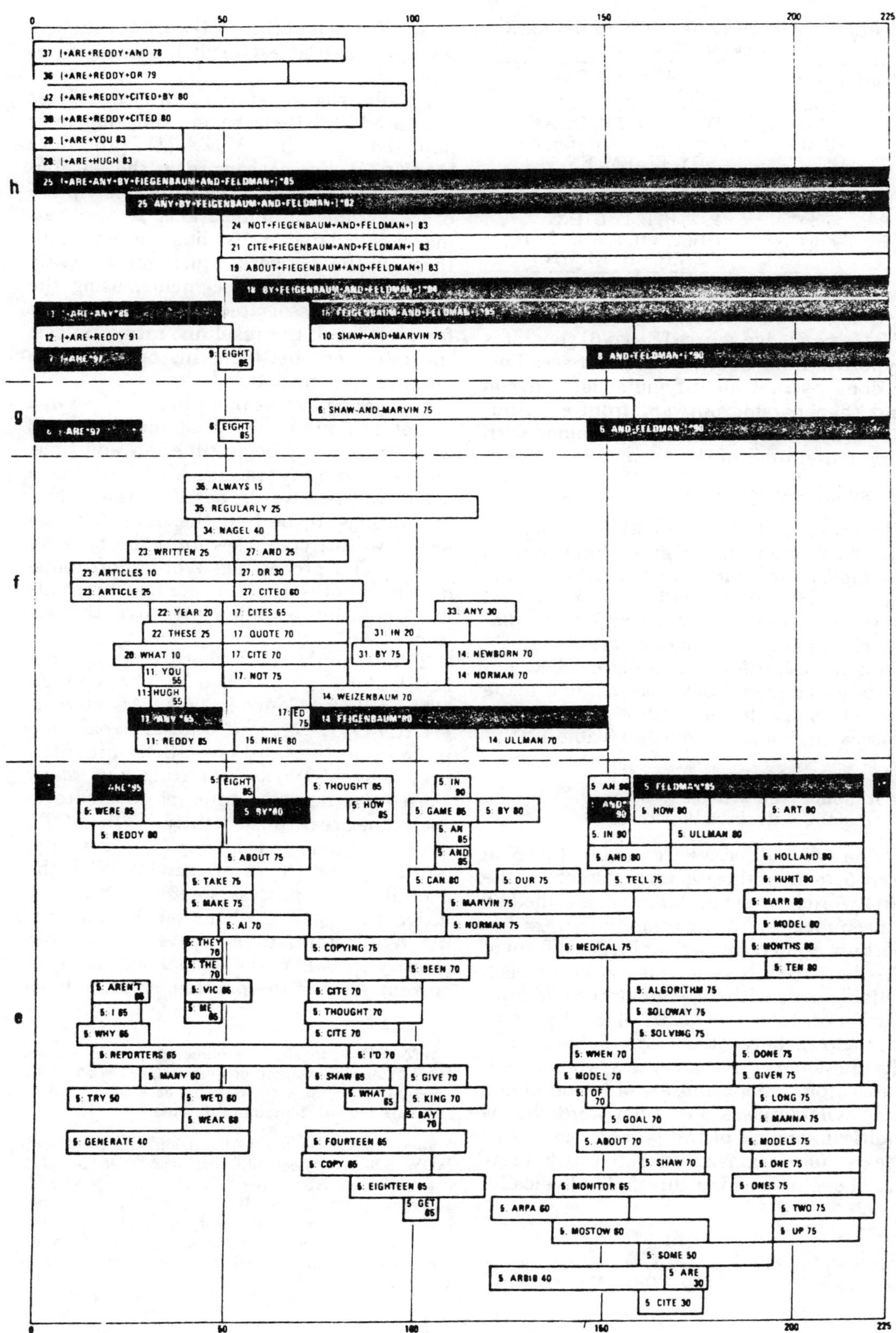
0
50
100
150
200
225
h
37 [+ARE+REDDY+AND 78
36 [+ARE+REDDY+OR 79
32 [+ARE+REDDY+CITED+BY 80
30 [+ARE+REDDY+CITED 80
29 [+ARE+YOU 83
28 [+ARE+HUGH 83
25 [+ARE+ANY+BY+FEIGENBAUM+AND+FELDMAN+]*85
25 ANY+BY+FEIGENBAUM+AND+FELDMAN+]*82
24 NOT+FEIGENBAUM+AND+FELDMAN+] 83
21 CITE+FEIGENBAUM+AND+FELDMAN+] 83
19 ABOUT+FEIGENBAUM+AND+FELDMAN+] 83
18 BY+FEIGENBAUM+AND+FELDMAN+]*84
17 [+ARE+ANY*86
16 FEIGENBAUM+AND+FELDMAN+]*85
12 [+ARE+REDDY 91
10 SHAW+AND+MARVIN 75
7 [+ARE*97
9 EIGHT 85
8 AND+FELDMAN+]*90
g
6 SHAW+AND+MARVIN 75
4 [+ARE*97
6 EIGHT 85
6 AND+FELDMAN+]*90
f
36 ALWAYS 15
35 REGULARLY 25
34 NAGEL 40
23 WRITTEN 25
27 AND 25
23 ARTICLES 10
27 OR 30
23 ARTICLE 25
27 CITED 60
22 YEAR 20
17 CITES 65
33 ANY 30
22 THESE 25
17 QUOTE 70
31 IN 20
20 WHAT 10
17 CITE 70
31 BY 75
14 NEWBORN 70
11 YOU 55
17 NOT 75
14 NORMAN 70
11 HUGH 55
14 WEIZENBAUM 70
11 ANY*65
17 ED 75
14 FEIGENBAUM*80
11 REDDY 85
15 NINE 80
14 ULLMAN 70
e
5 ARE*95
5 EIGHT 85
5 THOUGHT 85
5 IN 90
5 AN 90
5 FELDMAN*85
5 WERE 85
5 BY*80
5 HOW 85
5 GAME 85
5 BY 80
5 AND*90
5 HOW 80
5 ART 80
5 REDDY 80
5 AN 85
5 IN 90
5 ULLMAN 80
5 ABOUT 75
5 AND 85
5 AND 80
5 HOLLAND 80
5 TAKE 75
5 CAN 80
5 OUR 75
5 TELL 75
5 HUNT 80
5 MAKE 75
5 MARVIN 75
5 MARR 80
5 AI 70
5 NORMAN 75
5 MODEL 80
5 THEY 70
5 COPYING 75
5 MEDICAL 75
5 MONTHS 80
5 THE 70
5 BEEN 70
5 TEN 80
5 AREN'T 85
5 VIC 85
5 CITE 70
5 ALGORITHM 75
5 I 85
5 ME 85
5 THOUGHT 70
5 SOLOWAY 75
5 WHY 85
5 CITE 70
5 SOLVING 75
5 REPORTERS 65
5 I'D 70
5 WHEN 70
5 DONE 75
5 MANY 60
5 SHAW 85
5 GIVE 70
5 MODEL 70
5 GIVEN 75
5 TRY 50
5 WE'D 60
5 WHAT 65
5 KING 70
5 OF 70
5 LONG 75
5 WEAK 60
5 BAY 70
5 GOAL 70
5 MANNA 75
5 GENERATE 40
5 FOURTEEN 65
5 ABOUT 70
5 MODELS 75
5 COPY 85
5 SHAW 70
5 ONE 75
5 EIGHTEEN 65
5 MONITOR 65
5 ONES 75
5 GET 65
5 ARPA 60
5 TWO 75
5 MOSTOW 60
5 UP 75
5 SOME 50
5 ARBIB 40
5 ARE 30
5 CITE 30

TABLE 1. PHONE CLASSES USED TO DEFINE THE SYLLABLE CLASSES

Code	Phone Class	Phones in Class
A	A-like	AE, AA, AH, AO, AX
I	I-like	IY, IH, EY, EH, IX, AY
U	U-like	OW, UH, U, UW, ER, AW, OY, EL, EM, EN
L	Liquid	Y, W, R, L
N	Nasal	M, N, NX
P	Stop	P, T, K, B, D, G, DX
F	Fricative	HH, F, TH, S, SH, V, DH, Z, ZH, CH, JH, WH

Using the labeled segments as input, the *POM* knowledge source [SMIT76] generates hypotheses for likely syllable classes. This is done by first identifying syllable nuclei and then parsing outward from each nucleus, using a probabilistic grammar with production rules of the form:

syllable-class → segment-sequence.

The rules and their probabilities are induced by an off-line program that trains on manually segmented and labeled utterances. For each nucleus position, several (typically three to eight) competing syllable-class hypotheses may be generated.

Figure 5d shows the syllable-class hypotheses created. Each class name is made up of single-letter codes representing classes of phones, as given in Table 1.

Step 5. KS: MOW.
Stimulus: New syllable hypotheses.[6]
Action: Create word hypotheses.

The syllable classes are used by MOW in step 5 to hypothesize words. Each of the 1011 words in the vocabulary is specified by a pronunciation description. For word hypothesization purposes, an inverted form of the dictionary is kept; this associates each syllable class with all words whose pronunciation contains it. The *MOW* KS [SMIT76] looks up each hypothesized syllable class in the dictionary and generates word candidates from among those words containing that syllable class. For each word that is multisyllabic, all of the syllables in one of the pronunciations must match with a rating above a specified threshold. Typically, about 50 words of the 1011-word vocabulary are generated at each syllable nucleus position.

Finally, the generated word candidates are rated and their begin- and end-times adjusted by the *WIZARD* procedure [McKE77]. For each word in the vocabulary, WIZARD has a network description of its possible pronunciations. A word rating is calculated by finding the one path through the network which most closely matches the labeled segments, using the probabilities associated with the segment for each label; the resultant rating reflects the difference between this optimal path and the segment labels.[7]

Processing to this point has resulted in a set of bottom-up word candidates. Each word includes a begin-time, an end-time, and a credibility rating. MOW selects a subset of these words, based on their times and ratings, to be hypothesized; these selected word hypotheses form the base for the top-end processing. Words not immediately hypothesized are retained internally by MOW for possible later hypothesization.[8]

The amount of hypothesization that MOW does is controlled by the *WORD-CTL* (Word Control) KS. At step 2, WORD-CTL created initial goal hypotheses at the word level; these are interpreted by MOW as indicating how many word hypotheses to attempt to create in each time area. Subsequently, WORD-CTL may retrigger and modify the goal hypotheses (and thus retrigger MOW) if the overall search process stagnates; this condition is recognized when there are no waiting KS instantiations above a threshold priority or when the global measures of current state of the problem solution have

[6] MOW will also be reinvoked upon a modification to the word goal hypotheses by WORD-CTL.

[7] WIZARD is, in effect, a miniature version of the HARPY speech-recognition system (see Section 2.3), except that it has a network for each word, rather than one network containing all sentences.

[8] Since the September 1976 version, the POM and MOW KSs have been replaced by *NOAH* [SMIT77, SMIT81]. This KS outperforms, in both speed and accuracy, POM and MOW (with WIZARD) on the 1011-word vocabulary and is able to handle much larger vocabularies; its performance degradation is only logarithmic in vocabulary size, in the range of 500 to 19,000 words.

not improved in the last several KS executions.

WORD-CTL (and WORD-SEQ-CTL) are examples of KSs not directly involved in the hypothesizing and testing of partial solutions. Instead, these KSs control the search by influencing the activations of other KSs. These *policy* KSs impose global search strategies on the basic priority scheduling mechanism. For example, MOW is a generator of word hypotheses (from the candidates it creates internally) and WORD-CTL controls the number to be hypothesized. This clear separation of policy from mechanism has facilitated experimentation with various control schemes. A trivial change to WORD-CTL such that goal hypotheses are generated only at the start of the utterance (left-hand end) results in MOW creating word hypotheses only at the start, thus forcing all top-end processing to be left-to-right (see Section 3.2).

In this example four words (ARE, BY, AND, and FELDMAN) of the six in the utterance were correctly hypothesized; 86 incorrect hypotheses were generated (see Figure 5e). The 90 words that were hypothesized represent approximately 1.5 percent of the 1011-word vocabulary for each one of the six words in the utterance.

In addition, two unique word-level hypotheses are generated before the first and after the last segment of the utterance to denote the start and end of utterance, respectively. They are denoted by [and].

Step 6. KS: WORD-SEQ.
Stimulus: New words created bottom-up.
Action: Create four word-sequence hypotheses:
[–ARE*(97, 0:28),
AND–FELDMAN–]*(90, 145:225),
EIGHT(85, 48:57).
SHAW–AND–MARVIN(75, 72:157),

The *WORD-SEQ* knowledge source [LESS77a] has the task of generating, from the bottom-up word hypotheses, a small set (about three to ten) of word-sequence hypotheses. Each of these sequences, or *islands*, can be used as the basis for expansion into larger islands, which it is hoped will culminate in a hypothesis spanning the entire utterance. Multiword islands are used rather than single-word islands because of the relatively poor reliability of ratings of single words. With multiword islands, syntactic and coarticulation constraints can be used to increase the reliability of the ratings.

WORD-SEQ uses three kinds of knowledge to generate multiword islands efficiently:

(1) A table derived from the grammar indicates for every ordered pair of words in the vocabulary (1011 × 1011) whether that pair can occur in sequence within some sentence of the defined language. This binary table, whose density of ones for the X05 grammar is 1.7 percent, defines a *language-adjacent* relation.
(2) Acoustic-phonetic knowledge, embodied in the *JUNCT* (juncture) procedure [CRON77], is applied to pairs of word hypotheses and is used to decide if that pair might be considered to be *time-adjacent* in the utterance. JUNCT uses the dictionary pronunciations, and examines the segments at their juncture (gap or overlap) in making its decision.
(3) Statistical knowledge is used to assess the credibility of generated alternative word sequences and to terminate the search for additional candidates when the chance of finding improved hypotheses drops. The statistics are generated from previously observed behavior of WORD-SEQ and are based on the number of hypotheses generable from the given bottom-up word hypotheses and their ratings.

WORD-SEQ takes the highest rated single words and generates multiword sequences by expanding them with other hypothesized words that are both time- and language-adjacent. This expansion is guided by credibility ratings generated by using the statistical knowledge. The best of these word sequences (which occasionally includes single words) are hypothesized.

The *WORD-SEQ-CTL* (Word-Sequence-Control) KS controls the amount of hypothesization that WORD-SEQ does by creating "goal" hypotheses that WORD-SEQ interprets as indicating how many hypotheses to create. This provides the same kind of separation of policy and mechanism achieved in the MOW/WORD-CTL pair of KSs. WORD-SEQ-CTL fired at the start of processing, at step 3, in order to create the goal hypotheses. Subsequently, WORD-SEQ-CTL may trigger if stagnation is recognized; it then modifies the word-sequence goal hypotheses, thus stimulating WORD-SEQ to generate new islands from which the search may prove more fruitful. WORD-SEQ may generate the additional hypotheses by decomposing word sequences already on the blackboard or by generating islands previously discarded because their ratings seemed too low.

Step 6 results in the generation of four multiword sequences (see Figure 5g). These are used as initial, alternative anchor points for additional searching. Note that two of these islands are correct, each representing an alternative search path that potentially can lead to a correct interpretation of the utterance. This ability to derive the correct interpretation in multiple ways makes the system more robust. For example, there have been cases in which a complete interpretation could not be constructed from one correct island because of KS errors but was derived from another island.

High-level processing on the multiword sequences is accomplished by the following KSs: PARSE, PREDICT, VERIFY, CONCAT, STOP, and WORD-SEQ-CTL. Since an execution of the VERIFY KS will often immediately follow the execution of the PREDICT KS (each on the same hypothesis), we have combined the descriptions of the two KS executions into one step for ease of understanding.

Because the syntactic constraint used in the generation of the word sequences is only pairwise, a sequence longer than two words might not be syntactically acceptable. The *PARSE* knowledge source [HAYE77b] can parse a word sequence of arbitrary length, using the full grammatical constraints. This parsing does not require that the word sequence form a complete nonterminal in the grammar or that the sequence be sentence-initial or sentence-final; the words need only occur contiguously in some sentence of the language. If a sequence hypothesis does not parse, it is marked as "rejected." Otherwise a phrase hypothesis is created. Associated with the phrase hypothesis is the word sequence that supports it, as well as information about the parse(s).

Steps 7 through 10 show the PARSE KS processing each of the multiword sequences. In this example all four multiword sequences were verified as valid language fragments. However, if a multiword sequence had been rejected, the WORD-SEQ KS might have been reinvoked to generate additional multiword sequences in the time area of the rejected one. WORD-SEQ would generate the additional hypotheses by decomposing (shortening) word-sequence islands already on the blackboard or by regenerating islands which may not have been hypothesized initially owing to low ratings. Additional word-sequence hypotheses might also be generated in response to the modification of "goal" hypotheses at the word-sequence level by the WORD-SEQ-CTL. Such a structuring of a KS as a *generator* is a primary mechanism in Hearsay-II for limiting the number of hypotheses created on the blackboard and thereby reducing the danger of a combinatorial explosion of KS activity in reaction to those hypotheses.

The scheduling strategy is parameterized to delay phrase-level processing until an adequate number of highly rated phrase hypothesis islands is generated. This strategy is not built directly into the scheduler, but rather is accomplished by (1) appropriately setting external scheduling parameters (i.e., the high setting of the priorities of WORD-SEQ and PARSE KS actions in contrast to those of PREDICT, VERIFY, and CONCAT),[9] and (2) taking into account the current state of hypotheses on the phrase level of the blackboard in evaluating the usefulness of potential KS actions as described by their response frames.

Step 7. KS: PARSE*.
Stimulus: [-ARE* (word sequence).
Action: Create phrase: [+ARE* (97, 0:28).

Step 8. KS: PARSE*.
Stimulus: AND-FELDMAN-]* (word sequence).

---

[9] These settings are determined empirically by observing a number of training runs. They are not adjusted during test runs of the system.

Action: Create phrase:
AND+FELDMAN+]* (90, 145:225).

Step 9. KS: PARSE.
Stimulus: EIGHT (word sequence).
Action: Create phra[illegible] EIGHT (85, 48:57).

Step 10. KS: PARSE.
Stimulus: SHAW–AND–MARVIN (word sequence).
Action: Create phrase: SHAW+AND+MARVIN (75, 72:157).

Each of the four executions of the PARSE KS (steps 7–10) results in the creation of a phrase hypothesis; these are shown in Figure 5h. Each of these hypotheses causes an invocation of the PREDICT KS.

The *PREDICT* knowledge source [HAYE 77b] can, for any phrase hypothesis, generate predictions of all words which can immediately precede and all which can immediately follow that phrase in the language. In generating these predictions this KS uses the parsing information attached to the phrase hypothesis by the parsing component. The action of PREDICT is to attach a "word-predictor" attribute to the hypothesis which specifies the predicted words. Not all of these PREDICT KS instantiations are necessarily executed (and thus indicated as a step in the execution history). For instance, further processing on the phrases [+ARE and AND+FELDMAN+] is sufficiently positive that the scheduler never executes the instantiation of PREDICT for the phrase SHAW+AND+MARVIN (created in step 10).

The *VERIFY* KS can attempt to verify the existence of or reject each such predicted word in the context of its predicting phrase. If verified, a confidence rating for the word is also generated. The verification proceeds as follows: First, if the word has been hypothesized previously and passes the test for time-adjacency (by the JUNCT procedure), it is marked as verified and the word hypothesis is associated with the prediction. (Note that some word hypotheses may thus become associated with several different phrases.) Second, a search is made of the internal store created by MOW to see if the prediction can be matched by a previously generated word candidate which had not yet been hypothesized. Again, JUNCT makes a judgment about the plausibility of the time-adjacency relationship between the predicting phrase and the predicted word. Finally, WIZARD compares its word-pronunciation network with the segments in an attempt to verify the prediction.

For each of these different kinds of verification, the approximate begin-time (end-time if verifying an antecedent prediction) of the word being predicted following (preceding) the phrase is taken to be the end-time (begin-time) of the phrase. The end-time (begin-time) of the predicted word is not known, and in fact one function of the verification step is to generate an approximate end-time (begin-time) for the verified word. In general, it is possible to generate several different "versions" of the word which differ primarily in their end-times (begin-times); since no context following (preceding) the predicted word is given, several different estimates of the end (beginning) of the word may be plausible solely on the basis of the segmental information. These alternatives give rise to the creation of competing hypotheses.

VERIFY is invoked when a KS (PREDICT) places a "word-predictor" attribute on a phrase hypothesis. For each word on the attribute list that it verifies, it creates a word hypothesis (if one does not already exist), and the word is placed on a "word-verification" attribute of the phrase hypothesis. Word hypotheses created by VERIFY are shown in Figure 5f.

The *CONCAT* KS [HAYE77b] is invoked on phrase hypotheses which have word-verification attributes attached. For each verified word, the phrase and new word are parsed together and a new, extended phrase hypothesis is created (as shown in Figure 5h). The new hypothesis receives a rating based on the ratings of its component words. If all word predictions preceding or following the phrase had been rejected, the phrase hypothesis itself would be marked as "rejected." Similarly, the underlying word-sequence hypothesis is rejected if all the phrase hypotheses it supports are rejected. (This action would retrigger WORD-SEQ to generate more word sequences.)

Step 11. KS: PREDICT & VERIFY*.
Stimulus: [+ARE* (phrase).

Action: Predict (from the grammar) 292 words following. Reject (using the acoustic information) 277 of them. The four highest rated of the 15 verified words are
REDDY(85, 26:52),
ANY*(65, 24:49),
HUGH(55, 30:39), and
YOU(55, 28:39).

Step 12. KS: CONCAT.
Stimulus: [+ARE* (phrase), REDDY (word).
Action: Create phrase: [+ARE+REDDY (91, 0:52).

Step 13. KS: CONCAT*.
Stimulus: [+ARE* (phrase), ANY* (word).
Action: Create phrase: [+ARE+ANY* (86, 0:49).

In steps 11 through 13 the highly rated phrase [+ARE is extended and results in the generation of the additional phrases [+ARE+REDDY and [+ARE+ANY. These phrases, however, are not immediately extended because the predicted words REDDY and ANY are not rated sufficiently high. Instead, the scheduler, pursuing a strategy more conservative than strict best-first, investigates phrases that look almost as good as the best one. This scheduling strategy results in the execution of the PREDICT and VERIFY KSs on two of the other initial phrase islands: AND+FELDMAN+] and EIGHT.

Step 14. KS: PREDICT & VERIFY*.
Stimulus: AND+FELDMAN+]* (phrase).
Action: Predict 100 words preceding. Reject 76 of them. The best of the verified 24 (in descending rating order) are
FEIGENBAUM*(80, 72:150),
WEIZENBAUM(70, 72:150),
ULLMAN(70, 116:150),
NORMAN(70, 108:150), and
NEWBORN(70, 108:150).

Step 15. KS: PREDICT & VERIFY.
Stimulus: EIGHT (phrase).
Action: Predict the word NINE following and verify it (80, 52:82). Predict SEVEN preceding, but reject this because of mismatch with the acoustic segments.

The attempt to extend the phrase EIGHT at step 15 is not successful; none of the grammatically predicted words are acoustically verified, even using a lenient threshold. Thus this phrase is marked rejected and is dropped from further consideration.

Step 16. KS: CONCAT*.
Stimulus: FEIGENBAUM* (word), AND+FELDMAN+]* (phrase).
Action: Create phrase: FEIGENBAUM+AND+FELDMAN+]* (85, 72:225).

Beginning with step 16, extending the phrase AND+FELDMAN+] with the highly rated word FEIGENBAUM looks sufficiently promising for processing to continue now in a more depth-first manner along the path FEIGENBAUM+AND+FELDMAN+] through step 25.[10] Processing on the path [+ARE+REDDY does not resume until step 26.

Step 17. KS: PREDICT & VERIFY*.
Stimulus: FEIGENBAUM+AND+FELDMAN+]* (phrase).
Action: Predict eight preceding words. Reject one (DISCUSS). Find two already on the blackboard:
BY*(80, 52:72) and
ABOUT(75, 48:72).
Verify five others:
NOT(75, 49:82),
ED(75, 67:72),
CITE(70, 49:82),
QUOTE(70, 49:82),
CITES(65, 49:82).

In steps 18 through 24, alternative word extensions of FEIGENBAUM+AND+FELDMAN+] are explored. As a result of this exploration the phrase BY+FEIGENBAUM+AND+FELDMAN+] is considered the most credible.

Step 18. KS CONCAT*.
Stimulus: BY* (word), FEIGENBAUM+AND+FELDMAN+]* (phrase).
Action: Create phrase: BY+FEIGENBAUM+AND+FELDMAN+]* (84, 52:225).

Step 19. KS: CONCAT.
Stimulus: ABOUT (word), FEIGENBAUM+AND+FELDMAN+]* (phrase).
Action: Create phrase: ABOUT+FEIGENBAUM+AND+FELDMAN+] (83, 48:225).

Step 20. KS: PREDICT & VERIFY.
Stimulus:
ABOUT+FEIGENBAUM+AND+ FELDMAN+] (phrase).

---

[10] The rating on a hypothesis is only one parameter used by the scheduler to assign priorities to waiting KS instantiations. In particular, the length of a hypothesis is also important. Thus, FEIGENBAUM with a rating of 80 looks better than REDDY with a rating of 85 because it is much longer.

Action: Predict one preceding word: WHAT. Verify it (10, 20:49).

Step 21. KS: CONCAT
Stimulus: CITE (word), FEIGENBAUM+AND+FELDMAN+] (phrase).
Action: Create phrase: CITE+FEIGENBAUM+AND+FELDMAN+] (83, 49:225).

Step 22. KS: PREDICT & VERIFY.
Stimulus: CITE+FEIGENBAUM+AND+FELDMAN+] (phrase).
Action: Predict four preceding words. Reject two of them: BOOKS, PAPERS. Verify
THESE (25, 28:49),
YEAR (20, 30:49).

Step 23. KS: PREDICT & VERIFY*.
Stimulus: BY+FEIGENBAUM+AND+FELDMAN+]* (phrase).
Action: Predict ten preceding words. Reject five: ABSTRACTS, ARE, BOOKS, PAPERS, REFERENCED. Find two already on the blackboard:
ANY* (65, 24:49),
THESE (25, 28:49).
Verify three more:
ARTICLE (25, 9:52),
WRITTEN (25, 24:52),
ARTICLES (10, 9:52).

Step 24. KS: CONCAT.
Stimulus: NOT (word), FEIGENBAUM+AND+FELDMAN+]*.
Action: Create phrase: NOT+FEIGENBAUM+AND+FELDMAN+] (83, 49:225).

Step 25. KS: CONCAT*.
Stimulus: ANY* (word), BY+FEIGENBAUM+AND+FELDMAN+]* (phrase).
Action: Create phrase: ANY+BY+FEIGENBAUM+AND+FELDMAN+]* (82, 24:225).
[+ARE+ANY+BY+FEIGENBAUM+AND+FELDMAN+]* (85, 0:225) is also created, from [+ARE+ANY and BY+FEIGENBAUM+ AND+FELDMAN+].

In step 25 the word ANY is concatenated onto the phrase BY+FEIGENBAUM+AND+FELDMAN+]. However, instead of only creating this new combined phrase, the CONCAT KS also notices that the word ANY is the last word of the phrase [+ARE+ANY; this leads the CONCAT KS to merge the two adjacent phrases [+ARE+ANY and BY+FEIGENBAUM+AND+FELDMAN+] into a single phrase, after first ascertaining that the resulting phrase is grammatical. This merging bypasses the several single-word PREDICT, VERIFY, and CONCAT actions needed to generate the enlarged hypothesis from either of the two original hypotheses in an incremental fashion. Thus the recognition process is sped up in two ways: (1) several single-word actions are eliminated, and (2) the scheduler postpones KS actions on competing (incorrect) hypotheses since these potential actions seem less attractive than actions on the new, enlarged hypothesis. Such mergings occur in approximately half of the runs on the 1011-word grammar with the small branching factor (X05); in grammars with higher branching factors, the merging of phrase hypotheses occurs with even higher frequency.

It has been our experience that just as a multiword island is more credible than the individual words that compose it, so a merged phrase hypothesis is more credible than its two constituent phrases. For example, about 80 percent of the mergings in X05 runs produce correct hypotheses. In more complex grammars this statistic drops to about 35 percent, but correspondingly more phrase mergings occur.

The newly created merged phrase also happens to be a complete sentence; i.e., it has begin- and end-of-utterance markers as its extreme constituents. Thus it is a candidate for the interpretation of the utterance.

Step 26. KS: STOP.
Stimulus: [+ARE+ANY+BY+FEIGENBAUM+AND+FELDMAN+]* (complete sentence).
Action: Deactivation of several dozen competing hypotheses.

These start- and end-of-utterance "words" (denoted by [and]) appear in the syntactic specification of the language as the first and last terminals of every complete sentence. Thus any verified phrase that includes these as its extreme constituents is a complete sentence and spans the entire utterance. Such a sentence becomes a candidate for selection as the system's recognition result.

In general, the control and rating strategies do not guarantee that the first such complete spanning hypothesis found will have the highest rating of all possible spanning sentence hypotheses that might be found if the search were allowed to continue, so the system does not just stop with the first one generated.[11] However the characteristics of such a hypothesis are used by the *STOP* knowledge source to prune from further consideration other partial hypotheses which, because of their low ratings, are unlikely to be extendible into spanning hypotheses with ratings higher than the best already-discovered spanning sentence. This heuristic pruning procedure is based on the form of the ratings function (i.e., how the rating of the phrase is derived from its constituent words). The pruning procedure considers each partial phrase and uses the ratings of other word hypotheses in the time areas not covered by the phrase to determine if the phrase might be extendible to a phrase rated higher than the spanning hypothesis; if not, the partial phrase is pruned. This pruning process and the rating and halting policies are discussed in MOST77.

Of the hypotheses not discarded, extensions to the phrase [+ARE now appear as the most likely candidates to produce new and better complete phrases. This search for better complete phrases results, in steps 27 through 36, in the examination of numerous alternative extensions, each of which is promising.

Step 27. KS: PREDICT & VERIFY.
Stimulus: [+ARE+REDDY.
Action: Predict three following words. Verify CITED (60, 52:86), OR (30, 52:67), AND (25, 52:82).

Step 28. KS: CONCAT.
Stimulus: [+ARE* (phrase), HUGH (word).
Action: Create phrase: [+ARE+HUGH (83, 0:39).

Step 29. KS: CONCAT.
Stimulus: [+ARE (phrase), YOU (word).
Action: Create phrase: [+ARE+YOU (83, 0:39).

Step 30. KS: CONCAT.
Stimulus: [+ARE+REDDY (phrase), CITED (word).
Action: Create phrase: [+ARE+REDDY+CITED (80, 0:86).

Step 31. KS: PREDICT & VERIFY.
Stimulus: [+ARE+REDDY+CITED (phrase).
Action: Predict two following words. Verify BY(75, 83:98), IN(20, 86:114).

Step 32. KS: CONCAT.
Stimulus: [+ARE+REDDY+CITED (phrase), BY (word).
Action: Create phrase: [+ARE+REDDY+CITED+BY (80, 0:98).

Step 33. KS: PREDICT & VERIFY.
Stimulus: [+ARE+REDDY+CITED+BY (phrase).
Action: Predict one following word. Verify ANY (30, 105:126).

Step 34. KS: PREDICT & VERIFY.
Stimulus: [+ARE+HUGH (phrase).
Action: Predict one following word. Verify NAGEL (40, 42:63).

Step 35. KS: PREDICT & VERIFY.
Stimulus: [+ARE+YOU (phrase).
Action: Predict three following words. Reject USUALLY. Verify
REGULARLY (25, 39:116),
ALWAYS (15, 39:72).

Step 36. KS: CONCAT.
Stimulus: [+ARE+REDDY (phrase), OR (word).
Action: Create phrase: [+ARE+REDDY+OR (79, 0:67).

Step 37. KS: CONCAT.
Stimulus: [+ARE+REDDY (phrase), AND (word).
Action: Create phrase: [+ARE+REDDY+AND (78, 0:82).

Step 38. KS: STOP.
Stimulus: Stagnation
Action: Stop search and accept [+ARE+ANY+BY+FEIGENBAUM+AND+FELDMAN+]*.

The recognition processing finally halts in one of two ways: First, there may be no more partial hypotheses left to consider for prediction and extension. Because of the combinatorics of the grammar and the likelihood of finding some prediction rated at least above the absolute rejection threshold, this termination happens when the heuristic pruning procedure used by STOP and RPOL has eliminated all competitors. Such a halt occurs here as STOP decides to terminate the search process and accept the phrase [+ARE+ANY+BY+FEIGEN-

---

[11] An alternative control strategy based on the Shortfall Density scoring function and assumptions of the completeness of processing at the word level can guarantee that the first complete interpretation generated is the best possible (see Section 2.1). This results in a more conservative, breadth-first search, in which more alternatives are explored.

BAUM+AND+FELDMAN+] as the correct interpretation. In general there might be more than one complete sentence hypothesis at this point; STOP would select the one with the highest rating.

A second kind of halt occurs if the system expends its total allowed computing resources (time or space). (The actual thresholds used are set according to the past performance of the system on similar sentences, i.e., of the given length and over the same vocabulary and grammar.) In that case a selection of several of the highest rated phrase hypotheses is the result of the recognition process, with the selection biased toward the longest phrases which overlap (in time) the least.

Step 39. KS: SEMANT*.
Stimulus: Recognized utterance: [+ARE+ANY+BY+FEIGENBAUM+AND+FELDMAN+]*.
Action: Generate an interpretation for the database retrieval system.

The *SEMANT* knowledge source [FOX77] takes the word sequence(s) result of the recognition process and constructs an interpretation in an unambiguous format for interaction with the database that the speaker is querying. The interpretation is constructed by actions associated with "semantically interesting" nonterminals (which have been prespecified for the grammar) in the parse tree(s) of the recognized sequence(s). In our example the following structure is produced:

```
F:[U:([ARE ANY BY FEIGENBAUM AND
       FELDMAN])
   N:($PRUNE!LIST
       S:($PRUNE!LIST!AUTHOR   K:(A:
       ((FEIGENBAUM • FELDMAN)))))]
```

F denotes the total message. U contains the utterance itself. N indicates the main type of the utterance (e.g., PRUNE a previously specified list of citations, REQUEST, HELP), S the subtype (e.g., PRUNE a list according to its author). K denotes the different attributes associated with the utterance (e.g., A is the author, T is the topic).

If recognition produces more than one partial sequence, SEMANT constructs a maximally consistent interpretation based on all of the partial sentences, taking into account the rating, temporal position, and semantic consistency of the partial sentences.

The *DISCO* (discourse) knowledge source [HAYE77c] accepts the formatted interpretation of SEMANT and produces a response to the speaker. This response is often the display of a selected portion of the queried database. In order to retain a coherent interpretation across sentences, DISCO maintains a finite-state model of the ongoing discourse.

2. COMPARISON WITH OTHER SPEECH-UNDERSTANDING SYSTEMS

In addition to Hearsay-II, several other speech-understanding systems were also developed as part of the Defense Advanced Research Projects Agency (DARPA) research program in speech understanding from 1971 to 1976 [MEDR78]. As a way of concretely orienting the research, a common set of system performance goals, shown in Figure 6, was established by the study committee that launched the project [NEWE73]. All of the systems are based on the idea of diverse, cooperating KSs to handle the uncertainty in the signal and processing. They differ in the types of knowledge, interactions of knowledge, representation of search space, and control of the

FIGURE 6. DARPA speech-understanding-system performance goals set in 1971. [After NEWE73 and MEDR78.]

The system should
- Accept connected speech
- from many
- cooperative speakers of the General American Dialect
- in a quiet room
- using a good-quality microphone
- with slight tuning per speaker
- requiring only natural adaptation by the user
- permitting a slightly selected vocabulary of 1000 words
- with a highly artificial syntax and highly constrained task
- providing graceful interaction
- tolerating less than 10 percent semantic error
- in a few times real time on a 100-million-instructions-per-second machine
- and be demonstrable in 1976 with a moderate chance of success.

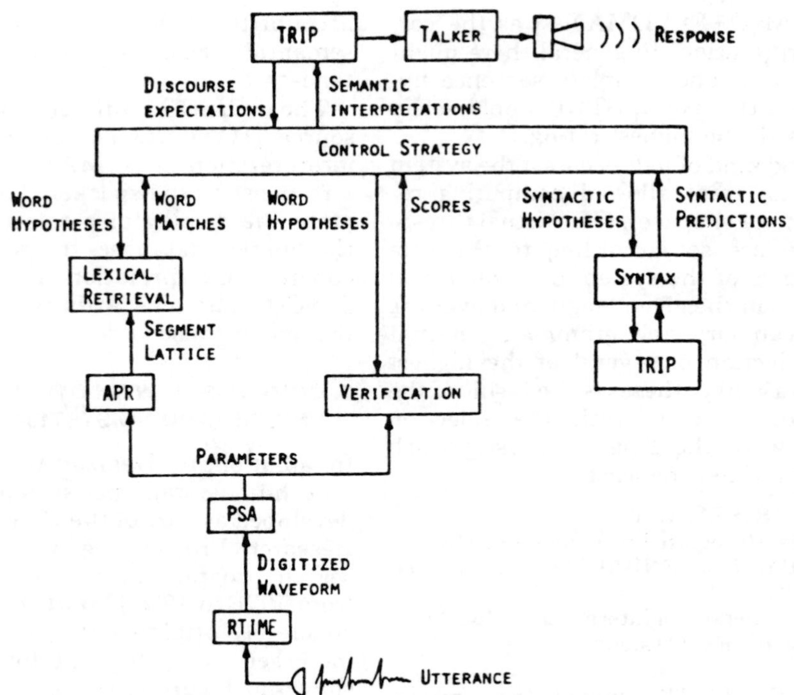

FIGURE 7. Structure of HWIM. [From WOLF80.]

search. (They also differ in the tasks and languages handled, but we do not address those here.) In this section we describe three of these systems, Bolt Beranek and Newman's (BBN's) HWIM, Stanford Research Institute's (SRI's) system, and Carnegie-Mellon University's (CMU's) HARPY, and compare them with Hearsay-II along those dimensions. For consistency we will use the terminology developed in this paper in so far as possible, even though it is often not identical to that used by the designers of each of the other systems.[12]

Although the performance specifications had the strong effect of pointing the various efforts in the same directions, the backgrounds and motivations of each group led to different emphases. For example, BBN's expertise in natural-language processing and acoustic-phonetics led to an emphasis on those KSs; SRI's interest in semantics and discourse strongly influenced its system design; and CMU's predilection for system organization placed that group in the central position (and led to the Hearsay-II and HARPY structures).

2.1 BBN's HWIM System

Figure 7 shows the structure of BBN's *HWIM* (Hear What I Mean) system [WOOD76, WOLF80]. In overall form, HWIM's general processing structure is strikingly similar to that of Hearsay-II. Processing of a sentence is bottom-up through audio signal digitization, parameter extraction, segmentation and labeling, and a scan for word hypotheses; this phase is roughly similar to Hearsay-II's initial bottom-up processing up through the MOW KS.

Following this initial phase, the Control Strategy module takes charge, calling the Syntax and Lexical Retrieval KSs as subroutines:

- The grammar is represented as an augmented transition network [WOOD70], and, as in Hearsay-II, includes semantic

[12] IBM has been funding work with a somewhat different objective [BAHL76]. Its stated goals mandate little reliance on the strong syntactic/semantic/task constraints exploited by the DARPA projects. This orientation is usually dubbed *speech recognition* as distinguished from *speech understanding*.

and pragmatic knowledge of the domain (in this case, "travel planning"). The Syntax KS combines the functions of Hearsay-II's PREDICT and CONCAT KSs. Like them, it handles contiguous sequences of words in the language, independently of the phrase structure nonterminal boundaries, as well as the merging of phrase hypotheses (i.e., island collision).

- The Lexical Retriever functions in this phase much like Hearsay-II's VERIFY KS, rating the acoustic match of a predicted word at one end of a phrase. Some configurations of HWIM also have a KS which does an independent, highly reliable, and very expensive word verification; that KS is also called directly by the Control Strategy.
- The Control Strategy module schedules the Syntax and Lexical Retrieval KSs opportunistically. To this end it keeps a task agenda that prioritizes the actions on the most promising phrase hypotheses. The task agenda is initialized with single-word phrase hypotheses constructed from the best word hypotheses generated in the bottom-up phase.

Given these similarities between HWIM and Hearsay-II, what besides the content of the KSs (which we do not address) are the differences? The most significant differences involve the mechanisms for instantiating KSs, scheduling KSs (i.e., selective attention for controlling the search), and representing, accessing, and combining KS results. These differences stem primarily from differing design philosophies:

- The Hearsay-II design was based on the assumption that a very general and flexible model for KS interaction patterns was required because the type, number, and interaction patterns of KSs would change substantially over the lifetime of the system [LESS75, LESS77b]. Thus we rejected an explicit subroutine-like architecture for KS interaction because it reduces modularity. Rather, the implicit data-directed approach was taken, in which KSs interact uniformly and anonymously via the blackboard.
- The HWIM design evolved out of an *incremental simulation* methodology [WOOD73]. In this methodology the overall system is implemented initially with some combination of computer programs and human simulators, with the latter filling the role of components (i.e., KSs and scheduling) not fully conceptualized. As experience is gained, the human simulators are replaced by computer programs. Thus by the time the system has evolved into a fully operational computer program, the type of KSs and their interaction patterns are expected to be stable. Modifications after this point aim to improve the performance of individual KSs and their scheduling, with only minor changes expected in KS interaction patterns. From this perspective, developing specific explicit structures for explicit KS interactions is reasonable.

Thus HWIM has an explicit control strategy, in which KSs directly call each other, and in which the scheduler has built-in knowledge about the specific KSs in the system. The Hearsay-II scheduler has no such built-in knowledge but rather is given an abstract description of each KS instantiation by its creator condition program.

Similarly, one KS communicates with another in HWIM via ad hoc KS-specific data structures. The introduction of a new KS is expected to occur very rarely and requires either that it adopt some other KS's existing data representation or that its new formats be integrated into those KSs that will interact with it. Hearsay-II's blackboard, on the other hand, provides a uniform representation which facilitates experimentation with new or highly modified KSs.

When one KS in a hierarchical structure like that in HWIM calls another, it provides the called KS with those data it deems relevant. The called KS also uses whatever data it has retained internally plus what it might acquire by calling other KSs. Hearsay-II's blackboard, on the other hand, provides a place for all data known to all the KSs; one KS can use data created by a previous KS execution without the creator of the data having to know which KS will use the data and without the user KS having to know which KS might be able to create the data.

The ability to embed into the HWIM system a detailed model of the KSs and their interaction patterns has had its most profound effect on the techniques developed for scheduling. Several alternative scheduling policies were implemented in the Control Strategy module. The most interesting of these, the "shortfall density scoring strategy" [WOOD77], can be shown formally to guarantee that the first complete sentence hypothesis constructed by the system is the best possible (i.e., highest rated) such hypothesis that it will ever be able to construct. Heuristic search strategies with this property are called *admissible* [NILS71]. This contrasts with the *approximate* Hearsay-II scheduling strategy, in which there is no guarantee at any point that a better interpretation cannot be found by continued search. Thus Hearsay-II requires a heuristic stopping decision, as described in Section 1.2. In HWIM an admissible strategy is possible because the scheduler can make some strong assumptions about the nature of KS processing: in particular, the algorithms used by the Lexical Retriever KS are such that it does not subsequently generate a higher rating for a predicted word than that of the highest rated word predicted in that utterance location by the initial, bottom-up processing.

An admissible strategy eliminates errors which an approximate strategy may make by stopping too soon. However, even when an admissible strategy can be constructed, it may not be preferable if it generates excessive additional search in order to guarantee its admissibility. More discussion of this issue in speech understanding can be found in WOLF80, WOOD77, MOST77, and HAYE80. Discussions of it in more general cases can be found in POHL70, HARR74, and POHL77.

Given that hypotheses are rated by KSs, combining on a single hypothesis several ratings generated by different KSs is a problem. A similar problem also occurs within a KS when constructing a hypothesis from several lower level hypotheses; the rating of the new one should reflect the combination of ratings of its components. Hearsay-II uses ad hoc schemes for such rating combinations [HAYE77d]. HWIM takes a formal approach, using an application of Bayes' theorem. To implement this, each KS's ratings are calibrated by using performance statistics gathered on test data. This uniform scheme for calibration and combination of ratings facilitates adding and modifying KSs. The issue of evaluating the combination of evidence from multiple sources is a recurrent problem in knowledge-based systems [SHOR75, DUDA78].

2.2 SRI's System

The SRI system [WALK78, WALK80], though never fully operational on a large vocabulary task, presents another interesting variant on structuring a speech-understanding system. Like the HWIM system, it uses an explicit control strategy with, however, much more control being centralized in the Control Strategy module. The designers of the system felt there was "a large potential for mutual guidance that would not be realized if all knowledge source communication was indirect" [WALK78, p. 84]. Part of this explicit control is embedded within the rules that define the phrases of the task grammar; each rule, in addition to defining the possible constituent structure for phrases in an extended form of BNF, contains procedures for calculating attributes of phrases and factors used in rating phrases. These procedures may, in turn, call as subroutines any of the knowledge sources in the system. The attributes include acoustic attributes related to the input signal, syntactic attributes (e.g., mood and number), semantic attributes such as the representation of the meaning of the phrase, and discourse attributes for anaphora and ellipsis. Thus the phrase itself is the basic unit for integrating and controlling knowledge-source execution.

The interpreter of these rules (i.e., the Syntax module) is integrated with the scheduling components to define a high-level Control Strategy module. Like Hearsay-II and HWIM, this control module opportunistically executes the syntax rules to predict new phrases and words from a given phrase hypothesis and executes the word verifier to verify predicted words. This module maintains a data structure, the "parse-net," containing all the word and phrase hypotheses constructed, and the at-

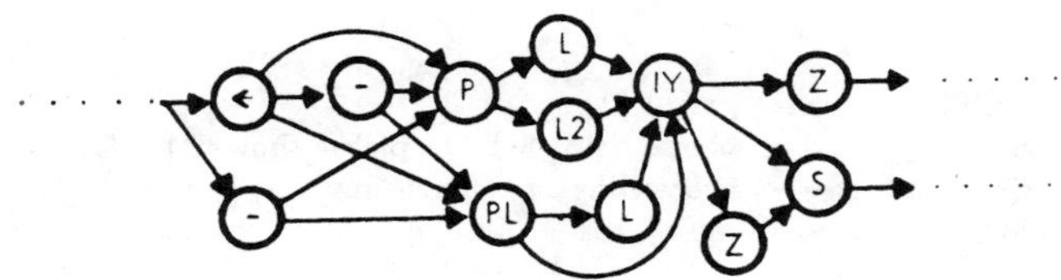

FIGURE 8. HARPY pronunciation network for the word "Please." [After LOWE80.]

tributes and factors associated with each hypothesis. This data structure is similar to a Hearsay-II blackboard restricted to the word and phrase levels. Like the blackboard, it serves to avoid redundant computation and facilitates the detection of possible island collisions.

As with Hearsay-II and HWIM, the SRI Control Strategy module is parameterized to permit a number of different strategies, such as top-down, bottom-up, island-driving, and left-to-right. Using a simulated word recognizer, SRI ran a series of experiments with several different strategies. One of the results, also substantiated by BBN experiments with HWIM, is that island-driving is inferior to some forms of left-to-right search. This appears to be in conflict with the Hearsay-II experimental results, which show island-driving clearly superior [LESS77a]. We believe the difference to be caused by the reliability of ratings of the initial islands: Both the HWIM and SRI experiments used single-word islands, but Hearsay-II uses multiword islands, which produce much higher reliability. (See the discussion at step 6 in Section 1.2 and in HAYE78b.) Single-word island-driving proved inferior in Hearsay-II as well.

2.3 CMU's HARPY System

In the systems described so far, knowledge sources are discernible as active components during the understanding process. However, if one looks at Hearsay-II, HWIM, and the SRI system in that order, there is clearly a progression of increasing integration of the KSs with the control structure. The HARPY system [LOWE76, LOWE80] developed at Carnegie-Mellon University is located at the far extreme of that dimension: Most of the knowledge is precompiled into a unified structure representing all possible utterances; a relatively simple interpreter then compares the spoken utterance against this structure to find the utterance that matches best. The motivation for this approach is to speed up the search so that a larger portion of the space may be examined explicitly. In particular, the hope is to avoid errors made when portions of the search space are eliminated on the basis of characteristics of small partial solutions; to this end, pruning decisions are delayed until larger partial solutions are constructed.

To describe HARPY, we describe the knowledge sources, their compilation, and the match (search) process. The *parameterization* and *segmentation* KSs are identical to those of Hearsay-II [GOLD77, GILL78]; these are not compiled into the network but, as in the other systems, applied to each utterance as it is spoken. As in Hearsay-II, the *syntax* is specified as a set of context-free production rules; HARPY uses the same task and grammar definitions. *Lexical* knowledge is specified as a directed pronunciation graph for each word; for example, Figure 8 shows the graph for the word "please." The nodes in the graph are names of the phonelike labels also generated by the labeler KS. A graph is intended to represent all possible pronunciations of the word. Knowledge about phonetic phenomena at *word junctures* is contained in a set of rewriting rules for the pronunciation graphs.

For a given task language, syntax and lexical and juncture knowledge are combined by a *knowledge compiler* program to form a single large network. First, the grammar is converted into a directed graph, the "word network," containing only terminal symbols (i.e., words); because of heuristics

⟨SENT⟩	::==	[⟨SS⟩]
⟨SS⟩	::==	please help ⟨M⟩ | please show ⟨M⟩ ⟨Q⟩
⟨Q⟩	::==	everything | something
⟨M⟩	::==	me | us

FIGURE 9. A tiny example grammar. [After LOWE80.]

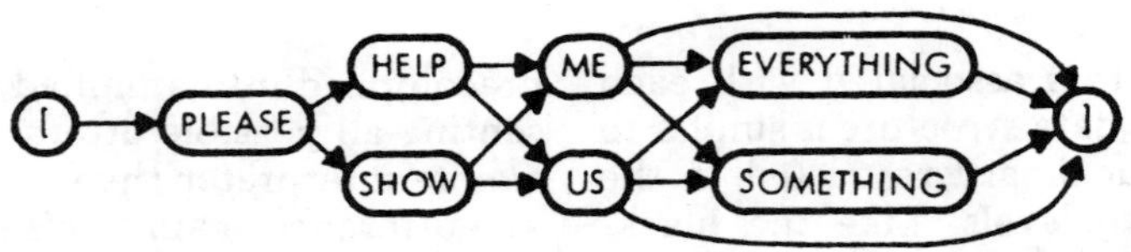

FIGURE 10. Word network for example language. [After LOWE80.]

used to compact this network, some of the constraint of the original grammar may be lost. Figure 9 shows a toy grammar, and Figure 10 the resulting word network. Next, the compiler replaces each word by a copy of its pronunciation graph, applying the word-juncture rules at all the word boundaries. Figure 11 shows part of the network for the toy example. The resulting network has the name of a segment label at each node. For the same 1011-word X05 language used by Hearsay-II, the network has 15,000 nodes and took 13 hours of DEC PDP-10(KL10) processing time to compile.

In the network each distinct path from the distinguished start node to the distinguished end node represents a sequence of segments making up a "legal" utterance. The purpose of the search is to find the sequence which most closely matches the segment sequence of the input spoken utterance. For any given labeled segment and any given node in the network, a primitive match algorithm can calculate a score for matching the node to the segment. The score for matching a sequence of nodes with a sequence of segments is just the sum of the corresponding primitive matches.

The search technique used, called *beam search*, is a heuristic form of dynamic programming, with the input segments processed one at a time from left to right and matched against the network. At the beginning of the ith step, the first $i - 1$ segments have been processed. Some number of nodes in the network are *active*; associated with each active node is a path to it from the start node and the total score of the match between that path and the first $i - 1$ segments of the utterance. All nodes

FIGURE 11. Partial final network for example language. [After LOWE80.]

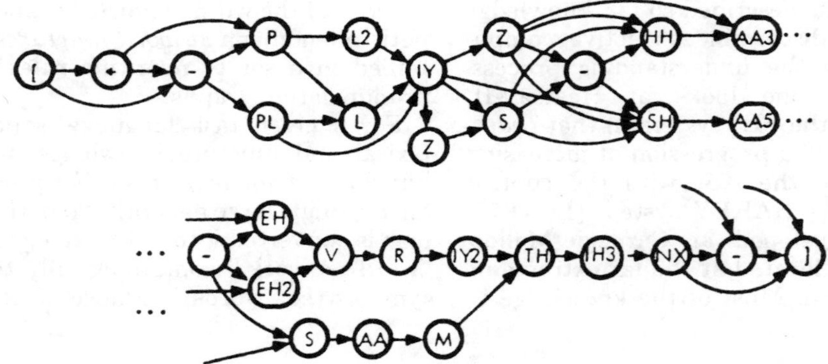

in the network that are successors of the active nodes are matched against the ith segment and become the new active nodes. The score for a new active node is the best path score that reaches the node at the ith segment, i.e., the sum of the primitive match at the segment plus the best path score to any of its predecessor nodes.

The best path score among all the new active nodes is taken as the target, and any new active nodes with path scores more than some threshold amount from the target are pruned away. This pruning rule is the heuristic heart of the search algorithm. It reduces the number of active nodes at each step and thus reduces the amount of processing time (and storage) needed in the search; typically only about 3 percent of the nodes in the net need to be matched. Note that the heuristic does not fix the number of active nodes retained at each step but allows it to vary with the density of competitors with scores near the best path. Thus in highly uncertain regions, many nodes are retained, and the search slows down; in places where one path is significantly better than most others, few competitors are kept, and the processing is rapid. The search strategy, therefore, is automatically cautious or decisive in response to the partial results. The threshold, i.e., the "beam width," is tuned ad hoc from test runs.

There are two major concerns about the extensibility of HARPY. First, the compilation process requires all knowledge to be represented in a highly stylized form; adding new kinds of knowledge strains the developer's ingenuity. So far, however, several kinds of knowledge have been added within the basic framework of expanding a node by replacing it with a graph. For example, as mentioned previously, phonetic phenomena at word junctures are handled. Also, the expected length of each segment is stored at each node and influences the match score. The second concern is with the size and compilation cost of the compiled network; both grow very large as the task language becomes more complex. There have been proposals that the word network not be expanded explicitly, but rather that the word pronunciation graphs be interpreted dynamically, as needed. An alternative response to this concern is that computer memory and processing costs continue to decline, so that using larger networks becomes increasingly feasible.

HARPY's novel structure is also interesting in its own right and is beginning to have effects beyond speech-understanding systems. Newell has done a speculative but thorough analysis of HARPY as a model for human speech understanding, using the production system formalism [NEWE80]; Rubin has successfully applied the HARPY structure to an image-understanding task [RUBI78].

3. SYSTEM PERFORMANCE AND ANALYSIS

3.1 Overall Performance of Hearsay-II

Overall performance of the Hearsay-II speech-understanding system at the end of 1976 is summarized in Table 2 in a form paralleling the goals given in Figure 6.

TABLE 2. HEARSAY-II PERFORMANCE

Number of speakers	One
Environment	Computer terminal room (>65 dB)
Microphone	Medium-quality, close-talking
System speaker-tuning	20–30 training utterances
Speaker adaptation	None required
Task	Document retrieval
Vocabulary	1011 words, with no selection for phonetic discriminability
Language constraints	Context-free semantic grammar, based on protocol analysis, with static branching factor of 10
Test data	23 utterances, brand-new to the system and run "blind." 7 words/utterance average, 2.6 seconds/utterance average, average fanout[a] of 40 (maximum 292)
Accuracy	9 percent sentence semantic error,[b] 19 percent sentence error (i.e., not word-for-word correct)
Computing resources	60 MIPSS (million instructions per second of speech) on a 36-bit PDP-10

[a] The *static branching factor* is the average number of words that can follow any initial sequence as defined by the grammar. The *fanout* is the number of words that can follow any initial sequence in the test sentences.

[b] An interpretation is *semantically correct* if the query generated for it by the SEMANT KS is identical to that generated for a sentence which is *word-for-word* correct.

Active development of the Hearsay-II speech system ceased at the end of 1976 with the conclusion of the speech-understanding program sponsored by DARPA [MEDR78, KLAT77]. Even though the configuration of KSs at that point was young, having been assembled in August 1976, the performance described in Table 2 comes close to meeting the ambitious goals, shown in Figure 6, established for the DARPA program in 1971 [NEWE73]. This overall performance supports our assertion that the Hearsay-II architecture can be used to integrate knowledge for resolving uncertainty. In the following sections we relate some detailed analyses of the Hearsay-II performance to the resolution of uncertainty. We finish with some comparison with the performances of the other systems described in Section 2.

3.2 Opportunistic Scheduling

In earlier KS configurations of the system, low-level processing (i.e., at the segment, syllable, and word levels) was not done in the serial, lock-step manner of steps 1, 4, and 5 of the example, that is, level-to-level, where each level is completely processed before work on the next higher level is begun. Rather, processing was opportunistic and data-directed as in the higher levels; as interesting hypotheses were generated at one level, they were immediately propagated to and processed by KSs operating at higher and lower levels. We found, however, that opportunistic processing at the lower levels was ineffective and harmful because the credibility ratings of hypotheses were insufficiently accurate to form hypothesis islands capable of focusing the search effectively. For example, even at the relatively high word level, the bottom-up hypotheses created by MOW include only about 75 percent of the words actually spoken; and the KS-assigned ratings rank each correct hypothesis on the average about 4.5 as compared with the 20 or so incorrect hypotheses that compete with it (i.e., which overlap it in time significantly). It is only with the word-sequence hypotheses that the reliability of the ratings is high enough to allow selective search.

Several experiments have shown the effectiveness of the opportunistic search. In one [HAYE77a] the opportunistic scheduling was contrasted with a strategy using no ordering of KS activations. Here, all KS precondition procedures were executed, followed by all KS activations they created; this cycle was repeated. For the utterances tested, the opportunistic strategy had a 29 percent error rate (word for word), compared with a 48 percent rate for the non-opportunistic. Also, the opportunistic strategy took less than half as much processing time.[13]

In another experiment [LESS77a] the island-driving strategy, which is opportunistic across the whole utterance, was compared with a left-to-right strategy, in which the high-level search was initiated from single-word islands in utterance-initial position. For the utterances tested, the opportunistic strategy had a 33 percent error rate as compared with 53 percent for the left-to-right; for those utterances correctly recognized by both strategies, the opportunistic one used only 70 percent as much processing time.

3.3 Use of Approximate Knowledge

In several places the Hearsay-II system uses approximate knowledge, as opposed to its more complete form also included in the system. The central notion is that even though the approximation increases the likelihood of particular decisions being incorrect, other knowledge can correct those errors, and the amount of computational resources saved by first using the approximation exceeds that required for subsequent corrections.

The organization of the POM and MOW KSs is an example. The bottom-up syllable and word-candidate generation scheme approximates WIZARD matching all words in the vocabulary at all places in the utterance, but in a fraction of the time. The errors show up as poor ratings of the can-

[13] The performance results given here and in the following sections reflect various configurations of vocabularies, grammars, test data, halting criteria, and states of development of the KSs and underlying system. Thus the absolute performance results of each experiment are not directly comparable to the performance reported in Section 3.1 or to the results of the other experiments.

grammar:	05	15	F
vocabulary			
S 250 words	err = 5.9 percent comp = 1.0 fanout = 10	err = 20.6 percent comp = 2.7 fanout = 17	err = 20.6 percent comp = 3.4 fanout = 27
M 500 words	err = 5.9 percent comp = 1.1 fanout = 18		
X 1011 words	err = 11.8 percent comp = 2.0 fanout = 36		

err = = semantic error rate
comp = = average ratio of execution time to that of S05 case, for correct utterances
fanout = = fanout of the test sentences (see note a of Table 2, Section 3.1)
N = 34 utterances

FIGURE 12. Hearsay-II performance under varying vocabularies and grammars.

didate words and as missing correct words among the candidates. The POM-MOW errors are corrected by applying WIZARD to the candidates to create good ratings and by having the PREDICT KS generate additional candidates.

Another example is the WORD-SEQ KS. Recall that it applies syntactic and acoustic-phonetic knowledge to locate sequences of words within the lattice of bottom-up words and statistical knowledge to select a few most credible sequences. The syntactic knowledge only approximates the full grammar, but takes less than 1 percent as much processing time to apply. The errors WORD-SEQ makes because of the approximation (i.e., generating some nongrammatical sequences) are corrected by applying the full grammatical knowledge of the PARSE KS, but only on the few, highly credible sequences WORD-SEQ identifies.

3.4 Adaptability of the Opportunistic Strategy

The opportunistic search strategy adapts automatically to changing conditions of uncertainty in the problem-solving process by changing the breadth of search. The basic mechanism for this is the interaction between the KS-assigned credibility ratings on hypotheses and scheduler-assigned priorities of pending KS activations. When hypotheses have been rated approximately equal, KS activations for their extension are usually scheduled together. Thus where there is ambiguity among competing hypotheses, the scheduler automatically searches with more breadth. This delays the choice among competing hypotheses until further information is brought to bear.

This adaptiveness works for changing conditions of uncertainty, whether it arises from the data or from the knowledge. The data-caused changes are evidenced by large variations in the numbers of competing hypotheses considered at various locations in an utterance, and by the large variance in the processing time needed for recognizing utterances. The results of changing conditions of knowledge constraint can be seen in Figure 12, which shows the results of one experiment varying vocabulary sizes and grammatical constraints.[14]

3.5 Performance Comparisons

It is extremely difficult to compare the reported performances of existing speech-understanding systems. Most have operated in different task environments and hence can apply different amounts of constraint

[14] Note that Figure 12 shows imperfect correlation between fanout and performance; compare, for example, X05 and SF. Fanout is an approximate measure of language complexity that reflects the average uncertainty between adjacent words. While X05 has a large fanout, it may be a simpler language to interpret than SF because most of the fanout is restricted to a few loci in the language, as opposed to the lower but more uniform uncertainty of SF.

GOAL: ACCEPT CONTINUOUS SPEECH FROM MANY COOPERATIVE SPEAKERS,

HARPY:	tested with	184	sentences from	3 Male, 2 Female	Speakers
Hearsay-II:		22		1 Male	
HWIM:		124		3 Male	
SDC:		54		1 Male	

GOAL: IN A QUIET ROOM, WITH A GOOD MIC, AND SLIGHT TUNING/SPEAKER.

HARPY:	in a computer terminal room, with a close-talking mic,	and	20	training sentences per speaker,
Hearsay-II:			20	
HWIM:			NO	
SDC:	in a quiet room, with a good mic,	and	NO	

GOAL: ACCEPTING 1000 WORDS, USING AN ARTIFICIAL SYNTAX & CONSTRAINING TASK,

HARPY:	1011 words, context-free grammar,	BF = 33	for document retrieval,
Hearsay-II:		BF = 33, 46	
HWIM:	1097 words, restricted ATN grammar,	BF = 196,	for travel planning,
SDC:	1000 words, context-free grammar,	BF = 105,	for data retrieval,

GOAL: YIELDING <10% SEMANTIC ERROR, IN A FEW TIMES REAL-TIME (=300 MIPSS)

HARPY:	yielding	5%	semantic error, using	28	million instructions per second of speech (MIPSS)
Hearsay-II:		9%,26%		85	
HWIM:		56%		500	
SDC:		76%		92	

FIGURE 13. Goals and performance for final (1976) DARPA systems. [After LEA79.]

from the task language to help the problem solving. Although some progress has been made [GOOD76, SOND78, BAHL78], there is no agreed-upon method for calibrating these differences. Also, the various systems use different speakers and recording conditions. And finally, none of the systems has reached full maturity; the amount that might be gained by further debugging and tuning is unknown, but often clearly substantial.

LEA79 contains an extensive description of the systems developed in the DARPA speech-understanding project and includes the best existing performance comparisons and evaluations. Figures 13 and 14, reproduced here from that report, show some comparison of the performances of Hearsay-II, HARPY, HWIM, and the SDC system [BERN76].[15]

The Hearsay-II and HARPY results are directly comparable, the two systems having been tested on the same tasks using the same test data. HARPY's performance here dominates Hearsay-II's in both accuracy and computation speed. And, in fact, HARPY was the only system clearly to meet and exceed the DARPA specifications (see Figure 6). It is difficult to determine the exact reasons for HARPY's higher accuracy, but we feel it is caused primarily by a combination of three factors:

(1) Because of its highly compiled efficiency, HARPY can afford to search a relatively large part of the search space. In particular, it can continue pursuing partial solutions even if they contain several low-rated segments (and its pruning threshold is explicitly set to ensure this). Thus HARPY is less prone to catastrophic errors, that is, pruning away the correct path. Hearsay-II, on the other hand, cannot afford to delay pruning decisions as long and thus is more likely to make such errors.

(2) Some knowledge sources are weaker in Hearsay-II than in HARPY. In particular, Hearsay-II's JUNCT KS has only a weak model of word juncture phenomena as compared with the more

[15] Performance of the SRI system is not included because that system was run only with a simulated bottom-end. Also, there are slight differences between the Hearsay-II performance shown in Figure 13 and that of Section 3.1; the former shows results from the official end of the DARPA project in September 1976, while the latter reflects some slight improvements made in the subsequent three months.

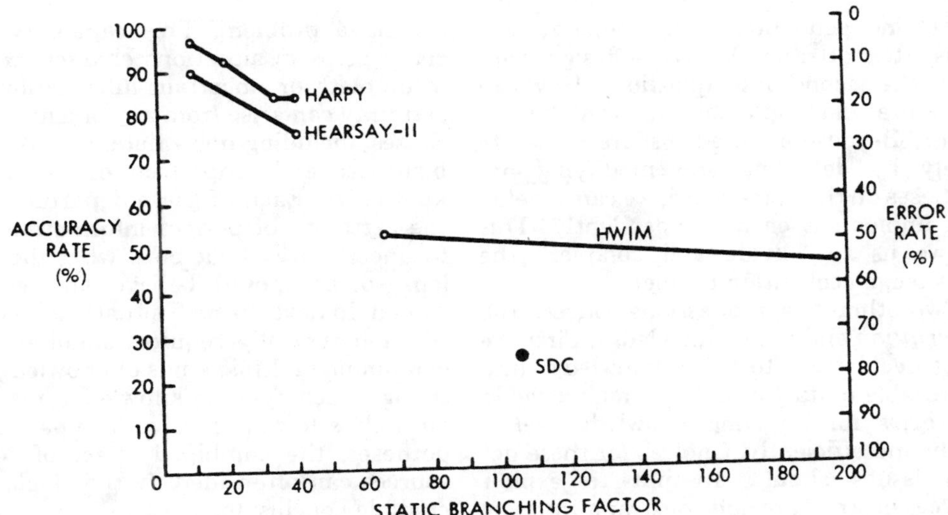

FIGURE 14 Effects of static branching factor on recognition error rate. [After LEA79.]

comprehensive and sophisticated juncture rules in HARPY. This disparity is an accident of the systems' development histories; there is no major conceptual reason why HARPY's juncture rules could not be employed by Hearsay-II.

(3) HARPY was debugged and tuned much more extensively than Hearsay-II (or any of the other DARPA SUSs, for that matter).This was facilitated by the lower processing costs for running tests. It was also helped by fixing the HARPY structure at an earlier point; Hearsay-II's KS configuration underwent a massive modification very late in the DARPA effort, as did HWIM's.

It seems clear that for a performance system in a task with a highly constrained and simply structured language, the HARPY structure is an excellent one. However, as we move to tasks that require more complex kinds of knowledge to constrain the search, we expect conceptual difficulties incorporating those kinds of knowledge into HARPY's simple integrated network representation.

4. CONCLUSIONS

Hearsay-II represents a new approach to problem solving that will prove useful in many domains other than speech. Thus far, however, we have focused on the virtues, and limitations, of Hearsay-II as a solution to the speech-understanding problem per se. In this section we consider what Hearsay-II suggests about problem-solving systems in general. To do so, we identify aspects of the Hearsay-II organization that facilitate development of "expert systems." Before concluding, we point out some apparent deficiencies of the current system that suggest avenues of further research. A more detailed discussion of these issues can be found in LESS77b.

4.1 Problem-Solving Systems

The designer of a knowledge-based problem-solving system faces several typical questions, many of which motivate the design principles evolved by Hearsay-II. The designer must first represent and structure the problem in a way that permits decomposition. A general heuristic for solving complex problems is to "divide and conquer" them. This requires methods to factor subproblems and to combine their eventual solutions. Hearsay-II, for example, divides the understanding problem in two ways: It breaks the total interpretation into separable hypotheses, and it modularizes different types of knowledge that can operate independently and cooperatively. This latter attribute helps the designer address the second basic question, "How can I acquire and implement relevant knowledge?" Because knowledge sources operate solely by detecting and modifying hypotheses on the blackboard, we can develop and implement each independently. This allows us to "divide and conquer" the knowledge acquisition problem.

Two other design questions concern the *description* and *use* of knowledge. First, we must decide how to break knowledge into executable units. Second, we must develop strategies for applying knowledge selectively and efficiently. Choices for these design issues should attempt to exploit sources of structure and constraint intrinsic to the problem domain and knowledge available about it. In the current context this means that a speech-understanding system should exploit many alternative types of speech knowledge to reduce uncertainty inherent in the signal. Moreover, the different types of knowledge should apply, ideally, in a best-first manner. That is, the most credible hypotheses should stimulate searches for the most likely adjoining hypotheses first. To this end, the Hearsay-II focusing scheduler considers the quality of hypotheses and potential predictions in each temporal interval and then selectively executes only the most marginally productive KS actions. Accomplishing this type of control required several new sorts of mechanisms. These included explicit interlinked hypothesis representations, declarative descriptions of KS stimulus and response frames, a dynamic problem state description, and a prioritized schedule of pending KS instantiations.

4.2 Specific Advantages of Hearsay-II as a Problem-Solving System

This paper has covered an extensive set of issues and details. From these we believe the reader should have gained an appreciation of Hearsay-II's principal benefits, summarized briefly as follows.

Multiple Sources of Knowledge

Hearsay-II provides a framework for diverse types of knowledge to cooperate in solving a problem. This capability especially helps in situations characterized by incomplete or uncertain information. Uncertainty can arise from any of a number of causes, including noisy data, apparent ambiguities, and imperfect or incomplete knowledge. Each of these departures from the certainty of perfect information leads to uncertainty about both what the problem solver should believe and what it should do next. In such situations finding a solution typically requires simultaneously combining multiple kinds of knowledge. Although each type of knowledge may rule out only a few alternative (competing) hypotheses, the combined effect of several sources can often identify the single most credible conclusion.

Multiple Levels of Abstraction

Solving problems in an intelligent manner often requires using descriptions at different levels of abstraction. After first finding an approximate or gross solution, a problem solver may work quickly toward a refined, detailed solution consistent with the rough solution. In its use of multiple levels of abstraction, Hearsay-II provides rudimentary facilities for such variable-granularity reasoning. In the speech task particularly, the different levels correspond to separable domains of reasoning. Hypotheses about word sequences must satisfy the constraints of higher level syntactic phrase-structure rules. Once these are satisfied, testing more detailed or finely tuned word juncture relations would be justified. Of course the multiple levels of abstraction also support staged decision making that proceeds from lower level hypotheses up to higher levels. Levels in such bottom-up processing support a different type of function, namely, the sharing of intermediate results, discussed separately in the following paragraph.

Shared Partial Solutions

The blackboard and hypothesis structures allow the knowledge sources to represent and share partial results. This proves especially desirable for complex problems where no a priori knowledge can reliably foretell the best sequence of necessary decisions. Different attempts to solve the same problem may require solving identical subproblems. In the speech domain these problems correspond to comparable hypotheses (same level, type, time). Hearsay-II provides capabilities for the KSs to recognize a hypothesis of interest and to incorporate it into alternative competing hypotheses at higher levels. Subsequent changes to the partial result then propagate to all of the higher level constructs that contain it.

Independent Knowledge Sources Limited to Data-Directed Interactions

Separating the diverse sources of knowledge into independent program modules provides several benefits. Different people can create, test, and modify KSs independently. In addition to the ordinary benefits of modularity in programming, this independence allows human specialists (e.g., phoneticians, linguists) to operationalize their diverse types of knowledge without concern for the conceptual framework and detailed behavior of other possible modules. Although the programming style and epistemological nature of several KSs may vary widely, Hearsay-II provides for all of them a single uniform programming environment. This environment constrains the KSs to operate in a data-directed manner—reading hypotheses from the blackboard when situations of interest occur, processing them to draw inferences, and recording new or modified hypotheses on the blackboard for others to process further. This paradigm facilitates problem-oriented interactions while minimizing complicated and costly design interactions.

Incremental Formation of Solutions

Problem solving in Hearsay-II proceeds incrementally through the accretion and integration of partial solutions. KSs generate hypotheses based on current data and knowledge. By integrating adjacent and consistent hypotheses into larger composites, the system develops increasingly credible and comprehensive partial solutions. These in turn stimulate focused efforts that drive the overall system toward the final goal, one most credible interpretation spanning the entire interval of speech. By allowing information to accumulate in this piecemeal fashion, Hearsay-II provides a convenient framework for heuristic problem solving. Diverse heuristic methods can contribute various types of assistance in the effort to eliminate uncertainty, to recognize portions of the sequence, and to model the speaker's intentions. Because these diverse methods exist in the form of independent, cooperating KSs, each addition to the current problem solution consists simply of an update to the blackboard.

Opportunistic Problem-Solving Behavior

Whenever good algorithms do not exist for solving a problem, we must apply heuristic methods or "rules-of-thumb" to search for a solution. In problems where a large number of data exist to which a large number of alternative heuristics potentially apply, we need to choose each successive action carefully. We refer to a system's ability to exploit selectively its best data and most promising methods as "opportunistic" problem solving [NII78, HAYE79b]. Hearsay-II developed several mechanisms to support such opportunistic behavior. In particular, its focus policies and prioritized scheduling allocate computation resources first to those KSs that exploit the most credible hypotheses, promise the most significant increments to the solution, and use the most reliable and inexpensive methods. Similar needs to focus intelligently will arise in many comparably rich and complex problem domains.

Experimentation in System Development

Whenever we attempt to solve a previously unsolved problem, the need for experimentation arises. In the speech-understanding task, for example, we generated several different types of KSs and experimentally tested a variety of alternative system configurations (specific sets of KSs) [LESS77b]. A solution to the overall problem depended on both developing powerful individual KSs and organizing multiple KSs to cooperate effectively to reduce uncertainty. These requirements necessitated a trial-and-error evaluation of alternative system designs. Throughout these explorations, the basic Hearsay-II structure proved robust and sufficient. Alternative configurations were constructed with relative ease by inserting or removing specific KSs. Moreover, we could test radically different high-level control concepts (e.g., depth-first versus breadth-first versus left-to-right searches) simply by changing the focus policy KS. The need for this kind of flexibility will probably arise in many future state-of-the-art problem-solving tasks. To support this flexibility, systems must be able to apply the same KSs in different orders and to schedule them according to varying selection criteria. These requirements directly motivate KS data-directed independence, as well as autonomous scheduling KSs that can evaluate the probable effects of potential KS actions. Because it supports these needs, Hearsay-II provides an excellent environment for experimental research and development in speech and other complex tasks.

4.3 Disadvantages of the Hearsay-II Approach

We can identify two different but related weaknesses of the Hearsay-II approach to problem solving. One weakness derives from the system's generality, and the other concerns its computational efficiency. Each of these is considered briefly in turn.

Generality Impedes Specialization and Limits Power

The Hearsay-II approach suggests a very general problem-solving paradigm. Every inference process reads data from the blackboard and places a new hypothesis also on the blackboard. Thus blackboard accesses mediate each decision step. While this proved desirable for structuring communications between different KSs, it proved undesirable for most intermediate decision tasks arising within a single KS. Most KSs employed private, stylized internal data structures different from the single uniform blackboard links and hypotheses. For example, the word recognizer used specialized sequential networks, whereas the word sequence recognizer exploited a large bit-matrix of word adjacencies. Each KS also stored intermediate results, useful for its own internal searches, in appropriately distinctive data structures. Attempts to coerce these specialized activities into the general blackboard-mediated style of Hearsay-II either failed completely or caused intolerable performance degradation [LESS77b].

Interpretive Versus Compiled Knowledge

Hearsay-II uses knowledge interpretively. That is, it actively evaluates alternative actions, chooses the best for the current situation, and then applies the procedure associated with the most promising KS instantiation. Such deliberation takes time and requires many fairly sophisticated mechanisms; its expense can be justified whenever an adequate, explicit algorithm does not exist for the same task. Whenever such an algorithm emerges, equal or greater performance and efficiency may be obtained by compiling the algorithm and executing it directly. For example, recognizing restricted vocabulary and grammatical spoken sentences from limited syntax can now be accomplished faster by techniques other than those in Hearsay-II. As described in Section 2.3, by compiling all possible interlevel substitutions (sentence to phrase to word to phone to segment) into one enormous finite-state Markov network, the HARPY system uses a modified dynamic programming search to find the one network path that most closely approximates the segmented speech signal. This type of systematic, compiled, and broad search becomes increasingly desirable as problem-solving knowledge improves. Put another way, once a satisfactory specific method for solving any problem is found, the related procedure can be "algorithmetized," compiled, and applied repetitively. In such a case the flexibility of a system like Hearsay-II may no longer be needed.

4.4 Other Applications of the Hearsay-II Framework

Both the advantages and disadvantages of Hearsay-II have stimulated additional research. Several researchers have applied the general framework to problems outside the speech domain, and others have begun to develop successors to the Hearsay-II system. We will briefly discuss one of these new applications and then mention the other types of activities underway.

Although the Hearsay-II framework developed around an understanding task, B. and F. Hayes-Roth et al. have extended many of its principal features to develop a model of planning [HAYE79b, HAYE79c]. While understanding tasks require "interpretive" or "analytic" processes, planning belongs to a complementary set of "generative" or "synthetic" activities. The principal features of the Hearsay-II system which make it attractive as a problem-solving model for speech understanding also suggest it as a model of planning.

The planning application shares all the principal features of the Hearsay-II system summarized in Section 4.2, but, as Figure 15 suggests, the planning model differs from the Hearsay-II framework in several ways. In particular, the designers found it convenient to distinguish five separate blackboard "planes," reflecting five qualitatively different sorts of decisions. The Plan plane corresponds most closely to Hearsay-II's single blackboard, holding the decisions that combine to form a solution to the planning problem, i.e., what low-level operations can be aggregated to achieve the high-level outcomes of the plan. These kinds of decisions in generative tasks can be thought of as the dual of the successively higher level, more aggregated hypotheses constituting the blackboard for interpretation tasks. In the speech task, corresponding hypotheses ex-

FIGURE 15 The planning blackboard and the actions of illustrative knowledge sources. [From HAYE79b.]

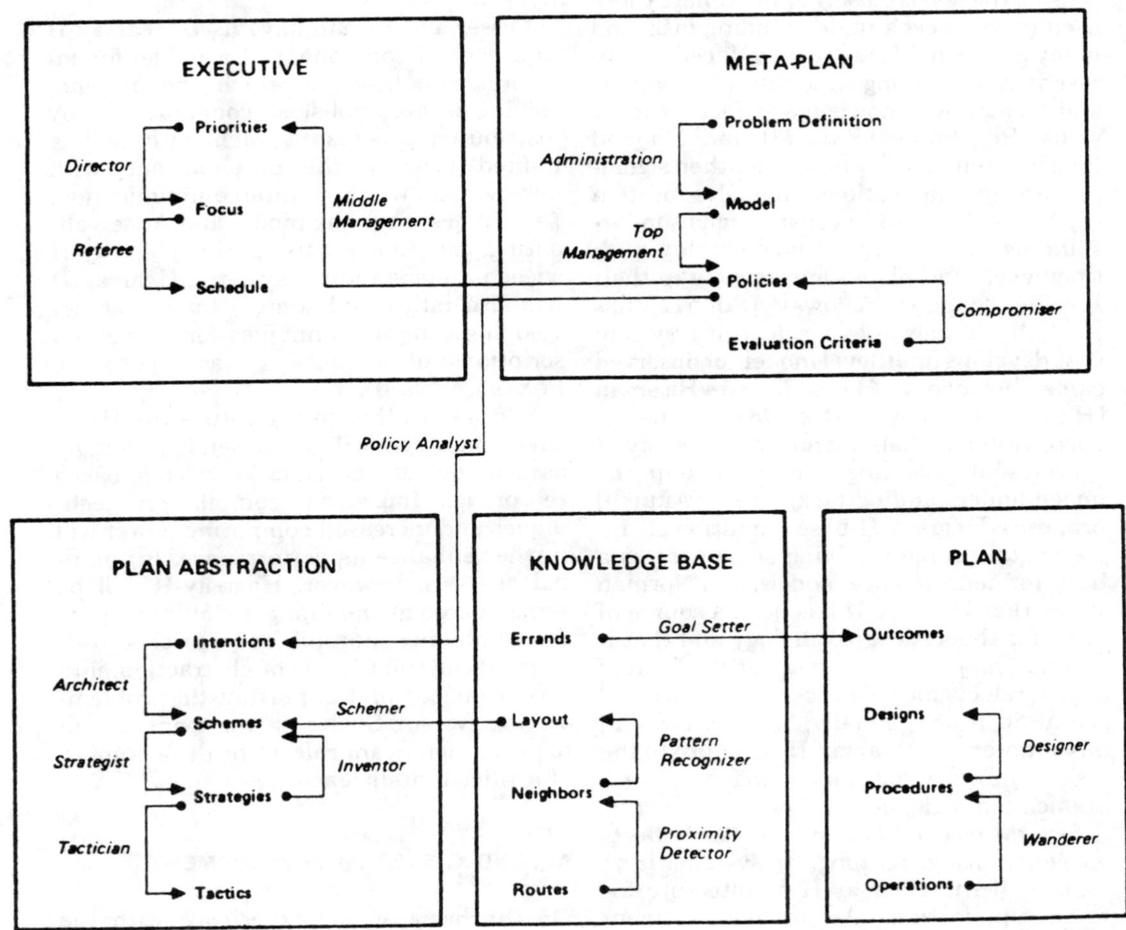

press how low-level segments and phones can be aggregated to form the high-level phrases and sentences intended by the speaker. The other four planes of the planning blackboard hold intermediate decisions that enter into the planning process in various ways. For example, based on the Hearsay-II experience with selective attention strategies, resource allocation strategies were formalized and associated explicitly with an Executive plane.

Although the planning model is the only current application of the Hearsay-II framework to generative tasks, several interesting applications that transfer the approach to other interpretation problems have been made. Rumelhart [RUME76] has proposed to apply the Hearsay-II framework to model human reading behavior. In this application only one blackboard plane is used, the levels closely approximate those used in the speech-understanding task, and many additional KSs are introduced to represent how varying amounts of linguistic and semantic knowledge affect reading skills. Engelmore [ENGE77] and Nii and Feigenbaum [NII78] describe other signal-processing applications, namely, protein crystallography and acoustic signal understanding. These applications employ multiple levels and planes appropriate to their specific domains. Soloway [SOLO77] has used the framework in a learning system that develops multilevel models of observed game behaviors. Hanson and Riseman [HANS78] and Levine [LEVI78] have developed systems that mirror the Hearsay-II speech-understanding components in the image-understanding task. Arbib [ARBI79] proposes Hearsay-II-based multilevel, incremental problem-solving structures as a basis for neuroscience models, and Norman states that Hearsay-II has been a source of ideas for theoretical psychology and that it "fulfills [his]. . .intuitions about the form of a general cognitive processing structure" [NORM80, p. 383]. Finally, Mann [MANN79] has adapted the Hearsay-II structure to the task of interpreting human-machine communication dialogues.

Several researchers have focused efforts on generalizing, refining, or systematizing aspects of the Hearsay-II architecture for wider application. As previously mentioned, B. and F. Hayes-Roth have formalized some aspects of meta-planning and executive control and have treated this type of problem solving within one uniform framework. Nii [NII79] has developed a system that assists a programmer in developing a new special-purpose variant of a Hearsay-II system suitable for some particular new task. Balzer and others [BALZ80] have implemented a more formalized, domain-independent version of Hearsay-II and are applying it to an automatic-programming-like task. This system uses one blackboard for interpretation and another for scheduling decisions, in a manner akin to that proposed for the Executive decisions in the Hayes-Roth planning system. In a similar way, Stefik uses three distinct planes to record the plan, meta-plan, and executive decisions arising in a system that incrementally plans genetic experiments [STEF80].

Lesser and Erman have used Hearsay-II as a central component in a model for interpretation tasks in which the problem solving is accomplished cooperatively by distributed processors, each with only a limited view of the problem and with narrow-bandwidth intercommunication; LESS79 describes the model and some validating experiments using the Hearsay-II speech-understanding system. Hearsay-II has also influenced some attempts at developing general techniques for formal descriptions of complex systems [FOX79a, FOX79b, LESS80].

We predict that in the future the Hearsay-II paradigm will be chosen increasingly as a model of heuristic, knowledge-based reasoning. Improved compilation techniques and increased computing power will further enhance its performance. In the final analysis, however, Hearsay-II will be remembered as the first general framework for combining multiple sources of knowledge, at different levels of abstraction, into a coordinated and opportunistic problem-solving system. Such systems seem certain to play a significant role in the development of artificial intelligence.

APPENDIX. SYSTEM DEVELOPMENT

On the basis of our experience with the Hearsay-I system [REDD73a, REDD73b], at the beginning of the Hearsay-II effort in 1973 we expected to require and evolve types of knowledge and interaction patterns whose details could not be anticipated. Because of this, the development of the system was marked by much experimentation and redesign. This uncertainty characterizes the development of knowledge-based systems. Instead of designing a specific speech-understanding system, we considered Hearsay-II as a model for a class of systems and a framework within which specific configurations of that general model could be constructed and studied [LESS75, ERMA75].

On the basis of this approach a high-level programming system was designed to provide an environment for programming knowledge sources, configuring groups of them into systems, and executing them. Because KSs interact via the blackboard (triggering on patterns, accessing hypotheses, and making modifications) and the blackboard is uniformly structured, KS interactions are also uniform. Thus one set of facilities can serve all KSs. Facilities are provided for

- defining levels on the blackboard,
- configuring groups of KSs into executable systems,
- accessing and modifying hypotheses on the blackboard,
- activating and scheduling KSs,
- debugging and analyzing the performance of KSs.

These facilities collectively form the Hearsay-II "kernel." One can think of the Hearsay-II kernel as a high-level system for programming speech-understanding systems of a type conforming to the underlying Hearsay-II model.

Hearsay-II is implemented in the SAIL programming system [REIS76], an Algol-60 dialect with a sophisticated compile-time macro facility as well as a large number of data structures (including lists and sets) and control modes which are implemented fairly efficiently. The Hearsay-II kernel provides a high-level environment for KSs at compile-time by extending SAIL's data types and syntax through declarations of procedure calls, global variables, and macros. This extended SAIL provides an explicit structure for specifying a KS and its interaction with other KSs (through the blackboard). The high-level environment also provides mechanisms for KSs to specify (usually in nonprocedural ways) information used by the kernel when configuring a system, scheduling KS activity, and controlling researcher interaction with the system.

The knowledge in a KS is represented using SAIL data structures and code, in whatever stylized form the KS developer chooses. The kernel environment provides the facilities for structuring the interface between this knowledge and other KSs, via the blackboard. For example, the syntax KS contains a grammar for the specialized task language to be recognized; this grammar is coded in a compact network form. The KS also contains procedures for searching this network, for example, to parse a sequence of words. The kernel provides facilities (1) for triggering this KS when new word hypotheses appear on the blackboard, (2) for the KS to read those word hypotheses (in order to find the sequence of words to parse), and (3) for the KS to create new hypotheses on the blackboard, indicating the structure of the parse.

Active development of Hearsay-II extended for three years. About 40 KSs were developed, each a one- or two-person effort lasting from two months to three years. The KSs range from about 5 to 100 pages of source code (with 30 pages typical), and each KS has up to about 50 kbytes of information in its local database.

The kernel is about 300 pages of code, roughly one-third of which is the declarations and macros that create the extended environment for KSs. The remainder of the code implements the architecture: primarily activation and scheduling of KSs, maintenance of the blackboard, and a variety of other standard utilities. During the three years of active development, an average of about two full-time-equivalent research programmers were responsible for the implementation, modification, and maintenance of the kernel. Included during this period were a half-dozen major reimplementations and scores of minor ones; these changes usually were specializations or selective optimizations, designed as experience with the system led to a better understanding of the usage of the various constructs. During this same period about eight full-time-equivalent researchers were using the system to develop KSs.

Implementation of the first version of the kernel began in the autumn of 1973, and was completed by two people in four months. The first major KS configuration, though incomplete, was running in early 1975. The first complete configuration, "C1," ran in January 1976. This configuration had very poor performance, with more than 90 percent sentence errors over a 250-word vocabulary. Experience with this configuration led to a substantially different KS configuration, "C2," completed in September 1976. C2 is the configuration described in this paper.

Implementing a general framework has a potential disadvantage: the start-up cost is relatively high. However, if the framework is suitable, it can be used to explore different configurations within the model more easily than if each configuration were built in an ad hoc manner. Additionally, a natural result of the continued use of any high-level system is its improvement in terms of enhanced facilities, increased stability, reliability, and efficiency, and greater familiarity on the part of the researchers using it.

Hearsay-II has been successful in this respect; we believe that the total cost of creating the high-level system and using it to develop KS configurations C1 and C2 (and intermediate configurations) was less than it would have been to generate them in an ad hoc manner. It should be stressed that the construction of even one configuration is itself an experimental and evolving process. The high-level programming system provides a framework, both conceptual and physical, for developing a configuration in an incremental fashion. The speed with which C2 was developed is some indication of the advantage of this system-design approach. A more detailed description of the development philosophy and tools can be found in ERMA78, and a discussion of the relationships between the C1 and C2 configurations can be found in LESS77b.

ACKNOWLEDGMENTS

The success of the Hearsay-II project depended on many persons, especially the following members of the Carnegie-Mellon University Computer Science Department "Speech Group": Christina Adam, Mark Birnbaum, Robert Cronk, Richard Fennell, Mark Fox, Gregory Gill, Henry Goldberg, Gary Goodman, Bruce Lowerre, Paul Masulis, David McKeown, Jack Mostow, Linda Shockey, Richard Smith, and Richard Suslick. Daniel Corkill, David Taylor, and the reviewers made helpful comments on early drafts of this paper.

Figure 1 is adapted from A. Newell, "A tutorial on speech understanding systems," in *Speech recognition: Invited papers of the IEEE symposium*, D. R. Reddy, Ed., Academic Press, New York, 1975. Figure 6 is adapted from M. F. Medress et al., "Speech understanding systems, Report of a steering committee," *Artif. Intell.* **9** (1978). Figure 7 is reprinted from J. J. Wolf and W. A. Woods, "The HWIM speech understanding system," in *Trends in speech recognition*, W. A. Lea, Ed., © 1980, by permission of Prentice-Hall, Inc., Englewood Cliffs, N.J. Figures 8–11 are reprinted from B. T. Lowerre and R. Reddy, "The HARPY speech understanding system," in *Trends in speech recognition*, W. A. Lea, Ed., © 1980, by permission of Prentice-Hall, Inc., Englewood Cliffs, N.J. Figure 15 originally appeared in B. Hayes-Roth and F. Hayes-Roth, "A cognitive model of planning," *Cognitive science*, 1979, **3** 275–310. Ablex Publishing Corporation, Norwood, N.J.

REFERENCES

ARBI79 ARBIB, M. A., AND CAPLAN, D. "Neurolinguistics must be computational," *Behav. Brain Sci.* **2**, 3 (1979).

BAHL76 BAHL, L. R., BAKER, J. K., COHEN, P. S., DIXON, N. R., JELINEK, F., MERCER, R. L., AND SILVERMAN, H. F. "Preliminary results on the performance of a system for the automatic recognition of continuous speech," in *1976 IEEE Int. Conf. Acoustics, Speech, and Signal Processing*, Philadelphia, Apr. 1976, pp. 425–433.

BAHL78 BAHL, L. R., BAKER, J. K., COHEN, P. S., COLE, A. G., JELINEK, F., LEWIS, B. L., AND MERCER, R. L. "Automatic recognition of continuously spoken sentences from a finite state grammar," in *Proc. IEEE Int. Conf. Acoustics, Speech, and Signal Processing*, Tulsa, Okla., Apr. 1978, pp. 418–421.

BALZ80 BALZER, R., ERMAN, L. D., AND WILLIAMS, C. *Hearsay-III: A domain-independent base for knowledge-based problem-solving*, Tech. Rep., USC/Information Sciences Institute, Marina del Rey, Calif., 1980. To appear.

BARN77 BARNETT, J. A., AND BERNSTEIN, M. I. *Knowledge-based systems: A tutorial*, Tech. Rep. TM-(L)-5903/000/00 (NTIS: AD/A-044-883), System Development Corp., Santa Monica, Calif., June 1977.

BERN76 BERNSTEIN, M. I. *Interactive systems research: Final report to the Director, Advanced Research Projects Agency*, Tech. Rep. TM-5243/006/00, System Development Corp., Santa Monica, Calif., Sept. 1976.

BURT76 BURTON, R. R. *Semantic grammar: An engineering technique for constructing natural language understanding systems*, Tech. Rep. BBN Rep. No. 3453, Bolt Beranek and Newman, Cambridge, Mass., 1976.

CMU77 CMU COMPUTER SCIENCE SPEECH GROUP. *Summary of the CMU five-year ARPA effort in speech understanding research*, Tech. Rep., Computer Science Dep., Carnegie-Mellon Univ., Pittsburgh, Pa., 1977.

CRON77 CRONK, R. "Word pair adjacency acceptance procedure in Hearsay-II," in CMU77, pp. 15–16.

DUDA78 DUDA, R. O., HART, P. E., NILSSON, N. J., AND SOUTHERLAND, G. L. "Semantic network representation in rule-based inference systems," in *Pattern-directed inference systems*, D. A. Waterman and F. Hayes-Roth, Eds., Academic Press, New York, 1978, pp. 203–222.

ENGE77 ENGELMORE, R. S., AND NII, H. P. *A knowledge-based system for the interpretation of protein X-ray crystallographic data*, Tech. Rep. Stan-CS-77-589, Computer Science Dep., Stanford Univ., Stanford, Calif., 1977.

ERMA75 ERMAN L. D., AND LESSER, V. R. "A multi-level organization for problem solving using many diverse cooperating sources of knowledge," in *Proc. 4th Int. Jt. Conf. Artificial Intelligence*, Tbilisi, USSR, 1975, pp. 483–490.

ERMA78 ERMAN, L. D., AND LESSER, V. R. "System engineering techniques for artificial intelligence systems," in *Computer vision systems*, A. Hanson and E. Riseman, Eds., Academic Press, New York, 1978, pp. 37–45.

ERNS69 ERNST, G., AND NEWELL, A. *GPS: A case study in generality and problem solving*, Academic Press, New York, 1969.

FEIG71 FEIGENBAUM, E. A., BUCHANAN, B. G., AND LEDERBERG, J. "On generality and problem solving: A case study using the DENDRAL program," in *Machine intelligence 6*, D. Michie, Ed., Edinburgh Univ. Press, Edinburgh, Scotland, 1971.

FEIG77 FEIGENBAUM, E. A. "The art of artificial intelligence: Themes and case studies of knowledge engineering," in *Proc. 5th Int. Jt. Conf. Artificial Intelligence*, Cambridge, Mass., 1977, pp. 1014–1029.

FOX77 FOX, M. S., AND MOSTOW, D. J. "Maximal consistent interpretations of errorful data in hierarchically modelled domains," in *Proc. 5th Int. Jt. Conf. Artificial Intelligence*, Cambridge, Mass., 1977, pp. 65–171.

FOX79a FOX, M. S. "An organizational view of distributed systems," in *Proc. Int. Conf. Systems and Cybernetics*, Denver, Colo., Oct. 1979.

FOX79b FOX, M. S. *Organization structuring: Designing large, complex software*, Tech. Rep. CMU-CS-79-115, Computer Science Dep., Carnegie-Mellon Univ., Pittsburgh, Pa., 1979.

GILL78 GILL, G., GOLDBERG, H., REDDY, R., AND YEGNANARAYANA, B. *A recursive segmentation procedure for continuous speech*, Tech. Rep. CMU-CS-78-134, Computer Science Dep., Carnegie-Mellon Univ., Pittsburgh, Pa., May 1978.

GOLD77 GOLDBERG, H., REDDY, R., AND GILL, G. "The ZAPDASH parameters, feature extraction, segmentation, and labeling for speech understanding systems," in CMU77, pp. 10–11.

GOOD76 GOODMAN, G. *Analysis of languages for man-machine voice communication*, Tech. Rep., Computer Science Dep., Carnegie-Mellon Univ., Pittsburgh, Pa., May 1976.

HANS78 HANSON, A. R., AND RISEMAN, E. M. "VISIONS: A computer system for interpreting scenes," in *Computer vision systems*, A. Hanson and E. Riseman, Eds., Academic Press, New York, 1978, pp. 303–333.

HARR74 HARRIS, L. R. "The heuristic search under conditions of error," *Artif. Intell.* **5**, 3 (1974), 217–234.

HAYE75 HAYES-ROTH, F., AND MOSTOW, D. J. "An automatically compilable recognition network for structured patterns," in *Proc. 4th Int. Jt. Conf. Artificial Intelligence*, Tbilisi, USSR, 1975, pp. 246–252.

HAYE77a HAYES-ROTH, F., AND LESSER, V. R. "Focus of attention in the Hearsay-II system," in *Proc. 5th Int. Jt. Conf. Artificial Intelligence*, Cambridge, Mass., 1977, pp. 27–35.

HAYE77b HAYES-ROTH, F., ERMAN, L. D., FOX, M., AND MOSTOW, D. J. "Syntactic processing in Hearsay-II," in CMU77, pp. 16–18.

HAYE77c HAYES-ROTH, F., GILL, G., AND MOSTOW, D. J. "Discourse analysis and task performance in the Hearsay-II speech understanding system," in CMU77, pp. 24–28.

HAYE77d HAYES-ROTH, F., LESSER, V. R., MOSTOW, D. J., AND ERMAN, L. D. "Policies for rating hypotheses, halting, and selecting a solution in Hearsay-II," in CMU77, pp. 19–24.

HAYE78a HAYES-ROTH, F., WATERMAN, D. A., AND LENAT, D. B. "Principles of pattern-directed inference systems," in *Pattern-directed inference systems*, D. A. Waterman and F. Hayes-Roth, Eds., Academic Press, New York, 1978.

HAYE78b HAYES-ROTH, F. "The role of partial and best matches in knowledge systems," in *Pattern-directed inference systems*, D. A. Waterman and F. Hayes-Roth, Eds., Academic Press, New York, 1978.

HAYE79a HAYES-ROTH, B., AND HAYES-ROTH, F. *Cognitive processes in planning*, Tech. Rep. R-2366-ONR, The RAND Corp., Santa Monica, Calif., 1979.

HAYE79b HAYES-ROTH, B., AND HAYES-ROTH, F. "A cognitive model of planning," *Cognitive Sci.* **3** (1979), 275–310.

HAYE79c HAYES-ROTH, B., HAYES-ROTH, F., ROSENSCHEIN, S., AND CAMMARATA, S. "Modeling planning as an incremental opportunistic process," in *Proc. 6th Int. Jt.*

Conf. Artificial Intelligence, Tokyo, 1979, pp. 375–383.

HAYE80 HAYES-ROTH, F. "Syntax, semantics, and pragmatics in speech understanding," in *Trends in speech recognition*, W. A. Lea, Ed., Prentice-Hall, Englewood Cliffs, N.J., 1980.

ITAK75 ITAKURA, F. "Minimum prediction residual principle applied to speech recognition," *IEEE Trans. Acoust., Speech, Signal Proc.* **23** (1975), 67–72.

KLAT77 KLATT, D. H. "Review of the ARPA speech understanding project," *J. Acoust. Soc. Am.* **62** (Dec. 1977), 1345–1366.

LEA79 LEA, W. A., AND SHOUP, J. E. *Review of the ARPA SUR Project and survey of current technology in speech understanding*, Final Rep., Office of Naval Research Contract No. N00014-77-C-0570, Speech Communications Research Lab., Los Angeles, Calif., Jan. 1979.

LEA80 LEA, W. A., ED. *Trends in speech recognition*, Prentice-Hall, Englewood Cliffs, N.J., 1980.

LESS75 LESSER, V. R., FENNELL, R. D., ERMAN, L. D., AND REDDY, D. R. "Organization of the Hearsay-II speech understanding system," *IEEE Trans. Acous., Speech, Signal Proc.* **23** (1975), 11–23.

LESS77a LESSER, V. R., HAYES-ROTH, F., BIRNBAUM, M., AND CRONK, R. "Selection of word islands in the Hearsay-II speech understanding system," in *Proc. IEEE Int. Conf. Acoustics, Speech, and Signal Processing*, Hartford, Conn., 1977, pp. 791–794.

LESS77b LESSER, V. R., AND ERMAN, L. D. "A retrospective view of the Hearsay-II architecture," in *Proc. 5th Int. Joint Conf. Artificial Intelligence*, Cambridge, Mass., 1977, pp. 790–800.

LESS79 LESSER, V. R., AND ERMAN, L. D. "An experiment in distributed interpretation," in *1st Int. Conf. Distributed Computing Systems*, IEEE Computer Society, Huntsville, Ala., Oct. 1979, pp. 553–571.

LESS80 LESSER, V. R., PAVLIN, J., AND REED, S. *Quantifying and simulating the behavior of knowledge-based systems*, Tech. Rep., Dep. Computer and Information Sciences, Univ. Massachusetts, Amherst, Mass., 1980.

LEVI78 LEVINE, M. D. "A knowledge-based computer vision system," in *Computer vision systems*, A. Hanson and E. Riseman, Eds., Academic Press, New York, 1978, pp. 335–352.

LOWE76 LOWERRE, B. T. *The HARPY speech recognition system*, Ph.D. thesis, Computer Science Dep., Carnegie-Mellon Univ., Pittsburgh, Pa., 1976.

LOWE80 LOWERRE, B. T., AND REDDY, R. "The HARPY speech understanding system," in *Trends in speech recognition*, W. A. Lea, Ed., Prentice-Hall, Englewood Cliffs, N.J., 1980, Chap. 15.

LOWR80 LOWRANCE, J. *Dependence-graph models of evidential support*, Ph.D. thesis, Dep. Computer and Information Sciences, Univ. Massachusetts, 1980 (forthcoming).

MANN79 MANN, W. C. "Design for dialogue comprehension," in *17th Ann. Meeting Assoc. Computational Linguistics*, La Jolla, Calif., Aug. 1979.

MCKE77 MCKEOWN, D. M. "Word verification in the Hearsay-II speech understanding system," in *Proc. IEEE Int. Conf. Acoustics, Speech, and Signal Processing*, Hartford, Conn., 1977, pp. 795–798.

MEDR78 MEDRESS, M. F., COOPER, F. S., FORGIE, J. W., GREEN, C. C., KLATT, D. H., O'MALLEY, M. H., NEUBURG, E. P., NEWELL, A., REDDY, D. R., RITEA, B., SHOUP-HUMMEL, J. E., WALKER, D. E., AND WOODS, W. A. "Speech understanding systems: Report of a steering committee," *Artif. Intell.* **9** (1978), 307–316.

MOST77 MOSTOW, D. J. "A halting condition and related pruning heuristic for combinatorial search," in CMU77, pp. 158–166.

NEWE69 NEWELL, A. "Heuristic programming: Ill-structured problems," in *Progress in operations research 3*, J. Aronofsky, Ed., Wiley, New York, 1969, pp. 360–414.

NEWE73 NEWELL, A., BARNETT, J., FORGIE, J., GREEN, C., KLATT, D., LICKLIDER, J. C. R., MUNSON, J., REDDY, R., AND WOODS, W. *Speech understanding systems: Final report of a study group*, North-Holland, Amsterdam, 1973.

NEWE75 NEWELL, A., "A tutorial on speech understanding systems," in *Speech recognition: Invited papers of the IEEE symposium*, D. R. Reddy, Ed., Academic Press, New York, 1975, pp. 3–54.

NEWE77 NEWELL, A., MCDERMOTT, J., AND FORGIE, C. *Artificial intelligence: A self-paced introductory course*, Computer Science Dep., Carnegie-Mellon Univ., Pittsburgh, Pa., 1977.

NEWE80 NEWELL, A. "HARPY, production systems and human cognition," in *Perception and production of fluent speech*, R. Cole, Ed., L. Erlbaum, Hillsdale, N.J., 1980, Chap. 11.

NII78 NII, H. P., AND FEIGENBAUM, E. A. "Rule-based understanding of signals," in *Pattern-directed inference systems*, D. A. Waterman and F. Hayes-Roth, Eds., Academic Press, New York, 1978.

NII79 NII, H. P., AND AIELLO, N. "AGE (Attempt to Generalize): A knowledge-based program for building knowledge-based programs," in *Proc. 6th Int. Jt. Conf. Artificial Intelligence*, Tokyo, Feb. 1979, pp. 645–655.

NILS71 NILSSON, N. *Problem-solving methods in artificial intelligence*, McGraw-Hill, New York, 1971.

NORM80 NORMAN, D. A. "Copycat science or does the mind really work by table look-up?," in *Perception and production of fluent speech*, R. Cole, Ed., L. Erlbaum, Hillsdale, N.J., 1980, Chap. 12.

POHL70 POHL, I. "First results on the effects of error in heuristic search," in *Machine in-*

telligence 5, B. Meltzer and D. Michie, Eds., Edinburgh Univ. Press, Edinburgh, Scotland, 1970.

POHL77 POHL, I. "Practical and theoretical considerations in heuristic search algorithms," in *Machine intelligence 8*, E. Elcock and D. Michie, Eds., Ellis Horwood, Chichester, England, 1977.

REDD73a REDDY, D. R., ERMAN, L. D., AND NEELY, R. B. "A model and a system for machine recognition of speech," *IEEE Trans. Audio and Electroacoustics* **AU-21** (1973), 229–238.

REDD73b REDDY, D. R., ERMAN, L. D., FENNELL, R. D., AND NEELY, R. B. "The Hearsay speech understanding system: An example of the recognition process," in *Proc. 3rd Int. Jt. Conf. Artificial Intelligence*, Stanford, Calif., 1973, pp. 185–193.

REDD75 REDDY, D. R., ED. *Speech recognition: Invited papers presented at the 1974 IEEE Symposium*, Academic Press, New York, 1975.

REDD76 REDDY, D. R. "Speech recognition by machine: A review," *Proc. IEEE* **64** (Apr. 1976), 501–531.

REIS76 REISER, J. F. *SAIL*, Tech. Rep. AIM-289, AI Lab., Stanford Univ., Stanford, Calif., 1976.

RUBI78 RUBIN, S. *The ARGOS image understanding system*, Ph.D. thesis, Computer Science Dep., Carnegie-Mellon Univ., Pittsburgh, Pa., 1978.

RUME76 RUMELHART, D. E. *Toward an interactive model of reading*, Tech. Rep. 56, Center for Human Information Processing, Univ. California, San Diego, 1976.

SACE74 SACERDOTI, E. E. "Planning in a hierarchy of abstraction spaces," *Artif. Intell.* **5** (1974), 115–135.

SHOR75 SHORTLIFFE, E. H., AND BUCHANAN, B. G. "A model of inexact reasoning in medicine," *Math. Bio. Sci.* **23** (1975).

SHOR76 SHORTLIFFE, E. *Computer-based medical consultation: MYCIN*, Elsevier, New York, 1976.

SMIT76 SMITH, A. R. "Word hypothesization in the Hearsay-II speech system," in *Proc. IEEE Int. Conf. Acoustics, Speech, and Signal Processing*, Philadelphia, Pa., 1976, pp. 549–552.

SMIT77 SMITH, A. R. *Word hypothesization for large-vocabulary speech understanding systems*, Ph.D. thesis, Computer Science Dep., Carnegie-Mellon Univ., Pittsburgh, Pa., 1977.

SMIT81 SMITH, A. R., AND ERMAN, L. D. "NOAH: A bottom-up word hypothesizer for large-vocabulary speech-understanding systems," *IEEE Trans. Pattern Anal. Mach. Intell.* (1981), to be published.

SOLO77 SOLOWAY, E. M., AND RISEMAN, E. M. "Levels of pattern description in learning," in *Proc. 5th Int. J. Conf. Artificial Intelligence*, Cambridge, Mass., 1977, pp. 801–811.

SOND78 SONDHI, M. M., AND LEVINSON, S. E. "Computing relative redundancy to measure grammatical constraint in speech recognition tasks," in *Proc. IEEE Int. Conf. Acoustics, Speech, and Signal Processing*, Tulsa, Okla., Apr. 1978.

STEF80 STEFIK, M. *Planning with constraints*, Ph.D. thesis, Computer Science Dep., Stanford Univ., Stanford, Calif., Jan. 1980.

WALK78 WALKER, D. E., ED. *Understanding spoken language*, Elsevier North-Holland, New York, 1978.

WALK80 WALKER, D. E. "SRI research on speech understanding," in *Trends in speech recognition*, W. A. Lea, Ed., Prentice-Hall, Englewood Cliffs, N.J., 1980, Chap. 13.

WOLF80 WOLF, J. J., AND WOODS, W. A. "The HWIM speech understanding system," in *Trends in speech recognition*, W. A. Lea, Ed., Prentice-Hall, Englewood Cliffs, N.J., 1980, Chap. 14.

WOOD70 WOODS, W. A. "Transition network grammars for natural language analysis," *Commun. ACM* **13**, 10 (Oct. 1970), 591–606.

WOOD73 WOODS, W. A., AND MAKHOUL, J. "Mechanical inference problems in continuous speech understanding," in *Proc. 3rd Int. Jt. Conf. Artificial Intelligence*, Stanford, Calif., 1973, pp. 73–91, also *Artif. Intell.* **5**, 1 (Spring 1974), 73–91.

WOOD76 WOODS, W., BATES, M., BROWN, G., BRUCE, B., COOK, C., KLOVSTAD, J., MAKHOUL, J., NASH-WEBBER, B., SCHWARTZ, R., WOLF, J., AND ZUE, V. *Speech understanding systems: Final technical progress report*, Tech. Rep. 3438, Bolt Beranek and Newman, Cambridge, Mass., Dec. 1976 (in five volumes).

WOOD77 WOODS, W. A. "Shortfall and density scoring strategies for speech understanding control," in *Proc. 5th Int. Jt. Conf. Artificial Intelligence*, Cambridge, Mass., 1977, pp. 13–26.

Using Patterns and Plans in Chess

David Wilkins
SRI International, Menlo Park, CA, U.S.A.

ABSTRACT

The purpose of this research is to investigate the extent to which knowledge can replace and support search in selecting a chess move and to delineate the issues involved. This has been carried out by constructing a program, PARADISE (PAttern Recognition Applied to DIrecting SEarch), which finds the best move in tactically sharp middle game positions from the games of chess masters. It encodes a large body of knowledge in the form of production rules. The actions of the rules post concepts in the data base while the conditions match patterns in the chess position and data base. The program uses the knowledge base to discover plans during static analysis and to guide a small tree search which confirms that a particular plan is best. The search is "small" in the sense that the size of the search tree is of the same order of magnitude as a human master's search tree (tens and hundreds of nodes, not thousands to hundreds of thousands as in many computer chess programs).

Once a plan is formulated, it guides the tree search for several ply and expensive static analyses (needed to analyze a new position) are done infrequently. PARADISE avoids placing a depth limit on the search (or any other artificial effort limit). By using a global view of the search tree, information gathered during the search, and the analysis provided by the knowledge base, the program produces enough terminations to force convergence of the search. PARADISE has found combinations as deep as 19 ply.

1. Introduction

One of the central concerns of artificial intelligence is expressing knowledge and reasoning with it. Chess has been one of the most popular domains for AI research, yet brute force searching programs with little chess knowledge play better chess than programs with more chess knowledge. There is still much to be learned about expressing and using the kind of knowledge involved in playing chess. CHESS 4.7 is probably the best chess program, and its authors make the following comments in [12]:

> But why is the program so devoid of chess knowledge? It is not because we are deliberately trading it for speed of execution.... It is not quite true to say that we don't know how to feed additional knowledge to the program.... Our problem is that the programming tools we are presently using are not adequate to the task. Too much work is needed to encode the sizable body of knowledge needed to significantly improve the quality of play.

Human masters, whose play is still much better than the best programs, appear to use a knowledge intensive approach to chess (see [2]). They seem to have a huge number of stored 'patterns,' and analyzing a position involves matching these patterns to suggest plans for attack or defense. This analysis is verified and possibly corrected by a small search of the game tree. Unlike the searches conducted by most programs, the human master's search usually has specific goals to accomplish and returns useful information which affects the analysis of other lines. The purpose of this research is to investigate the issues involved in expressing and using pattern-oriented knowledge to analyze a position, to provide direction for the search, and to communicate useful results from the search.

To reduce the amount of knowledge that must be encapsulated, the domain of the program has been limited to tactically sharp middle game positions. The phrase 'tactically sharp' is meant to imply that success can be judged by the gain of a material rather than a positional advantage. The complexity of the middle game requires extensive search, providing a good testing ground for attempts to replace search with knowledge and to use knowledge to guide the search and communicate discoveries from one part of the tree to another.

Since, in our chosen domain, the attacking side can generally win material with correct play, the program uses different models for the offensive and defensive players during its search of the game tree. The offensive player uses a large amount of knowledge, suggests many esoteric attacks, and invests much effort in making sure a plan is likely to work before suggesting it. The defensive player uses much less knowledge and effort, tries any defense that might possibly work, and tries only obvious counter attacks. Trying every reasonable defense enables the offense to satisfy itself that a line really does win. The size of the tree is kept small because the offensive player finds the best move immediately in most cases.

For a knowledge based program to achieve master level performance, it seems necessary that the knowledge base be amenable to modifications and additions. PARADISE provides for easy modification of and addition to its knowledge base (without adversely affecting program performance), thus allowing the knowledge to be built up incrementally and tuned to eliminate errors. This is accomplished by having the knowledge base composed of largely independent production rules which are written in a straightforward Production-Language [13].

The goal is to build an expert knowledge base and to reason with it to discover plans and verify them with a small tree search. As long as this goal is reached, the amount of execution time used is not important. It is a design decision to sacrifice efficient execution in order to use knowledge whenever reasonable. When a desired level of performance is reached, the program could be speeded up considerably by switching to a more efficient representation at the cost of transparency and ease of modification.

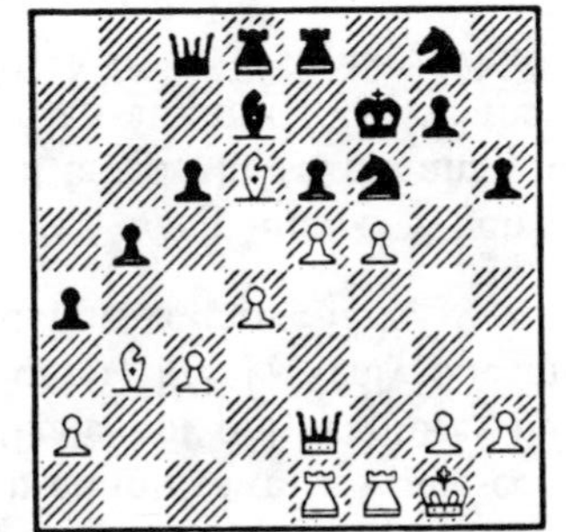

1.	Q–R5ch	N × Q
2.	P × Pch	K–N3
3.	B–B2ch	K–N4
4.	R–B5ch	K–N3
5.	R–B6ch	K–N4
6.	R–N6ch	K–R5
7.	R–K4ch	N–B5
8.	R × Nch	K–R4
9.	P–N3	any
10.	R–R4 mate	

FIG. 0. White to move.

Because it grows small trees, PARADISE can find deeper combinations than most chess programs. The position in Fig. 0 is an example of such a combination from an actual master game. White can mate by sacrificing his queen and playing nine additional moves (against black's line of longest resistance), the next to last move not being a check or capture. Thus the search tree must go at least 19 ply deep to find this combination. This is considerably deeper than any other current chess program could probe in a reasonable amount of time, but PARADISE solves this problem after generating a search tree of 109 nodes, in 20 minutes of CPU time on a DEC KL-10. (PARADISE is written in MacLisp.) The fact that PARADISE can accurately analyze all relevant lines in only 109 nodes shows that the program makes good use of its knowledge.

2. Overview of PARADISE

PARADISE uses a knowledge base consisting of about 200 production rules to find the best move in chess positions. Every production has a pattern (i.e., a complex, interrelated set of features) as its condition. Each production can be viewed as searching for all instances of its condition pattern in the position. For each instance found, the production may, as its action, post zero or more concepts in the data base for use by the system in its reasoning processes. A concept consists of a concept name, instantiations for a number of variables, and a list of reasons why the concept has been posted. The data base can be considered as a global blackboard where productions write information. The productions are built up by levels, with more primitive patterns (e.g., a pattern which matches legal moves) being used as building blocks for more complex patterns. A search tree (the major component of most chess programs) is used to show that one move suggested by the pattern-based analysis is in fact the best.

Fig. 1 shows one of the simplest productions in PARADISE. It attempts to find an offensive plan which attacks a trapped defensive piece. The first three lines in Fig. 1 constitute the pattern or condition of the production rule while the

```
((DMP1)
(NEVER (EXISTS (SQ) (PATTERN MOBIL DMP1 SQ)))
(NEVER (EXISTS (P1) (PATTERN ENPRIS P1 DMP1)))
(ACTION ATTACK ((OTHER-COLOR DMP1) (LOCATION DMP1)) (THREAT (WIN DMP1))
(LIKELY 0)))
```

FIG. 1. Production rule in PARADISE which recognizes trapped pieces.

fourth line constitutes the action. The first line specifies one variable that must be instantiated. Because of its name, the variable must be instantiated to a defensive piece that is not a pawn. The next two lines in the production access two more primitive patterns that have already been matched, MOBIL and ENPRIS. The MOBIL pattern matches each legal move that can be made without losing the moving piece. If there are no squares which match MOBIL when DMP1 is the first argument, then DMP1 is trapped. Only in this case will there be any possible instantiations for DMP1 after the second line in Fig. 1 is matched. The third line prevents the pattern from matching if the trapped piece is a ready en prise. The idea is that in this case DMP1 should be captured outright rather than attacked. Thus this production matches only trapped pieces which are not en prise.

In Fig. 1, the action of the production rule posts an ATTACK concept. This concept gives instantiations for two variables and tells the system that the opposite color of DMP1 would do well to attack the square which is DMP1's location. In addition one reason is given for suggesting this concept. This reason consists of attributes describing the threat of the concept and how likely it is to succeed. Concepts are discussed in more detail later in this paper. The more primitive patterns (such as MOBIL) and the language in which productions are written are described in detail in [13].

To offset the expense of searching for patterns in the position, problems must be solved with small search trees. In fact, PARADISE can be viewed as shifting some of its search from the usual chess game tree to the problem of matching patterns. PARADISE shows that its pattern-oriented knowledge base can be used in a variety of ways to significantly reduce the part of the game tree which needs to be searched. This reduction is large enough that a high level of expertise can be obtained using a large but still reasonable amount of resources. This reduction is also large enough that PARADISE avoids placing a depth limit (or any other artificial effort limit) on its search. The various ways in which the knowledge base is used are briefly mentioned below.

Calculating primitives. PARADISE's knowledge base contains about twenty patterns (productions without actions) which are primitives used to describe a chess position. These patterns are matched once for each position. They range from matching legal moves to matching patterns like MOBIL and ENPRIS. The primitives are relatively complex and calculating them is expensive.

Static analysis. Given a new position, PARADISE does an expensive in-depth static analysis which uses, on the average, 12 seconds of cpu time on a DEC KL-10. This analysis uses a large number of productions in the knowledge base to look for threats which may win material. It produces plans which should guide the search for several ply and should give information which can be used to stop the search at reasonable points.

Producing plans. The knowledge base is used to produce plans during static analysis and at other times. Through plans, PARADISE uses its knowledge to understand a new position created during the search on the basis of positions previously analyzed along that line of play, thus avoiding a static analysis. Plans guide the search and a static analysis is only occasionally necessary in positions created during the search. Producing a plan is not as simple as suggesting a move, it involves generating a large amount of useful information to help avoid static analyses along many different lines and to help detect success or failure of the plan as it is executed. (Examples are given later in this paper.)

Executing plans. The execution of a plan during the tree search requires using the knowledge base to solve goals specified in the plan. This use of the knowledge base could be viewed as a static analysis where the system's attention is focused on a particular goal or aspect of the position. Such a focused analysis can be done at a fraction of the cost of a full analysis which examines all aspects of the position.

Generating defensive moves. PARADISE does static analyses and executes plans only for the offense (the side for which it is trying to win material). To prove that an offensive plan succeeds, the search must show a winning line for all reasonable (i.e., any move which might be effective) defensive moves. Productions in the knowledge base are used to generate all the reasonable defenses.

Quiescence searches. When a node is a candidate for termination of the search, PARADISE uses a quiescence search to determine its value. This quiescence search may return information which will cause the termination decision to be revoked. Productions in the knowledge base provide much of the knowledge used in PARADISE's quiescence search. Quiescence searches in PARADISE investigate not only captures but forks, pins, multi-move mating sequences and other threats. Only one move is investigated at each node except when a defensive move fails.

Analysis of problem upon failure. When either the defense or offense has tried a move that failed, the search analyzes the information backed up with the refutation in an attempt to solve the problem. The knowledge base is used in this analysis to suggest plans which thwart the opponent's refutation. In this way PARADISE constructs new plans using the information gained from searching an unsuccessful plan.

Answering questions. The search often requests certain kinds of information about the current position. The knowledge base is used to provide such information. The most frequent requests ask if the position is quiescent and if there are any obviously winning moves in the position.

The above list describes eight general functions the knowledge base performs for PARADISE. This paper explains how plans are produced and executed. The productions, the static analysis, the tree search, and mechanisms for communicating information from one part of the tree to another are discussed in [13].

3. The Need for Concepts

To understand a chess position, a successful line of play must be found. Human masters understand concepts which cover many ply in order to find the best move. A knowledge based program must also have the ability to reason with concepts that are higher level than the legal moves in a chess position. The following position from [1] illustrates this.

FIG. 2. White to move.

In the above position, most computer chess programs would search the game tree as deep as their effort limit allowed and decide to play K–K3 which centralizes the king. They cannot search deep enough to discover that white can win since white's advantage would take more than 20 ply to show up in most evaluation functions used by computer programs. The point is that the solver of the above problem uses conceptual reasoning to solve it, and the concepts must be higher level than the legal moves in a chess position. A human master would recognize the following features (among others) in the above position: the black king must stay near his KB1 to prevent white's king bishop pawn from queening, the pawns form a blockade which the kings can't penetrate, and the kings can bypass this blockade only on the queen rook file.

For a knowledge based program to solve this problem, it must be able to express concepts at the level of conceptualization used above. The system must combine and reason with these concepts in unforeseen ways. In the above example, the blockading concept would be used to develop the plan of moving the white king to the queen rook file in order to bypass the blockade, but if both black and white had pawns on their QN4 then the blockading concept would be used to decide that neither king can invade the other's territory. Expressing and using concepts is a major problem for a knowledge-based chess program.

To clarify the problems involved in used concepts to reason about chess, a comparison to a well-known 'expert' system such as MYCIN is helpful. The following phrase is the action part of a typical MYCIN production rule (from [4]):

then there is suggestive evidence (0.7) that the identity of the organism is bacteroides

Such an action effectively adds to the plausibility score for some possible answer. This presupposes that any one writer of all the rules knows every possible solution since such rules will never create a diagnosis that has not been mentioned in the action part of some rule.

Using actions similar to those used in MYCIN rules would be similar to a chess system where the action part of each rule was to add to the plausibility score of either

(1) one or more of the legal moves in the position, or

(2) some prespecified object which could lead (through other rules) to recommending a legal move.

Such an approach is not satisfactory for the type of chess reasoning needed in the above problems. Concepts at a higher level than legal moves must be used in this reasoning, and objects cannot be prespecified (e.g., the extent of blockade must be created dynamically). Thus, PARADISE must reason by linking concepts to create plans instead of filling in prespecified slots.

In most current expert production systems (such as MYCIN), the action parts of the rules are in some sense part of the solution or a pointer to something which can produce a solution. In chess the system must discover lines of play that were not implicit in the knowledge base. Thus the word 'create' is used. MYCIN has a small solution set (120 organisms) and can mention each solution in its rules, while a chess program must discover an enormous number of lines using a set of productions which is much smaller in size (by an order of magnitude or more) than the number of plans it must recognize. This can be seen by looking at the actual production rules: MYCIN's actions mention the names of objects while PARADISE's actions involve many variables whose instantiation is not determined until execution of the action.

4. Knowledge Sources and Concepts

When a production in PARADISE matches, it may have an action part which posts various concepts in the data base. The program is able to express and use concepts by dividing its knowledge base into various *Knowledge Sources*. Each Knowledge Source (KS) provides the knowledge necessary to understand and reason about a certain abstract concept. In its simplest form, a KS is a group of productions which knows about some abstract concept, and a list of variables such that an instantiation of the variables represents a specific concept which corresponds to this abstract concept. For example, the production in Fig. 1 posts an ATTACK concept which corresponds to the ATTACK KS. The ATTACK KS in PARADISE has two variables, COL and SQ, and contains productions which know how to attack a particular square SQ for the side COL. (The ATTACK KS has more structure than this, but it is irrelevant to the present discussion.) With this KS, the system can use the abstract concept of attacking a square in its reasoning, in the expression of plans, and in the communication of discoveries from the tree search.

If one production knows about more than one abstract concept, it may be in more than one KS. When a concept in the data base (described below) has a corresponding KS (i.e., they have the same name), PARADISE will eventually treat that concept as a subgoal and use the corresponding KS to solve the subgoal in an attempt to produce a plan to realize that concept. (This may be done by creating other concepts.) There may also be concepts that have no corresponding KS and are not treated as subgoals. Such concepts are inspected by patterns attempting to match and by the searching routines. When a concept corresponds to a KS, it will sometimes be referred to as a goal or subgoal.

Concepts are posted in the data base by the actions in production rules. KSes then use the information in these concepts as subgoals to eventually produce a plan of action. When a new KS is executed, the patterns which matched in previous KSes can no longer be accessed. Thus concepts in the data base must contain all the information that will be needed to execute other KSs and to guide the search. Each KS expects a certain amount of information in a concept which it executes. (A concept is 'executed' when it is used as a goal by its corresponding KS.) At the very least, a KS expects an instantiation of its arguments (such as COL and SQ in the ATTACK KS). The ATTACK KS also expects some information on what the intentions of COL are once SQ is attacked. This information is needed so that the reason for wanting to attack SQ will not be destroyed or negated by an attempt to attack. Among other things, KSs usually expect information on how likely a goal is to succeed and on how threatening a goal is (this is useful in deciding if a sacrifice is warranted).

PARADISE stores information about concepts on a list of attribute-value pairs (or property list). A particular concept is expressed by giving its name, an instantiation of its arguments, and a list of attribute-value pairs, called an *attribute list.* Frequently, instances of a concept with identical argument instantiations but different attribute lists are posted for different reasons by different productions. Since many productions do not care about the values in the attribute lists, it is imperative to treat all concepts with the same name and instantiation (though different attribute lists) as just one concept. Otherwise, many productions would needlessly be executed repeatedly on different versions of the same goal. Some productions do access the information in the attribute lists, and it is necessary to keep each attribute list distinct for these productions. For these reasons, all concepts in PARADISE with the same instantiation are combined into one concept (which is executed as a goal only once), but the attribute list of this one concept is replaced by a list of attribute lists, one for each reason the concept was suggested.

The productions can access this structure as one concept but can still access the necessary information about each attribute list. When a production accesses the values of attributes, it may not care which list the values come from, or it may require that the values for each attribute come from the same list, or it may want the 'best' (in some sense) value for each attribute whether the different values come from the same list or not, or it may want values for one attribute to come from lists which have some particular value for another attribute. This accessing of the information in a concept is so complex that it can be looked on as pattern matching in itself. Thus the productions in a KS can be looked upon as matching patterns in the given chess position and matching patterns in different concepts.

Concepts and their accessing are quite complex. Intuitively, the productions in PARADISE are not making deductions, per se, but coming up with ideas that may or may not be right. Thus there are no 'facts' that have certain deduced values that can be reasoned with. The complexity of later analysis requires that a production essentially put down 'why' it thought of an idea. In this way, other productions can decide if the idea still looks right in light of what is known at that time. Most production systems avoid this complexity because the firing of a production is a deduction which adds a new piece of knowledge to the system. This piece of knowledge is assumed right and the system is not prepared to later decide that it wasn't right to make that deduction.

To summarize, KSs provide abstract concepts that are at a higher level than the productions themselves, and form the language in which PARADISE thinks. Concepts and KSs are used in the static analysis reasoning process, to formulate plans for communicating knowledge down the tree, to quickly access relevant productions during execution of a plan, and to communicate discoveries made during the search.

5. Plans

The goal of the static analysis process in PARADISE is to produce plans. Plans seem to play an important role in the problem solving process of move selection for good human chess players. Alexander Kotov in his book ***Think Like a Grandmaster*** Kotov [7, p. 148] writes:

> . . . it is better to follow out a plan consistently even if it isn't the best one than to play without a plan at all. The worst thing is to wander about aimlessly.

Most computer chess programs certainly do not follow Kotov's advice. In a knowledge based program, the cost of processing the knowledge should be offset by a significantly smaller branching factor in the tree search. Plans help reduce the cost of processing knowledge by immediately focusing the program's attention on the critical part of a new position created during the search, thus avoiding a complete re-analysis of this new position. Having plans also reduces the branching factor in the search by giving direction to the search. Consider, for example, that most programs may try the same poor move at every alternate depth in the tree, always re-discovering the same refutation. PARADISE can detect when a plan has been tried earlier along a line of play and avoid searching it again if nothing has changed to make it more attractive. Most programs also suffer because they intersperse moves which are irrelevant to each other and work towards different goals. PARADISE avoids this by following a single idea (its plan) down the tree.

Plans in PARADISE can be considered as special instances of concepts since each plan has a list of attribute lists. Instead of a list of instantiations for a set of variables (as in a concept), a plan has an expression in the *Plan-Language.* The Plan-Language expresses plans of action for the side about to move, called the offense. In general, the offense wants to have a reply ready for every defensive alternative. A plan cannot therefore be a linear sequence of goals or moves but must contain conditional branches depending on the opponent's reply. When the offense is on move, a specific move or goal is provided by the plan. When the defense is on move, a list of alternative sub-plans for the offense may be given. Each alternative begins with a template for matching the move made by the defense. Only alternatives whose template matches the move just made by the defense are tried in the search. PARADISE has the following templates which adequately describe defensive moves in terms of their effects on the purpose of the plan being executed (P and SQ are variables which will be instantiated in an actual plan to particular pieces and squares, respectively):

(P SQ) matches when the defense has moved the piece P to the square SQ.
(NIL SQ) matches when the defense has moved any piece to SQ.
(P NIL) matches when the defense has moved P (to any square).
(ANYBUT P) matches when the defense has moved some piece other than P.
NIL matches any defensive move.

The plan for an offensive move can be one of two things: a particular move or a goal. A particular move is simply the name of a piece and a square. Such a plan causes PARADISE to immediately make that move with no analysis of the position other than checking that the move is legal. A goal is simply the name of a KS followed by an instantiation for each argument of the KS. When executing a goal, PARADISE will post a concept corresponding to the KS in the data base by using the given instantiations and the attribute lists of this plan as a whole. The KS will then be executed for this concept. Any plan produced by this execution will replace the goal in the original plan and this modified plan will be used. This process expands and ellaborates plans. If executing the KS does not produce a plan then the original plan has failed.

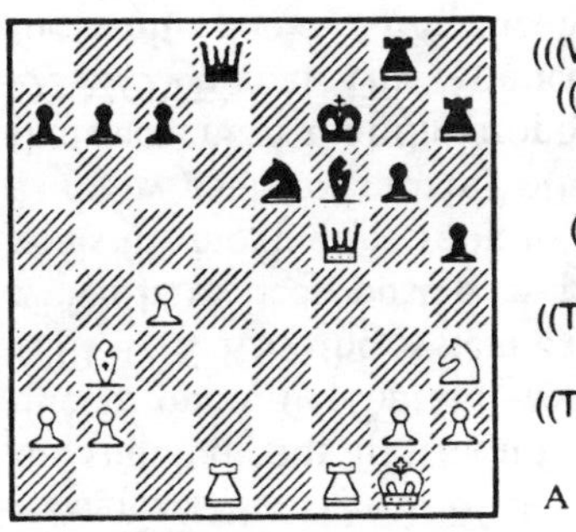

FIG. 3. White to move.

```
(((WN N5)
  (((BN N4) (SAFEMOVE WR Q7)
    (((BK NIL) (SAFECAPTURE WR BR))
     ((ANYBUT BK) (SAFECAPTURE WR BK))))
   ((BN N4) (CHECKMOVE WR Q7) (BK NIL) (SAFECAPTURE
                                          WR BQ) )))
 ((THREAT (PLUS (EXCHVAL WN N5) (FORK WR BK BR)))
                                          (LIKELY 0))
 ((THREAT (PLUS (EXCHVAL WN N5) (EXCH WR BQ)))
                                          (LIKELY 0)))
```

A plan produced by PARADISE

Fig. 3 shows a problem and one of the plans PARADISE's static analysis produces for it. ('WN' means white knight, 'N5' means the square N5, etc.) The internal representation of PARADISE has not been printed unambiguously since the term 'WR' does not specify which white rook. However, it should be obvious to which piece the names refer. The last two lines of the plan are attribute lists. The first five lines are the Plan-Language expression for the plan which can be read as follows:

> *Play N–N5. If black captures the knight with his knight, attempt to safely move the rook on Q1 to Q7. Then, if black moves his king anywhere try to safely capture the black rook on R7, and if black moves any piece other than his king, try to safely capture the king with the rook. A second alternative after black captures the knight is to attempt to safely move the rook on Q1 to Q7 with check. Then, if black moves his king anywhere try to safely capture the black queen with the rook.*

SAFEMOVE, SAFECAPTURE, and CHECKMOVE are all KSs in PARADISE. After playing N–N5 and N×N for black in the tree search, PARADISE will execute either the CHECKMOVE goal or the SAFEMOVE goal. Executing the SAFEMOVE goal executes the SAFEMOVE KS which knows about safely moving a piece to a square. This KS will see that R–Q7 is safe and produce this as the continuation of the original plan, causing the system to play R–Q7 with no further analysis. If for some reason R–Q7 was not safe then the SAFEMOVE KS will try to make Q7 safe for the rook (by posting a SAFE concept). If some plan is found, the original plan will be 'expanded' by replacing the SAFEMOVE goal with the newly found plan. In general, the newly found plan will contain (SAFEMOVE WR Q7) though it may come after a sacrificial decoy or some other tactic. If posting the SAFE concept does not produce a plan, then the SAFEMOVE goal has failed, and the alternative CHECKMOVE goal will be tried. If it also fails, a complete analysis of the position must be done. If black had answered N–N5 with a king move, it would not match the template (BN N4) and a complete analysis of the position would be undertaken without attempting to make Q7 safe for the rook.

By use of conditionals, a plan can handle a number of possible situations which may arise. The most important feature of the Plan-Language is that offensive plans are expressed in terms of the KSs. This has many advantages. Relevant productions are immediately and directly accessed when a new position is reached. The system has one set of abstract concepts it understands (the KSs) and does not need to use a different language for plans and static analysis. The system has been designed to make the writing of productions and thus the forming of KSs reasonable to do. Thus the range of plans that can be expressed is not fixed by the Plan-Language. By forming new KSs, the range of expressible plans may be increased without any new coding (in the search routines or anywhere else) to understand the new plans. This is important since the usefulness of the knowledge base is limited by its ability to communicate what it knows (e.g., through plans).

Given a number of plans to execute, the tree search must make decisions about which plan to search first, when to forsake one plan and try another, when to be satisfied with the results of a search, and other such things. To make such decisions, it must have information about what a plan expects to gain and why. Such information was available to the productions which matched to produce the plan and must be communicated in the attribute lists of the plan so as to provide many different types of access to this knowledge. Unlike most search-based chess programs, PARADISE must use its information about a plan at other nodes in the tree since it executes a plan without analyzing the newly created positions.

To use the information about plans in an effective manner, PARADISE divides a plan's effects into four different categories which are kept separately (i.e., their values are not combined in any way). These four categories are:

THREAT which describes what a plan threatens to actively win.

SAVE which describes counterthreats of the opponent a plan actively prevents,

LOSS which describes counterthreats of the opponent not defended against and functions the first piece to move in a plan will give up by abandoning its current location (thus providing new threats for the opponent), and

LIKELY which describes the likelihood that a plan will succeed.

These four categories have emerged during the development of PARADISE. Experience seems to indicate the system must have at least these four dimensions along which to evaluate plans in order to adequately guide the tree search.

Since the values for these categories must evaluate correctly at different nodes in the tree, they cannot be integers. Instead they (except for LIKELY) are expressions in the Threat-Language [13] which can describe threats in a sophisticated manner. These expressions are evaluated in the context of the current position and may return different values for different positions. The value of LIKELY is an integer. This integer represents the number of unforced moves the defense has before the offense can accomplish its plan. The most likely plans to succeed have a LIKELY of zero (every move is forcing). Both attribute lists in Fig. 3 have a likelihood of zero.

6. Creating Plans

A detailed description of the static analysis process in PARADISE is given in [13]. The concepts and KSs used to produce the plan in Fig. 3 are briefly described here. The system begins by posting a THREAT concept, the THREAT KS having productions which look for threats. Two different productions in THREAT post MOVE concepts for moving the white rook to Q7. (One recognizes the skewer of the black king to the rook, and the other recognizes the simultaneous attack on the king and queen where any king move leaves the queen open to capture with check.) After executing the THREAT and ATTACK KSs, the system executes the MOVE KS on the 50 MOVE concepts which have been posted by productions. In addition to Q7, there are MOVE goals for moving the rook to QB7, K7, KB8, Q6, QB6, QN6, and QR6 as well as many goals for moving other white pieces. A production in the MOVE KS, that recognizes that the proposed move is unsafe, matches for the white rook to Q7 MOVE goal. This production posts a SAFE concept for making Q7 safe for the white rook. After the MOVE KS is finished, 7 SAFE goals have accumulated. While executing the SAFE KS for the white rook to Q7 goal, one production notices that the black knight blocks the white queen's protection of Q7. This production posts a DECOY goal in order to decoy the black knight so that the queen can support the white rook on Q7. The DECOY KS is executed on the 7 DECOY goals which have been produced, and one production posts a FORCE goal suggesting N–N5 as a move to decoy black's knight. It is up to the FORCE KS to decide if N–N5 is forcing enough to provoke a move by the black knight. There are 9 FORCE goals in all and the production which finds N–N5 forcing posts an INITIAL-PLAN concept which is exactly like the plan shown in Fig. 3.

After executing the CAPTURE KS, the INITIAL-PLAN KS is executed on the 5 INITIAL-PLAN goals which have been produced. (Most of the MOVE goals failed without leading to the posting of a plan.) This KS looks for functions given up by a plan or threats not defended against by a plan. Since the plan of Fig. 3 checks the opposing king, a production posts a FINALPLAN concept for this plan. While executing a different goal, the INITIAL-PLAN KS notices that the white queen is under attack and is not defended by the plan in question. This causes execution of the DEFENDOFFENSE KS which produces 6 DEFENDTHREAT goals to save the white queen. The DEFENDTHREAT KS in turn posts 6 INITIAL-PLAN concepts, and executing the INITIAL-PLAN KS a second time produces a total 10 FINALPLAN concepts for the position in Fig. 3. The attribute lists of these plans rate only two of them as being likely to win material. These two are the one in Fig. 3, and a plan starting with R–Q7 immediately. The plan in Fig. 3 is rated highest and is tried first. This static analysis took more than 24 seconds of cpu time on a DEC KL-10. The static analysis process is very expensive, and PARADISE uses its plan to avoid doing such analyses.

Each static analysis is done entirely by the production rules which can easily be modified to increase or make more precise the knowledge available to the system. Each concept (and plan) produced has a REASON attribute listing each production that matched in the process of suggesting the concept. (REASONs have been omitted in Fig. 3.) This provides a good explanation of exactly why PARADISE believes something and is helpful for quick debugging and easy modification. The attribute lists of each concept contain enough information so that the system essentially knows 'why' it is doing something. Thus wrong ideas can be discarded readily and combinations of ideas that are antithetical to each other can be avoided. Few ridiculous plans are suggested.

7. How Detailed Should Plans Be?

The system must quickly recognize when a plan is not working and abandon it before effort is wasted investigating poor lines. On the other hand, it is expensive to completely analyze a position, so the system wants to use its plan as long as possible. To achieve a balance, plans must adequately express the purpose they intend to achieve. Productions must carefully formulate their Plan-Language expressions at the right level of detail using appropriate goals and descriptions of defensive moves. When executing a plan, the system will retrieve a goal or move from the plan to apply to a new position. Care must be taken to ensure that this move or goal is reasonable in the new position. Plans may become unreasonable when they are too general or too specific. In either case, they have failed to express their purpose.

The example of Fig. 3 illustrates the issues involved. Consider the first three ply of the plan as ((WN N5) (BN N4) (SAFEMOVE WR Q7)). Suppose this had been expressed as ((WN N5) NIL (WR Q7)). Playing R–Q7 after N × N is reasonable but if black moves his king instead, playing R–Q7 will lead the search down a blind alley. Thus, (WR Q7) is too specific and does not express white's purpose. This problem can be cured by a more specific description of black's reply (e.g., (BN N4) instead of NIL) since the template for black's move will not match if black moves his king. In actual fact, PARADISE does not know for sure that R–Q7 will be safe after N–N5 and N × N (although in this particular position it is). To avoid mistakenly playing R–Q7 when it is not safe, PARADISE uses a SAFEMOVE goal to more accurately express the purpose of the plan. For example, the plan could be ((WN N5) NIL (SAFEMOVE WR Q7)). If black answers N–N5 with N × N then the SAFEMOVE goal is reasonable and quickly produces R–Q7 as the move to play after verifying its safety. If black answers with a king move then the SAFEMOVE goal is not what white wants to do, but little is lost since R–Q7 is not safe and the line will be rejected without searching. However, if likely plans had existed for making Q7 safe, the search may still have been led astray. For this reason, PARADISE uses (BN N4) as the template in this plan. The purpose of N–N5 is to decoy the black knight to his KN4 and this template most accurately expresses this purpose.

Now let us consider the following more general plan: ((WN N5) NIL (SAFELY-ATTACK BK)). If black answers with N × N then the SAFELY-ATTACK KS should generate R–Q7 as a safe attack on the black king. If, instead, black moves his king then this KS should generate a check by the white queen or knight which would also be reasonable. Thus this plan produces reasonable moves for every black reply without ever causing a re-analysis of the new position. This would be a good plan if PARADISE knew (from its patterns) that it could get the black king in trouble after any reply. However, it only knows of the skewer of the black king to the rook, the threat of capturing the queen with check, and the fact that the white knight threatens the black king, rook, and knight from N5. It is accidental that the SAFELY-ATTACK goal works after black retreats his king. In the general case, such a goal would produce many worthless checks that would mislead the search. Thus this plan is too general to describe white's actual purpose.

It is very important to get the correct level of detail in a plan. The plan should handle as many replies as possible without causing a re-analysis, but it should avoid suggesting poor moves. The templates for describing defensive moves in the Plan-Language and the various KSs have been developed to allow PARADISE's plans to accurately express their purpose. The results have been quite satisfying: the productions in PARADISE now create plans which rarely suggest poor moves but which can still be used for as many ply as a human might use his original idea.

8. Using Plans to Guide the Search

PARADISE's tree searching algorithm is described in detail in [13]. Only a brief overview is given here in order to provide background for an example problem solution by the program. PARADISE's tree searching algorithm uses different strategies at the top level to show that one move is best. Once a strategy is selected, a best-first search is done. The value of each move is a range within which PARADISE thinks the 'true' value of the move lies. The program narrows these ranges by doing best-first searches until it can show that one move is best. By using the knowledge base to control the search and by using information discovered during previous searches, PARADISE produces enough cutoffs to force convergence of its search without a depth limit or other artificial effort limit.

Fig. 4 shows position 49 from [9]. PARADISE does a static analysis on this position which uses 18 seconds of cpu time and suggests two plans. Fig. 4 shows the plan suggested as best. To show how such plans are used to guide the search, PARADISE's search for this position is sketched below.

PARADISE begins by doing a best-first search of the above plan. Execution of this plan commences by playing Q × Pch and producing a new board position. The defense suggests both legal moves, K × Q and K–B1, but tries K × Q first. Since this move matches the (BK R2) template in the plan, PARADISE has ((CHECKMOVE WR R5) (BK NIL) (ATTACKP BK)) as its best plan at ply 3 of the search. Since it is in the middle of executing a plan, PARADISE does not look for better alternatives at this point. The best-first search only looks for better alternatives when a new plan is being selected.

Execution of the CHECKMOVE KS produces ((WR R5) (BK NIL) (ATTACKP BK)) as a plan which causes R–R5ch to be played. Black plays his only legal-move at ply 4, K–N1, which matches the (BK NIL) template in the plan, and leaves (ATTACKP BK) as the current plan. Thus the original plan is still guiding the search at ply 5. Executing the ATTACKP KS posts many concepts, including MOVE and SAFE concepts, and ((WN N6) ((NIL (SAFEMOVE WR R8)) (NIL (SAFEMOVE WN K7))) is produced as the best

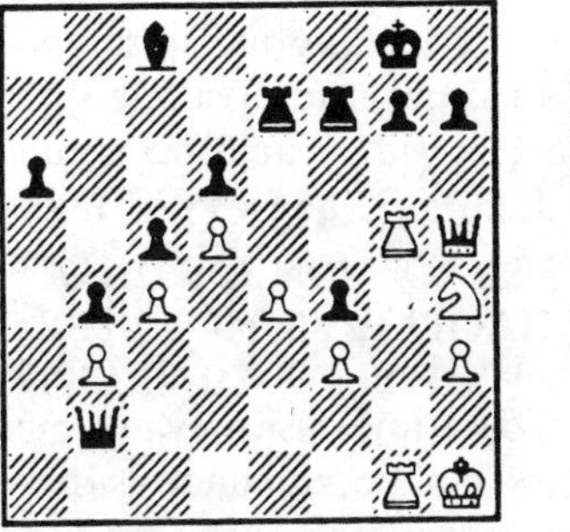

FIG. 4. White to move.

(PLY 1)
BESTPLAN:
(((WQ R7) (BK R2) (CHECKMOVE WR R5) (BK NIL)
(ATTACKP BK))
((HINT 1) (THREAT (PLUS (WIN BK) (EXCHVAL WQ R7)))
(LIKELY 1)))

A plan produced by PARADISE

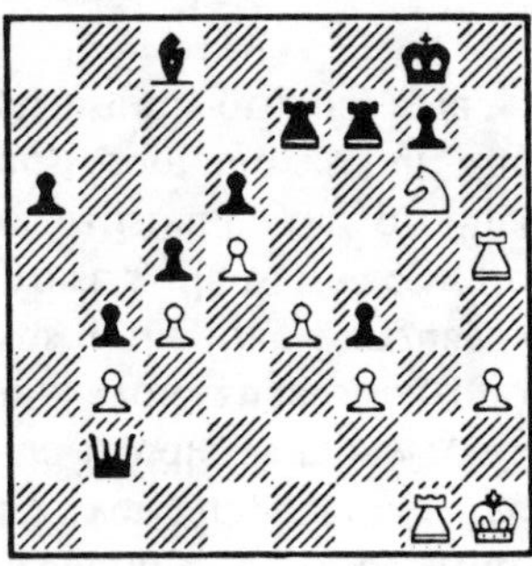

(PLY 6)
INITIAL DEFENSIVE MOVES:
((BR R6) (BB Q2) (BB N2) (BR B4) (BR B3) (BR B1))

FIG. 5.

plan in this position. This replaces (ATTACKP BK) in the current plan, thus elaborating it. After playing N–N6, the position in Fig. 5 is reached.

Productions which know about defending against R–R8 suggest the 6 black moves in Fig. 5. Black plays B × P first in an effort to save the bishop from the ensuing skewer. At this point the plan branches. Since both branches begin with a null template, they both match any black move at ply 6. Thus PARADISE has two plans at ply 7: (SAFEMOVE WR R8) and (SAFEMOVE WN K7). Before executing a plan for the offense, PARADISE executes the QUIESCENCE KS which looks for obviously winning moves. (This was done at plys 3 and 5 also, but did not suggest any moves.) Here R–R8 is suggested by the QUIESCENCE KS which causes the (SAFEMOVE WR R8) plan to be executed immediately. PARADISE plays R–R8, finds that black is mated, and returns to ply 6 knowing that black's B × P leads to mate. All this has been accomplished without a static analysis; the original plan has guided the search.

At ply 6, black uses KSs to refute the mating line. This involves analysis of the information produced by the previous search. No new moves are found since all reasonable defenses have already been suggested. PARADISE has a causality facility (see [14]) which determines the possible effects a move might have on a line of play. Using information generated during the search of the mating line, the causality facility looks for effects a proposed move might have (such as blocking a square which a sliding piece moved over, vacating an escape square for the king, protecting a piece which was attacked, etc.). The causality facility recognizes that neither B–Q2 nor B–N2 can affect the mating line found for B × P so they are rejected without searching.

Black plays R–B4 next, the causality facility having recognized that this move opens a flight square for the black king. Again PARADISE has both (SAFEMOVE WR R8) and (SAFEMOVE WN K7) as plans at ply 7. Both SAFEMOVE goals would succeed, but R–R8 has a higher recommendation and is played first. Black plays his only legal move at ply 8, K–B2.

The original plan no longer provides suggestions at ply 9. PARADISE must now look for better alternatives or do an expensive static analysis to suggest a new plan. Before trying either of these, the program executes the QUIESCENCE KS in an attempt to find an obviously winning move. R–KB8 is suggested and PARADISE immediately plays this move without doing a static analysis. This is mate so PARADISE returns to ply 6 to look for other defenses.

Both R–B3 and R–B1 are tried and both are quickly refuted by playing R–R8 from the SAFEMOVE goal of the original plan, K–B2, and R–KB8 from the QUIESCENCE KS. The search then returns to ply 2 and tries K–B1 in answer to Q × Pch. The template in the original plan does not match K–B1 so there is no plan at ply 3. However, the QUIESCENCE KS quickly suggests Q–R8 and PARADISE returns from the search convinced that Q × Pch will mate. This result shows that Q × Pch is best, so no other best-first searches are initiated.

PARADISE's plans are not always so accurate but space prevents presentation of a longer search. The above analysis uses about 130 seconds of cpu time on a DEC KL-10. It goes to a depth of 9 ply while creating only 21 nodes in the tree. Because of the guidance provided by the original plan, no static analysis was performed except on the original position. By comparison, the TECH2 program (an improved version of TECH [6]) at a depth setting of 6 discovers that it can win material with Q × Pch although the horizon effect hides the mate from it. For this analysis, TECH2 uses 210 seconds of cpu time on a KL-10 and creates 439,459 nodes by making legal moves (as well as making 544,768 illegal moves which are retracted).

9. A Typical Medium-Sized Search

This section presents the actual protocol produced by PARADISE while solving problem 82 in [9]. (The program prints squares in algebraic notation to avoid confusion.) This is a typical protocol produced by PARADISE while solving a problem in which the program finds the best line immediately. Problem 82 in [9] was chosen so that comparisons can be made with the search tree produced

FIG. 5.1. White to move.

by the CAPS program which is given in [1]. Such a comparison is interesting since CAPS has more knowledge about tactics than any other program that plays a full game of chess.

PARADISE's initial static analysis on the above position uses about 20 seconds of cpu time, and produces 7 plans. The one beginning with (WB H7) has a LIKELY of 0 and is searched first. The other six plans have a LIKELY of 1 and begin with the following moves: (WQ A3) (WR H7) (WR H8) (WQ F2) (WQ F3) (WQ E1). The protocol which follows was printed by PARADISE as it analyzed this problem. Explanatory comments have been added in a smaller font.

In the search, the program refuses to search plans that are not likely to succeed when it has already achieved a significant success. This is done because it is not reasonable to invest large amounts of effort trying ideas which don't seem likely to succeed when a winning line has already been found. The validity of this cutoff rests on PARADISE's accurate calculation of LIKELY values (see [13]). This could produce errors, though not serious ones since the errors would be the selection of a winning move which was not the 'best' winning move. No such errors have been made in any position PARADISE has analyzed.

(TOPLEVEL (VALUE . 0))
PLY 1 (EXPECT . 320)
BESTPLAN: (WB H7) (BK F8) (WQ A3))
NEWBOARD: (E4 WB H7)

The value of the initial position is 0. (White is trying to achieve a positive score.) The best plan specifies moving the WB to H7 and if black replies by moving his king to F8, the WQ–A3 is played. The reasoning behind the suggestion of this plan is fairly specific. PARADISE knows that after B–H7 black must move his king either to H8 where white has a discovered check, or to F8 where white can deliver a second check to which black's king cannot move in reply. The expectation of this plan (after 'EXPECT'), which is calculated from the attribute lists of the plan, is 320 (90 is the value of a queen, so 320 threatens mate). Wherever the word 'NEWBOARD' occurs, PARADISE constructs a new board position by playing a legal move.

(PLY: 2) DEFMOVES: ((BK F8) (BK H8))
NEWBOARD: (G8 BK F8)

The word 'DEFMOVES' labels the list of moves under consideration by the defensive search. (Each move is the first part of a plan under consideration.)

TRY CURRENT PLAN
PLY 3 (VALUE . 0) BESTPLAN: ((WQ A3))
NEWBOARD: (G3 WQ A3)

The phrase 'TRY CURRENT PLAN' means that the program is obtaining the next move by executing a plan that was inherited from an earlier analysis. In this example the current plan specifies an actual move rather than a goal, so the move is made immediately without calculating the primitives in this position. Applying the evaluation function to this position yields 0 (given after the word 'VALUE').

(PLY: 4) DEFMOVES: ((BR E7))
NEWBOARD: (E8 BR E7)

PARADISE knows (BR D6) will not help; CAPS searches it after refuting (BR E7).

NULL PLAN (VALUE . 0) (STATIC-ANALYSIS 20.4 SECONDS) (4 PLANS)
PLY 5 BESTPLAN: (((WB D3) ((NIL (CHECKMOVE WR H8)) (NIL (SAFECAPTURE WB BQ))
(NIL (SAFEMOVE WR H8) (((BK NIL) (SAFECAPTURE WR BR))
((ANYBUT BK) (SAFECAPTURE WR BK)))))))
(NEWEXPECT . 90)
NEWBOARD: (H7 WB D3)

The current plan is finished so the system does a static analysis which takes 20.4 seconds of cpu time and produces 4 plans. The best one begins with (WB D3) and continues with either a rook check on H8 threatening mate, the capture of the black queen by the bishop, or the rook move to H8 followed by a skewer of the black king to the black rook. Once again the static analysis accurately recommends the winning plan. This is an improvement over the performance of CAPS which finally suggested B–D3 as a defensive move since it protected the white pawn and white rook which are both en prise. The expectation is now 90, having been recalculated from the new current plan which only expects to win the black queen.

(PLY: 6) DEFMOVES: ((BR D3) (BR D3) (BQ D3) (BQ F1) (BP G5) (BQ D3) (BK G8))
NEWBOARD: (D8 BR D3)

TRY OBVIOUSLY WINNING MOVE
PLY 7 (VALUE . –33) BESTPLAN: ((WR H8))
(NEWEXPECT . 607)
NEWBOARD: (H4 WR H8)
(EXIT OFFENSE (VALUE 1300 . 1300))

The system finds R–H8 as an obviously winning move. It knows the move will mate (although it plays it to make sure), so it doesn't check the current plan. If the system hadn't been sure of the mate, it would have executed the current plan after noticing that R–H8 duplicates the

(CHECKMOVE WR H8) goal in the current plan. A range is returned as the value, but both the top and bottom of the range are 1300 (the value for mate) since the value has been exactly determined.

(PLY 6) REFUTE: ((WR H8))
(PLY: 6) DEFMOVES: ((BQ D3) (BQ F1) (BP G5) (BQ D3) (BK G8))
CAUSALITY: (BQ D3) LINE: (D8 BR D3) NO
NEWBOARD: (E2 BQ F1)

PARADISE backs up to ply 6. A counter-causal analysis tries to refute the move R–H8 by white but no new moves are suggested. The causality facility compares the proposed Q–D3 move to the tree produced for the R–D3 move and determines that Q–D3 cannot help. Q–D3 is therefore rejected without searching and Q–F1 is played (the causality facility approves it). The causality facility makes use of considerable information returned by the searching process. CAPS, which also has a causality facility, searches both R–D3 and Q–D3 in this position. In fact, more than half the moves rejected by causality in the remainder of this protocol are searched by CAPS.

OBVIOUSLY WINNING MOVE DUPLICATED
TRY CURRENT PLAN
PLY 7 (VALUE . −50) BESTPLAN: ((WB F1))
NEWBOARD: (D3 WB F1)

B–F1 is suggested as a winning move, but it duplicates the SAFECAPTURE goal in the current plan (and is not a sure mate) so the current plan is tried.

(PLY: 8) DEFMOVES: ((BP D1))
NEWBOARD: (D8 BR D1)

(VALUE . 49) TRY QUIESCENCE SEARCH
(PLY: 9) NEWBOARD: (H4 WR H8)
(QUIESCENCE VALUE (1300 . 1300))

The current plan is finished so the offense tries a quiescence search to see if the value holds up. A value of 1300 is returned so the search backs up with success for white.

(PLY 8) REFUTE: ((WR H8))
(PLY: 8) DEFMOVES: ((BP G5) (BR D2) (BR D7) (BP G6) (BP F5) (BP F6) (BK E8) (BK G8))
NEWBOARD: (G7 BP G5)

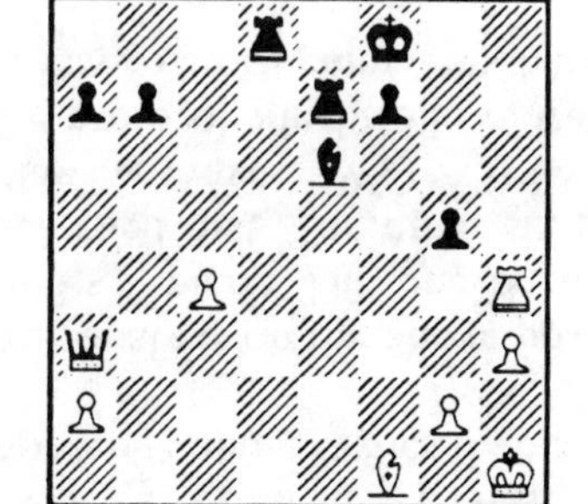

(VALUE .49) TRY QUIESCENCE SEARCH
(PLY: 9) NEWBOARD: (H4 WR H8)
DEFENDING MOVE SELECTED
(PLY: 10) NEWBOARD: (F8 BK G7)
(PLY: 11) NEWBOARD: (H8 WR D8)
DEFENDING MOVE SELECTED
(PLY: 12) NEWBOARD: (E7 BR D7)
(PLY: 13) NEWBOARD: (D8 WR D7)
(PLY: 14) NEWBOARD: (E6 BB D7)
(PLY: 15) NEWBOARD: (A3 WQ A7)
DEFENDING MOVE SELECTED
(PLY: 16) NEWBOARD: (D7 BB C6)
(QUIESCENCE VALUE (109 . 109))
(EXIT OFFENSE (VALUE 109 . 109))

A quiescence search to a depth of 16 shows that P–G5 fails for black. The quiescence search knows that white is ahead and that the white rook on H4 is not in danger, yet it plays aggressive moves (at plys 9 through 15) instead of being satisfied. This seems to generate nodes unnecessarily. PARADISE does this because it is a cheap way to get better results. The quiescence search is very inexpensive compared to the regular search. The system thinks it has enough information, yet it may be necessary to search this line again if the 'true' value is not found. Since PARADISE sees an inexpensive way (quiescence searching) to improve the result, it risks generating a few unnecessary (though inexpensive) nodes in order to avoid a possible re-search later.

(PLY 8) REFUTE: ((WR H8))
(PLY: 8) DEFMOVES: ((BR D2) (BR D7) (BP G6) (BP F5) (BP F6) (BK E8) (BK G8))
CAUSALITY: (BR D2) LINE: (D8 BR D1) NO
CAUSALITY: (BR D7) LINE: (D8 BR D1) NO
CAUSALITY: (BP G6) LINE: (G7 BP G5) NO
NEWBOARD: (F7 BP F5)

Black tries other moves at ply 8. Causality rejects R–D2 and R–D7 on the basis of the tree generated for R–D1, and it rejects P–G6 using the P–G5 tree.

(VALUE . 49) TRY QUIESCENCE SEARCH
(PLY: 9) NEWBOARD: (H4 WR H8)
DEFENDING MOVE SELECTED
(PLY: 10) NEWBOARD: (E6 BB G8)

(PLY: 11) NEWBOARD: (A3 WQ A7)
(QUIESCENCE VALUE (59 . 59))
(EXIT OFFENSE (VALUE 59 . 90))

Again the quiescence search confirms the offensive success. This time the value of 59 does not meet the expectation so the offensive search returns a range of 59 to 90 since the expectation of 90 may have been achieved if a static analysis had been done. PARADISE notes in the tree that searching here again may improve the value from 59 to 90.

(PLY 8) REFUTE: ((WR H8))
(PLY: 8) DEFMOVES: ((BP F6) (BK E8) (BK G8))
CAUSALITY: (BP F6) LINE: (F7 BP F5) NO
NEWBOARD: (F8 BK E8)

(VALUE . 49) TRY QUIESCENCE SEARCH
(PLY: 9) NEWBOARD: (A3 WQ A7)
(QUIESCENCE VALUE (59 . 59))
(EXIT OFFENSE (VALUE 59 . 90))

(PLY 8) REFUTE: ((WQ A7))
(PLY: 8) DEFMOVES: ((BK G8) (BR A8) (BP A6) (BP A5) (BP B6))
CAUSALITY: (BK G8) LINE: (F8 BK E8) NO
CAUSALITY: (BR A8) LINE: (D8 BR D1) NO
CAUSALITY: (BP A6) LINE: (D8 BR D1) NO
CAUSALITY: (BP A5) LINE: (D8 BR D1) NO
CAUSALITY: (BP B6) LINE: (F8 BK E8) NO
DEFMOVES: ( )

PLY 7 BESTPLAN: ((CHECKMOVE WR H8))
TERMINATE: PLAN SUCCEEDED
(EXIT OFFENSE (VALUE 59 . 90))

The offensive search terminates since a significant gain has been achieved. PARADISE again notes in the tree that searching other plans here may improve the value. The range of 59 to 90 is returned.

(PLY 6) REFUTE: ((WR H8) (WR H8) (WR H8) (WB F1))
(PLY: 6) DEFMOVES: ((BP G5) (BK G8))
NEWBOARD: (G7 BP G5)

OBVIOUSLY WINNING MOVE DUPLICATED
TRY CURRENT PLAN
PLY 7 (VALUE . 0) BESTPLAN: ((WB E2))
NEWBOARD: (D3 WB E2)

(PLY: 8) DEFMOVES: (BP H4))
NEWBOARD: (G5 BP H4)

(VALUE . 49) TRY QUIESCENCE SEARCH
(PLY: 9) NEWBOARD: (A3 WQ A7)
(QUIESCENCE VALUE (59 . 59))
(EXIT OFFENSE (VALUE 59 . 90))

(PLY: 8) DEFMOVES: ( )
PLY 7 BESTPLAN: ((CHECKMOVE WR H8))
TERMINATE: ALPHA BETA

(PLY 6) REFUTE: ((WB E2))
(PLY: 6) DEFMOVES: ((BQ E3) (BQ D2) (BQ E5) (BQ G2) (BQ A2) (BK G8))
CAUSALITY: (BQ E3) LINE: (D8 BR D3) NO
CAUSALITY: (BQ D2) LINE: (D8 BR D3) NO
CAUSALITY: (BQ E5) LINE: (D8 BR D3) NO
NEWBOARD: (E2 BQ G2)

TRY OBVIOUSLY WINNING MOVE
PLY 7 (VALUE . −10) BESTPLAN: ((WK G2))
NEWBOARD: (H1 WK G2)
(PLY: 8) DEFMOVES: ( )

The defensive search now does a null move analysis (see Wilkins [13]). It has no idea what to do so it lets the offense make two moves in a row. However, the offense calls the quiescence search which knows it is the defense's move. It decides the defense can escape from the threat of R–H8 so it calls the position quiescent.

(VALUE . 89) TRY QUIESCENCE SEARCH
assumed escape from (WR H8)
(QUIESCENCE VALUE (89 . 89))
(EXIT OFFENSE (VALUE 89 . 89))

(PLY: 8) DEFMOVES: ()
(PLY: 6) REFUTE: ((WK G2))
(PLY: 6) DEFMOVES: ((BQ A2) (BK G8))
CAUSALITY: (BQ A2) LINE: (D8 BR D3) NO
CAUSALITY: (BK G8) LINE: (G7 BP G5) NO
(PLY: 6) DEFMOVES: ()

PLY 5 BESTPLAN: ((WQ A5) NIL (CHECKMOVE WQ D8))
no unlikelys after success: quit
(EXIT OFFENSE (VALUE 59 . 89))

The search backs up to ply 5 and tries the next plan suggested by the static analysis. This plan has a LIKELY of 1 and the result already achieved is so successful that PARADISE rejects the unlikely plan without searching.

(PLY 4) REFUTE: ((WR H8) (WB D3))
(PLY: 4) DEFMOVES: ()
PLY 3 LAST PLAN
(EXIT OFFENSE (VALUE 59 . 320))

The search backs up to ply 3. There are no more plans to execute here, but a static analysis has not yet been done so the program makes a note of this. The top of the value range is changed to 320 to reflect the possibility of achieving the original expectation by doing a static analysis to find plans.

(PLY 2) REFUTE: ((WQ A3))
(PLY: 2) DEFMOVES: ((BK H8))
NEWBOARD: (G8 BK H8)

NULL PLAN (VALUE . 0) (STATIC-ANALYSIS 14.2 SECONDS) (2 PLANS)
PLY 3 BESTPLAN: ((WB D3))
(NEWEXPECT . 320)
NEWBOARD: (H7 WB D3)

The defense tries K–H8 at ply 2 and the original plan does not match this move so a static analysis is undertaken. Again PARADISE finds the right idea immediately. To compare, CAPS did not have the necessary knowledge and tried 3 other moves first, generating 80 nodes to disprove them, before stumbling onto B–D3.

(PLY: 4) DEFMOVES: ((BK G8))
NEWBOARD: (H8 BK G8)

(VALUE . 0) TRY OBVIOUSLY WINNING MOVE
PLY 5 BESTPLAN: ((WB E2))
(NEWEXPECT . 90)
NEWBOARD: (D3 WB E2)

(PLY: 6) DEFMOVES: ()
(VALUE . 99) TRY QUIESCENCE SEARCH
(QUIESCENCE VALUE (99 . 99))
(EXIT OFFENSE (VALUE 99 . 99))

(PLY: 6) DEFMOVES: () PLY 5 LAST PLAN
(EXIT OFFENSE (VALUE 99 . 320))
(PLY 4) REFUTE: ((WB E2)) (PLY: 4) DEFMOVES: ()

PLY 3 BESTPLAN: ((WB E4))
(NEWEXPECT . 10)
TERMINATE: FORWARD PRUNE
(EXIT OFFENSE (VALUE 99 . 320))

The search backs up to ply 3 and the offense tries B–E4 which has been suggested by the static analysis. Its expectation is 10 and B–D3 has already achieved 99 so a forward prune occurs.

(PLY 2) REFUTE: ((WB D3))
(PLY: 2) DEFMOVES: ()

PLY 1 BESTPLAN: ((WQ A3) NIL (CHECKMOVE WB H7))
no unlikelys after success: quit

The search returns to the top level to try the next plan but it is terminated because it has a LIKELY of 1 and the search is over. CAPS invests much effort at this point searching other offensive moves.

BEST MOVE: (E4 WB H7) VALUE: (59 . 320)
PRINCIPAL VARIATION:
1 (E4 WB H7) (G8 BK F8)
2 (G3 WQ A3) (E8 BR E7)

3 (H7 WB D3) (E2 BQ F1)
4 (D3 WB F1) (F7 BP F5)
5 (H4 WR H8) (E6 BB G8)
6 (A3 WQ A7)

TOTAL TIME: 297 SECONDS
NODES CREATED: 36 (22 REGULAR, 14 QUIESCENCE)
STATIC ANALYSES: 2

WHERE TIME WAS SPENT:
49% calculating primitives
33% quiescence searching (overlaps primitive calculations for 14 nodes)
11% static analysis
9% defense determining initial move
3% disk IO
0% causality facility, evaluation function, creating board positions

Many things should be noticed in this example. The plans do an excellent job of guiding the search: only two static analyses are done in the entire search. The plans are so accurately specified by the analysis that they never once lead the search off the correct line. White's play in the search is error-free. The causality facility makes good use of information returned from the search. Many black moves which would otherwise have been searched are eliminated in this manner. The range values accurately express the potential of each node so that the system does not have to waste effort determining the 'true' values. The best first search strategy plays a minor role in this example.

On this problem, CAPS generated a tree of 489 nodes in 115 seconds to obtain a principal variation of B–R7ch, K–B1, Q–R3ch, R–K2, B–Q3, Q × Rch, B × Q, R–Q8. This is slightly inaccurate since there is a mate in one for white at the end of this variation which CAPS's quiescence analysis did not recognize, but it is clear that CAPS understands the problem and its solution. PARADISE generates only 36 nodes to CAPS's 489 for the following three reasons (primarily):

—PARADISE has more knowledge available during static analysis and can accurately analyze a position and produce good plans. CAPS generates many nodes by not playing the correct offensive move first on some occasions.

—PARADISE returns more useful information from its search and can therefore use its causality facility to eliminate moves that CAPS searches.

—PARADISE has a best-first search strategy while CAPS is committed to finding the 'true' value (within alpha-beta) of each node it searches. This enables PARADISE to terminate as soon as some information is discovered without having to look for better alternatives.

This comparison shows the advances PARADISE has made in the use of knowledge. It is not meant to belittle CAPS which pioneered some of the techniques basic to this approach. In fact, CAPS is the only program with which a comparison is appropriate. For example, on this problem CHESS 4.4 (running on a CDC-6400) produces a tree with 30,246 nodes in 95 seconds of cpu time without finding the solution (which is too deep for it). Looking at the details of such a tree would not be helpful.

10. Measuring PARADISE's performance

To aid in evaluating performance, PARADISE was tested on positions in the book *Win At Chess* [9]. This book contains tactically sharp positions from master games which are representative of tactical problems of reasonable difficulty. PARADISE's knowledge base was developed by writing productions which would enable the program to solve, in a reasonable manner, fifteen chosen positions from among the first 100 in *Win At Chess*. The 85 positions not chosen were not considered during this development. This development process produced one version of the program, called PARADISE-0. Six positions were then picked at random from the remaining 85 and accurate records were kept on the work involved in getting the program to solve these reasonably. The version of the program which solves all 21 positions is called PARADISE.

PARADISE's performance on a problem is classified into one of three categories:

(1) problem solved as is (possibly with a minor bug fix),

(2) problem not solvable without a change to the program or a major change to the knowledge base, or

(3) problem solvable with a small addition to the knowledge base.

Category 3 helps measure the modifiability of the knowledge base. It is meant to include solutions which require no changes whatsoever to the program and only a small addition to the knowledge base. Small means that it takes less than 20 minutes total of human time to identify the problem and write or modify one production which will enable PARADISE, with no other changes, to solve the problem in a reasonable way (i.e., no ad hoc solutions).

Of the six positions chosen at random, two were in category 1, three were in category 3, and one was in category 2. The latter one inspired the only program changes between PARADISE-0 and PARADISE. These results speak well for the modifiability of the knowledge base, but shed little light on the generality of the program. To better test generality, PARADISE has been tested on the first 100 positions. These positions are divided into 5 groups of 20 and Reinfeld claims an increase in difficulty with increase in group number. (Eight end-game positions were eliminated, so the groups actually have 18, 19, 18, 20, and 17 positions.) PARADISE is considered to solve only the problems in category 1, while PARADISE-2 solves both category 1 and 3 problems. PARADISE would become PARADISE-2 simply by leaving in the productions written to solve problems in category 3.

Since the 21 developmental problems had not all been solved by one version of the program, these were tried first. Adding new knowledge during program development would (hopefully) not adversely affect performance on earlier problems, but this had to be confirmed. For example, productions added to the knowledge base to solve the last 5 developmental problems might produce so many suggestions in the first 5 problems that the search would become untractable in those problems. The testing proved that the new knowledge had no adverse effects. All 21 problems fell into category 1; thus the same version of the program solves them all. In every case, the analysis is either the same as or sharper than that produced by developmental versions of the program. This result provides strong evidence that the knowledge base is easily modifiable. If productions are written carefully and intelligently (a skill the author developed while writing productions for the developmental set), they do not appear to adversely affect the system's performance on positions unrelated to the new productions. This is an essential quality for a modifiable knowledge base.

Table 1 shows what percentage of these problems can be solved by PARADISE, PARADISE-2, CAPS (Berliner [1]), TECH (Gillogly [6]), CHESS 4.4 (Slate [12]) running on a CDC 6400, and a human player rated as class A (Berliner [1]). PARADISE was limited to forty-five minutes of cpu time per problem while the other programs were limited to five minutes.

PARADISE already exhibits more generality in this domain than programs like TECH and CAPS. PARADISE-2 outperforms all the programs and the human. This shows that these problems do not push the limits of the expressibility of the production language nor the ability of the program to control the tree search. PARADISE does well on Group III because seven of those twenty problems are in the twenty-one problems on which PARADISE was developed.

There are twenty problems solved by PARADISE-2 but not by PARADISE, but only thirteen productions were written to solve them. In two instances, an already existing production was modified. In five instances the same production solved two different category three problems. This is a strong indication that the productions being written are fairly general and not tailored to the specific problem. These results indicate that the generality of PARADISE is reasonable and that the modifiability of the knowledge base is excellent. There are three problems not solved by PARADISE-2 which are discussed in the next section.

TABLE 1. Percentage of problems solved by various chess players

	PARADISE	PARADISE–2	CAPS	TECH	CHESS 4.4	Class A human
Group I	78%	100%	67%	78%	94%	89%
Group II	68%	95%	74%	84%	95%	95%
Group III	94%	100%	61%	61%	78%	94%
Group IV	70%	95%	50%	40%	70%	80%
Group V	65%	94%	41%	47%	76%	53%
All 92	75%	97%	59%	61%	83%	83%

TABLE 2. Comparison of average tree size on first 100 problems (for solved problems)

	PARADISE-2	CAPS	CHESS 4.4
Group I	19.8	167.8	24,907.3
Group II	28.7	226.4	34,726.0
Group III	35.0	206.1	24,200.1
Group IV	58.4	453.6	31,538.1
Group V	48.4	285.3	25,917.5
All 100	38.1	260.6	28,496.8

PARADISE uses more cpu time and produces trees with considerably fewer nodes than the other programs. The example search in Section 8 is a problem from Group III, and tree sizes of 21 nodes for PARADISE and 439, 459 for TECH-2 are fairly typical. Table 2 compares the average tree size (in number of nodes) for PARADISE-2, CAPS and CHESS 4.4 on the problems they solved in these 100.

PARADISE attempts to use knowledge whenever possible in order to produce trees of the same order of magnitude as those produced by human masters. Table 2 shows that this has been accomplished for the most part. CAPS uses a lot of knowledge but invests only about one-fifth of a second per node calculating. CAPS relies on the search to correct mistakes made by inadequate knowledge and this results in trees one order of magnitude larger than those produced by PARADISE. CHESS 4.4 has little chess knowledge and relies almost entirely on search to discriminate between moves. It generates trees that are three orders of magnitude larger than those generated by PARADISE. The two knowledge-oriented programs (CAPS and PARADISE) grow larger trees for the deeper combinations (Groups IV and V), just as most humans would. CHESS 4.4's tree size seems unrelated to the depth of the combination. CHESS 4.4 is of course the best chess player of these three programs.

Table 3 shows where PARADISE invests its resources. The statistics are

TABLE 3. Resource investment in PARADISE (89 solved problems)

	Mean	Highest	Lowest	Standard Deviation
CPU time for whole problem:	332.9	1958	19	396.6
Nodes created during search:	38.06	215	3	41.9
% CPU time calculating primitives:	52.85	74.3	34.1	8.47
CPU time per static analysis:	12.22	26.5	2.2	5.14
Number of static analyses per problem:	3.73	35	0	5.96
% CPU time doing static analysis:	11.61	33.7	0.0	10.04
% nodes requiring static analysis:	8.95	33.3	0.0	8.07
% CPU time executing knowledge base:	91.6	97.7	81.5	2.92

compiled over the 89 problems which PARADISE-2 solved. They give some idea of the size of tree PARADISE grows, the amount of time it spends, and where this time is spent. (CPU time is in seconds on a KL-10 processor.)

Table 3 shows that calculating primitives is PARADISE's most computationally significant activity. The fact that less than 9% of the nodes generated had static analyses done on them shows that the plans do a good job of guiding the search. Because of this, static analyses are not a major overall expense even though an average one takes more than twelve seconds of cpu time. The different cpu time limit given to PARADISE in Table 1 is due to the availability of statistics, but is not as unfair as it seems. As Table 3 shows, PARADISE-2 uses an average of only 5.5 minutes of cpu time on the 89 problems it solves. Also, PARADISE could probably be speeded up by a factor of 2 or more with more efficient production matching. As Table 3 shows, the program spends more than 91% of its time in the inefficient production interpreter.

11. How PARADISE Goes Wrong

PARADISE-2 was not able to solve 3 of the 92 problems after small additions to the knowledge base. A failure by PARADISE can be classified in one of the three following categories:

(1) The best plan is never suggested. PARADISE tries every plan that has been suggested and then quits without having achieved an acceptable result since it has run out of ideas. This can be cured by filling a hole in the program's knowledge so that the best plan will be suggested.

(2) The search becomes unbounded. If a position is rich in possible attacks and defenses, with most combinations running many ply before a quiescent position is reached, then PARADISE may use an unreasonable amount of time searching. During testing, PARADISE was limited to 45 minutes of cpu time per problem.

(3) A mistake is made in the analysis. For example, PARADISE may not solve a problem (even though recommending the best move) because the causality facility has eliminated a good defensive move which should have been searched, or because the quiescence analysis has made a large error (small errors must be tolerated).

Of the twenty problems solved by PARADISE-2 but not by PARADISE, 19 fell into category 1 initially. One fell into category 3 because of a mistaken quiescence analysis, but an added production fixed the problem. There were no failures caused by the search becoming unbounded. The 3 problems which PARADISE-2 could not solve are shown in Fig. 6, and are examined in detail below.

In problem 31, white plays P–Q6 and wins the black bishop which must move to save the black rook. If Q × R is played immediately, black replies B × Pch and wins white's queen. (White still has a won position after this, but it is an

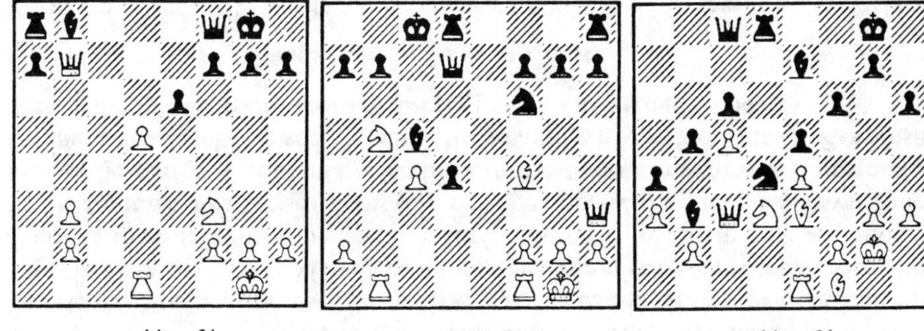

FIG. 6. Problems not solved by PARADISE-2.

involved pawn ending which goes well beyond the depth to which any current program can reasonably search.) PARADISE-2 could easily solve this problem by including a production which tries to block a checking move by a piece blocking a support of an en prise piece. Such a production could be expressed in only a few lines in the production-language. However, this is unacceptable because it is an ad hoc solution. The 'correct' way to find P–Q6 is by analyzing the refutation of Q × R. This move is suggested by PARADISE's counter-causal analysis but is not searched because offensive counter-causal moves are tried only if they are caputures (see [13]). Changing this restriction would involve a program change, so PARADISE-2 cannot solve this problem. This problem would be classified as a category 3 failure.

Problem 71 is a category 1 failure. The initial static analysis does not suggest N × RPch which wins for white by enabling the white queen to move to QR3 and then up the queen rook file. The static analysis has the goal of moving the white queen to QR3 and then up the queen rook file, so a fairly simple production in the MOVE KS suggests N × RP at the top level. With this new production PARADISE-2 at first got the correct answer, but a bug in one of the productions in the DEFENDMOVE KS prevents some good defensive moves from being tried at ply 4. When this defensive production is fixed, the search becomes unbounded (i.e., uses more than 45 minutes of cpu time) because of the many defensive and offensive possibilities. This is the only example of a category 2 failure during testing of the program.

Position 91 is also a category 1 failure. Black can win a pawn and a much superior position by playing B–K3. Black threatens mate with his queen and knight and white must play B × N to avoid it, allowing P × B, 2. Q–any P × Pch winning a pawn. Whenever PARADISE suggests mating sequences, it first expends a large amount of effort doing a sensitive analysis of the upcoming possibilities. Problem 91 must be understood on a similar level of specificity, since PARADISE uses this specific analysis to control the search. However, such a specific production would require more than thirty minutes of human effort to design and implement so PARADISE-2 was not given credit for this problem.

12. Comparison to Plans in Robot Problem Solving

Plans are used in many domains of AI research, especially robot problem solving. ABSTRIPS (Sacerdoti [10]), NOAH (Sacerdoti [11]), and BUILD (Fahlman [5]) are examples of planning systems in robot problem solving environments. Plans in these systems are very different from those in chess so a general description of these differences is more appropriate than a detailed comparison. Robot planning is frequently done in abstracted spaces which have been defined. These abstracted spaces omit details such as whether a door is open or not. There are a small number of such details, and the problem solver has some specific knowledge for each such detail which it can apply when required. For example, the problem solver has a procedure for opening a door should the door be closed when the robot wants to go through it. Such an approach is much more difficult in chess, at least with mankind's current understanding of the game. It is not clear how to define abstracted spaces. Small details are very important in chess and cannot be readily ignored, even for determining the first step of a plan. For example, a chess planner should not ignore the fact that a piece is pinned on the assumption that it can be unpinned when the plan calls for it to move. Thus plans in PARADISE are all at the same, very detailed level.

In the robot planning systems, the effects of an action are well defined. The program can easily and quickly determine the exact state of the world after it has moved a blue block. In chess, moves (actions) may subtly affect everything on the board. For example, a piece that was safe may no longer be (even though the move made has no direct effect on the piece), and the system may need to make an expensive calculation to determine this. Chess plans cannot make many assumptions about the state of the world in the future, but must describe the expected features of new states in the plan itself and then test for these features while executing the plan. Consider the monkey and bananas problem. If the experimenter is sinister, he could connect the bananas to the box by pulleys and rope, invisible to the monkey, so that when the box is pulled under the bananas, the bananas are pulled up so they cannot be reached from atop the box. In a sense, the robot planners assume that no such crazy side effects will happen, while a chess plan must prepare for such things. This manifests itself in PARADISE in at least two ways. First, plans are not composed of simple actions but are goals which may require the knowledge in many productions to be interpreted. This postponement of evaluation permits checking of many complex features in the current world state. Second, PARADISE has been designed to make it easy to produce new concepts (by writing productions and forming KSs) for expressing plans whenever they are needed to handle new 'crazy side effects.'

In most robot planning systems, tests for having achieved the goal or the preconditions of an action are trivial and give well defined answers. In chess, there may be only very subtle differences between a position where a particular action is good and positions where the same action is wrong. It is also hard to know when a goal has been achieved, since there is always a chance of obtaining a larger advantage (except when the opponent has been checkmated). Thus in chess it is necessary for the plan to provide a considerable amount of information to help in the making of these decisions. This is done in PARADISE through the attribute lists in plans.

The number of things PARADISE can consider doing at any point in a plan is about an order of magnitude larger than the number of things most robot problem solvers usually contend with. There are an average of about 38 legal moves in a chess position (see [3]). A robot usually has a much smaller number of possible actions which cannot be easily eliminated (for example, going to one of a few rooms or picking up one of a few objects). When planning farther in the future than just the first action, the chess planner has many more choices than the 38 legal moves. The inability to make assumptions about future states often prevents mentioning actual moves in a plan. Instead a description of the intent is needed, and the number of such descriptions is much larger than the number of legal moves that might be made. A robot usually has a much smaller number of possible actions, so the two types of plans explode at very different rates.

To summarize, the robot planners have the flavor of establishing a sequence from a small number of well-understood operations until the correct order is found, while chess planners have more a flavor of 'creating' the correct plan from the many possibilities. For this reason, a system which produces good chess plans needs a large amount of knowledge and non-trivial reasoning processes to produce plans.

Probably the most important idea PARADISE has for the robot problem solvers is that a plan may be viewed as a way to control what parts of a large knowledge base will be used to analyze each situation during plan execution. Plans in PARADISE can be viewed as telling the system what knowledge to use in analysis, thus defining a perspective for the system to use in new situations. Some amount of analysis from this new perspective is almost always done before the plan can continue executing. In most robot planning systems plans are more accurately viewed as telling the system what action to take. PARADISE tries to delay execution in order to bring more knowledge to bear.

13. Comparison to Plans in Chess

Pitrat's program [8], which solves chess combinations, is the most important example of the use of plans in chess. The language Pitrat uses for expressing plans has four statements with the move statement and modification statement being the most important. The move statement specifies that the piece on one particular square should move to another particular square. It may also be specified that the move must be a capture. The modification statement describes a modification to be made to a particular square. This can be one of four things: removal of a friend, removal of an enemy, moving a friend to the square, or getting an enemy to move to the square.

Plans in PARADISE provide much more flexibility in expression that Pitrat's move statement. In PARADISE, types of moves other than captures can be specified (e.g., safe moves and safe capture moves). Also, particular squares do not need to be named in PARADISE since it can use a variety of goals to express the plan. The important square to move to may change depending on the opponent's move so it is not always possible to specify such a square in advance. For example, if white makes a move which traps and attacks black's queen then (after some desperado move by black) white would like to capture black's queen wherever it may be. PARADISE can express the plan of capturing the queen anywhere, while Pitrat's move statement cannot since the planner does not know which particular square the queen will be on.

Pitrat's modification statement is a goal which the system tries to accomplish. These modifications are too simple to express the purposes behind their suggestion. For example, the system may want to decoy the black queen to make a square that it protects safe for white. Pitrat would express this goal as removing an enemy from the black queen's location which does not express the purpose of the plan. It will work well for the winning combination but will also allow many wrong moves since the queen may be decoyed to a square from which she can still protect the square in question. PARADISE can avoid this since it has the ability to express its purposes. It can specify that the black queen must be decoyed to make the particular square safe, and only decoys which remove the black queen's protection will be considered. PARADISE would also specify that the move after the decoy should be safe so it will not be tried unless the preparations have accomplished their purpose. PARADISE attempts to express the purpose of each plan while Pitrat's plans express side effects that will happen if the purpose is accomplished (e.g., a square becoming vacant). Unfortunately, the same side effects may also happen when the purpose is not accomplished, causing the system to waste effort searching poor lines.

Plans in PARADISE have two more major advantages over the plans in Pitrat's system. First, PARADISE has conditionals which allow specification of different plans for different replies by the opponent. The advantages of this are obvious: the system can immediately try the correct plan instead of searching an inappropriate plan and backtracking to correct itself. Second, PARADISE's plan language is modifiable. Simply by writing new productions, new goals and concepts can be created for expressing plans and the system will automatically understand these new plans. This property is necessary for any system that wishes to extend its domain or incrementally increase its expertise. Significant additions to Pitrat's plan language would seem to require a major programming effort.

Despite the shortcomings of the plans in Pitrat's program, they are much more sophisticated than any plans previously used in computer chess programs. Pitrat's program performs well in its domain. It processes nodes much faster than PARADISE and therefore can handle larger trees. The plans do an adequate job given these constraints. It may be the case that programs will obtain better performance by using Pitrat's approach of larger trees and less sophisticated plans, but the use of knowledge is only starting to be investigated by programs such as PARADISE and it is too early to draw conclusions.

14. Summary

PARADISE exhibits expert performance on positions it has the knowledge to understand, showing that a knowledge-based approach can solve some problems that the best search based programs cannot solve because the solutions are too deep. The knowledge base is organized into KSs which provide concepts for PARADISE to use in its reasoning processes. These concepts are higher level than the ideas produced by simply matching patterns. A single pattern cannot recognize a whole plan of action in a complex chess position; both pattern-level ideas and these higher level concepts are necessary in the reasoning process.

The concepts provided by the KSs are used to create plans during static analysis. The concepts communicate enough information that they can be rejected after being posted. This keeps antithetical ideas from being combined to produce ridiculous plans. The same concepts are used to express plans for guiding the search, and the KSs execute the plans during the search. By communicating plans down the tree, PARADISE can understand new positions on the basis of its analysis of previous positions. By having particular goals in mind when looking at a new position, the system quickly focuses on the relevant part of the knowledge base. Plans in PARADISE express their purpose fairly well, without being too general or too specific. They contain enough additional information to enable the system to decide when a line has succeeded or failed. Because of the successful communication of knowledge through plans, PARADISE is able to solve a number of chess combinations with small trees and without a depth limit on its search.

PARADISE's knowledge base is amenable to modification. Production rules (and therefore KSs) can be quickly written and inserted in the knowledge base to improve system performance without adverse affects. Since KSs are used in both planning and static analysis, modifications can improve both without program changes. The range of expressible plans can easily be increased.

15. Issues

One of the major issues in creating concepts is their generality. How 'high-level' should a concept be? If the concepts are too general then too many details are lost, and the system does not have the necessary facts to do certain reasoning. If not general enough, the system leans toward the extreme of needing a production for every possible chess position. The concepts in PARADISE have been constructed to be as general as possible without sacrificing expert-level performance to the loss of detail. The factor limiting generality is the ability to communicate details in the attribute lists of concepts. The generality in PARADISE has made concepts in the data base so complex that productions must essentially match patterns in these concepts.

The tradeoff of generality and specificity in concepts is closely related to the tradeoff of search and knowledge. With much specific knowledge the use of knowledge becomes expensive, but fewer mistakes need to be corrected in the search. Such a knowledge-based approach can solve deep problems (e.g., PARADISE has no depth limit), but may not be able to solve many problems, even easy ones, because of holes in its knowledge. With more general knowledge, analysis is cheaper but more time must be spent correcting mistakes in the search. Such a search-based approach often leads to a program which does a full width search. Such programs almost always solve problems within their depth limit, but cannot solve deep problems and suffer from problems like the horizon effect (see Berliner [1]).

PARADISE uses a mix of search and knowledge which involves more knowledge and less search than previous programs which include chess middle games in their domain. The strength of the program depends on the completeness of the knowledge base. Programs like CAPS and Pitrat's do not search all legal moves and may also have holes in their knowledge. One might expect PARADISE to miss combinations more often than these two programs since its more specific knowledge suggests fewer moves, but this has not been the case in the comparison of CAPS and PARADISE on the test postions. PARADISE recognizes mating attacks that both CAPS and Pitrat's program miss. PARADISE's knowledge base appears complete enough to outperform CAPS on the first 100 positions in Reinfeld [9], even on positions within CAPS' depth limit. PARADISE-2's knowledge base is complete enough to outperform CHESS 4.4 on these problems.

The primary justification for the cpu time used by PARADISE and the biggest advantage of the approach used in PARADISE is the extendability of the knowledge base. This means the effect of holes in the knowledge can easily be reduced in PARADISE. The play of most programs cannot be noticeably improved with easily made program or knowledge modifications. Improved play would involve programming a more sophisticated analysis, or controlling the search better so that it could search deeper. (Play can, of course, be improved by switching to a significantly faster computer in most cases.) It would be hard to incrementally improve performance of a program by increasing its depth limit since each increment of one ply multiplies the effort required by the branching factor (usually about 5 or 6 for programs with full width searches that have a reasonable move ordering for alpha-beta). The possibility of incremental improvement through improved analysis is discussed below.

Programming a more sophisticated static analysis in any of the programs mentioned in this paper (except PARADISE) would probably not be easy for the programmer. Even if it were, these programs are committed (by tree size) to limit the amount of processing per node. CAPS spends more time per node than the others, but still processes five nodes per second of cpu time. CHESS 4.7 processes around 3600 nodes per second on a Cyber 176. If CHESS 4.7 spent even an additional ten milliseconds per node in analysis, the size of the tree it could search in a given amount of time would be greatly reduced. Easy incremental improvement of CHESS 4.7 (and similar search-based programs) by making analysis progressively more sophisticated does not seem possible. This means the theoretical limitations imposed by the depth limit cannot easily be overcome.

The time constraints on CAPS and Pitrat's program would permit slight increases in the time spent on analysis. Such slight increases cannot involve very specific knowledge, so any knowledge which recognizes a new tactic would suggest more moves to be searched in many positions. This increases the size of the search tree exponentially. These programs are already running efficiently and would either have to develop new search control mechanisms, or use significantly more cpu time to cope with this increase in branching factor.

For PARADISE's knowledge base to achieve the completeness needed to rival the best search-based programs (in middle game tactics), many productions may yet have to be added. There is no evidence that suggests large numbers of productions will harm PARADISE's performance (although problems may arise). New productions do not seem to significantly increase the branching factor when the added productions are at the right level of specificity (see Wilkins [13]). New productions do not significantly increase the analysis effort largely because plans guide PARADISE's search so well that a static analysis is done at less than nine percent of the nodes generated. Thus most new productions will rarely be executed. Even when executed, productions usually do not match and the system can often determine this with little effort. Even when matched, well-written productions take only a few milliseconds to a few hundred milliseconds to match. Compared to the 12 seconds of cpu time PARADISE spends on a typical analysis, this is not significant. The limiting factor in PARADISE's incremental improvement appears to be the ability to recognize more complex tactics at the correct level of specificity.

Weighing the above tradeoffs in order to judge which approach is best depends on the current technology. With developments such as faster machines, parrallelism, or better hashing techniques, programs which rely on search can search deeper and perform better. The development of better pattern recognizers might increase the power of PARADISE's production language allowing PARADISE to perform better. There is little doubt that with current machines and our current understanding of how to use knowledge, good search-based programs solve a larger class of problems with less expense than do the best knowledge-based programs. However, techniques for using knowledge are only beginning to be developed and understood. This research shows ways to effectively use a large knowledge base which can be easily extended. As progress is made in representing and using knowledge, a knowledge-based program may eventually be able to approach (and even surpass) the performance of human chess masters.

ACKNOWLEDGEMENTS

The author is indebted to Hans Berliner for his continuing assistance and counsel during this research, and to the Stanford Artificial Intelligence Laboratory which provided the necessary environment and tools for doing this research.

REFERENCES

1. Berliner, H., Chess as problem solving: The development of a tactics analyzer, Unpublished doctoral thesis, Carnegie-Mellon University (1974).
2. Charness, H., Human chess skill, in: P. Frey (Ed.), *Chess Skill in Man and Machine* (Springer, Berlin, 1977), Chapter 2.
3. De Groot, A. D., *Thought and Choice in Chess* (The Hague: Mouton, 1965).
4. Davis, R., Applications of meta level knowledge to the construction, maintenance and use of large knowledge bases, AIM-283, Computer Science Department, Stanford University, 1976.
5. Fahlman, S. E., A planning system for robot construction tasks, *Artificial Intelligence* **5** (1974) 1–49.
6. Gillogly, J., The technology chess program, *Artificial Intelligence* **3** (1972) 145–163.
7. Kotov, A., *Think Like a Grandmaster* (Chess Digest, Dallas, 1971).
8. Pitrat, J., A chess combination program which uses plans, *Artificial Intelligence* **8** (1977) 275–321.
9. Reinfeld, F., *Win At Chess* (Dover Books, 1958).
10. Sacerdoti, E. D., Planning in a hierarchy of abstraction spaces, *Artificial Intelligence* **5** (1974) 115–135.
11. Sacerdoti, E. D., The nonlinear nature of plans, Stanford Research Institute Technical Note 101 (January 1975).
12. Slate, D. and Atkin, L., CHESS 4.5—The Northwestern University chess program, in: P. Frey (Ed.), *Chess Skill in Man and Machine* (Springer, Berlin, 1977).
13. Wilkins, D. E., Using patterns and plans to solve problems and control search, AIM-329, Computer Science Department, Stanford University (1979).
14. Wilkins, D. E., Causality analysis in chess, *Proceedings of Third Conference Canadian Society for Computational Study of Intelligence, Victoria, May* 1980.

Interactive Transfer of Expertise: Acquisition of New Inference Rules

Randall Davis*

Computer Science Department, Stanford University, Stanford, CA 94305, U.S.A.

ABSTRACT

TEIRESIAS *is a program designed to provide assistance on the task of building knowledge-based systems. It facilitates the interactive transfer of knowledge from a human expert to the system, in a high level dialog conducted in a restricted subset of natural language. This paper explores an example of* TEIRESIAS *in operation and demonstrates how it guides the acquisition of new inference rules. The concept of* meta-level knowledge *is described and illustrations given of its utility in knowledge acquisition and its contribution to the more general issues of creating an intelligent program.*

1. Introduction

Where much early work in artificial intelligence was devoted to the search for a single, powerful, domain-independent problem solving methodology (e.g., GPS [14]), more recent efforts have stressed the use of large stores of domain-specific knowledge as a basis for high performance. The knowledge base for this sort of program (e.g., DENDRAL [11], MACSYMA [13]) is traditionally assembled by hand, an ongoing task that typically involves numerous man-years of effort. A key element in constructing a knowledge base is the transfer of expertise from a human expert to the program. Since the domain expert often knows nothing about programming, the interaction between the expert and the performance program usually requires the mediation of a human programmer.

We have sought to create a program that could supply much the same sort of assistance as that provided by the programmer in this transfer of expertise task. The result is a system called TEIRESIAS[1] [5–8], a large INTERLISP [19] program designed to offer assistance in the interactive transfer of knowledge from a human expert to the knowledge base of a high performance program (Fig. 1).

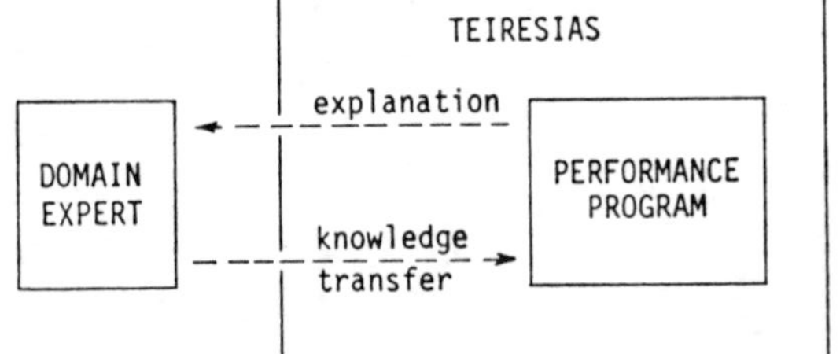

FIG. 1. Interaction between the expert and the performance program is facilitated by TEIRESIAS.

Information flow from right to left is labelled *explanation*. This is the process by which TEIRESIAS clarifies for the expert the source of the performance program's results and motivations for its actions. This is a prerequisite to knowledge acquisition, since the expert must first discover what the performance program already knows and how it used that knowledge. Information flow from left to right is labelled *knowledge transfer*. This is the process by which the expert adds to or modifies the store of domain-specific knowledge in the performance program.

Work on TEIRESIAS has had two general goals. We have attempted first to develop a set of tools and empirical methods for knowledge base construction and maintenance, and sought to abstract from them a methodology applicable to a range of systems. The second, more general goal has been the development of an intelligent assistant. This task involves confronting many of the traditional problems of AI and has resulted in the exploration of a number of solutions reviewed below.

This paper describes a number of the key ideas in the development of TEIRESIAS and discusses their implementation in the context a specific task (acquisition of new inference rules[2]) for a specific performance program (a rule-based computer consultant). While the discussion deals with one particular task, system and knowledge representation, several of the main ideas are applicable to more general issues concerning the creation of intelligent programs.

2. Meta-Level Knowledge

A central theme that runs through this and related papers [5–8] is the concept of *meta-level knowledge*. This takes several different forms as its use is explored, but can be summed up generally by saying that a program can "know what it knows". That is, a program can not only use its knowledge directly, but may also be able to examine it, abstract it, reason about it, and direct its application.

* Author's current address: 545 Technology Square, MIT, Cambridge, MA 02138, U.S.A.

This work was supported in part by the Advanced Research Projects Agency under ARPA Order 2494; by a Chaim Weizmann Postdoctoral Fellowship for Scientific Research, and by grant MCS 77-02712 from the National Science Foundation. It was carried out on the SUMEX Computer System, supported by the NIH Grant RR-00785.

[1] The program is named for the blind seer in *Oedipus the King*, since, as we will see, the program, like the prophet, has a form of "higher order" knowledge.

[2] Acquisition of new conceptual primitives from which rules are built is discussed in [7], while the design and implementation of the explanation capability suggested in Fig. 1 is discussed in [5].

To see in general terms how this might be accomplished, recall that one of the principal problems of AI is the question of representation and use of knowledge about the world, for which numerous techniques have been developed. One way to view what we have done is to imagine turning this in on itself, and using some of these same techniques to describe the program itself.

The resulting system contains both *object-level* representations describing the external world, and *meta-level* representations which describe the internal world of representations. As the discussion of "rule models" in Section 7 will make clear, such a system has a number of interesting capabilities.

3. Perspective on Knowledge Acquisition

We view the interaction between the domain expert and the performance program as *interactive transfer of expertise*. We see it in terms of a teacher who continually challenges a student with new problems to solve and carefully observes the student's performance. The teacher may interrupt to request a justification of some particular step the student has taken in solving the problem or may challenge the final result. This process may uncover a fault in the student's knowledge of the subject (the debugging phase) and result in the transfer of information to correct it (the knowledge acquisition phase).

Other approaches to knowledge acquisition can be compared to this by considering their relative positions along two dimensions: (i) the sophistication of their debugging facilities and (ii) the independence of their knowledge acquisition mechanism.

The simplest sort of debugging tool is characterized by a program like DDT, which is totally passive (in the sense that it operates only in response to user commands), is low level (since it operates at the level of machine or assembly language), and knows nothing about the application domain of the program.

Debuggers like BAIL [16] and INTERLISP's break package [19] are a step up from this since they function at the level of programming languages like SAIL and INTERLISP.

The explanation capabilities in TEIRESIAS, in particular the "how" and "why" commands (see [5] and [9] for examples), represent another step, since they function at the level of the control structure of the application program. The guided debugging which TEIRESIAS can also provide (illustrated in Section 6) represents yet another step, since here the debugger is taking the initiative and has enough built-in knowledge about the control structure that it can track down the error. It does this by requesting from the expert an opinion on the validity of a few selected rules from among the many that were invoked.

Finally, at the most sophisticated level are knowledge-rich debuggers like the one found in [2]. Here the program is active, high-level, and informed about the application domain, and is capable of independently localizing and characterizing bugs.

By independence of the knowledge acquisition mechanism, we mean the degree of human cooperation necessary. Much work on knowledge acquisition has emphasized a highly autonomous mode of operation. There is, for example, a large body of work aimed at inducing the appropriate generalizations from a set of test data (see, e.g., [3] and [12]). In these efforts user interaction is limited to presenting the program with the data and perhaps providing a brief description of the domain in the form of values for a few key parameters; the program then functions independently.

Winston's work on concept formation [21] relied somewhat more heavily on user interaction. There the teacher was responsible for providing an appropriate sequence of examples (and non-examples) of a concept.

In describing our work, we have used the phrase "interactive transfer of expertise" to indicate that we view knowledge acquisition as information transfer from an expert to a program. TEIRESIAS does not attempt to derive knowledge on its own, but instead tries to "listen" as attentively as possible and comment appropriately, to help the expert augment the knowledge base. It thus requires the strongest degree of cooperation from the expert.

There is an important assumption involved in the attempt to establish this sort of communication: we are assuming that it is possible to distinguish between basic *problem-solving paradigm* and *degree of expertise*, or equivalently, that control structure and representation in the performance program can be considered separately from the content of its knowledge base. The basic control structure(s) and representations are assumed to be established and debugged, and the fundamental approach to the problem assumed acceptable. The question of *how* knowledge is to be encoded and used is settled by the selection of one or more of the available representations and control structures. The expert's task is to enlarge *what* it is the program knows.

There is a corollary assumption, too, in the belief that the control structures and knowledge representations can be made sufficiently comprehensible to the expert (at the conceptual level) that he can (a) understand the system's behavior in terms of them and (b) use them to codify his own knowledge. This insures that the expert understands system performance well enough to know what to correct and can then express the required knowledge, i.e., he can "think" in those terms. Thus part of the task of establishing the link shown in Fig. 1 involves insulating the expert from the details of implementation, by establishing a discourse at a level high enough that we do not end up effectively having to teach him how to program.

4. Design of the Performance Program

4.1. Program architecture

Fig. 2 shows a slightly more detailed picture of the sort of performance program that TEIRESIAS is designed to help construct. (The performance program described here is modelled after the MYCIN program [17, 9], which provided the context within which TEIRESIAS was actually developed. We have abstracted out here just the essential elements of MYCIN's design.) The *knowledge base* is the program's store of task specific knowledge that makes possible high performance. The *inference engine* is an interpreter that uses the knowledge base to solve the problem at hand.

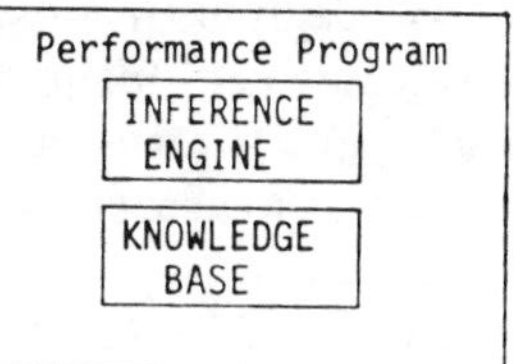

FIG. 2. Architecture of the performance program.

The main point of interest in this very simple design is the explicit division between these two parts of the program. This design is in keeping with the assumption noted above that the expert's task would be to augment the knowledge base of a program whose control structure (inference engine) was assumed both appropriate and debugged.

Two important advantages accrue from keeping this division as strict as possible. First, if all of the control structure information has been kept in the inference engine, then we can engage the domain expert in a discussion of the knowledge base and be assured that the discussion will have to deal only with issues of domain specific expertise (rather than with questions of programming and control structures). Second, if all of the task-specific knowledge has been kept in the knowledge base, then it should be possible to remove the current knowledge base, "plug in" another, and obtain a performance program for a new task.[3] The explicit division thus offers a degree of domain independence.

It does not mean, however, that the inference engine and knowledge base are totally independent: knowledge base content is strongly influenced by the control paradigm used in the inference engine. It is this unavoidable interaction which motivates the important assumption noted in Section 3 that the control structure and knowledge representation are comprehensible to the expert, at least at the conceptual level.

In this discussion we assume the knowledge base contains information about selecting an investment in the stock market; the performance program thus functions as an investment consultant. MYCIN, of course, deals with infectious disease diagnosis and therapy selection, and the rules and dialog shown later dealt with that subject initially. The topic has been changed to keep the discussion phrased in terms familiar to a wide range of readers, and to emphasize that neither the problems attacked nor the solutions suggested are restricted to a single domain of application or performance program design. The dialog is a real example of TEIRESIAS in action with a few words substituted in a medical example: e.g., *E. coli* became *AT&T*, *infection* became *investment*, etc.

An example of the program in action is shown in Section 6. The program interviews the user, requesting various pieces of information that are relevant to selecting the most appropriate investment, then prints its recommendations. In the remainder of this paper the "user" will be an expert running the program in order to challenge it, offering it a difficult case, and observing and correcting its performance.

4.2. The knowledge base

The knowledge base of the performance program contains a collection of decision rules of the sort shown in Fig. 3. (The rule is stored internally in the INTERLISP form, the English version is generated from that with a simple template-directed mechanisms.) Each rule is a single "chunk" of domain specific information indicating an *action* (in this case a conclusion) which is justified if the conditions specified in the *premise* are fulfilled.

The rules are judgmental, i.e., they make inexact inferences. In the case of the rule in Fig. 3, for instance, the evidence cited in the premise is enough to assert the conclusion shown with only a weak degree of confidence (0.4 out of 1.0). These numbers are referred to as *certainty factors*, and embody a model of confirmation described in detail in [18]. The details of that model need not concern us here; we need only note that a rule typically embodies an inexact inference rather than an exact rule.

```
RULE 027

If   [1.1] the time scale of the investment is long-term,
     [1.2] the desired return on the investment is greater than 10%, and
     [1.3] the area of the investment is not known,
then AT&T is a likely (0.4) choice for the investment.

PREMISE  ($AND (SAME OBJCT TIMESCALE LONG-TERM)
               (GREATER OBJCT RETURNRATE 10)
               (NOTKNOWN OBJCT INVESTMENT-AREA))

ACTION   (CONCLUDE OBJCT STOCK-NAME AT&T 0.4)
```

FIG. 3. Example of a rule.

Finally, a few points of terminology. The premise is a Boolean combination of one or more *clauses*, each of which is constructed from a *predicate function* with an *associative triple* (*attribute*, *object*, *value*) as its argument. For the first clause in Fig. 3, for example, the predicate function is SAME, and the triple is "*timescale* of *investment* is *long-term*". (The identifier OBJCT is used as a placeholder for the

[3] Two experiments of this sort have been performed with the MYCIN system, and suggest that this sort of "plug compatibility" of knowledge bases is a realistic possibility for a range of tasks.

specific object to be referred to; the actual binding is established each time the rule is invoked.)

4.3. The inference engine

The rules are invoked in a simple backward-chaining fashion that produces an exhaustive depth-first search of an and/or goal tree (Fig. 4). Assume that the program is attempting to determine which stock would make a good investment. It retrieves (the precomputed list of) all rules which make a conclusion about that topic (i.e., they mention STOCK-NAME in their action), and invokes each one in turn, evaluating each premise to see if the conditions specified have been met. For the example shown in Fig. 4, this means first determining what the timescale of the investment ought to be. This is in turn set up as a subgoal, and the process recurs.

The search is thus depth-first (because each premise condition is thoroughly explored in turn); the tree that is sprouted is an and/or goal tree (because rules may have OR conditions in their premise); and the search is exhaustive (because the rules are inexact, so that even if one succeeds, it was deemed to be a wisely conservative strategy to continue to collect all evidence about the subgoal.)

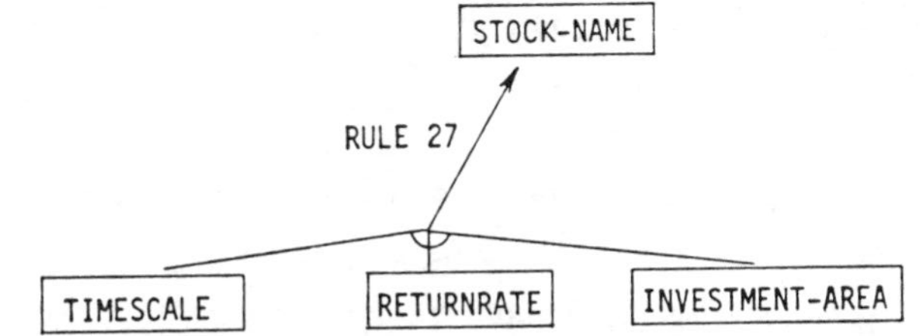

FIG. 4. Control structure of the performance program is an exhaustive, depth-first search of an and/or goal tree.

We have noted earlier that the expert must have at least a high-level understanding of the operation of the inference engine and the manner of knowledge representation to enable him to express new knowledge for the performance program. That level of understanding is well supplied by the information in Sections 4.2 and 4.3, together with an equally brief summary of the model of confirmation described in [18]. This should make plausible the assumption in Section 3 that the expert might indeed be able to understand these things sufficiently without having to deal with details of implementation. Note too that TEIRESIAS's basic design and the notion of interactive transfer of expertise does not depend on this particular control structure, only on the (non-trivial) assumption that an equally comprehensible explanation can be found for whatever control structure is actually used in the inference engine.

5. A Word about Natural Language

Natural language has not been a major focus of this work, and for the most part the simplest techniques have been used that would support the level of performance required. For instance, all questions and responses from TEIRESIAS are either preformed, or manufactured by filling in templates with appropriate words (as evidenced the occasional appearance of phrases like "a area"). Where answers are free text (rather than multiple choice), the system relies primarily on the keyword- and template-oriented techniques described in Section 7.3.4. There is no parser in the system, in part to minimize processing time, and in part because users often give ungrammatical responses.

6. Example of TEIRESIAS in Operation

In the interaction shown below, the expert is challenging the investment advisory program with a particular case, observing the program's performance, and then making the necessary correction to the knowledge base. The bug encountered here was created by deleting an existing rule from the knowledge base and removing all references to it. The expert then repairs the bug by tracking down the source of the problem and teaching the system the "new" rule.

The deleted rule was chosen to make possible an acquisition example that displays a large number of TEIRESIAS's capabilities in a single example. It is special in no other sense, however, and offers a real trace of the system in action.

In the trace below, computer output is in mixed upper and lower case in this font, user responses follow a double asterisk and are in **BOLD CAPITALS**, and commentary appears as {*indented italics inside braces*}. The example is also divided into five phases for later reference.

Investment Advisory Program

User?
**** RD**

Hello, Randy.

> {*The expert identifies himself to the program, and then, responding to the program's inquiries, describes a particular case as a test of performance.*}

(1) Investor's name?
****FRED SMITH**

(2) Age?
****40**

(3) Present taxable income?
****40,000**

(4) Number of dependents?
**3

(5) Occupation?
**LAWYER

(6) Amount of previous investment experience? (slight = less than one year; moderate = 2 to 4 years; extensive = more than 4 years)
**MODERATE

(7) Does the investor subscribe to the Wall Street Journal, or any securities market newsletters?
**Y

.
.
.

{*Most of the consultation with the performance program has been edited out for brevity (see* [5] *for a complete example). The interaction continues with the program printing out its conclusions.*}

The following investments appear to be the most appropriate at this time:
Varian-Corporation
American-Telephone-and-Telegraph

{*At this point* TEIRESIAS *steps in, and since the interaction is with an expert (rather than an ordinary user), it requests an evaluation of the performance program's results.*
From here on the dialog takes place between TEIRESIAS *and the expert, with the performance program in the background being manipulated by* TEIRESIAS.}

{**Phase I: tracking down the bug**}

{*The expert indicates that the results are incorrect . . .*}

Are all these correct?
++**N

{*. . . and then specifies the problems.*}

Are there any missing?
++**Y
Which one(s)?
++** DIGITAL-EQUIPMENT DATA-GENERAL
Are there any that shouldn't have appeared?
++** Y
Which one(s)?
++** AT&T

Do you want to
(1) track down the problem yourself, or
(2) allow me to guide the debugging, or
(3) ignore it for now and fix it another time?
Type 1, 2 or 3
++** 2

{*The first option allows the expert to use the explanation facilities described in* [5] *to track down the problem. The facility indicated by the second option is based on a model of the control structure of the performance program that allows a simple algorithmic search for the error, and will be demonstrated here. The third is for human engineering purposes, and allows the expert to sidestep this whole process if desired.*}

We'll start with the AT&T first.

{*Heuristics derived from our experience in debugging rule-based systems are built into* TEIRESIAS. *One such heuristic suggests that the best approach is to* (1) *track down one problem at a time, and* (2) *start with a result that shouldn't have appeared (if there is one). Experience indicates that this class of bug is often a manifestation of a deeper bug causing several problems, so curing it will often solve several problems at once.*}

The following rules were used in deducing that the investment should be AT&T:

RULE 027

Since [1.1] the area of the investment is not known, and
[1.2] the desired return on the investment is greater than 10%, and
[1.3] the time scale of the investment is long-term,
then AT&T is a likely (0.4) choice for the investment.

Is this rule correct?
++** Y
Should its premise have failed for this case?
++** Y
Which clause of the premise should have been false? [give #]
++** 1

{*The expert indicates that this rule should have failed, so the debugging continues by looking further back in the chain. Had he indicated that rule 27 had been invoked properly, then* TEIRESIAS *would have indicated that the problem was probably a missing rule which tended to* ***rule out*** *AT&T.*}

No conclusions were reached concerning the area of the investment.

Should it have been possible to conclude an area?
++** Y

{*The error might have been a failure to rule out an investment area.*}

Which one?
++** **HIGH TECHNOLOGY**

There were no rules successfully invoked in the attempt to deduce that the area of the investment should be high-technology.

The following (potentially applicable) rules were NOT executed because the starred [**] clause failed:

RULE 116

If (1) the desired return on the investment is greater than 10%,
(2) the time scale of the investment is long-term,
(3) the number of dependents of the client is less than 3,
(4) the age (in years) of the client is less than or equal to 35
then there is evidence (0.4) that the area of the investment should be high-technology.

RULE 050

If (1) the time scale of the investment is long-term,
(2) the desired return on the investment is greater than 10%,
(3) the risk class of the investment is speculative
then there is evidence (0.6) that the area of the investment should be high-technology.

Are all these rules correct?
++** **Y**
Should any of them have been successfully invoked?
++** **N**

{This would have been the case if one of the starred premise clauses were false because it was "stepped on" by yet another rule further back in the chain.}

Is there a rule missing?
++** **Y**

Ok, then I need a rule that would allow me to deduce that the area of the investment should be high-technology.

Would you like to give me such a rule now?
++** **Y**
Good . . .

{To review briefly: the expert is tracking down the reason why the system incorrectly concluded that the stock to invest in was AT&T. Shown below is the sequence of rules which were involved:

```
  RETURN
  TIME SCALE
**DEPENDENTS**
  AGE           —RULE 116→|
                          |→AREA
  TIME SCALE—RULE 050→    |  RETURN      —RULE 027→AT&T
  RETURN                     TIME SCALE
**RISK CLASS**
```

AT&T appeared because the system executed Rule 27 successfully.
This occurred in part because investment area was unknown.
Investment area was unknown because all rules to conclude it (Rules 50 and 116) failed.

Since the expert believes all existing rules are correct, the knowledge base must be missing a rule that will conclude about investment area, in particular, that the area should be high-technology. Such a rule will cause area to be known, inhibiting Rule 27, fixing at least this first problem.

Note how sharply focussed the issue has become, for both the expert and TEIRESIAS, *as a result of the large amount of contextual information available. The expert is not being asked to "discuss the stock market"; instead the system can at this point say*

. . . I need a rule that would allow me to deduce that the area of the investment should be high technology.

and it must be a rule which is invokable in the current situation. Thus it is easier for the expert to specify a rule that may never before have been explicitly stated or recognized as such. This can be an important advantage in any domain where the knowledge is not yet fully formalized.

The contextual information is useful for TEIRESIAS *as well. The information provides a number of expectations about the content of the rule which are used both in understanding what the expert types in, and in checking the new rule to make sure that it does indeed solve the problem at hand. Details of this process are explained below.*

The trace continues with the expert typing in the rule . . .}

{**Phase II: interpreting the rule**}

The new rule will be called RULE 383

If: 1. **THE CLIENT'S INCOME TAX BRACKET IS 50%**
and 2. **THE CLIENT IS FOLLOWING UP ON MARKET TRENDS CAREFULLY**
and 3.
Then: 1. **THERE IS EVIDENCE (0.8) THAT THE INVESTMENT AREA SHOULD BE HIGH TECHNOLOGY**
and 2.

This may take a few moments . . .

{*Generally on the order of* 10 *to* 30 *seconds of cpu time.*}

This is my understanding of your rule:

RULE 383

If (1) The client's income-tax bracket is 50%, and
(2) The market has followed an upward trend recently, and
(3) The client manages his assets carefully,
then there is evidence (0.8) that the area of the investment should be high-technology

{TEIRESIAS's *initial interpretation is not entirely correct (and the example was chosen in part for this reason). The first line of text and the conclusion have been interpreted correctly, but the second line has been turned into two clauses (numbers* 2 *and* 3) *in the system's initial attempt at understanding. (The expert occassionally types what should be two separate clauses as one line of text. The system is capable of handling this, but this same capability at times produces spurious clauses like No.* 3).

This level of performance results primarily from the system's simple word-by-word approach to meaning. While the result is in part incorrect, it will become clear below that the interpretations are both "reasonable" and "consistent" in light of the techniques used.}

{**Phase III: modifying the interpretation**}

Okay? (Yes or No)
++** N

{*The expert indicates there is a problem with the interpretation, and uses* TEIRESIAS's *rule editor to specify the changes needed.*}

Change premise?
++** Y

What clause should be changed in premise? (type HELP for list of commands)
++** CHANGE 2

Suppose (2) were changed to read:
(2) The client follows the market carefully
Would that be ok?
++** Y

{*Several simple heuristics are invoked to select the next most likely interpretation, based on the English source of this clause and the set of interpretations already rejected. In this case the second choice is correct.*}

Then you'll probably want to delete:
(3) The client manages his assets carefully
Correct?
++** Y

{TEIRESIAS *enforces certain consistency constraints on its interpretation of the English text. One of these constraints indicates that if the new interpretation of clause No.* 2 *is correct, then clause No.* 3 *must have arisen spuriously* (*since, among other things, it requires a different interpretation for the word* carefully).}

Anything else?
++**?
(1) the client's income-tax bracket is 50%
and (2) the client follows the market carefully
and (3) ⟨deleted⟩

Anything else?
++** N

Change action?
++** N

This is my understanding of your rule:

RULE 383

If: (1) the client's income-tax bracket is 50%, and
(2) the client follows the market carefully,
then there is evidence (0.8) that the area of the investment should be high-technology.

Okay? (Yes or No)
++** Y

{*This is the standard test of comprehension: the original English text has been turned into a rule coded in* LISP, *and is then retranslated back into English for approval. Compare the results with the expert's original input. Now that the expert is satisfied that* TEIRESIAS *understands the rule that he entered,* TEIRESIAS *checks several things about the rule to see if* **it** *is satisfied with the rule content.*}

{**Phase IV: "second guessing"**}

I hate to criticize, Randy, but did you know that most rules about what the area of an investment might be, that mention:
the income-tax bracket of the client, and
how closely the client follows the market
LSO mention:

[A] The amount of investment experience of the client
Shall I try to write a clause to account for [A]?
++** **Y**

{The mechanism that makes possible this sort of "second guessing" by the system is explained in detail below. Briefly, the system maintains a model of its own knowledge. In checking to see how this new piece of information "fits in" to that model, it discovers that its expectations have been only partially met. It indicates to the expert what expectations were left unfulfilled, and asks if it should attempt to fill in the missing parts.}

How about:
[A] The amount of investment experience of the client is moderate
Ok?
++** **Y**

{The expert agreed to the inclusion of the new clause and TEIRESIAS *is able to construct a plausible guess as to its content. Note that it must be possible to invoke the new rule in the current situation, in order to fix the known bug.* TEIRESIAS *uses this fact to guide its construction of the new clause. Details of this process are explained below.}*

Also, most rules about what the area of an investment might be ALSO conclude about:
[A] The desired risk classification of the investment
Shall I try to write a clause to account for [A]?
++** **N**

{The system noticed another unfulfilled expectation concerning the action part of the rule, but the expert always has the option of overriding the system's suggestions, and does so.}

{**Phase V: final checkout, bookkeeping, rerunning the consultation**}

The rule now reads:

RULE 383

If (1) the income-tax bracket of the client is 50%, and
(2) the client follows the market carefully, and
(3) the amount of investment experience of the client is moderate,
then there is evidence (0.8) that the area of the investment should be high-technology.

Please describe briefly why you added (or changed) this rule.
Type an empty line when done.

++THE SYSTEM FAILED TO REALIZE IT COULD CONCLUDE**
++INVESTMENT AREA, AND THIS ALLOWED RULE 027 TO BE**
++INVOKED INAPPROPRIATELY**
++**

{Experience suggests that in building any large knowledge base it is very useful to keep fairly detailed records about the source of various contributions. The new rule is automatically tagged with a range of such information (including author, date, and a record of the consultation which prompted its creation), along with any comments which the expert may care to make for his own future reference.}

RULE 383 has now been added to the knowledge base.

I will now rerun the consultation to check the effectiveness of your new rule. Get comfortable, since this may take a bit.

Also, new questions may be asked as a result of this new rule. If a question is printed, please answer it with reference to this current client.

.
.
.

{The consultation is then rerun, but all the previous answers are saved, so the expert can in most cases just watch it proceed. This has been edited out here for brevity.}

The following investments appear to be the most appropriate at this time:

Varian-Corporation
Data-General
Digital-Equipment

Well, it appears that things are straightened out.

{The new conclusions are the ones the expert indicated earlier as the correct answers. This does not go unnoticed.}

Are all these values correct now?
++** **Y**

{As always, however, the expert gets the last word, and TEIRESIAS *waits for approval before proceeding.}*

Good, then the problem's been fixed.

{How is it that three errors disappeared with the addition of one rule? This is explained schematically below:

```
*RULE 116*
*RULE 050*
 RULE 383→AREA—*RULE 027*→AT&T
                — RULE 084 →DATA-GENERAL
                            DIGITAL-EQUIPMENT
```

As before, Rules 116 *and* 50 *failed (hence the **'s), but now the new rule,* 383, *has succeeded, supplying a value for investment area. This in turn means that Rule* 27 *now fails, as hoped.*

However, Rule 84, *which requires a value of area, failed last time because the system was unable to deduce one. Now that Rule* 383 *supplies one, Rule* 84 *can fire, and it turns out to yield the missing answers.*}

7. How it all Works

7.1. Overview of the main ideas

Before reviewing the trace in more detail, we describe the ideas which make possible the capabilities displayed. The list below serves primarily to name and briefly sketch each in turn; the details are supplied in reviewing the example.

7.1.1. *Knowledge acquisition in context*

Performance programs of the sort TEIRESIAS helps create will typically find their greatest utility in domains where there are no unifying laws on which to base algorithmic methods. In such domains there is instead a collection of informal knowledge based on accumulated experience. This means an expert specifying a new rule may be codifying a piece of knowledge that has never previously been isolated and expressed as such. Since this is difficult, anything which can be done to ease the task will prove very useful.

In response, we have emphasized knowledge acquisition in the context of a shortcoming in the knowledge base. To illustrate its utility, consider the difference between asking the expert

> *What should I know about the stock market?*

and saying to him

> *Here is an example in which you say the performance program made a mistake. Here is all the knowledge the program used, here are all the facts of the case, and here is how it reached its conclusions. Now,* **what is it that you know and the system doesn't** *that allows you to avoid making that same mistake?*

Note how much more focussed the second question is, and how much easier it to answer.

7.1.2. *Building expectations*

The focussing provided by the context is also an important aid to TEIRESIAS. In particular, it permits the system to build up a set of expectations concerning the knowledge to be acquired, facilitating knowledge transfer and making possible several useful features illustrated in the trace and described below.

7.1.3. *Model-based understanding*

Model-based understanding suggests that some aspects of understanding can be viewed as a process of matching: the entity to be understood is matched against a collection of prototypes, or models, and the most appropriate model selected. This sets the framework in which further interpretation takes place, as that model can then be used as a guide to further processing.

While this view is not new, TEIRESIAS employs a novel application of it, since the system has a model of the knowledge it is likely to be acquiring from the expert.

7.1.4. *Giving a program a model of its own knowledge*

We will see that the combination of TEIRESIAS and the performance program amounts to a system which has a picture of its own knowledge. That is, it not only knows something about a particular domain, but in a primitive sense it knows what it knows, and employs that model of its knowledge in several ways.

7.1.5. *Learning as a process of comparison*

We do not view learning as simply the addition of information to an existing base of knowledge, but instead take it to include various forms of comparison of the new information with the old. This of course has its corollary in human behavior: A student will quickly point out discrepancies between newly taught material and his current stock of information. TEIRESIAS has a similar, though very primitive, capability: It compares new information supplied by the expert with the existing knowledge base, points out inconsistencies, and suggests possible remedies.

7.1.6. *Learning by experience*

One of the long-recognized potential weaknesses of any model-based system is dependence on a fixed set of models, since the scope of the program's "understanding" of the world is constrained by the number and type of models it has. As will become clear, the models TEIRESIAS employs are not hand-crafted and static, but are instead formed and continually revised as a by-product of its experience in interacting with the expert.

7.2. Phase I: tracking down the bug

To provide the debugging facility shown, TEIRESIAS maintains a detailed record of the actions of the performance program during the consultation, and then interprets this record on the basis of an exhaustive analysis of the performance program's control structure (see [5] for details). This presents the expert with a comprehensible task because (a) the backward-chaining technique used by the performance program is sufficiently straightforward and intuitive, even to a non-programmer;

and (b) the rules are designed to encode knowledge at a reasonably high conceptual level. As a result, even though TEIRESIAS is running through an exhaustive case-by-case analysis of the preceding consultation, the expert is presented with a task of debugging *reasoning* rather than *code*.

The availability of an algorithmic debugging process is also an important factor in encouraging the expert to be as precise as possible in his responses. Note that at each point in tracking down the error the expert must either approve of the rules invoked and conclusions made, or indicate which one was in error and supply the correction. This is extremely useful in domains where knowledge has not yet been formalized, and the traditional reductionist approach of dissecting reasoning down to observational primitives is not yet well established.[4]

TEIRESIAS further encourages precise comments by keeping the debugging process sharply focussed. For instance, when it became clear that there was a problem with the inability to deduce investment area, the system first asks which area it should have been. It then displays only those rules appropriate to that answer, rather than all of the rules on that topic which were tried.

Finally, consider the extensive amount of contextual information that is now available. The expert has been presented with a detailed example of the performance program in action, he has available all of the facts of the case, and has seen how the relevant knowledge has been applied. This makes it much easier for him to specify the particular chunk of knowledge which may be missing. This contextual information will prove very useful for TEIRESIAS as well. It is clear, for instance, what the *effect* of invocation of the new rule must be (as TEIRESIAS indicates, it must be a rule that will "deduce that the area of the investment should be high-technology"), and it is also clear what the *circumstances* of its invocation must be (the rule must be invokable for the case under consideration, or it won't repair the bug). Both of these will be seen to be quite useful (see Sections 7.3.3 and 7.6).

7.3. Phase II: interpreting the rule

As is traditional, "understanding" the expert's natural language version of the rule is viewed in terms of converting it to an internal representation, and then re-translating that into English for the expert's approval. In this case the internal representation is the INTERLISP form of the rule, so the process is also a simple type of code generation.

There were a number of reasons for rejecting a standard natural language understanding approach to this problem. First, as noted, understanding natural language is well known to be a difficult problem, and was not a central focus of this research. Second, our experience suggested that experts frequently sacrifice precise grammar in favor of the compactness available in the technical language of the domain. As a result, approaches that were strongly grammar-based might not fare well. Finally, technical language often contains a fairly high percentage of unambiguous words, so a simpler approach that includes reliance on keyword analysis has a good chance of performing adequately.

As will become clear, our approach to analyzing the expert's new rule is based on both simple keyword spotting and predictions TEIRESIAS is able to make about the likely content of the rule. Code generation is accomplished via a form of template completion that is similar in some respects to template completion processes that have been used in generating natural language. Details of all these processes are given below.

7.3.1. *Models and model-based understanding*

To set the stage for reviewing the details of the interpretation process, we digress for a moment to consider the idea of models and model-based understanding, then explore their application in TEIRESIAS.

In the most general terms, a model can be seen as a *compact, high-level description of structure, organization, or content* that may be used both to *provide a framework for lower-level processing*, and *to express expectations about the world.* One particularly graphic example of this idea can be found in the work on computer vision by Falk [10] in 1970. The task there was the standard one of understanding blocks-world scenes: the goal was to determine the identity, location, and orientation of each block in a scene containing one or more blocks selected from a known set of possibilities.

The key element of his work of interest here is the use of a set of *prototypes* for the blocks, prototypes that resembled wire frame models. While it oversimplifies slightly, part of the operation of his system can be described in terms of two phases. The system first performed a preliminary pass to detect possible edge points in the scene and attempted to fit a block model to each collection of edges. The model chosen was then used in the second phase as a guide to further processing. If, for instance, the model accounted for all but one of the lines in a region, this suggested that the extra line might be spurious. If the model fit well except for some line missing from the scene, that was a good hint that a line had been overlooked and indicated as well where to go looking for it.

While it was not a part of Falk's system, we can imagine one further refinement in the interpretation process and explain it in these same terms. Imagine that the system had available some *a priori* hints about what blocks might be found in the next scene. One way to express those hints would be to bias the matching process. That is, in the attempt to match a model against the data, the system might (depending on the strength of the hint) try the indicated models first, make a greater attempt to effect a match with one of them, or even restrict the set of possibilities to just those contained in the hint.

[4] The debugging process does allow the expert to indicate that while the performance program's results are incorrect, he cannot find an error in the reasoning. This choice is offered only as a last resort and is intended to deal with situations where there may be a bug in the underlying control structure of the performance program (contrary to our assumption in Section 3).

Note that in this system, (i) the models supply a compact, high-level description of structure (the structure of each block), (ii) the description is used to guide lower level processing (processing of the array of digitized intensity values), (iii) expectations can be expressed by a biasing or restriction on the set of models used, and (iv) "understanding" is viewed in terms of a matching and selection process (matching models against the data and selecting one that fits).

7.3.2. *Rule models*

Now recall our original task of interpreting the expert's natural language version of the rule, and view it in the terms described above. As in the vision example, there is a signal to be processed (the text), it is noisy (words can be ambiguous), and there is context available (from the debugging process) that can supply some hints about the likely content of the signal. To complete the analogy, we need a model, one that could (a) capture the structure, organization, or content of the expert's reasoning, (b) be used to guide the interpretation process, and (c) be used to express expectations about the likely content of the new rule.

Where might we get such a thing? There are interesting regularities in the knowledge base that might supply what we need. Not surprisingly, rules about a single topic tend to have characteristics in common — there are "ways" of reasoning about a given topic. From these regularities we have constructed *rule models*. These are abstract descriptions of subsets of rules, built from empirical generalizations about those rules, and are used to characterize a "typical" member of the subset.

Rule models are composed of four parts (Fig. 5). They contain, first, a list of EXAMPLES, the subset of rules from which this model was constructed.

EXAMPLES	the subset of rules which this model describes
DESCRIPTION	characterization of a "typical" member of this subset characterization of the premise characterization of the action which attributes "typically" appear correlations of attributes
MORE GENERAL	pointers to models describing more general
MORE SPECIFIC	and more specific subsets of rules

FIG. 5. Rule model structure.

Next, a DESCRIPTION characterizes a typical member of the subset. Since we are dealing in this case with rules composed of premise-action pairs, the DESCRIPTION currently implemented contains individual characterizations of a typical premise and a typical action. Then, since the current representation scheme used in those rules is based on associative triples, we have chosen to implement those characterizations by indicating (a) which attributes "typically" appear in the premise (action) of a rule in this subset, and (b) correlations of attributes appearing in the premise (action).[5]

Note that the central idea is the concept of *characterizing a typical member of the subset*. Naturally, that characterization would look different for subsets of rules, procedures, theorems, or any other representation. But the main idea of characterization is widely applicable and not restricted to any particular representational formalism.

The two remaining parts of the rule model are pointers to models describing more general and more specific subsets of rules. The set of models is organized into a number of tree structures, each of the general form shown in Fig. 6. At the root of each tree is the model made from all the rules which conclude about ⟨attribute⟩ (e.g., the INVESTMENT-AREA model), below this are two models dealing with all affirmative and all negative rules (e.g., the INVESTMENT-AREA-IS model), and below this are models dealing with rules which affirm or deny specific values of the attribute.

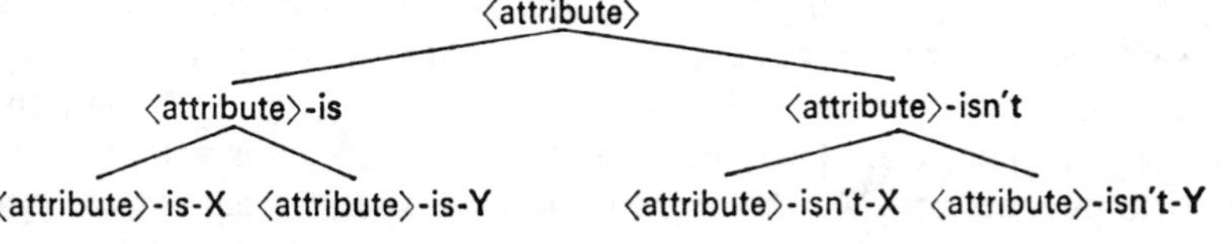

FIG. 6. Organization of the rule models.

These models are not hand-tooled by the expert. They are instead assembled by TEIRESIAS on the basis of the current contents of the knowledge base, in what amounts to a very simple (i.e., statistical) form of concept formation. The combination of TEIRESIAS and the performance program thus presents a system which has a model of its own knowledge, one which it forms itself.

The rule models are the primary example of meta-level knowledge in this paper (for discussion of other forms, see [5] and [8]). This form of knowledge and its generation by the system itself have several interesting implications illustrated in later sections.

Fig. 7 shows a rule model; this is the one used by TEIRESIAS in the interaction shown earlier. (Since not all of the details of implementation are relevant here, this discussion will omit some. See [5] for a full explanation.) As indicated above, there is a list of the rules from which this model was constructed, descriptions characterizing the premise and the action, and pointers to more specific and more general models. Each characterization in the description is shown split into its two parts, one concerning the presence of individual attributes and the other describing correlations. The first item in the premise description, for instance, indicates that "most" rules about what the area of an investment should be mention

[5] Both (a) and (b) are constructed via simple thresholding operations.

the attribute *rate of return* in their premise; when they do mention it they "typically" use the predicate functions SAME and NOTSAME; and the "strength", or reliability, of this piece of advice is 3.8 (see [5] for precise definition of the quoted terms).

The fourth item in the premise description indicates that when the attribute *rate of return* appears in the premise of a rule in this subset, the attribute *timescale of the investment* "typically" appears as well. As before the predicate functions are those typically associated with the attributes, and the number is an indication of reliability.

```
INVESTMENT-AREA-IS
EXAMPLES        (RULE116 0.3)
                (RULE050 0.7)
                (RULE037 0.8)
                (RULE095 0.9)
                (RULE152 1.0)
                (RULE140 1.0))
DESCRIPTION
  PREMISE       ((RETURNRATE SAME NOTSAME 3.8)
                 (TIMESCALE SAME NOTSAME 3.8)
                 (TREND SAME 2.8)

                 ((RETURNRATE SAME) (TIMESCALE SAME) 3.8)
                 ((TIMESCALE SAME) (RETURNRATE SAME) 3.8)
                 ((BRACKET SAME) (FOLLOWS NOTSAME SAME)
                                         (EXPERIENCE SAME) 1.5))
  ACTION        ((INVESTMENT-AREA CONCLUDE 4.7)
                 (RISK CONCLUDE 4.0)

                 ((INVESTMENT-AREA CONCLUDE) (RISK CONCLUDE) 4.7))
MORE-GENL       (INVESTMENT-AREA)
MORE-SPEC       (INVESTMENT-AREA-IS-UTILITIES)
```

FIG. 7. Example of a rule model.

7.3.3. *Choosing a model*

It was noted earlier that tracking down the bug in the knowledge base provides useful context, and, among other things, serve to set up TEIRESIAS's expectations about the sort of rule it is about to receive. As suggested, these expectations are expressed by restricting the set of models which will be considered for use in guiding the interpretation. At this point TEIRESIAS chooses a model which expresses what it knows thus far about the kind of rule to expect, and in the current example it expects a rule that will "deduce that the area of the investment should be high-technology."

Since there is not necessarily a rule model for every characterization, the system chooses the closest one. This is done by starting at the top of the tree of models, and descending until either reaching a model of the desired type, or encountering a leaf of the tree. In this case, the process descends to the second level (the INVESTMENT-AREA-IS model), notices that there is no model for INVESTMENT-AREA-IS-HIGH-TECHNOLOGY at the next level, and settles for the former.[6]

7.3.4. *Using the rule model: guiding the natural language interpretation*

TEIRESIAS uses the rule models in two different ways in the acquisition process. The first is as a guide in understanding the text typed by the expert, and is described here. The second is as a means of allowing TEIRESIAS to see whether the new rule "fits in" to its current model of the knowledge base, and is described in Section 7.5.

To see how the rule models are used to guide the interpretation of the text of the new rule, consider the second line of text typed by the expert. Each word is first reduced to a canonical form by a process that can recognize plural endings and that has access to a dictionary of synonyms. We then consider the possible connotations that each word may have (Fig. 8a). Here connotation means the word might be referring to one or more of the conceptual primitives from which rules are built (i.e., it might refer to a predicate function, attribute, object, or value). One set of connotations is shown.[7]

Code generation is accomplished via a "fill-in-the-blank" mechanism. Associated with each predicate function is a *template*, a list structure that resembles a simplified procedure declaration, and gives the order and generic type of each argument to a call of that function (Fig. 8b). Associated with each of the primitives that make up a template (e.g., ATTRIBUTE, VALUE, etc.) is a procedure capable of scanning the list of connotations to find an item of the appropriate type to fill in that blank.

The whole process is begun by checking the list of connotations for the predicate function implicated most strongly (in this case, SAME; see [5] for details), retrieving the template for that function, and allowing it to scan the connotations and "fill itself in" using the procedures associated with the primitives. The set of

[6] This technique is used in several places throughout the knowledge transfer process, and in general supplies the model which best matches the current requirements, by accommodating varying levels of specificity in the stated expectations. If, for instance, the system had known only that it expected a rule which concluded about investment area, it would have selected the first node in the model tree without further search.

TEIRESIAS also has techniques for checking that the appropriate model has been chosen and can advise the expert if a discrepancy appears. See [5] for an example.

[7] The connotations of a word are determined by a number of pointers associated with it, which are in turn derived from the English phrases associated with each of the primitives. For instance, one of the primitives—the attribute TREND—has associated with it the phrase *the general trend.* Hence when the English word *trends* is found in the text of the rule, it is first changed to *trend* by the canonicalization process, then the connotation pointers are checked, yielding the attribute TREND.

It is possible to have sets of interpretations other than the one shown and TEIRESIAS considers them all. The number of possibilities is kept constrained by enforcing several types of consistency This and other details are omitted here for the sake of brevity; see [5] for a complete description.

connotations in Fig. 8a produces the LISP code in Fig. 8c. The ATTRIBUTE routine finds the attribute TREND, the VALUE routine finds an appropriate value (UPWARD), and the OBJect routine finds the corresponding object type (MARKET) (but following the convention noted earlier, returns the variable name OBJCT to be used in the actual code).

```
THE CLIENT  IS  FOLLOWING  UP  ON  MARKET  TRENDS  CAREFULLY
            ↓              ↓        ↓        ↓
   PREDICATE FUNCTION     VALUE    OBJ    ATTRIBUTE
```

FIG. 8a. Connotations.

```
FUNCTION    TEMPLATE
SAME        (OBJ ATTRIBUTE VALUE)
```

FIG. 8b. Template for the predicate function SAME.

```
(SAME OBJCT TREND UPWARD)
The general trend of the market is upward
```

FIG. 8c. The resulting code.

There are several points to note here. First, the interpretation in Fig. 8c is incorrect (the system has been misled by the idiom "following up"); we'll see in a moment how it is corrected. Second, there are typically several plausible (syntactically valid) interpretations available from each line of text, and TEIRESIAS generates all of them. Each is assigned a score (the "text score") indicating how likely it is, based on how strongly it was implicated by the text (details in [5]). Finally, we have not yet used the rule models, and it is at this point that they are employed.

We can view the DESCRIPTION part of the rule model selected earlier as a set of predictions about the likely content of the new rule. In these terms the next step is to see how well each interpretation fulfills those predictions. Note, for example, that the third line of the premise description in Fig. 7 "predicts" that a rule about investment area will contain the attribute *market trend*, and the clause generated from the connotations in Fig. 8a fulfills this prediction. Each interpretation is scored (employing the "strength of advice" number in the rule model) according to how many predictions it fulfills, yielding the "prediction satisfaction score".

This score is then combined with the text score to indicate the most likely interpretation. Because more weight is given to the prediction score, the system tends to "hear what it expects to hear" (and that leads it astray in this case).

7.3.5. *Rule interpretation: sources of performance*

While our approach to natural language is very simple, the overall performance of the interpretation process is adequate. The problem is made easier, of course, by the fact that we are dealing with a small amount of text in a restricted context, written in a semi-formal technical language, rather than with large amounts of text in unrestricted dialog written in unconstrained English. Even so, the problem of interpretation is substantial. TEIRESIAS's performance is based on both the application of the ideas noted in Section 7.1 (notably the ideas of building expectations and model-based understanding) and the use of two additional techniques: the intersection of data-driven and model-driven processing, and the use of multiple sources of knowledge.

First, the interpretation process proceeds in what has been called the "recognition" mode: it is the intersection of a bottom-up (data-directed) process (the interpretations suggested by the connotations of the text) with a top-down (goal-directed) process (the expectations set up by the choice of a rule model). Each process contributes to the end result, but it is the combination of them that is effective.

This intersection of two processing modes is important where the interpretation techniques are as simple as those employed here, but the idea is more generally applicable as well. Even with more powerful interpretation techniques, neither direction of processing is in general capable of eliminating all ambiguity and finding the correct answer. By moving both top-down and bottom-up, we make use of all available sources of information, resulting in a far more focussed search for the answer. This technique is applicable across a range of different interpretation problems, including text, vision, and speech.

Second, in either direction of processing, TEIRESIAS uses a number of different sources of knowledge. In the bottom-up direction, for example, distinct information about the appropriate interpretation of the text comes from (a) the connotations of individual words (interpretation of each piece of data), (b) the function template (structure for the whole interpretation), and (c) internal consistency constraints (interactions between data points), as well as several other sources (see [5] for the full list). Any one of these knowledge sources alone will not perform very well, but acting in concert they are much more effective (a principle developed extensively in [15]).

The notion of program-generated expectations is also an important source of power, since the selection of a particular rule model supplies the focus for the top-down part of the processing. Finally, the idea of model-based understanding offers an effective way of using the information in the rule model to effect the top-down processing.

Thus our relatively simple techniques supply adequate power because of the synergistic effect of multiple, independent sources of knowledge, because of the focussing and guiding effect of intersecting data-directed and goal-directed processing, and because of the effective mechanism for interpretation supplied by the idea of model-based understanding.

7.4. Phase III: modifying the interpretation

TEIRESIAS has a simple rule editor that allows the expert to modify existing rules or (as in this example) indicate changes to the system's attempts to understand a new rule. The editor has a number of simple heuristics built into it to make the rule modification process as effective as possible. In dealing with requests to change a particular clause of a new rule, for instance, the system re-evaluates the alternative interpretations, taking into account the rejected interpretation (trying to learn from its mistakes), and making the smallest change possible (using the heuristic that the original clause was probably close to correct). In this case this succeeds in choosing the correct clause next (Fig. 8d shows the correct connotations and resulting code).

```
THE CLIENT  IS   FOLLOWING  UP ON MARKET TRENDS  CAREFULLY
     ↓       ↓       ↓                                ↓
    OBJ    SAME  ATTRIBUTE                          VALUE

              (SAME OBJCT FOLLOWS CAREFULLY)
              The client follows the market carefully
```

FIG. 8d. The correct interpretation.

There are also various forms of consistency checking available. One obvious but effective constraint is to ensure that each word of the text is interpreted in only one way. In the trace shown earlier, for instance, accepting the new interpretation of clause 2 means clause 3 must be spurious, since it attempts to use the word *carefully* in a different sense.

7.5. Phase IV: "second guessing", another use of the rule models

After the expert indicates that TEIRESIAS has correctly understood what he said, the system checks to see if *it* is satisfied with the content of the rule. The idea is to use the rule model to see how well this new rule "fits in" to the system's model of its knowledge—i.e., does it "look like" a typical rule of the sort expected?

In the current implementation, an incomplete match between the new rule and the rule model triggers a response from TEIRESIAS. Recall the last line of the premise description in the rule model of Fig. 7:

((BRACKET SAME) (FOLLOWS NOTSAME SAME)
(EXPERIENCE SAME) 1.5)

This indicates that when the tax BRACKET of the client appears in the premise of a rule of this sort, then how closely he FOLLOWS the market, and how much investment EXPERIENCE he has typically appear as well. Note that the new rule has the first two of these, but is missing the last, and the system points this out.

If the expert agrees to the inclusion of a new clause, TEIRESIAS attempts to create it. Since in this case the agreed upon topic for the clause was the amount of investment EXPERIENCE of the client, this must be the attribute to use. The rule model suggests which predicate function to use (SAME, since that is the one paired with EXPERIENCE in the relevant line of the rule model), and the template for this function is retrieved. It is filled out in the usual way, except that TEIRESIAS checks the record of the consultation when seeking items to fill in the template blanks. In this case only a VALUE is still missing. Note that, as the answer to question 6 of the consultation, the expert indicated that the amount of experience was **MODERATE**, so TEIRESIAS uses this as the value. The result is a plausible guess, since it ensures that the rule will in fact work for the current case (note the further use of the "debugging in context" idea). It is not necessarily correct, of course, since the desired clause may be more general, but it is at least a plausible attempt.

It should be noted that there is nothing in this concept of "second guessing" which is specific to the rule models as they are currently designed, or indeed to associative triples or rules as a knowledge representation. The fundamental point was that mentioned above of testing to see how the new knowledge "fits in" to the system's current model of its knowledge. At this point the system might perform any kind of check, for violations of any established prejudices about what the new chunk of knowledge should look like. Additional kinds of checks for rules might concern the strength of the inference, number of clauses in the premise, etc. Checks used with, say, a procedural encoding might involve the number and type of arguments passed to the procedure, use of global variables, presence of side effects, etc. In that case, for example, we can imagine adding a new procedure to a system which then responds by remarking that "*. . . most procedures that do hash-table insertion also have the side effect of incrementing the variable* NUMBRELEMENTS. *Shall I add the code to do this?*" In general, this "second guessing" process can involve any characteristic which the system may have "noticed" about the particular knowledge representation in use.

Note also that this second use of the rule model is quite different than the first. Where earlier we were concerned about interpreting text and determining what the expert actually said, here the task is to see what he plausibly *should have* said. Since, in assembling the rule models, TEIRESIAS may have noticed regularities in the reasoning about the domain that may not yet have occurred to the expert himself, the system's suggestions may conceivably be substantive and useful.

Finally, all this is in turn an instance of the more general notion of using meta-level knowledge in the process of knowledge acquisition: TEIRESIAS does not simply accept the new rule and add it to the knowledge base, but instead uses the rule model to evaluate the new knowledge in light of its current knowledge base. In a very simple way, learning is effected as a process of examining the relationships between what is already known and the new information being taught.

7.6. Phase V: final checkout, bookkeeping, rerunning the consultation

Now that both the expert and TEIRESIAS are satisfied, there is one final sequence of tests to be performed, reflecting once again the benefit of knowledge acquisition in context.

At this point, TEIRESIAS examines several things about the rule, attempting to make sure that it will in fact fix the problem uncovered. In this case, for instance, the action of the new rule should be a conclusion about investment area, the area mentioned should be high technology, and the conclusion should be affirmative. The premise should not contain any clauses which are sure to fail in the context in which the rule will be invoked. All these are potential sources of error which would make it obvious that the rule will not fix the bug.

The rule in the current example passes all the tests, but note what would have happened if the user had (perhaps accidentally) typed *the client's income tax bracket is* 20%.

The rule now reads:

RULE 383

If (1) the client's income tax bracket is 20%, and
  (2) the client follows the market carefully, and
  (3) the amount of investment experience is moderate,
then there is evidence (0.8) that the area of the investment should be high-technology.

Sorry, but this won't work. For Fred Smith, clause No. 1 ("the client's income tax bracket is 20%") is sure to fail.
Would you like to change the rule?
++**

(Since the answer to question 3 of the consultation indicated that the client had a taxable income of $40,000, TEIRESIAS is able to determine [by referring to the appropriate tables] that his tax bracket would not be 20%, hence the rule can't succeed). The expert then has the option of either editing the current rule or writing a new one (since the one he wrote may be correct, only inapplicable to the current problem). If he edits it, the tests are run again, until TEIRESIAS is satisfied that there is nothing obviously wrong with the rule.

There are also a number of straightforward bookkeeping tasks to be performed, including hooking the new rule into the knowledge base so that it is retrieved and invoked appropriately (e.g., in this case it gets added to the list of rules that conclude about INVESTMENT-AREA),[8] and tagging it with information which will make it easier to maintain the large and constantly changing body of rules (e.g., the name of the rule author, date of creation, author's justification for adding the rule, a pointer to the consultation which prompted its creation, etc.).

At this point, the system also performs any necessary recomputation of rule models. The operation is very fast, since it is clear from the action part of the rule which models may need to be recomputed, and the EXAMPLES part of the model then supplies the names of the other relevant rules.

TEIRESIAS then reruns the performance program as a sub-process, and checks the results to see if all the problems have been repaired.

[8] Note that these tests require the ability to dissect and partially evaluate the rule. The same function template which is used as a pattern for constructing rules is also used as a guide in this dissection and partial evaluation process. See [5] for details.

8. Other Uses for the Rule Models

Two other uses have been developed for the rule models, which demonstrate capabilities made possible by meta-level knowledge.

8.1. "Knowing what you know"

The MYCIN system has the ability to answer simple natural language questions about the knowledge base. In response to a question like "*How do you determine the identity of an organism causing an infection?*", that system will print the relevant rules. But a rule model, as a generalization of an entire class of rules, answers the question, too. Fig. 9 shows one example, taken from the stock market example we have been using.

****HOW DO YOU DECIDE THAT THE UTILITIES GROUP IS AN APPROPRIATE AREA FOR INVESTMENT?**

Rules which conclude that an appropriate area for investment is the utilities group generally use one or more of the following pieces of information:

the desired rate of return of the investment
the income-tax bracket of the client
the time-scale of the investment

Furthermore, the following relationships hold:
If a rule mentions the income-tax bracket of the client, it also typically mentions the time scale of the investment as well.

RULE 247, RULE 45, RULE 123, and RULE 206 conclude that an appropriate area for investment is the utilities group. Which of these (if any) would you like to see?
**

FIG. 9. "Knowing what you know."

By simply "reading" the rule model to the user, TEIRESIAS can supply an overview of the knowledge in the relevant rules. This suggests the structure of global trends in the knowledge of the expert who assembled the knowledge base, and thus helps to make clear the overall approach of the system to a given topic.

8.2. "Knowing what you don't know"

Another use of the models demonstrates that, in a primitive fashion, they give TEIRESIAS a model of what it *doesn't* know. There are models in the current system made from between 2 (the defined minimum) and 35 rules. We have defined a metric to measure the "strength" of a model, and base it on both the total number of rules from which the model was constructed and the strength of the inference of each of those rules. The entire model set is kept ordered from weakest to strongest, giving the system some indication of its likely competence on a range of subjects. In a very primitive way, it thus gains a knowledge of where it is ignorant.

This makes possible a new option for the expert. Instead of adding a rule to fix a bug, he can ask the system what it would like to learn.

– – ** **WHAT WOULD YOU LIKE TO KNOW?**
Answer
  -Y for yes
  -N for no, or
  -Q to quit this.
There are only 2 rules for concluding that the name of the stock to invest in would be Homestake-Mining.
Would you like to give me a rule for that? [Y, N, Q]
+ + ** **N**
There are only 2 rules for concluding that the risk class of an investment should be speculative.
Would you like to offer a rule for that? [Y, N, Q] + + ** **Y**
The new rule will be called RULE 384
    If (1)

FIG. 10. "Knowing what you don't know."

The system cycles through the rule models in order, indicating the weakest topics first. This is, of course, a first order solution to the problem of giving the system an indication of its areas of ignorance. A better solution would supply an indication of how much the system knows about a subject, compared with how much there is to know. There surely are subjects for which three or four rules exhaust the available knowledge, while for others a hundred or more rules may not suffice. The issue is related to work described in [4] on closed vs. open sets. That paper offers some interesting strategies for allowing a program to decide when it is ignorant and how it might reason in the face of the inability to store every fact about a given topic.

There appear to be no easy ways to deduce the incompleteness of the knowledge base using only the information stored in it. It is not valid to say, for instance, that there ought to be even a single rule for every attribute (how could an investor's name be deduced?). Nor is there a well-defined set of attributes for which no rules are likely to exist. Nor is it clear what sort of information would allow the incompleteness to be deduced.

The issue is a significant one, since a good solution to the problem would not only give TEIRESIAS a better grasp of where the performance program was weak, but would also provide several important capabilities to the performance program itself. It would, for example, permit the use of the "if it were true I would know" heuristic in [4]. Roughly restated, this says that "if I know a great deal about subject S, and fact F concerns an important aspect of S, then if I don't already know that F is true, it's probably false." Thus, in certain circumstances a lack of knowledge about the truth of a statement can plausibly be used as evidence suggesting that the statement is false.[9]

9. Assumptions and Limitations

The work reported here can be evaluated with respect to both the utility of its approach to knowledge acquisition and its success in implementing that approach.

9.1. The interactive transfer of expertise approach

As noted, our approach involves knowledge transfer that is interactive, that is set in the context of a shortcoming in the knowledge base, and that transfers a single rule at a time. Each of these has implications about TEIRESIAS's range of applicability.

Interactive knowledge transfer seems best suited to task domains involving problem solving that is entirely or primarily a high level cognitive task, based on a number of distinct, specifiable principles. Consultations in medicine or investments seem to be appropriate domains, but the approach would not seem well suited to those parts of, say, speech understanding or scene recognition in which low level process play a significant role.

The transfer of expertise approach presents a useful technique for task domains that do not permit the use of programs (like those noted in Section 3) which autonomously induce new knowledge from test data. The autonomous mode may most commonly be inapplicable because the data for a domain simply don't exist yet. In quantitative domains (like mass spectrum analysis [3]) or synthesized ("toy") domains (like the line drawings in [12]), a large body of data points is easily assembled. This is not currently true for many domains, consequently induction techniques cannot be used. In such cases interactive transfer of expertise offers a useful alternative.[10]

[9] This is another useful form of meta-level knowledge.

[10] Where the autonomous induction technique can be used, it offers the interesting advantage that the knowledge we expect the system to acquire need not be specified ahead of time, nor indeed even known. Induction programs are in theory capable of inducing "new" information (i.e., information unknown to their author) from their set of examples. Clearly the interactive transfer of expertise approach requires that the expert know and be able to specify precisely what it is the program is to learn.

Knowledge acquisition in context appears to offer useful guidance wherever knowledge of the domain is as yet ill-specified, but the context need not be a shortcoming in the knowledge base uncovered during a consultation, as is done here. Our recent experience suggests that an effective context is also provided by examining certain subsets of rules in the knowledge base and using them as a framework for specifying additional rules. The overall concept is limited, however, to systems that already have at least some minimal amount of information in their knowledge base. Earlier than this, there may be insufficient information to provide any context for the acquisition process.

Finally, the rule-at-a-time approach is a limiting factor. The example given earlier works well, of course, because the bug was manufactured by removing a single rule. In general, acquiring a single rule at a time seems well suited to the later stages of knowledge base construction, in which bugs may indeed be caused by the absence of one or a few rules. We need not be as lucky as the present example, in which one rule repairs three bugs; the approach will also work if three independent bugs arise in a consultation. But early in knowledge base construction, where large sub-areas of a domain are not yet specified, it appears more useful to deal with groups of rules, or, more generally, with larger segments of the basic task (as in [20]).

In general then, the interactive transfer of expertise approach seems well suited to the later stages of knowledge base construction for systems performing high-level tasks, and offers a useful technique for domains where extensive sets of data points are not available.

9.2. TEIRESIAS as a program

Several difficult problems remain unsolved in the current implementation of the program. There is, for instance, the issue of the technique used to generate the rule models. This process could be made more effective even without using a different approach to concept formation. While an early design criterion suggested keeping the models transparent to the expert, making the process interactive would allow the expert to evaluate new patterns as they were discovered by TEIRESIAS. This might make it possible to distinguish accidental correlations from valid interrelations, and increase the utility and sophistication of TEIRESIAS's second guessing ability. Alternatively, more sophisticated concept formation techniques might be borrowed from existing work.

There is also a potential problem in the way the models are used. Their effectiveness in both guiding the parsing of the new rule and in "second guessing" its content is dependent on the assumption that the present knowledge base is both correct and a good basis for predicting the content of future rules. Either of these can at times be false and the system may then tend to continue stubbornly down the wrong path.

The weakness of the natural language understanding technique presents a substantial barrier to better performance. Once again there are several improvements that could be made to the existing approach (see [5]), but more sophisticated techniques should also be considered (this work is currently underway; see [1]).

There is also the difficult problem of determining the impact of any new or changed rule on the rest of the knowledge base, which we have considered only briefly (see [5]). The difficulty lies in establishing a formal definition of inconsistency for inexact logics, since, except for obvious cases (e.g., two identical rules with different strengths), it is not clear what constitutes an inconsistency. Once the definition is established, we would also require routines capable of uncovering them in a large knowledge base. This can be attacked by using an incremental approach (i.e., by checking every rule as it is added, the knowledge base is kept consistent and each consistency check is a smaller task), but the problem is still substantial.

10. Conclusions

The ideas reviewed above each offer some contribution toward achieving the two goals set out at the beginning of this paper: the development of a methodology of knowledge base construction via transfer of expertise, and the creation of an intelligent assistant.

In the near-term they provide a set of tools and ideas to aid in the construction of knowledge-based programs and represent a few empirical techniques of knowledge engineering. Their contribution here may arise from their potential utility as case studies in the development of a methodology for this discipline.

Knowledge acquisition in the context of a shortcoming in the knowledge base, for instance, has proved to be a useful technique for achieving transfer of expertise, offering advantages to both the expert and TEIRESIAS. It offers the expert a framework for the explication of a new chunk of domain knowledge. By providing him with a specific example of the performance program's operation, and forcing him to be specific in his criticism, it encourages the formalization of previously implicit knowledge. It also enables TEIRESIAS to form a number of expectations about the knowledge it is going to acquire, and makes possible several checks on the content of that knowledge to insure that it will in fact fix the bug.

In addition, because the system has a *model of its own knowledge*, it is able to determine whether a newly added piece of knowledge "fit into" its existing knowledge base.

A second contribution of the ideas reviewed above lies in their ability to support a number of intelligent actions on the part of the assistant. While those actions have been demonstrated for a single task and system, it should be clear that none of the underlying ideas are limited to this particular task, or to associative triples or rules as a knowledge representation. The foundation for many of these ideas is the concept of meta-level knowledge, which has made possible a program with a limited form of introspection.

The idea of *model-based understanding*, for instance, found a novel application in the fact that TEIRESIAS has a model of the knowledge base and uses this to guide acquisition by interpreting it as predictions about the information it expects to receive.

The idea of *biasing the set of models* to be considered offers a specific mechanism for the general notion of *program-generated expectations*, and makes possible an assistant whose understanding of the dialog was more effective.

TEIRESIAS is able to "second guess" the expert with respect to the content of the new knowledge by using its models to *see how well the new piece of knowledge "fits in" to what it already knows.* An incomplete match between the new knowledge and the system's model of its knowledge prompts it to make a suggestion to the expert. With this approach, learning becomes more than simply adding the new information to the knowledge base; TEIRESIAS examines as well the relationship between new and existing knowledge.

The concept of meta-level knowledge makes possible *multiple uses of the knowledge in the system:* information in the knowledge base is not only used directly (during the consultation), but is also examined and abstracted to form the rule models (see [8] for additional examples).

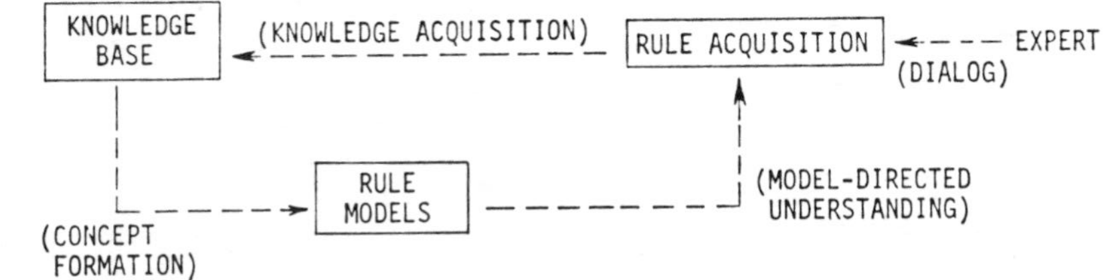

FIG. 11. Model-directed understanding and learning by experience combine to produce a useful feedback loop.

TEIRESIAS also represents a synthesis of the ideas of model-based understanding and learning by experience. While both of these have been developed independently in previous AI research, their combination produces a novel sort of feedback loop (Fig. 11). Rule acquisition relies on the set of rule models to effect the model-based understanding process. This results in the addition of a new rule to the knowledge base, which in turn prompts the recomputation of the relevant rule model(s).[11]

This loop has a number of interesting implications. First, performance on the acquisition of the next rule may be better, because the system's "picture" of its knowledge base has improved — the rule models are now computed from a larger set of instances, and their generalizations are more likely to be valid.

Second, since the relevant rule models are recomputed each time a change is made to the knowledge base, the picture they supply is kept constantly up to date, and they will at all times be an accurate reflection of the shifting patterns in the knowledge base. This is true as well for the trees into which the rule models are organized: they too grow (and shrink) to reflect the changes in the knowledge base.

Finally, and perhaps most interesting, the models are not hand-tooled by the system architect, or specified by the expert. They are instead formed by the system itself, and formed as a result of its experience in acquiring rules from the expert. Thus despite its reliance on a set of models as a basis for understanding, TEIRESIAS's abilities are not restricted by the existing set of models. As its store of knowledge grows, old models can become more accurate, new models will be formed, and the system's stock of knowledge about its knowledge will continue to expand. This appears to be a novel capability for a model-based system.

[11] The models are recomputed when any change is made to the knowledge base, including rule deletion or modification, as well as addition.

ACKNOWLEDGMENTS

The work described here was performed as part of a doctoral thesis supervised by Bruce Buchanan, whose assistance and encouragement were important contributions.

REFERENCES

1. Bonnett, A., BAOBAB, a parser for a rule-based system using a semantic grammar, Stanford University HPP Memo 78-10, Stanford CA, U.S.A. (1978).
2. Brown, J. S. and Burton, R. R., Diagnostic models for procedural bugs in mathematical skills, *Cognitive Science* **2** (April–June 1978), pp. 155–192.
3. Buchanan, B. G. and Mitchell, T., Model-directed learning of production rules, in: Waterman and Hayes-Roth (Eds.), *Pattern-Directed Inference Systems* (Academic Press, New York, 1978), pp. 297–312.
4. Carbonell, J. R. and Collins, A. M., Natural semantics in artificial intelligence, Proc. Third International Joint Conference on AI, Stanford, CA (August 1973), pp. 344–351.
5. Davis, R., Applications of meta-level knowledge to the construction, maintenance, and use of large knowledge bases, Stanford University HPP Memo 76-7 (July 1976).
6. Davis, R., Generalized procedure calling and content-directed invocation, Proc. of the Symposium on Artificial Intelligence and Programming Languages, *SIGART/SIGPLAN* (combined issue, August 1977), pp. 45–54.
7. Davis, R. Knowledge acquisition in rule based systems—knowledge about representations as a basis for system construction and maintenance, in: D. Waterman and F. Hayes-Roth (Eds.), *Pattern-Directed Inference Systems* (Academic Press, New York, 1978), pp. 99–134.
8. Davis, R. and Buchanan, B. G., Meta-level knowledge: overview and applications, Proc. Fifth International Joint Conference on AI, Cambridge, MA (August 1977), pp. 920–927.
9. Davis, R., Buchanan, B. and Shortliffe, E. H., Production rules as a representation for a knowledge-based consultation system, *Artificial Intelligence* **8** (February 1977), pp. 15–45.
10. Falk, G., Computer interpretation of imperfect line data, Stanford University AI Memo 132 (August 1970).
11. Feigenbaum, E. A., et al. On generality and problem solving, *Machine Intelligence* **6** (1971), pp. 165–190.
12. Hayes-Roth, F. and McDermott, J., Knowledge acquisition from structural descriptions Proc. Fifth International Joint Conference on AI, Cambridge, MA (1977), pp. 356–362.

13. Mathlab Group, The MACSYMA Reference Manual, MIT Lab. for Computer Science (September 1974).
14. Newell, A. and Simon, H., *Human Problem Solving* (Prentice-Hall, Englewood Cliffs, NJ, 1972).
15. Reddy, D. R., et al. The HEARSAY speech-understanding system: an example of the recognition process, Proc. 3rd IJCAI, Stanford, CA (1973), pp. 185–193.
16. Reiser, J. F., BAIL—A debugger for SAIL, AI Memo 270, Stanford University, AI Lab. (October 1975).
17. Shortliffe, E. H., MYCIN: *Computer-based Consultations in Medical Therapeutics* (American Elsevier, New York, 1976).
18. Shortliffe, E. H. and Buchanan, B. G., A model of inexact reasoning in medicine, *Mathematical Biosciences* **23** (1975), pp. 351–379.
19. Teitelman, W., *The* INTERLISP *Reference Manual*, Xerox Corp. (1975).
20. Waterman, D., Exemplary programming, in: D. Waterman and F. Hayes-Roth (Eds.), *Pattern-Directed Inference Systems* (Academic Press, New York 1978), pp. 261–280.
21. Winston, P. H., Learning structural descriptions from examples, Project MAC TR-76, MIT, Cambridge, MA (September 1970).

5 / Advanced Topics

The performance of many AI expert systems has attained impressive levels, but they are still rather "brittle" in many important respects. Most of their defects center upon their inability to reason about either their own knowledge or that of others. For example, PROSPECTOR cannot tell its users the kinds of things it knows about. Perhaps more importantly, it does not know that it does not know certain things. PROSPECTOR cannot modify its behavior to take account of what the user already knows about geology in general—and about the specific prospect under consideration. The papers in this chapter of the volume are examples of research on many fundamental problems that need to be solved before AI systems can become truly flexible and adaptable.

Topics having to do with the representation and use of knowledge can properly be considered to lie within the area of philosophy called *epistemology*, the study of knowledge. AI research is helping to clarify several important and long-standing philosophical problems; conversely, the perspective and traditions of philosophical analysis can help guide AI research. The paper by McCarthy and Hayes is a classic study of AI approaches to philosophical problems. It raises and discusses many important issues involved in the development of planning and decision-making systems.

Several extensions of first-order logic have been suggested to increase its expressive power. Some of these extensions, on close analysis, turn out to be syntactic variants of ordinary first-order logic rather than fundamentally different logical systems. Many of these variants elevate some important implementation details (such as indexing) to the level of the syntax of the language. Frame systems and semantic networks are two examples of representational systems that were proposed originally as alternatives to logic. Hayes's paper examines one of these frame-based systems and shows how it can be interpreted as a system of first-order logic.

McCarthy's articles in this chapter of the volume are about epistemological issues. In his 1977 paper, he describes several problems that he believes are fundamental to progress in AI. He also gives brief summaries of his work on two of these problems, namely, the *qualification problem* (how to limit the class of objects to consider in solving a problem) and the problem of representing and reasoning about another agent's knowledge. He proposes a method of reasoning called *circumscription* for dealing with the qualification problem. McCarthy's 1980 article treats circumscription in detail.

Several researchers have recognized the importance of representing and reasoning about the knowledge (and the beliefs and goals) of other agents. A standard approach to this problem has been to introduce a modal operator to represent such concepts as knowledge, belief, and want. (McCarthy's 1977 paper presents an alternative approach.) Moore's paper describes a way of expressing the possible-world semantics of modal logic in first-order logic. He is thus able to employ a technique for reasoning about knowledge and action entirely within the realm of ordinary first-order logic.

Knowledge, beliefs, and wants comprise part of what might be called the *cognitive state* of an agent. Natural language is an important medium by which humans can affect one another's cognitive states. The paper by Cohen and Perrault shows how "speech acts" (written or spoken statements, questions, and commands) can be regarded as the articulated result of deliberate, planned behavior designed to affect cognitive states in predictable ways. They define several speech acts in terms of operators similar to those used by the STRIPS planning system.

We have seen several examples in this volume in which databases of assertions are expanded to include deduced statements. A problem arises when changes are made in the original database of assertions, because some of the deduced statements may then no longer be valid. Doyle's paper proposes a technique for "truth maintenance" that efficiently computes the status of deduced statements. The problem of truth maintenance is related to the problem of *nonmonotonic* reasoning discussed in McCarthy's 1980 paper.

Most people associate "learning" with "intelligence," but AI research cannot claim many genuinely impressive achievements in building programs that learn. We have certainly not yet succeeded in designing programs that can *learn* to perform a task better than programs that have been specifically equipped with all the knowledge needed to solve that task. Mitchell's paper serves the very useful role of providing a framework for comparing a variety of approaches to a significant problem in learning—that of generalizing, retaining, and applying the important common features that characterize classes of observables. Mitchell's technique depends upon search and search strategies for establishing a generalization that is compatible with the positive training instances and incompatible with the negative ones. Here the search space consists of all the possible generalizations of any set of training instances, while the search strategy consists in using those instances to converge upon a consistent, useful generalization.

Some Philosophical Problems from the Standpoint of Artificial Intelligence

J. McCarthy
Computer Science Department
Stanford University

P. J. Hayes
Metamathematics Unit
University of Edinburgh

Abstract

A computer program capable of acting intelligently in the world must have a general representation of the world in terms of which its inputs are interpreted. Designing such a program requires commitments about what knowledge is and how it is obtained. Thus, some of the major traditional problems of philosophy arise in artificial intelligence.

More specifically, we want a computer program that decides what to do by inferring in a formal language that a certain strategy will achieve its assigned goal. This requires formalizing concepts of causality, ability, and knowledge. Such formalisms are also considered in philosophical logic.

The first part of the paper begins with a philosophical point of view that seems to arise naturally once we take seriously the idea of actually making an intelligent machine. We go on to the notions of metaphysically and epistemologically adequate representations of the world and then to an explanation of *can*, *causes*, and *knows* in terms of a representation of the world by a system of interacting automata. A proposed resolution of the problem of freewill in a deterministic universe and of counterfactual conditional sentences is presented.

The second part is mainly concerned with formalisms within which it can be proved that a strategy will achieve a goal. Concepts of situation, fluent, future operator, action, strategy, result of a strategy and knowledge are formalized. A method is given of constructing a sentence of first-order logic which will be true in all models of certain axioms if and only if a certain strategy will achieve a certain goal.

The formalism of this paper represents an advance over McCarthy (1963) and Green (1969) in that it permits proof of the correctness of strategies that contain loops and strategies that involve the acquisition of knowledge; and it is also somewhat more concise.

The third part discusses open problems in extending the formalism of part 2.

The fourth part is a review of work in philosophical logic in relation to problems of artificial intelligence and a discussion of previous efforts to program 'general intelligence' from the point of view of this paper.

1. PHILOSOPHICAL QUESTIONS

Why artificial intelligence needs philosophy

The idea of an intelligent machine is old, but serious work on the problem of artificial intelligence or even serious understanding of what the problem is awaited the stored-program computer. We may regard the subject of artificial intelligence as beginning with Turing's article 'Computing Machinery and Intelligence' (Turing 1950) and with Shannon's (1950) discussion of how a machine might be programmed to play chess.

Since that time, progress in artificial intelligence has been mainly along the following lines. Programs have been written to solve a class of problems that give humans intellectual difficulty: examples are playing chess or checkers, proving mathematical theorems, transforming one symbolic expression into another by given rules, integrating expressions composed of elementary functions, determining chemical compounds consistent with mass-spectrographic and other data. In the course of designing these programs intellectual mechanisms of greater or lesser generality are identified sometimes by introspection, sometimes by mathematical analysis, and sometimes by experiments with human subjects. Testing the programs sometimes leads to better understanding of the intellectual mechanisms and the identification of new ones.

An alternative approach is to start with the intellectual mechanisms (for example, memory, decision-making by comparisons of scores made up of weighted sums of sub-criteria, learning, tree search, extrapolation) and make up problems that exercise these mechanisms.

In our opinion the best of this work has led to increased understanding of intellectual mechanisms and this is essential for the development of artificial intelligence even though few investigators have tried to place their particular mechanism in the general context of artificial intelligence. Sometimes this is because the investigator identifies his particular problem with the field as a whole; he thinks he sees the woods when in fact he is looking at a tree. An old but not yet superseded discussion on intellectual mechanisms is in Minsky (1961); see also Newell's (1965) review of the state of artificial intelligence.

There have been several attempts to design a general intelligence with the same kind of flexibility as that of a human. This has meant different things to different investigators, but none has met with much success even in the sense of general intelligence used by the investigator in question. Since our criticism of this work will be that it does not face the philosophical problems discussed in this paper we shall postpone discussing it until a concluding section.

However, we are obliged at this point to present our notion of general intelligence.

It is not difficult to give sufficient conditions for general intelligence. Turing's idea that the machine should successfully pretend to a sophisticated observer to be a human being for half an hour will do. However, if we direct our efforts towards such a goal our attention is distracted by certain superficial aspects of human behaviour that have to be imitated. Turing excluded some of these by specifying that the human to be imitated is at the end of a teletype line, so that voice, appearance, smell, etc., do not have to be considered. Turing did allow himself to be distracted into discussing the imitation of human fallibility in arithmetic, laziness, and the ability to use the English language.

However, work on artificial intelligence, expecially general intelligence, will be improved by a clearer idea of what intelligence is. One way is to give a purely behavioural or black-box definition. In this case we have to say that a machine is intelligent if it solves certain classes of problems requiring intelligence in humans, or survives in an intellectually demanding environment. This definition seems vague; perhaps it can be made somewhat more precise without departing from behavioural terms, but we shall not try to do so.

Instead, we shall use in our definition certain structures apparent to introspection, such as knowledge of facts. The risk is twofold: in the first place we might be mistaken in our introspective views of our own mental structure; we may only think we use facts. In the second place there might be entities which satisfy behaviourist criteria of intelligence but are not organized in this way. However, we regard the construction of intelligent machines as fact manipulators as being the best bet both for constructing artificial intelligence and understanding natural intelligence.

We shall, therefore, be interested in an intelligent entity that is equipped with a representation or model of the world. On the basis of this representation a certain class of internally posed questions can be answered, not always correctly. Such questions are

1. What will happen next in a certain aspect of the situation?
2. What will happen if I do a certain action?
3. What is 3+3?
4. What does he want?
5. Can I figure out how to do this or must I get information from someone else or something else?

The above are not a fully representative set of questions and we do not have such a set yet.

On this basis we shall say that an entity is intelligent if it has an adequate model of the world (including the intellectual world of mathematics, understanding of its own goals and other mental processes), if it is clever enough to answer a wide variety of questions on the basis of this model, if it can get additional information from the external world when required, and can perform such tasks in the external world as its goals demand and its physical abilities permit.

According to this definition intelligence has two parts, which we shall call the epistemological and the heuristic. The epistemological part is the representation of the world in such a form that the solution of problems follows from the facts expressed in the representation. The heuristic part is the mechanism that on the basis of the information solves the problem and decides what to do. Most of the work in artificial intelligence so far can be regarded as devoted to the heuristic part of the problem. This paper, however, is entirely devoted to the epistemological part.

Given this notion of intelligence the following kinds of problems arise in constructing the epistemological part of an artificial intelligence:

1. What kind of general representation of the world will allow the incorporation of specific observations and new scientific laws as they are discovered?
2. Besides the representation of the physical world what other kind of entities have to be provided for? For example, mathematical systems, goals, states of knowledge.
3. How are observations to be used to get knowledge about the world, and how are the other kinds of knowledge to be obtained? In particular what kinds of knowledge about the system's own state of mind are to be provided for?
4. In what kind of internal notation is the system's knowledge to be expressed?

These questions are identical with or at least correspond to some traditional questions of philosophy, especially in metaphysics, epistemology and philosophic logic. Therefore, it is important for the research worker in artificial intelligence to consider what the philosophers have had to say.

Since the philosophers have not really come to an agreement in 2500 years it might seem that artificial intelligence is in a rather hopeless state if it is to depend on getting concrete enough information out of philosophy to write computer programs. Fortunately, merely undertaking to embody the philosophy in a computer program involves making enough philosophical presuppositions to exclude most philosophy as irrelevant. Undertaking to construct a general intelligent computer program seems to entail the following presuppositions:

1. The physical world exists and already contains some intelligent machines called people.
2. Information about this world is obtainable through the senses and is expressible internally.
3. Our common-sense view of the world is approximately correct and so is our scientific view.

4. The right way to think about the general problems of metaphysics and epistemology is not to attempt to clear one's own mind of all knowledge and start with 'Cogito ergo sum' and build up from there. Instead, we propose to use all of our own knowledge to construct a computer program that knows. The correctness of our philosophical system will be tested by numerous comparisons between the beliefs of the program and our own observations and knowledge. (This point of view corresponds to the presently dominant attitude towards the foundations of mathematics. We study the structure of mathematical systems–from the outside as it were–using whatever metamathematical tools seem useful instead of assuming as little as possible and building up axiom by axiom and rule by rule within a system.)
5. We must undertake to construct a rather comprehensive philosophical system, contrary to the present tendency to study problems separately and not try to put the results together.
6. The criterion for definiteness of the system becomes much stronger. Unless, for example, a system of epistemology allows us, at least in principle, to construct a computer program to seek knowledge in accordance with it, it must be rejected as too vague.
7. The problem of 'free will' assumes an acute but concrete form. Namely, in common-sense reasoning, a person often decides what to do by evaluating the results of the different actions he can do. An intelligent program must use this same process, but using an exact formal sense of of *can*, must be able to show that it has these alternatives without denying that it is a deterministic machine.
8. The first task is to define even a naïve, common-sense view of the world precisely enough to program a computer to act accordingly. This is a very difficult task in itself.

We must mention that there is one possible way of getting an artificial intelligence without having to understand it or solve the related philosophical problems. This is to make a computer simulation of natural selection in which intelligence evolves by mutating computer programs in a suitably demanding environment. This method has had no substantial success so far, perhaps due to inadequate models of the world and of the evolutionary process, but it might succeed. It would seem to be a dangerous procedure, for a program that was intelligent in a way its designer did not understand might get out of control. In any case, the approach of trying to make an artificial intelligence through understanding what intelligence is, is more congenial to the present authors and seems likely to succeed sooner.

Reasoning programs and the Missouri program

The philosophical problems that have to be solved will be clearer in connection with a particular kind of proposed intelligent program, called a reasoning program or RP for short. RP interacts with the world through input and output devices some of which may be general sensory and motor organs (for example, television cameras, microphones, artificial arms) and others of which are communication devices (for example, teletypes or keyboard-display consoles). Internally, RP may represent information in a variety of ways. For example, pictures may be represented as dot arrays or a lists of regions and edges with classifications and adjacency relations. Scenes may be represented as lists of bodies with positions, shapes, and rates of motion. Situations may be represented by symbolic expressions with allowed rules of transformation. Utterances may be represented by digitized functions of time, by sequences of phonemes, and parsings of sentences.

However, one representation plays a dominant role and in simpler systems may be the only representation present. This is a representation by sets of sentences in a suitable formal logical language, for example *w*-order logic with function symbols, description operator, conditional expressions, sets, etc. Whether we must include modal operators with their referential opacity is undecided. This representation dominates in the following sense:

1. All other data structures have linguistic descriptions that give the relations between the structures and what they tell about the world.
2. The subroutines have linguistic descriptions that tell what they do, either internally manipulating data, or externally manipulating the world.
3. The rules that express RP's beliefs about how the world behaves and that give the consequences of strategies are expressed linguistically.
4. RP's goals, as given by the experimenter, its devised subgoals, its opinion on its state of progress are all linguistically expressed.
5. We shall say that RP's information is adequate to solve a problem if it is a logical consequence of all these sentences that a certain strategy of action will solve it.
6. RP is a deduction program that tries to find strategies of action that it can prove will solve a problem; on finding one, it executes it.
7. Strategies may involve subgoals which are to be solved by RP, and part or all of a strategy may be purely intellectual, that is, may involve the search for a strategy, a proof, or some other intellectual object that satisfies some criteria.

Such a program was first discussed in McCarthy (1959) and was called the Advice Taker. In McCarthy (1963) a preliminary approach to the required formalism, now superseded by this paper, was presented. This paper is in part an answer to Y. Bar-Hillel's comment, when the original paper was presented at the 1958 Symposium on the Mechanization of Thought Processes, that the paper involved some philosophical presuppositions.

Constructing RP involves both the epistemological and the heuristic parts of the artificial intelligence problem: that is, the information in memory must be adequate to determine a strategy for achieving the goal (this strategy may involve the acquisition of further information) and RP must be clever enough to find the strategy and the proof of its correctness. Of course, these problems interact, but since this paper is focused on the epistemological part, we mention the Missouri program (MP) that involves only this part.

The Missouri program (its motto is, 'Show me') does not try to find strategies or proofs that the strategies achieve a goal. Instead, it allows the experimenter to present it proof steps and checks their correctness. Moreover, when it is 'convinced' that it ought to perform an action or execute a strategy it does so. We may regard this paper as being concerned with the construction of a Missouri program that can be persuaded to achieve goals.

Representations of the world

The first step in the design of RP or MP is to decide what structure the world is to be regarded as having, and how information about the world and its laws of change are to be represented in the machine. This decision turns out to depend on whether one is talking about the expression of general laws or specific facts. Thus, our understanding of gas dynamics depends on the representation of a gas as a very large number of particles moving in space; this representation plays an essential rôle in deriving the mechanical, thermal electrical and optical properties of gases. The state of the gas at a given instant is regarded as determined by the position, velocity and excitation states of each particle. However, we never actually determine the position, velocity or excitation of even a single molecule. Our practical knowledge of a particular sample of gas is expressed by parameters like the pressure, temperature and velocity fields or even more grossly by average pressures and temperatures. From our philosophical point of view this is entirely normal, and we are not inclined to deny existence to entities we cannot see, or to be so anthropocentric as to imagine that the world must be so constructed that we have direct or even indirect access to all of it.

From the artificial intelligence point of view we can then define three kinds of adequacy for representations of the world.

A representation is called metaphysically adequate if the world could have that form without contradicting the facts of the aspect of reality that interests us. Examples of metaphysically adequate representations for different aspects of reality are:

1. The representation of the world as a collection of particles interacting through forces between each pair of particles.
2. Representation of the world as a giant quantum-mechanical wave function.
3. Representation as a system of interacting discrete automata. We shall make use of this representation.

Metaphysically adequate representations are mainly useful for constructing general theories. Deriving observable consequences from the theory is a further step.

A representation is called epistemologically adequate for a person or machine if it can be used practically to express the facts that one actually has about the aspect of the world. Thus none of the above-mentioned representations are adequate to express facts like 'John is at home' or 'dogs chase cats' or 'John's telephone number is 321–7580'. Ordinary language is obviously adequate to express the facts that people communicate to each other in ordinary language. It is not, for instance, adequate to express what people know about how to recognize a particular face. The second part of this paper is concerned with an epistemologically adequate formal representation of common-sense facts of causality, ability and knowledge.

A representation is called heuristically adequate if the reasoning processes actually gone through in solving a problem are expressible in the language. We shall not treat this somewhat tentatively proposed concept further in this paper except to point out later that one particular representation seems epistemologically but not heuristically adequate.

In the remaining sections of the first part of the paper we shall use the representations of the world as a system of interacting automata to explicate notions of causality, ability and knowledge (including self-knowledge).

The automaton representation and the notion of 'can'

Let S be a system of interacting discrete finite automata such as that shown in figure 1

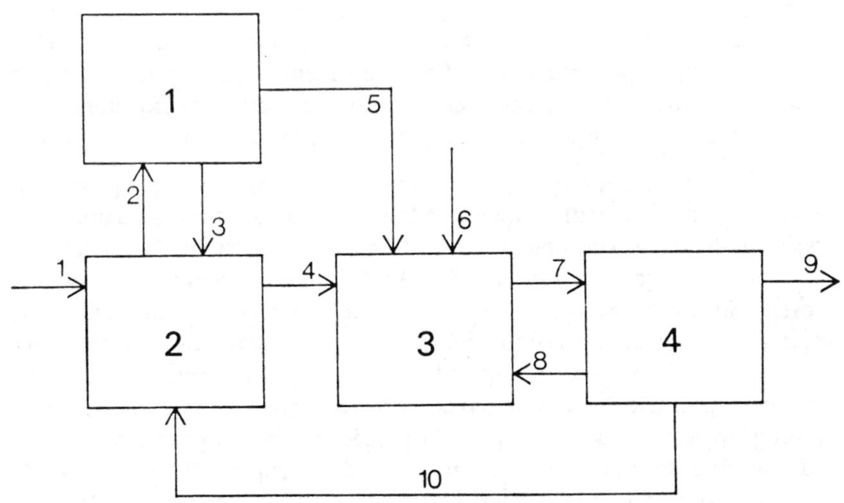

Figure 1

Each box represents a subautomaton and each line represents a signal. Time takes on integer values and the dynamic behaviour of the whole automaton is given by the equations:

$$\begin{aligned}
(1)\ & a_1(t+1) = A_1(a_1(t), s_3(t)) \\
& a_2(t+1) = A_2(a_2(t), s_1(t), s_2(t), s_{10}(t)) \\
& a_3(t+1) = A_3(a_3(t), s_4(t), s_5(t), s_6(t)) \\
& a_4(t+1) = A_4(a_4(t), s_7(t))
\end{aligned}$$

$$\begin{aligned}
(2)\ & s_2(t) = S_2(a_1(t)) \\
& s_3(t) = S_3(a_2(t)) \\
& s_4(t) = S_4(a_2(t)) \\
& s_5(t) = S_5(a_1(t)) \\
& s_7(t) = S_7(a_4(t)) \\
& s_8(t) = S_8(a_4(t)) \\
& s_9(t) = S_9(a_4(t)) \\
& s_{10}(t) = S_{10}(a_4(t))
\end{aligned}$$

The interpretation of these equations is that the state of any automaton at time $t+1$ is determined by its state at time t and by the signals received at time t. The value of a particular signal at time t is determined by the state at time t of the automaton from which it comes. Signals without a source automaton represent inputs from the outside and signals without a destination represent outputs.

Finite automata are the simplest examples of systems that interact over time. They are completely deterministic; if we know the initial states of all the automata and if we know the inputs as a function of time, the behaviour of the system is completely determined by equations (1) and (2) for all future time.

The automaton representation consists in regarding the world as a system of interacting subautomata. For example, we might regard each person in the room as a subautomaton and the environment as consisting of one or more additional subautomata. As we shall see, this representation has many of the qualitative properties of interactions among things and persons. However, if we take the representation too seriously and attempt to represent particular situations by systems of interacting automata we encounter the following difficulties:

1. The number of states required in the subautomata is very large, for example $2^{10^{10}}$, if we try to represent someone's knowledge. Automata this large have to be represented by computer programs, or in some other way that does not involve mentioning states individually.
2. Geometric information is hard to represent. Consider, for example, the location of a multi-jointed object such as a person or a matter of even more difficulty – the shape of a lump of clay.
3. The system of fixed interconnections is inadequate. Since a person may handle any object in the room, an adequate automaton representation would require signal lines connecting him with every object.
4. The most serious objection, however, is that (in our terminology) the automaton representation is epistemologically inadequate. Namely, we do not ever know a person well enough to list his internal states. The kind of information we do have about him needs to be expressed in some other way.

Nevertheless, we may use the automaton representation for concepts of *can*, *causes*, some kinds of counterfactual statements ('If I had struck this match yesterday it would have lit') and, with some elaboration of the representation, for a concept of *believes*.

Let us consider the notion of *can*. Let S be a system of subautomata without external inputs such as that of figure 2. Let p be one of the subautomata, and suppose that there are m signal lines coming out of p. What p can do is defined in terms of a new system S_p, which is obtained from the system S by disconnecting the m signal lines coming from p and replacing them by m external input lines to the system. In figure 2, subautomaton 1 has one output, and in the system S_1 this is replaced by an external input. The new system S_p always has the same set of states as the system S. Now let π be a condition on the state such as, 'a_2 is even' or '$a_2 = a_3$'. (In the applications π may be a condition like 'The box is under the bananas'.)

We shall write

$$can(p, \pi, s)$$

which is read, 'The subautomaton p *can* bring about the condition π in the situation s' if there is a sequence of outputs from the automaton S_p that will eventually put S into a state a' that satisfies $\pi(a')$. In other words, in determining what p can achieve, we consider the effects of sequences of its actions, quite apart from the conditions that determine what it actually will do.

In figure 2, let us consider the initial state a to be one in which all subautomata are initially in state 0. Then the reader will easily verify the following propositions:

1. Subautomaton 2 *will* never be in state 1.
2. Subautomaton 1 *can* put subautomaton 2 in state 1.
3. Subautomaton 3 *cannot* put subautomaton 2 in state 1.

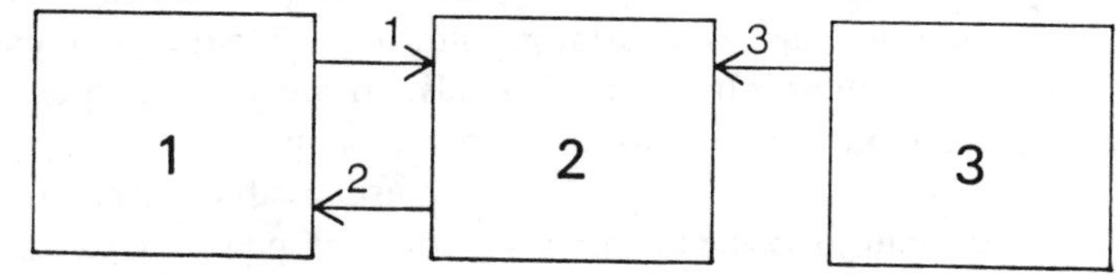

Figure 2. System S

$$\begin{aligned}
& a_1(t+1) = a_1(t) + s_2(t) \\
& a_2(t+1) = a_2(t) + s_1(t) + 2s_3(t) \\
& a_3(t+1) = \textbf{if } a_3(t) = 0 \textbf{ then } 0 \textbf{ else } a_3(t) + 1
\end{aligned}$$

$s_1(t) = \textbf{if } a_1(t) = 0 \textbf{ then } 2 \textbf{ else } 1$
$s_2(t) = 1$
$s_3(t) = \textbf{if } a_3(t) = 0 \textbf{ then } 0 \textbf{ else } 1$

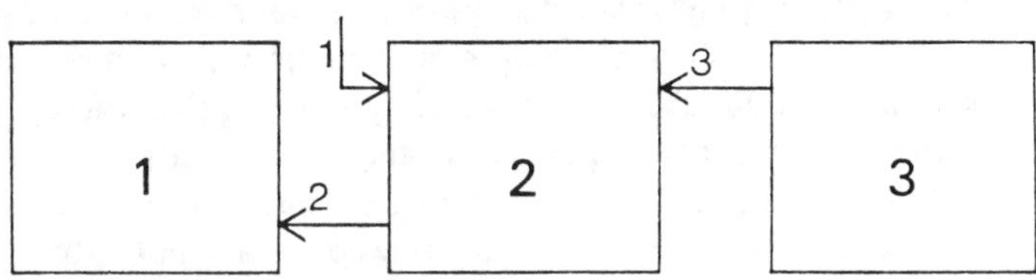

System S_1

We claim that this notion of *can* is, to a first approximation, the appropriate one for an automaton to use internally in deciding what to do by reasoning. We also claim that it corresponds in many cases to the common sense notion of *can* used in everyday speech.

In the first place, suppose we have an automaton that decides what to do by reasoning, for example suppose it is a computer using an RP. Then its output is determined by the decisions it makes in the resoning process. It does not know (has not computed) in advance what it will do, and, therefore, it is appropriate that it considers that it can do anything that can be achieved by some sequence of its outputs. Common-sense reasoning seems to operate in the same way.

The above rather simple notion of *can* requires some elaboration both to represent adequately the commonsense notion and for practical purposes in the reasoning program.

First, suppose that the system of automata admits external inputs. There are two ways of defining *can* in this case. One way is to assert $can(p,\pi,s)$ if p can achieve π regardless of what signals appear on the external inputs. Thus, instead of requiring the existence of a sequence of outputs of p that achieves the goal we shall require the existence of a strategy where the output at any time is allowed to depend on the sequence of external inputs so far received by the system. Note that in this definition of *can* we are not requiring that p have any way of knowing what the external inputs were. An alternative definition requires the outputs to depend on the inputs of p. This is equivalent to saying that p can achieve a goal provided the goal would be achieved for arbitrary inputs by some automaton put in place of p. With either of these definitions *can* becomes a function of the place of the subautomaton in the system rather than of the subautomaton itself. We do not know which of these treatments is preferable, and so we shall call the first concept *cana* and the second *canb*.

The idea that what a person can do depends on his position rather than on his characteristics is somewhat counter-intuitive. This impression can be mitigated as follows: Imagine the person to be made up of several subautomata; the output of the outer subautomaton is the motion of the joints. If we break the connection to the world at that point we can answer questions like, 'Can he fit through a given hole?' We shall get some counter-intuitive answers, however, such as that he can run at top speed for an hour or can jump over a building, since there are sequences of motions of his joints that would achieve these results.

The next step, however, is to consider a subautomaton that receives the nerve impulses from the spinal cord and transmits them to the muscles. If we break at the input to this automaton, we shall no longer say that he can jump over a building or run long at top speed since the limitations of the muscles will be taken into account. We shall, however, say that he can ride a unicycle since appropriate nerve signals would achieve this result.

The notion of *can* corresponding to the intuitive notion in the largest number of cases might be obtained by hypothesizing an 'organ of will', which makes decisions to do things and transmits these decisions to the main part of the brain that tries to carry them out and contains all the knowledge of particular facts. If we make the break at this point we shall be able to say that so-and-so cannot dial the President's secret and private telephone number because he does not know it, even though if the question were asked could he dial that particular number, the answer would be yes. However, even this break would not give the statement, 'I cannot go without saying goodbye, because this would hurt the child's feelings'.

On the basis of these examples, one might try to postulate a sequence of narrower and narrower notions of *can* terminating in a notion according to which a person can do only what he actually does. This notion would then be superfluous. Actually, one should not look for a single best notion of *can*; each of the above-mentioned notions is useful and is actually used in some circumstances. Sometimes, more than one notion is used in a single sentence, when two different levels of constraint are mentioned.

Besides its use in explicating the notion of *can*, the automaton representation of the world is very suited for defining notions of causality. For, we may say that subautomaton p caused the condition π in state s, if changing the output of p would prevent π. In fact the whole idea of a system of interacting automata is just a formalization of the commonsense notion of causality.

Moreover, the automaton representation can be used to explicate certain counterfactual conditional sentences. For example, we have the sentence, 'If I had struck this match yesterday at this time it would have lit'. In a suitable automaton representation, we have a certain state of the system yesterday at that time, and we imagine a break made where the nerves lead from my head or perhaps at the output of my 'decision box', and the appropriate signals to strike the match having been made. Then it is a definite and decidable question about the system S_p, whether the match lights or not, depending on whether it is wet, etc. This interpretation of this kind of counterfactual sentence seems to be what is needed for RP to learn from its mistakes, by accepting or generating sentences of the form, 'had I done thus-and-so I would have been successful, so I should alter my procedures in some way that would have produced the correct action in that case'.

In the foregoing we have taken the representation of the situation as a system of interacting subautomata for granted. However, a given overall situation might be represented as a system of interacting subautomata in a number of ways, and different representations might yield different results about what a given subautomaton can achieve, what would have happened if some subautomaton had acted differently, or what caused what. Indeed, in a different representation, the same or corresponding subautomata might not be identifiable. Therefore, these notions depend on the representation chosen.

For example, suppose a pair of Martians observe the situation in a room. One Martian analyses it as a collection of interacting people as we do, but the second Martian groups all the heads together into one subautomaton and all the bodies into another. (A creature from momentum space would regard the Fourier components of the distribution of matter as the separate interacting subautomata.) How is the first Martian to convince the second that his representation is to be preferred? Roughly speaking, he would argue that the interaction between the heads and bodies of the same person is closer than the interaction between the different heads, and so more of an analysis has been achieved from 'the primordial muddle' with the conventional representation. He will be especially convincing when he points out that when the meeting is over the heads will stop interacting with each other, but will continue to interact with their respective bodies.

We can express this kind of argument formally in terms of automata as follows: Suppose we have an autonomous automaton A, that is an automaton without inputs, and let it have k states. Further, let m and n be two integers such that $m,n \geqslant k$. Now label k points of an m-by-n array with the states of A. This can be done in $\binom{mn}{k}!$ ways. For each of these ways we have a representation of the automaton A as a system of an m-state automaton B interacting with an n-state automaton C. Namely, corresponding to each row of the array we have a state of B and to each column a state of C. The signals are in 1–1 correspondence with the states themselves; thus each subautomaton has just as many values of its output as it has states. Now it may happen that two of these signals are equivalent in their effect on the other subautomaton, and we use this equivalence relation to form equivalence classes of signals. We may then regard the equivalence classes as the signals themselves. Suppose then that there are now r signals from B to C and s signals from C to B. We ask how small r and s can be taken in general compared to m and n. The answer may be obtained by counting the number of inequivalent automata with k states and comparing it with the number of systems of two automata with m and n states respectively and r and s signals going in the respective directions. The result is not worth working out in detail, but tells us that only a few of the k state automata admit such a decomposition with r and s small compared to m and n. Therefore, if an automaton happens to admit such a decomposition it is very unusual for it to admit a second such decomposition that is not equivalent to the first with respect to some renaming of states. Applying this argument to the real world, we may say that it is overwhelmingly probable that our customary decomposition of the world automaton into separate people and things has a unique, objective and usually preferred status. Therefore, the notions of *can*, of causality, and of counterfactual associated with this decomposition also have a preferred status.

In our opinion, this explains some of the difficulty philosophers have had in analysing counterfactuals and causality. For example, the sentence, 'If I had struck this match yesterday, it would have lit' is meaningful only in terms of a rather complicated model of the world, which, however, has an objective preferred status. However, the preferred status of this model depends on its correspondence with a large number of facts. For this reason, it is probably not fruitful to treat an individual counterfactual conditional sentence in isolation.

It is also possible to treat notions of belief and knowledge in terms of the automaton representation. We have not worked this out very far, and the ideas presented here should be regarded as tentative. We would like to be able to give conditions under which we may say that a subautomaton p believes a certain proposition. We shall not try to do this directly but only relative to a predicate $B_p(s,w)$. Here s is the state of the automaton p and w is a proposition; $B_p(s,w)$ is true if p is to be regarded as believing w when in state s and is false otherwise. With respect to such a predicate B we may ask the following questions:

1. Are p's beliefs consistent? Are they correct?
2. Does p reason? That is, do new beliefs arise that are logical consequences of previous beliefs?
3. Does p observe? That is, do true propositions about automata connected to p cause p to believe them?
4. Does p behave rationally? That is, when p believes a sentence asserting that it should do something, does p do it?
5. Does p communicate in language L? That is, regarding the content of a certain input or ouput signal line as a text in language L, does this line transmit beliefs to or from p?
6. Is p self-conscious? That is, does it have a fair variety of correct beliefs about its own beliefs and the processes that change them?

It is only with respect to the predicate B_p that all these questions can be asked. However, if questions 1 thru 4 are answered affirmatively for some predicate B_p, this is certainly remarkable, and we would feel fully entitled to consider B_p a reasonable notion of belief.

In one important respect the situation with regard to belief or knowledge is the same as it was for counterfactual conditional statements: no way is provided to assign a meaning to a single statement of belief or knowledge, since for any single statement a suitable B_p can easily be constructed. Individual statements about belief or knowledge are made on the basis of a larger system which must be validated as a whole.

2. FORMALISM

In part 1 we showed how the concepts of ability and belief could be given formal definition in the metaphysically adequate automaton model and indicated the correspondence between these formal concepts and the corresponding commonsense concepts. We emphasized, however, that practical systems require epistemologically adequate systems in which those facts which are actually ascertainable can be expressed.

In this part we begin the construction of an epistemologically adequate system. Instead of giving formal definitions, however, we shall introduce the formal notions by informal natural-language descriptions and give examples of their use to describe situations and the possibilities for action they present. The formalism presented is intended to supersede that of McCarthy (1963).

Situations

A situation s is the complete state of the universe at an instant of time. We denote by *Sit* the set of all situations. Since the universe is too large for complete description, we shall never completely describe a situation; we shall only give facts about situations. These facts will be used to deduce further facts about that situation, about future situations and about situations that persons can bring about from that situation.

This requires that we consider not only situations that actually occur, but also hypothetical situations such as the situation that would arise if Mr Smith sold his car to a certain person who has offered $250 for it. Since he is not going to sell the car for that price, the hypothetical situation is not completely defined; for example, it is not determined what Smith's mental state would be and therefore it is also undetermined how quickly he would return to his office, etc. Nevertheless, the representation of reality is adequate to determine some facts about this situation, enough at least to make him decide not to sell the car.

We shall further assume that the laws of motion determine, given a situation, all future situations.*

In order to give partial information about situations we introduce the notion of fluent.

* This assumption is difficult to reconcile with quantum mechanics, and relativity tells us that any assignment of simultaneity to events in different places is arbitrary. However, we are proceeding on the basis that modern physics is irrelevant to common sense in deciding what to do, and in particular is irrelevant to solving the 'free will problem'.

Fluents

A *fluent* is a function whose domain is the space *Sit* of situations. If the range of the function is (*true*, *false*), then it is called a *propositional fluent*. If its range is *Sit*, then it is called a *situational fluent*.

Fluents are often the values of functions. Thus $raining(x)$ is a fluent such that $raining(x)(s)$ is true if and only if it is raining at the place x in the situation s. We can also write this assertion as $raining(x,s)$ making use of the well-known equivalence between a function of two variables and a function of the first variable whose value is a function of the second variable.

Suppose we wish to assert about a situation s that person p is in place x and that it is raining in place x. We may write this in several ways each of which has its uses:

1. $at(p,x)(s) \wedge raining(x)(s)$. This corresponds to the definition given.
2. $at(p,x,s) \wedge raining(x,s)$. This is more conventional mathematically and a bit shorter.
3. $[at(p,x) \wedge raining(x)](s)$. Here we are introducing a convention that operators applied to fluents give fluents whose values are computed by applying the logical operators to the values of the operand fluents, that is, if f and g are fluents then

   $$(f \ \mathbf{op} \ g)(s) = f(s) \ \mathbf{op} \ g(s)$$

4. $[\lambda s' . at(p,x,s') \wedge raining(x,s')](s)$. Here we have formed the composite fluent by λ-abstraction.

Here are some examples of fluents and expressions involving them:

1. $time(s)$. This is the time associated with the situation s. It is essential to consider time as dependent on the situation as we shall sometimes wish to consider several different situations having the same time value, for example, the results of alternative courses of actions.
2. $in(x,y,s)$. This asserts that x is in the location y in situation s. The fluent *in* may be taken as satisfying a kind of transitive law, namely:

   $$\forall x . \forall y . \forall z . \forall s . in(x,y,s) \wedge in(y,z,s) \supset in(x,z,s)$$

   We can also write this law

   $$\forall x . \forall y . \forall z . \forall . in(x,y) \wedge in(y,z) \supset in(x,z)$$

   where we have adopted the convention that a quantifier without a variable is applied to an implicit situation variable which is the (suppressed) argument of a propositional fluent that follows. Suppressing situation arguments in this way corresponds to the natural language convention of writing sentences like, 'John was at home' or 'John is at home' leaving understood the situations to which these assertions apply.
3. $has(Monkey,Bananas,s)$. Here we introduce the convention that capitalized words denote proper names, for example, 'Monkey' is the

name of a particular individual. That the individual is a monkey is not asserted, so that the expression *monkey*(*Monkey*) may have to appear among the premisses of an argument. Needless to say, the reader has a right to feel that he has been given a hint that the individual Monkey will turn out to be a monkey. The above expression is to be taken as asserting that in the situation s the individual *Monkey* has the object *Bananas*. We shall, in the examples below, sometimes omit premisses such as *monkey*(*Monkey*), but in a complete system they would have to appear.

Causality

We shall make assertions of causality by means of a fluent $F(\pi)$ where π is itself a propositional fluent. $F(\pi,s)$ asserts that the situation s will be followed (after an unspecified time) by a situation that satisfies the fluent π.

We may use F to assert that if a person is out in the rain he will get wet, by writing:

$$\forall x\,.\,\forall p\,.\,\forall s\,.\,raining(x,s) \wedge at(p,x,s) \wedge outside(p,s) \supset F(\lambda s'\,.\,wet(p,s'),s)$$

Suppressing explicit mention of situations gives:

$$\forall x\,.\,\forall p\,.\,\forall\,.\,raining(x) \wedge at(p,x) \wedge outside(p) \supset F(wet(p)).$$

In this case suppressing situations simplifies the statement.

F can also be used to express physical laws. Consider the law of falling bodies which is often written

$$h = h_0 + v_0\,.\,(t-t_0) - \tfrac{1}{2}g\,.\,(t-t_0)^2$$

together with some prose identifying the variables. Since we need a formal system for machine reasoning we cannot have any prose. Therefore, we write:

$$\forall b\,.\,\forall t\,.\,\forall s\,.\,falling(b,s) \wedge t \geqslant 0 \wedge height(b,s) + velocity(b,s)\,.\,t - \tfrac{1}{2}gt^2 > 0$$
$$\supset$$
$$F(\lambda s'\,.\,time(s') = time(s) + t \wedge falling(b,s') \wedge height(b,s') = height(b,s) + velocity(b,s)\,.\,t - \tfrac{1}{2}gt^2, s)$$

Suppressing explicit mention of situations in this case requires the introduction of real auxiliary quantities v, h and τ so that the sentence takes the following form

$$\forall b\,.\,\forall t\,.\,\forall \tau\,.\,\forall v\,.\,\forall h.$$

$$falling(b) \wedge t \geqslant 0 \wedge h = height(b) \wedge v = velocity(b) \wedge h + vt - \tfrac{1}{2}gt^2 > 0 \wedge time = \tau \supset F(time = t + \tau \wedge falling(b) \wedge height = h + vt - \tfrac{1}{2}gt^2)$$

There has to be a convention (or declarations) so that it is determined that *height*(b), *velocity*(b) and *time* are fluents, whereas t, v, τ and h denote ordinary real numbers.

$F(\pi,s)$ as introduced here corresponds to A. N. Prior's (1957, 1968) expression $F\pi$.

The use of situation variables is analogous to the use of time-instants in the calculi of world-states which Prior (1968) calls *U-T* calculi. Prior provides many interesting correspondences between his *U-T* calculi and various axiomatizations of the modal tense-logics (that is, using this F-operator: see part 4). However, the situation calculus is richer than any of the tense-logics Prior considers.

Besides F he introduces three other operators which we also find useful; we thus have:

1. $F(\pi,s)$. For some situation s' in the future of s, $\pi(s')$ holds.
2. $G(\pi,s)$. For all situations s' in the future of s, $\pi(s')$ holds.
3. $P(\pi,s)$. For some situations s' in the past of s, $\pi(s')$ holds.
4. $H(\pi,s)$. For all situations s' in the past of s, $\pi(s')$ holds.

It seems also useful to define a situational fluent $next(\pi)$ as the next situation s' in the future of s for which $\pi(s')$ holds. If there is no such situation, that is, if $\neg F(\pi,s)$, then $next(\pi,s)$ is considered undefined. For example, we may translate the sentence 'By the time John gets home, Henry will be home too' as *at*(*Henry*,*home*(*Henry*),*next*(*at*(*John*,*home*(*John*)),*s*)). Also the phrase 'when John gets home' translates into *time*(*next*(*at*(*John*,*home*(*John*)),*s*)).

Though next(π,s) will never actually be computed since situations are too rich to be specified completely, the values of fluents applied to next(π,s) will be computed.

Actions

A fundamental rôle in our study of actions is played by the situational fluent

$$result(p,\sigma,s)$$

Here, p is a person, σ is an action or more generally a strategy, and s is a situation. The value of $result(p,\sigma,s)$ is the situation that results when p carries out σ, starting in the situation s. If the action or strategy does not terminate, $result(p,\sigma,s)$ is considered undefined.

With the aid of *result* we can express certain laws of ability. For example:

$$has(p,k,s) \wedge fits(k,sf) \wedge at(p,sf,s) \supset open(sf,result(p,opens(sf,k),s))$$

This formula is to be regarded as an axiom schema asserting that if in a situation s a person p has a key k that fits the safe *sf*, then in the situation resulting from his performing the action *opens*(*sf*,*k*), that is, opening the safe *sf* with the key k, the safe is open. The assertion *fits*(k,*sf*) carries the information that k is a key and *sf* a safe. Later we shall be concerned with combination safes that require p to *know* the combination.

Strategies

Actions can be combined into strategies. The simplest combination is a finite sequence of actions. We shall combine actions as though they were

ALGOL statements, that is, procedure calls. Thus, the sequence of actions, ('move the box under the bananas', 'climb onto the box', and 'reach for the bananas') may be written:

begin *move*(*Box*,*Under-Bananas*); *climb*(*Box*); *reach-for*(*Bananas*) **end**;

A strategy in general will be an ALGOL-like compound statement containing actions written in the form of procedure calling assignment statements, and conditional **go to**'s. We shall not include any declarations in the program since they can be included in the much larger collection of declarative sentences that determine the effect of the strategy.

Consider for example the strategy that consists of walking 17 blocks south, turning right and then walking till you come to Chestnut Street. This strategy may be written as follows:

```
begin
    face(South);
    n:=0;
b:  if n=17 then go to a;
    walk-a-block, n:=n+1;
    go to b;
a:  turn-right;
c:  walk-a-block;
    if name-on-street-sign≠'Chestnut Street' then go to c
end;
```

In the above program the external actions are represented by procedure calls. Variables to which values are assigned have a purely internal significance (we may even call it mental significance) and so do the statement labels and the **go to** statements.

For the purpose of applying the mathematical theory of computation we shall write the program differently: namely, each occurrence of an action α is to be replaced by an assignment statement $s{:=}\mathit{result}(p,\alpha,s)$. Thus the above program becomes

```
begin
    s:=result(p,face(South),s);
    n:=0;
b:  if n=17 then go to a;
    s:=result(p,walk-a-block,s);
    n:=n+1;
    go to b;
a:  s:=result(p,turn-right,s);
c:  s:=result(p,walk-a-block,s);
    if name-on-street-sign(s)≠'Chestnut Street' then go to c.
end;
```

Suppose we wish to show that by carrying out this strategy John can go home provided he is initially at his office. Then according to the methods of Zohar Manna (1968a, 1968b), we may derive from this program together with the initial condition $\mathit{at}(\mathit{John},\mathit{office}(\mathit{John}),s_0)$ and the final condition $\mathit{at}(\mathit{John},\mathit{home}(\mathit{John}),s)$, a sentence W of first-order logic. Proving W will show that the procedure terminates in a finite number of steps and that when it terminates s will satisfy $\mathit{at}(\mathit{John},\mathit{home}(\mathit{John}),s)$.

According to Manna's theory we must prove the following collection of sentences inconsistent for arbitrary interpretations of the predicates q_1 and q_2 and the particular interpretations of the other functions and predicates in the program:

$$\begin{aligned}
&\mathit{at}(\mathit{John},\mathit{office}(\mathit{John}),s_0),\\
&q_1(0,\mathit{result}(\mathit{John},\mathit{face}(\mathit{South}),s_0)),\\
&\forall n\,.\,\forall s\,.\,q_1(n,s)\supset \textbf{if } n=17\\
&\qquad\qquad \textbf{then } q_2(\mathit{result}(\mathit{John},\mathit{walk\text{-}a\text{-}block},\mathit{result}(\mathit{John},\mathit{turn\text{-}right},\\
&\qquad\qquad s)))\\
&\qquad\qquad \textbf{else } q_1(n+1,\mathit{result}(\mathit{John},\mathit{walk\text{-}a\text{-}block},s)),\\
&\forall s\,.\,q_2(s)\supset \textbf{if } \mathit{name\text{-}on\text{-}street\text{-}sign}(s)\neq\text{'}\mathit{Chestnut\ Street}\text{'}\\
&\qquad \textbf{then } q_2(\mathit{result}(\mathit{John},\mathit{walk\text{-}a\text{-}block},s))\\
&\qquad \textbf{else } \neg\mathit{at}(\mathit{John},\mathit{home}(\mathit{John}),s)
\end{aligned}$$

Therefore the formula that has to be proved may be written

$$\begin{aligned}
&\exists s_0\{\mathit{at}(\mathit{John},\mathit{office}(\mathit{John}),s_0)\wedge q_1(0,\mathit{result}(\mathit{John},\mathit{face}(\mathit{South}),s_0))\}\\
&\qquad\supset\\
&\exists n\,.\,\exists s\,.\,\{q_1(n,s)\wedge \textbf{if } n=17\\
&\qquad\qquad \textbf{then } \wedge q_2(\mathit{result}(\mathit{John},\mathit{walk\text{-}a\text{-}block},\mathit{result}(\mathit{John},\mathit{turn\text{-}}\\
&\qquad\qquad \mathit{right},s)))\\
&\qquad\qquad \textbf{else } \neg q_1(n+1,\mathit{result}(\mathit{John},\mathit{walk\text{-}a\text{-}block},s))\}\\
&\qquad\vee\\
&\exists s\,.\,\{q_2(s)\wedge \textbf{if } \mathit{name\text{-}on\text{-}street\text{-}sign}(s)\neq\text{'}\mathit{Chestnut\ Street}\text{'}\\
&\qquad \textbf{then } \neg q_2(\mathit{result}(\mathit{John},\mathit{walk\text{-}a\text{-}block},s))\\
&\qquad \textbf{else } \mathit{at}(\mathit{John},\mathit{home}(\mathit{John}),s)\}
\end{aligned}$$

In order to prove this sentence we would have to use the following kinds of facts expressed as sentences or sentence schemas of first-order logic:

1. Facts of geography. The initial street stretches at least 17 blocks to the south, and intersects a street which in turn intersects Chestnut Street a number of blocks to the right; the location of John's home and office.
2. The fact that the fluent name-on-street-sign will have the value 'Chestnut Street' at that point.
3. Facts giving the effects of action α expressed as predicates about $\mathit{result}(p,\alpha,s)$ deducible from sentences about s.
4. An axiom schema of induction that allows us to deduce that the loop of walking 17 blocks will terminate.

5. A fact that says that Chestnut Street is a finite number of blocks to the right after going 17 blocks south. This fact has nothing to do with the possibility of walking. It may also have to be expressed as a sentence schema or even as a sentence of second-order logic.

When we consider making a computer carry out the strategy, we must distinguish the variable s from the other variables in the second form of the program. The other variables are stored in the memory of the computer and the assignments may be executed in the normal way. The variable s represents the state of the world and the computer makes an assignment to it by performing an action. Likewise the fluent name-on-street-sign requires an action, of observation.

Knowledge and ability

In order to discuss the rôle of knowledge in one's ability to achieve goals let us return to the example of the safe. There we had

1. $has(p,k,s) \land fits(k,sf) \land at(p,sf,s) \supset open(sf,result(p,opens(sf,k),s))$,

which expressed sufficient conditions for the ability of a person to open a safe with a key. Now suppose we have a combination safe with a combination c. Then we may write:

2. $fits2(c,sf) \land at(p,sf,s) \supset open(sf,result(p,opens2(sf,c),s))$,

where we have used the predicate *fits*2 and the action *opens*2 to express the distinction between a key fitting a safe and a combination fitting it, and also the distinction between the acts of opening a safe with a key and a combination. In particular, $opens2(sf,c)$ is the act of manipulating the safe in accordance with the combination c. We have left out a sentence of the form $has2(p,c,s)$ for two reasons. In the first place it is unnecessary: if you manipulate a safe in accordance with its combination it will open; there is no need to have anything. In the second place it is not clear what $has2(p,c,s)$ means. Suppose, for example, that the combination of a particular safe sf is the number 34125, then $fits(34125, sf)$ makes sense and so does the act $opens2(sf, 34125)$. (We assume that $open(sf,result(p,opens2(sf,34111),s))$ would not be true.) But what could $has(p,34125,s)$ mean? Thus, a direct parallel between the rules for opening a safe with a key and opening it with a combination seems impossible.

Nevertheless, we need some way of expressing the fact that one has to know the combination of a safe in order to open it. First we introduce the function $combination(sf)$ and rewrite 2 as

3. $at(p,sf,s) \land csafe(sf) \supset open(sf,result(p,opens2(sf,combination(sf),s)))$

where $csafe(sf)$ asserts that sf is a combination safe and $combination(sf)$ denotes the combination of sf. (We could not write $key(sf)$ in the other case unless we wished to restrict ourselves to the case of safes with only one key.)

Next we introduce the notion of a feasible strategy for a person. The idea is that a strategy that would achieve a certain goal might not be feasible for a person because he lacks certain knowledge or abilities.

Our first approach is to regard the action $opens2(sf,combination(sf))$ as infeasible because p might not know the combination. Therefore, we introduce a new function $idea\text{-}of\text{-}combination(p,sf,s)$ which stands for person p's idea of the combination of sf in situation s. The action $opens2(sf,idea\text{-}of\text{-}combination(p,sf,s))$ is regarded as feasible for p, since p is assumed to know his idea of the combination if this is defined. However, we leave sentence 3 as it is so we cannot yet prove $open(sf,result(p,opens2(sf,idea\text{-}of\text{-}combination(p,sf,s)),s))$. The assertion that p knows the combination of sf can now be expressed as

5. $idea\text{-}of\text{-}combination(p,sf,s) = combination(sf)$

and with this, the possibility of opening the safe can be proved.

Another example of this approach is given by the following formalization of getting into conversation with someone by looking up his number in the telephone book and then dialling it.

The strategy for p in the first form is

```
begin
  lookup(q,Phone-book);
  dial(idea-of-phone-number(q,p))
end;
```

or in the second form

```
begin
  s:=result(p,lookup(q,Phone-book),s0);
  s:=result(p,dial(idea-of-phone-number(q,p,s)),s)
end;
```

The premisses to write down appear to be

1. $has(p,Phone\text{-}book,s_0)$
2. $listed(q,Phone\text{-}book,s_0)$
3. $\forall s . \forall p . \forall q . has(p,Phone\text{-}book,s) \land listed(q,Phone\text{-}book,s) \supset phone\text{-}number(q) = idea\text{-}of\text{-}phone\text{-}number(p,q,result(p,lookup(q,Phone\text{-}book),s))$
4. $\forall s . \forall p . \forall q . \forall x . at(q,home(q),s) \land has(p,x,s) \land telephone(x) \supset in\text{-}conversation(p,q,result(p,dial(phone\text{-}number(q)),s))$
5. $at(q,home(q),s_0)$
6. $telephone(Telephone)$
7. $has(p,Telephone,s_0)$

Unfortunately, these premisses are not sufficient to allow one to conclude that

$in\text{-}conversation(p,q,result(p,\textbf{begin}\ lookup(q,Phone\text{-}book);\ dial(idea\text{-}of\text{-}phone\text{-}number(q,p))\ \textbf{end};, s_0))$.

The trouble is that one cannot show that the fluents $at(q,home(q))$ and $has(p,Telephone)$ still apply to the situation $result(p,lookup(q,Phone\text{-}book),s_0)$. To make it come out right we shall revise the third hypothesis to read:

$$\forall s . \forall p . \forall q . \forall x . \forall y . at(q,y,s) \wedge has(p,x,s) \wedge has(p,Phone\text{-}book,s) \wedge listed(q,Phone\text{-}book) \supset [\lambda r. at(q,y,r) \wedge has(p,x,r) \wedge phone\text{-}number(q) = idea\text{-}of\text{-}phone\text{-}number(p,q,r)]\ (result(p,lookup(q,Phone\text{-}book),s)).$$

This works, but the additional hypotheses about what remains unchanged when p looks up a telephone number are quite *ad hoc*. We shall treat this problem in a later section.

The present approach has a major technical advantage for which, however, we pay a high price. The advantage is that we preserve the ability to replace any expression by an equal one in any expression of our language. Thus if $phone\text{-}number(John) = 3217580$, any true statement of our language that contains 3217580 or $phone\text{-}number(John)$ will remain true if we replace one by the other. This desirable property is termed referential transparency.

The price we pay for referential transparency is that we have to introduce $idea\text{-}of\text{-}phone\text{-}number(p,q,s)$ as a separate *ad hoc* entity and cannot use the more natural $idea\text{-}of(p,phone\text{-}number(q),s)$ where $idea\text{-}of(p,\phi,s)$ is some kind of operator applicable to the concept ϕ. Namely, the sentence $idea\text{-}of(p,phone\text{-}number(q),s) = phone\text{-}number(q)$ would be supposed to express that p knows q's phone-number, but $idea\text{-}of(p,3217580,s) = 3217580$ expresses only that p understands that number. Yet with transparency and the fact that $phone\text{-}number(q) = 3217580$ we could derive the former statement from the latter.

A further consequence of our approach is that feasibility of a strategy is a referentially opaque concept since a strategy containing $idea\text{-}of\text{-}phone\text{-}number(p,q,s)$ is regarded as feasible while one containing $phone\text{-}number(q)$ is not, even though these quantities may be equal in a particular case. Even so, our language is still referentially transparent since feasibility is a concept of the metalanguage.

A classical poser for the reader who wants to solve these difficulties to ponder is, 'George IV wondered whether the author of the Waverley novels was Walter Scott' and 'Walter Scott is the author of the Waverley novels', from which we do not wish to deduce, 'George IV wondered whether Walter Scott was Walter Scott'. This example and others are discussed in the first chapter of Church's *Introduction to Mathematical Logic* (1956).

In the long run it seems that we shall have to use a formalism with referential opacity and formulate precisely the necessary restrictions on replacement of equals by equals; the program must be able to reason about the feasibility of its strategies, and users of natural language handle referential opacity without disaster. In part 4 we give a brief account of the partly successful approach to problems of referential opacity in modal logic.

3. REMARKS AND OPEN PROBLEMS

The formalism presented in part 2 is, we think, an advance on previous attempts, but it is far from epistemological adequacy. In the following sections we discuss a number of problems that it raises. For some of them we have proposals that might lead to solutions.

The approximate character of *result* (p, σ, s).

Using the situational fluent $result(p,\sigma,s)$ in formulating the conditions under which strategies have given effects has two advantages over the $can(p,\pi,s)$ of part 1. It permits more compact and transparent sentences, and it lends itself to the application of the mathematical theory of computation to prove that certain strategies achieve certain goals.

However, we must recognize that it is only an approximation to say that an action, other than that which will actually occur, leads to a definite situation. Thus if someone is asked, 'How would you feel tonight if you challenged him to a duel tomorrow morning and he accepted?' he might well reply, 'I can't imagine the mental state in which I would do it; if the words inexplicably popped out of my mouth as though my voice were under someone else's control that would be one thing; if you gave me a long-lasting belligerence drug that would be another'.

From this we see that $result(p,\sigma,s)$ should not be regarded as being defined in the world itself, but only in certain representations of the world; albeit in representations that may have a preferred character as discussed in part 1.

We regard this as a blemish on the smoothness of interpretation of the formalism, which may also lead to difficulties in the formal development. Perhaps another device can be found which has the advantages of ***result*** without the disadvantages.

Possible meanings of 'can' for a computer program

A computer program can readily be given much more powerful means of introspection than a person has, for we may make it inspect the whole of its memory including program and data to answer certain introspective questions, and it can even simulate (slowly) what it would do with given initial data. It is interesting to list various notions of $can(Program,\pi)$ for a program.

1. There is a sub-program σ and room for it in memory which would achieve π if it were in memory, and control were transferred to σ. No assertion is made that *Program* knows σ or even knows that σ exists.
2. σ exists as above and that σ will achieve π follows from information in memory according to a proof that *Program* is capable of checking.
3. *Program*'s standard problem-solving procedure will find σ if achieving π is ever accepted as a subgoal.

The frame problem

In the last section of part 2, in proving that one person could get into conversation with another, we were obliged to add the hypothesis that if a person has a telephone he still has it after looking up a number in the telephone book. If we had a number of actions to be performed in sequence, we would have quite a number of conditions to write down that certain actions do not change the values of certain fluents. In fact with n actions and m fluents we might have to write down mn such conditions.

We see two ways out of this difficulty. The first is to introduce the notion of frame, like the state vector in McCarthy (1962). A number of fluents are declared as attached to the frame and the effect of an action is described by telling which fluents are changed, all others being presumed unchanged.

This can be formalized by making use of yet more ALGOL notation, perhaps in a somewhat generalized form. Consider a strategy in which p performs the action of going from x to y. In the first form of writing strategies we have $go(x,y)$ as a program step. In the second form we have $s:=result(p,go(x,y),s)$. Now we may write

$$location(p):=tryfor(y,x)$$

and the fact that other variables are unchanged by this action follows from the general properties of assignment statements. Among the conditions for successful execution of the program will be sentences that enable us to show that when this statement is executed, $tryfor(y,x)=y$. If we were willing to consider that p could go anywhere we could write the assignment statement simply as

$$location(p):=y.$$

The point of using *tryfor* here is that a program using this simpler assignment is, on the face of it, not possible to execute, since p may be unable to go to y. We may cover this case in the more complex assignment by agreeing that when p is barred from y, $tryfor(y,x)=x$.

In general, restrictions on what could appear on the right side of an assignment to a component of the situation would be included in the conditions for the feasibility of the strategy. Since components of the situation that change independently in some circumstances are dependent in others, it may be worthwhile to make use of the block structure of ALGOL. We shall not explore this approach further in this paper.

Another approach to the frame problem may follow from the methods of the next section; and in part 4 we mention a third approach which may be useful, although we have not investigated it at all fully.

Formal literatures

In this section we introduce the notion of formal literature which is to be contrasted with the well-known notion of formal language. We shall mention some possible applications of this concept in constructing an epistemologically adequate system.

A formal literature is like a formal language with a history: we imagine that up to a certain time a certain sequence of sentences have been said. The literature then determines what sentences may be said next. The formal definition is as follows.

Let A be a set of potential sentences, for example, the set of all finite strings in some alphabet. Let $Seq(A)$ be the set of finite sequences of elements of A and let $L:Seq(A)\rightarrow\{\mathbf{true},\mathbf{false}\}$ be such that if $\sigma\in Seq(A)$ and $L(\sigma)$, that is, $L(\sigma)=\mathbf{true}$, and σ_1 is an initial segment of σ then $L(\sigma_1)$. The pair (A,L) is termed a *literature*. The interpretation is that a_n may be said after $a_1,\ldots,a_{n-1}$, provided $L((a_1,\ldots,a_n))$. We shall also write $\sigma\in L$ and refer to σ as a string of the literature L.

From a literature L and a string $\sigma\in L$ we introduce the derived literature L_σ. Namely, $\tau\in L_\sigma$ if and only if $\sigma*\tau\in L$, where $\sigma*\tau$ denotes the concatenation of σ and τ.

We shall say that the language L is universal for the class Φ of literatures if for every literature $M\in\Phi$ there is a string $\sigma(M)\in L$ such that $M=L_{\sigma(M)}$; that is, $\tau\in M$ if and only if $\sigma(M)*\tau\in L$.

We shall call a literature computable if its strings form a recursively enumerable set. It is easy to see that there is a computable literature U_C that is universal with respect to the set C of computable literatures. Namely, let e be a computable literature and let c be the representation of the Gödel number of the recursively enumerable set of e as a string of elements of A. Then, we say $c*\tau\in U_C$ if and only if $\tau\in e$.

It may be more convenient to describe natural languages as formal literatures than as formal languages: if we allow the definition of new terms and require that new terms be used in accordance with their definitions, then we have restrictions on sentences that depend on what sentences have previously been uttered. In a programming language, the restriction that an identifier not be used until it has been declared, and then only consistently with the declaration, is of this form.

Any natural language may be regarded as universal with respect to the set of natural languages in the approximate sense that we might define French in terms of English and then say 'From now on we shall speak only French'.

All the above is purely syntactic. The applications we envisage to artificial intelligence come from a certain kind of interpreted literature. We are not able to describe precisely the class of literatures that may prove useful, only to sketch a class of examples.

Suppose we have an interpreted language such as first-order logic perhaps including some modal operators. We introduce three additional operators: $consistent(\phi)$, $normally(\phi)$, and $probably(\phi)$. We start with a list of sentences as hypotheses. A new sentence may be added to a string σ of sentences according to the following rules:

1. Any consequence of sentences of σ may be added.
2. If a sentence ϕ is consistent with σ, then *consistent*(ϕ) may be added. Of course, this is a non-computable rule. It may be weakened to say that *consistent*(ϕ) may be added provided ϕ can be shown to be consistent with σ by some particular proof procedure.
3. *normally*(ϕ), *consistent*$(\phi) \vdash$ *probably*(ϕ).
4. $\phi \vdash$ *probably*(ϕ) is a possible deduction.
5. If $\phi_1, \phi_2, \ldots, \phi_n \vdash \phi$ is a possible deduction then *probably*$(\phi_1), \ldots,$ *probably*$(\phi_n) \vdash$ *probably*(ϕ) is also a possible deduction.

The intended application to our formalism is as follows:

In part 2 we considered the example of one person telephoning another, and in this example we assumed that if p looks up q's phone-number in the book, he will know it, and if he dials the number he will come into conversation with q. It is not hard to think of possible exceptions to these statements such as:

1. The page with q's number may be torn out.
2. p may be blind.
3. Someone may have deliberately inked out q's number.
4. The telephone company may have made the entry incorrectly.
5. q may have got the telephone only recently.
6. The phone system may be out of order.
7. q may be incapacitated suddenly.

For each of these possibilities it is possible to add a term excluding the difficulty in question to the condition on the result of performing the action. But we can think of as many additional difficulties as we wish, so it is impractical to exclude each difficulty separately.

We hope to get out of this difficulty by writing such sentences as

$$\forall p \,.\, \forall q \,.\, \forall s.\ at(q, home(q), s) \supset normally(in\text{-}conversation(p, q, result(p, dials(phone\text{-}number(q)), s)))$$

We would then be able to deduce

$$probably(in\text{-}conversation(p, q, result(p, dials(phone\text{-}number(q)), s_0)))$$

provided there were no statements like

$$kaput(Phone\text{-}system, s_0)$$

and

$$\forall s.\ kaput(Phone\text{-}system, s) \supset \neg in\text{-}conversation(p, q, result(p, dials(phone\text{-}number(q)), s))$$

present in the system.

Many of the problems that give rise to the introduction of frames might be handled in a similar way.

The operators *normally*, *consistent* and *probably* are all modal and referentially opaque. We envisage systems in which *probably*(π) and *probably* $(\neg\pi)$ and therefore *probably*(**false**) will arise. Such an event should give rise to a search for a contradiction.

We hereby warn the reader, if it is not already clear to him, that these ideas are very tentative and may prove useless, especially in their present form. However, the problem they are intended to deal with, namely the impossibility of naming every conceivable thing that may go wrong, is an important one for artificial intelligence, and some formalism has to be developed to deal with it.

Probabilities

On numerous occasions it has been suggested that the formalism take uncertainty into account by attaching probabilities to its sentences. We agree that the formalism will eventually have to allow statements about the probabilities of events, but attaching probabilities to all statements has the following objections:

1. It is not clear how to attach probabilities to statements containing quantifiers in a way that corresponds to the amount of conviction people have.
2. The information necessary to assign numerical probabilities is not ordinarily available. Therefore, a formalism that required numerical probabilities would be epistemologically inadequate.

Parallel processing

Besides describing strategies by ALGOL-like programs we may also want to describe the laws of change of the situation by such programs. In doing so we must take into account the fact that many processes are going on simultaneously and that the single-activity-at-a-time ALGOL-like programs will have to be replaced by programs in which processes take place in parallel, in order to get an epistemologically adequate description. This suggests examining the so-called simulation languages; but a quick survey indicates that they are rather restricted in the kinds of processes they allow to take place in parallel and in the types of interaction allowed. Moreover, at present there is no developed formalism that allows proofs of the correctness of parallel programs.

4. DISCUSSION OF LITERATURE

The plan for achieving a generally intelligent program outlined in this paper will clearly be difficult to carry out. Therefore, it is natural to ask if some simpler scheme will work, and we shall devote this section to criticising some simpler schemes that have been proposed.

1. L. Fogel (1966) proposes to evolve intelligent automata by altering their state transition diagrams so that they perform better on tasks of greater

and greater complexity. The experiments described by Fogel involve machines with less than 10 states being evolved to predict the next symbol of a quite simple sequence. We do not think this approach has much chance of achieving interesting results because it seems limited to automata with small numbers of states, say less than 100, whereas computer programs regarded as automata have 2^{10^5} to 2^{10^7} states. This is a reflection of the fact that, while the representation of behaviours by finite automata is metaphysically adequate – in principle every behaviour of which a human or machine is capable can be so represented – this representation is not epistemologically adequate; that is, conditions we might wish to impose on a behaviour, or what is learned from an experience, are not readily expressible as changes in the state diagram of an automaton.

2. A number of investigators (Galanter 1956, Pivar and Finkelstein 1964) have taken the view that intelligence may be regarded as the ability to predict the future of a sequence from observation of its past. Presumably, the idea is that the experience of a person can be regarded as a sequence of discrete events and that intelligent people can predict the future. Artificial intelligence is then studied by writing programs to predict sequences formed according to some simple class of laws (sometimes probabilistic laws). Again the model is metaphysically adequate but epistemologically inadequate.

In other words, what we know about the world is divided into knowledge about many aspects of it, taken separately and with rather weak interaction. A machine that worked with the undifferentiated encoding of experience into a sequence would first have to solve the encoding, a task more difficult than any the sequence extrapolators are prepared to undertake. Moreover, our knowledge is not usable to predict exact sequences of experience. Imagine a person who is correctly predicting the course of a football game he is watching; he is not predicting each visual sensation (the play of light and shadow, the exact movements of the players and the crowd). Instead his prediction is on the level of: team A is getting tired; they should start to fumble or have their passes intercepted.

3. Friedberg (1958, 1959) has experimented with representing behaviour by a computer program and evolving a program by random mutations to perform a task. The epistemological inadequacy of the representation is expressed by the fact that desired changes in behaviour are often not representable by small changes in the machine language form of the program. In particular, the effect on a reasoning program of learning a new fact is not so representable.

4. Newell and Simon worked for a number of years with a program called the General Problem Solver (Newell *et al.* 1959, Newell and Simon 1961). This program represents problems as the task of transforming one symbolic expression into another using a fixed set of transformation rules. They succeeded in putting a fair variety of problems into this form, but for a number of problems the representation was awkward enough so that GPS could only do small examples. The task of improving GPS was studied as a GPS task, but we believe it was finally abandoned. The name, General Problem Solver, suggests that its authors at one time believed that most problems could be put in its terms, but their more recent publications have indicated other points of view.

It is interesting to compare the point of view of the present paper with that expressed in Newell and Ernst (1965) from which we quote the second paragraph:

> We may consider a problem solver to be a process that takes a problem as input and provides (when successful) the solution as output. The problem consists of the problem statement, or what is immediately given; and auxiliary information, which is potentially relevant to the problem but available only as the result of processing. The problem solver has available certain methods for attempting to solve the problem. These are to be applied to an internal representation of the problem. For the problem solver to be able to work on a problem it must first transform the problem statement from its external form into the internal representation. Thus (roughly), the class of problems the problem solver can convert into its internal representation determines how broad or general it is; and its success in obtaining solutions to problems in internal form determines its power. Whether or not universal, such a decomposition fits well the structure of present problem solving programs.

In a very approximate way their division of the problem solver into the input program that converts problems into internal representation and the problem solver proper corresponds to our division into the epistemological and heuristic parts of the artificial intelligence problem. The difference is that we are more concerned with the suitability of the internal representation itself.

Newell (1965) poses the problem of how to get what we call heuristically adequate representations of problems, and Simon (1966) discusses the concept of 'can' in a way that should be compared with the present approach.

Modal logic

It is difficult to give a concise definition of modal logic. It was originally invented by Lewis (1918) in an attempt to avoid the 'paradoxes' of implication (a false proposition implies any proposition). The idea was to distinguish two sorts of truth: *necessary* truth and mere *contingent* truth. A contingently true proposition is one which, though true, could be false. This is formalized by introducing the modal operator $\Box$ (read 'necessarily') which forms propositions from propositions. Then p's being a necessary truth is expressed by $\Box p$'s being true. More recently, modal logic has become a much-used tool for analysing the logic of such various propositional operators as belief, knowledge and tense.

There are very many possible axiomatizations of the logic of $\Box$, none of which seem more intuitively plausible than many others. A full account of the main classical systems is given by Feys (1965), who also includes an excellent bibliography. We shall give here an axiomatization of a fairly simple modal logic, the system M of Feys-Von Wright. One adds to any full axiomatization of propositional calculus the following:

Ax. 1: $\Box p \supset p$

Ax. 2: $\Box(p \supset p) \supset (\Box p \supset \Box q)$

Rule 1: from p and $p \supset q$, infer q

Rule 2: from p, infer $\Box p$.

(This axiomatization is due to Gödel).

There is also a dual modal operator $\Diamond$, defined as $\neg\Box\neg$. Its intuitive meaning is 'possibly': $\Diamond p$ is true when p is at least possible, although p may be in fact false (or true). The reader will be able to see the intuitive correspondence between $\neg\Diamond p$ – p is impossible, and $\Box \sim p$ – that is, p is necessarily false.

M is a fairly weak modal logic. One can strengthen it by adding axioms, for example, adding *Ax*. 3: $\Box p \supset \Box\Box p$ yields the system called $S4$; adding *Ax*. 4: $\Diamond p \supset \Box\Diamond p$ yields $S5$; and other additions are possible. However, one can also weaken all these systems in various ways, for instance by changing *Ax*. 1 to *Ax*. 1′: $\Box p \supset \Diamond p$. One easily sees that *Ax*. 1 implies *Ax*. 1′, but the converse is not true. The systems obtained in this way are known as the *deontic* versions of the systems. These modifications will be useful later when we come to consider tense-logics as modal logics.

One should note that the truth or falsity of $\Box p$ is not decided by p's being true. Thus $\Box$ is not a truth-functional operator (unlike the usual logical connectives, for instance) and so there is no direct way of using truth-tables to analyse propositions containing modal operators. In fact the decision problem for modal propositional calculi has been quite nontrivial. It is just this property which makes modal calculi so useful, as belief, tense, etc., when interpreted as propositional operators, are all nontruthfunctional.

The proliferation of modal propositional calculi, with no clear means of comparison, we shall call the *first problem* of modal logic. Other difficulties arise when we consider modal predicate calculi, that is, when we attempt to introduce quantifiers. This was first done by Barcan-Marcus (1946).

Unfortunately, all the early attempts at modal predicate calculi had unintuitive theorems (*see* for instance Kripke 1963a), and, moreover, all of them met with difficulties connected with the failure of Leibniz' law of identity, which we shall try to outline.

Leibniz' law is

$L: \forall x . \forall y.\ x=y \supset (\Phi(x) \equiv \Phi(y))$

where Φ is any open sentence. Now this law fails in modal contexts. For instance, consider this instance of L:

$L_1: \forall x . \forall y.\ x=y \supset (\Box(x=x) \equiv \Box(x=y))$

By rule 2 of M (which is present in almost all modal logics), since $x=x$ is a theorem, so is $\Box(x=x)$. Thus L_1 yields

$L_2: \forall x . \forall y.\ x=y \supset \Box(x=y)$

But, the argument goes, this is counterintuitive. For instance the morning star is in fact the same individual as the evening star (the planet Venus). However, they are not *necessarily* equal: one can easily imagine that they might be distinct. This famous example is known as the 'morning star paradox'.

This and related difficulties compel one to abandon Leibniz' law in modal predicate calculi, or else to modify the laws of quantification (so that it is impossible to obtain the undesirable instances of universal sentences such as L_2). This solves the purely formal problem, but leads to severe difficulties in interpreting these calculi, as Quine has urged in several papers (cf. Quine 1964).

The difficulty is this. A sentence $\Phi(a)$ is usually thought of as ascribing some property to a certain individual a. Now consider the morning star; clearly, the morning star is necessarily equal to the morning star. However, the evening star is not necessarily equal to the morning star. Thus, this one individual – the planet Venus – both has and does not have the property of being necessarily equal to the morning star. Even if we abandon proper names the difficulty does not disappear: for how are we to interpret a statement like $\exists x . \exists y(x=y \wedge \Phi(x) \wedge \neg\Phi(y))$?

Barcan-Marcus has urged an unconventional reading of the quantifiers to avoid this problem. The discussion between her and Quine in Barcan-Marcus (1963) is very illuminating. However, this raises some difficulties – see Belnap and Dunn (1968) – and the recent semantic theory of modal logic provides a more satisfactory method of interpreting modal sentences.

This theory was developed by several authors (Hintikka 1963, 1967a; Kanger 1957; Kripke 1963a, 1963b, 1965), but chiefly by Kripke. We shall try to give an outline of this theory, but if the reader finds it inadequate he should consult Kripke (1963a).

The idea is that modal calculi describe several *possible worlds* at once, instead of just one. Statements are not assigned a single truth-value, but rather a spectrum of truth-values, one in each possible world. Now, a statement is necessary when it is true in *all* possible worlds – more or less. Actually, in order to get different modal logics (and even then not all of them) one has to be a bit more subtle, and have a binary relation on the set of possible worlds – the alternativeness relation. Then a statement is necessary in a world when it is true in all alternatives to that world. Now it turns out that many common axioms of modal propositional logics correspond directly to conditions on this relation of alternativeness. Thus for instance in the system M above, *Ax*. 1 corresponds to the reflexiveness of the alternativeness relation; *Ax*. 3($\Box p \supset \Box\Box p$) corresponds to its transitivity. If we make the alternativeness relation into an equivalence relation, then this is just like not having one at all; and it corresponds to the axiom: $\Diamond p \supset \Box \Diamond p$.

This semantic theory already provides an answer to the first problem of modal logic: a rational method is available for classifying the multitude of propositional modal logics. More importantly, it also provides an intelligible interpretation for modal predicate calculi. One has to imagine each possible world as having a set of individuals and an assignment of individuals to names of the language. Then each statement takes on its truthvalue in a world s according to the particular set of individuals and assignment associated with s. Thus, a possible world is an interpretation of the calculus, in the usual sense.

Now, the failure of Leibniz' law is no longer puzzling, for in one world the morning star – for instance – may be equal to (the same individual as) the evening star, but in another the two may be distinct.

There are still difficulties, both formal – the quantification rules have to be modified to avoid unintuitive theorems (see Kripke, 1963a, for the details) – and interpretative: it is not obvious what it means to have the *same* individual existing in *different* worlds.

It is possible to gain the expressive power of modal logic without using modal operators by constructing an ordinary truth-functional logic which describes the multiple-world semantics of modal logic directly. To do this we give every predicate an extra argument (the world-variable; or in our terminology the situation-variable) and instead of writing '$\Box\ \Phi$', we write

$$\forall t\,.\,A(s,t) \supset \Phi(t),$$

where A is the alternativeness relation between situations. Of course we must provide appropriate axioms for A.

The resulting theory will be expressed in the notation of the situation calculus; the proposition Φ has become a propositional fluent $\lambda s\,.\,\Phi(s)$, and the 'possible worlds' of the modal semantics are precisely the situations. Notice, however, that the theory we get is weaker than what would have been obtained by adding modal operators directly to the situation calculus, for we can give no translation of assertions such as $\Box\pi(s)$, where s is a situation, which this enriched situation calculus would contain.

It is possible, in this way, to reconstruct within the situation calculus subtheories corresponding to the tense-logics of Prior and to the knowledge-logics of Hintikka, as we shall explain below. However, there is a qualification here: so far we have only explained how to translate the propositional modal logics into the situation calculus. In order to translate quantified modal logic, with its difficulties of referential opacity, we must complicate the situation calculus to a degree which makes it rather clumsy. There is a special predicate on individuals and situation – $exists(i,s)$ – which is regarded as true when i names an individual existing in the situation s. This is necessary because situations may contain different individuals. Then quantified assertions of the modal logic are translated according to the following scheme:

$$\forall x\,.\,\Phi(x) \rightarrow \forall x\,.\,exists(x,s) \supset \Phi(x,s)$$

where s is the introduced situation variable.

We shall not go into the details of this extra translation in the examples below, but shall be content to define the translations of the propositional tense and knowledge logics into the situation calculus.

Logic of knowledge

The logic of knowledge was first investigated as a modal logic by Hintikka in his book *Knowledge and belief* (1962). We shall only describe the knowledge calculus. He introduces the modal operator Ka (read 'a knows that'), and its dual Pa, defined as $\neg Ka \neg$. The semantics is obtained by the analogous reading of Ka as: 'it is true in all possible worlds compatible with a's knowledge that'. The propositional logic of Ka (similar to $\Box$) turns out to be $S4$, that is, $M + Ax\,.\,3$; but there are some complexities over quantification. (The last chapter of the book contains another excellent account of the overall problem of quantification in modal contexts.) This analysis of knowledge has been criticized in various ways (Chisholm 1963, Follesdal 1967) and Hintikka has replied in several important papers (1967b, 1967c, 1969). The last paper contains a review of the different senses of 'know' and the extent to which they have been adequately formalized. It appears that two senses have resisted capture. First, the idea of 'knowing how', which appears related to our 'can'; and secondly, the concept of knowing a person (place, etc.), when this means 'being acquainted with' as opposed to simply knowing *who* a person *is*.

In order to translate the (propositional) knowledge calculus into 'situation' language, we introduce a three-place predicate into the situation calculus termed 'shrug'. $Shrug(p,s_1,s_2)$, where p is a person and s_1 and s_2 are situations, is true when, if p is in fact in situation s_2, then for all he knows he might be in situation s_1. That is to say, s_1 is an *epistemic alternative* to s_2, as far as the individual p is concerned – this is Hintikka's term for his alternative worlds (he calls them model-sets).

Then we translate $K_p q$, where q is a proposition of Hintikka's calculus, as $\forall t\,.\,shrug(p,t,s) \supset q(t)$, where $\lambda s\,.\,q(s)$ is the fluent which translates q. Of course we have to supply axioms for *shrug*, and in fact so far as the pure knowledge-calculus is concerned, the only two necessary are

$$K1\colon \forall s\,.\,\forall p\,.\,shrug(p,s,s)$$

and $K2\colon \forall p\,.\,\forall s\,.\,\forall t\,.\,\forall r\,.\,(shrug(p,t,s) \wedge shrug(p,r,t)) \supset shrug(p,r,s)$

that is, reflexivity and transitivity.

Others of course may be needed when we add tenses and other machinery to the situation calculus, in order to relate knowledge to them.

Tense logics

This is one of the largest and most active areas of philosophic logic. Prior's book *Past, present and future* (1968) is an extremely thorough and lucid account of what has been done in the field. We have already mentioned the four propositional operators F, G, P, H which Prior discusses. He regards these as modal operators; then the alternativeness relation of the semantic theory is simply the time-ordering relation. Various axiomatizations are given, corresponding to deterministic and nondeterministic tenses, ending and nonending times, etc; and the problems of quantification turn up again here with renewed intensity. To attempt a summary of Prior's book is a hopeless task, and we simply urge the reader to consult it. More recently several papers have appeared (see, for instance, Bull 1968) which illustrate the technical sophistication tense-logic has reached, in that full completeness proofs for various axiom systems are now available.

As indicated above, the situation calculus contains a tense-logic (or rather several tense-logics), in that we can define Prior's four operators in our system and by suitable axioms reconstruct various axiomatizations of these four operators (in particular, all the axioms in Bull (1968) can be translated into the situation calculus).

Only one extra nonlogical predicate is necessary to do this: it is a binary predicate of situations called *cohistorical*, and is intuitively meant to assert of its arguments that one is in the other's future. This is necessary because we want to consider some pairs of situations as being not temporally related at all. We now define F(for instance) thus:

$$F(\pi,s)\equiv\exists t\,.\,\mathit{cohistorical}(t,s)\wedge \mathit{time}(t)>\mathit{time}(s)\wedge\pi(t).$$

The other operators are defined analogously.

Of course we have to supply axioms for 'cohistorical' and time: this is not difficult. For instance, consider one of Bull's axioms, say $Gp\supset GGp$, which is better (for us) expressed in the form $FFp\supset Fp$. Using the definition, this translates into:

$$(\exists t\,.\,\mathit{cohistorical}(t,s)\wedge \mathit{time}(t)>\mathit{time}(s)\wedge\exists r\,.\,\mathit{cohistorical}(r,t)$$
$$\wedge\,\mathit{time}(r)>\mathit{time}(t)\wedge\pi(r))\supset(\exists r\,.\,\mathit{cohistorical}(r,s)$$
$$\wedge\,\mathit{time}(r)>\mathit{time}(s)\wedge\pi(r))$$

which simplifies (using the transitivity of '>') to

$$\forall t\,.\,\forall r\,.\,(\mathit{cohistorical}(r,t)\wedge\mathit{cohistorical}(t,s))\supset\mathit{cohistorical}(r,s)$$

that is, the transitivity of 'cohistorical'. This axiom is precisely analogous to the $S4$ axiom $\Box p\supset\Box\Box p$, which corresponded to transitivity of the alternativeness relation in the modal semantics. Bull's other axioms translate into conditions on 'cohistorical' and time in a similar way; we shall not bother here with the rather tedious details.

Rather more interesting would be axioms relating 'shrug' to 'cohistorical' and time; unfortunately we have been unable to think of any intuitively plausible ones. Thus, if two situations are epistemic alternatives (that is, $\mathit{shrug}(p,s_1,s_2)$) then they may or may not have the same time value (since we want to allow that p may not know what the time is), and they may or may not be cohistorical.

Logics and theories of actions

The most fully developed theory in this area is von Wright's action logic described in his book *Norm and Action* (1963). Von Wright builds his logic on a rather unusual tense-logic of his own. The basis is a binary modal connective T, so that pTq, where p and q are propositions, means '*p,then q*'. Thus the action, for instance, of opening the window is: (*the window is closed*)T(*the window is open*). The formal development of the calculus was taken a long way in the book cited above, but some problems of interpretation remained as Castañeda points out in his review (1965). In a more recent paper von Wright (1967) has altered and extended his formalism so as to answer these and other criticisms, and also has provided a sort of semantic theory based on the notion of a life-tree.

We know of no other attempts at constructing a single theory of actions which have reached such a degree of development, but there are several discussions of difficulties and surveys which seem important. Rescher (1967) discusses several topics very neatly, and Davidson (1967) also makes some cogent points. Davidson's main thesis is that, in order to translate statements involving actions into the predicate calculus, it appears necessary to allow actions as values of bound variables, that is (by Quine's test) as real individuals. The situation calculus of course follows this advice in that we allow quantification over strategies, which have actions as a special case. Also important are Simon's papers (1965, 1967) on command-logics. Simon's main purpose is to show that a special logic of commands is unnecessary, ordinary logic serving as the only deductive machinery; but this need not detain us here. He makes several points, most notably perhaps that agents are most of the time not performing actions, and that in fact they only stir to action when forced to by some outside interference. He has the particularly interesting example of a serial processor operating in a parallel-demand environment, and the resulting need for interrupts. Action logics such as von Wright's and ours do not distinguish between action and inaction, and we are not aware of any action-logic which has reached a stage of sophistication adequate to meet Simon's implied criticism.

There is a large body of purely philosophical writings on action, time, determinism, etc., most of which is irrelevant for present purposes. However, we mention two which have recently appeared and which seem interesting: a paper by Chisholm (1967) and another paper by Evans (1967), summarizing the recent discussion on the distinctions between states, performances and activities.

Other topics

There are two other areas where some analysis of actions has been necessary: command-logics and logics and theories of obligation. For the former the best reference is Rescher's book (1966) which has an excellent bibliography. Note also Simon's counterarguments to some of Rescher's theses (Simon 1965, 1967). Simon proposes that no special logic of commands is necessary, commands being analysed in the form 'bring it about that p!' for some proposition p, or, more generally, in the form 'bring it about that $P(x)$ by changing x!', where x is a *command* variable, that is, under the agent's control. The translations between commands and statements take place only in the context of a 'complete model', which specifies environmental constraints and defines the command variables. Rescher argues that these schemas for commands are inadequate to handle the *conditional command* 'when p, do q', which becomes ' bring it about that $(p \supset q)$!': this, unlike the former, is satisfied by making p false.

There are many papers on the logic of obligation and permission. Von Wright's work is oriented in this direction; Castañeda has many papers on the subject and Anderson also has written extensively (his early influential report (1956) is especially worth reading). The review pages of the *Journal of Symbolic Logic* provide many other references. Until fairly recently these theories did not seem of very much relevance to logics of action, but in their new maturity they are beginning to be so.

Counterfactuals

There is, of course, a large literature on this ancient philosophical problem, almost none of which seems directly relevant to us. However, there is one recent theory, developed by Rescher (1964), which may be of use. Rescher's book is so clearly written that we shall not attempt a description of his theory here. The reader should be aware of Sosa's critical review (1967) which suggests some minor alterations.

The importance of this theory for us is that it suggests an alternative approach to the difficulty which we have referred to as the frame problem. In outline, this is as follows. One assumes, as a rule of procedure (or perhaps as a rule of inference), that when actions are performed, *all* propositional fluents which applied to the previous situation also apply to the new situation. This will often yield an inconsistent set of statements about the new situation; Rescher's theory provides a mechanism for restoring consistency in a rational way, and giving as a by-product those fluents which change in value as a result of performing the action. However, we have not investigated this in detail.

The communication process

We have not considered the problems of formally describing the process of communication in this paper, but it seems clear that they will have to be tackled eventually. Philosophical logicians have been spontaneously active here. The major work is Harrah's book (1963); Cresswell has written several papers on 'the logic of interrogatives', see for instance Cresswell (1965). Among other authors we may mention Åqvist (1965) and Belnap (1963); again the review pages of the *Journal of Symbolic Logic* will provide other references.

Acknowledgements

The research reported here was supported in part by the Advanced Research Projects Agency of the Office of the Secretary of Defense (SD-183), and in part by the Science Research Council (B/SR/2299)

REFERENCES

Anderson, A.R. (1956) The formal analysis of normative systems. Reprinted in *The Logic of decision and action* (ed. Rescher, N.). Pittsburgh: University of Pittsburgh Press.

Åqvist, L. (1965) *A new approach to the logical theory of interrogatives, part I.* Uppsala: Uppsala Philosophical Association.

Barcan-Marcus, R.C. (1946) A functional calculus of the first order based on strict implication. *Journal of Symbolic Logic*, **11,** 1–16.

Barcan-Marcus, R.C. (1963) Modalities and intensional languages. *Boston studies in the Philosophy of Science.* (ed. Wartofsky, W.). Dordrecht, Holland.

Belnap, N.D. (1963) *An analysis of questions.* Santa Monica.

Belnap, N.D. & Dunn, J.M. (1968) The substitution interpretation of the quantifiers. *Noûs*, **2,** 177–85.

Bull, R.A. (1968) An algebraic study of tense logics with linear time. *Journal of Symbolic Logic*, **33,** 27–39

Castañeda, H.N. (1965) The logic of change, action and norms. *Journal of Philosophy*, **62,** 333–4.

Chisholm, R.M. (1963) The logic of knowing. *Journal of Philosophy*, **60,** 773–95.

Chisholm, R.M. (1967) He could have done otherwise. *Journal of Philosophy*, **64**, 409–17.

Church, A. (1956) *Introduction to Mathematical Logic.* Princeton: Princeton University Press.

Cresswell, M.J. (1965). The logic of interrogatives. *Formal systems and recursive functions.* (ed. Crossley, J.N. & Dummett, M.A.E.). Amsterdam: North-Holland.

Davidson, D. (1967) The logical form of action sentences. *The logic of decision and action.* (ed. Rescher, N.). Pittsburgh: University of Pittsburgh Press.

Evans, C.O. (1967) States, activities and performances. *Australasian Journal of Philosophy*, **45,** 293–308.

Feys, R. (1965) *Modal Logics.* (ed. Dopp, J.). Louvain: Coll. de Logique Math. série B.

Fogel, L.J., Owens, A.J. & Walsh, M.J. (1966) *Artificial Intelligence through simulated evolution.* New York: John Wiley.

Føllesdal, D. (1967) Knowledge, identity and existence. *Theoria*, **33,** 1–27.

Friedberg, R.M. (1958) A learning machine, part I. *IBM J. Res. Dev.*, **2,** 2–13.

Friedberg, R.M., Dunham, B., & North, J.H. (1959) A learning machine, part II. *IBM J. Res. Dev.*, **3,** 282–7.

Galanter, E. & Gerstenhaber, M. (1956). On thought: the extrinsic theory. *Psychological Review*, **63,** 218–27

Green, C. (1969) Theorem-proving by resolution as a basis for question-answering systems. *Machine Intelligence 4*, pp.183–205 (eds Meltzer, B. & Michie, D.). Edinburgh: Edinburgh University Press.

Harrah, D. (1963) *Communication: a logical model.* Cambridge, Massachusetts: MIT press.

Hintikka, J. (1962) *Knowledge and belief: an introduction to the logic of the two notions.* New York: Cornell University Press.

Hintikka, J. (1963) The modes of modality. *Acta Philosophica Fennica*, **16,** 65–82.

Hintikka, J. (1967a) A program and a set of concepts for philosophical logic. *The Monist*, **51,** 69–72.

Hintikka, J. (1967b) Existence and identity in epistemic contexts. *Theoria*, **32,** 138–47.

Hintikka, J. (1967c) Individuals, possible worlds and epistemic logic. *Noûs*, **1,** 33–62.

Hintikka, J. (1969) Alternative constructions in terms of the basic epistemological attitudes *Contemporary philosophy in Scandinavia* (ed. Olsen, R.E.) (to appear).

Kanger, S. (1957) A note on quantification and modalities. *Theoria*, **23,** 133–4.

Kripke, S. (1963a) Semantical considerations on modal logic. *Acta Philosophica Fennica*, **16,** 83–94.

Kripke, S. (1963b) Semantical analysis of modal logic I. *Zeitschrift für math. Logik und Grundlagen der Mathematik*, **9,** 67–96.

Kripke, S. (1965) Semantical analysis of modal logic II. *The theory of models* (eds Addison, Henkin & Tarski). Amsterdam: North-Holland.

Lewis, C.I. (1918) *A survey of symbolic logic.* Berkeley: University of California Press.

Manna, Z. (1968a) *Termination of algorithms.* Ph.D Thesis, Carnegie-Mellon University.

Manna, Z. (1968b) *Formalization of properties of programs.* Stanford Artificial Intelligence Report: Project Memo AI-64.

McCarthy, J. (1959) Programs with common sense. *Mechanization of thought processes*, Vol. I. London: HMSO

McCarthy, J. (1962) Towards a mathematical science of computation. *Proc. IFIP Congress* 62. Amsterdam: North-Holland Press.

McCarthy, J. (1963) *Situations, actions and causal laws.* Stanford Artificial Intelligence Project: Memo 2.

Minsky, M. (1961) Steps towards artificial intelligence. *Proceedings of the I.R.E.*, **49,** 8–30.

Newell, A., Shaw, V.C. & Simon, H.A. (1959) Report on a general problem-solving program. *Proceedings ICIP.* Paris: UNESCO House.

Newell, A. & Simon H.A. (1961) GPS – a program that simulates human problem-solving. *Proceedings of a conference in learning automata.* Munich: Oldenbourgh.

Newell, A. (1965) Limitations of the current stock of ideas about problem-solving. *Proceedings of a conference on Electronic Information Handling*, pp. 195–208 (eds Kent, A. & Taulbee, O.). New York: Spartan.

Newell, A. & Ernst, C. (1965) The search for generality. *Proc. IFIP Congress* 65.

Pivar, M. & Finkelstein, M. (1964). *The Programming Language LISP: its operation and applications* (eds Berkely, E.C. & Bobrow, D.G.). Cambridge, Massachusetts: MIT Press.

Prior, A.N. (1957) *Time and modality.* Oxford: Clarenden Press.

Prior, A.N. (1968) *Past, present and future.* Oxford: Clarendon Press.

Quine, W.V.O. (1964) Reference and modality. *From a logical point of view.* Cambridge, Massachusetts: Harvard University Press.

Rescher, N. (1964) *Hypothetical reasoning.* Amsterdam: North-Holland.

Rescher, N. (1966) *The logic of commands.* London: Routledge.

Rescher, N. (1967) Aspects of action. *The logic of decision and action* (ed. Rescher, N.). Pittsburgh: University of Pittsburgh Press.

Shannon, C. (1950) Programming a computer for playing chess. *Philosophical Magazine*, **41.**

Simon, H.A. (1965) The logic of rational decision. *British Journal for the Philosophy of Science*, **16,** 169–86.

Simon, H.A. (1966) *On Reasoning about actions.* Carnegie Institute of Technology: Complex Information Processing Paper 87.

Simon, H.A. (1967) The logic of heuristic decision making. *The logic of decision and action* (ed. Rescher, N.). Pittsburgh: University of Pittsburgh Press.

Sosa, E. (1967) Hypothetical reasoning. *Journal of Philosophy*, **64,** 293–305.

Turing, A.M. (1950) Computing machinery and intelligence. *Mind*, **59,** 433–60.

von Wright, C.H. (1963) *Norm and action: a logical enquiry.* London: Routledge.

von Wright, C.H. (1967) The Logic of Action – a sketch. *The logic of decision and action* (ed. Rescher, N.). Pittsburgh: University of Pittsburgh Press.

P. J. HAYES

The Logic of Frames

Introduction: Representation and Meaning

Minsky introduced the terminology of 'frames' to unify and denote a loose collection of related ideas on knowledge representation: a collection which, since the publication of his paper (Minsky, 1975) has become even looser. It is not at all clear now what frames are, or were ever intended to be.

I will assume, below, that frames were put forward as a (set of ideas for the design of a) formal language for expressing knowledge, to be considered as an alternative to, for example, semantic networks or predicate calculus. At least one group have explicitly designed such a language, KRL (Bobrow/Winograd, 1977a, 1977b), based on the frames idea. But it is important to distinguish this from two other possible interpretations of what Minsky was urging, which one might call the metaphysical and the heuristic (following the terminology of (McCarthy/Hayes, 1968)).

The "metaphysical" interpretation is, that to use frames is to make a certain kind of assumption about what entities shall be assumed to exist in the world being described. That is, to use frames is to assume that a certain *kind* of knowledge is to be represented by them. Minsky seems to be making a point like this when he urges the idea that visual perception may be facilitated by the storage of explicit 2-dimensional view prototypes and explicit rotational transformations between them. Again, the now considerable literature on the use of 'scripts' or similar frame-like structures in text understanding systems (Charniak, 1977; Lehnert, 1977; Schank, 1975) seems to be based on the view that what might be called "programmatic" knowledge of stereotypical situations like shopping-in-a-supermarket or going-somewhere-on-a-bus is necessary in order to understand English texts about these situations. Whatever the merits of this view (its proponents seem to regard it as simply *obvious*, but see (Feldman, 1975) and (Wilks, 1976) for some contrary arguments), it is clearly a thesis about what sort of things a program needs to know, rather than about *how* those things should or can be *represented*. One could describe the sequence of events in a typical supermarket visit as well in almost any reasonable expressive formal language.

The "heuristic", or as I would prefer now to say, "implementation", interpretation is, that frames are a computational device for organising stored representations in computer memory, and perhaps also, for organising the processes of retrieval and inference which manipulate these stored representations. Minsky seems to be making a point like this when he refers to the computational ease with which one can switch from one frame to another in a frame-system by following pointers. And many other authors have referred with evident approval to the way in which frames, so considered, facilitate certain retrieval operations. (There has been less emphasis on undesirable computational features of frame-like hierarchical organisations of memory.) Again, however, none of this discussion engages representational issues. A given representational language can be implemented in all manner of ways: predicate calculus assertions may be implemented as lists, as character sequences, as trees, as networks, as patterns in an associative memory, etc: all giving different computational properties but all encoding the same representational language. Indeed, one might almost characterise the art of programming as being able to deploy this variety of computational techniques to achieve implementations with various computational properties. Similarly, any one of these computational techniques can be used to implement many essentially different representational languages. Thus, circuit diagrams, perspective line drawings, and predicate calculus assertions, three entirely distinct formal languages (c.f. Hayes, 1975), can be all implemented in terms of list structures. Were it not so, every application of computers would require the development of a new specialised programming language.

Much discussion in the literature seems to ignore or confuse these distinctions. They are vital if we are to have any useful taxonomy, let alone theory, of representational languages. For example, if we confuse representation with implementation then LISP would seem a universal representational language, which stops all discussion before we can even begin.

One can characterise a representational language as one which has (or can be given) a semantic theory, by which I mean an account (more or less formal, more or less precise — this is not the place to argue for a formal model theory, but see Hayes, 1977) of how expressions of the language relate to the individuals or relationships or actions or configurations, etc., comprising the world, or worlds about which the language claims to express knowledge. (Such an account may — in fact must — entail making some metaphysical assumptions, but these will usually be of a very general and minimal kind (for example, that the world consists of individual entities and relationships of one kind or another which hold between them: this is the ontological committment needed to understand predicate logic)). Such a semantic theory defines the *meanings* of expressions of the language. That's what makes a formal language into a representational language: its expressions carry meaning. The semantic theory should explain the way in which they do this carrying. To sum up, then, although frames are sometimes understood at the metaphysical level, and sometimes at the computational level, I will discuss them as a representational proposal: a proposal for a language for the representation of knowledge, to be compared with other such representational languages: a language with a meaning.

What Do Frames Mean?

A frame is a data structure — we had better say *expression* — intended to represent a 'stereotypical situation'. It contains named '*slots*', which can be filled with other expressions — *fillers* — which may themselves be frames, or presumably simple names or identifiers (which may themselves be somehow associated with other frames, but not by a slot-filler relationship: otherwise the trees formed by filling slots with frames recursively, would always be infinitely deep). For example, we might have a frame representing a typical house, with slots called *kitchen*, *bathroom*, *bedrooms*, *lavatory*, *room-with-TV-in-it*, *owner*, *address*, etc.. A particular house is then to be represented by an *instance* of this *house* frame, obtained by filling in the slots with specifications of the corresponding parts of the particular house, so that, for example, the *kitchen* slot may be filled by an instance of the frame *contemporary-kitchen* which has slots *cooker*, *floorcovering*, *sink*, *cleanliness*, etc., which may contain in turn respectively an instance of the *split-level* frame, the identifier *vinyl*, an instance of the *double-drainer* frame, and the identifier '13' (for "very clean"), say. Not all slots in an instance need be filled, so that we can express doubt (e.g. "I dont't know where the lavatory is"), and in real 'frame' languages other refinments are included, e.g. descriptors such as "which-is-red" as slot fillers, etc. We will come to these later. From examples such as these (c.f. also Minsky's birthday-party example in Minsky, 1975), it seems fairly clear what frames mean. A frame instance denotes an individual, and each slot denotes a relationship which may hold between that individual and some other. Thus, if an instance (call it G00097) of the *house* frame has its slot called *kitchen* filled with a frame instance called, say G00082, then this means that the relationship *kitchen* (or, better, *is kitchen of*) holds between G00097 and G00082. We could express this same assertion (for it is an assertion) in predicate calculus by writing: is kitchen of (G00097, G00082).

Looked at this way,frames are essentially bundles of properties. *House* could be paraphrased as something like $\lambda x.$ (kitchen (x, y_1) & bathroom (x, y_2) & ...) where the free variables y_i correspond to the slots. Instantiating *House* to yield a particular house called *Dunroamin* (say), corresponds to applying the λ-expression to the identifier *Dunroamin* to get kitchen (dunroamin, y_1) & bathroom (dunroamin, y_2) & ... which, once the "slots" are filled, is an assertion about Dunroamin.

Thus far, then, working only at a very intuitive level, it seems that frames are simply an alternative syntax for expressing relationships between individuals, i.e. for predicate logic. But we should be careful, since although the meanings may appear to be the same, the inferences sanctioned by frames may differ in some crucial way from those sanctioned by logic. In order to get more insight into what frames are supposed to mean we should examine the ways in which it is suggested that they be *used*.

Frame Inference

One inference rule we have already met is *instantiation:* given a frame representing a concept, we can generate an instance of the concept by filling in its slots. But there is another, more subtle, form of inference suggested by Minsky and realised explicitly in some applications of frames. This is the "criteriality" inference. If we find fillers for all the slots of a frame, then this rule enables us to infer that an appropriate instance of the concept does indeed exist. For example, if an entity has a kitchen and a bathroom and an address and ..., etc.; then it must be a house. Possession of these attributes is a sufficient as well as necessary condition for an entity to qualify as a house, criteriality tells us.

An example of the use of this rule is in perceptual reasoning. Suppose for example the concept of a letter is represented as a frame, with slots corresponding to the parts of the letter (strokes and junctions, perhaps), in a program to read handwriting (as was done in the Essex Fortran project (Brady/Wielinga, 1977)). Then the discovery of fillers for all the slots of the 'F' frame means that one has indeed found an 'F' (the picture is considerably more complicated than this, in fact, as all inferences are potentially subject to disconfirmation: but this does not affect the present point.).

Now one can map this understanding of a frame straightforwardly into first-order logic also. A frame representing the concept C, with slot-relationships $R_1, \ldots, R_n$, becomes the assertion

$$\forall x\ (C(x) \equiv \exists y_1, \ldots, y_n.\ R_1(x, y_1)\ \&\ \ldots\ \&\ R_n(x, y_n))$$

or, expressed in clausal form:

$$\begin{aligned}&\forall x\ C(x) \supset R_1(x, f_1(x))\\ &\&\ \forall x\ C(x) \supset R_2(x, f_2(x))\\ &\&\ \qquad \vdots\\ &\&\ \forall x y_i\ R_1(x, y_1)\ \&\ R_2(x, y_2)\ \&\ \ldots\ \&\ R_n(x, y_n). \supset C(x)\end{aligned}$$

The last long clause captures the criteriality assumption exactly. Notice the Skolem functions in the other clauses: they have a direct intuitive reading, e.g. for *kitchen*, the corresponding function is *kitchenof*, which is a function from houses to their kitchens. These functions correspond exactly to the *selectors* which would apply to a frame, considered now as a data structure, to give the values of its fields (the fillers of its slots). All the variables here are universally quantified. If we assume that our logic contains equality, then we could dispense altogether with the slot-relations R_i and express the frame as an assertion using equality. In many ways this is more natural. The above then becomes:

$$\begin{aligned}&C(x) \supset \exists y.\ y = f_1(x)\\ &\&\ \text{etc.}\\ &f_1(x) = y_1\ \&\ \ldots\ \&\ f_n(x) = y_n. \supset C(x)\end{aligned}$$

(Where the existential quantifiers are supposed to assert that the functions are applicable to the individual in question. This assumes that the function symbols f_i denote partial functions, so that it makes sense to write $\neg \exists y$.) $f_1(x)$. Other notations are possible.)

We see then that criterial reasoning can easily be expressed in logic. Such expression makes clear, moreover (what is sometimes not clear in frames literature) whether or not criteriality is being assumed. A third form of frames reasoning has been proposed, often called *matching* (Bobrow/Winograd, 1977a). Suppose we have an instance of a concept, and we wish to know whether it can plausibly be regarded as also being an instance of another concept. Can we view John Smith as a dog-owner?, for example, where J.S. is an instance of the Man frame, let us suppose, and Dogowner is another frame. We can rephrase this question: can we find an instance of the dog-owner frame which *matches* J.S.? The sense of *match* here is what concerns us. Notice that this cannot mean a simple syntactic unification, but must rest — if it is possible at all — on some assumptions about the domain about which the frames in question express information.

For example, perhaps Man has a slot called *pet*, so we could say that a sufficient condition for J.S.'s being matchable to Dog-owner is that his *pet* slot is filled with as object known to be canine. Perhaps Dog-owner has slots *dog* and *name:* then we could specify how to build an instance of dog-owner corresponding to J.S.: fill the *name* slot with J.S.'s name (or perhaps with J.S. himself, or some other reference to him) and the *dog* slot with J.S.'s pet. KRL has facilities for just this sort of transference of fillers from slots in one frame to another, so that one can write routines to actually perform the matchings.

Given our expressions of frames as assertions, the sort of reasoning exemplified by this example falls out with very little effort. All we need to do is express the slot-to-slot transference by simple implications, thus: Isdog (x) & petof (x, y). ⊃ dogof (x, y) (using the first formulation in which slots are relations). Then, given:

name (J.S., "John Smith") (1)
& pet (J.S., Fido) (2)
& Isdog (Fido) (3)

(the first two from the J.S. instance of the 'man' frame, the third from general world-knowledge: or perhaps from Fido's being in fact an instance of the Dog frame) it follows directly that

dogof (J.S., Fido) (4)

whence, by the criteriality of Dogowner, from (1) and (4), we have:

Dogowner (J.S.)

The translation of this piece of reasoning into the functional notation is left as an exercise for the reader.

All the examples of 'matching' I have seen have this rather simple character. More profound examples are hinted at in (Bobrow/Winograd, 1977b), however. So far as one can tell, the processes of reasoning involved may be expressible only in higher-order logic. For example, it may be necessary to construct new relations by abstraction during the "matching" process. It is known (Huet, 1972; Pietrzykowski/Jensen, 1973) that the search spaces which this gives rise to are of gr complexity, and it is not entirely clear that it will be possible to automate this process in a reasonable way.)

This reading of a frame as an assertion has the merit of putting frames, frame-instances and 'matching' assumptions into a common language with a clear extensional semantics which makes it quite clear what all these structures *mean*. The (usual) inference rules are clearly correct, and are sufficient to account for most of the deductive properties of frames which are required. Notice, for example, that no special mechanism is required in order to see that J.S. is a Dogowner: it follows by ordinary first-order reasoning.

One technicality is worth mentioning. In KRL, the same slot-name can be used in different frames to mean different relations. For example, the *age* of a person is a number, but his *age* as an airline passenger (i.e. in the traveller frame) is one of {infant, child, adult}. We could not allow this conflation, and would have to use different names for the different relations. It is an interesting exercise to extend the usual first-order syntax with a notion of name-scope in order to allow such pleasantries. But this is really nothing more than syntactic sugar.

Seeing As

One apparently central intuition behind frames, which seems perhaps to be missing from the above account, is the idea of *seeing* one thing *as though* it were another: or of specifying an object by comparison with a known prototype, noting the similarities and points of difference (Bobrow/Winograd, 1977a). This is the basic analogical reasoning behind MERLIN (Moore/Newell, 1973), which Minsky cites as a major influence.

Now this idea can be taken to mean several rather different things. Some of them can be easily expressed in deductive-assertional terms, others less easily.

The first and simplest interpretation is that the 'comparison' is filling-in the details. Thus, to say JS is a man tells us something about him, but to say he is a bus conductor tells us more. The bus conductor frame would presumably have slots which did not appear in the Man frame (*since-when* for example, and *bus-company*), but it would also have a slot to be filled by the Man instance for JS (or refer to him in some other way), so have access to all his slots. Now there is nothing remarkable here. All this involves is asserting more and more restrictive properties of an entity. This can all be done within the logical framework of the last section.

The second interpretation is that a frame represents a 'way of looking' at an entity, and this is a *correct* way of looking at it. For example a Man may also be a Dog-owner, and neither of these is a *further* specification of the other: each has slots not possessed by the other frame. Thus far, there is nothing here more remarkable than the fact that several properties may be true of a single entity. Something may be both a Man *and* a Dog-owner, of course: or both a friend *and* an employee, or both a day *and* a birthday. And each of these pairs can have its own independent criteriality.

However, there is an apparent difficulty. A single thing may have apparently contradictory properties, seen from different points of view. Thus, a man viewed as a working colleague may be suspicious and short tempered; but viewed as a family man, may have a sweet and kindly disposition. One's views of oneself often seem to change depending on how one perceives one's social role, for another example. And in neither case, one feels, is there an outright contradiction: the different viewpoints 'insulate' the parts of the potential contradiction from one another.

I think there are three possible interpretations of this, all expressible in assertional terms. The first is that one is really asserting different properties in the two frames: that 'friendly' at work and 'friendly' at home are just different notions. This is analogous to the case discussed above where 'age' means different relations in two different contexts. The second is that the two frames somehow encode an extra parameter: the time or place, for example: so that Bill really is unfriendly *at work* and friendly *at home*. In expressing the relevant properties as assertions one would be obliged then to explicitly represent these parameters as extra arguments in the relevant relations, and provide an appropriate theory of the times, places, etc. which distinguish the various frames. These may be subtle distinctions, as in the self seen-as-spouse or the self seen-as-hospital-patient or seen-as-father, etc., where the relevant parameter is something like interpersonal role. I am not suggesting that I have any idea what a theory of these would be like, only that to introduce such distinctions, in frames or any other formalism, is to assume that there *is* such a theory- perhaps a very simple one. The third interpretation is that, after all, the two frames contradict one another. Then of course a faithful translation into assertions will also contain an explicit contradiction.

The assertional language makes these alternatives explicit, and forces one who uses it to choose which interpretation he means. And one can always express that interpretation in logic. At worst, *every* slot-relation can have the name of its frame as an extra parameter, if really necessary.

There is however a third, more radical, way to understand seeing-as. This is to view a seeing-as as a metaphor or analogy, without actually asserting that it is *true*. This is the MERLIN idea. Example: a man may be looked at as a pig, if you think of his home as a sty, his nose as a snout, and his feet as trotters. Now such a caricature may be useful in reasoning, without its being taken to be veridically true. One may *think of* a man as a pig, knowing perfectly well that as a matter of fact he isn't one.

MERLIN's notation and inference machinery for handling such analogies are very similar respectively to frames and "matching", and we have seen that this is merely first-order reasoning. The snag is that we have no way to distinguish a 'frame' representing a mere caricature from one representing a real assertion. Neither the old MERLIN (in which *all* reasoning is this analogical reasoning) nor KRL provide any means of making this rather important distinction.

What does it *mean* to say that you can look at a man as a pig? I think the only reasonable answer is something like: certain of the properties of (some) men are preserved under the mapping defined by the analogy. Thus, perhaps, pigs are greedy, illmannered and dirty, their snouts are short, upturned and blunt, and they are rotund and short-legged. Hence, a man with these qualities (under the mapping which defines the analogy: hence, the man's *nose* will be upturned, his *house* will be dirty) may be plausibly be regarded as pig-like. But of course there are many other properties of pigs which we would *not* intend to transfer to a men under the analogy: quadrupedal gait, being a source of bacon, etc. (Although one of the joys of using such analogies is finding ways of extending them: "Look at all the little piggies ... sitting down to eat their bacon" [G. Harrison]). So, the intention of such a caricature is, that some -not all- of the properties of the caricature shall be transferred to the caricaturee. And the analogy is correct, or plausible, when these transferred properties do, in fact, hold of the thing caricatured: when the man *is* in fact greedy, slovenly, etc....

This is almost exactly what the second sense of seeing-as seemed to mean: that the man 'matches' the pig frame. The difference (apart from the systematic rewriting) is that here we simply cannot assume criteriality of this pig frame. To say that a man *is* a pig is false: yet we have assumed that this fellow does fit this pig frame. Hence the properties expressed in this pig frame cannot be criterial for pig. To say that a man *is* a pig is to use criteriality incorrectly.

This then helps to distinguish this third sense of seeing-as from the earlier senses: the failure of criteriality. And this clearly indicates why MERLIN and KRL cannot distinguish caricatures from factual assertions; for criteriality is not made explicit in these languages. We can however easily express a non-criterial frame as a simple assertion.

One might wonder what use the 'frame' idea is when criteriality is abandoned, since a frame is now merely a conjunction. Its boundaries appear arbitrary: why conjoin just these properties together? The answer lies in the fact that not *all* properties of the caricature are asserted of the caricaturee, just those bundled together in the seeing-as frame. The bundling here is used to delimit the scope of the transfer. We could say that these properties were criterial for *pig-likeness* (rather than *pig-hood*).

In order to express caricatures in logic, then, we need only to define the systematic translations of vocabulary: nose — snout, etc., this seems to require some syntactic machinery which logic does not provide: the ability to substitute one relation symbol for another in an assertion. This kind of "analogy mapping" was first developed some years ago by R. Kling and used by him to express analogies in mathematics. Let ϕ be the syntactic mapping 'out' of the analogy (e.g. ⌜snout⌝ → ⌜nose⌝, ⌜sty⌝ → ⌜house⌝), and suppose $\lambda x.\ \psi(x)$ is the defining conjunction of the frame of Pig-likeness:

$$\text{Pig-like}(x) \equiv \psi(x)$$

(Where ψ may contain several existentially bound variables, and generally may be a complicated assertion). Then we can say that Pig-like (Fred) is true just when $\phi(\psi)$ holds for Fred, i.e. the asserted properties are *actually* true of Fred, when the relation names are altered according to the syntactic mapping ϕ. So, a caricature frame needs to contain, or be somehow associated with, a specification of how its vocabulary should be altered to fit reality. With this modification, all the rest of the reasoning involved is first-order and conventional.

Defaults

One aspect of frame reasoning which is often considered to lie outside of logic is the idea of a default value: a value which is taken to be the slot filler in the absence of explicit information to the contrary. Thus, the default for the *home-port* slot in a traveller frame may be the city where the travel agency is located (Bobrow et al. 1977).

Now, defaults certainly seem to take us outside first-order reasoning, in the sense that we cannot express the assumption of the default value as a simple first-order consequence of there being no contrary information. For if we could, the resulting inference would have the property that $p \vdash q$ but $(p \,\&\, r) \vdash \neg q$ for suitable p, q and r (p does not deny the default: q represents the default assumption: r overrides the default), and no logical system behaves this way (Curry [1956] for example, takes $p \vdash q \Rightarrow p \,\&\, r \vdash q$ to be the fundamental property of *all* 'logistic' systems).

This shows however only that a *naive* mapping of default reasoning into assertional reasoning fails. The moral is to distrust naivety. Let us take an example. Suppose we have a Car frame and an instance of it for my car, and suppose it has a slot called *status*, with possible values {*OK*, *struggling*, *needs-attention*, *broken*}, and the default is OK. That is, in the absence of contrary information, I assume the car is OK. Now I go to the car, and I see that the tyre is flat: I am surprised, and I conclude that (contrary to what I expected), the correct filler for the *status* slot is *broken*. But, it is important to note, my state of knowledge has changed. I was previously making an assumption — that the car was OK — which was reasonable *given my state of knowledge at the time*. We might say that if ψ represented my state of knowledge, then status (car) = OK was a reasonable inference from ψ: $\psi \vdash$ status (car) = OK. But once I know the tyre is flat, we have a new state of knowledge ψ_1, and of course $\psi_1 \vdash$ status (car) = broken. In order for this to be deductively possible, it must be that ψ_1 is got from ψ not merely by adding new beliefs, but also by removing some old ones. That is, when I see the flat tyre I am *surprised*: I had expected that it was OK. (This is not to say that I had explicitly considered the possiblity that the tyre might be flat, and rejected it. It only means that my state of belief was such that the tyres being OK was a consequence of it). And of course this makes sense: indeed, I was surprised. Moreover, there is no contradiction between my earlier belief that the car was OK and my present belief that it is broken. If challenged, I would not say that I had previously been irrational or mad, only misinformed (or perhaps just *wrong*, in the sense that I was entertaining a false belief).

As this example illustrates, default assumptions involve an implicit reference to the whole state of knowledge at the time the assumption was generated. Any event which alters the state of knowledge is liable therefore to upset these assumptions. If we represent these references to knowledge states explicitly, then 'default' reasoning can be easily and naturally expressed in logic. To say that the default for *home-port* is Palo Alto is to say that unless the current knowledge-state says otherwise, then we will assume that it is Palo Alto, *until the knowledge-state changes*. Let us suppose we can somehow refer to the current knowledge-state (denoted by NOW), and to a notion of derivability (denoted by the turnstile $\vdash$). Then we can express the default assumption by:

∃y. NOW ⊢ ⌜*homeport* (traveller, = y⌝ ∨ *homeport* (traveller) = Palo Alto. The conclusion of which allows us to infer that *homeport* (traveller) = Palo-Alto *until the st. te of knowledge changes*. When it does, we would have to establish this conclusion for the new knowledge state.

I believe this is intuitively plausible. Experience with manipulating collections of beliefs should dispel the feeling that one can predict all the ways new knowledge can affect previously held beliefs. We do not have a theory of this process, nor am I claiming that this notation provides one.* But *any* mechanism — whether expressed in frames or otherwise — which makes strong assumptions on weak evidence needs to have some method for unpicking these assumptions when things go wrong, or equivalently of controlling the propagation of inferences from the assumptions. This inclusion of a reference to the knowledge-state which produced the assumption is in the latter category. An example of the kind of axiom which might form part of such a theory of assumption-transfer is this. Suppose $\phi \vdash p$, and hence p, is in the knowledge-state ϕ, and suppose we wish to generate a new knowledge-state ϕ' by adding the observation q. Let ψ be $\phi -$ ⌜$\phi \vdash p$⌝ and all inferred consequences of ⌜$\phi \vdash p$⌝. Then if $\psi \cup \{q\} \nvdash \neg p$, define ϕ' to be $\psi \cup$ ⌜$\psi \vdash p$⌝, ⌜q⌝. This can all be written, albeit rather rebarbitively, in logic augmented with notations for

* Recent work of Doyle, McDermott and Reiter is providing such a theory: see (Doyle, 1978) (McDermott/Doyle, 1978) (Reiter, 1978)

describing constructive operations upon knowledge-states. It would justify for example the transfer of *status* (car) = OK past an observation of the form, say, that the car was parked in an unusual position, provided that the belief state did not contain anything which allowed one to conclude that an unusual parking position entailed anything wrong with the car. (It would also justify transferring it past an observation like *it is raining*, or *my mother is feeling ill*, but these transfers can be justified by a much simpler rule: if p and q have no possible inferential connections in ϕ — this can be detected very rapidly from the 'connection graph' (Kowalski 1973) — then addition of q cannot affect p.)

To sum up, a close analysis of what defaults mean shows that they are intimately connected with the idea of *observations*: additions of fresh knowledge into a data-base. Their role in *inference* — the drawing of consequences of assumptions — is readily expressible in logic, but their interaction with observation requires that the role of the state of the system's own knowledge is made explicit. This requires not a new *logic*, but an unusual *ontology*, and some new primitive relations. We need to be able to talk *about the system itself*, in its own language, and to involve assumptions about itself in its own processes of reasoning.

Reflexive Reasoning

We have seen that most of 'frames' is just a new syntax for parts of first-order logic. There are one or two apparently minor details which give a lot of trouble, however, especially defaults. There are two points worth making about this. The first is, that I believe that this complexity, revealed by the attempt to formulate these ideas in logic, is not an artefact of the translation but is intrinsic to the ideas involved. Defaults just *are* a complicated notion, with far-reaching consequences for the whole process of inference-making. The second point is a deeper one.

In both cases — caricatures and defaults — the necessary enrichment of logic involved adding the ability to talk about the system itself, rather than about the worlds of men, pigs and travel agents. I believe these are merely two relatively minor aspects of this most important fact: much common-sense reasoning involves the reasoner in thinking about himself and his own abilities as well as about the world. In trying to formalise intuitive common-sense reasoning I find again and again that this awareness of one's own internal processes of deduction and memory is crucial to even quite mundane arguments. There is only space for one example.

I was once talking to a Texan about television. This person, it was clear, knew far more about electronics than I did. We were discussing the number of lines per screen in different countries. One part of the conversation went like this.

Texan: You have 900 lines in England, don't you?
Me: No, 625.
Texan (confidently): I *thought* it was 900.
Me (somewhat doubtfully): No, I think it's 625.
(pause)
Say, they couldn't change it without altering the sets, could they? I mean by sending some kind of signal from the transmitter or ....
Texan: No, they'd sure have to alter the receivers.
Me (now confident): Oh, well, it's definitely 625 lines then.

I made a note of my own thought processes immediately afterwards, and they went like this. I *remembered* that we had 625 lines in England. (This remembering cannot be introspectively examined: it *seems* like a primitive ability, analogous to FETCH in CONNIVER. I will take it to be such a primitive in what follows. Although this seems a ludicrously naive assumption, the internal structure of remembering will not concern us here, so we might as well take it to be primitive.) However, the Texan's confidence shook me, and I examined the belief in a little more detail. Many facts emerged: I remembered in particular that we had changed from 405 lines to 625 lines, and that this change was a long, expensive and complicated process. For several years one could buy dual-standard sets which worked on either system. My parents, indeed, had owned such a set, and it was prone to unreliability, having a huge multigang sliding-contact switch: I had examined its insides once. There had been newspaper articles about it, technical debates in the popular science press, etc.. It was not the kind of event which could have passed unnoticed. (It was this *richness of detail*, I think, which gave the memory its subjective confidence: I couldn't have imagined all *that*, surely?) So if there had been another, subsequent, alteration to 900 lines, there would have been another huge fuss. But I had no memory at all of any such fuss: so it couldn't have happened. (I had a definite subjective impression of *searching* for such a memory. For example, I briefly considered the possibility that it had happened while my family and I were in California for 4 months, being somehow managed with great alacrity that time: but rejected this when I realised that our own set still worked, unchanged, on our return). Notice how this conclusion was obtained. It was the kind of event I would remember; but I don't remember it; so it didn't happen. This argument crucially involves an explicit assertion about my own memory. It is not enough that I didn't remember the event: I had to *realise* that I didn't remember it, and *use* that realisation in an argument.

The Texan's confidence still shook me somewhat, and I found a possible flaw in my argument. *Maybe* the new TV sets were constructed in a new sophisticated way which made it possible to alter the number of lines by remote control, say, by a signal from the transmitter. (This seems quite implausible to me now; but my knowledge of electronics is not rapidly accessible, and it did seem a viable possibility at the moment). How to check whether this was possible? Why, ask the expert: which I did, and his answer sealed the only hole I could find in the argument.

This process involves taking a previously constructed argument — a proof, or derivation — as an object, and inferring properties of it: that a certain step in it is weak (can be denied on moderately plausible assumption), for example. Again, this is an example of *reflexive reasoning:* reasoning involving descriptions of the self.

Conclusion

I believe that an emphasis on the analysis of such processes of reflexive reasoning is one of the few positive suggestions which the 'frames' movement has produced. Apart from this, there are no new insights to be had there: no new processes of reasoning, no advance in expressive power.

Nevertheless, as an historical fact, 'frames' have been extraordinarily influential. Perhaps this is in part because the original idea was interesting, but vague enough to leave scope for creative imagination. But a more serious suggestion is that the *real* force of the frames idea was not at the representational level at all, but rather at the implementation level: a suggestion about how to organise large memories. Looked at in this light, we could sum up 'frames' as the suggestion that we should *store* assertions in nameable 'bundles' which can be retrieved via some kind of indexing mechanism on their names. In fact, the suggestion that we should store assertions in non-clausal form.

Acknowledgements

I would like to thank Frank Brown and Terry Winograd for helpful comments on an earlier draft of this paper.

Appendix: Translation of KRL-ϕ into Predicate Logic

KRL	*many-sorted predicate logic*
Units	
(i) Basic	Unary predicate (sort predicate: assuming a disjoint sort structure.)
(ii) Specialisation	Unary predicate
(iii) Abstract	Unary predicate
(iv) Individual	name (individual constant)
(v) Manifestation	sometimes a λ-expression λx. P(x) & ... & Q(x) sometimes an ∈-expression ∈x. P(x) & ... & Q(x) (i.e. a variable over the set {x: P(x) & ... & Q(x)}
(vi) Relation	relation
Slot	binary relation or unary function
Descriptors	
(i) direct pointer	name
(ii) Perspective e.g. (a trip with destination = Boston airline = TWA)	λ-expression e.g. λx. trip (x) & destination (x) = Boston & airline (x) = TWA (in this case both fillers are unique. If not we would use a relation, e.g. airline (x, TWA))
(iii) Specification e.g. (the actor from Act E17 (a chase ...))	ι-expression e.g. ιx. actor (E17) = x or ιx. actor (E17) = x & Act (E17)
(iv) predication	λ-expression
(v) logical boolean	non-atomic expression
(vi) restriction e.g. (the one (a mouse) (which owns (a dog)))	ι-expression e.g. ιx. mouse (x) & ∃y.dog (y) & owns (x, y)
(vii) selection e.g. (using (the age from Person this one) select from (which is less than 2) ~ Infant (which is at least 12) ~ Adult otherwise child	ι-expression with conditional body e.g. ιx. (age (this one) < 2 & x = infant) ∨ (age) (this one) ≥ 12 & x = adult) ∨ (age (this one) < 2 & age (this one) ≥ 12 & x = child)
(viii) set specification	λ-expression (sets coded as predicates) or set specification (if we use set theory. Only very simple set theory is necessary)
(ix) contingency e.g. (during state 24 then (the topblock from (a stack with height = 3)))	ι-expression or ∈-expression whose body mentions a state or has a bound state variable. e.g. ιx.∃y. is stack (y, state 24) & height (y) = 3 & topblock (y, x) where I have taken stack to be a contingent property: other choices are possible (e.g. stacks always "exist" but have zero height in some states).

Examples

Traveller (x) ⊃	Person (x) & (category (x) = infant ∨ category (x) = child ∨ category (x) = adult) & ∃y. airport (y) & preferredairport (x, y)
Person (x) ⊃	string (first name (x)) & string (last name (x)) & integer (age (x)) & city (nametown (x)) & address (streetaddress (x))

```
Person (G0043)
  & firstname (G0043) = "Juan"
  & foreignname (lastname (G0043))
  & firstcharacter (lastname (G0043)) = "M"
  & age (G0043) > 21
Traveller (G0043)
  & category (G0043) = Adult
  & preferredairport (G0043, SJO)
```

References

Bobrow, D.G., Kaplan, R.M., Norman, D.A., Thompson, H. and Winograd, T.
1977
"GUS, a Frame-Driven Dialog System", *Artificial Intelligence* 8, 155–173.

Bobrow, D.G. and Winograd, T.
1977a
"An Overview of KRL", *Cognitice Science* 1, 3–46.
1977b
"Experience with KRL-O: One Cycle of a Knowledge Representation Language", Proc. 5th Int. Joint Conf. on AI, MIT, (vol 1), 213–222.

Brady, J.M. and Wielinga, B.J.
1977
"Reading the Writing on the Wall", Proc. Workshop on Computer Vision, Amherst Mass.

Charniak, E.
1977
"Ms. Malaprop, a Language Comprehension Program", Proc. 5th Int. Joint Conf. on AI, MIT, (vol 1), 1–8.

Curry, H.B.
1956
Introduction to Mathematical Logic (Amsterdam: Van Nostrand)

Doyle, J.
1978
Truth Maintenance System for Problem Solving, Memo TR-419, A.I. Laboratory, MIT

Feldman, J.
1975
"Bad-Mouthing Frames", Proc. Conf. on Theor. Issues in Natural Language Processing", Cambridge Mass, 102–103.

Hayes, P.J.
1975
"Some Problems and Non-problems in Representation Theory", Proc. 1st AISB Conf., Brighton Sussex.
1977
"In Defence of Logic", 5 Int. Joint Conf. on AI, MIT, (vol 2), 559–565.

Huet, G.P.
1972
Constrained Resolution: a Complete Method for Type Theory, Jenning's Computer Science, Report 1117, Cace Western University.

Kowalski, R.
1973
An Improved Theorem-Proving System for First Order Logic, DCL Memo 65, Edinburgh.

Lehnert, W.
1977
"Human and Computational Question Answering", *Cognitive Science* 1, 47–73.

McCarthy, J. and Hayes, J.P.
1969
"Some Philosophical Problems from the Standpoint of Artificial Intelligence", *Machine Intelligence* 4, 463–502.

McDermott, D. and Doyle, J.
1978
Non-monotonic logic I, Memo AI-486, A.I. Laboratory, MIT

Minsky, M.
1975
"A Framework for Representing Knowledge", in P. Winston (Ed.) *The Psychology of Computer Vision*, (New York: McGraw-Hill), 211–277.

Moore, J. and Newell, A.
1973
"How Can MERLIN Understand?", in L. Gregg (Ed.) *Knowledge and Cognition* (Hillsdale New York: Lawrence Erlbaum Assoc), 201–310.

Pietrzykowski, T. and Jensen, D.
1973
Mechanising W-Order Type Theory through Unification, Dept. of Applied Analysis and Comp. Science, Report CS-73-16, University of Waterloo.

Reiter, R.
1978
"On Reasoning by Default", Proc. 2nd Symp. on Theor. Issues in Natural Language Processing, Urbana, Illinois.

Schank, R.
1975
"The Structure of Episodes in Memory", in D.G. Bobrow and A. Collins (Eds) *Representation and Understanding*, (New York: Academic Press), 237–272.

Wilks, Y.
1976
"Natural Language Understanding Systems within the AI Paradigm: a Survey", in M. Penny (Ed) *Artificial Intelligence and Language Comprehension*, (National Institute of Education, Washington, Oc).

EPISTEMOLOGICAL PROBLEMS OF ARTIFICIAL INTELLIGENCE

John McCarthy
Computer Science Department
Stanford University
Stanford, California 94305

Introduction

In (McCarthy and Hayes 1969), we proposed dividing the artificial intelligence problem into two parts - an epistemological part and a heuristic part. This lecture further explains this division, explains some of the epistemological problems, and presents some new results and approaches.

The epistemological part of AI studies what kinds of facts about the world are available to an observer with given opportunities to observe, how these facts can be represented in the memory of a computer, and what rules permit legitimate conclusions to be drawn from these facts. It leaves aside the heuristic problems of how to search spaces of possibilities and how to match patterns.

Considering epistemological problems separately has the following advantages:

1. The same problems of what information is available to an observer and what conclusions can be drawn from information arise in connection with a variety of problem solving tasks.

2. A single solution of the epistemological problems can support a wide variety of heuristic approaches to a problem.

3. AI is a very difficult scientific problem, so there are great advantages in finding parts of the problem that can be separated out and separately attacked.

4. As the reader will see from the examples in the next section, it is quite difficult to formalize the facts of common knowledge. Existing programs that manipulate facts in some of the domains are confined to special cases and don't face the difficulties that must be overcome to achieve very intelligent behavior.

We have found first order logic to provide suitable languages for expressing facts about the world for epistemological research. Recently we have found that introducing concepts as individuals makes possible a first order logic expression of facts usually expressed in modal logic but with important advantages over modal logic - and so far no disadvantages.

In AI lit ure, the term *predicate calculus* is usually extended to cover the whole of first order logic. While predicate calculus includes just formulas built up from variables using predicate symbols, logical connectives, and quantifiers, first order logic also allows the use of function symbols to form terms and in its semantics interprets the equality symbol as standing for identity. Our first order systems further use conditional expressions (non-recursive) to form terms and λ-expressions with individuaal variables to form new function symbols. All these extensions are logically inessential, because every formula that includes them can be replaced by a formula of pure predicate calculus whose validity is equivalent to it. The extensions are heuristically non-trivial, because the equivalent predicate calculus may be much longer and is usually much more difficult to understand - for man or machine.

The use of first order logic in epistemological research is a separate issue from whether first order sentences are appropriate data structures for representing information within a program. As to the latter, sentences in logic are at one end of a spectrum of representations; they are easy to communicate, have logical consequences and can be logical consequences, and they can be meaningful in a wide context. Taking action on the basis of information stored as sentences, is slow and they are not the most compact representation of information. The opposite extreme is to build the information into hardware, next comes building it into machine language program, then a language like LISP, and then a language like MICROPLANNER, and then perhaps productions. Compiling or hardware building or "automatic programming" or just planning takes information from a more context independent form to a faster but more context dependent form. A clear expression of this is the transition from first order logic to MICROPLANNER, where much information is represented similarly but with a specification of how the information is to be used. A large AI system should represent some information as first order logic sentences and other information should be compiled. In fact, it will often be necessary to represent the same information in several ways. Thus a ball player habit of keeping his eye on the ball is built into his "program", but it is also explicitly represented as a sentence so that the advice can be communicated.

Whether first order logic makes a good programming language is yet another issue. So far it seems to have the qualities Samuel Johnson ascribed to a woman preaching or a dog walking on its hind legs - one is sufficiently impressed by seeing it done at all that one doesn't demand it be done well.

Suppose we have a theory of a certain class of phenomena axiomatized in (say) first order logic. We regard the theory as adequate for describing the epistemological aspects of a goal seeking process involving these phenomena provided the following criterion is satisfied:

Imagine a robot such that its inputs become sentences of the theory stored in the robot's data-base, and such that whenever a sentence of the form "*I should emit output X now*" appears in its data base, the robot emits output *X*. Suppose that new sentences appear in its data base only as logical consequences of sentences already in the data base. The deduction of these sentences also use general sentences stored in the data base at the beginning constituting the theory being tested. Usually a data-base of sentences permits many different deductions to be made so that a deduction program would have to choose which deduction to make. If there was no program that could achieve the goal by making deductions allowed by the theory no matter how fast the program ran, we would have to say that the theory was epistemologically inadequate. A theory that was epistemologically adequate would be considered heuristically inadequate if no program running at a reasonable speed with any representation of the facts expressed by the data could do the job. We believe that most present AI formalisms are epistemologically inadequate for general intelligence; i.e. they wouldn't achieve enough goals requiring general intelligence no matter how fast they were allowed to run. This is because the epistemological problems discussed in the following sections haven't even been attacked yet.

The word "epistemology" is used in this paper substantially as many philosophers use it, but the problems considered have a different emphasis. Philosophers emphasize what is potentially knowable with maximal opportunities to observe and compute, whereas AI must take into account what is knowable with available observational and computational facilities. Even so, many of the same formalizations have both philosophical and AI interest.

The subsequent sections of this paper list some epistemological problems, discuss some first order formalizations, introduce concepts as objects and use them to express facts about knowledge, describe a new mode of reasoning called circumscription, and place the AI problem in a philosphical setting.

Epistemological problems

We will discuss what facts a person or robot must take into account in order to achieve a goal by some strategy of action. We will ignore the question of how these facts are represented, e.g., whether they are represented by sentences from which deductions are made or whether they are built into the program. We start with great generality, so there many difficulties. We obtain successively easier problems by assuming that the difficulties we have recognized don't occur until we get to a class of problems we think we can solve.

1. We begin by asking whether solving the problem requires the co-operation of other people or overcoming their opposition. If either is true, there are two subcases. In the first subcase, the other people's desires and goals must be taken into account, and the actions they will take in given circumstances predicted on the hypothesis that they will try to achieve their goals, which may have to be discovered. The problem is even more difficult if bargaining is involved, because then the problems and indeterminacies of game theory are relevant. Even if bargaining is not involved, the robot still must "put himself in the place of the other people with whom he interacts". Facts like a person wanting a thing or a person disliking another must be described.

The second subcase makes the assumption that the other people can be regarded as machines with known input-output behavior. This is often a good assumption, e.g., one assumes that a clerk in a store will sell the goods in exchange for their price and that a professor will assign a grade in accordance with the quality of the work done. Neither the goals of the clerk or the professor need be taken into account; either might well regard an attempt to use them to optimize the interaction as an invasion of privacy. In such circumstances, man usually prefers to be regarded as a machine.

Let us now suppose that either other people are not involved in the problem or that the information available about their actions takes the form of input-output relations and does not involve understanding their goals.

2. The second question is whether the strategy involves the acquisition of knowledge. Even if we can treat other people as machines, we still may have to reason about what they know. Thus an airline clerk knows what airplanes fly from here to there and when, although he will tell you when asked without your having to motivate him. One must also consider information in books and in tables. The latter information is described by other information.

The second subcase of knowledge is according to whether the information obtained can be simply plugged into a program or whether it enters in a more complex way. Thus if the robot must telephone someone, its program can simply dial the number obtained, but it might have to ask a question, "*How can I get in touch with Mike?*" and reason about how to use the resulting information in conjunction with other information. The general distinction may be according to whether new sentences are generated or whether values are just assigned to variables.

An example worth considering is that a sophisticated air traveler rarely asks how he will get from the arriving flight to the departing flight at an airport where he must change planes. He is confident that the information will be available in a form he can understand at the time he will need it.

If the strategy is embodied in a program that branches on an environmental condition or reads a numerical parameter from the environment, we can regard it as obtaining knowledge, but this is obviously an easier case than those we have discussed.

3. A problem is more difficult if it involves concurrent events and actions. To me this seems to be the most difficult unsolved epistemological problem for AI - how to express rules that give the effects of actions and events when they occur concurrently. We may contrast this with the sequential case treated in (McCarthy and Hayes 1969). In the sequential case we can write

1) $s' = result(e, s)$

where s' is the situation that results when event e occurs in situation s. The effects of e can be described by sentences relating s', e and s. One can attempt a similar formalism giving a *partial situation* that results from an event in another partial situation, but it is difficult to see how to apply this to cases in which other events may affect with the occurrence.

When events are concurrent, it is usually necessary to regard time as continuous. We have events like *raining until the reservoir overflows* and questions like *Where was his train when we wanted to call him*?.

Computer science has recently begun to formalize parallel processes so that it is sometimes possible to prove that a system of parallel processes will meet its specifications. However, the knowledge available to a robot of the other processes going on in the world will rarely take the form of a Petri net or any of the other formalisms used in engineering or computer science. In fact, anyone who wishes to prove correct an airline reservation system or an air traffic control system must use information about the behavior of the external world that is less specific than a program. Nevertheless, the formalisms for expressing facts about parallel and indeterminate programs provide a start for axiomatizing concurrent action.

4. A robot must be able to express knowledge about space, and the locations, shapes and layouts of objects in space. Present

programs treat only very special cases. Usually locations are discrete - block A may be on block B but the formalisms do not allow anything to be said about where on block B it is, and what shape space is left on block B for placing other blocks or whether block A could be moved to project out a bit in order to place another block. A few are more sophisticated, but the objects must have simple geometric shapes. A formalism capable of representing the geometric information people get from seeing and handling objects has not, to my knowledge, been approached.

The difficulty in expressing such facts is indicated by the limitations of English in expressing human visual knowledge. We can describe regular geometric shapes precisely in English (fortified by mathematics), but the information we use for recognizing another person's face cannot ordinarily be transmitted in words. We can answer many more questions in the presence of a scene than we can from memory.

5. The relation between three dimensional objects and their two dimensional retinal or camera images is mostly untreated. Contrary to some philosophical positions, the three dimensional object is treated by our minds as distinct from its appearances. People blind from birth can still communicate in the same language as sighted people about three dimensional objects. We need a formalism that treats three dimensional objects as instances of patterns and their two dimensional appearances as projections of these patterns modified by lighting and occlusion.

6. Objects can be made by shaping materials and by combining other objects. They can also be taken apart, cut apart or destroyed in various ways. What people know about the relations between materials and objects remains to be described.

7. Modal concepts like *event e1 caused event e2* and *person e can do action a* are needed. (McCarthy and Hayes 1969) regards ability as a function of a person's position in a causal system and not at all as a function of his internal structure. This still seems correct, but that treatment is only metaphysically adequate, because it doesn't provide for expressing the information about ability that people actually have.

8. Suppose now that the problem can be formalized in terms of a single state that is changed by events. In interesting cases, the set of components of the state depends on the problem, but common general knowledge is usually expressed in terms of the effect of an action on one or a few components of the state. However, it cannot always be assumed that the other components are unchanged, especially because the state can be described in a variety of co-ordinate systems and the meaning of changing a single co-ordinate depends on the co-ordinate system. The problem of expressing information about what remains unchanged by an event was called *the frame problem* in (McCarthy and Hayes 1969). Minsky subsequently confused matters by using the word "frame" for patterns into which situations may fit. (His hypothesis seems to have been that almost all situations encountered in human problem solving fit into a small number of previously known patterns of situation and goal. I regard this as unlikely in difficult problems).

9. The *frame problem* may be a subcase of what we call the *qualification problem*, and a good solution of the qualification problem may solve the frame problem also. In the *missionaries and cannibals* problem, a boat holding two people is stated to be available. In the statement of the problem, nothing is said about how boats are used to cross rivers, so obviously this information must come from common knowledge, and a computer program capable of solving the problem from an English description or from a translation of this description into logic must have the requisite common knowledge. The simplest statement about the use of boats says something like, "*If a boat is at one point on the shore of a body of water, and a set of things enter the boat, and the boat is propelled to the another point on the shore, and the things exit the boat, then they will be at the second point on the shore*". However, this statement is too rigid to be true, because anyone will admit that if the boat is a rowboat and has a leak or no oars, the action may not achieve its intended result. One might try amending the common knowledge statement about boats, but this encounters difficulties when a critic demands a qualification that the vertical exhaust stack of a diesel boat must not be struck square by a cow turd dropped by a passing hawk or some other event that no-one has previously thought of. We need to be able to say that the boat can be used as a vehicle for crossing a body of water unless something prevents it. However, since we are not willing to delimit in advance possible circumstances that may prevent the use of the boat, there is still a problem of proving or at least conjecturing that nothing prevents the use of the boat. A method of reasoning called *circumscription*, described in a subsequent section of this paper, is a candidate for solving the qualification problem. The reduction of the frame problem to the qualification problem has not been fully carried out, however.

Circumscription - a way of jumping to conclusions

There is an intuition that not all human reasoning can be translated into deduction in some formal system of mathematical logic, and therefore mathematical logic should be rejected as a formalism for expressing what a robot should know about the world. The intuition in itself doesn't carry a convincing idea of what is lacking and how it might be supplied.

We can confirm part of the intuition by describing a previously unformalized mode of reasoning called *circumscription*, which we can show does not correspond to deduction in a mathematical system. The conclusions it yields are just conjectures and sometimes even introduce inconsistency. We will argue that humans often use circumscription, and robots must too. The second part of the intuition - the rejection of mathematical logic - is not confirmed; the new mode of reasoning is best understood and used within a mathematical logical framework and co-ordinates well with mathematical logical deduction. We think *circumscription* accounts for some of the successes and some of the errors of human reasoning.

The intuitive idea of *circumscription* is as follows: We know some objects in a given class and we have some ways of generating more. We jump to the conclusion that this gives all the objects in the class. Thus we *circumscribe* the class to the objects we know how to generate.

For example, suppose that objects a, b and c satisfy the predicate P and that the functions $f(x)$ and $g(x,y)$ take arguments satisfying P into values also satisfying P. The first order logic expression of these facts is

2) $P(a) \wedge P(b) \wedge P(c) \wedge (\forall x)(P(x) \supset P(f(x))) \wedge (\forall x\ y)(P(x) \wedge P(y) \supset P(g(x,y)))$.

The conjecture that everything satisfying P is generated from a, b and c by repeated application of the functions f and g is expressed by the sentence schema

3) $\Phi(a) \wedge \Phi(b) \wedge \Phi(c) \wedge (\forall x)(\Phi(x) \supset \Phi(f(x))) \wedge (\forall x\ y)(\Phi(x) \wedge \Phi(y) \supset \Phi(g(x, y))) \supset (\forall x)(\Phi(x) \supset P(x))$,

where Φ is a free predicate variable for which any predicate may be substituted.

It is only a conjecture, because there might be an object d such that $P(d)$ which is not generated in this way. (3) is one way of writing *the circumscription* of (2). The heuristics of circumscription - when one can plausibly conjecture that the objects generated in known ways are all there are - are completely unstudied.

Circumscription is not deduction in disguise, because every form of deduction has two properties that circumscription lacks - transitivity and what we may call *monotonicity*. Transitivity says that if $p \vdash r$ and $r \vdash s$, then $p \vdash s$. Monotonicity says that if $A \vdash p$ (where A is a set of sentences) and $A \subset B$, then $B \vdash p$ for deduction. Intuitively, circumscription should not be monotonic, since it is the conjecture that the ways we know of generating P's are all there are. An enlarged set B of sentences may contain a new way of generating P's.

If we use second order logic or the language of set theory, then circumscription can be expressed as a sentence rather than as a schema. In set theory it becomes.

3') $(\forall \Phi)(a \in \Phi \wedge b \in \Phi \wedge c \in \Phi \wedge (\forall x)(x \in \Phi \supset f(x) \in \Phi) \wedge (\forall x\ y)(x \in \Phi \wedge y \in \Phi \supset g(x, y) \in \Phi)) \supset P \subset \Phi)$,

but then we will still use the comprehension schema to form the set to be substituted for the set variable Φ.

The axiom schema of induction in arithmetic is the result of applying circumscription to the constant 0 and the successor operation.

There is a way of applying circumscription to an arbitrary sentence of predicate calculus. Let p be such a sentence and let Φ be a predicate symbol. The *relativization* of p with respect to Φ (written p^{Φ}) is defined (as in some logic texts) as the sentence that results from replacing every quantification $(\forall x)E$ that occurs in p by $(\forall x)(\Phi(x) \supset E)$ and every quantification $(\exists x)E$ that occurs in p by $(\exists x)(\Phi(x) \wedge E)$. The circumscription of p is then the sentence

4) $p^{\Phi} \supset (\forall x)(P(x) \supset \Phi(x))$.

This form is correct only if neither constants nor function symbols occur in p. If they do, it is necessary to conjoin $\Phi(c)$ for each constant c and $(\forall x)(\Phi(x) \supset \Phi(f(x)))$ for each single argument function symbol f to the premiss of (4). Corresponding sentences must be conjoined if there are function symbols of two or more arguments. The intuitive meaning of (4) is that the only objects satisfying P that exist are those that the sentence p forces to exist.

Applying the circumscription schema requires inventing a suitable predicate to substitute for the symbol Φ (inventing a suitable set in the set-theoretic formulation). In this it resembles mathematical induction; in order to get the conclusion, we must invent a predicate for which the premiss is true.

There is also a semantic way of looking at applying circumscription. Namely, a sentence that can be proved from a sentence p by circumscription is true in all minimal models of p, where a deduction from p is true in all models of p. Minimality is defined with respect to a containment relation $\leq$. We write that $M1 \leq M2$ if every element of the domain of $M1$ is a member of the domain of $M2$ and on the common members all predicates have the same truth value. It is not always true that a sentence true in all minimal models can be proved by circumscription. Indeed the minimal model of Peano's axioms is the standard model of arithmetic, and Gödel's theorem is the assertion that not all true sentences are theorems. Minimal models don't always exist, and when they exist, they aren't always unique.

(McCarthy 1977a) treats circumscription in more detail.

Concepts as objects

We shall begin by discussing how to express such facts as "*Pat knows the combination of the safe*", although the idea of treating a concept as an object has application beyond the discussion of knowledge.

We shall use the symbol *safe1* for the safe, and *combination(s)* is our notation for the combination of an arbitrary safe *s*. We aren't much interested in the domain of combinations, and we shall take them to be strings of digits with dashes in the right place, and, since a combination is a string, we will write it in quotes. Thus we can write

5) *combination(safe1)* = "45–25–17"

as a formalization of the English "*The combination of the safe is* 45–25–17". Let us suppose that the combination of *safe2* is, coincidentally, also 45-25-17, so we can also write

6) *combination(safe2)* = "45–25–17".

Now we want to translate "*Pat knows the combination of the safe*". If we were to express it as

7) **knows(pat, combination(safe1))*,

the inference rule that allows replacing a term by an equal term in first order logic would let us conclude

8) **knows(pat, combination(safe2))*,

which mightn't be true.

This problem was already recognized in 1879 by Frege, the founder of modern predicate logic, who distinguished between direct and indirect occurrences of expressions and would consider the occurrence of *combination(safe1)* in (7) to be indirect and not subject to replacement of equals by equals. The modern way of stating the problem is to call *Pat knows* a referentially opaque operator.

The way out of this difficulty currently most popular is to treat *Pat knows* as a *modal operator*. This involves changing the logic so that replacement of an expression by an equal expression is not allowed in opaque contexts. Knowledge is not the only operator that admits modal treatment. There is also belief, wanting, and logical or physical necessity. For AI purposes, we would need all the above modal operators and many more in the same system. This would make the semantic discussion of the resulting modal logic extremely complex. For this reason, and because we want functions from material objects to concepts of them, we have followed a different path - introducing concepts as individual objects. This has not been popular in philosophy, although I suppose no-one would doubt that it could be done.

Our approach is to introduce the symbol *Safe1* as a name for the concept of safe1 and the function *Combination* which takes a concept of a safe into a concept of its combination. The second operand of the function *knows* is now required to be a concept, and we can write

9) *knows(pat, Combination(Safe1))*

to assert that Pat knows the combination of safe1. The previous trouble is avoided so long as we can assert

10) *Combination(Safe1)* ≠ *Combination(Safe2)*,

which is quite reasonable, since we do not consider the concept of the combination of *safe1* to be the same as the concept of the combination of *safe2*, even if the combinations themselves are the same.

We write

11) *denotes(Safe1, safe1)*

and say that *safe1* is the denotation of *Safe1*. We can say that Pegasus doesn't exist by writing

12) ¬(∃x)(*denotes(Pegasus, x)*)

still admitting *Pegasus* as a perfectly good concept. If we only admit concepts with denotations (or admit partial functions into our system), we can regard denotation as a function from concepts to objects - including other concepts. We can then write

13) *safe1* = *den(Safe1)*.

The functions *combination* and *Combination* are related in a way that we may call extensional, namely

14) (∀S)(*combination(den(S))* = *den(Combination(S))*,

and we can also write this relation in terms of *Combination* alone as

15) (∀S1 S2)(*den(S1)* = *den(S2)* ⊃ *den(Combination(S1))* = *den(Combination(S2))*),

or, in terms of the denotation predicate,

16) (∀S1 S2 s c)(*denotes(S1, s)* ∧ *denotes(S2, s)* ∧ *denotes(Combination(S1), c)* ⊃ *denotes(Combination(S2), c)*).

It is precisely this property of extensionality that the above-mentioned *knows* predicate lac' in its second argument; it is extensional in its first argument.

Suppose we now want to say "*Pat knows that Mike knows the combination of safe1*". We cannot use *knows(mike, Combination(Safe1))* as an operand of another *knows* function for two reasons. First, the value of *knows(person, Concept)* is a truth value, and there are only two truth values, so we would either have Pat knowing all true statements or none. Second, English treats knowledge of propositions differently from the way it treats knowledge of the value of a term. To know a proposition is to know that it is true, whereas the analog of knowing a combination would be knowing whether the proposition is true.

We solve the first problem by introducing a new knowledge function *Knows(Personconcept, Concept)*. *Knows(Mike, Combination(Safe1))* is not a truth value but a *proposition*, and there can be distinct true propositions. We now need a predicate *true(proposition)*, so we can assert

17) *true(Knows(Mike, Combination(Safe1))*

which is equivalent to our old-style assertion

18) *knows(mike, Combination(Safe1))*.

We now write

19) *true(Knows(Pat, Knows(Mike, Combination(Safe1))))*

to assert that Pat knows *whether* Mike knows the combination of safe1. We define

20) (∀ *Person, Proposition*)(*K(Person, Proposition)* = *true(Proposition) and Knows(Person, Proposition)*),

which forms the proposition *that* a person knows a proposition from the truth of the proposition and that he knows whether the proposition holds. Note that it is necessary to have new connectives to combine propositions and that an equality sign rather than an equivalence sign is used. As far as our first order logic is concerned, (20) is an assertion of the equality of two terms. These matters are discussed thoroughly in (McCarthy 1977b).

While a concept denotes at most one object, the same object can be denoted by many concepts. Nevertheless, there are often useful functions from objects to concepts that denote them. Numbers may conveniently be regarded has having *standard concepts*, and an object may have a distinguished concept relative to a particular person. (McCarthy 1977b) illustrates the use of functions from objects to concepts in formalizing such chestnuts as Russell's, "*I thought your yacht was longer than it is*".

The most immediate AI problem that requires concepts for its successful formalism may be the relation between knowledge and ability. We would like to connect Mike's ability to open safe1 with his knowledge of the combination. The proper formalization of the notion of *can* that involves knowledge rather than just physical possibility hasn't been done yet. Moore (1977) discusses the relation between knowledge and action from a similar point of view, and the final version of (McCarthy 1977b) will contain some ideas about this.

There are obviously some esthetic disadvantages to a theory that has both *mike* and *Mike*. Moreover, natural language doesn't make such distinctions in its vocabulary, but in rather roundabout ways when necessary. Perhaps we could manage with just *Mike* (the concept), since the *denotation* function will be available for referring to *mike* (the person himself). It makes some sentences longer, and we have to use and equivalence relation which we may call *eqdenot* and say "*Mike eqdenot Brother(Mary)*" rather than write "*mike* = *brother(mary)*", reserving the equality sign for equal concepts. Since many AI programs don't make much use of replacement of equals by equals, their notation may admit either interpretation, i.e., the formulas may stand for either objects or concepts. The biggest objection is that the semantics of reasoning about objects is more complicated if one refers to them only via concepts.

I believe that circumscription will turn out to be the key to inferring non-knowledge. Unfortunately, an adequate formalism has not yet been developed, so we can only give some ideas of why establishing non-knowledge is important for AI and how circumscription can contribute to it.

If the robot can reason that it cannot open safel, because it doesn't know the combination, it can decide that its next task is to find the combination. However, if it has merely failed to determine the combination by reasoning, more thinking might solve the problem. If it can safely conclude that the combination cannot be determined by reasoning, it can look for the information externally.

As another example, suppose someone asks you whether the President is standing, sitting or lying down at the moment you read the paper. Normally you will answer that you don't know and will not respond to a suggestion that you think harder. You conclude that no matter how hard you think, the information isn't to be found. If you really want to know, you must look for an external source of information. How do you know you can't solve the problem? The intuitive answer is that any answer is consistent with your other knowledge. However, you certainly don't construct a model of all your beliefs to establish this. Since you undoubtedly have some contradictory beliefs somewhere, you can't construct the required models anyway.

The process has two steps. The first is deciding what knowledge is relevant. This is a conjectural process, so its outcome is not guaranteed to be correct. It might be carried out by some kind of keyword retrieval from property lists, but there should be a less arbitrary method.

The second process uses the set of "relevant" sentences found by the first process and constructs models or circumscription predicates that allow for both outcomes if what is to be shown unknown is a proposition. If what is to be shown unknown has many possible values like a safe combination, then something more sophisticated is necessary. A parameter called the value of the combination is introduced, and a "model" or circumscription predicate is found in which this parameter occurs free. We used quotes, because a one parameter family of models is found rather than a single model.

We conclude with just one example of a circumscription schema dealing with knowledge. It is formalization of the assertion that all Mike knows is a consequence of propositions P and Q.

21) $\Phi(P0) \wedge \Phi(Q0) \wedge (\forall P\ Q)(\Phi(P) \wedge \Phi(P\ implies\ Q) \supset \Phi(Q)) \supset (\forall P)(knows(Mike, P) \supset \Phi(P))$.

Philosophical Notes

Philosophy has a more direct relation to artificial intelligence than it has to other sciences. Both subjects require the formalization of common sense knowledge and repair of its deficiencies. Since a robot with general intelligence requires some general view of the world, deficiencies in the programmers' introspection of their own world-views can result in operational weaknesses in the program. Thus many programs, including Winograd's SHRDLU, regard the history of their world as a sequence of situations each of which is produced by an event occuring in a previous situation of the sequence. To handle concurrent events, such programs must be rebuilt and not just provided with more facts.

This section is organized as a collection of disconnected remarks some of which have a direct technical character, while others concern the general structure of knowledge of the world. Some of them simply give sophisticated justifications for some things that programmers are inclined to do anyway, so some people may regard them as superfluous.

1. Building a view of the world into the structure of a program does not in itself give the program the ability to state the view explicitly. Thus, none of the programs that presuppose history as a sequence of situations can make the assertion "*History is a sequence of situations*". Indeed, for a human to make his presuppositions explicit is often beyond his individual capabilities, and the sciences of psychology and philosophy still have unsolved problems in doing so.

2. Common sense requires scientific formulation. Both AI and philosophy require it, and philosophy might even be regarded as an attempt to make common sense into a science.

3. AI and philosophy both suffer from the following dilemma. Both need precise formalizations, but the fundamental structure of the world has not yet been discovered, so imprecise and even inconsistent formulations need to be used. If the imprecision merely concerned the values to be given to numerical constants, there wouldn't be great difficulty, but there is a need to use theories which are grossly wrong in general within domains where they are valid. The above-mentioned *history-as-a-sequence-of-situations* is such a theory. The sense in which this theory is an approximation to a more sophisticated theory hasn't been examined.

4. (McCarthy 1977c) discusses the need to use concepts that are meaningful only in an approximate theory. Relative to a Cartesian product co-ordinatization of situations, counterfactual sentences of the form "*If co-ordinate x had the value c and the other co-ordinates retained their values, then p would be true*" can be meaningful. Thus, within a suitable theory, the assertion "*The skier wouldn't have fallen if he had put his weight on his downhill ski*" is meaningful and perhaps true, but it is hard to give it meaning as a statement about the world of atoms and wave functions, because it is not clear what different wave functions are specified by "*if he had put his weight on his downhill ski*". We need an AI formalism that can use such statements but can go beyond them to the next level of approximation when possible and necessary. I now think that circumscription is a tool that will allow drawing conclusions from a given approximate theory for use in given circumstances without a total commitment to the theory.

5. One can imagine constructing programs either as empiricists or as realists. An empiricist program would build only theories connecting its sense data with its actions. A realist program would try to find facts about a world that existed independently of the program and would not suppose that the only reality is what might somehow interact with the program.

I favor building realist programs with the following example in mind. It has been shown that the Life two dimensional cellular automaton is universal as a computer and as a constructor. Therefore, there could be configurations of Life cells acting as self-reproducing computers with sensory and motor capabilities with respect to the rest of the Life plane. The program in such a computer could study the physics of its world by making theories and experiments to test them and might eventually come up with the theory that its fundamental physics is that of the Life cellular automaton.

We can test our theories of epistemology and common sense reasoning by asking if they would permit the Life-world computer to conclude, on the basis of experiments, that its physics was that of Life. If our epistemology isn't adequate for such a simple universe, it surely isn't good enough for our much more complicated universe. This example is one of the reasons for preferring to build realist rather than empiricist programs. The empiricist program, if it was smart enough, would only end up with a statement that "*my experiences are best organized as if there were a Life cellular automaton and events isomorphic to my thoughts occurred in a certain subconfiguration of it*". Thus it would get a result equivalent to that of the realist program but more complicated and with less certainty.

More generally, we can imagine a *metaphilosophy* that has the same relation to philosophy that metamathematics has to mathematics. Metaphilosophy would study mathematical systems consisting of an "epistemologist" seeking knowledge in accordance with the epistemology to be tested and interacting with a "world". It would study what information about the world a given philosophy would obtain. This would depend also on the structure of the world and the "epistemologist"'s opportunities to interact.

AI could benefit from building some very simple systems of this kind, and so might philosophy.

References

McCarthy, J. and Hayes, P.J. (1969) Some Philosophical Problems from the Standpoint of Artificial Intelligence. *Machine Intelligence* 4, pp. 463-502 (eds Meltzer, B. and Michie, D.). Edinburgh: Edinburgh University Press.

McCarthy, J. (1977a) Minimal Inference - A New Way of Jumping to Conclusions (to be published).

McCarthy, J. (1977b) First Order Theories of Individual Concepts (to be published).

McCarthy, J. (1977c) Ascribing Mental Qualities to Machines (to be published).

Moore, Robert C. (1977) Reasoning about Knowledge and Action, 1977 *IJCAI Proceedings*.

Circumscription—A Form of Non-Monotonic Reasoning

John McCarthy

Stanford University, Stanford, CA, U.S.A.

ABSTRACT

Humans and intelligent computer programs must often jump to the conclusion that the objects they can determine to have certain properties or relations are the only objects that do. Circumscription *formalizes such conjectural reasoning.*

1. Introduction . The Qualification Problem

McCarthy [6] proposed a program with 'common sense' that would represent what it knows (mainly) by sentences in a suitable logical language. It would decide what to do by deducing a conclusion that it should perform a certain act. Performing the act would create a new situation, and it would again decide what to do. This requires representing both knowledge about the particular situation and general common sense knowledge as sentences of logic.

The 'qualification problem', immediately arose in representing general common sense knowledge. It seemed that in order to fully represent the conditions for the successful performance of an action, an impractical and implausible number of qualifications would have to be included in the sentences expressing them. For example, the successful use of a boat to cross a river requires, if the boat is a rowboat, that the oars and rowlocks be present and unbroken, and that they fit each other. Many other qualifications can be added, making the rules for using a rowboat almost impossible to apply, and yet anyone will still be able to think of additional requirements not yet stated.

Circumscription is a rule of conjecture that can be used by a person or program for 'jumping to certain conclusions'. Namely, *the objects that can be shown to have a certain property P by reasoning from certain facts A are all the objects that satisfy P*. More generally, circumscription can be used to conjecture that the tuples $\langle x, y, \ldots, z \rangle$ that can be shown to satisfy a relation $P(x, y, \ldots, z)$ are all the tuples satisfying this relation. Thus we *circumscribe* the set of relevant tuples.

We can postulate that a boat can be used to cross a river unless 'something' prevents it. Then circumscription may be used to conjecture that the only entities that can prevent the use of the boat are those whose existence follows from the facts at hand. If no lack of oars or other circumstance preventing boat use is deducible, then the boat is concluded to be usable. The correctness of this conclusion depends on our having 'taken into account' all relevant facts when we made the circumscription.

Circumscription formalizes several processes of human informal reasoning. For example, common sense reasoning is ordinarily ready to jump to the conclusion that a tool can be used for its intended purpose unless something prevents its use. Considered purely extensionally, such a statement conveys no information; it seems merely to assert that a tool can be used for its intended purpose unless it can't. Heuristically, the statement is not just a tautologous disjunction; it suggests forming a plan to use the tool.

Even when a program does not reach its conclusions by manipulating sentences in a formal language, we can often profitably analyze its behavior by considering it to *believe* certain sentences when it is in certain states, and we can study how these *ascribed beliefs* change with time (see [9]). When we do such analyses, we again discover that successful people and programs must jump to such conclusions.

2. The Need for Non-Monotonic Reasoning

We cannot get circumscriptive reasoning capability by adding sentences to an axiomatization or by adding an ordinary rule of inference to mathematical logic. This is because the well known systems of mathematical logic have the following *monotonicity property*. If a sentence q follows from a collection A of sentences and $A \subset B$, then q follows from B. In the notation of proof theory: if $A \vdash q$ and $A \subset B$, then $B \vdash q$. Indeed a proof from the premisses A is a sequence of sentences each of which is a either a premiss, an axiom or follows from a subset of the sentences occurring earlier in the proof by one of the rules of inference. Therefore, a proof from A can also serve as a proof from B. The semantic notion of entailment is also monotonic; we say that A entails q (written $A \models q$) if q is true in all models of A. But if $A \models q$ and $A \subset B$, then every model of B is also a model of A, which shows that $B \models q$.

Circumspection is a formalized *rule of conjecture* that can be used along with the *rules of inference* of first order logic. *Predicate circumscription* assumes that entities satisfy a given predicate only if they have to on the basis of a collection of facts. *Domain circumscription* conjectures that the 'known' entities are all there are. It turns out that domain circumscription, previously called *minimal inference*, can be subsumed under predicate circumscription.

We will argue using examples that humans use such 'non-monotonic' reasoning and that it is required for intelligent behavior. The default case reasoning of many computer programs [11] and the use of THNOT in MICROPLANNER [12] programs are also examples of non-monotonic reasoning, but possibly of a different kind from those discussed in this paper. Hewitt [5] gives the basic ideas of the PLANNER approach.

The result of applying circumscription to a collection A of facts is a sentence schema that asserts that the only tuples satisfying a predicate $P(x, \ldots, z)$ are those whose doing so follows from the sentences of A. Since adding more sentences to A might make P applicable to more tuples, circumscription is not monotonic. Conclusions derived from circumscription are conjectures that A includes all the relevant facts and that the objects whose existence follows from A are all the relevant objects.

A heuristic program might use circumscription in various ways. Suppose it circumscribes some facts and makes a plan on the basis of the conclusions reached. It might immediately carry out the plan, or be more cautious and look for additional facts that might require modifying it.

Before introducing the formalism, we informally discuss a well known problem whose solution seems to involve such non-monotonic reasoning.

3. Missionaries and Cannibals

The *Missionaries and Cannibals* puzzle, much used in AI, contains more than enough detail to illustrate many of the issues.

> "Three missionaries and three cannibals come to a river. A rowboat that seats two is available. If the cannibals ever outnumber the missionaries on either bank of the river, the missionaries will be eaten. How shall they cross the river"

Obviously the puzzler is expected to devise a strategy of rowing the boat back and forth that gets them all across and avoids the disaster.

Amarel [1] considered several representations of the problem and discussed criteria whereby the following representation is preferred for purposes of AI, because it leads to the smallest state space that must be explored to find the solution. A state is a triple comprising the numbers of missionaries, cannibals and boats on the starting bank of the river. The initial state is 331, the desired final state is 000, and one solution is given by the sequence (331, 220, 321, 300, 311, 110, 221, 020, 031, 010, 021, 000).

We are not presently concerned with the heuristics of the problem but rather with the correctness of the reasoning that goes from the English statement of the problem to Amarel's state space representation. A generally intelligent computer program should be able to carry out this reasoning. Of course, there are the well known difficulties in making computers understand English, but suppose the English sentences describing the problem have already been rather directly translated into first order logic. The correctness of Amarel's representation is not an ordinary logical consequence of these sentences for two further reasons.

First, nothing has been stated about the properties of boats or even the fact that rowing across the river doesn't change the numbers of missionaries or cannibals or the capacity of the boat. Indeed it hasn't been stated that situations change as a result of action. These facts follow from common sense knowledge, so let us imagine that common sense knowledge, or at least the relevant part of it, is also expressed in first order logic.

The second reason we can't *deduce* the propriety of Amarel's representation is deeper. Imagine giving someone the problem, and after he puzzles for a while, he suggests going upstream half a mile and crossing on a bridge. "What bridge," you say. "No bridge is mentioned in the statement of the problem." And this dunce replies, "Well, they don't say there isn't a bridge." You look at the English and even at the translation of the English into first order logic, and you must admit that "they don't say" there is no bridge. So you modify the problem to exclude bridges and pose it again, and the dunce proposes a helicopter, and after you exclude that, he proposes a winged horse or that the others hang onto the outside of the boat while two row.

You now see that while a dunce, he is an inventive dunce. Despairing of getting him to accept the problem in the proper puzzler's spirit, you tell him the solution. To your further annoyance, he attacks your solution on the grounds that the boat might have a leak or lack oars. After you rectify that omission from the statement of the problem, he suggests that a sea monster may swim up the river and may swallow the boat. Again you are frustrated, and you look for a mode of reasoning that will settle his hash once and for all.

In spite of our irritation with the dunce, it would be cheating to put into the statement of the problem that there is no other way to cross the river than using the boat and that nothing can go wrong with the boat. A human doesn't need such an ad hoc narrowing of the problem, and indeed the only watertight way to do it might amount to specifying the Amarel representation in English. Rather we want to avoid the excessive qualification and get the Amarel representation by common sense reasoning as humans ordinarily do.

Circumscription is one candidate for accomplishing this. It will allow us to conjecture that no relevant objects exist in certain categories except those whose existence follows from the statement of the problem and common sense knowledge. When we *circumscribe* the first order logic statement of the problem together with the common sense facts about boats etc., we will be able to conclude that there is no bridge or helicopter. "Aha," you say, "but there won't be any oars either." No, we get out of that as follows: It is a part of common knowledge that a boat can be used to cross a river *unless there is something wrong with it or something else prevents using it*, and if our facts do not require that there be something that prevents crossing the river, circumscription will generate the conjecture that there isn't. The price is introducing as entities in our language the 'somethings' that may prevent the use of the boat.

If the statement of the problem were extended to mention a bridge, then the circumscription of the problem statement would no longer permit showing the non-existence of a bridge, i.e., a conclusion that can be drawn from a smaller collection of facts can no longer be drawn from a larger. This non-monotonic character of circumscription is just what we want for this kind of problem. The statement, "*There is a bridge a mile upstream, and the boat has a leak.*" doesn't contradict the text of the problem, but its addition invalidates the Amarel representation.

In the usual sort of puzzle, there is a convention that there are no additional objects beyond those mentioned in the puzzle or whose existence is deducible from the puzzle and common sense knowledge. The convention can be explicated as applying circumscription to the puzzle statement and a certain part of common sense knowledge. However, if one really were sitting by a river bank and these six people came by and posed their problem, one wouldn't take the circumscription for granted, but one *would* consider the result of circumscription as a hypothesis. In puzzles, circumscription seems to be a rule of inference, while in life it is a rule of conjecture.

Some have suggested that the difficulties might be avoided by introducing probabilities. They suggest that the existence of a bridge is improbable. The whole situation involving cannibals with the postulated properties cannot be regarded as having a probability, so it is hard to take seriously the conditional probability of a bridge given the hypotheses. More to the point, we mentally propose to ourselves the normal non-bridge non-sea-monster interpretation *before* considering these extraneous possibilities, let alone their probabilities, i.e. we usually don't even introduce the sample space in which these possibilities are assigned whatever probabilities one might consider them to have. Therefore, regardless of our knowledge of probabilities, we need a way of formulating the normal situation from the statement of the facts, and non-monotonic reasoning seems to be required. The same considerations seem to apply to fuzzy logic.

Using circumscription requires that common sense knowledge be expressed in a form that says a boat can be used to cross rivers unless there is something that prevents its use. In particular, it looks like we must introduce into our *ontology* (the things that exist) a category that includes *something wrong with a boat* or a category that includes *something that may prevent its use*. Incidentally, once we have decided to admit *something wrong with the boat*, we are inclined to admit a *lack of oars* as such a something and to ask questions like, "*Is a lack of oars all that is wrong with the boat?*"

Some philosophers and scientists may be reluctant to introduce such *things*, but since ordinary language allows "*something wrong with the boat*" we shouldn't be hasty in excluding it. Making a suitable formalism is likely to be technically difficult as well as philosophically problematical, but we must try.

We challenge anyone who thinks he can avoid such entities to express in his favorite formalism, "*Besides leakiness, there is something else wrong with the boat.*" A good solution would avoid counterfactuals as this one does.

Circumscription may help understand natural language, because if the use of natural language involves something like circumscription, it is understandable that the expression of general common sense facts in natural language will be difficult without some form of non-monotonic reasoning.

4. The Formalism of Circumscription

Let A be a sentence of first order logic containing a predicate symbol $P(x_1, \ldots, x_n)$ which we will write $P(\bar{x})$. We write $A(\Phi)$ for the result of replacing all occurrences of P in A by the predicate expression Φ. (As well as predicate symbols, suitable λ-expressions are allowed as predicate expressions).

Definition *The circumscription of P in $A(P)$* is the sentence schema

$$A(\Phi) \wedge \forall\bar{x}.(\Phi(\bar{x}) \supset P(\bar{x})) \supset \forall\bar{x}.(P(\bar{x}) \supset \Phi(\bar{x})). \tag{1}$$

(1) can be regarded as asserting that the only tuples $(\bar{x})$ that satisfy P are those that have to—assuming the sentence A. Namely, (1) contains a predicate parameter Φ for which we may substitute an arbitrary predicate expression. (If we were using second order logic, there would be a quantifier $\forall\Phi$ in front of (1).) Since (1) is an implication, we can assume both conjuncts on the left, and (1) lets us conclude the sentence on the right. The first conjunct $A(\Phi)$ expresses the assumption that Φ satisfies the conditions satisfied by P, and the second $\forall\bar{x}.(\Phi(\bar{x}) \supset P(\bar{x}))$ expresses the assumption that the entities satisfying Φ are a subset of those that satisfy P. The conclusion asserts the converse of the second conjunct which tells us that in this case, Φ and P must coincide.

We write $A \vdash_P q$ if the sentence q can be obtained by deduction from the result of circumscribing P in A. As we shall see $\vdash_P$ is a non-monotonic form of inference, which we shall call *circumscriptive inference*.

A slight generalization allows circumscribing several predicates jointly; thus jointly circumscribing P and Q in $A(P, Q)$ leads to

$$A(\Phi, \Psi) \wedge \forall\bar{x}.(\Phi(\bar{x}) \supset P(\bar{x})) \wedge \forall\bar{y}.(\Psi(\bar{y}) \supset Q(\bar{y})) \\ \supset \forall\bar{x}.(P(\bar{x}) \supset \Phi(\bar{x})) \wedge \forall\bar{y}.(Q(\bar{y}) \supset \Psi(\bar{y})) \tag{2}$$

in which we can simultaneously substitute for Φ and Ψ. The relation $A \vdash_{P,Q} q$ is defined in a corresponding way. Although we do not give examples of joint circumscription in this paper, we believe it will be important in some AI applications.

Consider the following examples:

Example 1. In the blocks world, the sentence A may be

$$isblock\ A \wedge isblock\ B \wedge isblock\ C \tag{3}$$

asserting that A, B and C are blocks. Circumscribing *isblock* in (3) gives the schema

$$\Phi(A) \wedge \Phi(B) \wedge \Phi(C) \wedge \forall x.(\Phi(x) \supset isblock\ x) \supset \forall x.(isblock\ x \supset \Phi(x)). \tag{4}$$

If we now substitute

$$\Phi(x) \equiv (x = A \vee x = B \vee x = C) \tag{5}$$

into (4) and use (3), the left side of the implication is seen to be true, and this gives

$$\forall x.(isblock\ x \supset (x = A \vee x = B \vee x = C)), \tag{6}$$

which asserts that the only blocks are A, B and C, i.e. just those objects that (3) requires to be blocks. This example is rather trivial, because (3) provides no way of generating new blocks from old ones. However, it shows that circumscriptive inference is non-monotonic since if we adjoin *isblock* D to (3), we will no longer be able to infer (6).

Example 2. Circumscribing the disjunction

$$\textit{isblock}\ A \vee \textit{isblock}\ B \tag{7}$$

leads to

$$(\Phi(A) \vee \Phi(B)) \wedge \forall x.(\Phi(x) \supset \textit{isblock}\ x) \supset \forall x.(\textit{isblock}\ x \supset \Phi(x)). \tag{8}$$

We may then substitute successively $\Phi(x) \equiv (x = A)$ and $\Phi(x) \equiv (x = B)$, and these give respectively

$$(A = A \vee A = B) \wedge \forall x.(x = A \supset \textit{isblock}\ x) \supset \forall x.(\textit{isblock}\ x \supset x = A), \tag{9}$$

which simplifies to

$$\textit{isblock}\ A \supset \forall x.(\textit{isblock}\ x \supset x = A) \tag{10}$$

and

$$(B = A \vee B = B) \wedge \forall x.(x = B \supset \textit{isblock}\ x) \supset \forall x.(\textit{isblock}\ x \supset x = B), \tag{11}$$

which simplifies to

$$\textit{isblock}\ B \supset \forall x.(\textit{isblock}\ x \supset x = B). \tag{12}$$

(10), (12) and (7) yield

$$\forall x.(\textit{isblock}\ x \supset x = A) \vee \forall x.(\textit{isblock}\ x \supset x = B), \tag{13}$$

which asserts that either A is the only block or B is the only block.

Example 3. Consider the following algebraic axioms for natural numbers, i.e., non-negative integers, appropriate when we aren't supposing that natural numbers are the only objects.

$$\textit{isnatnum}\ 0 \wedge \forall x.(\textit{isnatnum}\ x \supset \textit{isnatnum succ}\ x). \tag{14}$$

Circumscribing *isnatnum* in (14) yields

$$\Phi(0) \wedge \forall x.(\Phi(x) \supset \Phi(\textit{succ}\ x)) \wedge \forall x.(\Phi(x) \supset \textit{isnatnum}\ x) \supset \forall x.(\textit{isnatnum}\ x \supset \Phi(x)). \tag{15}$$

(15) asserts that the only natural numbers are those objects that (14) forces to be natural numbers, and this is essentially the usual axiom schema of induction. We can get closer to the usual schema by substituting $\Phi(x) \equiv \Psi(x) \wedge \textit{isnatnum}\ x$. This and (14) make the second conjunct drop out giving

$$\Psi(0) \wedge \forall x.(\Psi(x) \supset \Psi(\textit{succ}\ x)) \supset \forall x.(\textit{isnatnum}\ x \supset \Psi(x)). \tag{16}$$

Example 4. Returning to the blocks world, suppose we have a predicate $on(x, y, s)$ asserting that block x is on block y in situation s. Suppose we have another predicate $above(x, y, s)$ which asserts that block x is above block y in situation s. We may write

$$\forall x\, y\, s.(on(x, y, s) \supset above(x, y, s)) \tag{17}$$

and

$$\forall x\, y\, z\, s.(above(x, y, s) \wedge above(y, z, s) \supset above(x, z, s)), \tag{18}$$

i.e., *above* is a transitive relation. Circumscribing *above* in (17) and (18) gives

$$\begin{aligned} &\forall x\, y\, s.(on(x, y, s) \supset \Phi(x, y, s)) \\ &\wedge \forall x\, y\, z\, s.(\Phi(x, y, s) \wedge \Phi(y, z, s) \supset \Phi(x, z, s)) \\ &\wedge \forall x\, y\, s.(\Phi(x, y, s) \supset above(x, y, s)) \\ &\quad \supset \forall x\, y\, s.(above(x, y, s) \supset \Phi(x, y, s)) \end{aligned} \tag{19}$$

which tells us that *above* is the transitive closure of *on*.

In the preceding two examples, the schemas produced by circumscription play the role of axiom schemas rather than being just conjectures.

5. Domain Circumscription

The form of circumscription described in this paper generalizes an earlier version called *minimal inference*. Minimal inference has a semantic counterpart called *minimal entailment*, and both are discussed in [8] and more extensively in [3]. The general idea of minimal entailment is that a sentence q is minimally entailed by an axiom A, written $A \models_m q$, if q is true in all *minimal models* of A, where one model if is considered less than another if they agree on common elements, but the domain of the larger many contain elements not in the domain of the smaller. We shall call the earlier form *domain circumscription* to contrast it with the *predicate circumscription* discussed in this paper.

The domain circumscription of the sentence A is the sentence

$$Axiom(\Phi) \wedge A^{\Phi} \supset \forall x.\Phi(x). \tag{20}$$

where A^{Φ} is the relativization of A with respect to Φ and is formed by replacing each universal quantifier $\forall x.$ in A by $\forall x.\Phi(x) \supset$ and each existential quantifier $\exists x.$ by $\exists x.\Phi(x) \wedge$. $Axiom(\Phi)$ is the conjunction of sentences $\Phi(a)$ for each constant a and sentences $\forall x.(\Phi(x) \supset \Phi(f(x)))$ for each function symbol f and the corresponding sentences for functions of higher arities.

Domain circumscription can be reduced to predicate circumscription by relativizing A with respect to a new one place predicate called (say) *all*, then circumscribing *all* in $A^{all} \wedge Axiom(all)$, thus getting

$$Axiom(\Phi) \wedge A^{\Phi} \wedge \forall x.(\Phi(x) \supset all(x)) \supset \forall x.(all(x) \supset \Phi(x)). \quad (21)$$

Now we justify our using the name all by adding the axiom $\forall x.all(x)$ so that (21) then simplifies precisely to (20).

In the case of the natural numbers, the domain circumscription of true, the identically true sentence, again leads to the axiom schema of induction. Here *Axiom* does all the work, because it asserts that 0 is in the domain and that the domain is closed under the successor operation.

6. The Model Theory of Predicate Circumscription

This treatment is similar to Davis's [3] treatment of domain circumscription. Pat Hayes [4] pointed out that the same ideas would work.

The intuitive idea of circumscription is saying that a tuple $\bar{x}$ satisfies the predicate P only if it has to. It has to satisfy P if this follows from the sentence A. The model-theoretic counterpart of circumscription is *minimal entailment*. A sentence q is minimally entailed by A, iff q is true in all minimal models of A, where a model is minimal if as few as possible tuples $\bar{x}$ satisfy the predicate P. More formally, this works out as follows.

Definition. Let $M(A)$ and $N(A)$ be models of the sentence A. We say that *M is a submodel of N in P*, writing $M \leqslant_P N$, if M and N have the same domain, all other predicate symbols in A besides P have the same extensions in M and N, but the extension of P in M is included in its extension in N.

Definition. A model M of A is called *minimal in P* iff $M' \leqslant_P M$ only if $M' = M$. As discussed by Davis [3], minimal models do not always exist.

Definition. We say that *A minimally entails q with respect to P*, written $A \models_P q$ provided q is true in all models of A that are minimal in P.

Theorem. *Any instance of the circumscription of P in A is true in all models of A minimal in P, i.e., is minimally entailed by A in P.*

Proof. Let M be a model of A minimal in P. Let P' be a predicate satisfying the left side of (1) when substituted for Φ. By the second conjunct of the left side, P is an extension of P'. If the right side of (1) were not satisfied, P would be a proper extension of P'. In that case, we could get a proper submodel M' of M by letting M' agree with M on all predicates except P and agree with P' on P. This would contradict the assumed minimality of M.

Corollary. *If $A \vdash_P q$, then $A \models_P q$.*

While we have discussed minimal entailment in a single predicate P, the relation $<_{P,Q}$, models minimal in P and Q, and $\models_{P,Q}$ have corresponding properties and a corresponding relation to the syntactic notion $\vdash_{P,Q}$ mentioned earlier.

7. More on Blocks

The axiom

$$\forall x\, y\, s.(\forall z.\ \neg prevents(z, move(x, y), s) \supset on(x, y, result(move(x, y), s))) \quad (22)$$

states that unless something prevents it, x is on y in the situation that results from the action $move(x, y)$.

We now list various 'things' that may prevent this action.

$$\forall x\, y\, s.(\neg isblock\ x \vee \neg isblock\ y$$
$$\supset prevents(NONBLOCK, move(x, y), s)) \quad (23)$$

$$\forall x\, y\, s.(\neg clear(x, s) \vee \neg clear(y, s)$$
$$\supset prevents(COVERED, move(x, y), s)) \quad (24)$$

$$\forall x\, y\, s.(tooheavy\ x \supset prevents(weight\ x, move(x, y), s)). \quad (25)$$

Let us now suppose that a heuristic program would like to move block A onto block C in a situation $s0$. The program should conjecture from (22) that the action $move(A, C)$ would have the desired effect, so it must try to establish $\forall z. \neg prevents(z, move(A, C), s0)$. The predicate $\lambda z.prevents(z, move(A, C), s0)$ can be circumscribed in the conjunction of the sentences resulting from specializing (23), (24) and (25), and this gives

$$(\neg isblock\ A \vee \neg isblock\ C \supset \Phi(NONBLOCK))$$
$$\wedge\ (\neg clear(A, s0) \vee \neg clear(C, s0) \supset \Phi(COVERED))$$
$$\wedge\ (tooheavy\ A \supset \Phi(weight\ A))$$
$$\wedge\ \forall z.(\Phi(z) \supset prevents(z, move(A, C), s0))$$
$$\supset \forall z.(prevents(z, move(A, C), s0) \supset \Phi(z)) \quad (26)$$

which says that the only things that can prevent the move are the phenomena described in (23)–(25). Whether (26) is true depends on how good the program was in finding all the relevant statements. Since the program wants to show that nothing prevents the move, it must set $\forall z.(\Phi(z) \equiv false)$, after which (26) simplifies to

$$(isblock\ A \wedge isblock\ B \wedge clear(A, s0) \wedge clear(B, s0) \wedge \neg tooheavy\ A$$
$$\supset \forall z. \neg prevents(z, move(A, C), s0). \quad (27)$$

We suppose that the premisses of this implication are to be obtained as follows:

(1) *isblock A* and *isblock B* are explicitly asserted.

(2) Suppose that the only *on*ness assertion explicitly given for situation *s*0 is $on(A, B, s0)$. Circumscription of $\lambda x\, y. on(x, y, s0)$ in this assertion gives

$$\Phi(A, B) \wedge \forall x\, y.(\Phi(x, y) \supset on(x, y, s0)) \supset \forall x\, y.(on(x, y, s0) \supset \Phi(x, y)), \tag{28}$$

and taking $\Phi(x, y) \equiv x = A \wedge y = B$ yields

$$\forall x\, y.(on(x, y, s0) \supset x = A \wedge y = B). \tag{29}$$

Using

$$\forall x\, s.(clear(x, s) \equiv \forall y. \neg on(y, x, s)) \tag{30}$$

as the definition of *clear* yields the second two desired premisses.

(3) $\neg tooheavy(x)$ might be explicitly present or it might also be conjectured by a circumscription assuming that if x were too heavy, the facts would establish it.

Circumscription may also be convenient for asserting that when a block is moved, everything that cannot be proved to move stays where it was. In the simple blocks world, the effect of this can easily be achieved by an axiom that states that all blocks except the one that is moved stay put. However, if there are various sentences that say (for example) that one block is attached to another, circumscription may express the heuristic situation better than an axiom.

8. Remarks and Acknowledgments

(1) Circumscription is not a 'non-monotonic logic.' It is a form of non-monotonic reasoning augmenting ordinary first order logic. Of course, sentence schemata are not properly handled by most present general purpose resolution theorem provers. Even fixed schemata of mathematical induction when used for proving programs correct usually require human intervention or special heuristics, while here the program would have to use new schemata produced by circumscription. In [10] we treat some modalities in first order logic instead of in modal logic. In our opinion, it is better to avoid modifying the logic if at all possible, because there are many temptations to modify the logic, and it would be very difficult to keep them compatible.

(2) The default case reasoning provided in many systems is less general than circumscription. Suppose, for example, that a block x is considered to be on a block y only if this is explicitly stated, i.e., the default is that x is not on y. Then for each individual block x, we may be able to conclude that it isn't on block A, but we will not be able to conclude, as circumscription would allow, that there are no blocks on A. That would require a separate default statement that a block is clear unless something is stated to be on it.

(3) The conjunct $\forall \bar{x}.(\Phi(\bar{x}) \supset P(\bar{x}))$ in the premiss of (1) is the result of suggestions by Ashok Chandra [2] and Patrick Hayes [4] whom I thank for their help. Without it, circumscribing a disjunction, as in the second example in Section 4, would lead to a contradiction.

(4) The most direct way of using circumscription in AI is in a heuristic reasoning program that represents much of what it believes by sentences of logic. The program would sometimes apply circumscription to certain predicates in sentences. In particular, when it wants to perform an action that might be prevented by something, it circumscribes the prevention predicate in a sentence A representing the information being taken into account.

Clearly the program will have to include domain dependent heuristics for deciding what circumscriptions to make and when to take them back.

(5) In circumscription it does no harm to take irrelevant facts into account. If these facts do not contain the predicate symbol being circumscribed, they will appear as conjuncts on the left side of the implication unchanged. Therefore, the original versions of these facts can be used in proving the left side.

(6) Circumscription can be used in other formalisms than first order logic. Suppose for example that a set a satisfies a formula $A(a)$ of set theory. The circumscription of this formula can be taken to be

$$\forall x.(A(x) \wedge (x \subset a) \supset (a \subset x)). \tag{31}$$

If a occurs in $A(a)$ only in expressions of the form $z \in a$, then its mathematical properties should be analogous to those of predicate circumscription. We have not explored what happens if formulas like $a \in z$ occur.

(7) The results of circumscription depend on the set of predicates used to express the facts. For example, the same facts about the blocks world can be axiomatized using the relation *on* or the relation *above* considered in Section 4 or also in terms of the heights and horizontal positions of the blocks. Since the results of circumscription will differ according to which representation is chosen, we see that the choice of representation has epistemological consequences if circumscription is admitted as a rule of conjecture. Choosing the set of predicates in terms of which to axiomatize as set of facts, such as those about blocks, is like choosing a co-ordinate system in physics or geography. As discussed in [9], certain concepts are definable only relative to a theory. What theory admits the most useful kinds of circumscription may be an important criterion in the choice of predicates. It may also be possible to make some statements about a domain like the blocks world in a form that does not depend on the language used.

(8) This investigation was supported in part by ARPA Contract MDA–903–76–C–0206, ARPA Order No. 2494, in part by NSF Grant MCS 78–00524, in part by the IBM 1979 Distinguished Faculty Program at the T. J. Watson Research Center, and in part by the Center for Advanced Study in the Behavioral Sciences.

REFERENCES

1. Amarel, S., On representation of problems of reasoning about actions, in D. Michie (Ed.) *Machine Intelligence* 3 (Edinburgh University Press, Edinburgh, 1971), pp. 131–171.
2. Chandra, A., personal conversation (August 1979).
3. Davis, M., Notes on the mathematics of non-monotonic reasoning. *Artificial Intelligence*, this issue.

4. Hayes, P., personal conversation (September 1979).
5. Hewitt, C., Description and theoretical analysis (using schemata) of PLANNER: a language for proving theorems and manipulating models in a robot, MIT AI Laboratory TR-258 (1972).
6. McCarthy, J., Programs with common sense, in: *Proceedings of the Teddington Conference on the Mechanization of Thought Processes* (H.M. Stationery Office, London, 1960).
7. McCarthy, J., and Hayes, P., Some philosophical problems from the standpoint of Artificial Intelligence, in: D. Michie (Ed.), *Machine Intelligence* **4** (American Elsevier, New York, NY, 1969).
8. McCarthy, J., Epistemological problems of artificial intelligence, in: *Proceedings of the Fifth International Joint Conference on Artificial Intelligence* (MIT, Cambridge, MA, 1977).
9. McCarthy, J., Ascribing mental qualities to machines, in: M. Ringle (Ed.), *Philosophical Perspectives in Artificial Intelligence* (Harvester Press, July 1979).
10. McCarthy, J., First order theories of individual concepts and propositions, in: D. Michie (Ed.), *Machine Intelligence* **9** (University of Edinburgh Press, Edinburgh, 1979).
11. Reiter, R., A logic for default reasoning, *Artificial Intelligence*, this issue.
12. Sussman, G. J., Winograd, T., and Charniak, E., Micro-Planner Reference Manual, AI Memo 203, MIT AI Lab. (1971).

REASONING ABOUT KNOWLEDGE AND ACTION

Robert C. Moore
Artificial Intelligence Laboratory
Stanford University
Stanford, California 94305

Abstract

This paper discusses the problems of representing and reasoning with information about knowledge and action. The first section discusses the importance of having systems that understand the concept of knowledge, and how knowledge is related to action. Section 2 points out some of the special problems that are involved in reasoning about knowledge, and section 3 presents a logic of knowledge based on the idea of possible worlds. Section 4 integrates this with a logic of actions and gives an example of reasoning in the combined system. Section 5 makes some concluding comments.

1. Introduction

One of the most important concepts an intelligent system needs to understand is the concept of knowledge. AI systems need to understand what knowledge they and the systems or people they interact with have, what knowledge is needed to achieve particular goals, and how that knowledge can be obtained. This paper develops a formalism that provides a framework for stating and solving problems like these. For example, suppose that there is a safe that John wants to open. The common sense inferences that we would like to make might include:

> If John knows the combination, he can immediately open the safe.
>
> If John does not know the combination, he cannot immediately open the safe.
>
> If John knows where the combination is written, he can read the combination and then open the safe.

In thinking about this example, consider how intimately the concept of knowledge is tied up with action. Reasoning about knowledge alone is of limited value. We may want to conclude from the fact that John knows A and B that he must also know C and D, but the real importance of such information is usually that it tells us something about what John can do or is likely to do. A major goal of my research has been to work out some of the interactions of knowing and doing.

That this area has received little attention in AI is somewhat surprising. It is frequently stated that good interactive AI programs will require good models of the people they are communicating with. Surely, one of the most important aspects of a model of another person is a model of what he knows. The only serious work on these problems in AI which I am aware of is a brief disscussion in McCarthy and Hayes (1969), and some more recent unpublished writings of McCarthy. In philosophy there is a substantial literature on the logic of knowledge and belief. A good introduction to this is Hintikka (1962) and papers by Quine, Kaplan, and Hintikka in Linsky (1971). Many of the ideas I will use come from these papers.

In representing facts about knowledge and actions, I will use first-order predicate calculus, a practice which is currently unfashionable. It seems to be widely believed that use of predicate calculus necessarily leads to inefficient reasoning and information retrieval programs. I believe that this is an over-reaction to earlier attempts to build domain-independent theorem provers based on resolution. More recent research, including my own M.S. thesis (Moore, 1975), suggests that predicate calculus can be treated in a more natural manner than resolution and combined with domain-dependent control information for greater efficiency. Furthermore, the problems of reasoning about knowledge seem to require the full ability to handle quantifiers and logical connectives which only predicate calculus posseses.

Section 2 of this paper attempts to bring out some of the special problems involved in reasoning about knowledge. Section 3 presents a formalism which I believe solves these problems, and Section 4 integrates this with a formalism for actions. Section 5 makes some concluding comments.

2. Problems in Reasoning about Knowledge

Reasoning about knowledge presents special difficulties. It turns out that we cannot treat "know" as just another relation. If we can represent "Block1 is on Block2" by On(Block1,Block2), we might be tempted to represent "John knows that P" simply by Know(John,P). This approach glosses over a number of problems. We might be suspicious from the first, since P is not the name of an object but is rather a sentence (or proposition). The semantics of predicate calculus forbid the arbitrary intermingling of sentences and terms for good reason. For one thing, the second argument position of Know is a *referentially opaque context*. Ordinarily in logic we can freely substitute an expression for one that is extensionally equivalent (i.e., one that has the same referent or truth value), without affecting the truth of the formula that contains the expression. This is called *referential transparency*. For example, if X + Y = 7 and X = 3, then 3 + Y = 7. This pattern of reasoning is not valid with Know. We cannot infer from Know(John,(X + Y = 7)) and X = 3 that Know(John,(3 + Y = 7)) is true, since John might not know the value of X.

One possible solution to this problem is to make the second argument of Know the name of a formula rather than the formula itself. This is essentially the same idea as Goedel numbering, although it is not necessary to use such an obscure encoding as the natural numbers. We won't specify exactly how the encoding is done, but simply use "P" to represent a term denoting the formula P. The representation of "John knows that P" now becomes Know(John,"P"). We are no longer in any danger of infering Know(John,"P(A)") from Know(John,"P(B)") and A = B, because A is not contained in "P(A)". Only the name of A, i.e. "A", is contained, and since "A" does not equal "B", there is no problem.

There is, however, a more serious problem, the fact that people can reason with their knowledge. We would expect a reasoning system to have built into it the ability to conclude B from A and A ⊃ B. But if we treat Know as just an ordinary predicate, we will have no reason to suppose that Know(John,"A") and Know(John,"A ⊃ B") might suggest Know(John,"B"). This problem is emphasised by the fact that there is no formal connection between a formula and its name. The fact that we regard "P" as the name of P is entirely outside the system. To get around this, it is necessary to re-axiomatize the rules of logic within the system, e.g. ∀a,p,q(Know(a,"p ⊃ q") ∧ Know(a,"p") ⊃ Know(a,"q")). But if we hope to do automated reasoning, this amounts to re-programming the deductive system in first-order logic, and using the top-level inference routines as the interpreter. When we consider the complexities of quantification and matching, it seems likely that this would be an inefficient process.

A different idea which initially seems very appealing is to use the multiple data-base capabilities of advanced AI languages to set up a separate data base for each person whose knowledge we have some information about. We then can record what we know about his knowledge in that data base, and simulate his reasoning by running our standard inference routines in that data base. This idea seems to have wide currency in AI circles, and I advocated it myself in an earlier paper (Moore, 1973).

Unfortunately, it doesn't work very well. It can handle simple statements of the form "John knows that P," but more complicated expressions cause trouble. Consider "John knows that P or John knows that Q." We can't represent this by simply adding "P or Q" to the data base representing John's knowledge, because this would mean "John knows that P or Q," - something quite different. We could try setting up two data bases, DB1 and DB2, add "P" to one and "Q" to the other, and then assert in the main data base "DB1 represents John's knowledge, or DB2 represents John's knowledge." However, if we also wanted to assert "John knows that C, or John knows that D, or John knows that E," we would need *six* data bases to represent all the possibilites for John's knowledge - one for each of the combinations "A" and "C", "B" and "C", "A" and "D", etc. As we add more disjunctive assertions, we get a combinatorial explosion in the number of data bases.

We also have a problem in representing "John doesn't know that P." We can't add "not P" to John's data base, because this would be asserting "John knows that not P," and simply omitting "P" from John's data base means that *we* don't know whether John knows that P. So it seems that what John doesn't know has to be kept separate from what he does know. But there are inferences that require looking at both. For example, if we have "John doesn't know that P," and "John knows that Q implies P," we might want to conclude that "John doesn't know that Q," is probably true. This is representative of a class of inferences that the data base approach doesn't capture. There seems to be a fundamental problem in saying things about a person's knowledge that go beyond simply enumerating what he knows.

3. Reasoning about Knowledge via Possible Worlds

While there may be ways to directly attack the difficulties we have been discussing, there is a way to avoid them entirely by reformulating the problem in terms of possible worlds. When we want to reason about someone's knowledge, rather than talking about what facts he knows, we will talk about which of the various possible worlds might be, so far as he knows, the real world. A person is never completely sure which possible world (or possible state of *the* world) he is in, because his knowledge is incomplete. We will be willing to conclude that a person knows a particular fact, if the fact is true in all the worlds that are possible according to what he knows. This idea is due to Hintikka (1969), and is an adaptation of the semantics for modal logic developed chiefly by Kripke (1963).

Hintikka uses these ideas about possible worlds to provide a model theory for a modal logic of knowledge. In order to use this theory directly for reasoning, we will axiomatize it in first-order logic. To do this, we must encode a language that talks about knowing facts (which we will call the object language) into term expressions of a first-order language that talks about possible worlds (which we will call the meta-language). Then we will have a relation T, such that T(W,P) means the object-language formula denoted by P is true in the possible world denoted by W. So that we can talk more easily about truth in the actual world, we will have a predicate True, such that True(P) ≡ T(W0,P), where W0 is a constant which refers to the actual world. We will also have a relation K(A,W1,W2), which means that W2 is a world which is possible according to what A knows in W1. The fundamental axiom of knowledge is then ∀w1,a,p(T(w1,Know(a,p) ≡ ∀w2(K(a,w1,w2) ⊃ T(w2,p)). This simply says that a person knows the facts that are true in every world that is possible according to what he knows.

One problem with this axiom is that it is not universally true. For a person to know everything that is true in all worlds which are possible as far as he knows, he would have to know all the logical consequences of his knowledge. Of course, he can know only some of them. But in any particular case, if we can see that a certain conclusion follows from someone's knowledge, we are probably justified in assuming that he can see this also. So we can regard this axiom as a rule of plausible inference, using it when needed, but being prepared to retract our conclusions if they generate contradictions. I will not attempt here to devlop a general theory of plausible reasoning, but I believe that a theory can be worked out that will allow us to use this axiom in essentially its current form.

I should clarify what type of possible worlds I have in mind. Rather than all logically possible worlds, we will consider only those worlds which are possible according to "common knowledge". So, I will feel free to say that facts like "Fish live in water," are true in all possible worlds. This gives us an easy way of saying that not only does everyone know something, but everyone knows that everyone knows it, and everyone knows that everyone knows that everyone knows, etc.

We can now give the full axiomatization of knowledge in terms of possible worlds:

L1. True(p1) ≡ T(W0,p1)
L2. T(w1,(p1 And p2)) ≡ (T(w1,p1) ∧ T(w1,p2))
L3. T(w1,(p1 Or p2)) ≡ (T(w1,p1) ∨ T(w1,p2))
L4. T(w1,(p1 => p2)) ≡ (T(w1,p1) ⊃ T(w1,p2))
L5. T(w1,(p1 <=> p2)) ≡ (T(w1,p1) ≡ T(w1,p2))
L6. T(w1,Not(p1)) ≡ ¬T(w1,p1)

K1. T(w1,Know(a1,p1)) ≡ ∀w2(K(a1,w1,w2) ⊃ T(w2,p1))
K2. K(a1,w1,w1)
K3. K(a1,w1,w2) ⊃ (K(a1,w2,w3) ⊃ K(a1,w1,w3))
K4. K(a1,w1,w2) ⊃ (K(a1,w1,w3) ⊃ K(a1,w2,w3))

Axioms L1 - L6 just translate the logical connectives from the object language to the meta-language, using the ordinary Tarski definition of truth. For instance, according to L2, (A And B) is true in a world if and only if A is true in the world and B is true in the world. K1 is the fundamental axiom of knowledge which we already looked at. says that each world is possible as far as anyone in that world can tell, which is another way of saying that if something is known then it is true. Although it may not be obvious, K3 and K4 imply that everyone knows whether he knows a certain fact. K2 - K4 imply that for fixed A, K(A,w1,w2) is an equivalence relation. This makes our logic of knowledge isomorphic to the modal logic S5. The correspondence between various modal logics and and possible-worlds models for them is discussed in Kripke(1963).

This representation gives us what we need. The meta-language translations of the object-language statements have a structure that reflects their logical properties. To illustrate the use of these axioms, we can prove that people can do simple inferences:

Given: True(Know(A,P) And Know(A,(P => Q)))

Prove: True(Know(A,Q))

```
 1. True(Know(A,P) And Know(A,(P => Q)))          Given
 2. T(W0,(Know(A,P) And Know(A,(P => Q))))        L1,1
 3. T(W0,Know(A,P)) ∧ T(W0,Know(A,(P => Q)))      L2,2
 4. T(W0,Know(A,P))                               3
 5. K(A,W0,w1) ⊃ T(w1,P)                          K1,4
 6. T(W0,Know(A,(P => Q)))                        3
 7. K(A,W0,w1) ⊃ T(w1,(P => Q))                   K1,6
 8.    K(A,W0,w1)                                 Ass
 9.    T(w1,P)                                    5,8
10.    T(w1,(P => Q))                             7,8
11.    T(w1,P) ⊃ T(w1,Q)                          L4,10
12.    T(w1,Q)                                    11,9
13. K(A,W0,w1) ⊃ T(w1,Q)                          Dis(8,12)
14. T(W0,Know(A,Q))                               K1,13
15. True(Know(A,Q))                               L1,14
```

Proofs in this paper use natural deduction. The right hand column gives the axioms and preceding lines which justify each step. Indented sections are subordinate proofs, and **Ass** marks the assumptions on which these subordinate proofs are based. **Dis** indicates the discharge of an assumption.

This proof is completely straight-forward. Lines 1 - 7 simply expand the given facts into possible-worlds notation. Then we pick w1 as a typical world which is possible according to what A knows. In lines 9 - 12, we do the inference that we want to attribute to A. Since this inference can be done in an abitrarily chosen member of the set of worlds which are possible for A, it must be valid in all of them (line 13). From this we conclude that A can probably do the inference also (lines 14 - 15).

So far I have avoided dealing with the problem of quantifiers. Exactly what do expressions like ∃x(Know(A,P(x))). mean? This is not a simple assertion that someone knows a certain fact, so its intuitive meaning may not be clear. The best paraphrase seems to be "There is something that A knows has property P." It is a matter of great dispute in philosophy exactly how to handle this. I will take a pragmatic approach. To say that a person knows of something that it has property P means that he can name something that has property P. Furthermore, just any sort of name won't do. "The thing that has property P" is no good, for instance. We will say that A must know the standard name of the thing that has P. This is, of course, a simplification. Not all things have standard names, and some things have different standard names in different contexts, but we will ignore these difficulties to preserve the simplicity of the ordinary case. Abstract entities usually have unproblematical standard names - "23" is the standard name of 23, "15 + 8" is not.

Turning to the model theory, the interpretation of the formula we are considering would be that there is something that is P in all worlds compatible with what A knows. That means that standard names must refer to the same thing in all possible worlds. There is a term for this in philosophy, *rigid designator*. We can greatly simplify our formalism if we require that all ordinary terms in the object language be rigid designators. We would then have to have a special notation for non-rigid designators, but this will not come up in our examples, so I will not develop that idea here. We can now give the axioms for quantifiers and equality:

L7. T(w1,Exist(v1,P)) ≡ ∃x(T(w1,P[x/v1]));
    provided x is not free in P

L8. T(w1,All(v1,P)) ≡ ∀x(T(w1,P[x/v1]))
    provided x is not free in P

L9. T(w1,Eq(x1,x2)) ≡ (x1 = x2)

L7 and L8 are axiom schemas relative to P and x, and v1 is a meta-language variable that ranges over object-language variables. P[x/v1] means the result of substituting x for v1 in P.

These three axioms may seem somewhat peculiar in that they appear to say that individuals in the world can be part of object-language expressions. In L7 and L8, we took x, a variable ranging over real objects, and inserted it into P, the name of a sentence, implying that objects can be contained in sentences. To preserve the simplicity of the notation, without this apparent absurdity, we will make the interpretation that all functions which represent atomic predicates in the object language (e.g. **Eq**) take individuals as arguments and return expressions containing the standard names of those individuals.

4. Integrating Knowledge and Action

In order to integrate knowledge with actions, we need to formalize a logic of actions in terms comparable to our logic of knowledge. Happily, the standard AI way of looking at actions does just that. Most AI programs that reason about actions view the world as a set of possible situations, and each action determines a binary relation on situations, one situation being the outcome of performing the action in the other situation. We will integrate knowledge and action by identifying the possible worlds in our logic of knowledge with the possible situations in our logic of actions.

First, we need to define our formalism for actions exactly parallel to our formalism for knowledge. We will have an object-language relation **Res(E,P)** which says that it is possible for event E to occur, and P would be true in the resulting situation. In the meta-language, we will have the corresponding relation R(E,W1,W2) which says that W2 is a possible situation/world which could result from event E happening in W1. These two concepts are related in the following way:

R1. T(w1,Res(e1,p1)) ≡
    (∃w2(R(e1,w1,w2)) ∧ ∀w2(R(e1,w1,w2) ⊃ T(w2,p1)))

The existential clause on the right side of R1 says that it is possible for the event to occur, and the universal clause says that in every possible outcome the condition of interest is true. There is a direct parallel here with concepts of program correctness, the first clause expressing termination, and the second, partial correctness.

We can extend the parallel with programming-language semantics to the structure of actions. We will have a type of event which is an actor performing an action, Do(A,C). (C stands for "command".) Actions can be built up from simpler actions using loops, conditionals, and sequences:

R2. T(w1,Res(Do(a1,Loop(p1,c1)),p2) ≡
    T(w1,Res(Do(a1,If(p1,(c1;Loop(p1,c1)),Nil)),p2))

R3. T(w1,Res(Do(a1,If(p1,c1,c2)),p2) ≡
    ((T(w1,Know(a1,p1)) ∧ T(w1,Res(Do(a1,c1),p2))) ∨
    (T(w1,Know(a1,Not(p1))) ∧ T(w1,Res(Do(a1,c2),p2))))

R4. T(w1,Res(Do,a1,(c1;c2)),p1)) ≡
T(w1,Res(Do(a1,c1),Res(Do(a1,c2),p1)))

N1. R(Do(a1,Nil),w1,w2) ≡ (w1 = w2)

R2 defines the step-by step expansion of while-loops: if the test is true, execute the body and repeat the loop, else do nothing. To prove general results we would need some sort of induction axiom. R3 defines the execution of a conditional action. Notice that being able to execute a conditional requires *knowing* whether the test condition is true. This differs from ordinary program conditionals, where the test condition is either assumed to be a decidable primitive, or is itself a piece of code to be executed. R4 says that the result of carrying out a sequence of actions is the result of executing the first action, and then executing the rest. N1 simply defines the no-op action we need for the definition of **Loop**.

One of the most important problems we want to look at is how knowledge affects the ability to achieve a goal. Part of the answer is given in the definition of the notion **Can**. We will say that a person can bring about a condition if and only if there is an action which he knows will achieve the condition:

C1. T(w1,Can(a1,p1)) ≡ ∃c1(T(w1,Know(a1,Res(Do(a1,c1),p))))

The idea is that to achieve something, a person must know of a plan for achieving it, and then be able to carry out the plan.

We have seen a couple of ways that knowledge affects the possibility of action in R3 and C1. We now want to describe how actions affect knowledge. For actions that are not information-acquiring, we can simply say that the actor knows that he has performed the action. Since our axiomatization of particular actions implies that everyone knows what their effects are, this is sufficient. For information-acquiring actions, like looking at something, we will also add that the information has been acquired. This is best explained by a concrete example. Below, we will work out an example about opening safes, so we will now look at the facts about dialing combinations:

D1. ∃w2(R(Do(a1,Dial(x1,x2)),w1,w2) ≡
(T(w1,Comb(x1)) ∧ T(w1,Safe(x2)) ∧ T(w1,At(a1,x2)))

D2. R(Do(a1,Dial(x1,x2)),w1,w2) ⊃
((T(w1,Is-comb-of(x1,x2)) ⊃ T(w2,Open(x2))) ∧
((¬T(w1,Is-comb-of(x1,x2)) ∧ ¬T(w1,Open(x2)) ⊃
¬T(w2,Open(x2))) ∧
(T(w1,Open(x2)) ⊃ T(w2,Open(x2)))

D3. R(Do(a1,Dial(x1,x2)),w1,w2) ⊃
(K(a1,w2,w3) ≡ ((T(w2,Open(x2)) ≡ T(w3,Open(x2))) ∧
∃w4(K(a1,w1,w4) ∧ R(Do(a1,Dial(x1,x2)),w4,w3)))

D1 says that an actor can perform a dialing action if the thing he is dialing is a combination, the thing he is dialing it on is a safe, and he is at the same place as the safe. D2 tells how dialing a combination affects whether the safe is open: if the combination is the combination of the safe, then the safe will be open; if it is not the combination of the safe and the safe was locked, the safe stays locked; if the safe was already open, it stays open.

D3 describes how dialing affects the knowledge of the dialer. Roughly it says that the actor knows he has done the dialing, and he now knows whether the safe is open. More precisely, it says that the worlds that are now possible as far as he knows are exactly those which are the result of doing the action in some previously possible world and in which the information acquired matches the actual world. Notice that by making the consequent of D3 a bi-conditional, we have said that the actor has not acquired any other information by doing the action. Also notice that D3 is more subtle than just saying that whatever he knew before he knows now. This is not strictly true. He might have known before that the safe was locked, and now know that the safe is open. According to D3, if the actor knew before the action "P is true", after the action he knows "P was true before I did this action."

Having presented the basic formalism, I would now like to work out a simple example to illustrate its use. Simply stated, what I will show is that if a person knows the combination of a safe, and he is where the safe is, he can open the safe. Besides the axioms for **Dial**, we will need two more domain-specific axioms:

A1. T(w1,Is-comb-of(x1,x2)) ⊃
(T(w1,Comb(x1)) ∧ T(w1,Safe(x2)))

A2. T(w1,At(a1,x1)) ⊃ T(w1,Know(a1,At(a1,x1))

A1 says that if one thing is the combination of another, the first thing is a combination and the second thing is a safe. A2 says that a person knows what is around him. The proof is as follows:

Given: True(At(John,Sf))
True(Exists(X1,Know(John,Is-comb-of(X1,Sf))))

Prove: True(Can(John,Open(Sf)))

1.	True(Exists(X1,Know(John,Is-comb-of(X1,Sf))))	Given
2.	T(W0,Exists(X1,Know(John,Is-comb-of(X1,Sf))))	L1,1
3.	T(W0,Know(John,Is-comb-of(C,Sf)))	L7,2
4.	K(John,W0,w1) ⊃ T(w1,Is-comb-of(C,Sf))	K1,3
5.	True(At(John,Sf))	Given
6.	T(W0,At(John,Sf))	L1,5
7.	T(W0,Know(John,At(John,Sf)))	A2,6
8.	K(John,W0,w1) ⊃ T(w1,At(John,Sf))	K1,7
9.	K(John,W0,w1)	Ass
10.	T(w1,Is-comb-of(C,Sf))	4,9
11.	T(w1,Comb(C))	A1,10
12.	T(w1,Safe(Sf))	A1,10
13.	T(w2,At(John,Sf))	8,9
14.	∃w2(R(Do(John,Dial(C,Sf)),w1,w2)	D1,11,12,13
15.	R(Do(John,Dial(C,Sf)),w1,w2)	Ass
16.	T(w1,Is-comb-of(C,Sf)) ⊃ T(w2,Open(Sf))	D2,15
17.	T(w2,Open(Sf))	16,10
18.	R(Do(John,Dial(C,Sf)),w1,w2) ⊃ T(w2,Open(Sf))	Dis(15,17)
19.	T(w1,Res(Do(John,Dial(C,Sf)),Open(Sf)))	R1,14,18
20.	K(John,W0,w1) ⊃ T(w1,Res(Do(John,Dial(C,Sf)),Open(Sf)))	Dis(9,19)
21.	T(W0,Know(John,Res(Do(John,Dial(C,Sf)),Open(Sf))))	K1,20
22.	T(W0,Can(John,Open(Sf)))	C1,21
23.	True(Can(John,Open(Sf)))	L1,22

The proof is actually simpler than it may look. The real work is done in the ten steps between 10 and 19; the other steps are the overhead involved in translating between the object language and the meta language. Notice that we did not have to say explicitly that someone needs to know the combination in order to open a safe. Instead we said something more general, that it is necessary to know a procedure in order to do anything. In this case, the combination is part of that procedure. It may also be interesting to point out what would have happened if we had said only that John knew the safe had a combination, but not that he knew what it was. If we had done that, the existential quantifier in the second assertion would have been inside the scope of **Know**. Then the Skolem constant **C** would have depended on the variable **w1**, and the step from 20 to 21 would have failed.

5. Conclusions

In summary, the possible-worlds approach seems to have two major advantages as a tool for reasoning about knowledge. First, it allows "lifting" reasoning in knowledge contexts into the basic deductive system, eliminating the need for separate axioms or rules of inference for these contexts. Second, it permits a very elegant integration of the logic of knowledge with the logic of actions.

This approach seems to work very well as far as we have taken it, but there are some major issues we have not discussed. I have said nothing so far about procedures for reasoning automatically about knowledge. I have some results in this area which appear very promising, but they are too fragmentary for inclusion here. I have also avoided bringing up the frame problem, by not looking at any sequences of action. I am also working in this area, and I consider it one of the largest IOU's generated by this paper. However, the possible-worlds approach has an important advantage here. Whatever method is used to handle the frame problem, whether procedural or axiomatic, knowledge contexts will be handled automatically, simply by applying the method uniformly to all possible worlds. This should eliminate any difficulties of representing what someone knows about the frame problem.

6. References

Hintikka, J. (1963) *Knowledge and Belief*. Ithica, New York: Cornell University Press.

Hintikka, J. (1969) Semantics for Propositional Attitudes, in Linsky (1971), 145-167.

Kripke, S. (1963) Semantical Considerations on Modal Logic, in Linsky (1971), 63-72.

Linsky, L. (ed.) (1971) *Reference and Modality*. London: Oxford University Press.

McCarthy, J. and Hayes, P. J. (1969) Some Philosophical Problems from the Standpoint of Artificial Intelligence, in B. Meltzer and D. Michie (eds.) *Machine Intelligence 4*, 463-502. Edinburgh: Edinburgh University Press.

Moore, R. C. (1973) D-SCRIPT: A Computational Theory of Descriptions. *Advance Papers of the Third International Joint Conference on Artificial Intelligence*, 223-229.

Moore, R. C. (1975) *Reasoning from Incomplete Knowledge in a Procedural Deduction System*. MIT Artificial Intelligence Laboratory, AI-TR-347.

Elements of a Plan-Based Theory of Speech Acts*

PHILIP R. COHEN
Bolt Beranek and Newman Inc.
AND
C. RAYMOND PERRAULT
University of Toronto

This paper explores the truism that people think about what they say. It proposes that, to satisfy their own goals, people often *plan* their speech acts to affect their listeners' beliefs, goals, and emotional states. Such language use can be modelled by viewing speech acts as operators in a planning system, thus allowing both physical and speech acts to be integrated into plans.

Methodological issues of how speech acts should be defined in a plan-based theory are illustrated by defining operators for requesting and informing. Plans containing those operators are presented and comparisons are drawn with Searle's formulation. The operators are shown to be inadequate since they cannot be composed to form questions (requests to inform) and multiparty requests (requests to request). By refining the operator definitions and by identifying some of the side effects of requesting, compositional adequacy is achieved. The solution leads to a metatheoretical principle for modelling speech acts as planning operators.

1. INTRODUCTION

The Sphinx once challenged a particularly tasty-looking student of language to solve the riddle: "How is saying 'My toe is turning blue,' as a request to get off my toe, similar to slamming a door in someone's face?" The poor student stammered that in both cases, when the agents are trying to communicate something, they have analogous intentions. "Yes indeed" countered the Sphinx, "but what are those intentions?" Hearing no reply, the monster promptly devoured the poor student and sat back smugly to wait for the next oral exam.

*The research described herein was supported primarily by the National Research Council of Canada, and also by the National Institute of Education under Contract US-NIE-C-400-76-0116, the Department of Computer Science of the University of Toronto, and by a summer graduate student associateship (1975) to Cohen from the International Business Machines Corporation.

Contemporary philosophers have been girding up for the next trek to Giza. According to Grice (1957)[1], the slamming of a door communicates the slammer's anger only when the intended observer of that act realizes that the slammer wanted both to slam the door in his face and for the observer to believe that to be his intention. That is, the slammer intended the observer to recognize his intentions. Slamming caused by an accidental shove or by natural means is not a communicative act. Similarly, saying "My toe is turning blue" only communicates that the hearer is to get off the speaker's toe when the hearer has understood the speaker's intention to use that utterance to produce that effect.

Austin (1962) has claimed that speakers do not simply produce sentences that are true or false, but rather perform speech actions such as requests, assertions, suggestions, warnings, etc. Searle (1969) has adapted Grice's (1957) recognition of intention analysis to his effort to specify the necessary and sufficient conditions on the successful performance of speech acts. Though Searle's landmark work has led to a resurgence of interest in the study of the pragmatics of language, the intentional basis of communicative acts requires further elaboration and formalization; one must state for any communicative act, precisely which intentions are involved and on what basis a speaker expects and intends those intentions to be recognized.

The Sphinx demands a competence theory of speech act communication—a theory that formally models the possible intentions underlying speech acts. This paper presents the beginnings of such a theory by treating intentions as plans and by showing how plans can link speech acts with nonlinguistic behavior. In addition, an adequacy test for plan-based speech act theories is proposed and applied.

1.1 A Plan-based Theory of Speech Acts

Problem solving involves pursuing a goal state by performing a sequence of actions from an initial state. A human problem-solver can be regarded as "executing" a *plan* that prespecifies the sequence of actions to be taken. People can construct, execute, simulate, and debug plans, and in addition, can sometimes infer the plans of other agents from their behavior. Such plans often involve the communication of beliefs, desires and emotional states for the purpose of influencing the mental states and actions of others. Furthermore, when trying to communicate, people expect and want others to recognize their plans and may attempt to facilitate that recognition.

Formal descriptions of plans typically treat actions as *operators*, which are defined in terms of applicability conditions, called *preconditions*, *effects* that will be obtained when the corresponding actions are executed, and *bodies* that describe the means by which the effects are achieved. Since operators are repre-

[1]See also (Strawson, 1964; Schiffer, 1972)

sentations, their preconditions, effects, and bodies are evaluated relative to the problem-solver's model of the world. We hypothesize that people maintain, as part of their models of the world, symbolic descriptions of the world models of other people. Our plan-based approach will regard speech acts as operators whose effects are primarily on the models that speakers and hearers maintain of each other.[2]

Any account of speech acts should answer questions such as:

—Under what circumstances can an observer believe that a speaker has sincerely and successfully performed a particular speech act in producing an utterance for a hearer? (The observer could also be the hearer or speaker.)

—What changes does the successful performance of a speech act make to the speaker's model of the hearer, and to the hearer's model of the speaker?

—How is the meaning (sense/reference) of an utterance *x* related to the acts that can be performed in uttering *x*?

To achieve these ends, a theory of speech acts based on plans should specify at least the following:

—A planning system: a formal language for describing states of the world, a language for describing operators, a set of plan construction inferences, a specification of legal plan structures. Semantics for the formal languages should also be given.

—Definitions of speech acts as operators in the planning system. What are their effects? When are they applicable? How can they be realized in words?

As an illustration of this approach, this paper presents a simple planning system, defines the speech acts of requesting and informing as operators within that system, and develops plans containing direct requests, informs and questions (which are requests to inform). We do not, however, discuss how those speech acts can be realized in words.

We argue that a plan-based theory, unlike other proposed theories of speech acts, provides formal adequacy criteria for speech act definitions: given an initial set of beliefs and goals, the speech act operator definitions and plan construction inferences should lead to the generation of plans for those speech acts that a person could issue appropriately under the same circumstances.[3] This adequacy criterion should be used in judging whether speech act definitions pass certain tests, in particular, the test of compositionality. For instance, since a speaker can request that a hearer do some arbitrary action, the operator definitions should show how a speaker can request a hearer to perform a speech act. Similarly, since one can inform a hearer that an action was done, the definitions should capture a speaker's informing a hearer that a speech act was performed. We show how a number of previous formulations of requesting and informing are compositionally inadequate, and then develop definitions of informing that can be composed into questions.

Another goal of this research is to develop metatheoretical principles that state how to formulate speech act definitions to pass these adequacy tests. This paper proposes such a principle and shows how its application leads to compositionally adequate definitions for multiparty requests (as in "Ask Tom to open the door").

To simplify our problems in the early stages of theory construction, several restrictions on the communication situation that we are trying to model have been imposed:

—Any agent's model of another will be defined in terms of "facts" that the first believes the second believes, and goals that the first believes the second is attempting to achieve. We are not attempting to model obligations, feelings, etc.

—The only speech acts we try to model are requests, informs, and questions since they appear to be definable solely in terms of beliefs and goals. Requesting and informing are prototypical members of Searle's (1976) "directive" and "representative" classes, respectively, and are interesting since they have a wide range of syntactic realizations, and account for a large proportion of everyday utterances.

—We have limited ourselves to studying "instrumental dialogues"—conversations in which it is reasonable to assume that the utterances are planned and that the topic of discourse remains fixed. Typically, such dialogues arise in situations in which the conversants are cooperating to achieve some task-related goal (Deutsch, 1974), for example, the purchasing of some item. The value of studying such conversations relative to the structure of a task is that the conversants' plans can be more easily formalized.

1.2 A Competence Theory of Speech Acts

At least two interdependent aspects of a plan-based theory should be examined—the plans themselves, and the methods by which a person could construct or recognize those plans. This paper will be concerned with theories of the first aspect, which we shall term *competence* theories, analogous to competence theories of grammar (Chomsky, 1965). A plan-based competence theory of speech acts describes the *set of possible plans* underlying the use of particular kinds of speech acts, and thus states the conditions under which speech acts of those types are appropriate. Such descriptions are presented here in the form of a set of operator definitions (akin to grammatical "productions") and a specification of the ways in which plans are created from those operators.

The study of the second aspect aims for a *process* theory, which concerns *how* an ideal speaker/hearer chooses one (or perhaps more than one) plan out of the set of possible plans. Such a theory would characterize how a speaker decides what speech act to perform and how a hearer identifies what speech act was performed by recognizing the plan(s) in which that utterance was to play a part.

By separating out these two kinds of theoretical endeavors we are not claiming that one can study speech act competence totally divorced from issues of processing. On the contrary, we believe that for a (careful) speaker to issue a particular speech act appropriately, she must determine that the hearer's speech

[2]This approach was inspired by Bruce and Schmidt (1974), Bruce (1975), and Schmidt (1975). This paper can be viewed as supplying methodological foundations for the analyses of speech acts and their patterned use that they present.

[3]Though this could perhaps be an empirical criterion, it will be used intuitively here.

act recognition process(es) will correctly classify her utterance. Thus, a competence theory would state the conditions under which a speaker can make that determination—conditions that involve the speaker's beliefs about the hearer's beliefs, goals, and inferential processes.

Our initial competence theory has been embodied in a computer program (Cohen, 1978) that can construct most of the plans presented here. Programs often point out weaknesses, inconsistencies, and incorrect assumptions in the statement of the competence theory, and can provide an operational base from which to propose process theories. However, we make no claims that computational models of plan construction and recognition are cognitive process theories; such claims would require empirical validation. Moreover, it is unclear whether there could be just one process theory of intentional behavior since each individual might use a different method. A more reasonable goal, then, is to construct computational models of speech act use for which one could argue that a person could employ such methods and converse successfully.

1.3 Outline of the Paper

The thread of the paper is the successive refinement of speech act definitions to meet the adequacy criteria. First, we introduce in sections 2 and 3 the tools needed to construct plans: the formal language for describing beliefs and goals, the form of operator definitions, and a set of plan construction inferences.

As background material, section 4 summarizes Austin's and Searle's accounts of speech acts. Then, Searle's definitions of the speech acts of requesting and informing are reformulated as planning operators in section 5 and plans linking those speech acts to beliefs and goals are given. These initial operator definitions are shown to be compositionally inadequate and hence are recast in section 6 to allow for the planning of questions. Section 7 shows how the definitions are again inadequate for modelling plans for composed requests. After both revising the preconditions of requests and identifying their side effects, compositional adequacy for multiparty requests is achieved. The solution leads to a metatheoretical "point of view" principle for use in formulating future speech act definitions within this planning system. Finally, section 8 discusses the limitations of the formalism and ways in which the approach might be extended to handle indirect speech acts.

2. ON MODELS OF OTHERS

In this section, we present criteria that an account of one agent's (AGT1) model of another's (AGT2's) beliefs and goals ought to satisfy.[4] A theory of speech acts need not be concerned with what is actually true in the real world; it should describe language use in terms of a person's beliefs about the world. Accordingly, AGT1's model of AGT2 should be based on "believe" as described, for example, in Hintikka (1962; 1969). Various versions of the concept "know" can then be defined to be agreements between one person's beliefs and another's.

2.1 Belief

Apart from simply distinguishing AGT1's beliefs from his beliefs about AGT2's beliefs, AGT1's belief representation ought to allow him to represent the fact that AGT2 knows *whether* some proposition P is true, without AGT1's having to know which of P or ~ P it is that AGT2 believes. A belief representation should also distinguish between situations like the following:

1. AGT2 believes that the train leaves from gate 8.
2. AGT2 believes that the train has a departure gate.
3. AGT2 knows what the departure gate is for the train.

Thus, case 3 allows AGT1 to believe *that* AGT2 knows what the departure gate is without AGT1's actually knowing which gate AGT2 thinks that is. This distinction will be useful for the planning of questions and will be discussed further in section 6.

Following Hintikka (1969), belief is interpreted as a model operator A BELIEVE(P), where A is the believing agent, and P the believed proposition.[5] This allows for an elegant, albeit too strong, axiomatization and semantics for BELIEVE. We shall point out uses of various formal properties of BELIEVE as the need arises.

A natural question to ask is how many levels of belief embedding are needed by an agent capable of participating in a dialogue? Obviously, to be able to deal with a disagreement, AGT1 needs two levels (AGT1 BELIEVE and

[4]The representations used by Meehan (1976), and Schank and Abelson (1977) do not, in a principled way, maintain the distinctions mentioned here for belief or want.

[5]The following axiom schemata will be assumed:

B.1 aBELIEVE(all axioms of the predicate calculus)
B.2 aBELIEVE(P) => aBELIEVE(aBELIEVE(P))
B.3 aBELIEVE(P) OR aBELIEVE (Q) => aBELIEVE(P OR Q)
B.4 aBELIEVE(P&Q) <=>aBELIEVE(P) & aBELIEVE(Q)
B.5 aBELIEVE(P) => ~ aBELIEVE(~ P)
B.6 aBELIEVE(P => Q) => (aBELIEVE(P) => aBELIEVE(Q))
B.7 ∃x aBELIEVE(P(x)) => aBELIEVE(∃x P(x))
B.8 all agents believe that all agents believe B.1 to B.7

These axioms unfortunately characterize an idealized "believer" who can make all possible deductions from his beliefs, and doesn't maintain contradictory beliefs. Clearly, the logic should be weakened. However, we shall assume the usual possible worlds semantics of BELIEVE in which the axioms are satisfied in a model consisting of a *universe* U, a subset A of U of *agents*, a set of *possible worlds* W, and *initial world* WO in W, a *relation* R on the cross-product A × W × W, and for each world w and predicate P, a subset Pw of U called the *extension* of P in w. The truth functional connectives *and, or, not,* and = have their usual interpretations in all possible worlds. aBELIEVE(P) is true in world w if P is true in all worlds w1 such that R(a', w,w1), where a' is the interpretation of a in w. ∃x P(x) is true in world w if there is some individual i in U such that P(x) is true in w when all free occurrences of x in P are interpreted as i. The resulting semantics for "quantifying into" BELIEVE is notoriously contentious.

AGT1 BELIEVE AGT2 BELIEVE). If AGT1 successfully lied to AGT2, he would have to be able to believe some proposition P, while believing that AGT2 believes that AGT1 believes P is false (i.e., AGT1 BELIEVE AGT2 BELIEVE AGT1 BELIEVE (~ P)). Hence, AGT1 would need at least three levels. However, there does not seem to be any bound on the possible embeddings of BELIEVE. If AGT2 believes AGT1 has lied, he would need four levels. Furthermore, Lewis (1969) and Schiffer (1972) have shown the ubiquity of *mutual belief* in communication and face-to-face situations—a concept that requires an infinite conjunction of beliefs.[6] Cohen (1978) shows how a computer program that plans speech acts can represent beliefs about mutual beliefs finitely.

2.2 Want

Any representation of AGT2's goals (wants) must distinguish such information from: AGT2's beliefs, AGT1's beliefs and goals, and (recursively) from AGT2's model of someone else's beliefs and goals. The representation for WANT must also allow for different scopes of quantifiers. For example, it should distinguish between the readings of "AGT2 wants to take a train" as "There is a specific train that AGT2 wants to take" or as "AGT2 wants to take any train." Finally, it should allow arbitrary embeddings with BELIEVE. Wants of beliefs (as in "AGT1 WANTS AGT2 BELIEVE P") become the reasons for AGT1's telling P to AGT2, while beliefs of wants (i.e., AGT1 BELIEVES AGT1 WANTS P) will be the way to represent AGT1's goals P.[7] In modelling planning behavior, we are not concerned with goals that the agent does not think he has, nor are we concerned with the subtleties of "wish," "hope," "desire," and "intend" as these words are used in English. The formal semantics of WANT, however, are problematic.

3. MODELS OF PLANS

In most models of planning (e.g., Fikes & Nilsson, 1971; Newell & Simon, 1963), real world actions are represented by *operators* that are organized into plans.[8] To execute a plan, one performs the actions corresponding to the operators in that plan. An operator will be regarded as transforming the planner's model of the world, the *propositions* that the planner believes, in correspondence with the changes to the real world made by the operator's associated action.[9] An operator is *applicable* to a model of the world in which that operator's *preconditions* hold. Operators can be defined in terms of others, as stated in their *bodies* (Sacerdoti, 1975). The changes that an operator makes to the world model in which it is evaluated to produce a new world model are called that operator's *effects*.

We shall view plans for an arbitrary agent S to be constructed using (at least) the following heuristic principles of purposeful behavior:

At the time of S's planning:

1. S should not introduce in the plan actions whose effects S believes are (or will be) true at the time the action is initiated.
2. If E is a goal, an operator A that achieves E can be inserted into the plan.
3. If an operator is not applicable in the planner's belief model, all the preconditions of that operator that are not already true can be added to the plan.

   The previous two inferences reflect an agent's reasoning "in order to do this I must achieve that."

4. If the planner needs to know the truth-value of some proposition, and does not, the planner can create a goal that it know whether that proposition is true or false.
5. If the planner needs to know the value of some description before planning can continue, the planner can create a goal that it find out what the value is.

   The previous two inferences imply that the planner does not have to create an entire plan before executing part of it.

6. Everyone expects everyone else to act this way.

   Since agents can sometimes recognize the plans and goals of others, and can adopt others' goals (or their negations) as their own, those agents can plan to facilitate or block someone else's plans. Bruce and Newman (1978) and Carbonell (1978) discuss these issues at length.

The process of planning to achieve a goal is essentially a search through this space of inferences to find a temporal sequence of operators such that the first operator in the sequence is applicable in the planner's current world model and the last produces a world model in which the goal is true. A new world model is obtained by the execution of each operator.

3.1 The Form of Operators

Early approaches to problem-solving based on first order logic (Green, 1969; McCarthy & Hayes, 1969) have emphasized the construction of provably correct

[6]Lewis (1969) and Schiffer (1972) talk only about mutual or common knowledge, but the extension to mutual belief is obvious.

[7]This also allows a third place to vary quantifier scope, namely:

$$\exists x \text{ aBELIEVE aWANT } P(x)$$
$$\text{aBELIEVE } \exists x \text{ aWANT } P(x),$$
$$\text{aBELIEVE aWANT } \exists x P(x)$$

[8]One usually generalizes operators to *operator schemata* in correspondence with *types* of actions; operator instances are then formed by giving values to the parameters of an operator schema. Since only operator instances are contained in plans we will not distinguish between the operator schema and its instances unless necessary. The same schema/instance, type/token distinction applies as well to speech acts modelled as planning operators.

[9]We are bypassing the fact that people need to observe the success or failure of their actions before being able to accurately update their beliefs. The formalism thus only deals with operators and models of the world rather than actions and the real world. Operators names will be capitalized while their corresponding actions will be referred to in lower case.

plans. Such approaches formalize the changes an action makes to the state of the world model by treating an operator as a predicate of one whose arguments is a *state variable*, which ranges over states of the world model. Unfortunately, to be able to reason about what is true in the world after an action is executed, one must give axiom schemata that describe which aspects of the state of the world are *not* changed by each operator. For instance, calling someone on the telephone does not change the height of the Eiffel Tower. This thorny "frame problem" (McCarthy & Hayes, 1969) occurs because individual states of the world are not related to one another *a priori*.

To overcome this problem, Fikes and Nilsson (1971) in their STRIPS planning system assume that all aspects of the world stay constant except as described by the operator's effects and logical entailments of those effects. Such an assumption is not formalized in the reasoning system, making it difficult to prove the correctness of the resulting plans. Nevertheless, it has become the standard assumption upon which to build problem-solvers. We too will make it and thus shall describe an operator's effects by the propositions that are to be added to the model of the world.[10]

All operator schemata will have two kinds of preconditions—"cando" and "want" preconditions. The former, referred to as CANDO.PRs, indicate proposition schemata that, when instantiated with the parameter values of an operator instance, yield propositions that must be true in the world model for that operator instance to be applicable. We do not discuss how they can be proven true. The "want" precondition, henceforth WANT.PR, formalizes a principle of intentional behavior—the agent of an action has to want to do that action.

The following example serves to illustrate the form of such definitions.

MOVE(AGT,SOURCE,DESTINATION)

CANDO.PR:	LOC(AGT,SOURCE)
WANT.PR:	AGT BELIEVE AGT WANT move-instance
EFFECT:	LOC(AGT, DESTINATION)

The parameters of an operator scheme are stated in the first line of the definitions and it is assumed that values of these parameters satisfy the appropriate selectional restrictions, (here, a person, and two locations, respectively). The WANT.PR uses a parameter "move-instance" that will be filled by any instance of the MOVE operator schema that is currently being planned, executed, or recognized. The CANDO.PR states that before an agent can move from the SOURCE location, he must be located there. The EFFECT of the MOVE indicates that the agent's new location is the DESTINATION.

S's plan to achieve goal G is pictured schematically in Figure 1 (P and Q are arbitrary agents, A1 and A2 are arbitrary actions). Instead of indicating the entire state of the planner's beliefs after each operator, those propositions that are effects of an operator and are preconditions of some other operator in the plan are presented.

[10]Those propositions that need to be deleted (or somehow made "invisible" in the *current* worlmodel) will not be discussed here.

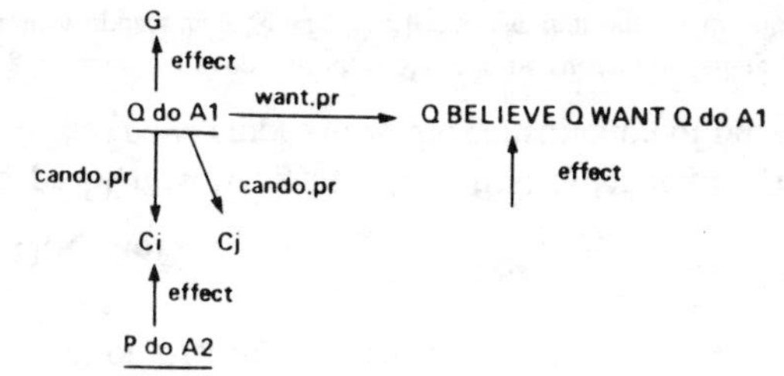

Figure 1. A schematic of S's plan to achieve G.

This diagram illustrates the building block of plans—given goal G, S applies an inference of type 2 and selects operator A1, whose agent is Q as a producer of that effect. That operator is applicable when preconditions Ci and Cj hold and when agent Q wants to perform A1. Type 3 inferences allow each of the preconditions to be achieved by other actions (e.g., A2), which may be performed by another agent (e.g., P). This chaining of operators continues until all preconditions are satisfied. Plan diagrams are thus read from "top" to "bottom".

To indicate that this schematic is part of agent S's plan, the plan components are "embedded" in what S BELIEVE S WANTs. The truth or falsity of preconditions is evaluated with respect to S's beliefs. For example, verifying the WANT.PR of operator A1 (i.e., Q BELIEVE Q WANT Q do A1) would involve establishing that S BELIEVE Q BELIEVE Q WANT Q do A1. If Q is the same person as S (i.e., S is planning her own action A1) then this condition is trivially true since A1 is already part of S's plan, and since for all agents R, we assume that if R BELIEVE (P) then R BELIEVE R BELIEVE (P). However, if Q is not the same as S, the WANT.PR also needs to be achieved, leading, as we shall see, to S's planning a speech act.

4. SPEECH ACTS

4.1 Austin's Performatives

Austin (1962) notes a peculiar class of declarative utterances, which he termed *performatives*, that do not state facts but rather constitute the performance of an action. For instance saying, "I hereby suggest you leave" is an act of suggesting. Unlike the usual declaratives, such sentences are not true or false, but rather are subject to the same kinds of failures ("infelicities") as nonlinguistic actions—such as being applied in the wrong circumstances or being performed insincerely.

Generalizing further, Austin claims that in uttering any sentence, one performs three types of speech acts: the *locutionary*, *illocutionary*, and *perlocution-*

ary acts. A speaker performs a *locutionary* act by making noises that are the uttering of words in language satisfying its vocabulary and grammar, and by the uttering of sentences with definite meaning (though perhaps having more than one). Such acts are used in the performance of *illocutionary acts* which are those acts performed *in* making utterances. For instance, stating, requesting, warning, ordering, apologizing, are claimed to be different types of illocutionary acts, each of which is said to have a unique *illocutionary force* that somehow characterizes the nature of the act. Each illocutionary act contains *propositional content* that specifies what is being requested, warned about, ordered, etc.

New distinctions, however, bring new problems. Frequently, when performative verbs are not used, the utterance's illocutionary force is not directly interpretable from its content. For example, to understand the force of the utterance "The door," the hearer may need to use his beliefs that the door is currently closed, that the speaker has two arm-loads of groceries, and that he wants to be on the other side of the door in determining that the speaker has requested that the door be opened. Furthermore, a speaker may appear to be performing one illocutionary act, and actually may be trying to use it to do something else. Thus, "We have to get up early tomorrow" may simply be an assertion but when said at a party, may be intended as an excuse to the host for leaving, *and* may be intended as a request that the hearer leave. Such *indirect speech acts* (Gordon & Lakoff, 1971; Searle, 1975) are the touchstone of any theory of speech acts.

The last major kind of act identified by Austin is the *perlocutionary* act—the act performed *by* making an utterance. For instance, with the illocutionary act of asserting something, I may *convince* my audience of the truth of the corresponding proposition (or *insult* or *frighten* them). Perlocutionary acts produce *perlocutionary effects*: convincing produces belief and frightening produces fear. While a speaker often has performed illocutionary acts with the goal of achieving certain perlocutionary effects, the actual securing of those effects is beyond his control. Thus, it is entirely possible for a speaker to make an assertion, and for the audience to recognize the force of the utterance as an assertion and yet not be convinced.

4.2 Speech Acts à la Searle

Searle (1969) presents a formulation of the structure of illocutionary acts (henceforth referred to simply as speech acts) by suggesting a number of necessary and sufficient conditions on their successful performance. He goes on to state rules corresponding to these conditions, for a speaker's using any "indicator of illocutionary force" to perform a particular speech act.

As an example, let us consider Searle's conditions for a speaker S, in uttering T, to request that some hearer H do action A. The conditions are grouped as follows:

Normal Input/Output Conditions. These include such conditions as: H is not deaf and S is not mute, joking, or acting.

Propositional Content Conditions. Literal speech acts only use propositions of certain forms. The restrictions on these forms are stated in the *propositional content conditions*. For a request, the proposition must predicate a future act of H.

Preparatory Condition. A preparatory condition states what must be true in the world for a speaker to felicitously issue the speech act. For a request, the preparatory conditions include:

—H is able to do A.
—S believes H is able to do A.
—It is not obvious to S and H that H will do A in the normal course of events (the "non-obviousness" condition).

Searle claims the non-obviousness condition is not peculiar to illocutionary acts. This paper will support his claim by showing how the condition can be applied more generally to rational, intentional behavior.

Sincerity Condition. A *sincerity condition* distinguishes a sincere performance of the speech act from an insincere one. In the case of a request, S must want H to do A; for a promise, S must intend to do the promised action; for an assertion, S must believe what he is asserting.

Essential Condition. An *essential condition* specifies what S was trying to do. For a request, the act is an attempt to get H to do A.

Force Condition (our terminology). The purpose of the *force condition* is to require that the speaker utter a speech act only if he intends to communicate that he is performing that act. "Intending to communicate" involves having certain intentions regarding how the hearer will recognize the force of the utterance. The basic idea is that it is intended that the hearer recognize that the speaker is trying to bring about the satisfaction of the essential condition. For a request this amounts to the speaker's wanting the hearer to realize the speaker intends for him to do A.

5. A FIRST REFORMULATION OF SEARLE'S CONDITIONS

Searle (1969) unfortunately does not supply justifications for the adequacy of his definitions for various kinds of speech acts. A primary goal of this paper is to show how a plan-based theory provides the basis for such adequacy criteria by allowing one to see clearly how changes in speech act definitions affect the plans that can be generated.

A second, more specific point of this formulation exercise is to show which of Searle's conditions are better regarded as pertaining to more general aspects of intentional behavior than to particular speech acts. In this spirit, we show how the sincerity condition, which we shall argue is a misnomer, and the propositional content and "non-obviousness" conditions arise during the course of planning. Concerning the remaining conditions, we assume the "normal input/output conditions," but have chosen not to deal with the force condition until we have a better understanding of the plans for speech acts and how they can be recognized. The remaining conditions, the preparatory and essential conditions, will be mapped into the formalism as the preconditions and effects of speech act operators.

5.1 First Definition of REQUEST

Searle claims the preparatory conditions are required for the "happy" performance of the speech act—where "happy" is taken to be synonymous with Austin's use of "felicitous." Austin was careful to distinguish among infelicities, in particular, misapplications (performing the act in the wrong circumstances), and flaws (incorrectly performing the act). We take Searle's preparatory conditions as conditions guaranteeing applicability rather than successful performance, allowing them to be formalized as preconditions. Thus if an operator's preconditions are not satisfied when it is performed, then the operator was "misapplied." Before expressing preconditions in a formalism, a systematic "point of view" must be adopted. Since the applicability conditions affect the planning of that speech act, the preconditions are stated as conditions on the speaker's beliefs and goals. Correspondingly, the effects describe changes to the hearer's mental state.[11] We establish a *point-of-view principle*, that is intended to be a guideline for constructing speech act definitions in *this* planning system—namely: preconditions begin with "speaker believe" and effects with "hearer believe."

Let us consider Searle's preparatory conditions for a request: H is able to do ACT, and S believes H is able to do ACT. From our discussion of "belief," it should be clear what H can *in fact* do, i.e., what the real world is like is not essential to the success of a request. What may be relevant is that S and/or H thinks H can do ACT. To formalize "is able to do A," we propose a predicate CANDO (Q,ACT) that is true if the CANDO.PR's of ACT are true (with person Q bound to the agent role of ACT).[12]

The essential condition, which is modeled as the EFFECT of a REQUEST,

[11]This does not violate our modelling just one person's view since a speaker, after having issued a speech act, will update his beliefs to include the effects of that speech act, which are defined in terms of the hearer's beliefs.

[12]This should be weakened to ". . . are true or are easily achievable"—i.e. if Q can plan to make them true.

is based on a separation of the illocutionary act from its perlocutionary effect. Speakers, we claim, cannot influence their hearers' beliefs and goals directly. The EFFECTs of REQUEST are modeled so that the hearer's actually wanting to do ACT is not essential to the successful completion of the speech act. Thus, the EFFECT is stated as the hearer's believing the speaker wants him to do the act. For important reasons, to be discussed in section 5.7, this formulation of the essential condition will prove to be a major stumbling block.

The operator REQUEST from SPEAKER to HEARER to do action ACT, which represents a literal request, can now be defined as:

```
REQUEST(SPEAKER,HEARER,ACT)
CANDO.PR:     SPEAKER BELIEVE HEARER CANDO ACT
                 AND
              SPEAKER BELIEVE
                 HEARER BELIEVE HEARER CANDO ACT
WANT.PR:      SPEAKER BELIEVE SPEAKER WANT request-instance
EFFECT:       HEARER BELIEVE
                 SPEAKER BELIEVE SPEAKER WANT ACT
```

5.2 Mediating Acts and Perlocutionary Effects

To bridge the gap between REQUESTs and the perlocutionary effect for which they are planned, a mediating step named CAUSE-TO-WANT is posited, that models what it takes to get someone to want to do something. Our current analysis of this "act" trivializes the process it is intended to model by proposing that to get someone to want to do something, one need only get that person to know that you want them to do it.

The definition of an agent's (AGT1) causing another agent (AGT) to want to do ACT is:

```
CAUSE-TO-WANT (AGT1,AGT,ACT)
CANDO.PR:     AGT BELIEVE
                 AGT1 BELIEVE AGT 1 WANT ACT
EFFECT:       AGT BELIEVE AGT WANT ACT
```

The plan for a REQUEST is now straightforward. REQUEST supplies the necessary precondition for CAUSE-TO-WANT (as will other act combinations). When the WANT.PR of some action that the speaker is planning for someone else to perform, is not believed to be true, the speaker plans a REQUEST. For example, assume a situation in which there are two agents, SYSTEM[13](S) and JOHN, who are located inside a room (i.e., they are at location INROOM). Schematically, to get JOHN to leave the room by moving himself to location

[13]The agent who creates plans will often be referred to as "SYSTEM," which should be read as "planning system."

OUTROOM, the plan would be as in Figure 2. Notice that the WANT.PR of the REQUEST itself, namely

```
S BELIEVE
S WANT
  REQUEST(S,JOHN,MOVE(JOHN,INROOM,OUTROOM))
```

is trivially true since that particular REQUEST is already part of S's plan. The CANDO.PR's of the REQUEST are true if S believes JOHN is located INROOM and if it believes JOHN thinks so too. Thus, once the planner chooses someone else, say H, to do some action that it believes H does not yet want to do, a directive act (REQUEST) may be planned.

5.3 Comparison with Searle's Conditions for a REQUEST

Searle's "non-obviousness" condition for the successful performance of a request stated that it should not be obvious to the speaker that the hearer is about to do the action being requested, independently of the request. If that were obvious to the speaker, the request would be pointless. However, as Searle noted, the non-obviousness condition applies more generally to rational, intentional behavior than to speech acts alone. In our formalism, it is the WANT.PR of the act being requested (goal "++" in Figure 2). If the planning system believed the WANT.PR were already true, i.e., if it believed that John already wanted to leave the room, then the plan would proceed no further; no REQUEST would take place.

Searle's "sincerity" condition, stated that the speaker had to want the requested act to be performed. The sincerity condition in the plan of Figure 2 is the goal labeled "+." The speaker's wanting the hearer to move is the reason for planning a REQUEST.

Notice also that the propositional content of the REQUEST, a future act to be performed by the hearer, is determined by prior planning—i.e., by a combination of that act's WANT.PR, the mediating act CAUSE-TO-WANT, and by the EFFECT of a REQUEST. Searle's propositional content condition thus seems to be a function of the essential condition (which is approximated by the EFFECTs of the speech act operator), as Searle claimed. So far, we have factored out those aspects of a request that Searle suggested were eliminable. Future revisions will depart more significantly.

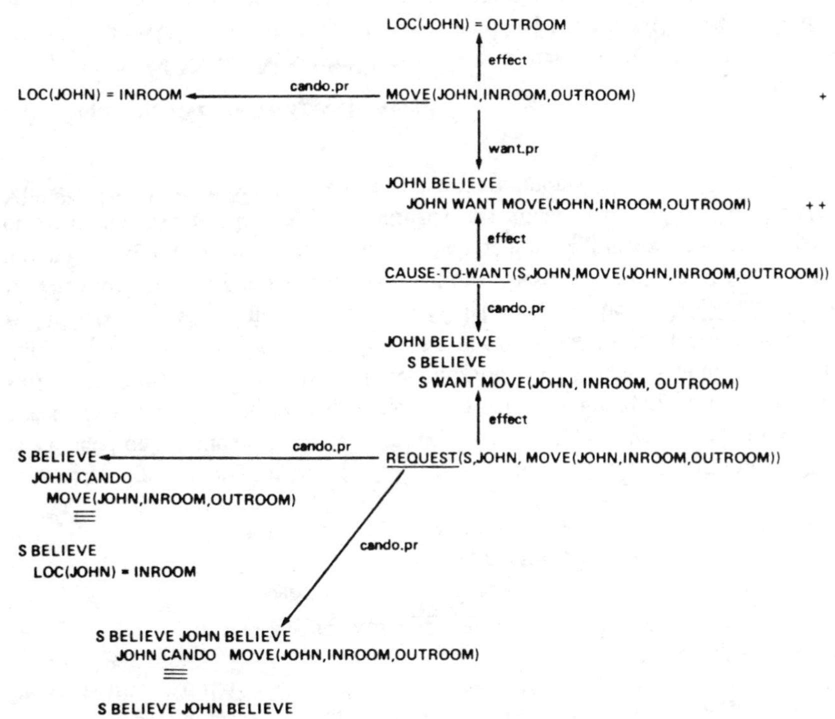

Figure 2. A plan for a REQUEST.

5.4 Definition of INFORM

The speech act of informing is represented by the operator INFORM, which is defined as a speaker's stating a proposition to a hearer for the purpose of getting the hearer to believe that the speaker believes that proposition to be true. Such acts will usually be planned on the basis of wanting the hearer to believe that proposition. For a SPEAKER to INFORM a HEARER that proposition PROP is true, we have:

```
INFORM(SPEAKER, HEARER, PROP)
CANDO.PR:    SPEAKER BELIEVE PROP
WANT.PR:     SPEAKER BELIEVE
               SPEAKER WANT inform-instance
EFFECT:      HEARER BELIEVE
               SPEAKER BELIEVE PROP
```

The CANDO.PR simply states that the only applicability condition to INFORMing someone that proposition PROP is true is that the speaker believes PROP.[14] The EFFECT of an INFORM is to communicate what the speaker believes. This allows for the hearer to refuse to believe the proposition without

[14]Other preconditions to the INFORM act could be added—for instance, to talk to someone one must have a communication link (Schank & Abelson, 1977); which may require telephoning or going to that person's location, etc. However, such preconditions would apply to *any* speech act, and hence probably belong on the locutionary act of making noises to someone.

invalidating the speaker's action as an INFORM. Therefore, an intermediate "act," termed CONVINCE, is necessary to get the hearer to believe the proposition.

For a person AGT 1 to CONVINCE another person AGT that proposition PROP is true, we define:

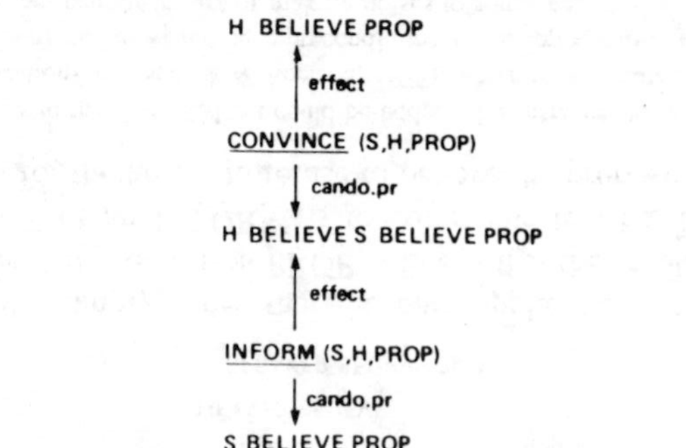

CONVINCE(AGT1, AGT, PROP)

CANDO.PR: AGT BELIEVE
AGT1 BELIEVE PROP

EFFECT: AGT BELIEVE PROP

This operator says that for AGT 1 to convince AGT of the truth of PROP AGT need only believe that AGT1 thinks PROP is true. Though this may be a necessary prerequisite to getting someone to believe something, it is clearly not sufficient. For a more sophisticated precondition of CONVINCE, one might state that before AGT will be convinced, she needs to know the justifications for AGT1's belief, which may require that AGT believe (or be CONVINCE of) the justifications for believing those justifications, etc. Such a chain of reasons for believing might be terminated by mutual beliefs that people are expected to have or by a belief AGT believes AGT1 already has. Ideally, a good model of CONVINCE would allow one to plan persuasive arguments.[15]

5.5 Planning INFORM Speech Acts

The planning of INFORM speech acts now becomes a simple matter. For any proposition PROP, S's plan to achieve the goal H BELIEVE PROP would be that of Figure 3. Notice that it is unnecessary to state as a precondition to inform, that the hearer H does not already believe PROP. Again, this non-obviousness condition that can be eliminated by viewing speech acts in a planning context.

What would be Searle's sincerity condition for the INFORM above (S BELIEVE PROP) turns out to be a precondition for the speech act rather than a reason for planning the act as we had for REQUEST's sincerity condition, (i.e., SPEAKER BELIEVE SPEAKER WANT HEARER do ACT). If we were to use REQUEST as a model, the sincerity condition for an INFORM would be SPEAKER BELIEVE SPEAKER WANT HEARER BELIEVE PROP. One may then question whether Searle's sincerity condition is a consistent naming of distinctive features of various kinds of speech acts. Insincerity is a matter of falsely claiming to be in a psychological state, which for this model is either belief or want. By this definition, both conditions, SPEAKER BELIEVE PROP

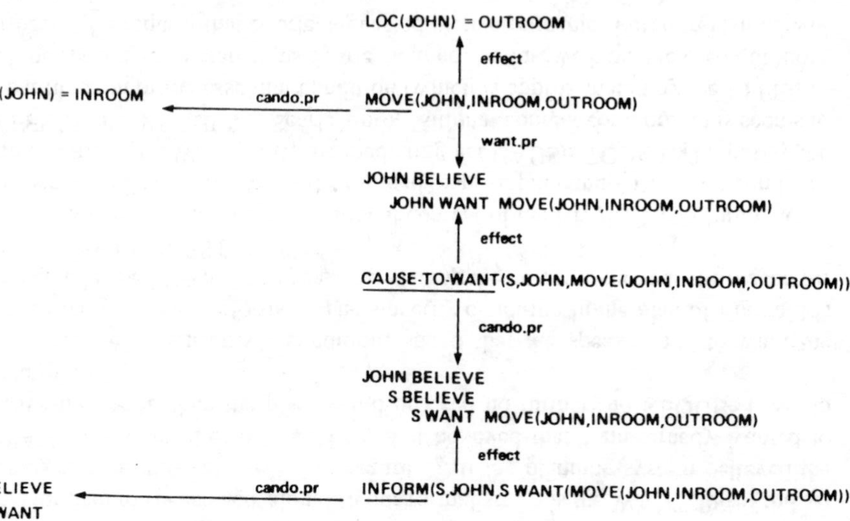

Figure 3. A plan for an INFORM.

and SPEAKER BELIEVE SPEAKER WANT HEARER BELIEVE PROP, are subject to insincerity.

5.6 Planning an INFORM of a WANT

As stated earlier, there are other ways to satisfy the precondition to CAUSE-TO-WANT. Since REQUEST was taken as a prototypical directive act, all members of that class share the same EFFECT (Searle's (1976) "illocutionary point"). However, issuing an INFORM of a WANT, as in "I want you to do X," also achieves it. Another plan to get John to move appears in Figure 4.

S BELIEVE S WANT:

LOC(JOHN) = OUTROOM

effect

LOC(JOHN) = INROOM ← cando.pr — MOVE(JOHN,INROOM,OUTROOM)

want.pr

JOHN BELIEVE
JOHN WANT MOVE(JOHN,INROOM,OUTROOM)

effect

CAUSE-TO-WANT(S,JOHN,MOVE(JOHN,INROOM,OUTROOM))

cando.pr

JOHN BELIEVE
S BELIEVE
S WANT MOVE(JOHN,INROOM,OUTROOM)

effect

S BELIEVE S WANT MOVE(JOHN,INROOM,OUTROOM) ← cando.pr — INFORM(S,JOHN,S WANT(MOVE(JOHN,INROOM,OUTROOM)))

Figure 4. A plan for an INFORM of a WANT.

[15] Without a specification of the justifications for a belief, this operator allows one to become convinced of the truth of one's own lie. That is, after speaker S lies to hearer H that P is true, and receives H's acknowledgment indicating H has been convinced, S can decide to believe P because he thinks H thinks so. Further research needs to be done on CONVINCE and BELIEVE to eliminate such bizarre behavior.

The initial stages of this plan are identical to that of Figure 2 through the CANDO.PR of CAUSE-TO-WANT. This precondition is achieved by an INFORM whose propositional content is S WANT MOVE (JOHN, INROOM, OUTROOM). In this instance, the planning system does not need to proceed through CONVINCE since an INFORM of a WANT produces the necessary effects. Testing the CANDO.PR of INFORM determines if the system believes this proposition, which it does since the MOVE by John is already one of its goals. The WANT.PR of INFORM is trivially true, as before, and thus the plan is complete.

5.7 REQUEST vs. INFORM of WANT

Searle claimed that the conditions he provided were necessary and jointly sufficient for the successful and nondefective performance of various illocutionary acts. Any behavior satisfying such a set of conditions was then said to be a particular illocutionary act. Thus, if two utterances have the same illocutionary force, they should be equivalent in terms of the conditions on their use. We believe that the two utterances "please open the door" and "I want you to open the door (please)" *can* have the same force as directives, differing only in their politeness. That is, they both *can be* planned for the same reasons. However, our treatment does not equate the literal speech acts that could realize them when they should be equated. The condition on REQUEST that distinguishes the two cases is the precondition SPEAKER BELIEVE HEARER BELIEVE HEARER CANDO ACT. Since there is no corresponding precondition in the plan for the INFORM of a WANT, there is no reason to check the hearer's beliefs.

In order to force an equivalence between a REQUEST and an INFORM of a WANT, various actions need to be redefined. We shall remove the above condition as a CANDO.PR from REQUEST and add it as a new CANDO.PR to CAUSE-TO-WANT. In other words, the new definition of CAUSE-TO-WANT would say that you can get a person to decide to want to do some action if she believes you want her to do it and if she believes she can do it. With these changes, both ways of getting someone to want to do some action would involve her believing she is able to do it. More formally, we now define:

```
REQUEST (SPEAKER, HEARER, ACT)
CANDO.PR:   SPEAKER BELIEVE HEARER CANDO ACT
WANT.PR:    SPEAKER BELIEVE SPEAKER WANT request-instance
EFFECT:     HEARER BELIEVE
               SPEAKER BELIEVE SPEAKER WANT ACT
```

and

```
CAUSE-TO-WANT (AGT1, AGT, ACT)
CANDO.PR:   AGT BELIEVE
               AGT1 BELIEVE AGT1 WANT ACT
                 AND
            AGT BELIEVE AGT CANDO ACT
EFFECT:     AGT BELIEVE AGT WANT ACT
```

Though REQUEST and INFORM of a WANT can achieve the same effect, they are not interchangeable. A speaker (S), having previously said to a hearer (H) "I want you to do X," can deny having the intention to get H to want to do X by saying "I simply told you what I wanted, that's all." It appears to be much more difficult, however, after having requested H to do X, to deny the intention of H's wanting to do X by saying "I simply requested you to do X, that's all." S usually plans a request for the purpose of getting H to want to do some act X by means of getting H to believe that S wants H to do it. While maintaining the distinction between illocutionary acts and perlocutionary effects, thus allowing for the possibility that H could refuse to do X, we need to capture this distinction between REQUEST and INFORM of WANT. The solution (Allen, 1979; Perrault & Allen, forthcoming) lies in formulating speech act bodies as plans achieving the perlocutionary effect—plans that a hearer is intended to recognize.

In the next two sections, we investigate the compositional adequacy of these operator definitions via the planning of REQUESTs that a hearer perform REQUEST or INFORM speech acts.

6. COMPOSITIONAL ADEQUACY: QUESTIONS

We are in agreement with many others, in proposing that questions be treated as requests for information. In terms of speech act operators, the questioner is performing a REQUEST that the hearer perform an INFORM. That is, the REQUEST leads to the satisfaction of INFORM's "want precondition." However, for a wh-question, the INFORM operator as defined earlier cannot be used since the questioner does not know the full proposition of which he is to be informed. If he did know what the proposition was there would be no need to ask; he need only decide to believe it.

Intuitively, one plans a wh-question to find out the value of some expression and a yes/no question to find out whether some proposition is true. Such questions are planned, respectively, on the basis of believing *that* the hearer knows what the value of that expression is or *that* the hearer knows whether the proposition is true, without the speaker's having to know what the hearer believes.

Earlier we stated that a person's (AGT1) belief representation should represent cases like the following distinctly:

1. AGT2 believes the Cannonball Express departs at 8 p.m.
2. AGT2 believes the Cannonball Express has a departure time.
3. AGT2 knows what the departure time for the Cannonball Express is.

Case 1 can be represented by a proposition that contains no variables. Case 2 can be represented by a belief of a quantified proposition—i.e.,

AGT2 BELIEVE
∃x (the y : DEPARTURE-TIME(CANNONBALL-EXPRESS,y)) = x)

However, Case 3 can be approximated by a *quantified belief*, namely,

∃x AGT2 BELIEVE
(the y : DEPARTURE-TIME(CANNONBALL-EXPRESS,y)) = x),

where "the y : P(y)," often written "iy P(y)," is the logical description operator read "the y which is P." This formula is best paraphrased as "there is something which AGT2 believes to be the departure time for the Cannonball Express."[16] Typical circumstances in which AGT1 might acquire such quantified beliefs are by understanding a definite description uttered by AGT2 referentially (Donnellan, 1966). Thus, if AGT2 says "the pilot of TWA 461 on July 4," AGT1 might infer that AGT2 knows who that pilot is.

Quantified beliefs often become goals when a planner needs to know the values of the parameters of an operator and when these parameters occur in that operator's preconditions.[17] We show how, when a quantified belief is a goal for AGT, AGT can plan a wh-question.

6.1 Planning Wh-Questions

First, a new operator, INFORMREF, and its associated mediating act CONVINCEREF, are needed.[18]

INFORMREF(SPEAKER,HEARER, λxDx) (i.e., D is a predicate of one argument)

CANDO.PR: ∃y SPEAKER BELIEVE (ixDx) = y

WANT.PR: SPEAKER BELIEVE SPEAKER WANT informref-instance

EFFECT: ∃y HEARER BELIEVE SPEAKER BELIEVE (ixDx) = y

Thus, before a speaker will inform a hearer of the value of some description, there must be some individual that the speaker believes is the value of the description, and the speaker must want to say what it is. The effect of performing this act is that there is then some individual that the hearer thinks the speaker believes to be the value of the description. As usual, we need a mediating act to model the hearer's then believing that individual to be the value of the description. To this end, we define AGT1's convincing AGT of the referent of the description as:

CONVINCEREF(AGT1,AGT, λxDx)

CANDO.PR: ∃y AGT BELIEVE AGT1 BELIEVE (ixDx) = y

EFFECT: ∃y AGT BELIEVE (ixDx) = y

Using these operators, if the planning system wants to know where Mary is and believes that Joe knows where she is, it can create the plan underlying the question "Where is Mary?" as is shown in Figure 5. After the system plans for Joe to tell it Mary's location, on the basis of believing that he knows where she is, it must get Joe to want to perform this act. In the usual fashion, this leads to a REQUEST and hence the construction of a question. The precondition to

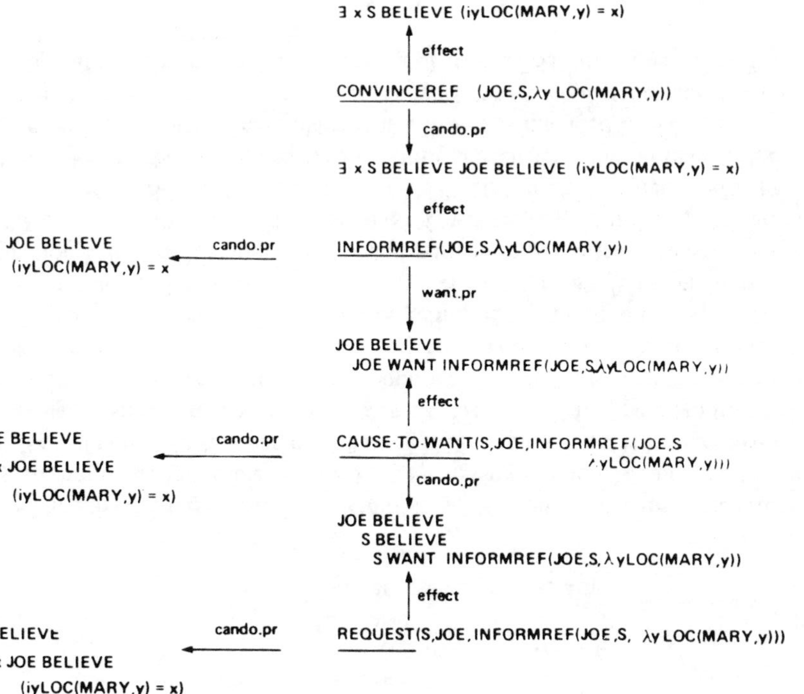

Figure 5. A plan for a wh-question.

[16]Another conjunction can be added to the representation of (3) as suggested by Allen (1979) to refine our representations of "AGT2's knowing what the value of the description is," namely:

$$\exists x \left[(\text{the } y\text{: } D(y) = x \ \& \ \text{AGT2 BELIEVE } ((\text{the } y\text{: } D(y)) = x)\right]$$

We shall, however, use the simpler quantified belief formulation.

[17]We would prefer to formalize declaratively that "the agent of an action must know the values of the parameters of the action." One way of doing this is suggested by Moore (1979).

[18]In Cohen (1978) we achieved the same effect by parameterizing INFORM and CONVINCE so that different sets of preconditions and effects were used if the original goal was a quantified belief. In addition, Cohen (1978) did not use descriptions. We believe the formulation that follows, due to J. Allen, is clearer. The actual names for these acts were suggested by W. Woods.

CAUSE-TO-WANT, namely, JOE BELIEVE JOE CANDO the INFORMREF is actually:

```
JOE BELIEVE
  ∃y JOE BELIEVE
     ixLOC(MARY,x) = y
```

which is implied by

```
∃y JOE BELIEVE ixLOC(MARY,x) = y
```

that was asserted, for this example, to be one of the planning system's beliefs. Notice, that the planning of this question depends upon the system's having chosen Joe to tell it the answer, and upon its having chosen itself to get Joe to want to perform the INFORM. Section 7 discusses what happens when different decisions are made.

6.2 Plans for Yes/No Questions

To plan a yes/no question about some proposition P, one should think that the hearer knows whether P is true or false (or, at least "might know"). An approximate representation of AGT2's knowing whether P is true or false is OR (AGT2 BELIEVE P, AGT2 BELIEVE ~ P)).[19] Such goals are often created, as modelled by our type 4 inference, when a planner does not know the truth-value of P. Typical circumstances in which an agent may acquire such disjunctive beliefs about another are telephone conversations, in which AGT1 believes that there are certain objects in AGT2's view. AGT1 then probably believes that AGT2 knows whether certain visually derivable (or easily computable) properties of those objects are true, such as whether object A is on top of object B.

To accommodate yes/no questions into the planning system, a third INFORM, called INFORMIF, and its associated mediating act CONVINCEIF are defined as follows:

```
INFORMIF(SPEAKER,HEARER,P)
CANDO.PR:   OR(SPEAKER BELIEVE P, SPEAKER BELIEVE ~ P)
EFFECT:     OR(HEARER BELIEVE SPEAKER BELIEVE P,
              HEARER BELIEVE SPEAKER BELIEVE ~ P)
WANT.PR:    SPEAKER BELIEVE SPEAKER WANT informif-instance

CONVINCEIF(AGT,AGT1,P)
CANDO.PR:   OR(AGT BELIEVE AGT1 BELIEVE P,
              AGT BELIEVE AGT1 BELIEVE ~ P)
EFFECT:     OR(AGT BELIEVE P, AGT BELIEVE ~ P)
```

[19]Allen (1979) also points out that another conjunct can be added to the representation of "knowing whether" as a disjunctive belief, to obtain (P & AGT2 BELIEVE (P)) OR (~ P & AGT2 BELIEVE (~ P)).

The plan for a yes/no question to Joe is now parallel to that of a wh-question.[20] That is, in the course of planning some other act, if the system wants proposition P to be true or to be false, and if the truth-value of proposition P is unknown to it, it can create the goal OR(SYSTEM BELIEVE P, SYSTEM BELIEVE ~ P). For instance if P were LOC(MARY,INROOM), the illocutionary acts underlying the question to Joe "Is Mary in the room?" can be planned provided the planning system believes that Joe either believes P is true or he believes P is false. That disjunctive belief could be stated directly or could be inferred from a belief like ∃y JOE BELIEVE(ixLOC(MARY,x)) = y—i.e., there is something Joe believes is Mary's location. But if it had some idea where Joe thought Mary was, say OUTROOM, then it would not need to ask.

6.3 Summary

A plan for a question required the composition of REQUEST and INFORM and led to the development of two new kinds of informing speech acts, INFORMREF and INFORMIF, and their mediating acts. The INFORMREF acts lead to "what," "when," and "where" questions while INFORMIF results in a yes/no question.[21] The reason for these new acts is that, in planning a REQUEST that someone else perform an INFORM act, one only has incomplete knowledge of their beliefs and goals; but an INFORM, as originally defined can only be planned when one knows what is to be said.

7. COMPOSITIONAL ADEQUACY AND THE POINT OF VIEW PRINCIPLE

Earlier, a guiding "Point of View Principle" (POVP) for defining speech acts as planning operators was proposed: the preconditions of the operator should be stated from the speaker's point of view, i.e., in terms of the speaker beliefs; the effects should be stated from the hearer's point of view. We now wish to judge the adequacy of speech act definitions formulated along these lines. The test case

[20]Searle (1969) suggested there were different speech acts for real and teacher-student (or exam) questions, where in the latter case, the questioner just wants to know what the student thinks is the answer. Since teacher-student questions seem to have similar conditions on their appropriateness as real questions, save the questioner's intention to be convinced, we have good reason for factoring the mediating acts out of each of the three INFORM act types. This leaves the INFORM acts neutral with respect to what kind of question they are contained in. In general, if the perlocutionary effects of an INFORM were incorporated into the act's definition, then we would need two new primitive teacher-student question speech acts. For now, we opt for the former.

[21]The language for stating operators needs to be extended to account for "which," "how," and "why" questions. For instance, "why" and "how" questions involve quantifying over actions and/or plans.

will be the composing of REQUESTs, i.e., the planning of a REQUEST that some third party himself perform a REQUEST. For instance, the utterance "Ask Tom to tell you where the key is" is an example of such a third party request.

The current definitions of speech acts will be shown to be compositionally inadequate since they force speakers to have unnecessary knowledge about intermediaries' beliefs. Achieving compositional adequacy, however, requires more than a simple restatement of the point of view principle; the side effects of speech act operators also must be considered.

Our scrutiny will be focused upon the seemingly innocent precondition to REQUEST, SPEAKER BELIEVER HEARER CANDO ACT whose form depended on the POVP. The goal is to show how the POVP leads us astray and how a formulation of that precondition according to a new POVP that suggests a more neutral point of view for speech act definitions sets us back on course. From here on, the two versions of the precondition will be referred to as the "speaker-based" and "neutral" versions.

7.1 Plans for Multiparty Speech Acts

Multiparty speech acts can arise in conversations where communication is somehow restricted so as to pass through intermediaries.[22] The planning system, since it is recursive, can generate plans for such speech acts using any number of intermediaries provided that appropriate decisions are made as to who will perform what action.

Let us suppose that the planning system wants to know where a particular key is and that it must communicate through John. We shall use the speaker-based precondition on REQUEST for this example, and for readibility, the following abbreviations:

SYSTEM—S	TOM—T	JOHN—J
BELIEVE—B	WANT—W	LOC(KEY23,y)—D(y)

Figure 6 shows the plan for the specific three-party speech act underlying "Ask Tom to tell me where the key is."

S develops the plan in the following fashion: T is chosen to tell S the key's location since, we shall assume, he is believed to know where it is. Since T is not believed to already want to tell, and since S cannot communicate directly with T (but T can communicate with S), J is chosen to be the one to talk T into telling. Since J is not believed to already want to do that, S plans a REQUEST that J perform a REQUEST, namely REQUEST(S,J,REQUEST (J,T,INFORMREF (T,S,λyLOC (KEY23,y)))). J, then, is an intermediary who is just expected to do what he is asked; his status will be discussed soon.

[22]For instance, in the Stanford Research Institute Computer-based Consultant research (Deutsch, 1974) communication between an expert and an apprentice was constrained in this way. The apprentice typically issued such speech acts, while the expert did not.

The preconditions that need to be satisfied in this plan are:

S BELIEVE:

(P1) ∃y T BELIEVE [ιxLOC(KEY23,x)=y]
(P2) T BELIEVE (P1) (implied by P1)
(P3) J BELIEVE (P1)
(P4) J BELIEVE J BELIEVE (P1) (implied by P3)
(P5) S BELIEVE J BELIEVE (P1) (implied by P3)

S BELIEVE S WANT:

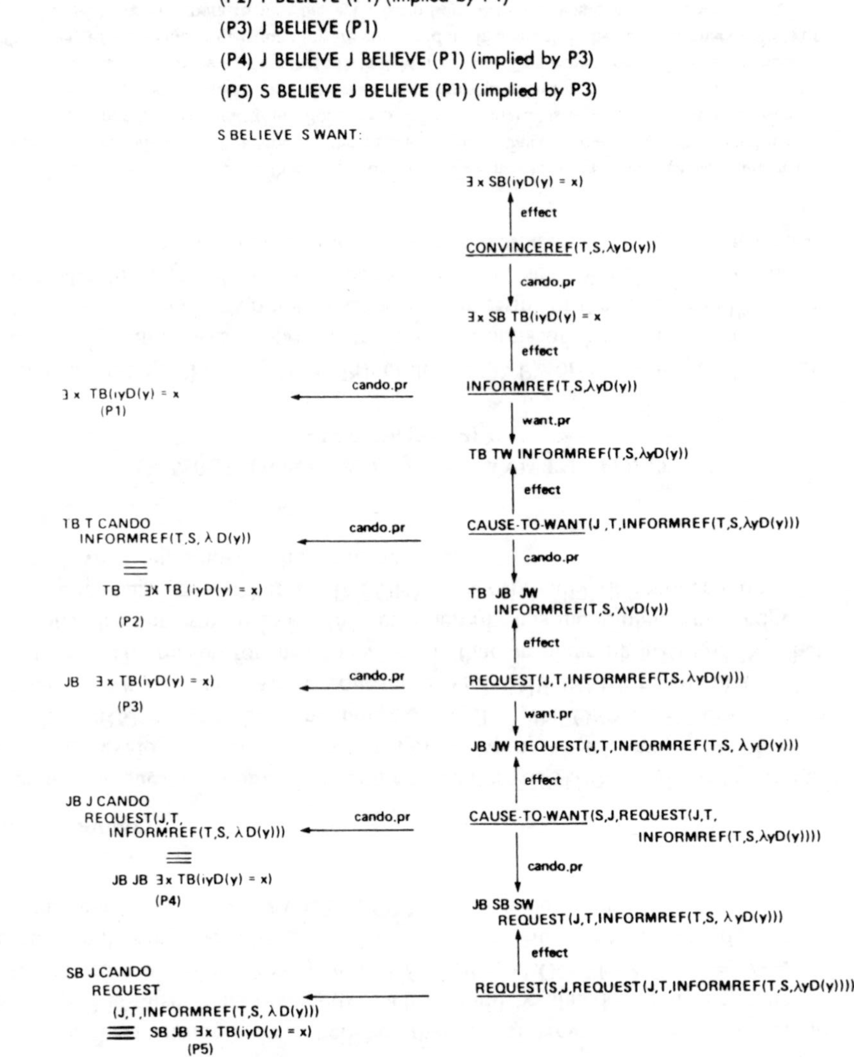

Figure 6. A plan for a third party REQUEST.

While the plan appears to be straightforward, precondition P3 is clearly unnecessary—S ought to be able to plan this particular speech act without having any *prior* knowledge of the intermediary's beliefs. This prior knowledge requirement comes about because precondition P5 is constructed by composing

REQUEST's precondition schema with precondition P3, and P3 is similarly constructed from P1.

The problem can be eliminated by reformulating REQUEST's precondition as HEARER CANDO ACT. Consider a general plan for three-party REQUESTs, as in Figure 7. T's INFORMREF has been generalized to "ACT(T)" whose precondition is "P."

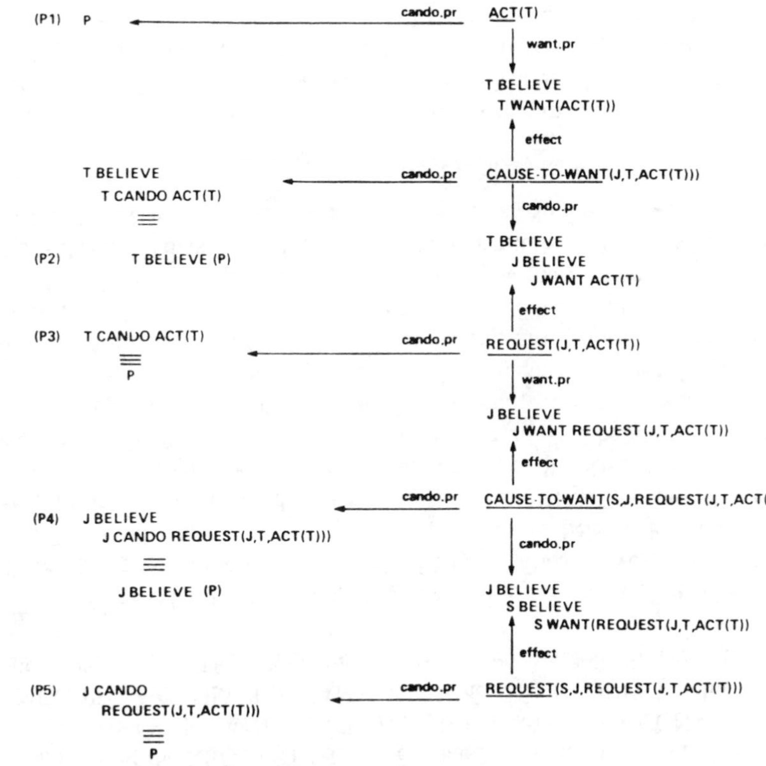

Figure 7. A third party REQUEST using the "neutral" precondition.

The preconditions that have to be satisfied in S's plan are:

S BELIEVE:
(P1) P (also P3 and P5)
(P2) T BELIEVE (P)
(P4) J BELIEVE (P)

Conditions P3 and P5 are the same as P1, and thus the preconditions to the REQUESTs in the plan, are independent of the speaker's beliefs; they depend only on *the planner's* beliefs. While the use of the neutral precondition eliminates prior knowledge requirements for REQUESTs *per se*, condition P4 still requires, as a precondition to CAUSE-TO-WANT, that the planner have some knowledge of the intermediary's beliefs. The next section shows why the planner need not have such beliefs at the time of plan construction.

7.2 Side Effects

The performance of a speech act has thus far been modeled as resulting in an EFFECT that is specific to each speech act type. But, by the very fact that a speaker has attempted to perform a particular speech act, a hearer learns more—on identifying which speech act was performed, a hearer learns that the speaker believed the various preconditions in the *plan* that led to that speech act held. The term *side effect* will be used to refer to the hearer's acquisition of such beliefs by way of the performance of a speech act. Since the plan the hearer infers for the

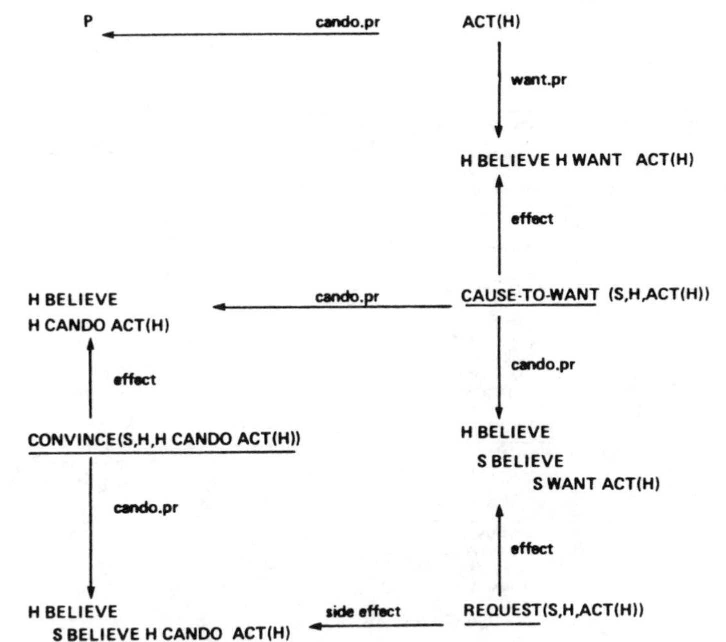

Figure 8. A REQUEST with side effects.

speaker depends upon his beliefs about the speaker's beliefs and goals, the side effects of a speech act cannot be specified in advance. However, the hearer is minimally entitled to believe the speaker thought her speech act's preconditions held (Bruce, 1975; Bruce & Schmidt, 1974).[23] Furthermore, not only do hearers make such assumptions about speakers' beliefs, but speakers know that and often depend on those assumptions for the success of their plans. Figure 8 is a schematic of a simple plan by S to REQUEST H to do action ACT that illustrates this situation.

The minimal side effect is that the hearer believes the speaker believes the precondition of the REQUEST holds, i.e., that HEARER BELIEVE SPEAKER BELIEVE HEARER CANDO ACT. This goal satisfies, via a CONVINCE, the CANDO.PR of CAUSE-TO-WANT, and hence the REQUEST achieves two goals in the plan.[24] The schematic can be applied twice in Figure 7 to obtain Figure 9.

After the side effects of J's REQUEST to T take hold, T would think J believes the preconditions to J's REQUEST (P) obtain. We claim that it is because T thinks that J believes P that T comes to believe P. In this way, precondition (P2) is satisfied as a result of J's REQUEST. Naturally, the side effect argument applies equally to J as the hearer of S's REQUEST. That is, J comes to believe P (precondition (P4)) because he thinks S believes P. S's belief that the preconditions to action A hold thus gets "passed" down the line of intermediaries, whatever its length, to the final agent of A. In this way S can issue the third party REQUEST without having any prior knowledge of J's beliefs about P; S's REQUEST provides all the necessary information!

An interesting aspect of this transmission is that, while J may come to believe P and, by making a REQUEST to T, transmit this belief, T's belief *that* P may be of little use to T. Consider Figure 9 again. Suppose P were

∃y T BELIEVE (ixLOC(KEY23,x))= y

which we are loosely paraphrasing as T knows where the key is. S's REQUEST conveys S's belief *that* T knows where the key is. Though J, to decide to perform his REQUEST, need only think *that* T knows where the key is, T actually has to know where it is before he can do A.[25] J's conveying his belief does no good

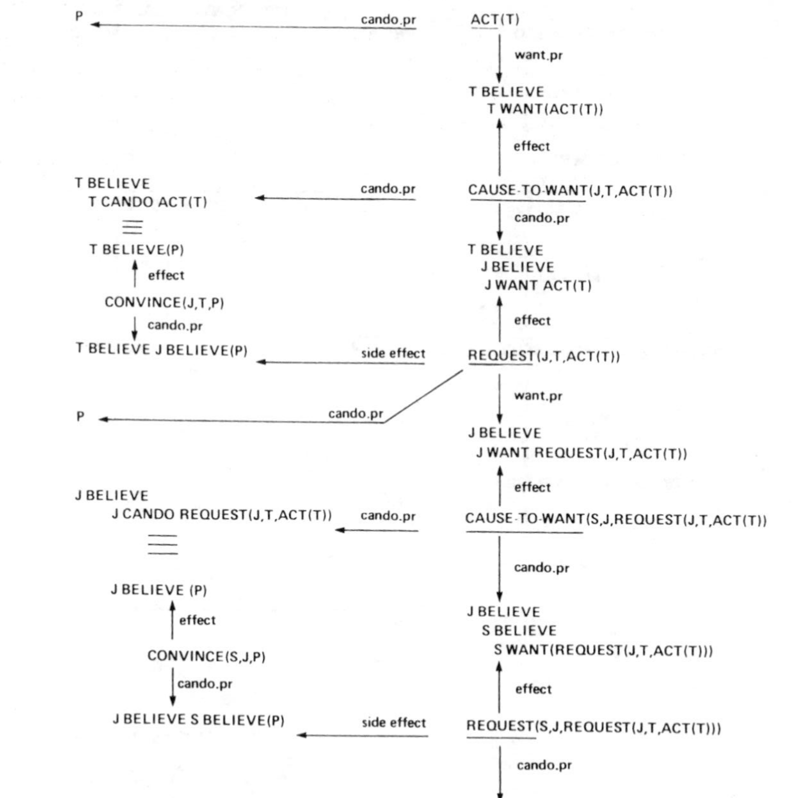

Figure 9. A third party REQUEST using the "neutral" precondition and side effects.

since he has supplied information for a CONVINCE, but T needs information sufficient for a CONVINCEWH. A planning system has to be able to realize this and to plan, by making the same choices as before, the additional REQUEST that John perform an INFORM, e.g., "Tell Tom that the key is in the closet."[26]

7.3 A New Point-of-View Principle

In addition to considering side effects for speech acts, we are led to propose a new point-of-view principle:

> The "Cando" preconditions and effects of speech acts should be defined in a way that does not depend on who the speaker of that speech act is. That is, no CANDO.OR or EFFECT should be stated as a proposition beginning with "SPEAKER BELIEVE."

[23]The hearer may in fact believe those preconditions are false.

[24]The simple backward-chaining planning algorithm described in Cohen (1978) could not easily construct this plan since it ignores intermediate states of the world model that would be created after each operator's execution (i.e., after S's, and J's, REQUESTs).

[25]T cannot obtain that information from believing P since

∃y T BELIEVE ixLOC(KEY23,x) = y cannot be inferred from
T BELIEVE ∃y T BELIEVE ixLOC(KEY23,x) = y, by B.2 and B.7 (footnote 5).

If CONVINCE can be defined so that AGT1 cannot be convinced by AGT2 that AGT1 believes something, then J could not CONVINCE T that ∃y T BELIEVE ixLOC(KEY23,x) = y on the basis of T's thinking that J believes it.

[26]The side effects again figure in this additional three-party REQUEST—John comes to believe that the key is in the closet by believing that S thinks so.

The CANDO.PRs of speech acts defined according to this principle not only resolve our difficulties with composite speech acts, but they also behave as desired for the usual noncomposite cases since preconditions now depend only on the *planner's* beliefs, and the planner is often the speaker. Thus speech act operator definitions are intimately bound to the form of the planning system.

The only result the new principle has on the form of the EFFECTs of speech acts is to make clear whose beliefs should be updated with those EFFECTs. After successfully executing a speech act to H, the speaker can update his model of H with the speech act's EFFECTs. But, for a composite speech act *ultimately* directed to H, the initial planner must observe or assume the success of the rest of the multiparty plan in order to conclude that the EFFECTs of the final speech act to H hold.

While the new principle guarantees that the EFFECTs of speech acts are independent of the use of intermediaries, hearers have every right to believe that the speakers of those speech acts believe that the preconditions hold. Because side effects are stated in terms of the hearer's beliefs about the speaker's beliefs, intermediaries are vulnerable to a charge of insincerity if they brazenly execute the speech acts they were requested to perform. It is to avoid such a charge, and thus make intermediaries "responsible for" the speech acts they execute, that we place the condition on CAUSE-TO-WANT stating that AGT BELIEVE AGT CANDO ACT.

Finally, to complete the reexamination of speech act definitions we point out that the WANT.PR also has a SPEAKER BELIEVE on it. One cannot, in the spirit of "housecleaning," remove the SPEAKER BELIEVE SPEAKER WANT from the WANT.PR of speech acts since a speaker's goal cannot be characterized independently of the speaker's beliefs, unless one is willing to model someone's "unconscious" goals. We are not.[27]

7.4 New Definitions of REQUEST and INFORM

Using this principle, REQUEST is redefined as:

```
REQUEST(SPEAKER,HEARER,ACT)
CANDO.PR:    HEARER CANDO ACT
WANT.PR:     SPEAKER BELIEVE
               SPEAKER WANT request-instance
EFFECT:      HEARER BELIEVE
               SPEAKER BELIEVE SPEAKER WANT ACT
```

The principle applied to the definition of the operator INFORM results in a CANDO.PR stated as PROP rather than as SPEAKER BELIEVE PROP.[28] Such a change allows one to plan to request an intermediary, say a child, to tell someone else that the key is in the closet without the planner's having to believe, at the time of planning, that the child thinks so. The new definition of INFORM then becomes:

```
INFORM(SPEAKER,HEARER,PROP)
CANDO.PR:    PROP
WANT.PR:     SPEAKER BELIEVE
               SPEAKER WANT inform-instance
EFFECT:      HEARER BELIEVE
               SPEAKER BELIEVE PROP
```

Regarding the other informing speech acts, the principle cannot be used to justify the deleting of the SPEAKER BELIEVE from the CANDO.PR of INFORMREF and INFORMIF since the highest elements of those conditions are "$\exists$" and "OR", respectively. Intuitively speaking, this is a sensible result since a speaker SP cannot plan for an intermeriary, INT, to tell H whether P is true, or what the value of description D is unless INT is believed to have that information.

7.5 Summary

The appropriate planning of composite speech acts has turned out to be a powerful test of the adequacy of speech act definitions. To meet its demands on the planning of questions and multiparty speech acts, two new speech acts, INFORMREF and INFORMIF have been defined, and the preconditions to REQUEST and INFORM have been reformulated according to a point-of-view principle. Since these last two speech acts were taken to be prototypes of Searle's (1976) "directive" and "representative" classes, the principle will find wide application.

A side effect of direct requests was identified and used in planning multiparty speech acts. Side effects, however, cannot be calculated until the hearer has recognized the speaker's plan and thus has classified the observed utterance as a particular speech act type. Thus the minimal side effect formulation given here should be further justified on the basis of what a hearer needs to assume about the speaker's beliefs in order to identify an utterances's illocutionary force.

There may be other ways to meet compositional adequacy. For instance, one could state explicitly that an action's preconditions should be true at the time the action is to be done (Bruce, 1975). For our multiparty REQUESTS, such an approach (using a speaker-based precondition) produces preconditions like: S believes J will believe P will be true when ACT is to be done, which seems reasonable. However, the minimal side effect of S's REQUEST then becomes: J now believes that (before that REQUEST) S *expected* J to believe that P would be true when ACT is done (where "now" is just after the REQUEST was made). As yet, we do not have an analogue of CONVINCE that would allow J to then come to believe that P would be true. Again, if REQUEST is defined using the neutral precondition, this problem does not arise.

[27]The fact that a WANT.PR is found on *every* intentional act makes us suspect that it belongs on some single "element" that is present for every act.

[28]Of course, what must be satisfied in any plan for INFORM is that the planner believe PROP.

8. CONCLUDING REMARKS

It has been argued that a theory of speech acts can be obtained by modelling them in a planning system as operators defined, at least, in terms of the speakers' and hearers' beliefs, and goals. Thus, speech acts are treated in the same way as physical acts, allowing both to be integrated into plans. Such an approach suggests new areas for application. It may provide a more systematic basis for studying real dialogues arising in the course of a task—a basis that would facilitate the tracking of conversants' beliefs and intentions as dialogue and task proceed. A similar analysis of characters' plans has also been shown (Bruce & Newman, 1978) to be essential to a satisfactory description of narrative. Finally, Allen (1979) and Cohen (1978) have suggested how computer conversants might plan their speech acts and recognize those of their users.

Given this range of application, the methodological issues of how speech acts should be modelled in a planning system become important. Specifically, a plan-based competence theory, given configurations of beliefs and goals, speech act operators, and plan construction inferences should generate plans for all and only those speech acts that are appropriate in those configurations. This paper developed tests that showed how various definitions of the speech acts of requesting and informing were inadequate, especially to the demand that they generate appropriate plans when composed with other speech acts to form questions and multiparty requests.

To resolve the difficulties, two ''views'' of INFORM to be used in constructing questions were defined, allowing the questioner to have incomplete knowledge of the hearer's beliefs. After revising both the form of speech act preconditions and identifying some speech act side effects, compositional adequacy for multiparty REQUESTS was achieved. The solution led to a metatheoretical ''point-of-view'' principle for use in defining future speech acts as operators within this planning system.

Our approach has both assumed certain idealized properties of speaker/hearers, and has been restricted in its scope. The preconditions and effects of our operators are stated in the language of logic, not because of any desire to perform logically valid inferences, but because the conditions in the plans should have well-defined semantics. While this has been partially realized through the adoption of the possible-worlds sematics for belief, the semantics is too strong to be a faithful model of human beliefs. For instance, it leads here to requiring a questioner to have very strong, though incomplete, knowledge of the hearer's beliefs. To reflect human beliefs more accurately, one needs to model (at least): degrees of belief, justifications, the failure to make deductions, inductive leaps, and knowing what/who/where something is. These refinements, though needed by a theory of speech acts, are outside its scope. Finally, the semantics for WANT and for actions are lacking (but see Moore (1979) for an interesting approach to the latter).

Only two kinds of speech acts, prototypes of Searle's (1976) directive and representative classes, have been examined here, but the approach can be extended to other members of those classes (Bruce, 1975) and perhaps to the commissive class that includes promises. However, in order to model promises and warnings, a better understanding of the concepts of benefit and obligation is necessary.

Finally, we have so far discussed how a planning system can select illocutionary force and propositional content of a speech act, but not how utterances realizing it can be constructed nor how illocutionary acts can be identified from utterances. Extending the plan-based approach to the first area means investigating the extent of ''pragmatic influence'' of linguistic processing. An important supbroblem here is the planning of referring expressions involved in performing illocutionary acts (Perrault & Cohen, forthcoming; Searle, 1969). Regarding speech act identification, the acid-test of a plan-based approach is its treatment of indirect speech acts (Searle, 1975). Gordon and Lakoff (1971) proposed ''conversational postulates'' to account for the relation between the direct or literal and the indirect illocutionary forces of an utterance. But, as Morgan (1977) notes, by calling them ''postulates,'' one implies they cannot be explained by some other independently motivated analysis.

We suggest that the relation between direct and indirect readings can be largely accounted for by considering the relationship between actions, their preconditions, effects, and bodies, and by modelling how language users can recognize plans, which may include speech acts, being executed by others. The ability to recognize plans is seemingly required in order to be *helpful*, independent of the use of indirect speech acts. For instance, hearers often understand a speaker's utterance literally but go beyond it, inferring the speaker's plans and then performing acts that would enable the speaker's higher level goals to be fulfilled. Indirect speech acts arise because speakers can intend hearers to perform helpful inferential processing and they intend for hearers to know this. Allen (1979) and Perrault and Allen (forthcoming) formalize this process of intended plan-recognition (and thus Searle's force condition) extending our plan-based approach to the interpretation of indirect speech acts.

ACKNOWLEDGMENTS

We would like to thank Marilyn Adams, James Allen, Ron Brachman, Chip Bruce, Sharon Oviatt, Bill Woods and the referees for their comments, and Brenda Starr, Jill O'Brien, and Beverly Tobiason for their tireless assistance in the paper's preparation. Special thanks are extended to Brenda Starr for her invaluable editorial help.

REFERENCES

Allen, J. A plan-based approach to speech act recognition. Ph.D. Thesis, Technical Report No. 131/79, Dept. of Computer Science, University of Toronto, January, 1979.

Austin, J. L. *How to do things with words*. J. O. Urmson (Ed.), Oxford University Press, 1962.

Bruce, B. Belief systems and language understanding. Report No. 2973, Bolt Beranek and Newman, Inc. January, 1975.

Bruce, B., & Newman, D. Interacting plans. *Cognitive Science*, 1978, *2*, 195–233.

Bruce, B., & Schmidt, C. F. Episode understanding and belief guided parsing. Presented at the Association for Computational Linguistics Meeting at Amherst, Massachusetts (July 26–27, 1974).

Carbonell, J. G. Jr. POLITICS: Automated idealogical reasoning. *Cognitive Science*, 1978, *2*, 27–51.

Chomsky, N. *Aspects of the theory of syntax*. Cambridge, Mass. MIT Press, 1965.

Cohen, P. R. On knowing what to say: Planning speech acts. Ph.D. Thesis, Technical Report No. 118, Department of Computer Science, University of Toronto, January 1978.

Deutsch, B. G. The structure of task-oriented dialogues. In L. D. Erman (Ed.), *Proceedings of the IEEE symposium on speech recognition*. Pittsburgh, PA: Carnegie-Mellon University, 1974.

Donnellan, K. Reference and definite description. In *The Philosophical Review*, v. 75, 1960, 281–304. Reprinted in Steinberg & Jacobovits (Eds.), *Semantics*, Cambridge University Press, 1966.

Fikes, R., & Nilsson, N. J. STRIPS: A new approach to the application of theorem proving to problem solving. *Artificial Intelligence*, 1971, *2*, 189–208.

Gordon, D., & Lakoff, G. Conversational postulates. *Papers from the Seventh Regional Meeting*, Chicago Linguistic Society, 1971, 63–84.

Green, C. Application of theorem-proving techniques to problem-solving. In D. E. Walker & L. M. Norton (Eds.), *Proceedings of the international joint conference on artificial intelligence*. Washington, D.C., May 1969.

Grice, H. P. Meaning. In *The Philosophical Review*, 1957, *66*, 377–388. Reprinted in D. A. Steinberg & L. A. Jacobovits (Eds.), *Semantics: An interdisciplinary reader in philosophy, linguistics, and psychology*. New York: Cambridge University Press, 1971.

Hintikka, J. *Knowledge and belief*. Ithaca: Cornell University Press, 1962.

Hintikka, J. Semantics for propositional attitudes. In J. W. Davis et al. (Eds.), *Philosophical logic*. Dordrecht-Holland: D. Reidel Publishing Co., 1969. Reprinted in L. Linsky (Ed.), *Reference and modality*. New York: Oxford University Press, 1971.

Lewis, D. K. *Convention: A philosophical study*. Cambridge, Mass: Harvard University Press, 1969.

McCarthy, J., & Hayes, P. J. Some Philosophical Problems from the Standpoint of Artificial Intelligence. In B. Meltzer & D. Michie (Eds.) *Machine intelligence 4*, New York: American Elsevier, 1969.

Meehan, J. R. Tale-spin, an interactive program that writes stories. In *Proceedings of the fifth international joint conference on artificial intelligence*, Cambridge, Mass., 91–98.

Moore, R. C. Reasoning about knowledge and action. Ph.D. Thesis, Artificial Intelligence Laboratory, Department of Electrical Engineering and Computer Science, Massachusetts Institute of Technology, February, 1979.

Morgan, J. Conversational postulates revisited. *Language*, 1977, 277–284.

Newell, A., & Simon, H. A. GPS, A program that simulates human thought. In E. A. Feigenbaum & J. Feldman (Eds.), *Computers and thought*. New York: McGraw Hill, 1963.

Perrault, C. R., & Allen, J. F. A plan-based analysis of indirect speech acts. Forthcoming.

Perrault, C. R., & Cohen, P. R. Inaccurate Reference, *Proceedings of the workshop on computational aspects of linguistic structure and discourse setting*, Joshi, A. K., Sag, I. A., & Webber, B. L. (Eds.), Cambridge University Press, forthcoming.

Sacerdoti, E. D. A structure for plans and behavior. Ph.D. Thesis, Technical Note 109, Artificial Intelligence Center, Stanford Research Institute, Menlo Park, California, August 1975.

Schank, R., & Abelson, R. *Scripts, plans, goals, and understanding*. Hillsdale, N.J.: Lawrence Erlbaum Associates, 1977.

Schiffer, S. *Meaning*. Oxford: Oxford University Press, 1972.

Searle, J. R. A taxonomy of illocutionary acts. In K. Gunderson (Ed.), *Language mind and knowledge*, University of Minnesota Press, 1976.

Searle, J. R. Indirect speech acts. In P. Cole & J. L. Morgan (Eds.), *Syntax and semantics*, (Vol. 3), *Speech acts*. New York: Academic Press, 1975.

Searle, J. R. *Speech acts: An essay in the philosophy of language*. Cambridge: Cambridge University Press, 1969.

Strawson, P. F. Intention and convention in speech acts. In *The Philosophical Review*, v: lxxiii, 1964. Reprinted in *Logico-linguistic papers*, London: Methuen & Co., 1971.

A Truth Maintenance System*

Jon Doyle

Massachusetts Institute of Technology, Artificial Intelligence Laboratory, Cambridge, MA, U.S.A.

ABSTRACT

To choose their actions, reasoning programs must be able to make assumptions and subsequently revise their beliefs when discoveries contradict these assumptions. The Truth Maintenance System *(TMS) is a problem solver subsystem for performing these functions by recording and maintaining the reasons for program beliefs. Such recorded reasons are useful in constructing explanations of program actions and in guiding the course of action of a problem solver. This paper describes (1) the representations and structure of the TMS, (2) the mechanisms used to revise the current set of beliefs, (3) how dependency-directed backtracking changes the current set of assumptions, (4) techniques for summarizing explanations of beliefs, (5) how to organize problem solvers into "dialectically arguing" modules, (6) how to revise models of the belief systems of others, and (7) methods for embedding control structures in patterns of assumptions. We stress the need of problem solvers to choose between alternative systems of beliefs, and outline a mechanism by which a problem solver can employ rules guiding choices of what to believe, what to want, and what to do.*

In memory of **John Sheridan Mac Nerney**

1. Introduction

Computer reasoning programs usually construct computational models of situations. To keep these models consistent with new information and changes in the situations being modelled, the reasoning programs frequently need to remove or change portions of their models. These changes sometimes lead to further changes, for the reasoner often constructs some parts of the model by making inferences from other parts of the model. This paper studies both the problem of how to make changes in computational models, and the underlying problem of how the models should be constructed in order to make making changes convenient. Our approach is to record the reasons for believing or using each program belief, inference rule, or procedure. To allow new information to displace previous conclusions, we employ "non-monotonic" reasons for beliefs, in which one belief depends on a lack of belief in some other statement. We use a program called the *Truth Maintenance System*[1] (TMS) to determine the current set of beliefs from the current set of reasons, and to update the current set of beliefs in accord with new reasons in a (usually) incremental fashion. To perform these revisions, the TMS traces the reasons for beliefs to find the consequences of changes in the set of assumptions.

* This research was conducted at the Artificial Intelligence Laboratory of the Massachusetts Institute of Technology. Support for the Laboratory's artificial intelligence research is provided in part by the Advanced Research Projects Agency of the Department of Defense under Office of Naval Research contract number N00014-75-C-0643, and in part by NSF grant MCS77-04828.

1.1. The essence of the theory

Many treatments of formal and informal reasoning in mathematical logic and artificial intelligence have been shaped in large part by a seldom acknowledged view: the view that the process of reasoning is the process of deriving new knowledge from old, the process of discovering new truths contained in known truths. This view, as it is simply understood, has several severe difficulties as a theory of reasoning. In this section, I propose another, quite different view about the nature of reasoning. I incorporate some new concepts into this view, and the combination overcomes the problems exhibited by the conventional view.

Briefly put, the problems with the conventional view of reasoning stem from the *monotonicity* of the sequence of states of the reasoner's beliefs: his beliefs are true, and truths never change, so the only action of reasoning is to augment the current set of beliefs with more beliefs. This monotonicity leads to three closely related problems involving commonsense reasoning, the frame problem, and control. To some extent, my criticisms here of the conventional view of reasoning will be amplifications of Minsky's [36] criticisms of the logistic approach to problem solving.

One readily recalls examples of the ease with which we resolve apparent contradictions involving our commonsense beliefs about the world. For example, we routinely make assumptions about the permanence of objects and the typical features or properties of objects, yet we smoothly accommodate corrections to the assumptions and can quickly explain our errors away. In such cases, we discard old conclusions in favor of new evidence. Thus, the set of our commonsense beliefs changes non-monotonically.

Our beliefs of what is current also change non-monotonically. If we divide the trajectory of the temporally evolving set of beliefs into discrete temporal situations, then at each instant the most recent situation is the set of current beliefs, and the preceding situations are past sets of beliefs. Adjacent sets of beliefs in this trajectory are usually closely related, as most of our actions have only a relatively small set of effects. The important point is that the trajectory does not form a sequence of monotonically increasing sets of beliefs, since many actions change what we expect is true in the world. Since we base our actions on what we currently believe, we must continually update our current set of beliefs. The problem of describing and performing this updating efficiently is sometimes called the *frame problem*. In

[1] As we shall see, this term not only sounds like Orwellian Newspeak, but also is probably a misnomer. The name stems from historical accident, and rather than change it here, I retain it to avoid confusion in the literature.

connection with the frame problem, the conventional view suffers not only from monotonicity, but also from *atomicity*, as it encourages viewing each belief as an isolated statement, related to other beliefs only through its semantics. Since the semantics of beliefs are usually not explicitly represented in the system, if they occur there at all, atomicity means that these incremental changes in the set of current beliefs are difficult to compute.

The third problem with the conventional view actually subsumes the problem of commonsense reasoning and the frame problem. The problem of control is the problem of deciding what to do next. Rather than make this choice blindly, many have suggested that we might apply the reasoner to this task as well, to make inferences about which inferences to make. This approach to the problem of control has not been explored much, in part because such control inferences are useless in monotonic systems. In these systems, adding more inference rules or axioms just increases the number of inferences possible, rather than preventing some inferences from being made. One gets the unwanted inferences together with new conclusions confirming their undesirability.

Rather than give it up, we pursue this otherwise attractive approach, and make the deliberation required to choose actions a form of reasoning as well. For our purposes, we take the desires and intentions of the reasoner to be represented in his set of current beliefs as beliefs about his own desires and intention. We also take the set of inference rules by which the reasoning process occurs to be represented as beliefs about the reasoner's own computational structure. By using this self-referential, reflexive representation of the reasoner, the inference rules become rules for self-modification of the reasoner's set of beliefs (and hence his desires and intentions as well). The control problem of choosing which inference rule to follow takes the form "Look at yourself as an object (as a set of beliefs), and choose what (new set of beliefs) you would like to become."

The language of such inference rules, and the language for evaluating which self-change to make, are for the most part outside the language of inference rules encouraged by the conventional view of reasoning. For example, when the current set of beliefs is inconsistent, one uses rules like "Reject the smallest set of beliefs possible to restore consistency" and "Reject those beliefs which represent the simplest explanation of the inconsistency." These sorts of rules are all we have, since we cannot infallibly analyze errors or predict the future, yet these rules are non-monotonic, since they lead to removing beliefs from the set of current beliefs.

To repeat, one source of each of these problems is the monotonicity inherent in the conventional view of reasoning. I now propose a different view, and some new concepts which have far reaching consequences for these issues.

Rational thought is the process of finding reasons for attitudes.

To say that some attitude (such as belief, desire, intent, or action) is rational is to say that there is some acceptable reason for holding that attitude. Rational thought is the process of finding such acceptable reasons. Whatever purposes the reasoner may have, such as solving problems, finding answers, or taking action, it operates by constructing reasons for believing things, desiring things, intending things, or doing or willing things. The actual attitude in the reasoner occurs only as a by-product of constructing reasons. The current set of beliefs and desires arises from the current set of reasons for beliefs and desires, reasons phrased in terms of other beliefs and desires. When action is taken, it is because some reason for the action can be found in terms of the beliefs and desires of the actor. I stress again, the only *real* component of thought is the current set of reasons—the attitudes such as beliefs and desires arise from the set of reasons, and have no independent existence.

One consequence of this view is that to study rational thought, we should study justified belief or reasoned argument, and ignore questions of truth. Truth enters into the study of extra-psychological rationality and into what commonsense truisms we decide to supply to our programs, but truth does not enter into the narrowly psychological rationality by which our programs operate.

Of course, this sort of basic rationality is simpler to realize than human belief. Humans exhibit "burn-in" phenomena in which long-standing beliefs come to be believed independently of their reasons, and humans sometimes undertake "leaps of faith" which vault them into self-justifying sets of beliefs, but we will not study these issues here. Instead, we restrict ourselves to the more modest goal of making rational programs in this simpler sense.

The view stated above entails that for each statement or proposition P just one of two states obtains: Either

(a) P has at least one currently acceptable (*valid*) reason, and is thus a member of the current set of beliefs, or

(b) P has no currently acceptable reasons (either no reasons at all, or only unacceptable ones), and is thus not a member of the current set of beliefs.

If P falls in state (a), we say that P is *in* (the current set of beliefs), and otherwise, that P is *out* (of the current set of beliefs). These states are not symmetric, for while reasons can be constructed to make P *in*, no reason can make P *out*. (At most, it can make $\neg$P *in* as well.)

This shows that the proposed view also succumbs to monotonicity problems, for the set of reasons grows monotonically, which (with the normal sense of "reason") leads to only monotonic increases in the set of current beliefs. To solve the problem of monotonicity, we introduce novel meanings for the terms "a reason" and "an assumption".

Traditionally, a reason for a belief consists of a set of other beliefs, such that if each of these basis beliefs is held, so also is the reasoned belief. To get off the ground, this analysis of reasons requires either circular arguments between beliefs (and the appropriate initial state of belief) or some fundamental type of belief which grounds all other arguments. The traditional view takes these fundamental beliefs, often called assumptions (or premises), as believed without reason. On this view, the reasoner makes changes in the current set of beliefs by removing some of the current assumptions and adding some new ones.

To conform with the proposed view, we introduce meanings for "reason" and "assumption" such that assumptions also have reasons. A *reason* (or justification) for a belief consists of an ordered pair of sets of other beliefs, such that the reasoned belief is *in* by virtue of this reason only if each belief in the first set is *in*, and each belief in the second set is *out*. An *assumption* is a current belief one of whose valid reasons depends on a non-current belief, that is, has a non-empty second set of antecedent beliefs. With these notions we can create "ungrounded" yet reasoned beliefs by making assumptions. (E.g. give P the reason ({ }, {¬P}).) We can also effect non-monotonic changes in the set of current beliefs by giving reasons for some of the *out* statements used in the reasons for current assumptions. (E.g. to get rid of P, justify ¬P.) We somewhat loosely say that when we justify some *out* belief supporting an assumption, (e.g. ¬P), we are *denying* or *retracting* the assumption (P).

These new notions solve the monotonicity problem. Following from this solution we find ways of treating the commonsense reasoning, frame, and control problems plaguing the conventional view of reasoning. Commonsense default expectations we represent as new-style assumptions. Part of the frame problem, namely how to non-monotonically change the set of current beliefs, follows from this non-monotonic notion of reason. However, much of the frame problem (e.g. how to give the "laws of motion" and how to retrieve them efficiently) lies outside the scope of this discussion. The control problem can be dealt with partially by embedding the sequence of procedural states of the reasoner in patterns of assumptions. We will treat this idea, and the rest of the control problem, in more detail later.

Other advantages over the conventional view also follow. One of these advantages involves how the reasoner retracts assumptions. With the traditional notion of assumption, retracting assumptions was unreasoned. If the reasoner removed an assumption from the current set of beliefs, the assumption remained out until the reasoner specifically put it back into the set of current beliefs, even if changing circumstances obviated the value of removing this belief. The new notions introduce instead the *reasoned retraction of assumptions*. This means that the reasoner retracts an assumption only by giving a reason for why it should be retracted. If later this reason becomes invalid, then the retraction is no longer effective and the assumption is restored to the current set of beliefs.

The reasoned retraction of assumptions helps in formulating a class of backtracking procedures which revise the set of current assumptions when inconsistencies are discovered. The paradigm procedure of this sort we call dependency-directed backtracking after Stallman and Sussman [53]. It is the least specialized procedure for revising the current set of assumptions in the sense that it only operates on the reasons for beliefs, not on the form or content of the beliefs. In short, it traces backwards through the reasons for the conflicting beliefs, finds the set of assumptions reached in this way, and then retracts one of the assumptions with a reason involving the other assumptions. (We describe the procedure in detail later.) Dependency-directed backtracking serves as a template for more specialized revision procedures. These specialized procedures are necessary in almost all practical applications, and go beyond the general procedure by taking the form of the beliefs they examine into account when choosing which assumption to reject.

1.2. Basic terminology

The TMS records and maintains arguments for potential program beliefs, so as to distinguish, at all times, the current set of program beliefs. It manipulates two data structures: *nodes*, which represent beliefs, and *justifications*, which represent reasons for beliefs. We write St(N) to denote the statement of the potential belief represented by the node N. We say the TMS believes in (the potential belief represented by) a node if it has an argument for the node and believes in the nodes involved in the argument. This may seem circular, but some nodes will have arguments which involve no other believed nodes, and so form the base step for the definition.

As its fundamental actions,

(1) the TMS can create a new node, to which the problem solving program using the TMS can attach the statement of a belief (or inference rule, or procedure, or data structure). The TMS leaves all manipulation of the statements of nodes (for inference, representation, etc.) to the program using the TMS.

(2) It can add (or retract) a new justification for a node, to represent a step of an argument for the belief represented by the node. This argument step usually represents the application of some rule or procedure in the problem solving program. Usually, the rules or procedures also have TMS nodes, which they include in the justifications they create.

(3) Finally, the TMS can mark a node as a *contradiction*, to represent the inconsistency of any set of beliefs which enter into an argument for the node.

A new justification for a node may lead the TMS to believe in the node. If the TMS did not believe in the node previously, this may in turn allow other nodes to be believed by previously existing but incomplete arguments. In this case, the TMS invokes the *truth maintenance* procedure to make any necessary revisions in the set of beliefs. The TMS revises the current set of beliefs by using the recorded justifications to compute non-circular arguments for nodes from premises and other special nodes, as described later. These non-circular arguments distinguish one justification as the *well-founded supporting justification* of each node representing a current belief. The TMS locates the set of nodes to update by finding those nodes whose well-founded arguments depend on changed nodes.

The program using the TMS can indicate the inconsistency of the beliefs represented by certain currently believed nodes by using these nodes in an argument for a new node, and by then marking the new node as a contradiction. When this happens, another process of the TMS, *dependency-directed backtracking*, analyzes the well-founded argument of the contradiction node to locate the *assumptions* (special types of nodes defined later) occurring in the argument. It then makes a record of the inconsistency of this set of assumptions, and uses this record to change one of the assumptions. After this change, the contradiction node is no longer believed. We explain this process in Section 4.

The TMS employs a special type of justification, called a *non-monotonic justification*, to make tentative guesses. A non-monotonic justification bases an argument for a node not only on current belief in other nodes, as occurs in the most familiar forms of deduction and reasoning, but also on lack of current belief in other nodes. For example, one might justify a node N–1 representing a statement P on the basis of lack of belief in node N–2 representing the statement ¬P. In this case, the TMS would hold N–1 as a current belief as long as N–2 was not among the current beliefs, and we would say that it had assumed belief in N–1. More generally, by an *assumption* we mean any node whose well-founded support is a non-monotonic justification.

As a small example of the use of the TMS, suppose that a hypothetical office scheduling program considers holding a meeting on Wednesday. To do this, the program assumes that the meeting is on Wednesday. The inference system of the program includes a rule which draws the conclusion that due to regular commitments, any meeting on Wednesday must occur at 1:00 P.M. However, the fragment of the schedule for the week constructed so far has some activity scheduled for that time already, and so another rule concludes the meeting cannot be on Wednesday. We write these nodes and rule-constructed justifications as follows:

Node	*Statement*	*Justification*	*Comment*
N–1	DAY (M) = WEDNESDAY	(SL ( ) (N–2))	*an assumption*
N–2	DAY (M) ≠ WEDNESDAY		*no justification yet*
N–3	TIME (M) = 13:00	(SL (R–37 N–1) ( ))	

The above notation for the justifications indicates that they belong to the class of *support-list* (SL) justifications. Each of these justifications consists of two lists of nodes. A SL-justification is a *valid* reason for belief if and only if each of the nodes in the first list is believed and each of the nodes in the second list is not believed. In the example, if the two justifications listed above are the only existing justifications, then N–2 is not a current belief since it has no justifications at all. N–1 is believed since the justification for N–1 specifies that this node depends on the lack of belief in N–2. The justification for N–3 shows that N–3 depends on a (presumably believed) node R–37. In this case, R–37 represents a rule acting on (the statement represented by) N–1.

Subsequently another rule (represented by a node R–9) acts on beliefs about the day and time of some other engagement (represented by the nodes N–7 and N–8) to reject the assumption N–1.

N–2 DAY (M) ≠ WEDNESDAY (SL (R–9 N–7 N–8) ( ))

To accommodate this new justification, the TMS will revise the current set of beliefs so that N–2 is believed, and N–1 and N–3 are not believed. It does this by tracing "upwards" from the node to be changed, N–2, to see that N–1 and N–3 ultimately depend on N–2. It then carcfully examines the justifications of each of these nodes to see that N–2's justification is valid (so that N–2 s *in*). From this it follows that N–1's justification is invalid (so N–1 is *out*), and hence that N–3's justification is invalid (so N–3 is *out*).

2. Representation of Reasons for Beliefs

2.1. States of belief

A node may have several justifications, each justification representing a different reason for believing the node. These several justifications comprise the node's *justification-set*. The node is believed if and only if at least one of its justifications is *valid*. We described the conditions for validity of SL-justifications above, and shortly will introduce and explain the other type of justification used in the TMS. We say that a node which has at least one valid justification is *in* (the current set of beliefs), and that a node with no valid justifications is *out* (of the current set of beliefs). We will alternatively say that each node has a *support-status* of either *in* or *out*. The distinction between *in* and *out* is not that between *true* and *false*. The former classification refers to current possession of valid reasons for belief. *True* and *false*, on the other hand, classify statements according to truth value independent of any reasons for belief.

In the TMS, each potential belief to be used as a hypothesis or conclusion of an argument must be given its own distinct node. When uncertainty about some statement (e.g. P) exists, one must (eventually) provide nodes for both the statement and its negation. Either of these nodes can have or lack well-founded arguments, leading to a four-element belief set (similar to the belief set urged by Belnap [2]) of neither P nor ¬P believed, exactly one believed, or both believed.

The literature contains many proposals for using three-element belief sets of *true*, *false*, and *unknown*. With no notion of justified belief, these proposals have some attraction. I urge, however, that systems based on a notion of justified belief should forego three-valued logics in favor of the four-valued system presented here, or risk a confusion of truth with justified belief. Users of justification-based three-valued systems can avoid problems if they take care to interpret their systems in terms of justifications rather than truth-values, but the danger of confusion seems greater when the belief set hides this distinction. One might argue that holding contradictory beliefs is just a transient situation, and that any stable situation uses only three belief states: *true*—only P believed, *false*—only ¬P believed, and *unknown*—neither believed. But the need for the four-element system cannot be dismissed so easily. Since we make the process of revising beliefs our main interest, we concern ourselves with those processes which operate during the transient situation. For hard problems and tough decisions, these "transient" states can be quite long-lived.

2.2. Justifications

Justifications, as recorded in the TMS, have two parts; the external form of the justification with significance to the problem solver, and the internal form of significance to the TMS. For example, a justification might have the external form (Modus Ponens A $A \supset B$) and have the internal form (SL (N–1 N–2 N–3) ( )), supposing that N–1 represents the rule Modus Ponens, N–2 represents A, and N–3 represents $A \supset B$. The TMS never uses or examines the external forms of justifications, but merely records them for use by the problem solver in constructing externally meaningful explanations. Henceforth, we will ignore these external forms of justifications.

Although natural arguments may use a wealth of types of argument steps or justifications, the TMS forces one to fit all these into a common mold. The TMS employs only two (internal) forms for justifications, called *support-list* (SL) and *conditional-proof* (CP) justifications. These are inspired by the typical forms of arguments in natural deduction inference systems, which either add or subtract dependencies from the support of a proof line. A proof in such a system might run as follows:

Line	*Statement*	*Justification*	*Dependencies*
1.	$A \supset B$	Premise	{1}
2.	$B \supset C$	Premise	{2}
3.	A	Hypothesis	{3}
4.	B	MP 1, 3	{1, 3}
5.	C	MP 2, 4	{1, 2, 3}
6.	$A \supset C$	Discharge 3, 5	{1, 2}

Each step of the proof has a line number, a statement, a justification, and a set of line numbers on which the statement depends. Premises and hypotheses depend on themselves, and other lines depend on the set of premises and hypotheses derived from their justifications. The above proof proves $A \supset C$ from the premises $A \supset B$ and $B \supset C$ by hypothesizing A and concluding C via two applications of Modus Ponens. The proof of $A \supset C$ ends by discharging the assumption A, which frees the conclusion of dependence on the hypothesis but leaves its dependence on the premises.

This example displays justifications which sum the dependencies of some of the referenced lines (as in line 4) and subtract the dependencies of some lines from those of other lines (as in line 6). The two types of justifications used in the TMS account for these effects on dependencies. A support-list justification says that the justified node depends on each node in a set of other nodes, and in effect sums the dependencies of the referenced nodes. A conditional-proof justification says that the node it justifies depends on the validity of a certain hypothetical argument. As in the example above, it subtracts the dependencies of some nodes (the hypotheses of the hypothetical argument) from the dependencies of others (the conclusion of the hypothetical argument). Thus we might rewrite the example in terms of TMS justifications as follows (here ignoring the difference between premises and hypotheses, and ignoring the inference rule MP):

N–1	$A \supset B$	(SL ( ) ( ))	*Premise*
N–2	$B \supset C$	(SL ( ) ( ))	*Premise*
N–3	A	(SL ( ) ( ))	*Premise*
N–4	B	(SL (N–1 N–3) ( ))	*MP*
N–5	C	(SL (N–2 N–4) ( ))	*MP*
N–6	$A \supset C$	(CP N–5 (N–3) ( ))	*Discharge*

CP-justifications, which will be explained in greater detail below, differ from ordinary hypothetical arguments in that they use two lists of nodes as hypotheses, the *in*hypotheses and the *out*hypotheses. In the above justification for N–6, the list of *in*hypotheses contains just N–3, and the list of *out*hypotheses is empty. This difference results from our use of non-monotonic justifications, in which arguments for nodes can be based both on *in* and *out* nodes.

2.3. Support-list justifications

To repeat the definition scattered throughout the previous discussion, the support-list justification has the form

(SL ⟨*in*list⟩ ⟨*out*list⟩),

and is valid if and only if each node in its *in*list is *in*, and each node in its *out*list is *out*. The SL-justification form can represent several types of deductions. With empty *in*list and empty *out*list, we say the justification forms a *premise* justification. A premise justification is always valid, and so the node it justifies will always be *in*. SL-justifications with nonempty *in*lists and empty *out*lists represent normal deductions. Each such justification represents a monotonic argument for the node it justifies from the nodes of its *in*list. We define *assumptions* to be nodes whose supporting-justification has a nonempty *out*list. These assumption justifications can be interpreted by viewing the nodes of the *in*list as comprising the reasons for wanting to assume the justified node; the nodes of the *out*list represent the specific criteria authorizing this assumption. For example, the reason for wanting to assume "The weather will be nice" might be "Be optimistic about the weather"; and the assumption might be authorized by having no reason to believe "The weather will be bad." We occasionally interpret the nodes of the *out*list as "denials" of the justified node, beliefs which imply the negation of the belief represented by the justified node.

2.4. Terminology of dependency relationships

I must pause to present some terminology before explaining CP-justifications. The definitions of dependency relationships introduced in this section are numerous, and the reader should consult Tables 1, 2 and Fig. 1 for examples of the definitions.

TABLE 1. A sample system of six nodes and seven justifications.

Node	Justification	Justification name
1	(SL (3) ( ))	J1
2	(SL ( ) (1))	J2
3	(SL (1) ( ))	J3
4	(SL (2) ( ))	J4a
4	(SL (3) ( ))	J4b
5	(SL ( ) ( ))	J5
6	(SL (3 5) ( ))	J6

TABLE. 2. All the dependency relationships implicit in the system of Table 1. Dashed entries are empty. All other entries are lists of nodes in the dependency relationship to the node given at the top of the column.

Dependency	Node 1	Node 2	Node 3	Node 4	Node 5	Node 6
Support-status	out	in	out	in	in	out
Supporting-justification	—	J2	—	J4a	J5	—
Supporting-nodes	3	1	1	2	—	3
Antecedents	—	1	—	2	—	—
Foundations	—	1	—	1, 2	—	—
Ancestors	1, 3	1, 3	1, 3	1, 2, 3	—	1, 3
Consequences	2, 3	4	1, 4, 6	—	6	—
Affected-consequences	2, 3	4	1, 6	—	—	—
Believed-consequences	2	4	—	—	—	—
Repercussions	1, 2, 3, 4, 6	4	1, 2, 3, 4, 6	—	—	—
Believed-repercussions	2, 4	4	—	—	—	—

As mentioned previously, the TMS singles out one justification, called the *supporting-justification*, in the justification-set of each *in* node to form part of the non-circular argument for the node. For reasons explained shortly, all nodes have only SL-justifications as their supporting-justifications, never CP-justifications. The set of *supporting-nodes* of a node is the set of nodes which the TMS used to determine the support-status of the node. For *in* nodes, the supporting-nodes are just the nodes listed in the *in*list and *out*list of its supporting-justification, and in this case we also call the supporting-nodes the *antecedents* of the node. For the supporting-nodes of *out* nodes, the TMS picks one node from each justification in the justification-set. From SL-justifications, it picks either an *out* node from the *in*list or an *in* node from the *out*list. From CP-justifications, it picks either an *out* node from the *in*hypotheses or consequent or an *in* from the *out*hypotheses. We define the supporting-nodes of *out* nodes in this way so that the support-status of the node in question cannot change without either a change in the support-status of one of the supporting nodes, or without the addition of a new valid justification. We say that an *out* node has no antecedents. The TMS keeps the supporting-nodes of each node as part of the node data-structure, and computes the antecedents of the node from this list.

The set of *foundations* of a node is the transitive closure of the antecedents of the node, that is, the antecedents of the node, their antecedents, and so on. This set is the set of nodes involved in the well-founded argument for belief in the node. The

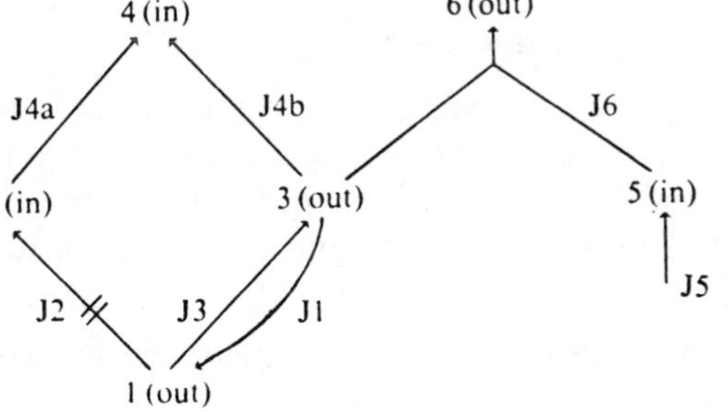

FIG. 1. A depiction of the system of Table 1. All arrows represent justifications. The uncrossed arrows represent *in*lists, and only the crossed line of J2 represents an *out*list. We always visualize support relationships as pointing upwards.

set of *ancestors* of a node, analogously, is the transitive closure of the supporting-nodes of the node, that is, the supporting-nodes of the node, their supporting-nodes, and so on. This set is the set of nodes which might possibly affect the support-status of the node. The ancestors of a node may include the node itself, for the closure of the supporting-nodes relation need not be well-founded. The TMS computes these dependency relationships from the supporting-nodes and antecedents of nodes.

In the other direction, the set of *consequences* of a node is the set of all nodes which mention the node in one of the justifications in their justification-set. The *affected-consequences* of a node are just those consequences of the node which contain the node in their set of supporting-nodes. The *believed-consequences* of a node are just those *in* consequences of the node which contain the node in their set of antecedents. The TMS keeps the consequences of each node as part of the node data-structure, and computes the affected- and believed-consequences from the consequences.

The set of *repercussions* of a node is the transitive closure of the affected-consequences of the node, that is, the affected-consequences of the node, their affected-consequences, and so on. The set of *believed-repercussions* of a node is the transitive closure of the believed-consequences of the node, that is, the believed-consequences of the node, their believed-consequences, and so on. The TMS computes all these relationships from the consequences of the node.

In all of the following, I visualize the lines of support for nodes as directed upwards, so that I look up to see repercussions, and down to see foundations. I say that one node is of lower level than another if its believed-repercussions include the other node.

2.5. Conditional-proof justifications

With this terminology, we can now begin to explain conditional-proof justifications. The exact meaning of these justifications in the TMS is complex and difficult to describe, so the reader may find this section hard going, and may benefit by referring back to it while reading Sections 3.3, 4, and 5. CP-justifications take the form

(CP ⟨consequent⟩ ⟨*in*hypotheses⟩ ⟨*out*hypotheses⟩).

A CP-justification is valid if the consequent node is *in* whenever
(a) each node of the *in*hypotheses is *in* and
(b) each node of the *out*hypotheses is *out*. Except in a few esoteric uses described later, the set of *out*hypotheses is empty, so normally a node justified with a CP-justification represents the implication whose antecedents are the *in*hypotheses and whose consequent is the consequent of the CP-justification. Standard conditional-proofs in natural deduction systems typically specify a single set of hypotheses, which corresponds to the *in*hypotheses of a CP-justification. In the present case, the set of hypotheses must be divided into two disjoint subsets, since nodes may be derived both from some nodes being *in* and other nodes being *out*. Some deduction systems also employ multiple-consequent conditional-proofs. We forego these for reasons of implementation efficiency.

The TMS handles CP-justifications in special ways. It can easily determine the validity of a CP-justification only when the justification's consequent and *in*hypotheses are *in* and the *out*hypotheses are *out*, since determining the justification's validity with other support-statuses for these nodes may require switching the support-statuses of the hypothesis nodes and their repercussions to set up the hypothetical situation in which the validity of the conditional-proof can be evaluated. This may require truth maintenance processing, which in turn may require validity checking of further CP-justifications, and so the whole process becomes extremely complex. Instead of attempting such a detailed analysis (for which I know no algorithms), the TMS uses the opportunistic and approximate strategy of computing SL-justifications currently equivalent to CP-justifications. At the time of their creation, these new SL-justifications are equivalent to the CP-justifications in terms of the dependencies they specify, and are easily checked for validity. Whenever the TMS finds a CP-justification valid, it computes an equivalent SL-justification by analyzing the well-founded argument for the consequent node of the CP-justification to find those nodes which are not themselves supported by any of the *in*hypotheses or *out*hypotheses but which directly enter into the argument for the consequent node along with the hypotheses. Precisely, the TMS finds all nodes N in the foundations of the consequent such that N is not one of the hypotheses or one of their repercussions, and N is either an antecedent of the consequent or an antecedent of some other node in the repercussions of the hypotheses. The *in* nodes in this set form the *in*list of the equivalent SL-justification, and the *out* nodes of the set form the *out*list of the equivalent SL-justification. The TMS attaches the list of SL-justifications computed in this way to their parent CP-justifications, and always prefers to use these SL-justifications in its processing. The TMS checks the derived SL-justifications first in determining the support-status of a node, and uses them in explanations. It uses only SL-justifications (derived or otherwise) as supporting-justifications of nodes.

2.6. Other types of justifications

My experience with the TMS indicates that yet more forms of justifications would be useful. A *general-form* (GF) justification merges the above two forms into one in which the nodes in an *in*list and an *out*list are added to the result of a conditional-proof. We might notate this as

(GF ⟨*in*list⟩ ⟨*out*list⟩ ⟨consequent⟩ ⟨*in*hypotheses⟩ ⟨*out*hypotheses⟩).

I also suggest a *summarization* (SUM) justification form,

(SUM ⟨consequent⟩ ⟨*in*hypotheses⟩ ⟨*out*hypotheses⟩),

which abbreviates

(GF ⟨*in*hypotheses⟩ ⟨*out*hypotheses⟩ ⟨consequent⟩ ⟨*in*hypotheses⟩ ⟨*out*hypotheses⟩).

This form adds the hypotheses of a conditional-proof back into the result of the conditional-proof, thus summarizing the argument for the consequent by excising the intermediate part of the argument. Section 5 explains this technique in detail. I use SUM-justifications there for expository convenience, although I have not implemented them in the TMS.

3. Truth Maintenance Mechanisms

3.1. Circular arguments

Suppose a program manipulates three nodes as follows:

F	$(=(+X\ Y)\ 4)$	. . .	*omitted*
G	$(=X\ 1)$	(SL (J) ( ))	
H	$(=Y\ 3)$	(SL (K) ( )).	

(We sometimes leave statements and justifications of nodes unspecified when they are not directly relevant to the presentation. We assume that all such omitted justifications are valid.) If J is *in* and K is *out*, then the TMS will make F and G *in*, and H *out*. If the program then justifies H with

(SL (F G) ( )),

the TMS will bring H *in*. Suppose now that the TMS makes J *out* and K *in*, leading to G becoming *out* and H remaining *in*. The program might then justify G with

(SL (F H) ( )).

If the TMS now takes K *out*, the original justification supporting belief in H becomes invalid, leading the TMS to reassess the grounds for belief in H. If it makes its decision to believe a node on the basis of a simple evaluation of each of the justifications of the node, then it will leave both G and H *in*, since the two most recently added justifications form circular arguments for G and H in terms of each other.

These circular arguments supporting belief in nodes motivate the use of well-founded supporting justifications, since nodes imprudently believed on tenuous circular bases can lead to ill-considered actions, wasted data base searches, and illusory inconsistencies which might never have occurred without the misleading, circularly supported beliefs. In view of this problem, the algorithms of the TMS must ensure that it believes no node for circular reasons.

Purported arguments for nodes can contain essentially three different kinds of circularities. The first and most common type of circularity involves only nodes which can be taken to be *out* consistently with their justifications. Such circularities arise routinely through equivalent or conditionally equivalent beliefs and mutually constraining beliefs. The above algebra example falls into this class of circularity.

The second type of circularity includes at least one node which must be *in*. Consider, for example

F	TO–BE	(SL ( ) (G))
G	¬TO–BE	(SL ( ) (F)).

In the absence of other justifications, these justifications force the TMS either to make F *in* and G *out*, or G *in* and F *out*. This type of circularity can arise in certain types of sets of alternatives.

In unsatisfiable circularities, the third type, no assignment of *in* or *out* to nodes is consistent with their justifications. Consider

F . . . (SL ( ) (F)).

With no other justifications for F, the TMS must make F *in* if and only if it makes F *out*, an impossible task. Unsatisfiable circularities sometimes indicate real inconsistencies in the beliefs of the program using the truth maintenance system, and can be manifest, for example, when prolonged backtracking rules out all possibilities. The current version of the TMS does not handle unsatisfiable circularities (it goes into a loop), as I removed the occasionally costly check for the presence of such circularities to increase the normal-case efficiency of the program. A robust implementation would reinstate this check. Step 5 in Section 3.2 discusses this problem in more detail.

3.2. The truth maintenance process

The truth maintenance process makes any necessary revisions in the current set of beliefs when the user adds to or subtracts from the justification-set of a node. Retracting justifications presents no important problems beyond those of adding justifications, so we ignore retractions to simplify the discussion. We first outline the procedure, and then present it in greater detail. The details will not be crucial in the following, so the casual reader should read the overview and then skip to Section 4.

In outline, the truth maintenance process starts when a new justification is added to a node. Only minor bookkeeping is required if the new justification is invalid, or if it is valid but the node is already *in*. If the justification is valid and the node is *out*, then the node and its repercussions must be updated. The TMS makes a list containing the node and its repercussions, and marks each of these nodes to indicate that they have not been given well-founded support. The TMS then examines the justifications of these nodes to see if any are valid purely on the basis of unmarked nodes, that is, purely on the basis of nodes which do have well-founded support. If it finds any, these nodes are brought *in* (or *out* if all their justifications are invalid purely on the basis of well-founded nodes). Then the marked consequences of the nodes are examined to see if they too can now be given well-founded support. Sometimes, after all of the marked nodes have been examined in this way, well-founded support-statuses will have been found for all nodes. Sometimes, however, some nodes will remain marked due to circularities. The TMS then initiates a constraint-relaxation process which assigns support-statuses to the remaining nodes. Finally, after all this, the TMS checks for contradictions and CP-justifications, performs dependency-directed backtracking and CP-justification processing if necessary, and then signals the user program of the changes in support-statuses of the nodes involved in truth maintenance.

In detail, the steps of the algorithm are as follows. We enclose comments in bracket-asterisk pairs (E.g. [*This is a comment.*])

Step 1 (*Adding a new justification*). Add the new justification to the node's justification-set and add the node to the set of consequences of each of the nodes mentioned in the justification. If the justification is a CP-justification, add the node to the *CP-consequent-list* of the consequent of the CP-justification, for use in Step 6. If the node is *in*, we are done. If the node is *out*, check the justification for validity. If invalid, add to the supporting-nodes either an *out* node from the *in*list, or an *in* node from the *outlist*. If valid, proceed to Step 2.

Step 2 (*Updating beliefs required*). Check the affected-consequences of the node. If there are none, change the support-status to *in*, and make the supporting-nodes the sum of the *in*list and *out*list; then stop. Otherwise, make a list L containing the node and its repercussions, record the support-status of each of these nodes, and proceed to Step 3. [*We must collect all the repercussions of the node to avoid constructing circular arguments which use repercussions of a node in its supposedly well-founded supporting argument.*]

Step 3 (*Marking the nodes*). Mark each node in L with a support-status of *nil*, and proceed to Step 4. [*Nodes can have a support-status of *nil* only during truth maintenance. This mark distinguishes those nodes with well-founded support from those for which well-founded support has not been determined.*]

Step 4 (*Evaluating the nodes' justifications*). For each node in L, execute the following subprocedure. When all are done, proceed to Step 5.

Step 4(*a*) (*Evaluating the justification-set*). If the node is either ***in*** or *out*, do nothing. Otherwise, keep picking justifications from the justification-set, first the SL-justifications and then the CP-justifications, checking them for well-founded validity or invalidity (to be defined shortly) until either a valid one is found or the justification-set is exhausted. [*The TMS tries justifications in chronological order, oldest first.*] If a valid justification is found, then (1) install it as the supporting-justification (first converting it to SL form if it is a CP-justification), (2) install the supporting-nodes as in Step 2, (3) mark the node *in*, and (4) recursively perform Step 4(a) for all consequences of the node which have a support-status of *nil*. If only well-founded invalid justifications are found, mark the node *out*, install its supporting-nodes as in Step 1, and recursively perform Step 4(a) for all *nil*-marked consequences of the node. Otherwise, the processing of the node is temporarily deferred; the subprocedure is finished. [*An SL-justification is *well-founded valid* if each node in the *in*list is *in* and each node of the *out*list is *out*; it is *well-founded invalid* if some node of the *in*list is *out* or some node of the *out*list is *in*. CP-justifications are well-founded valid if all *in*hypotheses are *in*, all *out*hypotheses are *out*, and the consequent is *in*; they are well-founded invalid if all *in*hypotheses are *in*, all *out*hypotheses are *out*, and the consequent is *out*.*]

[* This step may find well-founded supporting-justifications for some nodes in L, but may leave the support-status of some nodes undetermined due to circularities in potential arguments. These leftover nodes are handled by Step 5 below. If it were not for CP-justifications, Step 4 could be dispensed with entirely, as Step 5 effectively subsumes it. However, we include Step 4 both to handle CP-justifications and to improve (we hope) the efficiency of the algorithm by getting the solidly supported nodes out of the way first. *]

Step 5 (*Relaxing circularities*). For each node in L, execute the following subprocedure. On completion, proceed to Step 6.

Step 5(*a*) (*Evaluating the justification-set*). If the node is either ***in*** or *out*, do nothing. Otherwise, continue to select justifications from the SL-justifications (ignoring the CP-justifications) and to check them for not-well-founded validity or invalidity [* which assumes that all nodes currently marked ***nil*** will eventually be marked *out*, as explained shortly *] until either a valid justification is found or the justification-set is exhausted. If all justifications are invalid, mark the node *out*, install its supporting-nodes as in Step 1, and recursively perform Step 5(a) for all *nil*-marked consequences of the node. If a valid justification is found, then a special check must be made to see if the node already has affected-consequences. If the node does have affected-consequences, then all of them, and the node as well, must be re-marked with *nil* and re-examined by the loop of Step 5. [* We do this because the procedure may have previously determined the support-status of some other node on the assumption that this node was *out*. *] If there are no affected-consequences, then install the valid justification as the supporting-justification, install the supporting-nodes as in Step 2, mark the node *in*, and then recursively perform Step 5(a) for all consequences of the node which have a support-status of *nil*. [* All justifications will be either not-well-founded valid or invalid; there is no third case. An SL-justification is *not-well-founded valid* if each node in the *in*list is *in* and no node of the *out*list is *in*; otherwise, it is *not-well-founded invalid*. This evaluation of nodes assumes that a support-status of *nil* is the same as *out*, i.e. that all currently unassigned nodes will eventually be marked *out*. *]

[* If step 5 terminates, it finds well-founded support for all nodes in L. It will not terminate if unsatisfiable circularities exist. These circularities can be detected by checking to see if a node is its own ancestor after finding a not-well-founded valid justification for it in Step 5(a). If the node is its own ancestor, an unsatisfiable circularity exists in which the argument for belief in the node depends on lack of belief in the node. Unfortunately, this sort of non-termination can also occur with a satisfiable set of nodes and justifications which requires making changes to nodes not in the list L to find this satisfiable assignment of support-statuses. For example, if *F* is *in* but not in L, and if *G* has only the justification (SL (*F*) (*G*)) and is in L, then the procedure will not be able to assign a well-founded support-status to *G* without going outside L to change the support-status of *F*. In consequence, if truth maintenance is done properly it must be non-incremental in such cases.

This relaxation procedure finds one assignment of support-statuses to nodes, but there may be several such assignments possible. A more sophisticated system would incorporate some way in which to choose between these alternatives, since guidance in what the program believes will typically produce guidance in what the program does. Some versions of the TMS (e.g. [14]) incorporated rudimentary analysis facilities, but the current version lacks any such ability. It appears that this relaxation step must be fairly blind in choosing what revision to make. Methods for choosing between alternate revision must have some idea of what all the alternate revisions are, and these are very hard to determine accurately. One can approximate the set of alternate revisions by revisions including some particular belief, but after several such approximations this adds up to just trying some partial revision and seeing if it works out. *]

Step 6 (*Checking for CP-justifications and contradictions*). Call each of the following subprocedures for each of the nodes in L, and then proceed to Step 7. [* This step attempts to derive new SL-justifications from CP-justifications, and to resolve any inconsistencies appearing in the new set of beliefs. Since Step 5 leaves all nodes in L either *in* or *out*, it may now be possible to evaluate some CP-justifications which were previously unevaluable, and to resolve newly apparent contradictions. *]

Step 6(*a*) (*Check for CP-justifications*). Do nothing if the node is *out* or has an empty CP-consequent list. Otherwise, for each node in the CP-consequent-list, check its CP-justifications for validity, and if any are valid, derive their currently equivalent SL-justifications and justify the node with the resulting justification. If this justification is new and causes truth maintenance (Steps 1 through 5), start Step 6 over, otherwise return.

Step 6(*b*) (*Check for contradiction*). Ignore the node unless it is *in* and is marked as a contradiction, in which case call the dependency-directed backtracking system on the node. If truth maintenance (Steps 1 through 5) occurs during backtracking, start Step 6 over, otherwise return.

[* This step halts only when no new SL-justifications can be computed from CP-justifications, and no contradictions exist or can be resolved. *]

Step 7 (*Signalling changes*). Compare the current support-status of each node in L with the initial status recorded in Step 2, and call the user supplied *signal-recalling functions* and *signal-forgetting functions* to signal changes from *out* to *in* and from *in* to *out*, respectively. [* The user must supply two global functions which, if not overridden by a local function that the user might attach to the changed node, are called with the changed node as the argument. However, if the user has attached local function to the changed node, the TMS will call that function instead. *]

End of the truth maintenance procedure.

For more detail, I recommend the chapter on data dependencies in [4], which presents a simplified LISP implementation of a TMS-like program along with a proof of its correctness. McAllester [30] presents an alternative implementation of a truth maintenance system with a cleaner organization than the above. Doyle [15] presents a program listing of one version of the TMS in an appendix.

3.3. Analyzing conditional-proofs

The *Find Independent Support* (FIS) procedure computes SL-justifications from valid CP-justifications by finding those nodes supporting the consequent which do not depend on the hypotheses. Repeating our earlier explanation of what this means, FIS finds all nodes N in the foundations of the consequent of the conditional-proof justification such that

(1) N is not one of the hypotheses or one of their repercussions, and

(2) N is either an antecedent of the consequent or an antecedent of some node in the repercussions of the hypotheses. The *in* nodes in this set form the *in*list of the equivalent SL-justification, and the *out* nodes of the set form the *out*list of the equivalent SL-justification.

Let (CP C IH OH) be a valid CP-justification, where C is the consequent node, IH is the list of *in*hypotheses, and OH is the list of *out*hypotheses. The steps of FIS are as follows:

Step 1 (*Mark the hypotheses*). Mark each of the nodes in IH and OH with both an E (*examined*) mark and a S (*subordinates*) mark, then proceed to Step 2. [* The E mark means that the node has been examined by the procedure. We use it to make the search through the foundations of C efficient. The S mark means that the node is either one of the hypotheses or a repercussion of one of the hypotheses. *]

Step 2 (*Mark the foundations*). Call the following subprocedure on C, and proceed to Step 3.

Step 2(*a*) (*Mark the repercussions of the hypotheses*). If the node has an E mark, return. If the node has no E mark, mark it with the E mark, and call Step 2(a) on each of the antecedents of the node. If any of the antecedent nodes is marked with an S mark, mark the current node with an S mark. Finally, return. [* This step marks those nodes in both the foundations of C and the repercussions of the hypotheses. *]

Step 3 (*Unmark the foundations*). Using a recursive scan, similar to Step 2(a), remove the E marks from the foundations of C and proceed to Step 4.

Step 4 (*Remark the hypotheses*). As in Step 1, mark the hypotheses with E marks, this time ignoring their S marks. Proceed to Step 5.

Step 5 (*Collect the net support*). Call the following subprocedure on C and proceed to Step 6.

Step 5(*a*) (*Skip repercussions and collect support*). If the node has an E mark, return. Otherwise, mark the node with an E mark. If the node has no S mark, add it to IS if it is *in*, and to OS if it is *out*, then return. If the node has an S mark, execute Step 5(a) on each of its antecedents, then return. [* This step collects just those nodes in the foundations of C which are not hypotheses or their repercussions, and which directly support (are antecedents of) repercussions of the hypotheses. These nodes are exactly the nodes necessary to make the argument go through for C from the hypotheses. *]

Step 6 (*Clean up and return the result*). Repeat Step 3, removing both E and S marks, remove all marks from the nodes in IH and OH, and return the justification (SL IS OS).

End of the Find Independent Support procedure.

4. Dependency-Directed Backtracking

When the TMS makes a contradiction node *in*, it invokes dependency-directed backtracking to find and remove at least one of the current assumptions in order to make the contradiction node *out*. The steps of this process follow. As above, we enclose commentary in bracket-asterisk pairs ([*, *]).

Step 1 (*Find the maximal assumptions*). Trace through the foundations of the contradiction node C to find the set $S = \{A_1, \ldots, A_n\}$, which contains an assumption A if and only if A is in C's foundations and there is no other assumption B in the foundations of C such that A is in the foundations of B. [* We call S the set of the *maximal* assumptions underlying C. *]

[* Just as the TMS relies on the problem solving program to point out inconsistencies by marking certain nodes as contradictions, it also relies on the problem solver to use non-monotonic assumptions for any beliefs to which backtracking might apply. Because the TMS does not inspect the statements represented by its nodes, it foregoes the ability, for example, to retract premise justifications of nodes. *]

Step 2 (*Summarize the cause of the inconsistency*). If no previous backtracking attempt on C discovered S to be the set of maximal assumptions, create a new node NG, called a *nogood*, to represent the inconsistency of S. [* We call S the *nogood-set*. *] If S was encountered earlier as a nogood-set of a contradiction, use the previously created nogood node. [* Since C represents a false statement, NG represents

$$\mathrm{St}(A_1) \wedge \cdots \wedge \mathrm{St}(A_n) \supset \mathit{false},$$

or

$$\neg(\mathrm{St}(A_1) \wedge \cdots \wedge \mathrm{St}(A_n)) \tag{1}$$

by a simple rewriting. *]

Justify NG with

$$(\mathrm{CP}\ C\ S\ (\ )). \tag{2}$$

[* With this justification, NG will remain *in* even after Step 3 makes one of the assumptions *out*, since the CP-justification means that NG does not depend on any of the assumptions. *]

Step 3 (*Select and reject a culprit*). Select some A_i, the *culprit*, from S. Let $D_1, \ldots, D_k$ be the *out* nodes in the *out*list of A_i's supporting-justification. Select D_j from this set and justify it with

$$(\mathrm{SL}\ (NG\ A_1 \cdots A_{i-1}\ A_{i+1} \cdots A_n)\ (D_1 \cdots D_{j-1}\ D_{j+1} \cdots D_k)). \tag{3}$$

[* If one takes these underlying D nodes as "denials" of the selected assumption, this step recalls *reductio ad absurdum*. The backtracker attempts to force the culprit *out* by invalidating its supporting-justification with the new justification, which is valid whenever the nogood and the other assumptions are *in* and the other denials of the culprit are *out*. If the backtracker erred in choosing the culprit or denial, presumably a future contradiction will involve D_j and the remaining assumptions in its foundations. However, if the *out*list of the justification (3) is nonempty, D_j will be an assumption, of higher level than the remaining assumptions, and so will be the first to be denied.

The current implementation picks the culprit and denial randomly from the alternatives, and so relies on blind search. Blind search is inadequate for all but the simplest sorts of problems, for typically one needs to make a guided choice among the alternative revisions of beliefs. I will return to this problem in Section 8. *]

Step 4 (*Repeat if necessary*). If the TMS finds other arguments so that the contradiction node C remains *in* after the addition of the new justification for D_j, repeat this backtracking procedure. [* Presumably the previous culprit A_i will no longer be an assumption. *] Finally, if the contradiction becomes *out*, then halt; or if no assumptions can be found in C's foundations, notify the problem solving program of an unanalyzable contradiction, then halt.

End of the dependency-directed backtracking procedure.

As an example, consider a program scheduling a meeting, to be held preferably at 10 A.M. in either room 813 or 801.

N–1	TIME(M) = 1000	(SL ( ) (N–2))
N–2	TIME(M) ≠ 1000	
N–3	ROOM(M) = 813	(SL ( ) (N–4)
N–4	ROOM(M) = 801	

With only these justifications, the TMS makes N–1 and N–3 *in* and the other two nodes *out*. Now suppose a previously scheduled meeting rules out this combination of time and room for the meeting by supporting a new node with N–1 and N–3 and then declaring this new node to be a contradiction.

N–5 CONTRADICTION (SL (N–1 N–3) ( ))

The dependency-directed backtracking system traces the foundations of N–5 to find two assumptions, N–1 and N–3, both maximal.

N–6	NOGOOD N–1 N–3	(CP N–5 (N–1 N–3) ( ))	*here* ≡ (SL ( ) ( ))
N–4	ROOM(M) = 801	(SL (N–6 N–1) ( ))	

The backtracker creates N–6 which means, in accordance with form (1) of Step 2,

$$\neg(\mathrm{TIME}(M) = 1000 \wedge \mathrm{ROOM}(M) = 813)$$

and justifies N–6 according to form (2) above. It arbitrarily selects N–3 as the culprit, and justifies N–3's only *out* antecedent, N–4, according to form (3) above. Following this, the TMS makes N–1, N–4 and N–6 *in*, and N–2, N–3 and N–5 *out*. N–6 has a CP-justification equivalent to a premise SL-justification, since N–5 depends directly on the two assumptions N–1 and N–3 without any additional intervening nodes.

A further rule now determines that room 801 cannot be used after all, and creates another contradiction node to force a different choice of room.

N–7	CONTRADICTION	(SL (N–4) ( ))	
N–8	NOGOOD N–1	(CP N–7 (N–1) ( ))	*here*≡(SL (N–6) ( ))
N–2	TIME(M) ≠ 1000	(SL (N–8) ( ))	

Tracing backwards from N–7 through N–4, N–6 and N–1, the backtracker finds that the contradiction depends on only one assumption, N–1. It creates the nogood node N–8, justifies it with a CP-justification, in this case equivalent to the SL-justification (SL (N–6) ( )), since N–7's foundations contain N–6 and N–1's repercussions do not. The loss of belief in N–1 carried N–5 away as well, for the TMS makes N–2, N–3, N–6 and N–8 *in*, and N–1, N–4, N–5 and N–7 *out*.

5. Summarizing Arguments

Long or extremely detailed arguments are usually unintelligible. When possible, able expositors make their explanations intelligible by structuring them into clearly separated levels of detail, in which explanations of major points consist of several almost-major points, and so on, with each item explained in terms of the level of detail proper to the item. Structuring arguments in this way serves much the same purpose as structuring plans of action into levels of detail and abstraction. Users of the TMS, or any other means for recording explanations, must take care to convert raw explanations into structured one, if the explanations lack structure initially. Consider, as an exaggerated example, a centralized polling machine for use in national elections. At the end of Election Day, the machine reports that John F. Kennedy has won the election, and when pressed for an explanation of this decision, explains that Kennedy won because Joe Smith voted for him, and Fannie Jones voted for him, and Bert Brown voted for him, et cetera, continuing in this way for many millions of voters, pro and con. The desired explanation consists of a summary total of the votes cast for Kennedy, Nixon, and the other candidates. If pressed for further explanations, breakdowns of these totals into state totals follow. The next level of explanation expands into city totals, and only if utterly pressed should the machine break the results into precincts or individual voters for some place, say Cook County.

One can summarize the arguments and explanations recorded in the TMS by using conditional-proofs to subtract nodes representing "low-level" details from arguments. Summarizations can be performed on demand by creating a new node, and justifying this node with a CP-justification mentioning the node to be explained as its consequent, and the set of nodes representing the unwanted low-level beliefs as its *in* and *out*hypotheses. The effective explanation for the new node, via a SL-justification computed from the CP-justification, will consist solely of those high-level nodes present in the well-founded argument being summarized.

Explanations can be generalized or made more abstract by this device as well, by justifying the original node in terms of the new node, or by justifying the original node with the new SL-justification computed for the new node. This new justification will not mention any of the low-level details subtracted from the original argument, and so will support the conclusion as a general result, independent of the particular low-level details used to derive it. For example, an electronic circuit analysis program might compute the voltage gain of an amplifier by assuming a typical input voltage, using this voltage to compute the other circuit voltages including the output voltage, computing the voltage gain as the ratio of the output voltage to the input voltage, and finally justifying the resulting value for the gain using a conditional-proof of the output voltage value given the hypothesized input voltage value. This would leave the gain value depending only on characteristics of the circuit, not on the particular input voltage value used in the computation.

Returning to the election example above, summarizing the election result by subtracting out all the individual voter's ballots leaves the argument empty, for presumably the intermediate results were computed solely in terms of the ballots. In order to summarize an explanation, one must know the form of the desired summarization. While this analytical knowledge is frequently unavoidable, we typically can reduce its scope by introducing structure into arguments during their creation. To illustrate this point, we explain how one simple structuring technique works smoothly with so-called structured descriptions to easily produce perspicuous explanations.

For this discussion, we take a structured description to consist of a description-item (sometimes termed a "node" in the knowledge-representation literature; but we reserve this term for TMS nodes), a set of roles-items representing the parts of the description, and a set of local inference rules. These roles frequently represent entities associated with the description. For example, a PERSON description may have a MOTHER role, and an ADDER description may have roles for ADDEND, AUGEND, and SUM.

To structure explanations, we draw an analogy between the parts of a description and the calling sequence of a procedure. We associate one TMS node with each description-item and two TMS nodes with each role-item. We will use the node associated with a description-item to mark the arguments internal to the description, as explained shortly. We separate the nodes for role-items into two sets, corresponding to the external "calling sequence" and the internal "formal parameters" of the procedure. We use one of the nodes associated with each role-item to represent the external system's view of that "argument" to the procedure call, and the other node associated with the role-item to represent the procedure's view of that "formal parameter" of the procedure. Then we organize the problem solving program so that only the procedure and its internal rules use or justify the internal set of nodes, and that all other descriptions and procedures use or justify only the external set of nodes. The motivation for this separation of the users and justifiers of two sets of nodes into internal users and external users is that we can structure arguments by transmitting information between these two sets of nodes in a special way, as we now describe.

Let D be the node associated with the description, and let E_i and I_i be corresponding external and internal role-item nodes. We justify D to indicate the reason for the validity of the description. To distinguish internal arguments from external arguments, we justify I_i with

(SL (DE_i) ( )).

This makes all portions of arguments internal to the description depend on D. With the internal arguments marked in this way, we can separate them from other arguments when transmitting information from the internal nodes to the external nodes. We justify E_i with

(SUM I_i (D) ( )).

This justification subtracts all internal arguments from the explanation of E_i, and replaces them with the single node D.

For example, suppose the hypothetical voting program above computed the vote total for Somewhere, Illinois by summing the totals from the three precincts A, B, and C. The program isolates this level of the computation from the precinct computations by using an ADDER description to sum these subtotals.

N–1	ADDER DESCRIPTION AD	...	*Somewhere, IL*
N–2	EXTERNAL A OF AD = 500	...	*Precinct A*
N–3	EXTERNAL B OF AD = 200	...	*Precinct B*
N–4	EXTERNAL C OF AD = 700	...	*Precinct C*

Here the computations for the precinct totals justify the three precinct totals. The program then transmits these values to nodes representing the internal components of the adder description, and a local rule of the description computes the value of the sum component.

N–5	INTERNAL A OF AD = 500	(SL (N–1 N–2) ( ))
N–6	INTERNAL B OF AD = 200	(SL (N–1 N–3) ( ))
N–7	INTERNAL C OF AD = 700	(SL (N–1 N–4) ( ))
N–8	A + B OF AD = 700	(SL (N–5 N–6) ( )) *intermediate result*
N–9	INTERNAL SUM OF AD = 1400	(SL (N–7 N–8) ( ))

The program transmits this value for the sum to the node representing the external form of the result.

N–10	EXTERNAL SUM OF AC = 1400	(SUM N–9 (N–1) ( )) *here* ≡ (SL (N–1 N–2 N–3 N–4) ( ))

The SUM-justification for N–10 subtracts all dependence on any internal computations made by the adder, N–1. The resulting explanation for N–10 includes only N–1, N–2, N–3 and N–4. In cases involving more complex procedures than adders, with large numbers of internal nodes and computations of no interest to the external system, the use of this technique for structuring explanations into levels of detail might make the difference between an intelligible explanation and an unintelligible one.

6. Dialectical Arguments

Quine [41] has stressed that we can reject any of our beliefs at the expense of making suitable changes in our other beliefs. For example, we either can change our beliefs to accommodate new observations, or can reject the new observations as hallucinations or mistakes. Notoriously, philosophical arguments have argued almost every philosophical conclusion at the expense of other propositions. Philosophers conduct these arguments in a discipline called dialectial argumentation, in which one argues for a conclusion in two steps; first producing an argument for the conclusion, then producing arguments against the arguments for the opposing conclusion. In this discipline, each debater continually challenges those proposed arguments which he does not like by producing new arguments which either challenge one or more of the premises of the challenged arguments, or which challenge one or more steps of the challenged argument. We can view each debater as following this simplified procedure:

Step 1 (*Make an argument*). Put forward an argument A for a conclusion based on premises thought to be shared between debaters.

Step 2 (*Reply to challenges*). When some debater challenges either a premise or a step of A with an argument B, either (1) make a new argument for the conclusion of A, or (2) make an argument for the challenged premise or step of A challenging one of the premises or steps of B.

Step 3 (*Repeat*). Continue to reply to challenges, or make new arguments.

In this section we show how to organize a problem solving program's use of the TMS into the form of dialectical argumentation. Several important advantages and consequences motivate this. As the first consequence, we can reject any belief in a uniform fashion, simply by producing a new, as yet unchallenged, argument against some step or premise of the argument for the belief. We were powerless to do this with the basic TMS mechanisms in any way other than physically removing justifications from the belief system. This ability entails the second consequence, that we must explicitly provide ways to choose what to believe, to select which of the many possible revisions of our beliefs we will take when confronting new information. Quine has urged the fundamentally pragmatic nature of this question, and we must find mechanisms for stating and using pragmatic belief revision rules. As the third consequence of adopting this dialectial program organization, the belief system becomes additive. The system never discards arguments, but accumulates them and uses them whenever possible. This guides future debates by keeping them from repeating past debates. But the arguments alone comprise the belief system, since we derive the current set of beliefs from these arguments. Hence all changes to beliefs occur by adding new arguments to a monotonically growing store of arguments. Finally, as the fourth consequence, the inference system employed by the program becomes modular. We charge each component of the inference system with arguing for its conclusion and against opposing conclusions. On this view, we make each module be a debater rather than an inference rule.

We implement dialectial argumentation in the TMS by representing steps of arguments both by justifications and by beliefs. To allow us to argue against argument steps, we make these beliefs assumptions.

Suppose some module wants to justify node N with the justification (SL I O). Instead of doing this directly, the module creates a new node, J, representing the statement that I and O SL-justify N; in other words, that belief in each node of I and lack of belief in each node of O constitute a reason for believing in N. The module justifies N with the justification (SL $J+I$ O), where $J+I$ represents the list I augmented by J. The TMS will make N *in* by reason of this justification only if J is *in*. The nodule then creates another new node, $\neg J$, representing the statement that J represents a challenged justification. Finally, the module justifies J with the justification (SL ( ) ($\neg J$)). In this way, the module makes a new node to represent the justification as an explicit belief, and then assumes that the justification has not been challenged.

For example, suppose a module wishes to conclude that $X = 3$ from $X+Y = 4$ and $Y = 1$. In the dialectical use of the TMS, it proceeds as follows:

N–1	$X+Y = 4$	...
N–2	$Y = 1$	...
N–3	$X = 3$	(SL (N–4 N–1 N–2) ( ))
N–4	(N–1) AND (N–2) SL–JUSTIFY N–3	(SL ( ) (N–5))
N–5	N–4 IS CHALLENGED	*no justifications yet*

Since N–5 has no justifications, it is *out*, so N–4, and hence N–3, are *in*.

In this discipline, conflicts can be resolved either by challenging premises of arguments, or by challenging those justifications which represent arguments steps. Actually, premise justifications for nodes now become assumptions, for the explicit form of the premise justification is itself assumed. In either case, replies to arguments invalidate certain justifications by justifying the nodes representing the challenges. The proponent of the challenged argument can reply by challenging some justification in the challenging argument.

This way of using the TMS clearly makes blind dependency-directed backtracking useless, since the number of assumptions supporting a node becomes very large. Instead, we must use more refined procedures for identifying certain nodes as the causes of inconsistencies. I will return to this issue in Section 8.

7. Models of Others' Beliefs

Many problem solving tasks require us to reason about the beliefs of some agent. For example, according to the speech act theory of purposeful communication, I must reason about your beliefs and wants, and about your beliefs about my beliefs and wants [5, 49]. This requirement entails the ability to reason about embedded belief and want spaces, so called because these are sets of beliefs reported as compound or embedded statements of belief, for example, "I believe that you believe that it is raining." In fact, I must frequently reason about my own system of beliefs and wants. In planning, I must determine what I will believe and want after performing some actions, and this requires my determining how the actions affect my beliefs and wants. In explaining my actions, I must determine what I believed and wanted at some time in the past, before performing the intervening actions. And when choosing what to do, want or believe, I must reason about what I now am doing, wanting, or believing.

In making a problem solver which uses such models of belief systems, we face the problem of how to describe how additions to these models affect the beliefs contained in them, how belief revision proceeds within a model of a belief system. It would be extremely convenient if the same mechanism by which the program revises its own beliefs, namely the TMS, could be applied to revising these models as well. Fortuitously, the mechanism of representing justifications as explicit beliefs introduced in Section 6 lets us do just that.

To represent a belief system within our own, we use beliefs in our own system about the beliefs and justifications in the other system. We then mirror the other system's justifications of its beliefs by making corresponding justifications in our system's TMS of our beliefs about the other system's beliefs. For each node N in an agent U's belief system, we make two nodes, UB[N] and $\neg$UB[N], one representing that U believes in N, and the other representing that U doesn't believe in N. We justify $\neg$UB[N] with

(SL ( ) (UB[N])),

thus assuming that all nodes in U's system are *out* until given valid justifications. For each SL-justification J (= (SL I O)) for N in U's belief system, we make a node UB[J] representing that U's belief system contains J. We then justify UB[N] with the justification (SL L ( )), where L contains the node UB[J], the nodes UB[M] for each node M in I, and the nodes $\neg$UB[M] for each node M in O.

We might view this technique as embodying an observation of traditional modal logics of belief. Most of these logics include an axiom schema about the belief modality Bel of the form

$$\text{Bel}(p \supset q) \supset (\text{Bel}(p) \supset \text{Bel}(q)).$$

When we mirror embedded justifications with TMS justifications, we are making an inference analogous to the one licensed by this axiom.

For example, suppose the program believes than an agent U believes A, that U does not believe B, and that U believes C because he believes A and does not believe B. If we looked into U's TMS we might see the following nodes and justifications.

A	· · ·	· · ·
B	· · ·	· · ·
C	· · ·	(SL (A) (B))

Our program represents this fragment of U's belief system as follows:

N–1	UB[A]	· · ·	*UB means "U believes"*
N–2	¬UB[B]	(SL ( ) (N–3))	
N–3	UB[B]		*no justification yet*
N–4	UB[(A) AND (B) SL–JUSTIFY C]	· · ·	
N–5	UB[C]	(SL (N–4 N–1 N–2) ( ))	

In this case, N–1, N–2, N–4 and N–5 are *in*, and N–3 is *out*. If the program revises its beliefs so that N–2 is *out*, say by the addition of a new justification in U's belief system,

N–5	UB[· · · SL–JUSTIFY B]	· · ·
N–2	UB[B]	(SL (N–5 · · ·) ( ))

then the TMS will make N–5 *out* as well. In this way, changes made in particular beliefs in the belief system lead automatically to other changes in beliefs which represent the implied changes occurring within the belief system.

Of course, we can repeat this technique at each level of embedded belief spaces. To use this technique we must require the inference rules which draw conclusions inside a belief space to assert the corresponding beliefs about justifications for those conclusions. One frequently assumes that others have the same set of inference rules as oneself, that they can draw the same set of inferences from the same set of hypotheses. This assumption amounts to that of assuming that everyone operates under the same basic "program" but has different data or initial beliefs. I am currently exploring a formalization of this assumption in an "introspective" problem solver which has a description of itself as a program, and which uses this self-description as the basis of its models of the behavior of others [16].

8. Assumptions and the Problem of Control

How a problem solver revises its beliefs influences how it acts. Problem solvers typically revise their beliefs when new information (such as the expected effect of an action just taken or an observation just made) contradicts previous beliefs. These inconsistencies may be met by rejecting the belief that the action occurred or that the observation occurred. This might be thought of as the program deciding it was hallucinating. Sometimes, however, we choose to reject the previous belief and say that the action made a change in the world, or that we had made some inappropriate assumption which was corrected by observation. Either of these ways of revising beliefs may be warranted in different circumstances. For example, if during planning we encounter a contradiction by thinking through a proposed sequence of actions, we might decide to reject one of the proposed actions and try another action. On the other hand, if while carrying out a sequence of actions we encounter a contradiction in our beliefs, we might decide that some assumption we had about the world was wrong, rather than believe that we never took the last action. As this example suggests, we might choose to revise our beliefs in several different ways. Since we decide what to do based on what we believe and what we want, our choice of what to believe affects what we choose to do.

How can we guide the problem solver in its choice of what to believe? It must make its choice by approximating the set of possible revisions by the set of assumptions it can change directly, for it cannot see beforehand all the consequences of a change without actually making that change and seeing what happens. We have studied two means by which the problem solver can decide what to believe, the technique of encoding control information into the set of justifications for beliefs, and the technique of using explicit choice rules. Both of these approaches amount to having the reasoner deliberate about what to do. In the first case, the reasoning is "canned." In the second, the reasoning is performed on demand.

We encode some control information into the set of justifications for beliefs by using patterns of non-monotonic justifications. We can think of a non-monotonic justification (SL ( ) (N–2 N–3)) for N–1 as suggesting the order in which these nodes should be believed, N–1 first, then N–2 or N–3 second. On this view, each non-monotonic justification contributes a fragment of control information which guides how the problem solver revises its beliefs. In Sections 8.1, 8.2 and 8.3, we illustrate how to encode several standard control structures in patterns of justifications, namely default assumptions, sequences of alternatives, and a way of choosing representatives of equivalence classes useful in controlling propagation of constraints (a deduction technique presented by [53]). These examples should suggest how other control structures such as decision trees or graphs might be encoded.

Even with these fragments of control information, many alternative revisions may appear possible to the problem solver. In such cases, we may wish to provide the problem solver with rules or advice about how to choose which revision to make. If we are clever (or lazy), we might structure the problem solver so that it uses the same language and mechanisms for these revision rules as for rules for making other choices, such as what action to perform next, how to carry out an action, or which goal to pursue next. In [11] my colleagues and I incorporated this suggestion into a general methodology which we call *explicit control of reasoning*, and implemented AMORD, a language of pattern-invoked procedures controlled by the TMS. I am currently studying a problem solver architecture, called a *reflexive interpreter*, in which the problem solver's structure and behavior are themselves domains for reasoning and action by the problem solver [16]. This sort of interpreter represents its own control state to itself explicitly among its beliefs as a *task network* similar to that used in McDermott's [34] NASL, in which problems or intentions are represented as *tasks*. The interpreter also represents to itself its own structure as a program by means of a set of *plans*, abstract fragments of task network. It represents the important control state of having to make a choice by creating a *choice task*, whose carrying out involves making a choice. The interpreter can then treat this choice task as a problem for solution like any other task. In this framework, we formulate rules for guiding belief revision as plans for carrying out choice tasks. We index these revision plans by aspects of the problem solver state, for example, by the historical state, by the control state, by the state of the problem solution, by the domain, by the action just executed, and by other circumstances. Each revision plan might be viewed as a specialization of the general dependency-directed backtracking procedure. Such refinements of the general backtracking procedure take the form of the beliefs (and thus the problem solver state) into account when deciding which assumptions should be rejected. I will report the details of my investigation in my forthcoming thesis.

8.1. Default assumptions

Problem solving programs frequently make specifications of default values for the quantities they manipulate, with the intention either of allowing specific reasons for using other values to override the current values, or of rejecting the default if it leads to an inconsistency. (See [45] for a lucid exposition of some applications.) The example in Section 1.2 includes such a default assumption for the day of the week of a meeting.

To pick the default value from only two alternatives, we justify the default node non-monotonically on the grounds that the alternative node is *out*. We generalize this binary case to choose a default from a larger set of alternatives. Take $S = \{A_1, \ldots, A_n\}$ to be the set of alternative nodes, and if desired, let G be a node which represents the reason for making an assumption to choose the default. To make A_i the default, justify it with

$$(\mathrm{SL}\,(G)\,(A_1 \cdots A_{i-1}\, A_{i+1} \cdots A_n)).$$

If no additional information about the value exists, none of the alternative nodes except A_i will have a valid justification, so A_i will be *in* and each of the other alternative nodes will be *out*. Adding a valid justification to some other alternative node causes that alternative to become *in*, and invalidates the support of A_i, so A_i goes *out*. When analyzing a contradiction derived from A_i, the dependency-directed backtracking mechanism recognizes A_i as an assumption because it depends on the other alternative nodes being *out*. The backtracker may then justify one of the other alternative nodes, say A_j, causing A_i to go *out*. This backtracker-produced justification for A_j will have the form

(SL ⟨various nodes⟩ ⟨remainder nodes⟩)

where ⟨remainder nodes⟩ is the set of A_k's remaining in S after A_i and A_j are taken away. In effect, the backtracker removes the default node from the set of alternatives, and makes a new default assumption from the remaining alternatives. As a concrete example, our scheduling program might default a meeting day as follows:

N-1	PREFER W. TO M. OR F.	...
N-2	DAY(M) = MONDAY	
N-3	DAY(M) = WEDNESDAY	(SL (N-1) (N-2 N-4))
N-4	DAY(M) = FRIDAY	

The program assumes Wednesday to be the day of the meeting M, with Monday and Friday as alternatives. The TMS will make Wednesday the chosen day until the program gives a valid reason for taking Monday or Friday instead.

We use a slightly different set of justifications if the complete set of alternatives cannot be known in advance but must be discovered piecemeal. This ability to extend the set of alternatives is necessary, for example, when the default is a number, due to the large set of possible alternatives. Retaining the above notation, we represent the negation of St(A_i) with a new node, $\neg A_i$. We arrange for A_i to be believed if $\neg A_i$ is *out*, and set up justifications so that if A_j is distinct from A_j, A_j supports $\neg A_i$. We justify A_i with

$$(\mathrm{SL}\,(G)\,(\neg A_i)),$$

and justify $\neg A_i$ with a justification of the form

$$(\mathrm{SL}\,(A_j)\,(\ ))$$

for each alternative A_j distinct from A_i. As before, A_i will be assumed if no reasons for using any other alternative exist. Furthermore, new alternatives can be added to the set S simply by giving $\neg A_i$ a new justification corresponding to the new alternative. As before, if the problem solving program justifies an unselected alternative, the TMS will make the default node *out*. Backtracking, however, has a new effect. If A_i supports a contradiction, the backtracker may justify $\neg A_i$ so as to make A_i become *out*. When this happens, the TMS has no way to select an alternative to take the place of the default assumption. The extensible structure requires an external mechanism to construct a new default assumption whenever the current default is ruled out. For example, a family planning program might make assumptions about the number of children in a family as follows:

N-1	PREFER 2 CHILDREN	...
N-2	#-CHILDREN(F) = 2	(SL (N-1) (N-3))
N-3	#-CHILDREN(F) ≠ 2	(SL (N-4) ( ))
		(SL (N-5) ( ))
□		(SL (N-6) ( ))
		(SL (N-7) ( ))
N-4	#-CHILDREN(F) = 0	
N-5	#-CHILDREN(F) = 1	
N-6	#-CHILDREN(F) = 3	
N-7	#-CHILDREN(F) = 4	

With this system of justifications, the TMS would make N–2 *in*. If the planning program finds some compelling reason for having 5 children, it would have to create a new node to represent this fact, along with a new justification for N–3 in terms of this new node.

8.2. Sequences of alternatives

Linearly ordered sets of alternatives add still more control information to a default assumption structure, namely the order in which the alternatives should be tried. This extra heuristic information might be used, for example, to order selections of the day of the week for a meeting, of a planning strategy, or of the state of a transistor in a proposed circuit analysis.

We represent a sequence of alternatives by a controlled progression of default assumptions. Take $\{A_1, \ldots, A_n\}$ to be the heuristically-ordered sequence of alternative nodes, and let G be a node which represents the reason for this heuristic ordering. We justify each A_i with

$$(\mathrm{SL}\,(G \neg A_{i-1})\,(\neg A_i)).$$

A_1 will be selected initially, and as the problem solver rejects successive alternatives by justifying their negations, the TMS will believe the successive alternatives in turn. For example, our scheduling program might have:

N–1	SEQUENCE N–2 N–4 N–6	...
N–2	DAY(M) = WEDNESDAY	(SL (N–1) (N–3))
N–3	DAY(M) ≠ WEDNESDAY	
N–4	DAY(M) = THURSDAY	(SL (N–1 N–3) (N–5))
N–5	DAY(M) ≠ THURSDAY	
N–6	DAY(M) = TUESDAY	(SL (N–1 N–5) ( ))

This would guide the choice of day for the meeting M to Wednesday, Thursday and Tuesday, in that order.

Note that this way of sequencing through alternatives allows no direct way for the problem solving program to reconsider previously rejected alternatives. If, say, we wish to use special case rules to correct imprudent choices of culprits made by the backtracking system, we need a more complicated structure to represent linearly ordered alternatives. We create three new nodes for each alternative A_i: PA_i, which means that A_i is a possible alternative, NSA_i, which means that A_i is not the currently selected alternative, and ROA_i, which means that A_i is a ruled-out alternative. We suggest members for the set of alternatives by justifying each PA_i with the reason for including A_i in the set of alternatives. We leave ROA_i unjustified, and justify each A_i and NSA_i with

A_i: (SL (PA_i $NSA_1 \cdots NSA_{i-1}$) (ROA_i))
NSA_i: (SL ( ) (PA_i))
(SL (ROA_i) ( )).

Here the justification for A_i is valid if and only if A_i is an alternative, no better alternative is currently selected, and A_i is not ruled out. The two justifications for NSA_i mean that either A_i is not a valid alternative, or that A_i is ruled out. With this structure, different parts of the problem solver can independently rule in or rule out an alternative by justifying the appropriate A or ROA node. In addition, we can add new alternatives to the end of such a linear order by constructing justifications as specified above for the new nodes representing the new alternative.

8.3. Equivalence class representatives

Problem solvers organized to encourage modularity and additivity frequently contain several different methods or rules which compute values for the same quantity or descriptions for the same object. We call these multiple results *coincidences*, after [9, 59]. If the several methods compute several values, we can often derive valuable information by checking these competing values for consistency. With polynomials as values, for example, this consistency checking sometimes allows solving for the values of one or more variables. After checking the coincidence for consistency and new information, prudent programs normally use only one of the suggested values in further computation, and retain the other values for future reference. The various values form an *equivalence class* with respect to the propagation of the value in other computations, and one of the values in this class must be chosen as the representative for propagation. We could choose the representative with a default assumption, but this would lead to undesirable backtracking behavior. For instance, if the backtracking system finds the equivalence class representative involved in an inconsistency, then it should find some way of rejecting the representative as a proper value, rather than letting it stand and selecting a new representative. This means the backtracker should find the choice of representative invisible, and this requirement rules out using either the default assumption or sequence of alternatives representations.

We select equivalence class representatives by using conditional-proof justifications to hide the choice mechanism from the backtracking system. For each node R_i representing an equivalence class member, we create two new nodes: PR_i, which means that R_i is a possible representative, and SR_i, which means that R_i is the selected representative. Rather than the program deriving justifications for the R nodes directly, it should instead suggest these values as possible representatives by justifying the corresponding PR nodes instead. With this stipulation we justify each R_i and SR_i as follows:

SR_i: (SL (PR_i) ($SR_1 \cdots SR_{i-1}$))
R_i: (CP SR_i ( ) ($SR_1 \cdots SR_{i-1}$))

Here the justification for SR_i means that R_i has been suggested as a member of the equivalence class, and that no other member of the class has been selected as the representative. This justification constitutes a default assumption of R_i as the selected representative. However, the justification for R_i means that the reason for believing R_i will be the reason for both suggesting and selecting R_i (the argument for SR_i), minus the reason for selecting it (the default assumption), thus leaving only the reason for which R_i was suggested, namely the antecedents of PR_i. In this way the equivalence class selector picks alternatives as the representative in the order in which they were added to the set of alternatives, while hiding this selection from the backtracking system.

For example, suppose a commodity analysis program derives two values for the predicted number of tons of wheat grown this year and notices this coincidence.

N–1	SUGGEST WHEAT (1979) = $5X+3000$	(SL (R–57 · · ·) ( ))
N–2	SUGGEST WHEAT (1979) = $7Y$	(SL (R–60 · · ·) ( ))
N–3	$Y = (5X+3000)/7$	(SL (N–1 N–2) ( ))

These suggested values correspond to possible equivalence class representatives. To avoid using both values in further computations, the program chooses one.

N–4	N–1 SELECTED	(SL (N–1) ( ))
N–5	WHEAT (1979) = $5X+3000$	(CP N–4 ( ) ( ))
		here=(SL (N–1) ( ))
N–6	N–2 SELECTED	(SL (N–2) (N–4))
N–7	WHEAT (1979) = $7Y$	(CP N–6 ( ) (N–4))

Since N–1 is *in* and it is the first in the ordering imposed by the selection justifications, it is selected to be the value propagated, and the TMS makes N–4 and N–5 *in*. Suppose now that some contradiction occurs and has N–5 in its foundations, and that the dependency-directed backtracker denies some assumption in N–1's foundations. Consequently, the TMS makes N–1 (and N–3) *out*, and N–6 and N–7 *in*, with N–7's CP-justification equivalent in this case to (SL(N–2)( )). Thus the pattern of justifications leads to selecting the second suggested value. If the program then finds a third value,

N–8	SUGGEST WHEAT (1979) = $4X+100$	· · ·
N–9	$Y = (4X+100)/7$	(SL (N–2 N–8) ( ))
N–10	N–8 SELECTED	(SL (N–8) (N–4 N–6))
N–11	WHEAT (1979) = $4X+100$	(CP N–10 ( ) (N–4 N–6))

it will derive any new information possible from the new value, then add the new value to the list of waiting alternative values for propagation. In this case, N–8 and N–9 are *in*, and N–10 and N–11 are *out*.

9. Experience and Extensions

We have experience with the TMS in a number of programs and applications. I implemented the first version of the TMS in September 1976, as an extension (in several ways) of the "fact garbage collector" of Stallman and Sussman's [53] ARS electronic circuit analysis program. After that, I took the program through many different versions. Howard Shrobe and James Stansfield also made improvements in the program. Truth maintenance techniques have been applied in several other circuit analysis and synthesis programs, including SYN [12] and QUAL [10], and in Steele and Sussman's [56] constraint language. We organized our rule-based problem solving system AMORD [11] around the TMS, and used AMORD in developing a large number of experimental programs, ranging from blocks world problem solvers to circuit analysis programs and compilers. McAllester [31] uses his own truth maintenance system in a program for symbolic algebra, electronic circuit analysis, and programming. In addition, Weiner [62] of UCLA used AMORD to implement an explanation system in studying the structure of natural explanations, and Shrobe [50] uses AMORD in a program-understanding system.

Several researchers have extended the basic belief-revision techniques of the TMS by embedding them in larger frameworks which incorporate time, certainty measures, and other problem solving concepts and processes. Friedman [19] and Stansfield [54] merge representations of continuous degrees of belief with truth maintenance techniques. London [29] and Thompson [60] add chronological contexts to a dependency-based framework. London also presents many detailed examples of the use of dependency networks in the modelling component of a problem solving program.

Improvements in the basic truth maintenance process have also been suggested. McAllester [30] describes a relative of the TMS based on a three-valued belief set, with multi-directional clauses as justifications. Thompson [60] generalizes the node-justification structure of the TMS to non-clausal arguments and justifications. Shrobe (in [50] and in personal communications) has suggested several ways in which the problem solver can profit by reasoning about the structure of arguments, particularly in revising its set of goals after solving some particular goal. These ideas suggest other improvements including (1) modification of the TMS to make use of multiple supporting-justifications whenever several well-founded arguments can be found for a node, (2) use of the TMS to signal the problem solver whenever the argument for some node changes, and (3) development of a language for describing and efficiently recognizing patterns in arguments for nodes, well-founded or otherwise. How to incorporate truth maintenance techniques into "virtual-copy" representational systems [17] also seems worth study.

The TMS continually checks CP-justifications for validity, in hopes of deriving new equivalent SL-justifications. This makes the implementation considerably more complex than one might imagine. I expect that a simpler facility would be more generally useful, namely the TMS without CP-justifications, but with the Find Independent Support procedure isolated as a separate, user invoked facility. Practical experience shows that in most cases, one only expects the CP-justification to be valid in the situation in which it is created, so it seems reasonable to make the user responsible for calling FIS directly rather than letting the TMS do it.

Finally, a cluster of problems center about incrementality. The TMS normally avoids examining the entire data base when revising beliefs, and instead examines only the repercussions of the changed nodes. However, apparently unsatisfiable circularities can occur which require examining nodes not included in these repercussions. In another sense of incrementality, some circumstances can force the TMS to examine large numbers of nodes, only to leave most of them in their original state after finding alternate non-circular arguments for the supposedly changed nodes. Latombe [27] has investigated ways of avoiding this, but these difficulties deserve further study. One particularly enticing possibility is that of adapting the ideas of Baker's [1] real-time list garbage-collection algorithms to the case of truth maintenance.

10. Discussion

The TMS solves part of the belief revision problem, and provides a mechanism for making non-monotonic assumptions. Artificial intelligence researchers recognized early on that AI systems must make assumptions, and many of their systems employed some mechanism for this purpose. Unfortunately, the related problem of belief revision received somewhat less study. Hayes [21] emphasized the importance of the belief revision problem, but with the exception of Colby [6], who employed a belief system with reasons for some beliefs, as well as measures of credibility and emotional importance for beliefs, most work on revising beliefs appears to have been restricted to the study of backtracking algorithms operating on rather simple systems of states and actions. The more general problem of revising beliefs based on records of inferences has only been examined in more recent work, including Cox's [7] graphical deduction system, Crocker's [8] verification system, de Kleer's [9] electronic circuit analysis program, Fikes' [18] deductive modelling system, Hayes' [22] travel planning system, Katz and Manna's [24] program modification system, Latombe's [26, 27] design program, London's [29] planning and modelling system, McDermott's [32, 33, 34] language understanding, data base, and design programs, Moriconi's [39] verification system, Nevins' [40] theorem prover, Shrobe's [50] program understanding system, the MDS/AIMDS/BELIEVER programs [47, 51, 52], and Sussman and Stallman's [53, 59] electronic circuit analysis programs. Berliner's [3] chess program employed "lemmas" for recording interesting facts about partial board analyses of conditional-proofs, but the program derives these lemmas through a perturbation technique rather than through analysis of arguments and justifications.

In addition, the philosophical literature includes many treatments of belief revision and related problems. Many writers study evaluative criteria for judging which belief revisions are best, based on the connections between beliefs. Quine and Ullian [43] survey this area. Other writers study the problems of explanations, laws, and counterfactual conditions. Rescher [44] builds on Goodman's [20] exposition of these problems to present a framework for belief revision motivated by Quine's [41, 42] "minimum mutilation" principle. Lewis [28] and Turner [61] propose means for filling in this framework. Scriven [48] relates these questions to the problem of historical explanation in a way quite reminiscent of our non-monotonic arguments for beliefs. Suppes [57] surveys work on learning and rational changes of belief. The view of reasoning proposed in Section 1.1 is connected with many topics in the theories of belief, action, and practical reasoning. Minsky [37] presents a theory of memory which includes a more general view of reasoning.

Kramosil [25] initiated the mathematical study of non-monotonic inference rules, but reached pessimistic conclusions. More recently, McDermott and I [35] attempt to formalize the logic underlying the TMS with what we call *non-monotonic logic*. We also survey the history of such reasoning techniques. Weyhrauch [63] presents a framework for meta-theoretic reasoning in which these reasoning techniques and others can be expressed. Hintikka [23] presents a form of possible-world semantics for modal logics of knowledge and belief. Moore [38] combines this semantics for knowledge with a modal logic of action, but ignores belief and belief revision.

One might hope to find clues about how to organize the TMS's analysis of potential arguments for beliefs by studying what types of arguments humans find easy or difficult to understand. Statman [55] indicates that humans have difficulty following arguments which have many back-references to distant statements. He attempts to formalize some notions of the complexity of proofs using measures based on the topology of the proof graph. Wiener [62] catalogues and analyzes a corpus of human explanations, and finds that most exhibit a fairly simple structure. De Kleer [10] studies causal explanations of the sort produced by engineers, and discovers that a few simple principles govern a large number of these explanations.

I have used the term "belief" freely in this paper, so much so that one might think the title "Belief Revision System" more appropriate, if no less ambitious, than "Truth Maintenance System." Belief, however, for many people carries with it a concept of grading, yet the TMS has no non-trivial grading of beliefs. (Section 9 mentioned some extensions which do.) Perhaps a more accurate label would be "opinion revision system," where I follow Dennett [13] in distinguishing between binary judgemental assertions (opinions) and graded underlying feelings (beliefs). As Dennett explains, this distinction permits description of those circumstances in which reasoned arguments force one to assert a conclusion, even though one does not believe the conclusion. Hesitation, self-deception, and other complex states of belief and opinion can be described in this way. I feel it particularly apt to characterize the TMS as revising opinions rather than beliefs. Choosing what to "believe" in the TMS involves making judgements, rather than continuously accreting strengths or confidences. A single new piece of information may lead to sizable changes in the set of opinions, where new beliefs typically change old ones only slightly.

I also find this distinction between binary judgements and graded approximations useful in distinguishing non-monotonic reasoning from imprecise reasoning, such as that modelled by Zadeh's [64] fuzzy logic. I view the non-monotonic capabilities of the TMS as capabilities for dealing with incomplete information, but here the incompleteness is "exact": it makes binary statements about (typically) precise statements. Any approximation in the logic enters only when one views the set of current beliefs as a whole. In the logics of imprecise reasoning, the incompleteness is "inexact": the statements themselves are vague, and the vagueness need not be a property of the entire system of beliefs. While both approaches appear to be concerned with related issues, they seem to be orthogonal in their current development, which suggests studies of their combination. (Cf. [19].)

One final note: the overhead required to record justifications for every program belief might seem excessive. Some of this burden might be eliminated by using the summarization techniques of Section 5 to replace certain arguments with smaller ones, or by adopting some (hopefully well-understood) discipline of retaining only essential records from which all discarded information can be easily recomputed. However, the pressing issue is not the expense cf keeping records of the sources of beliefs. Rather, we must consider the expense of *not* keeping these records. If we throw away information about derivations, we may be condemning ourselves to continually rederiving information in large searches caused by changing irrelevant assumptions. This original criticism of MICRO-PLANNER (in [58]) applies to the context mechanisms of CONNIVER and QA4 as well. If we discard the sources of beliefs, we may make impossible the correction of errors in large, evolving data bases. We will find such techniques not just desirable, but necessary, when we attempt to build truly complex programs and systems. Lest we follow the tradition of huge, incomprehensible systems which spawned Software Engineering, we must, in Gerald Sussman's term, make "responsible" programs which can explain their actions and conclusions to a user. (Cf. [46].)

ACKNOWLEDGEMENTS

This paper is based on a thesis submitted in partial fulfillment of the degree of Master of Science to the department of Electrical Engineering and Computer Science of the Massachusetts Institute of Technology on May 12, 1977. Sections 6 and 7 contain material not reported in that thesis. Although I have held the views expressed in Section 1.1 for several years, I found my prior attempts at explaining them unsatisfactory, so these views appear here for the first time as well. I thank Gerald Jay Sussman (thesis advisor), Johan de Kleer, Scott Fahlman, Philip London, David McAllester, Drew McDermott, Marvin Minsky, Howard Shrobe, Richard M. Stallman, Guy L. Steele, Jr., and Alan Thompson for ideas and comments. de Kleer, Steele, Marilyn Matz, Richard Fikes, Randall Davis, Shrobe, and the referees of the Journal *Artificial Intelligence* gave me valuable editorial advice. I thank the Fannie and John Hertz Foundation for supporting my research with a graduate fellowship.

REFERENCES

1. Baker, H. G. Jr., List processing in real time on a serial computer, *C. ACM*, **21** (4) (April 1978) 280–294.
2. Belnap, N. D., How a computer should think, in: Gilbert Ryle (Ed.), *Contfempoorary Aspects Philosophy* (Oriel, Stocksfield, 1976).
3. Berliner, H. J., Chess as problem solving: The development of a tactics analyzer, CMU Computer Science Department (1974).
4. Charniak, E., Riesbeck, C. and McDermott, D., *Artificial Intelligence Programming* (Lawrence Erlbaum, Hillsdale, New Jersey, 1979).
5. Cohen, P. R., On knowing what to say: Planning speech acts, Department of Computer Science, University of Toronto, TR-118 (1978).
6. Colby, K. M., Simulations of belief systems, in: R. C. Schank and K. M. Colby (Eds.) *Computer Models of Thought and Language* (W. H. Freeman, San Francisco, 1973) pp. 251–286.
7. Cox, P. T., Deduction plans: A graphical proof procedure for the first-order predicate calculus, Department of Computer Science, University of Waterloo, Research Report CS-77-28 (1977).
8. Crocker, S. D., State deltas: A formalism for representing segments of computation, University of Southern California, Information Sciences Institute, RR–77–61 (1977).
9. De Kleer, J., Local methods for localization of failures in electronic circuits, MIT AI Lab, Memo 394 (November 1976).
10. De Kleer, J., Causal and teleological reasoning in circuit recognition, Ph.D. Thesis, MIT Department of Electrical Engineering and Computer Science (1979).
11. De Kleer, J., Doyle, J., Steele, G. L. Jr., and Sussman, G. J., Explicit control of reasoning, *Proc. ACM Symp. on Artificial Intelligence and Programming Languages* (Rochester, New York, 1977), also MIT AI Lab, Memo 427 (1977).
12. De Kleer, J. and Sussman, G. J., Propagation of constraints applied to circuit synthesis, MIT AI Lab, Memo 485 (1978).
13. Dennett, D. C., How to change your mind, in: *Brainstorms* (Bradford, Montgomery, VT, 1978), pp. 300–309.
14. Doyle, J., The use of dependency relationships in the control of reasoning, MIT AI Lab, Working Paper 133 (1976).
15. Doyle, J., Truth maintenance systems for problem solving, MIT AI Lab, TR–419 (1978).
16. Doyle, J., Reflexive interpreters, MIT Department of Electrical Engineering and Computer Science, Ph.D. proposal (1978).
17. Fahlman, S. E., NETL: *A System for Representing and Using Real World Knowledge* (MIT Press, Cambridge, 1979).
18. Fikes, R. E., Deductive retrieval mechanisms for state description models, *Proc. Fourth International Joint Conference on Artificial Intelligence* (1975) pp. 99–106.
19. Friedman, L., Plausible inference: A multi-valued logic for problem solving, Jet Propulsion Laboratory, Pasadena, CA, Report 79–11 (1979).
20. Goodman, N., The problem of counterfactual conditionals, in: *Fact, Fiction, and Forecast* (Bobbs-Merrill, NY, 1973) pp. 3–27.
21. Hayes, P. J., The frame problem and related problems in artificial intelligence, in: A. Elithorn and D. Jones (Eds.), *Artificial and Human Thinking* (Josey-Bass, San Francisco, 1973).
22. Hayes, P. J., A representation for robot plans, *Proc. Fourth IJCAI* (1975), pp. 181–188.
23. Hintikka, J., *Knowledge and Belief* (Cornell University Press, Ithica, 1962).
24. Katz, S. and Manna, Z., Logical analysis of programs, C. *ACM* **19** (4) (1976) 188–206.
25. Kramosil, I., A note on deduction rules with negative premises, *Proc. Fourth IJCAI* (1975) 53–56.
26. Latombe, J.-C., Une application de l'intelligence artificielle a la conception assistée par ordinateur (TROPIC), Université Scientifique et Médicale de Grenôble, Thesis D.Sc. Mathematiques (1977).
27. Latombe, J.-C., Failure processing in a system for designing complex assemblies, *Proc. Sixth IJCAI* (1979).
28. Lewis, D., *Counterfactuals* (Basil Blackwell, London, 1973).
29. London, P. E., Dependency networks as a representation for modelling in general problem solvers, Department of Computer Science University of Maryland, TR–698 (1978).

30. McAllester, D. A., A three-valued truth maintenance system, MIT AI Lab., Memo 473 (1978).
31. McAllester, D. A., The use of equality in deduction and knowledge representation, MIT Department of Electrical Engineering and Computer Science, M.S. Thesis (1979).
32. McDermott, D., Assimilation of new information by a natural language understanding system, MIT AI Lab., AI–TR–291 (1974).
33. McDermott, D., Very large PLANNER-type data bases, MIT AI Lab. AI Memo 339 (1975).
34. McDermott, D., Planning and acting, *Cognitive Science* **2** (1978) 71–109.
35. McDermott, D. and Doyle, J., Non-monotonic logic I, MIT AI Lab., Memo 486 (1978).
36. Minsky, M., A framework for representing knowledge, MIT AI Lab., Memo 306 (1974).
37. Minsky, M., *K*-lines: A theory of memory, MIT AI Lab., Memo 516 (1979).
38. Moore, R. C., Reasoning about knowledge and action, Ph.D. Thesis MIT, Department of Electrical Engineering and Computer Science (1979).
39. Moriconi, M., A system for incrementally designing and verifying programs, University of Southern California, Information Sciences Institute, RR–77–65 (1977).
40. Nevins, A. J., A human-oriented logic for automatic theorem proving, *J. ACM* **21** (4) (October 1974) 606–621.
41. Quine, W. V., Two dogmas of empiricism, in: *From a Logical Point of View* (Harvard University Press, Cambridge, 1953).
42. Quine, W. V., *Philosophy of Logic* (Prentice-Hall, Englewood Cliffs, 1970).
43. Quine, W. V. and Ullian, J. S., *The Web of Belief* (Random House, NY, 1978).
44. Rescher, N., *Hypothetical Reasoning* (North-Holland, Amsterdam, 1964).
45. Reiter, R., On reasoning by default, *Proc. Second Symp. on Theoretical Issues in Natural Language Processing* (Urbana, IL, 1978).
46. Rich, C., Shrobe, H. E., and Waters, R. C., Computer aided evolutionary design for software engineering, MIT AI Lab., Memo 506 (1979).
47. Schmidt, C. F. and Sridharan, N. S., Plan recognition using a hypothesize and revise paradigm: An example, *Proc. Fifth IJCAI* (1977) 480–486.
48. Scriven, M., Truisms as the grounds for historical explanations, in: P. Gardiner (Ed.) *Theories of History* (Free Press, New York, 1959).
49. Searle, J. R., *Speech Acts* (Cambridge University Press, 1969).
50. Shrobe, H. E., Dependency directed reasoning for complex program understanding, MIT AI Lab., TR–503 (1979).
51. Sridharan, N. S. and Hawrusik, F., Representation of actions that have side-effects, *Proc. Fifth IJCAI* (1977) 265–266.
52. Srinivasan, C. V., The architecture of coherent information system: A general problem solving system, *IEEE Trans. Computers* **C–25** (4) (April 1976) 390–402.
53. Stallman, R. M. and Sussman, G. J., Forward reasoning and dependency-directed backtracking in a system for computer-aided circuit analysis, *Artificial Intelligence* **9** (2) (October 1977) 135–196.
54. Stansfield, J. L., Integrating truth maintenance systems with propagation of strength of belief as a means of addressing the fusion problem, MIT AI Lab., draft proposal (1978).
55. Statman, R., Structural complexity of proofs, Stanford University Department of Mathematics, Ph.D. Thesis (1974).
56. Steele, G. L. Jr. and Sussman, G. J., Constraints, MIT AI Lab., Memo 502 (1978).
57. Suppes, P., A survey of contemporary learning theories, in: R. E. Butts and J. Hintikka (Eds.), *Foundational Problems in the Special Sciences* (D. Reidel, Dordrecht, 1977).
58. Sussman, G. J. and McDermott, D., From PLANNER to CONNIVER—A genetic approach, *Proc. AFIPS FJCC* (1972) 1171–1179.
59. Sussman, G. J. and Stallman, R. M., Heuristic techniques in computer-aided circuit analysis *IEEE Trans. Circuits and Systems* **CAS–22** (11) (November 1975) 857–865.
60. Thompson, A., Network truth maintenance for deduction and modelling. *Proc. Sixth IJCAI* (1979).
61. Turner, R., Counterfactuals without possib'e worlds, University of Essex (1978).
62. Weiner, J., The structure of natural explanations: Theory and applications, Ph.D. Thesis, University of California, Los Angeles (1979).
63. Weyhrauch, R. W., Prolegomena to a theory of formal reasoning, Stanford AI Lab., AIM–315 (1978).
64. Zadeh, L., Fuzzy logic and approximate reasoning, *Synthese* **30** (1975) 407–428.

Generalization as Search

Tom M. Mitchell

Computer Science Department
Rutgers University
New Brunswick, NJ 08903

1 Introduction

"Learning" is a broad term covering a wide range of processes. We learn (memorize) multiplication tables, learn (discover how) to walk, learn (build up an understanding of, then an ability to synthesize) languages. Many subtasks and capabilities are involved in these various kinds of learning.

One capability central to many kinds of learning is the ability to generalize: to take into account a large number of specific observations, then to extract and retain the important common features that characterize classes of these observations. This generalization problem has received considerable attention for two decades in the fields of Artificial Intelligence, Psychology, and Pattern Recognition (e.g., [Bruner, 1956], [Nilsson, 1965], [Minsky, 1969], [Hunt, 1975], [Plotkin, 1970], [Waterman, 1970], [Winston, 1975], [Brown, 1973], [Michalski, 1973], [Hayes-Roth, 1975], [Mitchell, 1977], [Buchanan, 1978], [Vere, 1978]). The results so far have been tantalizing: partially successful generalization programs have been written for problems ranging from learning fragments of spoken English to learning rules of chemical spectroscopy. But comparing alternative strategies, and developing a general understanding of techniques has been difficult because of differences in data representations, terminology, and problem characteristics.

The purpose of this paper is to compare various approaches to generalization in terms of a single framework. Toward this end, generalization is cast as a search problem, and alternative methods for generalization are characterized in terms of the search strategies that they employ. This characterization uncovers similarities among approaches, and leads to a comparison of relative capabilities and computational complexities of alternative approaches. The characterization allows a precise comparison of systems that utilize different representations for learned generalizations.

2 The Problem

The class of generalization problems considered here can be described as follows: A program accepts input observations (instances) represented in some language, which we shall call the instance language. Learned generalizations correspond to sets of these instances, and are formulated by the program as statements in a second language, which we shall call the generalization language. In order to associate instances with generalizations, the program must possess a matching predicate that tests whether a given instance and generalization match (i.e., whether the given instance is contained in the instance set corresponding to the given generalization).

Given the instance language, generalization language, and matching predicate, the generalization problem is to infer the identity of some unknown "target" generalization by observing a sample set of its training instances. Each training instance is an instance from the given language, along with its classification as either an instance of the target generalization (positive instance) or not an instance of the target generalization (negative instance). This generalization problem can be summarized as follows:

Generalization Problem:

Given:

1. A language in which to describe instances.
2. A language in which to describe generalizations.
3. A matching predicate that matches generalizations to instances.
4. A set of positive and negative training instances of a target generalization to be learned.

Determine: Generalizations within the provided language that are consistent with the presented training instances (i.e., plausible descriptions of the target generalization).

Here, a generalization is considered to be consistent with a set of training instances if and only if it matches every positive instance and no negative instance in the set. With this strict definition of consistency, we assume (1) that the training instances contain no errors and (2) that it is possible to formulate a correct description of the target generalization within the given generalization language. Although several of the systems discussed in this paper have attempted to deal with learning from inconsistent training data, an analysis of performance in such cases is beyond the scope of this paper.

Throughout this paper we shall refer to a simple example of the above class of generalization problems, in order to illustrate several approaches to learning. In this problem, the instances are unordered pairs of simple objects characterized by three properties. Each object is described by its shape (e.g., square, circle, triangle), its color (e.g., red, orange, yellow), and its size (e.g., large, small). The instance language will describe each instance as an unordered pair of feature vectors, each of which specifies the size, color, and shape of an object. For example, Instance1 below describes an instance in this language.

Instance1: { (Large Red Square) (Small Yellow Circle) }

Generalizations of these instances will be represented in a similar fashion, except that we may indicate that the color, size, or shape of an object is unimportant by replacing the value of that feature by a question mark. Thus, the following generalization represents the set of all instances containing one small circle and one large object.

Generalization1: { (Small ? Circle) (Large ? ?) }

We define the matching predicate for this instance language and generalization language so that a generalization matches an instance provided the features specified in the generalization have counterparts in the features specified in the instance. Thus, Generalization1 matches Instance1 (note the instances and generalizations are <u>unordered</u> pairs). More precisely, in this example problem we will say that a generalization, g, matches an instance, i, if and only if there is a mapping from the pair of feature vectors of g onto the pair of feature vectors of i, such that the restrictions on feature values given in g are consistent with the feature values of i. Here a feature restriction in g is consistent with a feature value in i if either (a) the feature restriction in g is identical to the feature value in i, or (b) the feature restriction in g is a question mark.

3 Generalization as Search

The above generalization problem is essentially a search problem. The generalization language corresponds to an hypothesis space (search space) of possible solutions, and the learning task is to examine this hypothesis space, subject to constraints imposed by the training instances, to determine plausible generalizations. This characterization of generalization as search is used below to describe generalization <u>methods</u>, independent of the particular generalization and instance languages used. This characterization leads to a useful classification and comparison of various systems.

3.1 The Partial Ordering

A key characteristic of the above generalization problem is that there is an important structure inherent to the generalization language for <u>every</u> such problem. This structure, which has been described previously for individual generalization languages [Plotkin, 1970], [Michalski, 1973], [Hayes-Roth, 1974], [Vere, 1975], [Mitchell, 1977], is based on the relation "more-specific-than", defined as follows:

> <u>More-specific-than relation:</u> Given two generalizations, G1 and G2, G1 is "more-specific-than" G2 if and only if $\{i \in I \mid M(G1,i)\} \subset \{i \in I \mid M(G2,i)\}$, where I is the set of all instances describable in the instance language, and M is the matching predicate.

In other words, G1 is "more-specific-than" G2 if and only if G1 matches a proper subset of the instances that G2 matches. This relation partially orders the hypothesis space through which the learning program must search. Notice the above definition of this relation is extensional - based upon the instance sets that the generalizations represent. In order for the more-specific-than relation to be practically computable by a computer program, it must be possible to determine whether G1 is more-specific-than G2 by examining the descriptions of G1 and G2, without computing the (possibly infinite) sets of instances that they match. This requirement places restrictions upon the nature of generalization languages for which some of the methods below are suited.

A portion of the partially ordered generalization language for the

Section 3.1

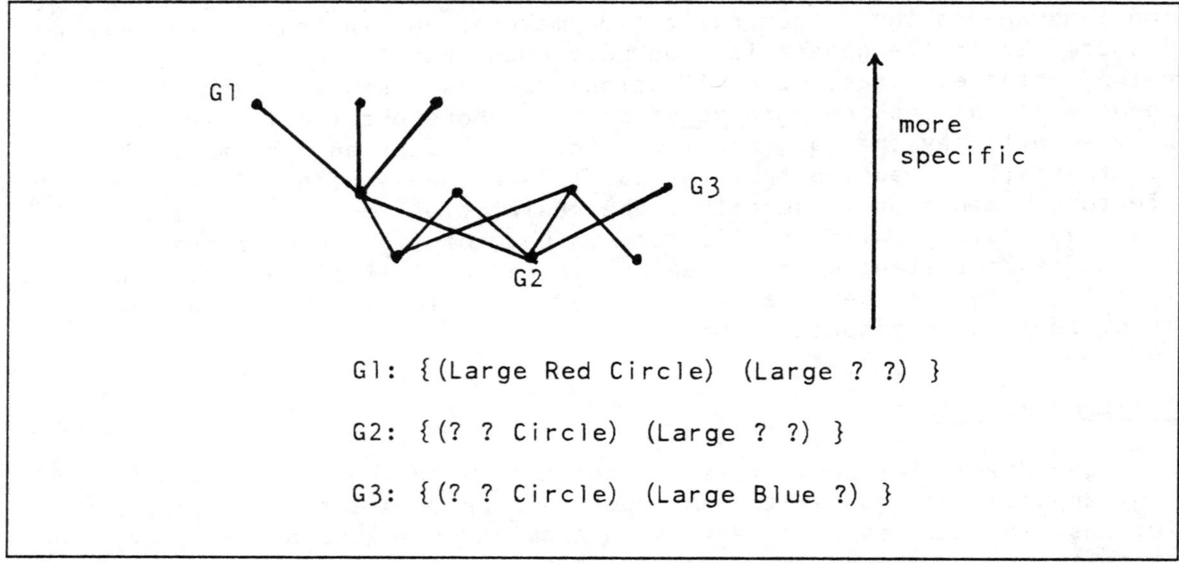

Figure 1. Portion of Partially Ordered Generalization Language.

example problem is shown in Figure 1. Here, G1 is more-specific-than G2: the constraints in G2 are logically implied by those in G1, and therefore any instance which matches G1 must also match G2. In contrast, G3 and G1 are not comparable generalizations according to the more-specific-than relation: although the sets of instances characterized by G3 and G1 intersect, neither set contains the other.

The more-specific-than relation defined above imposes a partial ordering over the generalizations in the hypothesis space. This partial ordering is important because it provides a powerful basis for organizing the search through the hypothesis space. Note that the definition of this relation (and the corresponding partial ordering) is dependent only on the defined instance language, generalization language, and matching predicate. It is independent of the particular generalization to be learned and the particular training instances presented.

4 Three Data-Driven Generalization Strategies

If generalization is viewed as a search problem, then generalization methods can be characterized in terms of the search strategies that they employ. Many generalization programs employ search strategies that are data-driven, in the sense that they consider discrepancies between the current hypothesis and available data in order to determine appropriate revisions to the current hypothesis. Although no two of these programs employ exactly the same strategy, it is informative to group them into classes whose members employ similar strategies and therefore possess similar performance characteristics. The aim of this section is not to compare alternative generalization learning programs, but rather alternative classes of data-driven strategies that existing programs implement in various ways, for

Section 4

various generalization languages. We consider three such classes of search strategies here. A prototypical program is described for each class, and the characteristics of the prototype examined. The capabilities and efficiency of the classes are then compared in terms of these prototypes.

4.1 Depth-first Search

```
Initialize the current best hypothesis, CBH, to some generalization
that is consistent with the first observed positive training instance.

FOR EACH subsequent instance, i, BEGIN

IF i is a negative instance, and i matches CBH

    THEN  BEGIN

        Consider ways of making CBH more specific so that i no longer
        matches it.

        Test these possible revisions to find those that match all
        earlier positive instances.

        Choose one acceptable revision as the new CBH.

        END

ELSE IF i is a positive instance, and i does not match CBH,

    THEN  BEGIN

        Consider ways of making CBH more general so that i matches it.

        Test these possible revisions to find those that do not match
        any earlier negative instance.

        Choose one acceptable revision as the new CBH.

        END

IF none of the considered revisions to CBH result in a generalization
        consistent with previous instances as well as i,

    THEN Backtrack to an earlier version of CBH, and try a different
         branch in the search, and reprocess instances that have
         been processed since that point.

END
```

Figure 2. Depth-First Search Strategy.

Section 4.1

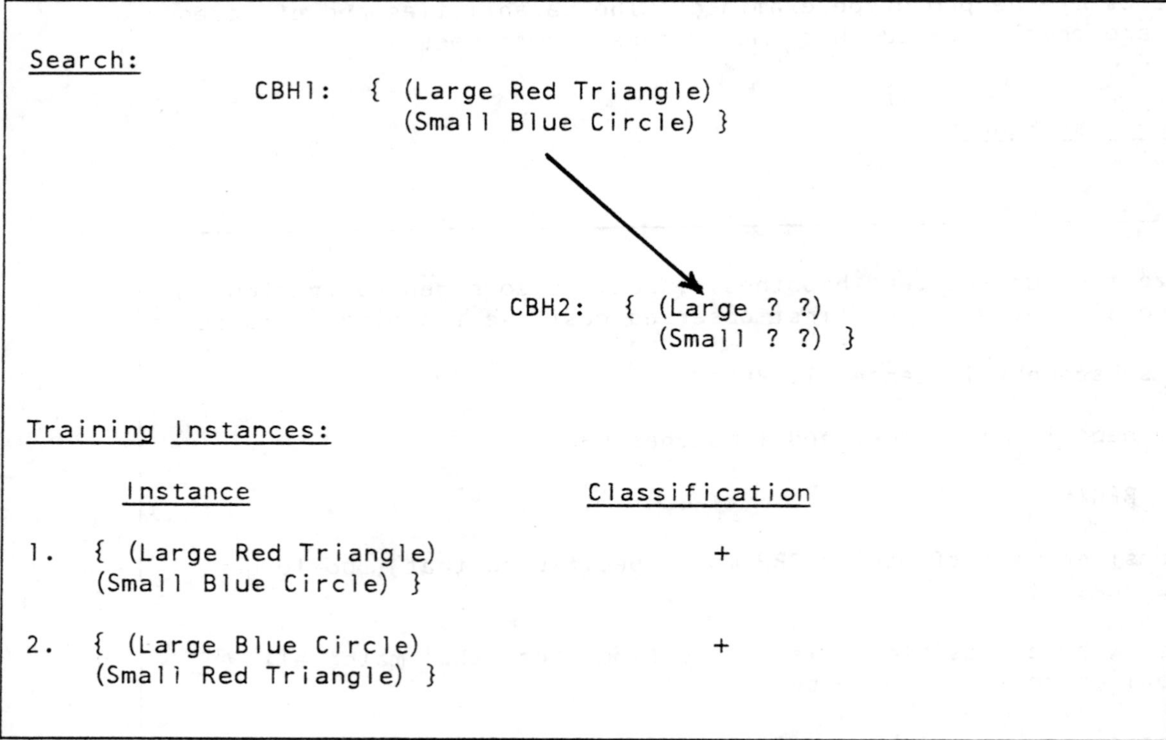

Figure 3. Depth-First Search Example.

One data-driven strategy for generalizing from examples is depth-first search through the hypothesis space. Programs that can be characterized in this way include [Winston, 1975] and the RULEMOD portion of the Meta-DENDRAL program as described in [Buchanan, 1978]. In this strategy, a single generalization is chosen as the current best hypothesis for describing the identity of the target generalization. This current hypothesis is then tested against each newly presented training instance, and is altered as needed so that the resulting generalization is consistent with each new instance. Each such alteration yields a a new current hypothesis, and corresponds to one step in a data-driven, depth-first search through the hypothesis space.

A prototypical depth-first search strategy can be described as shown in Figure 2.

Figure 3 illustrates the Depth-First Search strategy in the context of the example problem described earlier. This figure shows the effect of two positive training instances. Here, the first positive training instance leads to initializing the current best hypothesis to CBH1, which matches no instances other than the first positive instance. When the second positive instance is observed, CBH1 must be revised so that it will match the new positive instance. Notice that there are many plausible revisions to CBH1 in addition to CBH2, shown in the figure. Systems such as [Winston, 1975] and [Buchanan, 1978] use domain-specific heuristics to determine which of the possible revisions to select when many are plausible.

Section 4.1

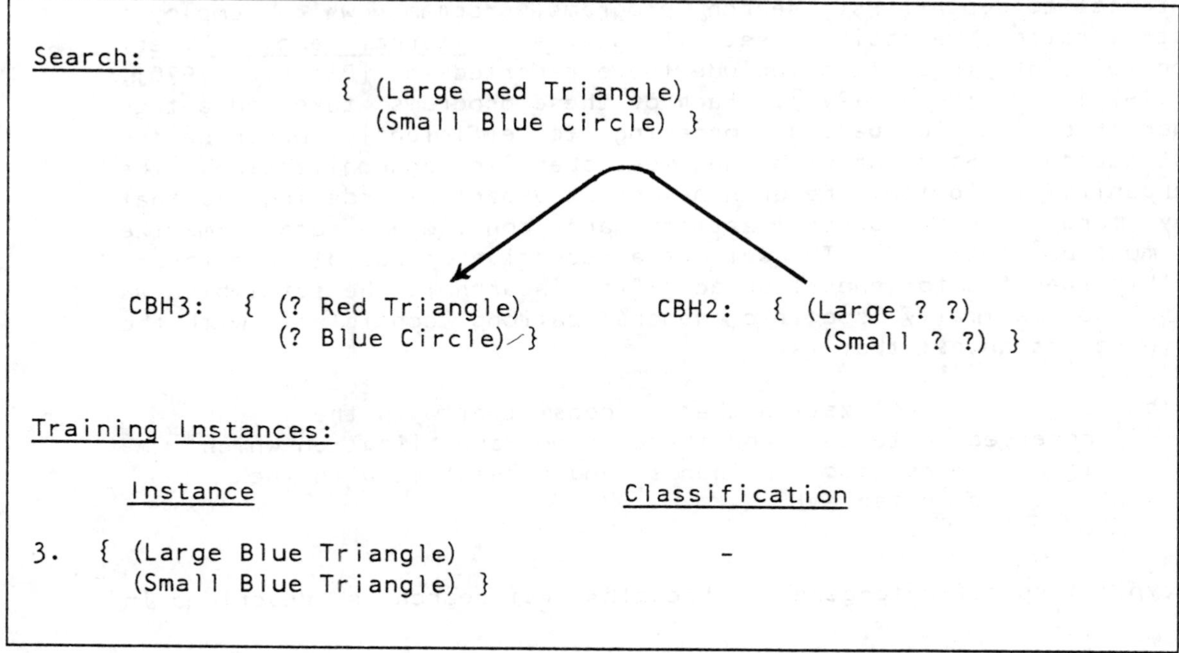

Figure 4. Depth-First Search Example Continued.

Figure 4 illustrates the effect of a third training instance which conflicts with CBH2. In this case, although CBH2 could be specialized to exclude the new negative instance, no such revision is consistent with the observed positive instances. Therefore, the system must backtrack to an earlier version of the CBH, reconsidering its previous revisions to determine a revision that will be consistent with the new negative instance as well as the observed positive instances. This backtracking step is shown schematically in Figure 4, and results in this case in the new current hypothesis CBH3.

There are two awkward characteristics of this depth-first search strategy:

1) Cost of maintaining consistency with past instances: It is costly to test each alteration to the current hypothesis for consistency with past training instances. Some systems (e.g., [Winston, 1975]) sacrifice assured consistency with past instances by not reexamining them when the current hypothesis is altered. Others (e.g., [Buchanan, 1978]) test past instances, and therefore require progressively longer computations for each successive training instance.

2) Need to backtrack: Once the program has determined a set of acceptable alterations to the current generalization, it must choose one of these as the new current hypothesis. In the event that subsequent instances reveal an incorrect choice has been made, the program must backtrack to reconsider previously processed training instances and generalizations.

Section 4.2

4.2 Specific-to-General Breadth-first Search

In contrast to depth-first search programs, programs which employ a breadth-first strategy maintain a set of several alternative hypotheses. Systems which fall into this class include those reported in [Plotkin, 1970], [Hayes-Roth, 1974], and [Vere, 1975]. Each of these programs takes advantage of the general-to-specific partial ordering to efficiently organize the breadth-first search. Starting with the most specific generalizations, the search is organized to follow the branches of the partial ordering so that progressively more general generalizations are considered each time the current set must be modified. The set of alternative plausible hypotheses computed by this specific-to-general breadth-first search is the set (which we shall call S) of maximally specific generalizations consistent with the observed training instances; that is

S = {s | s is a generalization that is consistent with the observed instances, and there is no generalization which is both more specific than s, and consistent with the observed instances}.

A prototypical specific-to-general breadth-first search is described in Figure 5.

```
Initialize the set of current hypotheses, S, to the set of maximally
specific generalizations that are consistent with the first
observed positive training instance.

FOR EACH subsequent instance, i, BEGIN

IF i is a negative instance,

    THEN  Retain in S only those generalizations which do not
          match i.

ELSE IF i is a positive instance,

    THEN  BEGIN

          Generalize members of S that do not match i, along each branch
          of the partial ordering, but only to to the extent required to
          allow them to match i.

          Remove from S any element that either (1) is more general than
          some other element in S, or (2) matches a previously observed
          negative instance.

END
```

Figure 5. Breadth-First Search Strategy.

Section 4.2

Notice that this algorithm involves comparing generalizations in order to determine whether one is more general than another. The generalization language must allow making this test efficiently; that is, the test should be made by examining the descriptions of the two generalizations directly, without having to consider explicitly the sets of instances that they represent. This requirement represents a restriction on the kind of generalization languages for which this approach is practical.

Figure 6 illustrates this search strategy, using the same two positive instances considered in Figure 3. The set S1 is determined in response to the first positive instance. It contains the most specific generalization consistent with the observed instance. S1 is then revised in response to the second positive instance, as shown in Figure 6. Here, the generalization in S1 is generalized along each branch of the partial ordering, to the extent needed to match the new positive instance. The resulting set, S2, is the set of maximally specific describable generalizations consistent with the two observed positive instances.

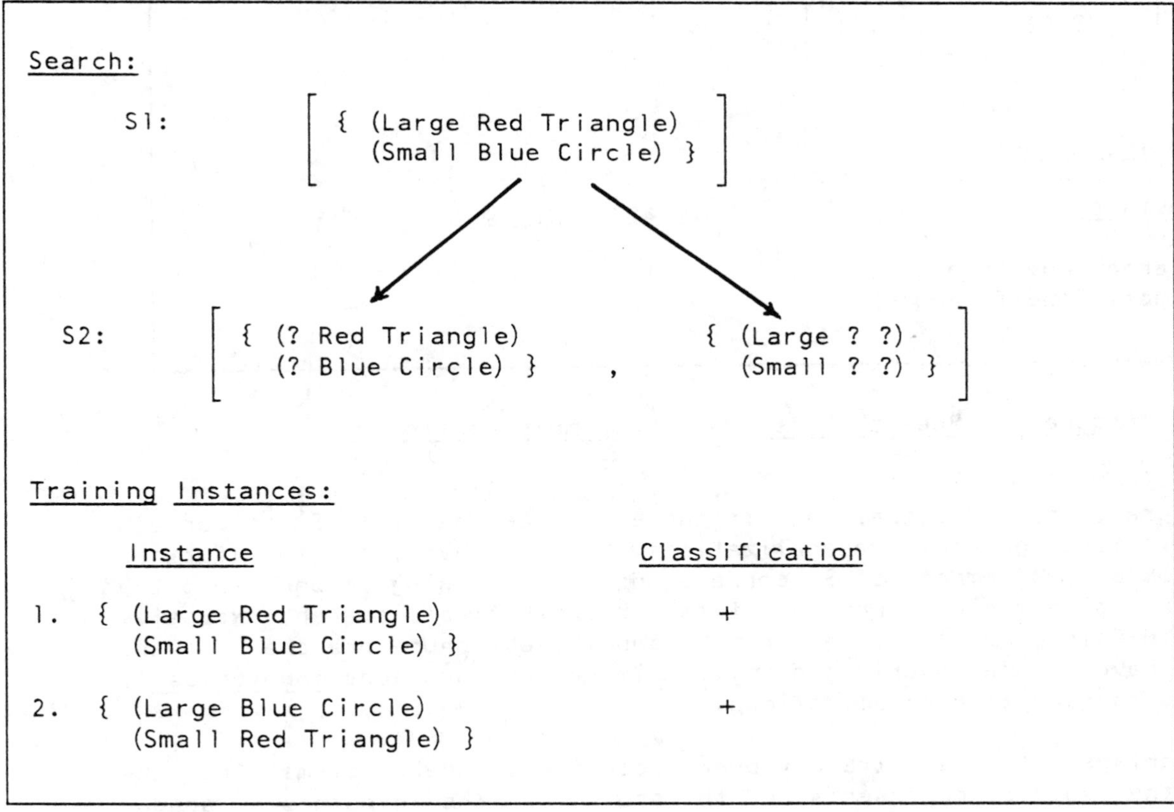

Figure 6. Specific-to-General Breadth-First Search Example.

Section 4.2

Figure 7 illustrates the effect of a subsequent negative training instance. In this case, one of the members of S2 was found to match the negative instance, and was therefore removed from the revised set of current hypotheses, S3. Notice that there is no possibility of finding an acceptable specialization of the offending generalization, since by definition, no more specific generalization is consistent with the observed positive instances. At the same time, no further generalization is acceptable since this will also match the new negative instance.

```
S2:  [ { (? Red Triangle)          { (Large ? ?)
         (? Blue Circle) }    ,      (Small ? ?) } ]

S3:  [ { (? Red Triangle)
         (? Blue Circle) } ]
```

Training Instances:

Instance	Classification
3. { (Large Blue Triangle) (Small Blue Triangle) }	-

Figure 7. Breadth-First Search Example Continued.

In general, positive training instances force the set S to contain progressively more general generalizations. Each revision to (further generalization of) a member of S corresponds to searching deeper into the partial ordering along one branch of the breadth-first search. Negative instances eliminate generalizations from S, and thereby prune branches of the search which have become overly general. This search proceeds monotonically from specific to general generalizations.

One advantage of this strategy over depth-first search stems from the fact that the set S represents a threshold in the hypothesis space. Generalizations more specific than this threshold are not consistent with all the observed positive instances, whereas those more general than this threshold are. Thus, when a generalization in S must be revised, it can only be made more general, and this revision therefore need not be tested for consistency with past positive instances. Revisions must still, however, be tested against previous negative instances to assure that that the revised generalization is not overly general.

Section 4.3

4.3 Version Space Strategy

The version space strategy for examining the hypothesis space involves representing and revising the set of all hypotheses that are describable within the given generalization language and that are consistent with the observed training instances. This set of generalizations is referred to as the version space of the target generalization, with respect to the given generalization language and observed training instances. The term version space is used to refer to this set because it contains all plausible versions of the emerging concept.

This strategy begins by representing the set of all generalizations consistent with the first positive training instance, then eliminates from consideration any generalization found inconsistent with subsequent instances. Programs that implement this strategy for various generalization languages are described in [Mitchell, 1977], [Mitchell, 1978], and [Mitchell, 1980].

The version space approach is feasible because the general-to-specific ordering of generalizations allows a compact representation for version spaces. In particular, a version space can be represented[2] by two sets of generalizations: the set S as defined above, and the dual set G, where

G = {g | g is consistent with the observed instances, and
there is no generalization which is both more
general than g, and consistent with the instances }.

Together, the sets S and G precisely delimit the version space[3]. It is thus possible to determine whether a given generalization is contained in the version space delimited by sets S and G:

A generalization, x, is contained in the version space represented by S and G

if and only if

(1) x is more specific than or equal to some member of G, and
(2) x is more general than or equal to some member of S.

The set S is computed in a manner similar to that described for the specific-to-general breadth-first search strategy described above. The set G can be computed by conducting a second, complementary, breadth-first search from general to specific generalizations. The version space strategy can thus be viewed as an extension of the above breadth-first search strategy into a bi-directional search, and can be described as shown in Figure 8.

---

2 The version space is "represented" in the sense that it is possible to generate and recognize any generalization in the version space by examining its representation.

3 The version space relative to any given set of training instances forms a convex set with respect to the partial ordering of the search space. For a formal description and analysis of this approach, see [Mitchell, 1978].

Section 4.3

```
Initialize the sets S and G, respectively, to the sets of maximally
specific and maximally general generalizations that are
consistent with the first observed positive training instance.

FOR EACH subsequent instance, i, BEGIN

IF i is a negative instance,

    THEN  BEGIN

          Retain in S only those generalizations which do not
          match i.

          Make generalizations in G that match i more specific,
          only to to the extent required so that they no longer match i,
          and only in such ways that each remains more general than
          some generalization in S.

          Remove from G any element that is more specific than some other
          element in G.

      END

ELSE IF i is a positive instance,

    THEN  BEGIN

          Retain in G only those generalizations which match i.

          Generalize members of S that do not match i, only to to the
          extent required to allow them to match i, and only in such
          ways that each remains more specific than some generalization
          in G.

          Remove from S any element that is more general that some other
          element in S.

      END
END
```

Figure 8. Version Space Strategy.

Figure 9 shows the effect of the same two positive instances shown in the previous examples. The situation is very similar to that for the breadth-first search, except that the additional set G is initialized as shown. The generalization used to initialize the set G is the most general generalization describable within the given language, and matches every possible instance. Because it is consistent with the two positive training instances shown in this figure, the set G is unaltered by these instances.

Section 4.3

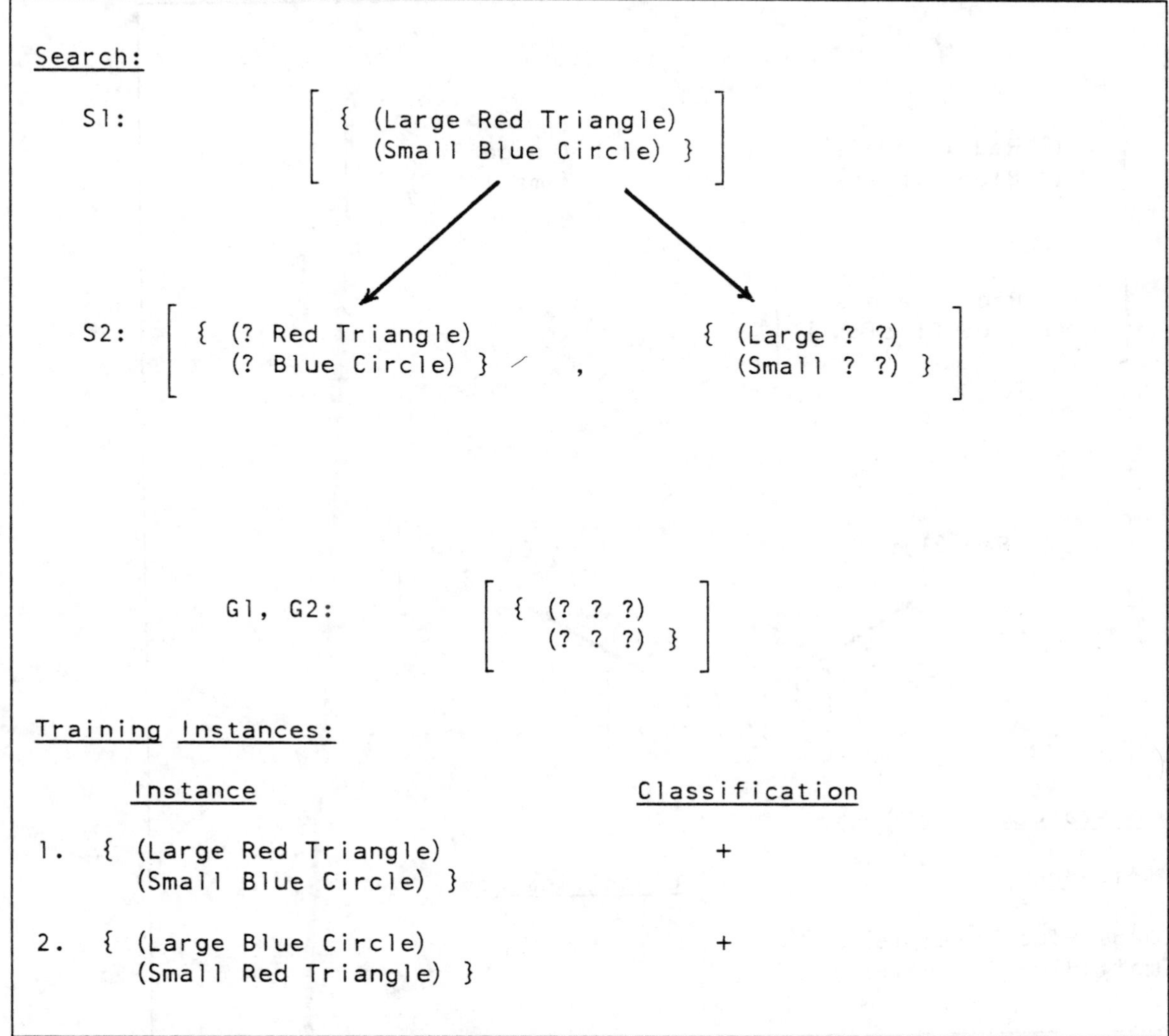

Figure 9. Version Space Example.

Figure 10 illustrates the effect of a negative training instance on the version space. Here, the set S2 is revised as in the breadth-first search. The set G2 is also revised since the negative instance reveals that the current member of G2 is overly general. The generalization in G2 is therefore specialized along all possible branches of the partial ordering that lead toward some member of S3. Along each such branch, it is specialized only to the extent required so that the generalization no longer matches the new negative instance.

The revised S and G sets illustrated in Figure 10 represent the version space of all generalizations in the provided language which are consistent with the three observed training instances. The version space at this point contains the members of S3 and G3, as well as all generalizations that lie between these two sets in the partially ordered hypothesis space. Subsequent

Section 4.3

Search:

S2: [{ (? Red Triangle) (? Blue Circle) } , { (Large ? ?) (Small ? ?) }]

S3: [{ (? Red Triangle) (? Blue Circle) }]

G3: [{ (? Red ?) (? ? ?) } , { (? ? Circle) (? ? ?) }]

G2: [{ (? ? ?) (? ? ?) }]

Training Instances:

Instance	Classification
3. { (Large Blue Triangle) (Small Blue Triangle) }	-

Figure 10. Version Space Example Continued.

positive training instances may force S to become more general, while subsequent negative training instances may force G to become more specific. Given enough additional training instances, S and G may eventually converge to sets containing the same description. At this point the system will have converged to the only consistent generalization within the given generalization language.

As with specific-to-general breadth first search, the version space approach is practical only for problems in which the "more-specific-than" relation can be computed by direct examination of described generalizations. There is also a minor theoretical restriction on the form of the generalization language: in order for the sets S and G to correctly delimit any version space that can arise, every chain in the partially ordered generalization language must have a most specific and most general member.

Section 4.3

The advantage of the version space strategy lies in the fact that the set G summarizes the information implicit in the negative instances that bounds the acceptable level of generality of hypotheses, while the set S summarizes the information from the positive instances that limits the acceptable level of specialization of hypothesis. Therefore, testing whether a given generalization is consistent with all the observed instances <u>is logically equivalent</u> to testing whether it lies between the sets S and G in the partial ordering of generalizations.

The version space method is assured to find all generalizations (within the given generalization language) that are consistent with the observed training instances, independent of the order of presentation of training instances. The sets S and G represent the version space in an efficient manner, summarizing the information from the observed training instances so that no training instances need be stored for later reconsideration.

4.4 Capabilities

In comparing alternative strategies for generalization, the important issues concern relative capabilities rather than efficiency. The major differences in capabilities among the above three data-driven strategies derive from the number of plausible generalizations carried along at each step, and from the use of the partial ordering in guiding the search. Below, we consider two desirable capabilities for a generalization program.

1) The ability to detect the point at which the target generalization is completely determined by the training instances, and, when necessary, to use incompletely determined generalizations in a reasonable manner.

2) The ability to direct the presentation of training instances to obtain informative instances.

4.4.1 Using Incompletely Learned Generalizations

One important capability for learning programs is the ability to detect when the observed training data are sufficient to precisely determine the target generalization. That is, to detect the point at which only a single generalization from the provided language remains consistent with the observed data. Of course the generalization is "learned" at this point only under the assumption that the generalization language contains a correct description of the generalization, and that the training instances are correct. The capability to detect this condition is important if the learned information is to be later applied to classify unknown instances. Equally important is the capability to make use of incompletely learned generalizations when only limited training data are available.

The version space strategy provides an easy method for detecting the point at which a generalization is completely determined by a set of training instances, with respect to the given generalization language. This condition is satisfied if and only if the computed sets S and G are equal and contain only one generalization. In contrast, it is difficult to recognize this condition when maintaining only a single current hypothesis, as with the depth-first search strategy, or when maintaining only the set S, as with the breadth-first search strategy.

Because availability of training instances is limited in many domains, and because for some generalization languages no finite set of training instances is sufficient to determine a unique generalization[4], it is crucial to be able to apply incompletely learned generalizations in a reasonable way. For example, suppose that the training instances shown in the previous figures are the only training instances available for that problem. Consider the task of using what has been learned thus far in order to classify the three new instances shown in Figure 11 as positive or negative.

```
instance1: {(Small Red Triangle) (Large Blue Circle)}

instance2: {(Large Blue Triangle) (Small Blue Square)}

instance3: {(Small Red Circle) (Small Blue Circle)}
```

Figure 11. Instances with Unknown Classification.

The sets S and G that represent the version space provide a handle on the problem of representing and using incompletely learned generalizations. Even though the exact identity of the target generalization is not fully determined by the three training instances in the preceding example, it is assumed that the correct description of the target generalization lies somewhere within the version space delimited by S3 and G3 of Figure 10. Therefore, if a new instance matches every generalization in the version space (equivalently, if it matches every element in the set S), then it can be classified as a positive instance with the same certainty as if a unique generalization had been determined by the training instances. This is the case for Instance1 in Figure 11.

Similarly, if the instance matches no generalization in the version space (i.e., it matches no element of the set G), then it is certain that the instance does not match any description of the target generalization that would be determined by examining additional instances. This is the case for Instance2 in Figure 11. Thus, for such instances it is possible to obtain classifications that are just as unambiguous as if the learned generalization had been completely determined by the training instances.

In contrast, instances that match some, but not all generalizations in the version space cannot be unambiguously classified until further training instances are available. This is the case for Instance3 in Figure 11. Of course, by considering outside knowledge or by examining the proportion of

4 Finite sets of training instances from an infinite instance language are not in general sufficient to determine a unique generalization.

Section 4.4.1

generalizations in the version space which match the instance, one might still estimate the classification of such instances.

When an instance is unambiguously classified by the version space, then regardless of which member of the version space is the correct description of the target generalization, the classification of the given instance will be the same. All the observed training instances will therefore receive an unambiguous classification by the associated version space. Surprisingly, even instances which have not been observed during training may receive an unambiguous classification, as does Instance2 in Figure 11. If the instance has not been observed as a training instance by the learning system, then how can the system produce an unambiguous classification of this instance? Are such unambiguous classifications reliable?

It can be proven that any such unambiguous classification is a correct classification, provided that (1) the observed training instances were correct, and (2) the generalization language allows describing the target generalization. Notice that the generalization language used in our example is biased, in the sense that it does not allow describing every possible set of instances. This biased generalization language, together with the observed data leads to an unambiguous classification of Instance2. Provided that this biased generalization language allows describing the correct generalization, the unambiguous classification of Instance2 is the correct classification. This example provides an interesting insight into the significance of initial biases for allowing inductive leaps during generalization. [Mitchell, 1980a] contains a discussion of the importance of and sources of biases for learning and generalization.

Because the specific-to-general breadth-first strategy computes the set S, this strategy allows unambiguously classifying the same positive instances as the version space strategy. Since it does not compute the set G, however, it cannot distinguish between instances which the version space strategy would classify as negative instances, and those which cannot be unambiguously classified. The breadth-first strategy would therefore be able to classify Instance1 from Figure 11 as a positive instance, but would not allow a reliable classification of either Instance2 or Instance3.

4.4.2 Selecting New Training Instances

A further capability afforded by computing the sets S and G is the selection of informative new training instances. Consider the following problem: after processing some sequence of training instances, a program is provided a set of further instances, without their classifications as positive or negative instances, and is allowed to request the correct classification of any one of them.

The instance whose classification should be requested in this case (the instance which will provide on the average the most useful information) is the instance which comes closest to matching one half of the generalizations in the version space. Regardless of its classification, finding out its classification will allow rejecting one half of the currently plausible generalizations. Thus, by testing each instance to determine what proportion of the generalizations in the version space it matches, the most informative training instance can be selected.

Section 4.4.2

If instead of selecting from a list of possible instances, the program is able to itself generate at each step an instance that matches half the generalizations in the current version space, then the program can itself generate an optimal[5] sequence of training instances for learning the target generalization.

As a simple illustration of using the represented version space to direct the presentation of training instances, suppose that after being shown the three training instances in the example problem above, the learning program is allowed to request the classification of any one of the instances shown in Figure 11. In this case, Instance3 is an instance whose classification would be useful to know -- it is an instance that matches some, but not all the members of the current version space. On the other hand, since the classifications of Instance1 and Instance2 are already determined by the version space, no new information would be obtained by requesting their classification. Thus, the instances whose classification would be informative are precisely those that cannot be reliably classified by the current version space.

The breadth-first strategy also provides some information for selecting new training instances. The strategy of selecting instances which match half the generalizations in the computed set S is reasonable, although less complete than the strategy which takes into account the entire version space.

4.5 Complexity and Efficiency

The overall space and time efficiency of each approach is determined by a number of factors, including the order of presentation of training instances, the chosen generalization language and the branching of the associated partial ordering, the cost of matching generalizations to training instances, and the amount of space needed to store generalizations and observed instances.

A complete analysis is beyond the scope of this paper, but it is possible to characterize the time and space complexity as a function of the number of training instances, under reasonable assumptions. In particular, we assume that positive and negative instances are distributed uniformly throughout the sequence of training instances.

Under this assumption, bounds on the time and space complexity of the prototype data-driven strategies described earlier are summarized in Table 1. Here p indicates the number of positive training instances, n indicates the number of negative training instances, s indicates the largest size obtained by the set S, and g represents the largest size obtained by the set G. The time complexity bounds indicate bounds on the number of comparisons between generalizations and instances, and comparisons between generalizations. Notice that for some generalization and instance languages, each such comparison may itself be an NP problem. For example, some structural

5 This strategy determines the identity of the target generalization in the shortest possible number of training instances, assuming no prior knowledge of the identity of the target generalization. Choosing instances under this handicap is a much different problem than the problem faced by a teacher who knows the generalization, and must choose good instances. Results from information theory involving optimal binary codes apply here.

Section 4.5

Table 1

Bounds on processing time and maximum storage costs.

Strategy	Processing Time	Storage Space
Depth-first search	$O(pn)$	$O(p+n)$
Specific-to-general Breadth-first search	$O(spn + s^2p)$	$O(s+n)$
Version space strategy	$O(sg(p+n) + s^2p + g^2n)$	$O(s+g)$

This table describes the complexity of the various prototype algorithms, under assumptions described in the text.

description languages (e.g., that used in Meta-DENDRAL) involve testing subgraph isomorphism (an NP-complete problem) as part of this comparison.

The complexity of the depth-first strategy stems from the need to reexamine past instances after each revision to the current generalization. Note from the earlier description of this strategy that each time a positive instance forces a change to the current hypothesis, all past negative instances must be examined. Thus, time requirements are $O(n)$ for each such positive instance, or $O(pn)$ in total. Revising the current hypothesis in response to negative instances yields a similar result. Because all instances must be stored for later reexamination, the space requirements are linear with the number of observed instances, $O(p+n)$.

For the prototype specific-to-general breadth-first strategy, only negative instances need be stored for later examination, so that space requirements are $O(s+n)$. In the time complexity, the term $O(spn)$ arises because each time that a positive instance alters the set S, each altered hypothesis must be compared against all past negative instances. The term $O(s^2p)$ arises because each revised element of S must be tested to determine whether it is more general than another element of S.

Since the version space strategy computes both S and G, no training instances need be saved, and space complexity is $O(s+g)$. Notice that for this strategy, processing time grows linearly with the number of training instances $(p+n)$, whereas for the other two strategies time grows as the product pn. However, in this case processing time grows as the square of both S and G.

Section 4.5

In interpreting the above results it is important to know how the sizes of the sets S and G vary over the training sequence. For the generalization languages for which the version space strategy has been implemented, these sets have been observed to first grow in size, then level off, and finally decrease in size as the version space converges toward the correct description of the target generalization. Under such conditions, the dominant term in determining time complexity is the first term in each of the expressions in table 1. The exact sizes of the sets S and G depend, of course, upon the nature of the generalization language.

A further consideration in determining overall efficiency which has not been considered here is the effect of ordering and selection of training instances. Short, informative training sequences certainly lower demand for computer resources, as well as demands on the supplier of these instances. By investing some time in ordering or selecting training instances, it is possible that a program might lower its total resource requirements. A related issue is the (not well understood) possibility of controlling the sizes of the sets S and G by prudent ordering and selection of training instances.

5 Other Generalization Strategies

The generalization strategies surveyed in the previous section are data-driven in the sense that revisions to current hypotheses are made in response to -- and directed by -- observed discrepancies with the data. This section notes two other classes of generalization strategies that have been used successfully in various domains.

5.1 Generate-and-Test Strategies

Data-driven search involves considering discrepancies between the current hypotheses and available data, in order to determine appropriate revisions to the current hypotheses. An alternative class of search strategies, which we shall call generate-and-test strategies, generates new hypotheses according to a predetermined procedure that is independent of the input data[6]. Each newly generated hypothesis is then tested against the entire set of available training data, and identified as either an acceptable generalization, a node to be expanded further by the generator, or node to be pruned from the search.

Generate-and-test strategies typically consider all available training instances at each step of the search to test newly generated hypotheses. Because they judge the generated hypotheses by their performance over many instances, rather than making decisions based upon individual training instances, they can accommodate quite severe errors in the training data. On the other hand, generate-and-test strategies are not well suited to incremental processing of training data -- should unexpected data become

---

6 This distinction between generate-and-test and data-driven methods is similar to the distinction in [Simon, 1973] between "the rule induction version of the generate and test method" and the "rule induction version of the heuristic search method".

Section 5.1

available, the generate-and-test search may have to be completely reexecuted. Furthermore, since the generation of hypotheses is not influenced by the data, the search can be quite branchy and expensive.

An interesting combination of generate-and-test and data-driven search procedures is found in the Meta-DENDRAL program [Buchanan, 1978]. One portion of the program, called RULEGEN [Buchanan, 1978], conducts a coarse, generate-and-test search to form approximate rules of mass spectroscopy based upon highly unreliable training instances. These approximate rules are then used as starting points for a data-driven strategy (either RULEMOD [Buchanan, 1978] or VS [Mitchell, 1978]) which conducts a more detailed search to refine each rule, using both the original training data and additional available data. Thus, the advantages of generate-and-test search for dealing with inconsistent data are blended with the advantages of data-driven search for a more focused search based on incremental use of the data.

Some generate-and-test strategies for generalization follow the partial ordering of the hypothesis space to control hypothesis generation. [Banerji, 1980] describes and compares two such generalization strategies - one that searches from general to specific hypotheses, and one that searches from specific to general. Figure 12 shows the relationship among the search strategies employed by several existing generalization programs.

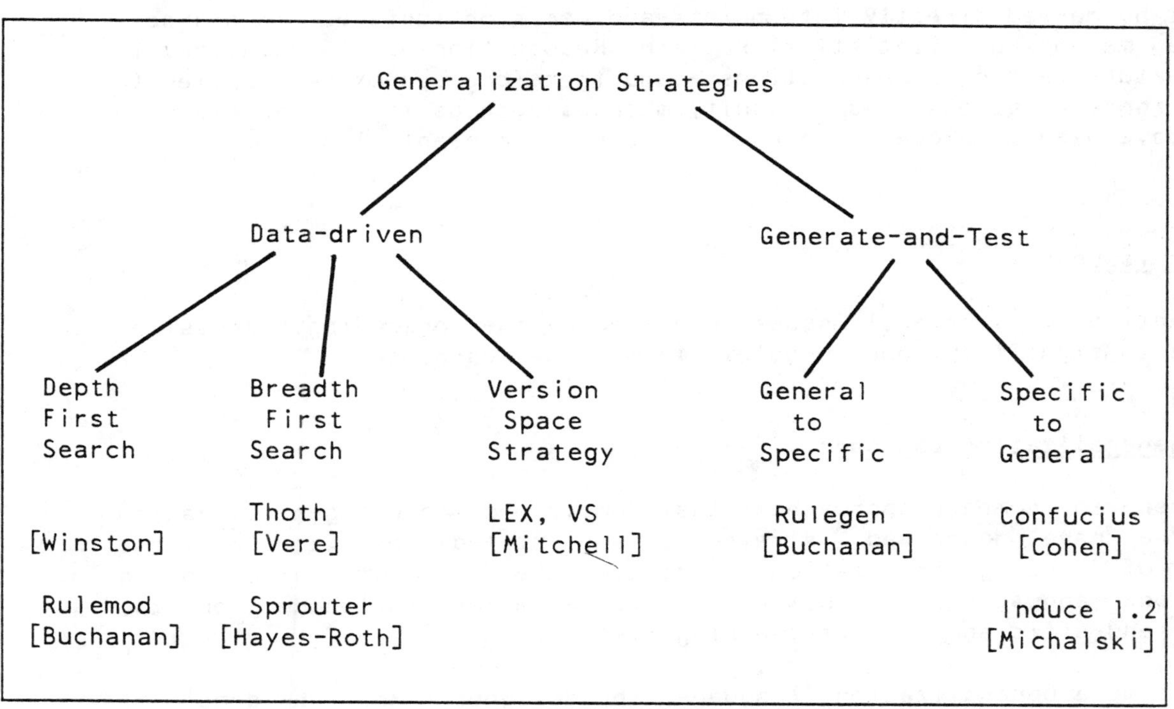

Figure 12. Some Classes of Search Strategies for Generalization.

Section 5.1

5.2 Statistical Pattern Recognition

The field of statistical pattern recognition deals with one important subclass of generalization problems. In this subclass, the instances are represented by points in n-space, and the generalizations are represented by decision surfaces in n-space (e.g., hyperplanes, polynomials of specified degree). The matching predicate corresponds to determining whether a given point (instance) lies on one side or another of a given decision surface (generalization). The field of Statistical Pattern Recognition has developed very good generalization methods for particular classes of decision surfaces. Many of these methods are relatively insensitive to errors in the data and some have well understood statistical convergence properties, under certain assumptions about the probability distribution of input instances.

In contrast to work in Statistical Pattern Recognition, work on the generalization problem within Artificial Intelligence has focused on problems involving a different class of instance and generalization languages. These languages are incompatible with numerically oriented representations that describe objects as feature vectors in n-space. For example, Winston's program [Winston, 1975] for learning descriptions of simple block structures such as arches and towers, represents instance block structures in terms of their component blocks and relationships among these. In this domain, the natural representation for instances is a generalized graph rather than a feature vector. Even the simple generalization problem used as an example in this paper cannot be mapped directly into points and decision surfaces in n-space. Many of the methods of Statistical Pattern Recognition are specialized to numerical feature vector representations, and therefore cannot be applied to these other representations. As a result, methods such as those described in this paper have been developed to handle these new representations.

6 Further Issues

This section notes several issues suggested by the preceding discussion, which relate to significant open problems in machine learning.

6.1 The Generalization Language

In order to compare approaches that employ different generalization languages, we have described strategies and stated results in terms independent of the generalization language used. The choice of a generalization language does, however, have a major influence on the capabilities and efficiency of the learning system.

In choosing a generalization language, the designer fixes the domain of generalizations which the program may describe, and therefore learn. Most current systems employ generalization languages that are biased in the sense that they are capable of representing only <u>some</u> of the possible sets of describable instances. With the choice of a generalization language, the system designer builds in his biases concerning useful and irrelevant generalizations in the domain. This bias constitutes both a strength and a weakness for the system: If the bias is inappropriate, it can prevent the system from ever inferring correct generalizations. If the bias is appropriate, it can provide the basis for important inductive leaps beyond information directly available from the training instances. The effect of a biased generalization language on classifying unobserved instances was illustrated in the earlier section on utilizing partially learned generalizations. [Mitchell, 1980a] provides a general discussion of the importance of bias in learning.

The choice of "good" generalization languages, and the impact of this choice on the selection of a good learning strategy is poorly understood at present. Methods by which a program could automatically detect and repair deficiencies in its generalization language would represent a significant advance in this field.

In addition to influencing system capabilities, the choice of generalization language also has a strong influence on the resource requirements of the system. For example, the complexity of the matching predicate for generalizations represented by graphs can be exponential, while the complexity for generalizations represented by feature vectors is linear. Secondly, a language for which the general-to-specific ordering is shallow and branchy will typically yield larger sets S and G than a language in which the ordering is narrow but deep. In particular, the introduction of disjunction into the generalization language greatly increases the branching in the partial ordering, thereby aggravating the combinatorial explosion faced by the learning program.

6.2 Using Expectations and Prior Knowledge

In this discussion we defined "acceptable" generalizations primarily in terms of consistency with the training data. Generalizations may also be judged in terms of consistency with prior knowledge or expectations. As noted above, one method of imposing such expectation-based, or model-based constraints on a learning system is to build them into the generalization language. A second method is to build them into the generator of hypotheses, as is done in some generate-and-test searches. In most existing programs the blending of expectations together with constraints imposed by the training data is either done in an ad hoc manner or not done at all. In complex systems the constraints imposed by prior knowledge may be critical to making appropriate inductive leaps, and to controlling the combinatorics inherent in learning. Developing general methods for combining prior knowledge effectively with training data to constrain learning is a significant open problem.

6.3 Inconsistency

In order to simplify the analysis attempted above, it has been necessary to consider only problems in which the generalization language contains some generalization consistent with every training instance. This condition might not be satisfied if either (1) the generalization language is insufficient to describe the target generalization, or (2) the training instances contain errors. In general, there will be no way for the program to determine which of these two problems is the cause of the inconsistency. In such cases, the learning program must be able to detect inconsistency, and recover from it in a reasonable way.

Section 6.3

Statistical methods typically deal with inconsistency better than the descriptive methods considered here. As noted earlier, generate-and-test search procedures appear better suited to deal with inconsistency since they base the selection among alternative hypotheses on sets of training instances rather than single instances. Some data-driven strategies have been extended to deal with inconsistent data [Hayes-Roth, 1974], [Mitchell, 1978]. Inconsistency is unavoidable in many real-world applications. Well understood methods for learning in the presence of such inconsistency are needed.

6.4 Partially Learned Generalizations

As a practical matter, it is essential to develop methods for representing and reasoning about "partially" learned generalizations. It is unlikely in realistic applications that sufficient training data will be available to fully determine every needed generalization. Therefore, the problem of representing and utilizing incompletely learned generalizations is critical to using generalization methods for practical applications. The techniques noted above for dealing with this issue constitute an initial approach to the problem. Extending these ideas to take advantage of prior knowledge of the domain, and to operate in the presence of inconsistency are important open problems.

7 Summary

The problem of generalization may be viewed as a search problem involving a large hypothesis space of possible generalizations. The process of generalization can be viewed as examining this space under constraints imposed by the training instances, as well as prior knowledge and expectations. In this light, it is informative to characterize alternative approaches to generalization in terms of the strategy that each employs in examining this hypothesis space.

A general-to-specific partial ordering gives structure to the hypothesis space for generalization problems. Several data-directed generalization strategies have been described and compared in terms of the way in which they organize the search relative to this partial ordering. This examination leads to a comparison of their relative capabilities and computational complexity, as well as to a useful perspective on generalization and significant topics for future work.

8 Acknowledgments

The ideas presented in this paper have evolved over discussions with many people. John S. Brown, Bruce Buchanan, John Burge, Rick Hayes-Roth, and Nils Nilsson have provided especially useful comments on various drafts of this paper. This work has been supported by NIH under grant RR-643-09, and by NSF under grant MCS80-08889.

References

[Banerji, 1980]
Banerji, R.B., and T.M. Mitchell, Description languages and learning algorithms: A paradigm for comparison. International Journal of Policy Analysis and Information Systems, special issue on Knowledge Acquisition and Induction, vol. 4, p. 197, 1980.

[Brown, 1973]
Brown, J. S., Steps toward automatic theory formation. Procedings of IJCAI3, Stanford University, 1973, pp. 20-23.

[Bruner, 1956]
Bruner, J. S., J. J. Goodnow, and G. A. Austin, A Study of Thinking. Wiley, New York, 1956.

[Buchanan, 1978]
Buchanan B. G., and T. M. Mitchell, Model-directed learning of production rules, In Pattern-Directed Inference Systems (D. A. Waterman and F. Hayes-Roth, Eds.), Academic Press, New York, 1978.

[Hayes-Roth, 1974]
Hayes-Roth, F., Schematic classification problems and their solution. Pattern Recognition, 6, pp. 105-113 (1974).

[Hayes-Roth, 1975]
Hayes-Roth F., and D Mostow, An automatically compilable recognition network for structured patterns. IJCAI4, Cambridge, MA, September 1975, pp. 356-362.

[Hunt, 1975]
Hunt, E. B., Artificial Intelligence. Academic Press, New York, 1975.

[Michalski, 1973]
Michalski, R. S., AQVAL/1 - Computer implementation of a variable valued logic system VL1 and examples of its application to pattern recognition. Procedings 1st International Joint Conference on Pattern Recognition, Washington, D.C., 1973, pp. 3-17.

[Minsky, 1969]
Minsky M., and S. Papert, Perceptrons, MIT Press, Cambridge, Mass., 1969.

[Mitchell, 1977]
Mitchell, T. M., Version Spaces: A candidate elimination approach to rule learning. IJCAI5, MIT, Cambridge, MA, August 1977, pp. 305-310.

[Mitchell, 1978]
Mitchell, T. M., Version Spaces: An approach to concept learning. Ph.D. thesis, Stanford University, December, 1978. Also Stanford CS report STAN-CS-78-711, HPP-79-2.

[Mitchell, 1980]
Mitchell, T.M., P.E., Utgoff, and R.B. Banerji, Learning problem-solving heuristics by experimentation. Proceedings of the Workshop on Machine Learning, C-MU, July, 1980.

[Mitchell, 1980a]
Mitchell, T.M., The need for biases in learning generalizations. Rutgers Computer Science Technical Report CBM-TR-117.

[Nilsson, 1965]
Nilsson, N.J., Learning Machines McGraw-Hill, New York, 1965.

[Plotkin, 1970]
Plotkin, G. D. A note on inductive generalization, Machine Intelligence 5 (B. Meltzer and D. Michie, Eds.), Edinburgh University Press, Edinburgh, 1970, pp. 153-163.

[Popplestone, 1970]
Popplestone, R. J., An Experiment in Automatic Induction. Machine Intelligence - 5 (B. Meltzer and D. Michie, Eds.), Edinburgh University Press, 1970, pp. 204-215.

[Simon, 1973]
Simon H. A., and G. Lea, Problem solving and rule induction: a unified view. Knowledge and Cognition (L.W. Gregg, Ed.), Lawrence Erlbaum Associates, Potomac, Maryland, 1974, pp. 105-127.

[Vere, 1975]
Vere, S. A., Induction of concepts in the predicate calculus. IJCAI4, Tbilisi, USSR, 1975, pp. 281-287.

[Vere, 1978]
Vere, S. A., Inductive learning of relational productions. Pattern-Directed Inference Systems (D.A. Waterman and F. Hayes-Roth, Eds.), Academic Press, New York, 1978.

[Waterman, 1970]
Waterman, D. A., Generalization learning techniques for automating the learning of heuristics. Artificial Intelligence, 1(1,2), pp. 121-170 (1970).

[Winston, 1975]
Winston, P. H., (Ed.), The Psychology of Computer Vision, McGraw-Hill, New York, 1975.

INDEX

Al